Lecture Notes in Computer Science 2652

Edited by G. Goos, J. Hartmanis, and J. van Leeuwen

Springer-Verlag Berlin Heidelberg GmbH

Francisco José Perales
Aurélio J. C. Campilho
Nicolás Pérez de la Blanca
Alberto Sanfeliu (Eds.)

Pattern Recognition and Image Analysis

First Iberian Conference, IbPRIA 2003
Puerto de Andratx, Mallorca, Spain, June 4-6, 2003
Proceedings

 Springer

Volume Editors

Francisco José Perales
Department of Mathematics and Computer Science
C/Valldemossa km 7.5, PC 07122, Palma de Mallorca, Spain
E-mail: paco.perales@uib.es

Aurélio J. C. Campilho
Universidade do Porto, Faculdade de Engenharia
INEB - Instituto de Engenharia Biomédica
Rua Dr. Roberto Frias, 4200-465 Porto, Portugal
E-mail: campilho@fe.up.pt

Nicolás Pérez
Universidad de Granada, E.T. S. Ing. Informática
Departamento de Ciencias da la Computacíon e I.A.
18071 Granada, Spain
E-mail: nicolas@decsai.ugr.es

Alberto Sanfeliu
IRI, Institut de Robòtica i Informàtida Industrial
Technological Park of Barcelona, U. Building
St. LLorens i Artigas 4-6 2nd Floor, 08028 Barcelona, Spain
E-mail: asanfeliu@iri.upc.es

Cataloging-in-Publication Data applied for

A catalog record for this book is available from the Library of Congress

Bibliographic information published by Die Deutsche Bibliothek
Die Deutsche Bibliothek lists this publication in the Deutsche Nationalbibliographie;
detailed bibliographic data is available in the Internet at <http://dnb.ddb.de>.

ISBN 978-3-540-40217-6   ISBN 978-3-540-44871-6 (eBook)
DOI 10.1007/978-3-540-44871-6

http://www.springer.de

© Springer-Verlag Berlin Heidelberg 2003

Originally published by Springer-Verlag Berlin Heidelberg New York in 2003.

Typesetting: Camera-ready by author, data conversion by DA-TeX Gerd Blumenstein
Printed on acid-free paper   SPIN: 10933381   06/3142   5 4 3 2 1 0

Preface

IbPRIA 2003 (Iberian Conference on Pattern Recognition and Image Analysis) was the first of a series of similar events organized every two years, by AER-FAI (Asociación Española de Reconocimento de Formas y Análisis de Imágenes) and APRP (Associação Portuguesa de Reconhecimento de Padrões). In 2003 it was hosted by the Universitat de les Illes Balears, Departament de Ciències Matemàtiques i Informàtica. It provides an international forum for presentation of ongoing research in computer vision, image analysis, pattern recognition and speech recognition. Taking into account the new frontiers of information society programs where images and audio are fundamental in the communication process, new applications are also being addressed, namely videoconferencing, motion detection, human tracking and speech applications. The response to the call for papers for this conference was very good. From 185 full papers submitted, 130 were accepted, 72 being presented as oral presentations and 58 as posters. The review process was carried out by the Program Committee, each being paper assessed by at least two reviewers. We are specially indebted to the Program Committee and the reviewers for the effort and the high quality of the reviews, which allowed us to prepare this book. An acknowledgement is also due to the authors for responding to our call and for sharing with us their work, their views and enthusiasm.

The conference benefited from the collaboration of the invited speakers Prof. J. Aggarwal from the Computer & Vision Research Center University of Texas at Austin (USA), Prof. L.I. Kuncheva from the School of Informatics, University of Wale at Bangor (UK), and Prof. A. Zisserman, Department of Engineering Science, University of Oxford (UK). We also would like to express to the invited speakers our sincere gratitude.

We are very grateful to all the members of the organizing committee. Their intensive work allowed a smooth organization of the conference and of this proceedings. Finally, we are very pleased to welcome all the delegates who attended in the conference. For those did not attend, we hope this book provides a broad but detailed view of the research presented during the conference. Looking forward to meeting you at the next IbPRIA conference, in Portugal, 2005.

June 2003   F.J. Perales and A.J.C. Campilho

Organization

IbPRIA 2003 was organized by AERFAI (Spanish Association for Pattern Recognition and Image Analysis) and APRP (Associação Portuguesa de Reconhecimento de Padrões), and, as the local organizer of this edition, the department of Mathematics and Computer Science, Universitat de les Illes Balears (UIB).

General Conference Co-chairs:	F.J. Perales López, Computer Graphics and Vision Group, Mathematics and Computer Science Department, UIB (Spain)
	Aurelio J.C. Campilho, INEB, Instituto de Engenharia Biomédica, Faculdade de Engenharia Universidade do Porto (Portugal)
Organizing Chairs:	A. Amengual, J.M. Buades, G. Fontanet, M. González, A. Igelmo, A. Juanico, C.S. Manresa, R. Mas, M. Mascaró Portells, A. Mir, G. Oliver, A. Ortiz, P. Palmer (UIB, Spain), J. Marti (U. Girona, Spain), F. Pla (U. Jaime I, Spain)

Program Committee

Reviewers

Abásolo, M.J.	Universitat de les Illes Balears, Spain
Alves, J.	APRP, Portugal
Baldrich, R.	Univ. Autònoma de Barcelona-CVC, Spain
Barbosa, J.	FEUP, Portugal
Baumela, L.	AERFAI, Spain
Benedi, J.M.	AERFAI, Spain
Corte, L.	APRP, Portugal
El-Sakka, M.	University of Western Ontario, Canada
Garrido, A.	University of Granada, Spain
González, M.	Universitat de les Illes Balears, Spain
González, Y.	Universitat de les Illes Balears, Spain
Igelmo, A.	Universitat de les Illes Balears, Spain
Juan, A	Polytechnical University of Valencia, Spain
López, M.A.	University of Jaime I, Spain
Martí, E.	Univ. Autònoma de Barcelona-CVC, Spain
Martí, J.	University of Girona, Spain
Mas, R.	Universitat de les Illes Balears, Spain
Mendonça, A.	APRP, Portugal
Monteiro, J.	APRP, Portugal
Oliver, G.	Universitat de les Illes Balears, Spain
Otazu, X.	Univ. Autònoma de Barcelona-CVC, Spain
Peinado, A.M.	University of Granada, Spain
Pimenta, A.	APRP, Portugal
Pina, P.	CVRM/IST, Portugal
Pinho, A.	APRP, Portugal
Radeva, P.	Univ. Autònoma de Barcelona-CVC, Spain
Roca, X.	Univ. Autònoma de Barcelona-CVC, Spain
Rubio, A.J.	University of Granada, Spain
Salvador, J.	APRP, Portugal
Sanchiz, J.M.	University of Jaime I, Spain
Segura, J.C.	University of Granada, Spain
Sequeira, J.	APRP, Portugal
Serrat, J.	Univ. Autònoma de Barcelona-CVC, Spain
Sotoca, J.M.	University of Jaime I, Spain
Sousa, B.	APRP, Portugal
Traver, V.J.	University of Jaime I, Spain
Vanrell, M.	Univ. Autònoma de Barcelona-CVC, Spain
Varona, X.	Univ. Autònoma de Barcelona-CVC, Spain
Velhote, M.	FEUP, Portugal

Sponsoring Institutions

MCyT (Ministerio de Ciencia y Tecnología, Spanish Goverment),
TIC2002-10616-E
Mathematics and Computer Science Department, Universitat de les Illes Balears
(UIB)
IAPR (International Association for Pattern Recognition)
Conselleria d'Innovació i Energia (Govern de les Illes Balears)
European Union (Human Potential Programme)

Table of Contents

Solids Characterization Using Modeling Wave Structures

Miguel Adan[1] and Antonio Adan[2]

[1] E.U.I.T.Agrícola, UCLM
Miguel.Adan@uclm.es
[2] E.S. Informática, UCLM
Paseo de la Universidad 4, 13071 Ciudad Real, Spain
Antonio.Adan@uclm.es

Abstract. This paper introduces a characterization study on solid and 3D shapes based-on the recent Modeling Wave (MW) topological organization. The MW establishes a whole n-connectivity relationship in 3D objects modeling meshes. Now an extended use of MW is carried out. Through a new feature called Cone-Curvature, which originates from the MW concept, a flexible and extended surroundings geometry knowledge for every point of the solid surface is given. No-local nor no-global but a half-connectivity has been used for defining a robust 3D similarity measure. The method presented has been successfully tested in our lab over range data in a wide variety of shapes. Consequently, extended research on 3D objects clustering will be accomplished in the near future.

1   Introduction

Similarity and recognition are two words that frequently appear in papers devoted to Computer Vision research. To tell the truth, similarity studies are less frequent than recognition ones. In fact 'recognition' is a word excessively used for talking about pattern, pose, matching, identification or objects discrimination. Nevertheless an efficient way of dealing with recognition/similarity is through an efficient representation model.

One of the keys in this environment is the search for invariant features to scale, translation and rotation. At this point, both, local and global strategies can be found. In local approaches, every point of the surface of the object has knowledge of the features of its immediate neighbours. For mesh representation, this means that a given node is handled as a single item isolated from the complete mesh and without any relationship to the remaining nodes. Local invariants like Gaussian and mean curvatures are widely used. Analytic expressions, curvature estimations [1] or local parametric representations [2] that use raw data have appeared in the last years. In [3] a representation which captures surface curvature information from certain points produces images, called "surface signatures", at these points. For mesh models representations several geometrical features have been also defined such as the simplex angle

F.J. Perales et al. (Eds.): IbPRIA 2003, LNCS 2652, pp. 1–10, 2003.

([4], [5]), curvature index [6] and integral Gaussian curvature ([7], [8]). Despite their utility, local features curvatures are very sensible to noise. In these methods, keeping local and unlinked information could be insufficient for efficiently characterizing an object and carrying out a similarity procedure. In Shum et al. [9] the correspondence between two original shapes can be obtained by minimizing a specific distance based-on spherical representations.

On the contrary, global approaches consider features that define the whole shape and not correlated with the observer viewpoint. So, avoiding the use of local strategies, new directions have been accomplished through global invariant features. In [10] Canonical Length and Weighted Principal Directions features give a solution for 3D free-form object discrimination/identification problem whereas random measures between points are presented in [11]. There are also several studies which consider both local-global strategies [12]. Therefore global features can be efficiently used as discriminant parameters, but it would be a weak procedure to analyze similarity when a partial view of the object is handled.

No-local no-global strategies are rarely considered in literature. In this case, every point of the object surface has an extended knowledge of its surroundings and it is possible to define extended-local invariants. The main difficulty in using that idea in a solid modeling environment is to define a model with an appropriated topology and connectivity. MWS structure [13] has been designed to maintain new and wider relationships among subsets of mesh nodes. In this sense, typical 3-connectivity is just another relationship.

This paper is devoted to showing a new 3D shape characterization study based on extended knowledge that goes from local to global knowledge using MWS. In Section 2, MWS is briefly defined whereas Section 3 is devoted to defining and analysing Cone-Curvature as an extended-local invariant. Experimentation and future works are shown in the last section.

2   MWS Concept

The *Modeling Wave Set* (MWS) concept has been published lately as a new topological organization where an n-connectivity relationship is established [13]. With MWS, an object is simultaneously modeled in n subspaces of features, corresponding to n different viewing directions of the object. In this section a brief explanation of MWS is carried out.

Our solid representation model is defined on a mesh of n nodes from the tessellation of the unit sphere. Let T_I be this initial tessellation that can be considered standard and includes an implicit coordinate system. In practice, one way to obtain T_I is by projecting the vertices of regular polyhedral over the unit sphere. So it is possible to obtain a three-neighbour relationship as a local topology.

The procedure for building a model T_M through T_I is as follows: first T_I is deformed to fit the normalized surface of the object; then several geometric features can be extracted from the deformed mesh and finally, these features are mapped into T_I. So, T_I is implemented as a valid data structure for representing 3D objects in a simplified and normalized manner. Additionally, it is used for mapping some features of the same object on it.

From the initial tessellation T_I, a new topological structure called *Modeling Wave* (MW) and a more complex multidimensional data structure MWS will be defined next.

MW structure organizes the nodes of T_I in disjoint subsets following a new relationship. Each subset contains a group of nodes spatially disposed over the sphere as a closed quasi-circle, resulting in subsets that look like concentric rings on the sphere. Since this organization resembles the shape of a wave, this has been called *Modeling Wave (MW)*. Consequently each of the disjoint subsets is known as *Wave Front (WF)*. Of course, MW structure remains after the modeling process has finished. In others words, the WF structures are in T_M (see Figure 1).

To build a MW, a first node of the tessellated sphere must be chosen as the origin of the structure. This node, called *Initial Focus*, constitutes the first *Wave Front*, F^1, and identifies the MW. Consequently, F^j is the j-th WF that will be contiguous to F^{j+1}. Thus, two new relationships are established for the nodes: a neighbourhood relationship defined among WFs, and a belonging relationship of each node to one, and only one, WF.

From the previous definition it can be deduced that any node of T_I may be *Initial Focus* and, therefore, it can generate its MW. In that case, $\text{ORD}(T_I)$ different MWs can be generated. Let us call all the possible MWs that can be generated over a given tessellated sphere T_I *Modeling Wave Set (MWS)*.

Due to the multidimensional nature of our MWS structure, when we map any local or global feature onto T_I we obtain n different feature subspaces for the same object, i.e. one subspace for each MW. Each subspace supplies a feature map of the object arranged by the corresponding *Wave Fronts*. Details about the MW and MWS concepts can be seen in [13]

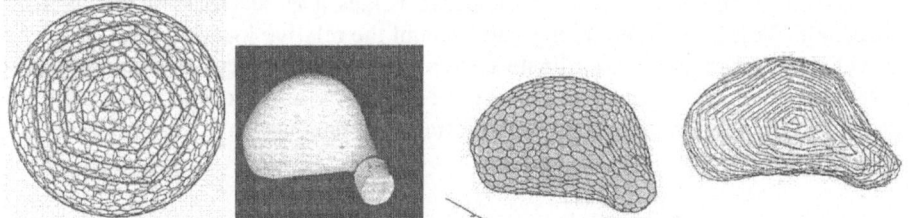

Fig. 1. MW drawn over T_I (left) and an example of representation model using MWs. On the right, the first WFs are plotted over the model mesh

3   Cone-Curvature

3.1   Definition

Cone-Curvature (CC) is defined as a new and intuitive feature based on MW structure taking into account the location of the WFs inside the model. We will start talking about the jth CC which will mean CC of the jth WF, F^j.

Let N be the *Initial Focus* of a particular MW. In order to define *j*th CC of the node N, we consider firstly two elements: the barycentre of the nodes of the *j*th WF, C^j, and the least squares fitted plane to the *j*th WF, R^j, $\vec{n}^j$ being its associate normal vector. Let us consider, for every trio $\{C^j, N, N_i\}, N_i \in F^j\}, C^j \in R^j$, the angle $\gamma^j{}_i = \angle C^j NN_i \in [0, \pi]$ and finally the average of these angles, β^j.

The geometric meaning of β^j can be considered as the angle of the cone which is closed to the *j*th WF, *N* being the vertex, and NC^j being the cone axis. Values next to $\pi/2$ correspond to low curvature zones whereas values next to 0 or π, correspond to high curvature zones. Note that the set of values $\{\beta^1, \beta^2, \beta^3, ...\beta^j\}$ gives an extended curvature information around N until the *j*th WF, where the word 'curvature' has a no-local meaning. Nevertheless it makes sense to consider only the first WFs around N which will be seen joined to N from a specific viewpoint. This concept is illustrated in Figure 2.

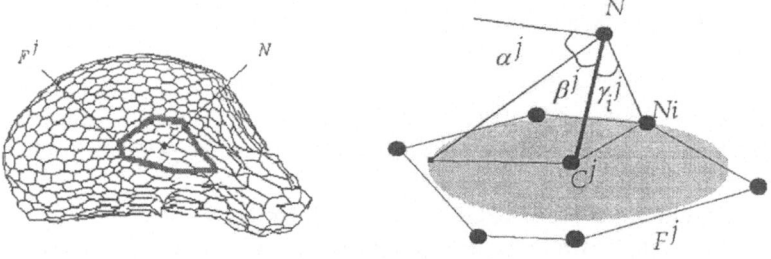

Fig. 2. Definition of *j*th CC

In order to distinguish convex and concave values it is necessary to define a sign for each WF. This is assigned taking into account the relative location of O, R^j, and N, where O is the origin of the coordinate system fixed to the object. In other words, if O and N are in the same side of Rj there exist concavity and the opposite case corresponds to convexity. The last idea can be formally defined as:

$$sign(F^j) = sign\left(\left(\vec{n}^j \cdot \overrightarrow{C^j N}\right) * \left(\vec{n}^j \cdot \overrightarrow{OC^j}\right)\right)$$

Finally we take the formal definition of jth Cone-Curvature of a node N as:

$$\alpha^j = sign(F^j) * \left|\frac{\pi}{2} - \beta^j\right|$$

where the term $\left|\pi/2 - \beta^j\right|$ allows to fix $\alpha^j \in [-\pi/2, \pi/2]$. Therefore, negative values are for concave zones, values next to zero correspond to flat areas and positive values correspond to convex zones. Obviously, the CC concept gives a kind of signed curvature measure for specific areas, growing around the node chosen from the *1*st to the *j*th WF.

Coming back to the whole representation in the sphere T_I, it can be said that a set of correspondences $c^j : T_I \rightarrow [-\pi/2, \pi/2]$ $j = 1,...q$, q being the number of *Wave Front* considered, is established for all the nodes of T_I. So for each node N a set of q values $\{\alpha^1, \alpha^2, ...\alpha^q\}$ could be used for exploring its surroundings (see Figure 3). Next, some examples are included to explain in more detail the last concepts.

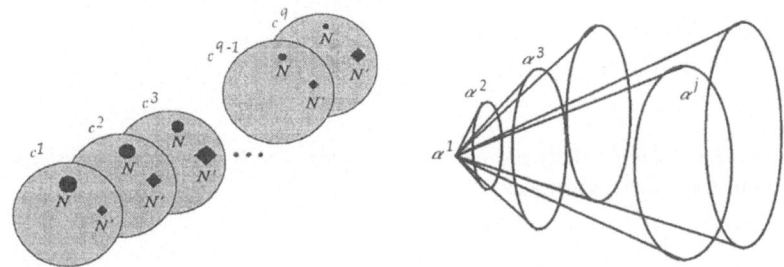

Fig. 3. CCs Mapping Set of over T_I (left) and visualization of CCs for a node N

3.2   Analysing an Example

Figure 4 plots *2*nd to *18*th CCs for three different nodes of the mesh. As it can be seen the location of N(612), N(370) and N(344) in the mesh correspond to different areas. Note that their CC distributions are very distant. Nevertheless if the nodes are in the same zone, the corresponding CC distributions are nearer, except in the *2*nd and *3*rd order. Obviously this is due to the fact that for the first WFs the measure of CC is more sensible to errors. Therefore, small variations in the location of the nodes involves high variations in first orders of CC whereas for upper orders such variations do not meaningfully affect it. Errors are mainly due to the 3D sensor resolution, the modeling process and the effects of mesh discretization/resolution.

Keeping this in mind, local features are not suitable enough for characterizing an object unless errors are minimum. Therefore we will characterize objects taking half-order CCs.

Figure 5 shows the set of correspondences c^j for j=2...18. In this case, for each *j*th CC their values are plotted in an ordered manner. So, a whole representation of the object can be seen. Note that label A corresponds to several concave zones, label B to low values of CC and C to convex zones.

Another visualization of the *j*th CC can be appreciated in the next figure (Figure 6) where the CC value is plotted over the own mesh as a specific grey level. The colour is assigned to the patch through the CC's average of their nodes. Several coloured meshes corresponding to several CC orders are plotted. At this point it is necessary to remark on how a consistent representation of the object implies low frequency components or colour continuity in a mathematical sense. In other words, high frequency implies that some kind of error is present in the 3D image. This circumstance can be seen especially for c^2 where the discontinuity is evident whereas for upper orders no high frequency components are appreciated.

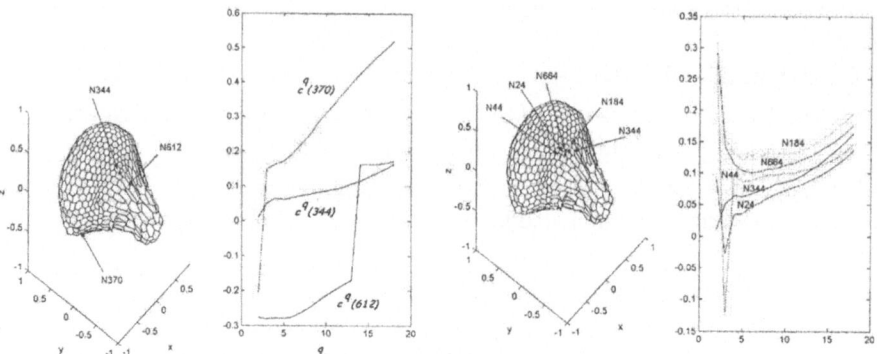

Fig. 4. CjCs for scattered (left) and near (right) nodes. The X-axis and Y-axis correspond to CC-order and CC value respectively.

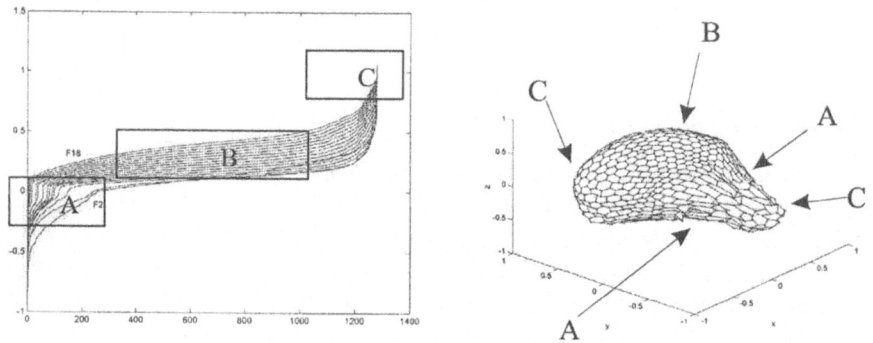

Fig. 5. Set of correspondences c^j for j=2…18 plotted in a sorted manner

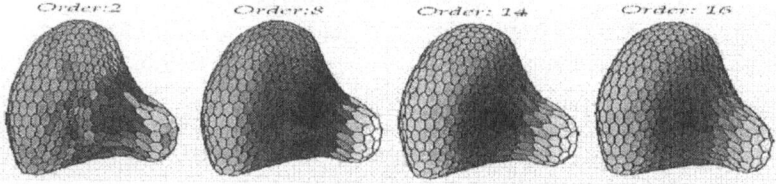

Fig. 6. Illustration of 2nd, 8th, 14th and 16th CCs. Note the discontinuity in 2nd CC and the continuity for the rest

4   Experimentation and Future Works

Our solid characterization method has been tested on database of around 100 real items including both polyhedral and curve-shaped objects. The object database has been created using a *Gray Range Finder* sensor though several synthetic objects have been used. The system has worked with objects of small dimensions (5 to 15 cm) located in front of the sensor, over a controlled device which allows us to take different poses of the object. The average error of the acquired range information is around 1 mm.

In order to prove the invariance of the CC feature we have checked this representation for the database at different poses and we have compared them taking a WF range from 2nd to 18th orders. It can be said that the procedure works in all the cases in that, for each object, similar jth CC's distributions have been obtained when j>3. For 2nd and 3rd orders, CC's distributions for the same object present an irregular disparity. As it has been said before, this is due to CC of N is highly sensible to the noise in the neighbourhood of N.

Figure 7-left shows the 8th CC distributions for five objects when four pose are taken for each one. A detail is included on the right. The X-axis and Y-axis correspond to node number and CC value respectively. In this figure two things can be obviously appreciated. Firstly, the nearness of the four plots for each object which proves the invariance of CC in our spherical model. Secondly the disparity between the distributions corresponding to different objects, which means that through CCs it is possible to accomplish an efficient solid similarity study.

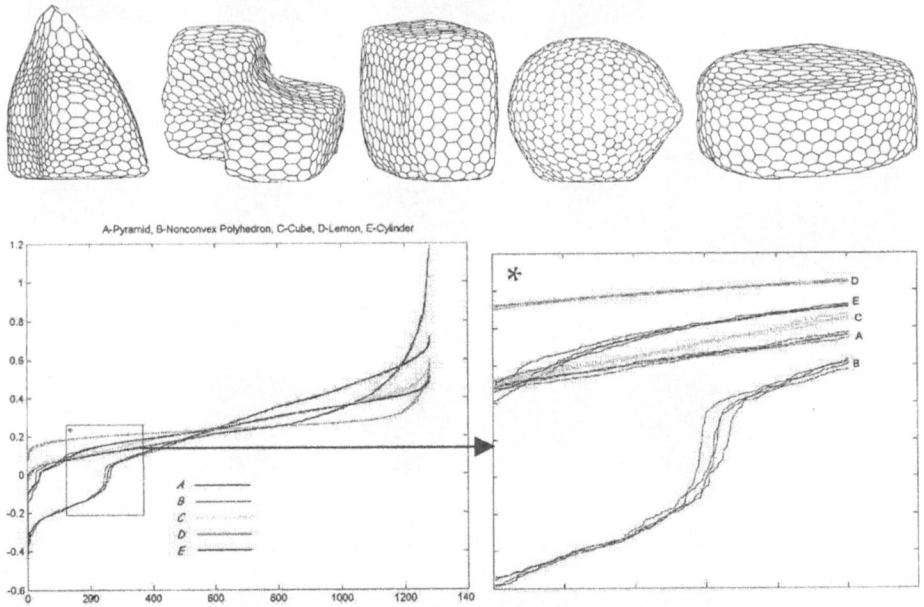

Fig. 7. Modeling meshes (above) and their corresponding 8th CC distributions for four poses (below)

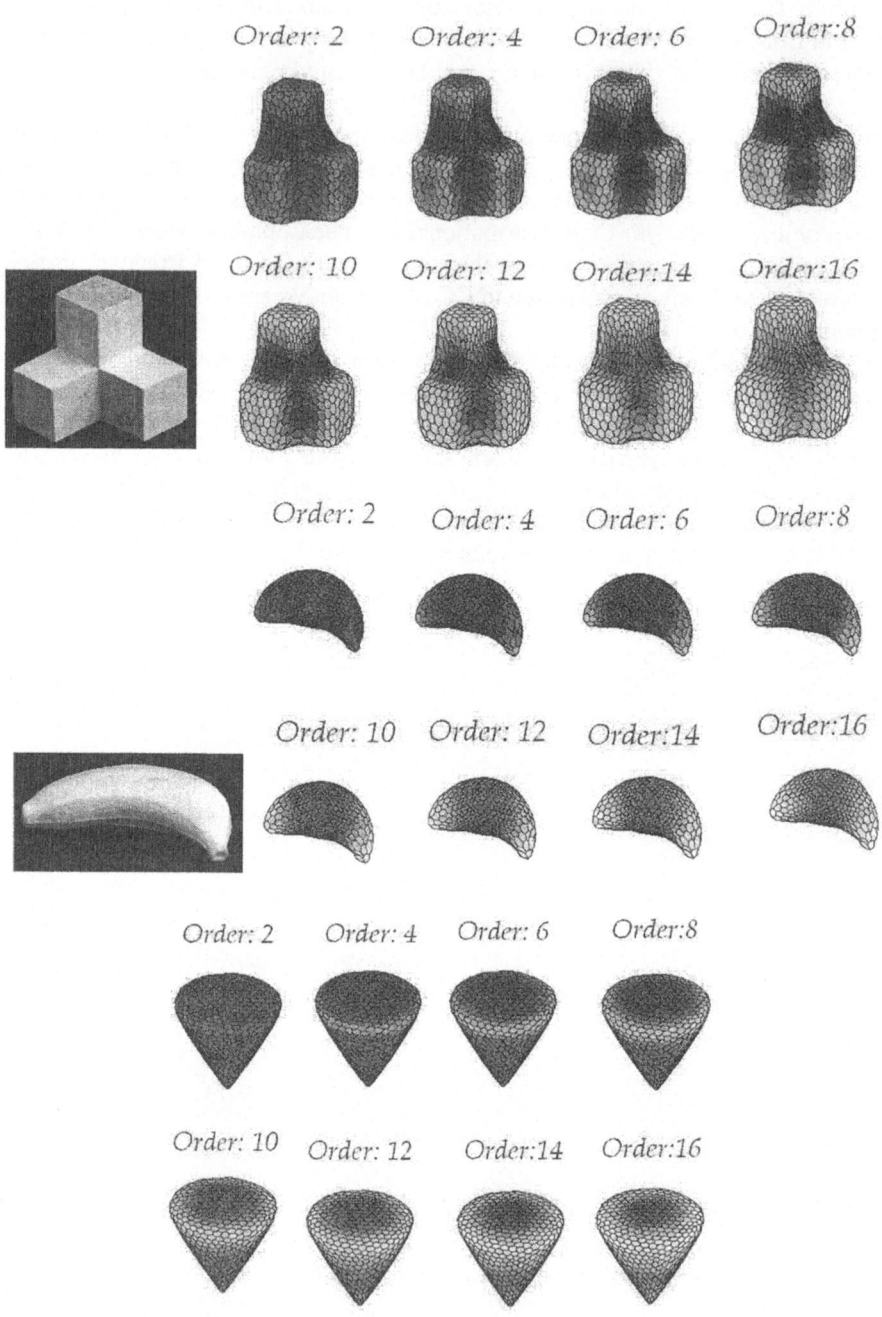

Fig. 8. CC models for several orders. The continuity of CC for each patch of the mesh when the order grows can be appreciated

In fact, we have defined a distance based on CC concept which allows us to measure how much an object is similar to another one. Since the present paper is devoted to defining the characterization through CC it is not possible to explain in detail this similarity measure, its consequent analysis and experimentation. Briefly, we will say that, for two objects A and B, it is possible to define a jth distance, d^j, for their corresponding jth CCs. The expression is the following

$$d^j(A,B) = \sqrt{\sum_{k=1}^{n}(c_A^j(k) - c_B^j(k))^2}$$

Note that the sum is extended to all the nodes of the mesh. With this expression it is possible to analyse the efficiency of using CCs for low and high values of j, in other words the suitability of considering near or far information.

Finally, there is another detail which requires attention. Although a reference about the continuity of the correspondence $c^j : T_I \rightarrow [-\pi/2, \pi/2]$ $j = 1,...q$ has been made before (see Fig 6), it can be said that there is also continuity in the set of q values $\{\alpha^1, \alpha^2, ...\alpha^q\}$ for each node N of the model. In Fig 8 a sequence of models for several orders is presented. It can be appreciated that every patch of the mesh smoothly changes its grey level when j grows.

This kind of representation, based on the MW structure with CC as a feature, is being used for carrying out 3D shapes similarity studies and new solid classification algorithms.

Acknowledgements

This research has been supported by the CICYT Spanish project PDI2002-03999-C02-01.

References

[1]   Hameiri, E., Shimshoni I.: Estimating the Principal Curvatures and the Darboux Frame from Real 3D Range Data. 1st Int. Symp. On 3D Data Processing Visualization and Transmission. Padova. (2002) 258-267

[2]   Johnson, A., Hebert, M.: Using Spin Images for Efficient Object Recognition in Cluttered 3D Scenes. PAMI 21(5) (1999) 433-449

[3]   Yamany, S.M., Farag, A.A.: Surface Signatures: An Orientation Independent Free-Form Surface Representation Scheme for the Purpose of Objects Registration and Matching. Pattern Analysis and Machine Intelligence, 24(8) (2002) 1105-1120

[4]   Delinguette, H.: Simplex Meshes: A General Representación for 3D Shape Reconstruction. Technical Report 2214, INRIA, France (1994)

[5]   Hebert, M., Ikeuchi, K., Delingette, H.: A Spherical Representation for Recognition of Free-form Surfaces. IEEE Trans. Pattern Anal. Mach. Intell. 17(7) (1995) 681-690

[6]   Koenderink, J.J., Van Doorn, A.J.: Surface shape and curvature scales. Image and Vision Computing, 10(8) (1992) 557-56

[7]   Dyn, N., Hormann, K., Kim, S-J., Levin, D.: Optimizing 3D Triangulations Using Discrete Curvature Analysis. Mathematical Methods for Curves and Surfaces. Vanderbilt University Press, (2000) 135-146

[8]   Alboul, L., Van Damme, R.: Polyhedral metrics in surface reconstruction. In: Mullineux, G. (ed.): The Mathematics of Surfaces VI. Clarendon Press, Oxford (1996) 171-200

[9]   Shum, H., Hebert, M., Ikeuchi, K.: On 3D Shape Similarity, Technical. Report, CMU, (1995)

[10]   Adán, A., Cerrada, C., Feliú, V.: Global shape invariants: a solution for 3D free-form object discrimination/identification problem. Pattern Recognition 34 (2001) 1331-1348

[11]   Osada, R., Funkhouser, T., Chazelle, B., Dobkin, D.: Matching 3D models with shape distributions. Proceeding of Shape Modeling International. Genova, (2001)

[12]   Vandeborre, J-P., Couillet, V., Daoudi, M.: A practical approach for 3D model indexing by combining local and global invariants. 1st Int. Symp. On 3D Data Processing Visualization and Transmission. Padova. (2002) 644-647

[13]   Adán, A., Cerrada, C., Feliú, V.: Modeling Wave Set: Definition and Application of a new Topological Organization for 3D Object Modeling. Computer Vision and Image Understanding, 79 (2000) 281-307

A Probabilistic Model
for the Cooperative Modular Neural Network

Luís A. Alexandre[1,2*], Aurélio Campilho[2,3], and Mohamed Kamel[4]

[1] Departamento de Informática, Universidade da Beira Interior
Covilhã, Portugal
lfbaa@di.ubi.pt
[2] INEB – Instituto de Engenharia Biomédica
Laboratório de Sinal e Imagem Biomédica
Campus da FEUP, Rua Roberto Frias
s/n, 4200-465 Porto, Portugal
[3] Universidade do Porto, Faculdade de Engenharia
Departamento de Engenharia Electrotécnica e Computadores
Porto, Portugal
campilho@fe.up.pt
[4] Department of Systems Design Engineering
University of Waterloo, Ontario, Canada mkamel@uwaterloo.ca

Abstract. This paper presents a model for the probability of correct classification for the Cooperative Modular Neural Network (CMNN). The model enables the estimation of the performance of the CMNN using parameters obtained from the data set. The performance estimates for the experiments presented are quite accurate (less than 1% relative difference). We compare the CMNN with a multi-layer perceptron with equal number of weights and conclude that the CMNN is preferred for complex problems. We also investigate the error introduced by one of the CMNN voting strategies.

1   Introduction

The basic idea behind a modular neural network (MNN) architecture [1,2,3,4,5] is the combination of several small networks that are trained to solve a specific part of the full problem. The output of these networks can be combined using, amongst others, rules such as the simple and weighted averages or the product [6,7,8] or alternatively, one of the outputs can be selected as the correct result.

Intuitively, a MNN architecture should perform better than a single network for problems that can be separated into several subproblems. In this case, there is a decoupling of the neurons (and weights) used for learning each subproblem when compared to the case of using a single network to solve the entire problem.

---

* We acknowledge the support of project number POSI/35590/SRI/2000 approved by the Portuguese 'Fundação para a Ciência e Tecnologia'(FCT) and POSI and partially financed by FEDER.

F.J. Perales et al. (Eds.): IbPRIA 2003, LNCS 2652, pp. 11–18, 2003.

This paper introduces a model for the probability of correct classification for the cooperative MNN (CMNN) [1,9,10]. This model enables a better understanding of the way this MNN works. It also enables the estimation of the performance of the CMNN using parameters estimated from the data set. We show empirically that these estimates are accurate. We compare the CMNN with a multi-layer perceptron (MLP) with equal number of weights and conclude that the CMNN is preferred for complex problems. We also investigate the error introduced by one of the voting strategies.

Section 2 introduces the CMNN architecture and the model for the probability of correct classification (PCC). Section 3 includes the several voting strategies that can be associated with the CMNN. Section 4 contains experiments, illustrating the ideas presented in the previous sections and confirming the validity of the developed model. In the last section, the results are discussed and the conclusions posted.

2   CMNN Architecture

In this section we describe the CMNN architecture. Consider a classification problem with L classes. C_n represents class n. The input feature vector is X. The CMNN consists of k expert NNs, $g_i(X)$, $i = 1, \ldots, k$, that are trained to solve a particular subproblem of the total problem, and also to recognize when the input data does not belong to its own subproblem. A classifier g_i outputs a vector of estimates of the posterior probabilities, $p_i(X \in C_n | X)$,

$$g_i(X) = (p_i(X \in C_n | X), \ldots, p_i(X \in C_{n-1+\#I_i} | X)), n, \ldots, n-1+\#I_i \in I_i \quad (1)$$

with I_i being the set of indexes that correspond to the classes that classifier g_i can deal with and $\#I_i$ the number of corresponding classes.

We define the set containing the indexes of all the experts as

$$H = \{1, \ldots, k\} \quad (2)$$

and also

$$H_j = H \backslash \{j\}, \ j \in H \quad (3)$$

Each expert g_i has also a set of $k - 1$ outputs, $o_{i,j}$, $j \in H_i$, corresponding to the other experts in the architecture. These outputs have values in $[0, 1]$. A higher value represents more confidence on the fact that the classifier g_j should be selected to produce the final decision.

For each input X, each expert NN produces a vector of posterior probabilities on the I_i outputs corresponding to the classes of its own subproblem, and tries to guess which classifier should be used to classify this pattern, using the remaining $k - 1$ outputs.

The final decision consists on the class with the largest posterior probability from the classifier that is selected by the votes of the $o_{i,j}$ outputs of all classifiers. Several voting strategies can be considered.

This architecture is represented in figure 1.

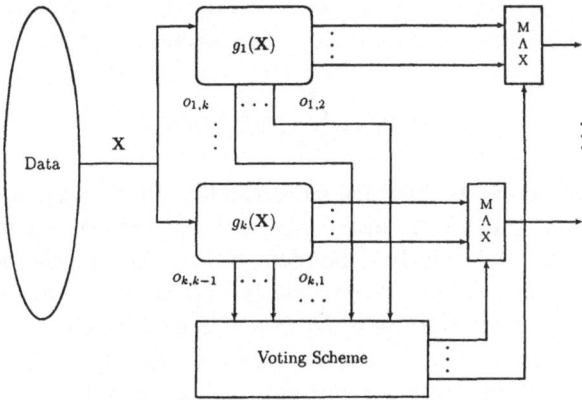

Fig. 1. The CMNN architecture

2.1 General Case

We extend the operator 'max' to work with vectors: it outputs the largest component of the vector. The set of points in which the event 'class n has the largest posterior probability for classifier g_i ' occurs will be represented as $B_{n,i}$:

$$B_{n,i} = \{X : p_i(X \in C_n|X) = \max g_i(X)\} \qquad (4)$$

The set of points in which the event 'classifier g_i makes a correct classification' occurs will be represented by D_i:

$$D_i = \bigcup_{n \in I_i} (B_{n,i} \cap \{X : X \in C_n\}) \qquad (5)$$

To simplify, will call $B_{n,i}$ an event and not the set of points where this event takes place. This will also be done for the set D_i and others to be defined below.

The event 'classifier g_i is elected as the one which will output the final decision' will be represented by F_i.

This way, the probability of correct classification for this architecture comes as

$$PCC = P\left(\bigcup_{i=1}^{k} \bigcup_{n \in I_i} (B_{n,i} \cap \{X \in C_n\} \cap F_i)\right) \qquad (6)$$

Using expression 5 results

$$PCC = P\left(\bigcup_{i=1}^{k} (D_i \cap F_i)\right) \qquad (7)$$

Since the events D_i are disjoint, so is the intersection $(D_i \cap F_i)$, and expression 7 can be written as

$$PCC = \sum_{i=1}^{k} P(D_i \cap F_i) \qquad (8)$$

To simplify the last expression we will assume that the events D_i and F_i are independent. This leads to the following expression for PCC

$$PCC = \sum_{i=1}^{k} P(D_i)P(F_i) \qquad (9)$$

This assumption can be justified since the fact that classifier g_i is the chosen one for classifying the input (event F_i) is dependent of the majority of the classifiers, thus not particularly dependent of classifier g_i (the dependence that may exist, since classifier g_i also votes, is decreased as the total number of experts increases). Since the event D_i depends exclusively of classifier g_i, it is not a strong assumption to consider its independence from F_i.

The different voting strategies will now be considered.

3 Different Voting Strategies

These are the voting strategies proposed by the original author of the CMNN architecture [9]. We present them in a formal manner using the events defined above and also defining new ones.

3.1 Plurality Vote

In this case, each expert g_i votes only for one (other) expert: the one with the highest value of $o_{i,j}$. The expert with more votes wins.

The number of votes that classifier g_i receives is T_i:

$$T_i = \sum_{j \in H_i} \mathbb{I}_{\{\max_{n \in H_j} o_{j,n} = o_{j,i}\}} \qquad (10)$$

where $\mathbb{I}_{\{A\}}$ denotes the indicator function, which gives one if the event A is true and zero otherwise.

Using this definition, we can write $F_i = \{T_i = \max_{j \in H} T_j\}$.

3.2 Borda Count

The $o_{j,i}$ are ranked and a value of $k - 2$ is assigned to the largest output of classifier g_j, $k - 3$ to the second largest and so on, such that the smallest output receives a value of zero.

The values are summed for each classifier and the one with the largest sum is elected.

We define the function $r(o_{j,i}) : H \times H \mapsto \{1, \ldots, k - 1\}$ that gives the rank of $o_{j,i}$.

The total value assigned to classifier g_i is

$$BC_i = \sum_{j \in H_i} (k - 1 - r(o_{j,n})) \qquad (11)$$

The event F_i is thus $F_i = \{BC_i = \max_{j \in H} BC_j\}$.

3.3 Fuzzy Vote

In this case, the elected classifier is the one with the largest summation over all values of the votes $o_{j,i}$.

We define

$$S_i = \sum_{j \in H_i} o_{j,i} \tag{12}$$

In this case, the event F_i comes as $F_i = \{S_i = \max_{j \in H} S_j\}$.

3.4 Nash Vote

Nash vote is similar to fuzzy vote but instead of having a sum of the $o_{j,i}$ we have the product.

We define

$$Pd_i = \prod_{j \in H_i} o_{j,i} \tag{13}$$

In this case, we have $F_i = \{Pd_i = \max_{j \in H} Pd_j\}$.

4 Experiments

4.1 A 17 Class Artificial Problem

An artificial problem with 2 features and 17 classes that are roughly clustered in 5 groups was produced. The classes were generated using Gaussian distributions. The data is plotted in figure 2. Each class has 150 data points, hence, the data set has 2550 data points.

The CMNN architecture consists of 5 MLPs with topologies [2:22:7] for the 3 groups with 3 classes (the other 4 outputs are for the voting scheme) and [2:20:8] for the 2 groups with 4 classes (again using 4 outputs for the voting scheme). The voting strategy used was the plurality vote. We trained a single multi-layer perceptron (MLP) with the same number of weights as the CMNN architecture (topology [2:56:17]) to give an idea of the improvement that can be obtained with the CMNN over a single MLP. Since both the CMNN and the MLP use the same number of weights, the differences of performance are related to the way the weights are connected and not to their number. All networks were trained using resilient back-propagation for 100 epochs.

Table 1 presents the average classification error and standard deviation, both in percentage, for the 10 repetitions of the leave-k-out cross-validation, with $k = 255$.

Notice that there is a third line in the table for an CMNN-IV. This is the same as the CMNN but assuming that the voting was ideal, i.e., that the experts always made the correct choice of the expert that should made the final decision.

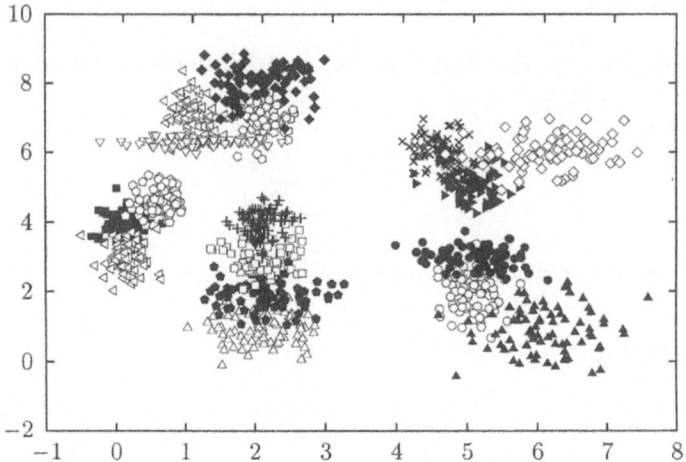

Fig. 2. The data set for the artificial problem

Table 1. Average classification errors and corresponding standard deviations, for the artificial problem

Architecture	Error [%]	St. Dev. [%]
MLP	17.61	2.95
CMNN	14.55	3.26
CMNN-IV	13.80	3.22

It has slight better performance than the CMNN giving an idea of the error introduced by the voting scheme, which is about 0.75%.

During testing, the values of $P(D_i)$ and $P(F_i)$ were estimated. These values were then used with the model for the PCC, yielding the value of 86.44%. This is equivalent to an error of 100-86.44=13.56% . This is in good agreement with the obtained value of 14.55% error for the CMNN (the difference is 0.89% out of 14.55%), thus asserting that the model developed is accurate.

4.2   A 2 Group, 4 Class Real Problem

To test the prediction capabilities of our bounds on real problems we used a data set for a vowel discrimination problem. The data consists of the first and second formants of the vowels 'i','I','a' and 'A' produced by 76 speakers (33 males, 28 females and 15 children). Each vowel was repeated twice by each speaker, giving a total number of 608 data points. It is a subset of the Peterson and Barney data set referred in [3] and is represented in figure 3. Both features were linearly scaled by dividing by 1000.

The CMNN architecture consists of 2 multi-layer perceptrons (MLPs) with topologies [2:15:3] - 2 outputs for each class in each group and the other for

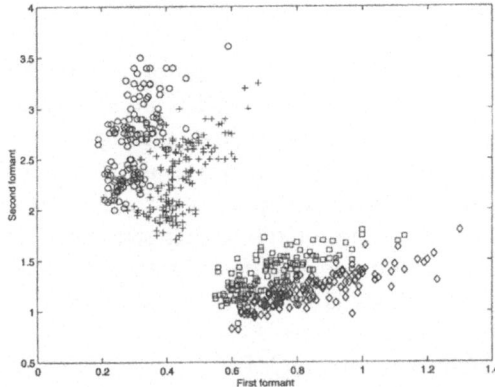

Fig. 3. Data set for a 4 class, 2 group problem

Table 2. Average classification errors and corresponding standard deviations, for the real problem

Architecture	Error [%]	St. Dev. [%]
MLP	6.41	2.04
CMNN	8.39	3.22
CMNN-IV	8.22	2.88

the output used for the voting strategy. The voting strategy used was again the plurality vote. We trained a single multi-layer perceptron (MLP) with the same number of weights as the CMNN architecture (topology [2:26:4]) to give an idea of the improvement that can be obtained with the CMNN over a single MLP. The networks were again trained using resilient back-propagation for 100 epochs. Table 2 presents the average classification error and standard deviation, both in percentage, for the 8 repetitions of the leave-k-out cross-validation, with $k = 76$.

The CMNN-IV has again, and as expected, a slight better performance than the CMNN. In this case, the error introduced by the voting scheme against the CMNN with the ideal voting scheme is 0.17%.

With the estimated values of $P(D_i)$ and $P(F_i)$ replaced in the model, we obtain an estimate for the PCC of 91.64%. This is equivalent to an error of 100-91.64=8.36% . This is again in good agreement with the obtained value of 8.39% error for the CMNN. Once again the model for the PCC yields a good estimate: the difference of the estimate to the true value is only 0.03%.

In this case the MLP outperformed the CMNN. We believe that this happened because the problem was too simple for the CMNN. Some of the weights used in the voting scheme were better used by the MLP in approximating the problem as a whole.

5 Conclusions

This paper presents a model for the probability of correct classification for the cooperative modular neural network (CMNN) architecture. The validity of the presented model was confirmed by experiments using both artificial and real data sets. Its predictions of the CMNN error rates, using some estimated parameters from the data sets, were in good accordance with the empirical errors.

The error introduced by one of the voting strategies, the plurality vote, as compared with the ideal vote was also investigated. We concluded that the error the voting scheme introduces is small when compared with the error of the experts in their subproblems.

Finally, a multilayer perceptron (MLP) with equal number of weights as the CMNN was used. This makes the differences in accuracy of these two classifiers to be only due to the way the weights are connected and not to their number. The results suggest that the CMNN produces better results with problems involving several groups, i.e., if the problem is simple, a simple architecture should be used.

References

1. Auda, G., Kamel, M.: Modular neural network classifiers: A comparative study. J. Intel. Robotic Systems (1998) 117–129
2. De Bollivier, M., Gallinari, P., Thiria, S.: Cooperation of neural nets and task decomposition. In: Int. Joint Conf. on Neural Networks. Volume 2., Seattle, USA (1991) 573–576
3. Jacobs, R., Jordan, M., Nowlan, S., Hinton, G.: Adaptive mixtures of local experts. Neural Computation (1991) 79–87
4. Jacobs, R., Peng, F., Tanner, M.: A bayesian approach to model selection in hierarchical mixtures-of-experts architectures. Neural Networks **10** (1997) 231–241
5. Wanas, N., Kamel, M., Auda, G., Karray, F.: Feature-based decision aggregation in modular neural network classifiers. Pattern Recognition Letters **20** (1999) 1353–1359
6. Alexandre, L., Campilho, A., Kamel, M.: Combining independent and unbiased classifiers using weighted average. In: Proceedings of the 15th International Conference on Pattern Recognition. Volume 2., Barcelona, Spain, IEEE Press (2000) 495–498
7. Alexandre, L., Campilho, A., Kamel, M.: On combining classifiers using sum and product rules. Pattern Recognition Letters **22** (2001) 1283–1289
8. Kittler, J., Hatef, M., Duin, R., Matas, J.: On combining classifiers. IEEE Trans. PAMI **20** (1998) 226–239
9. Auda, G., Kamel, M.: CMNN: Cooperative modular neural networks for pattern recognition. Pattern Recognition Letters **18** (1997) 1391–1398
10. Auda, G., Kamel, M., Raafat, H.: Voting schemes for cooperative neural network classifiers. In: IEEE Int. Conference on Neural Networks. Volume 3., Australia (1995) 1240–1243

Robust Learning Algorithm
for the Mixture of Experts*

Héctor Allende[1], Romina Torres[1,3], Rodrigo Salas[1], and Claudio Moraga[2]

[1] Universidad Técnica Federico Santa María; Dept. de Informática;
Casilla 110-V; Valparaíso-Chile
{hallende,romina,rsalas}@inf.utfsm.cl
[2] University of Dortmund; Department of Computer Science;
D-44221 Dortmund; Germany;
moraga@cs.uni-dortmund.de
[3] Global Software Group – Chile, Motorola

Abstract. The Mixture of Experts model (ME) is a type of modular artificial neural network (MANN) whose architecture is composed by different kinds of networks who compete to learn different aspects of the problem. This model is used when the searching space is stratified. The learning algorithm of the ME model consists in estimating the network parameters to achieve a desired performance. To estimate the parameters, some distributional assumptions are made, so the learning algorithm and, consequently, the parameters obtained depends on the distribution. But when the data is exposed to outliers the assumption is not longer valid, the model is affected and is very sensible to the data as it is showed in this work. We propose a robust learning estimator by means of the generalization of the maximum likelihood estimator called M-estimator. Finally a simulation study is shown, where the robust estimator presents a better performance than the maximum likelihood estimator (MLE).

Keywords: Artificial Neural Networks, Mixtures of Experts, Robust Learning.

1   Introduction

Artificial Neural Networks (ANN) are a very useful and important model with many applications in a broad field, they have been very successful in areas like classification, diagnosis, regression, compression, feature selection, time series modeling, and others. ANN are capable of modeling many non-linear functions. Some of the task cannot be modeled by a single network and it is very difficult to incorporate an a priori knowledge of the problem.

The brain is formed by a collection of modules, where each one is specialized to an specific function. This theory has two important hypothesis: there

---

* This work was supported in part by Research Grant Fondecyt 1010101 and 7010101, in part by Research Grant CHL-99/023 from the German Ministry of Education and Research (BMBF) and in part by Research Grant DGIP-UTFSM

F.J. Perales et al. (Eds.): IbPRIA 2003, LNCS 2652, pp. 19–27, 2003.

exists a correspondence between structure and function, i.e., there exist diverse structural regions in the brain, where the function takes place. The second hypothesis considers that different brain regions compete for the capacity of doing some task. So, different regions of the brain become very specialize in the task where its structure is more adequate [5].

Based on this idea, a modular architecture known as Mixture of Experts (ME) was developed by Jacobs, Jordan, Nowlan and Hinton [6]. This Architecture consists of two types of neural networks with different functions, the experts and the gating neural network. The experts networks compete for the learning of the training data and the gating network decides which expert networks are more capable to model the pattern. The learning process of the ME model combines associative and competitive aspects of the learning.

The learning problem can be seen as a parameter estimation problem based on the gradient ascent algorithms. An alternative method to estimate the maximum likelihood (ML-estimate) was presented by Jordan and Jacobs [8]. They introduced an expectation maximization algorithm (EM) for the ME models.

There are several factors affecting ML-estimate. First of all, the selection of training samples as initial estimates can affect the convergence to a great extent. Another factor that affects the performance of the ML-estimate is the presence of statistical outliers. Statistical outliers are defined as those observations that are substantially different from the distributions of the mixture models. The problem of outliers is not uncommon in practical applications. For example, in remote sensing, a scene usually contains pixel of unknown origin which form "information noise", the statistical distributions of theses pixels may be significantly different from those of training classes and constitute statistical outliers.

Unfortunately, the ME models are very sensitive to the presence of the outliers as it is shown in this work, motivating the research of robustness for this models. We propose to robustify the learning process of the ME models by using a special function that is insensible to the presence of outliers in the model's parameter estimation process.

In recent years there have been studies on Robustness of feedforward artificial neural networks, [1], [2]) but the authors are unaware of the existence of any study of the robustness of the ME models, in particular, when the estimation is based on the M-estimators.

2   Mixture of Experts Models Architecture

The modular architecture, specified in [7], consists in K modules called *experts* or *local experts*, where each one solves an approximation problem over a local region of the input space. Each expert has a probability model that associated an input vector $\underline{x} \in \mathbb{R}^n$ with an output vector $\underline{y} \in \mathbb{R}^m$, $P(\underline{y}|\underline{x}, \underline{w}_j)$, $\quad j = 1, 2, \ldots K$, where $\underline{w}_j$ represents the parameter of the expert j.

Consider the figure 1, where each expert ε_i generates the output $\underline{\mu}_i = f(\underline{x}, \underline{w}_i)$ with probability $P(\underline{y}|\underline{x}, \underline{w}_i)$, where $\underline{\mu}_i$ is the conditional expectation, $\underline{\mu}_i = E[\underline{y}|\underline{x}, \underline{w}_i]$ under the probability model $P(\underline{y}|\underline{x}, \underline{w}_i)$.

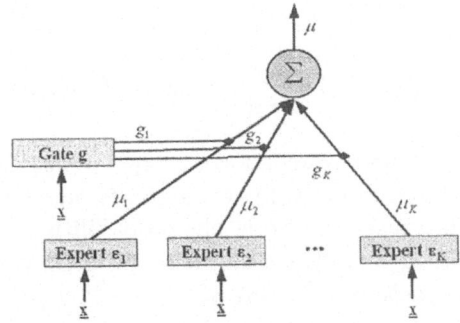

Fig. 1. Mixtures of Experts Architecture (ME): This architecture consists in a set of experts networks and a gating network. The experts compete for the learning of the problem and the gating mediates the competence

We suppose that different kinds of neural networks are appropriate in different regions of the domain space, so such form that the architecture needs a mechanism to identify for each input $\underline{x}$ which experts are more adequate to model the desire output. This is done by a gating network, which divides the input space in regions by a set of scalar coefficients g_i (output of the gating network) which depends on the input $\underline{x}$, and the output is the mixture of the contribution of each expert. There exists a probability vector $[g_1, g_2, \ldots, g_K]^T$ for each data point of the input space. Generally, the network implements a parameterized function $\xi(\underline{x}, \eta)$ and a normalize function $g_i(\xi)$ which maps from $\mathbb{R}^K$ to $\mathbb{R}^K$. The objective is to force the probability restrictions as was presented in [6], where a *softmax* function was used given by $g_i = \frac{\exp \xi_i}{\sum_j \exp \xi_j}$. So, it is easy to check that the g_i's are non-negative and their sum is one. The probabilistic interpretation of the ξ_i is that they are discriminant surfaces for a classification problem and the gating network is a *classification* system which maps the input $\underline{x}$ to the probabilities of some experts being able to generate the desire output (based only on the knowledge of $\underline{x}$), where $g_i \geq 0$ and $\sum_{i=1}^{K} g_i = 1$.

2.1   Mixture of Experts Model Specification

Assuming that the training set $\chi = \{(\underline{x}^{(n)}, \underline{y}^{(n)})\}_{n=1}^{N}$ is generated by the following procedure: given a data point $\underline{x}$, an expert ε_i is chosen with probability $P(\varepsilon_i | \underline{x}, \eta^*)$, given the expert ε_i and the input $\underline{x}$, it is assumed that the desired output $\underline{y}$ is generated with probability $P(\underline{y} | \underline{x}, \underline{w}_i^*)$. The data is assumed to be independent and identically distributed.

The *experts* model different processes and the *gating* network models the decision of using some of these different processes. The output $\underline{y}$ can be generated by the total probability of y given $\underline{x}$ obtained by the sum of the weighted contribution of all experts ε_i:

$$P(\underline{y}|\underline{x}, \underline{\Theta}^*) = \sum_{i=1}^{K} P(\varepsilon_i|\underline{x}, \underline{\eta}^*) P(\underline{y}|\underline{x}, \underline{w}_i^*) \tag{1}$$

where $\underline{\Theta}^*$ denotes the true parameter vector ($\underline{\Theta}^* = [\underline{w}_1^{*T}, \underline{w}_2^{*T}, \ldots, \underline{w}_K^{*T}, \underline{\eta}^{*T}]^T$). The density in the equation (1) is known as *finite mixture density*.

The gating network task is to model the probabilities $P(\varepsilon_i|\underline{x}, \underline{\eta}^*)$, constructed as a probability class in a multi-classification problem of the input $\underline{x}$, parameterizing by softmax function obtaining $g_i^* = P(\varepsilon_i|\underline{x}, \underline{\eta}^*)$.

The moments of the mixture density are directly calculated. The conditional media $\underline{\mu}^* = E[\underline{y}|\underline{x}, \underline{\Theta}^*]$ is obtained by taking the expectation of the equation (1),

$$\underline{\mu}^* = \sum_i g_i^* \underline{\mu}_i^* \tag{2}$$

where $\underline{\mu}_i^*$ is the conditional media associated to the probability distribution $P(\underline{y}|\underline{x}, \underline{w}_i^*)$ corresponding to the experts output ε_i. The modular architecture output is a weighted sum of the experts output.

3   Learning Algorithm

The learning problem is treated as parameter estimation process of the ME architecture. The parameters are chosen in the way that they maximize the joint probability given in the equation (1). This process is known as maximum likelihood estimation (MLE). The data of the learning set χ are assumed to be generated independently by the mixture density. The likelihood function of the learning set for a specific sample vector $\chi = \{(\underline{x}^{(n)}, \underline{y}^{(n)})\}_{n=1}^{N}$ is given by

$$L(\chi, \underline{\Theta}) = P(\{\underline{y}^{(n)}\}_1^N | \{\underline{x}^{(n)}\}_1^N) = \begin{array}{l} \prod_{n=1}^{N} P(\underline{y}^{(n)}|\underline{x}^{(n)}) \\ \prod_{n=1}^{N} \sum_{i=1}^{K} g_i(\underline{x}, \underline{\eta}) P(\underline{y}^{(n)}|\underline{x}^{(n)}, \underline{w}_i) \end{array} \tag{3}$$

The MLE consists in maximize the equation (3) or equivalently, maximize the log-likelihood

$$l(\chi, \underline{\Theta}) = \sum_{n=1}^{N} \log \sum_{i=1}^{K} g_i(\underline{x}, \underline{\eta}) P(\underline{y}^{(n)}|\underline{x}^{(n)}, \underline{w}_i) \tag{4}$$

To estimate the ME model parameters $\underline{\Theta}^*$, techniques based on gradient ascent are applied (see [6] and [7]). An alternative method is the algorithm of expectation maximization (EM) that was generalized to the ME architecture by Jordan y Jacobs in [8]. This algorithm is very useful to Models where the experts and the gating networks have a simple parametric form.

4 Robust Learning Algorithm

The learning process of the ME model is done by means of the maximum likelihood estimator (MLE) described by the equation (3).

The robust learning process based on the random sample $\{(\underline{x}^{(n)}, \underline{y}^{(n)})\}_{n=1}^{N}$ with common distribution $P(\underline{y}|\underline{x})$, consists in minimizing the functional cost given by the equation (5) to find the parameter M-estimator $\hat{\underline{\Theta}}_{N}^{M}$ of the parameters $\underline{\Theta}^{*}$ in the ME model by the equation (6).

$$
\begin{aligned}
RL_N(\chi, \underline{\Theta}) &= \sum_{n=1}^{N} \rho(\underline{y}^{(n)}, \underline{\Theta}|\underline{x}^{(n)}) \\
&= \sum_{n=1}^{N} \rho\left(\sum_{i=1}^{K} g_i(\underline{x}, \underline{\eta}) P(\underline{y}^{(n)}|\underline{x}^{(n)}, \underline{w}_i) \right)
\end{aligned}
\tag{5}
$$

$$
\hat{\underline{\Theta}}_{N}^{M} = \arg\min_{\underline{\Theta} \in \mathbb{R}^d} \{RL_N(\chi, \underline{\Theta})\}
\tag{6}
$$

where ρ is the robust function that introduces a bound to the influence due to the presence of the outlier in the data.

Assuming that ρ is differentiable whose derivative is given by $\psi(y, \underline{\Theta}|\underline{x}) = \frac{\partial \rho(y, \underline{\Theta}|\underline{x})}{\partial \underline{\Theta}}$, or, alternatively, the estimated parameter can be obtained by solving the first order equation:

$$
\sum_{n=1}^{N} \psi(\underline{y}^{(n)}, \hat{\underline{\Theta}}_{N}^{M}|\underline{x}) = \sum_{n=1}^{N} \psi\left(\sum_{i=1}^{K} g_i(\underline{x}, \underline{\eta}) P(\underline{y}^{(n)}|\underline{x}^{(n)}, \underline{w}_i) \right) = \underline{0}
\tag{7}
$$

4.1 Selecting the Robust Function

In [4] some special functions for M-estimation are discussed. The goal is to weight each observation according to the magnitude of likelihood evaluated at the observation. Samples with low likelihood are likely to be regarded as outliers and are downweighted. In particular, for the location problem, data that are far away must have a bounded impact in the estimation algorithm, so there are several functions that can be use, for example the Huber function given by

$$
\rho_H(z) = \begin{cases} z + \frac{1}{2}\log(2\pi) & \text{if } z \geq \frac{1}{2}(-k^2 - \log(2\pi)) \\ -k\{-2z - \log(2\pi)\}^{\frac{1}{2}} - \frac{1}{2}k^2 & \text{otherwise} \end{cases}
\tag{8}
$$

$$
\psi_H(z) = \begin{cases} 1 & \text{if } z \geq \frac{1}{2}(-k^2 - \log(2\pi)) \\ k\{-2z - \log(2\pi)\}^{-\frac{1}{2}} & \text{otherwise} \end{cases}
\tag{9}
$$

where z is the log-likelihood given by the equation (4) evaluated at the point $(\underline{x}, \underline{y})$.

4.2 Robust Learning Algorithm Based on the Gradient Techniques

To obtain the neural networks parameters, the function given by the equation (5) must be minimized through a neural network learning process. In this work gradient descent is applied to minimize the equation (5).

Let $\zeta = \sum_i g_i(\underline{x}, \eta) P(\underline{y}^{(n)}|\underline{x}^{(n)}, \underline{w}_i)$, so by taking derivatives of $RL_N(\Theta)$ with respect to $\underline{\mu}_i$ and ξ_i, the following expression are obtained:

$$
\begin{aligned}
\frac{\partial RL_N(\Theta)}{\partial \mu_i} &= \sum_n \psi(\zeta) g_i P(\underline{y}^{(n)}|\underline{x}^{(n)}, \underline{w}_i) \frac{\partial}{\partial \mu_i} \ln\left\{ (P(\underline{y}^{(n)}|\underline{x}^{(n)}, \underline{w}_i) \right\} \\
\frac{\partial RL_N(\Theta)}{\partial \xi_i} &= \sum_n \psi(\zeta) g_i \left\{ P(\underline{y}^{(n)}|\underline{x}^{(n)}, \underline{w}_i) - \sum_k g_k P(\underline{y}^{(n)}|\underline{x}^{(n)}, \underline{w}_k) \right\}
\end{aligned}
\tag{10}
$$

where $\psi = \frac{\partial \rho}{\partial \zeta}$, g_i is the softmax function, and

$$
\frac{\partial g_k}{\partial \xi_i} = \begin{cases}
-\frac{\exp \xi_k \exp \xi_i}{(\sum_j \exp\{\xi_j\})^2} = -g_k g_i & if \ i \neq k \\
g_i - \left(\frac{\exp \xi_i}{\sum_j \exp\{\xi_j\}} \right)^2 = g_i - g_i^2 \ if \ i = k
\end{cases}
\tag{11}
$$

The parameter estimation problem in ME-models has been addressed in [9], [11] and [12], in particular they considered that, the experts and the gating networks are linear. Furthermore the ME-models is assumed with multidimensional Gaussian conditional densities, in this case, the conditional density satisfy:
$P(\underline{y}|\underline{x}, \underline{w}_i) = \frac{1}{(2\pi)^{m/2}|\Sigma_i|^{1/2}} \exp\{-\frac{1}{2}(\underline{y}^{(n)} - \underline{\mu}_i)^T \Sigma_i^{-1}(\underline{y}^{(n)} - \underline{\mu}_i)\}$,
where $\underline{\mu}_i = f(\underline{x}, \underline{w}_i) = \underline{w}_i^T \underline{x}$ is the output of the i-th expert. The gating network is also considered linear, $\xi = \eta^T \underline{x}$, and then a softmax function is applied to obtain the output of this network that weight the experts output. When the covariance matrix is the identity matrix $\Sigma_i = I$, the conditional distribution is $P(\underline{y}|\underline{x}, \underline{w}_i) = \frac{1}{(2\pi)^{m/2}} \exp\{-\frac{(\underline{y}-\underline{\mu}_i)^T(\underline{y}-\underline{\mu}_i)}{2}\}$. Finally by using gradient ascent in the functional cost, we obtain the parameter update of the net given by the following expression:

$$
\begin{aligned}
\Delta \underline{w}_i &= \alpha \psi(\zeta) g_i \frac{1}{(2\pi)^{m/2}} \exp\left\{ -\frac{(\underline{y}^{(n)}-\underline{\mu}_i)^T(\underline{y}^{(n)}-\underline{\mu}_i)}{2} \right\} (\underline{y}^{(n)} - \underline{\mu}_i) \underline{x}^{(n)T} \\
\Delta \underline{\eta}_i &= \alpha \psi(\zeta) g_i \left\{ P(\underline{y}^{(n)}|\underline{x}^{(n)}, \underline{w}_i) - \sum_k g_k P(\underline{y}^{(n)}|\underline{x}^{(n)}, \underline{w}_k) \right\} \underline{x}^{(n)T}
\end{aligned}
\tag{12}
$$

where α is the learning rate.

5 Simulations Results Applied to the Building Data

The robust learning of the ME models where evaluated on a real life data consisting on a prediction problem. The *Building2* data set was obtained from the

Table 1. Results obtained for the ME and robust ME models for the second experiment

#experts	Train. ME	Train. robust ME	Test ME	Test robust ME
3	0.0081	0.0037	0.0082	0.0042
4	0.0069	0.0036	0.0076	0.0040
10	0.0039	0.0034	0.0043	0.0038
20	0.0036	0.0034	0.0040	0.0038
25	0.0035	0.0034	0.0039	0.0038
30	0.0034	0.0035	0.0039	0.0039

PROBEN1 benchmark set [10]. The problem is to predict the hourly consumption of electrical energy, hot water, and cold water, based on the date, day of the week, time of day, outside temperature, outside air humidity, solar radiation, and wind speed. The data set is spread over six month from September to February. So, the input vector is dimension 14 and the output vector is 3. The data consists in 4208 samples.

The experiment consisted in that the data set was divided in three groups: the learning set with 1462 samples, the validation set with 1464 samples and the test set with 1282 samples. The performance of the networks obtained was evaluated by using the mean square error (MSE). The importance of this experiment is that the learning and the validation sets belong to different phase of the year (Winter - Spring). The results obtained are shown in the table 1 for the ME, using the classical MLE for the learning algorithm, and robust ME models, using the Huber function introduced in the subsection 4.1.

As can be observed, the robust ME model outperforms the model proposed in [11], it is shown that MELG obtained a MSE of 0.0072. The mean square error for the ME model is correlated to the number of experts, if the number of experts is increased, the MSE decreased. In [11] it is shown that the number of experts can be found in an adaptive form, but this algorithm is time consuming and depends on the initialization.

For the robust ME model, empirically can be seen that with a robust learning the model complexity is lower, because the number of experts needed to obtain a desire performance is much less than the classical ME model as can be appreciated in the figure 2.

6 Concluding Remarks

In this work it is shown that the ME models with robust learning outperforms the results presented in similar works where ME models based on the gradient ascend techniques were used. On the other side, we extend our comparative study to the localized ME model for the gating network, by showing that if the *softmax* function is used, then the function is decomposed in different soft regions in the way that each expert network models some region. For the experiments studied

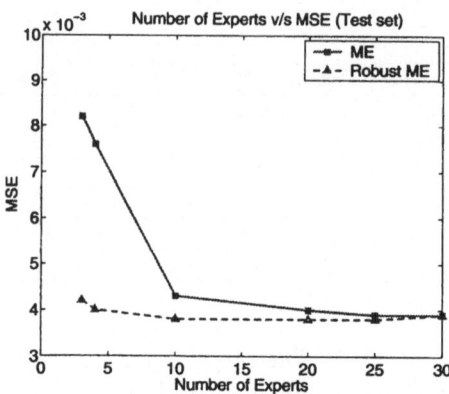

Fig. 2. Number of Experts vs. MSE

in this work, it is not necessary to introduce more complexity by using localized model with robust learning, because less numbers of experts are required to obtain a desired performance, and the convergence of the learning algorithm is faster.

It may be observed that, from the point of view of Fuzzy logic, the weighted sum (of experts outputs), if normalized, represents a form of aggregation (see e.g. [3]). This suggest the possibility to generalize the ME model by considering other aggregation operations and evaluating their performance.

References

[1] H. Allende, C. Moraga, and R. Salas. Neural model identification using local robustness analysis. *Lecture Notes in Computer Science. Fuzzy Days 2001*, 2206:162–173, Nov 2001.

[2] H. Allende, C. Moraga, and R. Salas. Robust estimator for the learning process in neural networks applied in time series. *LNCS*, 2415:1080–1086, Aug 2002.

[3] D. Dubois and H. Prade. A review of fuzzy set aggregation connectives. *Information Sciences*, 36:85–121, 1985.

[4] F. R. Hampel, E. M. Ronchetti, P. J. Rousseeuw, and W. A. Stahel. *Robust Statistics*. Wiley Series in Probability and Mathematical Statistics, 1986.

[5] R. A. Jacobs. Computational studies of the development of functionally specialized neural modules. *Trends in Cognitive Science*, 3(1):31–38, 1999.

[6] R. A. Jacobs, M. I. Jordan, S. J. Nowlan, and G. E. Hinton. Adaptive mixtures of local experts. *Neural Computation*, 3(1):79–87, 1991.

[7] M. Jordan and R. Jacobs. *Modular and hierarchical learning systems, The Handbook of Brain Theory and Neural Networks, Cambridge, MA*, volume 1. MIT Press, 1999.

[8] M. I. Jordan and R. A. Jacobs. Hierarchical mixtures of experts and the EM algorithm. *Neural Computation*, 6(2):181–214, 1994.

[9] P. Moerland. Mixtures of experts estimate a posteriori probabilities. *Proc. International Conference on Artificial Neural Networks ICANN-97, Laussanne Switzerland*, pages 499–504, 1997.

[10] L. Prechelt. Proben1 – a set of benchmarks and benchmarking rules for neural training algorithms. *Technical Report 21/94, Fakultaet fur Informatik, Universitaet Karlsruhe, D-76128 Karlsruhe, Germany*, September 1994.

[11] V. Ramamurti and J. Ghosh. Structurally adaptive localized mixtures of experts for non-stationary enviroments. Technical report, University of Texas at Austin, Austin, TX 78712-1084, 1996.

[12] S. Tadjudin and D. Landgrebe. Robust parameter estimation for mixture model. *IEEE Trans. on Geoscience and remote sensing*, 8(1):439–445, 2000.

A Robust and Effective Learning Algorithm for Feedforward Neural Networks Based on the Influence Function*

Héctor Allende[1,3], Rodrigo Salas[1], and Claudio Moraga[2]

[1] Universidad Técnica Federico Santa María
Dept. de Informática;
Casilla 110-V; Valparaíso-Chile;
{hallende, rsalas}@inf.utfsm.cl
[2] University of Dortmund; Department of Computer Science;
D-44221 Dortmund; Germany; moraga@cs.uni-dortmund.de
[3] Universidad Adolfo Ibañez; Facultad de Ciencia y Tecnología

Abstract. The learning process of the Feedforward Artificial Neural Networks relies on the data, though a robustness analysis of the parameter estimates of the model must be done due to the presence of outlying observations in the data. In this paper we seek the robust properties in the parameter estimates in the sense that the influence of aberrant observations or outliers in the estimate is bounded so the neural network is able to model the bulk of data. We also seek a trade off between robustness and efficiency under a Gaussian model. An adaptive learning procedure that seeks both aspects is developed. Finally we show some simulations results applied to the RESEX time series.
KEYWORDS: Feedforward Artificial Neural Networks, Robust Learning, Effective parameter estimate.

1 Introduction

In the last decades there have been a widespread interest in the use of artificial neural networks (ANN) in many different problems ranging from pattern classification to control engineering. A very important and widely applicable class of ANN models are the feedforward artificial neural networks (FANN) because they have been remarked as universal approximators of continous, bounded, nonlinear functions that can be trained from examples of input-output data.

The ANN are seen by researches as either highly parameterized models or nonparametric structures. ANN models are flexible, and have a demonstrated success in a variety of applications in which linear models fail to perform well. A statistical analysis has been made by considering ANN as nonlinear regression models and by casting network learning as a statistical estimation problem [6], [10].

* This work was supported in part by Research Grant Fondecyt 1010101 and 7010101, in part by Research Grant DGIP-UTFSM, and in part by Research Grant CHL-99/023 from the German Ministry of Education and Research (BMBF).

F.J. Perales et al. (Eds.): IbPRIA 2003, LNCS 2652, pp. 28–36, 2003.

The learning algorithm for the parameters estimation of the neural model relies on the data. When the data are contaminated with outliers, for example, observations that are substantially different to the bulk of data due to gross errors, they can influence badly bringing degradation in the estimates [1], [2], [5]. Full effectiveness can be achieved only when the data agree with the assumptions underlying the data generating process but not when deviations from them occurs (See [8]), aspect widely investigated in statistics, but very poorly in the ANN literature [2], [3], [4], [5]. In this work we seek a compromise in terms of statistical efficiency and robustness of learning procedures by applying M estimators introduced by Huber [8].

This paper is organized as follows. In section 2, we introduce the notation and architecture of the feedforward neural networks (FANN). In section 3, we develop a robust analysis of the Learning Algorithm for the FANN, and then we propose a robust and effective estimator for the FANN parameters (weights). We will give simulation results in section 4 where the procedure is applied to Time Series modeling, and a comparative analysis based on the performance of the different learning algorithms is made. Concluding remarks and future extensions are presented in section 5.

2   Feedforward Artificial Neural Networks

A FANN consists of elementary processing elements called neurons, organized in three type of layers, the input, the output and the hidden layers, where the latter is located between the input and the output layers. The number of input and output units are determined by the application. The links of the neurons are from one layer to the successive without any type of bridge, lateral or feedback connections. For simplicity, a single-hidden-layer architecture is considered in this paper, consisting in only one hidden layer and one output neuron, this class of neural models can be specified by the number of hidden neurons by $S_\lambda = \{g_\lambda(\underline{x}, \underline{w}) \in \mathbb{R}, \ \underline{x} \in \mathbb{R}^m, \ \underline{w} \in \mathcal{W}\}$, where $\mathcal{W} \subseteq \mathbb{R}^d$, $g_\lambda(\underline{x}, \underline{w})$ is a non-linear function of $\underline{x}$ with $\underline{w} = (w_1, w_2, ..., w_d)^T$ being its parameter vector, λ is the number of the hidden neurons and $d = (m + 2)\lambda + 1$ is the number of free parameters. The results presented in this paper can be easily extended to FANN with a higher number of layers and output neurons.

Given the sample of observations, the task of neural learning is to construct an estimator $g_\lambda(\underline{x}, \underline{w})$ of the unknown function $\varphi(\underline{x})$ by

$$\hat{y} = g_\lambda(\underline{x}, \underline{w}) = \gamma_2 \left(\sum_{j=1}^{\lambda} w_j^{[2]} \gamma_1 \left(\sum_{i=1}^{m} w_{ij}^{[1]} x_i + w_{m+1,j}^{[1]} \right) + w_{\lambda+1}^{[2]} \right) \qquad (1)$$

where $\underline{w}$ is a parameter vector to be estimated, γ'_s are linearity or non-linearity and λ is a control parameter (number of hidden units). An important factor in the specification of neural models is the choice of the 'activation' function γ'_s, these can be any non-linearity as long as they are continuous, bounded and differentiable. The activation function of the hidden neurons γ_1 typically is a squashing or a radial basis function. A special type of squashing function is the logistic function $\gamma_1(z) = [1 + exp\{-z\}]^{-1}$ and is one of the most commonly used. For the output neuron the function γ_2 could be a linear function $f(z) = z$, or squashing function.

The estimated parameter $\hat{w}_n^{LS}$ is obtained from the sample $\{\underline{x}^t, y_t\}_{t=1..n}$ of size n by minimizing iteratively a loss function $L_n(\underline{w})$, given for example by the ordinary least squares function (2). The loss function gives us a measure of accuracy with which the estimated model fits the observed data.

$$L_n(\underline{w}) = \frac{1}{2n} \sum_{t=1}^{n} \left(y_t - g_\lambda(\underline{x}^t, \underline{w})\right)^2 \tag{2}$$

3 Robust Analysis of FANN

In some earlier works is shown that FANN models are affected with the presence of outlying observations, in the way that the learning process and the prediction have a very poor performance (See [2], [5], [9]).

Let the data set $\chi = \{\underline{x}^t, y_t\}_{t=1..n}$ consists of an independent and identically distributed (i.i.d) sample of size n coming from the probability distribution $F(\underline{x}, y)$. A nonlinear function $y = \varphi(\underline{x})$ is approximated from the data by a feedforward artificial neural network, i.e., $y = g_\lambda(\underline{x}, \underline{w}^*) + r$, where $y \in \mathbb{R}$ is the desired output, $\underline{x} \in \mathbb{R}^m$ is the input vector, $\underline{w}^* \in W \subset \mathbb{R}^d$ is the unknown parameters vector and $r \in \mathbb{R}$ is the residual error.

Assuming that W is an open convex set and r_t are independent to the $\underline{x}^t$, $t = 1..n$, with symmetric density $h(r/\sigma_r)$, where $\sigma_r > 0$ is the scale parameter and $k(\underline{x})$ is the density function of the $\underline{x}$, then the joint density function $f(\underline{x}, y)$ is given by $f(\underline{x}, y) = \frac{1}{\sigma_r} h\left(\frac{y - g_\lambda(\underline{x}, \hat{w}_n)}{\sigma_r}\right) k(\underline{x})$.

An M-estimator $\hat{w}_n^M$ is defined by $\hat{w}_n^M = arg\ min\{RL_n(\underline{w}) : \underline{w} \in W\}, W \subseteq \mathbb{R}^d$, where $RL_n(\underline{w})$ is a robust functional cost given by the following equation,

$$RL_n(\underline{w}) = \frac{1}{n} \sum_{t=1}^{n} \rho\left(y_t - g_\lambda(\underline{x}^t, \underline{w})\right) \tag{3}$$

where ρ is the robust function that introduces a bound to the influence due to the presence of outliers in the data. Assuming that ρ is differentiable whose derivative is given by $\psi(r, \underline{w}) = \frac{\partial \rho(r, \underline{w})}{\partial r}$, an M-estimator $\hat{w}_n^M$ can be defined implicitly by the solution of the following equation,

$$\sum_{t=1}^{n} \psi\left(\frac{y_t - g_\lambda(\underline{x}_t, \underline{w})}{\sigma_r}\right) Dg_\lambda(\underline{x}_t, \underline{w}) = \underline{0} \tag{4}$$

where $\psi : \mathbb{R} \times \mathcal{W} \to \mathbb{R}$, $r_t = y_t - g_\lambda(\underline{x}^t, \hat{\underline{w}}_n^M)$ is the residual error and

$$Dg_\lambda(\underline{x}, \underline{w}) = \left(\frac{\partial}{\partial w_1} g_\lambda(\underline{x}, \underline{w}), \ldots, \frac{\partial}{\partial w_d} g_\lambda(\underline{x}, \underline{w}) \right)^T \qquad (5)$$

is the gradient of the FANN. We will denote $Dg_\lambda = Dg_\lambda(\underline{x}, \underline{w})$ for short.

3.1 The Influence Function of the M-estimator of the FANN

In order to study the robustness and effectiveness aspect of the M-estimator, we should analyze the *influence function* (IF) . The IF is a local measure introduced by Hampel [7] and describes the effect of an infinitesimal contamination at the point $(\underline{x}, y)$ on the estimate.

The IF of the M-estimator applied to the FANN model, $\hat{\underline{w}}_n^M$, and calculated at the distribution function $F(\underline{x}, y)$ is given by the following equation,

$$IF(\underline{x}, r; \underline{w}, F) = \psi(r, \underline{w}) M^{-1} Dg_\lambda(\underline{x}, \underline{w}) \qquad (6)$$

where r is the residual, $Dg_\lambda(\underline{x}, \underline{w})$ is given by equation (5) and

$$M = \int_{\mathbb{R}} (\psi'(r, \underline{w}) Dg_\lambda Dg_\lambda^T - \psi(r, \underline{w}) D^2 g_\lambda) dF(\underline{x}, y) = \mathbb{E}_F[H(r, \underline{x}, \underline{w})] \qquad (7)$$

where $H(r, \underline{x}, \underline{w}) = (\psi'(r, \underline{w}) Dg_\lambda Dg_\lambda^T - \psi(r, \underline{w}) D^2 g_\lambda)$ is the Hessian of $\rho(\cdot)$ with respect to the parameters $\underline{w}$ and $D^2 g_\lambda = [\frac{\partial^2 g_\lambda(\underline{x}, \underline{w})}{\partial w_i \partial w_j}]$ is the Hessian matrix of the FANN of side $d \times d$. In practice, M is not observable and must be estimated, White [10] demonstrated that a consistent estimator of M is $\hat{M}_n = \frac{1}{n} \sum_{t=1}^n H(r_t, \underline{x}_t, \hat{\underline{w}}_n^M)$, where $\hat{\underline{w}}_n^M$ are the parameters obtained from the data by the minimization of the risk function (3). With this result, we can estimate the influence at the point $(\underline{x}^*, y^*)$ by $\hat{IF}(\underline{x}^*, r^*; \hat{\underline{w}}_n^M) = \psi(r^*, \hat{\underline{w}}_n^M) \hat{M}_n^{-1} Dg_\lambda(\underline{x}^*, \hat{\underline{w}}_n^M)^T$.

3.2 Analyzing the Gaussian Case

As a special case we studied the case when the residual distribution is the standard normal, i.e., $h(r/\sigma_r) = \phi(r/\sigma_r)$, so the density function is given by $f(\underline{x}, y) = \phi(r/\sigma_r) k(\underline{x})$. If we assume a Gaussian model for the residuals and ψ is odd, then the second term in (7) can be neglected, so we get:

$$M = \mathbb{E}[\psi'] \mathbb{E}[Dg_\lambda Dg_\lambda^T] = \left(\int_{\mathbb{R}} \psi'(r) d\Phi(r) \right) \left(\int_{\mathbb{R}} Dg_\lambda Dg_\lambda^T dK(\underline{x}) \right) \qquad (8)$$

From the equation (6) and (8) we can realize that the IF can be decomposed as the product of two factors, one dependent on the residual known as *residual influence* (IR) and the *influence due to the position* (IP), obtaining the *total influence*:

$$IF(\underline{x}, r; \underline{w}, F) = IT(\underline{x}, r; \underline{w}, F) = IR(r; \underline{w}, \Phi) IP(\underline{x}; \underline{w}, K) \qquad (9)$$

where $IR(r; \underline{w}, \Phi) = \psi(r)/\mathbb{E}[\psi'(r)]$ and $IP(\underline{x}; \underline{w}, K) = (\mathbb{E}[Dg_\lambda Dg_\lambda^T])^{-1} Dg_\lambda$.

An important summary value based on the IF is the *gross error sensitivity* that measures the worst (approximate) influence which a small amount of contamination of fixed size can have on the value of the estimator. The gross outlier sensitivity is defined as $\gamma_u^*(\hat{\underline{w}}_n^M, F) := \sup_{\underline{x},r}\{\|IF(\underline{x}, r; \hat{\underline{w}}_n^M, F)\|\}$. It is a desirable feature that $\gamma_u^*(\hat{\underline{w}}_n^M, F)$ be finite obtaining a *B-robust* estimator.

In the Gaussian case, the gross error sensitivity is due to the residual and the position influence, i.e., $\gamma_u^*(\hat{\underline{w}}_n^M, F) = \sup_{\underline{x},r}\{|IR(r; \hat{\underline{w}}_n^M, \Phi)|\|IP(\underline{x}; \hat{\underline{w}}_n^M, K)\|\}$. When the classical Least Square estimator is used, the gross error sensitivity is $\gamma_u^*(\hat{\underline{w}}_n^{LS}, F) = \sup_{\underline{x},r}\{|r|\|IP(\underline{x}; \hat{\underline{w}}_n^{LS}, F)\|\} = \infty$, i.e., this procedure lacks of robustness by being sensible to the contamination in the residual error that relies on the data.

To obtain a B-robust estimator we analyzed the influence due to the position (IP) and the influence due to the residual (IR). The influence due to the position is bounded $(sup_{\underline{x}}\{\|IP(\underline{x}; \underline{w}, K)\|\} < \infty)$, when γ_1 is a logistic function and γ_2 is a logistic or a linear function, because the gradient of the FANN model, $Dg_\lambda(\underline{x}, \underline{w})$, has four types of derivatives:

$$\frac{\partial g_\lambda(\underline{x}, \hat{\underline{w}}_n)}{\partial w_{ij}^{[1]}} = \gamma_2'(\cdot) w_j^{[2]} \gamma_{1,j}'(\cdot) x_i, i = 1..m, j = 1..\lambda;$$

$$\frac{\partial g_\lambda(\underline{x}, \hat{\underline{w}}_n)}{\partial w_{m+1,j}^{[1]}} = \gamma_2'(\cdot) w_j^{[2]} \gamma_{1,j}'(\cdot), j = 1..\lambda;$$

$$\frac{\partial g_\lambda(\underline{x}, \hat{\underline{w}}_n)}{\partial w_j^{[2]}} = \gamma_2'(\cdot) \gamma_{1,j}(\cdot), j = 1..\lambda; \text{ and,}$$

$$\frac{\partial g_\lambda(\underline{x}, \hat{\underline{w}}_n)}{\partial w_{\lambda+1}^{[2]}} = \gamma_2'(\cdot),$$

because γ_2' is a constant if γ_2 is linear and $max_z\{\gamma_2'(z)\} = 0.25$ if γ_2 is a logistic function. Similarly for γ_1'. These factors decrease faster than x_i grows. The influence due to the residual must satisfy that $\sup_r\{|IR(r; \hat{\underline{w}}_n^M, \Phi)|\} = \sup_r\{|\psi(r)/\mathbb{E}[\psi'(r)]|\} < \infty$ to obtain a robust learning estimator that is insensible to the presence of outlying observations. For example the Huber and the Bisquare functions, given by equation (10) and (11) respectively, satisfy these requirements.

$$\psi_H(r, c) = sgn(r)min\{|r|, c\} \tag{10}$$

$$\psi_B(r, c) = \begin{cases} r(1 - (r/c)^2)^2 & r \in [-c, c] \\ 0 & r < -c \text{ or } r > c \end{cases} \tag{11}$$

By putting a bound on γ^* will often conflict with the aim of asymptotic effectiveness. In order to obtain an effective and robust estimator the value of the constant c of the $\psi - function$ should be estimated.

It is a well know fact that the LS estimator is the most effective estimator of the mean under a Gaussian model. By assuming that the residual has a distribution close to the Gaussian and outliers should appear in regions further than $3\sigma_r$. By assuming that $E[r] = 0$ and by considering a robust estimation of σ_r given by $\sigma_r = 1.483median\{|r - median\{r\}|\}$, we should look for a constant c such that the distance between $\psi_.(r^*, c)$ and $\psi_{LS}(r^*) = r^*$ is not bigger than

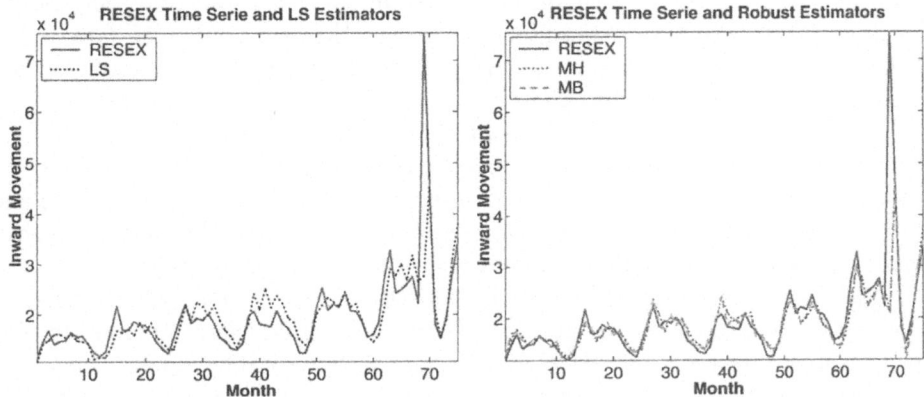

Fig. 1. a)(left) LS estimator. b)(right) Robust Learning Algorithm

a desired constant $k > 0$ given at some point r^* obtaining almost full efficacy inside the $[-r^*, r^*]$ region, and outside that point, the robust estimator start to have less efficacy than the LS estimator under Gaussianity.

The value of the constant c could be obtained analytically or by numeric methods, for example, in the Huber case, we choose $k = 0$, so the value of the constant is $c = r^*$ and for the Bisquare case, we take some small value for k and after some calculations and by using the absolute value as the distance metric, i.e., $|\psi_B(r, c) - r| = k$, we obtained $c = r^*/(\sqrt{1 - \sqrt{1 - k/r^*}})$.

Due to the fact that the estimation process is an adaptive learning algorithm σ_r varies while the model is approaching the training data, implying that $\sigma_r = \sigma_r(t)$ depends on the iteration t. The same holds for the constant $c = c(t)$.

4   Simulations Results Applied to the RESEX Data

In this section the procedure is applied to the Residence Telephone Extensions Inward Movement (Bell Canada) known as RESEX data. The chosen series is a monthly series of "inward movement" of residential telephone extensions of a fixed geographic area in Canada from January 1966 to May 1973, a total of 89 data points [1]. This serie has two extremely large values in November and December 1972 as it is shown in Figure 1. The two obvious outliers have a known cause, namely a bargain month (November) in which residence extensions could be requested free of charge. Most of the orders were filled during December, with the remainder being filled in January. This serie was identified as an ARIMA $(2, 0, 0) \times (0, 1, 0)_{12}$ model with the form $x_t = \phi_1 x_{t-1} + \phi_2 x_{t-2} + x_{t-12} + \phi_1 x_{t-13} + \phi_2 x_{t-14} + a_t$

After analyzing the performance of different architectures where the input and the hidden neurons where changed, good results were obtained for the FANN with lags X_{t-1}, X_{t-2}, X_{t-12}, X_{t-13}, X_{t-14} to predict X_t, i.e., five input neurons and one output neuron with linear activation function, and only one hidden neuron with logistic activation function. Due to the low number of data and in order to study the influence of the outlier in the learning algorithm, all the data were included in the training phase.

This architecture was trained using three different functional cost: the least square estimator (LS) described in (2), the M-estimators with the $\psi - function$ of Huber (MH) and the Tukey's bisquare (MB) given by the equation (10) and (11) respectively. To obtain the parameters that minimize the functional cost, the backpropagation with momentum algorithm was used [6].

The FANN were trained with all the data including the outliers (Serie 1) and with the data where the known outliers were edited (Serie 2). The training process was repeated 20 times.The results are shown in table 1 and 2, where the performance and the effectiveness of the prediction of the FANN trained with different estimators (first column) are shown. The performance was evaluated with the mean square error (MSE) and the effectiveness as the ratio between the MSE of the LS and the robust estimators.

The second and third column of both tables show the results of the FANN trained with Serie 1 and Serie 2 respectively. A fourth column was included to show the evaluation of FANN trained with the contaminated data (Serie 2) but evaluated by omitting the outliers. Finally in the table 1, two additional columns were added to show the peak value of the errors occurred in the location of the outliers data, the most importants contributors to the MSE.

As can be seen in table 2, the robust estimators shows almost full effectiveness under "uncontaminated" data (second column). Under the presence of outliers, the performance of the FANN with LS estimator was superior than the other two networks but as can be seen in the figure 1a), the model is separated to the bulk of data, so if we evaluate the networks without considering the outliers (fourth column), the FANNs with Robust learning over performed substantially the LS case with 212% of effectiveness (4th column of table 2). As a conclusion, first, the Robust networks approximated better the bulk of data meanwhile the FANN with LS learning tends to model the outliers, and, second, the MSE is a global measure of the prediction performance that introduce a distortion vision of the quality of the estimator because does not show the local behavior of the model.

Table 1. Performance of the learning process obtained for the different Learning algorithms ($\times 10^6$)

Est.	Serie 1	Serie 2	Serie 2 without out.	$error^2$ Out. Nov.	$error^2$ Out. Dec.
LS	2.3184 ± 1.4609	37.680 ± 0.0086	6.4264 ± 1.2678	2274.8	4.3
MH	2.3182 ± 0.0277	42.484 ± 0.0084	3.0203 ± 0.6122	2928.3	3.9
MB	2.3365 ± 0.0102	42.592 ± 0.0848	3.0304 ± 0.5806	2967.5	0.2

Table 2. Effectiveness of the Robust Learning compared to the LS case ($\frac{MSE_{LS}}{MSE_M}. * 100\%$) and square error of the outliers

Estimator	Serie 1	Serie 2	Serie 2 without out.
LS	—	—	—
MH	100.01%	88.69%	212.77%
MB	99.22%	88.47%	212.06%

5   Concluding Remarks

The learning process of the FANN, based on the Least Square for the parameters estimate, were shown to be sensible to the presence of outliers, where they tend to model gross outliers due to their influence in the training. A Robust Learning Algorithm based on M-estimator was developed where the influence of the outlier in the estimation process was bounded. The robustness of the estimator will often conflict with the aim of asymptotic effectiveness, therefore the shape of the functional cost were adapted during the training.

Simulations results on real Time Serie were developed to show the improvement of the Robust Learning Algorithm over conventional least squares fitting for the RESEX Time Series.

Different types of M-estimators could be used in the Robust Learning Algorithm, so further studies can be made to choose the proper function for the data in study. The Robust technique used in this paper can be used in a different scope other than neural networks in time series. Future work in robust techniques and Neural Networks will center around making neural networks robust to changes in the variance of the noise.

References

[1] H. Allende, C. Moraga, and R. Salas, *Artificial neural networks in time series forecasting: A comparative analysis*, Kybernetika **38** (2002), no. 6, 685–707.

[2] _____, *Robust estimator for the learning process in neural networks applied in time series*, ICANN 2002. LNCS **2415** (2002), 1080–1086.

[3] E. Capobianco, *Neural networks and statistical inference. Seeking robust and efficient learning*, Comp. Statistics & Data Analysis (2000), no. 32, 443–454.

[4] D. Chen and R. Jain, *A robust back propagation learning algorithm for function approximation*, IEEE Trans. on Neural Networks **5** (1994), no. 3, 467–479.

[5] J. T. Connor and R. D. Martin, *Recurrent neural networks and robust time series prediction*, IEEE Transactions of Neural Networks **2** (1994), no. 5, 240–253.

[6] Richard Golden, *Mathematical methods for neural networks analysis and design*, vol. 1, MIT Press, 1996.

[7] F. R. Hampel, E. M. Ronchetti, P. J. Rousseeuw, and W. A. Stahel, *Robust statistics*, Wiley Series in Probability and Mathematical Statistics, 1986.

[8] Peter J. Huber, *Robust statistics*, Wiley Series in probability and mathematical statistics, 1981.

[9] R. Salas, *Robustez en redes neuronales feedforward*, Master's thesis, Universidad Técnica Federico Santa María, 2002.

[10] Halbert White, *Artificial neural networks: Approximation and learning theory*, Basil Blackwell, Oxford, 1992.

Regularization of 3D Cylindrical Surfaces

Luis Alvarez, Carmelo Cuenca, and Javier Sánchez

Departamento de Informática y Sistemas
Universidad de Las Palmas de G.C.
Campus Universitario de Tafira
35017, Las Palmas
{lalvarez,ccuenca,jsanchez}@dis.ulpgc.es
http://serdis.dis.ulpgc.es/~{alvarez,jsanchez}

Abstract. In this paper we present a method for the regularization of 3D cylindrical surfaces. By a cylindrical surface we mean a 3D surface that can be expressed as an application $S(l, \theta) \rightarrow R^3$, where (l, θ) represents a cylindrical parametrization of the 3D surface. We built an initial cylindrical parametrization of the surface. We propose a new method to regularize such cylindrical surface. This method takes into account the information supplied by the disparity maps computed between pair of images to constraint the regularization of the set of 3D points. We propose a model based on an energy which is composed of two terms: an attachment term that minimizes the difference between the image coordinates and the disparity maps and a second term that enables a regularization by means of anisotropic diffusion. One interesting advantage of this approach is that we regularize the 3D surface by using a bi-dimensional minimization problem.

1 Introduction

This paper deals with the problem of 3D geometry reconstruction from multiple 2D views. Recently, a new accurate technique based on a variational approach has been proposed in [4]. Using a level set approach, this technique optimizes a 3D surface by minimizing an energy that takes into account the regularity of the set of points as well as the projection of the set of points on different images.

In this paper we propose a different approach which is also based on a variational formulation but only using a disparity estimation between images. We will assume that the 3D surface we want to recover has a cylindrical geometry, that is, it can be expressed as an application $S(l, \theta) \rightarrow R^3$, where (l, θ) represents a cylindrical parametrization of the 3D surface. Of course, this is an important limitation in term of the surface geometry, but it simplifies in a strong way the complexity of the problem and it can be applied in a lot of situations like for instance, human face reconstruction as we will show in the experimental results. We will also assume that the cameras are calibrated (see [3], [5] or [6]). Very accurate techniques to estimate the disparity map in a stereo pair of images have been proposed. To extend these techniques to the case of multiple views is not

F.J. Perales et al. (Eds.): IbPRIA 2003, LNCS 2652, pp. 37–44, 2003.
© Springer-Verlag Berlin Heidelberg 2003

a trivial problem. The 3D geometry estimation that we propose can be divided in the following steps:

- For every pair of consecutive images, we estimate a dense disparity map using the accurate technique developed in [1]. We estimate such disparity maps forward and backward. From these disparity maps we obtain a 3D surface for every pair of stereoscopic images.
- Based on the camera configuration we estimate a 3D cylinder and we project in such cylinder the 3D surfaces obtained in the previous step. From these projections we estimate an initial cylindrical parametrization of the surface. This cylindrical parametrization is based on the distance between the 3D point and the cylinder axis. In fact, for each cylinder coordinates (l, θ) we average such distance for all 3D points which are projected in (l, θ).
- Typically, the recovered set of 3D points is noisy, because of errors in the camera calibration process, errors in the disparity map estimations, etc., so some kind of regularization is needed. In this paper, we propose a new variational model to smooth cylindrical surfaces. This regularization model is based on the disparity estimations.

The regularization model we propose is based on a variational approach. We start with an energy that has two terms, an attachment and a regularizing term. The former minimizes the difference by respect to the disparity map computed for every pair of stereoscopic images. This term is responsible for maintaining the final 3D regularized point close to the information supported by the disparity maps. The latter enables a regularization by preserving discontinuities on the cylindrical function. The regularizing term is similar to the terms used in other fields like stereoscopic reconstruction [1], optical flow estimation [2], etc.

Deriving this energy yields a PDE (Partial Differential Equation) that is then embedded into a gradient descend method to look for the solution. We develop an explicit numerical scheme based on finite differences to implement the method.

In Sect. 2 we introduce the cylindrical coordinate system necessary for the representation of the cylindrical function and the relation with the projective camera model. In Sect. 3 we study the model by proposing an energy deriving it and embedding the resulting PDE into a gradient descend method. In Sect. 3.2 there is an explanation of the explicit numerical scheme. Finally in Sect. 4 we present the experimental results for the bust sequence.

2   The Cylinder Structure

2.1   The Cylindrical Coordinate System and the Projective Camera

Using the notation expressed in Fig. 1 we note by $\bar{N}_1, \bar{N}_2$ and $\bar{N}_3$ the orthogonal axis of the coordinate system and by $\bar{Q}_0$ the origin of the system. $\bar{N}_1$ represents the cylinder axis. The cylindrical coordinates are expressed by means of a list of three candidates (l, θ, r) where l is the displacement on the cylinder axis, θ is an angle (as it is outlined in Fig. 1) and r is the distance from a 3D point to the

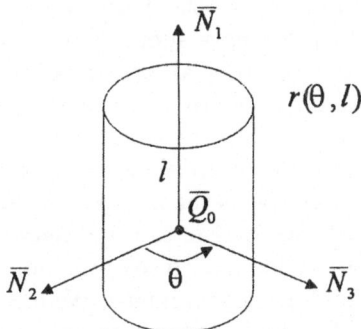

Fig. 1. Cylindrical and cartesian coordinate systems

cylinder axis. A cylindrical surface $S(l, \theta)$ will be given by a cylindrical function $r(\theta, l)$ in the following way :

$$S(l, \theta) = \bar{Q}_0 + l\bar{N}_1 + r(l, \theta)\left(\cos\theta\bar{N}_2 + \sin\theta\bar{N}_3\right) .\qquad(1)$$

With this relation we may transform a cylindrical function $r(l, \theta)$ into a function in the cartesian coordinate system. So, to provide a cylinder surface is equivalent to provide a cylinder function $r(l, \theta)$. We will see later that our method make use of the disparity maps between pairs of stereoscopic images to constraint the regularization of the cylindrical function. The disparity maps are expressed in image coordinates associated to every camera. We assume the projective model for the cameras. In our problem we have N_c different projective cameras and every camera is represented by a projection matrix $\mathbf{P}_c$ of dimensions $3x4$ that projects 3D points into the projection plane. In projective coordinates these projections can be represented as follows:

$$\tilde{m}_c(l, \theta) = \mathbf{P}_c \left(S(l, \theta), 1\right)^t .\qquad(2)$$

2.2   Building the Cylindrical Function

We suppose that for every stereoscopic pair we have a 3D surface. Our first problem is to transform the 3D surfaces into a unique cylindrical function. The main steps for computing the cylindrical function are:

1. Compute the coordinate system by estimating $\bar{Q}_0, \bar{N}_1, \bar{N}_2$ and $\bar{N}_3$.
2. Adapt the resolution of the cylindrical image. The cylindrical function will be represented through an image. This is what we call the cylindrical image. The rows and columns of this image are given by the $\bar{N}_1$ axis and the angle, θ, respectively.
3. Create the cylindrical function, $r(\theta, l)$. Once we have carried out the previous steps we have to merge the information of all the 3D surfaces in one function. We compute an average for all coincident 3D points projections in one pixel in the cylinder coordinate system (l, θ).

The first step is to estimate the position, $\bar{Q}_0$ and axis, $\bar{N}_1, \bar{N}_2$ and $\bar{N}_3$, of the cylindrical coordinate system. We have supposed that the camera configuration system is cylindrical in the sense that all the cameras are situated around the scene and looking at the center. We also suppose that the focus of the cameras are situated close to a common plane. $\bar{Q}_0$ is estimated as the average of the 3D points of all surfaces. $\bar{N}_1$ is the cylindrical axis and is computed accordingly to the configuration of the focuses, $\bar{N}_2$ is the unitary vector that points to the focus of the first camera and $\bar{N}_3$ is orthogonal to the others.

In the second step we are concern with the problem of representing the cylindrical function through a bi-dimensional image. We have to compute the dimensions of an image that will allocate the values of the 3D points in cylindrical coordinates. To calculate the number of rows the lowest and highest 3D points in the $\bar{N}_1$ component are computed. The difference between them defines the size of the cylindrical axis. The number of columns are estimated knowing that $2 \cdot \pi \cdot radius$ is the length for the cylinder. We adapt the value of $radius$ in order to obtain an image with regular pixels (same pixel height and width). This value depends on the dimension of the image in the $\bar{N}_1$ axis. This image represents the $r(\theta, l)$ function.

The last step consist of assigning a value to every pixel on the image. This process is carried out by representing the 3D points in cylindrical coordinates and computing an average for coincident points on a pixel. There may be some locations where no 3D point is projected, so a post-processing to fill these pixels is necessary. These are filled from the values of the surrounding pixels.

3   The Regularizing Method

3.1   Energy Minimization

The regularization of the cylindrical function $r(l, \theta)$ is equivalent to regularize the cylindrical surface $S(l, \theta)$. We propose a variational formulation to look for the regularized solution. This solution is the result of a minimization problem. Our model is composed of two terms: the attachment term that uses the disparity maps to constraint the process; and the regularizing term that is used to obtain a smooth solution. This term is designed to regularize the surface by preserving the discontinuities of the cylindrical function which are related to the varying depth of the 3D surface.

The energy model proposed is

$$
E(r) = \beta \left(\sum_{c=1}^{N} \int \int \left\| \bar{m}_{c+1}(l, \theta) - \bar{m}_c(l, \theta) - h_+^c(\bar{m}_c) \right\|^2 dl d\theta \right.
$$
$$
\left. + \sum_{c=1}^{N} \int \int \left\| \bar{m}_c(l, \theta) - \bar{m}_{c+1}(l, \theta) - h_-^c(\bar{m}_{c+1}) \right\|^2 dl d\theta \right)
$$
$$
+ \alpha \int \int \phi(\|\nabla r\|) \, dl d\theta. \tag{3}
$$

$\bar{m}_{c+1}(l, \theta)$ is the image coordinate for camera $c + 1$ denoted by (2) and $\bar{m}_c(l, \theta)$ is the correspondent for camera c. Vectors $\bar{h}^c_{+/-}(\bar{m}_c) = \begin{pmatrix} u_{+/-}(\bar{m}_c) \\ v_{+/-}(\bar{m}_c) \end{pmatrix}$ represent the optical flow estimations for pixel $\bar{m}_c$ on camera c. Sign $+$ corresponds to the optical flow from camera c to $c + 1$ and sign $-$ to the optical flow from camera c to camera $c - 1$.

After minimizing this energy we obtain the associated Euler–Lagrange equation that is given by the following PDE:

$$\beta \cdot \left(\sum_{c=1}^{N_c} \left((\bar{m}_{c+1} - \bar{m}_c - \bar{h}^c_+(\bar{m}_c))^t \cdot \left(\frac{\partial \bar{m}_{c+1}}{\partial r} - \frac{\partial \bar{m}_c}{\partial r} - \mathcal{J}\bar{h}^c_+ \frac{\partial \bar{m}_c}{\partial r} \right) \right) \right.$$

$$\left. + \sum_{c=1}^{N_c} \left((\bar{m}_c - \bar{m}_{c+1} - \bar{h}^{c+1}_-(\bar{m}_{c+1}))^t \cdot \left(\frac{\partial \bar{m}_c}{\partial r} - \frac{\partial \bar{m}_{c+1}}{\partial r} - \mathcal{J}\bar{h}^{c+1}_- \frac{\partial \bar{m}_{c+1}}{\partial r} \right) \right) \right)$$

$$-\alpha \cdot \operatorname{div} \left(\frac{\phi'(\|\nabla r\|)}{\|\nabla r\|} \nabla r \right) = 0 \tag{4}$$

where $\mathcal{J}\bar{h} = \mathcal{J} \begin{pmatrix} u(x, y) \\ v(x, y) \end{pmatrix} = \begin{pmatrix} \frac{\partial u}{\partial x} & \frac{\partial u}{\partial y} \\ \frac{\partial v}{\partial x} & \frac{\partial v}{\partial y} \end{pmatrix}$.

In order to search for the solution we implement a gradient descend method in the way $\frac{\partial r}{\partial t} = -\frac{\partial E(r)}{\partial r}$. The divergence term is well known and acts like a diffusion scheme. If we expand the divergence expression we obtain

$$\operatorname{div} \left(\frac{\phi'(\|\nabla r\|)}{\|\nabla r\|} \nabla r \right) = \frac{\phi'(\|\nabla r\|)}{\|\nabla r\|} r_{\xi\xi} + \phi''(\|\nabla r\|) r_{\eta\eta} \tag{5}$$

where $\eta = \frac{\nabla r}{\|\nabla r\|}$ and $\xi = \eta^{\perp}$ are the unitary vectors in the directions parallel and perpendicular to the gradient, respectively.

Playing with function $\phi(s)$ it is possible to achieve an anisotropic diffusion at contours. The first in proposing this kind of diffusion equation were Perona and Malik [7] in where they introduced a decreasing function to avoid diffusion at contours.

3.2 Numerical Scheme

In this section we are going to see how to implement an explicit numerical scheme for this method. We derive $\frac{\partial \bar{m}}{\partial r}$ analytically from (2). Regarding (5) the divergence is divided in two terms and the values for both of them are given by the following expressions:

$$r_{\xi\xi} = \frac{r_{xx}r_y^2 - 2r_x r_y r_{xy} + r_{yy}r_x^2}{r_x^2 + r_y^2}, \qquad r_{\eta\eta} = \frac{r_{yy}r_y^2 + 2r_x r_y r_{xy} + r_{xx}r_x^2}{r_x^2 + r_y^2}. \tag{6}$$

Fig. 2. Bust configuration: This figure shows the 3D reconstructed bust and the distribution of the projection planes corresponding to the 47 cameras

The first and second derivates on x and y and the derivates of the components of the optical flow, $\frac{\partial u}{\partial x}, \frac{\partial u}{\partial y}, \frac{\partial v}{\partial x}, \frac{\partial v}{\partial y}$ and $\frac{\partial u}{\partial x}$, have been approximated by finite differences.

The final numerical scheme is implemented by means of an explicit scheme in the following way:

$$
r_{t+1} = r_t + dt \cdot \left(\alpha \left(r_{\xi\xi} + g\left(\|\nabla r\| \right) r_{\eta\eta} \right) - \beta \left(\sum_{c=1}^{N_c} \left(\left(\bar{m}_c - \bar{m}_{c+1} - \bar{h}_-^{c+1}(\bar{m}_{c+1}) \right)^t \right. \right. \right.
$$

$$
\cdot \left(\frac{\partial \bar{m}_c}{\partial r} - \frac{\partial \bar{m}_{c+1}}{\partial r} - \mathcal{J}\bar{h}_-^{c+1} \frac{\partial \bar{m}_{c+1}}{\partial r} \right) \right) + \sum_{c=1}^{N_c} \left(\left(\bar{m}_{c+1} - \bar{m}_c - \bar{h}_+^c(\bar{m}_c) \right)^t
$$

$$
\left. \left. \left. \cdot \left(\frac{\partial \bar{m}_{c+1}}{\partial r} - \frac{\partial \bar{m}_c}{\partial r} - \mathcal{J}\bar{h}_+^c \frac{\partial \bar{m}_c}{\partial r} \right) \right) \right) \right). \tag{7}
$$

Function $g(s)$ is a decreasing function that disables isotropic diffusion for big values of the gradient.

4   Experimental Results

In this section we show the results of regularizing a bust sequence. In this case the sequence is composed of 47 images taken around a bust. Figure 2 shows the configuration of this sequence with the projection planes of the cameras. This is a close sequence in where the first and last images are correlatives.

In Fig. 4 we may see the original Bust reconstruction and a regularized version for $\alpha = 0, 1$ and $s = 0.1$.

From Fig. 5 we may appreciate several regularizations for $\alpha = 3, 0$ and different values of s. The β parameter is much smaller and is used to normalize the variation between the two terms. In these experiences $\beta = 10^{-4}$.

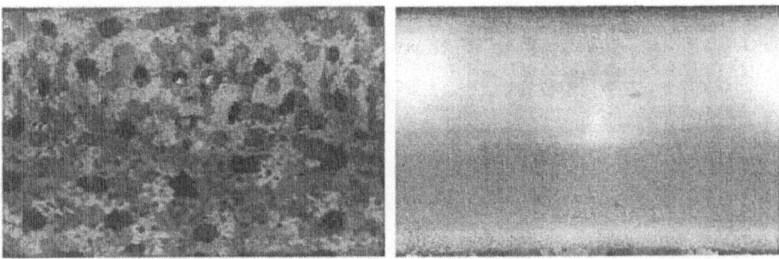

Fig. 3. The left image represents the texture of the Bust sequence projected on a cylindrical image. The right image is the cylindrical function represented in gray levels (the white color is associated to the highest values)

5   Conclusions

In this paper we have presented a novel and simple method for the representation and regularization of cylindrical surfaces. This method is ideally suited for convex surfaces and also be appropriated for surfaces that have not deep clefts. We have taken advantage of the simplicity of cylindrical coordinates to represent the set of 3D points. Once the cylindrical function is built the problem of regularizing the set of 3D points is reduced to the problem of regularizing a bi-dimensional function.

We have established an energy in a traditional attachment–regularizing couple of terms. From this energy we have derived a diffusion-reaction PDE. We have shown in the experiments that varying the α parameter results in a more regular set of points and varying the λ parameter implies a more regular set of points by preserving the cylindrical function discontinuities as we have expected from the results obtained in other fields. The use of α and λ parameters are

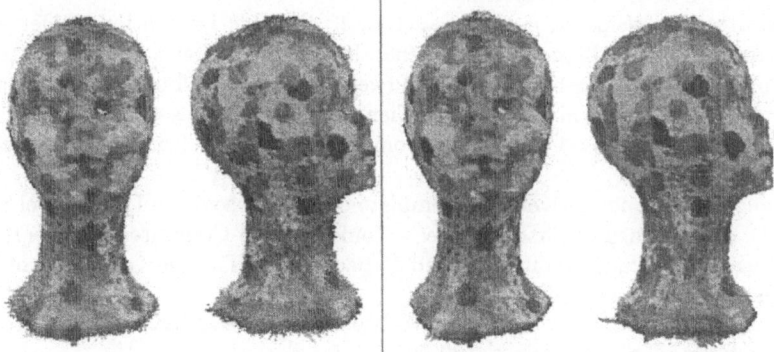

Fig. 4. Left two images: Front and profile views of the Bust reconstruction. Right two images: Front and profile views of a 3D regularization for the Bust sequence using $\alpha = 0, 1$ and $s = 0.1$

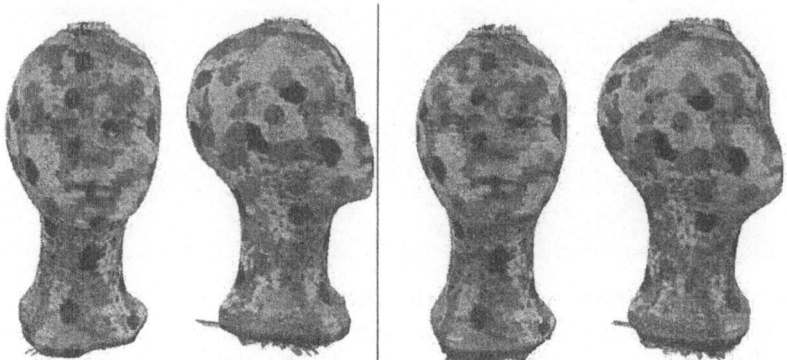

Fig. 5. Several views of different 3D regularizations for the Bust sequence. Left two images: $\alpha = 3, 0$ and $s = 0, 5$; Right two images: $\alpha = 3, 0$ and $s = 1, 0$

simple. α refers to the smoothness of the final set of points and λ refers to the way the regularization is carried out at the contours.

Acknowledgments

This work has been partially supported by the Spanish research project TIC 2000-0585 founded by the Ministerio de Ciencia y Tecnología and by the research project PI2002/193 founded by the Canary Islands Government.

References

[1] Alvarez, L., Deriche, R., Sánchez, J., and Weickert, J.: Dense disparity map estimation respecting image derivatives: a PDE and scale-space based approach. Journal of Visual Communication and Image Representation **13** (2002) 3–21. Also published as Inria Research Report n° 3874

[2] Alvarez, L., Weickert, J., and Sánchez, J.: Reliable Estimation of Dense Optical Flow Fields with Large Displacements. International Journal of Computer Vision, Vol. 39, **1** (2000) 41–56. An extended version maybe be found at Technical Report n°2 del Instituto Universitario de Ciencias y Tecnologías Cibernéticas

[3] Faugeras, O.: Three-Dimensional Computer Vision: A Geometric Viewpoint. MIT Press (1993)

[4] Faugeras, O. and Keriven, R.: Complete Dense Stereovision Using Level Set Methods. Proceedings of Fifth European Conference on Computer Vision (1998)

[5] Faugeras, O., and Luong, Q., and Papadopoulo, T.: The Geometry of Multiple Images. Mit Press (2001)

[6] Hartley, R. and Zisserman, A.: Multiple View Geometry in Computer Vision. Cambridge University Press (2000)

[7] Perona, P. and Malik, J.: Scale-Space and Edge Detection Using Anisotropic Diffusion. IEEE Transactions on Pattern Analysis and Machine Intelligence **12** (1990) 429–439

Non-rigid Registration of Vessel Structures
in IVUS Images

Jaume Amores and Petia Radeva*

Computer Vision Center, Dept. Inform àtica, UAB
Bellaterra, Spain
jaume@cvc.uab.es

Abstract. We present a registration and retrieval algorithm of medical images. Our algorithm is oriented in a general fashion towards gray level medical images of non-rigid bodies such as coronary vessels, where object shape information provide poor information. We use rich descriptors based on both local and global (contextual) information, and at the same time we use a cooperative-iterative strategy in order to get a good set of correspondences as well as a good final transformation. We focus on a novel application of registration of medical images: registration of IVUS, a promising technique of analyzing the coronary vessels.

1 Introduction

There is a wide range of applications of medical image registration and we refer to books such as [7] for detailed information. We apply registration to IntraVascular UltraSound images (IVUS), a powerful imaging modality for analysis and diagnosis of coronary vessels ([1]). In concrete we present a registration procedure to be used as a first step in a more general retrieval framework. The IVUS technique produces images with quite particularities and noise, difficult to analyze. Thus, creating a retrieval system of IVUS images is of high clinical interest for diagnosis purposes.

Although there is a huge number of works in the area of Registration and Retrieval of Medical Images [2, 7], matching of IVUS images and retrieving cases from an IVUS images database is a new problem to be solved. On the other hand, many works on medical image registration are focused on rigid parts that justifies rigid registration. Medical images of non-rigid bodies such as coronary vessels in IVUS present features quite different as they do not have any characteristic spatial configuration forced by the bony structure. We perform elastic matching with a variational approach for the transformation, given the high variability inter and intra subject of our medical images.

Registration consists on finding structures analog in a pair of images and compute a transformation that align them. We will follow point mapping as a general procedure of registration [5, 1].

---

* This work is supported by Ministerio de Ciencia y Tecnologia of Spain, grant TIC2000-1635-C04-04.

Opposite to many works on medical images such as brain MRIs, which take a grid of characteristic points over all the image, we only extract a small set of characteristic points from the boundaries of the salient regions we want to match. This approach makes the algorithm faster and avoids the necessity of employing a multi-resolution scheme. Given the type of images we deal with, we must choose quite a rich set of descriptors which not only take into account the local statistics near the characteristic point (local descriptors) but also the context of the point (global or contextual descriptors). This gives information of how other structures are located around the point, and at the same time takes account of where the point is located at its own structure. Graphs are the most traditional tool for taking into account the context of some object. However, they are very dependent on an accurate segmentation, and this makes them little robust.

Instead, we make use of the so-called correlograms (see [3]) in order to take account of the context of points, extending the shape-context descriptor of Belongie et al [3] to cope with gray level images. Correlograms in 2-D will allow us to match the couple of images coarsely coping with the spatial distribution of structures, but have the draw-back of including some information about the 2-D shape of the contours not interesting in our case. Thus we extend the contextual information using shape invariant 1-D correlograms after a coarse alignment. The use of these two types of context descriptors as well as local descriptors will make our feature space rich enough.

Yet, the set of correspondences obtained with this set of descriptors is not enough to compute directly the final transformation based on them. We use a cooperative-iterative scheme (see [5]) in searching a good final transformation, which consists on giving feedback from the transformation to compute a new set of correspondences, which at the same time will produce a new transformation and so on, iterating the algorithm. We use a feedback scheme similar to the one used by Rangarajan et al. in [6], but without an annealing framework, as the combination of contextual and local information give us enough information to seek for an accurate transformation in a more straightforward manner.

Summarizing, we extend and combine different important ideas into a single framework: incorporation of contextual information with correlograms modified to cope with gray level images, adding a second type of contextual information, shape invariant 1-D correlograms; a cooperative-iterative scheme similar to the one used by Rangarajan et al. [6] and the use of Thin Plate Splines (TPS) [4], allowing different degrees of regularization-approximation as the correspondences become better and better. The combination of these three factors give our algorithm robustness as well as accuracy.

The article is organized as follows: section 2 explains the description of the registration method, section 3 shows the results obtained and the paper finishes with conclusions and future work.

2   Description of the Method

Coronary vessels present all their structures of interest around the wall of the vessel. We first make an anisotropic diffusion [9] of the IVUS image and let a snake grow from its interior to the wall of the vessel. Then we sample the boundary points in order to take our set of characteristic points and finally we extract the feature vectors associated to each characteristic point.

2.1   Feature Space

We compute local feature vectors associated to each characteristic point and then based on them compute 2-D correlograms and 1-D correlograms. Local feature vectors aim at characterizing the biological structure where the point lies, whereas correlograms will put the points into context. Summarizing, associated to each characteristic point x_i we are going to use three different feature vectors: our local feature vector l_i, a 2-D correlogram v_i, an 1-D correlogram w_i. We will now describe each of them in turn.

In IVUS images regions such as calcium plaque are characterized by the gray level they have inside them and the gray level they cause outside them because of their echogenic impedance. Thus a good descriptor of the structure the point is at, is the gray level profile along the line perpendicular to the wall from the point towards the outside part of the vessel. We measure a set of statistics over this profile and its first derivative which conform our local feature vector [1].

Correlograms consist of partitioning the image in cells distributed radially around its origin, which is the current point we are describing. In fig. 1 we can see a correlogram, a partition of the image in sectors or cells, each one accounting for some part of the image at a specified range of angles and radius, taking as origin a characteristic point x_i. The radial length of the cells grows with logarithmical rate from the origin towards outside, giving more importance to the near context of the point.

In every cell of the correlogram we compute a statistic such as the mean over the local feature vectors of the points that lie inside the cell. Let v_i be the 2-D correlogram associated to x_i. Let $\{x_{u_1}, x_{u_2}, \ldots, x_{u_t}\}$ be the characteristic points which lie in the u cell of v_i. We take the local feature vectors associated to these characteristic points: $\{l_{u_1}, l_{u_2}, \ldots, l_{u_t}\}$ and compute a mean over each of their characteristics. Let every local feature vector l_k have d characteristics: $l_k = (l_{k1}, l_{k2}, \ldots, l_{kd})\ \forall k$. Let $c_{uj} = mean(\{l_{u_1 j}, l_{u_2 j}, \ldots, l_{u_t j}\})$, the mean over the j characteristic of the local feature vectors $\{l_{u_1}, l_{u_2}, \ldots, l_{u_t}\}$. If we have r cells for every correlogram, we can express the 2-D correlogram associated to the characteristic point x_i as $v_i = (c_{11}, c_{12}, \ldots, c_{1d}, c_{21}, c_{22}, \ldots, c_{2d}, \ldots, c_{r1}, c_{r2}, \ldots, c_{rd})$.

The 1-D correlogram is a division in cells but now of the contour curve where we have our characteristic points. Let w_i be the 1-D correlogram for the characteristic point x_i. We can express the contour curve as a function $\varphi : [0,1) \rightarrow \mathbb{R}^2$ depending on an intern parameter $s \in [0,1)$: $\varphi(s) = (x,y)$. We take as intern parameter s an approximation to the arc-length of the curve, and such that $\varphi(0) = x_i$. Then we take as cells of the 1-D correlogram a set of

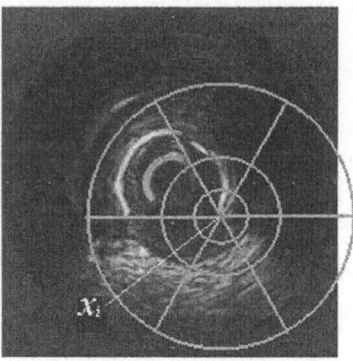

Fig. 1. Correlogram with 12 intervals of angles and 5 intervals of radius

intervals $I_u \subset [0,1) \forall u, \bigcup I_u = [0,1), I_u \cap I_v = \emptyset \leftrightarrow u \neq v$. This correlogram is not based on the local feature vectors directly but on a classification result of the characteristic points using these local feature vectors. For all the points that fall inside one cell of a correlogram w_i we count how many of these points belong to the same type of structure and this is the value associated to this cell.

The 1-D correlogram does not take into account the particular shape peculiarities of two structures to be aligned. Once we have put the structures close by using the 2-D correlogram, which take account of the 2-D distribution of structures, we finish an accurate matching of points from two analog structures by using the 1-D correlogram. This descriptor accounts mainly for the position of the point along the boundary of the structure it belongs to, saying intuitively if this point is at one extremum (and in which extremum it is) or if it is near the center of the structure. Thus extremum points from both structures are matched together, central points together, and so on.

2.2 Iterative Scheme and Final Algorithm

Once extracted a set of characteristic points, we apply a coarse alignment using as feature vectors only the 2-D correlograms, which accounts for the 2-D distribution of structures and put analog structures close enough.

After this coarse alignment, we perform a classification of the points. Let I_1 be the query image and I_2 be the complementary. For any pair $x_i \in I_1$, $y_j \in I_2$, the distance between them is computed as $d_{class} + d(w_i, w_j)$, where the distance $d(w_i, w_j)$ is the χ^2 distance (see [3]) between the 1-D correlograms of both points, and d_{class} is infinite if both points do not belong to the same type of structure (class), and 0 if they do. By adding d_{class} we are restricting the correspondences to match always points belonging to the same structure. Furthermore, we restrict the region where the matching point lies to be near the mapped characteristic point, $f(x_i)$, where f is the coarse transformation obtained in the first step. With these measures of distance between every couple of points we compute the final set of correspondences and based on them the final transformation. The computation of the transformations is done by adjusting a TPS to the set of correspondences obtained at each step.

For both steps we also use an iterative step that aims at doing cooperation between neighbor points in the computation of a reliable set of correspondences. The idea of cooperation is based on the fact that if one point x_i is matched with y_i, a neighbor point x_{i+1} of x_i should not be matched with a point y_j too far away from y_i. Let a couple of points $x_i \in I_1$ and $y_j \in I_2$, and let its distance in the feature space be d_{ij}. We have such a distance for every possible couple of points. After obtaining an initial set of correspondences based on these distances, we make a transformation by TPS. Let $f(x_i)$ be the mapping of x_i by the TPS. We recompute the distance between every couple of points $(x_i \in I_1, y_j \in I_2)$ as $d_{ij} + \alpha \| f(x_i) - y_j \|$. With these new distances we compute a new set of correspondences that produce a new transformation and this is iterated several steps. The TPS do not allow two neighbor points x_{i+1} of x_i to be mapped far away from each other. Thus, by adding the term $\alpha \| f(x_i) - y_j \|$ for the point x_i and $\alpha \| f(x_{i+1}) - y_j \|$ for the point x_{i+1} to the set of distances, we are biasing both points towards the same region of I_2. The parameter α indicates how much we rely on the last transformation. If the last transformation is very accurate, we take as α a high value, restricting the corresponding points $y_j \in I_2$ to be near the mapped points $f(x_i)$. Thus, as the process makes the transformations better, we must increase this parameter through the successive iterations, beginning with a small value. Also the regularization degree of the TPS becomes smaller as the set of correspondences is better, as a high regularization is only needed to approximate coarsely noisy correspondences. Thus we decrease the regularization through the successive iterations.

Both types of correlograms depend on the spatial distribution of the characteristic points. As the spatial distribution of the points become modified by the successive mappings, we must recompute these correlograms through successive iterations of the algorithm.

3   Results

We would like to show first the necessity of using contextual as well as local information, and the necessity of using as contextual information not only the 2-D correlograms but also 1-D correlograms. For an explanation of the parameters used see [1].

In fig. 2 we can see a first couple of IVUS images with two calcium plaques, one on the left and the other one on the right. The IVUS image of 2-(a) corresponds to the query image, and the IVUS image of 2-(b) to its complementary image. In fig. 2-(c) we show the anisotropic diffusion of the query image and superposed in red the boundary of the vessel from which we extract the characteristic points. In fig. 2-(d) we show the anisotropic diffusion of the complementary image and superposed in red the boundary of the vessel from which we extract the characteristic points. In fig. 6 we see the final set of correspondences.

In fig. 3 we compare the result of the first coarse transformation using contextual information (2-D correlograms) and using only local information (our local feature vectors). We show transformation results on the anisotropic diffusion of the images because it is visually more clear. In 3-(a) we show the anisotropic diffusion of the query transformed by the coarse mapping. In 3-(b) we show the complementary image with the edges of the transformed query image superposed in red. We can see how both calcium plaques are mapped close, as well as the adventitia tissue. In 3-(c) and 3-(d) we show the same coarse transformation using only local feature vectors. We can see that one of the calcium plaques has not been mapped closed to any of the calcium plaques of the complementary image.

In fig. 4 we see how the set of correspondences using only a 2-D correlogram is more noisy than using a combination of 1-D correlogram and local feature vectors.

If fig. 5 we compare the result of the transformation obtained in the second step using 1-D correlograms and including the classification information by the distance d_{class} (see previous section), with a transformation obtained by the same algorithm but using 2-D correlograms and including also the classification information. As can be seen the transformation using 2-D correlograms is more inaccurate and produce an irregular warping with the noise seen in the images. The irregular warping is due to be using a slow regularization degree of the TPS based on a too noisy a set of correspondences for such a small degree of regularization. Finally we see results for another couple in fig. 7.

4   Conclusions and Future Work

We apply a registration technique to a novel type of medical images, IVUS images of highly elastic bodies and quite difficult to analyze. These types of images need a rich feature space, using not only local information around the point but also providing context or global information relative to this point. We extend the work of Belongie et al. [3] using a modification of their correlograms in order to cope with gray level images, and adding a second contextual information, shape

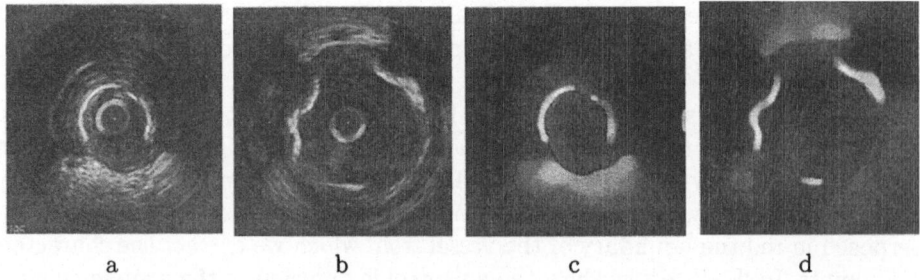

a   b   c   d

Fig. 2. Query and its complementary IVUS (a)-(b). Their anisotropic diffusion results (c)-(d)

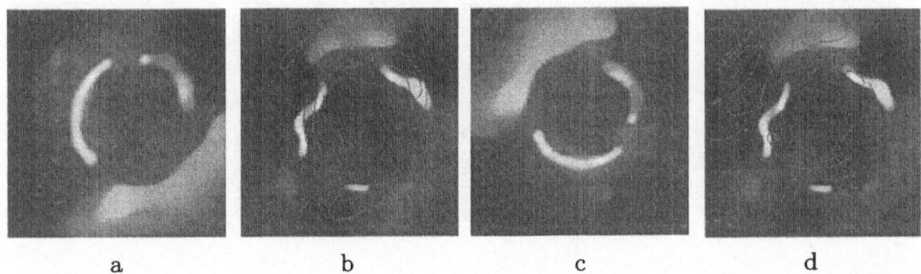

a   b   c   d

Fig. 3. Coarse alignment (first step of the algorithm) using first contextual information (a)-(b), and then only local information (c)-(d)

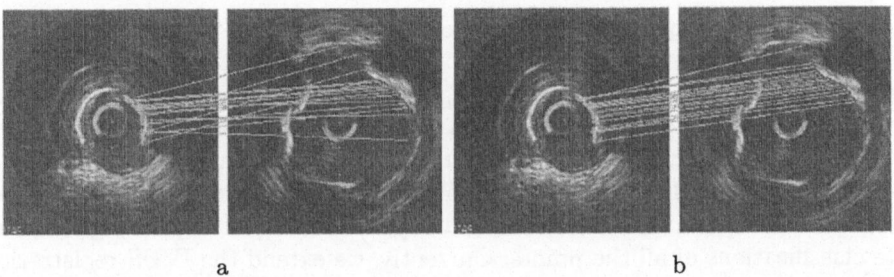

a   b

Fig. 4. Correspondences with only 2-D correlograms (a) and correspondences with 1-D correlograms and local feature vectors (b)

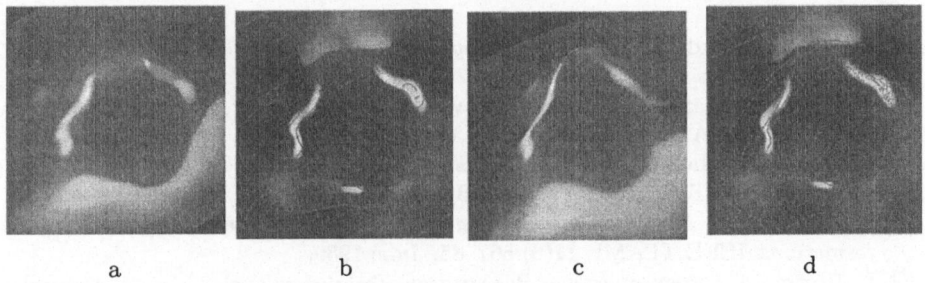

a   b   c   d

Fig. 5. Second transformation using first in 1-D correlograms (a)-(b), and then 2-D correlograms (c)-(d)

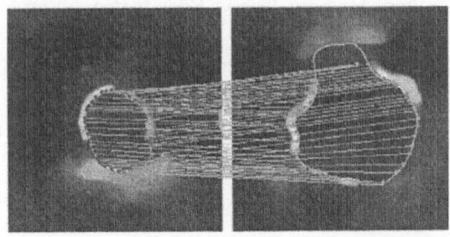

Fig. 6. Final set of correspondences of the first pair of images

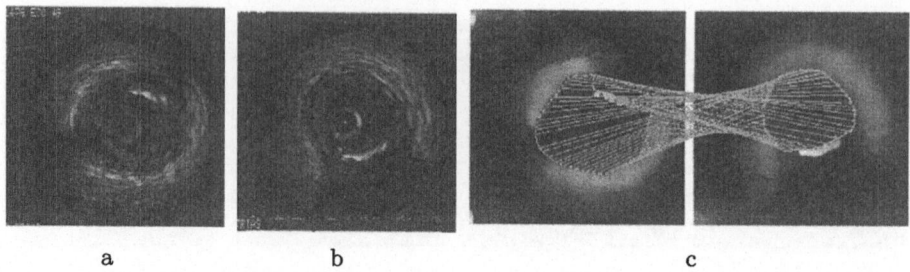

a   b   c

Fig. 7. Query (a), complementary (b), and final set of correspondences on their anisotropic diffusions (c)

invariant 1-D correlograms. We incorporate this rich set of descriptors into a cooperative-iterative scheme similar to the one used by Rangarajan et al. [6], but without the deterministic annealing framework they use, as the combination of contextual and local information gives us enough information to seek for an accurate transformation in a more straightforward manner. The combination of rich descriptors, TPS, and the use of an iterative-cooperative scheme gives our algorithm robustness as well as accuracy, the result not depending on accurate classifications of all the points. Currently, we extend the IVUS registration including textural information.

References

[1] J.Amores, P. Radeva. *Elastic Matching Retrieval in Medical Images using contextual information.* CVC. Tech Report 23. September 2002.
[2] J. B. Antoine-Mantz and M. A. Viergever. *A survey of medical image registration.* Medical Image Analysis (1998) Vol. 2, num. 1, pp 1-37.
[3] S.Belongie, J. Malik, and J.Puzicha. *Shape Matching and object recognition using shape contexts.* Technical Report UCB//CSD-00-1128, UC Berkeley, 2001.
[4] F. L. Bookstein. *Principal warps: Thin-plate splines and the decomposition of deformations.* IEEE TPAMI, 11(6):567585, June 1989.
[5] L. Brown. *A Survey of Image Registration Techniques.* Vol 24, no 4, December 1992.
[6] H. Chui and A. Rangarajan. *A new algorithm for non-rigid point matching.* Proc. CVPR, 2000, Vol. 2, pp. 40-51.
[7] Hajnal, Hill and Hawkes. *Medical Image Registration,* The Biomedical Engineering Series, 2001.
[8] A. Pentland and S. Sclaroff. *Closed-form solutions for physically based shape modelling and recognition.* IEEE. TPAMI 13(7):715-729.
[9] J.Weickert. *Anisotropic Diffusion in Image Processing.* PhD. Thesis, Kaiserslautern University, 1996.

Underwater Cable Tracking by Visual Feedback*

Javier Antich and Alberto Ortiz

Mathematics and Computer Science Department
University of the Balearic Islands, Spain
{javi.antich,alberto.ortiz}@uib.es

Abstract. Nowadays, the surveillance and inspection of underwater installations, such as power and telecommunication cables and pipelines, is carried out by trained operators who, from the surface, control a Remotely Operated Vehicle (ROV) with cameras mounted over it. This is a tedious, time-consuming and expensive task, prone to errors mainly because of loss of attention or fatigue of the operator and also due to the typical low quality of seabed images. In this study, the development of a vision system guiding an Autonomous Underwater Vehicle (AUV) able to detect and track automatically an underwater power cable laid on the seabed has been the main concern. The system has been tested using sequences from a video tape obtained by means of a ROV during several tracking sessions of various real cables. The average success rate that has been achieved is about 90% for a frame rate higher than 25 frames/second.

1   Introduction

The feasibility of an underwater installation can only be guaranteed by means of a suitable inspection program. This program must provide the company with information about potential hazardous situations or damages caused by the mobility of the seabed, corrosion, or human activities such as marine traffic or fishing. Nowadays, the surveillance and inspection of these installations are carried out using video cameras attached to ROVs normally controlled by operators from a support ship. Obviously, this is a tedious task because the operator has to concentrate for a long time in front of a console, which makes the task highly prone to errors mainly due to loss of attention and fatigue. Besides, the peculiar characteristics of the undersea images —blurring, low contrast, non-uniform illumination— increase the complexity of the operation. Therefore, the automation of any part of this process can constitute an important improvement in the maintenance of such installations with regard to errors, time and monetary costs.

The special visual features that artificial objects possess allow distinguishing them from the rest of objects present in a natural scenario even in very noisy images. In our case, the rigidity and shape of the underwater cable can be exploited

* This study has been partially supported by project CICYT-DPI2001-2311-C03-02 and FEDER fundings.

F.J. Perales et al. (Eds.): IbPRIA 2003, LNCS 2652, pp. 53–61, 2003.
© Springer-Verlag Berlin Heidelberg 2003

by a computer vision algorithm to discriminate it from the surrounding environment. This fact makes feasible the automatic guidance of an AUV by means of visual feedback to carry out maintenance/inspection tasks. Following this strategy, a first approach to the problem of detecting and tracking an underwater power cable by analysing the image sequence from a video camera attached to an AUV was described in [7], being afterwards improved and optimised in [8].

In this paper, a new version with similar success rate, better performance and lower complexity is proposed. The vision system has been tested using sequences from a video tape obtained in several tracking sessions of various real cables with a ROV driven from the surface. These cables were installed several years ago, so that the images do not present highly contrasted cables over a sandy seabed; on the contrary, these cables are partially covered in algae or sand, and are surrounded by algae and rocks, making thus the sequences highly realistic. The mean success rate that has been achieved is about 90% for a frame rate of more than 25 frames/second.

The rest of the paper is organized as follows: section 2 revises previous work on the subject; the proposed vision system is described in section 3; section 4 shows the results obtained; and, finally, section 5 presents some conclusions and future work.

2   Previous Work

In the literature about cable inspection, two main sensing devices can be distinguished: magnetometres and sonar. In general, both strategies require AUVs larger and more powerful than is needed because of the very size of the devices and due to the need of including extra batteries in the vehicle [5]. By using CCD cameras, however, this problem is considerably reduced, either in cost and in AUV size. In fact, throughout the last years, several research groups have shown the suitability of vision systems either for navigation and for mission tasks (see [9], among many others).

With regard to visual cable and pipeline tracking and inspection, several systems have been proposed so far. Matsumoto and Ito [6] developed a vision system able to follow electrical cables in underwater environments by using edge detectors, the Hough transform and some higher-level processing related to the line-like appearance of the cables. Hallset [5] presented another system able to follow pipelines using edge detectors and the Hough transform too, and a map of the pipeline network. At the University of Ancona, a system oriented towards helping human operators in the inspection of gas and oil pipelines was also implemented [10]. In this case, the system detected the pipes and some other accessories attached to them using statistical information obtained from selected areas of the image related to the position of the cable. More recently, Balasuriya et al. proposed a system based on predicting a Region Of Interest (ROI) in the image and applying the Hough transform to an edge map produced by a LoG operator [4]. An improved version using a rough 2D model of the cable appears in [3].

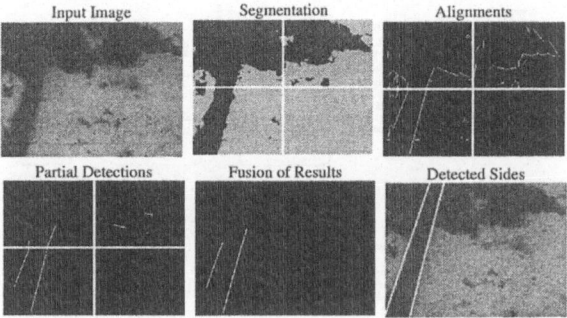

Fig. 1. Intermediate and final results for a real image split in 2 × 2 cells

3 The Vision System

Artificial objects usually present distinguishing features in natural environments. In the case of the cable, given its rigidity and shape, strong alignments of contour pixels can be expected near its sides. The vision system described in the paper exploits this fact to find the cable in the images.

In order to obtain the cable parameters, the system splits the image to be analysed in a grid of cells which are processed separately. This division pretends to reinforce the evidence of the cable in those areas of the image where it appears clearly defined. Different steps are carried out to locate the cable in every cell of the resultant grid. First, an optimised segmentation process is executed to find image regions as approximated as possible to the scene objects. Given the contours of such regions, alignments of contour pixels are determined. If among those alignments there is strong evidence of the location of the cable (mainly two alignments with a great number of pixels lined up and with a high degree of parallelism, even without discounting the perspective effect), then the cable is considered to have been located and its parameters are computed. After analysing all the cells of the grid, the partial results obtained are merged to achieve a global agreement about the real cable position and orientation in the image. By way of example, fig. 1 shows the cable detection process for a real image.

Once the cable has been detected, its location and orientation in the next image are predicted by means of a Kalman filter, which allows reducing the pixels to be processed to a small ROI. In this way, the computation time is considerably lowered together with the probability of misinterpretations of similar features appearing in the image.

When tracking the cable, a low or null evidence of its presence in the ROI can be obtained. In such a case, the image is discarded and a transient failure counter increased. If this anomalous situation continues throughout too many images, then it is attributed to a failure in the prediction of the ROI, resulting in two special actions: the Kalman filter is reset and the ROI is widened to the whole image.

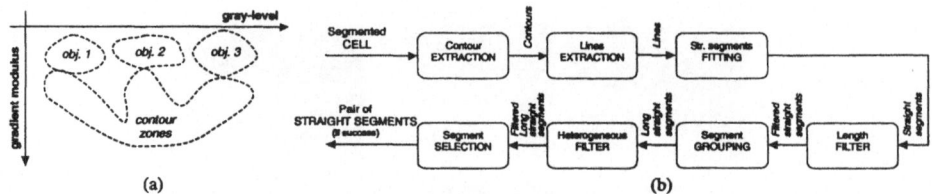

Fig. 2. (a) Ideal bidimensional histogram; (b) Flow diagram of the cable detection step

3.1 Segmentation Process

A gray-level thresholding technique has been applied to carry out the segmentation of every grid cell. It is based on a particular histogram where the relevant objects of the scene can be more easily distinguished than using the traditional gray-level histogram.

In order to obtain the mentioned histogram, the cell of the grid to be analysed is first transformed into the {gray-level, gradient modulus} space. This transformation consists in building a bidimensional histogram where one horizontal axis corresponds to gray-level, the other horizontal axis corresponds to a digital approximation of the modulus of gray-level gradient —the Sobel operator has been used—, and for every combination {gray-level, gradient modulus} the vertical axis is the number of pixels in the cell having that gray-level and that gradient modulus.

In the case of several objects with different gray-levels, the ideal bidimensional histogram should look like fig. 2(a). In effect, if the image can be approximated by a noisy piecewise constant bidimensional function, the interior of any object in the cell has gradient near zero, so that pixels in the interior zones are located in the lower part of the histogram, with regard to gradient. Border pixels among objects, however, are located in zones of higher gradient, joining the clusters corresponding to the interiors of such objects in a "fingers"-like fashion.

Once the bidimensional histogram has been built, it is projected onto the plane {gray-level, number of pixels}. The projection is cumulative and does not consider the pixels whose gradient is greater than a predefined threshold. Ideally, this parameter should reject the pixels that belong to the contour zones.

The next step partitions the cell into the regions that can be intuitively distinguished in the previously computed histogram, looking for its valleys.

3.2 Detection of the Cable

Once the cell has been segmented, the system proceeds to locate the cable executing the tasks enumerated in fig. 2(b). This step is carried out from the contours of the segmented cell, by looking for lines which can belong or be near the sides of the cable. In this context, a line is defined as a set of connected contour pixels not including branches. On the other hand, it is important to note that, unlike

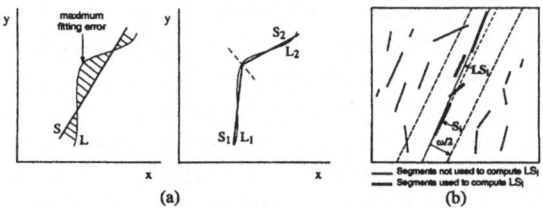

Fig. 3. (a) Splitting of a line L; (b) Co-linearity analysis

previous versions of the system [8], the detection step does not assume a vertical orientation of the cable in the image. This restriction is removed in order to use any evidence of the presence of the cable. However, it also increases the probability of erroneous detections.

Lines are obtained by scanning the segmented cell from bottom to top. The direction of scanning is important as the lower part of the image tends to be clearer than the upper part when the camera is not oriented towards the seabed, due to the properties of light propagation undersea. Once a contour pixel has been found, adjacent pixels are selected according to a prediction of the cable orientation produced by a Kalman filter applied over the past cable parameters. Using this information, the system favours looking for lines in directions similar to the predicted one. When, for a given contour pixel, there is no adjacent pixel in the preferred directions, the process of tracking the line finishes and a new one starts by resuming the scanning of the cell from the point it was left.

A straight segment fitting task follows next. This process can be seen as a low-pass filter to remove noise either due to the redefinition of the cable contours caused by the proliferation of flora on top of and by the cable, and due to the processes of acquisition and segmentation. Total least squares is used in the fitting. As the fitting error can become large in some cases, a control procedure is executed after each fitting. It is as follows: (1) for each point p_i belonging to the line L, its orthogonal distance to the fitted straight segment S, $d(p_i, S) \geq 0$, is computed; (2) if $d(p_j, S) = max\{d(p_i, S) \mid p_i \in L\} \geq k_e$, then L is split into two halves by the point of greatest local maximum error which is not an end of the line (k_e is a threshold). See fig. 3(a) for a typical example.

The resultant set of straight segments is filtered according to their length. In this context, the length of a straight segment is defined by means of the total number of contour points that it fits. The filter consists in keeping the N longest straight segments. In this way, it is intended to reduce the size of the problem in a controlled way. Besides, as the segments that supply more information are kept, a non-negative influence of the filter on the results obtained is expected.

Subsequently, a co-linearity analysis is applied to the set of straight segments obtained, in order to join the segments that can be considered as originally belonging to the same long straight contour. As an example of the analysis performed, consider the set of segments that have passed the length-based filtering process (see fig. 3(b)). For each straight segment S_i under analysis, a new long straight segment LS_i is calculated using again total least squares. This time, the points used in the fitting are those contour points corresponding to the straight segments which completely fall within a strip-shaped region aligned with S_i, whose width is w, the tolerated co-linearity error.

Immediately afterwards, the resultant set of straight segments is filtered again. Unlike the specific length filter, now each long straight segment is evaluated based on a suitable combination of four different criteria. Those segments that obtain an evaluation lower than a predefined threshold are removed. In this way, it is intended to reject straight segments with little probability of belonging to one side of the cable. The criteria used to assess such segments are as follows: length (C_1), fitting error (C_2), average of the gradient modulus of the contour pixels fitted by the straight segment considered (C_3), and the standard deviation of the differences among the gradient directions of the aforementioned contour pixels (C_4). The partial and normalised assessments obtained of each one of the previous criteria are weighted in order to compute the final one. Successful results have been achieved assigning a higher weight to the criteria C_1 and C_2.

The last task of the detection step consists in choosing the pair of long straight segments which are likely to correspond to the sides of the cable. Considering its morphological characteristics, the task mainly looks for two long and parallel straight lines. Initially, each possible pair of straight segments is checked according to the distance that separates them. Those pairs whose separation reasonably differs from the expected width of the cable in the images are discarded. Note that, using this new parameter, the system assumes that the width of the cable does not change significantly between images. This is just a matter of navigation control. The probability of erroneous detections thus is considerably reduced. Afterwards, three different criteria are used to evaluate each surviving pair of straight segments: degree of parallelism (C_5), average of the Euclidean length of both segments (C_6), and, finally, the average of the individual assessments obtained by such segments in the previous task (C_7). Once all the final weighted assessments have been computed, the pair with the highest one is selected. In case the maximum score is below a minimum value, it is considered there is not enough evidence of the cable in the cell.

3.3   Fusion of Partial Results

Once all the cells of the grid have been processed, each cell contributes to the computation of the global position and orientation of the cable using the resultant partial detections. Those cells for which two long parallel straight segments showing enough evidence of the presence of the cable have been found contribute with that pair. In the remaining cases, the contribution consists in the segments surviving the filtering tasks previous to the pairing. In this way, both sides of the cable are not required to lie in the same cell of the grid so as to be taken into account. Results are merged considering non-overlapping groups of 2×2 cells in a pyramidal way, reducing, at each iteration, the number of cells from $N \times M$ to $\lceil \frac{N}{2} \rceil \times \lceil \frac{M}{2} \rceil$. For every set of cells, the fusion of results is achieved by re-executing the segment grouping, heterogeneous filtering and segment selection

Table 1. Image sequence results

Sequence	Length (frames)	Frame rate achieved	Wrong detections	Success rate
1	253	61.76 f/s - 16 ms/f	37	85%
2	499	33.02 f/s - 30 ms/f	64	87%
3	386	39.93 f/s - 25 ms/f	11	97%
4	116	33.29 f/s - 30 ms/f	11	90%
5	113	36.75 f/s - 27 ms/f	11	90%
Average	1367	40.95 f/s - 24 ms/f	134	89.8%

tasks previously described (see fig. 2(b)). The merging process finishes when only one cell is left. In this case, the average of the pair of segments resulting from the segment selection task, if any, constitutes the output of the vision system.

3.4   Cable Tracking Strategy

The tracking stage is based on the hypothesis that the cable parameters are not going to change too much from one image to the next. Therefore, once the cable has been detected in the image sequence, the computed position and orientation are used to predict the new parameters in the next image. In this way, the image area where to look for the cable can be reduced to a ROI, increasing, thus, the probability of success. In case the system is not able to find enough evidence of the cable in the ROI, the recovery mechanism previously described is activated.

To predict the cable parameters, the system makes use of a linear Kalman filter for the main axis of the cable. Previous versions of the system carry out such prediction by means of two filters, one for every side of the cable (see [8] for details). The main axis has however shown to be more predictable than the sides. The state vector X contains the position and orientation of the main cable axis in the Hough plane (ρ, θ). The model of the filter is expressed as (1) $X(t+1) = X(t) + v(t)$ and (2) $Z(t+1) = X(t) + w(t)$, where v and w represent respectively the process and the measurement noises.

The ROI for the next image is computed as follows: first, the position and orientation of each cable side are estimated on the basis of the predicted main axis and the expected cable width in the images; afterwards, a small tolerance factor is added to both sides.

4   Experimental Results

To test the system, real image sequences coming from several ROV sessions recorded on video tape have been used. Specifically, five sequences were selected from that recorded material to carry out the experiments. Although they are

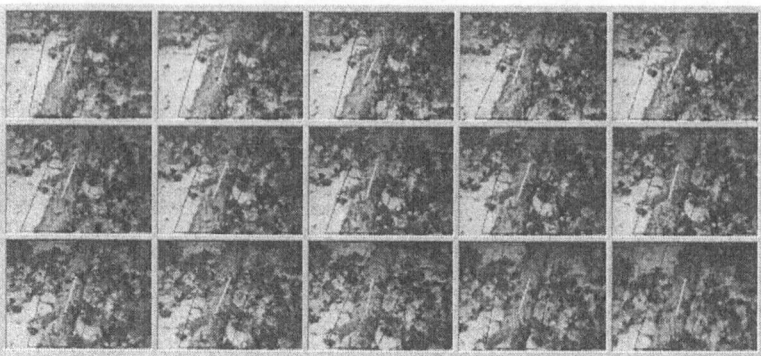

Fig. 4. Results for an excerpt of sequence 4 with the ROI superimposed. The white line represents the computed main cable axis and thus a possible command to the AUV navigation controller

not very lengthy, they cover a wide range of complexity: steep gradient in illumination, low contrast and blurring, objects overlapping the cable, instability in the vehicle motion, etc. Table 1 shows relevant information about every sequence. The success rate appearing in the table refers to those images for which the ROI wholly includes the cable and the system has been able to determine correctly its location. All the tests were run on an Intel Pentium III 800 MHz machine executing Windows XP Professional, and the resolution of the images was half-NTSC (320 × 240 pixels).

Fig. 4 shows results for an excerpt of sequence 4. In general, the system tends to return the main axis of the cable within the cable region of every image, as it can be seen in the figure, so that it can be said the position of the cable is correctly detected every time. The orientation measured, however, is sometimes affected by the noise present in the image, either in the form of small particles of algae and lack of contrast between cable and seabed. Consequently, sometimes deviates from the real orientation.

5   Conclusions and Future Work

A vision system for real-time underwater cable tracking has been presented. Using only visual information, the system is able to locate and follow a cable in an image sequence overcoming the typical difficulties of underwater scenes. Five highly realistic sequences have been used to test the system. The mean success rate that has been achieved is about 90% for a frame rate of more than 25 frames/second. Given the fact that the output of the system has not been used to correct the vehicle's course, which would give rise to softer movements of the camera, a higher success rate is still expected. Additional information about the vision system can be found in [2].

This study is included in a more ambitious project in which the inspection of underwater installations in connection with the proposed system is the main concern. At present, a first approximation to the control architecture for locating and tracking the cable autonomously on the basis of the vision system has been successfully implemented and validated. For a detailed description on the subject, the reader is referred to [1].

Acknowledgments

The authors of this study wish to thank GESA for supplying them the cable image sequences used to test the vision system.

References

[1] J. Antich and A. Ortiz. A behaviour-based control architecture for visually guiding an underwater cable tracker. In *Proceedings of the IFAC Workshop GCUV*, 2003.

[2] J. Antich and A. Ortiz. Behaviour-based control of an underwater cable tracker. Technical Report A-4-2003, Departament de Matemàtiques i Informàtica (UIB), 2003.

[3] A. Balasuriya and T. Ura. Multi-sensor fusion for autonomous underwater cable tracking. In *Proceedings of the MTS/IEEE Oceans*, pages 209–215, 1999.

[4] A. Balasuriya et al. Vision based autonomous underwater vehicle navigation: underwater cable tracking. In *Proceedings of the MTS/IEEE Oceans*, pages 1418–1424, 1997.

[5] J. O. Hallset. *Testing the Robustness of an Underwater Vision System*, pages 225–260. In Real-Time Imaging: theory, techniques, and applications. IEEE Press, 1996.

[6] S. Matsumoto and Y. Ito. Real-time vision-based tracking of submarine cables for AUV/ROV. In *Proceedings of the MTS/IEEE Oceans*, pages 1997–2002, 1995.

[7] A. Ortiz, G. Oliver, and J. Frau. A vision system for underwater real-time control tasks. In *Proceedings of the MTS/IEEE Oceans*, volume 2, pages 1425–1430, 1997.

[8] A. Ortiz, M. Simó, and G. Oliver. A vision system for an underwater cable tracker. *International Journal of Machine Vision and Applications*, 13(3):129–140, 2002.

[9] J. Santos-Victor and J. Sentieiro. The role of vision for underwater vehicles. In *Proceedings of the IEEE Symposium on AUV Technology*, pages 28–35, 1994.

[10] P. Zingaretti et al. Imaging approach to real-time tracking of submarine pipeline. In *Proceedings of the SPIE Electronic Imaging*, volume 2661, pages 129–137, 1996.

A Hierarchical Clustering Strategy and Its Application to Proteomic Interaction Data

Vicente Arnau[1] and Ignacio Marín[2]

[1] Departamento de Informática, Universidad de Valencia, Campus de Burjassot
Avda. Vicent Andrés Estellés, s/n. 46100 Burjassot, Valencia, Spain
vicente.arnau@uv.es
[2] Departamento de Genética, Universidad de Valencia, Campus de Burjassot
Calle Doctor Moliner, 50. 46100 Burjassot, Valencia, Spain
ignacio.marin@uv.es

Abstract. We describe a novel strategy of hierarchical clustering analysis, particularly useful to analyze proteomic interaction data. The logic behind this method is to use the information for all interactions among the elements of a set to evaluate the strength of the interaction of each pair of elements. Our procedure allows the characterization of protein complexes starting with partial data and the detection of "promiscuous" proteins that bias the results, generating false positive data. We demonstrate the usefulness of our strategy by analyzing a real case that involves 137 *Saccharomyces cerevisiae* proteins. Because most functional studies require the evaluation of similar data sets, our method has a wide range of applications and thus it can be established as a benchmark analysis for proteomic data[1].

1 Introduction

When we can define a distance measure among elements of a set, hierarchical clustering techniques are often very useful to define "natural" groups within that set [4]. However, the ability of such methods to obtain reasonable classifications depend on how are the distances among the elements. For example, when many pairs of elements are at the same distance, it is often impossible to unambiguously define the groups. This problem arises in many cases, as in the characterization of nets of irregular topology, in which distances are generally constrained to values between 1 and 5 [1]. The available data on protein-protein interactions generated in massive proteomic analyses [5-7, 13] can be similarly converted into distances, that measure the degree of metabolic or functional proximity within the cell. Again, those distances are constrained. For both prokaryotic and eukaryotic organisms, it has been found that

[1] This paper is supported by CICYT (Grant No. TIC2000-1151-C07-04), by Fundació *La Caixa* (Grant No. 01/080-00) and Generalitat Valencia (Gran. No. BM-011/2002). It is also part of the *NEUROGENOMICA* project, supported by an MCYT grant (GEN2001-4851-C06-02).

F.J. Perales et al. (Eds.): IbPRIA 2003, LNCS 2652, pp. 62-69, 2003.

distances have very often low values, suggesting that the cellular protein interaction network has "small world" properties, with a high degree of connectivity and closeness among components [8, 11].

It is therefore very interesting to generate methods able to deal with those difficult cases. In this work, we describe a fast, iterative hierarchical clustering algorithm that uses the information provided by the whole database of distances among elements of a set (that we will call from now on as *primary distances, d*) to evaluate the closeness of two particular elements. The algorithm converts the primary distances between two elements into *secondary distances (d')* that reflect the strength of the connection between two elements *relative to all the other elements in the set*. Those secondary distances can then be used again to perform a hierarchical clustering analysis.

In the following section, we will detail the new algorithm and we will show its properties by analyzing a simple case. Then, we will describe the results when the method is applied to a real case (a complex set of 137 interacting proteins of the baker's yeast *Saccharomyces cerevisiae*). The last section contains some concluding remarks about the advantages of this strategy.

2   A New Hierarchical Clustering Strategy

We start by defining the parameters used to perform a typical hierarchical clustering strategy (see also [10]). Let us consider a set of N elements. For each pair of elements, we have determined a distance value, that we will call *primary distance (d)*. Let us now establish in that set a partition P, formed by M clusters (A_1, A_2, ..., A_M). Each cluster A_i contains x_i elements (a_1, a_2, ..., a_{xi}). We can define then a cluster function for A_i ($F[A_i]$) as follows:

$$F(A_i) = \sum_{k=1}^{x_i-1} \sum_{j=k+1}^{x_i} d_{a_k a_j} \tag{1}$$

where d_{ij} is the primary distance between element a_i and element a_j. The number of primary distances within this cluster is:

$$n(A_i) = x_i (x_i - 1) / 2 \tag{2}$$

Similarly, we can define a function for the whole partition ($F[P]$) , that includes the distances among all elements:

$$F(P) = \sum_{i=1}^{N-1} \sum_{j=i+1}^{N} d_{ij} \tag{3}$$

The number of primary distances for the whole partition is:

$$n(P) = N (N - 1) / 2 \tag{4}$$

We can then define a global function ($F[G]$) that evaluates, once the clusters have been established, the average of the distances for pairs of elements included in the clusters respect to the average value of distances in the whole partition:

$$F(G) = [\ \frac{\sum_{i=1}^{M} F_{A_i}}{\sum_{i=1}^{M} \dfrac{x_i(x_i - 1)}{2}} \ ] \ / \ [\, F(P)/n(P)\,] \tag{5}$$

This F(G) value is minimum when the clustering obtained is optimal. Therefore, the problem to solve is to minimize the value of F(G) for a certain set of elements. A typical algorithm of hierarchical clustering is developed in [2]. Starting with N elements, a maximum number of N clusters are established. An F(A$_i$) value equal to zero is assigned to all single-element clusters (i. e. intraelement distances are zero). Then, the best grouping with N − 1 clusters is determined by examining all possible combinations among the N elements and putting together the two elements that have a minimum distance (equivalent to minimizing F[G] for that particular number of clusters). This procedure can be repeated for N-2, N-3, ..., up to 1 clusters. It is significant that the way that the F(G) values change every time a cluster is eliminated provides a hint of the quality of the clustering. When a large increment is obtained for the F(G) value when we pass from X to X - 1 clusters, we can conclude that the grouping is becoming artificial, i. e. is putting together elements that are too dissimilar for the clustering to be meaningful [3].

Let us consider now the situation when there are many identical primary distances between pairs of elements. This situation causes the additional problem that there are many identically optimal (i. e. with identical F[G] values), but totally unrelated solutions, both when the same or different numbers of clusters are established. A typical example will clearly show how this additional difficulty complicates the clustering procedure. In Table 1, we show a table of distances, generated for illustrative purposes.

In the set shown in Table 1, there are 8 elements, named A to H, and all primary distances have values ranging from 1 to 5. Thus, many of these distances are identical. When we apply the typical clustering strategy described above, we will find that several independent solutions, obtained by connecting elements that are separated by a distance equal to 1, yield identical, optimal F(G) values. Using the data in Table 1, if we make 20 hierarchical clusterings, we obtain four solutions with identical values of F(G) (Table 2, left).

Table 1. Matrix of distances among eight elements (A – H). The distances are constraines to values between 1 and 5

	A	B	C	D	E	F	G	H
A	-	1	1	2	3	4	5	5
B	1	-	1	1	2	3	4	5
C	1	1	-	2	3	4	5	5
D	2	1	2	-	1	2	3	4
E	3	2	3	1	-	1	3	2
F	4	3	4	2	1	-	1	1
G	5	4	5	3	3	1	-	1
H	5	5	5	4	2	1	1	-

Table 2. Four optimal solutions found using Table 1 distances

Optimal clusterings	No. of times found
(A, B, C) (D, E) (F, G, H)	15
(A, C) (B, D) (E, F) (G, H)	2
(A, C) (B, D) (E) (F, G, H)	2
(A, B, C) (D) (E, F) (G, H)	1

Table 3. Secondary distances among the eight elements analyzed

	A	B	C	D	E	F	G	H
A	-	5	1	21	21	21	21	21
B	5	-	5	17	21	21	21	21
C	1	5	-	21	21	21	21	21
D	21	17	21	-	6	21	21	21
E	21	21	21	6	-	18	21	21
F	21	21	21	21	18	-	4	4
G	21	21	21	21	21	4	-	1
H	21	21	21	21	21	4	1	-

The results of the multiple replicates can be used to evaluate the strength of the connection between two elements respect to the connections among all the elements in the partition. For example, if we apply the clustering algorithm 20 times, it is found that the four solutions are generated with different frequencies. One of the solutions is found in 75% of the analyzed cases (Table 2, right). Moreover, connections between particular pairs of elements occur in several final solutions (e. g. elements A and C are together in all 20 solutions shown in Table 2). Thus, the strength of the connection between two elements, respect to the whole set, can be evaluated by considering the number of times those two elements are found together in all alternative solutions and the frequency of each alternative solution. Thus, a new table of *secondary distances* (d') can be generated that contains the number of times that each pair of elements appear together for a large and randomly generated set of alternative optimal solutions. In our example, these secondary distances are shown in Table 3. This secondary distances are simply calculated as the number of times two elements do not appear together plus one. Thus, in our case, all elements that never appear together have a secondary distance of 21 and all those elements that go always together have a secondary distance of 1 (Table 3).

Table 4. Optimal clustering using secondary distances

(A, C) (B) (D) (E) (F) (G) (H)	F(G) = 0.06086957
(A, C) (B) (D) (E) (F) (G, H)	F(G) = 0.06086957
(A, C) (B) (D) (E) (F, G, H)	F(G) = 0.15217391
(A, C, B) (D) (E) (F, G, H)	F(G) = 0.20289855
(A, C, B) (D, E) (F, G, H)	F(G) = 0.22608696
(A, C, B, D, E) (F, G, H)	F(G) = 0.69297659
(A, C, B, D, E, F, G, H)	F(G) = 1

Once these secondary distances are established, we can now use them to make a new cluster analysis. As an example, we show, in Table 4, the groups obtained by taking the secondary distances shown in Table 3 and using the heuristic hierarchical clustering algorithm described above.

In Table 4, the small increments of F(G) up to the establishment to three clusters together with the large jump in the F(G) value, from 0.226 to 0.693, when two clusters are established suggest that three natural clusters are present. In fact, they correspond to those more frequently found in the original analysis using primary distances (Table 2). However, it would be most interesting to be able to *a priori* establish a cutoff value beyond which the clustering results will be considered unreliable. To do so, we have defined an *Affinity Coefficient (AC)*, as follows:

$$AC = 100 \{(1 - F[G]) / (1 - F[G_{min}])\} \quad\quad (6)$$

Where $F(G_{min})$ is the minimum value for the F(G) function. We thus will proceed to define a particular value of *AC* and then use it to establish the limit in which the clustering procedure is stopped. If *AC* = 100, then only optimal clustering will be considered. In a case as the one discussed above, that would mean that only elements with distances equal to 1 will be clustered together. However, by relaxing the conditions, that is using *AC* < 100, we will allow some level of non-optimal clustering to occur. As we will show in the next section, relaxing the conditions of clustering may be useful when considering incomplete and/or unreliable data, as those generated in massive proteomic projects.

For a total of R replicates for the hierarchical clustering analysis using primary distances, the clustering strategy may be described as follows:

```
Select AC value
Repeat_from N = 0
    Random ordering of elements;
    Hierarchical Clustering (d, AC);
    Increment d' counters according to the solution found;
    N = N + 1
To N = R
```

3   Application to Real Proteomic Data

Protein-protein interaction data are rapidly accumulating and the analysis of these data may provide very important hints about cellular function. In the yeast *Saccharomyces cerevisiae*, massive interaction data have been obtained using two different strategies, namely massive two-hybrid system analyses [7, 12] and affinity purification of complexes using tagged proteins [5, 6]. However, there are two problems with the information generated using those techniques. On one hand, false positive interactions are generated by proteins that are "promiscuous", that is, able, under the conditions of these experiments, to anomalously bind to multiple partners. The number of false positive interactions may be up to 50% [13]. On the other hand, purification of complexes using tagged proteins is often partial, that is, the complexes obtained do not contain all the proteins that constitute them *in vivo*. This is shown by the fact that different complexes that however share several, often many, subunits are found (data from [5, 6]).

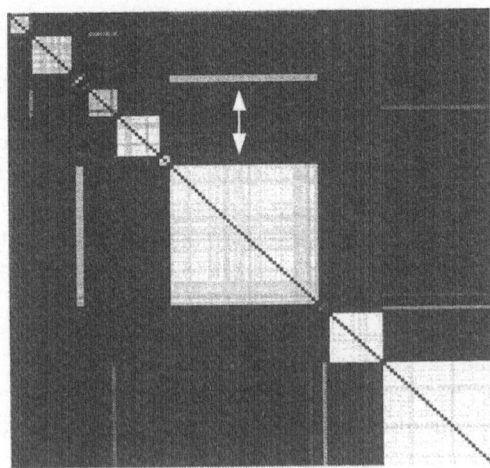

Fig. 1. Summary of results for septin-interacting proteins of *S. cerevisiae*, with *AC* = 100%. The light gray tones correspond to low secondary distances between proteins. Proteins that are part of a complex are shown consecutively in this figure. Asterisks indicate two examples of putative promiscuous proteins, characterized by having similar secondary distance values with proteins belonging to several different complexes. These results were obtained after 1000 replicates

Our clustering strategy may contribute to the resolution of these problems, especially for the data provided by complex purification experiments. In order to implement this strategy, we started by creating a simple measure of distance among proteins, that ranges from 1 (when direct interactions are known) to 5 (unrelated proteins) (Mars, Arnau and Marín, submitted). Once distances are determined for a set of relevant proteins, the clustering strategy detailed in the previous section allows to determine secondary distances among proteins. When a protein is promiscuous, it has primary distances of 1 with many proteins. This fact determines that the secondary distances of this protein with many others are similar and often much higher than expected for a protein that belongs to a particular complex. On the other hand, when different independent complexes are found that have several proteins in common, and thus most likely correspond to partial purifications of a same, bigger complex, those common proteins obtain values of distance equal to 1. When secondary distances are established, proteins of these complexes with common subunits have values that are much smaller that those found for proteins that belong to independent complexes.

We have used this strategy with the set of proteins that interact with a group of *S. cerevisiae* cytokinesis and cell cycle regulators, the proteins known as septins. Using data obtained by Gavin *et al.* and Ho *et al.* [5, 6], we established that septins interact with a total of 137 proteins that were purified as part of 13 complexes. We then generated a 137 x 137 matrix of distances by compiling all the information available for those proteins, and used our hierarchical clustering strategy to determine secondary distances among proteins under different *AC* values, ranging from 100% (only distances equal to 1 are used for clustering) to 70% (a much more relaxed condition, when proteins with distances equal to 2 or even 3 were allowed to cluster together). Figure 1 shows our results for $AC = 100\%$ using gray tones to represent secondary distances.

The first important result is that our analyses allowed the recognition of eleven of the thirteen complexes, demonstrating that the clustering strategy is correctly functioning. Moreover, our results also established the existence of a very strong link between proteins of the remnant two complexes, that suggests these complexes actually may be just partial purifications of a single, larger complex. Examination of the components of those two highly related complexes led us to the finding that they have related functions, and most likely are part of a single complex, which function would be to coordinately generate multiple aminoacyl-tRNAs in order to locally increase protein synthesis. A similar complex had been hitherto characterized in animals U (see [9] and references therein), but never in yeasts as *S. cerevisiae*. In summary, our method has demonstrated its usefulness to deal with real proteomic data, generating significant information to interpret complex interaction results.

4   Conclusions

In this paper, we propose a strategy of hierarchical clustering with two distinctive features: iterative generation of multiple solutions and control of the quality of the clustering, using the AC parameter. We also show that it can be used to analyze real proteomic data. It is known that protein complexes are often partially characterized and that a certain amount of false positives are obtained when massive interaction data are generated. Our strategy allows detection of those anomalies.

Our implementation of this method is relatively fast. Data presented above for 137 proteins generated a dataset of 9316 distances. A total of 1000 replicates to obtain reliable secondary distances from that dataset can be obtained in about an hour on an IBM-compatible PC computer running at 1.7 GHz. The examined dataset contains about 2.5×10^{-4} of all possible interactions in *S. cerevisiae* (that has about 6000 different protein products) and perhaps about 10^{-6} of all possible interactions in human cells (assuming 100000 different proteins, in part determined by alternative RNA processing). That means that analysis of the whole datasets for eukaryotic species would require parallelizing our algorithms. However, research of most scientists is focused on particular cellular processes that involve limited groups of proteins. Those applications require the analyses of much smaller datasets, as the one showed above, that can be easily performed on a standard personal computer in a short time. Thus, we think our strategy can be of very general use, and its simplicity allows it to potentially become established as a benchmark for proteomic data analysis.

References

[1] V. Arnau, J.M. Orduña, A. Ruiz, and J. Duato. "On the Characterization of Interconnection Networks with Irregular Topology: a New Model of Communication Cost", in Proceedings of the IASTED Internactonal Conference Parallel and Distributed Computing and Systems (PDCS'99) pp. 1-6, Massachusetts, 1999.

[2] R. O. Duda and P. E. Hart. "Pattern Classification and Scene Analysis", John Wiley and Sons, 1973.

[3] B. Everitt, "Cluster Analysis". John Wiley and Sons, New York, 1974.

[4] D. Fasulo. "An Analysis of Recent Works on Clustering Algorithms", Tech. Rep. # 01-03-02. Dpto. of Computer Science & Engineering, University of Washington, 1999.

[5] A.-C. Gavin, M. Bösche, R. Krause, P. Grandi, M. Marzioch et al. (38 authors), "Functional organization of the yeast proteome by systematic analysis of protein complexes", Nature, 415, 141-147, 2002.

[6] Y. Ho, A. Gruhler, A. Helibut, G. D. Bader, L. Moore et al. (46 authors), "Systematic identification of protein complexes in Saccharomyces cerevisiae by mass spectrometry", Nature, 415, 180-183, 2002.

[7] T. Ito, T. Chiba, R. Ozawa, M. Yoshida, M. Hattori, and Y. Sakaki, "A comprehensive two-hybrid analysis to explore the yeast protein interactome", Proc. Natl. Acad. Sci. USA, 98, 4569-4574, 2001.

[8] H. Jeong, S. P. Mason, A.-L. Barabási, and Z. N. Oltvai. "Lethality and centrality in protein networks", Nature 411, 41-42, 2001.

[9] L. Nathanson and M. P. Deutscher, "Active aminoacyl-tRNA synthetases are present in nuclei as a high molecular weight multienzyme complex", J. Biol. Chem. 41, 31559-31562, 2000.

[10] J.M. Orduña, V. Arnau, and J. Duato. "Characterization of Communications between Processes in Message-Passing Applications", in "IEEE International Conference on Cluster Computing (CLUSTER2000)", pp. 91-98, Chemnitz, Germany, 2000.

[11] J. C. Rain, L. Selig, H. De Reuse, V. Battaglia, C. Reverdy, et al. (13 authors), "The protein-protein interaction map of Helicobacter pylori", Nature 409, 211-215, 2001.

[12] P. Uetz, L. Giot, G. Cagney, T. A. Mansfield, R. S. Judson et al. (20 authors). "A comprehensive analysis of protein-protein interactions in Saccharomyces cerevisiae", Nature, 403, 623-627, 2000.

[13] C. von Mering, R. Krause, B. Snel, M. Cornell, S. G. Oliver, S. Fields, and P. Bork, "Comparative assessment of large-scale data sets of protein-protein interactions", Nature, 417, 399-403, 2002.

A New Optimal Classifier Architecture to Aviod the Dimensionality Curse

Paul M. Baggenstoss*

Naval Undersea Warfare Center
Newport RI, 02841
p.m.baggenstoss@ieee.org
http://www.npt.nuwc.navy.mil/csf

Abstract. In paper we present the theoretical foundation for optimal classification using class-specific features and provide examples of its use. A new PDF projection theorem makes it possible to project probability density functions from a low-dimensional feature space back to the raw data space. An M-ary classifier is constructed by estimating the PDFs of class-specific features, then transforming each PDF back to the raw data space where they can be fairly compared. Although statistical sufficiency is not a requirement, the classifier thus constructed will become equivalent to the optimal Bayes classifier if the features meet sufficiency requirements individually for each class. This classifier is completely modular and avoids the dimensionality curse associated with large complex problems. By recursive application of the projection theorem, it is possible to analyze complex signal processing chains. It is possible to automate the feature and model selection process by direct comparison of log-likelihood values on the common raw data domain. Pre-tested modules are available for a wide range of features including linear functions of independent random variables, cepstrum, and MEL cepstrum.

1 Introduction

1.1 Classical Classification Theory and the Dimensionality Problem

The so-called M-ary classification problem is that of assigning a multidimensional sample of data $\mathbf{x} \in \mathcal{R}^N$ to one of M classes. The statistical hypothesis that class j is true is denoted by H_j, $1 \leq j \leq M$. The statistical characterization of $\mathbf{x}$ under each of the M hypotheses is described completely by the probability density functions (PDFs), written $p(\mathbf{x}|H_j)$, $1 \leq j \leq M$. Classical theory as applied to the problem results in the so-called Bayes classifier, which simplifies to the Neyman-Pearson rule for equi-probable prior probabilities

$$j^* = \arg \max_j \ p(\mathbf{x}|H_j). \tag{1}$$

---

* This work was supported by the Office of Naval Research.

F.J. Perales et al. (Eds.): IbPRIA 2003, LNCS 2652, pp. 70–79, 2003.

Because this classifier attains the minimum probability of error of all possible classifiers, it is the basis of most classifier designs. Unfortunately, it does not provide simple solutions to the dimensionality problem that arises when the PDFs are unknown and must be estimated. The most common solution is to reduce the dimension of the data by extraction of a small number of information-bearing features $\mathbf{z} = T(\mathbf{x})$, then re-casting the classification problem in terms of $\mathbf{z}$:

$$j^* = \arg\max_j \ p(\mathbf{z}|H_j). \tag{2}$$

This leads to a fundamental trade-off - whether to discard features in an attempt to reduce the dimension to something manageable - or to include them and suffer the problems associated with estimating a PDF at high dimension. Unfortunately, there may be no acceptable compromise. Virtually all methods which attempt to find decision boundaries on a high-dimensional space are subject to this trade-off or "curse" of dimensionality. For this reason, many researchers have explored the possibility of using class-specific features [Frimpong-Ansah et al., 1989], [Kumar et al., 1999], [Kumar et al., 2000], [Watanabe et al., 1997],
[Belhumeur et al., 1997], [Sebald, 2001], [Oh et al., 2001].

The basic idea in using class-specific features is to extract M class-specific feature sets, $\mathbf{z}_j = T_j(\mathbf{x})$, $1 \leq j \leq M$, where the dimension of each feature set is small, then to arrive at a decision rule based only upon functions of the lower-dimensional features. Unfortunately, the classifier modeled on the Neyman-Pearson rule,

$$j^* = \arg\max_j \ p(\mathbf{z}_j|H_j), \tag{3}$$

is invalid because comparisons of densities on different feature spaces are meaningless. One of the first approaches that comes to mind is to computes for each class a likelihood ratio against a common hypothesis composed of "all other classes". While this seems beneficial on the surface, there is no theoretical dimensionality reduction since for each likelihood ratio to be a sufficient statistic, "all features" must be included when testing each class against a hypothesis that includes "all other classes". A number of other approaches have emerged in recent years to arrive at meaningful decision rules. Each method makes a strong assumption (such as that the classes fall into linear subspaces) that limits the applicability of the method or else uses ad-hoc method of combining the likelihoods of the various feature sets. In this paper, we present an extension to the classical theory that provides for an optimal architecture using class-specific features.

2   The PDF Projection Theorem

The PDF projection theorem allows us to *project* a PDF $p_z(\mathbf{z})$ from any feature space $\mathbf{z} = T(\mathbf{x})$ back to the original (raw) data space $\mathbf{x}$. Define

$$\mathcal{P}(T, p_z) = \{p_x(\mathbf{x}) : \mathbf{z} = T(\mathbf{x}) \ \text{and} \ \mathbf{z} \sim p_z(\mathbf{z})\},$$

that is, $\mathcal{P}(T, p_z)$ is the set of PDFs $p_x(\mathbf{x})$ which, through $T(\mathbf{x})$, generate PDF $p_z(\mathbf{z})$ on $\mathbf{z}$. If $T(\ )$ is many-to-one, $\mathcal{P}(T, p_z)$ will contain more than one member. Therefore, it is impossible to uniquely determine $p_x(\mathbf{x})$ from $T(\ )$ and $p_z(\mathbf{z})$. We can, however, find a particular solution if we constrain $p_x(\mathbf{x})$. In order to apply the constraint, it is necessary to make use of a reference hypothesis, H_0, for which we know the PDF of both $\mathbf{x}$ and $\mathbf{z}$. If we constrain $p_x(\mathbf{x})$ such that for every transform pair $(\mathbf{x}, \mathbf{z})$ we have

$$\frac{p_x(\mathbf{x})}{p_x(\mathbf{x}|H_0)} = \frac{p_z(\mathbf{z})}{p_z(\mathbf{z}|H_0)}, \tag{4}$$

or that the likelihood ratio (with respect to H_0) is the same in both the raw data and feature domains, we arrive at a satisfactory answer. We cannot offer a justification for this constraint other than it is a means of arriving at an answer. However, we will soon show that this constraint produces desirable properties. The particular form of $p_x(\mathbf{x})$ is uniquely defined by the constraint itself, namely

$$p_x(\mathbf{x}) = \frac{p_x(\mathbf{x}|H_0)}{p_z(\mathbf{z}|H_0)} \, p_z(\mathbf{z}); \quad \text{where} \quad \mathbf{z} = T(\mathbf{x}). \tag{5}$$

Theorem 1 states that not only is $p_x(\mathbf{x})$ a PDF, but that it generates $p_z(\mathbf{z})$ through $T(\mathbf{x})$.

Theorem 1. (PDF Projection Theorem). *Let H_0 be some fixed reference hypothesis with known PDF $p_x(\mathbf{x}|H_0)$. Let $\mathcal{X}$ be the region of support of $p_x(\mathbf{x}|H_0)$. In other words $\mathcal{X}$ is the set of all points $\mathbf{x}$ where $p_x(\mathbf{x}|H_0) > 0$. Let $\mathbf{z} = T(\mathbf{x})$ be a many-to-one transformation. Let $\mathcal{Z}$ be the image of $\mathcal{X}$ under the transformation $T(\mathbf{x})$. Let the PDF of $\mathbf{z}$ when $\mathbf{x}$ is drawn from $p_x(\mathbf{x}|H_0)$ exist and be denoted by $p_z(\mathbf{z}|H_0)$. It follows that $p_z(\mathbf{z}|H_0) > 0$ for all $\mathbf{z} \in \mathcal{Z}$. Now, let $p_z(\mathbf{z})$ be any PDF with the same region of support $\mathcal{Z}$. Then the function (5) is a PDF on $\mathcal{X}$, thus*

$$\int_{\mathbf{x} \in \mathcal{X}} p_x(\mathbf{x}) \, d\mathbf{x} = 1.$$

Furthermore, $p_x(\mathbf{x})$ is a member of $\mathcal{P}(T, p_z)$.
Proof: *These assertions are proved in reference [Baggenstoss, 2001].*

2.1   Usefulness and Optimality Conditions of the Theorem

The theorem shows that provided we know the PDF under some reference hypothesis H_0 at both the input and output of transformation $T(\mathbf{x})$, if we are given an arbitrary PDF $p_z(\mathbf{z})$ defined on $\mathbf{z}$, we can immediately find a PDF $p_x(\mathbf{x})$ defined on $\mathbf{x}$ that generates $p_z(\mathbf{z})$. While it is interesting that $p_x(\mathbf{x})$ generates $p_z(\mathbf{z})$, there are an infinite number of them and it is not yet clear that $p_x(\mathbf{x})$ is the best choice. However, suppose we would like to use $p_x(\mathbf{x})$ as an approximation to the PDF $p_x(\mathbf{x}|H_1)$. Define

$$\hat{p}_x(\mathbf{x}|H_1) \stackrel{\triangle}{=} \frac{p_x(\mathbf{x}|H_0)}{p_z(\mathbf{z}|H_0)} \, \hat{p}_z(\mathbf{z}|H_1), \tag{6}$$

where $\mathbf{z} = T(\mathbf{x})$. From Theorem 1, we see that (6) is a PDF. Furthermore, if $T(\mathbf{x})$ is a sufficient statistic for H_1 vs H_0, then as $\hat{p}_z(\mathbf{z}|H_1) \to p_z(\mathbf{z}|H_1)$, we have

$$\hat{p}_x(\mathbf{x}|H_1) \to p_x(\mathbf{x}|H_1).$$

This is immediately seen from the well-known property of the likelihood ratio which states that if $T(\mathbf{x})$ is sufficient for H_1 vs. H_0,

$$\frac{p_x(\mathbf{x}|H_1)}{p_x(\mathbf{x}|H_0)} = \frac{p_z(\mathbf{z}|H_1)}{p_z(\mathbf{z}|H_0)}. \tag{7}$$

Note that for a given H_1, the choice of $T(\mathbf{x})$ and H_0 are coupled, so they must be chosen *jointly*. Also note that the sufficiency condition is required for optimality, but is not necessary for 6 to be a valid PDF. Here we can see the importance of the theorem. The theorem, in effect, provides a means of creating PDF approximations on the high-dimensional input data space without dimensionality penalty using low-dimensional feature PDFs and provides a way to optimize the approximation by controlling both the reference hypothesis H_0 as well as the features themselves. This is the remarkable property of Theorem 1 - that the resulting function remains a PDF whether or not the features are sufficient statistics. Since sufficiency means optimality of the classifier, approximate sufficiency mean PDF approximation and approximate optimality.

Theorem 1 allows maximum likelihood (ML) methods to be used in the raw data space to optimize the accuracy of the approximation. Let $\hat{p}_z(\mathbf{z}|H_1)$ be parameterized by the parameter θ. Then, the maximization

$$\max_{\theta, T, H_0} \left\{ \frac{p_x(\mathbf{x}|H_0)}{p_z(\mathbf{z}|H_0)} \hat{p}_z(\mathbf{z}|H_1; \theta), \quad \mathbf{z} = T(\mathbf{x}) \right\}$$

is a valid ML approach and can be used for model selection (with appropriate data cross-validation).

2.2   Data-Dependent Reference Hypothesis

Under certain conditions, the reference hypothesis H_0, in (6), may be changed "on the fly". The advantage of a variable reference hypothesis is that H_0 may be made to more closely match the input data sample to avoid the PDF tails to avoid very small values of $p(\mathbf{z}|H_0)$. This is only allowed if the ratio $p(\mathbf{x}|H_0)/p(\mathbf{z}|H_0)$ is independent of H_0 as H_0 varies within a set $\mathcal{H}_z$. For every statistic $\mathbf{z}$, there is a *region of sufficiency* (ROS) $\mathcal{H}_z$. For example, let $\mathbf{z} = T(\mathbf{x})$ contain the sample variance:

$$\mathbf{z} = \left[\frac{1}{N} \sum_{i=1}^{N} x_i, \ *, \ * \dots \right]$$

Let $H_0(\sigma^2)$ be the hypothesis that $\mathbf{x}$ is a set of independent Gaussian samples of zero mean and variance σ_2. Then, it may be shown that the ratio $p(\mathbf{x}|H_0)/p(\mathbf{z}|H_0)$ is independent of σ^2 because as σ^2 varies, it traces out a ROS for $\mathbf{z}$. We are therefore justified in making the substitution $\sigma^2 = z_1$, which is the value of σ^2 which maximizes both the numerator and denominator of the ratio for each dtaa sample. This makes H_0 a function of the data $\mathbf{z}$. We therefore write

$$\hat{p}_x(\mathbf{x}|H_1) = \frac{p_x(\mathbf{x}|H_0(\mathbf{z}))}{p_z(\mathbf{z}|H_0(\mathbf{z}))}\hat{p}_z(\mathbf{z}|H_1), \tag{8}$$

where $\mathbf{z} = T(\mathbf{x})$. The reason for using a variable hypothesis is purely numerical - it has no statistical interpretation. It allows PDF approximations to be used in the denominator expression, such as the central limit theorem (CLT).

2.3   Asymptotic ML Theory

If H_0 is parameterized by a set of parameters θ, and $\mathbf{z}$ is a maximum likelihood estimator of θ, then we may use asymptotic ML theory and may approximate (8) using

$$\hat{p}_x(\mathbf{x}|H_1) = \frac{p_x(\mathbf{x};\hat{\theta})}{(2\pi)^{-\frac{P}{2}}|\mathbf{I}(\hat{\theta})|^{\frac{1}{2}}}\hat{p}_\theta(\hat{\theta}|H_1), \tag{9}$$

where $\hat{\theta}$ is the ML estimate of θ, and $\mathbf{I}(\theta)$ is the Fisher's information matrix. This expression agrees with the PDF approximation from asymptotic theory [Strawderman, 2000], [Durbin, 1980].

2.4   The Chain Rule

In many cases, it is difficult to derive the J-function for an entire processing chain. On the other hand, it may be quite easy to do it for one stage of processing at a time. In this case, the chain rule can be used to good advantage. The chain rule is just the recursive application of the PDF projection theorem. For example, consider a processing chain:

$$\mathbf{x} \xrightarrow{T_1(\mathbf{x})} \mathbf{y} \xrightarrow{T_2(\mathbf{y})} \mathbf{w} \xrightarrow{T_3(\mathbf{w})} \mathbf{z} \tag{10}$$

The recursive use of (6) gives:

$$p_x(\mathbf{x}|H_1) = \frac{p_x(\mathbf{x}|H_0(\mathbf{y}))}{p_y(\mathbf{y}|H_0(\mathbf{y}))}\frac{p_y(\mathbf{y}|H_0'(\mathbf{w}))}{p_w(\mathbf{w}|H_0'(\mathbf{w}))}\frac{p_w(\mathbf{w}|H_0''(\mathbf{z}))}{p_z(\mathbf{z}|H_0''(\mathbf{z}))}p_z(\mathbf{z}|H_1) \tag{11}$$

where $\mathbf{y} = T_1(\mathbf{x})$, $\mathbf{w} = T_2(\mathbf{y})$, $\mathbf{z} = T_3(\mathbf{w})$, and $H_0(\mathbf{y})$, $H_0'(\mathbf{w})$, $H_0''(\mathbf{z})$ are reference hypotheses (possibly data-dependent) suited to each stage in the processing chain. By defining the J-functions of each stage, we may write the above as

$$p_x(\mathbf{x}|H_1) = J(\mathbf{x}, T_1, H_0(\mathbf{y}))\ J(\mathbf{y}, T_2, H_0'(\mathbf{w}))\ J(\mathbf{w}, T_3, H_0''(\mathbf{z}))\ p_z(\mathbf{z}|H_1). \tag{12}$$

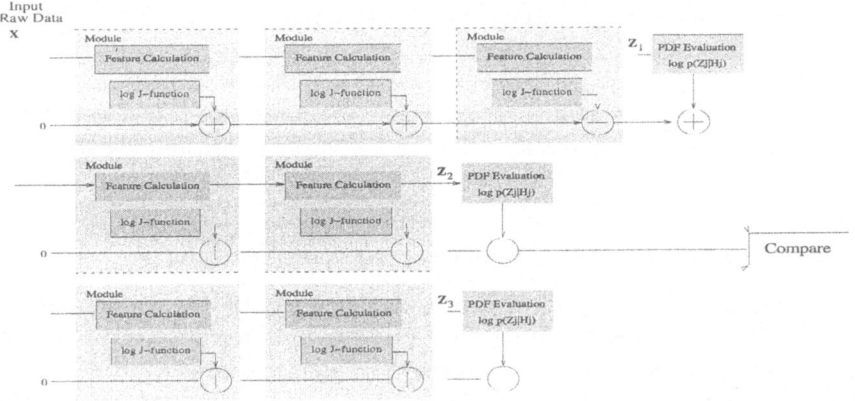

Fig. 1. Block diagram of a class-specific classifier

3   The Class-Specific Classifier

3.1   Classifier Architecture and the Class-Specific Module

Application of the PDF projection theorem to classification is simply a matter of substituting (8) into (1). In other words, we implement the classical Neyman-Pearson classifier, but with the class PDFs factored using the PDF projection theorem:

$$j^* = \arg\max_j \frac{p_x(\mathbf{x}|H_{0,j}(\mathbf{z}_j))}{p_z(\mathbf{z}_j|H_{0,j}(\mathbf{z}_j))} \, \hat{p}_z(\mathbf{z}_j|H_j), \tag{13}$$

where $\mathbf{z}_j = T_j(\mathbf{x})$, and we have allowed for class-dependent, data-dependent, reference hypotheses.

The chain-rule processor (11) is ideally suited to classifier modularization. Figure 1 is a block diagram of a class-specific classifier. The packaging of the feature calculation together with the J-function calculation is called the class-specific module. Each arm of the classifier is composed of a series of modules called a "chain".

A library of pre-tested modules are available at
http://www.npt.nuwc.navy.mil/csf . Some of the most important feature types include:

1. Linear functions of independent random variables. A widely-used combination of transformations in signal processing is to first apply an orthogonal linear transformation, perform a squaring operation (or magnitude-squared for complex RVs), then perform a linear transformation. These transformations include widely-used features such as MEL cepstrum [Picone, 1993], polynomial fits to power series and power spectra, and autocorrelation function - and through one-to-one transformations also autoregressive (AR) and reflection coefficients (RC).

2. Order statistics. Rather than applying linear filters to the chi-squared or exponential RVs at the output (magnitude-squared) of orthogonal transformations, it is often more apropriate to choose the largest set of "bins" - and regard the bin locations (frequencies) and amplitudes as features.
3. One-to-one transformations. A multitude of one-to-one transformations are used for feature conditioning including Levinson algorithm, log transformations, etc.

3.2   Feature Selectivity: Classifying without Training

The J-function and the feature PDF provide a factorization of the raw data PDF into trained and untrained components. The ability of the J-function to provide a "peak" at the "correct" feature set gives the classifier a measure of classification performance without needing to train. In fact, it is not uncommon that the J-function dominates, eliminating the need to train at all. This we call the *feature selectivity effect*. For a fixed amount of raw data, as the dimension of the feature set decreases, indicating a larger rate of data compression, the effect of the J-function compared to the effect of the feature PDF increases. An example where the J-function dominates is a bank of matched filter for known signals in noise. If we regard the matched filters as feature extractors and the matched filter outputs as scalar features, it may be shown that this method is identical to comparing only the J-functions. Let $z_j = |\mathbf{w}_j'\mathbf{x}|^2$ where $\mathbf{w}_j$ is a normalized signal template such that $\mathbf{w}_j'\mathbf{w}_j = 1$. Then under the white (independent) Gaussian noise (WGN) assumption, z_j is distributed $\chi^2(1)$. It is straightforward to show that the J-function is a monotonically increasing function of z_j. Signal waveforms can be reliably classified using only the J-function and ignoring the PDF of z_j under each hypothesis. The curse of dimensionality can be avoided if the dimension of $\mathbf{z}_j$ is small for each j. This possibility exists, even in complex problems, because $\mathbf{z}_j$ is required only to have information sufficient to separate class H_j from a specially-chosen reference hypothesis $H_{0,j}$.

3.3   J-function Verification

One thing to keep in mind is that it is of utmost importance that the J-function is accurate because this will insure that the resulting projected PDF is, in fact, a valid PDF. A fool-proof method of testing the J-function is to define a fixed hypothesis, denoted by H_s, for which we can compute the PDF $p(\mathbf{x}|H_s)$ readily, and for which we can synthesize raw data. Note that H_s is *not* a reference hypothesis. The synthetic data is converted into features and the PDF $\hat{p}(\mathbf{z}|H_s)$ is estimated from the synthetic features (using a Gaussian Mixture PDF, HMM, or any appropriate statistical model). Next, the theoretical PDF $p(\mathbf{x}|H_s)$ is compared with the projected PDF

$$\hat{p}(\mathbf{x}|H_s) = J(\mathbf{x}, T, H_0)\,\hat{p}(\mathbf{z}|H_s)$$

for each sample of synthetic data. The log-PDF values are plotted on each axis and the results should fall on the X=Y line.

4   Types of J-functions

We now summarize the various methods we have discussed for computing the J-function.

4.1   Fixed Reference Hypothesis

For modules using a fixed reference hypothesis, care must be taken in calculation of the J-function because the data is more often than not in the tails of the PDF. For fixed reference hypotheses the J function is

$$J(\mathbf{x}, T, H_0) = \frac{p_x(\mathbf{x}|H_0)}{p_z(\mathbf{z}|H_0)}. \tag{14}$$

The numerator density is usually of a simple form so it is known exactly. The denominator density $p_z(\mathbf{z}|H_0)$ must be known exactly or approximated carefully so that it is accurate even in the far tails of the PDF. The saddlepoint approximation (SPA), described in a recent publication [Kay et al., 2001], provides a solution for cases when the exact PDF cannot be derived, but the exact moment-generating function (MGF) is known. The SPA is known to be accurate in the far tails of the PDF [Kay et al., 2001].

4.2   Variable Reference Hypothesis Modules

For a variable reference hypotheses, the J function is

$$J(\mathbf{x}, T, H_0(\mathbf{z})) = \frac{p_x(\mathbf{x}|H_0(\mathbf{z}))}{p_z(\mathbf{z}|H_0(\mathbf{z}))}. \tag{15}$$

Modules using a variable reference are usually designed to position the reference hypothesis at the peak of the denominator PDF, which is approximated by the central limit theorem (CLT).

4.3   Maximum Likelihood Modules

A special case of the variable reference hypothesis approach is the maximum likelihood (ML) method, when $\mathbf{z}$ is an (ML) estimator (See section 2.3)

$$J(\mathbf{x}, T, H_0) = \frac{p(\mathbf{x}|\hat{\boldsymbol{\theta}})}{(2\pi)^{-\frac{P}{2}} |\mathbf{I}(\hat{\boldsymbol{\theta}})|^{\frac{1}{2}}}$$

4.4   One-to-One Transformations

One-to-one transformations do not change the information content of the data but they are important for feature conditioning prior to PDF estimation. Recall from Section 2 that Theorem 1 is a generalization of the change-of-variables theorem for 1:1 transformations. Thus, for 1:1 transformations, the J-function reduces to the absolute value of the determinant of the Jacobian matrix,

$$J(\mathbf{x}, T) = |\mathbf{J}_T(\mathbf{x})|.$$

5   Implemetation Problems

There are a wide range of pitfalls that must be avoided for proper implementation of a class-specific classifier.

1. Numerical errors in J-function calculation.
2. Proper selection of features and reference hypothesis.
3. Proper PDF estimation of features.
4. Data segmentation. Although the features of each class may use a different segmentation of the raw data, all features must represent exactly the same input data.
5. Normalization. By normalizing features, information relating to the scaling of the raw data is lost. If normalization is used, it must be applied equally to all dclasses, i.e. care must be taken to normalize the raw input data, which is processed by all feature transformations, rather than normalizing just a subset of the feature sets. As a rule of thumb, all energy present in the input data must find its way to the output of all feature transformations.

6   Conclusions

Space requirements do not permit any examples here. For examples and additional information, the reader is refered to the web site: http://www.npt.nuwc.navy.mil/csf. The PDF projection theorem represents a completely new paradigm in classification. Because it requires careful feature design for each data class, it is not just another method of making sense of the classification problem in a high-dimensional feature space. Thus, it is difficult to directly compare with a variety of approaches that operate on a given feature set. Furthermore, we are describing a new "method", not a new "algorithm". Therefore, proper implementation is necessary to insure that the results are valid. Results on real data have resulted in orders of magnitude reductions in false alarm rate in operational systems. Work is underway to compare the method with existing methods on standard databases of handwritten character.

We have introduced a powerful new theorem that opens up a wide range of new statistical methods for signal processing, parameter estimation, and hypothesis testing. Instead of needing a common feature space for likelihood comparisons, the theorem allows likelihood comparisons to be made on a common raw data space, while the difficult problem of PDF estimation can be accomplished in separate feature spaces. We have discussed the recursive application of the theorem which gives a hierarchical breakdown and allows processing streams to be analyzed in stages. For additional information on designing a classifier as well as a library of modules, the reader is referred to the class-specfific web site http://www.npt.nuwc.navy.mil/csf. A more detailed theoretical treatment of the method may be found in a recent publication [Baggenstoss, 2003].

References

[Baggenstoss, 2001] Baggenstoss, P. M. (2001). A modified Baum-Welch algorithm for hidden Markov models with multiple observation spaces. *IEEE Trans. Speech and Audio*, pages 411–416.

[Baggenstoss, 2003] Baggenstoss, P. M. (2003). The PDF projection theorem and the class-specific method. *IEEE Trans Signal Processing*, pages 672–685.

[Belhumeur et al., 1997] Belhumeur, P., Hespanha, J., and Kriegman, D. (1997). Eigenfaces vs. Fisherfaces: Recognition using class specific linear projection. *PAMI*, 19(7):711–720.

[Durbin, 1980] Durbin, J. (1980). Approximations for densities of sufficient estimators. *Biometrika*, 67(2):311–333.

[Frimpong-Ansah et al., 1989] Frimpong-Ansah, Pearce, K., Holmes, D., and Dixon, W. (1989). A stochastic/feature based recogniser and its training algorithm. *ICASSP-89*, 1:401–404.

[Kay et al., 2001] Kay, S. M., Nuttall, A. H., and Baggenstoss, P. M. (2001). Multidimensional probability density function approximation for detection, classification and model order selection. *IEEE Trans. Signal Processing*, pages 2240–2252.

[Kumar et al., 1999] Kumar, S., Ghosh, J., and Crawford, M. (1999). A versatile framework for labeling imagery with large number of classes. In *Proceedings of the International Joint Conference on Neural Networks*, pages 2829–2833, Washington, D. C.

[Kumar et al., 2000] Kumar, S., Ghosh, J., and Crawford, M. (2000). A hierarchical multiclassifier system for hyperspectral data analysis. In Kittler, J. and Roli, F., editors, *Multiple Classifier Systems*, pages 270–279. Springer.

[Oh et al., 2001] Oh, I.-S., Lee, J.-S., and Suen, C. Y. (2001). A class-modularity for character recognition. In *Proceedings of International Conference on Document Analysis and Recognition (ICDAR) 2001*, pages 64–68, Seattle, Washington.

[Picone, 1993] Picone, J. W. (1993). Signal modeling techniques in speech recognition. *Proceedings of the IEEE*, 81(9):1215–1247.

[Sebald, 2001] Sebald, D. (2001). Support vector machines and the multiple hypothesis test problem. *IEEE Trans. Signal Processing*, 49(11):2865–2872.

[Strawderman, 2000] Strawderman, R. L. (2000). Higher-order asymptotic approximation: Laplace, saddlepoint, and related methods. *Journal of the American Statistical Association*, 95(452):1358–1364.

[Watanabe et al., 1997] Watanabe, H., Yamaguchi, T., and Katagiri, S. (1997). Discriminative metric design for robust pattern recognition. *IEEE Trans. Signal Processing*, 45(11):2655–2661.

Learning from Imbalanced Sets through Resampling and Weighting*

R. Barandela[1,4], J.S. Sánchez[2], V. García[1], and F.J. Ferri[3]

[1] Instituto Tecnológico de Toluca
Av. Tecnológico s/n, 52140 Metepec, México
[2] Dept. Llenguatges i Sistemes Informàtics
U. Jaume I, 12071 Castelló, Spain
[3] Dept. d'Informàtica
U. València, 46100 Burjassot (València), Spain
[4] Instituto de Geografía
Vedado, La Habana, Cuba

Abstract. The problem of imbalanced training sets in supervised pattern recognition methods is receiving growing attention. Imbalanced training sample means that one class is represented by a large number of examples while the other is represented by only a few. It has been observed that this situation, which arises in several practical situations, may produce an important deterioration of the classification accuracy, in particular with patterns belonging to the less represented classes. In the present paper, we introduce a new approach to design an instance-based classifier in such imbalanced environments.

1 Introduction

Design of supervised pattern recognition methods is based on a training sample (TS), that is, a collection of examples previously analyzed by a human expert. Performance of the resulting classification system depends on both the quantity and the quality of the information contained in the TS. This dependency is particularly strong in the case of non-parametric classifiers since these systems do not rest upon any probabilistic assumption about the class models. Researchers have very early realized that the TS must satisfy some requirements in order to guarantee good classification results. From the start, two assumptions were established: 1) the set of c classes present in the TS covers the whole space of the relevant classes, and 2) the training instances used to teach the classifier how to identify each class are actually members of that class.

As the number of practical applications of these methods grows, experience has gradually indicated the necessity of some requisites for the system to reach satisfactory results. Among others, one can remark: 3) the TS represents the population, 4) the considered features must permit discrimination, and 5) the size/dimensionality rate of the sample is high enough.

* Partially supported by grants 32016-A (Mexican CONACyT), TIC2000-1703-C03-03 (Spanish CICYT), and P1-1B2002-07 (Fundació Caixa Castelló-Bancaixa).

F.J. Perales et al. (Eds.): IbPRIA 2003, LNCS 2652, pp. 80–88, 2003.
© Springer-Verlag Berlin Heidelberg 2003

An additional and interesting complication arises when the TS is *imbalanced*. A TS is said to be imbalanced if one of the classes is represented by a very small number of instances compared to the other classes. Throughout this paper, and consistently with the common practice [16, 10], we consider only two-class problems and therefore, the examples are said to be either positive or negative (that is, either from the minority class or the majority class, respectively). It has been observed that class imbalance may cause a significant deterioration in the performance attainable by standard supervised methods. High imbalance occurs in real-world domains where the decision system is to detect a rare but important case, such as fraudulent telephone calls [12], oil spills in satellite images [17], an infrequent disease [24], or text categorization [20, 18].

Most of the research efforts addressing this problem can be organized into three categories. One is to assign distinct costs to the classification errors for positive and negative examples [14, 8]. The second is to resample the original TS, either by over-sampling the minority class [19] and/or under-sampling the majority class [16] until the classes are approximately equally represented. The third consists in internally biasing the discrimination-based process so as to compensate for the class imbalance [21, 12, 11].

In an earlier study [2], we provided preliminary results of several techniques addressing the class imbalance problem. In such a work, we focused on resampling (by under-sampling the majority class) the TS and also on internally biasing the discrimination process, as well as on a combination of both methods. In the present paper, we introduce a new approach for a better and higher decrease in the number of negative examples. The technique proposed here is evaluated over four real datasets using a Nearest Neighbour (NN) classifier [6].

2 Related Works

The two basic methods for resampling the TS cause the class distribution to become more balanced. Nevertheless, both strategies have shown important drawbacks. Under-sampling throws out potentially useful data, while over-sampling increases the TS size and hence the time to design a classifier. Furthermore, since over-sampling typically replicates examples in the minority class, overfitting is more likely to occur. In the last years, research has focused on improving these basic methods. Kubat and Matwin [16] proposed an under-sampling technique that intelligently removes only those negative instances that are "redundant" or that "border" the minority prototypes (they assume that these bordering cases are noisy examples).

Chawla et al. [4] combine under-sampling and over-sampling methods and, instead of over-sampling by merely replicating positive prototypes, they form new minority instances by interpolating between several positive examples that lie close together. On the other hand, Chan and Stolfo [3] first run preliminary experiments to determine the best class distribution for learning and then generate *multiple TSs with such a distribution*. This is accomplished by including all the positive examples and some of the negative prototypes in each TS. Afterwards, they run a learning algorithm on each of the datasets and combine the induced classifiers to form a composite learner. This method ensures that all of the available training instances are used, since each negative example will be found in at least one of the TSs.

Pazzani et al. [21] take a slightly different approach when learning from an imbalanced TS by assigning different weights to prototypes of the different classes. On the other hand, Ezawa et al. [11] bias the classifier in favour of certain attribute relationships. Kubat et al. [17] use some counter-examples to bias the recognition process.

In a previous work [2], we presented some methods for under-sampling the majority class in the TS and a technique for biasing the classification procedure. Since downsizing the majority class can result in throwing away some useful information, this size reduction must be done carefully. One should be interested in using the removal of negative examples to eliminate the less valuable prototypes, that is, noisy or atypical cases, instances that are close to the decision boundaries, and redundant examples. For these purposes, we employed several well-known editing and condensing schemes [7] that offer a good alternative for removing all these examples. In [2], we tried three prototype selection algorithms. Two of them are in the group of editing: the classical Wilson's proposal [23] and the k-NCN (Nearest Centroid Neighbourhood) scheme [13]. Both aim at filtering the TS by deletion of noisy or atypical instances, generally increasing the NN accuracy. These two techniques were also used in an iterative manner.

For elimination of redundant prototypes, we have employed the Modified Selective (MS) [1] condensing. This method is based on the idea of creating a consistent subset [15], and guarantees a suitable approximation to the NN decision boundaries as they are defined by the whole TS. Finally, employment of the combined editing-condensing (Wilson + MS and k-NCN + MS) was also proposed as a way of downsizing the majority class in the TS to balance the class distribution.

For internally biasing the discrimination procedure, we proposed in [2] a weighted distance function to be used in the classification phase. Let $d_E(\cdot)$ be the Euclidean metric, and let Y be a new sample to be classified. Let x_0 be a training prototype from class i, let N_i be the number of prototypes from class i, let N be the TS size, and let m be the dimensionality of the feature space. Then, the weighted distance measure is defined as:

$$d_W(Y, x_0) = (\tfrac{N_i}{N})^{1/m} \cdot d_E(Y, x_0)$$

The basic idea behind this weighted distance is to compensate for the imbalance in the TS without actually altering the class distribution. Thus, weights are assigned, unlike in the usual weighted k-NN rule [9], to the respective classes and not to the individual prototypes. In such a way, since the weighting factor is higher for the majority class than for the minority one, the distance to positive instances becomes much lower than the distance to negative examples. This produces a tendency for the new patterns to find their nearest neighbour among the prototypes from the minority class.

3   Classifier Performance in Class Imbalance Problems

To evaluate the performance of learning systems, a confusion matrix like the one in Table 1 (for a two-class problem) is usually employed. The elements in this table characterize the classification behaviour of the given system. The columns are the actual class and the rows correspond to the predicted class. The sum of the two columns gives the total number of samples in each class which is $n^+ = TP + FN$ and $n^- = FP + TN$, respectively.

The standard evaluation measure in pattern recognition domain is the classification accuracy, defined as $acc = \frac{TP+TN}{n^++n^-}$. However, this form of classification accuracy assumes that the error costs (that is, the cost of a false positive and a false negative) are equal. This assumption has been criticized as being unrealistic. For instance, consider a domain where only 0.2% patterns are positive. In such a situation, labeling all new patterns as negative would give an accuracy of 99.8%, but failing on all positive cases. Classifiers that optimize for accuracy in these problems are of questionable value since they rarely predict the minority class. Consequently, in the presence of imbalanced datasets, it is more appropriate to use other performance measures.

Alternative criteria for evaluating classifier performance include ROC curves [22] and the geometric mean of accuracies [16]. These are good indicators of performance on imbalanced datasets because they are independent of the distribution of prototypes between classes, and are thus robust in circumstances where such a distribution might change with time or be different in the training and test sets. In particular, the geometric mean of accuracies measured separately on each class [16] is defined as $g = \sqrt{acc^+ \cdot acc^-}$, where $acc^+ = \frac{TP}{n^+}$ is the accuracy on the positive examples, and $acc^- = \frac{TN}{n^-}$ denotes the accuracy on the negative examples. This measure closely relates with the distance to perfect classification in the ROC space.

The rationale behind this measure is to maximize the accuracy on each of the two classes while keeping these accuracies balanced. For instance, a high acc^+ by a low acc^- will result in a poor g value. The g measure has the distinctive property of being nonlinear, that is, a change in acc^+ (or acc^-) has a different effect on g depending on the magnitude of acc^+: the smaller the value of acc^+, the greater the change of g. This means that the cost of misclassifying each positive pattern increases the more often positive examples are misclassified.

In this work, the g criterion will be used to evaluate the learning algorithms both because the interesting general properties of g and also because the pro-

Table 1. Confusion matrix

	Actual Positive	Actual Negative
Predict Positive	True Positive (TP)	False Positive (FP)
Predict Negative	False Negative (FN)	True Negative (TN)

posed classifiers do not directly have a changing parameter which properly justifies a ROC analysis.

4   The Weighted Wilson's Editing

As already explained, we have experimented with several methods [2] aimed at reducing the size of the majority class. Out of concern for the possibility of eliminating useful information, we have used the well-known Wilson's editing algorithm [23]. One of the contributions of our previous paper to the imbalance problem has been the application of this editing technique only to the majority class. Another idea also explored in [2] is the employment of a weighted distance when looking for the nearest prototype of a new pattern to be classified. Both proposals have produced a significant increase in performance.

Despite these important results, it was observed in [2] that the editing technique does not produce significant reductions in the size of the majority class. Accordingly, the imbalance in the TS is not diminished in an important way. It is worthy to consider that Wilson's technique essentially consists in a sort of classification system. The corresponding procedure works by applying the k-NN classifier to estimate the class label of all prototypes in the TS. Afterwards, those prototypes whose class label does not agree with the associated with the largest number of the k neighbours are discarded.

Of course, the k-NN classifier is also affected by the imbalance problem. When applied to prototypes from the majority class, the imbalance in the TS will cause a tendency to find most of their k neighbours into that majority class. Consequently, only a few of the negative instances will be removed from the TS. This means that the majority class is not completely cleaned of atypical cases and also that the balance in the TS is far from being reached.

To cope with this difficulty, in the present paper we introduce the employment of the weighted distance previously mentioned, not only in the classification phase but also in editing the majority class. That is, we apply the Wilson's editing procedure, but using the weighted distance function instead of the Euclidean metric. In such a way, the already explained tendency will be overturned.

This proposal is assessed with experiments carried out over four datasets from the UCI Database Repository (http://www.ics.uci.edu/~mlearn/). Five-fold cross-validation is used to obtain averaged results of the g criterion. Some datasets have required to be transformed into two-class problems, both to have a minority class and also to facilitate comparison with other published results [16].

The experimental results are shown in Table 2. The average g values obtained when classifying with the original TS, and with this TS after being processed with the idea of Kubat and Matwin [16], are also included for comparison purposes. Weighted editing of the majority class yields an improvement in performance (as measured by the g criterion). This improvement is more remarkable when the weighted distance is employed both in editing and classification. It is

Table 2. Average g value by processing the majority class

	Phoneme	Satimage	Glass	Vehicle
Original TS	73.8	70.9	86.7	55.8
Euclidean editing and classification	74.9	73.0	86.2	64.0
Euclidean editing and weighted classif.	75.7	76.2	87.9	65.8
Weighted editing and Euclidean classif.	75.0	74.5	86.2	65.6
Weighted editing and classification	75.3	77.8	87.9	67.2
Kubat and Matwin	74.4	71.7	86.4	61.0

Table 3. Average size before and after processing the majority class

	Phoneme	Satimage	Glass	Vehicle
Original TS	3,054.0	4,647.0	150.0	508.0
After Euclidean editing	2,882.8	4,471.6	147.2	414.8
After weighted editing	2,729.8	4,320.6	144.6	392.0

also important to note that the results from the procedure of Kubat and Matwin are excelled in all datasets.

The effects of the weighted Wilson's editing can be better analyzed by considering the number of negative examples that remain in the TS after its application (see Table 3). Results in this table suggest a higher decrease in the size of the majority class when it is processed with the weighted editing.

On the other hand, there is no reason to consider that the minority class is free from atypical prototypes, which certainly affect the classifier performance. However, none of the previously published works has reported attempts to eliminate noisy positive examples. Because of the relative small size of the minority class, positive prototypes are considered as very important and therefore, elimination of some of them is usually regarded as a very risky undertaking.

To explore the convenience of editing also the minority class, we have done some experiments applying the usual and the weighted editings to both classes simultaneously. In these experiments, both editing procedures have been applied only once since more iterations may lead to removal of all examples in the minority class. As can be seen in Table 4, both editing methods have produced an increase in the imbalance between the classes, although this increment is patently lower when the weighted editing was applied.

Despite this imbalance intensification, weighted editing of both classes produces enhancement of the g values, when compared with the usual editing technique (see Table 5). This is particularly true when the weighted distance is also employed to classify new patterns. These results indicate that the weighted distance for classification is able to cope with the imbalance increase (with the weighted editing) when it is moderate, as in Phoneme and Glass databases.

In these datasets, the g values now obtained exceed the best results shown in Table 2 (editing only the majority class).

5   Concluding Remarks and Further Work

In some real-world applications, the learning system has to work with just a few positive examples and a great number of negative instances. Traditional learning systems such as the NN rule can be misled when applied to such practical problems. This effect can become moderate by using some simple prototype selection techniques to under-sample the majority class and/or some kind of weighted distance to compensate the imbalance. In these directions, a new approach has been proposed in this paper. The idea of employing a weighted distance when editing the majority class has yield promising results: majority class gets a higher size reduction and the resulting TS is better cleaned from atypical prototypes.

The issue of cleaning also the minority class, through removal of noisy and redundant prototypes, deserves further attention. The resulting increase in the imbalance when both classes are processed may be diminished if the minority class is over-sampled after the application of the editing procedure. In our paper, we have shown that, when this increase is moderate, employment of the weighted distance in the classification stage is able to obtain accuracy improvement.

Despite the successful results, a problem common to most of the downsizing techniques is that they do not permit control on the number of prototypes to be removed. Therefore, eliminated examples can be too many or too few to adequately solve the class imbalance problem. Hence, experimentation with schemes that allow to control the number of resulting examples [5] could be of interest.

Table 4. Majority to minority ratio when both classes are processed

	Phoneme	Satimage	Glass	Vehicle
Original TS	2.41	9.29	6.25	2.99
After Euclidean editing	2.85	12.06	8.00	6.90
After weighted editing	2.52	10.37	7.23	5.49

Table 5. Average g values when processing both classes

	Phoneme	Satimage	Glass	Vehicle
Euclidean editing and classification	73.8	66.4	84.6	47.5
Euclidean editing and weighted classif.	76.7	69.5	86.4	51.5
Weighted editing and Euclidean classif.	75.1	70.1	84.6	52.3
Weighted editing and classification	76.4	72.2	88.7	56.1

References

[1] Barandela, R., Cortès, N., Palacios, A.: The nearest neighbor rule and the reduction of the training sample size, In: *Proc. 9th Spanish Symp. on Pattern Recognition and Image Analysis* **1** (2001) 103-108.

[2] Barandela, R., Sánchez, J. S., García, V., Rangel, E.: Strategies for learning in class imbalance problems, *Pattern Recognition* **36** (2003) 849-851.

[3] Chan, P., Stolfo, S.: Toward scalable learning with non-uniform class and cost distributions: a case study in credit card fraud detection, In: *Proc. 4th Int. Conf. on Knowledge Discovery and Data Mining* (1998) 164-168.

[4] Chawla, N. V., Bowyer, K. W., Hall, L. O., Kegelmeyer, W. P.: SMOTE: synthetic minority over-sampling technique, *Journal of Artificial Intelligence Research* **16** (2000) 321-357.

[5] Chen, C. H., Józwik, A.: A sample set condensation algorithm for the class sensitive artificial neural network, *Pattern Recognition Letters* **17** (1996) 819-823.

[6] Cover, T. M., Hart, P. E.: Nearest neighbor pattern classification, *IEEE Trans. on Information Theory* **13** (1967) 21-27.

[7] Dasarathy, B. V.: *Nearest Neighbor Norms: NN Pattern Classification Techniques*, IEEE Computer Society Press, Los Alamos, CA, 1991.

[8] Domingos, P.: Metacost: a general method for making classifiers cost-sensitive, In: *Proc. 5th Int. Conf. on Knowledge Discovery and Data Mining* (1999) 155-164.

[9] Dudani, S. A.: The distance-weighted k-nearest neighbor rule, *IEEE Trans. on Systems, Man, and Cybernetics* **6** (1976) 325-327.

[10] Eavis, T., Japkowicz, N.: A recognition-based alternative to discrimination-based multi-layer perceptrons, In: *Advances in Artificial Intelligence* **LNCS 1822**, Springer-Verlag (2000) 280-292.

[11] Ezawa, K. J., Singh, M., Norton, S. W.: Learning goal oriented Bayesian networks for telecommunications management, In: *Proc. 13th Int. Conf. on Machine Learning* (1996) 139-147.

[12] Fawcett, T., Provost, F.: Adaptive fraud detection, *Data Mining and Knowledge Discovery* **1** (1996) 291-316.

[13] Ferri, F. J., Sánchez, J. S., Pla, F.: Editing prototypes in the finite sample size case using alternative neighbourhoods, In: *Advances in Pattern Recognition* **LNCS 1451**, Springer-Verlag (1998) 620-629.

[14] Gordon, D. F., Perlis, D.: Explicitly biased generalization, *Computational Intelligence* **5** (1989) 67-81.

[15] Hart, P. E.: The condensed nearest neighbor rule, *IEEE Trans. on Information Theory* **14** (1968) 515-516.

[16] Kubat, M., Matwin, S.: Addressing the curse of imbalanced training sets: one-sided selection, In: *Proc. 14th Int. Conf. on Machine Learning* (1997) 179-186.

[17] Kubat, M., Holte, R., Matwin, S.: Machine learning for the detection of oil spills in satellite radar images, *Machine Learning* **30** (1998) 195-215.

[18] Lewis, D, Catlett, J.: Heterogeneous uncertainity sampling for supervised learning, In: *Proc. 11th Int. Conf. on Machine Learning* (1994) 148-156.

[19] Ling, C. X., Li, C.: Data mining for direct marketing: problems and solutions, In: *Proc. 4th Int. Conf. on Knowledge Discovery and Data Mining* (1998) 73-79.

[20] Mladenic, D., Grobelnik, M.: Feature selection for unbalanced class distribution and naive Bayes, In: *Proc. 16th Int. Conf. on Machine Learning* (1999) 258-267.

[21] Pazzani, M., Merz, C., Murphy, P., Ali, K., Hume, T., Brunk, C.: Reducing misclassification costs, In: *Proc. 11th Int. Conf. on Machine Learning* (1994) 217-225.
[22] Swets, J., Dawes, R., Monahan, J.: Better decisions through science, *Scientific American* (2000) 82-87.
[23] Wilson, D. L.: Asymptotic properties of nearest neighbor rules using edited data sets, *IEEE Trans. on Systems, Man and Cybernetics* **2** (1972) 408-421.
[24] Woods, K., Doss, C., Bowyer, K. W., Solka, J., Priebe, C., Kegelmeyer, W. P.: Comparative evaluation of pattern recognition techniques for detection of microcalcifications in mammography, *International Journal of Pattern Recognition and Artificial Intelligence* **7** (1993) 1417-1436.

Morphological Recognition of Olive Grove Patterns

Teresa Barata and Pedro Pina

CVRM / Centro de Geo-Sistemas, Instituto Superior Técnico
Av. Rovisco Pais, 1049-001 Lisboa, Portugal
{tbarata,ppina}@alfa.ist.utl.pt

Abstract. This paper presents a methodology to segment olive groves in high spatial resolution remotely sensed images. The developed algorithms exploit the typical spatial patterns presented by this forest cover and are mainly based on mathematical morphology operators. It consists on identifying firstly the olive groves followed by the recognition of their individual trees. The methodology is tested with ortophotomaps from a region in central Portugal.

1   Motivation and Objectives

The Mediterranean agricultural landscape is, since antiquity, characterised by the presence of the olive tree that has been preserved and intensively used by their people. On the agricultural and economical points of views, this species assumes a fundamental role, which presently receives an important financial support by the agricultural strategy of the European Union, constituting therefore an important natural resource, which is important to evaluate correctly. The main producer countries also dispose of informatics instruments to manage this resource, namely, through Geographical Information Systems where the information of the producers is introduced and updated in a periodic basis. Nevertheless, these tasks are presently performed, among other traditional methods, by using mainly the traditional techniques in forest inventories, *i.e.*, through the manual photo interpretation of aerial photographs by an expert, when these images exist, together with fieldwork missions.

Due to this situation and considering the current state-of-the-art in pattern recognition/image analysis, where several forest cover segmentation approaches have been published recently [2][3][6][7][9][12][13] but none on the specific olive trees cover, it was considered to develop a methodology to substitute the fastidious and incomplete present procedures of evaluating and upgrading olive groves.

From the spatial point of view, the olives trees are characterised by a regular spatial pattern along lines and rows where each tree can be identified by a circular region (its cupola) over a different background. This well-defined spatial arrangement, distinguishable in images with high spatial resolution gives the possibility of recognising directly this forest class without combining information where the spectral power is higher (for instance, from the Landsat TM bands).

The *methodology developed* and presented in this paper exploits the textural information at high spatial resolution scales in order to segment the olive groves and

F.J. Perales et al. (Eds.): IbPRIA 2003, LNCS 2652, pp. 89-96, 2003.

then to recognise each tree individually. It is mainly based on mathematical morphology operators by proposing a sequence that extracts the typical regular patterns presented by this type of tree. Mathematical morphology is an image analysis theory created in the middle 1960's by Georges Matheron and Jean Serra whose initial objective was to provide some tools to describe the geometric features of structures [10]. Its theoretical evolution over the last three decades, after the first applications in the geosciences scientific domain, has successfully reached new application areas and also remote sensing (a recent complete survey can be consulted in [11]).

2   Description of Data Available

The data available to develop the present methodology consists of ortophotomaps, *i.e.*, aerial photographs that were previously geometrically corrected and geo-referenced, from a region in central Portugal [1]. The respective digital input images are true colour ones (RGB) with a dimension of 2500 x 2500 pixels, each one with 256 grey levels digitised with a spatial resolution of 1 metre/pixel.

An example showing the general aspect view of an image is presented in fig. 1, where the different olive groves that occur in this view are magnified in order to have a better perception. Its regular patterns can be clearly noticed, where the olive trees, due to agricultural practices, are regularly aligned along rows and lines presenting standard distances between adjacent trees. On the contrary, the global shape of the olive groves varies from region to region depending upon several reasons (the relief of the terrain, the type of soil, the limits of the farms, etc.), being almost impossible to find two different olive groves presenting the same global geometry. Moreover, the land where these trees are located is seasonally cleaned, therefore showing homogeneous bare or almost bare soil.

3   Segmentation: Global Mask Construction

The first phase of this methodology consists of segmenting globally the olive groves. It aims on creating roughly a mask that contains the individual olive trees. Nevertheless, this kind of hull may, in this first step, contain more information than the olive trees. This way appears the necessity of later verifying if all the trees that construct these typical patterns belong to this forest cover type. The trees, or the structures, not located at standard distances from their adjacent neighbours are not considered as olive trees. The way of providing a sequence of transforms to answer that statement constitutes the second phase of the proposed methodology (section 4).

It seems, at once, that the olive trees can be segmented using the top-hat transform introduced by Meyer [8], since it identifies the local darker regions over a lighter background independently from its height location. The black or valley top-hat version, $BTH(f)$, is computed on thresholding T at adequate levels (t_1 and t_2) the function f resulting from the difference between the closing φ with a structuring element B of size λ of the initial image f and f itself.

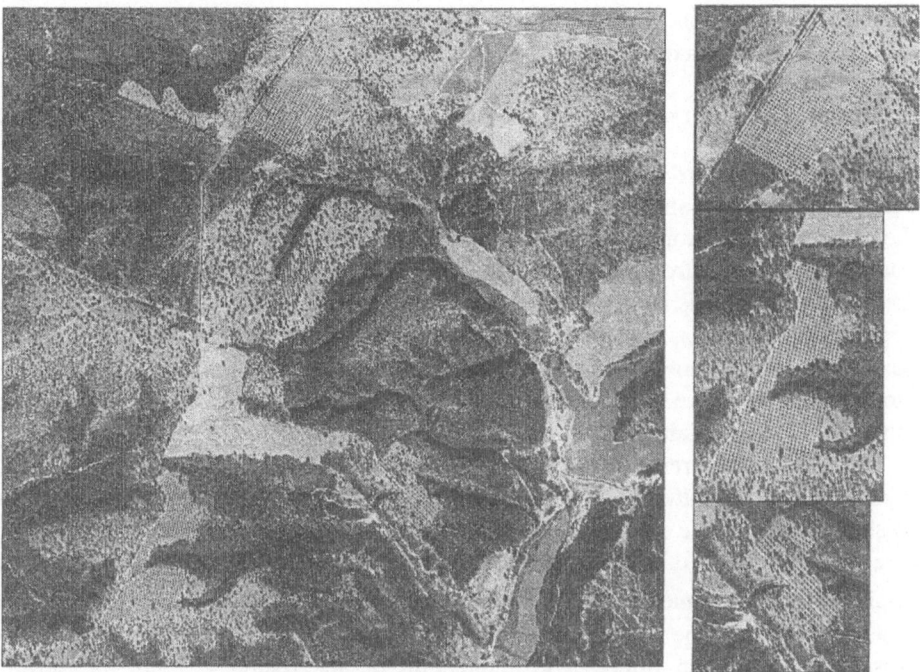

Fig. 1. Orthophotomap (area of 2500 m x 2500 m) with a spatial resolution of 1 metre/pixel and different olive groves occurring in the region, whose magnification is presented on the right side of the figure

Anyhow, the direct application of the black top-hat transform segments not only the desired sets of trees but also, with the exception of noise, the darker regions of the image that have the same size, *i.e.*, the valleys that correspond to directional structures like roads, water lines, or connected alignments of trees. No matter how long these structures are, they are always detected if their thickness is smaller than the diameter of the structuring element used. In fig. 2b an application of the black top-hat transform to the image of fig. 2a is presented, where the dark structures that have a size smaller or equal to the structuring element are segmented: the segmented image consists of the olive trees, some individual trees (mainly cork oak type in the region under study), some continuously aligned trees (see the black structure along the road in white that starts at the bottom left corner of the image in fig. 2a), and some bushes and vegeta-tion (Remark: for visualisation reasons, in the binary images the set X is represented in black, while the complementary X^c set appears in white).

In order to avoid the segmentation of directional or aligned structures, the top-hat transform should be modified. This modification follows the ideas proposed by Lay [5] to segment small black spots in the human retina. It consists of firstly computing the *inf* of the directional closings of the initial image f in the main directions of the digital grid used (in the hexagonal case the directions α, $\alpha+60°$ and $\alpha+120°$ are the ones used) with directional structuring elements l of the maximum diameter l of the trees. The following operations are the same of the classical top-hat transform, *i.e.*, consist of the difference between the *inf* image and the initial one *f*, thresholded *T* at adequate levels (t_1 and t_2):

$$X_1 = IBTH(f) = T\left[\inf\left[\varphi^{\lambda l}(f,\alpha), \varphi^{\lambda l}(f,\alpha+60°), \varphi^{\lambda l}(f,\alpha+120°)\right] - f\right]_{(t_1,t_2)} \quad (1)$$

The valleys that are filled in one direction are only retained if they are also filled in the other two directions, *i.e.*, if they present an isotropic shape. The thresholding of the image resulting from the difference operation between the *inf* image and the initial one produces the isotropic top-hat. The differences between the image obtained from the application of this isotropic black top-hat (fig. 2c) and the one resulting from the application of the classic top-hat transform (fig. 2b) are evident: only the isotropic dark structures are now segmented, resulting in a much cleaner image. Anyhow, although the olive grove is correctly segmented, there is some noise that is still included in the final image obtained at the end of this step.

To filter now the remaining undesired structures one has to take advantage of the regular pattern exhibited by the olive trees. It consists of the creation of a cluster or mask that contains the olive trees in order to filter the structures outside the mask. The creation of a cluster of olive trees is obtained by a closing operation φ with an isotropic structuring element λB of half of the size of the distance between adjacent trees in a line or row of the pattern (fig. 3a). This "strong" cluster is now able to resist to erosion-reconstruction filters. The application of an erosion ε with an isotropic structuring element will remove the smaller unwanted structures located outside the mask and will leave some regions that mark the mask of the olive trees (fig. 3b). These regions will serve now as markers for the reconstruction R of the final mask in the geodesics $\varphi^{\lambda B}(X_1)$. The reconstruction operation results from the application of the geodesical dilation δ of $\varepsilon^{\lambda B}(\varphi^{\lambda B}(X_1))$ in the geodesics $\varphi^{\lambda B}(X_1)$ performed till idempotence. The output of this transform can be seen in fig. 3c. The set intersection of this image with the initial one X_1, will provide as a result the olive grove (set X_2) but also some unwanted structures located between the olive trees (fig. 3d), that still have to be filtered (see next section):

$$X_2 = (R_{\varphi^{\lambda B}(X_1)}(\varepsilon^{\lambda B}(\varphi^{\lambda B}(X_1)))) \cap X_1 \quad (2)$$

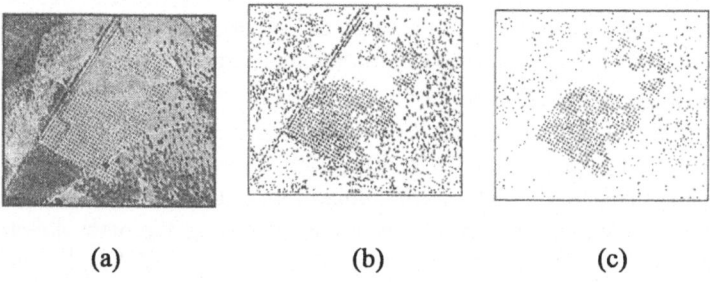

(a)   (b)   (c)

Fig. 2. Application of the top-hat transform: (a) initial image; (b) classic version; (c) isotropic version

(a)   (b)   (c)

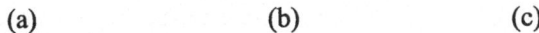

Fig. 2. Application of the top-hat transform: (a) initial image; (b) classic version; (c) isotropic version

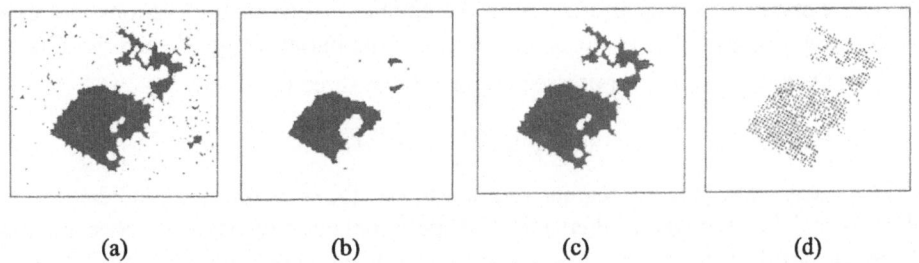

(a)   (b)   (c)   (d)

Fig. 3. Sequence to create a mask containing the olive grove: (a) closing; (b) erosion; (c) reconstruction; (d) set intersection

4   Recognition: Indirect Individual Tree Analysis

Although based on the typical pattern exhibited by the olive groves, their correct segmentation at each orthophotomap does not imply a totally correct identification of the trees that constitute them, since no verification of the structures located within each mask was directly performed. Thus, it is necessary to verify this point and, in case of missegmentation, to suppress "fake" trees.

Since the distance between adjacent trees in the terrain is standard, a simple solution to solve this problem could rest on analysing the distances measured between adjacent objects and filtering the ones not respecting the standard one. Although the solution is not straightforward, laying the major difficulty on the definition of adjacent structures, it is anyway a possible solution. Anyhow we propose to act globally on each olive grove through a sequence based on morphological operators.

The first step of this algorithm starts by identifying the geodesic centre of each structure or object belonging to each segmented olive grove (set X_3). It is obtained by a thinning ($\bigcirc$) with the letter D of Golay alphabet (see [10] for the details) performed till idempotence (the definition of geodesic centre is only valid for simply connected objects, being necessary to fill previously the occurring holes, to guarantee that all structures are correctly analysed). The following step consists of identifying the influence zone of each structure through an isotropic and homotopic thickening ($\otimes$) of the geodesic centres (the letter L of Golay alphabet [10] is the one used)(fig. 4a):

$$Y_1 = \left(\left(\left(X_3 \bigcirc D\right)_\infty\right) \otimes L\right)_\lambda \tag{3}$$

If the object belongs to the olive grove pattern then its influence zone presents a standard isotropic shape. On the other hand, the fragmented influence zones present different shapes, which signifies that they are competing for the same region and consequently indicate that not all of them belong to the regular pattern, *i.e.*, not all of them are olive trees. The identification of these "irregular" shapes is obtained through a granulometric approach by application of isotropic openings of increasing size. In order to distinguish isotropic from anisotropic objects, directional structuring elements have to be used in the opening trasform. It consists of computing the *sup* of openings by line segments of the specified size in the number of principal directions indicated by the sampling grid. The set difference between the initial image Y_2 and the filtered one permits to recover the suppressed regions by the directional openings:

$$Y_2 = \left(\sup_l(\gamma^{\lambda l}(Y_1))\right) \backslash Y_1 \tag{4}$$

These sets mark now the regions of interest, *i.e.*, the ones that are candidates to be olive trees. The recovery of their initial shape is obtained through its reconstruction R in the geodesics Y_2 (fig. 4b). Now these objects constitute isotropic influence zones divided by one or more lines of unitary thickness (one pixel in the digital images) being its merge performed by a unitary closing of size 1 (fig. 4c):

$$Y_3 = \varphi^{1B}\left(R_{Y_2}(Y_2)\right) \tag{5}$$

The geodesic centre of each one of these influence zones substitutes in the initial image the several geodesic centres obtained before:

$$Y_4 = (Y_3 \, O \, D)_\infty \cup \left(Y \backslash Y_3\right) \tag{6}$$

The resulting image constitutes now the correct olive grove where all its members are at standard distances being, indirectly, considering as olive trees (the respective influence zones are presented in fig. 4d).

5   Application of the Developed Methodology

The presented methodology was developed using an initial set of about 300 ortophotomaps from a region in central Portugal. In order to develop the methodology, 60 ortophotomaps were chosen as training set, while 30 images of those larger initial set were used as test set. The ground-truth images used to perform the comparison, *i.e.*, to compute the confusion matrixes, were obtained by expert photo-interpretation.

The analysis of table 1 demonstrates that the olive groves are identified with a high rate (59/66=0.8939). The errors committed (olive groves not identified) are related to: (i) some intrinsic features of the images (terrains not properly cleaned or presenting abundant vegetation result in images with lower contrast) and (ii) algorithmic options (the very small olive groves are filtered). There exist some structures presenting regular patterns similar to the olive groves that are identified into this forest cover (false positive), such as, vineyards or fruit trees.

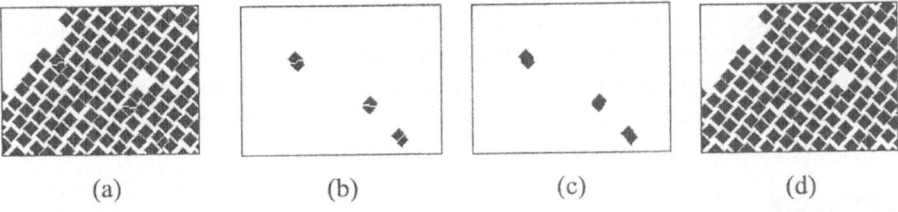

(a)   (b)   (c)   (d)

Fig. 4. Identification of possible "fake" olive trees (zoomed region): (a) influence zones; (b) candidates to "fake" trees; (c) closing; (d) influence zones of corrected olive trees

Table 1. Average classification rates of olive groves

	Ground-Truth	Developed methodology	
		Positive	False positive
Number of olive groves	66	59	7

Table 2. Average classification rates of olive trees

	Ground-Truth	Developed methodology	
		Positive	False positive
Number of olive trees	38266	36073	2497

The recognition of individual trees also reaches a high recognition level like table 2 shows (36073/38266=0.9427). The false positive ones, *i.e.*, the trees that are classified as olive trees, but are in fact other type of trees (the majority of them, are cork-oak, a common cover in the Portuguese region under study) appear normally in the neighbourhood of the olive groves being, during the application of the developed algorithm, captured and included within the constructed mask.

6   Conclusions

A novel methodology to segment and recognise olive groves in high spatial resolution remotely sensed images was presented. It is based on the assumption that they constitute typical patterns and is constructed into two main phases: the first one consists of segmenting the olive grove while the second one makes the recognition of each one of its individual olive trees. The algorithms developed appeal to mathematical morphology operators and exploit the typical spatial pattern exhibited by this forest cover type, using only intensity images (256 grey levels, 1 metre/pixel), and are independent the dimension, shape and orientation presented by the olive groves. The results obtained in the application of these algorithms to ortophotomaps of a central region in Portugal are highly satisfying, but still face some difficulties that may be solved by some improvements.

The major difficulty is related to the similarity of other regular patterns that may be confounded with olive groves, namely, the ones presented by fruit trees. Although the dimension and shape of the cupolas of the trees may be a good discriminator in some situations, it does not remain valid for some other situations. The use of spectral features is a hypothesis to exploit in future developments.

Moreover, a comparative study between images at different spatial scales is envisaged in order to evaluate the lower needed scale to perform the upgrading tasks.

References

[1]   Barata, T.: Classification of forest covers in remotely sensed images through a mathematical morphology based methodology (in portuguese), PhD thesis, Instituto Superior Técnico, Technical University of Lisboa, Lisboa (2001)

[2]   Ferro, C.J. and Warner, T.A.: Scale and texture in digital image classification. *Photogrammetric Engineering and Remote Sensing* 68 (1) (2002) 51-63

[3]   Gong, P., Mei, X., Biging, G.S. and Zhang, Z.: Improvement of oak canopy model extracted from digital photogrammetry, *Photogrammetric Engineering & Remote Sensing*, 68(9) (2002) 919

[4]   Gong, P., Sheng, Y. and Biging, G.S.: 3D model-based tree measurement from high-resolution aerial imagery, *Photogrammetric Engineering & Remote Sensing*, 68(11) (2002) 1203

[5]   Lay, B.: *Analyse automatique des images angiofluorographiques*, PhD thesis, École Nationale Supérieure des Mines de Paris, Paris (1983)

[6]   Lobo, A.: Image segmentation and discriminant analysis for the identification of landscape units in ecology, *IEEE Transactions on Geoscience and Remote Sensing*, 35(5) (1997) 1136-1145

[7]   Lobo, A., Moloney, K. and Chiariello, N.: Fine-scale mapping of grassland from digitized aerial photographs: an approach using image segmentation and discriminant analysis, *International Journal of Remote Sensing*, 19(1) (1998) 65-84

[8]   Meyer, F.: *Cytologie quantitative et morphologie mathématique*, PhD Thesis, École Nationale Supérieure des Mines de Paris, Paris (1979)

[9]   Oliver, C.J.: Rain forest classification based on SAR texture, *IEEE Transactions on Geoscience and Remote Sensing*, 38(2) (2000) 1095-1104

[10]   Serra, J.: *Image Analysis and Mathematical Morphology*, Academic Press, London (1982)

[11]   Soille, P. and Pesaresi, M.: Advances in mathematical morphology applied to geoscience and remote sensing, *IEEE Transactions on Geoscience and Remote Sensing*, 40(9) (2002) 2042-2055

[12]   Tripathi, N.K. and Gokhale, K.V.G.K.: Directional morphological image transforms for lineament extraction from remotely sensed images, *International Journal of Remote Sensing*, 21(17) (2000) 3281-3292

[13]   Uutera, J., Haara, A., Tokola, T. and Maltamo, M.: Determination of the spatial distribution of trees from digital aerial photographs, *Forest Ecology and Management*, 110 (1-3) (1998) 275-282

Combining Multi-variate Statistics and Dempster-Shafer Theory for Edge Detection in Multi-channel SAR Images*

D. Borghys and C. Perneel

Royal Military Academy, Signal & Image Centre
Av. de la Renaissance 30, B-1000 Brussels
Dirk.Borghys@elec.rma.ac.be

Abstract. A new scheme for detecting edges in multi-channel SAR images is proposed. The method is applied to a set of two full-polarimetric SAR images, i.e. a P-band and an L-band image. The first step is a low-level edge detector based on multi-variate statistical hypothesis tests. As the spatial resolution of the two SAR bands is not the same, the test is applied to the polarimetric information for each band separately. The multi-variate statistical hypothesis test is used to decide whether an edge of a given orientation passes through the current point. The test is repeated for a discrete number of orientations. Eight orientations are used. The response for the different orientations of the scanning rectangles as well as for different bands is combined using a method based on Dempster-Shafer Theory. The proposed scheme was applied to a multi-channel E-SAR image[1] and results are shown and evaluated.

1 Introduction

Synthetic Aperture Radar (SAR) image products are very important and useful for remote sensing applications because they can be acquired independent of time of day or weather conditions and because their characteristics (wavelength, polarisation, observation angle) can be chosen in function of the phenomenon under investigation. The first satellite-based SAR systems used for remote sensing were single-band mono-polarisation systems with a spatial resolution of a few tens of meters (e.g. 25m for ERS1, 30m for Radarsat). However, scene interpretation results can be greatly enhanced by combining different SAR images [1] e.g. multi-polarisation, multi-frequency, different aspect angles, multi-temporal, etc. In future satellite systems, the spatial resolution will be improved to a few meters and the systems will be capable to acquire high-resolution polarimetric and/or multi-frequency, i.e. multi-channel, data. Current airborne SAR systems are already capable to acquire multi-channel SAR images with a metric resolution. For the automatic interpretation of such images, adequate low-level image

---

* The presented research is done in the frame of a European project IST-2000-25044: SMART (Space and Airborne Mined Area Reduction Tools).
[1] The test image was provided to us by the German Aerospace Center (DLR).

F.J. Perales et al. (Eds.): IbPRIA 2003, LNCS 2652, pp. 97–107, 2003.

processing tools are needed. In this paper we propose an edge detection scheme for multi-channel SAR images. Current edge detectors were designed to work on low-resolution, single-band, multi-look SAR images. The most widely used edge detector for such SAR images is the ratio-detector [2]. It is based on the speckle distribution in uniform regions in single-band multi-look intensity images. In [3, 4] we proposed new edge detectors for polarimetric SAR images and based on multi-variate statistical hypothesis tests. The hypothesis test is applied for different orientations of a set of two scanning rectangles. In order to determine whether a vertical edge passes through a point P two vertical rectangles are constructed around the point P and the statistics of the pixels in both rectangles are compared using the hypothesis test. The test is repeated for a given number of different orientations of the scanning rectangles. Normally the maximum of the response over all orientations is considered as the global edge response. In this article we investigate a new and improved way to combine (fuse) the responses of statistical edge detectors. The method is based on Dempster-Shafer evidence theory [5, 6] which is briefly described in section 3. In a first step the fusion method is applied to combine the response of the statistical test over the different orientations of the scanning rectangles. In a second step the same fusion method is used to combine edge detection results obtained from the two frequency-bands. In section 2 the edge detector based on multi-variate statistical hypothesis is introduced, section 3 gives a brief summary of Dempster-Shafer evidence theory which is applied to the fusion of edge detection results in section 4. In section 5 results of applying the method on a set of two polarimetric SAR images, are shown and discussed. The last section presents the conclusions and the perspectives for further research.

2   An Edge Detector Based on Multi-variate Statistics

An obvious way to detect edges in multi-channel images is to fuse the results of existing detectors applied on each individual channel. An alternative is to use multi-variate statistical methods which treat the combined information from the different channels as a single input-vector. We have already successfully introduced such methods for detecting edges in polarimetric SAR images [3, 4]. Fig. 1 illustrates the two approaches that can be used for detecting edges in multi-channel SAR images. A comparative evaluation [7] has shown that the multi-variate methods outperform the fusion of uni-variate methods. The multi-variate hypothesis test for equality of variances that was used is the *Levene test* [8]. It is applied to the single-look complex data where differences in radar backscattering appear as differences in variance of a zero-mean normal distribution. The null-hypothesis H_o is that the samples from the two scanning rectangles are from populations with the same variance, the alternative hypothesis H_1 is that the population variances are different. In the Levene test the samples from the two scanning windows are first transformed in absolute deviations of sample means. In the case of a single-look complex polarimetric image with complex data of

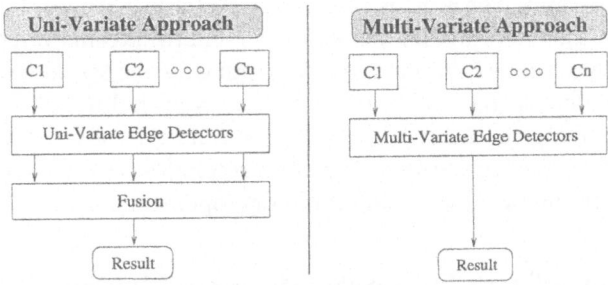

Fig. 1. Edge Detection in Polarimetric SAR

the type x^{HH}, x^{HV}, x^{VV} this results in:

$$\mathbf{L}_{ik} = \left[\,|\,\Re(x_{ik}^{HH} - \overline{x}_{k}^{HH})\,|,\,|\,\Im(x_{ik}^{HH} - \overline{x}_{k}^{HH})\,|,\,...,\,|\,\Im(x_{ik}^{VV} - \overline{x}_{k}^{VV})\,|\,\right]^{t}, \quad (1)$$

in which i is the index of the observations and k the index of the scanning window (k=1 or 2). The question whether two samples display significantly different amounts of variance is then transformed into a question of whether the transformed values show a significantly different mean. This can then be tested using a Hotellings T^2-test [9, 8]. The *Hotellings T^2-statistic* is defined as:

$$T^2 = \frac{n_1 n_2 (\overline{\mathbf{L_1}} - \overline{\mathbf{L_2}})^t \mathbf{C}^{-1}(\overline{\mathbf{L_1}} - \overline{\mathbf{L_2}})}{n1 + n2}, \quad (2)$$

with $\overline{\mathbf{L_k}}$ the average of the $\mathbf{L}_{ik}$ values in the kth window and $[C]$ the pooled covariance matrix estimated by:

$$\mathbf{C} = \frac{(n_1 - 1)\mathbf{C_1} + (n_2 - 1)\mathbf{C_2}}{n_1 + n_2 - 2}, \quad (3)$$

where C_1 and C_2 represent the covariance matrices estimated from the two scanning rectangles. The significance of T^2 is determined by using the fact that in the null-hypothesis of equal population means the transformed statistic

$$T_F = \frac{(n_1 + n_2 - p - 1)T^2}{(n_1 + n_2 - 2)p} \quad (4)$$

follows a Fisher-Snedecor distribution, F_{ν_1, ν_2} with degrees of freedom $\nu_1 = p$ and $\nu_2 = n_1 + n_2 - p - 1$. p is the number of variants, i.e. 6 in our case if the real and imaginary components for each polarisation are counted separately. From the theoretical distribution of the test statistic the theoretical $\alpha\%$ false alarm threshold θ_α for the detector can be determined. It is given by

$$P\{T_F \geq \theta_\alpha \mid H_o\} = \alpha. \quad (5)$$

The theoretical distribution of the test-statistic when the null-hypothesis is verified is used to transform the test-statistic in each point in the image into the corresponding p-value. For a value pf the test-statistic $T_F(x, y)$, found in a given pixel, the p-value is the probability that an even more extreme value can be found when the null-hypothesis is verified. A low p-value means the test-statistic is very extreme and indicates that the null-hypothesis is probably not verified, i.e. the region corresponding to the two scanning rectangles is not uniform, and there might be an edge passing between the two rectangles. Using p-values allows to compare and combine results of different edge operators.

3   Overview of the Dempster-Shafer Theory Framework

The aim of the fusion described in the current article is to combine the response of the edge detector for different orientations of the scanning rectangles as well as to combine the results obtained in different SAR images of the same scene. The proposed fusion method is based on *Dempster-Shafer (DS) theory* [5, 6] . Dempster-Shafer or evidence theory is a mathematical tool that allows to work with uncertain, imprecise and incomplete information. The uncertainty is taken into account by assigning masses to sets of different hypotheses. Several experts distribute their knowledge over these different hypotheses and a final decision is obtained after combining the masses assigned by each expert. In DS-theory a set of hypotheses is defined: $\Theta = \{H_1, H_2, ...H_n\}$. The different experts or sources of information distribute masses to sub-sets A_i of Θ. For each source of information a mass function is defined as:

$$m : 2^\theta \to [0, 1]$$
$$A_i \to m(A_i) \quad , \tag{6}$$

in which 2^θ is the set of all sub-sets of Θ and $m(A_i)$ represents the confidence that the information source has that the solution lies in the sub-set A_i. The attribution of masses for each information source is constrained by the following rules:

$$0 \le m(A_i) \le 1 \ ,$$
$$m(\Phi) = 0 \ , \tag{7}$$
$$\sum_{A_i \in 2^\Theta} m(A_i) = 1 \ ,$$

where Φ denotes the empty set. The solution is found by combining the masses attributed to the different sub-sets by the different experts. The combination of masses from different experts is done by Dempster's combination rule. Let m_1 and m_2 be the masses that were respectively attributed by expert 1 and expert 2, then the combination of the masses from these two is defined as:

$$m_{12}(A_i) = \sum_{A_p \cap A_q = A_i} m_1(A_p)m_2(A_q) \ . \tag{8}$$

Masses are thus attributed to the sub-set formed by the intersection of the different sub-sets. Depending on what happens when the intersection is empty, one distinguishes the closed world or the open world model. In the closed world one assumes that the solution corresponds necessarily to one of the defined sub-sets.

Any mass that would be combined into the empty set is therefore redistributed over all other sets and the mass of the empty set remains zero. In the open world model one allows the possibility that the solution is not part of the defined sub-sets. A mass that goes into the empty set can then be interpreted as a symptom of the fact that the solution is not within the sub-sets or that different experts have incompatible opinions. From the combined masses two functions can be derived that characterise the support to the final decision. The first is called the *belief* (*Bel*) and represents the degree of minimal support on sub-set A_i. The second is called *plausibility* (*Pls*) and corresponds to the maximal or potential support to a given sub-set in the final mass assignment [6]. They are defined as:

$$Bel(A_i) = \sum_{\substack{A_j \subseteq A_i \\ A_j \neq \Phi}} m(A_j) \quad , \quad Pls(A_i) = \sum_{A_j \cap A_i} m(A_j) \ . \tag{9}$$

In the design of a system for fusion of information based on DS-theory one distinguishes the following steps:

- Define the sub-sets relative to the problem
- Choose the model (closed or open)
- Define the mass functions used by each expert to distribute its confidence to the different sets

4   Application of DS-Theory to the Fusion of Edge Detection Results

4.1   Definition of the Sub-sets and the Strategy

The aim is to combine the response of the edge detector for different orientations of the scanning rectangles. The edge detector for each orientation of the windows is considered as an expert giving its opinion about the presence of an edge along that direction. A small p-value means the expert has a strong opinion about the presence of the edge and consequently a high confidence should be given to that direction. The larger the p-value, the less strong the opinion is and the less confidence should be given to that particular direction. We use 8 orientations $D_0..D_7$ (ranging from $D_0 = 0$ to $D_7 = 157.5°$ in steps of $22.5°$) of the scanning rectangles and we say that if a low p-value is found for a given direction, it does not necessarily mean an edge is located along that direction; it could be oriented along neighbouring directions. Even when we find an edge in a given orientation, we do not know whether there is, in the same point not also an edge along another orientation (a corner). Therefore we need to attribute also some mass to the other directions. We have defined the following sub-sets of directions:

- the singleton: $\{D_i\}$,
- the triplet: $\{D_{i-1}, D_i, D_{i+1}\}$,
- the complement of the direction $\overline{\{D_i\}}$
- the complete set of directions $\{D_0..D_7\}$

The open world model is the most convenient for our problem [13]. In general the mass of the empty set $m(\Phi)$ after combining the masses is an indication for a disagreement between experts or for the fact that the solution is not among the defined sub-sets. This mass should therefore be high at corners The mass of the complete set m_C indicates an indecisiveness of the experts. It will be low in edges or corners and high in the background. Three cases are distinguished:

- *Background:* If all p-values are "high", probably no edge is present, and we attribute most of the mass to the complete set of orientations, i.e. we know nothing to decide the orientation of an edge. The complete set will, when the masses are combined over different experts, not contribute to the mass of the empty set. Therefore the mass of the empty set will be very low.
- *Corners:* Here several experts may detect an intermediate p-value and we should find a high conflict between the experts and the mass of the empty set should be high.
- *Edges:* The p-value for the correct edge direction is very low while neighbouring directions will also have a low p-value. The mass of the complete set should be low because some experts are very sure, while there is some conflict due competing neighbouring directions.

4.2   Learning the System's Parameters

For determining the system's parameters a learning set with examples of edge (EP), corner (CP) and background points (BP) was selected.

Thresholds for the p-Values. In order to introduce a dependence of the mass assignment on the p-values that are obtained for the different orientations, the range of possible p-values was sub-divided into 5 sub-ranges corresponding to increasing p-value. The actual borders are fixed by studying the p-values of the set of learning points for a given edge direction. The thresholds are selected such that for the correct edge direction the p-values are very low or low; for corners they are intermediate or high and in the background the p-values are high or very high. The p-value thresholds that gave the best results for the Levene test are: $T_1 = 10^{-8}$, $T_2 = 10^{-7}$, $T_3 = 10^{-4}$, $T_4 = 10^{-2}$.

Optimisation of the Mass Functions. Even when the sub-sets are chosen and when we know what should be the result of the combination of masses from different experts, it is still difficult to design the mass functions consequently. We therefore determined the mass functions automatically on the basis of a small learning set. In order to find the optimal mass functions a cost function $C_{tot} = C_\Phi + C_C$ is defined as the sum of a cost function defined on the empty set and the complete set as:

$$C_\Phi = \frac{1}{N_{BP}} \sum_{p \in BP} [m_{\Phi,p} - 0.1]^2 + \frac{1}{N_{EP}} \sum_{p \in EP} [m_{\Phi,p} - 0.5]^2$$

$$+ \frac{1}{N_{CP}} \sum_{p \in CP} [m_{\Phi,p} - 0.9]^2 \, , \tag{10}$$

$$C_C = \frac{1}{N_{BP}} \sum_{p \in BP} [m_{C,p} - 0.5]^2 + \frac{1}{N_{EP}} \sum_{p \in EP} [m_{C,p} - 0.1]^2$$

$$+ \frac{1}{N_{CP}} \sum_{p \in CP} [m_{C,p} - 0.1]^2 \, . \tag{11}$$

The masses of the different sub-sets are adapted iteratively in order to minimise the cost function C_{tot} on the learning points. The optimisation is performed using the downhill simplex method of Nelder and Mead [10, 11]. Convergence is reached after 20 to 25 iterations. The resulting mass functions are shown in table 4.2. The general tendency for the resulting mass functions after optimisation is that for very low p-values most of the mass goes to the singleton. As p-value increases the mass of the triplet (neighbouring edge orientations) and the complement (a possible indication of corners) increases and finally, for very high p-values, most of the mass is concentrated in the complete set which corresponds to undeciveness (background). Masses in the table correspond to the value assigned when the p-value corresponds to the given thresholds; for p-values in between the thresholds, masses are linearly interpolated.

Table 1. Mass functions after optimisation of cost function

Sub-Set	Threshold					
	0.0	T_1	T_2	T_3	T_4	1.0
$\{D_i\}$	0.497	0.473	0.014	0.101	0.018	0.021
$\{D_{i-1}, D_i, D_{i+1}\}$	0.174	0.062	0.906	0.131	0.010	0.089
$\{D_i\}$	0.066	0.329	0.005	0.299	0.000	0.009
$\{D_0..D_7\}$	0.262	0.136	0.075	0.470	0.972	0.882

4.3 Fusion of Results from Different Frequency Bands

The test set used in this paper consists of two polarimetric images, respectively in P-band and L-band. The two images were acquired from two parallel flight paths and cover approximately the same region. However the spatial resolution of both images is not the same. Together with the SLC images we received transformation matrices that enable one to find the ground coordinates of each point in the SLC images. These were obtained by the German Space Agency

DLR by geocoding the SAR image using a DEM of the region. By combining the transformation matrices from the two bands it is thus possible to find the relationship between the positions in the two images. However, because of the difference in spatial resolution, this is not a one-to-one relationship. This is why we decided to apply the raw edge detector to each band separately and fuse only the results of the edge detection. In this paper we used the two images as two sets of experts voting for a given edge orientation in each pixel of the P-band image. The DS-based fusion is used to combine the different experts for different edge orientations as well as for the two bands. As a reference, the image with lowest resolution is used, i.e. the P-band image. The P-band image is scanned and in each pixel first the edge information from the different orientation experts is gathered and then the corresponding point in the L-band image is determined and the edge information from the L-band image at that point is also gathered. The DS-fusion is used to combine this joint information.

5   Results and Discussion

5.1   Fusion of Edge Orientations

In fig. 2 a part of the original P-band E-SAR image is shown on the left. The edge detector is applied to the three polarisations simultaneously. The dimension of the scanning rectangles is 10×50. The 2nd and 3rd image respectively show the mass of the empty set m_Φ and of the complete set m_C after combination of masses. High values for m_Φ correspond to corners and to other locations in the image with high uncertainty with respect to the orientation of edges, e.g. highly textured regions (built-up areas, forests or lines of trees). On the other hand m_C is low at the position of edges and corners. The decision whether a given point of the image corresponds to an edge (or corner) can thus be based on the combined information in m_Φ and m_C. If the point belongs to an edge, the orientation of the edge can be derived from the plausibility and the belief. The orientation corresponds to the singleton of directions for which the highest plausibility is found. The right image of fig. 2 represents the image of edge orientations.

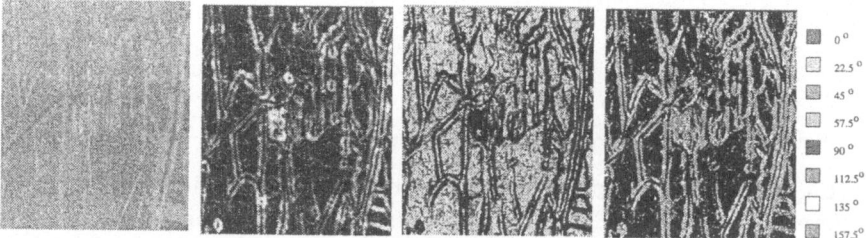

Fig. 2. Pband image results (from left to right: original image, m_Φ, m_C and image of edge orientations)

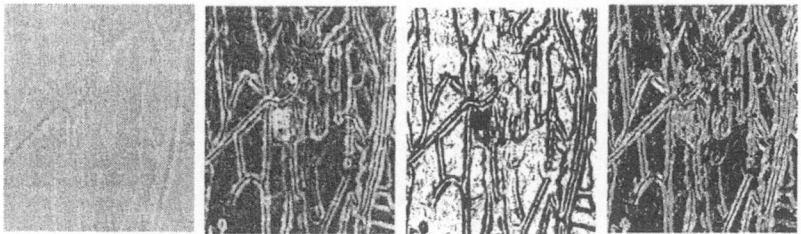

Fig. 3. Results of fusing the edge information of the two frequency bands (from left to right: original L-band image, results after fusion for m_Φ, m_C and edge orientation)

5.2 Fusion of Edge Detection Results from the Two Bands

In fig. 3 the results of fusing the edge information of the P- and L-band image are shown. Note that the L-band image in the figure was geometrically rescaled to the same size as the P-band image for display purposes. Results are also shown in the coordinates of the P-band image. Note that the image of the complete set shows more edge detail after the fusion.

5.3 Comparative Evaluation of the Results

The images above already show that the results after fusion of the two bands are better than without the fusion. In order to obtain a quantitative idea of the detector's performance we determined the *Receiver-Operator Characteristic (ROC)* curves for edge detection based on the P-band alone and after fusion of P-band and L-band. ROC curves show the probability of detection P_d of a detector versus its probability of false alarms P_f. P_d and P_f are determined on a test image in which the true edges are known. These "true" edges were indicated manually on the image. The ROC curve is generated by varying the detector's threshold. Fig. 4 shows the ROC curves obtained with and without fusion of the two bands. The curve found for the fusion is above the curve found for the P-band, indicating that the combination of the two bands indeed improves edge detection results.

6 Conclusions and Perspectives

In this article a new scheme for detecting edges in multi-frequency polarimetric SAR images is presented. It consists of two steps. The first step uses a multi-variate statistical hypothesis test to decide whether an edge of a given orientation passes through the current point. The test is repeated for a discrete number (8) of orientations. The multi-variate test is applied to the full-polarimetric image, but each frequency band is treated separately because their spatial resolution is

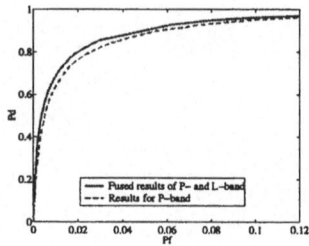

Fig. 4. ROC curve for edge detection results

different. The second step combines the edge detector response over the different orientations. For this combination an approach based on Dempster-Shafer theory was developed. The edge detector for each orientation behaves as an expert that gives an opinion about the presence of an edge in a set of possible directions. The confidence each expert assigns to each sub-set of orientations is determined using mass function. A cost function is defined to find masses in order to increase the distinction between edges, corners and background. The masses are automatically optimised using this cost function. The method is applied to a set of two full-polarimetric E-SAR images in resp. P- and L-band. In a next step we will investigate further how to incorporate local spatial information, i.e. taking into account neighbours of each pixel, to improve edge detection. In particular we will explore a method to increase further the confidence in a given edge pixel when neighbouring edge pixels in the higher-resolution image are found along the same edge direction. We will also investigate the use of active contours to improve detected edge structure and investigate synergy between our edge detector and speckle reduction methods.

References

[1] Ulaby, F.: Sar biophysical retrievals: Lessons learned and challenges to overcome. In: Retrieval of Bio- and Geophysical Parameters from SAR Data for Land Applications, ESTEC, NL (1998)
[2] Touzi, R., Lopes, A., Bousquet, P.: A statistical and geometrical edge detector for sar images. IEEE-GRS **26** (1988) 764–773
[3] Borghys, D., Perneel, C., Acheroy, M.: Contour detection in high-resolution polarimetric sar images. In: SPIE Conf. on SAR Image Anal. ,Modelling and Tech. III; Barcelona. (2000)
[4] Borghys, D., Perneel, C., Acheroy, M.: A multi-variate contour detector for high-resolution polarimetric sar images. In: Proc. ICPR 2000, Barcelona. Volume 3. (2000) 650–655
[5] Dempster, A.: A generalisation of bayesian inference. Journal of the Royal Statistical Society **30** (1968) 205–247
[6] Smets, P.: Belief functions. Technical Report TR/IRIDIA/89-4, IRIDIA, Universite Libre de Bruxelles, Brussels (1989)
[7] Borghys, D.: Interpretation and Registration of High-Resolution Polarimetric SAR Images. PhD thesis, ENST E 031, Paris (2001)

[8] Manly, B., ed.: Multivariate Statistical Methods. Chapman and Hall (1995)

[9] Anderson, T.: Introduction to Multivariate Statistical Analysis. J. Wiley & Sons (1958)

[10] Press, W.: Numerical Recipes in C. Cambridge University Press (1992)

[11] Coleman, T.: Optimization Toolbox for use with MATLAB. Matworks Inc. (1999)

[12] Fjörtoft, R.: Segmentation d'images radar par detection de contour. PhD thesis, Institut National Polytechnique de Toulouse, Toulouse (1999)

[13] Neveu, S., Boivin, V.: Contribution à la détection de contours sur des images sar: fusion de données par la théorie de dempster-shafer. Projet de fin détudes, Ecole Navale et Groupe des Ecoles Poulmic, Brest (2002)

High-Level Clothes Description Based on Colour-Texture and Structural Features

Agnés Borràs, Francesc Tous, Josep Lladós, and Maria Vanrell*

Computer Vision Center - Dept. Informàtica
UAB Bellaterra 08193, Spain
{agnesba,ftous,josep,maria}@cvc.uab.es
http://www.cvc.uab.es

Abstract. This work is a part of a surveillance system where content-based image retrieval is done in terms of people appearance. Given an image of a person, our work provides an automatic description of his clothing according to the colour, texture and structural composition of its garments. We present a two-stage process composed by image segmentation and a region-based interpretation. We segment an image by modelling it due to an attributed graph and applying a hybrid method that follows a split-and-merge strategy. We propose the interpretation of five cloth combinations that are modelled in a graph structure in terms of region features. The interpretation is viewed as a graph matching with an associated cost between the segmentation and the cloth models. Finally, we have tested the process with a ground-truth of one hundred images.

1 Introduction

In many application fields large volume of data appear in image form. The Content-Based Image Retrieval (CBIR) is the Computer Vision area in charge to handle and organize this great volume of data due to its visual content. Image retrieval from databases is usually formalized in terms of descriptors that combine salient visual features such as colour, texture, shape and structure. For any given feature there also exists multiple representations that characterize it from different perspectives. The reviews of Huang [11] and Forsyth [7] expose a wide variety of feature representations and image retrieval strategies.

This work is focused on the development of a content-based retrieval system where the image classification is done according to the presence and description of a certain object. The process involves two steps: an image segmentation and a region based interpretation. In the first step, the information of the segmented image is organized as an attributed graph which features characterize the regions and their relationships. We define certain operators that, following a split-and-merge scheme, allow the graph to evolve until finding the final solution. Image

---

* This work has been partially supported by the project TIC2000-0382 and the grant 2002FI-00724.

F.J. Perales et al. (Eds.): IbPRIA 2003, LNCS 2652, pp. 108–116, 2003.

segmentation techniques can be roughly classified into four groups: pixel based, boundary based, region based and hybrid techniques. Some understanding surveys on image segmentation are those of Haralick and Shapiro[9] and Muñoz[13]. Our segmentation strategy is classified as a hybrid method for combining clustering in the colour space, colour homogeneity and edge detection. In the second step of our process, image interpretation, the structure of the segmented regions is matched against a set of models of objects. These models are also represented as graphs that contain features such as colour, texture, size, shape and position. Hence, the interpretation step is performed as a matching procedure between the graph of the segmented image and the graph of the model objects. The best matching solution is chosen due to a cost measure provided by the matching operations on the model features.

We have tested our system by integrating it as a retrieval module of a general surveillance application. This application performs image retrieval in terms of people appearance and acts as a control mechanism of the people that enters in a building. It automatically constructs an appearance feature vector from an image acquired while people is checking-in in front of an entrance desk. This way, the system analyses some person characteristics, such as the height, the presence of glasses or the clothing, and stores the result in a database. Thus, a graphic based interface allows the security personnel of the building to perform an image retrieval of the registered people by formulating queries related on their appearance. The objective of our work is centred in the module that provides an automatic description of the people clothing. This description is given in natural language in terms of colour, texture and structural composition of the garments.

In the literature we can find several examples of strategies that, like the one which we have developed, combine region features and graph structure for database indexing [6][14]. However, in the concrete aim of the clothing description, the most similar approach consists in the Changs development of a computer-aided fashion design system [3]. However, this approach treats the clothing segmentation process but does not treat the interpretation one.

The paper is organized as follows: in section 2 we detail the image segmentation according to its graph-modelling and its strategy. In the section 3 we present how we model the clothing compositions as another graph of features and how we perform the matching to interpret the clothing regions. Next, in the section 4, we expose an example of the retrieval behaviour of our module. Finally, in the sections 5 and 6 we present some results and conclusions respectively.

2   Image Segmentation

2.1   Segmentation Modelling

Graph Representation. We model an image I as a set of non-overlapping regions R structured by an attributed graph G. The graph G is formed by a set of nodes N, a set of edges E, and two labelling functions over these nodes and edges. While each node identifies an image region r, each edge represents a relation between two regions r_i, r_j. The graph is also provided with two labelling functions, L_N and L_E. They are in charge to obtain and store the feature information F_N and F_E that identifies the nodes and edges respectively.

$$G = (N, E, L_N : N \to F_N, L_E : E \to F_E)$$

Node Features $F_N = \{BB(n), A(n), H(n), E(n), AC(n), AI(n), T(n)\}$: A region is described with its bounding box (BB), the area (A), the colour histogram (H), the edge presence (E), the average chromaticity (AC), the average intensity (AI), and the texture presence (T).

Edge Features $F_E = \{D(n_i, n_j), NH(n_i, n_j)\}$: The region relations are defined by the neighbourhood information (NH) and a similarity distance (D). In the next section 2.2 we detail how D is computed from the node features.

Graph Edition Operations. We define two graph operators that work over the graph structure and allow it to grow and to diminish. These operators are the fusion operator γ_F and the division operator γ_D. After a step of graph expansion or contraction, they are in charge to recalculate F_N and F_E and restructure G (remove obsolete edges, etc).

2.2   Segmentation Process

Algorithm Steps. As we illustrate in the Figure 1, our segmentation algorithm is a process that consists in three steps: initialisation, split and merge.

Starting from the source image I and a mask of the zone we want to segment, we create the initial graph G as a unique node. Then we expand G in two phases corresponding to a discrimination of the textured areas and a breaking of the plain ones. Thus, the division operator $\gamma_D(G)$ acts over the graph nodes due to some predefined split criteria SC based on the node features F_N. Finally we

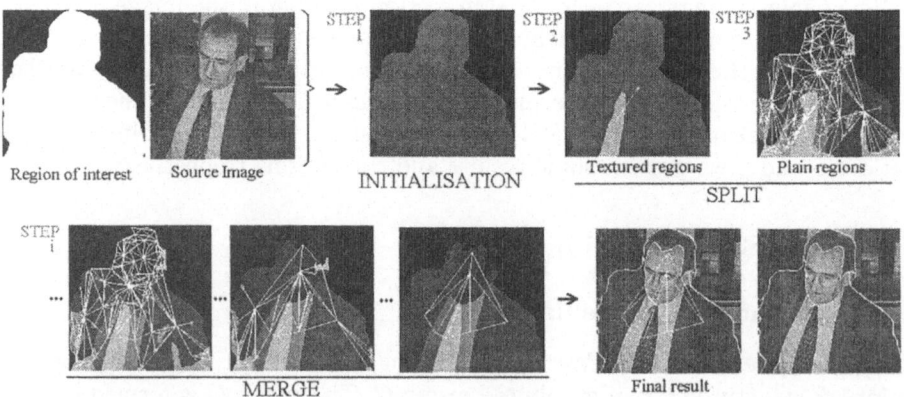

Fig. 1. Segmentation process guided by a graph structure

apply iteratively the fusion operator $\gamma_F(G)$ due to some merge criteria MC that deal with the edge features F_E of the graph. Next we expose the criteria we follow to apply the operators in the split and merge steps.

Split Criteria. We deal with homogeneity measures on the node features.

Texture Discrimination. We discriminate the texture zones by applying a statistical strategy inspired in the work of Karu[12] and in the MPEG-7 texture descriptor[5]. The general idea of our process is to consider as textured regions those image zones with a certain amount of area that present a high density of contours checked at certain frequencies. The exact detection steps are graphically showed in the Figure 2. The node feature E stores the edge information, and T indicates the texture presence.

Plain Regions Split. We apply a pixel-based technique that consists in a clustering of the colour space. A plain region will be formed by all the connected pixels in the image that belong to the same colour cluster. We have used the octree quantization algorithm of Gervautz and Purgathofer[8] that, given a number of colours nc, provides the palette of the ncth most usual colours of the image. This adaptability is very interesting to avoid the under segmentation when we deal with garment combinations of very similar colours. The quantization information is stored in the node feature H.

Merge Criteria. We allow the fusion of two adjacent regions if their similarity feature D is under a certain threshold. Being this value a measure between 0 and 1, the fusion operator will be applied iteratively to the pair of neighbouring regions with minimum distance.

Plain Regions Similarity. The shadows provided by the clothes folds are viewed as intensity changes that become especially critical in the case of the plain regions. Thus, we have developed a similarity distance that gives more tolerance to the intensity variations and allows the presence of progressive and smooth intensity degradation in a region. The similarity measure is computed by a combination of a chromatic distance and an intensity distance. The chromatic distance is computed from the AC node features as the Euclidean distance between the colour means on the chromatic plane. When two regions are adjacent, the intensity distance ID is computed from the E node features as the rate of edge

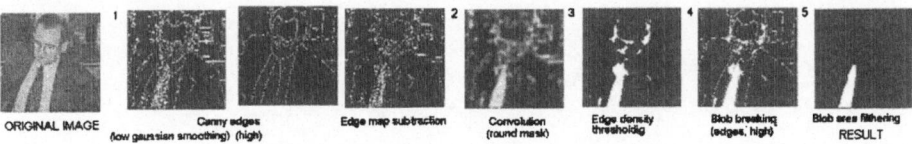

ORIGINAL IMAGE   Canny edges   Edge map subtraction   Convolution   Edge density   Blob breaking   Blob area filtering
                (low gaussian smoothing) (high)   (round mask)   thresholding   (edges, high)   RESULT

Fig. 2. The five steps of the texture discrimination process

pixels in the common boundary. Otherwise, we calculate ID as the Euclidean distance between the average intensity AI of the regions.

Textured Regions Similarity. We use the histograms of the two regions (H) as their texture descriptors. We use a similarity metric that treats simultaneously the distances of the histogram rates and the distances of the colours that they represent. This measure is commonly used for region based image retrieval and is defined as a similarity colour descriptor in the MPEG-7[5] encoding.

3   Interpretation

3.1   Interpretation Modelling

We attempt to distinguish between five types of clothing compositions that are combinations of two garments (buttoned or unbuttoned) and a tie. We understand the garments of a class composition as ordered layers from the most external to the most internal. For example we describe a person wearing an unbuttoned black jacket and a blue shirt, like a structure of two layers, the first black and the second blue. In terms of garment regions this can be seen as two black outer regions and one blue inner region.

We describe a clothing composition by a an ideal model structured as an attributed graph G_M where the nodes N_M represent the garment regions gr and the edges E_M their relationship (see Figure 3).

$$G_M = (N_M, E_M, L_{N_M} : N_M \rightarrow F_{N_M}, L_{E_M} : E_M \rightarrow F_{E_M})$$

Model Node Features $F_{N_M} = \{A(n_m), S(n_m), CL(n_m), CH(n_m)\}$: The model regions are defined by its ideal area (A) understood as the area rate with respect to the whole object. The region limits are analysed in order to identify a certain shape (S). Furthermore, we can set some colour restrictions by forcing the region to have a certain colour homogeneity (CH) and being this colour homogeneity of a certain label (CL) such as skin, grey, blue, pink, etc. We use the 25 colour label classification proposed by the colour naming method of Benavente[1].

Model Edge Features $F_{E_M} = \{SP(n_{mj}, n_{mk}), SI(n_{mj}, n_{mk})\}$: We need to add some similarity restrictions (SI) to those regions that, even thought of being apart, belong to the same garment (for instance the two regions that describe an unbuttoned jacket). We indicate the relative spatial positions between two

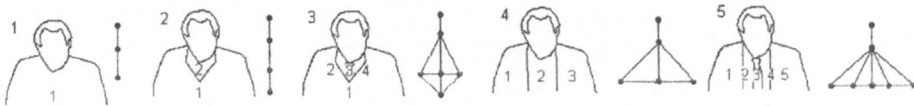

Fig. 3. Modeling of the five possible clothing compositions

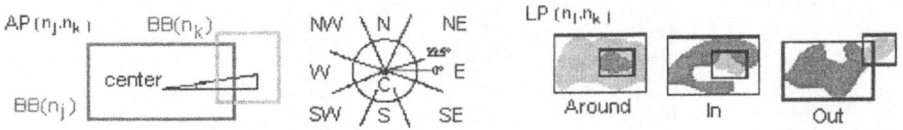

Fig. 4.   Spatial   position   labels: [AP∈{N,NW,W,SW,S,SE,E,NE,C}, LP∈{I,A,O}]

regions (SP) with a combination of two labels $[AP, LP]$. These labels are obtained from the region bounding boxes and are inspired in the iconic indexing techniques of Rs-String [10] and 2D String [4]. Figure 4 show them graphically.

3.2   Interpretation Process

The interpretation process consists in evaluating all the possible mapping solutions between a segmentation graph G and each model graphs G_M. Minimizing a cost value associated to matching operations chooses the best result. The interpretation process applies an n-to-one mapping between the image regions and the model regions. It also allows an image region not to take part in the solution. The procedure pretends to avoid the over segmentation problem and reject those intrusive regions (bags, wallets, etc.) that do not belong to the clothing.

Matching Cost. We compute the mapping between a graph G and a model G_{Mi} due to some cost functions. These functions evaluate how the node features and the edge features of the model are preserved when they are mapped to the image ones. The functions δ_A, δ_{CH}, δ_{CL}, and δ_S, evaluate $F_{N_{Mi}}$, and the functions δ_{SI} and δ_{SP}, evaluate $F_{E_{Mi}}$. Let us name $\delta_{F_{N_M}}(\{n\}_i, n_{mi})$ and $\delta_{F_{ME}}(e_i, e_{mi})$ the combination of the node costs and edge costs respectively. In a higher level, the function δ joins and weights them with the parameters, $\alpha_{N,i}$ and $\alpha_{E,i}$. These parameters enhance the significance of a model part or of a relationship.

$$\delta(G_k, G_{Mi}) = \sum_{i=1}^{\#N_{Mi}} \alpha_{N,i} * \delta_{F_{N_{Mi}}}(\{n\}_i, n_{mi}) + \sum_{i=1}^{\#E_M} \alpha_{E,i} * \delta_E(e_i, e_{mi}) \quad (1)$$

Next we define in a general way how we calculate the costs related with each feature. For more details, see Borràs[2]. The functions δ_A, δ_{SI} and δ_{CH} provide cost measures that vary in a range of goodness from 0 to 1 in reference to the area (A), similarity (SI) and colour homogeneity (CH) features. The area cost is computed as the ratio of the difference between the $\{n\}_l$ and mn_l areas. The similarity and cohesion costs are computed as the mean of the colour-texture distances defined in the section 2.2. In relation to the features with boolean

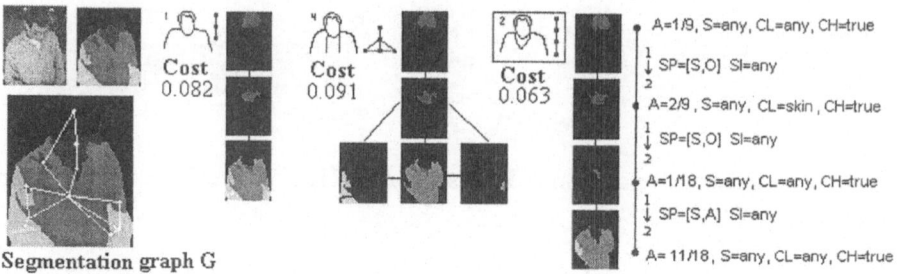

Fig. 5. Given a segmentation graph G the figure shows the three best matching for the graph-modelled classes: 1,4 and 2. There is no result for 3 and 5 due to the absence of tie shape. The image is classified as Class2 since it has the lowest matching cost

properties, their costs are set to 0 or ∞ according to its accomplishment. The function δ_{SP} checks the space labelling (SP) and δ_{CL} examines the colour labelling of a region (CL) using the colour naming method [1]. Finally δ_S analyses the shape with synthetic tie mask.

Matching Process. From graph G and a model graph G_{Mi}, we make an expansion in a depth-search priority of a decision tree. Each tree level represents the mapping of a region model with a set of segmented neighbouring regions. Each tree node has associated a cost mapping of the partial solution. At each step, we only expand the nodes with a cost value ≤ 1. When the process is done for all G_M we choose the segmentation solution G_i^k with minimum cost $C_{i,k}$ ≤ 1. Applying the matching process to the whole models and observing the minimum value of each best mapping, we decide the class classification of the clothing composition. Figure 5 exemplifies a graph matching solution.

4   Example

We exemplify the behaviour of our method in front of a query formulated against a database. This database contains the clothing descriptions that our method has generated from a set of 100 test images, as well as, the colour labelling of identified garments [1]. Then, we try it out with two queries which results are showed in the Figure 6. A first query would be formulated as: "We search a person wearing a clothing composition of two layers: the first opened, the second closed; with indistinct colour for the first layer, and white for the second layer". Then, a second query could refine the previous one adding a colour restriction for the first layer as: "...with black colour for the first layer...".

Fig. 6. Image retrieval: 1 to 7. Refined retrieval: 1,4,5 and 6. (a) Original image (b) Segmentation and colour naming (c) clothing regions of the structure identification

5   Evaluation of the Results

Starting from a set of one hundred images $\{I^j\}_{\{j:1..100\}}$ taken from a real environment, we have evaluated the whole process and their intermediate steps. We have chosen an empirical discrepancy method based on a set of ground truth information. We have used a synthetic segmentation of the images $SG = \{G^j\}$ and a manual labelling of their structure $SG_M = \{G^j_{Mi}\}$. According to them we have extract some statistics over two sets of structure results that we have obtained form two experiments. The first set, RG^I_M, is obtained by running our method starting from the original images. The second set, RG^{SG}_M, is obtained by running it from the synthetic segmented images.

Global Evaluation. Running our method form the original images we have obtained a success of 64% on the clothing classification ($SG_M \cap RG^I_M = 64\%$)

Segmentation Evaluation. We have compared the success on the structure identification starting from the original images and starting from the synthetic ones. Then we have obtained that $SG_M \cap RG^I_M = 64\%$ and $SG_M \cap RG^{SG}_M = 69\%$. Therefore we observe that the automatic segmentation influences the process by incrementing the structure misclassification in a rate of 5%. This way, we can evaluate the segmentation success in a rate of 92.75%.

Structure Description Evaluation. As we have seen in the previous results, the structure description method can be evaluated with a 69% of success without the segmentation influence. The mean reasons that introduce this 31% of error are given by altered positions if the person in the image scene and severe occlusions on the cloth zones provided by external objects.

6   Conclusions

We have developed a content-based image retrieval strategy that we have applied to a problem of people clothing identification. Our process consists in two stages, image segmentation and interpretation, both guided by a graph structure. Even thought the difficulties that the clothes segmentation carries (the shadows of their folds, the irregular textures, etc.), our segmentation method fulfils satisfactorily the objective. To perform the interpretation step, we have modelled five types of clothing compositions according to some region features. We use several cost functions to evaluate the best matching between the regions of the segmented image and the ideal regions of the clothes composition models. The process attempts to overcome the over segmentation problem by allowing an n-to-one region mapping. Our strategy can be adapted to recognize and describe in terms of regions any object due to their colour, texture and structure features.

References

[1] Benavente, R., Olivé, M. C., Vanrell, M., Baldrich, R.: Colour Perception: A Simple Method for Colour Naming. 2n Congrés Català d'IA, Barcelona (Spain) (October 1999) 340-347

[2] Borràs A.: High-Level Clothes Description Based on Color-Texture Features. Master Thesis. Computer Vision Center - Dept. Informàtica UAB (September 2002)

[3] Chang, C. C., Wang, L. L.: Color Texture Segmentation for Clothing in a Computer-Aided Fashion Design System. IVC Volume 14, Number 9 (1996) 685-702

[4] Chang, S. K., Shi, Q. Y., Yan, C. W.: Iconic Indexing by 2-D Strings. IEEE Trans. on PAMI Volume 9, (May 1987) 413-428

[5] Choi, Y., Won, C. S., Ro, Y.M, Manjunath, B. S.: Introduction to MPEG-7: Texture Descriptors (2002) 213-230

[6] Chen Y., Wang J.: A region-based fuzzy feature matching approach to content-based image retrieval. IEEE Trans. on PAMI Volume 24 (2002)

[7] Forsyth, D. A., Malik, J., Fleck, M. M., Greenspan, H., Leung, T. K., Belongie, S., Carson, C., Bregler, C.: Finding Pictures of Objects in Large Collections of Images. Object Representation in Computer Vision (1996) 335-360

[8] Gervautz, M., Purgathofer, W.: A simple method for color quantization: Octree quantization. Graphics Gems I (1990) 287-293

[9] Haralick, R. M., Shapiro, L. G.: Image Segmentation Techniques. CVGIP Volume 29, Number 1 (January 1985) 100-132

[10] Huang, P. W., Jean, Y. R.: Spatial Reasoning And Similarity Retrieval For Image Database Systems Based On Rs-Strings. PR Volume 29, (1996) 2103-2114

[11] Huang, T., Rui, Y.: Image retrieval: Past, present, and future. International Symposium on Multimedia Information Processing, (1997)

[12] Karu, K., Jain, A. K., Bolle, R. M.: Is There Any Texture in the Image. ICPR96 (1996) B94.3

[13] Muñoz, X.: Image Segmentation Integrating Color, Texture and Boundary Information. Master Thesis. Universitat de Girona (2001)

[14] Shearer, K., Bunke, H., Venkatesh, S.: Video indexing and similarity retrieval by largest common subgraph detection using decision trees. PR Volume 34, Number 5 (May 2001) 1075-1091

A New Method for Detection and Initial Pose Estimation Based on Mumford-Shah Segmentation Functional

Jose Maria Buades Rubio, Manuel González Hidalgo,
and Francisco José Perales López

Departamento de Matemáticas e Informática
Unidad de Gráficos y Visión
Universitat de les Illes Balears
{josemaria.buades,paco.perales,dmimgh0}@uib.es
http://dmi.uib.es/research/GV

Abstract. In this paper we describe a new method for detection and initial pose estimation of a person in a human computer interaction in an uncontrolled indoor environment. We used the Koepfler-Morel-Solimini mathematical formulation of Mumford-Shah segmentation functional adapted to color images. The idea is to obtain a system to detect the hands and face in a sequence of monocular or binocular images. The skin color is predefined and a procedure is parameterized to segment and recognize the homogeneous regions. Besides, we fit our results to a restriction that the two hands and face must be detected at the same time. We also use a biomechanical restriction to reach this initial estimation. So, the centroid of the blob is computed for every region. We explain the mathematical background segmentation, and region classification (hands, face, head and upper-torso). Finally, we present some interesting results and we implement the algorithm efficiently in order to obtain real time results processing standard video format.

1 Introduction

Human-Computer Interaction (HCI) is evolving towards devices that allow the user to interact without physical contact with the machine; this communication can be carried out with voice or user gesticulation capture. In gesture capture, it is possible to use different kinds of devices: black and white cameras, color cameras, infrared cameras, etc. Our research focuses on capturing human motion with color cameras. The user gesticulation analysis process involves various tasks: capture, user detection, tracking of interesting regions, gesture recognition and execution of the action specified by the user. In this work we focus on the capture process and user detection; we propose a new method to detect a user, recognize his/her clothes and other parameters that will be useful in the tracking task [10] in a future work.

Capture is carried out from color cameras; our system allows us to employ more than one camera to carry out a 3D reconstruction in a tracking step.

F.J. Perales et al. (Eds.): IbPRIA 2003, LNCS 2652, pp. 117-125, 2003.
© Springer-Verlag Berlin Heidelberg 2003

The global process must detect a new user entering the system and analyze him/her to determine parameters such as hair color and clothes. Once the user who is going to interact with the machine has been detected, the system starts to track interesting regions such as the head, hands, body and joints, using information obtained in the user detection task. The input data for the gesture interpretation process are the position and orientation of these regions. This process will determine which gesture the user has carried out. Next, these gesture data are sent to the execution process which ends the process by performing the action that has been specified, and so completing the feedback process.

In the following section, we explain briefly the mathematical background of the segmentation process based on the Mumford-Shah functional. This method is adapted to multichannel images (color images) and real time processing. Section 3 introduces the main method to detect the user in front of the camera and carefully explains the analysis process and parameters needed for a future tracking process. Finally, we conclude with some interesting results including a set of color images and conclusions, future works and references.

2   Multichannel Segmentation Algorithm

Image segmentation is the first step in data extraction for computer vision systems. Achieving good segmentation has turned out to be extremely difficult, and is a complex process. Moreover, it depends on the technique used to detect the uniformity of the characteristics sought between image pixels and to isolate regions of the image that have this uniformity. Multiple techniques have been developed to achieve this goal, such as contour detection, split and merging regions, histogram thresholding, clustering, etc. A Survey can be found in [1].

In color image processing, pixel color is usually determined by three values corresponding to R (red), G (green) and B (blue). The distinctive color sets [7] have been employed with different goals, and specific sets have even been designed to be used with specific segmentation techniques [1].

We define a color image as a scalar function $g = (g^1, g^2, g^3)$, defined over image domain $\Omega \subseteq \Re^2$ (normally a rectangle), in such a way that $g: \Omega \rightarrow \Re^3$. The image will be defined for three channels, under the hypothesis that they are good indicators of autosimilarity of regions. A segmentation of image g will be a partition of the rectangle in a finite number of regions; each one corresponding to a region of the image where components of g are approximately constant. As we will try to explicitly compute the region boundaries and of course control both their regularity and localization, we will employ the principles established in [2, 4] to define a good segmentation.

So, the functional E that we consider to segment color images must have control terms of autosimilarity for each region with respect to the channels chosen (that is, distinctive color used) and the size, localization and regularity of the boundaries. To achieve our goals we consider the functional defined by Mumford-Shah in [3] (to segment gray level images) which is expressed as:

$$E(u,B) = \int_{\Omega} \|u - g\|^2 \, d\mu + \lambda \ell(B) =$$

$$\int_{\Omega} \left\{ (u^1 - g^1)^2 + (u^2 - g^2)^2 + (u^3 - g^3)^2 \right\} dxdy + \lambda \ell(B) \tag{1}$$

where B is the set of boundaries of a homogenous region that define a segmentation and u (each u^k) is a mean value, or more generally a regularized version of g (of each g^k) in the interior of such areas. The scale parameter λ in the functional (1) can be interpreted as a measure of the amount of boundary contained in the final segmentation B: if λ is small, we allow for many boundaries in B, if λ is large we allow for few boundaries.

The segmentation properties defined for the previous functional has been studied by Koepfler-Morel-Solimini in [2, 4] and we can see the properties of the functional in [3, 4]. The use of multichannel images (eg. color images) can be seen in [4, 5].

A segmentation B of a color image g will be a finite set of piecewise affine curves - that is, finite length curves - in such a way that for each set of curves B, we are going to consider the corresponding u to be completely defined because the value of each u^i coordinate over each connected component of $\Omega \setminus B$ is equal to the mean value of g^i in this connected component. Unless stated otherwise, we shall assume that only one u is associated with each B. Therefore, we shall write in this case $E(B)$ instead of $E(u, B)$. We define the following concepts.

Definition 1. A set of curves B' is a subsegmentation of B if B' has been obtained from B by merging an arbitrary number of adjacent regions.

Definition 2. A segmentation B is normal if for each subsegmentation B' of B it is verified that E(B) < E(B').

A property which is easier to compute is defined as follows:

Definition 3. A segmentation B is called 2-normal if, for every pair of neighboring regions O_i y O_j , the new segmentation B' obtained by merging these regions satisfies E(B') > E(B).

A more detailed explanation of the concepts and their mathematical properties can be consulted in [2, 4, 6]. We shall consider only segmentations where the number of regions is finite, in other words $\Omega \setminus B$ has a finite number of connected components and the regions do not have internal boundaries.

Koepler-Morel-Solimini demonstrate that the set of 2-normal segmentation verifies the properties that are demanded in the image segmentation algorithm. Note that the results and boundary marks obtained by Morel-Solimini continue being valid when we are working with color images instead of gray level images, in other words, in the case of multichannel images[4]. We shall use a variation of segmentation algorithm by region merging described in [3] adapted to color images.

Obviously, it is not possible to directly find the global minimum of the energy by examining the whole set of possible segmentations. The principle of the computational method we use is to generate local transformations of a given segmentation and keep the ones which reduce the energy (lower energy means improvement of the segmentation). The tool to produce these transformations is to merge adjacent regions according to a region growing algorithm.

The concept of 2-normal segmentations synthesizes the concept of optimal segmentation we are looking for, and it lays on the basis of the computational method we use. In fact, if we follow the main idea of the region growing methods, we shall see that what they compute is precisely a 2-normal subsegmentation of a fine initial segmentation, obtained by recursive merging.

We now consider the problem of computing a 2-normal segmentation as defined above. The 2-normality property is well adapted for the construction of an algorithm based on region growing by merging neighboring regions. Two regions will be merged if this operation reduces the energy. At each step we need to compare the balance of energy if we remove a common boundary $\partial(O_i, O_j)$ of two neighboring regions O_i, O_j. If B is 2-normal, one has $E(B) \leq E(B - \partial(O_i, O_j))$, which, in the case of a piecewise constant function u, implies the balance

$$\lambda\ell(\partial(O_i, O_j)) \leq \frac{|O_i| \cdot |O_j|}{|O_i| + |O_j|} \left(\sum_{k=1}^{3} (u_i^k - u_j^k)^2 \right) \tag{2}$$

where $| \cdot |$ is the area measure and u_i, is the approximation of g on O_i to compute the data for evaluating the balance for each region O_i we associate its area $|O_i|$ and we can compute

$$u_i^k = \frac{\int_{O_i} g^k}{|O_i|} \text{ for } k=1, 2, 3.$$

We call equation (2) the merging criterium. We decide to remove the common boundary $\partial(O_i, O_j)$ of O_i and O_j if this equation is not satisfied. By repeating this step, that is, by comparing the balance energy for deciding to join any two neighboring regions, we finally obtain a 2-normal segmentation for the scale parameter λ, a segmentation, i.e., where no further elimination improves the energy. Then, we have implemented a multiscalar algorithm and data structure similar to that used in [2] and [6] but adapted to color images and real time processing.

The algorithm used the RGB components, because the segmentations obtained are very accurate to our goal. But the system is able to use another color space or color descriptor as we can see in [1]. Moreover, if it is needed it can weigh the channels used in order to obtain the segmentation.

3   User Detection and Initial Pose

The image is captured and segmented with the algorithm explained in the previous section and is then analyzed to determine whether it is a user or not, as we can see below in a work related with this topic [8]. If a user has been detected, the system studies him and obtains some parameters that will be useful in the tracking and analysis process [9]. By applying this process directly to segmented images without using information from previous frames, the system is robust to background changing and variable illumination. The parameters obtained from the segmentation task are fixed in order to user interactions with upper torso (body, arms, hands and head). The system obtains the upper torso configuration: shirt, hair, hands and face. User detection process is waiting for a user located opposite the camera, with hands separated and at the same height that head, then it recognizes and later analyzes user configuration.

Below we offer a more detailed explanation of this step.

This module receives a segmentation of the captured image, analyzes every region and marks as skin region if its RGB medium value is in a characteristic color range of skin. To achieve more homogenous regions, neighboring skin regions are merged. This merging is carried out to avoid detecting a hand or the face in two neighboring regions. To join a hand with the face or the other hand is not possible due to the expected initial position described above, following the merging criteria:

$$\forall O_i, O_j / Neighbour(O_i, O_j) \land Skin(O_i) \land Skin(O_j) \Rightarrow O_i \cup O_j \qquad (3)$$

where $Neighbor(O_i, O_j)$ means that two regions are neighbors and $Skin(O_i)$ means that is a skin region.

After this skin region merging, we obtain a skin region set, called β, where any pair of skin regions are separated.

For all ordered set of three regions included in β, we identify each one as face Z, left hand Y_1 and right hand Y_2, then we evaluate a criteria to determine whether this configuration is correct. The criteria is done by

$$\underset{i,j,k}{Max}\{\varphi(O_i, O_j, O_k): \forall O_i, O_j, O_k \in \beta\} \geq \alpha \qquad (4)$$

where α is a threshold probability and we call φ the user detection function. In this function we take into account the following:

1   The central region must be the biggest. $A(Z) > A(Y_1)$ and $A(Z) > A(Y_2)$, where $A(Z)$ is the area of Z.
2   Lateral regions, hands, have a similar area. $A(Y_1) \approx A(Y_2)$
3   Face region area $A(Z)$ must be between a minimum Z^- and a maximum Z^+
4   Hands area $A(Y_1)$ and $A(Y_2)$ must be between a minimum Y^- and a maximum Y^+
5   Vertical position Y_1 and Y_2 should be similar and nearest possible to Z

The user detection function returns a value between zero and one that measures the probability that a user has been detected. From all possible combinations of Z, Y_1 and Y_2 the one with the greatest value, greater than a reference minimum value α, is chosen as the best configuration.

In order to apply the above algorithm, we need to fix the following values: a color range of skin to detect hand and face regions, a threshold probability α to discriminate non expected initial positions. To avoid high differences of hands we include an area similarity criterion, a maximum size of hand area is also necessary. All these parameters are used in order to discriminate bad detections.

All threshold values are established in relation with camera to user distance and image resolution. This distance is predefined by initial application setup.

After a user has been detected, the same image is analyzed to determine hair and shirt color. Region proposed as hair, X is the upper neighboring region of Z if $A(X) / A(Z)$ relation is greater than a threshold, hair is discarded and is considered that it is a bald user.

To analyze shirt, the following algorithm is applied. Initially, shirt region W is the greatest region whose upper boundary is included in the boundary of Z (see Figure 1). Afterwards, neighboring regions of W are joined until Z is connected with Y_1 and Y_2 through W. A candidate region T_i chosen at every step i to be joined to W is in relation with: color space distance between mean color of T and W, and distance in pixels from T to Y_1 and Y_2.

With this process, the system detects a user and obtains useful data for the tracking system. In the following section some results are displayed.

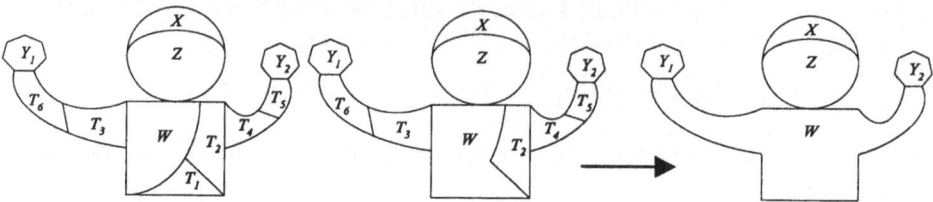

Fig. 1. Shirt region detection. W region is the initial region classified as shirt. In each step the algorithm merges a new region T_i until W joins Z with Y_1 and Y_2

4   Results

All capture software has been implemented with the API designed by Microsoft for Windows platform, this API called DirectShow permits the use of any camera (IEEE 1394, USB Web Cam, parallel port scanner, video file,...) as long as you have drivers for Windows. Any kind of these input devices is programmed in a transparently and independent hardware way, without the need to modify our application. This API has been chosen with the intention to cover the highest number of end users at a low cost without changing the capturing system.

We have implemented the above algorithm in C++. It has been tested in 320x240 resolutions (Figure 2) and 640x480 standard video resolution (Figure 3). We initialize the multichannel segmentation algorithm with an initial segmentation wich is a grid of size $T_x \times T_y$ on the image, usually we take $T_x = T_y = 1$, 2 or 4. From this initial segmentation, the algorithm determines a 2-normal segmentation for different values of the scale parameters λ, we increase from $\lambda = 2^0$ to $\lambda = 2^n$ following the merging criterion described in (2) and the specifications of the algorithm described at the end of section 2. The stopping criterion can be: if the last level $\lambda = 2^n$ has been reached or if there is just one region left or if the desired number of regions is reached. In our displayed experiments the stopping criterion is to achieve a fixed number of regions. Then, we apply the algorithm described in section 3 where the selected parameters are detailed: Skin range color in HLS ([0-10], [20-230], [62-255])

In the two sequences of pictures we can see in Green the boundaries of hair region. The color Red is used for boundaries of hand and face regions, the centroid of these regions is visualized with a solid red square. In Pink we display the upper-torso boundary and finally we use Black and White for other regions detected for the segmentation algorithm.

In the first sequence we take a 2x2 initial segmentation and the system runs at 5 frames/second in a P4 1.6GHz. We display several different initial positions and cloth configuration; and we can see how the proposed method detects the interesting regions. In the second sequence, Figure 3, we display the same initial pose image and the results obtained with different size of initial segmentation, from top to bottom we use 1x1, 2x2, 4x4 respectively. Left column pictures are 320x240 and right ones are 640x480. In the first case, the system runs at 0.32 frames/second, 1.41 frames/sec and 6.70 frames/sec; and in the second 0.08 frames/second, 0.30 frames/sec and 0.82 frames/sec respectively.

5   Conclusions and Future Work

In this paper we have proposed a new system for user detecting for HCI that does not use background substraction, therefore the system is robust to environment and illumination changes. Moreover, it analyzes the user to determine parameters that will be useful for a future tracking process. The region segmentation process based on the Mumford-Shah algorithm adapted to multichannel images is sufficiently good and beneficial for our aims. Besides, the process is carried out in real time. The software implementation is efficient and OOP. The result of this process is the input of a tracking and reconstruction of an intelligent human computer interaction system. It remains as future work to do tracking of interesting body parts and to interpret movements in order to carry out action recognition that the user is performing. At the moment, we are working on particle filter tracking with a biomechanical model to reduce the search space solutions. Moreover, a stereo version is proposed to improve final results. This paper is subsidized by the project IST-2001-32202 HUMODAN and CICYT TIC2001-0931.

References

[1]   [1] H.D. Cheng, X.H. Jiang, Y. Sun, JinGli Wang "Color Image Segmentation: Advances and Prospects", Journal of Pattern Recognition 34, (2001), pp. 2259-2281

[2]   [2] G. Koepler, J.M. Morel, and S. Solimini, "Segmentation by minimizing a functional and the merging methods", SIAM J. on Numerical Analysis, Vol 31, No 1, Feb. 1994

[3]   [3] D. Mumford and J. Shah, "Optimal approximations by piecewise smooth functions and variational problems", Communications on Pure and Applied Mathematics, XLII(4), 1989

[4]   [4] J.M. Morel and S. Solimini. "Variational Methods for Image Segmentation", Birkhauser Verlag. 1995

[5]   [5] M. Gonzalez "Segmentación de imágenes en Color por método variacional". Proc. Del XIV C.E.D.Y.A. y IV C.M.A. pp 287-288, 1995.

[6]   [6] C. Ballester, V. Caselles and M. Gonzalez, "Affine invariant segmentation by variational methods", SIAM J. Appl. Math., Vol. 56, No 1, pp. 294-325, 1996

[7]   [7] G. Wyszecki and W.S. Stiles "Color Science: Concepts and Methods. Quantitative data and Formulae" Wiley, 2nd Edition, 1982

[8]   [8] I. Haritaoglu, "W4: Real-Time Surveillance of People and Their Activities" IEEE Transactions on Pattern Analysis and Machine Intelligence, vol 22 No8, pp 809-830, 2000

[9]   [9] H. Sidenbladh, M.J. Black and D.J. Fleet "Stochastic Tracking of 3D Human Figures Using 2D Image Motion" ECCV 2000.
[10]   [10] J.M. Buades, R. Mas, F.J. Perales. "Matching a Human Walking Sequence with a VRML Syntehtic Model". AMDO 2000. Palma de Mallorca, September 2000. pp 145-158

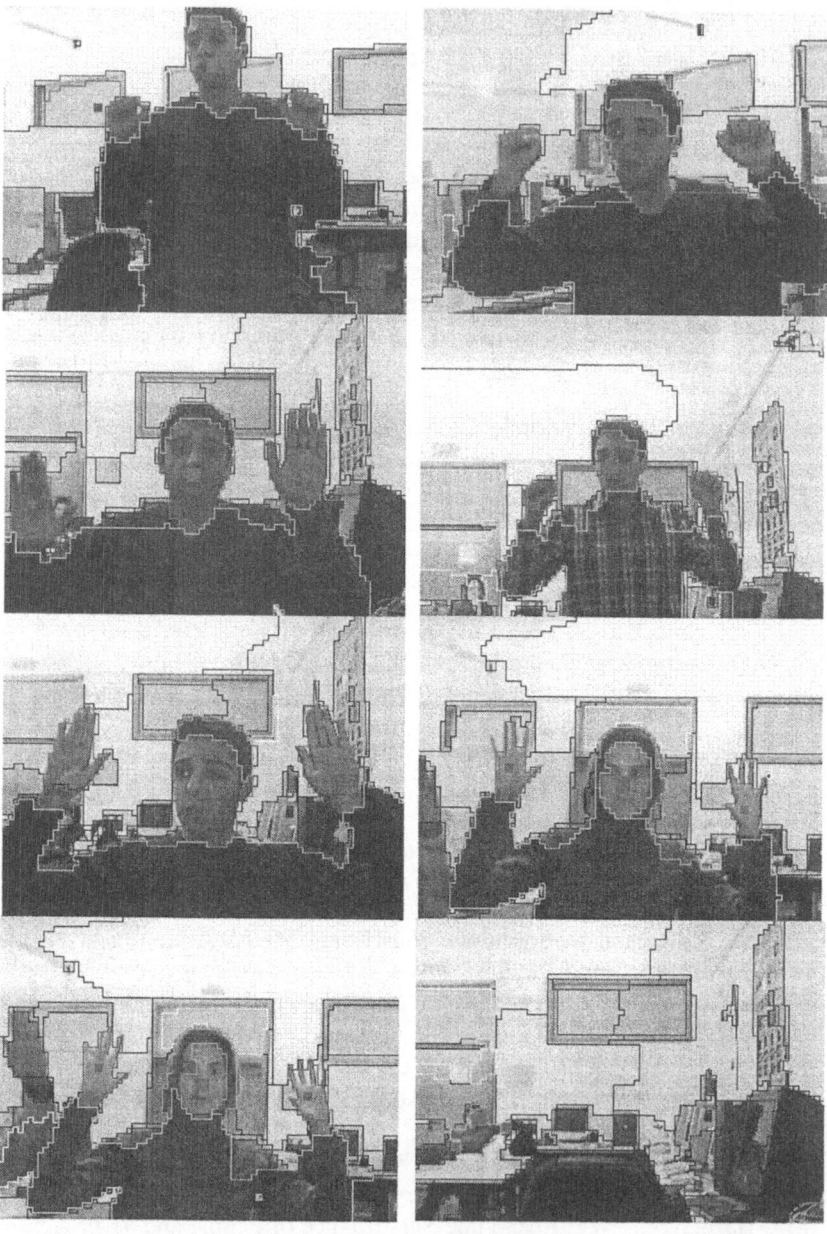

Fig. 2. Some results obtained in real time with a Sony VFW-V500 camera. Images are 320x240 resolution in RGB color

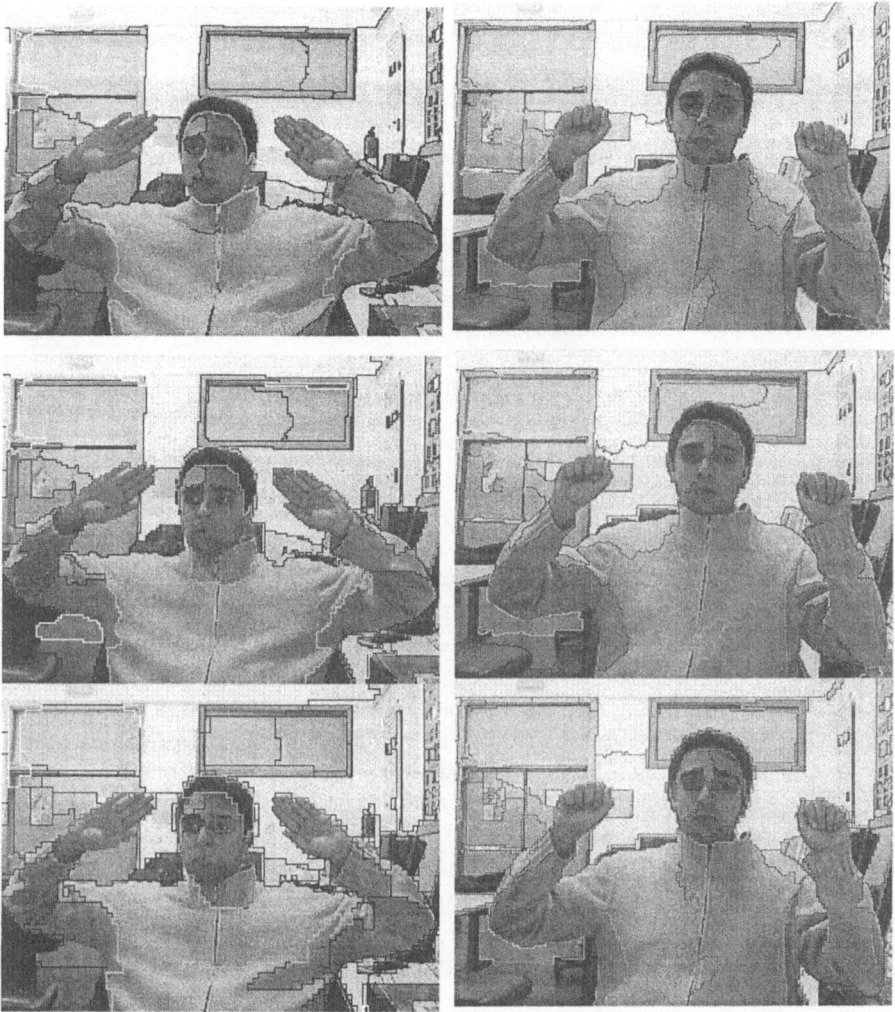

Fig. 3. Some results obtained with different size of initial segmentation

Tracking Heads Using Piecewise Planar Models

José M. Buenaposada, Enrique Muñoz, and Luis Baumela

Universidad Politécnica de Madrid, Departamento de Inteligencia Artificial
Campus de Montegancedo s/n, 28660 Madrid (Spain)
{jmbuena,kike}@dia.fi.upm.es, lbaumela@fi.upm.es

Abstract. We present a procedure for tracking a rigid object based on a piecewise planar model, and show how it can be used to track a human face. The tracking is performed using a single incremental SSD-based tracker. The main feature of the approach presented is that it can track a rigid set of arbitrarily small patches all of which could not be individually tracked.

1 Introduction

Three-dimensional head tracking is a basic component in many applications of computer vision. For instance, the construction of advanced computer interfaces deals with problems such as the identification of head gestures, face expression analysis or lip reading. It is also used in biometric applications, like face or iris-based recognition, for which a stable location of the face is critical. Also, for very low bit-rate communications, the MPEG-4 standard proposes the use of animated artificial face models in a wide range of applications from virtual videoconferencing to virtual actors. All these applications require a robust and efficient (i.e. real-time or near real-time) head tracker with no markers on it.

Various techniques have been proposed in the literature for head tracking. Some of them only track the 2D position of the face on the image plane [2, 5], others model the face as a plane, which can be affinely or projectively [7, 3, 6] tracked in 3D space. Finally, there is a third group of procedures which rely on a 3D model of the face. These are based on individually tracking a set of salient points [11], 2D image patches [8, 9, 12], or 3D surface-based head models [10].

Procedures based on individually tracking a set of features can be quite unstable as each feature, individually, may not provide enough information to be tracked. In order to cope with this problem some higher level process, like a Kalman filter [9, 12] or a set motion restrictions propagated on a network of features [8], are used to accumulate the information provided by the tracker of each feature/patch in order to estimate the motion of the head. This problem does not exist for methods which model the face with a single surface, but, on the other hand, those based on a single-plane are not able to track the head in presence of out-of-the-image plane rotations [7, 3, 6], whereas those which are based on a more complex head model, for example a cylinder [10], need computationally expensive warping algorithms.

F.J. Perales et al. (Eds.): IbPRIA 2003, LNCS 2652, pp. 126–133, 2003.

In this paper we present a procedure for model-based head tracking. The model is based on a set of image patches located in space with a known 3D structure. Our approach differs from previous feature/patch-based trackers [8, 9, 12] in that we track all features using a single incremental tracker [7, 6]. In this way we integrate in a single tracker the low level information provided by all patches in the image, enabling us to reliably track a set of arbitrarily small patches, all of which could not be individually tracked. In section 2 we briefly introduce the incremental image alignment paradigm. In section 3 we build the tracker. Finally in sections 4 and 5 some experiments are presented and conclusions drawn.

2   Incremental Image Registration

Let $\mathbf{x}$ represent the location of a point in an image and $I(\mathbf{x}, t)$ represent the brightness value of that location in the image acquired at time t. Let $\mathcal{R} = \{\mathbf{x}_1, \mathbf{x}_2, \ldots, \mathbf{x}_N\}$ be a set of N image points of the object to be tracked (*target region*), whose brightness values are known in the first image of a sequence, $I(\mathbf{x}, t_0)$.

Assuming that the brightness constancy assumption holds, then

$$I(\mathbf{x}, t_0) = I(\mathbf{f}(\mathbf{x}, \bar{\mu}_t), t) \; \forall \mathbf{x} \in \mathcal{R}, \tag{1}$$

where $I(\mathbf{f}(\mathbf{x}, \bar{\mu}_t), t)$ is the image acquired at time t rectified with motion model $\mathbf{f}$ and motion parameters $\bar{\mu} = \bar{\mu}_t$.

Tracking the object means recovering the motion parameter vector of the target region for each image in the sequence. This can be achieved by minimising the difference between the template and the rectified pixels of the target region for every image in the sequence

$$\min_{\bar{\mu}} \sum_{\forall \mathbf{x} \in \mathcal{R}} [I(\mathbf{f}(\mathbf{x}, \bar{\mu}), t) - I(\mathbf{x}, t_0)]^2 \tag{2}$$

This minimisation problem has been traditionally solved linearly by computing $\bar{\mu}$ incrementally while tracking. We can achieve this by making a Taylor series expansion of (2) at $(\bar{\mu}, t)$ and computing the increment in the motion parameters between two time instants. Different solutions to this problem have been proposed in the literature, depending on which term of equation (2) the Taylor expansion is made on and how the motion parameters are updated [1].

If we update the model parameters of the first term in equation (2) using an additive method, then the minimisation can be rewritten as [1, 4]

$$\min_{\delta\bar{\mu}} \sum_{\forall \mathbf{x} \in \mathcal{R}} [I(\mathbf{f}(\mathbf{x}, \bar{\mu}_t + \delta\bar{\mu}), t + \delta t) - I(\mathbf{x}, t_0)]^2, \tag{3}$$

where $\delta\bar{\mu}$ represents the estimated increment in the motion parameters of the target region between time instants t and $t + \delta t$.

– Offline computations:
  1. Compute and store $\mathbf{M}(\mathbf{x}, \mathbf{0})$.
  2. Compute and store $\mathbf{H}_0$.
– On line computations:
  1. Warp $I(\mathbf{z}, t + \delta t)$ to compute $I(\mathbf{f}(\mathbf{x}, \bar{\mu}_t), t + \delta t)$.
  2. Compute $\mathcal{E}(\mathbf{x}, t + \delta t)$.
  3. From (4) compute $\delta\bar{\mu}$.
  4. Update $\bar{\mu}_{t+\delta t} = \bar{\mu}_t + \delta\bar{\mu}$.

Fig. 1. Outline of the incremental tracking algorithm

The solution to this linear minimisation problem can be approximated by [4]

$$\delta\bar{\mu} = -\mathbf{H}_0^{-1} \sum_{\forall \mathbf{x} \in \mathcal{R}} \mathbf{M}(\mathbf{x}, \mathbf{0})^\top \mathcal{E}(\mathbf{x}, t + \delta t), \tag{4}$$

where $\mathbf{H}_0$ is

$$\mathbf{H}_0 = \sum_{\forall \mathbf{x} \in \mathcal{R}} \mathbf{M}(\mathbf{x}, \mathbf{0})^\top \mathbf{M}(\mathbf{x}, \mathbf{0}),$$

$\mathcal{E}(\mathbf{x}, t + \delta t)$ is the error in the estimation of the motion of pixel $\mathbf{x}$ of the target region

$$\mathcal{E}(\mathbf{x}, t + \delta t) = I(\mathbf{f}(\mathbf{x}, \bar{\mu}_t), t + \delta t) - I(\mathbf{x}, t_0),$$

and $\mathbf{M}(\mathbf{x}, \mathbf{0})$ is the Jacobian vector of pixel $\mathbf{x}$ with respect to the model parameters $\bar{\mu}$ at time instant t_0 (we will assume $\bar{\mu}_{t_0} = \mathbf{0}$). If $\mathbf{f}(\mathbf{x}, \mathbf{0}) = \mathbf{x}$, then $\mathbf{M}(\mathbf{x}, \mathbf{0})$ can be expressed as

$$\mathbf{M}(\mathbf{x}, \mathbf{0}) = \left. \frac{\partial I(\mathbf{f}(\mathbf{x}, \bar{\mu}), t_0)}{\partial \bar{\mu}} \right|_{\bar{\mu}=\mathbf{0}} = \nabla_{\mathbf{x}} I(\mathbf{x}, t_0)^\top \left[\frac{\partial \mathbf{f}(\mathbf{x}, \bar{\mu})}{\partial \bar{\mu}} \right]_{\bar{\mu}=\mathbf{0}},$$

where $\nabla_{\mathbf{x}} I(\mathbf{x}, t_0)$ is the template image gradient and $\frac{\partial \mathbf{f}(\mathbf{x}, \bar{\mu})}{\partial \bar{\mu}}$ is the Jacobian vector of the motion model.

The Jacobian of pixel $\mathbf{x}$ with respect to the model parameters in the reference template, $\mathbf{M}(\mathbf{x}, \mathbf{0})$, is a vector whose values are our *a priori* knowledge about target structure, i.e. how the brightness value of each pixel in the reference template changes as the object moves infinitesimally. It represents the information provided by each template pixel to the tracking process. Note that when $\mathbf{H}_0 = \sum_{\forall \mathbf{x} \in \mathcal{R}} \mathbf{M}(\mathbf{x}, \mathbf{0})^\top \mathbf{M}(\mathbf{x}, \mathbf{0})$ is singular the motion parameters cannot be recovered, this would be a generalisation of the so called *aperture problem* in the estimation of optical flow.

The on-line computation performed by this tracking procedure is quite small (see Fig. 1) and consists of a warping of N pixels, which can be made very fast by conventional software o even by specialised hardware, a subtraction of N pixels to compute $\mathcal{E}(\mathbf{x}, t + \delta t)$, the addition of N vectors multiplied by one constant, and the multiplication of this result by the $n \times n$ matrix $\mathbf{H}_0^{-1}$, where $n = \dim(\bar{\mu})$.

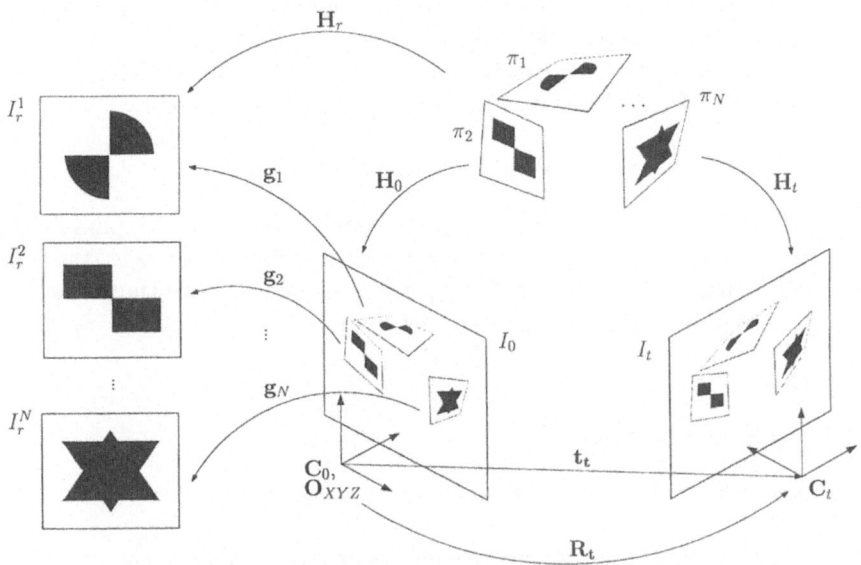

Fig. 2. Geometrical set up of the tracking process

3 The Tracker

In this section we will introduce the target region motion model, $\mathbf{f}$, and show how to compute the image Jacobian $\mathbf{M}(\mathbf{x}, \mathbf{0})$ with respect to the parameters of the model.

3.1 Motion Model

Let $\{\pi_i\}$ be a set of N planar patches in 3D space, each one containing a target region. Each patch, π_i, of this set can be described by equation $\pi_i \equiv \mathbf{n}_i^\top \mathbf{P} = 1$, where $\mathbf{n}_i = [a, b, c]^\top$ is a three-element vector containing the normal direction to the plane π_i, and $\mathbf{P} = [X, Y, Z]^\top \in \pi_i$ are the coordinates of a 3D point on that plane expressed in the reference system of the scene, O_{XYZ}. Each plane, π_i, will have a *reference template* or high-resolution image of the target region, I_r^i, associated to it. At the initial time instant, we will assume that the reference systems attached to the camera and scene are perfectly aligned.

The projection of a point on a planar patch $\mathbf{P}_{\pi_j}$ onto image I_i of the sequence is given by

$$\mathbf{x}_i^{\pi_j} = \underbrace{\mathbf{K}\,\mathbf{R}_i[\,\mathbf{I} - \mathbf{t}_i \mathbf{n}_j^\top\,]}_{\mathbf{H}_i}\,\mathbf{P}_{\pi_j}, \qquad (5)$$

where $\mathbf{K}$ is the camera intrinsics matrix, which is assumed to be known, $\mathbf{I}$ is the 3×3 identity matrix, $\mathbf{R}_i$, $\mathbf{t}_i$ represent the pose of the camera and $\mathbf{x}_i^{\pi_j}$ represents the homogeneous coordinates of the pixel projection. As we are dealing with 3D points that are located on planes, their projection model is a 2D linear projective transformation or *homography*, $\mathbf{H}_i$.

The motion model, $\mathbf{f}(\mathbf{x}, \bar{\mu})$, can be derived from (5) by considering the projection of 3D point $\mathbf{P}_{\pi_j}$ onto $I_0 \equiv I(\mathbf{x}_0, t_0)$ and onto $I_t \equiv I(\mathbf{x}_t, t)$

$$\mathbf{x}_t^{\pi_j} = \mathbf{K}\,\mathbf{R}_t [\,\mathbf{I} - \mathbf{t}_t \mathbf{n}_j^\top\,]\,\mathbf{K}^{-1} \mathbf{x}_0^{\pi_j},$$

where, $\mathbf{R}_t(\alpha, \beta, \gamma)$ and $\mathbf{t}_t(t_x, t_y, t_z)$ are the six parameters, $\bar{\mu} = (\alpha, \beta, \gamma, t_x, t_y, t_z)^\top$, of the motion model, which represent the pose of the camera with respect the first image in the sequence. Note that, since our scene is rigid, these motion parameters are common to all patches π_j in the model.

3.2 The Image Jacobian

In this subsection we will show how to compute the second element of our algorithm, $\mathbf{M}(\mathbf{x}, \mathbf{0})$.

Due to partial occlusions, perspective effects or low resolution, the projection of a target region onto I_0 may not provide enough information to accurately compute $\nabla_\mathbf{x} I(\mathbf{x}, t_0)$. In this case we use the reference template to compute it, through the following relation

$$\nabla_\mathbf{x} I(\mathbf{x}, t_0)|_{\forall \mathbf{x} \in \pi_i} = \left[\frac{\partial I_r^i(\mathbf{g}_i(\mathbf{x}, \bar{\mu}))}{\partial \mathbf{g}_i} \right]^\top \left[\frac{\partial \mathbf{g}_i(\mathbf{x}, \bar{\mu})}{\partial \mathbf{x}} \right],$$

where $\mathbf{g}_i$ is the warping function that transforms the projection of planar patch π_i in image I_0 onto reference template I_r^i, that is, $I_0(\mathbf{x}) = I_r^i(\mathbf{g}_i(\mathbf{x}, \bar{\mu}))\ \forall \mathbf{x} \in \pi_i$.

Finally, the Jacobian of the motion model with respect to the motion parameters is given by

$$\frac{\partial \mathbf{f}(\mathbf{x}, \bar{\mu})}{\partial \bar{\mu}}\bigg|_{\bar{\mu}=\mathbf{0}} = \left[\frac{\partial \mathbf{f}(\mathbf{x}, \bar{\mu})}{\partial \alpha}, \ldots, \frac{\partial \mathbf{f}(\mathbf{x}, \bar{\mu})}{\partial t_z} \right]_{\bar{\mu}=\mathbf{0}}, \tag{6}$$

where, for example

$$\frac{\partial \mathbf{f}(\mathbf{x}, \bar{\mu})}{\partial \alpha} = \mathbf{K} \begin{bmatrix} 0 & 0 & 0 \\ 0 & 0 & -1 \\ 0 & 1 & 0 \end{bmatrix} \mathbf{K}^{-1} \mathbf{x}_0; \quad \text{and} \quad \frac{\partial \mathbf{f}(\mathbf{x}, \bar{\mu})}{\partial t_x} = -\mathbf{K} \begin{bmatrix} 1 \\ 0 \\ 0 \end{bmatrix} \mathbf{K}^{-1} \mathbf{x}_0.$$

4 Experiments

We have carried out three experiments to test the tracking algorithm here presented, for each of which we have generated an image sequence (See videos at: http://www.dia.fi.upm.es/~lbaumela/FaceExpressionRecognition/research.html). Sequences A and B were generated using pov-ray[1] (see Fig 3

---

[1] A free ray tracer software, http://www.povray.org

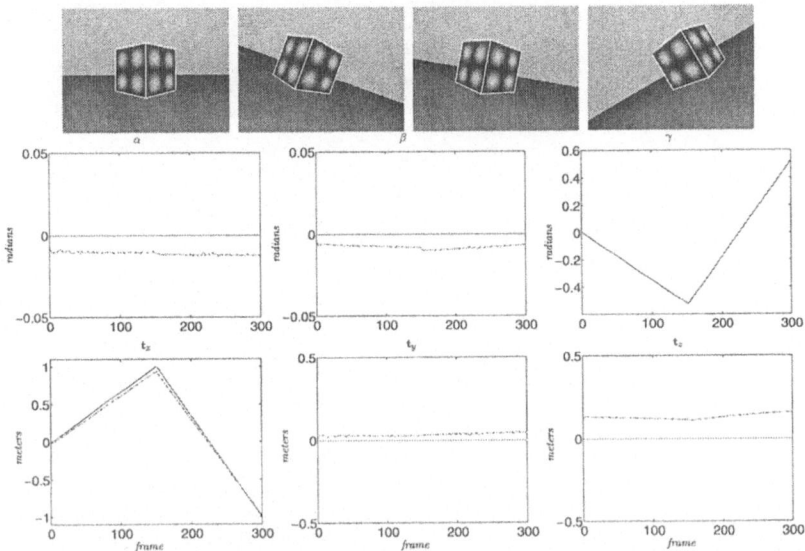

Fig. 3. Sequence A. First row: images 1, 100, 200 and 300 of the sequence. In white thick lines is shown the motion estimated by our tracker. Second and third rows: tracking parameters for sequence A. In solid line is shown the ground truth data and in dash-dot line is shown the motion estimated by the tracker

and 4), in order to have ground truth data of the motion of our target. Sequence C (see Fig. 5) was captured with a Sony VL-500 CCD colour camera with no gain and no gamma correction.

In the first experiment we test the accuracy of our tracker. For this test we have used sequence A (see Fig. 3), in which a cube located 4 meters away from the camera translates along the X axis (t_x varies) and rotates around the Z axis (γ varies). As can be seen in Fig. 3 the parameters estimated with our tracker coincide with the ground truth data. Note that as we are generating the sequences with synthetic ligths and we are warping the textures over the planar patches (with aliasing effects involved), the sequences are not noise free.

The second experiment compares the tracking procedure presented in this paper with a traditional patch-based tracker in which each of the patches is tracked individually. For this test we have generated sequence B (see Fig. 4) which is identical to sequence A except that now the moving object is composed of two planar patches with textures which individually do not provide enough information for tracking. As shown in Fig. 4 the individual tracker diverges after a few frames. This is caused by the ambiguity of the textures in the patches.

In the last experiment we test the performance of our tracker when following a human face. For this test we use sequence C. As shown in Fig. 5, the tracker accurately tracks the face even for moderate out-of-the-image plane rotations.

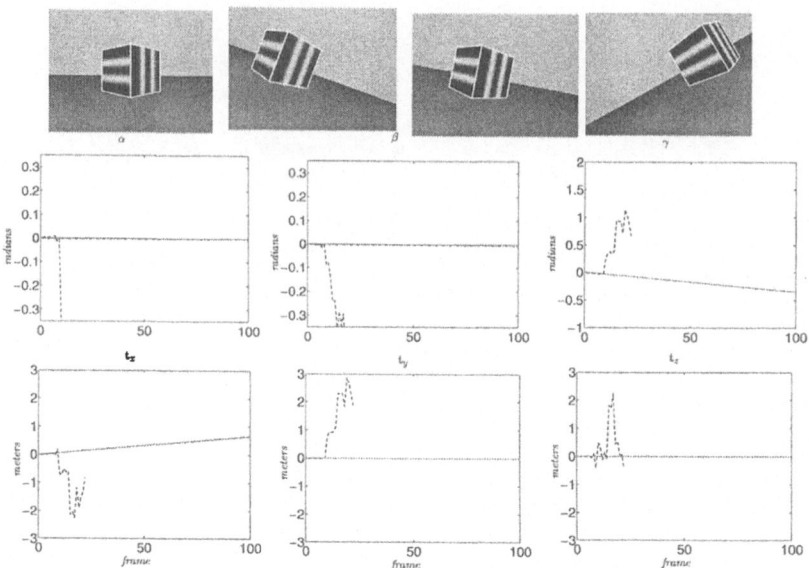

Fig. 4. Sequence B. First row: images 1, 100, 200 and 300 of the sequence. In white thick lines is shown the motion estimated by our tracker. Second and third rows: tracking parameters for the first 100 frames in sequence B. In solid line is shown the ground truth data, with dashed line is shown the estimation of the individual tracker, finally with dash-dot line is shown the motion estimated by our tracker

These rotations could be even larger just by including patches taken from the sides of the head.

5   Conclusions

We have presented a procedure for tracking a rigid object based on a set of image patches. By integrating low level information in a single tracker we have been able to reliably track in 3D a set of patches which individually could not provide enough information. With this algorithm we could also track a face with out-of-the-image plane rotations, even with a poor face model.

Another issue that should be addressed in the future is the speed of convergence of the tracker. This is related to the approximation made to solve (3) and to the dependencies (correlations) in the columns of the $\mathbf{H_0}$ matrix, which are, in turn, directly related to the ambiguities in the estimation of the tracking parameters and which may result in slow convergence, and eventually divergence, of the tracker. Other open issues are the invariance to illumination changes and to variation in the texture of the patches (e.g. variations in face appearance).

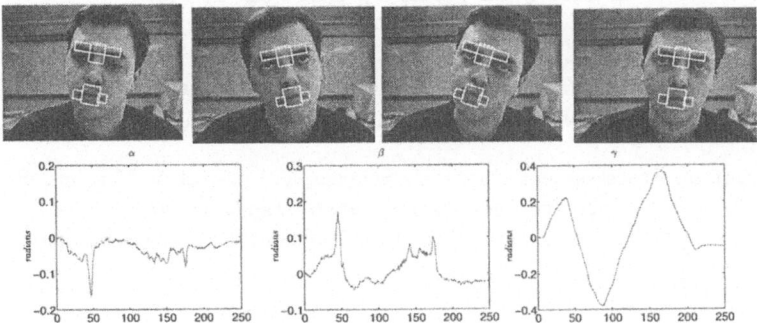

Fig. 5. Sequence C. Upper row: four images of the sequence. In white thick lines is shown the location of each feature estimated by the tracker. Bottom row: Estimated rotation parameters

References

[1] Simon Baker and Ian Matthews. Equivalence and efficiency of image alignment algorithms. In *Proc. of CVPR*, volume 1, pages 1090–1097. IEEE, 2001.

[2] Stan Birchfield. Elliptical head tracking using intensity gradients and color histograms. In *Proc, of CVPR*, pages 232–237. IEEE, 1998.

[3] Michael J. Black and Yasser Yacoob. Recognizing facial expressions in image sequences using local parameterized models of image motion. *Int. Journal of Computer Vision*, 25(1):23–48, 1997.

[4] José M. Buenaposada, Enrique Muñoz, and Luis Baumela. Incremental image alignment. Technical Report DIA-CV-2003-01, Computer Vision Lab, Faculty of Computer Science, UPM, January 2003.

[5] José M. Buenaposada and Luis Baumela. Variations of grey world for face tracking. *Image Processing and Communications*, 7(3-4):51–62, 2001.

[6] José M. Buenaposada and Luis Baumela. Real-time tracking and estimation of plane pose. In *Proc. of ICPR*, pages 697–700. IEEE, August 2002.

[7] Gregory D. Hager and Peter N. Belhumeur. Efficient region tracking with parametric models of geometry and illumination. *PAMI*, 20(10):1025–1039, 1998.

[8] Gregory D. Hager and Kentaro Toyama. X vision: Combining image warping and geometric constraints for fast visual tracking. In *Proc. of ECCV*, volume II, LNCS-1065, pages 507–517. Springer-Verlag, 1996.

[9] Tony S. Jebara and Alex Pentland. Parametrized structure from motion for 3d adaptive feedback tracking of faces. In *Proc. of CVPR'97*, pages 144–150. 1997.

[10] Marco La Cascia, Stan Sclaroff, and Vassilis V. Athitsos. Fast, reliable head tracking under varying illumination: An approach based on robust registration of texture-mapped 3d models. *PAMI*, 22(4):322–336, April 2000.

[11] Rainer Stiefelhagen, Yie Yang, and Alex Waibel. A model-based gaze tracking system. *Int. Journal of Artificial Intelligence Tools*, 6(2):193–209, 1997.

[12] Stephan Valente and Jean-Luc Dugelay. A visual analysis/synthesis feedback loop for accurate face tracking. *Signal Processing: Image Communications*, 16:585–608, 2001.

Support Vector Machines for Crop Classification Using Hyperspectral Data*

G. Camps-Valls[1], L. Gómez-Chova[1], J. Calpe-Maravilla[1],
E. Soria-Olivas[1], J. D. Martín-Guerrero[1], and J. Moreno[2]

[1] Grup de Processament Digital de Senyals, Universitat de València, Spain.
gustavo.camps@uv.es, http://gpds.uv.es/
[2] Departament de Termodinàmica, Universitat de València, Spain.

Abstract. In this communication, we propose the use of Support Vector Machines (SVM) for crop classification using hyperspectral images. SVM are benchmarked to well–known neural networks such as multilayer perceptrons (MLP), Radial Basis Functions (RBF) and Co-Active Neural Fuzzy Inference Systems (CANFIS). Models are analyzed in terms of efficiency and robustness, which is tested according to their suitability to real–time working conditions whenever a preprocessing stage is not possible. This can be simulated by considering models with and without a preprocessing stage. Four scenarios (128, 6, 3 and 2 bands) are thus evaluated.
Several conclusions are drawn: (1) SVM yield better outcomes than neural networks; (2) training neural models is unfeasible when working with high dimensional input spaces and (3) SVM perform similarly in the four classification scenarios, which indicates that noisy bands are successfully detected.

1 Introduction

The information contained in hyperspectral images allows the reconstruction of the energy curve radiated by the terrestrial surface throughout the electromagnetic spectrum. Hence, characterization, identification and classification of the observed material from their spectral curve is an interesting possibility. Pattern recognition methods have proven to be effective techniques in this kind of applications. In fact, classification of surface features in satellite imagery is one of the most important applications of remote sensing. It is often difficult and time--consuming to develop classifiers by hand, so many researchers have turned to techniques from the fields of statistics and machine learning to automatically generate classifiers [1–7]. Nevertheless, the main problem with supervised methods

* This research has been partially supported by the Information Society Technologies (IST) programme of the European Community. The results of this work will be applied in the "Smart Multispectral System for Commercial Applications" project (SmartSpectra, www.smartspectra.com). All the data used were acquired in the Scientific Analysis of the European Space Agency (ESA) Airborne Multi-Annual Imaging Spectrometer Campaign DAISEX (Contract ♯15343/01/NL/MM).

F.J. Perales et al. (Eds.): IbPRIA 2003, LNCS 2652, pp. 134–141, 2003.

is that the learning process heavily depends on the quality of the training data set and the input space dimensionality. Certainly, these are main issues to be addressed, given the high cost of true sample labelling, the high number of spectral bands, and the high variability of the earth surface. In practice, a pre–processing stage (feature selection/extraction) is time–consuming, scenario–dependent and needs *a priori* knowledge.

Therefore, the last objective in such a scheme is to process the data in order to extract valid, novel, potentially useful, and ultimately understandable structure in data, which constitutes a *data mining* approach [1]. In this context, we propose the use of Support Vector Machines (SVM) [10] to develop crop cover classifiers and to obtain a thematic map of the crops on the scene. SVM are not affected by the curse of dimensionality and offer solutions with an explicit dependence on the most informative patterns in the data. Previous works have shown succesful classification performance of hyperspectral data [5, 11] but further work must be carried out in order to study robustness in noisy situations (irrelevant bands) and changing environments (several images). We compare SVM to other well-known machine learning methods such as multilayer perceptrons (MLP), Radial Basis Functions (RBF) [6] and Co-Active Neural Fuzzy Inference System (CANFIS) [7]. Robustness and suitability to real–time working conditions are evaluated by considering models with and without a preprocessing stage.

The paper is outlined as follows. In Section 2, data collection and the experimental setup is presented. SVM are described in Section 3 and results shown in Section 4. We end up with some conclusions and further work.

2   Material and Experimental Setup

We have used six hyperspectral images acquired with the 128-bands HyMap spectrometer during the DAISEX-99 campaign (http://io.uv.es/projects/daisex/). More information about the data collection, Hymap calibration and atmospheric correction can be retrieved from [3, 4]. Six different classes were considered in the area (corn, sugar beet, barley, wheat, alfalfa, and soil), which were labelled from ♯1 to ♯6, respectively. In this sense, the task is referred to as a multiclassification pattern recognition problem. However, we are not only interested in the accuracy provided by each method but also in their suitability to real–time working conditions whenever a feature selection stage is not possible. This scenario is simulated by considering models without a pre-processing stage and thus using 128 bands. In addition, previous work [3, 4] in feature selection yielded three subsets of representative features (6, 3 and 2 bands), which induce three different pattern recognition problems, respectively. Two data sets (training and validation sets) were built (150 samples/class each) and models were selected using the cross-validation method. Finally, a test set consisting of the true map on the scene over complete images was used as the final performance indicator. In each one of the six images (700×670 pixels), the total number of test samples is 327,336 (corn 31,269; sugar beet 11,322; barley 124,768; wheat 53,400; alfalfa 24,726; and bare soil 81,851) and the rest is considered unknown.

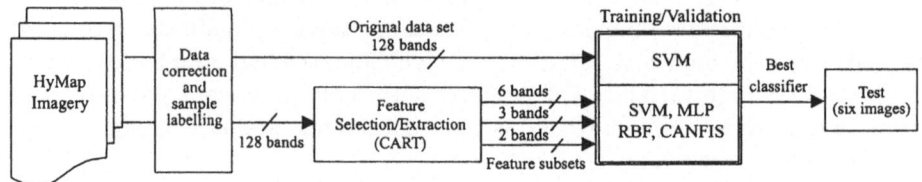

Fig. 1. Diagram of the hyperspectral data classification process. A training data set is extracted from the the six collected images and then a CART-based feature selection stage yields three representative subsets (consisting of 6, 3 and 2 bands, respectively) [4], which constitute three different pattern recognition problems, respectively. An additional scenario considering the whole training data set (128 bands) incorporates. Four classifiers are thus implemented and tested in the six whole images

Once the desired input-output mapping for training and validation are defined, usually a feature selection stage is used to reduce dimension of the input space. This can make the training process feasible and improve results by removing noisy irrelevant bands. However, design and application of a dimension-reduction techniques is time-consuming and scenario-dependent, which are evident problems to circumvent. In fact, we are not only interested in the classification accuracy provided by each method but also in their suitability to real-time working conditions whenever a feature selection stage is not possible. This scenario is simulated by considering models with and without a feature selection stage. The proposed learning scheme is shown in Fig. 1.

3   Support Vector Machines

Support Vector Machines have been recently proposed as a method for pattern classification and nonlinear regression. Their appeal lies in their strong connection to the underlying statistical learning theory where an SVM is an approximate implementation of the method of structural risk minimization [10]. SVM has many attractive features. For instance, the solution of the quadratic programming (QP) problem [2] is globally optimized while with neural networks the gradient based training algorithms only guarantee finding a local minima. In addition, SVM can handle large feature spaces (specially convenient when working with hyperspectral data), can effectively avoid overfitting by controlling the margin and can automatically identify a small subset made up of informative points, namely *support vectors* (SV). Consequently, they have been used for particle identification, face recognition, text categorization, time series prediction, bioinformatics, texture classification, etc. Visit http://www.kernel-machines.org for publications and application resources.

In the following, we summarize the "one-against-the-rest procedure" for classification purposes, in which, a classifier is obtained for each class. Given a labeled

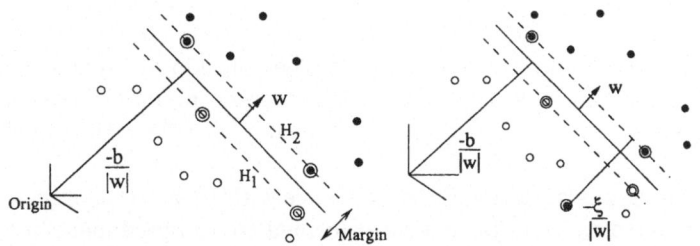

Fig. 2. Left: The Optimal Decision Hyperplane in a linearly separable problem. **Right:** Linear decision hyperplanes in nonlinearly separable data can be handled by including slack variables ξ_i. Figures adapted from [9]

training data set $((\mathbf{x}_1, y_1), \ldots, (\mathbf{x}_n, y_n)$, where $\mathbf{x}_i \in \mathbb{R}^d$ and $y_i \in \{+1, -1\})$ and a nonlinear mapping, $\phi(\cdot)$, usually to a higher dimensional space, $\mathbb{R}^d \xrightarrow{\phi(\cdot)} \mathbb{R}^H$ $(H > d)$, the SVM method solves:

$$\min_{\mathbf{w}, \xi_i, b} \left\{ \frac{1}{2} \|\mathbf{w}\|^2 + C \sum_i \xi_i \right\} \tag{1}$$

subject to the following constraints:

$$y_i(\phi^T(\mathbf{x}_i)\mathbf{w} + b) \geq 1 - \xi_i \qquad \forall i = 1, \ldots, n \tag{2}$$
$$\xi_i \geq 0 \qquad \forall i = 1, \ldots, n \tag{3}$$

where $\mathbf{w}$ and b define a linear regressor in the feature space, nonlinear in the input space unless $\phi(\mathbf{x}_i) = \mathbf{x}_i$. In addition, ξ_i and C are, respectively, a positive slack variable and the penalization applied to errors (Fig. 2). The parameter C can be regarded as a regularization parameter which affects the generalization capabilities of the classifier and is selected by the user. A larger C corresponds to assigning a higher penalty to the training errors.

An SVM is trained to construct a hyperplane $\phi^T(\mathbf{x}_i)\mathbf{w} + b = 0$ for which the margin of separation is maximized. Using the method of Lagrange multipliers, this hyperplane can be represented as:

$$\sum_i \alpha_i y_i \phi(\mathbf{x}_i) \cdot \phi(\mathbf{x}) = 0 \tag{4}$$

where the auxiliary variables α_i are Lagrange multipliers. Its solution reduces to: *Maximize:*

$$L_d \equiv \sum_i \alpha_i - \frac{1}{2} \sum_{i,j} \alpha_i \alpha_j y_i y_j \phi(\mathbf{x}_i) \cdot \phi(\mathbf{x}_j) \tag{5}$$

subject to the constraints:

$$0 \leq \alpha_i \leq C, \tag{6}$$

$$\sum_i \alpha_i y_i = 0 \tag{7}$$

Using the Karush-Kuhn-Tucker Theorem, the solution is a linear combination of training examples which lie closest to the decision boundary (the corresponding multipliers are non-zero). Only these examples, affect the construction of hyperplane.

The mapping ϕ is performed in accordance with Cover's theorem which guarranties that patterns, non-linearly transformed to a high–dimensionality space, are linearly separable. Working with high dimension converted patterns would, in principle, constitute an intractable problem but all the ϕ mappings used in the SVM occur in the form of an inner product. Accordingly, the solution is to replace all the occurrences of an inner product resulting from two mappings with the kernel function K defined as:

$$K(\mathbf{x}_i, \mathbf{x}_j) = \phi(\mathbf{x}_i) \cdot \phi(\mathbf{x}_j). \tag{8}$$

Then, without considering the mapping ϕ explicitly, a non-linear SVM can be constructed by selecting the proper kernel.

In order to solve problems with k classes we must reformulate the problem. Given a classifier $(\mathbf{w}^j, b^j)$, $j \in \{0, ..., k-1\}$ for each class, to assign a sample $\mathbf{x}$ to a certain k class we must calculate the output of the k classifiers and select the one with the highest output. We then proceede as in the binary case. Full details on the solution can be found in [8].

4   Classification Results

4.1   Training an SVM

Nonlinear classifiers are obtained by taking the dot product in kernel-generated spaces. Some common kernels are the linear $(K(\mathbf{x}_i,\mathbf{x}_j) = \mathbf{x}_i \cdot \mathbf{x}_j)$, polynomial $(K(\mathbf{x}_i,\mathbf{x}_j) = (\mathbf{x}_i \cdot \mathbf{x}_j + 1)^d)$, and Gaussian (RBF) $(K(\mathbf{x}_i,\mathbf{x}_j) = e^{-(\mathbf{x}_i \cdot \mathbf{x}_j)^2/\sigma^2})$. Note that one or more free parameters must be previously settled in the nonlinear kernels (polynomial degree d, Gaussian width σ) together with the trade-off parameter C, usually known as the *penalization* factor. Selection of the best subset of free parameters are usually done by cross validation methods but this can lead to poor generalization capabilities and lack of representation. We alleviate this problem using the V-fold cross-validation method[1] with the training data set.

Many discriminative methods, including neural networks and SVM, are often more accurate and efficient when dealing with two classes only. For large number of classes, higher-level multi-class methods utilize these two-class classification methods as the basic building blocks, namely "one-against-the-rest" procedures. However, such approaches lead to suboptimal solutions when dealing with multi-class problems and to the well-known problem of the "false positives". Therefore, we have used a multi–classification scheme for all the methods.

---

[1] The 8-fold cross validation uses 7/8 of data for training and 1/8 for validation purposes. This procedure is repeated eight times with different validation sets.

Table 1. Average recognition rates (RR [%]) of the six images in training, validation, and test sets for different models. The four subsets (128, 6, 3, 2 bands) are evaluated (except for neural networks in which the computational burden involved made training with 128 bands unfeasible), all of them containing 150 samples per class

METHOD	FEAT.	TRAIN	VALID	TEST
SVM128	Poly	100	98.78	95.53
SVM6	Poly	99.79	99.44	96.44
SVM3	RBF	91.22	91.00	85.16
SVM2	RBF	89.11	89.11	82.68
MLP6	6x5x6	99.33	99.44	94.53
MLP3	3x25x6	90.22	87.67	82.97
MLP2	2x27x6	88.00	85.67	81.95
RBF6	6x16x6	98.88	98.80	94.10
RBF3	3x31x6	88.20	87.00	81.44
RBF2	2x18x6	87.33	85.25	81.62
CANFIS6	6x2x7x6	98.68	96.66	94.22
CANFIS3	3x3x12x6	89.20	88.77	81.64
CANFIS2	2x8x15x6	86.33	86.00	81.82

4.2 Model Comparison

Table 1 shows the average recognition rate (RR[%]) of the six images in training, validation, and test sets. In all cases, we considered equiprobable classes for training and validation and thus no individual penalization parameter [8] in the case of SVM or heuristic rule in neural networks were necessary. However, test set contains highly unbalanced classes and thus, the latter practice could improve results if the training process was intentionally driven by priors. However, this would not be a fair assumption for our purposes, i.e. achiving an automatic scenario-independent classifier.

Some conclusions can be drawn from Table 1. SVM performs better than neural networks in all scenarios. Moreover, when a feature selection stage is not possible (128 bands used), the computational burden involved in the training process of neural networks make these methods unfeasible. Contrarily, SVM are not affected by input dimension and presence of noisy bands. Additionally, as the dimension of the input space is lower, neural networks degrade more rapidly than SVM do. In that sense, complexity[2] of all models increases as the input dimension decreases. In fact, RBF kernels and more than 15% of SVs are strictly necessary to attain significant results with less than six bands. Despite

---

[2] We evaluate model's complexity in terms of the kernel used and the number of SV in the SVM approach and in terms of the number of hidden neurons in the neural networks.

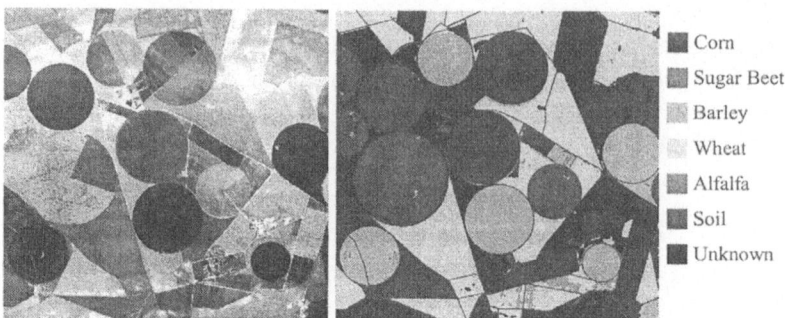

Fig. 3. **Left:** HyMap RGB composition, Barrax, Spain. **Right:** Classification of the whole scene yielded by the best SVM classifier

polynomial kernel has been claimed to be specially well-suited for hyperspectral data classification [5], it has yielded similar results to the linear kernel in our case (see next section for details). Finally, no numerical (RR<3%) or statistical (κ scores in the range [0.6,0.8]) differences are found between SVM with and without a step for dimensionality reduction prior to classification. This indicates that noisy bands have been successfully identified and their contribution to the final decision attenuated without decreasing the recognition rate.

Table 2 shows the confusion matrix of the best SVM. High recognition rates (RR[%]>90%) are achieved for all classes but SVM misclassify almost 6% of corn (class ♮1) as bare soil (class ♮6). This is due to that corn is in an early stage of maturity. Figure 3 shows the original and the classified samples for one of the collected images.

Table 2. Confusion matrix and recognition rate [RR %] in each class yielded by the best SVM classifier in the TEST set (whole scene)

Desired class	Predicted class						RR[%]
	♮1 Corn	♮2 Sugar beet	♮3 Barley	♮4 Wheat	♮5 Alfalfa	♮6 Soil	
♮1, corn	31,188	67	7	1	0	6	99.74
♮2, sugar beet	23	11,256	43	0	0	0	99.42
♮3, barley	732	702	120,874	1993	18	449	96.88
♮4, wheat	12	108	320	52,956	4	0	99.17
♮5, alfalfa	28	106	140	36	24,413	3	98.73
♮6, soil	4914	1003	1539	190	15	74,190	90.64

5 Conclusion

In this communication, we have proposed the use of kernel methods for both hyperspectral data classification. SVM have revealed very efficient in different situations when a preprocessing stage is not possible. This method can tolerate the presence of ambiguous patterns and features in the data set. Future work will consider boosting methods and combined forecasters.

References

[1] P. S. Bradley, U. M. Fayyad, and O. L. Mangasarian. Mathematical programming for data mining: formulations and challenges. *INFORMS Journal on Computing*, 11(3):217–238, 1999.

[2] R. Fletcher. *Practical Methods of Optimization*. John Wiley & Sons, Inc. 2nd Edition, 1987.

[3] L. Gómez, J. Calpe, J. D. Martín, E. Soria, E. Camps-Valls, and J. Moreno. Semi-supervised method for crop classification using hyperspectral remote sensing images. In *1st International Symposium. Recent Advantages in Quantitative Remote Sensing.*, Torrent, Spain., Set 2002.

[4] L. Gómez-Chova, J. Calpe, E. Soria, G. Camps-Valls, J. D. Martín, and J. Moreno. CART-based feature selection of hyperspectral images for crop cover classification. In *IEEE International Conference on Image Processing*, 2003.

[5] J. A. Gualtieri and S. Chettri. Support vector machines for classification of hyperspectral data. In *International Geoscience and Remote Sensing*, 2000.

[6] S. Haykin. *Neural Networks: A Comprehensive Foundation*. Prentice Hall, 1999.

[7] Jang Jyh-Shing Roger, Sun Chuen-Tsai, and Mizutani Eiji. *Neuro–Fuzzy and Soft–Computing*. Prentice Hall, 1997.

[8] Y. Lin, Y. Lee, and G. Wahba. Support Vector Machines for classification in non-standard situations. Department of Statistics TR 1016, University of Wisconsin-Madison, 2000.

[9] B. Schölkopf and A. Smola. *Learning with Kernels – Support Vector Machines, Regularization, Optimization and Beyond*. MIT Press Series, 2001. Partially available from http://www.learning-with-kernels.org.

[10] V. N. Vapnik. *Statistical Learning Theory*. John Wiley & Sons, New York, 1998.

[11] J. Zhang, Y. Zhang, and T. Zhou. Classification of hyperspectral data using support vector machine. In *IEEE International Conference on Image Processing*, pages 882–885, 2001.

Vehicle License Plate Segmentation
in Natural Images*

Javier Cano and Juan-Carlos Pérez-Cortés

Instituto Tecnológico de Informática, Universidad Politécnica de Valencia
Camino de Vera, s/n 46071 Valencia (SPAIN)
{jcano,jcperez}@iti.upv.es

Abstract. A robust method for plate segmentation in a License Plate
Recognition (LPR) system is presented, designed to work in a wide
range of acquisition conditions, including unrestricted scene environments, light, perspective and camera-to-car distance. Although this novel
text-region segmentation technique has been applied to a very specific
problem, it is extensible to more general contexts, like difficult text segmentation tasks dealing with natural images. Extensive experimentation
has been performed in order to estimate the best parameters for the task
at hand, and the results obtained are presented.

1 Introduction

Text-region segmentation has been largely studied over the last years, [9], [8], [5],
[2], [4], however, even today it remains an open field of work, interesting for many
different applications in which complex images are to be processed. Reasonable
advances have been actually achieved in the task of extracting text from some
kind of restricted images, as in the case of scanned documents, artificially edited
video, electronic boards, synthetic images, etc. In all of them, the text included
in the image has a number of "a priori" defined properties (localisation, intensity,
homogeneity) that makes possible to tackle the segmentation task using filters,
morphology or connectivity based approximations.

Historically, the methods devised to solve the text segmentation problem
fall into one of two different branches: a morphology and/or connectivity approach, most useful for dealing with the kind of images previously described,
and a textural (statistical) approach that has been successfully used to find text
regions over non-restricted natural images. This is the problem that arises in the
segmentation phase of an LPR system, where images are composed of a great
variety of objects and affected by illumination and perspective variations. All
these variable environment conditions result in a complex scene, where text regions are embedded within the scene and nearly impossible to identify by the
methods employed in the morphology approximation.

Thus, the task of text (license plate) segmentation in a LPR system is included in the second category. Moreover, due the nature of images (as we will

---

* Work partially supported by the Spanish CICYT under grant TIC2000-1703-CO3-01

F.J. Perales et al. (Eds.): IbPRIA 2003, LNCS 2652, pp. 142–149, 2003.

see in Section 2), it is also desirable to use a segmentation method capable of generating various hypothesis for each image in order to prevent the loss of any possible license plate region. In this way, it is possible to design a subsequent recognition phase that filters the final results without discarding beforehand any reasonable segmentation hypothesis.

The segmentation method proposed can be also useful for detecting any kind of text regions in natural and complex images. However, since we are concerned with a very particular task, all the parameters have been specifically adapted to improve the detection of text regions which match the constraints imposed by the shape and content of a typical vehicle license plate.

As it will be shown in the experiments section, very promising results have been achieved for the segmentation phase, therefore the next step in the design of a complete license plate recognition system requires further work on the design of a complementary recognition phase able to take advantadge of the multiple data (multiple hypothesis) provided by this segmentation.

The rest of the paper is organized as follows: Section 3 describes the data and their acquisition conditions. In Section 2, the proposed methodology is presented. Extensive experimentation and results are reported in Section 4, and finally, in Section 5, some conclusions are given and future work is proposed.

2 Corpus

A number of experiments have been performed in order to evaluate the performance of the novel segmentation technique. In other application areas, there are typically one or more standard databases which are commonly used to test different approaches to solve a specific task, and it is possible to compare results among them. This is not the case for our application, as far as we know, perhaps because license plate segmentation in non-restricted images is a fairly recent topic of interest in the pattern recognition community.

Therefore, we have used a locally acquired database. It is composed of 1307 color images of 640×480 pixels randomly divided into a test set of 131 and a training set of 1176 images. The experiments were carried out using only the gray-level information.

The scenes have been freely captured without any distance, perspective, illumination, position, background or framing constraints, except that the plate number has to be reasonably legible for a human observer. Several examples of images in the database are shown in Figure 1. In applications such as parking time control or police surveillance, the camera can be located in a vehicle and the images captured may be similar to the ones in this database. In other applications, such as access control or traffic surveillance, cameras are typically fixed in a place and thus the scene features (perspective, distance, background, etc.) are easily predictable.

A specific preprocessing step has to be performed prior to the training and test phases. This preprocessing task consists of a manual labelling, where each

Fig. 1. Four real example images from the test set. Different acquisition conditions are shown, as illumination, perspective, distance, background, etc.

license plate is located in the image and a four-sided polygon corresponding to the minimum inclusion box of the plate is defined and associated to that image.

3   Methodology

The aim of the segmentation phase is to obtain a rectangular window of a test image that should include the license plate of a vehicle present in a given scene. The task of detecting the skew and accurately finding the borders of the plate is left for the next phase, as well as the recognition proper, which is beyond the scope of this paper.

The method proposed for the automatic location of the license plate is based on a supervised classifier trained on the features of the plates in the training set. To reduce the computational load, a preselection of the candidate points that are more likely to belong to the plate is performed. The original image is subject to three operations. First, an histogram equalization is carried out to normalize the illumination. Next, a Sobel filter is applied to the whole image to highlight non-homogeneous areas. Finally, a simple threshold and a sub-sampling are applied to select the subset of points of interest. The complete procedure is depicted in Figure 2.

Fig. 2. Test image preprocess example. Upper-left: Original image. Upper-right: Equalization. Lower-left: Horizontal Sobel filter and Lower-right: Threshold binarization

3.1 Multi-hypothesis Scheme

Ideally, one segmentation hypothesis per image should be enough to detect a single vehicle plate, but because of the unrestricted nature of the images, it is possible that false positives appear when particular areas have features typically found in a license plate, like signs, advertisements and many other similarly textured regions. Therefore, it is important to save every hypothesis that can represent a plate region and leave the decision of discarding wrong hypotheses for the recognition phase, where all the details about the task are taken into account.

There is an additional important reason to adopt a multi-hypothesis scheme. Images have been acquired at different distances from the camera to the vehicle and, as a result, different sizes of plates can be seen in the images. This variability can be overcome using size-invariant features, including in the training set features from images of various sizes or using a multi-resolution scheme producing additional hypotheses. Informal tests have been performed that suggest that the first two options give rise to less accurate models of the "license plate texture" and thus lead to more false positives. For this reason, the third option has been

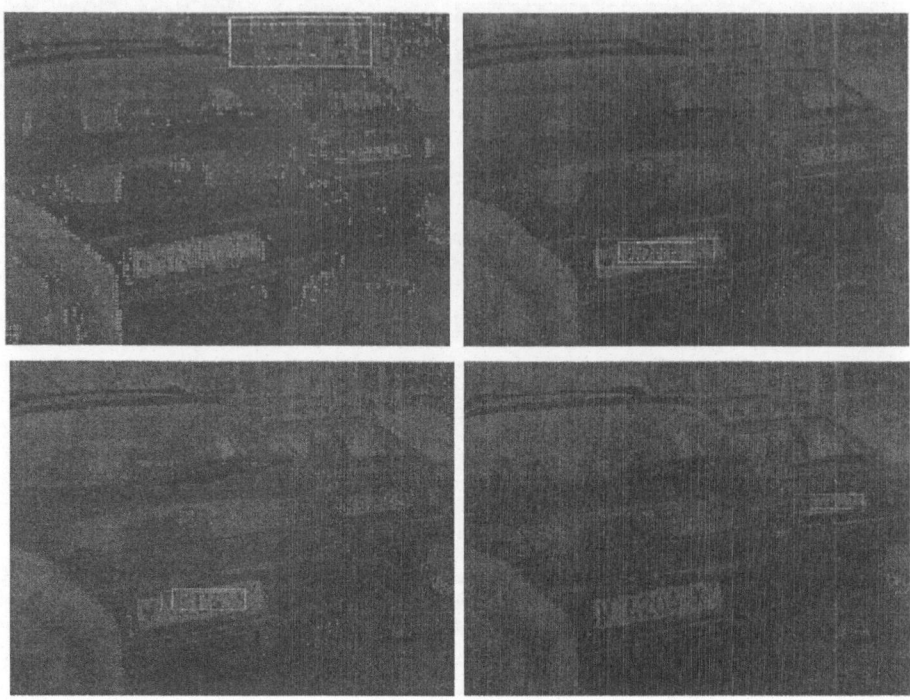

Fig. 3. Different hypothesis in a multi-resolution segmentation scheme. The brighter points indicate pixels classified as "license plate"

chosen. In Figure 3, an example of this multi-hypothesis detection procedure is shown.

3.2 Feature Vectors

A feature extraction technique that has proven its success in other image recognition tasks [3], [6] has been used in this case. It consists on using the gray values of a small local window centered on each pixel and applying a PCA transformation to reduce its dimensionality.

Each feature vector of the training set is labelled as belonging to one of two classes: positive (pixel in a license plate region), or negative (any other region). Obviously this gives rise to a huge set of negative samples, compared to the relatively small set of vectors of the "plate" class. Many of the negative samples can be very similar and add very little value to the "non-plate" class representation if they come from common background areas such as car bodies, buildings, etc.

To reduce the negative set, editing and condensing procedures can be probably used with good results, but we have applied a simpler and more efficient method that can be regarded as a bootstrapping technique. The procedure starts up with no negative samples in the training set and then proceeds by iteratively adding those training samples that are misclassified in each iteration. In the first iteration, since the train set it is only composed by positive samples, the classification relies on a threshold on the average distance of the k-nearest neighbours.

We have found that a more compact and accurate training set is built if another distance threshold is used to limit the number of misclassified samples included at each iteration.

3.3 Classification

A conventional statistical classifier based on the *k nearest neighbours rule* is used to classify every pixel of a test image to obtain a pixel map where well-differentiated groups of positive samples probably indicate the location of a license plate.

In order to achieve a reasonable speed, a combination of a *"kd-tree"* data structure and an *"approximate nearest neighbour"* search technique have been used. This data structure and search algorithm combination has been successfully used in other pattern recognition tasks, as in [7] and [1]. Moreover, the *"approximate"* search algorithm provides us with a simple way to control the tradeoff between speed and precision.

4 Experiments

The results of the proposed segmentation technique are highly dependent on the classifier performance, which in turn depends on the use of a complete and accurate training set. Several parameters in this regard have been varied in initial tests.

In Figure 4, the segmentation results are shown for four iterations of the bootstrap process. A clear improvement is found in the 3 first iterations, but after that the results do not improve significantly. In this experiment, a window size of 40×8 pixels and the training images scaled so as the plate has a similar size, have been tested. Larger values of the window size proved to add little classification improvement.

However, the most promising results have been obtained for a window size of 40×8 pixels and the training images scaled so as the plate is around three times as large in each dimension, as suggest the results in Figure 5. In the experiments reported in that figure, as receiver operating curves, the size of the window is fixed to 40×8 pixels, while the normalized plate size ranges from 40×8 to 160×40.

The best tradeoff between segmentation accuracy and cost is probably for a plate size of 100×25 pixels. Only slightly better results are found for higher plate sizes.

All the results are given at the pixel level. A simple post-processing procedure that isolates areas with a large number of pixels labelled as "license plate" with the correct size has to be applied before the plate recognitions phase. The shape

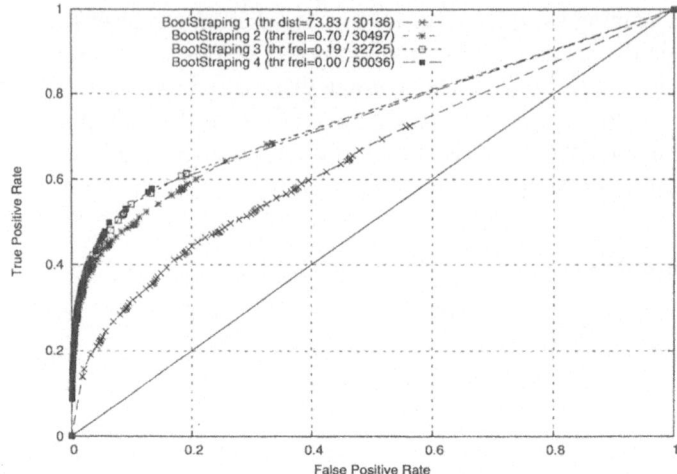

Fig. 4. Improvement of the classification performance in four bootstrap iterations

of that area must also be taken into consideration to minimize the number of false positives at the plate segmentation level.

5   Conclusions and Further Work

A robust text segmentation technique has been presented. This technique seems to be able to cope with highly variable acquisition conditions (background, illumination, perspective, camera-to-car distance, etc.) in a License Plate Recognitions task.

From the experiments performed, it can be concluded that a good tradeoff between segmentation accuracy and computation cost can be obtained for a plate normalization size of 100x25 pixels and a local window of 40x8 pixels for the feature vectors. In this conditions, a ratio of 0% False Positive Rate against a 40% True Positive Rate can be obtained with the most restrictive confidence threshold, that is, a 100% of classification reliability at the pixel level.

According to visual inspection of the whole set of 131 test images, the segmentation system has correctly located all the plates but two. Due to the unrestricted nature of the test set this can be considered a very promising result.

The computational resource demand of this segmentation technique is currently the main drawback, taking an average of 34 seconds the processing of a single 640x480 image on a AMD Athlon PC, at 1.2GHz in the conditions of the experiments reported. With some code and parameter optimizations, however, much shorter times, of only a few seconds are being already obtained in our laboratory.

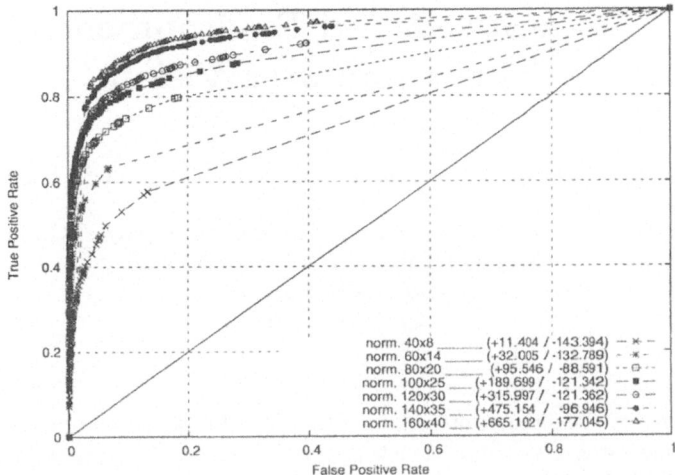

Fig. 5. Classification performance for a fixed local window size and a range of plate normalizations. Only the results of the last bootstrap iteration are presented

References

[1] J. Cano, J.C. Perez-Cortes, J. Arlandis, and R. Llobet. Trainig set expansion in handwritten character recognition. In *Workshop on Statistical Pattern Recognition SPR-2002*, Windsor (Canada), 2002.

[2] Paul Clark and Majid Mirmehdi. Finding text regions using localised measures. In Majid Mirmehdi and Barry Thomas, editors, *Proceedings of the 11th British Machine Vision Conference*, pages 675–684. BMVA Press, 2000.

[3] H. Ney D. Keysers, R. Paredes and E. Vidal. Combination of tangent vectors and local representations for handwritten digit recognition. In *Workshop on Statistical Pattern Recognition SPR-2002*, Windsor (Canada), 2002.

[4] A. Jain and S. Bhattacharjee. Text segmentation using gabor filters for automatic document processing. *Machine Vision and Applications*, 5:169–184, 1992.

[5] A. Jain and B. Yu. Automatic text location in images and video frames. In *Proceedings of ICPR*, pages 1497–1499, 1998.

[6] R. Paredes, J. Perez-Cortes, A. Juan, and E. Vidal. Face recognition using local representations and a direct voting scheme. In *Proc. of the IX Spanish Symposium on Pattern Recognition and Image Analysis*, volume I, pages 249–254, Benicassim (Spain), May 2001.

[7] J.C. Perez-Cortes, J. Arlandis, and R. Llobet. Fast and accurate handwritten character recognition using approximate nearest neighbours search on large databases. In *Workshop on Statistical Pattern Recognition SPR-2000*, Alicante (Spain), 2000.

[8] Wu and E. Riseman. Textfinder: An automatic system to detect and recognize text in images. *IEEE Transactions on pattern analysis and machine intelligence*, 21(11), 1999.

[9] Y. Zhong, K. Karu, and A. Jain. Locating text in complex color images. *Pattern Recognition*, 28(10):1523–1236, 1995.

High-Accuracy Localization
of an Underwater Robot
in a Structured Environment
Using Computer Vision

Marc Carreras, Pere Ridao, Joan Batlle, and David Ribas

Institute of Informatics and Applications, University of Girona
Campus Montilivi, 17071 Girona, Spain
marcc@eia.udg.es
http://iiia.udg.es

Abstract. This paper presents a vision-based localization approach for
an underwater robot in a structured environment. The system is based
on a coded pattern placed on the bottom of a water tank and an onboard down-looking camera. Main features are, absolute and map-based
localization, landmark detection and tracking, and real-time computation (12.5 Hz). The proposed system provides three-dimensional position and orientation of the vehicle. The paper details the codification
used in the pattern and the localization algorithm, which is illustrated
with some images. Finally, the paper shows results about the accuracy
of the system.

1   Introduction

The localization of an underwater robot is a big challenge. Techniques involving
inertial navigation systems, acoustic or optical sensors have been developed for
this purpose. However such techniques, which have been designed to be used
in unknown and unstructured environments, are inaccurate and have drift problems [3]. On the other hand, in structured environments the localization problem
can be drastically reduced allowing the experimentation with underwater robots
to be possible.

This papers proposes a vision-based localization system to estimate the position and orientation of an underwater robot in a structured environment. Main
features of this system are absolute and map-based localization, landmark detection and tracking, and real-time computation. The components of the system
are an onboard down-looking camera and a coded pattern placed on the bottom
of a water tank. The algorithm calculates the three-dimensional position and
orientation referred to the water tank coordinate system with a high accuracy
and drift-free.

The aim of the proposed localization system is to provide an accurate estimation of the position of URIS Autonomous Underwater Vehicle (AUV) in
the water tank, see Figure 1. The utility of this water tank is to experiment in

F.J. Perales et al. (Eds.): IbPRIA 2003, LNCS 2652, pp. 150–157, 2003.

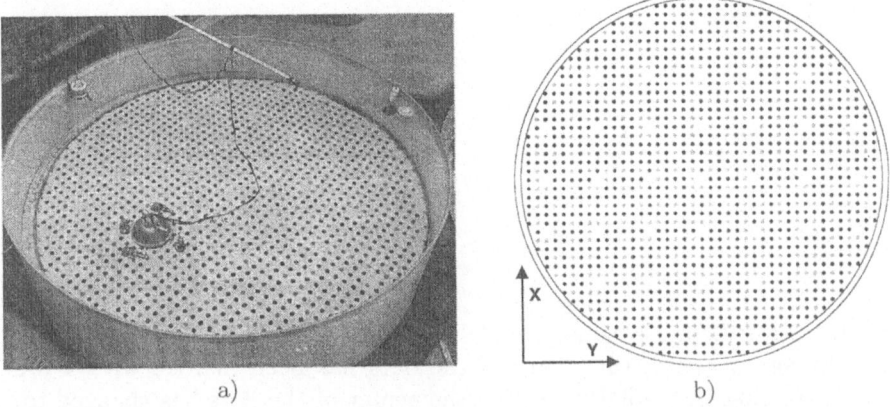

Fig. 1. a) URIS's experimental environment. b) Visually Coded pattern. The absence of a dot identifies a global mark. The dots marked here with a circle are used to find the orientation of the pattern

different research areas, like dynamics modelling or control architectures [1], in which the position or velocity of the vehicle are usually required.

The rest of the paper details the localization system in depth. Section 2 describes the experimental setup, emphasizing the down-looking camera and the visually coded pattern. In section 3, the algorithm phases are described and illustrated. And finally, some results and conclusions are given in section 4.

2   Experimental Setup

The robot for which has been designed the localization system is URIS. Its hull is composed of a stainless steel sphere with a diameter of 350mm. On the outside of the sphere there are two video cameras (forward and down looking) and 4 thrusters (2 in X direction and 2 in Z direction). Experiments with URIS are carried out in a water tank, see Figure 1,a. The shape of the tank is a cylinder with 4.5 meters in diameter and 1.2 meters in height. The localization system is composed by a coded pattern which covers the whole bottom of the tank and a down-looking camera attached on URIS.

2.1   Down-Looking Camera Model

The camera used by the localization system is an analog B/W camera. It provides a large underwater field of view (about 57° in width by 43° in height). The camera model that has been used is the Faugeras-Toscani [2] algorithm in which only a first order radial distortion has been considered. This model is based on the projective geometry and relates a three-dimensional position in the space with a two-dimensional position in the image, see Figure 2a. These are the equations of the model:

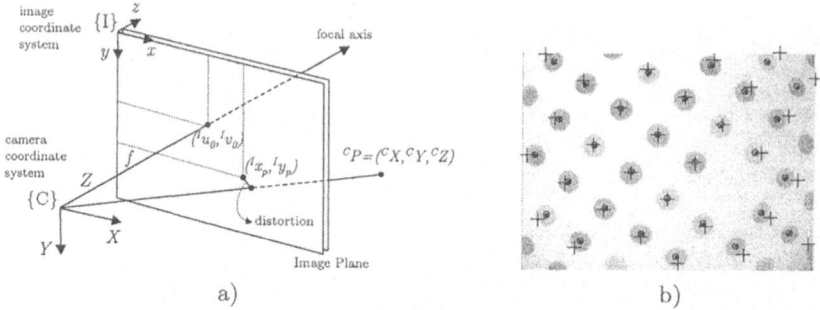

Fig. 2. Down-Looking camera model: a) Camera projective geometry. b) Acquired image in which the center of the dots has been marked with a round. After correcting the radial distortion the center of the dots has changed to the one marked with a cross

$$\frac{^C X}{^C Z} = \frac{(x_p - u_0)(1 + k_1 r^2)}{f k_u} \tag{1}$$

$$\frac{^C Y}{^C Z} = \frac{(y_p - v_0)(1 + k_1 r^2)}{f k_v} \tag{2}$$

$$r = \sqrt{\left(\frac{x_p - u_0}{k_u}\right)^2 + \left(\frac{y_p - v_0}{k_v}\right)^2} \tag{3}$$

where, $(^C X, ^C Y, ^C Z)$ are the coordinates of a point in the space respect the camera coordinate frame $\{C\}$ and (x_p, y_p) are the coordinates, measured in pixels, of this point projected in the image plane. And, as intrinsic parameters of the camera: (u_0, v_0) are the coordinates of the center of the image, (k_u, k_v) are the scaling factors, f is the focal distance, k_1 is the first order term of the radial distortion. Finally, r is the distance, in length units, between the projection of the point and the center of the image.

The calibration of the intrinsic parameters of the camera was done off-line using several representative images. In each of these images, a set of points were detected and its correspondent global position was found. Applying the Levenberg-Marquardt optimization algorithm, which is an iterative non-linear fitting method, the intrinsic parameters were estimated. Using these parameters, the radial distortion can be corrected, as it can be seen in Figure 2b. It can be appreciated that the radial distortion influences in more degree the pixels that are far from the center of the image (u_0, v_0).

2.2   Visually Coded Pattern

The main goal of the pattern is to provide a set of known global positions to estimate, by solving the projective geometry, the position and orientation of the underwater robot. The pattern is based on grey level colors and only round shapes appear on it to simplify the landmark detection, see Figure 1,b. Each

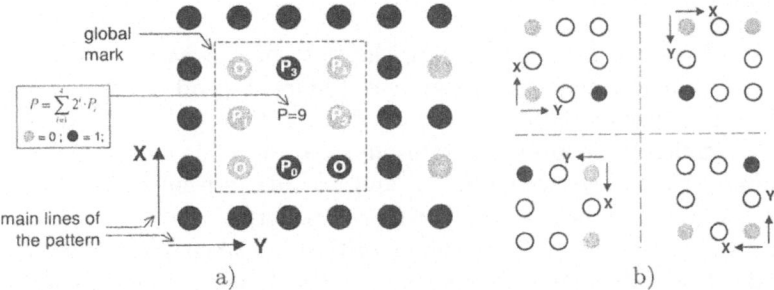

Fig. 3. Features of the pattern, a) the main lines of the target and details about the absolute marks are shown, b) the three orientation dots of a global mark indicate the direction of the X and Y axis

one of these rounds or dots will become a global position used in the position estimation. Only three colors appear on the pattern, white as background, and grey or black in the dots. The dots have been distributed among the pattern following the X and Y directions. All lines that are parallel to X and Y axis are called the *main lines of the pattern*, see Figure 3a.

The pattern contains some global marks, which encode a unique global position. These marks are recognized by the absence of one dot surrounded by 8 dots. From the 8 dots that surround the missing one, 3 are used to find the orientation of the pattern and 5 to encode the global position. The 3 dots which mark the orientation, appear in all the global marks in the same position and with the same colors. In Figure 3 a, these 3 dots are marked with the letter "o". Also, in Figure 3 b it can be seen how depending on the position of these 3 dots, the direction of the X and Y axis changes.

The global position is encoded in the binary color (grey or black) of the 5 remainder dots. Figure 3 a shows the position of these 5 dots and the methodology in which the global position is encoded. The maximum number of positions is 32. These global marks have been uniformly distributed on the pattern. A total number of 37 global marks have been used, repeating 5 codes in opposite positions on the pattern. In order to choose the distance between two neighbor dots several aspects were taken into account, like: the velocities and oscillations of the vehicle, the camera field of view and the range of depths in which the vehicle can navigate. The distance between each two neighbor dots that was finally chosen is 10 cm. The range of distances, between the center of the robot and the pattern, that were used in the design are from 50 cm to 80 cm.

3   Localization Procedure

Each position estimation requires a set of sequential tasks. Next subsections describe the phases that constitute the whole localization procedure.

3.1   Pattern Detection

The first phase consists in detecting the dots of the pattern. Binarization is first applied to the acquired image, see Figure 4a and 4b. Due to the non-uniform sensitivity of the camera in its field of view, a correction of the pixel grey level values is performed before binarization. This correction is based on the illumination-reflectance model [4] and provides a robust binarization of the pattern also under non-uniform lighting conditions.

Once the image is binarized, the algorithm finds the objects and checks the area and shape of them, dismissing the ones that do not match the characteristics of a dot object. Finally, for each detected dot, the algorithm classifies its grey level labelling them in three groups: *grey*, *black* or *unknown*. In case the label is unknown, the dot will be partially used in next phases, as Section 3.3 details. Figure 4c shows the original image with some marks on the detected dots.

3.2   Dots Neighborhood

The next phase in the localization system consists in finding the neighborhood relation among the detected dots. The first step is to compensate the radial distortion that affects the position of the detected dots in the image plane. In Figure 4d, the dots before distortion compensation are marked in black and, after the compensation, in grey. The new position of the dots in the image is based on the ideal projective geometry. This means that lines in the real world appear as lines in the image. Using this property, and also by looking at relative distances and angles, the main lines of the pattern are found. Figure 4d shows the detected main lines of the pattern. To detect the main lines, at least 6 dots must appear in the image.

Next step consists in finding the neighborhood of each dot. The algorithm starts from a central dot, and goes over the others according to the direction of the main lines. To assign the neighborhood of all the dots, a recursive algorithm was developed which also uses distances and angles between dots. After assigning all the dots, a network joining all neighbor dots can be drawn, see Figure 4e.

3.3   Dots Global Position

Two methodologies are used to identify the global position of the detected dots. The first one is used when a global mark is detected, what means that, a missing dot surrounded by 8 dots appears on the network and, any of them has the *unknown* color label, see Figure 4e. In this case, the algorithm checks the three orientation dots to find how the pattern is oriented. From the four possible orientations, only one matches the three colors. After that, the algorithm checks the five dots which encode a memorized global position. Then, starting from the global mark, the system calculates the position of all the detected dots using the dot neighborhood.

The second methodology is used when any global mark appears on the image, or when there are dots of the global mark which have the color label *unknown*.

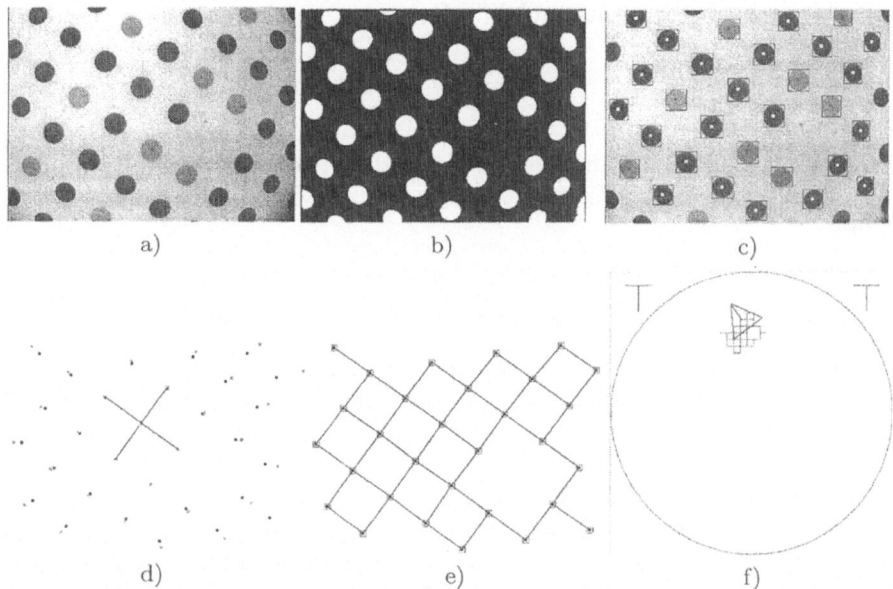

Fig. 4. Phases of the localization system: a) acquired image, b) binarization, c) detection of the dots, d) main lines of the pattern, e) dots neighborhood, f) estimated position and orientation

It consists on *tracking* the dots from one image to the next one. The dots that appear in the same zone in two consecutive images are considered to be the same, and therefore, the global position of the dot is transferred. The high speed of the localization system, compared with the slow dynamics of the underwater vehicle, assures the tracking performance. The algorithm distinguishes between grey and black dots, improving the robustness on the tracking.

3.4 Position and Orientation Estimation

Having the global positions of all the detected dots, the localization of the robot can be carried out. Equation 4 contains the homogeneous matrix which relates the position of one point (X_i, Y_i, Z_i) respect the camera coordinate system $\{C\}$, with the position of the same point respect to the water tank coordinate system $\{T\}$. The parameters of this matrix are the position $(^T X_C, {}^T Y_C, {}^T Z_C)$ and orientation $(r_{11}, ..., r_{33})$ of the camera respect $\{T\}$. The nine parameters of the orientation depend only on the values of *roll*, *pitch* and *yaw* angles.

$$
\begin{pmatrix} {}^T X_i \\ {}^T Y_i \\ {}^T Z_i \\ 1 \end{pmatrix} = \begin{pmatrix} r_{11} & r_{12} & r_{13} & {}^T X_C \\ r_{21} & r_{22} & r_{23} & {}^T Y_C \\ r_{31} & r_{32} & r_{33} & {}^T Z_C \\ 0 & 0 & 0 & 1 \end{pmatrix} \begin{pmatrix} {}^C X_i \\ {}^C Y_i \\ {}^C Z_i \\ 1 \end{pmatrix} \tag{4}
$$

For each dot i, the position $(^T X_i, ^T Y_i, ^T Z_i)$ is known, as well as the ratios:

$$\frac{^C X_i}{^C Z_i} \text{ and } \frac{^C Y_i}{^C Z_i} \tag{5}$$

which are extracted from Equations 1 and 2. These ratios can be applied to Equation 4 eliminating $^C X_i$ and $^C Y_i$. Also, $^C Z_i$ can be eliminated by using next equation:

$$(^T X_i - ^T X_j)^2 + (^T Y_i - ^T Y_j)^2 + (^T Z_i - ^T Z_j)^2 = \\ (^C X_i - ^C X_j)^2 + (^C Y_i - ^C Y_j)^2 + (^C Z_i - ^C Z_j)^2 \tag{6}$$

in which the distance between two dots, i and j, calculated respect $\{T\}$ is equal to the distance respect $\{C\}$. Using Equation 6 together with 4 and 5 for dots i and j, an equation with only the camera position and orientation is obtained. And repeating this operation for each couple of dots, a set of equations is obtained from which an estimation of the position and orientation can be performed. In particular, a two-phase algorithm has been applied. In the first phase, $^T Z_C$, *roll* and *pitch* are estimated using the non-linear fitting method proposed by Levenberg-Marquardt. In the second phase, $^T X_C$, $^T Y_C$ and *yaw* are estimated using a linear least square technique. Finally, the position and orientation calculated for the camera are recalculated for the vehicle. Figure 4f shows the vehicle position in the water tank marked with a triangle. Also the detected dots are marked on the pattern.

4   Results and Conclusions

The vision based localization system, that has been presented in this paper, offers a very accurate estimation of the position and orientation of URIS inside the water tank[1]. Main sources of error that affect the system are the imperfections of the pattern, the simplification on the camera model, the intrinsic parameters of the camera, the accuracy in detecting the centers of the dots and, the error of least-square and Levenberg-Marquardt algorithms on its estimations. After studying the nature of the source of errors, it has been assumed that the localization system behaves as an aleatory process in which the mean of the estimates coincides with the real position of the robot. It is important to note that the system estimates the position knowing the global position of the dots seen by the camera. In normal conditions, the tracking of dots and the detection of global marks never fails, what means that there is not drift in the estimates. By normal conditions we mean, when the water and bottom of the pool are clean, and there is indirect light of the Sun.

To find out the standard deviation of the estimates, the robot has been placed in 5 different locations. In each location, the robot was completely static and a set of 2000 samples was taken. Normalizing the mean of each set to zero and

---

[1] Some videos showing the performance of the system can be seen at: http://eia.udg.es/~marcc/research

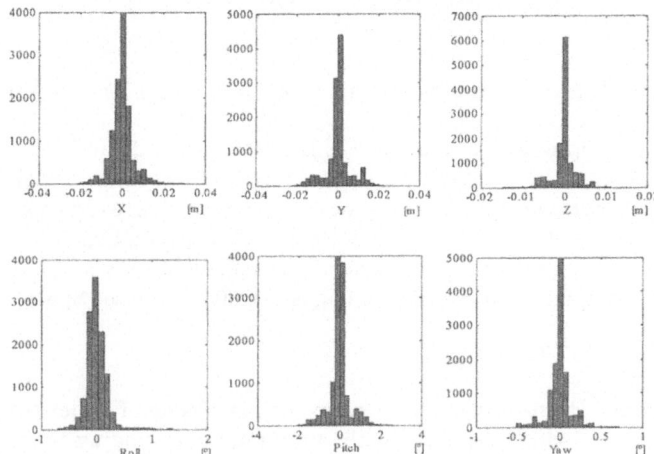

Fig. 5. Histogram of the estimated position and orientation

grouping all the samples, a histogram can be plotted, see Figure 5. From this data set, the standard deviation was calculated obtaining these values: 0.006[m] in X and Y, 0.003[m] in Z, 0.2[°] in *roll*, 0.5[°] in *pitch* and 0.2[°] in *yaw*.

The only drawback of the system is the pattern detection when direct light of the Sun causes shadows to appear in the image. In this case, the algorithm fails in detecting the dots. Any software improvement to have a robust system in front of shadows would increase the computational time, and the frequency of the algorithm would be too slow. However, the algorithm is able to detect these kind of situations, and the vehicle is stopped. The system is fully integrated on the vehicle's controller, giving new measures 12.5 times per second. Due to the high accuracy of the system, other measures like the heading from a compass sensor, or the depth from a pressure sensor, are not needed.

References

[1] M. Carreras, P. Ridao, J. Batlle, and T. Nicosevici. Efficient learning of reactive robot behaviors with a neural-q_learning approach. In *IEEE/RSJ International Conference on Intelligent Robots and Systems*, Lausanne, Switzerland, 2002.

[2] O. D. Faugeras and G. Toscani. The calibration problem for stereo. In *Proc. of the IEEE Computer Vision and Pattern Recognition*, pages 15–20, 1986.

[3] R. Garcia, J. Batlle, X. Cufi, and J. Amat. Positioning an underwater vehicle through image mosaicking. In *IEEE International Conference on Robotics and Automation*, pages 2779–2784, Rep.of Korea, 2001.

[4] R.C. Gonzalez and R.E. Woods. *Digital Image Processing*. Addison-Wesley, Reading, MA, 1992.

Determine the Composition of Honeybee Pollen by Texture Classification

Pilar Carrión[1], Eva Cernadas[1], Juan F. Gálvez[1], and Emilia Díaz-Losada[2]

[1] Dpto de Informática, E.S.E.I., Universidade de Vigo
Campus Universitario As Lagoas s/n, 32004 Ourense (Spain)
{pcarrion,galvez}@uvigo.es, cernadas@ei.uvigo.es
[2] Dpto de Bioloxía Vexetal e Ciencias do Solo
Facultad de Ciencias, Universidade de Vigo
Campus Universitario As Lagoas, 32004 Ourense (Spain)

Abstract. Humans are interested in the knowledge of honeybee pollen composition, which depends on the local flora surrounding the beehive, due to their nutritional value and therapeutical benefits. Currently, pollen composition is manually determined by an expert palynologist counting the proportion of pollen types analyzing the pollen of the hive with an optical microscopy. This procedure is tedious and expensive for its systematic application. We present an automatic methodology to discriminate pollen loads of various genus based on texture classification. The method consists of three steps: after selection non-blurred regions of interest (ROIs) in the original image, a texture feature vector for each ROI is calculated, which is used to discriminate between pollen types. An statistical evaluation of the algorithm is provided and discussed.

Keywords: Image analysis, Texture classification, Blurring, Pollen loads, Honeybee pollen

1 Introduction

Humans use products coming from the hive such as honey, royal jelly or apicultural pollen for different purposes. Despite of their nutritional value as nutritional complement for humans, they are appreciated for their therapeutical characteristics. Hence, they are recommended to treat many human complaints. Nowadays, honeybee pollen is sold in health food shops, supermarkets or food superstores. Their consumption in Spain and other countries is relatively recent, but in the last years it has been become economically very important.

Corbicula pollen is the essential feeding for the hive. The worker bees collect the pollen in the flower, form small balls, stick them to the corbiculas of their back legs and carry them to the hive. The pollen loads collected come from plants placed in the surrounding of the hive. So, the local flora surrounding the beehive influences the palynological composition of pollen loads. The presence of a specific combination of pollen types in a sample indicates its geographical origin. As a result, analyzing the proporcional representation of different pollen types

F.J. Perales et al. (Eds.): IbPRIA 2003, LNCS 2652, pp. 158–167, 2003.

allows the characterization of pollen from different areas. The current method to determine the floral origin is analyzing the pollen by an optical microscopy and then counting the number of pollen of vegetal species [3]. This procedure is tedious and requires expert personal. Industries are interested in the development of methodologies, which can systematically be applied on a chain of production, to classify pollen loads.

Investigations of the composition of pollen loads collected by honeybee have demonstrated [15] that bees forms pollen loads with monospecific pollen grains, i.e. pollen grains of only one plant specie. Each pollen plant has special physical characteristics such as colour, size, shape, texture, etc [4]. In particular, texture has qualitatively been described by some authors using stereoscopic microscope as thick, medium and thin texture [9], [8]. Differences in visual texture of pollen loads are due to the microtexture associated to pollen grain of each vegetable specie, which is related to the structure of its exine and the nature of pollenkit that covers it. So, pollen loads texture must be characteristic of each plant specie.

Our attempts are to design a methodology to characterize honeybee pollen marked in the northwestern of Iberian Peninsula (Galicia). In a preliminary work, [1], we have tested the performance of well-known texture classification features to discriminate *Rubus* and *Cytisus* pollen loads. The sensitivity reached was 78%. Unfortunately, when increasing the number of specie plants, system performance decreases until it is no useful for pollen load classification. Improvements of the methodology are presented. Results to discriminate pollen loads of the five most common specie plants of the northwestern Iberian Peninsula (Galicia) [14] (*Rubus, Cytisus, Castanea, Quercus* and *Raphanus*) are provided and discussed.

The paper have been organized as follows: section 2 presents a briefly description of previous research developed for this application. The proposed method is described in section 3. The results and discussion are included in section 4 and conclusions are provided in the last section.

2   Previous Research

In an initial work [1], we have tested a method to discriminate between *Rubus* and *Cytisus* genus. It is composed of the stages shown in figure 1. Images acquisition of pollen loads is carried out using the infrastructure of Biology Lab (a Nikon SMZ800 magnifying glass connected to a general purpose digital camera Nikon Coolpix E950). Afterwards, images are transferred to the PC by a serial cable. Curbicula pollen are digitized at spatial resolution of 480 point per mm, yielding an image of 1600×1200 pixels. Figure 2 shows images of every genus.

The pre-processing stage transforms the digital data into a suitable form to the next stage. As it can be observed in figure 2, pollen images are blurring in some parts due to corbicula pollen is not flat over the acquisition area. Then, the pre-processing step tries to extract *non-blurring* regions of interest (ROIs) in the *original image*. A texture feature extractor computes image properties on those ROIs that will be used for pollen load classification. First-order and second-order

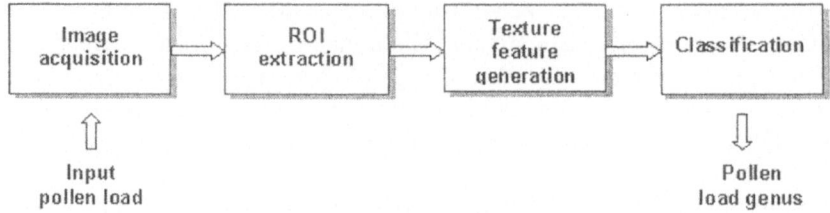

Fig. 1. The basic stages involved in the system operation

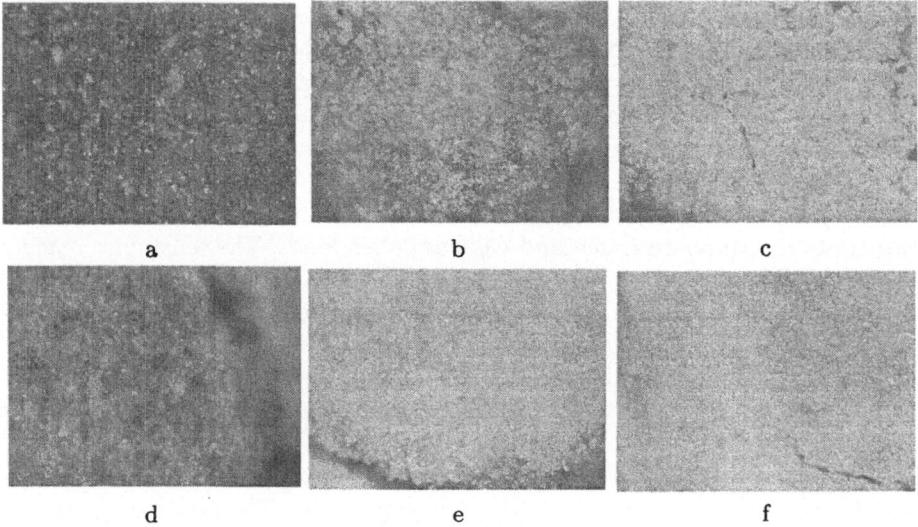

Fig. 2. Digital images of *Cytisus* (a), *Castanea* (b), *Quercus* (c), *Rubus* (d), *Raphanus* (e) pollen loads of the hive of Lobios and *Castanea* (f) pollen load of the hive of Viana

statistical features or wavelet packet signatures was used to discriminate between *Rubus* and *Cytisus* genus [1]. In particular, the following texture feature vectors were tested [1]: Haralick's coefficients (HC) (7 features) [6], [7], Grey Level Run Length Statistics (GLRLS) (5 features) [17], [16], Neighboring Gray Level Dependence Statistics (NGLDS) (5 features) [16], First-order statistics (FOS) (11 measures) [19], and energy and entropy features computed for three levels of decomposed wavelet packets (feature vectors WE and WH respectively with 12 features) [12], [10] using Daubechies wavelet of filter length 20 (D_{20}) [2].

The classifier uses these features to assign the pollen load to a specific plant genus. A minimum distance classifier was used.

3   Methods

As we have mentioned above, pollen images present random burred areas. Added to this fact, image grey level shade (visual appearance of pollen loads) can be influenced by many factors such as humidity, dried treatment, etc [4]. This fact can be observed comparing pollen loads coming from hives of different places (see images *b* and *f* of figure 2 for genus *Castanea*).

Our previous methodology consisted of three steps: ROIs extraction, texture feature generation and classification. The overall performance of the system may be improved redesigning some steps of this scheme and/or adding some one. In particular, we propose to normalize images before processing and we present some approaches to improve non-blurring ROI selection and to compute texture features. These approaches are described in the following subsections.

3.1   Image Normalization

The collection process of honeybee pollen and/or the geographical place of collection have an effect in the final appearance of grey level intensities of the final image. Nevertheless, palynologists believe that spatial structure of image is retained. This fact lead us to define a technique for image normalization that avoids the influence of this external conditions without biasing its spatial properties. The normalization process is inspired by the methods used to remove the effect of varying illumination environments [18]. Let $f(x, y)$ be the original image of size $N \times M$ and let μ and E are respectively the mean and energy of $f(x, y)$ given by

$$\mu = \frac{1}{MN} \sum_{x,y} f(x, y) \qquad E = \frac{1}{MN} \sum_{x,y} \left(f(x, y) \right)^2 \tag{1}$$

The normalized image is computed by

$$f_n(x, y) = \frac{f(x, y) - \mu}{\sqrt{E}} \tag{2}$$

3.2   Non-blurring ROIs Selection

The non-flat surface of pollen loads cause degradations on some parts of images. We are not interested in restoring that images but also in selecting non-degraded regions of interest (ROIs), which will be used for the pollen load texture classification. In spite of the methods proposed to image restoration in the literature [17], there is no measures to find non-degraded areas. These degradations look like smoothed or blurred areas, which present properties like smoother edges, lower entropy or lower spatial frequencies. We define the following three measures to quantify the level of blurring in a ROI, which can be respectively fallen into the categories of statistical, edge-based and filtering approaches:

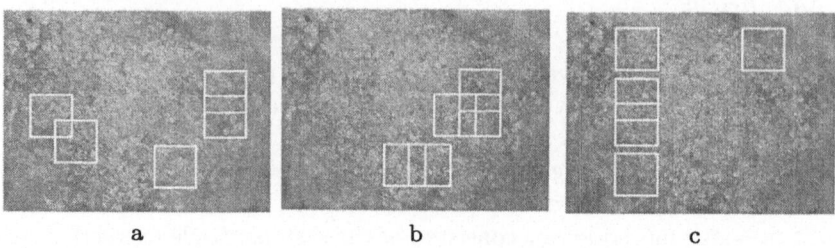

a   b   c

Fig. 3. ROIs extracted from an image of *Castanea* pollen load using the measure (a)Fourth Statistical Moment, (b)Edge Strength and (c)High Frequency

4SM: Fourth Statistical moment, which is a measure of histogram sharpness, has been satisfactory used in a previous work [1].

Edge Strength (ES): we define the edge strength as the mean value of an edge map, which is computed applying an edge operator to the original image (we use Sobel operator). ES will be higher when the image presents many sharp edges, i.e. images are less blurred.

High Frequency (HF): a discrete wavelet transform is based on the pyramidal algorithm which splits the image spectrum into four spatial frequency bands *ll*, *lh*, *hl* and *hh* (*l* means low and *h* means high) [12]. Each filtering is followed by a down-sampling by a factor of two which finally yields the four octave subbands. This procedure is repeatedly applied to each resulting low-frequency band resulting in a multiresolution decomposition. We use Daubechies family bases to define filters [2]. For each resolution i, only the wavelet coefficients hh_i (highs/highs) matrix were retained and these are relocated into a final matrix HH (with the same dimensions as the original image) given by:

$$HH = \sum_{i=1}^{n} \phi(hh_i) \qquad (3)$$

where n is the maximum depth of the pyramidal algorithm (we assume $n = 3$) and $\phi(.)$ is a matrix operation which returns an up-sampled copy of the input matrix hh_i. HF, which is a measure of the strength of high frequencies over every scale, is computed taking the mean value of HH. HF will be higher when the image presents sharp and lots of edges.

The method works as follows: images are sweeping out left to right and top to down and it is taken overlapping regions of $N \times N$ pixels (a shifting of 150 pixels is used and N is fixed to 256 pixels). Next, the mentioned measures are computed on every ROIs of an image and a set of ROIs, which have the highest values of the measures (4SM, ES and HF), are chosen. Figure 3 shows an example of the ROIs selected by each measure, where overlays of the boundary of regions are overlapped to the original image.

3.3   Texture Features Generation

Second-order statistics features exploit the spatial dependencies that character-ize the texture of an image. Alternative possibilities to extract texture-related spatial dependencies is applying Local Linear Transformations (LLT) to an im-age. The first-order statistics of the transformed image encode texture proper-ties. Laws [11], [17] suggests the following three basic convolution vectors: $V_A = [1, 2, 1]$, $V_E = [-1, 0, 1]$ and $V_S = [-1, 2, -1]$ for kernel size, $L = 3$. The first one corresponds to a local averaging operator, the second one to an edge detection operator and the third one to a spot detector. Calculating their cross-products (one each other) yield nine 2-D linear and shift-invariant (LSI) filters.

If we consider V_A, V_E and V_S as elementary vectors, higher dimensional vectors can be easily built from the elementary masks. Convolving these vectors with themselves and each other, one-dimensional vectors of the following order (B_L, $L = 5$) results:

$$B_L^{ij} = V_i * V_j \qquad i, j = A, E, S \tag{4}$$

Convolution of these vectors B_5^{ij} with each elementary vectors (V_A, V_E and V_S) yields the next order vectors (B_L, $L = 7$), and so on. In all cases, mutual multiplication of these vectors (B_L^{ij}) for each order L, considering the first term as a column vector and the second one as a row vector, yields 2-D masks of size $L \times L$.

What statistics and what neighbourhood (L) are suitable for solving our texture discrimination problem is a critical decision. It is basically due to the lack of intuitive understanding that humans have about texture parameters. This implies that many texture features are suggested in the literature and the only way to choose the best one for a specific application will be by experimental testing.

We compute for each image the following first order statistics: variance (μ_2), 3rd (μ_3) and 4th (μ_4) central moments, energy (m_2) and entropy ($Ent.$). Several texture feature vectors, LLT(L), are computed as a function of filtering neighbourhood ($L = 3, 5, 7, \ldots$).

3.4   Classification

Once textural feature are computed, the next issue is how to assign each query case to a pre-established class (in our case, *Rubus, Cytisus, Castanea, Quercus* and *Raphanus* genus). Minimum distance classifier is the simplest one in the literature [5]. Let M be the number of classes, L the number of corbicula pollens and J the number of regions of interest extracted from each corbicula pollen. Lets also $x_{lj}^n = [x_{lj1}, x_{lj2}, ..., x_{ljn}]$ be the feature vector of n elements that identifies uniquely the ROI j of image l. The metric used to measure the similarity between a query case and the mean class prototypes is the Mahalanobis distance to each class i, D_i, defined as:

$$D_i = (x_{lj}^n - m_i)^T \Sigma^{-1} (x_{lj}^n - m_i) \quad i = 1, ..., M \tag{5}$$

where Σ is the covariance matrix in the training set and m_i is the mean class prototype for each class i. Prototype class is calculated taking the mean vector on the training set. We assume the same covariance matrix for all classes. The training set is performed using $L-1$ pollen loads and the test is carried out using the excluded one (leave-one-image-out approach). If this is correctly classified a hit is counted. This is repeated L times, each excluding a different pollen load. The class of excluded one is derived by majority voting among the set of J ROIs extracted from each pollen load image. The percentage of correct classified pollen loads give us the *sensibility* of the system.

Some of texture features may have meaningless classification capabilities or do not improve overall system performance or even decrease it. In a previous work [1], we have tested different approaches to reduce or select the *optimal* features. They fall into three categories: global approaches (principal component analysis), scalar aproaches (maximum individual sensitivity) and vector approaches. Vector feature selectors have reported the best results. These approaches measure the capabilities of feature vectors (or subsets of the set of available features). We use the Floating Search Method (FSM) proposed by Pudil et al. [13]. FSM searches subsets of k elements out of the n available features ($k \leq n$). We assume k as the maximum between n and 20 features. The main drawback of FSM method is that it can drop in cicles. In this case, the algorithm is stopped.

4   Results and Discussion

System performance is tested using a dataset of 200 pollen loads collected in two places (Viana and Lobios). There are 40 pollen loads of each genus studied: *Rubus, Cytisus, Castanea, Quercus* and *Raphanus*. Of these 40 samples, 20 come from Viana and 20 from Lobios. Afterwards, 5 *non-blurring* 256×256 ROIs are extracted using the measures presented in section 3.2 from both the original image and the normalized image (see section 3.1). This procedure yields 6 possibilities (shown as columns in table 1) to extract the ROIs from each orignal image. It is very difficult to separately asses the performance of ROIs extraction process and the only way to quantify it is through the global system performance for pollen genus discrimination. Next, for each ROI, various texture feature vectors are compute. In this study, we test three filtering neigbourhoods ($L = 3, 5, 7$) (see section 3.3). So, there are five features by filtered image times 9, 25 and 36 masks result respectively in LLT(3)=45, LLT(5)=125 and LLT(7)=180 features. Results are also compared with those obtained using the texture features mentioned in section 2. Results are summarized in Table 1.

The main conclusions derived from table 1 are:

– Texture features based on local linear transformations (LLT) achieve normally higher sensitivities of the system than other texture features in all cases. The highest sensibility reached is 73%.

Table 1. Percentage of correct pollen loads classification

Texture features	N	ROIs selection					
		Original image			Normalized image		
		4SM	ES	HF	4SM	ES	HF
FOS	11	57	52	53	46	53	33
HC	7	55	52	40	48	47	45
NGLDS	5	47	47	38	51	46	39
GLRLS	5	48	42	36	52	51	40
SF	28	65	65	59	62	64	53
WE	12	55	63	49	44	56	36
WH	12	55	61	43	47	45	45
LLT(3)	45	65	72	55	57	64	50
LLT(5)	125	65	**73**	60	64	66	51
LLT(7)	180	67	73	57	66	67	54

N: Number of texture features
SF: union of FOS, HC, NGLDS and GLRLS

- Edge strength (ES) measure to extract the ROIs always provides better performance than other ones for every texture features or image pre-processing (original or normalized image).
- We believed that the normalization of images before processing must improve system performance. The experimental test led us to the contrary result. That may be due to this normalization process destroys partially structural properties of image, decreassing their capabilities to texture discrimination.

Confusion matrices help us to exactly determine how is system behavior in relation to both different pollen types and geographical locations of beehives. Table 2 shows the confusion matrix to the best method in table 1 (marked in bold type). Items in this table represent percentage of correct and error pollen loads classification of the observed class (class provided by the classifier) in relation to the expected class (true or actual classes). The percentage of correct pollen load classification provided by the system for every genus and every hive is quite uniform. Partial sensitivities range from 65% to 100% except to the *Cytisus* pollen of the hive of Viana.

5   Conclusion

A novel methodology to determine the genus of pollen loads using digital images taken by a magnifying glass is presented. It consists of four steps: image normalization, non-blurring ROIs extraction, texture feature generation, feature selection and classification. The highest sensibility reached to discriminate the five most common plants in the northwestern of Iberian Peninsula is 73%. It is achieved combining the measure of edge strength to extract ROIs with the texture filtering features. System behavior is quite uniform for every class.

Table 2. Confusion matrix of the combination that provides the highest sensitivity in table 1 (73%). Sucesses are in bold type and errors are in normal type

Predicted class	Actual Class									
	Cytisus		Rubus		Castanea		Quercus		Raphanus	
	L	V	L	V	L	V	L	V	L	V
Cytisus	**65**	**45**	10	15	5	0	0	0	0	0
Rubus	35	45	**80**	**85**	15	0	5	5	0	5
Castanea	0	5	0	0	**60**	**80**	15	0	0	0
Quercus	0	0	10	0	15	10	**70**	**65**	0	20
Raphanus	0	5	0	0	5	10	10	30	**100**	**75**

L and V mean respectively the hive of Lobios and Viana

The approach described is generic and flexible and it could be useful to other texture classification problems.

Acknowledgment

This investigation was supported by the Xunta de Galicia (regional government) project *Study of dairy selection of polineferas plant in apis mellifera and influence of protein content of pollenkit and texture of polen loads.*

References

[1] P. Carrión, E. Cernadas, P. Sá-Otero, and E. Díaz-Losada. Could the Pollen Origin be Determined using Computer Vision?. An Experimental Study. In *IASTED International Conference on Visualization, Imaging, and Image Processing*, pages 74–79, 2002.

[2] I. Daubechies. Ortonormal bases of compactly supported wavelets. *Commun. Pure Appl. Math.*, XLI:909–996, 1988.

[3] E. Diaz Losada, E. Fernández Gómez, C. Alvarez Carro, and M.P. Saa Otero. Aportación al conocimiento del origen floral y composición quimica del polen apicola de Galicia (Spain). *Boletin de la Real Sociedad Española de Historia Natural*, 92(1-4):195–202, 1996.

[4] E. Diaz Losada, A. V. González Porto, and M.P. Saa Otero. tude de la culeur du pollen apicole recueilli pa Apis mellifer L. en nord-ouest d'Espagne. (Galice). *Acta Botanica Gallica*, 145(1):39–48, 1998.

[5] R. O. Duda, P. E. Hart, and D. G. Stork. *Pattern Classification*. Jonh Wiley Sons, 2001.

[6] R. M. Haralick, K. Shanmugam, and I. Dinstein. Textural Features for Image Classification. *IEEE Trans. on Man and Cibernetics*, 3(6):610–621, 1973.

[7] R. M. Haralick and L. Shapiro. *Computer and Robot Vision*. Addison-Wesley, 1993.

[8] M.I. Hidalgo and M. L. Bootello. About some physical characteristics of the pollen loads collected by Apis mellifera L. . *Apicoltura*, 6:179–191, 1990.

[9] D. Hodges.   The pollen loads of the honeybee. In *Bee Research Association*, page 48. 1984.

[10] A. Laine and J. Fan. Texture classification by Wavelet Packet signatures. *IEEE Trans. on Pattern Analysis and Machine Intelligence*, 15(11):1186–1191, 1993.

[11] K. I. Laws. Rapid texture identification: image processing for missile guidance. In *SPIE*, volume 238, pages 376–380, 1980.

[12] S. Mallat. A threary for multiresolution signal descomposition: the wavelet representation. *IEEE Trans. on Pattern Analysis and Machine Intelligence*, 11(7):674–693, 1989.

[13] P. Pudil, J. Novovicova, and J. Kittler. Floating search methods in feature selection. *Pattern Recognition Letters*, 15:1119–1125, 1994.

[14] M. P. Sá-Otero, E. Diaz-Losada, and A. V. González-Porto. Relacin categorizada de especies de la flora gallega (NO de Espaa) que Apis Melifera L. utiliza como fuente de polen . *Boletin de la Real Sociedad Española de Historia Natural*, 96(3-4):81–89, 2001.

[15] P. Sá-Otero, P. Canal-Camba, and E. Diaz-Losada. Initial data on the specific heterogeneity foundin the bee pollen loads produced in the "Baixa-Limia-Serra do Xurés" Nature Park, 2002.

[16] L. H. Siew, R. M. Hodgson, and E. J. Wood. Texture Measures for Carpet Wear Assessment. *IEEE Trans. on Pattern Analysis and Machine Intelligence*, 10(1):92–104, 1988.

[17] M. Sonka, V. Hlavac, and R. Boyle. *Image Processing, Analysis, and Machine Vision*. International Thomsom Publishing (ITP), 1999.

[18] Bea Thai and Glenn Healey. Optimal spatial filter selection for illumination-invariant color texture discrimitation. *IEEE Transations on System, Man and Cybernetics*, 30(4):610–616, 2000.

[19] S. Theodoridis and K. Koutroumbas. *Pattern recognition*. Academic Press, 1999.

Automatic Word Codification for the RECONTRA Connectionist Translator *

Gustavo A. Casañ and M. Asunción Castaño

Dept. Ingeniería y Ciencia de los Computadores
Universidad Jaume I. Castellón, Spain.
{ncasan,castano}@icc.uji.es

Abstract. Previous work has shown that a simple recurrent neural model called RECONTRA is able to successfully approach simple text-to-text Machine Translation tasks in limited semantic domains. In order to deal with tasks of medium or large vocabularies, distributed representations of the lexicons are required in this translator. This paper shows a method for automatically extracting these distributed representations from perceptrons with output context.

1 Introduction

A simple neural translator called RECONTRA (REcurrent CONnectionist TRAnslator) has recently shown to successfully approach simple text-to-text limited-domain Machine Translation (MT) tasks [3]. In this approach the vocabularies involved in the translations can be represented according to (simple and clear) local codifications. However, in order to deal with large vocabularies, local representations would lead to networks with an excessive number of connections to be trained in a reasonable time. Consequently, distributed representations of both source and target vocabularies are required, as this type of codification can help to reduce the size of the networks. In previous experiments with RECONTRA [2][3], the distributed codifications adopted were hand-made and were not compact representations.

This paper focuses on how to automatically create adequate and compact distributed codifications for the vocabularies in the RECONTRA translator. The method presented in the paper approaches the problem through a multilayer perceptron (MP) in which output delays are included in order to take into account the context of the words to be coded.

The rest of the paper is organized as follows: Section 2 describes the connectionist architectures employed to infer the lexicons representations and to translate the languages, as well as the procedures used to train them, and the method used to extract the translations. Section 3 presents the tasks to be approached in the experimentation and Section 4 reports the translation performances obtained. Finally, Section 5 discusses the conclusions of the experimental process.

---

* Partially supported by the Spanish Fundación Bancaja, project P1·1B2002-1.

F.J. Perales et al. (Eds.): IbPRIA 2003, LNCS 2652, pp. 168-175, 2003.

2 The RECONTRA Translator and the Codification Generator

2.1 Network Architectures

The neural topology of the RECONTRA translator is a simple Elman network [8] in which time delays are included in the input layer, in order to reinforce the information about past and future events. Figure 1 illustrates this connectionist architecture.

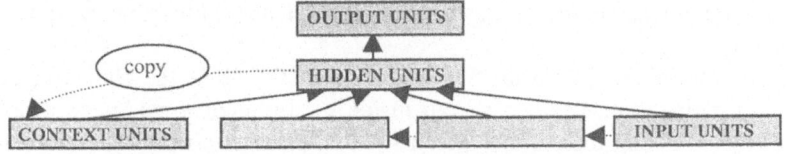

Fig. 1. Elman simple recurrent network with delayed inputs

In order to automatically obtain the lexicons representations for the RECONTRA translator, several neural techniques can be employed. It could be convenient to obtain representations with similar codifications for words which have similar syntactic and/or semantic contexts. Taking this into account there are several possible methods using artificial neural networks, as Elman networks [4] [7], RAAM (Recursive AutoAssociative Memory) machines [10] [6] or FGREP (Forming Global Representations with Extended backPropagation) [9].

The method adopted in this paper to encode the vocabularies uses a MP to produce the same output as the input (a word of the vocabulary to be encoded). The MP has as many input and output units as the number of words in the vocabulary, since we use a local codification of the vocabulary. When the MP is trained enough, the activations of the hidden units have developed its own representations of the input/output words and can be considered the codifications of the words in the vocabulary. Consequently, the size of the (unique) hidden layer of the MP determines the size of the distributed codifications obtained.

In order to take into account the context in which a word appears, the corresponding previous and following words in a sentence are also shown at the output of the MP. In addition, the importance of the input word over its context can be made equal, decreased or increased. When the emphasis is placed on the context of the input word, each output window includes one instance of the input word as well as one instance of the previous and following words in its context. According to this, the format of an output window of size 5 for an input word x is $x\text{-}2\ x\text{-}1\ x\ x\text{+}1\ x\text{+}2$, where $x\text{-}2$, $x\text{-}1$ are the two previous words in its context and $x\text{+}1$, $x\text{+}2$, the two following words. On the other hand, when the emphasis in the codification process is (equated or) on the input word over its context, such input word is repeated several times at the output window.

2.2 Training Procedure

The MP encoder was trained to produce the same output word (and its context) as the word presented at the input layer. To this end, an on-line version of the Backward-Error propagation (BEP) algorithm [11] was employed.

In the RECONTRA translator, the words of every input sentence were presented sequentially at the input layer of the net, while the model should provide the successive words of the corresponding translated sentence, until the end of such output sentence (identified by a special word) was recognized. The model was trained through an on-line and truncated version of the BEP algorithm mentioned above [11]. With regard to the translated message provided by RECONTRA, the net continuously generated (at each time cycle) output activations, that were interpreted by assuming that the net supplied the output word for which the pre-established codification in the target lexicon was nearest (using the Euclidean distance) to the corresponding output activations.

For the training of both the MP and the RECONTRA, the choice of the learning rate and momentum was carried out inside the bidimensional space which they defined, by analyzing the residual mean squared error of a network trained for 10 random presentations of the complete learning corpus (10 epochs). Training continued for the learning rate and momentum that led to the lowest mean squared error over the learning corpus. The learning process stopped after a certain number of epochs (1000 epochs for the encoder and 500 for the translator). A sigmoid function (0,1) was assumed as the non-linear function. Context activations of RECONTRA were initialized to 0.5 at the beginning of every input-output pair of sentences.

3   The Experimental Machine Translation Tasks

3.1   The MLA-MT Task

The first task chosen for testing the encoder described in the previous section was an extension of a simple pseudo-natural task called *Miniature Language Adquisition Machine Translation* (MLA-MT) task [5]. This task consisted in translating (from Spanish into English and vice versa) descriptions of simple visual scenes as well as removals of objects to or from a scene. Since many of the sentences are worded by using the passive voice, the degree of asynchrony between the Spanish and the corresponding English sentence is substantial. The sizes of the vocabularies involved in the original MLA-MT task were slightly increased for our experimentation, leading to 50 Spanish words and 38 English words. The medium sizes of the Spanish and English sentences were 16 and 15 words, respectively. Figure 2 shows one example of this task.

Spanish: se elimina el círculo grande que está encima del cuadrado y del triángulo claro
English: the large circle which is above the square and the light triangle is removed

---

Fig. 2. A pair of sentences from the MLA-MT task

3.2 The Traveller Task

The second task chosen in this paper was a subset of the Traveller MT task designed in the EuTrans project [1] which had larger vocabularies than the above task. The medium size of the sentences in Spanish is 8.6 and 8 for the English sentences. The task approaches typical situations of a Traveller at the reception of a hotel in a country whose language he/she does not speak. The subtask includes (Spanish to English) sentences in which the Traveller notifies his/her departure, asks for the bill, asks and complains about the bill and asks for his/her luggage to be moved. The subtask has 132 different Spanish words, and 82 English words. Both vocabularies include the categories $DATE and $HOUR which respectively represent generic dates and hours. Some examples of this subtask are shown in Figure 3.

Spanish: ¿Está incluido el recibo del teléfono en la factura?
English: Is the phone bill included in the bill?

Spanish: Me voy a ir el día $DATE a $HOUR de la mañana .
English: I am leaving on $DATE at $HOUR in the morning .

Fig. 3. Pairs of sentences from the Traveller task

4. Experimental Results

First, the MLA-MT task was approached using automatic codifications for the Spanish vocabulary provided by MPs in which the emphasis was placed on the context of the input word; the codifications of the English vocabulary was manually derived from the automatic Spanish ones. The experiment was repeated by using codifications in which the emphasis was equated or put on the input word to be encoded over its context. Later, the Traveller task was tackled adopting for the codifications of the Spanish vocabulary the kind of MPs which led to the best performances in the previous experiments. In a subsequent experiment, both Spanish and English codifications were automatically obtained. All these experiments were done using the Stuttgart Neural Network Simulator [12].

4.1 Training and Test Corpora

The corpora adopted in the translation tasks were sets of text-to-text pairs which consisted of a sentence in the source language and the corresponding sentence in the target language. For the MLA-MT task, a learning sample of 3,000 pairs was adopted to train the RECONTRA translators. The learned models were evaluated later on a different test set of 2,000 sentences. For the Traveller translation task a learning set of 5000 pairs of sentences and a test set of 1000 sentences were adopted.

The corpora used for the training of the MP encoders were sets of text-to-text pairs, each of them consisting of an input word and the same input word together with *its context (the preceding and following words in a sentence)* as output. All pairs were extracted from sentences which appeared in the training corpus employed for the translation task. All the repeated pairs extracted from the translation corpus appeared only once in the training set of the MP. If the context was zero, there were as many training pairs as words in the vocabulary, and as the context size increased, the number of pairs did too. There were no test corpora for the codification process; it was indirectly evaluated later in the translation process.

4.2 Features of the Networks

The MP for encoding the Spanish vocabulary in the ALM-MT task had a single hidden layer of 10 units (lower number of hidden neurons were also tried although they led to worse translation rates). An input word and several output words (1, 3, 4, 5, 6 or 8 words) were presented to the network using local codifications of 50 units for each one. If there was no right or left context of the input word, empty words were used instead.

The number of hidden units used in the above encoders (10 units) determined the size of the input and output layer of the RECONTRA translator to approach the ALM-MT task. In addition, 140 hidden units and an input window of 14 delayed words (with 6 words for the left context and 7 words for the right context) were adopted, since previous results obtained to approach this task with this architecture [2] led to adequate translation rates.

With regard to the features of the networks for tackling the Traveller task, previous experiments [3] showed that 50 and 37 units were adequate to (manually) encode the words of the Spanish and English vocabularies, respectively. In order to go further, in the experiments reported in this paper we tried to automatically encode both vocabularies with 25 units. Consequently, a MP with 132 inputs and 132 outputs (according to a local representation of the vocabulary), 25 hidden units and several (4, 6 or 8) output word delays was adopted for the Spanish vocabulary; a MP with 82 inputs, 82 outputs, 25 hidden neurons and 8 output delays was considered for the English vocabulary.

Due to the size of these encoders, the RECONTRA model used for approaching the Traveller MT task was a network with 25 input units and 25 outputs. In addition, taking previous experiments on this task [3] as a reference, the translator had 140 hidden neurons and a window of 6 delayed inputs (with 2 words for the left context and 3 words for the right context).

4.3   Results for the ALM-MT Task with One Instance of the Input Word into the Output of the MP Encoder

The first step in our approach to the ALM task was to obtain adequate codifications for the vocabularies. To this end, MPs with the features described in the previous section and with different output window sizes were trained. Each output window included one instance of the input word as well as one instance of the previous and following words in the context in which it appears. The codifications (of size 10) were then extracted from the learned MPs and used for representing the words in the

RECONTRA translator described above. The translators were later trained using the learning corpus of the translation task. The resulting learned networks were finally evaluated on the test corpora.

Table 1 shows the test sentence accuracy translation rates obtained. The results of two experiments using manual binary codifications are also included. One of them includes knowledge about parts of speech (gender and number) introduced by a human expert, and the other one corresponds to a random codification. The results of the table reveal that very poor translation performance rates were achieved with the codifications provided by the encoders.

Table 1. Test translation rates for the ALM-MT task using codifications provided by a MP with one instance of the input word into the output and using two manual codifications

MP Encoder		Accuracy Rates	
|Output window|	Output window format	Word	Sentence
1	x	50.40	0.30
3	x-1 x x+1	86.90	20.70
5	x-2 x-1 x x+1 x+2	83.26	10.60
Hand-made codifications		96.39	78.40
Random codifications		80.50	21.60

4.4 Results for the ALM-MT Task with Several Instances of the Input Word into the Output of the MP

The previous experiments were repeated, but this time the importance of the input word over its context was made equal or increased in the codification process.

Table 2 shows the test translation rates obtained. These results show that translation accuracies were considerably increased and were only slightly lower than those obtained using human knowledge.

Table 2. Test translation rates for the ALM-MT task using codifications provided by a MP with several instances of the input word into the output

MP Encoder		Accuracy Rates	
|Output window|	Output window format	Word	Sentence
4	x-1 x x x+1	93.66	61.80
6	x-1 x x x x x+1	95.21	72.70
8	x-2 x-1 x x x x x+1 x+2	96.06	74.40
8	x-1 x x x x x x x+1	94.46	70.30

4.5 Results for the Traveller Task

Taking into account the results achieved in the two previous sections, the Traveller task was approached using MPs in which several instances of the input word were presented at the output. Different MPs (described in Section 4.2) were trained and codifications (of size 25) were extracted for the Spanish and English vocabulary. In a first experiment, only the codifications obtained for the Spanish words were used. The codifications for the English vocabulary were manually derived from them (as in the experiments presented in the two previous sections). The RECONTRA translators with the features proposed in Section 4.2 for this task were trained and evaluated later. Table 3 shows the test accuracy translation rates obtained as well as the results of an experiment with (binary) manual codifications of the vocabularies.

Table 3. Test translation rates for the Traveller task using manual and automatic codifications for the Spanish vocabulary

MP Encoder		Accuracy Rates	
| Output window|	Output window format	Word	Sentence
4	x-1 **x x** x+1	99.48	97.30
6	x-1 **x x x x** x+1	99.30	97.70
8	x-2 x-1 **x x x x** x+1 x+2	99.39	96.30
8	x-1 **x x x x x x** x+1	99.49	97.10
Hand-made codifications		99.72	98.40

In a second experiment, both the Spanish and the English codifications which were automatically obtained from the MPs were used to train RECONTRA translators. These translators had the same features as those adopted in the previous experiment. Table 4 shows the test translation rates achieved. Very good rates (near to those obtained using manual codifications) were achieved; indeed using MPs to encode the English and Spanish lexicons the results seemed to be slightly better than those obtained using only automatic codifications for Spanish.

Table 4. Test translation rates for the Traveller task using automatic codifications for the Spanish and English vocabularies

MP Encoder		Accuracy Rates	
| Output window|	Output window format	Word	Sentence
4	x-1 **x x** x+1	99.64	98.00
6	x-1 **x x x x** x+1	99.59	97.70
8	x-2 x-1 **x x x x** x+1 x+2	99.54	97.60
8	x-1 **x x x x x x** x+1	99.51	96.70

5   Conclusions and Future Work

This paper proposes a method for automatically creating distributed codifications of the lexicons involved in a text-to-text MT task to be approached by the RECON-TRA translator. The method extracts such codifications of the hidden layer of a MP with output delays and the translation accuracies achieved are quite encouraging.

The results in this paper open an important area to be studied in the future: how to determine the size of the resulting codifications; algorithms for prunning the hidden neurons in the MP could be adopted for this subject. Further studies on the format of the output context of the MP encoder should be carried out. Finally, more complex text-to-text MT tasks with larger vocabularies will be approached.

References

1. J.C. Amengual et al. *The Eutrans Spoken Language System.* Machine Translation, vol. 15, pp. 75—102, 2000.
2. G. A. Casañ, M. A. Castaño. *Distributed Representation of Vocabularies in the RECONTRA Neural Translator.* Procs. of the 6th European Conference on Speech Communication and Technology, vol. 6, pp. 2423—2426. Budapest, 1999.
3 M. A. Castaño, F. Casacuberta. *Text-to-Text Machine Translation Using the RECONTRA Connectionist Model.* In "Lecture Notes in Computer Science: Applications of Bio-Inspired Artificial Neural Networks", vol. 1607, pp. 683—692, José Mira, Juan Vincente Sánchez-Andrés (Eds.), Springer-Verlag, 1999
4. M. A. Castaño. *Redes Neuronales Recurrentes para Inferencia Gramatical y Traducción Automática.* Ph.D. dissertation. Universidad Politécnica de Valencia, 1998.
5. A. Castellanos, I. Galiano, E. Vidal. *Applications of OSTIA to Machine Translation Tasks.* In "Lecture Notes in Computer Science—Lecture Notes in Artificial Intelligence: Grammatical Inference and Applications", vol. 862, pp. 93—105, R.C. Carrasco and J. Oncina (Eds.), Springer-Verlag, 1994.
6. D. J. Chalmers. *Syntactic Transformations on Distributed Representations.* Connection Science, vol. 2, pp.53—62, 1990.
7. J. L. Elman. *Distributed Representations, Simple Recurrent Networks, and Grammatical structure.* Machine Learning, vol. 7, pp. 195—225, 1991.
8. J. L. Elman. *Finding Structure in Time.* Cognitive Science, vol. 2, no. 4, pp. 279—311, 1990.
9. R. P. Miikkulainen, M. G. Dyer. *Natural Language Processing with Modular Neural Networks and Distributed Lexicon.* Cognitive Science, vol. 15, pp. 393—399, 1991.
10. J. B.Pollack. *Recursive Distributed Representations.* Artificial Intelligence, vol. 46, pp. 77—105, 1990.
11. D.E. Rumelhart, G. Hinton, R. Williams. *Learning Sequential Structure in Simple Recurrent Networks.* In "Parallel distributed processing: Experiments in the microstructure of cognition", vol. 1. Eds. D.E. Rumelhart, J.L. McClelland and the PDP Research Group, MIT Press, 1986.
12. A. Zell et al. *SNNS: Stuttgart Neural Network Simulator. User manual, Version 4.1.* Technical Report no. 6195, Institute for Parallel and Distributed High Performance Systems, University of Stuttgart, 1995.

The ENCARA System for Face Detection and Normalization

M. Castrillón, O. Déniz, M. Hernández

IUSIANI
Edificio Central del Parque Científico-Tecnológico
Campus Universitario de Tafira
Universidad de Las Palmas de Gran Canaria
35017 Las Palmas - Spain

Abstract

Facial image processing is becoming widespread in human-computer applications, despite its complexity. High-level processes such as face recognition or gender determination rely on low-level routines that must effectively detect and normalize the faces that appear in the input image. In this paper, a face detection and normalization system is described. The approach taken is based on a cascade of fast, weak clasifiers that together try to determine whether a frontal face is present in the image. The system is also able to obtain the position of facial features, such as mouth and eyes, and it operates in real-time. Comprehensive experiments carried out with real video sequences show that the system is faster than other approaches and effective in detecting frontal faces.

Keywords: computer vision, face detection, facial analysis, face recognition.

1 Introduction

Faces are the center of human-human communication, and have been object of analysis for centuries. It is evident, that the face conveys to humans such a wealth of social signals, and humans are expert at reading them. They tell us who is the person in front of us or help us to guess features that are interesting for social interaction such as gender, age, expression and more. That ability allows us to react differently with a person based on the information extracted visually from his/her face. For these and other reasons, computer-based facial analysis is becoming widespread, covering applications such as identity recognition, gender determination, facial expression detection, etc.

This work focus on real time face detection. Face detection must be a necessary preprocessing step in any automatic face recognition [1] or face expression analysis system [2]. However, the face detection problem commonly has not been considered in depth, being treated as a previous step in a more categorical system. Thus, many face recognition systems in the literature assume that a face has already been detected before performing the matching with the learned models

F.J. Perales et al. (Eds.): IbPRIA 2003, LNCS 2652, pp. 176-183, 2003.

[1]. This is evidenced by the fact that face detection surveys are very recent in the Computer Vision community [4,10].

The standard face detection problem given an arbitrary image can be defined as: *to determine any face -if any- in the image returning the location and extent of each* [4,10]. The whole procedure must perform in a robust manner for illumination, scale and orientation changes in the subject. It should be noticed that trying to build a system as robust as possible, i.e., detecting any possible facial pose at any size and under any condition, seems to be an extremely hard and certainly not trivial problem. As an example, a surveillance system can not expect that people show their faces clearly. Such a system must work continuously and should keep on looking at the person until he or she offers a good opportunity for the system to get a frontal view, or make use of multimodal information with an extended focus. Thus, robustness is a main aspect that must be taken into account by any system.

Face detection methods can be classified according to different criteria, and certainly some methods overlap different categories under any classification [4,10]. In this paper, these techniques are classified into two main families according to the information used to model faces:

- Pattern based (Implicit): These approaches work mainly on still gray images. They work searching a pattern at every position of the input image, applying the same procedure to the whole image.
- Knowledge based (Explicit): These approaches reduce processing costs taking into account face knowledge explicitly, exploiting and combining cues such as color, motion, face and facial features geometry, facial features appearance and temporal coherence for sequences.

The system presented here can be related to both categories, as it makes use of both implicit and explicit knowledge. The paper is organized as follows: in Section 2 the proposed system is described, in Section 3 results of experiments carried out with it are analyzed. Finally, in Section 4 the main conclusions of the work are outlined, as well as directions for future research.

2   The ENCARA system

Some facts have been considered during the development of the ENCARA face detection system. They can be summarized as follows:

1. ENCARA is designed to detect frontal faces in video streams. ENCARA is developed for providing fast performance in human-computer interaction applications where just soft recognition would be necessary.
2. ENCARA makes use only of visual information provided by a single camera. Its performance must be good enough using standard webcams.
3. ENCARA makes use of explicit and implicit knowledge.
4. ENCARA is based on a cascade hypothesis/verification classification schema.

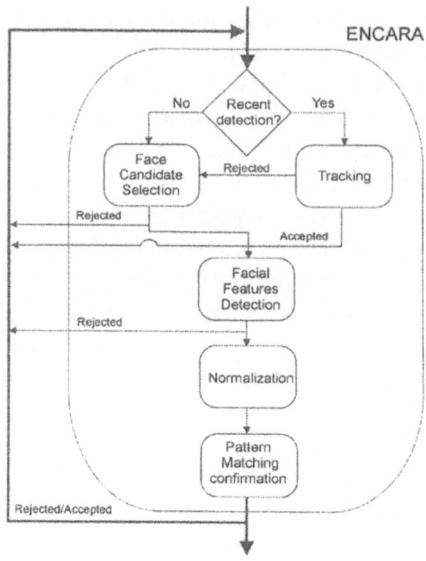

Figure 1. ENCARA general modules

5. Finally, the system is open to integrate new modules or modify the existing ones. This feature allows the system to incorporate improvements.

The process launches an initial face hypothesis on selected areas in the image. These areas present some kind of evidence that make them valid to assume that hypothesis. Later, the problem is tackled making use of multiple simple techniques applied opportunistically in a cascade approach in order to confirm/reject the initial frontal face hypothesis. In the first case, the module results are passed to the following module. In the second, the area is rejected. Those techniques are combined and coordinated with temporal information extracted from a video stream to improve performance. They are based on contextual knowledge about face geometry, appearance and temporal coherence.

ENCARA is described in terms of the main modules described in Figure 1. For each module the literature offers many valid techniques but in this implementation, the attention was paid to process at frame rate. The process is as follows:

1. *Tracking (M0):* ENCARA processes a video stream, if there was a recent frontal face detection, the system tries first to track facial features instead of detecting them again. If any of these tests is passed, the candidate is accepted as frontal. In any other case, the process continues.

   (a) *Last eye and mouth search:* The last detected patterns are searched in new frames.

   (b) *Test with previous:* If the tracked positions are similar to the one in previous frame, ENCARA applies the appearance test.

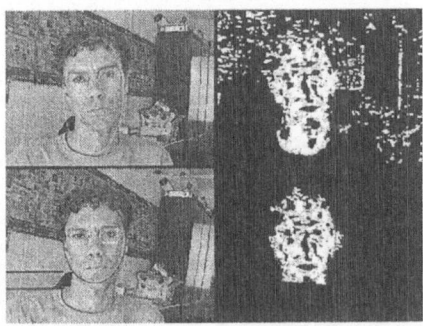

Figure 2. Example of resulting blob after neck elimination.

(c) *Majority test:* If the test with the previous frame is not passed, an extra test is performed to check if most patterns corresponding to facial features have not been lost and are located close to the previous position.

2. *Face Candidate Selection, M1:* The following steps are carried out to select areas of interest:

   (a) *Color Blob Detection:* Once the normalized red and green [9] image has been calculated, a simple schema based on defining a rectangular discrimination area on that color space is employed for skin color classification. Dilation is applied to the resulting blob image using a 3×3 element.

3. *Facial Features Detection, M2:* ENCARA searches facial features:

   (a) *Ellipse Approximation:* Major blobs detected as skin are fitted to a general ellipse using the technique described in [8] that returns the area, orientation and axis lengths of the ellipse in pixel units.

   (b) *Refusing Ellipses:* Before going further, some face candidates are rejected based on the dimensions of the ellipse detected and the axis.

   (c) *Rotation:* For this problem, it has been considered that a face can be rotated from its vertical position no more than 90 degrees, i.e., the hair is always over the chin. The orientation obtained from the ellipse fitted is employed for rotating the source image in order to get a face image where both eyes should lie on a horizontal line.

   (d) *Neck Elimination:* The quality of ellipse fitting mechanism is critical for the procedure. Clothes and hair styles affect the shape of the blob. If all these pixels that are not face such as neck and shoulders are not avoided, the rest of the process will be influenced by a bad estimation of the face area. This blob shape uncertainty will later affect the determination of possible positions for facial features, with higher risks of error.
   For eliminating the neck the system takes into account a range of possible ratios among the long and short axis of a face blob. On this range, the search is refined for the current subject. First, it is considered that most people present a narrower row in skin blob at neck level. Thus, starting from the ellipse center, the blob widest row is searched. Finally, the

narrowest blob row, that should be upper to the widest row, is located. A new ellipse is approximated to the cropped blob, see Figure 2.

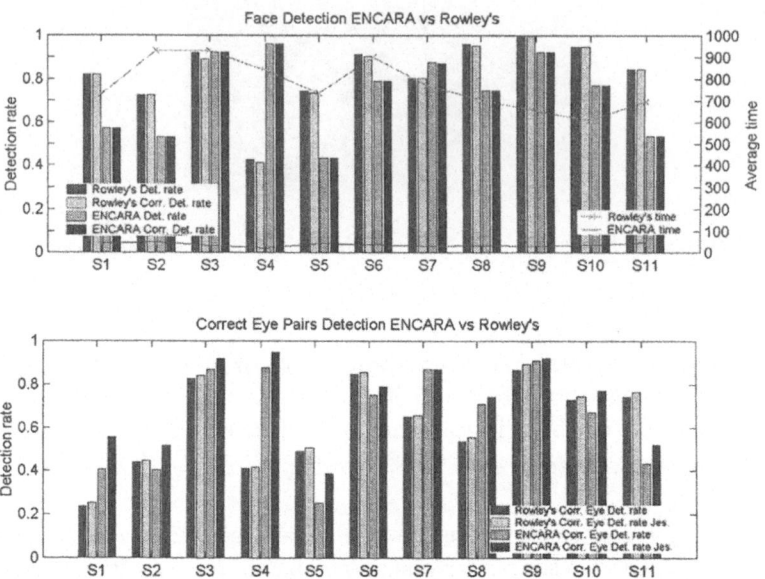

Figure 3. Results summary comparing ENCARA with Rowley's technique.

(e) *Eyes Detection:* At this point, the candidate has been rotated and cropped. As faces present geometric relations for features positions, the system searches each eye as a gray minimum in specific areas that have a coherent position for a frontal face. The search for each eye is bounded also by integrating integral projections. Each hemiface integral projection defines the upper y boundary of the search area, trying to avoid eyebrows. The minimal intereyes distance accepted in current version is 30 pixels.

(f) *Too Close Eyes Test:* If eyes detected using gray minima are too close in relation to ellipse dimensions, the closest one to ellipse center is refused. The search area $x's$ is modified avoiding the subarea where it was detected previously, searching the eye again.

(g) *Geometric tests:* Some tests are applied to gray level detected eyes:

   i. *Horizontal test:* Resulting eye candidates in transformed image should lie almost on a horizontal line if the ellipse orientation was correctly estimated. Using a threshold adapted to ellipse dimensions, candidate eyes that are too far from an horizontal line are refused.

   ii. *Intereye distance test:* Eyes should be at a certain distance coherent with ellipse dimension.

   iii. *Lateral test:* Face position is considered lateral if the distance from eyes to the closest border of the ellipse differs considerably.

4. *Normalization, M3:* A candidate set that verifies all the previous requirements is scaled and translated to fit a standard position and size (59×65).
   Finally, this normalized image is masked using an ellipse defined by means
   of normalized eye positions.
5. *Pattern Matching Confirmation, M4:* The appearance of the normalized image is tested in two steps.
   (a) *Eye appearance test:* A certain area (11×11) around both eyes in the nor-
       malized image is projected to a PCA eigenspace and reconstructed. The
       reconstruction error [3] provides a measure of its eye appearance, and
       could be used to identify uncorrect eye detections. The PCA eigenspace
       was built off-line using eyes marked manually from three different indi-
       viduals.
   (b) *Face appearance test:* A final appearance test applied to the whole nor-
       malized image in order to reduce false positives makes use of a Haar
       based operator [6].

For candidate areas that have reached this point, the system determines that
they are frontal faces. Then some actions are taken:

   (a) *Between eyes location:* The middle position between the eyes is com-
       puted.
   (b) *Mouth detection:* Once eyes have been detected, the mouth, i.e. a dark
       area, is searched down the eyes line according to intereyes distance. The
       located mouth position is accepted only if it fits the prototypical distance
       of the face from the eyes line.
   (c) *Nose detection:* Between eyes and mouth, ENCARA searches for another
       dark area using gray values for detecting nostrils. From nostrils upwards
       the brightest point found is selected as the nose.

3   Experimental results

In order to carry out empirical studies of the system, different video streams
were acquired and recorded using a standard webcam (320×240 pixels) at 15
Hz during 30 seconds. These sequences, labelled S1-S11, were acquired on different days without special illumination restrictions. The sequences, of 7 different
subjects, cover different gender, face sizes and hair styles. Ground data were
manually marked for each frame in all sequences for eyes and mouth center in
any pose. This gives $11 \times 450 = 4950$ images manually marked. All the frames
contain one individual but the pose is not restricted.

ENCARA performance is compared both with humans and a face detector system. On the one hand, the system is compared with manually marked or
ground data providing a measure of facial features detection accuracy in terms of
human precision. Whenever ENCARA detects a face, it provides eye positions.
These returned positions are compared with the manually marked. A correct
face detection is considered when for both eyes the distance to ground data or
manually marked eyes is lower than a threshold that depends on the actual distance between the eyes, *ground_data_inter_eyes_distance*/8. This threshold

is more restrictive than the one presented in [5] where the threshold established is twice the one presented here. Therefore, even if a face is roughly detected but its eyes are not correctly localized, this face detection will be considered incorrect. On the other hand, an excellent and widely used automatic face detector for frontal and profile faces [7] has been applied on these images.

The results achieved with both face detectors are provided in Figure 3. Top graph shows for all the sequences, S1-S11, the detected faces and correct detected faces for both approaches. Bottom graph indicates the rates for correctly detected eye pairs according to two different criteria as described above. For each sequence, the first two bars are referred to Rowley-Kanade's approach, while the last two to ENCARA performance. The polylines plotted present the average processing time in milliseconds using the standard C *clock()* function in a PIII 1Ghz for both approaches.

According to this Figure, ENCARA performs for the worst case, S10, 16.5 times and in the best case, S4, 39.8 faster than Rowley-Kanade's technique. Calculating the average excluding the best and the worst times gives and average of 22 times faster than Rowley's technique. However, the face detection rate is worst for ENCARA except for S3, S4 and S7.

This performance for ENCARA is accompanied by a correct eye pairs location rate according to Jesorsky's criterium greater than 97.5% (except for S5 which is 89.7%). This rate is generally better than the one provided by Rowley's technique, this fact can be explained due to this technique does not provide eye detections for every face detected.

For most sequences Rowley's technique detects more faces, however that difference is reduced if the comparison is carried out with the number of faces detected with both eye positions. Previous Figure reflects a performance for ENCARA that detects an average of 84% of the faces detected using Rowley-Kanade's technique but 22 times faster using standard acquisition and processing hardware. ENCARA provides also the added value of detecting facial features for each detected face.

4   Conclusions and future work

The current system implementation presents promising results in desktop scenarios providing frontal face detection and facial features localization data valid to be used by face processing techniques. The main goal established in the requirements of the system was real time processing. The final experiments present a rate of 20-25 Hz for the image sizes used in the experiments, using a PIII 1Ghz. Its performance is much faster but still not so reliable in comparison with Rowley-Kanade's technique. This rates are reached thanks to the combination of different fast techniques such as skin color detection and tracking. The system has been designed to be updated and improved according to ideas and/or techniques that could be integrated.

The development of a real time robust face detector system is a hard task. There are many different aspects that can be considered to improve ENCARA performance. Future work will necessarily pay attention to increasing color detection performance and adaptability. Current version depends on a first detection based on color which can be affected by illumination conditions and the existence of skin color in the background. In those situations the system avoids false detections thanks to the use of the appearance confirmation step.

Acknowledgments

The first author is supported by Consejería de Educación, Cultura y Deportes of the Comunidad Autónoma de Canarias, and Beleyma and Unelco through Fundación Canaria Universitaria de Las Palmas. The second author is supported by grant D260/54066308-R of Universidad de Las Palmas de Gran Canaria. This work was partially funded by research projects PI2000/042 of Gobierno de Canarias and UNI2002/16 of Universidad de Las Palmas de Gran Canaria.

References

1. R. Chellappa, C. Wilson, and S. Sirohey. Human and machine recognition of faces: A survey. *Proceedings IEEE*, 83(5):705–740, 1995.
2. Gianluca Donato, Marian Stewart Bartlett, Joseph C. Hager, Paul Ekman, and Terrence J. Sejnowski. Classifying facial actions. *IEEE Trans. on Pattern Analysis and Machine Intelligence*, 21(10), October 1999.
3. Erik Hjelmas and Ivar Farup. Experimental comparison of face/non-face classifiers. In *Procs. of the Third International Conference on Audio- and Video-Based Person Authentication. Lecture Notes in Computer Science 2091*, 2001.
4. Erik Hjelmas and Boon Kee Low. Face detection: A survey. *Computer Vision and Image Understanding*, 83(3), 2001.
5. Oliver Jesorsky, Klaus J. Kirchberg, and Robert W. Frischholz. Robust face detection using the hausdorff distance. *Lecture Notes in Computer Science. Procs. of the Third International Conference on Audio- and Video-Based Person Authentication*, 2091:90–95, 2001.
6. Stan Z. Li, Long Zhu, ZhenQiu Zhang, Andrew Blake, HongJiag Zhang, and Harry Shum. Statistical learning of multi-view face detection. In *European Conference Computer Vision*, 2002.
7. Henry A. Rowley, Shumeet Baluja, and Takeo Kanade. Neural network-based face detection. *IEEE Trans. on Pattern Analysis and Machine Intelligence*, 20(1):23–38, 1998.
8. Karin Sobottka and Ioannis Pitas. A novel method for automatic face segmentation, face feature extraction and tracking. *Signal Processing: Image Communication*, 12(3), 1998.
9. Christopher Wren, Ali Azarrbayejani, Trevor Darrell, and Alex Pentland. Pfinder: Real-time tracking of the human body. *IEEE Trans. on Pattern Analysis and Machine Intelligence*, 19(7), July 1997.
10. Ming-Hsuan Yang, David Kriegman, and Narendra Ahuja. Detecting faces in images: A survey. *Transactions on Pattern Analysis and Machine Intelligence*, 24(1):34–58, 2002.

Prediction and Discrimination of Pharmacological Activity by Using Artificial Neural Networks

M. J. Castro[1], W. Díaz[2], P. Aibar[3], and J. L. Domínguez[1]

[1] Dep. de Sistemes Informàtics i Computació, Universitat Politècnica de València
Camí de Vera s/n, 46071 València, Spain
mcastro@dsic.upv.es, jldoru@hotmail.com
[2] Dep. d'Informàtica, Universitat de València
Dr. Moliner, 50, 46100 Burjassot (València), Spain
Wladimiro.Diaz@uv.es
[3] Dep. de Llenguatges i Sistemes Informtics, Universitat Jaume I de Castelló
E-12071 Castelló, Spain
aibar@lsi.uji.es

Abstract. The design of new medical drugs is a very complex process in which combinatorial chemistry techniques are used. For this reason, it is very useful to have tools to predict and to discriminate the pharmacological activity of a given molecular compound so that the laboratory experiments can be directed to those molecule groups in which there is a high probability of finding new compounds with the desired properties. This work presents an application of Artificial Neural Networks to the problem of discriminating and predicting pharmacological characteristics of a molecular compound from its topological properties. A large amount of different configurations are tested, yielding very good performances.

1 Introduction

The design of new medical drugs possessing desired chemical properties is a challenging problem in the pharmaceutical industry. The traditional approach for formulating new compounds requires the designer to test a very large number of molecular compounds, to select them in a blind way, and to look for the desired pharmacological property. Therefore, it is very useful to have tools to predict and to discriminate the pharmacological activity of a given molecular compound so that the laboratory experiments can be directed to those molecular groups in which there is a high probability of finding new compounds with the desired properties.

The tools that have been developed for this purpose are based on finding the relationship between a molecule's chemical structure and its properties. Given that the properties of a molecule come from its structure, the way the molecular structure is represented has special relevance. In this work, the molecular structure is described by a reduced set of 62 topological indices. This paper describes

F.J. Perales et al. (Eds.): IbPRIA 2003, LNCS 2652, pp. 184–192, 2003.

a nefiural network based approach for solving the problem of activity prediction and discrimination based on the structural representation of the molecule.

Two discrimination problems and two prediction problems are studied, using multilayer perceptrons to discriminate/predict. A large amount of different configurations are tested, yielding to very good performances.

2   The Molecular Representation

The chosen set of molecular descriptors should adequately capture the phenomena underlying the properties of the compound. It is also important for these descriptors to be obtained without a lot of computational effort since they have to be computed for every molecule whose property needs to be predicted or discriminated.

The molecular topology is an alternative to the methods based on the "exact" description of the electronic attributes of a molecule calculated by mechanical-quantum methods. These molecular descriptors, which are based on graph theory, allow us to describe a molecule as a set of quantized numerical indices and it requires a lower calculation effort than other methods. They consider molecular structure as planar graphs where atoms are represented by vertices and chemical bonds are represented by edges. The topological indices have information about the number and kind of bonds that exist between the atoms as well as other structural attributes (size, branching factor, cycles, etc.) [1, 2, 3]. Searching for the set of indices which best adjust to this problem is a very complex task.

In this work, a set of 62 indices has been selected [4, 5]. Fourteen of these indices are related to the molecular attributes of the compound; for example, the total number of atoms of a certain element (carbon, nitrogen, oxygen, sulphur, fluorine, chlorine, ...), the total number of bonds of a certain type (simple, double or triple), the number of atoms with a specific vertex degree, distance between the bonds, etc...

The remaining forty-eight topological indices include different topological information, such as the number of double bonds at distance 1 or 2, and the minimum distance between pairs of atoms, which are counted as the number of bonds between atoms. These indices are classified into six groups which are associated to the most frequent elements that constitute the molecules with pharmacological activity: nitrogen, oxygen, sulphur, fluorine, chlorine, bromine, and a general group in which the distances between pairs of atoms are considered without identifying the type of atom.

As an example, the set of topological indices of a chemical compound so well-known as the acetylsalicylic acid (*aspirin*) is shown in Figure 1.

3   Activity Discrimination and Prediction Problems

The case studies are of interest in the field of medicine. Two discrimination problems and two prediction problems were studied using the topological descriptors of the molecules explained above.

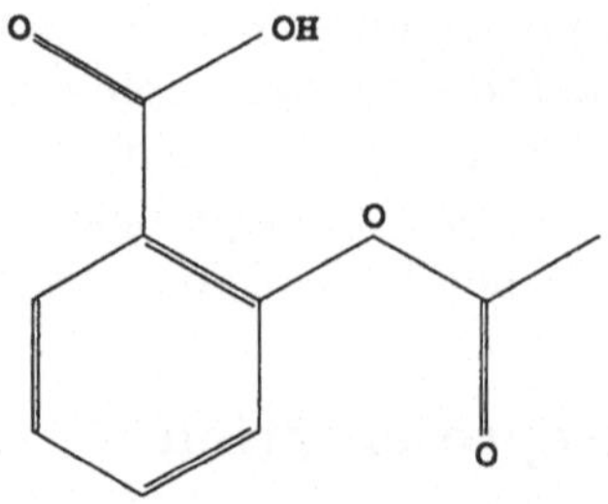

{ 9, 0, 4, 0, 0, 0, 0, 8, 5, 0, 4, 5, 4, 0, 4, 2, 0, 0, 0, 0, 0, 0, 0, 0, 5, 10, 8, 11, 7, 7, 0,

0, 0, 0, 0, 0, 0, 0, 0, 0, 0, 0, 0, 0, 0, 0, 0, 0, 0, 0, 0, 13, 17, 16, 15, 11, 6, 0, 0, 0, 0, 0, 0 }

Fig. 1. *Top.* Molecular structure of the acetylsalicylic acid (*aspirin*). The hydrogen-suppressed graph is shown, in which every unlabeled vertex represents a carbon atom and every double edge represents a double bond. *Bottom.* The set of topological indices: 9 carbon atoms, 4 oxygen atoms, 8 simple bonds, 5 double bonds, 4/5/4 atoms with a vertex degree equal to one, two and three, respectively, 4 double bonds at distance one, 2 double bonds at distance two, 5/10/8/11/7/7 atoms with a distance of one/two/three/four/five/six from the oxygen atoms, 13/17/16/15/11/6 atoms with a distance of one/two/three/four/five/six between them (Null values are skipped.)

3.1 Activity Discrimination Problems

The properties studied were analgesic and antidiabetic discrimination. The objective was to train a classifier and evaluate it.

– *Analgesic discrimination problem.* The purpose of this experiment was to determine whether a molecule has analgesic activity or not. A dataset of 985 samples with potential pharmacological activity was used.
– *Antidiabetic discrimination problem.* In this case, we wanted to determine whether a molecule presents antidiabetic activity. A dataset of 343 samples was used.

3.2 Activity Prediction Problems

The properties considered were antibacterial activity and solubility. The objective of the case studies was to implement a predictor and evaluate its performance.

– *Antibacterial activity prediction problem.* We wanted to predict the minimum inhibitory concentration of antibacterial activity. A dataset of 111 samples was used.
– *Solubility prediction problem.* In this case, we were interested in predicting the solubility capability of the molecules. A dataset of 92 samples was used.

Table 1. Datasets for the experimentation. For the activity discrimination problems, the active and inactive molecule percentages for each dataset are indicated in parenthesis

	Problem	Number of samples		Total
		Active	Inactive	
Activity	Analgesic	172 (17.5%)	813 (82.5%)	985
discrimination	Antidiabetic	180 (52.5%)	163 (47.5%)	343
Activity	Antibacterial			111
prediction	Solubility			92

3.3   Leaving-One-Out

The datasets for the four problems are shown in Table 1. In order to obtain statistically significant results, four different partitions (composed of 25% of the data) of each database were done for the final experiments. The partitions were performed randomly, taking into account that the percentages of active and inactive samples were homogeneous for the datasets of the activity discrimination problems.

The final experiments for each problem entailed four runs, using the *Leaving-One-Out* scheme [6]: training the neural model with the data of three partitions (out of this data, one partition was selected for validation) and testing with the data of the other partition. Therefore, the classification rates of the test sets reported in Section 5 are the average result of the four runs of each experiment.

4   Artificial Neural Networks for Structure-Activity Relationship Modeling

Classification of complex data has been addressed by various statistical and machine learning techniques. Although these methodologies have been successfully applied in a variety of domains, there are some classification tasks, particularly in medicine or chemistry, which require a more powerful, yet flexible and robust technique to cope with extra demands concerning limited datasets and complexity of interpretation. In this context, the use of artificial neural networks becomes an excellent alternative.

We used multilayer perceptrons (MLPs) for structure-activity discrimination and prediction. The number of input units was fixed by the number of topological descriptors of the molecules (62 topological indices). The input data of each dataset was discretized by dividing by the maximum value of all the indices.

There was only one output unit corresponding to the property being discriminated or predicted. The data for the activity discrimination problems were labeled with 1, -1, or 0: a value of 1 indicates that the molecule has pharmacological activity, a value of -1 indicates that the molecule is inactive, and a value of 0 indicates undetermined activity. Therefore, we use the hyperbolic tangent function, defined in the interval $[-1, 1]$, as the activation function.

Table 2. MLP topologies and learning algorithms studied

Topology:	One hidden layer: 2, 4, 8, 16, 32, 64
	Two hidden layers: 2-2, 4-4, 8-8, 16-16, 32-32, 64-64
Training algorithm:	Backpropagation without momentum term
	Learning rate: 0.1 0.2 0.4 0.7 0.9 1.5 2.0
Training algorithm:	Backpropagation with momentum term
	Learning rate: 0.1 0.2 0.4 0.7 0.9
	Momentum term: 0.1 0.2 0.4 0.7 0.9
Training algorithm:	Quickprop
	Learning rate: 0.1 0.2 0.3
	Quick rate: 1.75 2 2.25

The concentration and solubility levels for the activity prediction problems were discretized between 0 and 1, so we used the sigmoidal activation function.

The training of the MLPs was carried out using the neural net software package "SNNS: Stuttgart Neural Network Simulator" [7]. In order to successfully use neural networks, a number of considerations has to be taken into account, such as the network topology, the training algorithm, and the selection of the algorithm's parameters [8, 7, 9]. Experiments were conducted using different network topologies: a hidden layer with 2, 4, 8, 16, 32 and 64 units or two hidden layers with an equal number of hidden units (2, 4, 8, 16, 32 or 64). Several learning algorithms were also studied: the incremental version of the backpropagation algorithm (with and without momentum term) and the quickprop algorithm. Different combinations of learning rate (LR) and momentum term (MT) as well as different values of the maximum growth parameter (MG) for the quickprop algorithm were proved (see Table 2). In every case, a validation criterion was used to stop the learning process.

In order to select the best configuration of MLP for each problem, we performed all the above proofs using three partitions of the data: two partitions for training and one partition for validation. When we got the best configuration of topology, training algorithm and parameters (according to the validation data), we made the four-runs experiment: training an MLP of that configuration with the data of three partitions (two for training, one for validation) and testing with the data of the other partition.

In the experimentation with potential analgesic activity, the best performance on the validation data was achieved using an MLP of one hidden layer of 16 units, trained with the standard backpropagation algorithm with a learning rate equal to 0.1. For the antidiabetic activity discrimination problem, we reached the best performance on the validation data with an MLP of two hidden layers of 4 units each, trained with the backpropagation algorithm (LR=0.2 and MT=0.1).

The best performances on the validation data for the activity prediction problems were achieved, in both cases, by training with the standard backpropagation algorithm, using a learning rate equal to 0.1. For the antibacterial prediction,

Table 3. Best configurations for every problem

Problem		Best configuration MLP topology, algorithm and parameters	
Activity	Analgesic	{62−16−1}	Backpropagation (LR=0.1)
discrimination	Antidiabetic	{62−4−4−1}	Backpropagation (LR=0.2, MT=0.1)
Prediction	Antibacterial	{62−64−1}	Backpropagation (LR=0.1)
problem	Solubility	{62−32−1}	Backpropagation (LR=0.1)

the best topology was one hidden layer of 64 units; for the solubility prediction problem, the best performance on the validation data was achieved with an MLP of one hidden layer of 32 units.

For all the experiments, the best configurations of topology, training algorithm and parameters for the validation data are shown in Table 3.

5   Experimental Results

5.1   Activity Discrimination Problems Experiments

For the activity discrimination problems, the output values of the MLPs are between −1 and 1 (due to the hyperbolic tangent activation function). In the learning stage, −1 is assigned to the molecule that does not have pharmacological activity (analgesic or antidiabetic) and 1 to the molecule that do have it. After training the MLP models for the activity discrimination problems, the classification criterion was the following: if the molecule is *inactive* and the output achieved with the MLP is in the interval $[-1, -0.5]$, it is counted as correct; if the output is in the interval $]-0.5, 0[$ the result is counted as undetermined; finally, if the output is in the interval $[0, 1]$, it is an error. When testing an *active* molecule the classification criterion was similar: it is considered to be correctly classified when the output value of the MLP is between 1 and 0.5; if the output is in the interval $]0.5, 0[$, it is counted as undetermined; if the output is between 0 and −1, it is considered an error.

In the experimentation with potential analgesic activity, we trained four MLPs with the configuration shown in Table 3. We then tested these trained MLPs with the test data, obtaining the success percentages for the four runs shown in Table 4. In average, we achieved an overall classification rate equal to 82.44%, with no sample classified as undetermined. If we analyze these results (in average) considering the group (active or inactive), we get a success percentage of 54.65% in the active group and a success percentage of 88.31% in the inactive group.

For the antidiabetic activity discrimination problem, the obtained classification rates for each run of the experiment are also given in Table 4. In average, the percentage of classification was equal to 92.14% on the test data. If we analyze

Table 4. MLP performance (classification rate in %) for the discrimination problems

Discrimination problem	Run_1	Run_2	Run_3	Run_4	Average Active	Inactive	Total
Analgesic	86.18	76.83	83.33	83.40	54.65	88.31	**82.44**
Antidiabetic	94.19	88.37	91.86	94.12	91.67	92.61	**92.14**

the results considering the active and inactive groups we get a success percentage of 91.67% and 92.61%, respectively.

5.2 Activity Prediction Problems Experiments

Structure-activity prediction was achieved with high accuracy. For the antibacterial prediction problem, of all the networks tested, the most suitable one (on the validation data) turned out to be an MLP of one hidden layer of 64 units, trained with the standard backpropagation algorithm, using a learning rate equal to 0.1. This network was capable of predicting the minimum inhibitory concentration of antibacterial activity with a root-mean-square error (RMSE) lower (in average) than 1.66 on unseen data, the test dataset.[1]

The best performance on the validation data for the solubility prediction problem was achieved using an MLP of one hidden layer of 32 units, trained also with the standard backpropagation algorithm with a learning rate equal to 0.1. This MLP could predict the solubility capacity of a molecule with a RMSE of 0.18 on test data.

The results for each run of the experiment and the average error are shown in Table 5.

6   Conclusions and Future Work

In this work, the viability of the use of artificial neural networks for structure-activity discrimination and prediction have been shown based on the structural

---

[1] For the prediction problems, the MLPs have been trained using a sum-of-squares error (SSE) function, whereas for network testing it is more convenient to use a root-mean-square error (RMSE) of the form:

$$\text{RMSE} = \frac{\sum_n \|g(x^n; \omega) - t^n\|^2}{\sum_n \|t^n - \bar{t}\|^2}$$

where $g(x^n; \omega)$ denotes the output of the trained MLP given the input pattern x^n, and the sums run over the N patterns in the test set. The target for the n-th pattern is denoted as t^n and $\bar{t}$ is defined to be the average test set target vector. The RMSE has the advantage, unlike the SSE, that its value does not grow with the size of the test set. If it has a value of unity then the network is predicting the test data "in the mean" while a value of zero means perfect prediction of the test data [9].

Table 5. MLP root-mean-square error (RMSE) for the prediction problems

Precdiction problem	RMSE Run_1	Run_2	Run_3	Run_4	RMSE Average
Antibacterial	0.52	0.97	4.47	0.69	**1.66**
Solubility	0.14	0.21	0.20	0.17	**0.18**

representation of the molecules. Two discrimination problems and two prediction problems were studied, using multilayer perceptrons to discriminate and predict different properties of the molecular compounds.

The experiments performed with the analgesic group allow to determine whether a given molecule is active or inactive with a classification percentage of 82.44%. Better results were obtained with the antidiabetic group, with a success classification rate of 92.14%.

On the other hand, structure-activity prediction was achieved with high accuracy: antibacterial activity can be predicted with a root-mean-square error of 1.66; the solubility capacity of a molecule can be predicted with a 0.18 root-mean-square error.

Before ending we would like to remark that this work is only the first step towards an automatic methodology for designing new medical drugs. Thus, the following step will be the inverse problem of constructing a molecular structure given a set of desired properties [10].

Acknowledgements

We are grateful to Dr. Mr. Facundo Pérez and Dra. Ms. María Teresa Salabert, from the Chemistry and Physics Department of the Pharmacy Faculty of the Universitat de València, for their help in supplying the datasets and specially for their supervision in getting the topological indices and the elaboration of the samples used in the experimentation. The authors also wish to thank Cristina Adobes Martín for the software developed to calculate the topological indices.

Financial support for this work was provided by TIC2000-1153 of Spanish government.

References

[1] A. T. Balaban, ed. *Chemical Applications of Graph Theory*. Academic Press, 1976.
[2] N. Trinajstic. *Chemical Graph Theory*. CRC Press, 1976.
[3] L. B. Kier, L. H. Hall. *Molecular Connectivity in Structure-Activity Analysis*. John Willey, 1986.
[4] W. Díaz, M. J. Castro, C. Adobes, F. Pérez, M. T. Salabert. Discriminación de la actividad farmacológica utilizando técnicas conexionistas. In *Proc. IX CAEPIA*, p. 233–241, Gijón (Spain), 2001.

[5] J. L. Domínguez, M. J. Castro, W. Díaz.   Discriminación y predicción de propiedades de fármacos mediante redes neuronales. *Inteligencia Artificial. Revista Iberoamericana de Inteligencia Artificial,* 2003.

[6] R. O. Duda, P. E. Hart, D. G. Stork. *Pattern Classification.* John Wiley, 2001.

[7] A. Zell et al. *SNNS: Stuttgart Neural Network Simulator. User Manual, Version 4.2.* Univ. of Stuttgart, Germany, 1998.

[8] D. E. Rumelhart, G. E. Hinton, R. J. Williams. Learning internal representations by error propagation. *PDP: Computational models of cognition and perception, I,* p. 319–362. MIT Press, 1986.

[9] C. M. Bishop. *Neural networks for pattern recognition.* Oxford Univ. Press, 1995.

[10] V. Venkatasubramanian, K. Chan, J. M. Caruthers. Computer-Aided Molecular Design Using Neural Networks and Genetic Algorithms. *Computers and Chemical Engineering,* 18(9):833–844, 1994.

A Spatio-temporal Filtering Approach to Motion Segmentation

Jesús Chamorro-Martínez, J. Fdez-Valdivia, and Javier Martinez-Baena*

Department of Computer Science and Artificial Intelligence
University of Granada, Spain
{jesus,jfv,jbaena}@decsai.ugr.es

Abstract. In this paper, a new frequency-based approach to motion segmentation is presented. The proposed technique represents the sequence as a spatio-temporal volume, where a moving object corresponds to a three-dimensional object. In order to detect the "3D volumes" corresponding to significant motions, a new scheme based on a band-pass filtering with a set of logGabor spatio-temporal filters is used. It is well known that one of the main problems of these approaches is that a filter response varies with the spatial orientation of the underlying signal. To solve this spatial dependency, the proposed model allows to recombine information of motions that has been separated in several filter responses due to its spatial structure. For this purpose, motions are detected as invariance in statistical structure across a range of spatio-temporal frequency bands. This technique is illustrated on real and simulated data sets, including sequences with occlusion and transparencies.

Keywords: Motion segmentation, motion representation, motion pattern, logGabor filters, spatio-temporal models

1 Introduction

The motion segmentation, i.e. the process of dividing the scene into regions representing moving objects, is one of the most important problems in image sequence analisys. It has applications in fields such as optical flow estimartion, video coding or objects tracking.

The most common proposals to this problem relies on frame by frame analysis (for example, techniques based on optical flow estimates). Althought this kind of approaches works fine in many cases, it is well known they have problems in the presence of noise, occlusions or transparencies [1]. To overcome these problems, some authors propose to use extended features to find correspondeces beetween frames. None the less, the success of these models depends on the stability of detection of such features over multiple frames, and the way of solving the correspondence problem [2].

Unlike frame by frame analisys (or analisys over small number of frames), some approaches represents the sequence as a spatio-temporal volume. From this

---

* This work has been supported by the DGES (Spain) under grant PB98-1374

F.J. Perales et al. (Eds.): IbPRIA 2003, LNCS 2652, pp. 193–203, 2003.

point of view, a moving object may be observed as a three-dimensional object, where the axis x and y correspond to the spatial dimensions, and the third axis corresponds to the temporal dimension [3]. In this kind of methods, some important proposals are based on a band-pass filtering operation with a set of spatio-temporal filters [4, 5, 6, 7]. These approaches are derived by considering the motion problem in the Fourier domain, where the spectrum of a spatio-temporal translation lies in a plane whose orientation depends on the direction and velocity of the motion [8, 9]. Although these filters are a powerful tool to separate the motions presented in a sequence, it is nevertheless true that one of the main problems of these schemes is that components of the same motion with different spatial characteristics are separated in different responses. Moreover, a filter response will change if the spatial orientation or scale vary.

In this paper, we develop a methodology to motion segmentation on the basis of a spatio-temporal volumes detection. For this purpose, a new tehcnique based on a spatio-temporal filtering in the frequency domain is proposed. To solve the problems described above, we propose a new approach that groups the separated responses obtained by the filters in order to extract coherent and independent motions. Using a new distribution of 3D logGabor filters over the spatio-temporal spectrum, *a motion* is detected as an invariance in statistical structure across a range of spatio-temporal frequency bands. This new scheme recombines responses that, even with different spatial characteristics, have continuity in its motion.

2   The Proposed Method

The figure 1 shows a general diagram describing how the data flows through the proposed model. This diagram illustrates the analysis on a given sequence showing a clap of hands. The endpoint of analyzing this sequence is to separate the two hand motions. In a first stage, a three-dimensional representation is performed from the original sequence and then its Fourier transform is calculated. Given a bank of spatio-temporal logGabor filters, a subset of them is selected in order to extract significant spectral information. These selected filters are applied over the original spatio-temporal image in order to obtain a set of active responses.

In the second stage, for each pair of active filters, their responses are compared based on the distance between their statistical structure, computed over those points which form relevant points of the filters. As a result, a set of distances between active filters is obtained.

In a third stage, a clustering on the basis of the distance between the active filter responses is performed to highlight invariance of responses. Each of the cluster obtained in this stage defines a motion. In figure 1, two collections of filters have been obtained for the input sequence.

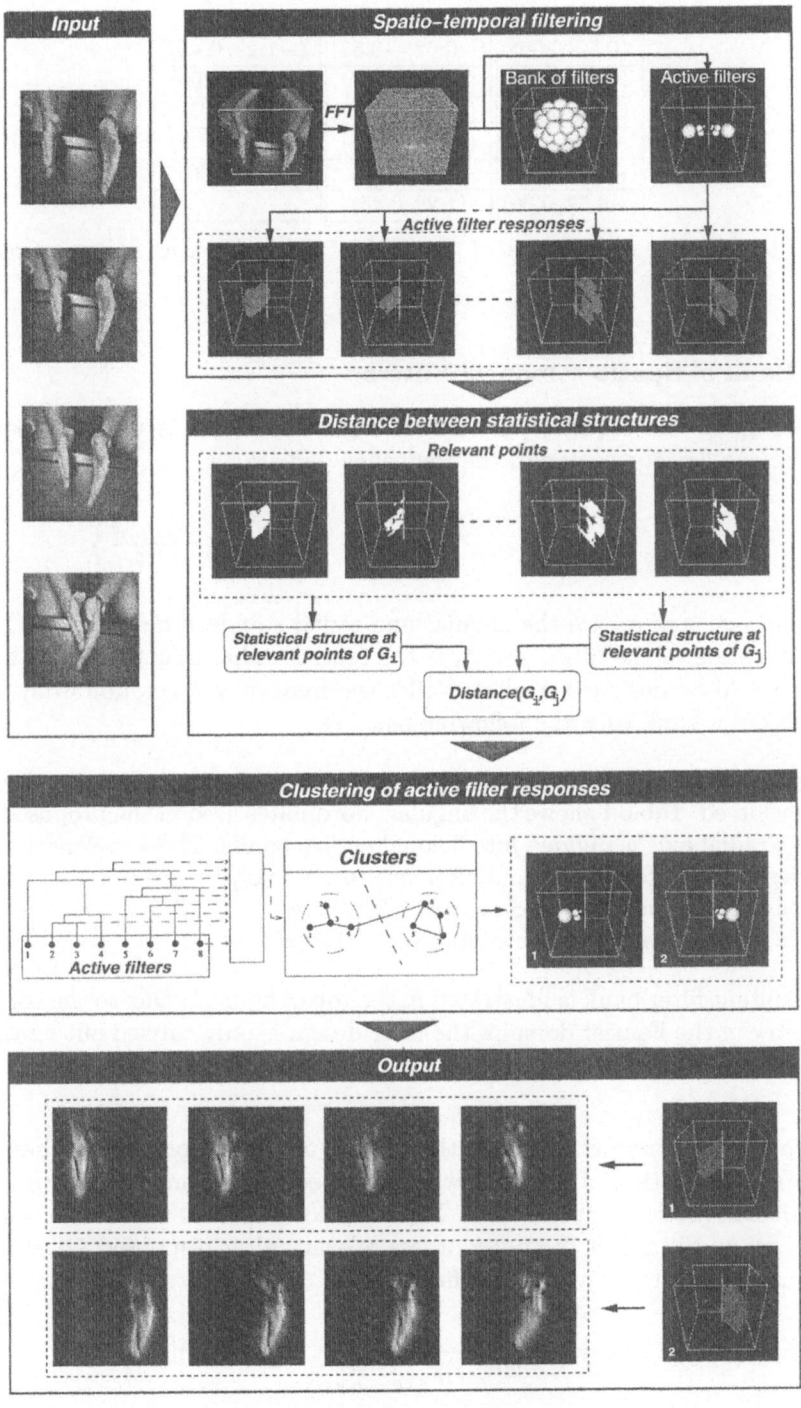

Fig. 1. A general diagram of the proposed model

(θ, φ)		
$(0.52, 0.00)$	$(-0.62, -0.53)$	$(-1.29, 0.45)$
$(0.62, 0.53)$	$(-1.08, 0.97)$	$(-1.05, 0.00)$
$(1.08, 0.97)$	$(1.08, -0.97)$	$(-1.29, -0.45)$
$(-1.08, 0.97)$	$(0.62, -0.53)$	$(1.29, -0.45)$
$(-0.62, 0.53)$	$(1.05, 0.00)$	$(1.57, 0.00)$
$(-0.52, 0.00)$	$(1.29, 0.45)$	

Table 1. Angular coordinates of the bank of filters (over an sphere of ratio 1)

2.1   Bank of Spatio-temporal Filters

To decompose the sequence, a bank of logGabor filters is used. A logGabor function can be represented in the frequency domain as:

$$\phi(\rho, \theta, \varphi) = e^{\left\{-\frac{\left(log\left(\frac{\rho}{\rho_o}\right)\right)^2}{2\left(log\left(\frac{\sigma_\rho}{\rho_o}\right)\right)^2}\right\}} e^{\left\{-\frac{(\theta - \theta_o)^2}{2\sigma_\theta^2}\right\}} e^{\left\{-\frac{(\varphi - \varphi_o)^2}{2\sigma_\varphi^2}\right\}} \tag{1}$$

where σ_θ , σ_φ and σ_ρ are the angular and radial standard deviation, (θ_o, φ_o) is the orientation of the filter, and ρ_o is the central radial frequency. The bank of filters should be designed so that it tiles the frequency space uniformly. Hence we consider a bank with the following features:

1. For each radial frequency, 17 spherical orientations over dynamic planes are considered. Table 1 shows the angular coordinates used in the proposed bank.
2. The radial axis is divided into 3 equal octave bands. The wavelength in each orientation is set at 3, 6 and 12 pixels respectively.
3. The radial bandwidth is chosen as 1.2 octaves
4. The angular bandwidth is chosen as 30 degrees

The resultant filter bank is illustrated in the top of figure 1. Due to the conjugate symmetry in the Fourier domain, the filter design is only carried out on the half 3D frequency space.

Active Filters In order to reduce the number of filter responses that have to be evaluated, a selection of filters that isolate spectral information corresponding to significant motions is performed. This selection allows to reduce the computational cost and it avoids the noisy or less relevant filter responses. Given a filter ϕ_i, a measure of its relevance is defined as:

$$w_i = \frac{1}{Card[V(i)]} \sum_{(\rho, \theta, \varphi) \in V(i)} |F(\rho, \theta, \varphi)| \tag{2}$$

where $|F(\rho, \theta, \varphi)|$ is the amplitude of the Fourier spectrum at (ρ, θ, φ), and $V(i)$ represents a spectral volume associated with the filter ϕ_i. To calculate $V(i)$, we consider that a point (ρ, θ, φ) in the spatio-temporal frequency domain will belong to $V(i)$ if

$$|\rho - \rho_o| \leq \sigma_\rho \; , \; |\theta - \theta_o| \leq \sigma_\theta \; y \; |\varphi - \varphi_o| \leq \sigma_\varphi \tag{3}$$

where σ_θ, σ_φ, σ_ρ and (θ_o, φ_o) are the logGabor filter parameters (let us remark that it is not necessary to calculate the responses of each filter to obtain these weights)

Using the filter relevance measure defined in (2), an unsupervised classification method is performed for each scale to group the filters into two classes: active ones and non-active ones. The cluster whose filters have the highest weights will determine the set of active filters (that will be noted *Active*). In our implementation, a hierarchical clustering [10] is used with a dissimilarity function between classes defined as

$$\delta(C_i, C_j) = |\mu_i - \mu_j| \tag{4}$$

where

$$\mu_k = \frac{1}{Card\,[C_k]} \sum_{r \in C_k} w_r \tag{5}$$

For each active filter, a set of 'relevant points' is computed. We calculate these points as local energy peaks on the filter responses [11]: given the response E_i of a filter ϕ_i, the maximal of E_i in the direction of the filter will determine the set of points which will focus our attention in the next stage.

2.2 Distance between Filter Responses

In this section, a distance between the statistical structures of a given pair of filter responses is proposed. To represent a statistical structure, we use the notions of *separable feature* and *integral feature* introduced in [12]. A separable feature is defined as any relevant characteristic that may be obtained for a point (phase, local contrast, energy, etc.). The combination of any subset of separable features will define an integral feature at a given point (x, y, z) . In this paper, the following five separable features proposed in [12] will be used: phase, local energy, local standard deviation, local contrast of the local energy, and local entropy.

Let $T^i(x, y, z) = \left[T_k^i(x, y, z)\right]_{k=1,2,\ldots L}$ be an integral feature at (x, y, z) which combines L separable features, noted as T_k^i, computed on the response of the filter ϕ_i. Let $\widehat{d}\left(T^i, T^j\right)$ be the distance between two integral features $T^i(x, y, z)$ and $T^j(x, y, z)$ given by the equation:

$$\widehat{d}\left(T^i, T^j\right) = \sum_{k=1}^{L} \frac{1}{Max_k} d(T_k^i, T_k^j) \tag{6}$$

with Max_k being a normalization factor [12], and $d(\cdot)$ a distance between separable features (this measure $d(\cdot)$ is defined for each separable feature in [12])

Based on the previous equation, a distance between the responses of two filters ϕ_i y ϕ_j is defined as:

$$\widehat{D}(\phi_i, \phi_j) = D\,[i,j]^2 + D\,[j,i]^2 \tag{7}$$

where

$$D\,[r,s] = \frac{1}{Card\,[P(r)]} \left(\sum_{P(r)} \left| \widehat{d}[T^r, T^s] \right|^\beta \right)^{\frac{1}{\beta}} \tag{8}$$

with $\widehat{d}[T^r, T^s]$ being the distance between integral features given by (6), and $P(r)$ the set of relevant points for the filter ϕ_r . The default value of the exponent β in (8) has been fixed to 3.

2.3   Clustering of Active Filters

In order to obtain a partition $C_1, C_2, ..., C_N$ of active filters, with C_i representing a motion, a clustering of the dataset $X = \{\phi_i \in Actives\}$ into an unknown number N of clusters is performed. For this purpose, a hierarchical clustering is used [10] with a dissimilarity function between classes defined on the basis of distances between statistical structures as

$$\delta(C_n, C_m) = min\left\{ \widehat{D}(\phi_i, \phi_j)\,,\ \phi_i \in C_n\,,\ \phi_j \in C_m \right\} \tag{9}$$

where $\widehat{D}(\phi_i, \phi_j)$ is given by the equation (7). Let us remark that the clustering is not performed for each point (x,y,t), but over the set of active filters X.

Selection of the Best Partition To select the level l of the hierarchy which will define the best partition $P^l = C_1, C_2, ..., C_N$, we propose the following function of goodness

$$f(P^l) = \frac{\gamma^*_{P^l}}{\varepsilon^*_{P^l}} \tag{10}$$

where $\varepsilon^*_{P^l}$ and $\gamma^*_{P^l}$ are two measures of the congruence and separation of the partition P^l respectively, given by the equations:

$$\varepsilon^*_{P^l} = max\left\{ \varepsilon_n \mid C_n \in P^l \right\} \tag{11}$$

$$\gamma^*_{P^l} = min\left\{ \gamma_n \mid C_n \in P^l \right\} \tag{12}$$

The congruence degree ε_n and separation degree γ_n of a cluster C_n are defined as

$$\varepsilon_n = max\left\{ cost(\mu^*_{i,j}) \mid \phi_i, \phi_j \in C_n \right\} \tag{13}$$

$$\gamma_n = min\{\delta(C_n, C_m) \mid m = 1, ..., N \ with\ m \neq n\} \tag{14}$$

where $\delta(C_n, C_m)$ is defined in (9), and $cost(\mu^*_{i,j})$ is the cost of the optimal path between two elements ϕ_i and ϕ_j in C_n calculated as follow: let $\prod_{ij}$ be the set of possibles paths linking ϕ_i and ϕ_j in C_n; given a path $\pi_{ij} \in \prod_{ij}$, its cost is defined as the greatest distance between two consecutive points on the path:

$$cost(\pi_{ij}) = max \left\{ \widehat{D}(\phi_r, \phi_{r+1}) \, / \, \phi_r, \phi_{r+1} \in \pi_{ij} \right\} \tag{15}$$

where ϕ_r and ϕ_{r+1} are two consecutive elements of π_{ij}, and $\widehat{D}(\phi_r, \phi_s)$ is defined in equation (7). The optimum path $\pi_{ij}^* \in \prod_{ij}$ between ϕ_i and ϕ_j is then defined as the path that links both filters with minimum cost:

$$\pi_{ij}^* = \underset{\pi_{i,j} \in \Pi_{i,j}}{argmin} \; \{cost(\pi_{i,j})\} \tag{16}$$

Due to the merging process of the hierarchical clustering and the distance between classes used in this case (equation (9)), the congruence degree ε_n equals to the distance between the two cluster which were merged together to obtain C_n [12]. Thus, the calculus of ε_n do not increase the computational cost of the clustering.

3   Results

In this section, the results obtained with real and synthetic sequences are showed to prove the performance of our model. For this purpose, several cases have been tested, from simple motion to occlusions and transparencies. In all the cases, the figures show the first and the last frame of the original sequence, and the motions detected in each case. Each motion, which has associated a cluster of filters, is represented by the sum of the filters responses (energy) of its cluster. In this representation, a high level of energy (white colour) corresponds to a high presence of motion.

A synthetic case of pure translational motion with constant speed is showed in figure 2(A). Specifically, the example shows three bars with velocities of (1,0), (-1,0) and (0,-1) pixels/frame respectively. Looking at the 3D representation of the original sequence, three independent planes can be seen corresponding to the three bars in motion. Our model separates each one of these planes into three different spatio-temporal outputs corresponding to the three motions. From this 3D representation, the sequence associated to each motion is extracted.

Figure 2(B) shows another synthetic example with a moving obtect with velocity of (1,1) pixels/frame. In this case, the object has the same texture that the background, so only the motion information allows to detect the object. As figure 2(B) shows, our model generates an output corresponding to the moving object.

The figure 2(C-D) shows two synthetic sequences which have been generated with Gaussian noise of mean 1 and variance 0. The first example (figure 2(C)) shows a sequence where a background pattern with velocity (-1,0) pixels/frame is occluded by a foreground pattern with velocity (1,0). The second example (figure 2(D)) shows two motions with transparency: an opaque background pattern

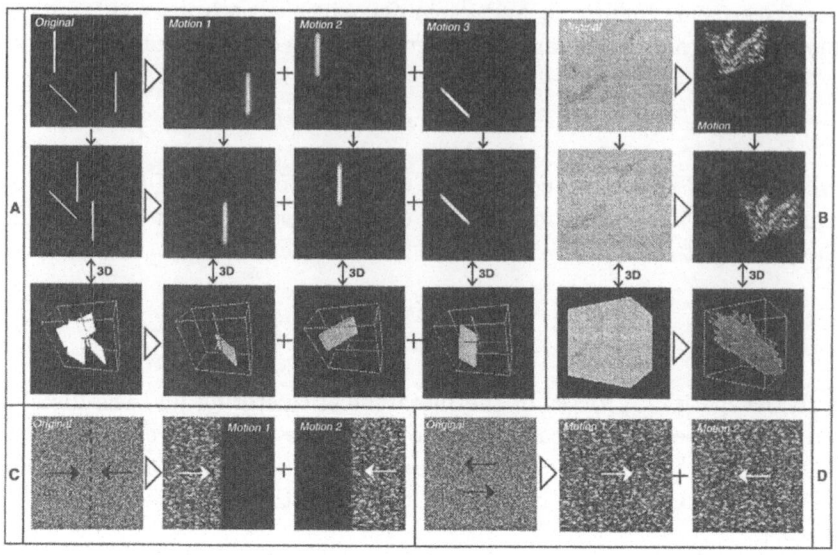

Fig. 2. Output of the model with synthetic sequences

with velocity (1,0), and a transparent foreground pattern with velocity (-1,0). In both cases, the figure shows the central frame of the sequence and the motions detected by the model (two in each case).

Figure 3(A-C) shows three examples with real sequences. In all the cases, boxes around the detected moving objects are showed over the original sequence. Each box is obtained from the energy representation (that is, the sum of the filters responses of the cluster associated to the motion) as the box which enclose the corresponding motion (to select the points with high level of energy a thresholding over the energy representation is performed). The first case corresponds to a double motion without occlusions where two hands are moving to clap. The second one shows an example of occlusion where a hand is crossing over another one. In this case, where the occlusion is almost complete in some frames, the motion combines translation and rotation without a constant velocity. The third case shows an example of transparency where a bar is occluded by a transparent object placed in the first plane. As figure 3 shows, in all the cases our model generates an output for each motion present in the sequence. Let us remark that the problem of the occlusion is solved by our model by mean of the spatio-temporal continuity of forms. Furthermore, this approach is capable of detecting motions even when different velocities and spatial orientations are present.

Figure 3(D) shows the result obtained with a noisy image sequence. This example has been generated by adding Gaussiam noise of mean 1 and variance 30 to the sequence of the figure 3(A). As figure 3(D) shows, our model segments the same two motions that were detected in the original sequence. That enlightens the consistency of the proposed algorithm in the presence of noise.

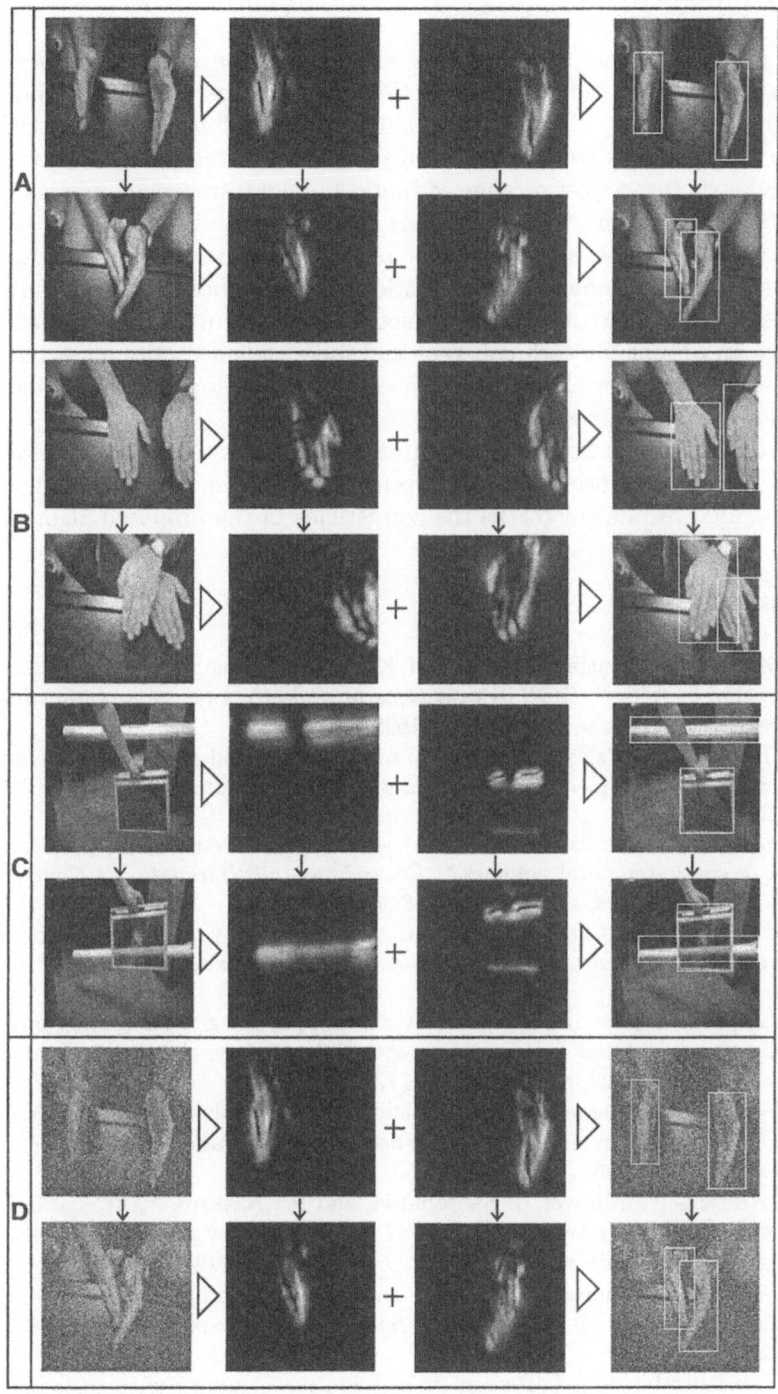

Fig. 3. Results with real sequences

4   Conclusions

In this paper, a new approach to motion segmentation in image sequences has been presented. The sequence has been represented as a spatio-temporal volume, where a moving object correspond to a three-dimensional object. Using this representation, a motion has been identified on the basis of invariance in statistical structure across a range of spatio-temporal frequency bands. To span the spatio-temporal spectrum, logGabor functions have been adopted as an appropriate method to construct filters of arbitrary bandwidth. The new approach allows to recombine information of motions that has been separated in several filter responses due to its spatial structure; as a result, the proposed model generates an output for each coherent and independent motion detected in the sequence, avoiding the classic problem associated with a representation based on spatio-temporal filters.

The technique has been illustrated on several data sets. Real and synthetic sequences combining occlusions and transparency have been tested. In all the cases, the final results enlightens the consistency of the proposed algorithm.

References

[1] F. Moscheni, S. Bhattacharjee, and M. Kunt, "Spatiotemporal segmentation based on region merging," *IEEE Transactions on Pattern Analysis and Machine Intelligence*, vol. 20, no. 9, pp. 897–915, 1998.

[2] D. Tweed and A Calway, "Integrated segmentation and depth ordering of motion layers in image sequences," *Image and Vision Computing*, vol. 20, pp. 709–724, 2002.

[3] K. Korimilli and S. Sarkar, "Motion segmentation based on perceptual organization of spatio-temporal volumes," *Proceedings.15th International Conference on Pattern Recognition*, vol. 3, pp. 844–849, 2000.

[4] E. H. Adelson and J. R. Bergen, "Spatiotemporal energy models for the perception of motion," *Journal of the Optical Society of America A.*, vol. 2, no. 2, pp. 284–299, Feb 1985.

[5] H. Liu, M. Hong, M. Herman, and A. Chellappa, "A general motion model and spatio-temporal filters for computing optical flow," *International Journal of Computer Vision*, vol. 22, no. 2, pp. 141–172, 1997.

[6] L. Wiskott, "Segmentation from motion: combining gabor and mallat wavelets to overcom de aperture and correspondence problem," *Pattern Recognition*, vol. 32, pp. 1751–1766, 1999.

[7] O . Nestares, C. Miravet, J. Santamaria, and R . Navarro, "Automatic segmentation of low visibility moving objects through energy analysis of the local 3d spectrum," *Proceedings of the SPIE'99*, vol. 3642, pp. 13–22, 1999.

[8] S.S Beauchemin and J.L. Barron, "On the fourier properties of discontinuous motion," *Journal of Mathematical Imaging and Vision*, vol. 13, pp. 155–172, 2000.

[9] S.S Beauchemin and J.L. Barron, "The frequency structure of 1d occluding image sequences," *IEEE Transactions on Pattern Analysis and Machine Intelligence*, vol. 22, no. 2, pp. 200–206, 2000.

[10] Anil K. Jain and Richard C. Dubes, *Algorithms for Clustering Data*, Prentice Hall, 1988.

[11] M. C. Morrone and R. A. Owens, "Feature detection from local energy," *Pattern Recognition Letters*, vol. 6, pp. 303–313, 1987.

[12] R. Rodriguez-Sanchez, J. A. Garcia, J. Fdez-Valdivia, and X. R. Fdez-Vidal, "The rgff representation model: A system for the automatically learned partitioning of 'visual patterns' in digital images," *IEEE Transactions on Pattern Analysis and Machine Intelligence*, vol. 21, no. 10, pp. 1044–1072, 1999.

Annotated Image Retrieval System
Based on Concepts and Visual Property

Junho Choi[1], Miyoung Cho[1], Mijin Yoon[1], Kyungsu Kim[2], Pankoo Kim[3]

[1] Dept. of Computer Science and Engineering
Chosun University, Gwangju 501-759 Korea
{spica, irune80,mjyoon}@mina.chosun.ac.kr
[2] Key Technology and Research Center,
Agency for Defense Development
arieskim@empal.com
[3] Corresponding Author, Dept. of CSE
Chosun University, Gwangju 501-759 Korea
pkkim@chosun.ac.kr

Abstract. Semantic content implies more than the simple identification of objects. Techniques for content-based image retrieval are not yet mature enough to recognize visual semantics completely. Therefore, it is necessary to use captions or text information attached to photos in the content-based information access of visual data. However, keyword-based retrieval is limited to the level of syntactic pattern matching. In other words, dissimilarity computation among terms is usually done by using string matching not concept matching. In this paper, we present a solution for retrieving images semantically, by means of the qualitative measurement of annotated keywords and also with the use of the spatial color distribution model.

1 Introduction

With the increasing use of image data, sophisticated techniques have become necessary to enable this information to be accessed based on its content. Indexing and retrieval of the visual content from image databases requires sophisticated content extraction techniques, content description methods, multi-dimensional data indexing methods and efficient similarity measurement techniques. To satisfy the demand for such advanced methods, recent research has produced many novel techniques for content-based visual information retrieval (CBVIR). CBVIR has emerged as a promising yet challenging research area in the past few years. However, as yet, no existing system is capable of completely understanding the semantics of visual information, even though the process of matching images, based on generic features such as color, size, texture, shape and object motion, is well within the realm of the technically possible.

F.J. Perales et al. (Eds.): IbPRIA 2003, LNCS 2652, pp. 204-211, 2003.

Semantic interpretation of image data would be incomplete without some mechanism for understanding the semantic content that is not directly visible. For this reason, human assisted content-annotation through natural language is the one of most commonly used methods, particularly in multimedia retrieval applications, and provides a means of exploiting syntactic, semantic as well as lexical information. A simple form of human-assisted semantic annotation is the attachment of a textual description (i.e., a keyword, or a simple sentence) to an image. Textual annotations can be used to convey the name of a visual object, or its properties.

Textual annotations in CBVIR systems are treated as a keyword list and use traditional text retrieval techniques. However, in classical text information retrieval systems, the relevant information will not be retrieved in response to a query, if the content and query representations do not share at least one term. This problem is known as 'term mismatch', and it results in users having to remember all of the keywords used in the annotation.

To resolve the problem of term mismatch, we propose a method for computerized conceptual similarity distance calculation in WordNet space. In this paper, we present a solution allowing for the qualitative measurement of concept-based retrieval of annotated images. The proposed similarity model considers edge, depth, link type, link density, as well as the existence of common ancestors. Therefore, the proposed methods provide a degree of conceptual dissimilarity between two concepts. We applied similarity measurement and the spatial distribution model of color to concept-based image retrieval.

This paper is organized as follows. Section 2 discusses related works. Section 3 describes semantic similarity measurement between concepts in WordNet. Section 4 presents an example of the application of similarity measurement to concept-based image retrieval. This paper concludes with Section 5.

2   Related Works

Our previous work presented in [4][8] introduces a semantic integrated visual information retrieval system that allows users to post both concepts and visual properties (i.e., sketch, color, etc.) as search criteria at the same time. Then, the system individually processes each search option and integrates them as results. Similar query processing can be found in [5], which proposes a terminology server architecture that manages semantic relations among words. The terminology server returns semantically similar terms for a semantic query processing operation. Both approaches utilize a lexical thesaurus as the mechanism for minimizing heterogeneity in keyword annotations, as well as a term rewriting mechanism. In the terminology server described in [5], terms are maintained using the correspondence between a semantic type and a relation, (i.e., "apple" *is-a* fruit). [4] uses WordNet™ [9] as a term management system that returns a set of terms considered to be similar (or related) to the given user search options and corresponding WordNet™ scene relations. With a set of words, query reformulation is required to process semantic query processing, which still performs pattern matching based query operation. However, query rewriting has some drawbacks in terms of its practical implementation. Since some abstract concepts, such as 'plant' or 'product name', may have hundreds of semantic entities, the resulting large number of logical relations in the WHERE clause may cause the performance of the associated query processing to be degraded. In addition, browsing and navigation of a database requires additional operations such as the tracking of semantic hierarchy.

One solution which has been proposed to tackle the above problem is to use similarity-based indexing and semantic distance[1][2] among terms in semantic query processing. In this approach, triangular inequality may improve the overall performance of the search. The problem of semantic distance computation on corpus statistics and lexical taxonomy has been the subject of considerable research over the last decade. However, only two distinct approaches have been reported in the literature. The first is the information content-based approach and the second is the edge-based approach.

3   A Hybrid Conceptual Distance Measure

3.1   The Existing Method

The information content-based approach[2] uses an entropy measure that is computed on the basis of the child node population. The information content of a conceptual entity, $H(c)$, is measured by using the number of words that are subsumed by c.

$$H(c) = -\log P(c) \tag{1}$$

where, $P(c)$ is the probability of encountering an instance of concept c. As the node's probability increases, its information content decreases. If there is a unique top node in the hierarchy, then its probability is 1, hence its information content is 0.

Resnik[2] proposed the following similarity measure between conceptual entities using information content.

$$sim(c_1, c_2) = \max_{c \in S(c_1, c_2)} [-\log p(c)] \tag{2}$$

where, $S(c_1, c_2)$ is the set of concepts that subsume both c_1 and c_2. To maximize the representative, the similarity value is the information content value of the node whose $H(c)$ value is the largest among those super classes.

The edge based approach is a more natural and direct way of evaluating semantic similarity in WordNet. It estimates the distance (e.g. edge length) between nodes. Sussna[1] defined the similarity distance between two conceptual entities as a weighted path length.

$$w(c_x \rightarrow_r c_y) = \max_r - \frac{\max_r - \min_r}{n_r(x)} \tag{3}$$

A weight between two conceptual entities is defined as follows:

$$w(c_i, c_j) = \frac{w(c_i \rightarrow_r c_j) + w(c_j \rightarrow_{r'} c_i)}{2d} \tag{4}$$

The symbols, $\rightarrow_r$ and $\rightarrow_{r'}$, represent a relation type r and its reverse. max_r and min_r are the maximum and minimum weights possible for a specific relation type r respectively. $n_r(x)$ is the number of relations of type r leaving a conceptual entity x. Therefore, the $w(c_i \rightarrow_r c_j)$ measurement considers both the density of the connections and the connection type. Finally, the similarity distance, d, between two concepts, is defined as the minimum path length.

3.2   The Combined Method

We propose a combined model that is derived from the edge-based notion by adding the information content. First of all, if the semantic distance between two adjacent nodes (one of them is a parent) is the following:

$$S_{ADJ}(c_i^l, c_j^{l-1}) = d(c_{j \rightarrow i}^l) \cdot f(d) \tag{5}$$

where, $f(d)$ is a function that returns a depth factor. As the depth level increases, the classification is based on finer and finer criteria. $d(c_{j \rightarrow i}^l)$ represents the density function. Since the overall semantic mass is of a certain amount for a given node, the density effect would suggest that the greater the density, the closer the distance between the nodes[3]. To explain this, as can be seen in Figure 1, it can be argued that the parent node, *Life_form*, is more strongly connected with the child nodes, *Animal*, *Plant*, and *Person*, than with the nodes *Aerobe* and *plankton*.

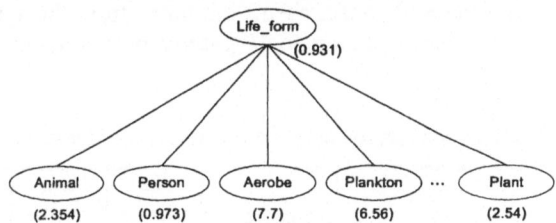

Fig. 1. Tree between Life_form and its child nodes

We will expand $S_{ADJ}(c_i^l, c_j^{l-1})$ to handle the case where more than one edges are in the shortest path between two concepts. Suppose we have the shortest path, p, from two concepts, c_i and c_j, such that $p = \{(t_0, c_0, c_1), (t_1, c_1, c_2)...(t_{n-1}, c_{n-1}, c_n)\}$. The shortest path, p, is the sum of the adjacent nodes. Therefore, the distance measure between c_i and c_j is as follows:

$$S_{edge}(c_i, c_j) = D(L_{j \rightarrow i}) \cdot \sum_{k=0}^{n} W(t_k) \cdot S_{ADJ}(c_k, c_{k+1}) \tag{6}$$

where, $D(L_{j \rightarrow i})$ is a function that returns a distance factor between c_i and c_j. The shorter the path from one node to the other, the more similar they are. $W(t_k)$ indicates the weight function that decides the weight value based on the link type. The simplest form of the weight function is the step function. If an edge type is IS_A then $W(t_k)$ returns 1 and otherwise returns a certain number that is less than 1.

Equation 6 only considers the link types and the number of edges. What is missing in equation 7 is a slot for shared concepts (as the number of shared concepts increases, the greater the similarity). To incorporate this into our similarity measurement, we propose the following equation.

$$S(c_i, c_j) = S_{edge} \cdot \max[H(C)] \tag{7}$$

where, $H(C)$ is the information content of the concept that subsumes both c_i and c_j. The above equation tells us that the total amount of similarity is proportional to the amount of shared information.

3.3   Comparison of the Measures

It would be reasonable to evaluate the performance of similarity measurements between concepts by comparing them with human ratings. The simplest way to implement this is to set up an experiment to rate the similarity of a set of word pairs, and examine the correlation between human judgment and machine calculations.

We used the noun portion of the version 1.6 of WordNet. It contains about 60,000 noun nodes(synsets). To make our experimental results comparable to those of other pervious methods, we used the results of each similarity rating measure for each word pair (Table 1). The M&C means are the average ratings for each pair as defined by Miller and Charles. And the replication means are taken from the special web site for word similarity.(http://www.cs.technion.ac.il/~gabr/resources/data/wordsim353/ ord-sim353.html).

Table 1. Comparison of Semantic Similarity Measures

Word pair		M&C means	Replica-tion means	Sim. means by node based	Sim. means by edge based	Sim. means by our system
car	automo-bile	3.92	8.94	7.45	32	11.95
gem	jewel	3.84	8.96	12.54	32	14.7
Journey	voyage	3.84	9.29	6.87	31	11.18
boy	lad	3.76	8.83	7.44	31	10.86
Rooster	voyage	0.08	0.62	0	0	1

To evaluate the similarity measurement of the proposed method, we use correlation values. For consistency in comparison, we will use semantic similarity measures rather than semantic distance measures.

Table 2. Summary of Experimental Results

Similarity Method	Correlation (r)
Human Judgment	0.9494
Node Based	0.8011
Edge Based	0.5789
Proposed Method	0.8262

Note that this conversion does not affect the result of the evaluation, since a linear transformation of each datum will not change the magnitude of the resulting correlation coefficient, although its sign may change from positive to negative. The correlation values between the similarity ratings and the mean ratings reported by Miller and Charles are listed in Table 2.

4   Implementation of Concept Based Image Retrieval

In the experiment, we used a sample image database containing nearly 2,300 selected images. The images we used in our experiments came from Microsoft's 'Design Gallery Live(http://dgl.microsoft.com)'. In this site, each image was categorized into one of approximately 50 categories, such as "Animals", "Plants", "Places", etc. Each image had three or four annotations. The search options selected for these experiments were:

1. Retrieval based on the proposed semantic similarity measurement
2. Retrieval based on the spatial distribution model of color

Our previous work on the feature extraction technique, called the spatial distribution model of color[4], is a good indicator of the color contents of images and forms the basis of an effective method of image indexing. Let us look at a few examples. A set of two experiments was conducted to search for similar images, (each containing a rose flower), as the target image. The first query is a simple search for images that look like the image that contains the picture of a rose(top-left image in Fig. 2). The search option is set such that we use the ontology with semantic similarity measurement, and the results of the retrieval are presented in Fig. 2. The value of each image is an average of the similarity measures between the annotated keyword of the image and the query keyword.

Fig. 3 represents the result of running the query with conceptual relativity and spatial color distribution. Note that, in Fig. 3, to the first 11 images, system rearranges the images on the basis of the spatial color distribution model. Starting from the 12'th retrieved image shown in Fig. 3, the images displayed here were relegated to 12'th place in favor of other images that the system found to be closer matches.

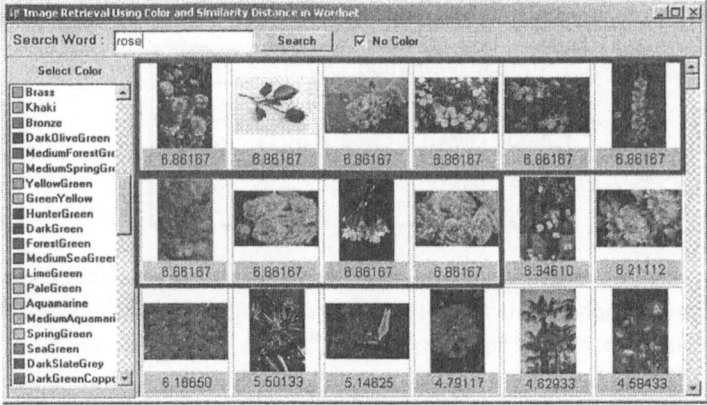

Fig. 2. Result of 'rose' Query using semantic similarity measurement without spatial color

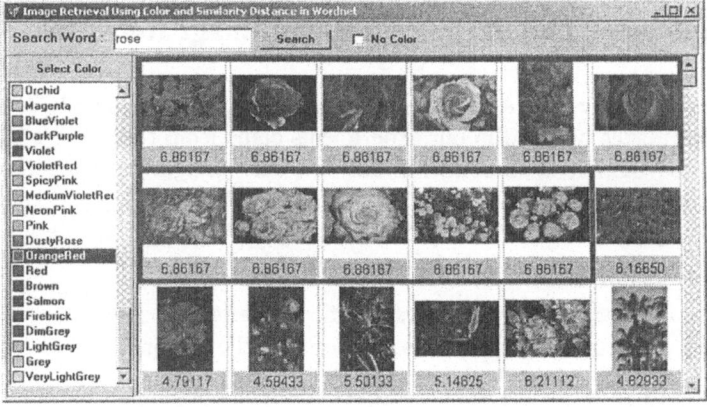

Fig. 3. Result of 'rose' Query using semantic similarity measurement with spatial color techniques for concept-based image retrieval with the spatial color distribution model can be extended to include multi-modal queries such as query by concept and color, or query by concept and shape

5   Conclusions

In this paper, we proposed a combined model that is derived from the edge-based approach by adding the information content. We consider the edge, depth, link type and density, as well as the existence of common ancestors. In particular, the proposed method provides a means of determining the link strength of an edge that links a parent node to a child node. The link strengths defined here are (1) the density(the number of child links that span out from a parent node), and (2) their topological location in WordNet space.

We also introduced a method of applying similarity measurement and the spatial color distribution model of color to concept-based image retrieval. With this method, it is possible to retrieve images by means of a conceptual approach based on keywords and the color distribution model. This is demonstrated by means of the experiments presented in section 4. Furthermore, the proposed method can be extended to include multi-modal queries, such as query by concept and shape, and query by concept and texture.

Acknowledgement

We would like to thank Dr. Youngchoon Park for his valuable comments.

References

[1]   Sussna "WordSense Disambiguation for Free-text Indexing Using a Massive Semantic Network" Proceedings of the Second International Conference on Information and Knowledge Management, CIKM'93.
[2]   Philip Resnik "Using Information Content to Evaluate Semantic Similarity in a Taxonomy" Proceedings of the 14th International Joint Conference on Artificial Intelligence, 1995.
[3]   R.Richardson, A.F. Smeaton "Using WordNet in a Knowledge-Based Approach to Information Retrieval", Working paper, CA-0395, School of Computer Applications, Dublin City University, Ireland, 1995
[4]   Forouzan Golshani and Youngchoon Park, "ImageRoadMap: A New Content-Based Image Retrieval System", Lecture Notes in Computer Science (LNCS) 1308, Springer-Verlag, pp. 225-239, 1997.
[5]   W.-S. Li, K.S. Candan, K. Hirata, and Y. Hara, "A Hybrid Approach to Multimedia Database Systems through Integration of Semantics and Media-based Search, LNCS - Worldwide Computing and Its Applications, T.Masuda, Y.Masunaga, M.Tsukamoto (Eds.), Springer-Verlag, Vol. 1274, P. 182-197, August, 1997.
[6]   Jay J Jiang, David W. Conrath "Semantic Similarity Based Corpus Statistics and Lexical Taxonomy", Proc. Of International Conference Research on Computational Linguistics, 1997.
[7]   J. Z. Wang, J. Li, D. Chan, G. Wiederhold, "Semantics-sensitive Retrieval or Digital Picture Libraries" D-Lib. Magazine, 1999.
[8]   Y.C. Park, F. Golshani, S. Panchanathan, "Conceptualization and Ontology: Tools for Efficient Storage and Retrieval of Semantic Visual Information", Internet Multimedia Management Systems Conference, 2000.
[9]   http://www.cogsci.princeton.edu/~wn/
[10]   K Barnard, D.A. Forsyth. "Learning the semantics of words and pictures" In int. Conf. on Computer Vision, 2001.
[11]   Guarino, N. and Welty, C. "Supporting Ontological Analysis of Taxonomic Relationships." Data and Knowledge Engineering (in press), 2001.

Multimodal Attention System
for an Interactive Robot

Oscar Déniz, Modesto Castrillón, Javier Lorenzo, Mario Hernández, and Juan
Méndez

Instituto Universitario de Sistemas Inteligentes (IUSIANI)
Univ. Las Palmas de Gran Canaria
Edif. Central del Parque Científico-Tecnológico. Campus de Tafira
35017 Las Palmas – Spain
odeniz@dis.ulpgc.es

Abstract. Social robots are receiving much interest in the robotics community. The most important goal for such robots lies in their interaction
capabilities. An attention system is crucial, both as a filter to center the
robot's perceptual resources and as a mean of letting the observer know
that the robot has intentionality. In this paper a simple but flexible and
functional attentional model is described. The model, which has been
implemented in an interactive robot currently under development, fuses
both visual and auditive information extracted from the robot's environment, and can incorporate knowledge-based influences on attention.

1   Introduction

In the last years the robotics community has sought to endow robots with social
and interaction abilities, with the first survey recently published [6]. Researchers
realized that robots that excelled in certain tasks were by no means considered intelligent by the general public. Social abilities are now considered very
important in order to make the robots more human. Emotion and multimodal
communication are also two related aspects that are still being researched.

In [11] the authors argue that a robot with attention would have a minimal
level of intentionality, since the attentional capacity involves a first level of goal
representations. Attention is a selection process whereby only a small part of the
huge amount of sensory information reaches higher processing centers. Attention
allows to divide the visual understanding problem into a rapid succession of local,
computationally less expensive, analysis problems. Human attention is divided
in the literature into two functionally independent stages: a preattentive stage,
which operates in parallel over the whole visual field, and an attentive stage, of
limited capacity, which only processes an item at a time. The preattentive stage
detects intrinsically salient stimuli, while the attentive stage carries out a more
detailed and costly process with each detected stimulus. The saliency values of
the attentive stage depend on the current task, acquired knowledge, etc [8, 10].

Probably the first robot that was explicitly designed to include some social
abilities is Kismet [1]. Kismet has had undeniable success in the robotics community because it has been a serious effort in making a robot sociable. Among

F.J. Perales et al. (Eds.): IbPRIA 2003, LNCS 2652, pp. 212–220, 2003.

other diverse modules, Kismet included an attention system, which is based on Wolfe's "Guided Search 2.0 (GS2)" model [15]. GS2 is based on extracting basic features (color, motion, etc.) that are linearly combined in a saliency map. In a winner-take-it-all approach, the region of maximum activity is extracted from the saliency map. The focus of attention (FOA) will then be directed to that region.

It is a well accepted fact that attention is controlled both by sensory salient and cognitive factors (knowledge, current task) [2]. The effect of the lower level subsystem (bottom-up influence) has been comprehensively studied and modelled. In contrast, the effect of higher level subsystems (top-down influence) in attention is not yet clear [9]. Hewett [8] also suggests that volitive processes should control the whole attention process, even though some of the controlled mechanisms are automatic in the human brain. Therefore, high-level modules should have total access to the saliency map. This would allow the attention focus to be directed by the point that a person is looking at, deictic gestures, etc. Fixations to the point that a person is looking at are useful for joint attention. In [14] an additional feature map is used for the purpose of assigning more saliency to zones of joint attention between the robot and a person.

In the third version of Wolfe's Guided Search [16] high-level modules act in two ways. On the one hand they can modify the combination weights. On the other hand, they can also act after each fixation, processing (recognizing, for example) the area of the FOA, after which an "inhibition of return" (IR) signal is generated. IR is a signal that inhibits the current FOA, so that it will not win in the saliency map for some time.

Top-down influences on attention are also accounted for in the FeatureGate model [5]. In this model, a function is used to produce a distance between the low-level observed features and those of the interest objects. In [13] the top-down influence is embedded in the changing parameters that control a relaxation and energy minimization process that produces the saliency map. Also, in [3] a neural network, controlled by high-level processes, is used to regulate the flow of information of the feature maps towards the saliency map. A model of attention similar to that of Kismet is introduced in [12] for controlling a stereo head. Besides the feature maps combination (color, skin tone, motion and disparity), space variant vision is used to simulate the human fovea. However, the system does not account for top-down influences. Moreover, it uses 9 Pentium processors, which is rather costly if the attention system is to be part of a complete robot.

In [7] an attention system is presented where high-level modules do influence (can act on) the whole saliency map. When, after a fixation, part of an object is detected, saliency is increased in other locations of the visual field where other parts of the object should be, considering also scaling and rotation. This would not be very useful in poorly structured and dynamic environments. In the same system, a suppression model equivalent to IR is used: after a fixation the saliency of the activated zone is decreased in a fixed amount, automatically.

The objective of this work was not to achieve a biologically faithful model, but to implement a functional model of attention for a social robot. This paper is organized as follows. Section 2 describes the proposed attention system, implemented for a social robot that is currently being developed. Experiments are described and analyzed in Section 3. Finally, the main conclusions are summarized in Section 4.

2   Attention Model

In all the citations made above, the effect of high-level modules is limited to a selection or guiding of the bottom-up influence (i.e. combination weights) and the modification of the relevance of the object in the FOA. We propose that the influence of high-level modules on attention should be more direct and flexible. Inhibition should be controlled by these modules, instead of being an automatic mechanism. The following situation is an example of such case: if I look at a particular person and I like her, inhibition should be low, in order to revisit her soon. There could even be no inhibition, which would mean that I would keep on looking at her. Note that by letting other processes control the saliency map joint attention and inhibition of return can be implemented. Also, the mechanism explained before that increases saliency in the zones where other parts of objects should be can be implemented. In fact, any knowledge-directed influence on attention can be included.

The objective of this work was to conceive a functional attention mechanism that includes sound and vision cues. Therefore, the model proposed here is simple to implement, being the most complex calculations done in the feature extraction algorithms. The activation (i.e. saliency) values are controlled by the following equation:

$$A(p,t) = \sum_i F_i(v_i \cdot f_i(p,t)) + \sum_j G_j(s_j \cdot g_j(p,t)) + K \cdot C(p,t) + T(p,t) \quad (1)$$

where F and G are functions that are applied to the vision-based (f_i) and sound-based (g_j) feature maps in order to group activity zones and/or to account for the error in the position of the detected activity zones. Spatial and temporal positions in the maps are represented by the p and t variables. v_i, s_j and K are constants. C is a function that gives more saliency to zones near the current FOA: $C(p,t) = e^{-\gamma|p-FOA(t-1)|}$. $T(p,t)$ represents the effect of high-level modules, which can act over the whole attention field. The maximum of the activation map defines the FOA, as long as it is larger than a threshold U:

$$FOA(t) = \begin{cases} \max_p A(p,t) & if \max_p A(p,t) > U \\ FOA(t-1) & otherwise \end{cases} \quad (2)$$

The model is depicted in Figure 1, using sound and vision for extracting feature maps. Note that a joint attention mechanism would use the component T of Equation 1, which for all practical purposes is equivalent to the approach taken in [14] that used a feature map for that end.

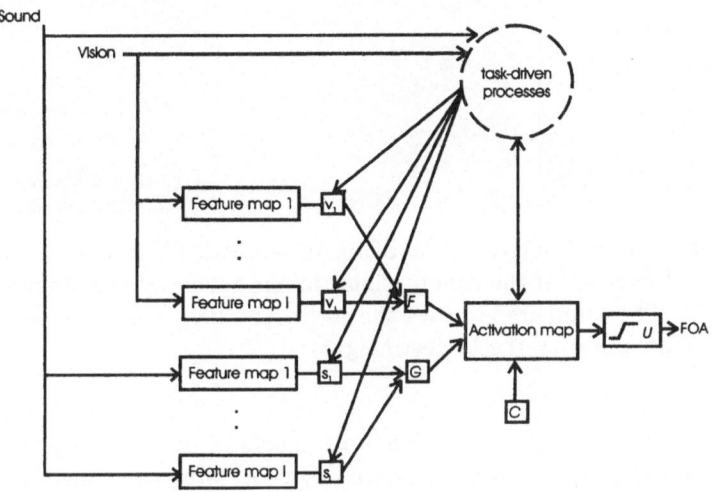

Fig. 1. Model of attention. The feature maps must represent the same physical space than the activation map. If sensors do not provide such values, a mapping would have to be done

The implementation presented in this paper will use an auditive feature map: the localization of a single sound source. Notwithstanding, this scheme can be used with multiple sources, as long as they are separated by another technique.

The visual feature map is extracted from images taken with an omnidirectional camera, using adaptive background differences. The aim was to detect blobs pertaining to people around the robot. The first step is to discard part of the captured image, as we want to watch only the frontal zone, covering 180 degrees from side to side (see Fig. 2). The background model is obtained as the mean value of a number of frames taken when no person is present in the room. The model M is updated with each input frame:

$$M(k+1) = M(k) + U(k) \cdot [I(k) - M(k)], \tag{3}$$

where I is the input frame. U is the updating function:

$$U(k) = exp(-\beta \cdot D(k)), \tag{4}$$

with:

$$D(k) = \alpha \cdot D(k-1) + (1-\alpha) \cdot |I(k) - I(k-1)|, \tag{5}$$

for α between 0 and 1. The parameters α and β control the adaptation rate.

The method of adaptive background differences described above still had a drawback. Inanimate objects should be considered background as soon as possible. However, as we are working at a pixel level, if we set the α and β parameters

Fig. 2. Left: the interactive robot being developed. Center: omnidirectional camera, placed in front of the robot. Right: image taken by the omnidirectional vision system. The numbers indicate the estimated height and the angle of the closest blob (the one with the largest height)

too low we run the risk of considering static parts of animate objects as background too. This problem can be alleviated by processing the image D. For each foreground blob, its values in D are examined. The maximum value is found, and all the blob values in D are set to that level. With this procedure the blob only enters the background model when all its pixels remain static. The blob does not enter the background model if at least one of its pixels has been changing.

As for the sound-based feature map, the aim was to detect the direction of sound sources (i.e. people). The signals gathered by a pair of microphones are amplified and preprocessed to remove noise. Then the angle in the horizontal of a sound source is extracted using the expression:

$$angle = \arcsin((s \cdot I/f)/d), \tag{6}$$

where s is the sound speed, f is the sampling frequency, d is the distance between the pair of microphones, and I is the interaural time difference (ITD). The ITD is a measure of the displacement between the signal gathered at one microphone and the signal gathered at the other, and is obtained through correlation. The implemented sound localization system is described in more detail in [4].

3 Implementation and Experiments

The attention model has been implemented on the robot head shown in Figure 2. This head includes an omnidirectional camera as a presence detector and a sound localization system based on a pair of microphones placed on both sides of the head. The feature and activation maps represent a half-plane in front of the robot. The FOA is used to command the pan and tilt motors of the robot's neck. For our particular implementation we decided that sound events should not change the FOA on their own, but they should make the nearest visual event win. Also, as a design decision we imposed that the effect of sound events should have precedence over the effect of C.

In our particular case the variable p takes values in the range $[0, 180]$ degrees and F will not be used. $v_1 = 1, f_1 = \{0, 1\}$ represents the effect of a visual feature map that detects foreground blobs using adaptive background differences and the omnidirectional camera. The visual feature maps are not actually 1-D, but 1 1/2-D, as for each angle we store the height of the blob, measured by the omnidirectional vision system. This height is used to move the tilt motor of the robot's neck. $g_1 = \{0, 1\}$ represents the output of the sound localization routine. The vision and sound localization modules communicate with the attention module through TCP/IP sockets. To account for errors in sound localization, G is a convolution with a function $e^{(-D \cdot |x|)}$, D being a constant. In order to meet these conditions the following should be verified:

- $s_1 < 1$ (the FOA will not be directly set by the sound event).
- Suppose that 2 blobs are anywhere in the activation map. Then a sound event is heard. One of the blobs will be closer to the sound source than the other. In order to enforce the preferences mentioned above, the maximum activation that the farthest blob could have should be less than the minimum activation that the nearest blob could have. This can be put as $1 + K + s_1 \cdot e^{(-D \cdot a)} <$ $1 + K \cdot e^{(-180 * \gamma)} + s_1 \cdot e^{(-D \cdot b)}$, b and a being the distances from the blobs to the sound source, the largest and the shortest one, respectively. That equation does not hold for $b < a$ but it can be verified for $b < a - \epsilon$, with a very small ϵ.

Operating with these two equations the following valid set of values was obtained: $D = 0.01, K = 0.001, s_1 = 0.9, \gamma = 0.15$. For those values $\epsilon = 0.67$ degrees, which we considered acceptable.

The effect of high-level processes (T) is not used in the implementation yet, as the robot is still under development. The simplicity of the model and of the implementation make the attention system efficient. With maps of 181 values, the average update time for the activation map was 0.27ms (P-IV 1.4Ghz). In order to show how the model performs, two foreground objects (a person and a coat stand) were placed near the robot. A sample image taken by the omnidirectional camera are shown in Figure 2. Initially, the FOA was at the coat stand. Then the person makes a noise and the FOA shifts, and remains fixating the person. In order to see what happens at every moment this situation can be divided into three stages: before the sound event, during the sound event and after the sound event.

Figure 3 shows the state of the feature maps and the activation map at each stage. Note that the vertical axis is shown in logarithmic coordinates, so that the effect of the C component, which is very small, can be seen. The exponential contributions thus appear in the figures as lines.

Before the sound event the FOA was at the blob on the left, approximately at 75 degrees, because it is the closest blob to the previous FOA (the robot starts working looking at his front, 90 degrees). This is shown in the first two figures. The two next figures show the effect of the sound event. The noise produces a peak near the blob on the right (the person). That makes activation rise near that blob, which in turn makes the blob win the FOA. The last two figures show how the FOA has been fixated to the person. In absence of other contributions the effect of the C component implements a tracking of the fixated object/person.

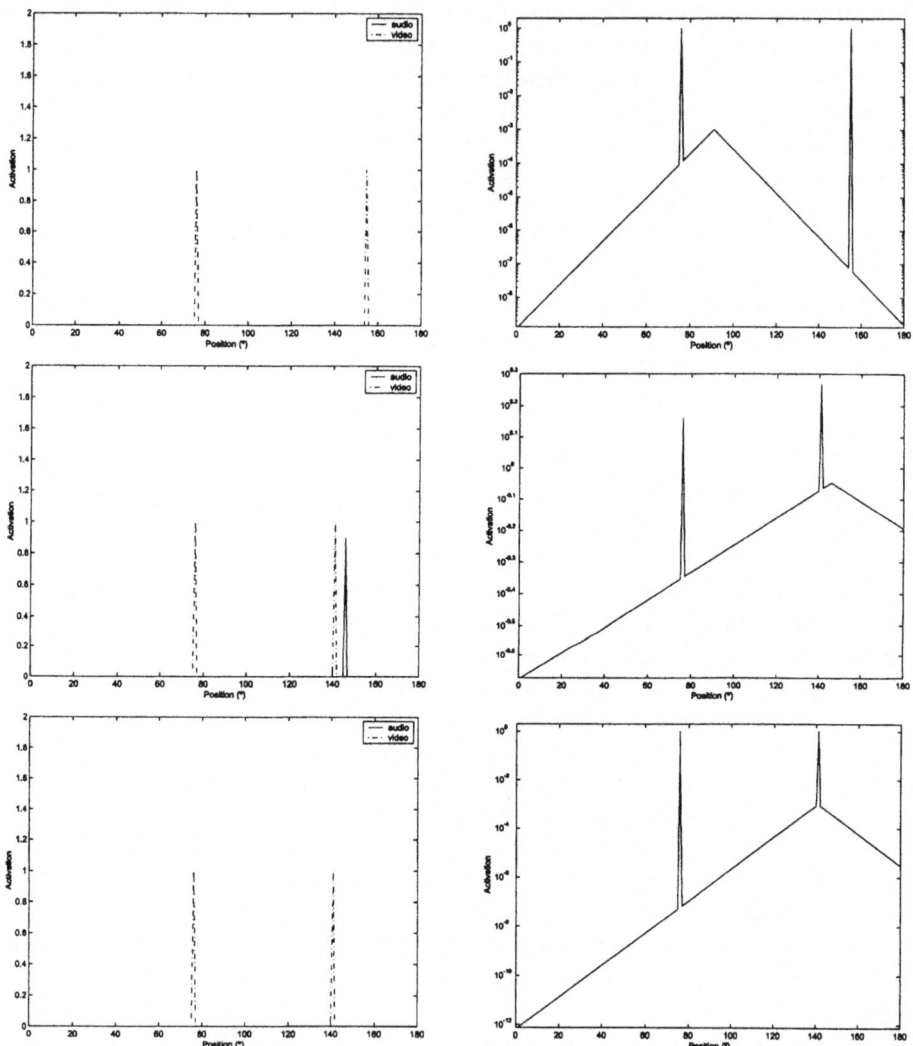

Fig. 3. State of the feature and activation maps. On the left column the figures show the visual and auditive feature maps. On the right column the figures show the resultant saliency map

4   Conclusions

An attentional system is a necessary module in a complex human-like robot. With it, the robot will be able to direct its attention to people in the environment, which is crucial for interaction. In this paper a simple yet functional model of attention has been described, drawing upon previous attentional systems for interactive robots. The model was implemented using both auditive and visual features extracted from a zone surrounding the robot. Visual features were extracted from video taken with an omnidirectional camera, which gives the robot a 180 degrees attentional span. The attentional system is currently running on a robotic head

The next step in our work will be to implement the high-level influences on the attention focus. This influence is to be defined by the robot's tasks and knowledge, which obviously need the completion of other modules, such as an action selection mechanism (with goals), memory and facial analysis.

Acknowledgments

The first author is supported by grant *D260/54066308-R* of Universidad de Las Palmas de Gran Canaria. This work was partially funded by research projects *PI2000/042* of Gobierno de Canarias and *UNI2002/16* of Universidad de Las Palmas de Gran Canaria.

References

[1] Cynthia L. Breazeal. *Designing social robots*. MIT Press, Cambridge, MA, 2002.
[2] M. Corbetta and G.L. Shulman. Control of goal-directed and stimulus-driven attention in the brain. *Nature reviews neuroscience*, 3:201–215, March 2002.
[3] P. Van de Laar, T. Heskes, and S. Gielen. Taks-dependent learning of attention. *Neural networks*, 10(6):981–992, 1997.
[4] O. Déniz, , J. Cabrera, and M. Hernández. Building a sound localization system for a robot head. *Inteligencia Artificial. Revista Iberoamericana de Inteligencia Artificial*, 2003. To appear.
[5] J.A. Driscoll, R.A. Peters II, and K.R. Cave. A visual attention network for a humanoid robot. In *IEEE/RSJ International Conference on Intelligent Robotic Systems*, Victoria, B.C., Canada, October 1998.
[6] T. Fong, I. Nourbakhsh, and K. Dautenhahn. A survey of socially interactive robots. *Robotics and Autonomous Systems*, 42(3-4), March 2003.
[7] T.D. Grove and R.B. Fisher. Attention in iconic object matching. In *Procs. of British Machine Vision Conference*, pages 293–302, Edinburgh, September 1996.
[8] D. Heinke and G.W. Humphreys. Computational models of visual selective attention: A review. In G. Houghton, editor, *Connectionist models in psychology*, 2001.
[9] L. Itti. Modeling primate visual attention. In J. Feng, editor, *Computational Neuroscience: A Comprehensive Approach*, Boca Ratón. CRC Press.
[10] L. Itti and C. Koch. Computational modeling of visual attention. *Nature reviews neuroscience*, 2(3):194–203, March 2001.

220   Oscar Déniz et al.

[11] L. Kopp and P. Gärdenfors. *Attention as a Minimal Criterion of Intentionality in Robots*, volume 89 of *Lund University Cognitive Studies*. 2001.

[12] G. Metta. An attentional system for a humanoid robot exploiting space variant vision. In *IEEE-RAS International Conference on Humanoid Robots*, pages 359–366, Tokyo, November 2001.

[13] R. Milanese, H. Wechsler, S. Gil, J.M. Bost, and T. Pun. Integration of bottom-up and top-down cues for visual attention using non-linear relaxation. In *Procs. IEEE Conf. on Computer Vision and Pattern Recognition*, pages 781–785, 1994.

[14] B. Scassellati. *Foundations for a Theory of Mind for a Humanoid Robot*. PhD thesis, MIT Department of Computer Science and Electrical Engineering, May 2001.

[15] J.M. Wolfe. Guided search 2.0: A revised model of visual search. *Psychonomic Bulletin and Review*, 1(2):202–238, 1994.

[16] J.M. Wolfe and G. Gancarz. *"Guided Search 3.0"*, pages 189–192. Basic and Clinical Applications of Vision Science. Kluwer Academic, Netherlands, 1996.

New Wavelet-Based Invariant Shape Representation Functions

Ibrahim El Rube[1], Maher Ahmed[2], and Mohamed Kamel[1]

[1] Systems Design Engineering, University of Waterloo
Waterloo, N2L 3G1, Ontario, Canada
ibrahim@watsup.uwaterloo.ca, mkamel@uwaterloo.ca
[2] Physics and Computer Science Department, Wilfrid Lurier University, Waterloo
N2L 3C5, Ontario, Canada
mahmed@wlu.ca

Abstract. In this paper, new wavelet-based affine invariant functions for shape representation are derived. These functions are computed from the wavelet approximation coefficients of the shape boundary. The first function is computed from applying a single wavelet transform, whereas the second function is computed from applying two different wavelet transforms. All the previously derived affine invariant functions were based on wavelet details coefficients which are sensitive to noise in the finer scale levels. The proposed invariant functions are more stable and less sensitive to noise than the details-based invariant functions.

1 Introduction

Wavelet analysis has become one of the important and powerful tools in many disciplines [6], [2]. In image processing and pattern recognition areas, wavelet is used in image enhancement, compression, feature extraction, and much more applications. One of the applications of wavelet transform is the shape representation. Shape representation is a crucial step in shape analysis and matching systems [9], [2]. If the representation of the shape does not change under certain geometric transformation, then this representation is said to be invariant to that transformation. Invariant representation functions can be computed either from the shape intensity or from the boundary of the shape [2]. Many researchers used the Wavelet Transform (WT) in shape representation. Some have attempted to apply the WT in 2-D domains (region-based techniques); others have chosen to apply the transform to 1-D shape boundary (contour-based techniques). Usually, region-based algorithms are greatly influenced by background variations (e.g., light and shading) and corrupted noise. Moreover, region-based techniques are usually very time consuming. On the other hand, contour representations provide better data reduction, and are usually less sensitive to noise than region-based techniques [7].

Wavelet representation contains information at different scales in which different shapes could have the same representation at a particular scale but not at all scale levels [13].

F.J. Perales et al. (Eds.): IbPRIA 2003, LNCS 2652, pp. 221–228, 2003.
© Springer-Verlag Berlin Heidelberg 2003

In this paper, two new affine invariant functions for shape representation are derived. One of these functions is derived from the approximation coefficients of the wavelet transform. The second function is derived from the approximation coefficients after applying two different wavelet transforms .

This paper is organized as follows: Section II gives a quick review of the related work. In sections III the proposed functions are derived. Section IV illustrates the experimental results. Finally section V gives the conclusions and the future work.

2   Related Work

In this section, the previously published papers that used wavelet transform in obtaining invariant shape representation are introduced. Since we are applying wavelet transform to the shape contour to obtain the affine invariant representation, the related publications only will be review. The affine invariant wavelet representations derived till now were based on the details coefficients. A quick overview of these functions is as follows:

- Alferez and Wang [1] proposed geometric and illumination invariants for object recognition depending on the details coefficients of the dyadic wavelet decomposition. They also showed that more complicated invariant functions could be constructed from more than two wavelet details scales.
- Tieng and Boles tried to derive more than one affine invariant function by applying the dyadic wavelet transform to the shape contour. In [12], and [13] they derived a relative invariant function from the approximations and the details coefficients of the shape contour.

$$I_1(i,k) = A_i x_k D_i y_k - A_i y_k D_i x_k \qquad (1)$$

where $A_i x_k$ are the approximation coefficients of the boundary sequence x_k and $D_i y_k$ are the details coefficients of the boundary sequence y_k. They found that the B-spline was the optimum wavelet function when compared to the Daubechies and Lamarie-Battle functions. Representation using the B-spline gave stable matching results and a small number of misclassifications. For classification purpose, they selected only two levels that have the largest energies concentrations.

In [10] they used complex Duabechies wavelet functions to calculate the invariant function. The Invariant function used here is the same as in [12] except that the approximation and the details are replaced by the real and the imaginary parts of the details coefficients, respectively.

In [11], they derived another invariant function by taking the wavelet coefficients of two different wavelet functions. The invariant function is given by

$$I_2(j,k) = D_j^1 x_k D_j^2 y_k - D_j^1 y_k D_j^2 x_k \qquad (2)$$

– Khalil and Bayoumi also tried to derive a wavelet-based affine invariant function using dyadic wavelet transform ([3], [4], and [5]). The invariant function is derived from the details coefficients generated from the wavelet transform of the shape boundary. The relative invariant function, using only two dyadic scale levels, is defined as:

$$I_3(i, j, k) = D_i \tilde{x}_k D_j \tilde{x}_k - D_i \tilde{y}_k D_j \tilde{x}_k \tag{3}$$

where $D_i \tilde{x}_k$ and $D_i \tilde{y}_k$ are the details signals of the affine transformed signals x_k and y_k at scale i and j respectively.

In [5], they continued their previous work in [4]. They showed that they can compute the invariant functions using 2, 3 , or 4 dyadic levels.

In [4], they derived an absolute wavelet-based conics invariant function that uses all the details scale levels (except the first two), which increased the discrimination power of the invariant function.

3   Wavelet-Based Affine Invariant Shape Representation Functions

The aim of this paper is to derive stable and robust wavelet-based invariant functions that can be used in shape representation. Wavelet-based invariant functions derived from the shape boundary were introduced by several authors. These functions were invariant to affine, or projective transformations. The derived affine and projective invariant functions were based either on the wavelet details coefficients only (as in [4, 1, 5, 12, 3] and [10]) or on the combination of the details and the approximations coefficients (as in [12, 13]).

A general framework for deriving affine invariant functions from wavelet decomposition is as follows:

For a 2-D shape represented by its contour sequences (x_k and y_k) and subjected to affine transformation, the relation between the original and the distorted sequences is

$$\begin{bmatrix} \tilde{x}_k \\ \tilde{y}_k \end{bmatrix} = \begin{bmatrix} c_{11} & c_{12} \\ c_{21} & c_{22} \end{bmatrix} \begin{bmatrix} x_k \\ y_k \end{bmatrix} + \begin{bmatrix} b_1 \\ b_2 \end{bmatrix} \tag{4}$$

where $c_{11}, c_{12}, c_{21}, c_{22}$, are the affine matrix coefficients and b_1, and b_2 represent the translation parameters. The translation parameters can be easily removed by subtracting the shape centroid from its extracted boundary.

By applying the wavelet transform to the distorted boundary sequences, these wavelet transformed sequences at scale level (i) are related by:

$$\begin{bmatrix} W_i \tilde{x}_k \\ W_i \tilde{y}_k \end{bmatrix} = \begin{bmatrix} c_{11} & c_{12} \\ c_{21} & c_{22} \end{bmatrix} \begin{bmatrix} W_i x_k \\ W_i y_k \end{bmatrix} \tag{5}$$

where $W_i x_k$ and $W_i y_k$ are the wavelet transformed original sequences at scale level i, and $W_i \tilde{x}_k$ and $W_i \tilde{y}_k$ are the wavelet transformed distorted sequences at scale level i. ($W_i x_k$ is either the detail or the approximation coefficients). For two different representations of x_k and y_k (i.e at different scale levels, or by two different coefficients types) and if the wavelet coefficients are subjected to the same geometric transformation,

$$\begin{bmatrix} W_i\tilde{x}_k & W_j\tilde{x}_k \\ W_i\tilde{y}_k & W_j\tilde{y}_k \end{bmatrix} = \begin{bmatrix} c_{11} & c_{12} \\ c_{21} & c_{22} \end{bmatrix} \begin{bmatrix} W_ix_k & W_jx_k \\ W_iy_k & W_jy_k \end{bmatrix} \tag{6}$$

An affine invariant function is computed by taking the determinant of equation 6, which means that

$$W_i\tilde{x}_k W_j\tilde{y}_k - W_i\tilde{y}_k W_j\tilde{x}_k = det(C)(W_ix_k W_jy_k - W_iy_k W_jx_k) \tag{7}$$

is a relative invariant function. Where C is the transformation matrix. Equation 7 tells us that almost all the affine invariant functions derived till now (from the published papers [4, 1, 5, 12, 13] and [3]) are computed from this function, where Wx_k and Wy_k are selected to be either the wavelet details coefficients(as in [4, 1, 5], and [3]) or the approximation and details coefficients (as in [12], and [13]).

It should be noted that the first 2 or 3 levels of the details coefficients are usually small in amplitude and are highly sensitive to noise. To overcome this problem these levels were avoided in computing the invariant functions that depend on the details coefficients (all the above systems). A less sensitive to small variations function is computed by considering the approximations coefficients only

$$I_4(i,j,k) = A_j\tilde{x}_k A_i\tilde{y}_k - A_i\tilde{x}_k A_j\tilde{y}_k = det(C)[A_jx_k A_iy_k - A_ix_k A_jy_k] \tag{8}$$

where $A_j\tilde{x}_k$, $A_i\tilde{x}_k$ are the distorted approximations coefficients of x_k at scales j and i, A_jx_k, A_ix_k are the original ones, $A_j\tilde{y}_k$, $A_i\tilde{y}_k$ are the distorted approximations coefficients of y_k at scales j and i, A_jy_k, A_iy_k are the original one, and $det(C)$ is the determinant of the transformation matrix.

This function is a relative invariant function (due to the existence of the determinant $det(C)$), and it can be made an absolute invariant function by dividing by another function computed from (at least one) different scale levels, or by dividing by any significant (non-zero) value from the same equation. (e.g. maximum value).

Another invariant function is derived from the approximation coefficients by applying two different wavelet transforms with different wavelet basis functions. The invariant function would look like:

$$I_5(i,j,k) = A_j^1\tilde{x}_k A_i^2\tilde{y}_k - A_i^2\tilde{x}_k A_j^1\tilde{y}_k = det(C)[A_j^1x_k A_i^2y_k - A_i^2x_k A_j^1y_k] \tag{9}$$

where $A_j^1\tilde{x}_k$ and $A_j^1\tilde{y}_k$ are the approximation coefficients of the distorted boundary after applying the first wavelet transform, $A_j^1x_k$ and $A_j^1y_k$ are the approximations of the original boundary resulted from the same transform, $A_j^2\tilde{x}_k$ and $A_j^2\tilde{y}_k$ are the approximation coefficients of the distorted boundary after applying the second wavelet transform, and $A_j^2x_k$ and $A_j^2y_k$ are the approximation coefficients of the original boundary resulted from the same transform.

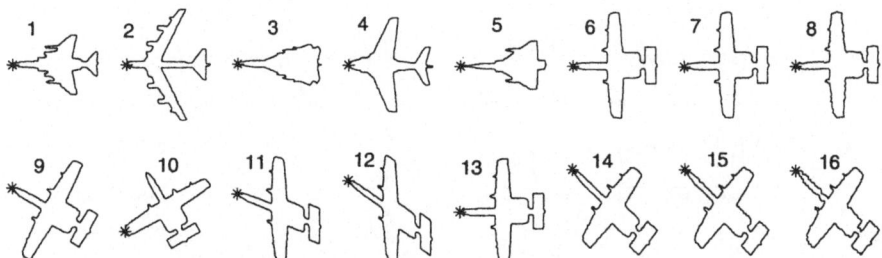

Fig. 1. Sample of the shapes used in our experiment, the asterisks show the boundary starting point

The advantages of using two different wavelet transforms with different basis functions is that the discrimination between shapes increases. This is because of the increase in the number of the invariant functions that can be obtained from this equation, which also helps in deriving higher order invariant functions using four (or more) different scale levels.

4   Experimental Results

Sample of the shapes used in our experiment are shown in figure 1. Shapes 1 to 6 are the boundaries extracted from 6 different shapes, while shapes 7 and 8 are noisy versions of shape 6. Shapes 9 to 14 are affine distorted shapes computed from shape 6 whereas shapes 15 and 16 are the noisy versions of shape 14. The affine distorted shapes $(9 - 14)$ are obtained by applying the transformation shown in equation 10 (the translation parameters are removed by calculating and subtracting the centroid of the shape)

$$\begin{bmatrix} \tilde{x} \\ \tilde{y} \end{bmatrix} = [T_{affine}] \begin{bmatrix} x \\ y \end{bmatrix} \tag{10}$$

where x and y are the pixel locations of the original 2-D shape, $\tilde{x}$ and $\tilde{y}$ are the distorted pixel locations, and T_{affine} [8] is the affine transformation matrix and is given by

$$T_{affine} = sc \begin{bmatrix} cos(\theta) & -sin(\theta) \\ sin(\theta) & cos(\theta) \end{bmatrix} \begin{bmatrix} 1 & sk \\ 0 & 1 \end{bmatrix} \tag{11}$$

Table 1. Affine transformation parameters and SNRs used in our experiment

Shape	1	2	3	4	5	6	7	8	9	10	11	12	13	14	15	16
sc	1	1	1	1	1	1	1	1	1	1	1	1	0.75	0.75	0.75	0.75
θ	0	0	0	0	0	0	0	0	30°	60°	0	0	0	45°	45°	45°
sk	0	0	0	0	0	0	0	0	0	0	0.3	0.7	0	0.4	0.4	0.4
SNR	-	-	-	-	-	-	39.2	33.1	-	-	-	-	-	-	38.3	32

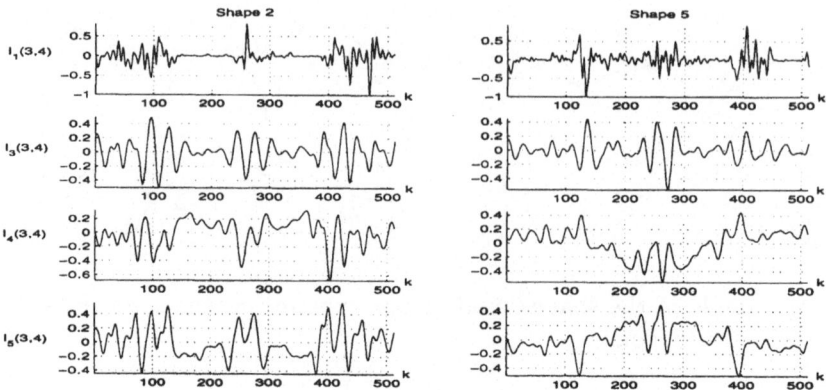

Fig. 2. The invariant functions of shapes 2, and 5 computed from scales 3 and 4

where sc is the scale, θ is the rotation angle, and sk is the skew parameter. The noisy shapes are obtained by adding a uniformly distributed noise to shapes 6 and 14. Table 1 shows the affine transformation parameters and the signal-to-noise ratios (SNRs) used in our experiment.

After extracting the boundary of each shape, the boundary sequences x_k and y_k are normalized to have the same length for all shapes before applying the WT. All shapes in our experiment are resampled to have 512 points, so the DWT decomposes the sequences x_k and y_k into 9 different scale levels. We used quadratic spline for the single WT, and quadratic spline and Daubechies (db12) for the two WT. The functions tested in this experiment are equations 1, 3, 8, and 9. Figures 2 illustrates the invariant functions computed for shapes 2 and 5 using the scale levels 3 and 4. Figure 3, illustrates these functions for the original (shape 6), and the affine and noisy (shape 15) shape for the scale levels 2 and 3. This figure shows that the degree of invariance of I_1 (equations 1), and I_3

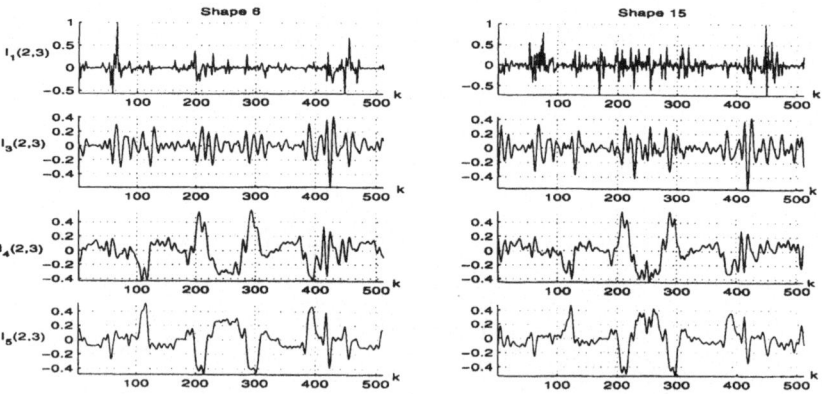

Fig. 3. The invariant functions of shapes 6, and 15 computed from scales 2 and 3

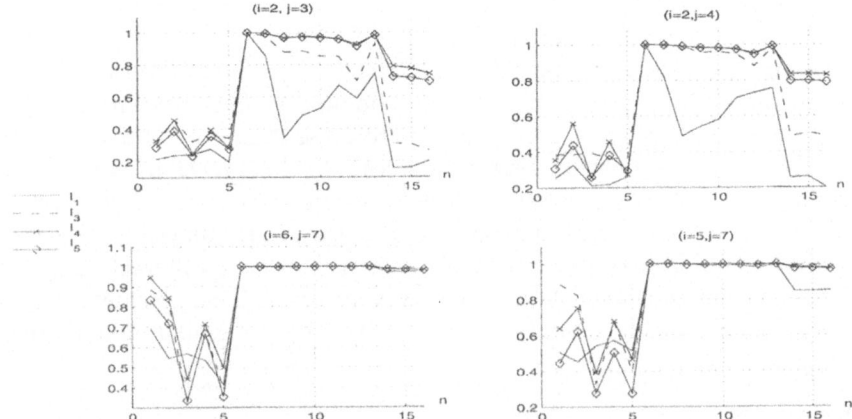

Fig. 4. The maximum correlation values computed between shape 6 and all other shapes (n=1 to 16) at different scale levels and differences, the first column is computed using $i - j = 1$ while the last column is computed for $i - j = 2$

(equation 3) decreases in the finer levels, and that these invariants are sensitive to small variations in these levels (even in the absence of added noise). While I_4 and I_5 (equations 8 and 9) appear to be less sensitive to these variations in theses levels.

The normalized correlation function defined in [4] is used in our experiment to measure the similarity between any two invariant functions. For two sequences a_k and b_k, the normalized correlation equals

$$R_{ab}(l) = \frac{\sum_l \sum_k a_k b_{k-l}}{\sqrt{\sum_k a_k^2 \sum_k b_k^2}} \tag{12}$$

Since the correlation is not translation invariant, one of the functions (a_k or b_k) is made periodic (for 3 periods) then the maximum value of the correlation is selected. This will reduce the effect of the starting point variation of the shape boundary on the calculations.

Figure 4 illustrates the maximum correlation values for the tested shapes. The shown maximum correlation values were computed between shape 6 and all other shapes. From these plots, it is clear that the derived functions (equations 8, and 9) can easily distinguish between different shapes and that equations 1, 3 fail to do this. This is because that equations 1, 3 are based on the the wavelet details which are highly sensitive to noise and small variations in the first scale levels. In the coarser scale levels, equation 3 has more discrimination between different shapes. This is because that the approximation coefficients capture global features and tends to be equal for globally similar shapes. The second column in figure 4 shows that the discrimination is improved by taking $i - j = 2$, which means that it will increase for large scale level differences (i.e. $i - j \geq 2$).

5 Conclusions

In this paper, we derived two affine invariant shape representation functions based on the approximations of the shape boundary. The experimental results show that these functions are less sensitive to noise than the details-based functions. Also the discrimination between shapes for these functions is increased by increasing the scale level differences. New invariant functions could be computed by combining the details and the approximations invariant functions. These functions will be used in measuring the dissimilarities between different shapes. The details-based functions will be used for measuring the local dissimilarities, and the approximations-based will be used in measuring the global dissimilarities.

References

[1] R. Alferez and Y. Wang. Geometric and illumination invariants for object recognition. *IEEE Transactions on Pattern Analysis and Machine Intelligence*, 21(6):505–536, June 1999.

[2] L. Costa and R. Cesar Jr. *Shape Analysis and Classification, Theory and Practice.* CRC Press LLC, 2001.

[3] M. Khalil and M. Bayoumi. Affine invariant object recogniton using dyadic wavelet transform. *2000 Canadian Conference on Electrical and Computer Engineering*, 1:421–425, 2000.

[4] M. Khalil and M. Bayoumi. A dyadic wavelet affine invariant function for 2-D shape recognition. *IEEE Transaction on Pattern Recognition and Machine Intelligence*, 23(10):1152–1164, October 2001.

[5] M. Khalil and M. Bayoumi. Affine invariants for object recognition using the wavelet transform. *Pattern Recognition Letters*, 23:57–72, 2002.

[6] S. Mallat. *A Wavelet tour of signal processing.* Academic Press, second edition, 1999.

[7] P. Otterloo. *A contour-Oriented Approach to Shape Analysis.* Printice Hall Int., 1991.

[8] T. Reiss. *Recognizing Planar Objects Using Invariant Image Features.* Springer-Verlag, 1991.

[9] M. Sonka, V. Hlavac, and R. Boyle. *Image Processing Analysis and Machine Vision.* PWS Publishing, 1999.

[10] Q. Tieng and W. Boles. Complex daubechies wavelet based affine invariant representation for object recognition. *IEEE International Conference, Image Processing*, 1:198–202, 1994.

[11] Q. Tieng and W. Boles. Object recognition using an affine invariant wavelet representation. *Proceedings of the 1994 Second Australian and New Zealand Conference on Intelligent Information Systems*, pages 307–311, 1994.

[12] Q. Tieng and W. Boles. An application of wavelet based affine invariant representation. *Pattern Recognition Letters*, 16:1287–1296, 1995.

[13] Q. Tieng and W. Boles. Wavelet based affine invariant representation: a tool for recognising planar objects in 3-D space. *IEEE Trans. Pattern Analysis and Machine Intelligence*, 19(8):846–857, Aug 1997.

A Feature Selection Wrapper for Mixtures*

Mário A. T. Figueiredo[1], Anil K. Jain[2], and Martin H. Law[2]

[1] Instituto de Telecomunicações, and
Departamento de Engenharia Electrotécnica e de Computadores.
Instituto Superior Técnico, 1049-001 Lisboa, PORTUGAL
mtf@lx.it.pt
[2] Department of Computer Science and Engineering, Michigan State University
East Lansing, MI 48824, U.S.A.
jain@cse.msu.edu, lawhiu@cse.msu.edu

Abstract. We propose a feature selection approach for clustering which extends Koller and Sahami's mutual-information-based criterion to the unsupervised case. This is achieved with the help of a mixture-based model and the corresponding expectation-maximization algorithm. The result is a backward search scheme, able to sort the features by order of relevance. Finally, an MDL criterion is used to prune the sorted list of features, yielding a feature selection criterion. The proposed approach can be classified as a *wrapper*, since it wraps the mixture estimation algorithm in an outer layer that performs feature selection. Preliminary experimental results show that the proposed method has promising performance.

1   Introduction

A great deal of research has been devoted to the *feature selection* (FS) problem in supervised learning [1, 2, 3] (a.k.a. *variable selection* or *subset selection* [4]). FS is important for a variety of reasons: it may improve the performance of classifiers learned from limited amounts of data; it leads to more economical (both in storage and computation) classifiers; in many cases, it leads to interpretable models. However, FS for unsupervised learning has not received much attention.

In mixture-based unsupervised learning (clustering [5]), each group of data is modelled as having been generated according to a probability distribution with known form. Learning then consists of estimating the parameters of these distributions, and is usually done via the *expectation-maximization* (EM) algorithm [6, 7, 8]. Although standard EM assumes that the number of components/groups is known, extensions which also estimate this number are also available (see recent work in [9] and references therein).

Here, we address the FS problem in mixture-based clustering, by extending the mutual-information based criterion proposed in [1] to the unsupervised context. The proposed approach can be classified as a *wrapper* [2], in the sense that

---

* Work partially supported by the Foundation for Science and Technology (Portugal), grant POSI/33143/SRI/2000, and the Office of Naval Research (USA), grant 00014-01-1-0266.

F.J. Perales et al. (Eds.): IbPRIA 2003, LNCS 2652, pp. 229–237, 2003.

the feature selection procedure is *wrapped around* the EM algorithm. This wrapper is able to sort the variables by order of relevance, using backward search. An MDL criterion is used to prune this sorted list leaving a set of *relevant* features.

Finally, let us briefly review previously proposed FS methods in unsupervised learning. In [10], a heuristic to compare the quality of different feature subsets, based on cluster separability, is suggested. A Bayesian approach used in [11] evaluates different feature subsets and numbers of clusters for multinomial mixtures. In [12], the clustering tendency of each feature is assessed by an entropy index. A genetic algorithm was used in [13] for FS in k-means clustering. Finally, [14] uses the notion of "category utility" for FS in a conceptual clustering task.

2   Mixture Based Clustering and the EM Algorithm

Mixture models allow a probabilistic approach to clustering ([6, 7, 8]) in which model selection issues (*e.g.*, number of clusters) can be formally addressed. Given n i.i.d. samples $\mathcal{Y} = \{\mathbf{y}_1, ..., \mathbf{y}_n\}$, the log-likelihood of a k-component mixture is

$$\log p(\mathcal{Y}|\boldsymbol{\theta}) = \log \prod_{i=1}^{n} p(\mathbf{y}_i|\boldsymbol{\theta}) = \sum_{i=1}^{n} \log \sum_{m=1}^{k} \alpha_m p(\mathbf{y}_i|\boldsymbol{\theta}_m), \tag{1}$$

where $\alpha_1, ..., \alpha_k \geq 0$ are the *mixing probabilities* ($\sum_m \alpha_m = 1$), $\boldsymbol{\theta}_m$ is the set of parameters of the m-th component, and $\boldsymbol{\theta} \equiv \{\boldsymbol{\theta}_1, ..., \boldsymbol{\theta}_k, \alpha_1, ..., \alpha_k\}$ is the full set of parameters. Each $\mathbf{y}_i$ is a d-dimensional vector of features $[y_{i,1}, ..., y_{i,d}]^T$, and we assume that all the components have the same form (*e.g.*, Gaussian).

Neither the *maximum likelihood* (ML), $\widehat{\boldsymbol{\theta}}_{\mathrm{ML}} = \arg\max_{\boldsymbol{\theta}} \log p(\mathcal{Y}|\boldsymbol{\theta})$, nor the *maximum a posteriori* (MAP), $\widehat{\boldsymbol{\theta}}_{\mathrm{MAP}} = \arg\max_{\boldsymbol{\theta}} \{\log p(\mathcal{Y}|\boldsymbol{\theta}) + \log p(\boldsymbol{\theta})\}$, estimates can be found analytically. The usual alternative is the EM algorithm [7, 8, 15, 16], which finds local maxima of $\log p(\mathcal{Y}|\boldsymbol{\theta})$ or $[\log p(\mathcal{Y}|\boldsymbol{\theta}) + \log p(\boldsymbol{\theta})]$.

EM is based on seeing $\mathcal{Y}$ as *incomplete* data, the *missing* part being a set of n labels $\mathcal{Z} = \{\mathbf{z}_1, ..., \mathbf{z}_n\}$, flagging which component produced each sample. Each label is a binary vector $\mathbf{z}_i = [z_{i,1}, ..., z_{i,k}]$, with $z_{i,m} = 1$ and $z_{i,p} = 0$, for $p \neq m$, meaning that $\mathbf{y}_i$ is a sample of $p(\cdot|\boldsymbol{\theta}_m)$. The complete log-likelihood (*i.e.*, given both $\mathcal{Y}$ and $\mathcal{Z}$) is

$$\log p(\mathcal{Y}, \mathcal{Z}|\boldsymbol{\theta}) = \sum_{i=1}^{n} \sum_{m=1}^{k} z_{i,m} \log[\alpha_m p(\mathbf{y}_i|\boldsymbol{\theta}_m)]. \tag{2}$$

The EM algorithm produces a sequence of estimates $\{\widehat{\boldsymbol{\theta}}(t), \ t = 0, 1, 2, ...\}$ by alternatingly applying two steps (until some convergence criterion is met):

• **E-step:** Compute the conditional expectation $\mathcal{W} = E[\mathcal{Z}|\mathcal{Y}, \widehat{\boldsymbol{\theta}}(t)]$, and plug it into $\log p(\mathcal{Y}, \mathcal{Z}|\boldsymbol{\theta})$, yielding the so-called Q-function: $Q(\boldsymbol{\theta}, \widehat{\boldsymbol{\theta}}(t)) = \log p(\mathcal{Y}, \mathcal{W}|\boldsymbol{\theta})$. Since the elements of $\mathcal{Z}$ are binary, their conditional expectations are given by

$$w_{i,m} \equiv E\left[z_{i,m}|\mathcal{Y}, \widehat{\boldsymbol{\theta}}(t)\right] = \Pr\left[z_{i,m} = 1|\mathbf{y}_i, \widehat{\boldsymbol{\theta}}(t)\right] \propto \widehat{\alpha}_m(t) \, p(\mathbf{y}_i|\widehat{\boldsymbol{\theta}}_m(t)) \tag{3}$$

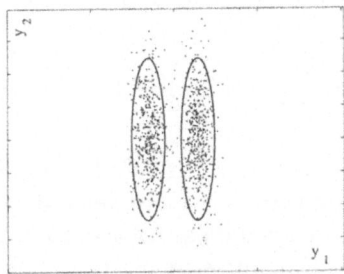

Fig. 1. Feature y_1 is relevant to the mixture nature of the data, while y_2 is not

(normalized such that $\sum_m w_{i,m} = 1$). Notice that α_m is the *a priori* probability that $z_{i,m} = 1$ (*i.e.*, that $\mathbf{y}_i$ belongs to cluster m) while $w_{i,m}$ is the corresponding *a posteriori* probability, after observing $\mathbf{y}_i$.

• **M-step:** Update the parameter estimates, $\widehat{\boldsymbol{\theta}}(t+1) = \arg\max_{\boldsymbol{\theta}} \{Q(\boldsymbol{\theta}, \widehat{\boldsymbol{\theta}}(t)) + \log p(\boldsymbol{\theta})\}$, in the case of MAP estimation, or without $\log p(\boldsymbol{\theta})$ in the ML case.

3   Feature Selection for Mixtures

3.1   Likelihood Formulation

Consider the example in Fig. 1: a 2-component bivariate Gaussian mixture. In this example, y_2 is clearly irrelevant for the "mixture nature" of the data. However, *principal component analysis* (PCA, one of the standard non-supervised feature sorting methods) of this data would declare y_2 as more relevant because it explains more data variance than y_1.

To address the FS problem for mixtures, we divide the available feature set $\mathbf{y} = [y_1, ..., y_d]$ into two subsets $\mathbf{y}_U$ and $\mathbf{y}_N$. Here, U and N (standing for "useful" and "non-useful") are two disjoint sub-sets of indices such that $U \cup N = \{1, 2, ..., d\}$. Our key assumption is that the non-useful features are independent of the useful ones, and their distribution is the same for all classes/clusters, *i.e.*,

$$p(\mathbf{y}|U, \boldsymbol{\theta}_U, \boldsymbol{\theta}_N) = p(\mathbf{y}_N|\boldsymbol{\theta}_N) \sum_{m=1}^{k} \alpha_m p(\mathbf{y}_U|\boldsymbol{\theta}_{m,U}), \tag{4}$$

where $\boldsymbol{\theta}_N$ is the set of parameters characterizing the distribution of the non-useful features, and $\boldsymbol{\theta}_U = [\boldsymbol{\theta}_{1,U}, ..., \boldsymbol{\theta}_{k,U}]$ is the set of parameters characterizing the mixture distribution of the useful features. Notice that we only need to specify U, because $N = \{1, 2, ..., d\} \backslash U$. The feature selection problem is then to find U and the corresponding parameter $\boldsymbol{\theta} = [\boldsymbol{\theta}_U, \boldsymbol{\theta}_N]$. Let us highlight some aspects of this formulation:

– Consider maximizing the log-likelihood, given observations $\mathcal{Y} = \{\mathbf{y}_1, ..., \mathbf{y}_n\}$,

$$\log p(\mathcal{Y}|U, \boldsymbol{\theta}_U, \boldsymbol{\theta}_N) = \sum_{i=1}^{n} \log p(\mathbf{y}_{i,N}|\boldsymbol{\theta}_N) + \sum_{i=1}^{n} \log \sum_{m=1}^{k} \alpha_m p(\mathbf{y}_{i,U}|\boldsymbol{\theta}_{m,U}), \quad (5)$$

with respect to U, $\boldsymbol{\theta}_U$ and $\boldsymbol{\theta}_N$. The result would be $U = \{1, ..., d\}$ (as noted in [11]), because a mixture is a more general model and so we can never decrease the likelihood by increasing the number of useful features. This shows that the problem requires some model selection criterion.

– Testing all possible 2^d partitions of $\{1, 2, ..., d\}$ into U and N is prohibitive, even for moderate d. The standard alternative is to use sub-optimal methods, such as sequential forward/backward search (SFS/SBS) schemes [3].

3.2   Connection with Feature Selection for Supervised Learning

Assume the class labels and the full feature vector follow some probability function $p(\mathbf{z}, \mathbf{y})$. A subset of features $\mathbf{y}_N$ is non-useful/irrelevant if it is conditionally independent of the labels, given the useful features $\mathbf{y}_U$ (see [1]), *i.e.*, if

$$p(\mathbf{z}|\mathbf{y}) = p(\mathbf{z}|\mathbf{y}_U, \mathbf{y}_N) = p(\mathbf{z}|\mathbf{y}_U). \quad (6)$$

Observation of the model in (4) reveals that we can look at the m-th mixture component as being $p(\mathbf{y}|\boldsymbol{\theta}_m) = p(\mathbf{y}_U|\boldsymbol{\theta}_{m,U})p(\mathbf{y}_N|\boldsymbol{\theta}_N)$. The outcome of the E-step of the EM algorithm (3), omitting the iteration counter (t) and the sample index i for notational economy, is then

$$w_m = \frac{\alpha_m\, p(\mathbf{y}_U|\boldsymbol{\theta}_{m,U})p(\mathbf{y}_N|\boldsymbol{\theta}_N)}{\sum_{j=1}^{k} \alpha_j\, p(\mathbf{y}_U|\boldsymbol{\theta}_{j,U})p(\mathbf{y}_N|\boldsymbol{\theta}_N)} = \frac{\alpha_m\, p(\mathbf{y}_U|\boldsymbol{\theta}_{m,U})}{\sum_{j=1}^{k} \alpha_j\, p(\mathbf{y}_U|\boldsymbol{\theta}_{j,U})}. \quad (7)$$

Recalling that $w_m = \mathrm{Prob}[\mathbf{y} \in \text{class } m|\mathbf{y}, \boldsymbol{\theta}]$, we can read (7) as: given $\mathbf{y}_U$, the probability that an observation belongs to any class m is independent of $\mathbf{y}_N$. This reveals the link between the likelihood (4) and the irrelevance criterion (6), based on conditional independence.

3.3   A Feature Usefulness Measure for Unsupervised Learning

In practice, there are no strictly non-useful features, but features exhibiting some degree of "non-usefulness". A natural measure of the degree of independence, as suggested in [1], is the expected value of the *Kullback-Leibler divergence* (KLD, or relative entropy [17]). The KLD between two probability mass functions $p_1(x)$ and $p_2(x)$, over a common (discrete) probability space Ω, is

$$\mathcal{D}_{KL}[p_1(x) \,\|\, p_2(x)] = \sum_{x \in \Omega} p_1(x) \log \frac{p_1(x)}{p_2(x)},$$

and satisfies $\mathcal{D}_{KL}[p_1(x) \parallel p_2(x)] \geq 0$, and $\mathcal{D}_{KL}[p_1(x) \parallel p_2(x)] = 0$, if and only if $p_1(x) = p_2(x)$, for all $x \in \Omega$. The relationship between conditional independence as stated in (6) and the KLD is given by the following implication

$$p(\mathbf{z}|\mathbf{y}_U, \mathbf{y}_N) = p(\mathbf{z}|\mathbf{y}_U) \quad \Rightarrow \quad \mathcal{D}_{KL}[p(\mathbf{z}|\mathbf{y}_U, \mathbf{y}_N)) \parallel p(\mathbf{z}|\mathbf{y}_U))] = 0, \qquad (8)$$

for all values of $\mathbf{y}_U$ and $\mathbf{y}_N$. To obtain a measure of usefulness of a feature set, we have to average this measure over all possible feature values, according to their distribution [1]. In practice, both the KLD and its average over the feature space are approximated by their sample versions on the training samples.

In unsupervised learning we only have the feature samples $\mathcal{Y} = \{\mathbf{y}_1, ..., \mathbf{y}_n\}$, but no labels $\mathcal{Z} = \{\mathbf{z}_1, ..., \mathbf{z}_n\}$. However, after running the EM algorithm we have their expected values $\mathcal{W} = \{w_{i,m}, \ m = 1, ..., k, \ i = 1, ..., n\}$. To build a sample-based feature usefulness measure, assume that $\mathcal{W}$ was obtained using the full feature set, and let $\widehat{\boldsymbol{\theta}}$ be the corresponding parameter vector. Now let $\mathcal{V}(N) = \{v_{i,m}(N), \ m = 1, ..., k, \ i = 1, ..., n\}$ be the expected label values obtained using only the features in the corresponding useful subset $U = \{1, ..., d\} \backslash N$, that is,

$$v_{i,m}(N) = \widehat{\alpha}_m \, p(\mathbf{y}_{i,U}|\widehat{\boldsymbol{\theta}}_{m,U}) \left(\sum_{j=1}^{k} \widehat{\alpha}_j \, p(\mathbf{y}_{i,U}|\widehat{\boldsymbol{\theta}}_{j,U}) \right)^{-1}. \qquad (9)$$

Then, a natural measure of the "non-usefulness" of the features in N is

$$\Upsilon(N) = \frac{1}{n} \sum_{i=1}^{n} \sum_{m=1}^{k} w_{i,m} \log \frac{w_{i,m}}{v_{i,m}(N)}, \qquad (10)$$

which is the sample mean of KLDs between the expected class labels obtained with and without the features in N. A low value of $\Upsilon(N)$ indicates that $\mathbf{y}_N$ is "almost" conditionally independent of the expected class labels, given $\mathbf{y}_U$.

4   A Sequential Backward Feature Sorting Algorithm

4.1   The Algorithm

Of course, evaluating $\Upsilon(N)$ for all 2^d possible subsets is unfeasible, even for moderate values of d. Instead, we propose a sequential backward search (SBS) scheme (Fig. 2) which starts with the full set of features set and removes them one by one in the order of irrelevance (according to the criterion (10)). This algorithm will produce an ordered set $I = \{i_1, ..., i_d\}$, which is a permutation of $\{1, 2, ..., d\}$ corresponding to a sorting of the features by increasing usefulness.

4.2   An Illustrative Example: Trunk's Data

To illustrate the algorithm, we use the problem suggested by Trunk [18]: two equiprobable d-variate Gaussian classes, with identity covariance and means

Input: Training data $\mathcal{Y} = \{\mathbf{y}^{(1)}, ..., \mathbf{y}^{(n)}\}$
Output: Set I of sorted feature indices.
  Initialization:
  $I \leftarrow \{\}$
  $U \leftarrow \{1, 2, ..., d\}$
  Run EM with all the features to get $\mathcal{W} = \{w_{i,m}, \ m = 1, ..., k, \ i = 1, ..., n\}$
  while $|I| < d$ **do**
    $\Upsilon_{\min} \leftarrow +\infty$
    for $i \in U$ **do**
      $I'_i \leftarrow \{i\} \cup I$
      Compute $\Upsilon(I'_i)$ according to (10)
      if $\Upsilon(I'_i) < \Upsilon_{\min}$ **then**
        $\Upsilon_{\min} \leftarrow \Upsilon(I'_i)$
        $i_{\min} \leftarrow i$
      end if
    end for
    $I \leftarrow \{i_{\min}\} \cup I$
    $U \leftarrow U \backslash \{i_{\min}\}$
    Update $\mathcal{W}$ by running EM using only the features in U.
  end while

Fig. 2. Feature sorting algorithm. Notice that the sets used in the algorithm are ordered sets and the set union preserves that ordering (*e.g.*, $\{c\} \cup \{b, a\} = \{c, b, a\} \neq \{a, b, c\}$)

$\boldsymbol{\mu}_1 = [1, 1/\sqrt{2}, 1/\sqrt{3}, ..., 1/\sqrt{d}]^T$ and $\boldsymbol{\mu}_2 = -\boldsymbol{\mu}_1$. Clearly, these features are already sorted in order of usefulness, and so any feature sorting scheme can be evaluated by how much it agrees with this ordering. In [3] (for supervised learning) a measure of the quality of the sorted set $I = \{i_1, ..., i_d\}$ was defined as

$$Q(I) = \frac{1}{d-1} \sum_{i=1}^{d-1} \frac{|I_1^i \cap \{1, ..., i\}| + |I_{i+1}^d \cap \{i+1, ..., d\}|}{d},$$

where $I_a^b = \{i_a, i_{a+1}, ..., i_b\}$. Note that $Q(I)$ is a measure of agreement between I and the optimal feature ordering $\{1, 2, ..., d\}$, with $Q(I) = 1$ meaning perfect agreement. Fig. 3 plots $Q(I)$ versus the sample set size, for $d = 20$, averaged over 5 data sets for each sample size. Remarkably, these values are extremely similar to those reported in [3], although here we are in an unsupervised learning scenario. Finally, the $\Upsilon_{\min}$ values are a measure of the relevance of each feature; in Fig. 3 we plot these values for the case of 500 samples per class.

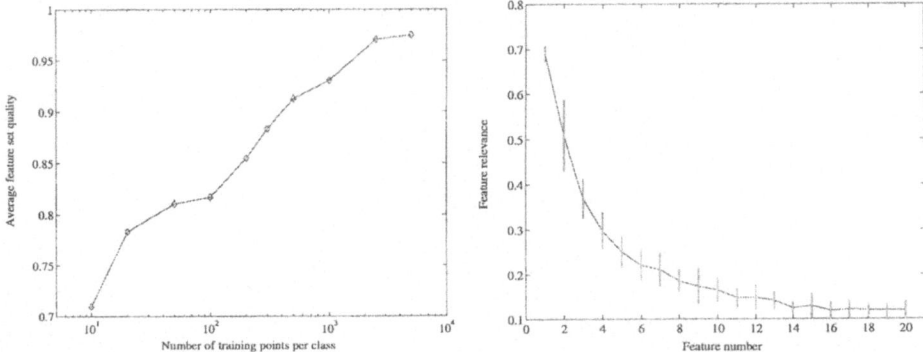

Fig. 3. Trunk data example. Left: feature sorting quality versus training set size. Right: feature relevance averaged over 20 data sets (vertical bars are $\pm$ 1 standard dev.)

5   Feature Selection by MDL

5.1   The Criterion

Having features sorted by order of relevance, we may now look for the best place to cut this sorted list, for a given data set. To this end, we return to the likelihood formulation (4), and to a comment made above: maximizing the likelihood leads to the selection of a full feature set. To avoid this over-fitting, we resort to the *minimum description length* (MDL) principle [19], criterion:

$$\widehat{U} = \arg\min_{U} \left\{ \min_{\boldsymbol{\theta}_U,\boldsymbol{\theta}_N} \left\{ -\log p(\mathcal{Y}|U,\boldsymbol{\theta}_U,\boldsymbol{\theta}_N) \right\} + \frac{|\boldsymbol{\theta}_U| + |\boldsymbol{\theta}_N|}{2} \log(n) \right\}, \quad (11)$$

where $\log p(\mathcal{Y}|U,\boldsymbol{\theta}_U,\boldsymbol{\theta}_N)$ is given in (5) and $|\boldsymbol{\theta}_U|$ and $|\boldsymbol{\theta}_N|$ are the total numbers of parameters in $\boldsymbol{\theta}_U$ and $\boldsymbol{\theta}_N$, respectively. Notice that the inner minimization simply corresponds to the ML estimate of $\boldsymbol{\theta}_U$ and $\boldsymbol{\theta}_N$ for a given U, obtained by the EM algorithm for $\boldsymbol{\theta}_U$ and by simple maximum likelihood estimates in the case of $\boldsymbol{\theta}_N$. The numbers of parameters $|\boldsymbol{\theta}_U|$ and $|\boldsymbol{\theta}_U|$ depend on the particular form of $p(\mathbf{y}_N|\boldsymbol{\theta}_N)$ and $p(\mathbf{y}_U|\boldsymbol{\theta}_{m,U})$. For example, with Gaussian mixtures with arbitrary mean and covariance, $|\boldsymbol{\theta}_U| = k(3u + u^2)/2$. With $p(\mathbf{y}_N|\boldsymbol{\theta}_N)$ also a Gaussian density with arbitrary mean and covariance, $|\boldsymbol{\theta}_N| = (3(d - u) + (d - u)^2)/2$.

This MDL criterion is used to select which features to keep, by searching for the solution of (11) among the following set of candidate subsets, produced by the feature sorting algorithm of Fig. 2: $\{I_1^q = \{i_1, ..., i_q\}; \ q = 1, ..., d\}$.

5.2   Illustrative Example

We *illustrate the behavior* of the feature selection algorithm with a simple synthetic example. Consider a three-component mixture in 8 dimensions

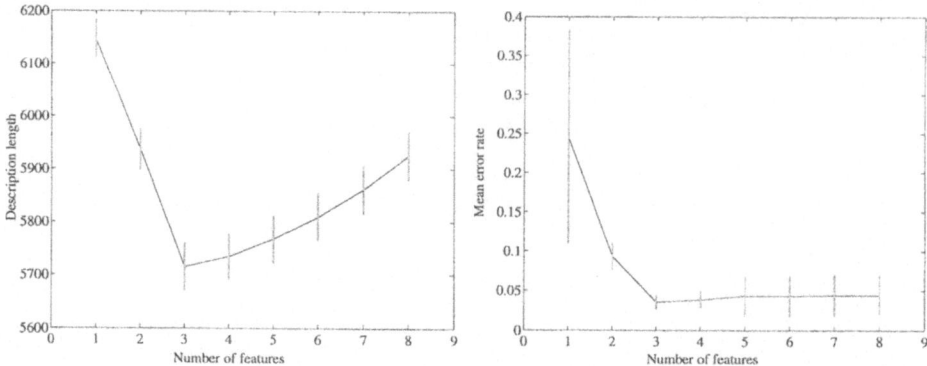

Fig. 4. MDL-based feature selection example. Left: description length, (11), as a function of the number of "useful" features (mean curve for 40 tests, ± one standard deviation). Right plot: mean error rate (also for 40 tests, ± one standard deviation)

with component means $\mu_1 = [3,0,0,0,...,0]^T, \mu_2 = [0,3,0,0,...,0]^T, \mu_3 = [0,0,3,0,...,0]^T$, and identity covariance matrices. Clearly, only the first three features are relevant to the mixture, features 4 to 8 are simply "noise". We have applied the feature sorting algorithm described above to 40 sets of 450 samples of this mixture (150 per class) and features 1, 2, and 3 were always placed ahead of the others in the sorted feature list. Next, we used the criterion in (11) to select the "optimal" number of features, and three features were always selected; the left plot in Fig. 4 shows the mean description length curve for the 40 tests, with ± one standard deviation bars. Since we have the true class labels for this data, we have computed error rates, which are plotted on the right side of Fig. 4 (again, mean over 40 test, ± one standard deviation bars); notice that the minimum error rate is achieved for the true number of relevant features; observe also that with too few or too many features, the obtained classifier becomes more instable (larger error bars).

6   Concluding Remarks

We have presented an approach to feature sorting and selection for mixture-based clustering. Tests on synthetic data show that the method is promising. Of course the method has yet to be extensively tested on real data, but assessing the quality of a feature selection method for unsupervised learning with real data is not an obvious task. Future developments will include extending the method to also estimate the number of clusters, by wrapping the feature selection procedure around a mixture-fitting algorithm that estimates the number of components (such as the one in [9]). Also, searching strategies other than backward search (*e.g.*, floating search [3]) will be considered in future work.

References

[1] D. Koller and M. Sahami, "Toward optimal feature selection," in *Proceedings of the International Conference on Machine Learning*, (Bari, Italy), pp. 284–292, 1996.

[2] R. Kohavi and G. John, "Wrappers for feature subset selection," *Artificial Intelligence*, vol. 97, no. 1-2, pp. 273–324, 1997.

[3] A. K. Jain and D. Zongker, "Feature selection: Evaluation, application, and small sample performance," *IEEE Transactions on Pattern Analysis and Machine Intelligence*, vol. 19, no. 2, pp. 153–158, 1997.

[4] T. Hastie, R. Tibshirani, and J. Friedman, *The Elements of Statistical Learning*. New York: Springer Verlag, 2001.

[5] A. K. Jain and R. Dubes, *Algorithms for Clustering Data*. Englewood Cliffs, N. J.: Prentice Hall, 1988.

[6] C. Fraley and A. Raftery, "Model based clustering, discriminant analysis, and density estimation," *Journal of the American Statist. Assoc.*, vol. 97, pp. 611–631, 2002.

[7] G. McLachlan and K. Basford, *Mixture Models: Inference and Application to Clustering*. New York: Marcel Dekker, 1988.

[8] G. McLachlan and D. Peel, *Finite Mixture Models*. New York: John Wiley & Sons, 2000.

[9] M. Figueiredo and A. K. Jain, "Unsupervised learning of finite mixture models," *IEEE Trans. on Pattern Analysis and Machine Intelligence*, vol. 24, pp. 381–396, 2002.

[10] J. Dy and C. Brodley, "Feature subset selection and order identification for unsupervised learning," in *Proc. 17th International Conf. on Machine Learning*, pp. 247–254, Morgan Kaufmann, San Francisco, CA, 2000.

[11] S. Vaithyanathan and B. Dom, "Generalized model selection for unsupervised learning in high dimensions," in *Advances in Neural Information Processing Systems 12* (S. Solla, T. Leen, and K.-R. Müller, eds.), MIT Press, 2000.

[12] M. Dash and H. Liu, "Feature selection for clustering," in *Proc. of Pacific-Asia Conference on Knowledge Discovery and Data Mining*, 2000.

[13] Y. Kim, W. Street, and F. Menczer, "Feature Selection in Unsupervised Learning via Evolutionary Search," in *Proceedings of the Sixth ACM SIGKDD International Conference on Knowledge Discovery and Data Mining*, 2000.

[14] M. Devaney and A. Ram, "Efficient feature selection in conceptual clustering," in *International Conference on Machine Learning*, pp. 92–97, 1997.

[15] A. Dempster, N. Laird, and D. Rubin, "Maximum likelihood estimation from incomplete data via the EM algorithm," *Journal of the Royal Statistical Society B*, vol. 39, pp. 1–38, 1977.

[16] G. McLachlan and T. Krishnan, *The EM Algorithm and Extensions*. New York: John Wiley & Sons, 1997.

[17] T. Cover and J. Thomas, *Elements of Information Theory*. New York: John Wiley & Sons, 1991.

[18] G. Trunk, "A problem of dimensionality: A simple example," *IEEE Trans. on Pattern Analysis and Machine Intelligence*, vol. 1, no. 3, pp. 306–307, 1979.

[19] J. Rissanen, *Stochastic Complexity in Stastistical Inquiry*. Singapore: World Scientific, 1989.

Tracking People
for Automatic Surveillance Applications

Luis M. Fuentes[1]* and Sergio A. Velastin[2]

[1] MoBiVA Group, Departamento de Óptica y Física Aplicada
Universidad de Valladolid
47071 Valladolid, Spain
luis.fuentes@computer.org,
[2] Digital Image Research Center, Kingston University
Penrhyn Road, Kingston upon Thames, Surrey KT1 2EE, UK

Abstract. The authors present a simple but robust real-time algorithm that allows tracking of multiple objects in complex environments. As the first stage, the foreground segmentation uses luminance contrast, reducing computation time avoiding the use colour information at this stage. Foreground pixels are then grouped into blobs analysing X-Y histograms. Tracking is achieved by matching blobs from two consecutive frames using overlapping information from bounding boxes and a linear prediction for the centroid's position. This method successfully solves blobs merging into groups and tracking them until they split again. Application in automatic surveillance is suggested by linking blob's information, in terms of trajectories and positions, with the events to be detected. Some examples in transport environments are outlined.

1 Introduction

The use of CCTV systems in surveillance has grown exponentially in the last decade. As noted by Norris [1] "the rise of CCTV surveillance system has to be seen in the context of underlying social, political and economic pressures which have led to the intensification of surveillance across a whole range of spheres and by a host of new technologies". In this context, experts predict an extensive application of CCTV surveillance system and its integration in a global surveillance network. However, this expansion requires technological aid to overcome the drawbacks associated with the huge amount of visual information generated by these surveillance systems [2]. Anything but reduced human monitoring became impossible by means of its physical and economic implications, and an advance towards an automated surveillance became the only solution. The concept of "advanced visual surveillance" involves not only the interpretation of a sequence of images but also the detection of predefined events susceptible of trigger an alarm. The use of constraints obtained from the knowledge of both, the task and the environment allows a greater computational efficiency [3]. However, intelligent surveillance systems have to deal with an especially difficult task

---

* This work was supported by UK's EPSRC founded project PerSec.

F.J. Perales et al. (Eds.): IbPRIA 2003, LNCS 2652, pp. 238–245, 2003.

when people and their behaviour are to be analysed. Some information may be obtained from the analysis of people trajectories and their interaction, involving, therefore, tracking. The analysis of a single blob position or trajectory can determine whether the person is standing in a forbidden area, running, jumping or hiding. Combining such information from two or more people may provide information about the interaction between them. In order to be successfully applied to security monitoring tasks, a visual surveillance system has to be able to process in real time more than one image channel. In certain environments, the number of CCTV surveillance cameras is so high that the idea of a dedicate PC for each one is simply unacceptable. Therefore, a simplification of the image processing stage is necessary in order to achieve real-time processing speed in four to eight image channels simultaneously. In the process leading from an acquired image to the information about objects in it, two steps are particularly important in computational terms: foreground segmentation and tracking. In this paper we present a foreground detection method based on luminance contrast and a straightforward tracking algorithm that relies only on blob matching information without using statistical descriptions to model or predict motion characteristics. Based on semantic description of predefined events, the system is able to detect them and rise an alert signal to the operator, the final decision-maker. In the approach presented here, the specific demands for CCTV surveillance systems applied to public transport environments will be analysed together with the appropriate image processing techniques in order to build an intelligence surveillance system being able to detect "potentially dangerous situations".

2   Related Work

Foreground detection algorithms are normally based on background subtraction algorithms (BSAs) [4, 5, 6]. These methods are based on extracting motion information by thresholding the differences between the current image and a reference image (background), which may be updated as to deal with changing lighting conditions [7, 8, 9], normally linked with outdoor environments. BSAs are widely used because they detect not only moving objects but also stationary objects not belonging to the scene. After the segmentation of the foreground pixels, some processing is needed to clean noisy pixels and define foreground objects. The cleaning process usually involves 3x3 median [8] or region-based [6] filtering, although some authors perform a filtering of both images -current and background- before computing the difference [5]. The proposed method is simpler. No model is needed for the background, just a single image. For outdoor applications this background image may be updated. Tracking algorithms establish a correspondence between the image structure of two consecutive frames. Typically the tracking process involves the matching of image features for non-rigid objects such as people, or correspondence models, widely used with rigid objects like cars. A description of different approaches can be found in Aggarwal's review, [10]. As the proposed tracking algorithm was developed for tracking people, we reduce the analysis of previous work to this particular field. Many approaches have been proposed for tracking a human body, as can be seen in some reviews [10], [11]. Some are applied in relatively controlled [5], [9], [12] or in variable outdoor environments [6], [8]. The proposed system works with blobs, defined as bounding boxes representing the foreground objects. Tracking is performed by matching boxes from two consecutive frames. The matching process uses the information of overlapping boxes [8], colour histogram back projection [13] or different blob features such as colour or distance between the blobs. In some approaches all these features are used to create the so-called matching matrices [4]. In many cases, Kalman filters are used to predict the position of the blob and match it with the closest blob [12]. The use of blob trajectory [12] or blob colour [8] helps to solve occlusion problems.

3   Segmentation

Foreground pixels detection is achieved using luminance contrast [14]. This method simplifies the background model, reducing it to a single image, and it also reduces computational time using just one coordinate in colour images. The central points of the method are described below.

3.1   Definition of Luminance Contrast

Luminance contrast is an important magnitude in psychophysics and the central point in the definition of the visibility of a particular object. Typically, luminance contrast is defined as the relative difference between object luminance, L_O, and surrounding background luminance, L_B. To apply this concept in foreground detection we propose an alternative contrast definition comparing the luminance coordinate in the YUV colour system 'y' of a pixel P(i,j) in both the current and the background images:

$$C(i,j) = \frac{y(i,j) - y_B(i,j)}{y_B(i,j)} \tag{1}$$

Luminance values are in the ranges [0,255] for images digitised in YUV format or [16,255] for images transformed from RGB coordinates [14]. Null (zero) values for background 'y' coordinate are changed to one because the infinite contrast value they produce has no physical meaning. With these possible luminance values, contrast will be in the non-symmetrical range [-1,254]. Values around zero are expected for background pixels, negative values for foreground pixels darker than their corresponding background pixels and positive values for brighter pixels. However, the highest values are obtained under the unusual circumstances of very bright objects against very dark backgrounds and values bigger than 10 are not likely to be obtained.

3.2   Foreground Detection and Blob Selection

According to the non-symmetrical distribution of contrast around zero, the foreground detection algorithm should use two different thresholds for positive C_P

and negative C_N values of contrast, depending on the nature of both the background and the objects to be segmented [14]. To simplify the discussion, we assume from now onwards a single contrast threshold C, that is $C_P = -C_N = C$. So, a pixel P(i,j) is set to foreground when the absolute value of its contrast is bigger than the chosen threshold C. Otherwise it is set to background. A median filter is applied afterwards to reduce noise and the remaining foreground pixels are grouped into an initial blob. This blob is divided horizontally and vertically using X-Y projected histograms, box size and height-to-width ratio. Resulting blobs are classified, according to their size and aspect, and characterised with the following features: bounding box, width, height and the centroid of foreground pixels in the box.

3.3   Tracking

The algorithm used here [15] is based on a two-way matching matrices algorithm (matching blobs from the current frame with those of the previous one and vice versa) with the overlapping of bounding boxes as a matching criterion. This criterion has been found to be effective in other approaches [8] and does not require the prediction of the blob's position since the visual motions of blobs were always small relative to their spatial extents. Due to its final application the algorithm works with relative positioning of blobs and their interaction forming or dissolving groups and does not keep the information of the blob's position when forming a group. However, the proposed system may be easily enhanced. Colour information may be used in the matching process and the predicted position can be used to track individual blobs while forming a group.

Matching Matrices Let us take two consecutive frames, F(t-1) and F(t). Foreground detection and blob identification algorithms result in N blobs in the first frame and M in the second. To find the correspondence between both sets of blobs, two matching matrixes are evaluated: the matrix matching the new blobs, $B_i(t)$, with the old blobs, $B_j(t-1)$, called M_t^{t-1} and the matrix matching the old blobs with the new ones M_{t-1}^t (2). To clarify the matching, the concept of "matching string" is introduced. Its meaning is clear, the numbers in column k show the blobs that match with the blob k, (3).

$$M_{t-1}^t(i,j) = Matching\{B_i(t-1), B_j(t)\}$$
$$M_t^{t-1}(i,j) = Matching\{B_i(t), B_j(t-1)\} \tag{2}$$

$$S_{t-1}^t(i) = \bigcup_j j \quad / \quad M_{t-1}^t(i,j) = 1 \tag{3}$$

It is possible for one blob to get a positive match with two blobs and, sometimes, with three. In this case, the corresponding string element has to store two or three values.

Fig. 1. An example of a tracking sequence and some trajectories in different scenarios

Tracking The algorithm solves the evolution of the blob from frame F(t-1) to frame F(t) by analysing the values of the matching strings of both frames. Simple events such as people entering or leaving the scenario, people merging into a group or a group splitting into two people are easily solved. An example of the correspondence between some events in the temporal evolution of the blobs and the matching strings, merging (4), is shown.

$$
B_i(t-1) \bigcup B_j(t-1) \equiv B_k(t) \qquad \Longrightarrow \qquad \begin{aligned} S_{t-1}^t(i) &= S_{t-1}^t(j) = k \\ S_t^{t-1}(k) &= i \bigcup j \end{aligned} \qquad (4)
$$

After classifying, the matching algorithm updates each new blob using the information stored in the old ones and keeps the position of the centroid to form a trajectory when the blob is being tracked. If two blobs merge to form a new one, this particular blob is classified as a group. This new group blob is tracked individually although the information about the two merged blobs is stored for future use. If the group splits again, the system uses speed direction and blob characteristics -like colour- to identify correctly the two splitting blobs. Tracking blobs centroid from frame to frame, trajectories of single persons or cars are easily obtained. Whenever it is necessary, an interpolation of the position of the tracked blob in the frames where it was forming part of a group may provide approximate complete trajectories. The interpolated centroids position is obtained using the median speed of previous frames and the centroid of the group blob.

4   Event Detection

Blob detection provides 2D information allowing an approximate positioning of people in the 3D scenario -a more precise positioning requires either a geometric camera calibration or stereo processing simultaneously analysing images from two cameras-. People position can be used to detect some position-based events characteristic of transport environment, such as unattended luggage, intrusion in forbidden areas, falls on tracks, etc. Further analysis using position information from consecutive frames, tracking, allows a basic analysis of people interaction and the detection of dynamic-based events, unusual movements in passageways, vandalism, attacks, etc. The following paragraph shows some examples of how event detection can be achieved using the position of the centroid, the characteristics of the blob and the tracking information. A low people-density situation is assumed.

1. Unattended luggage. A person carrying luggage leaves it and moves away:
   − Initial blob splits in two
   − One (normally smaller and horizontal) presents no motion, the other moves away from the first.
   − Temporal thresholding may be used to trigger the alarm.
2. Falls.
   − Blob wider than it is tall.
   − Slow or no centroid motion
   − Falls or tracks: centroid in forbidden area.
3. People hiding. People hide (from the camera-from other people)
   − Blob disappearing in many consecutive frames
   − Last centroid's position no close to a "gate" (to leave the scene)
   − Last centroid's position very close to a previously labelled "Hiding zone"
   − Temporal thresholding may be used to trigger the alarm.
4. Vandalism. People vandalising public property:
   − Isolation: only one person/group present in the scene
   − Irregular centroid motion
   − Possible changes in the background afterwards
5. Fights. People fighting move together and break away many times, fast movements:
   − Centroids of groups or persons move to coincidence
   − Persons/Groups merging and splitting
   − Fast changes in blob's characteristics

Frame-by-frame blob analysis and tracking provide enough information to detect some of the previous events and the possibility of others. In any case, the system only attracts the attention of the operator, who always decides whether an event is actually taking place.

5   Tracking Results

Due to final system requirements, a high processing speed is essential. Luminance contrast segmentation and its associated background model have been chosen because they provide an excellent performance with lower computational cost. Some important points concerning the influence of the chosen method in background subtraction and tracking has been previously discussed [14]. Some simulations have been used to test event detection -someone falling down the stairs, vandalism and people hiding, figure 2- whilst real footage has been used to test tracking algorithm and some position-based events -unattended luggage and intrusion into forbidden areas-.

Fig. 2. Tracking and event detection results on simulated events. Trajectories of someone scribbling graffiti and falling down the stairs

6   Conclusions

The presented real-time tracking system was implemented on an 850 MHz compatible PC running Windows 2000. It works with colour images in half PAL format 384x288. It has been tested with live video and image sequences in BMP and JPEG formats. The minimum processing speed observed is 10 Hz, from disk images in BMP format. Working with a video signal there is no perceptible difference between processed and un-processed video streaming. The system can successfully resolve blobs forming and dissolving groups and track one of them throughout this process. It can also be easily upgraded with background updating and tracking of multiple objects. With the proposed system, some predefined events have been detected, showing its suitability for security tasks, including surveillance and public areas monitoring, where the number of CCTV cameras mounted makes it impossible by means of its physical and economic implications. Reduced human monitoring is still needed to solve the raised alarms and to monitor system's selected video footage. Additional information like the number of people and crossing frequency in a certain area may also be obtained.

References

[1] Norris, C., Moran, J., Armstrong, G.: Surveillance, Closed Circuit Television and Social Control. Ashgate, UK (1998)

[2] Norris, C., Armstrong, G.: The Maximum Surveillance Society. The rise of CCTV. Berg Publishers, UK (1999)

[3] Buxton, H., Gong, S.: Visual surveillance in a dynamic and uncertain world. Artificial Intelligence **78** (1995) 431–459

[4] Intille, S. S., Davis, J. W., Bobick, A. F.: Real-time Closed-World Tracking. Proceedings of the IEEE Conference on Computer Vision and Pattern Recognition (CVPR'97) (1997) 697–703.

[5] De la Torre, F., Martinez, E., Santamaria, M. E., Moran, J. A.: Moving Object Detection and Tracking System: a Real-time Implementation. Proceedings of the Symposium on Signal and Image Processing GRETSI 97, Grenoble, (1997)

[6] Haritaoglu, I., Harwood, D., Davis, L. S.: W4: Real-Time Surveillance of People and Their Activities. IEEE Trans. Pattern Analysis and Machine Intelligence, **22(8)** (2000) 809–822

[7] Rota, N., Thonnat, M.: Video Sequence Interpretation for Visual Surveillance. Proceedings of The IEEE Workshop on Visual Surveillance, Dublin, (2000) 59–68.

[8] McKenna, S., Jabri, S., Duric, Z., Rosenfeld, A., Wechsler, H.: Tracking Groups of People. Computer Vision and Image Understanding **80** (2000) 42–56

[9] Wren, C. R., Azarbayejani, A., Darrel, T., Pentland, P.: Pfinder: Real-Time Tracking of the Human Body. Trans. Pattern Analysis and Machine Intelligence **17(6)** (1997) 780–785

[10] Aggarwal, J. K., Cai, Q.: Human Motion Analysis: A Review. Computer Vision and Image Understanding **73(3)** (1999) 428–440

[11] Gavrila, D. M.: The visual analysis of human movement: A survey. Computer Vision and Image Understanding **73** (1999) 82–98

[12] Rosales, R., Claroff, S.: Improved Tracking of Multiple Humans with Trajectory Prediction and occlusion Modelling. Proceedings of the IEEE Conf. On Computer Vision and Pattern Recognition (1998)

[13] Agbinya, J. I., Rees, D.: Multi-Object Tracking in Video. Real-Time Imaging **5** (1999) 295–304

[14] Fuentes, L. M., Velastin, S. A.: Foreground segmentation using luminance contrast. Proceedings of the WSES/IEEE Conference on Signal XXXX and Image Processing (2001).

[15] Fuentes, L. M., Velastin, S. A.: People Tracking in Surveillance Applications. 2nd IEEE International Workshop on Performance Evaluation of Tracking and Surveillance, PETS2001 (2001)

A User Authentication Technic
Using a Web Interaction Monitoring System

Hugo Gamboa[1] and Ana Fred[2]

[1] Escola Superior de Tecnologia de Setúbal,
Campo do IPS, Estefanilha, 2914-508 Setúbal, Portugal
hgamboa@est.ips.pt
[2] Instituto de Telecomunicações Instituto Superior Técnico
IST – Torre Norte, Piso 10,
Av. Rovisco Pais 1049-001 Lisboa Portugal afred@lx.it.pt

Abstract. User authentication based on biometrics has explored both physiological and behavioral characteristics. We present a system, called Web Interaction Display and Monitoring (WIDAM), that captures an user interaction on the web via a pointing device. This forms the basis of a new authentication system that uses behavioral information extracted from these interaction signals. The user interaction logs produced by WIDAM are presented to a sequential classifier, that applies statistical pattern recognition techniques to ascertain the identity of an individual - authentication system. The overall performance of the combined acquisition / authentication systems is measured by the global equal error rate, estimated from a test set. Preliminary results show that the new technique is a promising tool for user authentication, exhibiting comparable performances to other behavioural biometric techniques. Exploring standard human-computer interaction devices, and enabling remote access to behavioural information, this system constitutes an inexpensive and practical approach to user authentication through the world wide web.

1 Introduction

Personal identification / authentication plays an important role in current security and personalization systems. As opposed to traditional security systems, that based authentication on something *one has* or on something *one knows* (magnetic card, keys, etc. in the first case and passwords or personal identification numbers in the second), recent methodologies explore biometric characteristics. These methods are based on something *one is*, leading to increased reliability and immunity to authorization theft, loss or lent.

We can divide the biometric systems in two types [9]: (1) Identity verification (or authentication) occurs when a user claims who he is and the system accepts (or declines) his claim; (2) Identity identification (sometimes called search) occurs when the system establishes a subject identity (or fails to do it) without any prior claim.

F.J. Perales et al. (Eds.): IbPRIA 2003, LNCS 2652, pp. 246–254, 2003.
© Springer-Verlag Berlin Heidelberg 2003

Biometric techniques can also be classified according to the type of characteristics explored : (1) physiological — a physiological trait tends to be a stable physical characteristic, such as finger print, hand silhouette, blood vessel pattern in the hand, face or back of the eye. (2) behavioural — a behavioural characteristic is a reflection of an individual's psychology. Because of the variability over time of most behavioural characteristics, behavioural biometric systems need to be designed to be more dynamic and accept some degree of variability. On the other hand, behavioural biometrics are associated with less intrusive systems, leading to better acceptability by the users. Two examples of behavioural biometric techniques presently used are handwritten signature verification [6] and speaker recognition via voice prints [2].

The evaluation of a biometric technique requires the definition of metrics that can be used for the comparison of performance among different techniques [10], typically: False rejection rate (FRR) — rate of accesses where a legitim user is rejected by the system; False acceptance rate — rate of accesses where an impostor is accepted by the system; Equal error rate (EER) — the value at which FAR and FRR are equal.

In this paper we propose both a web based user interaction monitoring system called Web Interaction Display and Monitoring, WIDAM, and a new behavioural biometric technique based on web interaction via a pointing device, typically a mouse pointer. The normal interaction through this device is analyzed for extraction of behavioural information in order to link an identification claim to an individual.

In the following section we present the user interaction acquisition system, WIDAM. In section 3 we describe the authentication system, focusing on the sequential classifier. Section 4 presents experimental results obtained using the collected data. Conclusions are presented in section 5.

2   The Acquisition System

The acquisition system, WIDAM, (this system is presented with more detail in [4]) enables the user interaction monitoring, analysis and display on web pages. The system can be called as a remote display system that enables the synchronous and asynchronous observation of the user interaction, offering four different services : (1) Synchronous Monitoring Service — real-time monitoring of the user interaction; (2) Synchronous Display Service — real-time observation by other users; (3) Recording Service — storage of the user interaction information in the server database; (4) Playback Service — retrieval and playback of a stored monitored interaction.

WIDAM allows the usage of an interaction recording system directly over a web page, based on the Document Object Model [7] (DOM) of the web page. The system works in a normal web browser with java and javascript capabilities, without the need of any software installation. WIDAM is a light weight networked application using low bandwidth comparatively to image based remote display systems.

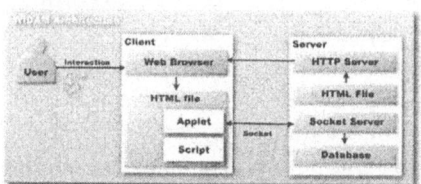

Fig. 1. The WIDAM Architecture

The WIDAM Architecture is composed by a client and server applications, as depicted in figure 1. The user accesses the WIDAM application via a web browser that connects to the server. Then, the server sends back to the user a web page that is capable of monitoring and displaying the user interaction. This page creates a connection to the server and selects one of the services provided by WIDAM. Then the client and the server exchange messages using a specific protocol.

The client works in any web browser capable of executing Javascript code and Java Applets, independent of the operating system. When the users enters into a page of the WIDAM system, an applet is launched. This applet creates a socket connection that enables the message passing from, and to the server. The client loads the html page and sends an handshaking message through the open socket, specifying which type of service is requested.

In the case of a Recording Service or Synchronous Monitoring Service, the script sends a request to the browser, asking for notification of the user interface events (a sub set of the events from the Document Object Model Events [11] listed in table 1).

In the case of a Synchronous Display Service or Playback Service, the web browser creates a virtual mouse pointer and waits for messages from the server specifying which event should be emulated in the web browser.

Table 1. DOM events captured by WIDAM

ID	Event handler	Event cause
0	onMouseMove	The user moves the cursor.
1	onMouseDown	The user presses a mouse button.
2	onKeyPress	The user presses a key.
3	onUnload	The user exits a document.
4	onMove	The window is moved.
5	onSelect	The user selects some text.
6	onResize	The window is resized.
7	onBlur	The window loses focus.
8	onFocus	The window receives focus.

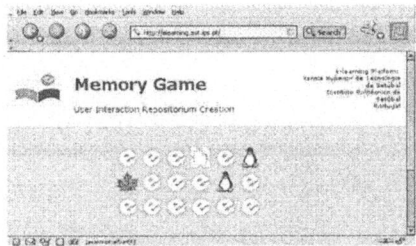
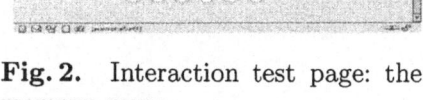

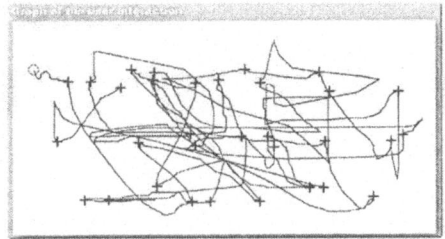

Fig. 2. Interaction test page: the memory game

Fig. 3. Graph of the user interaction in the memory game

For the purpose of the authentication technique being developed, the WIDAM system operated in the Recording Service mode, over a web page with the memory game: a grid of tiles, each tile having associated a hidden pattern, which is shown for a brief period of time upon clicking on it; the purpose of the game is to identify the matching tiles. The WIDAM system presents a web page to the user, asking for his identification (name, and a personal number). Then the system presents an *interaction acquisition page* with the memory game (that could be any html web page), depicted in figure 2. This page is monitored by the WIDAM application that records all the user interaction in a file stored in the web server. Figure 3 shows a graph of a user interaction while playing an entire memory game. The graph is produced by joining every sequential mouse movement with lines and using a cross mark to indicate a mouse click.

3   The Authentication System

An experimental system — the authentication system — was developed to verify the possibility of discriminating between users using their computer interaction information, specifically based on mouse movements performed between successive clicks, which we will call a *stroke* (see figure 4).

Figure 5 presents the acquisition and recognition systems and its respective building blocks. The acquisition system was addressed in the previous section. The recognition system comprises the following modules: (a) feature extraction; (b) feature selection; (c) parametrical learning; (d) statistical sequential classifier.

The recognition system reads the interaction data from the stored data files produced by the acquisition system. The interaction data passes a feature extraction procedure, creating a 63-dimensional vector, exploring both spatial (related to angle and curvature) and temporal (related to duration, position, velocity and acceleration) characteristics of the strokes. More details can be found in [5].

The system has an enrolment phase, where the global set of extracted features are used in an algorithm that selects a set of "best" features for each user, using *the equal error rate* as performance measure (feature selection block in figure 5), using the Sequential Forward Selection (SFS) [8] that selects the best single

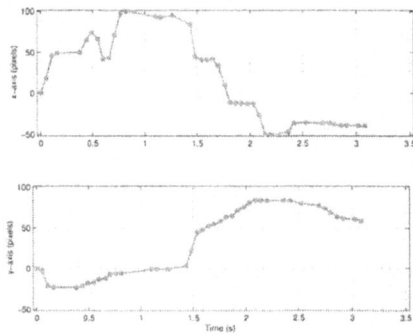

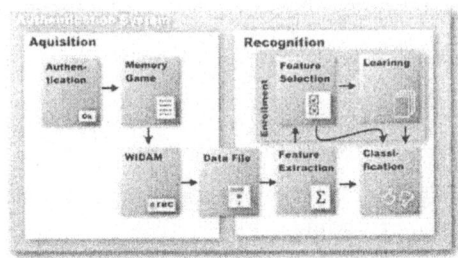

Fig. 4. Example of a stroke — input signals generated by the mouse move events between successive mouse clicks

Fig. 5. Authentication system architecture

feature and then adds one feature at time to a the vector of previously selected features. The algorithm stops when the equal error rate does not decrease.

The classification rule assumes a statistical model for the feature vectors. The learning phase consists of the estimation of the probability density functions, $p(X)$ (where X is the feature vector of a stroke), from each user's data. Considering that each user constitutes a recognition class, and assuming statistical independence between features, $p(X)$ factorizes into $p(X| user) = \prod p(x_i| user)$. We use as parametrical model for $p(x_i| user)$ the *weibull* [1] distribution ($p(x|a, b) = abx^{(b-1)}e^{(-ax^b)}$). Given the data from one user and one feature, maximum likelihood estimates of the parameters a and b are obtained.

The classifier's purpose is to decide if a user is who he claims to be, based on the patterns of interaction with the computer. We consider that the ith user is denoted by the class w_i, $i = 1, \ldots, L$, and L is the number of classes. As defined before, a feature vector is associated with one stroke. Given a sequence of n_s consecutive strokes executed by the user, w_i, interaction information is summarized in the vector $\mathbf{X} = X^1 \ldots X^{n_s}$, consisting of the concatenation of the feature vectors associated with each stroke. $X^j = x_1^j \ldots x_{n_{f_i}}^j$, the feature vector representing the jth stroke, has n_{f_i} elements, n_{f_i} being the number of features identified for user w_i in the feature selection phase.

Considering each stroke at a time, and assuming statistical independence between features, we can write $p(X_j|w_i) = \prod_{l=1}^{n_f} p(x_l^j|w_i)$. Considering stroke independence we can further write $p(\mathbf{X}|w_i) = \prod_{j=1}^{n_s} p(X_j|w_i)$.

The classifier will decide to accept or reject the claimed identity based on two distributions: the genuine distribution $p(\mathbf{X}|w_i)$, and the impostor distribution $p(\mathbf{X}| \overline{w_i})$ that is based on a mixture of distributions (weibull distributions), one for each other user not equal to i, expressed as $p(\mathbf{X}|\overline{w_i}) = \sum_{j \neq i} p(\mathbf{X}|w_i)\frac{1}{L}$. In the previous equation we assume that the classes are equiprobable, $p(w_i) =$

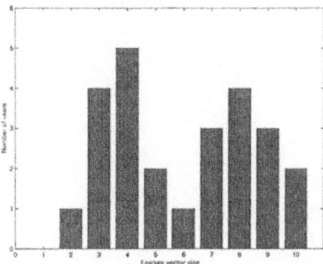

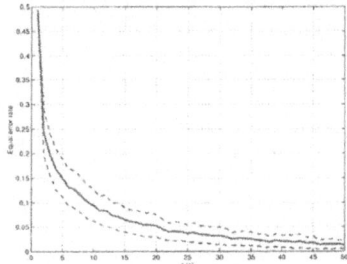

Fig. 6. User feature vectors size histogram

Fig. 7. Equal error rate results of the verification system. The solid line is the mean of the equal error rate of all users. The dashed lines are the mean plus and minus half standard deviation

$1/L$ $i = 1...L$. We can therefore express the posterior probability function as

$$p(w_i|\mathbf{X}) = \frac{p(\mathbf{X}|w_i)}{\sum_{k=1}^{L} p(\mathbf{X}|w_k)} = 1 - p(\overline{w_i}|\mathbf{X}).$$

Since $p(w_i|X_j)$ represents an estimate of the probability of the classification being correct, we establish a *limit*, λ, to select one of the decisions, using the decision rule in equation 1. To present result about the classifier performance we adjust λ to operate in the equal error rate point.

$$Accept(\mathbf{X} \in w_i) = \begin{cases} true & \text{if } p(w_i|\mathbf{X}) > \lambda \\ false & \text{otherwise} \end{cases} \tag{1}$$

4   Results

We asked 25 volunteers (engineering students) to use the developed system, playing several memory games during about 10-15 minutes. This way, we created an interaction repository of approximately 5 hours of interaction, providing more than 180 strokes per user. The acquisition system monitors the pointing device with a sample rate of 50 times per second, producing messages form the client to the server that require approximately 1 Kbytes/s (950 bytes per second) as the maximum bandwidth. For instance, the five hours of interaction occupies 18 Mbytes of disk space.

In order to use the same number of strokes per user in the tests performed, we randomly selected 180 strokes from each user. The set of strokes was divided into two equal parts, one for the training phase and other for the testing phase. Using the training set we learnt the parametrical distribution $p(x_i|user)$ for each user and each feature. Feature selection used the same data set and was tuned for each user, based on the performance of the system using sequences of 10

Table 2. Mean equal error rate (eer) and respective standard deviation (std) for different stroke sequence lengths (l)

l	eer	std
1	0.489	0.01
2	0.243	0.09
5	0.151	0.07
10	0.095	0.06
20	0.052	0.04
50	0.013	0.02
100	0.005	0.001

strokes. Figure 6 presents the histogram of the feature vector sizes for all the users; the average size of the feature vector is 6.

When testing the system for one user, we consider an imposter as one of the other users. The test function returns the equal error rate given N sequences of strokes of length l using the classifier tuned for user i. The input sequence of strokes of a test is composed of $N/2$ strokes randomly sampled from the testing set of the user, and $N/2$ strokes randomly sampled from the testing sets of all the other users.

One of the free variables of the system is the number of strokes that the system will use in the verification task. Bootstrap [3] estimates of the system performance as a function of the sequence stroke length (from 1 to 100 strokes) was obtained using 10000 bootstrap samples from the test set. The mean duration of a stroke is approximately 1 second. In table 2 we present the mean results of the equal error rate for all 25 users for several stroke sequence lengths. A graphical display of these results is shown in figure 7. As shown, the mean value and the standard deviation of the EER progressively tends to zero as more strokes are added to the decision rule. This illustrates the refinement of the performance obtained by the sequential classifier.

Table 3 presents EER values reported in the literature for several biometric techniques [12]. Preliminary results show that the proposed user authentication system, based on behavioural information extracted from the interaction with the computer, can achieve comparable performances with other biometric techniques.

5   Conclusion

We have explored the human computer interaction behavioural information to create a novel user behavioural biometric verification technique. For collecting the user interaction through the pointing device movements and clicks in a web page, we developed a system, WIDAM, working on the world wide web. This system comprises a user interaction acquisition module, responsible for the collection of user interaction data that is capable of synchronous and asynchronous recording and playback of web user interaction activity. The biometric technique

Table 3. Comparison between several biometric techniques

Biometric technique	Equal error rate
Retinal Scan	1:10 000 000
Iris Scan	1:131 000
Fingerprints	1:500
Hand Geometry	1:500
Signature Dynamics	1:50
Voice Dynamics	1:50
30s of User Interaction	1:50
60s of User Interaction	1:100
90s of User Interaction	1:200

is implemented in the authentication system that produces the user classification and estimates of the performance of the decision rule.

This authentication system is based on a sequential statistical classifier that receives the sequential data produced along the user interaction. A large set of features were initially extracted from the collected data, using both time domain related and spatial information from the mouse movement patterns. A feature selection procedure reduced this initial set to a small number of features, using a greedy search, and taking the classifier performance, measured by the EER, as objective function.

The results of the tests with 25 users and a total of 5 hours of interaction showed that this technique is a promising tool for user authentication, considering that the performance results are comparable to some of the behavioural biometric techniques and that it is an inexpensive technique that operates remotely using the human-computer interaction behaviour.

References

[1] Robert B. Abernethy. *The New Weibull Handbook*. Robert B. Abernethy, 2000.

[2] Mohamed F. BenZeghiba, Hervé Bourlard, and Johnny Mariethoz. Speaker verification based on user-customized password. Technical Report IDIAP-RR 01-13, Institut Dalle Molle d'Intelligence Artificial Perceprive, 2001.

[3] Bradley Efron and Robert J. Tibshirani. *An Introduction to the Bootstrap*. Chapman & Hall, 1993.

[4] Hugo Gamboa and Vasco Ferreira. WIDAM - Web Interaction Display and Monitoring. In *Proceedings of the 5th International Conference on Enterprise Information Systems*, volume 4, pages 21–27, 2003.

[5] Hugo Gamboa and Ana Fred. An Identity Authentication System Based On Human Computer Interaction Behaviour. In *Proceedings of the 3rd International Workshop on Pattern Recognition in Information Systems*, pages 46–55, 2003.

[6] J. Gupta and A. McCabe. A review of dynamic handwritten signature verification. Technical report, James Cook University, Australia, 1997.

[7] Arnaud Le Hors, Philippe Le Hgaret, and Lauren Wood. Document object model level 2 core. Technical report, W3C, 2000.

[8] Anil K. Jain, Robert P. W. Duin, and Jianchang Mao. Statistical pattern recognition: A review. *IEEE Transactions on Pattern Analysis and Machine Intelligence*, 22(1), 2000.

[9] Vaclav Matyas Jr and Zdenek Riha. Biometric authentication systems. Technical report, ECOM-MONITOR, 2000.

[10] Tony Mansfield and Gary Roethenbaugh. 1999 glossary of biometric terms. Technical report, Association for Biometrics, 1999.

[11] Tom Pixley. Document object model (dom) level 2 events specification. Technical report, W3C, 2000.

[12] Thomas Ruggles. Comparison of biometric techniques. Technical report, California Welfare Fraud Prevention System, 2002.

Recovering Camera Motion in a Sequence of Underwater Images through Mosaicking

Rafael Garcia, Xevi Cufí, and Viorela Ila

Computer Vision and Robotics Group, Institute of Informatics and Applications,
University of Girona, Campus de Montilivi
17071, Girona, Spain
{rafa,xcuf,viorela}@eia.udg.es

Abstract. A procedure for automatic mosaic construction over long image sequences is presented. This mosaic is used by an underwater vehicle to estimate its motion with respect to the ocean floor. The system exploits texture cues to solve the correspondence problem. The dynamic selection of a reference image extracted from the mosaic improves motion estimation, bounding accumulated error. Experiments with real images are reported.

1   Introduction

A composite image constructed by aligning and combining a set of smaller images is known as *mosaic* [1]. In most cases the construction of a mosaic involves recovering the relative motion between the camera and the scene. Mosaics of the ocean floor are very useful in undersea exploration, creation of visual maps, underwater navigation, etc. In this context an underwater vehicle carries a down-looking camera, taking images of the ocean floor to build a mosaic as it performs the mission. Quite often, the mosaicking systems found in the literature perform local gray level correlation [2] or compute optical flow [3] to align the images which form the mosaic. Although these techniques provide good results in standard images [4], they may lead to detection of incorrect correspondences in underwater sequences. The special properties of the medium makes underwater images difficult to process [5]: the elements of the image get blurred, some regions of interest present high clutter and lack of distinct features. Although most of the techniques neglect the use of textural information, considering only image intensity, texture provides a rich source of information to solve image alignment [6]. This paper extends our previous work [7, 8] to construct more accurate mosaics of the ocean floor and over longer image sequences. In [7], every image of the sequence was registered to the previous one. Therefore, when an inaccuracy is introduced in the transformation between both images, this error affects not only the current registration, but all the following ones.

In this paper, we address the problem of building mosaics of the ocean floor to reduce the error associated to the position of an underwater vehicle when it performs a mission. In particular, our mosaicking system has been upgraded

F.J. Perales et al. (Eds.): IbPRIA 2003, LNCS 2652, pp. 255–262, 2003.

in several ways to overcome the difficulties described above: (i) texture cues are considered to improve feature correspondences, thus reducing inaccuracies; and (ii) selection of a reference image extracted from the mosaic, in contrast to processing every pair of consecutive images.

The remainder of the paper is structured as follows: Section 2 outlines our mosaicking methodology, detailing the characterization procedure and the methodology applied to the selection of a reference image. Then, experimental results proving the validity of our proposal appear in Section 3. Finally, Section 4 presents the conclusions of this work.

2   Building a Mosaic

Our mosaicking system is divided into two main blocks, namely: *mosaic controller* and *mosaic engine*. The mosaic controller keeps the state of the mosaicking system and takes decisions according to this state. It is responsible of the mosaic data structure, *i.e.*, updating the mosaic image (I_m) according to the estimated motion. On the other hand, the motion is estimated by the mosaic engine. It considers the current image (I_c) and a reference image (I_r) and computes a planar homography which describes the motion between both. Selection of the reference image is performed by the mosaic controller. Figure 1 shows the relationship between both modules.

2.1   Mosaic Controller

This module aims to analyze how the vehicle is moving and generates the pertinent commands to control the mosaic engine. The mosaic controller provides the engine module with the images which will be used to estimate the motion of the vehicle. One of these images is the current frame acquired by the camera (I_c). The second one is a reference image (I_r), extracted from the mosaic image I_m by the controller.

Every iteration of the algorithm starts when current image I_c is acquired. Then, the geometric distortion caused by the lens (and the water-glass-air interface of the camera housing) is corrected through a simplification of the Faugeras-Toscani algorithm [9] to correct uniquely radial distortion, instead of performing full camera calibration [10]. Once lens distortion has been corrected, the current image at time instant k, denoted $I_c(k)$, is rotated and scaled so that its orientation and scale matches that of the reference image $I_r(k)$.

Consider a 3×3 matrix $^r\mathbf{H}_c(k)$ as the homography which transforms the coordinates of a point in image $I_c(k)$ into its corresponding coordinates in the reference image $I_r(k)$. The motion estimated at the previous time instant $^r\mathbf{H}_c(k-1)$ is assumed to be valid as an "a priori" motion estimation for instant k, since motion between two consecutive images is rather small due to the high frame-rate of the sequence. Then, images $I_r(k)$ and $I_c(k)$, together with "a priori" motion estimation matrix $^r\mathbf{H}_c(k-1)$ are passed to the mosaic engine, and it is told to execute. The output of the mosaic engine is the homography matrix $^r\mathbf{H}_c(k)$,

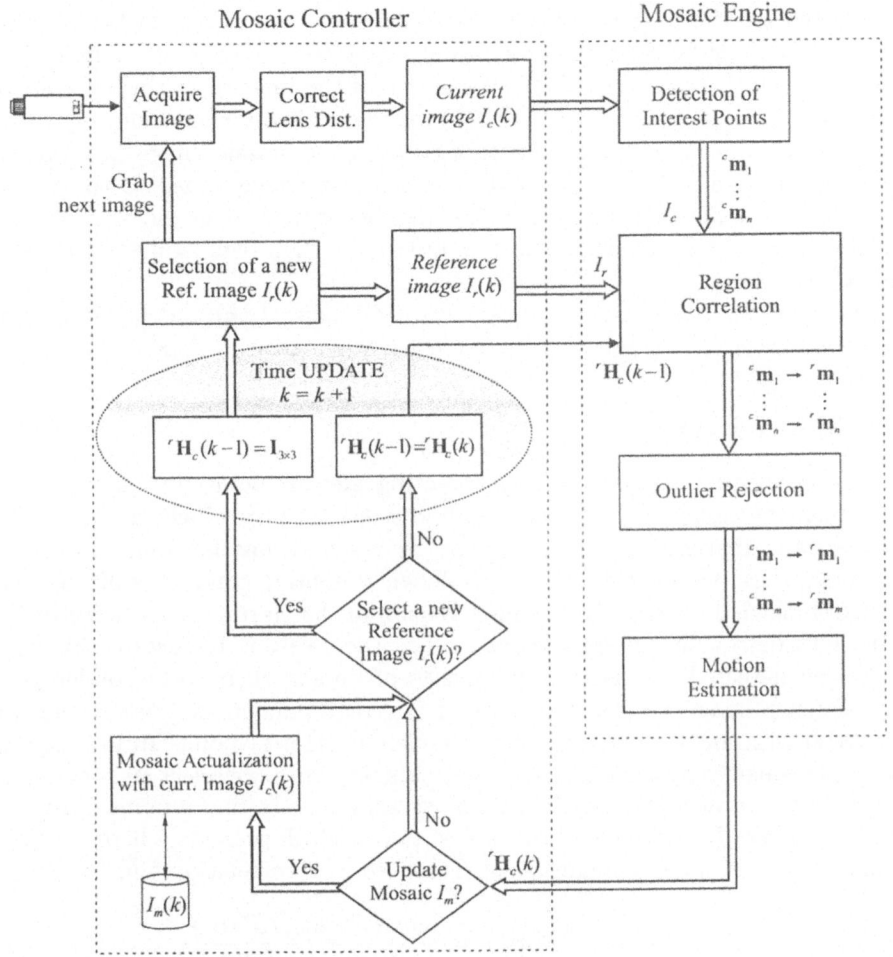

Fig. 1. Bloc diagram illustrating the relationship between the *mosaic controller* and the *mosaic engine*

which estimates the motion between $I_c(k)$ and $I_r(k)$ at time instant k. It should be noted that the engine is executed only when the controller requires it.

Once the engine has finished its execution, the controller decides if I_m should be updated. The controller can be configured to actualize the mosaic every α images, with $\alpha = 1..20$. It uses equation (1) to update the mosaic image $I_m(k)$ with the current image $I_c(k)$. I_m is only updated in those areas which have not been updated before by the previous images. Therefore, the first available information for every pixel is used to actualize the mosaic image. This strategy of using the less recent information to construct the mosaic is known in the literature as "use first" [2].

$$^m\mathbf{H}_c(k) = {}^m\mathbf{H}_r(k) \cdot {}^r\mathbf{H}_c(k) \tag{1}$$

The next step consists of deciding whether a new reference image I_r has to be selected for the next iteration. The controller uses matrix $^r\mathbf{H}_c(k)$ to check if the overlapping between the reference image $I_r(k)$ and current image $I_c(k)$ is below a given threshold (*e.g.* 40% of the size of the image). In this case, it has to select a new reference image $I_r(k+1)$ for the next iteration of the algorithm. The new reference image will be extracted from the mosaic image $I_m(k)$ at the same position and orientation as that of the last image added to the mosaic (at time $k - mod(k/\alpha)$). Following this methodology, drift in the estimation of the trajectory of the vehicle increases more slowly than registering every pair of consecutive images.

On the other hand, if the overlap between images $I_c(k)$ and $I_r(k)$ is bigger than the threshold, the reference image will not change, *i.e.* $I_r(k+1) = I_r(k)$.

2.2   Mosaic Engine

The engine begins its execution by detecting interest points in image I_c. The goal of the interest point detector is to find scene features which can be reliably detected and matched when the camera moves from one location to another. Moreover, these features should be stable when lighting conditions of the scene change somewhat. A slightly modified version of the Harris corner detector [11] is used to detect the interest points. Once the relevant features of image I_c have been detected, the next step consists of finding their correspondences in the reference image I_r. Before searching for correspondences, both images are smoothed with a 3×3 Gaussian mask. Given an interest point $^c\mathbf{m}$ in image I_c, instead of considering the point as an individual feature, we select an $n \times n$ region $R(^c\mathbf{m})$ centered at this point. Then, the system aims to find a point $^r\mathbf{m}$ in the reference image I_r, surrounded by an $n \times n$ area which presents a high degree of similarity to $^c\mathbf{m}$. This "similarity" is computed as a correlation function [4]:

$$\text{corr}\left\{R(^c\mathbf{m}), R(^r\mathbf{m})\right\} = \frac{\text{cov}\left\{R(^c\mathbf{m}), R(^r\mathbf{m})\right\}}{\sigma\left\{R(^c\mathbf{m})\right\} \cdot \sigma\left\{R(^r\mathbf{m})\right\}} \tag{2}$$

From equation (2) we can observe that the correlation between two points is defined as the covariance between the grey levels of region $R(^c\mathbf{m})$ in the current image and region $R(^r\mathbf{m})$ defined in I_r, normalized by the product of the standard deviation of these regions. In practice, these regions are subsampled by a factor q, reducing the processed pixels from $n \times n$ to $m \times m$, where $m = ((n-1)/q)+1$, and, therefore, decreasing the computational burden.

Equation (2) is computed for all the points of the reference image which fall inside a small search window. In order to locate this window, the system takes into account the previous estimated motion $^r\mathbf{H}_c(k-1)$. Consider an interest point $^c\widetilde{\mathbf{m}}$, defined in the current image and expressed in homogeneous coordinates. The search window is centered at $^r\widetilde{\mathbf{c}}$, as shown in equation (3).

$$^r\widetilde{\mathbf{c}} = {}^r\mathbf{H}_c(k-1) \cdot {}^c\widetilde{\mathbf{m}} \tag{3}$$

being $^r\tilde{\mathbf{c}}$ the projection of the interest point $^c\tilde{\mathbf{m}}$ into the reference image. The coordinates provided by $^r\tilde{\mathbf{c}}$ are uniquely used to open the window where equation (2) is applied to search for the correct correspondence $^r\tilde{\mathbf{m}}$ of interest point $^c\tilde{\mathbf{m}}$.

Equation (2) is normalized by substracting the mean and dividing by a factor which takes into account the dispersion of the gray levels in the considered regions. For this reason, this measurement of correlation is very adequate for underwater imaging, where lighting inhomogeneities are frequent. Unfortunately, although equation (2) produces good results in absence of rotations, its reliability decreases as images I_c and I_r present a higher rotational component. For this reason the mosaic controller rotates and scales the current image, prior to pass it to the engine.

According to equation (2), given an interest point $^c\mathbf{m}$ in the current image I_c, its correspondence $^r\mathbf{m}$ in I_r should be the point which has obtained the highest correlation score. Those pairs (*interest_point, matching*) which have obtained a correlation score lower than a given threshold are deleted. However, experimental work with underwater images has proved that in some cases the true correspondence is not the one with the highest correlation score [6]. Therefore, the incorrect correspondences (known as *"outliers"*) are detected through a two-step approach: first, discrimination of false matches through textural analysis; and next, elimination of points describing non-dominant motion by means of a *robust estimator*.

In order to characterize incorrect correspondences through textural analysis, the textural properties of the neighborhood of both the interest point $^c\mathbf{m}$ and its estimated correspondence $^r\mathbf{m}$ are computed. In this way, the regions $R(^c\mathbf{m})$ and $R(^r\mathbf{m})$ are characterized by two feature vectors ($^c\mathbf{v}$ and $^r\mathbf{v}$), which encode their textural properties. Some of the *Energy filters* defined by Laws (*e.g.* L5S5, E3E3, etc.) are used to perform the textural analysis [12]. Depending on the parametrization of the system, this textural characterization may consist, for instance, of measuring the texture at some neighboring locations $(g_0, g_1, ..., g_8)$ as shown in Figure 2. If the Euclidean distance between both vectors is smaller than a selected threshold, the pair (*interest_point, matching*) is considered to be an *outlier*. In fact, this approach is based in the assumption that interest points (and their correspondences) are located at the border between, at least, two regions with different textural properties. It is a reasonable assumption since interest points are detected by finding areas of high variation of the image gradient through a corner detector, *i.e.*, located in the border of different image textures.

The second step consists on applying a robust estimation method, the Least Median of Squares (LMedS), to detect those feature points describing a trajectory which is different from the dominant motion of the image [13]. These "bad" correspondences are in fact correctly matched points belonging to some moving object of the scene, such as a moving fish, algae, etc.

Next, the motion estimation $^r\mathbf{H}_c(k)$ between current and reference images is computed from the remaining pairs of points applying equation (4).

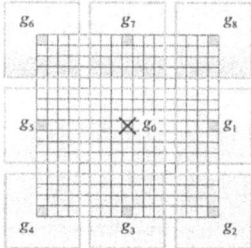

Fig. 2. Point characterization is performed by computing texture at 9 neighboring locations $(g_0, g_1, ..., g_8)$

$$^r\widetilde{m} = {}^r\mathbf{H}_c \cdot {}^c\widetilde{m} \quad \text{or} \quad \begin{bmatrix} \lambda \cdot {}^r x \\ \lambda \cdot {}^r y \\ \lambda \end{bmatrix} = \begin{bmatrix} h_{11} & h_{12} & h_{13} \\ h_{21} & h_{22} & h_{23} \\ h_{31} & h_{32} & 1 \end{bmatrix} \cdot \begin{bmatrix} {}^c x \\ {}^c y \\ 1 \end{bmatrix} \tag{4}$$

where λ is an arbitrary non-zero constant. Therefore, solving the homography of equation (4) involves the estimation of 8 unknowns. By using inhomogeneous coordinates instead of the homogeneous coordinates of the points, and operating the terms, the projective transformation of equation (4) can be written as:

$$\begin{bmatrix} {}^c x_1 & {}^c y_1 & 1 & 0 & 0 & 0 & -{}^r x_1 \cdot {}^c x_1 & -{}^r x_1 \cdot {}^c y_1 \\ 0 & 0 & 0 & {}^c x_1 & {}^c y_1 & 1 & -{}^r y_1 \cdot {}^c x_1 & -{}^r y_1 \cdot {}^c y_1 \\ \vdots & \vdots & \vdots & \vdots & \vdots & \vdots & \vdots & \vdots \\ {}^c x_n & {}^c y_n & 1 & 0 & 0 & 0 & -{}^r x_n \cdot {}^c x_n & -{}^r x_n \cdot {}^c y_n \\ 0 & 0 & 1 & {}^c x_n & {}^c y_n & 1 & -{}^r y_n \cdot {}^c x_n & -{}^r y_n \cdot {}^c y_n \end{bmatrix} \cdot \begin{bmatrix} h_{11} \\ h_{12} \\ h_{13} \\ h_{21} \\ h_{22} \\ h_{23} \\ h_{31} \\ h_{32} \end{bmatrix} = \begin{bmatrix} {}^r x_1 \\ {}^r y_1 \\ \vdots \\ {}^r x_n \\ {}^r y_n \end{bmatrix} \tag{5}$$

When the engine completes its execution, it gives back the control to the mosaic controller.

3   Experimental Results

In order to evaluate the proposed technique, several sea trials have been carried out under real conditions, using URIS, a small Unmanned Underwater Vehicle (UUV) developed at the University of Girona. The vehicle carries a downward-looking camera, which takes images of the seafloor. As the vehicle moves, the acquired images are sent to the surface through an umbilical tether, where they are stored on a tape to be processed off-line.

The sea trial reported here was carried out in July 2001. This experiment shows a trajectory performed by the vehicle in an area of the sea floor formed by rocks and algae. The original trajectory is formed by 4.380 images at a frame rate of 25 i.p.s. The sequence has been sub-sampled, taking only one image of every five, thus the mosaicking system processes 876 images.

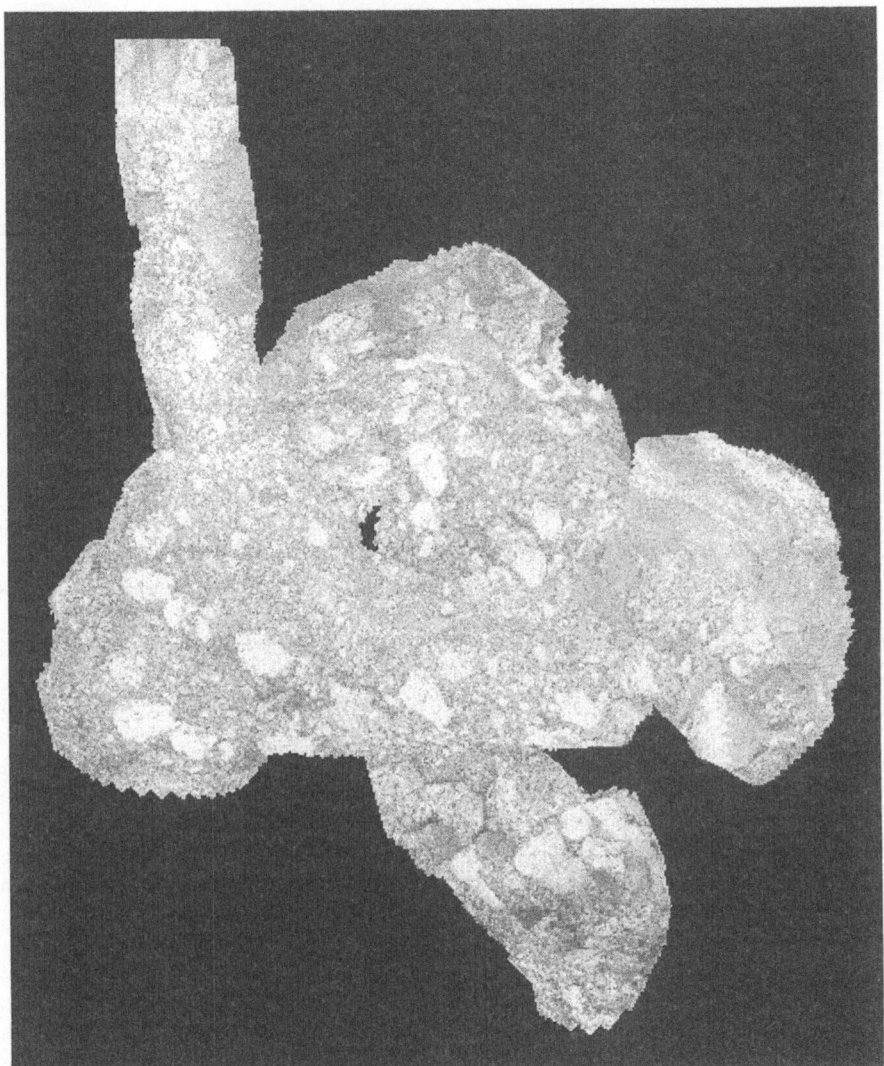

Fig. 3. Resulting mosaic after processing a sequence of 876 images. The vehicle starts its motion at the top-left of the image and then moves down performing several loops

Figure 3 shows the resulting mosaic. It can be observed in this Figure that image alignment is quite good, although the underwater terrain is not flat. Unfortunately, it is not possible to quantify the errors which are produced in real sea trials since the real trajectory cannot be recovered from any other sensors available in the UUV.

4   Conclusions

In this paper we have presented a methodology to construct mosaics of the ocean floor to estimate the motion of an underwater vehicle. The construction of visual mosaics of the floor can provide accurate position estimates for local navigation of the vehicle. A new texture-based characterization and matching methodology has been proposed, reducing the number of incorrect correspondences in image pairs. Moreover, a dynamic selection of the reference image improves, to a large extent, the performance of the system.

References

[1] R. Szeliski, Image mosaicing for tele-reality applications, in: IEEE Workshop on Applications of Computer Vision, 1994, pp. 44–53.

[2] N. Gracias, J. Santos-Victor, Underwater video mosaics as visual navigation maps, Computer Vision and Image Understanding 79 (1) (2000) 66–91.

[3] S. Negahdaripour, X. Xu, A. Khamene, A vision system for real-time positioning, navigation and video mosaicing of sea floor imagery in the application of ROVs/AUVs, in: IEEE Workshop on Applications of Computer Vision, 1998, pp. 248–249.

[4] A. Giachetti, Matching techniques to compute image motion, Image and Vision Computing 18 (3) (2000) 247–260.

[5] J. Jaffe, The domains of underwater visibility, in: SPIE Ocean Optics VIII, 1986, pp. 287–293.

[6] R. Garcia, X. Cufí, J. Batlle, Detection of matchings in a sequence of underwater images through texture analysis, in: IEEE International Conference on Image Processing, Vol. 1, Thessaloniki, Greece, 2001, pp. 361–364.

[7] R. Garcia, J. Batlle, X. Cufí, J. Amat, Positioning an underwater vehicle through image mosaicking, in: IEEE International Conference on Robotics and Automation, Vol. 3, Seoul, Rep. of Korea, 2001, pp. 2779–2784.

[8] X. Cufí, R. Garcia, P. Ridao, An approach to vision-based station keeping for an unmanned underwater vehicle, in: IEEE/RSJ International Conference on Intelligent Robots and Systems, Vol. 1, Lausanne, Switzerland, 2002, pp. 799–804.

[9] R. Garcia, J. Batlle, X. Cufí, A system to evaluate the accuracy of a visual mosaicking methodology, in: MTS/IEEE OCEANS Conference, Vol. 4, Honolulu, Hawaii, 2001, pp. 2570–2576.

[10] O. Faugeras, G. Toscani, The calibration problem for stereo, in: IEEE Conference on Computer Vision and Pattern Recognition, 1986, pp. 15–20.

[11] C. Harris, M. Stephens, A combined corner and edge detector, in: Alvey Vision Conference, Manchester, U.K., 1988, pp. 147–151.

[12] K. Laws, Textured image segmentation, Tech. Rep. 940, Image Processing Institute, University of Southern California, Los Angeles, California (1980).

[13] P. J. Rousseeuw, A. M. Leroy, Robust Regression and Outlier Detection, John Wiley and Sons, New York, 1987.

Best Achievable Compression Ratio
for Lossy Image Coding

Jose A. García[1], Joaquin Fdez-Valdivia[1],
Rosa Rodriguez-Sánchez[1], and Xose R. Fdez-Vidal[2]

[1] Depto. Ciencias de la Computación e I.A.,
E.T.S. de Ingeniería Informática, Univ. de Granada
18071 Granada. Spain.
{jags,J.Fdez-Valdivia,rosa}@decsai.ugr.es
[2] Depto. Física Aplicada. Facultad de Física, Univ. de. Santiago de Compostela.
15706 Santiago de Compostela. Spain.
faxose@usc.es

Abstract. The trade-off between image fidelity and coding rate is reached with several techniques, but all of them require an ability to measure distortion. The problem is that finding a general enough measure of perceptual quality has proven to be an elusive goal. Here, we propose a novel technique for deriving an optimal compression ratio for lossy coding based on the relationship between information theory and the problem of testing hypotheses. As an example of the proposed technique, we analyze the effects of lossy compression at the best achievable compression ratio on the identification of breast cancer microcalcifications.

1 Introduction

During the past two decades, various lossless and lossy image coding techniques have been developed (for a list of references see [2]). Typical lossless coders can attain compression ratios of only 2 : 1 or 3 : 1 for most images, thus users often prefer to deal with lossy algorithms which can achieve high compression rates, e.g., 50 : 1 or more. The problem is that high compression ratios are possible at the cost of imperfect source representation. Compression is lossy in that the decoded images are not exact copies of the originals but, if the properties of the human visual system are correctly exploited, original and decoded images will be almost indistinguishable. The trade-off between image distortion and coding rate may be stated as follows: [6] How much fidelity in the representation are willing to give up in order to reduce the storage or the number of bits required to transmit the data?

Here we propose a novel technique for deriving an optimal performance bound (it has been termed the "best achievable" compression ratio) based on the relationship between information theory and the problem of testing hypotheses. The best achievable compression ratio for lossy coders determines a boundary between achievable and non-achievable regions in the trade-off between source

F.J. Perales et al. (Eds.): IbPRIA 2003, LNCS 2652, pp. 263–270, 2003.

fidelity and coding rate. The resultant bounds are tight for situations of practical relevance. These performance bounds are directly achievable by a constructive procedure as suggested in a theorem, given in Section 2, which proves the relationship between the "best achievable" compression ratio and the Kullback-Leibler information gain [5].

Section 3 shows an example of the proposed technique for achieving optimal performance bounds, including lossy compression at the best achievable compression ratio in digitized mammograms. The main conclusions of the paper are summarized in Section 4.

2   The Best Achievable Compression Ratio

Let $X_1, X_2, \cdots, X_N$ be a sequence of N symbols from the set of gray levels $G = \{l | l = 1, 2, \cdots, l_{|G|}\}$. A 2D digital image can be interpreted as a sequence $X_1, X_2, \cdots, X_N$ of N symbols, with X_i being the gray level at pixel i. We use the notation I to denote a particular sequence of gray levels $x_1, \cdots, x_N$.

Let I be the original image; $I_{q(i)}$ be the reconstruction of the original image at compression ratio $q(i)$; P and $P_{q(i)}$ be the discrete probability distributions, with $P = (p(l/I))_l$ and $P_{q(i)} = (p(l/I_{q(i)}))_l$, that characterize the probability of occurrence of each gray level l in the original image I and the reconstruction $I_{q(i)}$, respectively.

Then $P_{q(1)}, P_{q(2)}, \cdots, P_{q(i)}, \cdots, P_{q(K)}$ denote the discrete probability distributions for the reconstructions of the original image at compression ratios $q(1), \cdots, q(i), \cdots, q(K)$, respectively; where if $i \leq j$ then, $q(i) \leq q(j)$; that is, $q(1)$ is the lowest compression ratio and $q(K)$ is the highest compression ratio.

In this setting, a classical statistical hypothesis testing to decide between any two distributions $P_{q(j)}$ and $P_{q(n)}$ can be stated as follows:

$$H_1 : P = P_{q(j)}$$
$$H_2 : P = P_{q(n)}$$

Consider the general decision function $g(x_1, \cdots, x_N)$ where $g(x_1, \cdots, x_N) = 1$ implies that H_1 is accepted and $g(x_1, \cdots, x_N) = 2$ implies that H_2 is accepted. The two probabilities of error are defined as:

$$\alpha_{j,n}^N = Pr\{g(x_1, \cdots, x_N) = 2/H_1 \text{ true}\}$$
$$\beta_{j,n}^N = Pr\{g(x_1, \cdots, x_N) = 1/H_2 \text{ true}\}. \tag{1}$$

In general, we wish to minimize both probabilities, but there is a trade-off. Thus we minimize the probability of error $\beta_{j,n}^N$ subject to a constraint on the other probability of error: $\alpha_{j,n}^N < \varepsilon$.

Let $\beta_{j,n}^{\varepsilon,N}$ be the lowest achievable probability of error $Pr\{g(x_1, \cdots, x_N) = 1/H_2 \text{ true}\}$ subject to $\alpha_{j,n}^N < \varepsilon$ for this problem. Note that more similar distributions $P_{q(j)}$ and $P_{q(n)}$ will produce higher values of the best achievable probability of error $\beta_{j,n}^{\varepsilon,N}$, and therefore, $\beta_{j,n}^{\varepsilon,N}$ may be interpreted as a measure of similarity between $P_{q(j)}$ and $P_{q(n)}$.

We have that, for each compression ratio $q(i)$, we can divide the set of distributions corresponding to the reconstructions of the original in two subsets: $\{P_{q(1)}, P_{q(2)}, \cdots, P_{q(i)}\}$ and $\{P_{q(i+1)}, \cdots, P_{q(K)}\}$. In the following, for each level of compression $q(i)$, we will define the probability of error over all the decision problems of hypothesis testing to decide between a distribution in $\{P_{q(i+1)}, \cdots, P_{q(K)}\}$ and any other in $\{P_{q(1)}, P_{q(2)}, \cdots, P_{q(i)}\}$.

Definition 1. For a given level $q(i)$, let $q(j)$ be any compression ratio such that $i < j$. Consider all the decision problems of hypothesis testing between two alternatives, $H_1 : P = P_{q(j)}$ and $H_2 : P = P_{q(n)}$, with n such that $1 \leq n \leq i$. Let $\beta_{j,n}^{\varepsilon,N}$, with $1 \leq n \leq i$, be the lowest achievable probability of error corresponding to each hypothesis test when the other individual probability of error $\alpha_{j,n}^N < \varepsilon$. Then the overall probability of error for these i decision problems is defined as the average sum of the individual probabilities of error $\beta_{j,n}^{\varepsilon,N}$, i.e.,

$$\beta_{\leftarrow}^{\varepsilon,N}(i,j) = \frac{1}{i} \sum_{1 \leq n \leq i} \beta_{j,n}^{\varepsilon,N}. \tag{2}$$

The overall probability of error $\beta_{\leftarrow}^{\varepsilon,N}(i,j)$ is essentially determined by the individual probability of error $\beta_{j,n}^{\varepsilon,N}$ for the hypothesis test between $P_{q(j)}$ and the distribution in $\{P_{q(1)}, \cdots, P_{q(n)}, \cdots, P_{q(i)}\}$ that is closest to $P_{q(j)}$ (for further details see [3]).

For a given level of compression $q(i)$, the best value in the overall probability of error $\beta_{\leftarrow}^{\varepsilon,N}(i,j)$, with j such that $i < j$, is simply given by:

$$\beta_{\leftarrow}^{\varepsilon,N}(i) = \min_{i < j \leq K} \{\beta_{\leftarrow}^{\varepsilon,N}(i,j)\}. \tag{3}$$

Thus, the best value $\beta_{\leftarrow}^{\varepsilon,N}(i)$ is given by the overall probability of error $\beta_{\leftarrow}^{\varepsilon,N}(i,j)$ for the distribution $P_{q(j)}$ in $\{P_{q(i+1)}, \cdots, P_{q(K)}\}$ that is furthest away from the subset $\{P_{q(1)}, P_{q(2)}, \cdots, P_{q(i)}\}$.

Similarly we can define, for each compression ratio $q(i)$, the probability of error over all the decision problems of hypothesis testing to decide between a distribution in $\{P_{q(1)}, P_{q(2)}, \cdots, P_{q(i)}\}$ and any other in $\{P_{q(i+1)}, P_{q(i+2)}, \cdots, P_{q(K)}\}$ as follows.

For a given level $q(i)$, let $q(l)$ be a compression ratio such that $l \leq i$; that is, $q(l) \leq q(i)$. Consider now all the decision problems of hypothesis testing between two alternatives:

$$H_1 : P = P_{q(m)}$$
$$H_2 : P = P_{q(l)}$$

with m such that $i < m \leq K$. Let $\beta_{m,l}^{\varepsilon,N}$ be the lowest achievable probability of error corresponding to each hypothesis test when the other individual probability of error $\alpha_{m,l}^N < \varepsilon$.

Definition 2. The overall probability of error for these new $K - i$ decision problems is given by:

$$\beta_{\rightarrow}^{\varepsilon,N}(l,i) = \frac{1}{K-i} \sum_{i<m\leq K} \beta_{m,l}^{\varepsilon,N} . \tag{4}$$

In this case, the overall probability of error $\beta_{\rightarrow}^{\varepsilon,N}(l,i)$ is essentially determined by the individual probability of error $\beta_{m,l}^{\varepsilon,N}$ for the hypothesis test between $P_{q(l)}$ and the distribution in $\{P_{q(i+1)}, \cdots, P_{q(m)}, \cdots, P_{q(K)}\}$ that is closest to $P_{q(l)}$ (see proof of Theorem 1 in [3]).

For a given compression ratio $q(i)$, the best value in the overall probability of error $\beta_{\rightarrow}^{\varepsilon,N}(l,i)$, with l such that $l \leq i$, is simply given by:

$$\beta_{\rightarrow}^{\varepsilon,N}(i) = \min_{1\leq l\leq i}\{\beta_{\rightarrow}^{\varepsilon,N}(l,i)\} . \tag{5}$$

Thus, the best value $\beta_{\rightarrow}^{\varepsilon,N}(i)$ is given by the overall probability of error $\beta_{\rightarrow}^{\varepsilon,N}(l,i)$ that corresponds to the distribution $P_{q(l)}$ in $\{P_{q(1)}, P_{q(2)}, \cdots, P_{q(i)}\}$ that is furthest away from the subset $\{P_{q(i+1)}, P_{q(i+2)}, \cdots, P_{q(K)}\}$.

For a given compression ratio $q(i)$ with $1 \leq i < K$, let $\beta^{\varepsilon,N}(i)$ be the average sum of the best overall probability of error $\beta_{\rightarrow}^{\varepsilon,N}(i)$ and the best overall probability of error $\beta_{\leftarrow}^{\varepsilon,N}(i)$, i.e.,

$$\beta^{\varepsilon,N}(i) = \frac{1}{2}\left[\beta_{\rightarrow}^{\varepsilon,N}(i) + \beta_{\leftarrow}^{\varepsilon,N}(i)\right] . \tag{6}$$

Levels of compression $q(i)$ that more clearly separate the set of distributions in two subsets $\{P_{q(1)}, P_{q(2)}, \cdots, P_{q(i)}\}$ and $\{P_{q(i+1)}, P_{q(i+2)}, \cdots, P_{q(K)}\}$, will produce lower values of the average sum $\beta^{\varepsilon,N}(i)$ of the best overall probabilities of error $\beta_{\rightarrow}^{\varepsilon,N}(i)$ and $\beta_{\leftarrow}^{\varepsilon,N}(i)$.

We will now define some new notation to express equality to first order in the exponent, as suggested in [1].

Definition 3. The notation $a_N \doteq b_N$ means

$$\lim_{N\to\infty} \frac{1}{N}\log\frac{a_N}{b_N} = 0$$

and therefore $a_N \doteq b_N$ implies that a_N and b_N are equal to the first order in the exponent. The logarithmic base 2 is used throughout this paper unless otherwise stated.

The best achievable compression ratio can now be defined as follows.

Definition 4. Best Achievable Compression Ratio. The best achievable compression ratio $q(i^*)$ is the highest level of compression that attains the asymptotically best value in $\beta^{\varepsilon,N}(i)$, i.e.,

$$\min_{1\leq i<K} \beta^{\varepsilon,N}(i) \doteq \beta^{\varepsilon,N}(i^*), \tag{7}$$

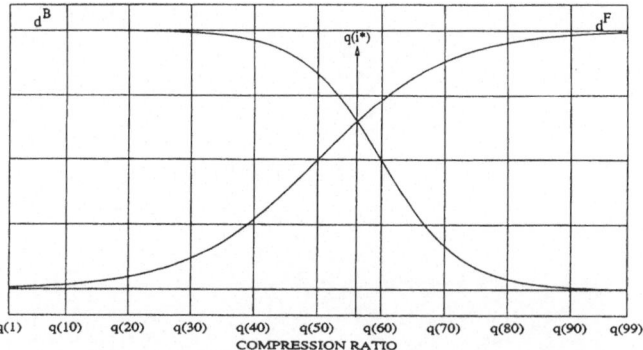

Fig. 1. $d^F(i)$ is non-decreasing and $d^B(i)$ is non-increasing; the maximum value of the minimum of $\{d^F(i), d^B(i)\}$ is attained if they are equal

and also verifies a condition of consistency

$$\beta^{\varepsilon,N}_{\rightarrow}(i^*) \doteq \beta^{\varepsilon,N}_{\leftarrow}(i^*). \tag{8}$$

The following result states the relationship between the best achievable compression ratio $q(i^*)$ and the Kullback-Leibler information gain.

Theorem 1. Let $q(i^*)$ be the highest compression ratio such that:

$$d^B(i^*) = d^F(i^*) \tag{9}$$

where

$$d^B(i) = \max_{i < j \le K} \left\{ \min_{1 \le n \le i} KL(P_{q(j)}, P_{q(n)}) \right\} \tag{10}$$

and

$$d^F(i) = \max_{1 \le l \le i} \left\{ \min_{i < m \le K} KL(P_{q(m)}, P_{q(l)}) \right\} \tag{11}$$

with $KL(P_{q(\dagger)}, P_{q(\ddagger)})$ being the Kullback-Leibler information gain [5] between $P_{q(\dagger)}$ and $P_{q(\ddagger)}$:

$$KL(P_{q(\dagger)}, P_{q(\ddagger)}) = \sum_l p(l/I_{q(\dagger)}) \log \frac{p(l/I_{q(\dagger)})}{p(l/I_{q(\ddagger)})},$$

where $P_{q(\dagger)} = (p(l/I_{q(\dagger)}))_l$ characterizes the probability of occurrence of each gray level l in the decoded image $I_{q(\dagger)}$ at compression ratio $q(\dagger)$.

Then, $q(i^*)$ is the best achievable compression ratio for the sequence of levels $q(1), q(2), \cdots, q(K)$.

Proof. See [3]. Figure 1 illustrates the functional shape of d^F and d^B.

This result implies that the performance bound given by the best achievable compression ratio is operational in that it is directly achievable by a constructive procedure. This optimal level will allow us to determine a boundary between achievable and non-achievable regions, and consequently, it provides useful information to benchmark specific applications.

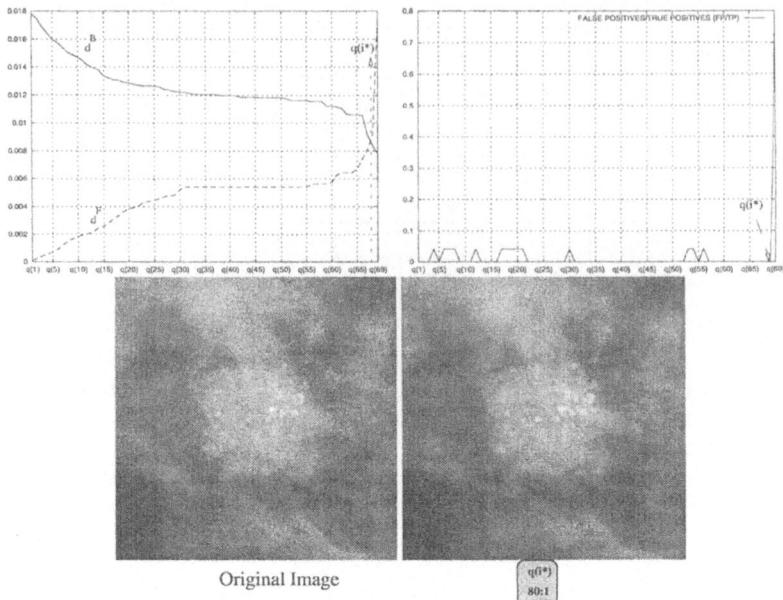

Original Image

Fig. 2. Plot of $d^B(i)$ and $d^F(i)$ for SPIHT; Best achievable compression ratio $q(i^*)$

3   Effects of Lossy Compression at Best Achievable Compression Ratio

This section analyzes the effects of lossy compression at the best achievable level on a test image corresponding to a digitized mammogram selected from the Nijmegen database [4] containing some clustered microcalcifications (see Figure 2).

The test image was coded at various compression ratios using the SPIHT algorithm operating through set partitioning in hierarchical trees [7] and accomplishing completely embedded coding. Figure 2 shows the obtained boundary between achievable and non-achievable regions, in which the best achievable compression ratio is obtained for the coder by using the constructive procedure given in Section 2. Figure 2 illustrates the plot of $d^B(i)$ and $d^F(i)$ for SPIHT. As suggested in Theorem 1 the best achievable compression ratio $q(i^*)$ is attained if $d^B(i^*) = d^F(i^*)$. For this test image *micro*, it happens at a high compression ratio of 80 : 1

Figure 2 also shows a plot of the false positive to true positive ratio (FP/TP) for microcalcification detection upon images reconstructed under various degrees of lossy compression using SPIHT. In order to derive the false positive to true positive detection ratio, the images reconstructed after compression were also reviewed to detect individual microcalcifications. This method can be used for characterizing compression losses using decoded images. Since it is rated diagnostic usefulness rather than general appearance or simply line or edge patterns,

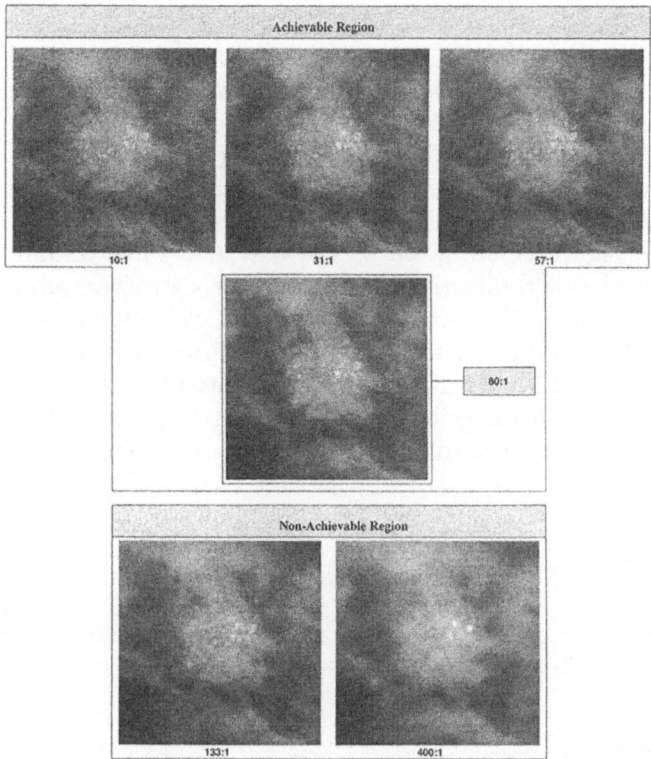

Fig. 3. Achievable and non-achievable regions using the SPIHT coder for micro

this method relates diagnostic accuracy to compression level. In fact, when the diagnostic usefulness of the reconstructed images significantly decreases, the false positive to true positive ratio also shows a significant increase. We show the plot of $d^B(i)$ and $d^F(i)$, the point at which $d^B(i^*) = d^F(i^*)$, the relationship between this point and the FP/TP ratio, as well as a reconstruction after compression at the best achievable ratio $q(i^*)$. As can be seen from Figure 2, the false positive to true positive ratio for the reconstruction at level $q(i^*)$ indicates that the imperfect source representation given by the image compressed at $q(i^*)$ is sufficient for evaluations that take into account diagnostic usefulness. Conversely, the diagnostic usefulness of images reconstructed at levels $q(i)$, with $i > i^*$, significantly decreases, i.e., the corresponding false positive to true positive rate shows a significant increase. This means that the best achievable compression ratio $q(i^*)$ determines a performance bound for the mammographic image micro; that is, it will allow us to distinguish between the best achievable operating points and those that are suboptimal or unachievable for the given image.

Both achievable and non-achievable regions using SPIHT for the test image are illustrated in Figure 3. For additional examples see [3].

4   Conclusions

The focus of this paper has been to a large extent the reformulation of the trade-off between image distortion and coding rate in terms of the derivation of an optimal compression level based on the relationship between information theory and the decision problems of hypothesis testing. This optimal level will allow us to determine a boundary between achievable and nonachievable regions, and consequently, it provides useful information to benchmark specific applications.

The performance bound given by the best achievable compression ratio is operational in that it is directly achievable by a constructive procedure, as suggested in Theorem 1. This theorem has stated the relationship between the best achievable compression ratio and the Kullback-Leibler information gain: the overall probabilities of error behave exponentially with exponents given by a function of the Kullback-Leibler gains, and therefore, the best achievable level of compression corresponds to the argument i that produces the worst value of these exponents.

Acknowledgments

This research was sponsored by the Spanish Board for Science and Technology (CICYT) under grant TIC2000-1421.

References

[1] Cover, T., and Thomas, J. *Elements of Information Theory*, Wiley Series in Telecommunications, John Wiley and Sons, Inc., (1991).

[2] Egger, O., Fleury, P., Ebrahimi, T., and Kunt, M. "High-performance compression of visual information–A Tutorial Review–Part I: Still Pictures", *Proceedings of the IEEE*, Vol. 87, No. 6, pp. 976-1013. (1999).

[3] Garcia, J. A., Fdez-Valdivia, J, Fdez-Vidal, X. R., and Rodriguez-Sanchez, R. "Best achievable compression ratio for lossy image coding", Technical report, Department of Computer Science and Artificial Intelligence, University of Granada, Spain, (2002) (avalaible in ftp://decsai.ugr.es/pub/diata/techrep/TR990324.ps.Z).

[4] Karssemeijer, N. "Adaptive noise equalization and image analysis in mammography." in *13th Int. Conf. Inform. Processing Med. Imag.*, pp. 472-486, (1992).

[5] Kullback, S. *Information theory and statistics*. Gloucester, Peter Smith (1978).

[6] A. Ortega and K. Ramchandran. "Rate-distortion methods for image and video compression." *IEEE Signal processing magazine*, Vol. 4. pp. 23-50, (1998).

[7] Said, A., and Pearlman, W. A., "A new fast and efficient image coder based on set partitioning in hierarchical trees." *IEEE Trans. on Circuits and Systems for Video Technology*, Vol. 6, pp. 243-250, (1996).

Performance and Improvements
of a Language Model
Based on Stochastic Context-Free Grammars*

José García-Hernandez, Joan Andreu Sánchez, and José Miguel Benedí

Depto. Sistemas Informáticos y Computación,
Universidad Politécnica de Valencia,
Camino de Vera, s/n. 46071-Valencia (Spain),
{jogarcia,jandreu,jbenedi}@dsic.upv.es

Abstract. This paper describes a hybrid language model defined as
a combination of a word-based n-gram, which is used to capture the
local relations between words, and a category-based SCFG with a word
distribution into categories, which is defined to represent the long-term
relations between these categories. Experiments on the UPenn Treebank
corpus are reported. These experiments have been carried out in terms
of the test set perplexity and the word error rate in a speech recognition
experiment.

1   Introduction

Language modeling is an important aspect to consider in the development of
speech and text recognition systems. The n-gram models are the most extensively
used for a wide range of domains [1]. The n-grams are simple and robust models
and adequately capture the local restrictions between words. Also, the estimation
the parameters and the integration of the model in speech recognition system
are well-known. However, the n-gram models cannot characterize the long-term
constraints of the sentences of the tasks.

Stochastic Context-Free Grammars (SCFGs) efficiently model long-term relations and have been successfully used on limited-domain tasks of low perplexity.
However, general-purpose SCFGs work poorly on large vocabulary tasks. The
main obstacles to using these models in complex real tasks are the difficulties of
learning and integrating SCFGs.

Several proposals have attempted to solve these problems by combining
a word n-gram model and a structural model in order to consider the syntactic
structure of the language [3, 9].

In the same way, we previously proposed a general hybrid language model [2].
This is defined as a linear combination of a word n-gram model, which is used to
capture the local relation between words, and a stochastic grammatical model,

---

* This work has been partially supported by the Spanish CICYT under contract
(TIC2002/04103-C03-03).

F.J. Perales et al. (Eds.): IbPRIA 2003, LNCS 2652, pp. 271–278, 2003.

which is used to represent the global relation between syntactic structures. In order to capture the long-term relations between syntactic structures and to solve the main problems derived from large-vocabulary complex tasks, we proposed a stochastic grammatical model defined by a category-based SCFG together with a probabilistic model of word distribution in the categories. Finally, experiments with a Penn Treebank corpus showed significant improvements in the test set perplexity with regard to the classical n-gram models.

The first part of this work is devoted to presenting the hybrid language model. In the second part we present the new improvements in the hybrid model together with the results of their evaluation process. The improvements have mainly focused on the estimation of better stochastic grammatical models. The evaluation process has been done using the Wall Street Journal part of the UPenn Treebank corpus. Two points of view have been considered: in order to compare results with other stochastic language models, an evaluation in terms of the *test set perplexity* results was carried out; in order to evaluate the behavior of this model in a speech recognition task, recognition performance in terms of the *word error rate* results were also reported.

2   The Language Model

An important problem related to language modeling is the computation of $\Pr(w_k|w_1\ldots w_{k-1})$ [4]. In order to calculate this probability, we proposed in [2] a general hybrid language model defined as a linear combination of a word n-gram model, which is used to capture the local relation between words, and a word stochastic grammatical model M_s which is used to represent the global relation between syntactic structures and which allows us to generalize the word n-gram model.

$$\Pr(w_k|w_1\ldots w_{k-1}) = \alpha\,\Pr(w_k|w_{k-n+1}\ldots w_{k-1})$$
$$+(1-\alpha)\,\Pr(w_k|w_1\ldots w_{k-1}, M_s), \qquad (1)$$

where $0 \leq \alpha \leq 1$ is a weight factor which depends on the task. Similar proposals have been presented by other authors [3, 9] along the same line.

The first term of expression (1) is the word probability of w_k given by the word n-gram model. The parameters of this model can be easily estimated, and the expression $\Pr(w_k|w_{k-n+1}\ldots w_{k-1})$ can be efficiently computed [4].

In order to capture long-term relations between syntactic structures and to solve the main problems derived from large vocabulary complex tasks, we proposed a stochastic grammatical model M_s defined as a combination of two different stochastic models: a category-based SCFG (G_c) and a stochastic model of word distribution into categories (C_w). Thus, the second term of the expression (1) can be written as: $\Pr(w_k|w_1\ldots w_{k-1}, G_c, C_w)$.

There are two important questions to consider: the definition and learning of G_c and C_w, and the computation of the probability $\Pr(w_k|w_1\ldots w_{k-1}, G_c, C_w)$.

Learning of the Models The parameters of the models G_c and C_w are estimated from a set of sentences from a training sample. We work with a Treebank corpus, where each word of the sentence is labeled with part-of-speech tags (POStag). From now on, these POStags are referred to as word categories in C_w and are the terminal symbols of the SCFG in G_c.

With regard to the learning of the G_c, several algorithms that learn SCFGs by means of estimation algorithms have been proposed. Some of the most widely-known methods for estimating SCFGs are: the Inside-Outside (IO) algorithm [6] and an algorithm based on the Viterbi score (VS algorithm). Alternatively, other algorithms, which only use a certain subset of derivations in the estimation process, have also been considered: from structural information content in a bracketed corpus (IOb algorithm [8] and VSb algorithm [11]) or from statistical information content in the $k-$best derivations [11]. Taking into account the good results achieved with category-based SCFGs on real tasks [11], some of these algorithms (VS, VSb and IOb) are considered in this work.

The parameters of the word-category distribution, $C_w = \Pr(w|c)$ are computed in terms of the number of times that the word w has been labeled with the POStag c. It is important to note that a word w can belong to different categories. In addition, it may happen that a word in a test set does not appear in the training set, and, therefore, its probability $\Pr(w|c)$ is not defined. We solve this problem by adding the term $\Pr(\text{UNK}|c)$ for all categories, where $\Pr(\text{UNK}|c)$ is the probability for unseen words of the test set.

Integration of the Model The computation of $\Pr(w_k|w_1 \ldots w_{k-1}, G_c, C_w)$ can be expressed as:

$$\Pr(w_k|w_1 \ldots w_{k-1}, G_c, C_w) = \frac{\Pr(w_1 \ldots w_k \ldots |G_c, C_w)}{\Pr(w_1 \ldots w_{k-1} \ldots |G_c, C_w)}, \tag{2}$$

where $\Pr(w_1 \ldots w_k \ldots |G_c, C_w)$ represents the probability of generating an initial substring given G_c and C_w.

This expression is computed by means of a simple adaptation [2] of two well-known algorithms: the LRI algorithm [5], to obtain the probability of generating an initial substring; and the Inside algorithm [6], to obtain the probability of generating a string.

3   Experiments with the UPenn Treebank Corpus

The corpus used in the experiments was the part of the Wall Street Journal (WSJ) which had been processed in the UPenn Treebank project[1] [7]. This corpus consists of English texts collected from the Wall Street Journal from editions of the late eighties. It contains approximately one million words distributed in

---

[1] Release 2 of this data set can be obtained from the Linguistic Data Consortium with Catalogue number LDC94T4B (http://www.ldc.upenn.edu/ldc/noframe.html)

Table 1. Characteristics of the WSJ corpus once it was divided into sentences

Data set	Directories	No. of senten.	No. of words
Training	00-20	42,075	1,004,073
Tuning	21-22	3,371	80,156
Test	23-24	3,762	89,537

25 directories. This corpus was automatically labelled, analyzed and manually checked as described in [7]. There are two kinds of labelling: a POStag labelling and a syntactic labelling. The size of the vocabulary is greater than 49,000 different words, the POStag vocabulary is composed of 45 labels[2] and the syntactic vocabulary is composed of 14 labels. The corpus was divided into sentences according to the bracketing. For the experiments, the corpus was divided into three sets: training, tuning and test. The main characteristics of these sets can be seen in Table 1. The sentences labeled with POStags were used to estimate the parameters of the category-based SCFGs, and the sentences labeled with both POStags and with words were used to estimate the parameters of the hybrid language model.

First, we present new improvements in the estimation of the stochastic grammatical models. Then, we describe the experiments which were carried out in order to test the hybrid language model.

3.1 Experiments Using Category-Based SCFGs

The parameters of an initial SCFG were estimated using the estimation methods described in the previous section. The initial grammar was in Chomsky Normal Form and it had the maximum number of rules which can be created with a given number of non-terminal symbols and 45 terminal symbols (the number of POStags).

The training set labeled with POStags was used to estimate the parameters of the models. In order to evaluate the proposed estimation methods, we reduced the computational effort by not considering the sentences with more than 50 words in the training set. Thus, the number of sentences was 41, 315 (98.2% over complete training) and the number of words was 959, 390 (95.6% over complete training).

The perplexity of the POStag part of the tuning set for different estimation algorithms (VS, VSb and IOb algorithms) and for different number of non-terminals was computed. In previous works [2], the number of non-terminals was chosen according to the number of syntactic tags defined in [7]. However, the obtained results were not satisfactory. Taking into account that the grammars are in Chomsky Normal Form, we consider that this number of non-terminals is not realistic. In order to test this hypothesis we increased this value progressively and the results can be seen in Table 2.

---

[2] There are 48 labels defined in [7], however, some of them do not appear in the corpus.

Table 2.   Number of non-terminals ($|N|$), tuning set perplexity (tsp) and number of rules of the final model (size) for the SCFG estimated with the VS, VSb and IOB algorithms

	VS		VSb		IOb	
$|N|$	tsp	size	tsp	size	tsp	size
14	20.13	195	21.10	256	13.34	471
20	20.42	255	19.38	406	12.33	888
25	17.59	407	16.93	499	11.86	1042
30	17.67	367	17.90	609	11.32	1454
35	16.92	600	16.64	789	10.24	1741

In general, the goodness of the model tended to decrease as the value of N increased. It can be observed that the best result was obtained by the IOb algorithm. For this algorithm, the percentage of improvement from 14 non-terminals to 35 non-terminals was 23.24%. However, it is important to note that time complexity of the estimation algorithms increases linearly with this value. With respect to the number of iterations needed to converge, the slowest algorithm was the IOb algorithm. Finally, it can be observed that the size of the final models increased with N and that the biggest models were obtained by the IOb algorithm.

3.2   Experiments with the Hybrid Language Model

First, we present perplexity results on the described task. These results are compared with the results obtained by other authors for the same task. Second, we present word error rate results on a speech recogniton experiment.

Perplexity Results In order to compare our model with other hybrid models, we carried out the experiments taking into account the restrictions considered in other works [3, 9]. The most remarkable restriction was that the vocabulary was restricted to the 10,000 most frequent words which appear in the training.

First, we describe the estimation of a 3-gram model to be used as both a baseline model and as a part of the hybrid language model. The parameters of a 3-gram model were estimated using the software tool described in [10][3]. Different smoothing techniques were tested, but we chose the one which provides a test set perplexity which is similar to the one presented in [3, 9]. Linear discounting was used as smoothing technique with the default parameters. The out-of-vocabulary words were used in the computation of the perplexity, and back-off from context cues was excluded. The tuning set perplexity with this model was 160.26 and the test set perplexity was 167.30.

Second, the category-based SCFGs (G_c) of the hybrid model was estimated with different algorithms such as we described previously. We selected the IOb

---

[3] Release 2.05 is available at http://svr-www.eng.cam.ac.uk/~prc14/toolkit.html.

Table 3. Test set perplexity with a 3-gram model and with the hybrid language model and percentage of improvement for different proposals

Model	Perplexity Trigram	Interpolated	α	% improvement
Previous model (IOb-14)	167.30	152.12	0.73	9.1
Current model (IOb-35)	167.30	142.29	0.65	13.2
(Chelba and Jelinek, 2000)	167.14	148.90	0.4	10.9
(Roark, 2001)	167.02	137.26	0.4	17.8

algorithm with 14 and 35 non-terminals for this experiment. In this way, we could compare the results obtained with the previous model (14 non-terminals) and the current model (35 non-terminals).

Finally, the parameters of the word-category distribution $C_w = \Pr(w|c)$ were computed from the POStags and the words of the training corpus. The unseen events of the test corpus were considered as the same word UNK and we conjectured that the unknown words were not equally distributed among categories, and we assigned a probability based on the classification of unknown words into categories in the tuning set. A small probability ϵ was assigned if no unseen event was associated to the category. The percentage of unknown words in the training set was 4.47% distributed in 31 categories and the percentage of unknown words in the tuning set was 5.53% distributed in 23 categories.

Once the parameters of the hybrid model were estimated, we applied expression (1). The tuning set was used in order to determine the best value of α for the hybrid model, and then the test set perplexity was computed. Table 3 shows the results obtained for different algorithms and the results obtained by other authors who define left-to-right hybrid language models of the same nature [3, 9]. It should be noted that the differences in the perplexity of the trigram model were due mainly to the different smoothing techniques[4]. It can be observed that the last results obtained by our model are very good, even better if you consider that both the models and their learning methods are well-consolidated. In addition, an important improvement of 4.50% was observed when we increased the number of non-terminals. The weight of the structural model of our proposal was less than the other models. This may be due to the fact that in the other models, the structural part has been constructed by using very rich linguistic information since they used the syntactic tagging and the bracketing to learn the model. In our model, we only used the bracketing information in the estimation process of our model G_c.

---

[4] Recently, important reductions in perplexity have been obtained, with the model proposed in [3], by using very different smoothing techniques. Their best results were: perplexity of the trigram model 145, perplexity of the interpolated model 130 and percentage of improvement 10.3%.

Table 4. Word error rate results for several models, with different training and vocabulary sizes, and the best language model factor

Model	Training Size	Vocabulary Size	LM Weight	WER
Lattice trigram	40M	20K	16	13.7
(Chelba and Jelinek, 2000)	20M	20K	16	13.0
(Roark, 2001)	1M	10K	15	15.1
Treebank trigram	1M	10K	5	16.6
No language model			0	16.8
Previous model	1M	10K	4	16.4
Current model	1M	10K	6	16.0

Word Error Rate Results Now, we describe preliminary speech recognition experiments which were carried out to evaluate the hybrid language model. Given that our hybrid language model is not integrated in a speech recognition system, we reproduced the experiments described in [3, 9] in order to compare our results with those reported in that works.

The experiment consisted of rescoring a list of n best hypotheses provided by the speech recognizer described in [3]. A better language model was expected to improve the results provided by a less powerful language model. In order to avoid the influence of the language model of the speech recognizer it is important to use a large value of n; however, for these experiments, this value was lower.

The experiments carried out was the DARPA '93 HUB1 test setup. This test consists of 213 utterances read from the *Wall Street Journal* with a total of 3,446 words. The corpus comes with a baseline trigram model, using a 20,000-word open vocabulary, and is trained on approximately 40 million words.

The 50 best hypotheses from each lattice were computed using Ciprian Chelba's A* decoder, along with the acoustic and trigram scores. Unfortunately, in many cases, 50 distinct string hypotheses were not provided [9]. An average of 22.9 hypotheses per utterance were rescored.

The LRI algorithm was used in order to compute the probability of each word in the list of hypotheses. The probability obtained with the hybrid language model was combined with the acoustic score and the results can be seen in Table 4 together with the results obtained for different language models.

We can observe that our language model slightly improved the results obtained by the baseline model, in accordance with the results obtained by other authors. However, our improvements were slight worst than the improvements obtained by other authors which used the same training corpus. This behavior was expected, given that the other models were structurally richer.

4   Conclusions

We have been described a hybrid language and results of its evaluation has also been provided. The test set perplexity results were as good as the ones obtained by other authors, even better if you consider that the models are very simple and their learning methods are well-known.

The word error rate results were slight worst than the ones obtained by other authors. However, we remark that these results tended to improve without including any additional linguistic information.

For future work, we propose to extend the experimentation by increasing the size of the training corpus in accordance with the work of other authors.

Acknowledgements

The authors would like to thank to Brian Roark for providing them the n-best lists for the HUB1 test set.

References

[1] L.R. Bahl, F. Jelinek, and R.L. Mercer. A maximum likelihood approach to continuous speech recognition. *IEEE Trans. Pattern Analysis and Machine Intelligence*, PAMI-5(2):179–190, 1983.

[2] J.M. Benedí and J.A. Sánchez. Combination of n-grams and stochastic context-free grammars for language modeling. In *Proc. COLING*, pages 55–61, Saarbrücken, Germany, 2000.

[3] C. Chelba and F. Jelinek. Structured language modeling. *Computer Speech and Language*, 14:283–332, 2000.

[4] F. Jelinek. *Statistical Methods for Speech Recognition*. MIT Press, 1998.

[5] F. Jelinek and J.D. Lafferty. Computation of the probability of initial substring generation by stochastic context-free grammars. *Computational Linguistics*, 17(3):315–323, 1991.

[6] K. Lari and S.J. Young. The estimation of stochastic context-free grammars using the inside-outside algorithm. *Computer, Speech and Language*, 4:35–56, 1990.

[7] M.P. Marcus, B. Santorini, and M.A. Marcinkiewicz. Building a large annotated corpus of english: the penn treebank. *Computational Linguistics*, 19(2):313–330, 1993.

[8] F. Pereira and Y. Schabes. Inside-outside reestimation from partially bracketed corpora. In *Proceedings of the 30th Annual Meeting of the Association for Computational Linguistics*, pages 128–135. University of Delaware, USA, 1992.

[9] B. Roark. Probabilistic top-down parsing and language modeling. *Computational Linguistics*, 27(2):249–276, 2001.

[10] R. Rosenfeld. The cmu statistical language modeling toolkit and its use in the 1994 arpa csr evaluation. In *ARPA Spoken Language Technology Workshop*, Austin, USA, 1995.

[11] J.A. Sánchez and J.M. Benedí. Learning of stochastic context-free grammars by means of estimation algorithms. In *Proc. EUROSPEECH'99*, volume 4, pages 1799–1802, Budapest, Hungary, 1999.

Segmentation of Curvilinear Objects Using a Watershed-Based Curve Adjacency Graph

Thierry Géraud

EPITA Research and Development Laboratory
14-16 rue Voltaire, F-94276 Le Kremlin-Bicêtre cedex, France,
thierry.geraud@lrde.epita.fr
http://www.lrde.epita.fr/

Abstract. This paper presents a general framework to segment curvilinear objects in 2D images. A pre-processing step relies on mathematical morphology to obtain a connected line which encloses curvilinear objects. Then, a graph is constructed from this line and a Markovian Random Field is defined to perform objects segmentation. Applications of our framework are numerous: they go from simple surve segmentation to complex road network extraction in satellite images.

1 Introduction

Many different methods have been proposed to segment curvilinear structures in 2D images. Let us just recall some of them which are, to our humble opinion, the most promising ones:

- tracking by active testing by Geman and Jedynak (1996);
- unifying snakes, region growing and energy/Bayes/MDL, so-called region competition, by Zhu and Yuille (1996);
- defining Markovian field on a set of segments by Tupin et al. (1998);
- dynamic programming for saliency optimization by Lindenbaum and Berengolts;
- using a Markov point process by Stoica et al. (2000).

These methods suffer from drawbacks. The saliency approach does not rely on a global optimization process. Tracking-like approaches cannot plainly take into account features extracted from image regions and require a starting point; these approaches are thus limited to rather easy segmentation problems. Markovian approaches are often computationally expensive due to the high number of primitives —small segments— they have to handle. Last, region competition is also an expensive approach where both the region and variational flavors are not often pertinent when objects are not regions.

In this paper we propose a general framework for curvilinear object segmentation that overcomes these drawbacks.

F.J. Perales et al. (Eds.): IbPRIA 2003, LNCS 2652, pp. 279–286, 2003.

This paper is organized as follows. The first section is a preliminary section that introduces the basic ideas and tools on which the proposed framework relies. Section 3 then describes the framework itself and illustrates its capabilities on road extraction in satellite images; afterwards, we conclude in section 4.

2   Preliminaries

2.1   Watershed Transform

The watershed transform (WT), as explained by Vincent and Soille (1991), is a morphological algorithm usually used for the purpose of segmentation. Considering a gray level image as a topographic map, let us denote by catchment basin associated with a regional minimum of this map, all points whose steepest slope paths reach this minimum. The watershed line is a closed one-pixel thick crest line which separates every adjacent catchment basins, i.e., regions.

2.2   Region Adjacency Graph and Markov Random Field

A now common framework to segment an image I or to extract objects from I is based on the watershed transform; it can be summarized as follows.

1. An image G of the gradient norm of I is computed. Contours in the gradient norm image (GNI) G have high intensity values whereas regions have low intensity values.
2. The watershed transform (WT) is applied to G which results in getting a partition of I into regions. The watershed line passes through crest lines of G, that is, objects contours. This partition, P, is an over-segmentation since G contains a number of minima greater than the effective number of objects/regions to segment.
3. The region adjacency graph (RAG) is extracted from P. A node corresponds to a region (more precisely, a catchment basin) and an edge between two nodes indicates that these regions are adjacent. Extra information are put into the graph; for instance they can be statistical estimations concerning regions of I which are then enclosed in graph nodes, or saliency values of contours estimated from I and added to graph nodes.
4. The last step aims at grouping regions according to given criterions in order to get a final segmentation. To that aim, a Markov Random Field (MRF) is defined onto the RAG and the segmentation process is handled by a Markovian relaxation.

This framework is powerful since it remains general —it can be applied to various imagery segmentation problems— and since the final segmentation results from a global process on high-level image primitives (regions in that case). Moreover, it enables operational segmentations even when images are over-sized and when objects are difficult to segment; for instance, Géraud et al.

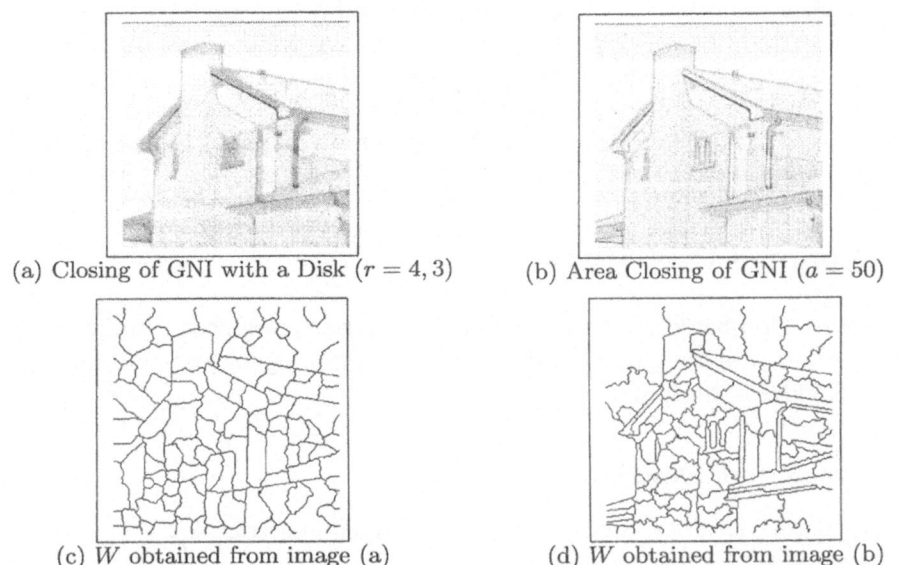

(a) Closing of GNI with a Disk $(r = 4, 3)$ (b) Area Closing of GNI $(a = 50)$

(c) W obtained from image (a)   (d) W obtained from image (b)

Fig. 1. Watershed Transform Results with the Same Final Number of Regions

(1995) succeed in segmenting internal brain structures from magnetic resonance images. Let us mention that this framework has been discussed by many authors such as Kim and Yang (1994); Haris et al. (1998); Bleau and Leon (2000); Sarkar et al. (2000), and a multi-scale version of this framework has been proposed by Gauch (1999).

2.3   Minima Suppression and Area Closing

A classic algorithm to suppress minima in images is the morphological closing operator. When these is no prior information about the shape of image objects, closing is usually performed with a structural element being a disk in order to preserve isotropy. However, artifacts appear in resulting images: in particular, crest lines can strongly move when one wants to remove many minima, that is, when filtering strength (i.e., the disk radius) increases.

Conversely, an area closing operator does not present this drawback. This operator is a "connected filter", as described by Salembier and Serra (1995), which removes minima whose area (influence zone) is less than a given threshold. A fast implementation of this operator is provided by Meijster and Wilkinson (2002).

Figure 1 illustrates the contour shifting / un-shifting properties of both "classical" and area closing operators. Starting from the classical HOUSE image, we apply closing operators to its gradient norm image (GNI); the negatives of the results are depicted by images (a) and (b). We then apply the watershed transform algorithm, which respectively leads to images (c) and (d). Please note that these segmentation results contain the same number of regions. However, contours are shifted when the classical closing is involved which is not the case with the area closing. Moreover, in the former case regions have more uniform sizes and are spread more uniformly over the image space than in the latter case. This is another drawback since we prefer segmentations that are more adapted to original image data.

3   Proposed Framework

Although region-based methods are not well suited to segment curvilinear objects, we now propose a framework which relies on a region segmentation algorithm to address this issue.

3.1   Framework Description

Our framework is very similar to the one described in section 2.2.

Pre-Processing. From an original image containing curvilinear objects we compute a gray level image where pixel values denote their potential of belonging to these objects. Curvilinear objects are thus located on some parts of the crest lines of this "potential" image.

Morphological Filtering. The filtering step consists in computing an area closing of the potential image and then running the watershed transform. The "closed" potential image has much less minima than the "original" potential image while properly retaining crest lines location (Cf. discussions of sections 2.1 and 2.3). Therefore, the resulting watershed line includes the curvilinear objects.

Curve Adjacency Graph. From the watershed line, we build a curve adjacency graph (CAG). A node of this graph (red bullets in the picture below) represents a shed, that is, a connected part of the watershed line separating two adjacent basins. An edge (green lines in the picture below) is drawn between two nodes/sheds if one end of the first shed is connected with a end of the second one through the watershed line.

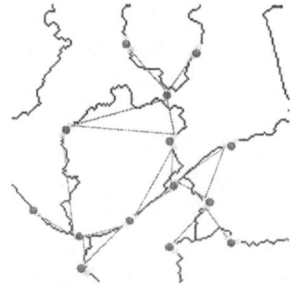

For every node we make the distinction between edges coming from connections to one shed end (yellow anchors) and those coming from connections to the other shed end. This distinction is symbolized by yellow and blue anchors in the picture above.

Markovian Relaxation Segmenting curvilinear objects now turns out to be a graph labeling problem. Upon the graph structure, we define a Markov random field. Let us denote by X the observation field, by Y the result field, by x_s and y_s their respective restriction to a given node s, by Y_{V_s} the restriction of Y to the neighborhood of s. The variable y_s has a Boolean realization where 1 means *object* and 0 means *not object*. Under the Markovian assumption we have:

$$p(y_s|X, Y - y_s) = \tfrac{1}{Z} \exp(-(U(x_s, y_s) + U(Y_{N_s}))).$$

The first energy term, $U(x_s, y_s)$, models *a priori* knowledge about curvilinear objects, and the second energy term, $U(Y_{N_s})$ deals with labeling contextual information. Since we have expressed the object segmentation problem as an energy minimization problem, a relaxation process is performed to finally get the segmentation result.

3.2 Framework Adaptation

In order to apply this framework to a given segmentation application, this framework should be adapted.

The first step depends on the particular application and on the original image data. For instance, when the original image contains a curve to be segmented and when this curve is dark pixels on white background, the potential image can be as simple as the original image once inverted. An other example is the case of road network extraction from a multi-channels satellite image; then the proper channels should be processed (fused) to build the potential image.

Setting the area parameter of the morphological filtering step also depends on both application and data. As explained in section 2.3, this parameter removes image local minima. Thus, considering the watershed transform result, this parameter has an effect of merging small catchment basins. When a curvilinear object contains a loop, this loop can disappear if its area is lower than the area parameter value.

Last, defining the energies for the Markov random field is also data dependent. Features associated with nodes —a *priori* knowledge about piece of curvilinear objects— are numerous; they can be the potential mean value along the piece of curve, a curvature measurement, its saliency as discussed by Najman and Schmitt, and so on. Features related to contextual energy express knowledge about the global shape of the curvilinear objects and the connections between its different parts; for instance, a feature can be a continuity measure when the object is a smooth curve or, in the contrary, a measure that ensures that the object is only composed of straight lines and $\pi/2$ breaks.

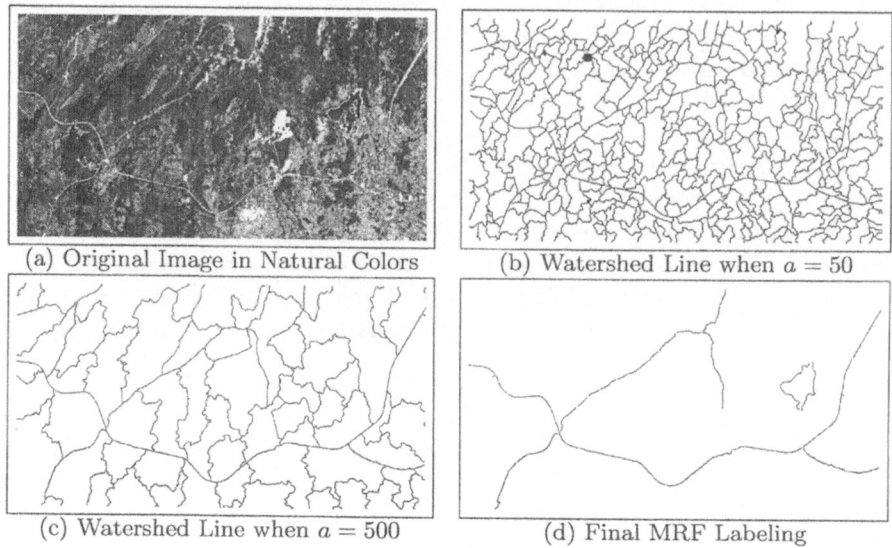

(a) Original Image in Natural Colors   (b) Watershed Line when $a = 50$

(c) Watershed Line when $a = 500$ (d) Final MRF Labeling

Fig. 2. Application to Road Network Extraction

3.3 Illustration

We have applied our framework to different image segmentation issues. In this section, we present a result in the field of road extraction network. It is illustrated with a small part (700×380 pixels) of a Landsat image from St-Johns city, Canada, having a 25 m resolution and 7 spectral channels; see figure 2. This original image is under *"Copyright © 2000. Government of Canada with permission from Natural Resources Canada"* (http://geogratis.cgdi.gc.ca/). Applying the whole road extraction process to an image having 2.10^6 pixels takes less than 20s on a 1,7 GHz personal computer running GNU/Linux and using our image processing library Olena (Cf. section "notes and Comments" after section 4) which provides fast implementation of algorithms.

As one can see on figures 2 (b) and 2 (c), with different values of the area parameter the resulting watershed line is more or less simplified but data of interest are not affected. Extra information about applying the proposed method to road network extraction are given in Géraud (2003).

4   Conclusion

We have presented a method to extract road network from satellite images. We have transposed the recognition scheme "WT + RAG + MRF", described in section 2.2 and which is dedicated to image segmentation, to the problematic of road network recognition. To that aim, we propose a recognition scheme that is, as far as we know, original: "area opening + WT + CAG + MRF".

This recognition scheme is a global optimization process so it provides robust and reproducible results. Moreover, it is general and can easily be adapted to various image processing fields where the recognition of curvilinear structures is involved.

Notes and Comments. Source code of our method is available on the Internet from the location `http://www.lrde.epita.fr`. It has been developed using OLENA, our generic image processing library. OLENA is free software under the GNU Public Licence (GPL) and information about this library are presented by Darbon et al. (2002).

References

A. Bleau and L. Leon. Watershed-based segmentation and region merging. *Computer Vision and Image Understanding*, 77:317–370, 2000.

J. Darbon, T. Géraud, and A. Duret-Lutz. Generic implementation of morphological image operators. In *Mathematical Morphology, Proceedings of the 6th International Symposium VI (ISMM)*, pages 175–184, Sydney, Australia, April 2002. Sciro Publishing.

J. Gauch. Image segmentation and analysis via multiscale gradient watershed hierarchies. *IEEE Trans. on Image Processing*, 8(1):69–79, January 1999.

D. Geman and B. Jedynak. An active testing model for traking roads in satellite images. *IEEE Trans. on Pattern Analysis and Machine Intelligence*, 18(1): 1–14, 1996.

T. Géraud. Fast road network extraction in satellite images using mathematical morphology and Markov random fields. In *Proceedings of the IEEE-EURASIP Workshop on Nonlinear Signal and Image Processing*, Grado, Italy, June 2003. To appear.

T. Géraud, J.-F. Mangin, I. Bloch, and H. Maître. Segmenting internal structures in 3D MR images of the brain by Markovian relaxation on a watershed based adjacency graph. In *Proc. of the IEEE Int. Conf. on Image Processing*, volume 3, pages 548–551, 1995.

K. Haris, S. Efstratiadis, N. Maglaveras, and A. Katsaggelos. Hybrid image segmentation using watersheds and fast region merging. *IEEE Trans. on Image Processing*, 7(12):1684–1699, December 1998.

I. Kim and H. Yang. A systematic way for region-based image segmentation based on Markov random field model. In *Pattern Recognition Letters*, volume 15, pages 969–976, October 1994.

M. Lindenbaum and A. Berengolts. A probabilistic interpretation of the saliency network. In *Proceedings of the European Conference on Computer Vision (2)*, volume 1843 of *Lecture Notes in Computer Science*, pages 257–272. Springer, 2000.

A. Meijster and M. Wilkinson. A comparison of algorithms for connected set openings and closings. *IEEE Trans. on Pattern Analysis and Machine Intelligence*, 24(4):484–494, 2002.

L. Najman and M. Schmitt. Geodesic saliency of watershed contours and hierarchical segmentation. *IEEE Trans. on Pattern Analysis and Machine Intelligence*, 18(12):1163–1173, December 1996.

P. Salembier and J. Serra. Flat zones filtering, connected operators, and filters by reconstruction. *IEEE Trans. on Image Processing*, 4(8):1153–1160, 1995.

A. Sarkar, M. Biswas, and K. Sharma. A simple unsurpervised MRF model based image segmentation approach. *IEEE Trans. on Image Processing*, 9(5): 801–812, May 2000.

R. Stoica, X. Descombes, and J. Zerubia. A Markov point process for road extraction in remote sensed images. Technical Report 3923, INRIA, 2000.

F. Tupin, H. Maître, J.-F. Mangin, J. Nicolas, and E. Pechersky. Detection of linear features in SAR images: Application to road network extraction. *IEEE Trans. on Geoscience and Remote Sensing*, 36(2):434–453, 1998.

L. Vincent and P. Soille. Watersheds in digital spaces: an efficient algorithm based on immersion simulations. *IEEE Trans. on Pattern Analysis and Machine Intelligence*, 13(6):583–598, June 1991.

S. C. Zhu and A. Yuille. Region competition: Unifying snakes, region growing, energy/bayes/MDL for multi-band image segmentation. *IEEE Trans. on Pattern Analysis and Machine Intelligence*, 18(9):884–900, September 1996.

Automatic Keyframing of Human Actions for Computer Animation

Jordi Gonzàlez, Javier Varona, F.Xavier Roca, and Juan José Villanueva

Computer Vision Center & Dept. d'Informàtica
Edifici O, Universitat Autònoma de Barcelona (UAB)
08193 Bellaterra, Spain
{poal,xaviv,xavir,villanueva}@cvc.uab.es
http://www.cvc.uab.es

Abstract. This paper presents a novel human action model based on *key-frames* which is suitable for animation purposes. By defining an action as a sequence of time-ordered body posture configurations, we consider that the most characteristic postures (called key-frames) are enough for modeling such an action. As characteristic postures are found to correspond to low likelihood values, we build a human action eigenspace, called *aSpace*, which is used to estimate the likelihood value for each posture. Once the key-frames have been found automatically, they are used to build a human action model called *p–action* by means of interpolation between key-frames. This parameterized model represents the time evolution of the human body posture during a prototypical action, and it can be used for computer animation. As a result, realistic and smooth motion is achieved. Furthermore, realistic virtual sequences involving several actions can be automatically generated.

1 Introduction

Keyframing is the process of automatic generation of intermediate frames based on a set of key-frames supplied by the animator. In computer animation, the term *key-frame* has been generalized to apply to any variable whose value is set at specific frames and from which values for the intermediate frames, called *in-betweens*, are interpolated according to some prescribed procedure [7]. Key-frames are created by specifying an appropriate set of parameter values, which is related to the body configuration, at a given time. This process of interpolation is important in creating effective animation, due to the fact that interpolation can occur in both space and time. Usually, most applications create a curved path between translation key-frames where possible. But the speed of the interpolation may be non-linear as well so that, for example, the change begins slowly, speeds up, and slows down into the next key-frame.

However, keyframing requires that the animator possesses a detailed understanding of how moving objects should behave over time as well as expresses that information through keyframed configurations. Standard interpolation algorithms (linear, cubic or spline) can be applied to generate the corresponding

F.J. Perales et al. (Eds.): IbPRIA 2003, LNCS 2652, pp. 287–296, 2003.

in-betweens. Consequently, given a sample action sequence, we can apply the keyframing technique with a minimum of human intervention in order to achieve automatic animation.

In this paper, we first describe shortly different developments found in the literature which consider key-frames. Next, we enhance the work presented in [5] (where a novel action eigenspace called *aSpace* was built based on a Point Distribution Model) to obtain a parametric representation of human actions. Subsequently, we select automatically the most characteristic body postures, i.e., the *key-frames*, for a given action. These postures constitute the basis of our final parametric human action model, called *p–action*. Facilities of such *p–actions* to animation are discussed. Experimental results and conclusions are lastly provided.

2   Background and Previous Work

We define an action as a sequence of time-ordered body posture configurations. If one considers the complete set of body postures for a given action sequence, it is obvious that the sequence contains redundant information: several postures are found to be repeated. A posterior analysis determines that there exists a more reduced group of human postures that do not appear as frequently as the redundant ones: they are found to *identify* an action. They give enough information to state, by only considering these reduced group of human postures, which action is being performed. But also, these characteristics human postures can be used to *discriminate* between different actions.

Such capabilities argue for representing an action by selecting few frames from the entire sequence. It can be found in the literature an increasing number of papers which attempt to perform human action tracking and recognition by only considering few poses. In [1], human motion tracking is applied during a gymnastic exercice which is known in advance. Tracking is performed by using a set of key-frames for each exercise, which are computed beforehand. Also in [2], few body poses are considered to achieve human action recognition. However, no criteria is used to select the key-frames, which are found randomly. In [9], human action tracking and recognition is performed by considering a set of stored key-frames. However, it is not clear how many key-frames are required for a given tennis stroke, due to the fact that they are provided beforehand.

In this paper, the set of key-frames for a given action is found automatically and is demonstrated to be suitable for representing such an action by performing animation.

3   Parametric Eigenspaces

Consider an action as a sequence of human postures. Each human posture model is based on a stick figure, which is composed of ten rigid parts and six joints, similar to that presented in [4]. A sequence of n frames corresponding to a performance of a given action was considered to be composed of a set of body posture configurations $\mathbf{S}_j = \{\mathbf{x}_1, \mathbf{x}_2, ..., \mathbf{x}_n\}$, where

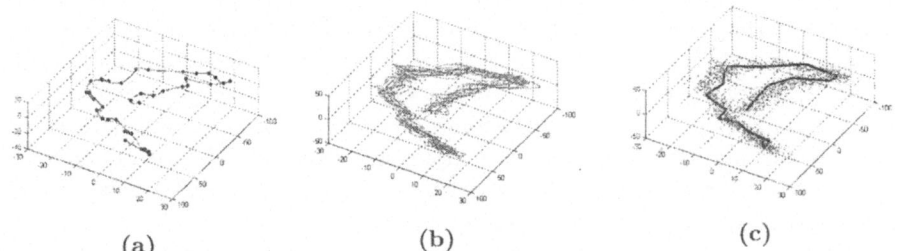

(a)   (b)   (c)

Fig. 1. Parametric eigenspace for the bending action. Only the three most prominent dimensions are displayed. **(a)** Manifold obtained by interpolation between the projections (black dots) of the postures of a single performance. **(b)** Manifolds obtained by interpolation between the projections of the postures of several performances. Each manifold corresponds to a performance. **(c)** Manifold (thick line) obtained by interpolation between the means of pose distributions [3]

$$\mathbf{x}_i = (\mathbf{u}_i, \mathbf{\Theta}_i)^T. \tag{1}$$

$\mathbf{\Theta}_i$ corresponds to the ten angle values which define the configuration of the stick figure, and $\mathbf{u}_i$ corresponds to the hip center coordinates.

An action $\mathbf{A}$ is learnt using r different sequences $\mathbf{A} = \{\mathbf{S}_1, \mathbf{S}_2, ..., \mathbf{S}_r\}$. In order to provide a proper learning set which is generic enough, the same action is performed several times by different actors of different sizes. For our experiments, 25 performances for each action were recorded. As a result, nearly 2000 frames are included for each action. Note that each performance sequence is not compulsory to contain the same number of frames.

Such a learning data set was used to compute the action class Ω_A called *aSpace* and defined as:

$$\Omega_A = (\mathbf{E}, \mathbf{\Lambda}, \bar{\mathbf{x}}), \tag{2}$$

where $\mathbf{E} = (\mathbf{e}_1, ..., \mathbf{e}_m)$ corresponds to the eigenvectors of the reduced space, $\mathbf{\Lambda}$ to the m largest eigenvalues and $\bar{\mathbf{x}}$ to the mean body posture configuration for that action. A detailed description about *aSpaces* can be found in [5]. Next, we enhance such a representation to cope with animation requirements.

If the acquisition rate of the camera is large enough to record smooth changes of the posture between frames, consecutive human postures become strongly correlated and, therefore, their projections in the *aSpace* become close to one another. Consequently, if we avoid drastic changes, a smoothly varying manifold in the *aSpace* can be computed, which is called the *parametric eigenspace representation* [3]. By means of parameterization, we attain a control mechanism over our *aSpaces* representation in order to generate a relatively natural sequence of postures which satisfies the requirements of the animator.

So first, each body human posture configuration $\mathbf{x}_i$ of a performance $\mathbf{S}_j$ of our learning set $\mathbf{A}$ is projected to the eigenspace Ω_A. Projections $\mathbf{y}_i$ of consecutive body postures are located on piece-wise smooth manifolds parameterized by the variation of the pose over time (see Fig. 1.(a)). This temporal variation of the posture is referred to as p, which is normalized for each performance, that is, $p \in [0, 1]$. Usually, p is given in percentage: for example, $p = 50\%$ refers to the human body posture configuration at the middle of an action performance. Thus, by varying p, we actually move along the manifold. The idea of describing the time evolution of the action model by using the normalized pose is similar to that proposed in [4] for the walking action.

Therefore, we consider the projections y_i of a given performance S_j as the control values for a interpolating curve $g_j(p)$, which is computed using a standard cubic-spline interpolation algorithm [8]. This process is repeated for each performance of the learning set, thus obtaining r manifolds. These manifolds are parameterized by the temporal variation of the posture (see Fig. 1.(b)):

$$g_j(p), \qquad 0 \le p \le 1, \qquad j = 1, ..., r. \tag{3}$$

For example, assume that an *aSpace* is well represented by the three largest eigenvalue eigenvectors, that is, $m = 3$. Then, the cubic polynomial would be defined as:

$$g_j(p) = (u_j(p), v_j(p), w_j(p)), \tag{4}$$

which, in fact, represents three equations, one for each dimension:

$$u_j(p) = a_u p^3 + b_u p^2 + c_u p + d_u. \tag{5}$$

Then, the mean manifold for the action Ω_A is found: for each performance S_j, points lying in the manifold $g_j(p)$ are indexed by their parameter p:

$$g(p) = [g_1(p), ..., g_r(p)]^T, \qquad 0 \le p \le 1. \tag{6}$$

Afterwards, the mean is computed for each index p. The mean manifold called $\bar{g}(p)$ is obtained by interpolating between these means using a standard cubic-spline interpolation algorithm. Fig. 1.(c) shows the point clouds in the *aSpace* corresponding to the bending action and its interpolated parametric curve $\bar{g}(p)$.

This action representation is not influenced by the duration of a performance (expressed in seconds or number of frames). It is obvious that the posture configurations presented during a performance do not change with any variations of speed [2]. Thus, only the temporal variation of the human posture is modeled.

Unfortunately, this resulting parametric manifold is influenced by noise factors, such as abnormal posture configurations presented during any action performance or imprecision in the location of the human body joints. These issues affect the mean calculation for each index p. As a result, the manifold presents abrupt changes of direction.

The problem arises from the fact that any subject performs an action in the way he or she is used to. Furthermore, it is highly unlikely that the same actor performs different times the same action in a completely similar manner. So we need to determine how a *prototypical action* representation can be derived by considering individual and highly variable performances as the learning set. And this is possible, since people can distinguish a given action despite of the performer. So only few human posture configurations are considered to represent a given action, which will constitute the *key-frame* set for that action.

4 Automatic Key-Frame Selection

Given an action $\mathbf{A}$, our goal consists in extracting the most characteristic body posture configurations, which will correspond to the set of key-frames for that action, i.e. $\mathbf{K}_A = \{\mathbf{k}_1, \mathbf{k}_2, ..., \mathbf{k}_k\}$. This set will be used to compute the in-betweens, that is, the intermediate frames between key-frames, by using interpolation algorithms.

As expounded before, when an action sequence is analyzed, quite few characteristic body postures can be found. From a probability point of view, characteristic postures are the least likely body postures exhibited during the action performances. This fact is simply a consequence of the very reduced number of frames where these postures appear. So we need to represent the action in terms of a probability distribution in order to compute the likelihood that a sample $\mathbf{x}_j$ is an instance of the action class Ω_A, that is, $P(\mathbf{x}_j|\Omega_A)$. Low values actually correspond to less repetitive samples, that is, very characteristic postures for that action. Thus, by selecting those samples that are less likely, we assure that they provide most entropy of such an action class.

The *aSpace* can also be used to compute the action class conditional density $P(\mathbf{x}_j|\Omega_A)$, assumed to be Gaussian [3]. Also, once the manifold $\bar{\mathbf{g}}(p)$ has been calculated, the mean action performance is described by the projections that lie in such a manifold. Consequently, we compute the likelihood values for the sequence of pose-ordered points $\mathbf{x}_j$ in such a manifold. Due to high-dimensionality of the data, Moghaddam and Pentland in [6] proposed a more efficient and robust manner to compute such a likelihood. As a result, an estimation of the Mahalanobis distance, which considers only the largest eigenvalue eigenvectors of the eigenspace, is applied for each point of the manifold $\bar{\mathbf{g}}(p)$. Thus, we obtain a distance function that estimates the likelihood value for each posture. Note that this distance measurement is also related to important changes of direction of the manifold.

Applying a pose ordering to each distance, peaks of this function correspond to locally maximal distances or, in other words, to the least likely samples. So each peak of the distance function corresponds to a key-frame $\mathbf{k}_i$, and the number of key-frames k is determined by the number of peaks. Thus, we obtain the set $\mathbf{K}_A$ of time-ordered key-frames for the action A. Examples of key-frames obtained from the manifold computed in running *aSpaces* are shown in Fig. 2.

Fig. 2. Key-frames generated for a running action

5   Parametric Action Representation or *P–action*

Once the key-frames have been selected, a new manifold is obtained by interpolating between the key-frame set using a standard cubic-spline interpolation
algorithm. This interpolated parametric curve is also defined to as a function of
the pose p:

$$\mathbf{f}^{A}(p), \qquad 0 \leq p \leq 1, \tag{7}$$

which can be written explicitly as (assuming that three eigenvectors are enough
for representing the *aSpace*):

$$\mathbf{f}^{A}(p) = (u(p), v(p), w(p)), \tag{8}$$

which represents three equations, one for each eigenvector (i.e. dimension of the
aSpace), similarly to the definition of $\bar{\mathbf{g}}(p)$ in Eq. (5).

As shown in Fig. 3, $\mathbf{f}^{A}(p)$ represents a manifold which *smooths* the manifold
$\bar{\mathbf{g}}(p)$: by using interpolation, we attain a reduction of the roughness derived from
the learning set. Mathematically, smoothness is determined by how many derivatives of the curve equation are continuous: by using cubic splines, second-order
continuity between segments is attained. Thus, points belonging to manifold
$\mathbf{f}^{A}(p)$ represent the typical postures exhibited for that action.

The break points of the spline correspond to the projections of the key-
frames found before. Consequently, the curve is made up of several segments,
which correspond to transitions between key-frames: each segment represents
how the body posture evolves from one key-frame to its next in temporal order.
Thus, the action as a whole is represented as a parametric curve, which consists
of a sequence of key-frames plus the transition between these key-frames.

We denote $\mathbf{f}^{A}(p)$ as the *parametric action representation* or *p–action*. A *p–
action* is also parameterized by the pose p, which represents the time evolution
of the human posture during a prototypical action. In consequence, pose-ordered
points lying in a *p–action* are the projections of a sequence of body postures that
viewers can recognize easily as a particular performance for that action.

Using characteristic postures (i.e., the key-frames) guarantees that the viewer
can recognize easily which action is being animated. Despite of the fact that the
manifold can include points used in the learning stage, it also contains human
body postures which were not learnt due to the cubic-spline interpolation step.
Thus, a smooth performance is achieved. Also, a mechanism of control over our
action representation is attained by considering the parameter p, which can be

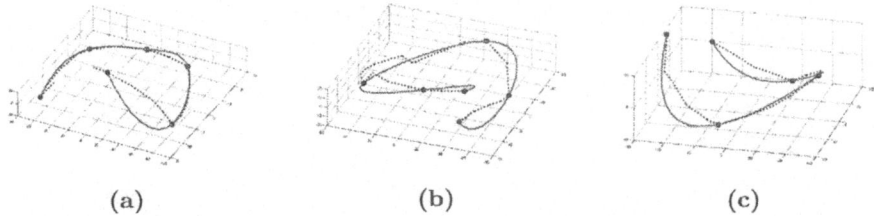

(a)   (b)   (c)

Fig. 3. *P-actions* obtained by interpolation (solid curve) of the key-frames (black dots) found in $\bar{\mathbf{g}}(p)$ (dot curve) for bending (**a**), punching (**b**) and running (**c**) actions

used to specify the temporal order of the postures during a new animated sequence. These characteristics justify the utilization of the *p–action* for animation purposes.

6 Animation Using *P–actions*

Animation can be achieved by sampling the *p–action* manifold, that is, considering those $\mathbf{y}_k \in \mathbf{f}^A(p)$. In fact, these points correspond to projections of human body posture configurations. Therefore, the original stick figure configuration $\mathbf{x}_k$ of Eq. (1) can be found as:

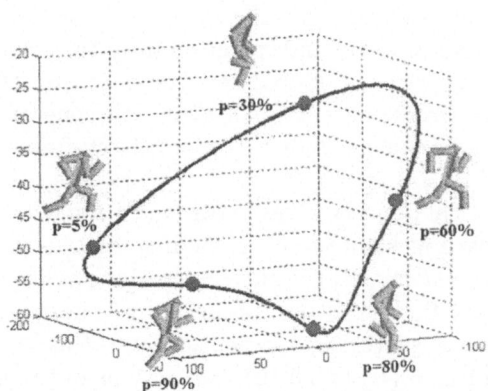

Fig. 4. *P-action* computed in the running *aSpace*: by varying the parameter pose p, we actually move along the manifold $\mathbf{f}^A(p)$, thus obtaining the temporal evolution of the human body posture during the prototypical performance of the running action

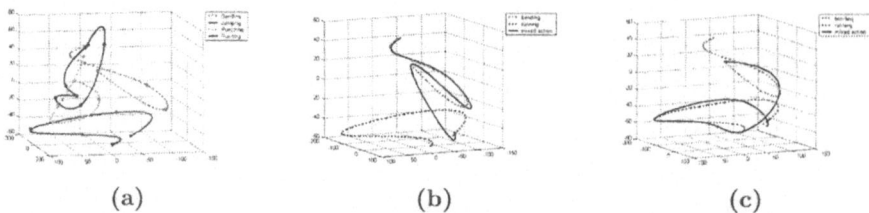

(a)   (b)   (c)

Fig. 5. Figure (a) shows the parametric curves in the *universal aSpace*. Figure (b) and Figure (c) corresponds to a mixed action (bending, running, and bending again). Figure (b) shows the resulting manifold by varying the parameter pose p from $p = 0\%$ to $p = 50\%$, and figure (c) shows the variation of p from $p = 50\%$ to $p = 90\%$. Due to the interpolation step, transitions between actions occur smoothly

$$\mathbf{x}_k = \sum_{i=1}^{m} \mathbf{e}_i \mathbf{y}_{ki} + \bar{\mathbf{x}}. \tag{9}$$

As a result, a 3D model can be built from $\mathbf{x}_k$ in order to generate a synthetic sequence. In Fig. 4, the manifold corresponding to the running action is shown. The action is satisfactorily synthesized by moving along that curve, thus providing realistic and smooth motion to computer-animated sequences.

In order to synthesize sequences with several actions involved, a *universal aSpace* is built. In this eigenspace, the learning samples correspond to the complete set of actions. As before, a manifold for each action is computed, as shown in Fig. 5.(a). Dots represent the key-frames for each action, and the curves describe the manifolds obtained by interpolation from these key-frames. Thus, the animator just need to select the desired key-frames of the actions being involved in the new sequence. Subsequently, the system will generate the corresponding in-betweens in order to change from one selected key-frame to the next one by interpolation.

Note that the critical point here lies in the transition between actions. Despite of the fact that no learning samples corresponding to action transitions have been included in the *universal aSpace*, the cubic spline interpolation step will generate physically meaningful body posture variations to change smoothly from one action to the next. Thus, switching between actions is feasible in a continuous and realistic manner. In Fig. 5.(b) and 5.(c), two actions in the *universal aSpace* are presented as dot curves. In Fig. 6, a sequence performance is shown, during which four actions are played: bending, punching, running and bending again. Note that there are some postures which were not learnt, that is, transitions between actions appear due to the interpolation nature of the manifold computation.

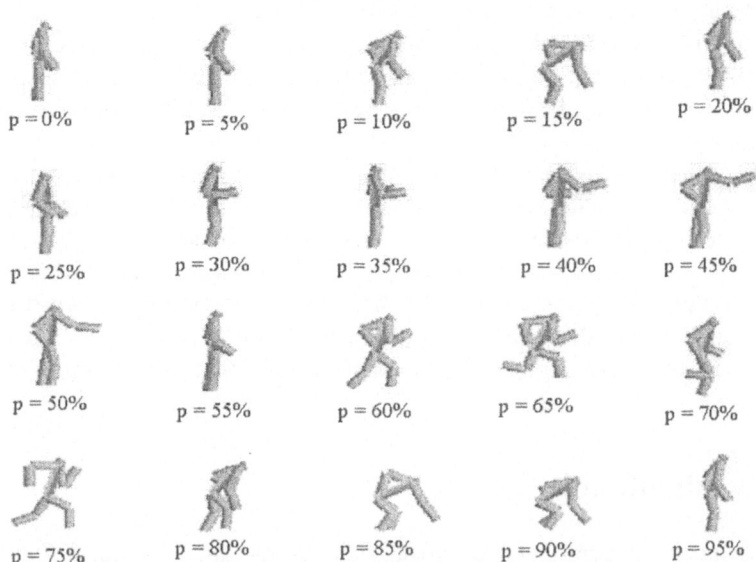

Fig. 6. Parametric curve in the *universal aSpace*: by varying the parameter pose p, the set of postures exhibited during the prototypical performance of several mixed actions is presented. First row corresponds to bending, second row to punching, third row to running, and fourth row to bending again. Note that $p = 20\%$, $p = 60\%$ and $p = 80\%$ correspond to transition frames between actions, which are generated due to the interpolation algorithm. See explaining text for details

7 Conclusions

We developed a novel human action model based on the keyframing technique. We consider the key-frame set of a given action as the most characteristic human body postures for such an action. A human posture is modeled as a stick figure and defined in terms of the global angle values of its body parts. Most characteristic postures are found automatically by computing the likelihood value for each body posture in a human action eigenspace called *aSpace*. These postures are found to identify such an action and to discriminate between different actions. Using interpolation between key-frames, a human action model called *p-action* is calculated. This parametric human action representation represents the time evolution of the human body posture during a prototypical action. In this paper, *p-actions* are used to perform computer animation, thus achieving realistic and smooth motion. Furthermore, virtual sequences with several actions involved can be generated by means of interpolation between the key-frames of the actions involved in such sequences. As a result, transitions between different actions (which involve to synthesize human body postures not presented in the learning set) are generated in a continuous and realistic manner.

The design of the *p–action* model is the first step for animation. At present, we have parameterized such a manifold in terms of the arc length. Thus, the relationship between the parametric value p and the corresponding distance along the manifold is known. As a result, the speed at which the animated sequence is synthesized can be controlled.

In the literature, key-frames are mostly used for tracking and recognition. Once our model has been presented as suitable to perform animation, extension to recognition is straightforward. By considering the key-frame set, which is the core of the *p–action* representation, existing key-frame-based human action recognition algorithms can be applied directly. Furthermore, as key-frames are found automatically, automatic action learning can be developed. Lastly, key-frames can incorporate additional information in order to be useful for tracking purposes.

Acknowledgements

This work has been supported by project TIC2000-0382 of spanish CICYT.

References

[1] K. Akita. Image sequence analysis of real world human motion. *Pattern Recognition*, 17(1):73–83, 1984.

[2] J. Ben-Aire, Z. Wang, P. Pandit, and S. Rajaram. Human activity recognition using multidimensional indexing. *IEEE Trans. Pattern Analysis and Machine Intelligence*, 24(8):1091–1104, 2002.

[3] H. Borotschnig, L. Paletta, M. Prantl, and A. Pinz. Appearance-based active object recognition. *Image and Vision Computing*, 18:715–727, 2000.

[4] J. Cheng and M.F. Moura. Capture and represention of human walking in live video sequences. *IEEE Transactions on Multimedia*, 1(2):144–156, 1999.

[5] J. Gonzàlez, X. Varona, F.X. Roca, and J.J. Villanueva. *aSpaces*: Action spaces for recognition and synthesis of human actions. In *Proc. Second International Workshop on Articulated Motion and Deformable Objects (AMDO 2002)*, pages 189–200, Palma de Mallorca, Spain, 2002.

[6] B. Moghaddam and A. Pentland. Probabilistic visual learning for object representation. *IEEE Trans. Pattern Analysis and Machine Intelligence*, 19(7):696–710, 1997.

[7] R. Parent. *Computer Animation. Algorithms and Techniques*. Morgan Kaufmann Publishers, San Francisco, CA, 2002.

[8] W. Press, B.P. Flannery, S.A. Teukolsky, and W.T. Vetterling. *Numerical Recipes in C*. Cambridge University Press, Cambridge, 1988.

[9] J. Sullivan and S. Carlsson. Recognizing and tracking human action. In *Proceedings of the seventh European Conference Computer Vision (ECCV'02)*, pages 629–644, Copenhagen, Denmark, 2002.

Robust Line Matching and Estimate of Homographies Simultaneously*

José J. Guerrero and Carlos Sagüés

Dpto. de Informática e Ingeniería de Sistemas, Univ. de Zaragoza
María de Luna 3, E-50018 ZARAGOZA (SPAIN)
:{jguerrer,csagues}@posta.unizar.es

Abstract. This paper addresses the robust matching of lines simultaneously to the computation of homographies between two views, when structure and motion are unknown. Using viewpoint non invariant measures, such as image dependent parameters, gives a lot of non matched or wrong matched features. The inclusion of projective transformations gives much better results with short computing overload. We use line features which can usually be extracted more accurately than points and they can be used in cases when there are partial occlusion. In the first stage, the lines are matched to the weighted nearest neighbor using brightness-based and geometric-based image parameters. From them, robust homographies can be computed, allowing to reject wrong matches, and growing also additional matches in the final stage. Although lines and points are dual features to compute homographies, some problems related to data representation and normalization using lines are considered. Results show that the robust technique turns out stable, and its application is useful in many situations. We have used it for robot homing and we also present automatic matching of lines at aerial images.

1 Introduction

In this paper we address the problem of robust matching of lines in two images when camera motion is unknown. Using lines instead of points has been considered by some researches [1]. Straight lines can be accurately extracted in noisy images, they capture more information than points, specially in man-made environments, and they may be used where occlusions occur.

However, line matching is more difficult than point matching because the end points of the extracted lines is not reliable. Besides that, there is not geometrical constraint, like the epipolar, for lines in two images. The putative matching of features based on image parameters has many drawbacks, giving non matched or wrong matched features. Previously the problem of wide baseline matching has been addressed establishing a viewpoint invariant affinity measure [2]. We use the homography in the matching process to select and to grow previous matches which have been obtained combining geometric and brightness image

---

* This work was supported by projects DPI2000-1265,DPI2000-1272.

F.J. Perales et al. (Eds.): IbPRIA 2003, LNCS 2652, pp. 297–307, 2003.
© Springer-Verlag Berlin Heidelberg 2003

parameters. Perspective images of plane scenes are usual in perception of man made environments, and the model to work with them is well known. Points or lines on the world plane in one image of the world plane are mapped to points or lines in the other image by a plane to plane homography [3]. This is an exact transformation for planar scenes or for small baseline image pairs. As known, there is no geometric constraint for infinite lines in two images, but the homography can be considered a first approximation for a general 3D scene.

To compute homographies, points and lines are dual geometric entities, however line-based algorithms are generally more difficult than point-based ones [4]. Thus, some particular problems related to data representation and normalization must be considered in practice. We compute homographies from corresponding lines in two images making use of classical normalization of point data [5], and avoiding singularities.

Robust estimate is actually unquestionable technique to obtain results in real situations where outliers and spurious data are present [6, 7]. In this paper the least median of squares method [8] has been used to estimate the homography. It provides not only the solution in a robust way, but also a list of previous matches that are in disagreement with it, which allows to reject wrong matches.

The simultaneous computation of matches and projective transformation between images is useful in many applications, but we have used it for robot homing. Our algorithm can also be applied in photogrammetry where points are the feature mostly used [9], but lines are plentiful in urban scenes. We have put into practice our matching with aerial images obtaining satisfactory results.

2 Basic Matching

In several works, the matching is made over close images. In this context, correspondence determination by tracking geometric information along the image sequence has been proposed as a good solution [10], [11]. We determine correspondences between lines in two images of large disparity without knowledge about motion or scene structure. We use not only the geometric parameters but also the brightness attributes supplied by the contour extractor (the lines are extracted using our implementation of the method proposed by Burns [12]). So, agl and c (average grey level and contrast) of the line are combined with geometric parameters of the segments such as midpoint coordinates (x_m, y_m), the line orientation θ (in 2π range with dark on the right and bright on the left) and the length l of the extracted line.

Significant motion between views or changes on light conditions and measurements noise makes that few or none of the defined line parameters remain invariant between images.

2.1 Similarity Measures

In the matching process two similarity measures are used, a geometric measure and a brightness measure. We name $\mathbf{r_g}$ the difference of geometric parameters between both images $(1, 2)$, $\mathbf{r_g} = [x_{m1} - x_{m2}, \ y_{m1} - y_{m2}, \ \theta_1 - \theta_2, \ l_1 - l_2]^T$.

As previously [11], we define the $\mathbf{R}$ matrix to express the uncertainty due to measurement noise in the extraction of features in each image

$$\mathbf{R} = \begin{bmatrix} \sigma_\perp^2 S^2 + \sigma_\parallel^2 C^2 & \sigma_\perp^2 CS - \sigma_\parallel^2 CS & 0 & 0 \\ \sigma_\perp^2 CS - \sigma_\parallel^2 CS & \sigma_\perp^2 C^2 + \sigma_\parallel^2 S^2 & 0 & 0 \\ 0 & 0 & 2\frac{\sigma_\perp^2}{l^2} & 0 \\ 0 & 0 & 0 & 2\sigma_\parallel^2 \end{bmatrix},$$

where $C = \cos\theta$ y $S = \sin\theta$. Location uncertainties of segment tips along the line direction and along the orthogonal direction are represented by $\sigma_\parallel$ and $\sigma_\perp$ respectively. With this geometric representation we can assume no correlation between midpoint location and θ and l parameters [10].

Additionally we define the diagonal matrix $\mathbf{P} = diag(\sigma_{x_m}^2, \sigma_{y_m}^2, \sigma_\theta^2, \sigma_l^2)$ to represent the uncertainty of variation of the geometric parameters due to camera motion and unknown scene structure.

Thus, from those matrixes we introduce $\mathbf{S} = \mathbf{R}_1 + \mathbf{R}_2 + \mathbf{P}$ to weigh the variations on the geometric parameters of corresponding lines due to both, line extraction noise ($\mathbf{R}_1$ in image 1 and $\mathbf{R}_2$ in image 2) and unknown structure and motion. Note in $\mathbf{R}$ that $\sigma_\parallel$ is bigger than $\sigma_\perp$. Therefore measurement noise of x_m and y_m are coupled and the line orientation shows the direction where the measurement noise is bigger (along the line). However, in $\mathbf{P}$ the orientation does not main because the evolution of the line between images is mainly due to camera motion which is not dependent on the orientation of the image line.

The matching technique in the first stage is made to the nearest neighbor. The similarity between the parameters can be measured with a Mahalanobis distance like, $\mathbf{d_g} = \mathbf{r_g}^T \mathbf{S}^{-1} \mathbf{r_g}$.

A second similarity measure has been defined for the brightness parameters. In this case we define the diagonal matrix $\mathbf{B} = diag(\sigma_{agl}^2, \sigma_c^2)$, where σ_{agl} and σ_c represent the uncertainty of variations of the agl and c. Both depend on measurement noise and on changes of illumination between images.

Naming $\mathbf{r_b}$ the variation of the brightness parameters between both images, $\mathbf{r_b} = [agl_1 - agl_2, c_1 - c_2]^T$, the Mahalanobis distance for the similarity between the brightness parameters is, $\mathbf{d_b} = \mathbf{r_b}^T \mathbf{B}^{-1} \mathbf{r_b}$.

2.2 Matching Criteria

Two image lines are stated as compatible when both, geometric and brightness variations are small. For one line in the second image to belong to the compatible set of a line in the first image, the following tests must be satisfied:

- *Geometric compatibility.* Assuming that the noise is Gaussian distributed, the similarity distance for the geometric parameters is distributed as a χ^2 with 4 d.o.f. Establishing a significance level of 5%, the compatible lines must fulfill, $\mathbf{d_g} \leq \chi_4^2(95\%)$.
- *Brightness compatibility.* Similarly, refereing to the brightness parameters, the compatible lines must fulfill, $\mathbf{d_b} \leq \chi_2^2(95\%)$.

A general Mahalanobis distance for the six parameters is not used because the correct weighting of so different information as brightness based and location based in a sole distance is difficult and could easily lead to wrong matches. Thus, compensation between high precision in some parameters with high error in other parameter is avoided.

A line in the first image can have more than one compatible line in the second image. From the compatible lines, the line having the smallest d_g is selected as putative match. The matching is carried out in both directions from first to second image and from second to first, in such a way that, a match (n_1, n_2) is considered valid when the line n_2 is the putative match of n_1 and simultaneously n_1 is the putative match of n_2.

In practice the parameters $\sigma_j (j = \perp, \|, x_m, y_m, \theta, l, agl, c)$ introduced in R, P, B must be tuned according to the estimated image noise, expected camera motions and illumination conditions, respectively.

3   From Lines to Homographies

The representation of a line in the projective plane is obtained from the analytic representation of a plane through the origin: $n_1 x_1 + n_2 x_2 + n_3 x_3 = 0$. The equation coefficients $n = (n_1, n_2, n_3)^T$ correspond to the homogeneous coordinates of the projective line. All the lines written as λn are the same than n. The case $n_3 = 0$ corresponds to a line through the origin of the virtual image plane. As cameras have a limited field of view, observed lines have usually n_3 close to 0. Similarly, an image point $p = (x, y, 1)^T$ is also an element of the projective plane and the equation $n \cdot p = n^T \cdot p = 0$ represents the belonging of point p to the line n, which shows the duality of points and lines.

A projective transformation between two projective planes (1 and 2) can be represented by a linear transformation T_{21}, in such a way that $p_2 = T_{21} p_1$. Considering the above equations for lines in both images, we have $n_2 = \left[T_{21}^{-1} \right]^T n_1$. A homography requires eight parameters to be completely defined, because there is an overall scale factor. A corresponding point or line gives two linear equations in terms of the elements of the homography. Thus, four corresponding lines assure a unique solution for T_{21}, if no three of them are parallel. To have an accurate solution it is interesting to have the lines as separate in the image as possible.

3.1   Computing Homographies from Corresponding Lines

Here, we obtain the projective transformation of points ($p_2 = T_{21} p_1$), but using matched lines. To deduce it, we suppose the start (s) and end (e) tips of a matched line segment to be $p_{s1}, p_{e1}, p_{s2}, p_{e2}$, which usually will not be corresponding points. The line in the second image can be computed as the cross product of two of its points (in particular the observed tips) as

$$n_2 = p_{s2} \times p_{e2} = \tilde{p}_{s2} p_{e2}, \tag{1}$$

where $\tilde{\mathbf{p}}_{s2}$ is the skew-symmetric matrix obtained from vector $\mathbf{p}_{s2}$.

As the tips belong to the line we have, $\mathbf{p}_{s2}^T \mathbf{n}_2 = 0$; $\mathbf{p}_{e2}^T \mathbf{n}_2 = 0$. As the tips of line in the first image once transformed also belong to the corresponding line in the second image, we can write, $\mathbf{p}_{s1}^T \mathbf{T}_{21}^T \mathbf{n}_2 = 0$; $\mathbf{p}_{e1}^T \mathbf{T}_{21}^T \mathbf{n}_2 = 0$. Combining with equation (1) we have,

$$\mathbf{p}_{s1}^T \mathbf{T}_{21}^T \tilde{\mathbf{p}}_{s2} \mathbf{p}_{e2} = 0 \; ; \; \mathbf{p}_{e1}^T \mathbf{T}_{21}^T \tilde{\mathbf{p}}_{s2} \mathbf{p}_{e2} = 0. \tag{2}$$

Therefore each couple of corresponding lines gives two homogeneous equations to compute the projective transformation, which can be determined up to a non-zero scale factor. Developing them in function of the elements of the projective transformation, we have

$$\begin{pmatrix} Ax_{s1} & Ay_{s1} & A & Bx_{s1} & By_{s1} & B & Cx_{s1} & Cy_{s1} & C \\ Ax_{e1} & Ay_{e1} & A & Bx_{e1} & By_{e1} & B & Cx_{e1} & Cy_{e1} & C \end{pmatrix} \mathbf{t} = \begin{pmatrix} 0 \\ 0 \end{pmatrix},$$

where $\mathbf{t} = (t_{11}\, t_{12}\, t_{13}\, t_{21}\, t_{22}\, t_{23}\, t_{31}\, t_{32}\, t_{33})^T$ is a vector with the elements of $\mathbf{T}_{21}$, and $A = y_{s2} - y_{e2}$, $B = x_{e2} - x_{s2}$ and $C = x_{s2}y_{e2} - x_{e2}y_{s2}$.

Using four corresponding lines, we can construct a 8×9 matrix $\mathbf{M}$. The solution corresponds with the eigenvector associated to the least eigenvalue (in this case the null eigenvalue) of the matrix $\mathbf{M}^T \mathbf{M}$. In order to have a reliable transformation, more than the minimum number of matches and an estimation method may be considered. Thus from n matches a $2n \times 9$ matrix $\mathbf{M}$ can be built, and the solution $\mathbf{t}$ can be obtained from SVD decomposition of this matrix [3]. In this case the relevance of each line depends on its observed length, because the cross product of the segment tips is related to the segment length.

It is known that a previous normalization of data avoids problems of numerical computation. As our formulation only uses image coordinates of observed tips, data normalization proposed for points [5] has been used.

3.2   Robust Estimation

The least squares method assumes that all the measures can be interpreted with the same model, which makes it to be very sensitive to out of norm data. Robust estimation tries to avoid the outliers in the computation of the estimate. From the existing robust estimation methods [6], we have chosen the least median of squares method. This method makes a search in the space of solutions obtained from subsets of minimum number of matches. The algorithm to obtain an estimate with this method can be summarized as follows:

1. A Monte-Carlo technique is used to randomly select m subsets of 4 features.
2. For each subset S, we compute a solution in closed form $\mathbf{T}_S$.
3. For each solution $\mathbf{T}_S$, the median M_S of the squares of the residue with respect to all the matches is computed.
4. We store the solution $\mathbf{T}_S$ which gives the minimum median M_S.

A selection of m subsets is good if at least in one subset the 4 matches are good. Assuming a ratio ϵ of outliers, the probability of one of them been good can be obtained [8] as, $P = 1 - \left[1 - (1 - \epsilon)^4\right]^m$. For example, if we want a probability $P = 0.999$ of having one good at least, with $\epsilon = 35\%$ of outliers, the number of subsets m should be 34.

Once the solution has been obtained, the outliers can be selected from those of maximum residue. As in [6] the threshold is fitted proportional to the standard deviation of the residue, estimated as [8], $\hat{\sigma} = 1.4826 \left[1 + 5/(n-4)\right]\sqrt{M_S}$. Assuming that the measurement error is Gaussian with zero mean and standard deviation σ, then the square of the residues follows a χ_2^2 distribution with 2 degrees of freedom. Taking, for example, that 95% probability is established for the line to fit in the homography (inlier) then the threshold will be fixed to $5.99\ \hat{\sigma}^2$.

4   Final Matches

From here on, we introduce the geometrical constraint introduced by the estimated homograpy to get a bigger set of matches. Actually we compute an only homography in the image. This would be right if the scene points were on a plane. Although this fails in some situations, the results are good when the distance from the camera to the scene is large enough with respect to the baseline. For example, this assumption gives very good results in robot homing, where image disparity is mainly due to camera rotation, and therefore the sole homography captures the robot orientation, that is the most useful information for a robot to correct its trajectory. We have also made some experiments to segment into several scene planes, to obtain line matching in more general situations. This segmentation of planes could be very useful to make automatic 3D model of urban scenes.

Our objective here is to obtain at the end of the process more good matches, also eliminating wrong matches given by the basic matching. Thus final matches are composed by two sets. The first one is obtained from the matches selected after the robust computation of the homography that passe additionally an overlapping test compatible with the transformation of the segment tips. The second set of matches is obtained taking all the segments not matched initially and those being rejected previously. With this set of lines a matching process similar to the basic matching is carried out. However, now the matching is made to the nearest neighbor segment transformed with the homography. The transformation is applied to the end tips of the image segments using the homography T_{21} to find, not only compatible lines but also compatible segments in the same line.

In the first stage of the matching process there was no previous knowing of camera motion. However in this second step the computed homography provides information about expected disparity and therefore the uncertainty of geometric variations can be reduced. A new tuning of σ_{x_m}, σ_{y_m}, σ_θ and σ_l, must be considered. To automate the process, a global reduction of these parameters has been proposed and tested in several situations, obtaining good results with reductions about 1/5. As the measurement noise ($\sigma_\parallel$ and $\sigma_\perp$) has not changed, the initial

Fig. 1. Images showing the final matches when the robot rotates 18 degrees. Only one match is no good (10), which is a wrong match as segment although good as line

tuning is maintained in this second step. Note that the brightness compatibility set is the initially computed, and therefore it must not be repeated.

5   Experimental Results

A set of experiments with different kind of images has been carried out to test the algorithm proposed. The images correspond to different applications: Indoor robot homing, architectural models and aerial images. In the algorithms there are extraction parameters which allows to obtain more or less lines according to its minimum length and minimum gradient. There are also parameters to match the lines, whose tuning has turned out simple and quite intuitive. In the experiments we have used some small variations with respect to the following tentative tuning parameters $\sigma_\perp = 1$, $\sigma_\parallel = 10$, $\sigma_{agl} = 8$, $\sigma_c = 4$, $\sigma_{xm} = 60$, $\sigma_{ym} = 20$, $\sigma_\theta = 2$, $\sigma_l = 10$. When these changes are important we indicate them in the particular experiment.

We have applied the algorithm presented for robot homing. In this application the robot must go to previously learnt positions using a camera [13]. The robot corrects its heading from the computed projective transformation between learnt and actual images.

In this experiment a set of robot rotations (from 2 to 20 degrees) has been made. The camera center is about 30 cm. out of the axis of rotation of the robot and therefore this camera motion has a short baseline. In Table 1 the number of matches in the three steps with this set of camera motions are shown. The number of lines extracted in the reference image is 112.

From this experiment the progressive advantage of the simultaneous computation of the homography and matching can be seen. When the image disparity is small, the robust estimation of the homography does not improve the basic matching. However, with a disparity close to 70% of the image size, the basic matching produces a high ratio of wrong matches ($> 30\%$), that are automat-

Table 1. Number of matches in the tree steps of the algorithm, with some robot rotation, indicating also the number of wrong matches (W). Here, the matches that are good as lines but wrong as segments (not overlapped) are considered wrong

Robot Rotation	σ_{xm}	Basic	After_$\mathbf{T}_{21}$	Final
4°	60	73 (5W)	56 (1W)	76 (0W)
8°	60	53 (6W)	31 (0W)	52 (0W)
12°	100	41 (9W)	30 (2W)	33 (1W)
16°	100	27 (9W)	17 (3W)	30 (1W)
20°	140	28 (10W)	17 (1W)	24 (0W)

ically corrected in the final matching. We observe that in this case the system also works even with a large image disparity.

To simplify, only the images corresponding to the 18 degrees of robot rotation are shown. A 38 % of wrong matches are given by the basic matching. At the final matching stage, all the matches are good when considered as lines, although one of them can be considered wrong as segment (Fig. 1).

Other experiments have been carried out indoor. In Fig. 2 we show the two images taken with a stereo system having $30cm.$ of baseline. The number of lines extracted are 83 and 93 respectively. The basic matching gives a 45 matches but 16% are wrong matches. After the computation of the homography all are good but only 35 matches remain. At the final stage 66 matches are given, and only two can been considered wrong as segment, although they are good as lines.

5.1   Aerial Images

In this experiment, two aerial images with quite large stereo between them are used (Fig. 3). In photogrammetry applications putative matching has usually a high ratio of spurious results. This is confirmed in our case, where the basic

Fig. 2. Images of other indoor scene showing the final matches (66). All of them are good when considered as lines, although two of them are wrong as segments.

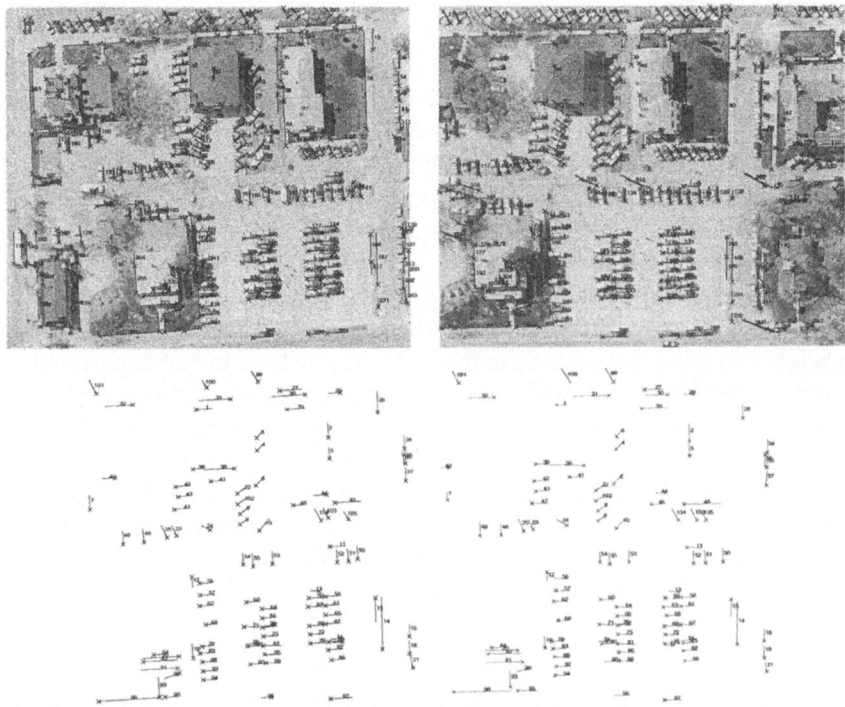

Fig. 3. Two aerial images with quite large stereo. The first row shows the lines extracted (approximately 300 lines/image). From them, the basic matching provides 121 matches (64 being wrong). Second row shows the matches at the final stage (105 matches, 3 being wrong that are corresponding to contiguous cars)

matching has given a ratio of wrong matches higher than 50% , which is the theoretical limit of least median of squares method. However, if we select a smaller percent of the squares of the residue instead of the median, the robust method works properly. The results in Fig. 3 have been obtained with a percent of 30%. The basic matching provides 121 matches, 64 of them being wrong. The robust computation of the homography provides 55 matches, 11 of them being wrong as segment but good as infinite line. Among the 105 final matches, there are only 3 wrong matches which correspond to contiguous cars. Note that the final matches are duplicated with respect to the matches obtained with the homography. Note also that the final matches selected are mainly located on the ground. There are some lines on the roofs of the buildings but they are nearly parallel to the flight of the camera which is coherent with the model of homography used.

6 Conclusions

We have presented and tested a method to automatically obtain matches of lines simultaneously to the robust computation of homographies. The robust computation works especially well to eliminate outliers which may appear when matching is based on image properties and there is no information of scene structure or camera motion. The homographies are computed from lines extracted and the use of lines has advantages with respect to the use of points. The geometric mapping between uncalibrated images provided by the homography turns out useful to grow matches and to eliminate wrong matches.

All the work is made automatically with only some previous tuning of parameters related to expected camera motion. As can be seen in the experiments, the proposed algorithm works with different types of scenes and the tuning phase is simple and intuitive. As limitation of this work, the matching depends on the mapping between the lines and the homography computed. So, plane scenes or situations where disparity is mainly due to rotation, give the best results. However, it is also possible to compute several homographies according to scene structure which is the goal we are actually working for.

References

[1] Schmid, C., Zisserman, A.: Automatic line maching across views. In: IEEE Conference on CVPR. (1997) 666–671
[2] Pritchett, P., Zisserman, A.: Wide baseline stereo matching. In: IEEE Conference on Computer Vision. (1998) 754–760
[3] Hartley, R., Zisserman, A.: Multiple View Geometry in Computer Vision. Cambridge University Press, Cambridge (2000)
[4] Quan, L., Kanade, T.: Affine structure from line correspondences with uncalibrated affine cameras. IEEE Trans. on Pattern Analysis and Machine Intelligence 19 (1997) 834–845
[5] Hartley, R.: In defense of the eight-point algorithm. IEEE Trans. on Pattern Analysis and Machine Intelligence 19 (1997) 580–593
[6] Zhang, Z.: Parameter estimation techniques: A tutorial with application to conic fitting. Rapport de recherche RR-2676, I.N.R.I.A., Sophia-Antipolis, France (1995)
[7] Torr, P., Murray, D.: The development and comparison of robust methods for estimating the fundamental matrix. International Journal of Computer Vision 24 (1997) 271–300
[8] Rousseeuw, P., Leroy, A.: Robust Regression and Outlier Detection. John Wiley, New York (1987)
[9] Habib, A., Kelley, D.: Automatic relative orientation of large scale imagery over urban areas using modified iterated hough transform. Journal of Photogrammetry and Remote Sensing 56 (2001) 29–41
[10] Deriche, R., Faugeras, O.: Tracking line segments. In: First European Conference on Computer Vision, Antibes, France (1990) 259–268
[11] Guerrero, J., Sagüés, C.: Tracking features with camera maneuvering for vision-based navigation. Journal of Robotic Systems 15 (1998) 191–206

[12] Burns, J., Hanson, A., Riseman, E.: Extracting straight lines. IEEE Trans. on Pattern Analysis and Machine Intelligence **8** (1986) 425–455
[13] Guerrero, J., Sagüés, C.: Robot homing from homographies. Technical report, D.I.I.S. Universidad de Zaragoza (2002)

Modeling High-Order Dependencies
in Local Appearance Models*

David Guillamet[1], Baback Moghaddam[2], and Jordi Vitrià[1]

[1] Computer Vision Center-Dept. Informàtica, Universitat Autònoma de Barcelona
08193 Bellaterra, Barcelona, Spain
{davidg,jordi}@cvc.uab.es
[2] Mitsubishi Electric Research Laboratories
Cambridge, MA 02139, USA
baback@merl.com

Abstract. We propose a novel local appearance modeling method for object detection and recognition in cluttered scenes. The approach is based on the joint distribution of local feature vectors at multiple salient points and their factorization with Independent Component Analysis (ICA). The resulting densities are simple multiplicative distributions modeled through adaptive Gaussian mixture models. This leads to computationally tractable joint probability densities which can model high-order dependencies. Our technique has been initially tested with natural and cluttered scenes with some degree of occlusions yielding promising results. We also propose a method to select a reduced set of learning samples in order to mantain the internal structure of an object to be able to use high-order dependencies reducing the computational load.

1 Introduction

For appearance based object modeling in images, the choice of method is usually a trade-off determined by the nature of the application or the availability of computational resources. Existing object representation schemes provide models either for global features [13], or for local features and their spatial relationships [10, 1, 12, 5]. With increased complexity, the latter provides higher modeling power and accuracy. Among various local appearance and structure models, there are those that assume rigidity of appearance and viewing angle, thus adopting more explicit models [12, 10, 9]; while others employ stochastic models and use probabilistic distance and matching metrics [5, 8, 1].

Recognition and detection of objects is achieved by the extraction of low level feature information in order to obtain accurate representations of objects. In order to obtain a good description of objects, extracted low level features

---

* This work is supported by Comissionat per a Universitats i Recerca del Departament de la Presidencia de la Generalitat de Catalunya and Ministerio de Ciencia y Tecnologia grant TIC2000-0399-C02-01.

F.J. Perales et al. (Eds.): IbPRIA 2003, LNCS 2652, pp. 308–316, 2003.

must be carefully selected and it is often necessary to use as many salient features as possible. But one of the most common problems in computer vision is the computational cost of dealing with high dimensional data as well as the intractability of joint distributions of multiple features.

We propose a novel local appearance and color modeling method for object detection and recognition in cluttered scenes. The approach is based on the joint distribution of local feature vectors at multiple salient points and factorization with Independent Component Analysis (ICA). Taking this new statistically independent space to create $k = 3$ tuples ($k = 3$ salient points) of the most salient points of an object, we are able to obtain a set of joint probability densities which can model high-order dependencies. In order to obtain a good estimation of the tuple space, we use an adaptive Gaussian mixture model based on the Minimum Description Length (MDL)[14] criterion to optimally represent our data.

We have tested our method in a real and complex environment where we detect a real object (the US Pentagon building) after 9/11/01. We demonstrate that our technique is able to detect a complex object with a damaged portion of the building and under different natural conditions but we have to select a properly number of training tuples. Our method is based on high-order dependencies but, since the object consists of several keypoints, the number of possible tuples for learning is extremely huge. Thus, we propose a method to select the learning tuples in order to be able to work with high-order dependencies using a reasonable amount of computational resources.

2   Methodology

We propose to use an adaptive Gaussian mixture model as a parametric approximation of the joint distribution of image features of local color and appearance information at multiple salient points.

Let i be the index for elementary feature components in an image, which can be pixels, corner/interest points [3, 4], blocks, or regions in an image. Let x_i denote the feature vector of dimension n at location i. x_i can be as simple as {R,G,B} components at each pixel location, some invariant feature vectors extracted at corner or interest points [7, 10, 11], transform domain coefficients at an image block, and/or any other local/ regional feature vectors.

For model-based object recognition, we use the *a posteriori* probability defined as $max_l P(M_l|T)$ where M_l is the object model and $T = \{x_i\}$ represents the features found in the test image. Equivalently, by assuming equal priors, classification/detection will be based on maximum likelihood testing:

$$max_l P(T|M_l) \tag{1}$$

For the class-conditional density in equation (1), it is intractable to model dependencies among all x_i's (even if correspondence is solved), yet to completely ignore these dependencies is to severely limit the modeling power of the probability densities. Objects frequently distinguish themselves not by individual regions

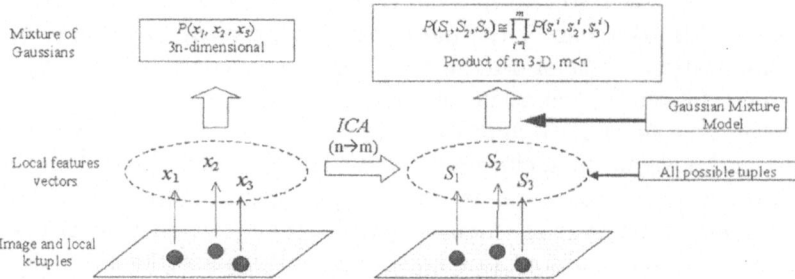

Fig. 1. System diagram for k-tuple density factorization using ICA and Gaussian mixture models

(or parts), but by the relative location and comparative appearance of these regions. A tractable compromise between these two modeling extremes (which does not require correspondence) is to model the joint density of all k-tuples of x_i's in T. Figure (1) shows a general scheme of our methodology.

2.1 Joint Distribution of k-Tuples

Instead of modeling the total joint likelihood of all $x_1, x_2, \ldots x_I$, which is an $(I \times n)$-dimensional distribution, we model the alternative distribution of all k-tuples as an approximation:

$$P(\{(x_{i_1}, x_{i_2}, \ldots, x_{i_k})\}|M_l) \tag{2}$$

This becomes a $(k \times n)$-dimensional distribution, which is still intractable (Note: $k < n$ and $k << I$). We can use multi-dimensional histograms as an approximation of the joint distribution of image features with, i.e 20 histogram bins along each dimension, and such a framework would require $20^{(k \times n)}$ bins. Therefore, a factorization of this distribution into a product of low-dimensional distributions is required. We achieve this factorization by transforming x into a new feature vector S whose components are (mostly) independent. This is where Independent Component Analysis (ICA) comes in.

2.2 Density Factorization with ICA

ICA originated in the context of blind source separation [2, 6] to separate "independent causes" of a complex signal or mixture. It is usually implemented by pushing the vector components away from Gaussianity by minimizing high-order statistics such as the 4th order cross-cumulants. ICA is in general not perfect therefore the IC's obtained are not guaranteed to be completely independent.

By applying ICA to $\{x_i\}$, we obtain the linear mapping

$$x \approx AS \tag{3}$$

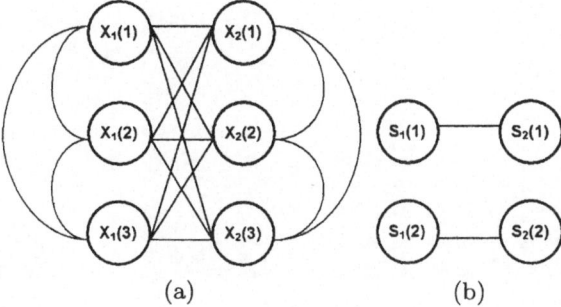

Fig. 2. Graphical models: (a) fully-connected graph denoting no independence assumptions (b) the ICA-factorized model with pair-wise only dependencies

and

$$P(\{(S_{i_1}, S_{i_2}, \ldots, S_{i_k})\}|M_l)$$

$$\approx \prod_{j=1}^{m} P(\{(s_{i_1}^j, s_{i_2}^j, \ldots, s_{i_k}^j)\}|M_l) \tag{4}$$

where A is a n-by-m matrix and S_i is the "source signal" at location i with nearly independent components (Note: $m < n$). The original high-dimensional distribution is now factorized into a product of m k-dimensional distributions, with only small distortions expected. We note that this differs from so-called "naive Bayes" where the distribution of feature vectors is assumed to be factorizable into 1D distributions for each component. Without ICA the model suffers since in general these components are almost certainly statistically dependent.

After factorization, each of the k dimensional factored distributions becomes manageable if k is small, e.g., $k = 2$ or 3. Moreover, matching can now be performed individually on these low-dimensional distributions and the scores are additively combined to form an overall score.

Figure (2) is a graphical model showing the dependencies between a pair of 3-dimensional feature vectors x_1, x_2. The joint distribution over all nodes is 6-dimensional and all nodes are (potentially) interdependent. The basic approach towards obtaining a tractable distribution is to remove intra-component dependencies (vertical and diagonal links) leaving only inter-component dependencies (horizontal links). Simultaneously, we seek to reduce the number of observed components from $n = 3$ to a smaller number $m = 2$ of "sources". Ideally, a perfect ICA transform results in the graphical model shown in the right diagram where the pair S_1, S_2 only have pair-wise inter-component dependencies. Therefore, the resulting factorization can be simply modeled by 2D histograms or Gaussian mixture models[1].

---

[1] We should note that in practice with an approximate ICA transform, the diagonal links of the original model are less likely to be removed than the vertical ones.

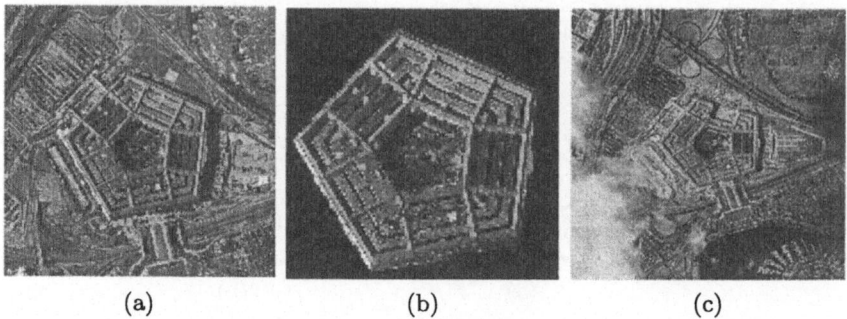

(a)   (b)   (c)

Fig. 3. (a) Satellite image of the US Pentagon building (prior to 9/11/01). (b) extracted building region used for learning. (c) a new test image of the same region taken after 9/11/01 under different natural conditions and with the damaged portion of the building missing (removed after site cleanup). (Note: All images have been rescaled for display purposes)

3   Experimental Results

Our experimental results have been focused on the use of $k = 3$ tuples in order to analyze the effect of choosing different learning tuples. We used a Harris operator [4, 11] to detect interest points and extracted the first 9 differential invariant jets [7] at each point as the corresponding feature vector x. Using these jets as our feature results in a local appearance model which is not only invariant to in-plane rotation (and translation) but is also robust with respect to partial occlusions. We must emphasize however that our methodology is not restricted to differential invariant jets and can in principal be used for any local set of features, for example, color, curvature, edge-intensity, texture moments. We then performed ICA to get $m < 9$ independent components for the feature vectors (jets). Using a $k = 3$ tuple model results in a set of $3D$ Gaussian mixture models which were used to model our 3-tuple joint component densities.

We tested our system with real and cluttered scenes where objects can be affected by different natural factors. This is the case presented in figure (3) which shows the modeling of the US Pentagon building before and after the September 11 terrorist attack. Figure (3.a) presents a real image of the pentagon building and figure (3.b) shows the extracted building used for our learning and modeling. Figure (3.c) depicts a test image which was taken after the bombing debris was cleared away by the cleanup crew (leaving a whole section of the building missing).

Image of figure (3.b) has been used as training and the number of extracted keypoints is approximately 250. All possible $k = 3$ tuples that we can generate from 250 keypoints is extremely huge (like $250 \times 249 \times 248 = 15438000$) and it is impossible to learn a mixture of Gaussians with this huge number of training tuples. Our idea is to select a subset of them in order to find a representative set of tuple candidates to learn the Gaussian mixture models and obtain a good

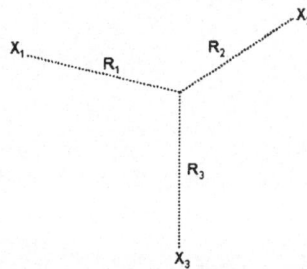

Fig. 4. Given 3 local features (x_1, x_2 and x_3) to create a $k = 3$ tuple, we obtain the middle point and when all the distances (R_1, R_2 and R_3) between the middle point to all the three features are less than a predefined radial value (R_{thr}), this tuple is considered for training

representation of the natural object. In order to manage with natural occlusions, tuples must be carefully selected. Thus, we defined a radial threshold (R_{thr}) and we only consider those tuples that the distance between each keypoint of the tuple with respect to the middle point of the tuple is less than R_{thr}. This idea is represented in figure (4) where we can see three local features (x_1, x_2 and x_3) and the middle point of the tuple. When all the three distances (R_1, R_2 and R_3) between each feature and the middle point are less than R_{thr}, the tuple will be considered for training. As can be seen, this idea comes out in order to consider tuples with close keypoints to mantain the object structure.

This present work shows that a good criterion to choose a set of learning tuples is fundamental in order to obtain satisfactory results. Our pentagon object used for learning is about 120×120 pixels and, as seen in figure (3), it consists of several structured parts but repeated along the object. After obtaining all the pentagon keypoints, we have considered a set of learning tuples with a radial threshold of $25, 30, 35, 40$ and 45 pixels because we need to mantain the structure of the object. For example, a radial threshold of 45 pixels is about a quarter of the pentagon and, as seen, it should be enough because our pentagon contains a repeated structure. In case that a learning object consists of several and different structured parts, the radial threshold for our learning tuples should be analyzed more carefully. Detection maps corresponding to different radial thresholds can be seen in figure (5) where we can appreciate that small radial thresholds lead to bad detection maps and big radial thresholds lead to good (or acceptable) detection maps. We should state that the number of training tuples when we use big radial thresholds are really huge and our adaptative gaussian mixture model needs a considerable amount of computational resources.

Since we are testing our method with an object with a missing part, see figure (3.c), detection maps of figure (5) are understandable in the sense that part of the pentagon may not be recognized properly. When using a $R_{thr} = 25$ pixels, results are not acceptable since the pentagon is not correctly detected and

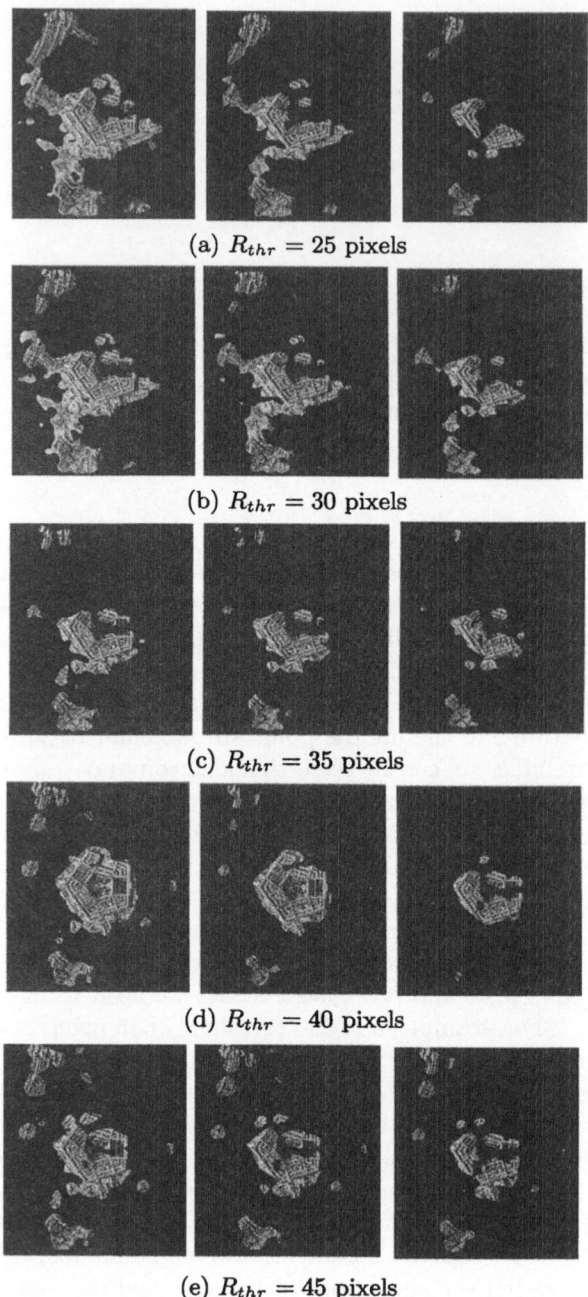

(a) $R_{thr} = 25$ pixels

(b) $R_{thr} = 30$ pixels

(c) $R_{thr} = 35$ pixels

(d) $R_{thr} = 40$ pixels

(e) $R_{thr} = 45$ pixels

Fig. 5.   Detection maps corresponding to different radial thresholds (from $R_{thr} = 25$ to $R_{thr} = 45$ pixels)

a lot of external regions are considered as the pentagon. But, when using $R_{thr} = 40$ pixels, pentagon is correctly detected and only a few external regions are considered as being part of the pentagon object.

4 Conclusions

A novel probabilistic modeling scheme was proposed based on the factorization of high-dimensional distributions of local image features. Our framework was tested using real imagery where the US Pentagon building is learned and detected in other natural conditions and with a damaged portion of the building missing. These experiments with complex and cluttered scenes demonstrate that this technique is well suited to object detection and localization tasks in natural environments. As seen, one of the problems is the huge number of training tuples obtained when considering high-order dependencies and the associated computational resources required that are extremely high. Thus, we propose a method to select a reduced set of learning tuples in order to mantain the internal structure of the object to be able to use high-order dependencies reducing the computational load.

References

[1] Chang P., Krumm, J.: Object recognition with color cooccurrence histograms. In Proc CVPR, 1999
[2] Comon P.: Independent component analysis - a new concept? Signal Processing, 36:287-314, 1994
[3] Deriche R., Giraudon G.: A computational approach for corner and vertex detection. International Journal Computer Vision, 10(2): 101-124, 1993.
[4] Harris C., Stephens M.: A combined corner and edge detector. In Alvey Vision Conf. 1988, pp. 147-151
[5] Huang J., Kumar S. R., Mitra M., Zhu W. J., Zabih R.: Image indexing using color correlograms. In Proc. of International Conference in Computer Vision and Pattern Recognition, 1997
[6] Jutten C., Herault J.: Blind separation of sources. Signal Processing, 24:1-10,1991
[7] Koenderink J. J., van Doorn A. J.: Representation of local geometry in the visual system. Biological Cybernetics, 55: 367-375, 1987
[8] Moghaddam B., Biermann H., Margaritis D.: Regions-of-Interest and Spatial Layout in Content based Image Retrieval. In Proc. of European Workshop on Content Based Multimedia Indexing, 1999
[9] Moghaddam B., Pentland A.: Probabilistic Visual Learning for Object Representation. IEEE Transactions on PAMI, 19(7): 696-710, 1997
[10] Schmid C., Mohr R.: Local grayvalue invariants for image retrieval. IEEE Trans. on Pattern Analysis and Machine Intelligence 19 (5), 530–534, 1997
[11] Schmid C., Mohr R., Bauckhage C.: Comparing and evaluating interest points. In Proc ICCV, 1998.
[12] Schneiderman H., Kanade T.: Probabilistic Modeling of Local Appearance and Spatial Relationships for Object Recognition. In Proc of CVPR, pp. 45-51, 1998.

[13] Swain, M. J., Ballard, D. H.: Color Indexing. International Journal of Computer Vision, vol. 7, pp. 11-32, 1991

[14] Tenmoto H., Kudo M., Shimbo M.: MDL-Based Selection of the Number of Components in Mixture Models for Pattern Recognition. In SSPR/SPR, pp. 831-836, 1998.

An Experimental Evaluation of K-nn for Linear Transforms of Positive Data*

David Guillamet and Jordi Vitrià

Computer Vision Center-Dept. Informàtica, Universitat Autònoma de Barcelona
08193 Bellaterra, Barcelona, Spain
{davidg,jordi}@cvc.uab.es

Abstract. We present an experimental evaluation of the subspaces obtained on positive data using the Principal Component Analysis (PCA), Non-negative Matrix Factorization (NMF) and Weighted Non-negative Matrix Factorization (WNMF) techniques in order to compare which technique provides a subspace that mantains the neighbourhood structure of the original space. Different distance metrics are used both in the original and the projected spaces in order to find which one is more adapted to our data. Results demonstrate that for our positive data (color histograms) a good candidate that preserves the original neighbourhood is NMF in conjunction with L_1 distance metric when the χ^2 metric is used in the original space. Since this is the most widely used distance metric when having histogram representations, our initial results seem to be relevant.

1 Introduction

Over the past few years, several pattern recognition systems for visual object recognition have been proposed based on principal component analysis (PCA) [8, 7, 14, 1, 12, 13]. Although details vary, these systems can all be described in terms of the same preprocessing and run-time steps. All of them are characterized by the learning of a set of feature vectors and finding a subspace representation that captures the structure of the data. Usually, when calculating the covariance matrix of the problem, eigenvectors are sorted by decreasing eigenvalue only taking the most representative ones which correspond to the directions of maximum variance. Once the subspace is fully-described by a projection matrix, the classification of a new feature vector is accomplished by projecting and finding the nearest neighbor in the subspace.

Recently, a new approach for obtaining a linear representation of data has been proposed. This new technique, called Non-negative Matrix Factorization (NMF), was used in the work of Lee and Seung [5] to find parts of objects in an unsupervised way. Non-negative Matrix Factorization differs from other methods

---

* This work is supported by Comissionat per a Universitats i Recerca del Departament de la Presidencia de la Generalitat de Catalunya and Ministerio de Ciencia y Tecnologia grant TIC2000-0399-C02-01.

F.J. Perales et al. (Eds.): IbPRIA 2003, LNCS 2652, pp. 317–325, 2003.

by its use of non-negativity constraints. Their work was tested with a set of faces [5] and the obtained NMF bases are localized features that correspond with intuitive notions of the parts of faces.

Both methods, PCA and NMF, can be viewed as maximum likelihood learning in a latent variable model. The space that is generated by a PCA transform can be associated to a natural metric [7]. Otherwise, since NMF generates a non-negative space, it does not exist a natural metric to use. This is the reason why a distance metric must be defined in this space in order to compare and classify projected data.

This paper presents experimental evaluations of traditional distance measures in the context of visual object recognition when using both PCA and NMF techniques. Also, a weighted version of NMF is introduced that outperforms results obtained using NMF. Since NMF is based on positive restrictions, we have used local color histograms as object features in order to verify which is the most suitable technique to represent our original data. An extended analysis of different distance metrics in the original space has been carried out in order to compare both techniques. Also, different distance metrics have been compared in the projected spaces obtained using PCA and NMF. An extended analysis to compare both projected spaces with the original space has been done noticing very interesting results.

2   PCA and NMF Techniques

2.1   Principal Component Analysis (PCA)

In the context of visual data classification, and due to the high dimensionality of data, similarity and distance metrics are computationally expensive and some compaction of the original data is usually needed. Principal Component Analysis is an optimal linear dimensionality reduction scheme with respect to the mean squared error (MSE) of the reconstruction. For a set of m training vectors $\mathbf{X} = \{\mathbf{x}^1, \ldots \mathbf{x}^m\}$ the mean ($\nu = \frac{1}{m} \sum_{j=1}^{m} \mathbf{x}^j$) and covariance matrix ($\Sigma = \frac{1}{m} \sum_{j=1}^{m} (\mathbf{x}^j - \nu)(\mathbf{x}^j - \nu)^T$) can be calculated. Given a projection matrix $\mathbf{E}$ composed of the r eigenvectors of Σ with highest eigenvalues, the r-dimensional representation of an original, n-dimensional vector $\mathbf{x}$, is given by the projection $\mathbf{y} = \mathbf{E}^T (\mathbf{x} - \nu)$.

2.2   Non-negative Matrix Factorization (NMF)

NMF is a method to obtain a representation of data using non-negativity constraints. These constraints lead to a part-based representation because they allow only additive, not subtractive, combinations of the original data [5]. Given an initial database expressed by a $n \times m$ matrix $\mathbf{V}$, where each column is an n-dimensional non-negative vector of the original database (m vectors), it is possible to find two non-negative matrices ($\mathbf{W}$ and $\mathbf{H}$) in order to approximate the original matrix $\mathbf{V}_{i\mu} \approx (\mathbf{WH})_{i\mu} = \sum_{a=1}^{r} \mathbf{W}_{ia} \mathbf{H}_{a\mu}$. The dimensions of the factorized matrices $\mathbf{W}$ and $\mathbf{H}$ are $n \times r$ and $r \times m$, respectively. Usually, r is chosen so that $(n+m)r < nm$. Each column of matrix $\mathbf{W}$ contains a basis vector while each column of $\mathbf{H}$ contains the weights needed to approximate the corresponding column in $\mathbf{V}$ using the bases from $\mathbf{W}$.

In order to estimate $\mathbf{W}$ and $\mathbf{H}$, an objective function has to be defined. A possible objective function is given by $F = \sum_{i=1}^{n} \sum_{\mu=1}^{m} [\mathbf{V}_{i\mu} \log(\mathbf{WH})_{i\mu} - (\mathbf{WH})_{i\mu}]$. This objective function can be related to the likelihood of generating training samples in $\mathbf{V}$ from the bases $\mathbf{W}$ and encodings $\mathbf{H}$ under a Poisson model. An iterative approach to reach a local maximum of this objective function is given by the following rules [5]: $\mathbf{W}_{ia} \leftarrow \mathbf{W}_{ia} \sum_{\mu} \frac{\mathbf{V}_{i\mu}}{(\mathbf{WH})_{i\mu}} \mathbf{H}_{a\mu}$, $\mathbf{W}_{ia} \leftarrow \frac{\mathbf{W}_{ia}}{\sum_{j} \mathbf{W}_{ja}}$, $\mathbf{H}_{a\mu} \leftarrow$
$\mathbf{H}_{a\mu} \sum_{i} \mathbf{W}_{ia} \frac{\mathbf{V}_{i\mu}}{(\mathbf{WH})_{i\mu}}$. Initialization is performed using positive random initial conditions for matrices $\mathbf{W}$ and $\mathbf{H}$. The convergence of the process is also ensured. See [5, 6] for more information.

Once a set of $\mathbf{W}$ bases is found to represent a certain data class, a new data vector is projected using the same iteration rules as explained before but taking the class matrix $\mathbf{W}$ as a constant reference. Thus, taking the constant matrix $\mathbf{W}$ of a data class and starting with a positive random matrix factor $\mathbf{H}$, we will obtain a set of projected coefficients ($\mathbf{H}$) that would be the projected coefficients of a new data vector expressed using the set of bases $\mathbf{W}$ of a given data class.

A weighted version of NMF can be introduced by considering a weight matrix $\mathbf{Q}$ that takes into account the probability of each training data vector over the whole set of training vectors. Iterative update rules are the same as the ones related before for the NMF with the addition of a new matrix $\mathbf{Q}$. This weighted model can be seen as the result of multiplying both sides of the factorization with a m by m diagonal weight matrix $\mathbf{Q}$ and to estimate the bases and encodings for the new factorization model, $\mathbf{VQ} \approx \mathbf{WHQ}$. Where the diagonal element q_{μ} corresponds to the weight of training vector μ, with $1 \leq \mu \leq m$. It is also assumed that all the weights sum to unity. The modified objective function in this case takes the form $F_Q = \sum_{\mu=1}^{m} q_{\mu} \sum_{i=1}^{n} [\mathbf{V}_{i\mu} \log((\mathbf{WH})_{i\mu} q_{\mu}) - (\mathbf{WH})_{i\mu}]$. Now, the iterative update rules to obtain the new matrices subject to this new objective function are defined by: $\mathbf{W}_{ia} \leftarrow \frac{\mathbf{W}_{ia}}{\sum_{\mu} q_{\mu} \mathbf{H}_{a\mu}} \sum_{\mu} \frac{q_{\mu} \mathbf{V}_{i\mu}}{(\mathbf{WH})_{i\mu}} \mathbf{H}_{a\mu}$, $\mathbf{W}_{ia} \leftarrow$
$\frac{\mathbf{W}_{ia}}{\sum_{j} \mathbf{W}_{ja}}$, $\mathbf{H}_{a\mu} \leftarrow \mathbf{H}_{a\mu} \sum_{i} \mathbf{W}_{ia} \frac{\mathbf{V}_{i\mu}}{(\mathbf{WH})_{i\mu}}$. See [3] for more information.

3   Distance Metrics

Five commonly used distance metrics are tested in this work: L_1, L_2, Cos, χ^2 and Histogram intersection. Assuming that we are working with n dimensional vectors, L_1 metric between two vectors x and y is defined as

$$\text{dist}_{L_1}(x, y) = \sum_{i=1}^{n} |x_i - y_i| \qquad (1)$$

L_2 metric between two vectors x and y is defined as

$$\text{dist}_{L_2}(x, y) = \sqrt{\sum_{i=1}^{n}(x_i - y_i)^2} \tag{2}$$

Cos metric between two vectors x and y is defined as

$$\text{dist}_{Cos}(x, y) = \frac{x^T y}{\| x \| \cdot \| y \|} \tag{3}$$

where $\| . \|$ denotes the norm. This measure is also defined as the cosine of the angle between two vectors and is usually used to extract a measure of correlation between vectors. χ^2 metric is usually used when we try to obtain a measure of similarity between histograms and is defined as

$$\text{dist}_{\chi^2}(x, y) = \frac{1}{2}\sum_{i=1}^{n}\frac{(x_i - y_i)^2}{x_i + y_i} \tag{4}$$

Finally, the histogram intersection [11] measure is not a true metric but it is usually used in the context of color histogram classification because it provides the best recognition results. Histogram intersection between two histograms x and y is defined as

$$\text{dist}_{Int}(x, y) = \sum_{i=1}^{n}\min(x_i, y_i) \tag{5}$$

4   Methodology

Since our intention is to compare three techniques used on the dimensionality reduction of the original space, it is interesting to compare which is the technique that mantains the neighbourhood of the original space. We analyze how two vectors that are close in the original space are related in the projected spaces of the analyzed techniques, NMF/WNMF and PCA, in order to find which is the technique that can reproduce the original space more exactly. Figure 1 shows a graphical example of this idea. Figure (1.a) shows a sample vector X_1 and its 5 neighbours in the original space using some distance d. When projecting the original space to a reduced one using some technique, NMF/WNMF or PCA in our particular case, the original space of figure (1.a) is transformed to the space represented in figure (1.b) where we can appreciate that only two original vectors, X_3 and X_7, mantain its neighbourhood with X_1. Figure (1.c) represents a projected space obtained using another technique where we can see that three original vectors, X_3, X_{32} and X_{21}, mantain its neighbourhood with X_1. With this example and only evaluating the neighbourhood of X_1, the projected space of figure (1.c) is closer to the original space than the one represented in figure (1.b).

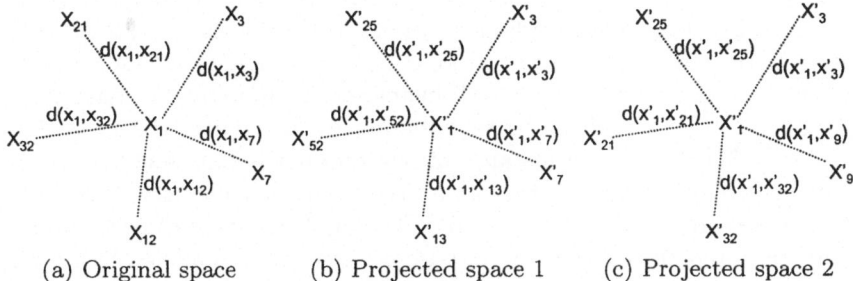

(a) Original space   (b) Projected space 1   (c) Projected space 2

Fig. 1. Considering a sample vector X_1 and its 5 neighbours, (a) represents the 5 nearest original vectors of X_1. Assuming that we used a technique to reduce the original space to another one, (b) represents the 5 nearest reduced vectors of the projected vector (X_1') of its original vector X_1. (c) represents the projection of the same original space to a reduced space using another technique. The first projected space (b) holds 2 vectors and (c) holds 3 vectors from the original space in its neighbourhood. Thus, the second projected space is closer to the original one for this specific vector X_1

5 Experimental Results

Our experiments are focused on the evaluation of 45 different pharmaceutical products having 6 different instances per product. These products present several color ambiguities (some products are nearly similar only differing in reduced regions) and, in all the images, the background color is black and the illumination is controlled. Figure (2.a) shows a subset of the pharmaceutical products used in the experiments. We used a Harris operator [4, 10] to detect interesting keypoints in our products. Once a keypoint is considered, we extract a local color

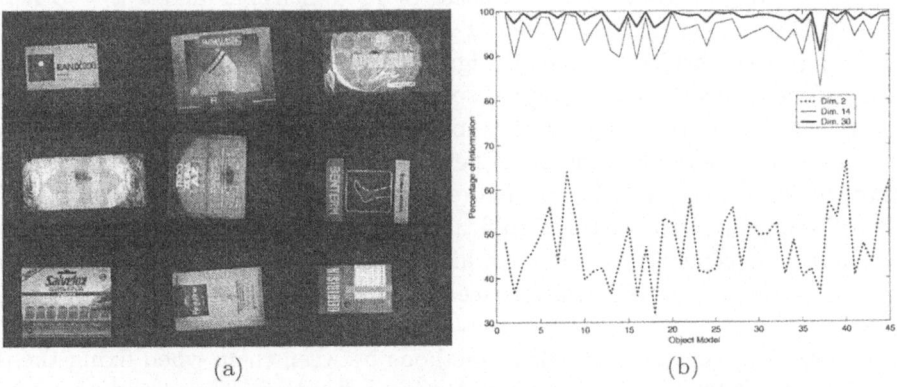

(a)   (b)

Fig. 2. (a) 9 of the 45 pharmaceutical products used in our experiments. (b) Amount of information captured using a PCA space and 3 different dimensions of the projected space (2, 14 and 30)

histogram from its neighborhood and we will use this color histogram as a salient feature of the object. Since we find desirable to be able to capture the objects at any rotation angle, the extracted local color histograms should be invariant to this feature. Thus, we extract each histogram from a circular mask from the neighborhood of a keypoint because it minimizes the rotational effects that the image can suffer. Once each instance of one product is represented by a collection of local color histograms, we join all the local color histograms that belong to the same product in one object class. Taking 3 instances of each product as training data and the other three as testing data, we join all the histograms of each set of data in one object model. Thus, each object class is represented by an average of 1000 local color histograms.

Each object model is projected to a PCA and a NMF/WNMF space using different dimensionalities of the projected space. We fixed these dimensionalities to: 2,6,10,14,18,22,26 and 30. Each local color histogram is represented by a 512 dimensional vector, but we have to note that nearly all the components of each histogram are null. Thus, using 30 dimensions to represent a projected space should be enough to capture the relevant information contained in each color histogram. With a PCA space, we are able to know the amount of information that can be captured by the projected space. Figure (2.b) shows the amount of information that is represented using three different dimensions of the PCA space with respect all the 45 object models of our database. It is clear that 2 dimensions is not enough to capture reliable information from the original space, but 30 dimensions should be enough since nearly all the objects mantain a 99% of the information of the original space.

In computer vision, one common task is to match two sets of data corresponding to two different objects in order to find a matching between them. Here, we reproduce this idea by having 45 different pharmaceutical products that we compare using different subspace representations, distance metrics and neighbourhoods. Figure 3 shows the graphical results when we compare the training data vectors of object 3 against the testing data vectors of object 6 using a dimensionality of the projected spaces of 22 dimensions and a $k = 5$ nearest neighbour classifier. Also, different distance metrics are used in the original space and in the projected spaces. Figure (3.a) gives us an idea of how a projected space is related to the original space using different distance metrics and, in this particular case, a L_2 distance in the projected space of PCA is the best combination to reproduce the same neighbourhood of the original space when using the L_2 metric. Also in this figure (3.a), it is interesting to note that the WNMF technique outperforms significantly the NMF results. This improvement is clearly manifested when using the histogram intersection, L_1 or a χ^2 test as a distance metric in the original space and using a L_1 metric in the projected space.

Figure (3.b) compares the three methods between them when fixing the dimensionality of the problem to 30 and using a fixed neighbourhood of $k = 13$. When comparing one object against another one, as in figure 3, we only take into account when one method represents the original space better than the other

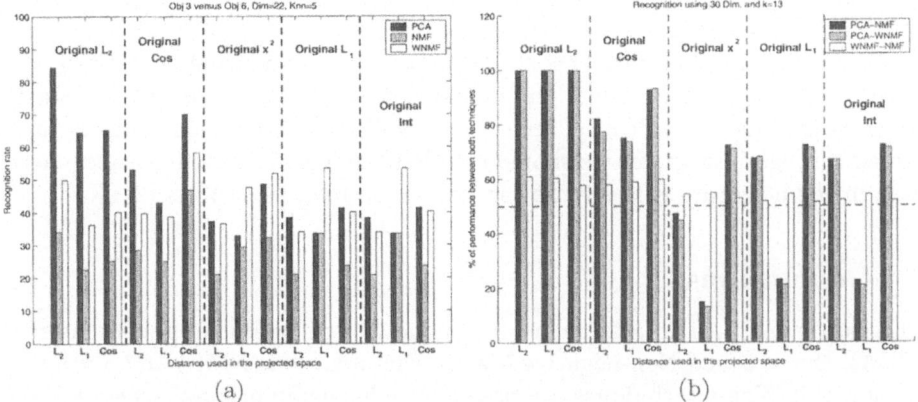

Fig. 3. (a) Comparison of object vectors of model 3 against the object vectors of model 6 using a projected space of 22 dimensions and a $K = 5$ nearest neighbour classifier using three different techniques: PCA, NMF and WNMF. Horizontal axis reflects the three different distance metrics used in the projected spaces of PCA, NMF and WNMF. Vertical axis reflects the percentage of vectors that mantains its neighborhood with the original space. (b) Graphical results obtained when comparing PCA versus NMF (black columns), PCA versus WNMF (gray columns) and WNMF versus NMF (white columns) when using 30 dimensions and $k = 13$ neighbours for a nearest neighbour classifier. When using a χ^2, L_1 or histogram interesection as distance metrics in the original space, NMF and WNMF are significantly better than PCA (performances below 50%). Also, since the white column (WNMF versus NMF) is always above 50% means that WNMF is better than NMF for all the cases

one, that is, if we compare PCA versus NMF (label *PCA-NMF* in figure (3.b)), we only take into account *when* PCA is better than NMF for each particular comparison. Since we have 45 pharmaceutical products, we have $45 \times 45 = 2025$ evaluations. Figure (3.b) shows that when one column is above 50% means that one method performs better than the other one out of these 2025 evaluations. Thus, this figure is useful for extracting some interesting conclusions of this work.

The first conclusion is that WNMF, as a modification of the original NMF, performs better than the NMF in all the comparisons. When using a L_2 metric in the original space of color histograms, PCA performs always better with respect to NMF and WNMF (100% in figure (3.b)).The best distance metric to use with PCA is L_2 and this is not a novelty since PCA creates its subspace as an optimal reduction scheme with respect to the mean squared error, so that, L_2 is the natural distance metric to use in the reduced space. When using the *Cos* metric in the original space, PCA starts decreasing its performance in front of NMF and WNMF, but it is still better because it has a percentage of 70% to 80% of performance as seen in figure 3. The most important conclusion is that *NMF or WNMF techniques are better than PCA when using the L_1 metric in* the subspace and compared to the χ^2, L_1 or the histogram intersection metrics used in the original space.

We should say that with this study, we are only comparing how a projected space is related to the original one in terms of neighbourhoods but not stating which is the best classification technique. Additionaly, since our data is represented through histograms we should say that the most common distance metric used in the literature is the χ^2 as can be seen in relevant studies [2, 9].

6 Conclusions

This paper analyzes an alternative technique to Principal Component Analysis (PCA), the so called Non-negative Matrix Factorization (NMF) and a weighted version of it. These techniques are based on reducing an original space to a subspace where dimensionality is lower and the main question is whether this new subspace representation can be used for classification/recognition purposes. This study is a first attempt in order to analyze how the subspaces obtained using PCA and NMF/WNMF are related to the original ones. We evaluated the neighbourhood of the original vectors with respect to their projections in the different subspaces of PCA and NMF/WNMF. Different distance metrics in the original space and in the subspaces are evaluated in order to find how to preserve the original neighbourhood. As a result, we state that the NMF technique combined with the L_1 norm is well suited for reproducing the neighbourhood of a given space when χ^2 is used. This is a very important result since our original data is represented using color histograms (positive data) and is a very common to use χ^2 when having histogram representations. Also, we can also experimentally state that WNMF performs slightly better than NMF for all the cases.

References

[1] Belhumeur, P. N., Hespanha J. P., Kriegman D. J.: Eigenfaces vs. fisherfaces: Recognition using class specific linear projection. IEEE Trans. PAMI,19(7):711-720,1997
[2] Belongie, S., Malik, J., Puzicha, J.: Shape Matching and Object Recognition Using Shape Contexts. IEEE Transactions on PAMI, 24(24):509-522, April 2002
[3] Guillamet D., Bressan M., Vitria J.: Weighted Non-negative Matrix Factorization for Local Representations. In Proc. CVPR, pp. 942-947, 2001
[4] Harris C., Stephens M.: A combined corner and edge detector. In Alvey Vision Conf. 1988, pp. 147-151
[5] Lee D., Seung H.: Learning the parts of objects by non-negative matrix factorization. Nature, 401:788-791, 1999
[6] Lee D., Seung H.: Algorithms for non-negative matrix factorization. In: Advances in Neural Information Processing Systems, 2000
[7] Moghaddam B., Pentland A. P.: Probabilisitc visual learning for object representation. IEEE Trans. on Pattern Analysis and Machine Intell., 19(7):696-710,1997
[8] Murase, H., Nayar, S.: Visual learning and recognition of 3d objects from appearance. International Journal of Computer Vision 14, 5-24, 1995

 [9] Schiele, B., Crowley, J. L.: Recognition without Correspondence using Multidimensional Receptive Field Histograms. IJCV 36(1):31-50, 2000
[10] Schmid C., Mohr R., Bauckhage C.: Comparing and evaluating interest points. In Proc ICCV, 1998
[11] Swain, M. J., Ballard, D. H.: Color Indexing. International Journal of Computer Vision, vol. 7, pp. 11-32, 1991
[12] Swets, D., Weng, J.: Using discriminant eigenfeatures for image retrieval. IEEE Trans. on Pattern Analysis and Machine Intelligence 18 (8), 831–836, 1996
[13] Swets, D., Weng, J.: Hierarchical discriminant analysis for image retrieval. IEEE Trans. on Pattern Analysis and Machine Intelligence 21 (5), 386–401, 1999
[14] Turk M., Pentland A. P.: Eigenfaces for recognition. Journal of Cognitive Neuroscience, 3(1):71-86, 1991

Wavelet Packet Image Coder Using Coefficients Partitioning for Remote Sensing Images

Su-Young Han[1] and Seong-Yun Cho[2]

[1] Dept. of Electronic Engineering, Hanyang University
17 Haengdang-dong, Seongdong-Gu Seoul, Korea, 133-791
yejiwon@ihanyang.ac.kr
[2] Dept. of Digital Media, Anyang University
Anyang 5-dong, Manan-gu Anyang, Kyonggi-do, Korea, 708-113
scho@aycc.anyang.ac.kr

Abstract. In this paper, a new embedded wavelet packet image coder algorithm is proposed for an effective image coder using correlation between partitioned coefficients. This new algorithm presents parent-child relationship for reducing image reconstruction error using relations between individual frequency sub-bands. By parent-child relationships, every coefficient is partitioned and encoded for the zerotree data structure. It is shown that the proposed wavelet packet image coder algorithm achieves lower bit rates than SPIHT. It also demonstrates higher PSNR under the same bit rate. The perfect rate control is compared with the conventional methods. These results show that the encoding and decoding processes of the proposed coder are simpler and more accurate than the conventional ones for texture images that include many mid and high-frequency elements such as aerial and satellite photograph images. The experimental results imply the possibility that the proposed method can be applied to real-time vision system, on-line image processing and image fusion which require smaller file size and better resolution.

Keywords: Wavelet Packet, SPIHT, Image Compression, CPSO

1   Introduction

Most of the images collected from airplanes or satellites are texture imagery containing plenty of middle frequency. Contrary to the dyadic wavelet transform which recursively decomposes low frequency components, the wavelet packet transform is suitable for analyzing or presenting non-stationary signals such as texture images by its adaptability to each frequency band [1]. In high altitude photograph images such as aerial or satellite photograph images, buildings and landscapes are usually represented as recursive textures. After FFT as a preprocessing, it is notified that high frequency components are dominated in these images. The wavelet packet transform usually shows better performance than the conventional wavelet transform in the processing of information which has high frequency component [2, 3, 4].

F.J. Perales et al. (Eds.): IbPRIA 2003, LNCS 2652, pp. 326–335, 2003.

However, the wavelet packet transformation should lose the multi-resolution structure of wavelet basis function. It is because that the zerotree method could not be directly introduced in the wavelet packet transform. That is, it is impossible to construct the tree that has its coefficients located in the same spatial relationship.

In this paper, a coefficient partitioning scanning order (CPSO) is newly defined using decomposition information, which is derived from wavelet packet decomposition. From this definition, a new wavelet packet image coder algorithm, which applies the zerotree by partitioning its coefficient, is developed. In the proposed algorithm, input images are transformed into wavelet packets using 9-7 biorthogonal filters over full bandwidth and optimal basis functions are selected on the basis of entropy. Then, parent-child relationships are defined in the packet-transformed coefficients depending upon its sub-band decomposition information and the essentiality of coefficients. From this relationship, CPSO is constructed. After partitioning the coefficients, each coefficient is quantized hierarchically and decoded.

This paper is organized as follows; the characteristics and the points of issue of the conventional algorithms are concerned in Section 2. Then, the proposed wavelet packet image coder algorithm is introduced in Section 3. In the Section 4, the improvement of the new algorithm over the conventional algorithms in bitrate and PSNR is demonstrated by the experimental results. Finally, Section 5 summarizes the results, discusses some technical issues and suggests some further research prospects.

2   Wavelet Packet Image Coder Algorithm

The wavelet packet image coder algorithm can be divided into three sections as shown in Fig. 1. First, input images are partitioned over all bandwidth using proper wavelet filters and based on the partitioned coefficients, and then input images are divided again by the wavelet packet or basis function, which provides optimal conditions for image coding. Second, quantize wavelet packet coefficients using scalar quantizer, vector quantizer or hierarchical quantizer. Third, we get the bit stream using entropy encoder such as Huffman Arithmetic encoder [6].

2.1   Wavelet Packet Transform

The image is first decomposed into the wavelet packet. In the wavelet packet transform for signal compression, several wavelet decomposition criteria such as entropy measurement, shareholding, rate-distortion tradeoff can be considered. Among these algorithms, the singletree algorithms introduced by Ramchandran and Vetterli is known as optimal in the sense of rate-distortion [2, 8]. However, this algorithm needs to be applied to all of the scalar quantizer for each node and calculate quantization distortion and bit rates, and then it finds out optimal basis using these calculation results. These calculations introduce the computational complexity, which makes real-time application difficult. And, because a scalar

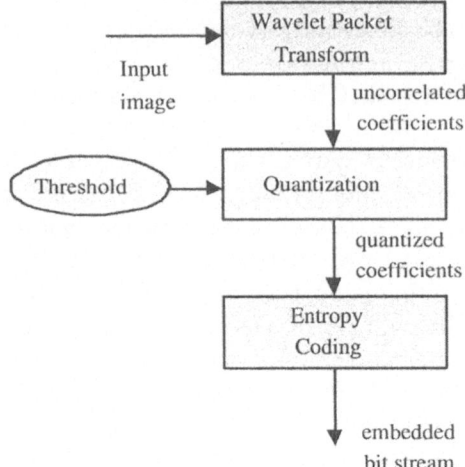

Fig. 1. Wavelet Packet Coding Algorithm

quantization process has been already included in the packet transformation scheme, multilevel quantization, which is a core technique of the zerotree wavelet popular in pyramid structure wavelet transform, cannot be applied. Therefore, in the embedding approach using additive successive quantization, it may be no longer optimal. In our research, we use an entropy-based algorithm with a simple scheme [6].

2.2   EZW and SPIHT Algorithm

EZW (Embedded Wavelet Transform) [3] algorithm has known as the most popular one among the other image wavelet code algorithms. In spite of it simplicity, it has good bit rate distortion performance and the embedding characteristic that the large and major coefficients re transferred earlier than other ones. This characteristic is very helpful to progressive transmission

SPIHT (Set Partitioning In Hierarchical Tree) is well known as an improved model of EZW [5]. In opposition to EZW which decides transfer order using the dominant and subordinate pass, SPIHT decides transfer order more effectively using the LIP (List of Insignificant Pixel) and LIS (List of Insignificant Sets).

These two algorithms construct a tree with zero quantized coefficients using the relationships between bilateral bandwidths. In conclusion, it introduces efficient reduction of the amount of data which are sent to decoder. However, because the hierarchical structure with multi-level resolutions is not clear in the wavelet packet, it is not easy to use the relationship between bilateral bandwidths. That is, in the wavelet packet, the parent-child relationship, which is used in the EZW or SPIHT, is not easy to maintain.

3   Coefficient Partitioning Wavelet Packet Coder Algorithm

In this section, CPSO is defined using the split information of sub-band, which is provided from wavelet packet decomposition, and then, a new wavelet packet coder algorithm that quantizes each coefficient with zerotree on CPSO is suggested.

3.1   Structure of Proposed Coder

The structure of the proposed coefficient partitioning algorithm and quantization procedure is as follows;

First of all, an input image is decomposed into wavelet packet using 9-7 tap biorthogonal filter and first-order entropy.

After the wavelet packet decomposition has done, each coefficient is partitioned depending on its split information and the essentiality of each coefficient, and processed with the successive quantization. During these processes, the new CPSO, which uses the relationships between individual bandwidths, is defined for applying the zerotree algorithm to the wavelet packet transform.

3.2   CPSO for Proposed Algorithm

In the dyadic wavelet transform, all of the parent nodes have always 4 children nodes, which have same frequency space, except the lowest frequency sub-band. However, in the wavelet packet transform, the children nodes cannot apply a conventional zerotree algorithm directly.

In this section, the new coefficient partition scanning order is defined using the parent-child relationship (the relationship of identical space) based on the zerotree method.

In the proposed algorithm, CPSO is defined as the next three conditions.

Condition 1. If child sub-band S is more decomposed than band P, which is related with the parent node, it does not have a child node. This bandwidth finds out the significant coefficients through the raster scan after finishing the P band threshold scanning as shown in the Figs. 2-a and 2-b. We call it CPSO0.

Condition 2. If child sub-band S is not decomposed, it has 4 children nodes. It is described in Fig. 2-c. Equation (1) describes condition 2. We call it CPSO4.

$$\{D(x,y) \mid S(x+i, y+j), \text{ where } i = 0, 1 \text{ and } j = 0, 1\}. \tag{1}$$

where $D(x,y)$ is the set of children nodes and $S(x,y)$ is a child node in sub-band.

Condition 3. If child sub-band S, in the higher resolution than P band of parent node, is decomposed into 4 sub-bands, each coefficient located in the same space of the sub-band becomes a child node. It is described in Equation (2) and Fig. 2-d. We call it CPSO1.

$$\{D(x,y) \mid S_k(x,y), \text{ where } k = 0, 1, 2, 3\}. \tag{2}$$

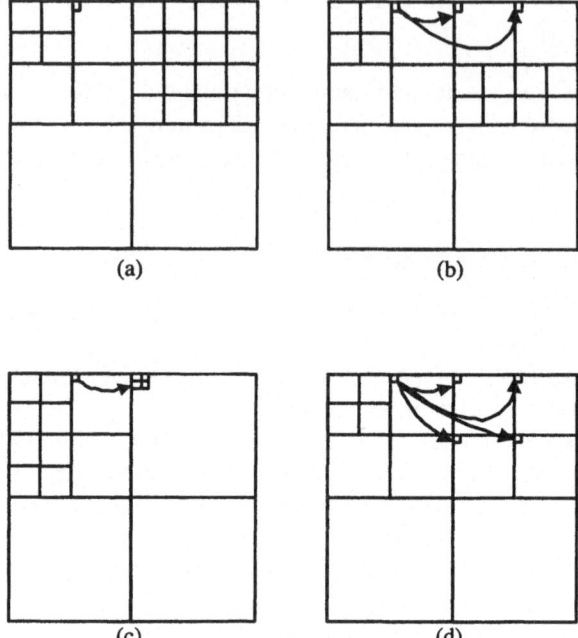

Fig. 2. Examples of CPSO in the wavelet packet transform; (a) example of CPSO0, (b) other example of CPSO0, (c) example of CPSO4, (d) example of CPSO1

where $D(x, y)$ is the set of children nodes and $S_k(x, y)$ is a child node in subband.

3.3 Coder Algorithm

In most of wavelet packet transforms except top-down algorithm, the information, which indicates each band's decomposition, has to be transferred with transformed coefficients in a header format.

In this paper, during the coding process, the child node scheme of each coefficient is verified using this information and CPSO is extracted depending on these results. In this list of decomposition information SM (Split Mark), 1 is assigned for the decomposed band and 0 for the un-decomposed band

Following is a pseudocode for the coding algorithm, excluding the wavelet packet decomposition and the entropy coding. The list of the detected coefficients DC saves the coordinate of coefficient which has bigger absolute value than the specific threshold in the list of waiting coefficients WC, and in the list of root of waiting coefficients WCR used with the SM, the split information of each node indicates a child or descendant represented as 1 or 0 for the variety of un-scanned descendant. $c_{x,y}$ is a wavelet transform coefficient for the coordinate of spatial dimension $\{x, y\}$ and the first threshold value T_0 for identifying a significant value, $T_0 = max\{c_{x,y}\}/2$.

while (up to target compression ratio)

    while (each coefficient saved in *WC*)

        if $|c_{x,y}| \geq T_0$

          then

              Output 1, output 1 or 0 for +/- bit,

                add coordinate to the list *DC* and delete from the *WC*

          else

              Output 0

        fi

    end

    while (each coefficient saved in *WCR*)

        if $|c_{x,y}| \geq T_0$

          then

              Output 1 and determine scanning order in children nodes according to *SM*.

              if (CPSO0)

                Add coordinate to the list *WCR*.

              fi

              if (CPSO1)

$$D(x,y) = \begin{cases} \text{each coefficient located in same with x, y} \\ \text{at } S_k(x,y) \end{cases}$$

              fi

              if (CPSO4)

$$D(x,y) = \begin{cases} (2^*x, 2^*y),\ (2^*x, 2^*y+1) \\ (2^*x+1, 2^*y),(2^*x+1, 2^*y+1) \end{cases}$$

              fi

              while (*in* $D(x,y)$)

                  if $|c_{x,y}| \geq T_0$

                    then

                      Output 1 and 1 or 0 for +/- bit,

                        add it to the *DC*.

                  else

                      Output 0, and it to the *WC*

                  fi

                  Determine scanning order in descendent nodes according to *SM*.

                  According to CPSO, determine $D(x,y)$ and move the tree to the *WCR*

              end

          else

              Output 0

        fi

    end

end

4   Experimental Results

In this chapter, the experimental results for 512 x 512 remote sensing images, which are sample-1 (see Fig. 3) and sample-2 (see Fig. 4) are summarized in Table 1 and in Figs. 7 and 8 for comparing the different algorithms. Figs. 5 and 6 are coefficients which are decomposed with wavelet transform packet. These samples are collected from www.spaceimaging.com web site, which supplies the most advanced satellite and aerial images. These images are selected to experiment and demonstrate for the superiority of the proposed algorithm against the conventional algorithm. These kinds of images are usually composed of simplified and recursive geometrical structures such as rectangular, circles, lines and groups of points by high altitude view. Most of high frequency component images have shown better performance in the partitioning of image using wavelet packet decomposition [7].

Two-dimensional separable length 9-7 biorthonormal wavelet filters were used for wavelet packet decomposition. After applying coefficient partitioning scanning order, the proposed algorithm in this paper is compared with the results of the conventional SPIHT algorithm.

Comparing the performance between the proposed algorithm and conventional algorithm has done by bit rate and PSNR (Peak Signal to Noise Ratio). PSNR, is defined as Equation (3).

$$PSNR = 10 \times log10 \frac{255^2}{MSE} dB \tag{3}$$

Bit rate directly refers to the size of file obtained from the coding procedure to be consistent with SPIHT coder.

In the proposed algorithm, such as SPIHT, all of output data of coder indicate only 1 or 0. That is, whether or significant coefficient, sign of coefficient and SM (split mark), which include the packet decomposition information coder also represent whether or decomposition using only 1 or 0.

Accordingly, the proposed algorithm can do bit operation for all of the output data and reduce the file size more than the conventional algorithm when it is saved.

Table 1 and Figs. 7 and 8 show the results of performance comparison between two algorithms. Bit rate for performance comparison uses the bit per pixel unit against size, including all of header information. In case of the sample images, the proposed coefficient partitioning wavelet packet method using CPSO shows 1 or 2 dB higher performance, compared to the SPIHT in the higher compression rates.

As concerns parent-child node relationship, which has usually applied in the wavelet packet, it cannot be utilized multi-resolution structure that the wavelet transform does. The result in Table 1 shows that the image adaptability of wavelet packet transform can compliment sufficiently the parent-child relationship at the wavelet packet for the images which have relatively middle or high bandwidth frequency signal such as aerial or satellite images.

Fig. 3. Satellite image of Fresno, USA as sample-1

Fig. 4. Satellite image of Carolina, USA as sample-2

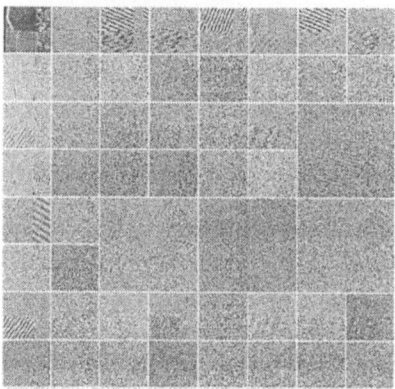

Fig. 5. Wavelet Packet Decomposition result of sample-1 as shown in Fig. 3 (Fresno)

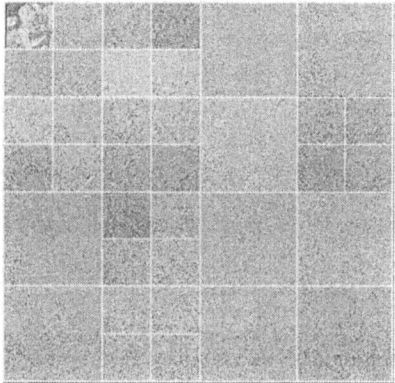

Fig. 6. Wavelet Packet Decomposition result of sample-2 as shown in Fig. 4 (Carolina)

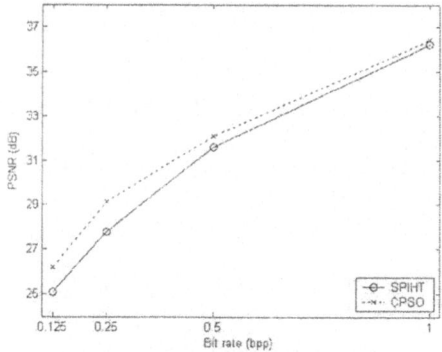

Fig. 7. PSNR of sample-1

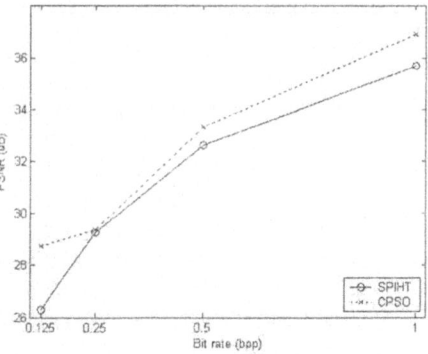

Fig. 8. PSNR of sample-2

Table 1. Results of the performance comparison between CPSO and SPIHT

Bit rate	Sample #1 (PSNR)		Sample #2 (PSNR)	
(bpp)	SPIHT	CPSO	SPIHT	CPSO
0.125	25.10	26.19	16.31	28.71
0.25	27.80	29.12	29.26	29.35
0.5	31.61	32.08	32.61	33.33
1.0	36.22	36.44	35.66	36.89

5   Conclusions

In this work, using the relationships between sub-bands, the new wavelet packet transform image coder algorithm is proposed. The proposed algorithm, CPSO, demonstrates improving the image compression algorithm that uses the conventional wavelet transform.

In the CPSO algorithm, the new parent-child relationship is extracted using the relationships between individual frequencies sub-bands at the wavelet packet transform, decide the coding order of coefficient to reduce image reconstruction error.

There are improvements in bit rate and distortion performance by decoding wavelet packet transform coefficient with the zerotree method.

The experimental results demonstrate very high PSNR at the bit rate and show a great improvement in total image compression time.

From these results, it is shown that the encoding and decoding processes of the proposed coder are simpler and more accurate than the conventional method for texture images, which include many mid and high-frequency elements such as aerial and satellite photograph images.

It shows that the proposed algorithm has a great possibility to improve real-time vision system, on-line image processing and JPEG2000.

References

[1] Pei-Yuan Huang, Long-Wen Chang: Digital Image Coding with Hybrid Wavelet Packet Transform. PCM 2001, LNCS 2195. (2001) 301–307
[2] Ramchandran K., M. Vetterli: Best wavelet packet bases in a rate-distortion sense. IEEE Trans. on Image Processing, 2(2) (1993) 1760-1785
[3] Shapiro J.: Embedded image coding using zerotree wavelet coefficients. IEEE Trans. on Signal Processing, 41 (1993) 3445–3462
[4] Meyer J., A. Averbuch, J. Stromberg: Fast adaptive wavelet packet image compression. IEEE Trans. on Image Processing. (1998)
[5] Said A., W. Pearlman: A new fast and efficient image codec based on set partitioning in hierarchical trees. IEEE Trans. on Circuits and Systems for Video Tech., 6 (1996) 243–250
[6] Coifman R., M. Wickerhauser: Entropy-based algorithms for best basis selection. IEEE Trans. on Information Theory, 38(2) (1992) 713–718

[7] Han S., C. Lim: Embedded wavelet packet image coder using set partitioning. Proc. of IEEE TENCON' 97, Brisbane, Australia. (1997)

[8] Li J., C. Kuo: Embedded wavelet packet image coder with fast rate-distortion optimized decomposition. Proc. of SPIE's International Symposium on Visual Comm. and Image, San Jose, CA. (1997) 1077–1088

Generation and Use of Synthetic Training Data in Cursive Handwriting Recognition

Muriel Helmers and Horst Bunke*

Institut für Informatik und angewandte Mathematik
Universität Bern, Neubrückstr. 10, CH-3012 Bern, Switzerland
bunke@iam.unibe.ch*

Abstract. Three different methods for the synthetic generation of hand-written text are introduced. These methods are experimentally evaluated in the context of a cursive handwriting recognition task, using an HMM-based recognizer. In the experiments, the performance of a traditional recognizer, which is trained on data produced by human writers, is compared to a system that is trained on synthetic data only. Under the most elaborate synthetic handwriting generation model, a level of performance comparable to, or even slightly better than, the system trained on the writing of humans was observed.

Keywords: handwriting recognition, cursive handwriting, classifier training, synthetic training data, hidden Markov model (HMM)

1 Introduction

Automatic handwriting recognition has become a major area of research [1]. Significant progress has been achieved and first commercial systems entered the market [2, 3]. Nevertheless there is still ample room for improvement. A serious problem in handwriting recognition is the dependency of all available recognition methods on large amounts of training data. Virtually any method for handwritten character, word, or sentence recognition (e.g. neural network, statistical classifier, hidden Markov model, or support vector machine) needs to be trained. As a rule of thumb, the larger the training set is, the better will be recognition rate of the system. However, the collection of training data in handwriting recognition is a tedious and expensive process with clear limitations.

In the area of machine printed character recognition it was proposed to use synthetic data for training. A number of successful activities in this direction have been reported in the literature. Using a character degradation model, Baird successfully constructed a Tibetan OCR system using training data that was initialized with real images but augmented by synthetic variations [4]. Using the same degradation model, a full-ASCII, 100- typeface classifier was developed

---

* corresponding author

F.J. Perales et al. (Eds.): IbPRIA 2003, LNCS 2652, pp. 336-345, 2003.
© Springer-Verlag Berlin Heidelberg 2003

using exclusively synthetic training data [5]. A recent review of document image degradation models and their use in synthetic data generation for OCR can be found in [6]. A system for machine printed Arabic OCR that was trained on synthetic data only is described in [7].

In the present paper we discuss a number of methods to generate synthetic handwritten text that can be used to train handwriting recognition systems. The basic idea is to use image templates of single characters and n-tuples of characters, and concatenate them to generate synthetic handwritten text. All templates are produced by human writers. A similar approach was reported in [8]. However, the aim in [8] was not to generate synthetic data for a recognition system, but just to produce naturally looking handwritten notes from ASCII text, to be used for personal communication. The methods proposed in the present paper are experimentally evaluated in the context of an HMM based sentence recognizer that was developed earlier [9, 10]. Aim of the experiments is to measure the recognition rate of the recognizer using synthetic training data and compare it to the performance achieved with training data produced by human writers. Other work on the synthetic generation of handwriting has been reported in [11–13].

2   Generation of Synthetic Training Data

In this section, we introduce a number of methods, with increasing degree of complexity, to generate synthetic training data for handwriting recognition systems.

2.1   Synthetic handwriting based on individual characters extracted from a form

The method described in this sub-section is based on a software tool for the generation of handwritten notes from ASCII files [14]. Each writer who contributes to the training set fills in one specially designed form. This form is divided into boxes. There exists one box for each character from the underlying alphabet. The forms filled in by the individual writers are scanned and an image is extracted for each character. Then, given an ASCII text and the character images extracted from a form as described before, a handwritten version of the ASCII text is generated by simply concatenating the corresponding character images. An example of a page of text, synthetically generated with this method, is shown in Fig. 2. For the purpose of comparison, the same text written by the writer who filled in the underlying form is shown in Fig. 1. Obviously, this approach is extremely simple. Consequently, there are some shortcomings in the synthetic text images. First, there are no ligatures[1]. Secondly, all instances of the same character in a text are always identical. This clearly restricts the usefulness of

---

[1] A ligature is a stroke that connects two consecutive characters

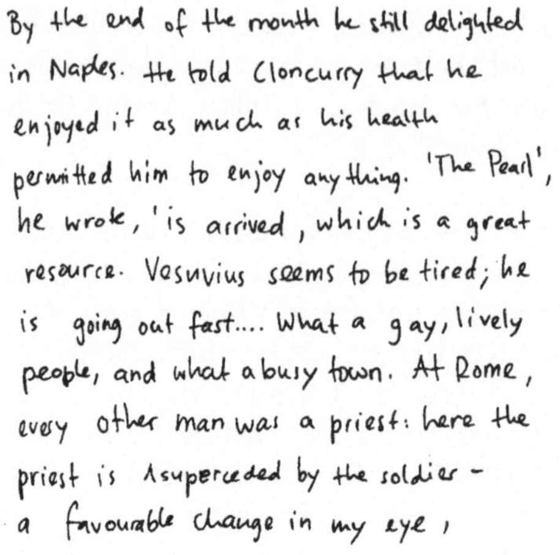

By the end of the month he still delighted
in Naples. He told Cloncurry that he
enjoyed it as much as his health
permitted him to enjoy anything. 'The Pearl',
he wrote, 'is arrived, which is a great
resource. Vesuvius seems to be tired; he
is going out fast.... What a gay, lively
people, and what a busy town. At Rome,
every other man was a priest: here the
priest is ʌsuperceded by the soldier –
a favourable change in my eye,

Fig. 1. Example of a text written by a human writer

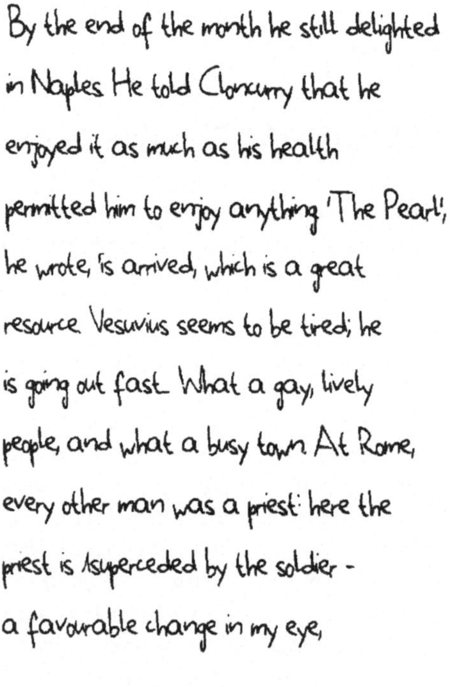

By the end of the month he still delighted
in Naples He told Cloncurry that he
enjoyed it as much as his health
permitted him to enjoy anything 'The Pearl',
he wrote, 'is arrived, which is a great
resource Vesuvius seems to be tired; he
is going out fast What a gay, lively
people, and what a busy town At Rome,
every other man was a priest: here the
priest is ʌsuperceded by the soldier –
a favourable change in my eye,

Fig. 2. Example of a synthetically generated text based on character templates produced by the same writer as in Fig. 1, using the method of Section 2.1

this method in the automatic generation of training data for handwriting recognition systems, as we shall se later in Section 3.

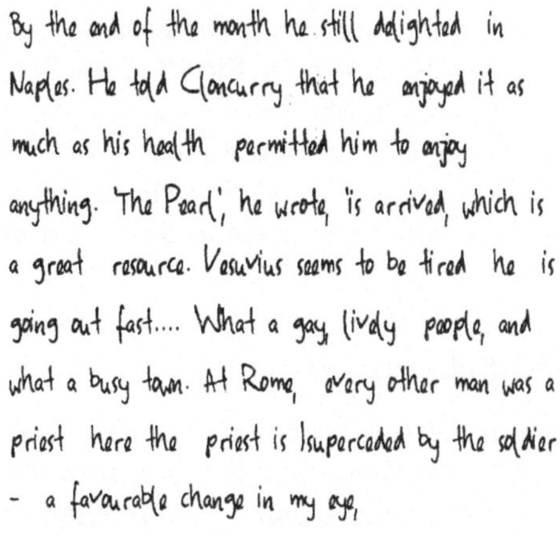

By the end of the month he still delighted in
Naples. He told Cloncurry that he enjoyed it as
much as his health permitted him to enjoy
anything. 'The Pearl', he wrote, 'is arrived, which is
a great resource. Vesuvius seems to be tired he is
going out fast.... What a gay lively people, and
what a busy town. At Rome, every other man was a
priest here the priest is superceded by the soldier
- a favourable change in my eye,

Fig. 3. Same example as in Fig. 2, but using the method of Section 2.2

2.2 Synthetic handwriting based on individual characters extracted from natural text

It is well known that the shape of a character depends on its context. From this point of view, the template images used in the method introduced in Section 2.1 are rather unnatural because all characters are written in isolation. Under the method described in this sub-section, each writer contributing to the training set not just fills isolated characters in the boxes on a form, but writes some given text, which typically consists of five to ten lines. The text to be written must be selected - or defined - in such a way that each character occurs at least once.

Once a writer has produced a text, it is scanned and preprocessed using the same procedures as described in [9]. That is, the skew of the page is detected and corrected, and the individual lines of text are extracted. Next, each text line is normalized. The normalization steps include slant correction, and normalizing the text line's width, height, and position with respect to the baseline.

After preprocessing, individual character subimages are extracted from a line of text. For this step, a semi-automatic procedure is applied. Under this procedure, the Hidden-Markov-Model (HMM) based recognizer described in [9, 10] is run on a line of text in the forced alignment mode. For more details on the forced alignment method for segmenting text lines into words and characters, the reader is referred to [15]. Finding the optimal alignment between the ground truth and the handwritten text line image is accomplished fully automatically. However, some misalignments are inevitable. To overcome these misalignments some manual correction is done in a postprocessing step.

Once an image template has been generated for each character of the underlying alphabet, synthetic handwritten text can be generated similarly to the method described in Section 2.1. That is, the handwritten version of a given

ASCII text is generated by concatenating the corresponding character images. An example of this method is shown in Fig. 3. Here the same ASCII text is used as in Fig. 2. Clearly, this method still has the shortcomings pointed out in Section 2.1, namely, lack of ligatures and identical prototype images for each character. Nevertheless, it may be argued that the shape of the individual characters is more natural than under the method described in 2.1.

2.3   Using n-tuples of characters

In [8] it was suggested to use n-tuples of characters as basic templates in order to generated naturally looking synthetic handwritten text. As a matter of fact, the two shortcomings pointed out before can be overcome if n-tuples of characters rather than individual characters are used as the elementary building blocks for the synthesized text. First, character n-tuples will normally include ligatures, and secondly, it is very likely that a character not only occurs in one, but in several n-tuples. Hence the synthetic handwritten text will usually include more than one instance per character. In the experiments described in Section 3, we used template images of 1-, 2-, and 3-tuples of characters. However, the method can be easily extended to tuples of higher order. In the following we describe the procedure greater detail.

First a dictionary of n-tuples is constructed. In [8] such a dictionary is compiled using the most frequent groups of letters appearing in the Brown corpus [16]. Here we adopted an alternative approach and extracted all 2- and 3- tuples of characters occurring in a subset of the texts that were used in the experiments. This set of 2- and 3-tuples was complemented by all 1-tuples, i.e. all individual characters of the alphabet. The total number of 2- and 3-tuples included in the dictionary is 712.

Given the dictionary of n-tuples, any text that is to be synthesized is subject to a parsing procedure that splits the text into a sequence of n-tuples from the dictionary. For this splitting process, a simple greedy parsing strategy is used [17].

Given an arbitrary ASCII text, its synthetic handwritten version is generated by first splitting it into a sequence of n-tuples from the dictionary using the greedy parsing strategy, and then concatenating the template images that correspond to the n-tuples. The template images of the n-tuples are extracted from handwritten text similarly to the forced alignment procedure described in Section 2.2. That is, the HMM forced alignment procedure yields the location of each character in the image of a line of text. From this information the n-tuples included in the dictionary can be extracted. As an example, the original text of Fig. 1, produced by the n-tuple method is shown in Fig. 4. Obviously, this version of the text looks more natural than its counterparts shown in Figs. 2 and 3

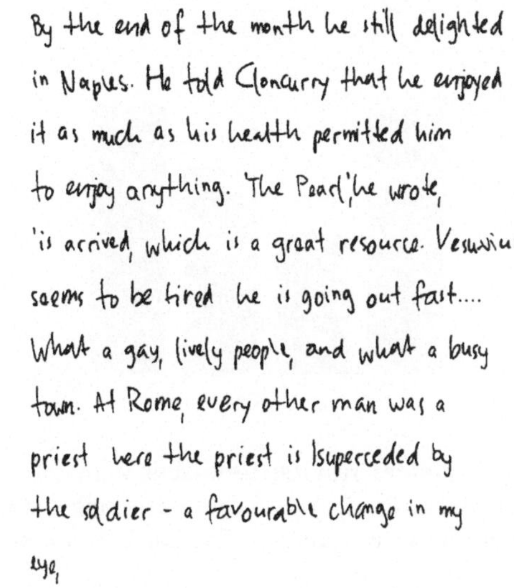

By the end of the month he still delighted
in Naples. He told Cloncurry that he enjoyed
it as much as his health permitted him
to enjoy anything. The Pearl,'he wrote,
'is arrived, which is a great resource. Vesuvius
seems to be tired he is going out fast....
What a gay, lively people, and what a busy
town. At Rome, every other man was a
priest here the priest is Isuperceded by
the soldier - a favourable change in my
eye,

Fig. 4. Same example as in Fig. 2, but using the method of Section 2.3

3   Experimental Results

The recognizer used in this work is the one described in [9, 10]. The main focus of the experiments described in this section is on the question how a recognizer, trained in the traditional way on data produced by human writers, will compare with one that is trained on synthetic data. For all experiments a subset of the IAM database was selected. A detailed description of this database can be found in [21].

For the experiments, nine different text fragments, each written on a separate sheet of paper by 16 different writers were selected. So the dataset selected for the experiments consists of a total of 144 text fragments. These text fragments include 1190 word instances over a vocabulary of 357 words. One of these text fragments is shown in Fig. 1.

The aim of the first experiment was to provide a figure of reference against which the various methods for synthetic training data generation could be measured. In this experiment the HMM classifier described in [9, 10] was trained and tested on natural, i.e. human produced, data exclusively. The 144 text fragments selected from the IAM database were split in a proportion of 80% − 20% into training and test set, respectively. All 16 writers were equally distributed over both the training and test set. A 5-fold cross-validation was conducted. In this experiment a recognition rate of 70.8% on the word level was measured. This experiment will be referred to as Experiment 1 in the following.

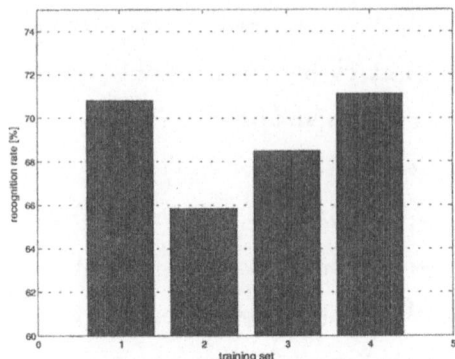

Fig. 5. Summary of experimental results; tests sets were all natural data; training sets varied: 1= natural training data; 2= synthetic training data according to Section 2.1; 3= synthetic training data according to Section 2.2; 4= synthetic training data according to Section 2.3

Next the performance of the classifier was measured using natural test data and training data synthetically generated by the method described in Section 2.1. In this experiment exactly the same protocol and the same dataset as in Experiment 1 were used. The only difference was in the training data. Here the same text fragments, but synthetically produced, using character templates from the writer who generated that natural training text fragment, replaced each natural handwritten text fragment. The test data in this experiment was the same as in Experiment 1, i.e. it was all natural. In this experiment, which will be referred to as Experiment 2 below, a recognition rate of 65.8% was measured. Thirdly, the synthetic handwriting method described in Section 2.2 was experimentally evaluated, using the same procedure as in Experiment 2 except for the different method to produce the synthetic training data. In this experiment, which will be referred to as Experiment 3 below, a recognition rate of 68.5% was achieved.

Finally the n-tuple method described in Section 2.3 was evaluated. The procedure was analogous to Experiments 2 and 3. This experiment will be referred to as Experiment 4 below. A recognition rate of 71.1% was measured.

A summary of all experimental results is shown in Fig. 5. Obviously, the recognition performance of the HMM classifier used in this work depends on the quality of the training data. First of all, we notice a clear performance drop if synthetic training data produced with the method described in Section 2.1 is used instead of natural handwriting. For synthetic training data, the increase from 65.8 to 68.5% indicates that single characters, written in isolation, are less suitable for the generation of useful training data than single characters extracted from whole words or sentences. Moreover, generating synthetic handwritten text with just one template per character class and without any ligatures (Experiments 2 and 3) seems not sufficient to achieve a level of performance similar to one obtained through the use of natural training data. However, under the more elaborate model presented in Section 2.3 the recognition performance of the system based on synthetic training data even slightly outperformed the system trained with natural data.

4   Summary and Conclusions

In this paper the generation of synthetic data for the development of handwriting recognition systems is proposed. The basic idea is to use templates of individual characters together with n-tuples of characters and concatenate them into words and sentences. All templates are extracted from handwriting probes of human writers. In a series of experiments it was shown that training a handwriting recognition system on synthetic data only can lead to a recognition performance as good, or even better, than that of a system trained in the traditional way using handwriting produced by humans.

The acquisition of training data in handwriting recognition is costly. This observation is confirmed by the fact that the repository of publicly available databases is quite limited. A potential danger of this limitation is the excessive use - and sometimes abuse - of these databases. Some of these databases are getting 'worn out'. The use of synthetic data in the development of handwriting recognition systems may be a promising way to overcome this dilemma. More-over, through synthetic generation almost unlimited amounts of training data can be generated. According to the results presented in [22–24], this may allow us to build recognizers with a very high recognition accuracy.

There are a number of issues to be potentially addressed in future research. First of all, the parameter space of the methods described in Section 2 hasn't been fully explored. For example, one could use n-tuples with n larger than 3, or an optimal parsing procedure when splitting a word into n-tuples. Secondly, one could provide not just a single template for each character and each n-tuple, but extract multiple templates and choose among them at random when pro-ducing some given text. In this way, more variation in the synthetic handwriting can be expected. Thirdly, it would be interesting to see how training on syn-thetic data compares with natural data in case of larger vocabularies, a larger number of writers, and for classifiers other than HMMs. Further issues to be addressed in future are the mixture of natural and synthetic training data, the use of synthetic data for testing, and the application of distortion models [4], [25].

References

1. Plamondon, R., Srihari, S.: On-line and off-line handwriting recognition: A com-prehensive survey, IEEE Trans. PAMI 22, 2000, 63 - 84

2. Kaltenmeier, A., Caesar, T., Gloger, J., Mandler, E.: Sophisticated topology of hidden Markov models for cursive script recognition, Proc. 2nd Int. Conf. on Document Analysis and Recognition, Vol. 2, 1997, 1097 - 1101

3. Impedovo,S., Wang, P., Bunke, H. (eds.): Automatic Bankcheck Processing, World Scientific, 1997

4. Baird, H.S.: Document image defect models, in Baird, H.S., Bunke, H., Yamamoto, K. (eds.): Structured Document Image Analysis, Springer, 1992, 546 - 556

5. Fossey, R., Baird, H.S.: A 100-Font Classifier, Proc. 1st Int. Conf. on Document Analysis and Recognition, 1991

6. Baird, H.S.: The state of the art of document image degradation modelling, Proc. 4th IAPR Int. Workshop on Document Image Analysis Systems, 2000, 1 - 13

7. Märgner, V., Pechwitz, M.: Synthetic data for Arabic OCR system development, Proc. 6th Int. Conf. on Document Analysis and Recognition, 2001

8. Guyon, I.: Handwriting synthesis from handwritten glyphs, Proc. of the 5th Int. Workshop Frontiers in Handwriting Recognition, 1996, 309 - 312

9. Marti, U.-V., Bunke, H.: Using a statistical language model to improve the performance of an HMM-based cursive handwriting recognition system, Int. Journal of Pattern Recognition and Art. Intelligence 15, 2001, 65 - 90

10. Marti, U.-V., Bunke, H.: Text line segmentation and word recognition in a system for general writer independent handwriting recognition, Proc. 6th Int. Conference on Document Analysis and Recognition, 2001, 159 - 163

11. Wang, J., Wu, C., Xu, Y.-Q., Shum, H.-Y., Ji, L.: Learning-based cursive handwriting synthesis, Proc. 8th Int. Workshop on Frontiers in Handwriting Recognition, 2002, 157 - 162

12. Setlur, S., Govindaraju, V.: Generating manifold samples from a handwritten word, Pattern Recognition Letters 15, 1994, 901 - 905

13. Plamondon, R., Guerfali, W.: The generation of handwriting with delta-lognormal synergies, Biological Cybernetics 78, 1998, 119 - 132

14. Frantzen B., Fürhauser W.: DATA BECKERs Goldene Serie: Meine Handschrift, DATA BECKER GmbH, 1999

15. Zimmermann, M., Bunke, H.: Automatic segmentation of the IAM off-line database for handwritten English text, Proc. 16th Int. Conference on Pattern Recognition, 2002, Vol IV, 35 - 39

16. Francis, W.N., Kucera, H.: Brown Corpus of Standard American English, Brown University, Providence, RI, 1961

17. Helmers, M.: Verwendung von künstlich erzeugten Texten in der Handschrifterkennung, diploma thesis, university of Bern, Switzerland, 2002

18. Johansson, S., Leech, G.N., Goodluck, H.: Manual of Information to accompany the Lancaster-Oslo/Bergen Corpus of British English, for use with digital Computers, Department of English, University of Oslo, Oslo, 1978

19. Young, S., Jansen, J., Odell, J., Ollason, D., Woodland, P.: The HTK Book, Entropic, 1999

20. Rabiner, L.R.: A tutorial on hidden Markov models and selected applications in speech recognition, Proceedings of the IEEE, 1989, 257 - 285

21. Bunke, H., Marti, U.-V.: The IAM-database: An English sentence database for off-line handwriting recognition, Int. Journal of Document Analysis and Recognition, 2002, 5:39-46

22. Rowley, H.A., Goyal, M., Bennett, J.: The effect of large training set sizes on online Japanese Kanji and English cursive recognizers, Proc. 8th Int. Workshop on Frontiers in Handwriting Recognition, 2002, 36 - 40

23. Smith, S.J.: Handwritten character classification using nearest neighbour in large databases, IEEE Trans. PAMI 16, 1994, 915 - 919
24. Cano, J., Perez-Cortes, J-C., Arlandis, J., Llobet, R.: Training set expansion in handwritten character recognition, in T. Caelli, A. Amin, R. Duin, M. Kamel, D. de Ridder (eds.): Structural, Syntactic, and Statistical Pattern Recognition, Springer, LNCS 2396, 2002, 548 - 556
25. Ha, T., Bunke H.: Off-line handwritten numeral recognition by perturbation method, IEEE Trans. PAMI 19, 1997, 535 - 539

Video-Sensor for Detection and Tracking of Moving Objects*

Elias Herrero[1], C. Orrite[1], A. Alcolea[1], A. Roy[1],
José J. Guerrero[2], and Carlos Sagüés[2]

[1] Aragon Institute of Engineering Research
jelias@posta.unizar.es
[2] Department of Computer Science and Systems Engineering
University of Zaragoza
María de Luna, 1, 50018, Zaragoza, Spain

Abstract. In this paper we present a complete chain of algorithms for detection and tracking of moving objects using a static camera. The system is based on robust difference of images for motion detection. However, the difference of images does not take place directly over the image frames, but over two robust frames which are continuously constructed by temporal median filtering on a set of last grabbed images, which allows working with slow illumination changes. The system also includes a Kalman filter for tracking objects, which is also employed in two ways: assisting to the process of object detection and providing the object state that models its behaviour. These algorithms have given us a more robust method of detection, making possible the handling of occlusions as can be seen in the experimentation made with outdoor traffic scenes.

1 Introduction

Detection of moving objects is an important problem in applications such as surveillance [1], object tracking [2], and video compression [3]. There exist a lot of related approaches. So, Haar-wavelet transform is used to describe an object class in terms of a dictionary of local, oriented and multi-scale intensity differences between adjacent regions [4] and it is applied to detect pedestrians in driver assistance systems. The AMOS method [3] is an active system that uses low-level segmentation and a high-level object tracking, although it needs an initial segmentation made manually by the user.

Nevertheless when detecting moving objects, methods based on difference are more often used, although they have also some drawbacks. Thus, the difference map is usually binarized by thresholding at some predefined value but, as known, that threshold is critical, since a too low threshold will swap the difference map with spurious changes, while a too high threshold will suppress significant changes. There are several thresholding techniques specifically designed to be effective in these cases [5], but they do not take into account the

---

* This work has been supported by the CICYT project COO1999AX014

F.J. Perales et al. (Eds.): IbPRIA 2003, LNCS 2652, pp. 346–353, 2003.

relation between frames in order to eliminate noise and they are, in general, computationally expensive. Additionally these approaches have some difficulties with small or slow-moving objects. In this sense, to make more robust the detection of changes, intensity characteristics of groups of pixels at the same location may be compared using an statistical approach [6].

All these works give good results, however in cases of occlusions or cluttered images their performance get worse. To solve this problem, some approaches employ techniques based on estimation or optical flow. In this context, some authors use a Kalman filter with snakes in order to track non-rigid objects [7]. In this case, the system detects and rejects spurious measurements, which are not consistent with previous estimations of motion. A Kalman filter and a neural system is used to avoid the gross errors in motion trajectories [8]. In other case, Kalman filter along with XT-slices (spatial-temporal) are used to analyze the human motion [9]. Sometimes the filter is used to recover lost regions when tracking vehicles in a road [2], or even, groups of filters each one specialized in a motion model are proposed in [10].

Our video-sensor is based on difference of images including long time information robustly filtered by the median of a set of images. This makes the method less sensible to the threshold, and changes of illumination have less influence. The pure segmentation algorithms work well in a few applications, but they fail in many cases. As commented, to solve these fails, researchers have used these algorithms together with estimation tools. In our video sensor we complement the idea of robust difference with a Kalman filter as an assistant to improve the system performance. Thus, the prediction provided by the Kalman filter is used to search on the difference map when the segmentation has failed. Besides that, the Kalman filter provides state information to control the object behaviour, avoiding problems when occlusions or slow moving objects are present.

The paper is organized in four sections. In the first one, we explain the detection of moving objects based on the robust difference of images. Secondly, we present the tracking algorithm working in two ways: assisting to detection, and providing object state. In the third section, we show the different experiments carried out and the obtained results. Finally, the conclusions are exposed in fourth section.

2   Detection and Segmentation Task

To search the object of interest, the proposed method analyzes changes over a sequence of images, instead of just between two images. This is carried out using the difference between a reference frame and current frame. The reference frame is obtained from a set of previous images in the sequence. The new frame is obtained from current frame and a shorter subset of neighbor images.

To obtain a noise-free reference frame we should use some smoothing. Linear filters suppress Gaussian noise but perform very poorly in case of noise patterns consisting of strong and spike-like components. This is the usual situation in a sequence of images where gray level of background pixels stays approximately constant except in a few, corrupted by noise. In these cases, the noise can be effectively rejected using a rank value filter. In particular, the median filter has become very useful in robust estimation in presence of outliers, in relation to other traditional methods like root mean square.

The reference frame M_k is obtained by a temporal median filter of an input sequence of n images [11], where every frame has $m \times p$ pixels. This noise-free reference frame, is given by:

$$M_k = \begin{bmatrix} median(1,1,k) & \cdots & median(1,p,k) \\ \cdots & \cdots & \cdots \\ median(m,1,k) & \cdots & median(m,p,k) \end{bmatrix} \tag{1}$$

Being $median(i,j,k) = median\{F(i,j,k-n-l+1), \ldots, F(i,j,k-l)\}$ the median of gray level (F) in the image, where $i = 1, \ldots, m$ and $j = 1, \ldots, p$. Besides, k denotes the current time, n is the number of images used to obtain the reference frame and it represents the horizon of background filtering, and l is the number of images used to obtain the current frame.

The parameter n should be properly selected to eliminate the noise. Thus, if n is high enough, we will obtain a reference frame even if there are moving objects in the initial images. This reference frame is updated with every new image and it takes into account the illumination changes in such a way that the object motion detection is not disturbed.

Similarly the current frame (N_k) is computed from a set of (l) previous images. This set represents the horizon of motion filtering, which is related with the minimum velocity to be detected. The "l" parameter should also be properly selected: high enough to eliminate noise, but not too high because fast small objects could be lost. Finally, the detection of the moving blobs is made by the definition of a $MOVIL_k$ frame, which is obtained from the thresholding difference between the current and the reference frames as:

$$MOVIL_k(i,j) = \begin{cases} 1 \text{ if } |M_k(i,j) - N_k(i,j)| > \sigma \\ 0 \text{ otherwise} \end{cases}, \sigma \text{ is the threshold.} \tag{2}$$

3   The Tracking Task

With the robust method exposed above, we have the moving blobs which correspond to the objects of interest. Sometimes, this method can fail because of illumination problems, poor contrast, etc, and certain *assistance* is required to reduce the effect of these problems.

We have been working with the problem of tracking to match lines in a navigation system [12], using the Kalman filter. As known, this filter is a mathematic equations set, which provides a very efficient least squares solution using a dynamic model. It results very powerful in several aspects. For example, it gives future estimate from past information, it can be used with maneuvering targets and it can manage different dynamic models in according to object behaviour [10]. Although in these works linear models are used, some authors work

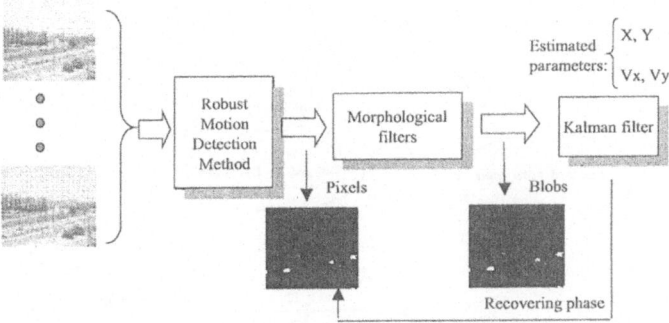

Fig. 1. Block diagram of the detection of moving objects

with a non-linear motion model to segment lines using the Extended Kalman filter [13] but our video-sensor proposes a tracking of objects based on standard Kalman filter.

To track moving objects we have chosen a state vector ($\mathbf{x}$) which is composed by four parameters: x and y positions and v_x and v_y velocities, which define the state of our objects. A constant velocity model with zero-mean random acceleration has been considered.

3.1   Kalman Filter: Working as Segmentation Assistant

The main mission of the filter is to track objects that have been detected by the previous task in order to avoid their loss. The threshold used in the process of image difference (Equation 2) may cause the loss of pixels of low contrast corresponding to moving objects. Besides, as commented in section 2 a morphological filtering has been used, which may eliminate some blob corresponding to "good" but small, far away placed or partially occluded moving objects.

The Kalman filter gives a predicted position and its covariance, in such a way that the full system (in the *Recovering phase*) may look for corresponding pixels in the difference image (Fig. 1). If these pixels are found, then their centroid is used as measurement of Kalman filter.

3.2   Kalman Filter: Controlling the State of the Object

The second novel use of the Kalman filter is the control and assessment of the state of the object (s_i). To model the behavior of the moving objects, six states and seven transitions have been defined (Fig. 2). The states are **Init, Localized_with_blob, Localized_without_blob, Stopped_&_localized, Lost**, and **Overlapped**. Five transitions are related to the evolution of moving objects and two are related to time conditions.

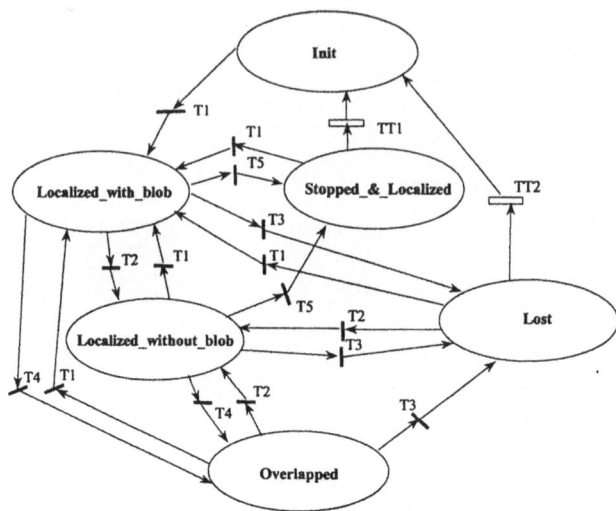

Fig. 2. Block diagram of states of the moving objects. The ellipses indicate the states and the transitions indicate the conditions to jump between states

Transitions The transitions related with the evolution of the moving object are:

- T1: This transition is fired when the blob associated to a moving object is detected after the morphological filter.
- T2: This transition is fired when the blob is not detected but the corresponding pixels are detected at the difference image (*Recovering phase*).
- T3: This transition is fired when the Kalman filter estimates the position of the moving object, but neither its blob can be detected after the morphological filter nor corresponding pixels can be found at the difference image.
- T4: This transition is fired when a moving object overlaps with other moving object. So, only one blob is detected after the morphological filter which is associated with the closest object.
- T5: This transition is fired when the object velocity supplied by Kalman filter gets down a certain value.

The transitions related to time conditions are

- TT1: Time transition from **Stopped_&_localized** state when the time at that state is higher than t_{Stop} time.
- TT2: Time transition from the **Lost** state when the time at that state is higher than t_{Lost}.

States An explanation for the different states follows:

– **Init.** This is the initial state, where the system looks for a new moving object. From this state there is just one output transition to **Localized_with_blob** state (T1). This happens when a new large enough blob is detected, being not close to the influence zone of an overlapping. Likewise, there are two input transitions from **Stopped_&_localized** (TT1) and **Lost** (TT2) states. When some of them is fired the component corresponding to the object is deleted.

– **Localized_with_blob.** In this state, the robust method is able to detect the blob because the blob is large enough. The centroide of this blob is used as measurement for the Kalman filter. When an object comes to this state from **Init**, a new component is created.

– **Localized_without_blob.** In this case, the detected blob after the morphological filtering is very small and it is eliminated. However some corresponding pixels are found at difference image around the position estimated by Kalman filter. So, the centroid of these pixels will be used as measurement for the Kalman filter (*Recovering phase*, Fig. 1).

– **Lost.** This is the state of the object whose blob has not been detected neither after the morphological filter nor in the *Recovering phase*. This normally happens when the moving object is occluded by a static object. In this state, Kalman filter continue estimating for t_{Lost} time without measurement.

– **Stopped_&_localized.** As told, the velocity of the object is given by the Kalman filter. According to this value, it is possible to deduce when the object is stopped. If the object remains in **Stopped_&_localized** state during a time $t > t_{Stop}$, it will be deleted and will evolve to **Init** state.

– **Overlapped.** This is the case in which a moving object is occluded by other moving object, and therefore both objects will evolve to this state. While this happens both objects will have the same measure due to the fact that only one blob is detected.

4 Experiments and Discussion

Due to the limited extension of this paper we present some images showing the algorithm working in different situations. In this sense, four example sequences are depicted in Fig. 3. Comments about this figure are included in the legend.

In these images, bounding boxes on the object of the image indicate that the corresponding blob has been detected. Likewise, the size of crosses is proportional to the estimation covariance, in such a way that we may have little cross when corresponding pixels are detected and a large cross when they have not been detected. In the last case, there is no measurement for the Kalman filter.

5 Conclusions

In this paper we have presented a complete chain of algorithms to detect and track moving objects using a static camera. The proposed system performs ro-

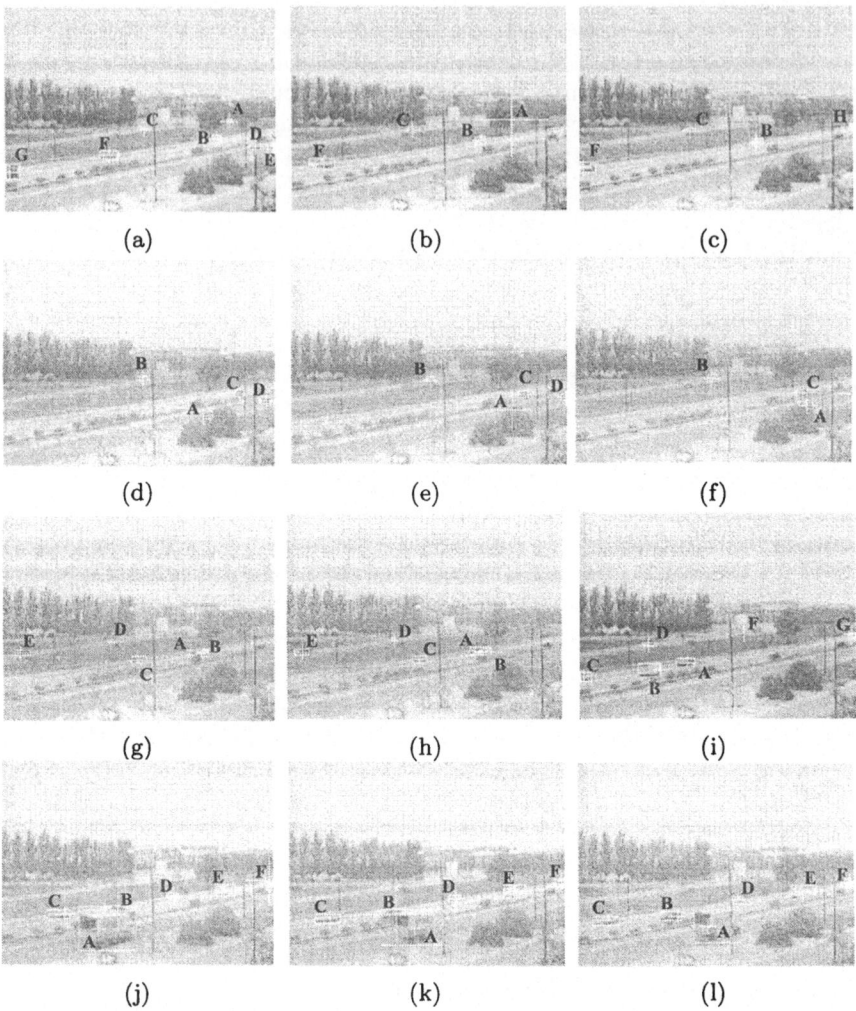

Fig. 3. **EXP.1** (a) The "A" object is in the **Localized_with_blob** state; (b) it evolves by the T3 transition to the **Lost** state; (c) finally, it evolves by TT2 to **Init** state. **EXP.2** (d) The "A" object is in the **Localized_with_blob** state; (e) it evolves by the T3 transition to the **Lost** state; (f) finally, it evolves by T1 to **Localized_with_blob** state. **EXP.3** (g) The "A" and "B" objects are both in the **Localized_with_blob** state; (h) both objects evolve by the T4 transition to the **Overlapped** state; (i) finally, the "A" object evolves by the T1 transition to the **Localized_with_blob** state, and the "B" object evolves by TT2 to the **Init** state. **EXP.4** (j) The "A" and "B" objects are both in the **Localized_with_blob** state; (k) the "A" object evolves by the T4 transition to the **Overlapped** state, while the "B" object evolves to the **Lost** state; (l) finally both objects evolve by the T1 transition to the **Localized_with_blob** state

bust motion detection and object tracking even with illumination changes, using no special hardware requirements. The motion algorithm is based on image difference between two median filtered frames. In contrast to other methods of difference, which need to take a background free of other moving objects, the smoothing of reference and current frames allows to detect moving objects even though there are moving objects at the initial background. The detection and segmentation algorithms are complemented with a Kalman filter to track and match different moving objects along the sequence. The Kalman filter is also used in two ways: Assisting to the motion detection, and providing information to model the behaviour of the objects. This results in a much better method of detection which also makes possible the handling of occlusions.

References

[1] P. Remagnino, T. Tan, and K. Baker, "Multi-agent visual surveillance of dynamic scenes," *Image and Vision Computing*, no. 6, pp. 529–532, 1998.

[2] J. Badenas, J. M. Sanchiz, and F. Pla, "Motion-based segmentation and region tracking in image sequences," *Pattern Recognition*, no. 34, pp. 16–18, 2001.

[3] D. Zhong and S. Chang, "Amos: An active system for mpeg-4 video object segmentation," *Int. Conference on Image Procesing*, pp. 647–651, 1998.

[4] C. Papageorgiou and T. Poggio, "A trainable system for object detection," *International Journal of Computer Vision*, vol. 38, no. 1, pp. 15–33, 2000.

[5] P. Rosin, "Thresholding for change detection," *Sixth International Conference on Computer Vision, Bombay, India*, pp. 274–279, January 1998.

[6] A. Jain, R. Duin, and J. Mao, "Statistical pattern recognition: A review," *IEEE Trans. on Pattern Analysis and Machine Intelligence*, vol. 22, pp. 4–37, January 2000.

[7] N. Peterfreund, "Robust tracking of position and velocity with kalman snakes," *IEEE Trans. on Pattern Analysis and Machine Intelligence*, vol. 21, pp. 564–569, June 1999.

[8] R. Mecke and B. Michaelis, "A robust method for motion estimation in image sequences," *AMDO 2000, Palma de Mallorca, SPAIN*, pp. 108–119, 2000.

[9] Y. Ricquebourg and P. Bouthemy, "Real-time tracking of moving persons by exploiting spatio-temporal image slices," *IEEE Trans. on Pattern Analysis and Machine Intelligence*, vol. 22, pp. 797–808, August 2000.

[10] P. Tissainayagam and D. Suter, "Visual tracking with automatic motion model switching," *Pattern Recognition*, vol. 34, pp. 641–660, 2001.

[11] C. Orrite, J. E. Herrero, and A. Alcolea, "Fast robust motion detection by temporal median filtering," *Proc. of the IX Spanish Symposium on Pattern Recognition and Image Analysis, Castellón , SPAIN*, May 2001.

[12] J. Guerrero and C. Sagues, "Tracking features with camera maneuvering for vision-based navigation," *Journal of Robotic Systems*, vol. 15, no. 4, pp. 191–206, 1998.

[13] G. Foresti, "A line segment based approach for 3d motion estimation and tracking of multiple objects," *Int. Journal of Pattern Recognition and Artificial Intelligence*, vol. 12, no. 6, pp. 881–900, 1998.

Estimation of Anti-bacterial Culture Activity from Digital Images

José Jasnau Caeiro[1,2] and Armando Ventura[2]

[1] INESC-ID, SIPS
Apartado 13069, 1000-029 LISBOA, Portugal
[2] Instituto Politécnico de Beja, ESTIG
P-7800-050 Beja, Portugal
j.caeiro@ieee.org, ajventura@netvisao.pt

Abstract. The purpose of this paper is to describe a method developed for estimation of the diameter of circular disks resulting from anti-bacterial cultures, immersed in a bacterial gel, using digital images of the growth recipients (Petri dishes). This methodology uses a chain of several image processing algorithms that are applied to the Petri dishes images until a set of diameter estimates are produced.

The experimental protocol is presented and the results are analyzed in terms of the best non-linear filtering method as a function of the diameter error estimate at the output of the system.

1 Introduction

One way of determining the effect of anti-bacterial cultures is to introduce them in fixed amounts in a bacteria culture and to observe, after pre-determined time intervals, how many bacteria have been killed. Since the area where bacteria are killed is approximately defined by a circular disk, the effect of the anti-bacterial culture may be determined by estimating the diameter of the disks. For each anti-bacterial culture a large set of samples must be created experimentally. The slow and error-prone human procedure for determination of the diameters of the disks can be replaced by procedures based on digital processing of the images bacteria cultures. Two basic approaches can be followed: region or contour based. It is fairly common the choice of area determination procedures using thresholded images but they suffer the problems resulting from imprecise border determination. Edge detection methods usually determine more accurately the position of the object borders.

Simple disk diameter estimation procedures are reliable enough to solve the problem, as is shown in this paper, although more complex methodologies could eventually increase the precision of the measurements. These methodologies include optimal fitting or voting/clustering approaches. The first group of methods are based on the optimization of an objective function. The second group of methods are more robust against outliers.

Using non-linear pre-filtering some improvement can be obtained in the precision of the measurements since the image properties that somehow lead to outliers are reduced (non-Gaussian type noise) by some of these filters.

F.J. Perales et al. (Eds.): IbPRIA 2003, LNCS 2652, pp. 354–359, 2003.
© Springer-Verlag Berlin Heidelberg 2003

Although the determination of anti-bacterial disk diameter estimation is an useful application of image processing techniques no mention of such a procedure in the available scientific literature, as far as we know.

This paper is organized as follows. In Section 2 we proceed to the input data characterization, presenting the origin of the images and shortly describing some of their properties. Section 3 the disk diameter estimation methodology is discussed and the constituting algorithms are reviewed. The input and output of each element of the system is elucidated. Section 4 is devoted to the presentation of the experimental protocol and the analysis of the experimental data. The paper ends with Section 5 where some general conclusions are taken from this work and some future research directions are pointed out.

2   Image Characterization

The diameter estimation system uses as input data digital images from bacteria cultures grown in standard 100mm Petri dishes. Several types of bacteria and anti-bacterial cultures form the set of images. Images present changes according to several factors: type of cultures; background illumination; room temperature; culture development time, etc.. To illustrate the type of data input to the system a sample of images is presented in Figure 1. These images were acquired with 768×576 spatial pixel resolution and a 8-bit gray-level intensity resolution. The image represented in Figure 2 shows several common properties of the set of images to be processed. The bacteria culture, (the image background represented as region R_1 in Figure 2), is formed by a mix of random processes. Bacteria colonies have a tendency to aggregate thus creating whiter parts. Anti-bacterial regions, R_2, share the same property. The histogram of the image represented on Figure 2 shows the presence of some noise due to the random growth of bacteria and the killing of the bacteria. The small black circular disk is where the anti-bacterial solution is introduced. A part of the agar is removed and replaced by this solution. The area where bacteria are killed is dark gray and of a circular shape. The more active the anti-bacterial solution is the bigger the diameter of this disk becomes. Usually these diameters are measured by humans using mechanical devices. It is slower and more error-prone than an image processing based method.

3   Diameter Estimation Methodology

The disk diameter estimation system is presented in Figure 3. The original image I is initially pre-processed by the non-linear filter system. It can be visually seen that the background region, R_b, due to the existence of different types of bacteria cultures presents different formation patterns. Streaks of small dark areas are mingled with a clearer background.

The first step in the procedure is the application of a non-linear filter to the input image I in order to smooth out the irregularities that arise in the images due to the growth of colonies of bacteria and the death of bacteria in these

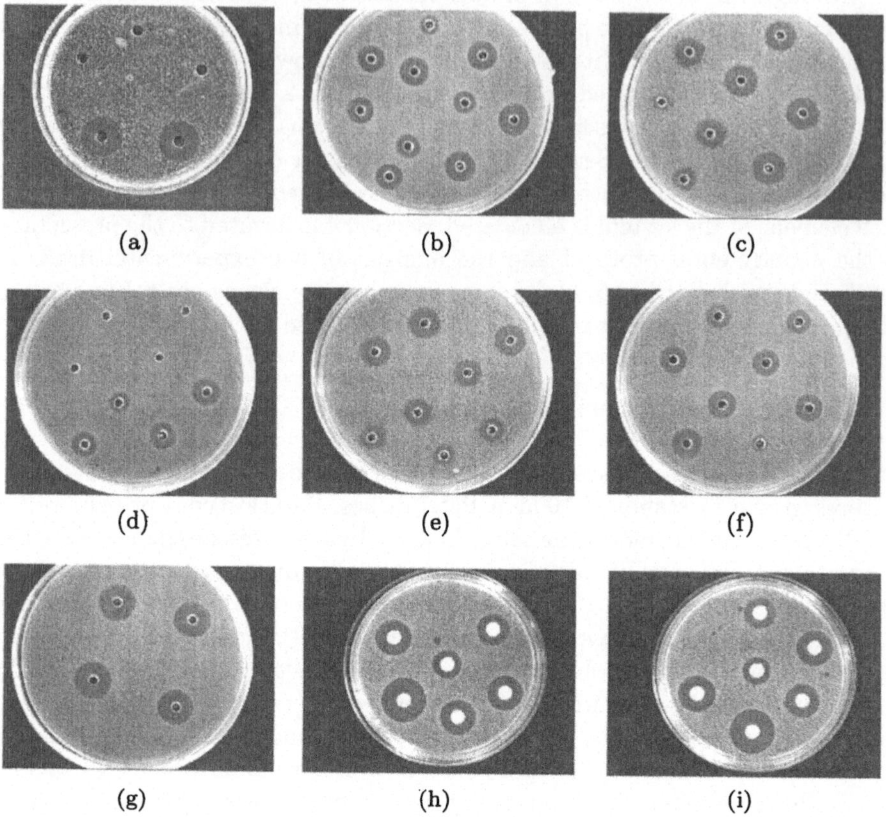

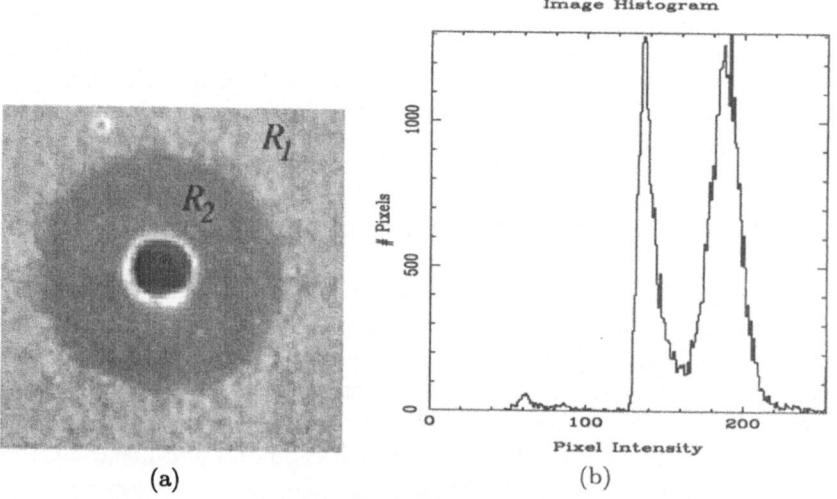

Fig. 1. Set of images from the anti-bacterial cultures grown in Petri dishes. All images were captured in a 768×576 image format

Fig. 2. Close-up of anti-bacterial culture growth area

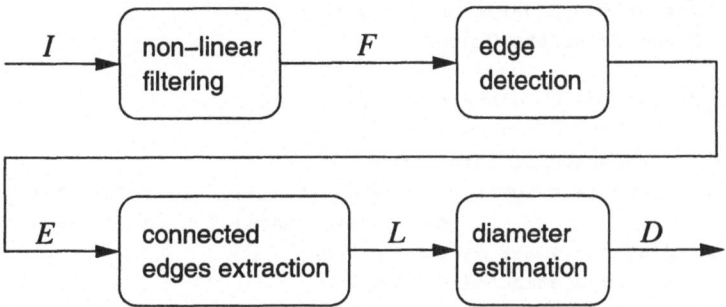

Fig. 3. Block diagram of the disk diameter estimation system using as data the digital images of anti-bacterial cultures

clusters. A set of non-linear filters was chosen from (Dougherty and Astola) [3], (Kuosmanen and Astola) [2] to be experimentally tested and includes: *modified nearest neighbor*; *Hodges-Lehman*; *comparison and selection*; *selective average*; *modified trimmed mean*; *C-filter*; *ranked-order* and *weighed order statistic*. The next step is the application of the widely used Canny edge detection method (Canny) [1] to the pre-processed image F. It consists in the application of a gradient amplitude estimation filter followed by non-maxima suppression and hysteresis thresholding. The derivative of Gaussian approximation was used for the gradient estimation filter since it is very widely used. After the edge detection procedure an edge map E is formed. This edge map is a binary image with values belonging to the set $V = \{Edge, NonEdge\}$. The input images allow relatively large values of the scale factor, σ, to be chosen since the disk circles are relatively far away from each other.

A connected components algorithm is then used to determine the objects present in the edge map (Haralick) [4]. The diameter and diameter variance are estimated for each connected object. Several methods were tested and the one which consistently presented the lowest diameter estimation variance across the range of images and non-linear filters was chosen.

Perimeter measurement and maximal and minimal diameter in OX and OY are simple methods of determining the diameter. Instead we chose the diameter estimation procedure represented by the pseudo-code in Figure 4. The diameter is estimated by searching, for each element (x_i, y_i) of the object S, the maximum distance max_{ik} to another element (x_k, y_k) of the same object S. All these individual maximum distances are added to the variable *distance*:

$$distance = \sum_i max_{ik},$$

and the diameter is estimated as $d = distance/N$, where N is the number of points constituting the object S. A simple procedure was setup to distinguish between objects that are circle shaped and non-circle shaped. All the objects for which the ratio of the highest maximum individual distance to diameter

```
Input: List of Coordinates of the object(X,Y)
Output: Diameter of the Object

let max_distance=0.0, distance=0.0, sum=0.0
for i=1 to NumberOfCoordinates
    for j=1 to NumberOfCoordinates
        let distance = sqrt( pow(coordinates[i].X - coordinates[j].X,2) +
                             pow(coordinates[i].Y - coordinates[j].Y,2) )
        if (distance > max_distance) then
            let max_distance=distance
    end
  let sum=sum+max_distance
  let max_distance=0.0, distance=0.0
end
let output=sum/NumberOfCoordinates
```

Fig. 4. Pseudo-code representing the diameter estimation procedure

estimate is found to be greater than 1.5, are considered to be non-circle shaped. More complex shape descriptors could be considered instead of this ratio but since the majority of objects in the images are fundamentally circles we chose not to.

4   Experimental Results

We determined the *selective average filter* to be the one that performed best in the diameter estimation procedure we propose. The experiment which lead to this conclusion was setup under the assumption that the estimate which consistently returned the lowest diameter estimate variance would be the best. We therefore chose the error at the output of the system for the performance evaluation. We used the same image for all the experiments and chose several scale factors, σ for the Canny edge detector. As for the *hysteresis thresholding* part of the Canny method the high threshold value was chosen to be $t_H = 90\%$ and the low threshold value $t_L = 10\%$.

We present in Table 1 a sample of the results of the application of some non-linear filters to the disk originated by the anti-bacterial culture on top of the image represented in Figure 1(e). Using a scale factor $\sigma = 3.5$ we get diameter estimates within the interval $[90.24, 93.63]$ (all diameters were measured in pixel units). The range of diameter variances is the interval $[1.88, 11.89]$. Other filters that performed well are the *weighed order statistic filter* and the *C-filter*. We should note that a 1.5 percent relative error is achieved with the best filter for the results presented in Table 1. The *selective average filter* is presented in the literature as a non-linear filter that may enhance the edge contrast properties. Many of the non-linear filters do not blur the edges.

Table 1. Estimated error in the determination of the diameter for the different non-linear filters for a scale factor for the Canny edge detection method $\sigma = 3.5$

non-linear filter	diameter	variance
selective average filter	91.94	1.88
weighed order statistic filter	93.63	2.06
C-filter	91.80	2.47
modified nearest neighbor filter	91.72	3.17
comparison and selection filter	92.06	3.60
ranked-order filter	91.62	11.50
Hodges-Lehman filter	90.24	11.75
modified trimmed mean filter	90.69	11.89

5   Conclusions

An application of image processing techniques was developed for the estimation of diameters of anti-bacterial cultures grown in Petri dishes. The method returns consistent values with low error on the output. The selective average filter was experimentally determined to be the best performing for this type of images.

Further work should include a better characterization of the stochastic processes originating the image regions (bacteria and anti-bacteria regions) thus allowing a more solid choice of pre-filtering methods. More robust methods for circle diameter estimation should also be studied, namely those based on the circle based Hough transform. Another research possibility is the application of circle fitting procedures using optimal approaches.

We wish to thank the following students of the Instituto Politécnico de Beja that implemented several of the algorithms used in this paper: Cristina Colaço, Helena Bentes, Eduardo Barbosa, Ricardo Sousa, Francisco Azedo, Paula Lampreia, Sidónio Cordeiro and Maria Vilhena.

This work was funded by the Fundação para a Ciência e Tecnologia of Portugal.

We wish also to remember the leading researcher of this team, Margarida Machado, of INETI (Instituto Nacional de Engenharia e Tecnologia Insdutrial) who has unfortunately died before the end of this work.

References

[1] Canny, John F.: A computational approach to edge detection. IEEE Trans. on Pattern Analysis and Machine Intelligence **8** (1986) 679–698
[2] Kuosmanen, Pauli, Astola, Jaako T.: Fundamentals of Nonlinear Digital Filtering. CRC Press (1997)
[3] Dougherty, Edward R., Astola, Jaako.: Nonlinear Filters for Image Processing. SPIE Press and IEEE Press (1999)
[4] Haralick, Robert, Shapiro, Linda.: Computer and Robot Vision, Addison-Wesley Publishing Company, Inc. (1992)

Robust Extraction of Vertices in Range Images by Constraining the Hough Transform

Dimitrios Katsoulas

Institute for Pattern Recognition and Image Processing, University of Freiburg
Georges-Koehler-Allee 52, D-79110 Freiburg, Germany
dkats@informatik.uni-freiburg.de

Abstract. We describe a technique for extracting vertices from range images of cluttered box-like objects. Edge detection is performed and an edge map is acquired. Extraction of vertices is carried out using the edge map and comprises two steps: Linear boundary detection in $3D$ and boundary grouping. In order to recover the four parameters of a $3D$ linear segment, we decompose the problem in two $2D$ subproblems, each recovering two line parameters. These subproblems are solved by means of the Hough Transform, constrained in this way so that accurate and efficient propagation of the edge points localization error is achieved. Pairs of orthogonal boundaries are grouped to form a vertex. The orthogonality of a boundary pair is determined by a simple statistical test. Our strategy comprises many advantages, the most important of which robustness, computational efficiency and accuracy, the combination of which is not to be found in existing approaches.

1 Introduction

Automatic unloading and sorting of piled objects is of great importance to the industry, because it undertakes a task that is very monotonous, strenuous and sometimes quite dangerous for humans. Objects which are often encountered in industrial sites and distribution centers are mainly rigid boxes as in Fig. 4 (a) or deformable box-like objects (sacks) full of material as in Fig. 5 (a). It is advantageous to employ range imagery for dealing with the problem mainly due to relative insensitivity on lighting conditions and object texture. It is since years known in the computer community that a three-dimensional visible vertex provides the strongest constraints for accurately determining the position of convex, three-dimensional objects and thus are very good approximations of the location of the objects in space. Since the objects we are dealing with are either boxes or box-like objects, their vertices can still be used for generating accurate object location hypotheses. For this reason the robust and accurate detection of object vertices in range images is of extreme importance to this application.

Although a variety of methods for detecting corners in intensity images have been reported, this is not the case for range images. The majority of the existing approaches (like [3],[1] and others) use region information to extract vertices. The disadvantage is that the objects need to expose more than one surfaces to

F.J. Perales et al. (Eds.): IbPRIA 2003, LNCS 2652, pp. 360–369, 2003.
© Springer-Verlag Berlin Heidelberg 2003

the sensor for accurate estimation of the vertex position. In [7], edge detection was performed on the input range image, object boundaries were detected using the Dynamic Generalized Hough Transform [8] and vertices were extracted by grouping orthogonal object boundaries. This allows for accurate vertex detection even if the objects expose only one surface. However the error in the localization of the edge points was not taken into consideration, which made the approach not as robust as desired.

The technique discussed in this paper comprises the same two parts, as was the case in [7]: Linear boundary detection and boundary grouping. However there are essential differences between the two approaches: The three dimensional linear object boundaries are recovered, via application of an iterative algorithm to the edge map of the range image: In each iteration Hough Transforms are executed and a set of models are recovered, followed by a model selection process which retains the best models in terms of accuracy. The Hough Transforms are constrained so that the edge points localization error is accurately propagated to the parameter space. Boundaries comprising a fixed fraction of the edge points are sought in each iteration. Finally, orthogonal pairs of boundaries are grouped to a vertex. The orthogonality of a pair of recovered linear boundaries is determined via a statistical test.

This strategy results in a variety of advantages over existing systems: Robustness due to introduction of error propagation which reduces the detection rate of false positives, and due to robust boundary grouping guided by a statistical test. Accuracy, due to the incorporation of a model selection process, which retains the most accurate boundaries. Computational efficiency since the algorithm's complexity is linear to the number of edge points. Low memory consumption since accumulations use one dimensional structures. Versatility since exposure of only one object surface is enough for vertex detection, so that the system can deal with jumbled or neatly placed configurations of boxes. And last but not least simplicity as the flow diagrams that follow indicate. Our approach is described in detail in the subsequent sections.

2   Detection of Linear Object Boundaries in 3D

Input of our system are range images acquired from a laser range finder. Edge detection is performed on the image and an edge map is created. Such a map is depicted in Fig. 4 (b) and corresponds to the intensity image of Fig. 4 (a). The sensor coordinate frame is attached to the edge map. A range edge point $\mathbf{D}$ is defined by the coordinates $\mathbf{D}(X_s, Y_s, Z_s)$. The values X_s, Z_s express its position on the two-dimensional image plane, Y_s expresses its depth value. We decided to use the detector of [6] which performs approximation of the image scan lines with linear and quadratic segments. The major advantages of this method with regard to local edge detectors are its computational efficiency and its accuracy. The latter is due to the fact that whether a range point is classified as edge *point or not does not* depend on local information but on the parameters of the approximated segments which intersect at the point, the determination of which is influenced by a big number of range points. However the localization accuracy of the edge points is still not satisfactory. The surface of the target objects can not be always well approximated by parabolic segments, especially in areas where small local surface deformations occur. This is not very likely to happen when the objects are rigid boxes or deformable but full of material. Additionally, error is introduced by the laser sensor data acquisition process. The problem we face is in which way can we robustly recover the parameters of the $3D$ linear object boundaries of the objects from the edge map.

2.1 Parameter Recovery with the Hough Transform

The Standard Hough Transform (SHT) is the most common method employed for recovering multiple parametric models from images. Despite this, the SHT technique in its original form does not address the problem of localization error. Another weakness of the SHT is its computational inefficiency when dealing with models with many degrees of freedom. Lets suppose the model sought has N parameters and each image point constraints p of them. For each image point, the SHT increments all the bins comprising a $N - p$ -dimensional manifold of an N -dimensional accumulator. In our case the models ($3D$ lines) have $N = 4$ degrees of freedom and each point constraints $p = 2$ line parameters. Applying the SHT, will be both memory consuming, since a $4D$ accumulator is needed, as well as computationally inefficient, since mapping of a single edge point requires updating a $2D$ manifold of the accumulator.

A plethora of algorithms have been proposed to address the computational inefficiency of the SHT. Lets suppose mainly for simplicity $p = 1$, that is, we regard $2D$ images. The idea is to decrease the number of required accumulator updates per mapping by constraining the pose of the model. This is done by simultaneously mapping k ($1 < k \leq N$) instead of one pixels to the parameter space. If so, the dimensionality of the manifold along which the accumulator must be updated drops from $N - 1$ to $N - k$. In [11],[2] $k = N$ is regarded which implies $N - k = 0$. In this case update of only one accumulator cell per mapping is needed. Unfortunately these approaches are not free of problems: Mapping large sets of pixels gives rise to a combinatorially explosive number of possible sets. Randomization techniques have been proposed to reduce the number of sets examined.

Other researchers propose a somewhat different solution, which is based on decomposing the Hough Transform into subproblems. Each subproblem is solved within the context of a trial: A set of points with cardinality $d(d < N)$ (distinguished set) is randomly selected. Random subsets of the remaining points with cardinality v (varying sets) are then considered, so that $d + v = N$. The union of the two sets is then mapped to the parameter space by updating one cell, since the points in the union fully constrain the pose of the model. After all the varying sets have been examined, the accumulator maxima are extracted. A trial is considered successful if those maxima satisfy user-defined criteria. The process finishes when a fixed number of trials t has been performed. There is a variety of algorithms which may result from this framework by assigning different values to the cardinality (d) of the distinguished set, the number of varying subsets (r) examined within a trial and the number of trials (t). Leavers [8] sets $d = 1$, r is automatically determined by the framework, and t is the number of connected components found in the edge map. More recently Olson with his RUDR (Recognition using Decomposition and Randomization) technique [9] considers $d = N - 1$ and $r = n - 1$ where n the number of edge pixels in the image. A trial is considered successful when at least m points lie on the model. Finally, if γ the probability of failure in finding a model in the image, then the number of trials is given by (1).

$$t = \frac{\log(\frac{1}{\gamma})}{(\frac{m}{n})^{N-1}} \tag{1}$$

The selection of the particular cardinality for the distinguished set results to the fact that in each trial the transform is constrained to lie on a one-dimensional manifold, that is a curve (Hough Curve), in the parameter space. Many advantages are gained from this selection: Firstly, one dimensional data structures are used for the accumulation process, so the memory requirements are reduced to $O(n)$. Secondly, the complexity is $O(tr)$ or $O(tn)$. Since all quantities in (1) are user-defined constants ($\frac{m}{n}$ is a constant fraction of the input data), the overall algorithm complexity turns out to be linear to the number of pixels. Thirdly, if localization error is considered, a set of pixels maps not exactly on the Hough Curve, but to an area (error cloud) of the parameter space which lies close to the Hough Curve. The projection of the cloud to the Hough Curve will thus be a good approximation of it. This allows for simple, accurate and efficient error propagation to the parameter space. The error is expressed in a straightforward way via square boundaries in the image space whose side length (δ) is measured in pixels. The combination of these benefits are not to be found in other approaches simultaneously, up to our knowledge, and for this reason the adoption of RUDR framework seems to be the best choice for dealing with our problem.

2.2 Line Detection in $3D$

In our case, each edge point constraints two out of the four line parameters. It is thus not possible to directly apply the decomposition technique discussed above, because we cannot select a particular cardinality of the distinguished set which will allow for constraining the transform to lie on an one-dimensional curve, as in the $2D$ case. Therefore we came to the idea to break the problem down to $2D$ subproblems, and the natural way to do it is to examine two such subproblems, each recovering two line parameters using the RUDR technique. In detail: A trial is initiated by randomly selecting a distinguished point $\mathbf{D}(X_d, Y_d, Z_d)$, which supposedly belongs to the linear boundary $\mathbf{L}$, shown in the edge map of Fig. 4 (c). At first, the two parameters of the $2D$ orthogonal projection of $\mathbf{L}$ to the image plane ($\mathbf{ZX}$) are estimated. Fig. 1 (a) illustrates: The orthogonal projections of all the edge points to the image plane are taken into account. Lets

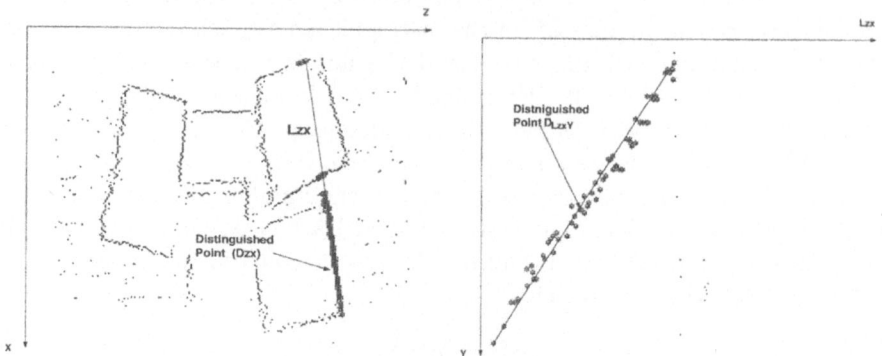

(a) Line detection in the image (**ZX**) plane   (b) Line detection in the $\mathbf{L_{zx}Y}$ plane

Fig. 1.   3D Line detection in two steps

consider $\mathbf{D_{zx}}$ the projection of $\mathbf{D}$. A two-dimensional RUDR trial is performed on the image plane with $\mathbf{D_{zx}}$ as distinguished point and the parameters of $\mathbf{L_{zx}}$ are retrieved. The corresponding range points to the pixels contributed to the accumulator's maximum (drawn as "*" in Fig. 1 (a)) are then projected to the plane defined by $\mathbf{L_{zx}}$ and the axis $\mathbf{Y}$ of the sensor coordinate system. Lets consider now $\mathbf{D_{L_{zx}Y}}$ the projection of $\mathbf{D}$ to this plane. A second two-dimensional RUDR trial is performed on this plane with $\mathbf{D_{L_{zx}Y}}$ as distinguished point to retrieve the remaining two parameters of $\mathbf{L}$. Fig. 1 (b) illustrates. The range points finally determined to belong to the line $\mathbf{L}$ correspond to the $2D$ points drawn as "*" in this figure. The flow diagram of the trial for detection of a $3D$ line is depicted in Fig. 2 (a).

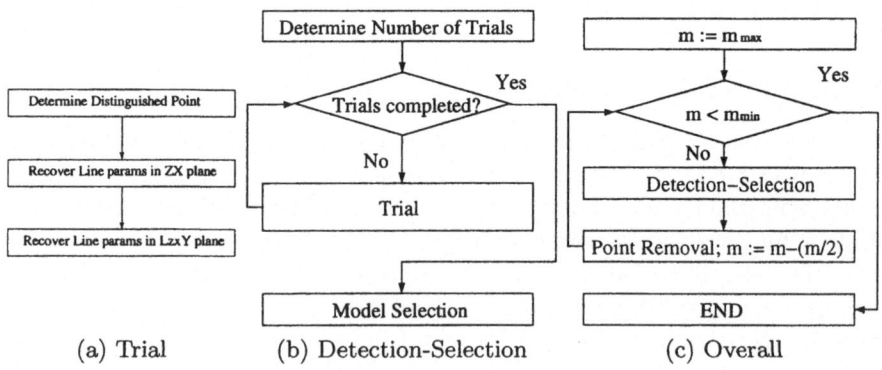

(a) Trial   (b) Detection-Selection   (c) Overall

Fig. 2.   Flow diagrams

2.3   Model Selection

Boundary detection to the edge map of Fig. 4 (b) is presented in Fig. 3 (a), where the detected lines are superimposed to the edge map. The problem observed, is that the line detection process outputs redundant lines. This is a consequence of the randomization. Our algorithm as is, cannot guarantee that more than one points belonging to the same boundary will not be used as distinguished pixels of the recovery process. Simply removing the range points determined to belong to a boundary after a successful trial and continue the process is questionable. We cannot assure that some of these points cannot be used by a later trial to recover a model which represents the boundary better. Instead of retaining a locally sufficient model it is preferable to wait until all the trials take place and retain the models which satisfy some global optimality criteria. It is logical to assume that a recovered model should be favored over another if it describes a bigger number of image points more accurately. The latter statement is a simplified version of the Minimum Description Length (MDL) principle for model selection, which has been used quite frequently in various computer vision applications, lately in [5], [10]. We adopt the strategy of in [5] p.123 for formalizing our approach, mainly due to its compactness and simplicity: Lets suppose that the recovery process outputs M models (in our case $3D$ lines). We regard a vector $\mathbf{m}$ of size M, the element m_i of which has the value 1 if the model i is contained in the final description and 0 if not. We consider as well a $M \times M$ matrix $\mathbf{Q}$, the diagonal terms q_{ii} of which express the benefit value for a model, while the others q_{ij} handle the interaction between the possibly overlapping models i and j. A model benefits when considered in the final description if it describes many data points with high accuracy as expressed by (2), where V_i the variance and $|M_i|$ the number of points of the model i, K_1, K_2 user defined constants.

$$q_{ii} = K_1|M_i| - K_2 V_i \tag{2}$$

We always penalize overlapping models, thus the benefit of overlapped models is negative and analogous to the number of points explained by both models, as expressed by (3).

$$q_{ij} = -\frac{K_1|M_i \cap M_j|}{2} \tag{3}$$

The function the maximization of which will result to the selection of the optimal set of models, is given by (4).

$$F(\mathbf{m}) = \mathbf{m}^T \mathbf{Q} \mathbf{m} \tag{4}$$

Many approaches can be applied for maximizing (4), among them simulated annealing or neural networks. A greedy algorithm of $O(M^2)$ is selected [5] for efficiency reasons. Fig. 3 (b) illustrates the results of model selection on the lines detected in Fig. 3 (a).

We name the process of line Detection followed by model Selection the **D-S** process, the flow diagram of which is illustrated in Fig. 2 (b). The algorithm's complexity is the complexity of the line detection plus the complexity of the

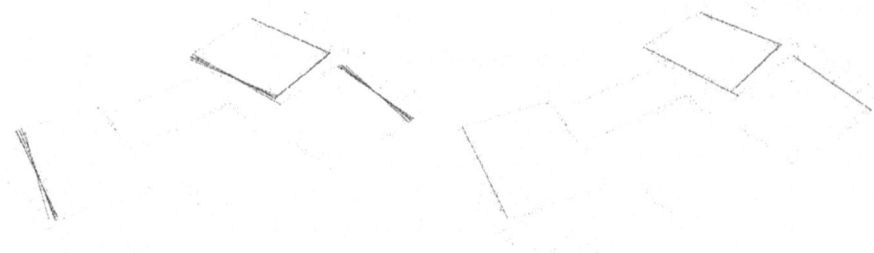

(a) Before segment selection   (b) After segment selection

Fig. 3. Effect of segment selection

selection that is $O(tn) + O(M^2) \approx O(n)$, since $t = O(1)$ and $n \gg M$. In terms of memory consumption, all we need is one dimensional accumulator of size $O(n)$ plus a two dimensional matrix of size $M \times M$. The **D-S** process inherits its robustness from the RUDR approach but it is more accurate because the best segments are retained by the selection process.

2.4   Acceleration via Point Removal

Our algorithm as is, performs t trials followed by model selection to extract $3D$ lines from the input edge map on which at least m points lie. The model selection, guarantees that the remaining linear segments describe the edge points to which they correspond in an optimal way. In other words, it is highly probable (this probability is given by the quantity $1 - \gamma$) that no other segments can be found comprising m or more points other than those already discovered. This observation results to a substantial algorithm acceleration: We adopt an iterative approach, every iteration of which comprises a **D-S** process retrieving lines with at least m points followed by a point removal, so that all the points determined by the **D-S** to lie on lines are eliminated from further consideration. We start by looking for long segments, so m is assigned a big value (m_{max}) and then we gradually reduce the number of points expected to be found on a segment by $\frac{m}{2}$ until a lower threshold (m_{min}) is reached. The execution time of the **D-S** step is proportional to the number of edge points in the image times the number of trials. The latter is inversely proportional to the number of points expected to lie in the lines. By looking for lines comprising many points first, we reduce the number of trials and thus the execution time of the current **D-S** step. By point removal reduction of execution time of the subsequent **D-S** steps is guaranteed. Thus an overall algorithm acceleration is realized. The flow diagram of the entire algorithm is depicted in Fig. 2 (b).

3   Boundary Grouping

We define a $3D$ vertex as an aggregate consisting of two orthogonal $3D$ linear segments and a vertex point defined by their intersection. In the ideal case, two linear segments $\mathbf{X},\mathbf{Y}$ comprise a vertex if the dot product of their direction vectors $\mathbf{x},\mathbf{y}$ is zero, that is: $r = \mathbf{x}^T\mathbf{y} = 0$. However due to uncertainty in the estimation of the segment parameters the dot product can never be exactly zero and a threshold must be introduced to determine the validity of a grouping hypothesis. The threshold depends on the uncertainty in the calculation of the line parameters and thus is difficult to define. The dot product is a bilinear function of the direction vectors. Thus rigorous uncertainty propagation can be achieved and a statistical test can determine whether the grouping hypothesis is to be rejected or not, based on a user defined significance value. In [4] a compact framework for testing uncertain geometric relations is presented, on which our method is based. If we assume Gaussian noise and if Σ_{xx} and Σ_{yy} the covariance matrices of the direction vectors $\mathbf{x}$ and $\mathbf{y}$ respectively, the variance of their dot product is given by the expression:

$$\sigma_r^2 = \mathbf{x}^\mathbf{T}\Sigma_{yy}\mathbf{x} + \mathbf{y}^\mathbf{T}\Sigma_{xx}\mathbf{y} \tag{5}$$

The optimal test statistic for the hypothesis $H_0 : r = 0$ is given by: $z = \frac{r}{\sigma_r} \sim N(0,1)$. We select a significance value α and compare the value z with the value $N_{1-\alpha}(0,1)$. If $z > N_{1-\alpha}(0,1)$, the grouping hypothesis is rejected. In all our experiments α was set to 0.05. The overall grouping algorithm has as follows: All possible pairs of detected lines are considered and those pairs passing the statistical test along with their intersection points are inserted to the set of the detected vertices.

4   Experimental Results

We applied our algorithm in various range images corresponding to piled objects. Two test cases are presented here: Rigid card-board boxes (Fig. 4) and sacks (bags) full of material (Fig. 5). The edge map, the recovered $3D$ line segments and the extracted vertices are as well depicted. In both cases all the objects linear boundaries were successfully recovered except those which were very noisy and comprised few number of points. For the boxes case we had $n = 1015$ edge points and assumed error of $\delta = 0.6$ pixels during the detection in the image plane and $\delta = 4$ pixels during line detection in the $\mathbf{L_{ZX}Y}$ plane. The corresponding values for the sacks test case were $n = 1260$, $\delta = 1$, and $\delta = 4$. In both cases, the probability of failure was $\gamma = 0.01$ and the model selection parameters were set to $K_1 = 1$, $K_2 = 0.1$. Two algorithm iterations were executed: The first detected lines comprising at least 60 and the second 30 range points. The execution time for vertex detection was about 12 seconds in both cases in a Pentium $3, 600MHz$. Note that if we execute only one iteration in the context of which lines comprising 30 points are sought from the first place, the execution time rises to about 19 seconds. This verifies that the iterative algorithm and point removal actually reduce the overall execution time.

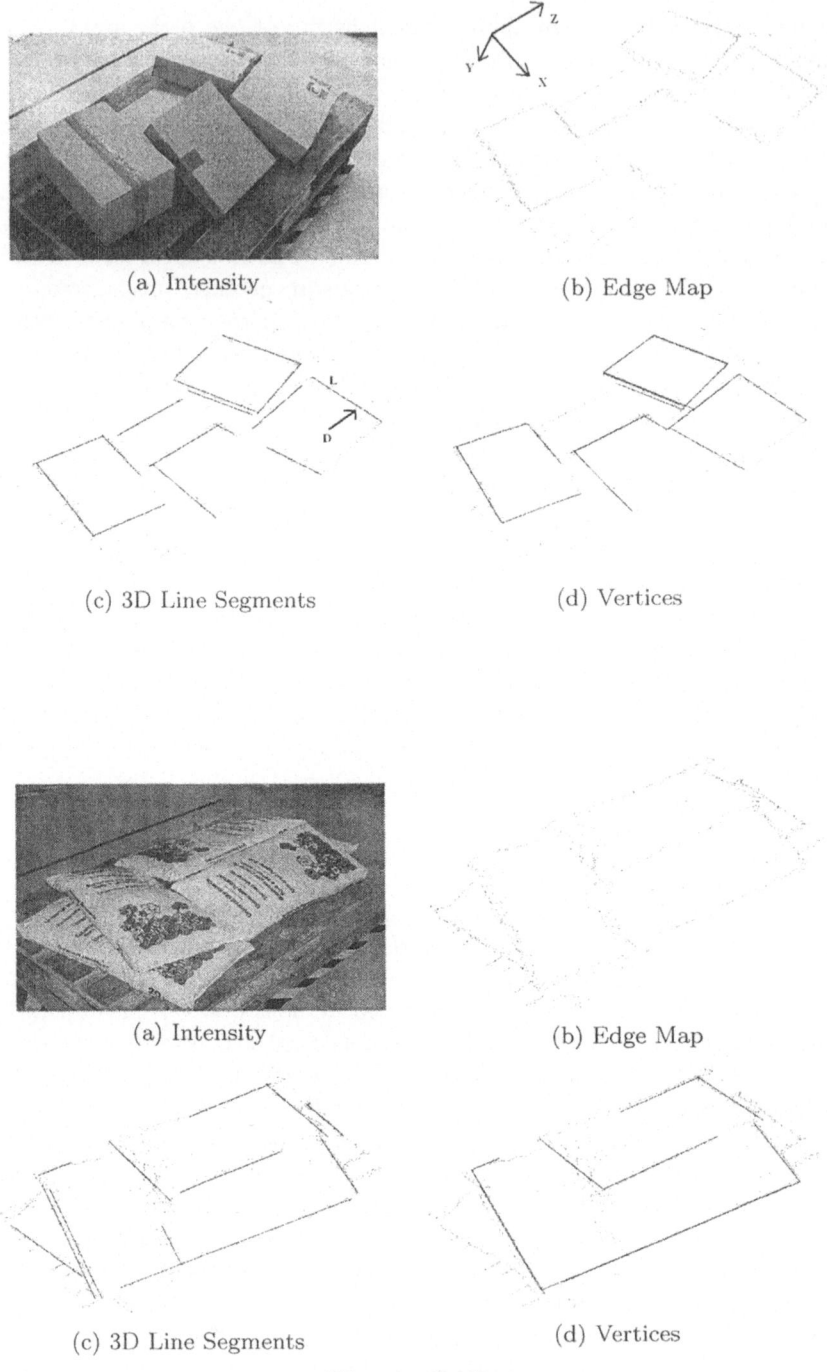

(a) Intensity

(b) Edge Map

(c) 3D Line Segments

(d) Vertices

(a) Intensity

(b) Edge Map

(c) 3D Line Segments

(d) Vertices

Fig. 5. Sacks

5 Conclusions

We presented a technique for detecting vertices in range images of cluttered objects in two steps: Boundary extraction and grouping. Recovery of the four parameters of the linear boundary segments was performed by a sequence of problem decomposition, model selection and point removal, integrated into an iterative framework. Efficient and accurate propagation of error to the parameter space was achieved so that robustness was realized. Boundary grouping via a statistical test contributed to the system's robustness. Vertex extraction corresponds to the recovery of a subset of the parameter set describing each object on the pallet. In the future we intend to use this framework as a starting point for the recovery of the remaining parameters of each object.

References

[1] A. J. Baerveldt. Robust *Singulation of Parcels with a Robot System using multiple sensors*. PhD thesis, Swiss federal institute of technology, 1993.

[2] R. C. Bolles and M. A. Fischler. A RANSAC-based approach to model fitting and its application to finding cylinders in range data. In *Proceedings of the 7th International Joint Conference on Artificial Intelligence (IJCAI '81)*, pages 637643 August 24-28 1991.

[3] C. H. Chen and A. C. Kak. A robot vision system for recognizing 3-D objects in low-order polynomial time. *IEEE Transactions on Systems, Man, and Cybernetics*, 19(6):1535-1563 November-December 1989.

[4] W. Foerstner, A. Brunn, and S. Heuel. Statistically testing uncertain geometric relations. In G. Sommer, N. Krueger, and Perwass Ch., editors, *Mustererkennung*, pages 17-26. Springer, September 2000.

[5] A. Jakliç A. Leonardis, and F. Solina. *Segmentation and recovery of Superquadrics*, volume 20 of *Computational imaging and vision*. Kluwer Academic Publishers, Dordrecht, 2000.

[6] X. Jiang and H. Bunke. Edge detection in range images based on scan line approximation. *Computer Vision and Image Understanding: CVIU* 73(2):183-199 February 1999.

[7] D. Katsoulas and L. Bergen. Efficient 3d vertex detection in range images acquired with a laser sensor. In B. Radig and S. Florczyk, editors, *Pattern Recognition, Proc. of 23rd DAGM Symposium*, number 2191 in LNCS Pattern Recognition, pages 116123. Springer, September 2001.

[8] V. F. Leavers. The dynamic generalized Hough transform: its relationship to the probabilistic Hough transforms and an application to the concurrent detection of circles and ellipses. *Computer Vision, Graphics, and Image Processing. Image Understanding*, 56(3):381-398 November 1992.

[9] C. F. Olson. A general method for geometric feature matching and feature extraction. *International Journal of Computer Vision*, 45(1):39-54 October 2001.

[10] S. Sclaroff and L. Liu. Deformable shape detection and description via model-based region grouping. *IEEE Transactions on Pattern Analysis and Machine Intelligence*, 23(5):475-489 2001.

[11] L. Xu and E. Oja. Randomized Hough transform (RHT): basic mechanisms, algorithms, and complexities. *Computer Vision, Graphics, and Image Processing: Image Understanding*, 57:131-154 1993.

Comparison of Log-linear Models and Weighted Dissimilarity Measures

Daniel Keysers[1], Roberto Paredes[2], Enrique Vidal[2], and Hermann Ney[1]

[1] Lehrstuhl für Informatik VI, Computer Science Department
RWTH Aachen – University of Technology, D-52056 Aachen, Germany
{keysers,ney}@informatik.rwth-aachen.de
[2] Instituto Tecnológico de Informática
Departemento de Sistemas Informáticos y Computación
Universidad Politécnica de Valencia, E-46022 Valencia, Spain
{rparedes, evidal}@iti.upv.es

Abstract. We compare two successful discriminative classification algorithms on three databases from the UCI and STATLOG repositories. The two approaches are the log-linear model for the class posterior probabilities and class-dependent weighted dissimilarity measures for nearest neighbor classifiers. The experiments show that the maximum entropy based log-linear classifier performs better for the equivalent of a single prototype. On the other hand, using multiple prototypes the weighted dissimilarity measures outperforms the log-linear approach. This result suggests an extension of the log-linear method to multiple prototypes.

1 Introduction

In this paper, we compare two classification algorithms that are both *discriminative*. Algorithms for classification of observations $x \in \mathbb{R}^D$ into one of the classes $k \in \{1, \ldots, K\}$ usually estimate some of their parameters in the training phase from a set of labeled training data $\{(x_n, k_n)\}$, $n = 1, \ldots, N$. The training procedure can take into account only the data from one class at a time or all of the competing classes can be considered at the same time. In the latter case the process is called discriminative. As discriminative training puts more emphasis on the decision boundaries, it often leads to better classification accuracy.

We examine the connection between two discriminative classification algorithms and compare their performance on three databases from the UCI and STATLOG repositories [5, 6].

The principle of maximum entropy is a powerful framework that can be used to estimate class posterior probabilities for pattern recognition tasks. It leads to log-linear models for the class posterior and uses the log-probability of the class posterior on the training data as training criterion. It can be shown that its combination with the use of first-order feature functions is equivalent to the discriminative training of single Gaussian densities with pooled covariance matrices [4].

F.J. Perales et al. (Eds.): IbPRIA 2003, LNCS 2652, pp. 370–377, 2003.

The use of weighted dissimilarity measures, where the weights may depend on the dimension and class and are trained according to a discriminative criterion, has shown high performance on various classification tasks [9]. Also for this method, a strong connection to the use of Gaussian densities can be observed if one prototype per class is used. For more than one prototype per class, the similarity leads to a mixture density approach. These connections to the Gaussian classifier are used to compare the two discriminative criteria.

2   Classification Framework

To classify an observation $x \in \mathbb{R}^D$, we use the Bayesian decision rule

$$x \longmapsto r(x) = \operatorname*{argmax}_{k} \{p(k|x)\} = \operatorname*{argmax}_{k} \{p(k) \cdot p(x|k)\} .$$

Here, $p(k|x)$ is the class posterior probability of class $k \in \{1, \ldots, K\}$ given the observation x, $p(k)$ is the a priori probability, $p(x|k)$ is the class conditional probability for the observation x given class k and $r(x)$ is the decision of the classifier. This decision rule is known to be optimal with respect to the number of decision errors, if the correct distributions are known. This is generally not the case in practical situations, which means that we need to choose appropriate models for the distributions.

If we denote by Λ the set of free parameters of the distribution, the maximum likelihood approach consists in choosing the parameters $\hat{\Lambda}$ maximizing the log-likelihood on the training data:

$$\hat{\Lambda} = \operatorname*{argmax}_{\Lambda} \sum_n \log p_\Lambda(x_n|k_n) \tag{1}$$

Alternatively, we can maximize the log-likelihood of the class posteriors,

$$\hat{\Lambda} = \operatorname*{argmax}_{\Lambda} \sum_n \log p_\Lambda(k_n|x_n) , \tag{2}$$

which is also called discriminative training, since the information of out-of-class data is used. This criterion is often referred to as mutual information criterion in speech recognition, information theory and image object recognition [2, 8].

Discriminative training was used in [9] to learn the weights of a weighted dissimilarity measure. This weighted measure was used in the nearest neighbor classification rule improving significantly the accuracy of the classifier in comparison to other distance measures, for which the parameters were not estimated using discriminative training.

3   Maximum Entropy, Gaussian and Log-linear Models

The principle of maximum entropy has origins in statistical thermodynamics, is related to information theory and has been applied to pattern recognition tasks such as language modeling [1] and text classification [7]. Applied to classification, the basic idea is the following: We are given information about a probability distribution by samples from that distribution (training data). Now, we choose the distribution such that it fulfills all the constraints given by that information (more precisely: the observed marginal distributions), but otherwise has the highest possible entropy. (This inherently serves as regularization to avoid overfitting.) It can be shown that this approach leads to log-linear models for the distribution to be estimated.

Consider a set of so-called feature functions $\{f_i\}, i = 1, \ldots, I$ that are supposed to compute 'useful' information for classification:

$$f_i \quad : \quad \mathbb{R}^D \times \{1, \ldots, K\} \longrightarrow \mathbb{R} \quad : \quad (x, k) \longmapsto f_i(x, k)$$

It can be shown that the resulting distribution that maximizes the entropy has the following log-linear or exponential functional form:

$$p_\Lambda(k|x) = \frac{\exp\left[\sum_i \lambda_i f_i(x, k)\right]}{\sum_{k'} \exp\left[\sum_i \lambda_i f_i(x, k')\right]}, \quad \Lambda = \{\lambda_i\}. \tag{3}$$

Interestingly, it can also be shown that the stated optimization problem is convex and has a unique global maximum. Furthermore, this unique solution is also the solution to the following dual problem: Maximize the log probability (2) on the training data using the model (3).

A second desirable property of the discussed model is that effective algorithms are known that compute the global maximum of the log probability (2) given a training set. These algorithms fall into two categories: On the one hand, we have an algorithm known as generalized iterative scaling [3] and related algorithms that can be proven to converge to the global maximum. On the other hand, due to the convex nature of the criterion (2), we can also use general optimization strategies as e.g. conjugate gradient methods.

The crucial problem in maximum entropy modeling is the choice of the appropriate feature functions $\{f_i\}$. In general, these functions depend on the classification task considered.

The straight forward way to define feature functions for classification purposes is to directly use the features provided for the specific task. Consider therefore the following first-order feature functions for log-linear classification:

$$f_{k,i}(x, k') = \delta(k, k') \, x_i \, ,$$
$$f_k(x, k') = \delta(k, k') \, ,$$

where $\delta(k, k') := 1$ if $k = k'$, and 0 otherwise denotes the Kronecker delta function. The Kronecker delta is necessary here to distinguish between the different classes. It can be shown that maximum entropy training using first-order features is equivalent to the discriminative training of single Gaussian densities with globally pooled covariance matrices using the criterion (2) [4]. Furthermore, we may also consider products of feature values for the feature functions (second-order features) by including

$$f_{k,i,j}(x, k') = \delta(k, k') \, x_i x_j \, , \quad i \geq j \, .$$

In this case, the maximum entropy training is equivalent to the discriminative training of single Gaussian densities with full, class-specific covariance matrices, where the constraint on the covariance matrices to be positive (semi-) definite is relaxed [4]. The correspondences can be derived by observing that the functional form of the class posterior

$$p(k|x) = \frac{p(k)\,\mathcal{N}(x|\mu_k, \Sigma_k)}{\sum_{k'} p(k')\,\mathcal{N}(x|\mu_{k'}, \Sigma_{k'})}$$

also leads to a log-linear expression like (3) for the appropriate choice of feature functions. These correspondences to Gaussian models with one prototype justify the classification of the log-linear approach to be a 'one-prototype' approach.

4   Class-Dependent Weighted Dissimilarity Measures

In [9], a *class-dependent* weighted dissimilarity measure for nearest neighbor classifiers was introduced. The squared distance is defined as

$$d^2(x, \mu) = \sum_d \left(\frac{x_d - \mu_d}{\sigma_{k_\mu d}} \right)^2 \quad , \ \Lambda = \{\sigma_{kd}, \mu_d\},$$

where d denotes the dimension index and k_μ is the class the reference vector μ belongs to. The parameters Λ are estimated with respect to a discriminative training criterion that takes into account the out-of-class information and can be derived from the minimum classification error criterion:

$$\hat{\Lambda} = \operatorname*{argmin}_{\Lambda} \sum_n \frac{\min\limits_{\mu:k_\mu = k_n} d_\Lambda(x_n, \mu)}{\min\limits_{\mu:k_\mu \neq k_n} d_\Lambda(x_n, \mu)} \tag{6}$$

In other words, the parameters are chosen to minimize the average ratio of the distance to the closest prototype of the same class with respect to the distance to the closest prototype of the competing classes.

To minimize the criterion, a gradient descent approach is used and a leaving one out estimation with the weighted measure is computed at each step of the gradient procedure. The weights selected by the algorithm are those weights with the best leaving one out estimation instead of the weights with the minimum criterion value. In the experiments, only the weights $\{\sigma_{kd}\}$ were estimated according to the proposed criterion. The references $\{\mu_k\}$ were chosen as the means for the one-prototype approach and in the multiple-prototype approach the whole training set was used.

Also in this approach, we have a strong relation to Gaussian models. Consider the use of one prototype per class. The distance measure then is a *class-dependent* Mahalanobis distance with class-specific, diagonal covariance matrices

$$\Sigma_k = \operatorname{diag}(\sigma_{k1}^2, \ldots, \sigma_{kD}^2).$$

Table 1. Corpus statistics for the three databases used in the experiments from the UCI and STATLOG repositories, respectively.

corpus name	MONK	DNA	LETTER
# classes	2	3	26
# features	17	180	16
# training samples	124	2 000	15 000
# test samples	432	1 186	5 000

The decision rule is then equivalent to the use of single Gaussian models in combination with an additional factor to compensate for the missing normalization factor of the Gaussian. In the case of multiple prototypes per class, the equivalence is extensible to mixtures of Gaussian densities.

5   Connection between the Two Classifiers

As discussed in the two previous sections, the two approaches are equivalent to the use of discriminative training for single Gaussian densities with some additional restrictions. This implies that the main difference between the classifiers is the criterion that is used to choose the class boundaries:

Gaussian Densities: criterion: maximum likelihood (1); decision boundary: linear (pooled covariance matrices) or quadratic (class-specific covariance matrices)

Log-linear Model: criterion: maximum mutual information (maximum likelihood of the posterior) (2); decision boundary: linear (first-order feature functions) or quadratic (second-order feature functions)

Weighted Dissimilarity Measures: criterion: intra-class distances versus inter-class distances (6); decision boundary: quadratic (one prototype per class) or piecewise quadratic (multiple prototypes per class)

6   Databases and Results

The experiments were performed on three corpora from the UCI and STATLOG database, respectively [5, 6]. The corpora were chosen to cover different properties with respect to the number of classes and features and with respect to the size. The statistics of the corpora are summarized in Table 1. MONK is an artificial decision task with categorical features also known as the monk's problem. For the experiments, the categorical features were transformed into binary features. For the DNA task, the goal is to detect gene intron/exon and exon/intron boundaries given part of a DNA sequence. Also for this task, the categorical features were transformed into binary features. Finally, the LETTER corpus consists of printed characters that were preprocessed and a variety of different features was extracted.

Table 2. Experimental results for the three databases used with different settings of the algorithms given as error rate (er) in %. The number of parameters (#param.) refers to the total number of parameters needed to completely define the classifier.

	MONK		DNA		LETTER	
method	er[%]	#param.	er[%]	#param.	er[%]	#param.
single Gaussian	28.5	51	9.5	720	41.6	432
log-linear, first-order	28.9	36	5.6	543	22.5	442
second-order	0.2	308	5.1	48 873	13.5	3 562
weighted dissimil., one prot.	16.7	68	6,7	1 080	24.1	832
multiple prot.	0.0	2 142	4.7	360 540	3.3	240 416
best other [5, 6]	0.0	-	4.1	-	3.4	-

Table 2 shows a summary of the results obtained with the two methods. The figures show the following tendencies:

- Considering the four approaches that can be labeled 'one-prototype' (single Gaussian, both log-linear models and the one-prototype weighted dissimilarity measure), the discriminative approaches generally perform better than the maximum likelihood based approach (single Gaussian).
- For the two log-linear approaches, the second-order features perform better than the first-order features.
- On two of the three corpora, the log-linear classifier with first-order features performs better than the one-prototype weighted dissimilarity measure using a smaller number of parameters.
- On all of the corpora, the log-linear classifier with second-order features performs better than the one-prototype weighted dissimilarity measure, but using a larger number of parameters.
- The weighted dissimilarity measures using multiple prototypes outperforms the other regarded ('one-prototype') approaches on all tasks and is competitive with respect to the best known results on each task.

Note that second-order features perform better here although estimation of full, class-specific covariance matrices is problematic for many tasks. This indicates a high robustness of the maximum entropy log-linear approach. Note further that both the one-prototype weighted dissimilarity classifier and the log-linear model with second-order features lead to quadratic decision boundaries, but the former does not take into account bilinear terms of the features, which is the case for the second-order features.

The high error rate of the log-linear model with first-order features on the MONK corpus was analyzed in more detail. As this task only contains binary features, also the one-prototype weighted dissimilarity classifier leads to linear decision boundaries here ($x^2 = x \Leftrightarrow x \in \{0, 1\}$). Therefore it is possible to infer the parameters for the log-linear model from the training result of the weighted dissimilarity classifier. This showed that the log-likelihood of the posterior (2) on the training data is lower than that resulting from maximum entropy training, which is not surprising as exactly this quantity is the training criterion for the log-linear model. But interestingly the same result holds for the *test* data as well. That is, the maximum entropy training result has higher prediction accuracy on the average for the class posterior, but this does not result in better classification accuracy. This may indicate that on this corpus with very few samples the weighted dissimilarity technique is able to better adapt the decision boundary as it uses a criterion derived from the minimum classification error criterion.

7   Conclusion

A detailed comparison of two discriminative algorithms on three corpora with different characteristics has been presented. The discriminative approaches generally perform better than the maximum likelihood based approach.

A direct transfer of the maximum entropy framework to multiple prototypes is difficult, as the use of multiple prototypes leads to nonlinearities and the log-linear model cannot be directly applied any more.

The consistent improvements obtained with weighted dissimilarity measures and multiple prototypes in combination with the improvements obtained by using second-order features suggest possible improvements that could be expected from a combination of these two approaches.

References

[1] A. L. Berger, S. A. Della Pietra, and V. J. Della Pietra. A maximum entropy approach to natural language processing. *Computational Linguistics*, 22(1):39–72, March 1996.

[2] J. Dahmen, R. Schlüter, and H. Ney. Discriminative training of Gaussian mixture densities for image object recognition. In *21. DAGM Symposium Mustererkennung*, pages 205–212, Bonn, Germany, September 1999.

[3] J. N. Darroch and D. Ratcliff. Generalized iterative scaling for log-linear models. *Annals of Mathematical Statistics*, 43(5):1470–1480, 1972.

[4] D. Keysers, F. J. Och, and H. Ney. Maximum entropy and Gaussian models for image object recognition. In *Pattern Recognition, 24th DAGM Symposium*, pages 498–506, Zürich, Switzerland, September 2002.

[5] C. J. Merz, P. M. Murphy, and D. W. Aha. *UCI Repository of Machine Learning Databases*. http://www.ics.uci.edu/~mlearn/MLRepository.html. University of California, Department of Information and Computer Science, Irvine CA, 1997.

[6] D. Michie, D. J. Spiegelhalter, C. C. Taylor (eds). *Machine Learning, Neural and Statistical Classification*. Ellis Horwood, 1994. Available at http://www.amsta.leeds.ac.uk/~charles/statlog/, datasets at http://www.liacc.up.pt/ML/statlog/datasets.html.

[7] K. Nigam, J. Lafferty, and A. McCallum. Using maximum entropy for text classification. In *IJCAI-99 Workshop on Machine Learning for Information Filtering*, pages 61–67, Stockholm, Sweden, August 1999.

[8] Y. Normandin. Maximum mutual information estimation of hidden Markov models. In C. H. Lee, F. K. Soong, and K. K. Paliwal, editors, *Automatic Speech and Speaker Recognition*, pages 57–81, Norwell, MA, Kluwer, 1996.

[9] R. Paredes and E. Vidal.   A class-dependent weighted dissimilarity measure for nearest-neighbor classification problems. *Pattern Recognition Letters*, 21(12):1027–1036, November 2000.

Motion Segmentation
Using Distributed Genetic Algorithms

Eun Yi Kim[1] and Se Hyun Park[2]*

[1]College of Internet and Media, Konkuk Univ.,
1 Hwayang-dong, Gwangjin-gu, Seoul, Korea
eykim@kkucc.konkuk.ac.kr
[2]Division of Computer Engineering,
College of Electronic and Information, Chosun Univ.,
375 Susuk-dong, Dong-gu, Gwangju, Korea
sehyun@chosun.ac.kr

Abstract This paper presents a Bayesian framework for simultaneous motion segmentation and estimation using genetic algorithms (GAs). The segmentation label and motion field are modeled by Markov random fields (MRFs), and a MAP estimate is used to identify the optimal label and motion field. In this paper, the motion segmentation and estimation problems are formalized as optimization problems of the energy function. And, the process for optimization of energy function is performed by iterating motion segmentation and estimation using a genetic algorithm, which is robust and effective to deal with combinatorial problems. The computation is distributed into chromosomes that evolve by distributed genetic algorithms (DGAs). Experimental results shows that our proposed method estimates an accurate motion field and segments a satisfactory label fields.

1   Introduction

Motion segmentation refers to labeling pixels, which are associated with different coherently moving objects or parts. It plays an important role in image sequence processing. In applications related to object recognition [1], the estimation of motion fields and their segmentations are often primary tasks for object tracking, object-based video compression and indexing, and so on. Motion segmentation is closely related to other problem, motion estimation. Motion estimation refers to assigning a parametric or nonparametric motion vector to each pixel in the image; it is an integral part of motion segmentation [2,3]. An accurate estimate of the motion is required to obtain a good segmentation result, while a good motion segmentation result is needed to accurately estimate the motion. Due to this reason, techniques that simultaneously estimate and segment motion has been intensively proposed [2-4]. Such approaches usually adopted a Bayesian approach, and pose the motion estimation and segmentation problem as a

---

* The corresponding author: Tel. +82-62-230-7021; Fax: +82-62-230-7021.

F.J. Perales et al. (Eds.): IbPRIA 2003, LNCS 2652, pp. 378-385, 2003.
© Springer-Verlag Berlin Heidelberg 2003

MAP (Maximum a posteriori) estimation of motion and segmentation given the observed images [2,3]. They can provide an elegant formalism, and easily incorporate mechanisms to achieve spatial and temporal continuity. However, Bayesian approaches suffer from higher computational complexity [2,3].

As a result, genetic algorithms (GAs) have been intensively investigated as a solution to this computational complexity [5]. GAs are stochastic search methods based on the mechanics of natural selection and genetics. These algorithms are robust, and can successfully deal with combinatorial problems. They are also attractive because they can achieve an efficient parallel exploration of search space without getting stuck in local optima [5,6].

This paper presents a Bayesian framework for simulation motion segmentation and estimation using GAs. The segmentation label and motion field are modeled by MRFs, and a MAP estimate is used to identify the optimal label and motion field. GAs are used as optimization algorithm to maximize a posterior probability, which performs segmentation and estimation alternately. The segmentation is computed according to the previous parameters, thereafter, a parameter is estimated using this segmentation. Experimental results demonstrate the effectiveness of the proposed method.

2   Problem Specifications

Let $S=\{(i,j):1\leq i\leq M_1,\ 1\leq j\leq M_2\}$ denote the $M_1\times M_2$ lattice, such that an element in S index an image pixel. And, let $d(i,j) = (u,v)$ denote a motion vector from the current frame to the reference frame. Then we consider the motion field $d(i,j)$ as the sum of a parametric field and a residual field as shown in Eg. (1).

$$d(i,j) = d_p(i,j) + d_r(i,j) \ , \tag{1}$$

where the $d_p(i,j)$ is the parametric motion vector and the $d_r(i,j)$ is the residual motion vector at the pixel (i,j). The residual field represents the discrepancy between the motion information characterized by the motion parameters and the true optical flow of the pixel. Let $\Lambda=\{\lambda_1, \ldots, \lambda_R\}$ denote the label set and $X=\{X_{ij}\}$ be a family of random variables defined on S. Let x denote a realization of X.

Our goal is to find u, v and x which maximizes the posteriori probability density function (pdf) for given two frames the current frame g_k and reference frame g_{k-1}. That is, we want to determine

$$\arg\max_{u,v,x} P(u,v,x \mid g_k, g_{k-1})$$

$$= \arg\max_{u,v,x} \frac{P(g_k \mid u,v,x,g_{k-1})\times P(u,v,x \mid g_{k-1})}{P(g_k \mid g_{k-1})} \ , \tag{2}$$

$$= \arg\max_{u,v,x} \frac{P(g_k \mid u,v,x,g_{k-1})\times P(u,v \mid x,g_{k-1})\times P(x \mid g_{k-1})}{P(g_k \mid g_{k-1})}$$

where the denominator is constant with respect to the unknowns. So, maximization of a posteriori pdf $P(u, v, x \mid g_k, g_{k-1})$ is equivalent to maximization the following posteriori pdf:

$$P(g_k \mid u, v, x, g_{k-1}) \times P(u, v \mid x, g_{k-1}) \times P(x \mid g_{k-1}) \tag{3}$$

Eq. (3) is divided into three components of the following: $P(g_k \mid u, v, x, g_{k-1})$, $P(u, v \mid x, g_{k-1})$, and $P(x \mid g_{k-1})$. The conditional pdf $P(g_k \mid u, v, x, g_{k-1})$ measures how well the motion and segmentation estimates fit the given frames, which is defined as follows:

$$
\begin{aligned}
&-\log P(g_k \mid u, v, x, g_{k-1}) \\
&= \sum_{(i,j) \in S} \mid I_k(i, j) - I_{k-1}(i + u(i, j), j + v(i, j)) \mid^2
\end{aligned}
\tag{4}
$$

The $P(u, v \mid x, g_{k-1})$ is the displacement field given the motion segmentation and the reference frame. If we ignore the dependence on the reference frame g_{k-1}, this pdf is defined as follows:

$$
\begin{aligned}
&-\log P(u, v \mid x, g_{k-1}) = -\log P(u, v \mid x) \\
&= \alpha_1 \sum_{(i,j) \in S} \| d(i, j) - d_p(i, j) \|^2 \\
&\quad + \alpha_2 \sum_{(i,j) \in S} \sum_{(k,l) \in N_{ij}} \| d(i, j) - d(k, l) \|^2 \cdot T(x(i, j), x(k, l))
\end{aligned}
\tag{5}
$$

where α_1 and α_2 control the weight of each terms, N_{ij} is the set of pixels neighboring (i, j), and T is defined as follows:

$$
T(x(i, j), x(k, l)) = \begin{cases} 1, & \text{if } x(i, j) = x(k, l) \\ 0, & \text{otherwise} \end{cases}
\tag{6}
$$

Finally, the $P(x \mid g_{k-1})$ is the a priori probability of the segmentation. If we ignore the dependence on the reference frame g_{k-1}, this pdf is defined as follows:

$$
-\log P(x \mid g_{k-1}) = -\log P(x) = \alpha_3 \sum_{(i,j) \in S} \sum_{(k,l) \in N_{ij}} V_c(x(i, j), x(k, l)) ,
\tag{7}
$$

where α_3 control the weight of this term, and the potential function $V_c = -1$ if the label is defined as follows:

$$
V_c(x(i, j), x(k, l)) = \begin{cases} -1, & \text{if } x(i, j) = x(k, l) \\ 1, & \text{otherwise} \end{cases}
\tag{8}
$$

Accordingly, Eq. (3) can be rewritten as follows, which is called as an energy function. Instead of maximizing the posterior distribution, the energy function is minimized to identify the optimal label.

$$f = \sum_{(i,j)\in S} |I_k(i,j) - I_{k-1}(i+u(i,j), j+v(i,j))|^2$$

$$+\alpha_1 \sum_{(i,j)\in S} \| d(i,j) - d_p(i,j) \|^2$$

$$+\alpha_2 \sum_{(i,j)\in S} \sum_{(k,l)\in N_{ij}} \| d(i,j) - d(k,l) \|^2 \cdot T(x(i,j), x(k,l))$$

$$+\alpha_3 \sum_{(i,j)\in S} \sum_{(k,l)\in N_{ij}} V_c(x(i,j), x(k,l))$$

$$(9)$$

3   Optimization of Energy Function

We formalize the motion segmentation and estimation problems as optimization problems of the energy function in the section II. In this paper, the process for optimization of energy function is performed by iterating motion segmentation and estimation using a genetic algorithm. To reduce computational time and eliminate a large percentage of local minima, a genetic algorithm is used as an optimization algorithm.

3.1   Overview of the Proposed Method

The proposed method consists of two levels: an estimation level and a segmentation level. These two levels are iterated until they converge to a stable optimization, which is then taken as the resulting segmented image. After segmenting regions by a GA, sufficient small regions are merged into a region with the most similar motion field in the adjacent regions, because the regions forming an object share some common temporal characteristics.

Estimation level update the motion field u, v given the estimate of the label field x. For an evaluation of this level, the following local energy function is used:

$$f_{u,v} = |I_k(i,j) - I_{k-1}(i+u(i,j), j+v(i,j))|^2$$

$$+\alpha_1 \| d(i,j) - d_p(i,j) \|^2$$

$$+\alpha_2 \sum_{(k,l)\in N_{(i,j)}} \| d(i,j) - d(k,l) \|^2 \cdot T(x(i,j), x(k,l))$$

$$(10)$$

where x is the label obtained by previous step.

Segmentation level update the label x, assuming the motion vector u, v is given. For an evaluation of this level, the following local energy function is used:

$$
\begin{aligned}
f_x = {} & \alpha_1 \| d(i,j) - d_p(i,j) \|^2 \\
& + \alpha_2 \sum_{(k,l) \in N_{(i,j)}} \| d(i,j) - d(k,l) \|^2 \cdot T(x(i,j), x(k,l)) \\
& + \alpha_3 \sum_{(k,l) \in N_{(i,j)}} V_c(x(i,j), x(k,l))
\end{aligned}
\tag{11}
$$

where u and v are components of the motion vector obtained by estimation level. The genetic operators in this level are same with the ones used in the estimation level.

The computation in each level is distributed into a set of chromosomes that evolve using the DGA. A generation is defined as an iteration of both the estimation and segmentation level. The stopping criterion is determined relative to the equilibrium, which is the ratio of pixels that have the same label in both the current and previous generations. The stopping criterion is reached when the equilibrium is above the equilibrium threshold.

3.2   A Chromosome

To apply GAs to any practical problem, an appropriate representation of the candidate solution is needed. The representation of a solution is an important choice in the algorithm because it determines the data structures that are to be modified in the crossover and mutation operators. In this paper, a binary base-2 coding is used, which is used in Goldberg's classical genetic algorithm (CGA) (Godlberg, 1989). Binary base-2 coding represents each chromosome as a string of elements of the set {0. 1} (bits), which transforms the m real numbers into integers whose base-2 representations are then stored sequentially in the string.

A chromosome consists of label field and motion field at pixel (i,j), and is represented by a bit string. The structure of chromosome is described in Fig. 1. And, the fitness of a chromosome is defined as Eq. (10) and Eq. (11).

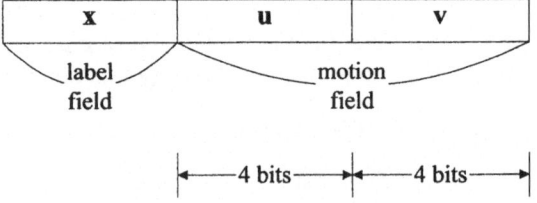

Fig.1 The structure of a chromosome

The chromosomes are evolved through iterating genetic operators until the stopping criterion is satisfied.

3.3   GA Operators

The genetic operators in estimation and segmentation level are illustrated below.

Selection. Replace each chromosome by a neighbor according to the fitness of the neighboring chromosomes. We use an elitist selection mechanism (Andrey and Tarroux, 1998; Goldberg, 1989; Kim et al., 1998). The chromosome whose fitness is the highest in the neighborhood is selected.

Crossover. For each chromosome, look for the neighbor which has the same label and recombine the current chromosome with this neighbor. We use one-point crossover, which is the most widely used crossover operator (Beasley et al., 1993; Goldberg, 1989; Holland, 1975; Kim et al., 1998; Manderick and Spiessens, 1989). In this operator, a single crossover point is positioned randomly between two consecutive bits, and all the bits coming after that point are exchanged between the two strings involved in the crossover process, yielding two new strings. The current chromosome is replaced by one of the two offspring.

Mutation. We randomly select any gene of each chromosome, at random. The bit corresponding to the gene is flipped, i.e., its value is changed from 0 to 1 or vice versa. During the early generations of any frame, mutation occurs in the label, as well as in the feature vector portion. However, during subsequent generations mutation occurs only in the feature vector portion.

3.4   Initialization

The values of the chromosomes are initialized through two steps. First, each label field is given a random label value uniformly chosen from a set of possible labels, and initial motion field is obtained by using a conventional block-matching algorithm. Second, given the initial motion field, a label field is evolved by using GAs[5], until they converge to a stable optimization, which is then taken as the resulting initial label field. The parametric motion field within these regions is represented by the affine parameters, which are updated by least squares estimation at the conclusion of the segmentation level.

4   Experimental Results

To assess the validity of the proposed method, it was tested on a well-known image sequence, namely "Table tennis". It should be noted that the DGA parameters, such as the window size and probabilities of the genetic operations, all have an influence on the performance of the algorithms. Accordingly, these parameters were determined empirically. The parameters were as follows: the window size was 5 by 5; mutation and crossover rates were 0.005 and 0.01, respectively; the maximal stability was 99.99%; the maximal number of generations was 1000. And, the parameters, which control the weight of the each term in Eq. (10) and (11), were set as follows: α_1 is 10; α_2 is 10; α_3 is 10.

The proposed method has been applied to two frames, 18th and 19th, of the sequence, shown in Fig. 2(a) and (b). The results of our proposed methods are shown in Fig. 2(c) and (d). In this sequence, there are five objects: the background, ball, arm, racquet, and hand with the racquet. As show in the results, the proposed method classifies the small difference of the motion filed of the racquet, and hand with the racquet. Moreover, this method classifies the arm and hand under an elbow joint as single segment, regardless of the movement of the shirt. Therefore, it can be seen that our proposed method estimates an accurate motion field and segments a satisfactory label fields.

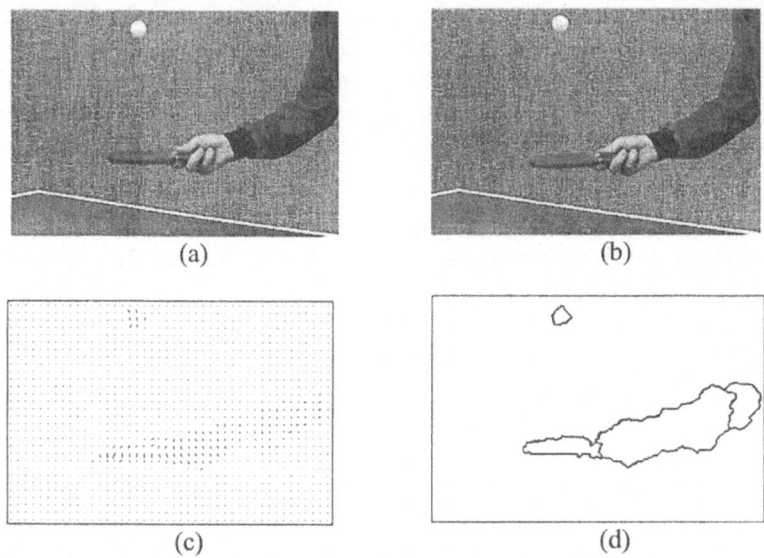

(a)   (b)

(c)   (d)

Fig 2. Segmentation Results of *Table Tennis*. (a) 18th frame. (b) 19th frame (c) estimated motion field (d) segmentation results

5   Conclusion

We presented a framework for simultaneous motion segmentation and estimation using genetic algorithms (GAs). The segmentation label and motion field were modeled by Markov random fields (MRFs), and the energy function of MRFs was optimized by GAs. It was used as optimization algorithm to maximize a posterior probability, which performs segmentation and estimation alternately. Experimental results demonstrated that our proposed method estimates an accurate motion field and segments a satisfactory label fields.

Acknowledgement

This work was supported by the Faculty Research Fund of Konkuk University in 2002.

References

[1]   H. S. Kim, E. Y. Kim and H. J. Kim, "Intelligent Network Camera For Video-Based Security System," *IEEE Symposium on Consumer Electronics*, Melaka, Malaysia, 1999, pp. 99-102

[2]   Michael M. Chang, A. Murat Tekalp, and Ibrahim Sezan, "Simultaneous Motion Estimation and Segmentation," *IEEE Trans. on Image Processing*, Vol. 6, No. 9, pp. 1326-1333, Sept. 1997

[3]   Fabrice Heitz and Patrick Bouthemy, "Motion Estimation and Segmentation Using a Global Bayesian Approach," *IEEE Conference on Acoustics, Speech, and Signal Processing*, Vol. 4, 1990

[4]   F. Moscheni, S. Bhattacnarjee, and Murat Kunt, "Spatiotemporal Segmentation Based on Region Merging," *IEEE Trans. on Pattern Anal. and Machine Intell.*, Vol. 20 No. 9, pp.897-915 Sept. 1998

[5]   H. J. Kim, E. Y. Kim, J. W. Kim, and S. H. Park, "MRF Model based Image Segmentation Using Hierarchical Distributed Genetic Algorithm," *IEE Electronics Letters*, Vol. 34 No. 25, pp. 2394-2395, 1998

[6]   D. E. Goldberg, Genetic Algorithms in Search, Optimization and Machine Learning. Addison Wesley, 1989

Supervised Locally Linear Embedding Algorithm for Pattern Recognition

Olga Kouropteva*, Oleg Okun, and Matti Pietikäinen

Machine Vision Group, Infotech Oulu and Department of Electrical and Information
Engineering
P.O.Box 4500, FIN-90014 University of Oulu, Finland
{kouropte,oleg,mkp}@ee.oulu.fi

Abstract. The dimensionality of the input data often far exceeds their intrinsic dimensionality. As a result, it may be difficult to recognize multidimensional data, especially if the number of samples in a dataset is not large. In addition, the more dimensions the data have, the longer the recognition time is. This leads to the necessity of performing dimensionality reduction before pattern recognition. Locally linear embedding (LLE) [5, 6] is one of the methods intended for this task. In this paper, we investigate its extension, called supervised locally linear embedding (SLLE), using class labels of data points in their mapping into a low-dimensional space. An efficient eigendecomposition scheme for SLLE is derived. Two variants of SLLE are analyzed coupled with a k nearest neighbor classifier and tested on real-world images. Preliminary results demonstrate that both variants yield identical best accuracy, despite of being conceptually different.

1 Introduction

In pattern recognition, raw data acquired by a camera or scanner are often fed as they are or after simple pre-processing to a recognition module. Though being straightforward, this approach suffers from several major drawbacks: a large data dimensionality makes recognition difficult and time-consuming and in combination with a small data set, the effect known as the curse of dimensionality unavoidably lowers the accuracy rate.

To eliminate unfavorable consequences of using multidimensional data for recognition, a kind of dimensionality reduction is wanted. One popular way to do this is to perform a transformation of the original data, lowering their dimension. PCA is undoubtly the most frequently used technique for this purpose. Despite of its simplicity and good results obtained in solving many tasks, PCA is essentially a linear technique, which can make it an inappropriate choice when the data possess intrinsic nonlinearity.

To overcome this problem, a new technique, called locally linear embedding (LLE) has been recently proposed [5, 6], which is able to do nonlinear dimensionality reduction in an unsupervised way. Among its advantages over many other

---

* Olga Kouropteva is grateful to the Infotech Oulu Graduate School.

F.J. Perales et al. (Eds.): IbPRIA 2003, LNCS 2652, pp. 386–394, 2003.

similar methods are 1) good preservation of local geometry of high-dimensional data in a low-dimensional space, 2) only two parameters to be set, 3) a single global coordinate system in the low-dimensional space, and 4) a non-iterative solution scaling well to large data sets due to a sparse eigenvector problem and thus avoiding local minima inherent to many iterative techniques.

For pattern recognition, however, a class membership of each sample in the training set is usually known in advance and this paved the way for the concept of a supervised LLE, where labels are employed [1, 3]. Thus, the dimensionality reduction became both nonlinear and supervised.

In this paper, we apply two variants of the supervised LLE (SLLE), proposed independently in [1] and [3], in combination with a k nearest neighbor classifier to handwritten digit recognition. The purpose is to see what one can reach while carrying out the recognition in a low-dimensional space generated by SLLE. In addition, we derive an efficient eigendecomposition scheme for SLLE.

2   LLE

As an input, LLE takes a set of N D-dimensional vectors (each of which may represent one image, for example) assembled in a matrix X of size DxN. Its output is another set of N d-dimensional vectors ($d \ll D$) assembled in a matrix Y of size dxN. As a result, the kth column vector of Y corresponds to the kth column vector of X. Further we will treat vectors as points either in $\mathbb{R}^D$ or in $\mathbb{R}^d$, depending on the context.

The original, unsupervised LLE consists of three steps:

1. Find K nearest neighbors of each point X_i in $\mathbb{R}^D$, $i = 1, \ldots, N$. The Euclidean distance is used as a similarity measure. Proximity information is collected in a matrix A (of size KxN). The jth column of A stores indices of K points closest to X_j (A_{1j} and A_{Kj} correspond to the highest and lowest proximity, respectively).
2. Assigning weights to pairs of neighboring points. Each weight W_{ij} characterizes a degree of closeness of X_i and X_j. The following optimization task must be solved [5]:

$$\varepsilon(W) = \sum_{i=1}^{N} \| X_i - \sum_{j=1}^{K} W_{ij \in A_i} X_{j \in A_i} \|^2 \, , \qquad (1)$$

subject to constraints $\sum_{j=1}^{K} W_{j \in A_i} = 1$ and $W_{ij} = 0$, if X_i and X_j are not neighbors.
3. Computing the low-dimensional embedding. Since the goal of LLE is to preserve a local linear structure of a high-dimensional space as accurately as possible in a low-dimensional space, weights W_{ij} are kept fixed and the following cost function is minimized [5]:

$$\delta(Y) = \sum_{i=1}^{N} \| Y_i - \sum_{j=1}^{K} W_{ij \in A_i} Y_{j \in A_i} \|^2 \qquad (2)$$

under constraints $\frac{1}{N}\sum_{i=1}^{N} Y_i Y_i^T = I$ (normalized unit covariance) and $\sum_{i=1}^{N} Y_i = 0$ (translation-invariant embedding), which provide a unique solution. To find the matrix Y under these constraints, a new matrix is constructed based on the matrix W: $M = (I - W)^T(I - W)$. LLE then computes the bottom $d + 1$ eigenvectors of M, associated with the $d + 1$ smallest eigenvalues. The first eigenvector (composed of 1's) whose eigenvalue is close to zero is excluded. The remaining d eigenvectors yield the final embedding Y.

3   Supervised LLE

Being unsupervised, the original LLE does not make use of class membership of each point to be projected. To complement the original LLE, a *supervised* LLE was proposed. Its name implies that membership information influences on which points are included in the neighborhood of each point. That is, the supervised LLE employs prior information about a task to perform dimensionality reduction.

So far, two approaches to the supervised LLE have been proposed. The first approach (abbreviated as SLLE1) forms the neighborhood of X_i *only* from points belonging to the same class as that of X_i [3]. The second approach (abbreviated as SLLE2) expands the interpoint distance if the points belong to different classes; otherwise, the distance remains unchanged [1]. Either approach modifies Step 1 of the original LLE, while leaving other two steps unchanged.

3.1   SLLE1

Suppose that the first N_1 columns of X are occupied by the data of the first class, the next N_2 columns are composed of the data of the second class, etc., i.e. data of a certain class are compactly stored in X. This does not affect the algorithm logic, but simplifies explanation. As a result, we can assume that X is composed of submatrices Ξ_i of size DxN_i, $i = 1, \ldots, L$, where L is the number of different classes.

The nearest neighbors for each $X_j \in \Xi_i$ are then sought in Ξ_i only. When applied to all X_j's $\in \Xi_1$, this procedure leads to a construction of the matrix A_1. By repeating the same for $\Xi_2, \ldots, \Xi_L$, matrices $A_2, \ldots, A_L$ are generated. Because each A_i contains indices of points and it was constructed independently of other matrices, it is obvious that several matrices can have identical elements, however, referring to different points.

To distinguish points belonging to different classes, we add a shift to values of all elements of the matrices starting from A_2. The shift value for A_i is computed as $\sum_{j=1}^{i-1} N_j$. Such a procedure guarantees that no two matrices A_i and A_j will make reference to the same point.

Having set elements of all matrices, we then concatenate A_i's into a single matrix A whose size is KxN, where now $N = \sum_{i=1}^{L} N_i$. We also concatenate Ξ_i's into a single matrix X whose size is DxN.

3.2 SLLE2

Another alternative consists of increasing the interpoint distance in $\mathbb{R}^D$ if points belong to different classes. In doing this, different classes can become more spatially separated. It implies that they will remain spatially separated in $\mathbb{R}^d$ after their mapping, i.e. this will facilitate classification in $\mathbb{R}^d$.

Let Ω be the initial matrix of interpoint distances in $\mathbb{R}^D$. Then a modification rule is

$$\Omega = \begin{cases} \Omega, & \text{if points belong to the same class} \\ \Omega + \alpha \max(\Omega), & \text{if points belong to different classes.} \end{cases}$$

That is, the magnitude of a distance expansion is parameterized by α which belongs to [0,1]. The smaller (larger) α, the less (more) class labels affect a choice of the nearest neighbors for each point.

After adjusting distances, K nearest neighbors are sought as in case of the original LLE.

4   Efficient Eigendecomposition for SLLE1

Because M is sparse, eigenvector computation is quite efficient, though for large N's it anyway remains the most time-consuming step. However, it is still possible to exploit the mathematical structure of M (at least in case of SLLE1) to efficiently compute eigendecompositions when N is large.

For SLLE1, M *always* has a block diagonal form, where one block corresponds to one class. That is, in general, if there are L classes, there are L blocks. This is because the data of each class are compactly stored in X so that nonzero entries in M are localized within a range of indices allocated for each class.

Let us consider M (of size $N \times N$) as in (3) when the number of classes is equal to 3 ($N = l + m + n$):

$$M = \begin{pmatrix} A^{l \times l} & 0^{l \times m} & 0^{l \times n} \\ 0^{m \times l} & B^{m \times m} & 0^{m \times n} \\ 0^{n \times l} & 0^{n \times m} & C^{n \times n} \end{pmatrix} , \tag{3}$$

where $A^{l \times l}$, $B^{m \times m}$, $C^{n \times n}$ are $l \times l$, $m \times m$, $n \times n$ blocks, respectively.

We chose three classes only for simplicity of explanation and everything discussed below is equally valid for an arbitrary number of classes.

Let us assume that the eigenproblems for all blocks are written as follows:

$$Ax = \lambda x, \quad By = \mu y, \quad Cz = \nu z , \tag{4}$$

where pairs $(x \, \lambda)$, $(y \, \mu)$ and $(z \, \nu)$ stand for the eigenvectors and eigenvalues for A, B and C, respectively.

Now let us show that the following proposition is true.

Proposition 1. *Given x, y and z as solutions of the respective eigenproblems in (4),*

1. *the vectors* $\tilde{x} = (x^{l \times 1} 0^{(m+n) \times 1})$, $\tilde{y} = (0^{l \times 1} y^{m \times 1} 0^{n \times 1})$, $\tilde{z} = (0^{(l+m) \times 1} z^{n \times 1})$
are the eigenvectors of M,
2. *the eigenvalues of* M *include those of* A, B *and* C.

Proof. Multiply first M by $\tilde{x}$:

$$M\tilde{x} = \begin{pmatrix} A^{l \times l} & 0^{l \times m} & 0^{l \times n} \\ 0^{m \times l} & B^{m \times m} & 0^{m \times n} \\ 0^{n \times l} & 0^{n \times m} & C^{n \times n} \end{pmatrix} \begin{pmatrix} x^{l \times 1} \\ 0^{m \times 1} \\ 0^{n \times 1} \end{pmatrix} = \begin{pmatrix} (Ax)^{l \times 1} \\ 0^{m \times 1} \\ 0^{n \times 1} \end{pmatrix} = \begin{pmatrix} \lambda x^{l \times 1} \\ 0^{m \times 1} \\ 0^{n \times 1} \end{pmatrix} = \lambda \tilde{x} .$$

(5)

Since $M\tilde{x} = \lambda\tilde{x}$, $\tilde{x}$ is the eigenvector of M and λ is the eigenvalue of M. Next, multiply M by $\tilde{z}$:

$$M\tilde{z} = \begin{pmatrix} A^{l \times l} & 0^{l \times m} & 0^{l \times n} \\ 0^{m \times l} & B^{m \times m} & 0^{m \times n} \\ 0^{n \times l} & 0^{n \times m} & C^{n \times n} \end{pmatrix} \begin{pmatrix} 0^{l \times 1} \\ 0^{m \times 1} \\ z^{n \times 1} \end{pmatrix} = \begin{pmatrix} 0^{l \times 1} \\ 0^{m \times 1} \\ (Cz)^{n \times 1} \end{pmatrix} = \begin{pmatrix} 0^{l \times 1} \\ 0^{m \times 1} \\ \nu z^{n \times 1} \end{pmatrix} = \nu \tilde{z} .$$

(6)

Since $M\tilde{z} = \nu\tilde{z}$, $\tilde{z}$ is the eigenvector of M and ν is the eigenvalue of M. Finally, multiply M by $\tilde{y}$:

$$M\tilde{y} = \begin{pmatrix} A^{l \times l} & 0^{l \times m} & 0^{l \times n} \\ 0^{m \times l} & B^{m \times m} & 0^{m \times n} \\ 0^{n \times l} & 0^{n \times m} & C^{n \times n} \end{pmatrix} \begin{pmatrix} 0^{l \times 1} \\ y^{m \times 1} \\ 0^{n \times 1} \end{pmatrix} = \begin{pmatrix} 0^{l \times 1} \\ (By)^{m \times 1} \\ 0^{n \times 1} \end{pmatrix} = \begin{pmatrix} 0^{l \times 1} \\ \mu y^{m \times 1} \\ 0^{n \times 1} \end{pmatrix} = \mu \tilde{y} .$$

(7)

Since $M\tilde{y} = \mu\tilde{y}$, $\tilde{y}$ is the eigenvector of M and μ is the eigenvalue of M. □

It means that M and block matrices composing it have common eigenvalues and the eigenvectors of M can be easily derived from those of the individual blocks by inserting zeroes in appropriate positions.

Remember that we need to compute the bottom $d + 1$ eigenvectors of M corresponding to the $d + 1$ smallest eigenvalues in order to find the embedding. According to [3], the value for d should be *less by one than the number of classes*. This condition leads to the minimal (zero) cost in (2), which we are interested in. However, how to select appropriate eigenvectors if we would like to work with blocks instead of the whole M?

It turned out that the smallest $d + 1$ eigenvalues of M are clustered near zero. When very small eigenvalues are sought as in our case, this may lead to ill-conditioned eigenvalues and eigenvectors, i.e. those sensitive to small perturbations in M. However, even if each individual eigenvector may be sensitive to such perturbations, the eigenspace spanned by *all* the eigenvectors associated with the clustered eigenvalues is not! This fact is confirmed by a large difference in magnitude for the smallest $(d + 1)$th and $(d + 2)$th (and next) eigenvalues of M.

SLLE1, applied to M, yields the bottom $d+1$ piecewise constant eigenvectors similar to pulse functions[1]. Each eigenvector has one "pulse" corresponding to

---

[1] Similar shapes of the eigenvectors were also observed while performing the spectral clustering [4] when the data were optimally partitioned into clusters according to a certain criterion. The respective eigenvalues were clustered as well [7].

the data of a certain class and different "pulses" do not intersect each other since the eigenvectors are mutually orthogonal. It implies that different classes are *linearly* separated in $\mathbb{R}^d$.

Now let us turn attention to the eigenproblems of the individual blocks of M. We figured out that each block has one distinct eigenvalue which is very small compared to others. It came as no surprise that the eigenvector associated with that eigenvalue belonged to the subspace found for M. As a result, we only have to compute *one* eigenvector (corresponding to the smallest eigenvalue) per block in M since the number of classes is equal to that of blocks.

By summarizing the abovementioned, an efficient decomposition for M in case of SLLE1 can be found in block-by-block fashion. The eigenvectors of the blocks are to be padded by zeroes. A precise location for padding is determined by a block index as shown in Proposion 1. In particular, if L is the number of blocks, then the eigenvector taken from the jth ($1 < j < L$) block should be padded by $\sum_{i=1}^{j-1} N_i$ zeroes from the front and $\sum_{i=j+1}^{L} N_i$ zeroes from the end, where N_i is the size of the ith block.

5   Experiments

To compare LLE, SLLE1 and SLLE2, we took all samples of "1", "3", "7", "8", and "9" from the MNIST database of handwritten digits [2]. Because of large memory requirements for LLE and SLLE2, only these five classes were used and the MNIST training/test sets were interchanged.

When picking classes, we aimed at selecting digits of similar shapes, such as 1 and 7 or 3, 8 and 9 in order to make the task of digit recognition more challenging. The training set comprised 5,000 samples whereas the test set consisted of 30,000 samples. Entries to the matrix X were raw grayscale pixel values without pre-processing.

We ran each algorithm in order to map the training set into $\mathbb{R}^d$ with $K=10$ and $d=4$ (because of 5 classes; see Sect. 4). Given such parameter values, *all* samples belonging to the same class were projected to one point in $\mathbb{R}^d$ in case of SLLE1 and SLLE2 ($\alpha = 0.3, \ldots, 1$). For LLE and SLLE2 ($\alpha = 0.1, \ldots, 0.2$), projections formed "clouds".

The samples from the test set were then mapped into $\mathbb{R}^d$ by using the non-parametric generalization [6] with K set to 10. Knowing the coordinates of the test samples in $\mathbb{R}^d$, a k ($k=15$) nearest neighbor classification was carried out in $\mathbb{R}^d$ to classify them (since d is small, such a large value for k almost did not affect the search time, while better classification was achieved). Results of classification are presented in Tables 1-4, where the last columns show the accuracy rates attained in classifying a certain class of digits.

One can see that with given parameters, the original LLE lost to both supervised algorithms when classifying data in the embedded space. The average accuracy rate for SLLE2 varied depending on α and attained the highest value at $\alpha=0.3$, which afterwards did not change as α grew. This highest rate is indentical to that achieved with the *non-parametric* SLLE1. Classification results for

Table 1. Confusion matrix (LLE). Average accuracy rate - 93.83%

	1	3	7	8	9	
1	6,654	27	34	22	5	98.7%
3	19	5,577	37	460	38	91.0%
7	66	11	5,870	22	296	93.7%
8	94	236	36	5,396	89	92.2%
9	17	73	198	95	5,566	93.6%

Table 2. Confusion matrix (identical for SLLE1 and SLLE2 with $\alpha = 0.3, \dots, 1$). Average accuracy rate - 95.86%

	1	3	7	8	9	
1	6,698	12	21	2	9	99.3%
3	149	5,847	49	61	25	95.4%
7	101	2	6,067	1	94	96.8%
8	265	95	16	5,410	65	92.5%
9	110	51	104	15	5,669	95.3%

Table 3. Confusion matrix (SLLE2 with $\alpha = 0.1$). Average accuracy rate - 95.48%

	1	3	7	8	9	
1	6,630	18	69	2	23	98.3%
3	16	5,669	46	315	85	92.5%
7	41	13	5,865	7	339	93.6%
8	63	25	63	5,594	106	95.6%
9	6	46	60	44	5,793	97.4%

Table 4. Confusion matrix (SLLE2 with $\alpha = 0.2$). Average accuracy rate - 94.66%

	1	3	7	8	9	
1	6,683	12	35	2	10	99.1%
3	27	5,675	378	35	16	92.6%
7	58	2	6,087	0	118	97.2%
8	111	35	452	5,218	35	89.2%
9	19	26	235	7	5,662	95.2%

Table 5. Confusion matrix (k nearest neighbors in $\mathbb{R}^D$). Average accuracy rate - 94.02%

	1	3	7	8	9	
1	6,701	15	16	1	9	99.4%
3	99	5,783	89	82	78	94.3%
7	175	4	5,950	3	133	95.0%
8	278	203	45	5,121	204	87.5%
9	63	79	202	19	5,669	93.9%

all methods depend on k. The Euclidean metric, lacking the robustness to noise and outliers, mainly attributed to the large k we used. As to K, only SLLE1 was truly insensitive to its choice while LLE and SLLE2 were completely or partly dependent on K.

Finally, in order to see to what extent the curse of dimensionality was reduced when doing the classification in $\mathbb{R}^d$, the k nearest neighbor classification was also done in $\mathbb{R}^D$ with $k = 15$ (Table 5). It turned out that the average accuracy rate when classifying in the LLE-reduced space was slightly worse than that in the original space. It means that LLE should not be employed for classification (this reasoning was also given in [1]). In contrast, the average accuracy achieved in the SLLE-reduced space was superior to that in $\mathbb{R}^D$, while the time spent was approximately the same in both cases.

6   Conclusion

In this paper, we compared two algorithms (SLLE1 and SLLE2) for supervised dimensionality reduction augmented with the capability to generalize to new data. Since they employ class labels when performing a mapping $\mathbb{R}^D \to \mathbb{R}^d$, they were coupled with a k nearest neighbor classifier in order to test their performance on handwritten digit images. Experiments demonstrated that SLLE and k nearest neighbors outperforms k nearest neighbors operating alone in the original space.

The efficient eigendecomposition scheme was also proposed in case of SLLE1. Such a scheme dramatically reduces memory requirements, since only one block at a time will be processed. It means that a large M is not a restriction for SLLE1. In addition, for large N's such a strategy can lower the time spent on the eigendecomposition.

References

[1] D. de Ridder and R. P. W. Duin. Locally linear embedding for classification. Technical Report PH-2002-01, Delft University of Technology, 2002.
[2] http://yann.lecun.com/exdb/mnist/index.html.

[3] O. Kouropteva, O. Okun, and M. Pietikäinen. Classification of handwritten digits using supervised locally linear embedding algorithm and support vector machine. In *Proc. of the 11th European Symp. on Artificial Neural Networks, Bruges, Belgium*, 2003.

[4] M. Meilă and J. Shi. Learning segmentation by random walks. In T. Leen, T. G. Dietterich, and V. Tresp, editors, *Advances in Neural Information Processing Systems*, volume 13, pages 873–879. MIT Press, Cambridge, MA, 2001.

[5] S. T. Roweis and L. K. Saul. Nonlinear dimensionality reduction by locally linear embedding. *Science*, 290(5500):2323–2326, 2000.

[6] L. K. Saul and S. T. Roweis. Think globally, fit locally: unsupervised learning of nonlinear manifolds. Technical Report MS CIS-02-18, University of Pennsylvania, 2002.

[7] J. Shawe-Taylor and N. Cristianini. One the concentration of spectral properties. In T. G. Dietterich, S. Becker, and Z. Ghahramani, editors, *Advances in Neural Information Processing Systems*, volume 14, pages 511–517. MIT Press, Cambridge, MA, 2002.

Hash–Like Fractal Image Compression with Linear Execution Time

Kostadin Koroutchev and José R. Dorronsoro*

Depto. de Ingeniería Informática and Instituto de Ingeniería del Conocimiento
Universidad Autónoma de Madrid, 28049 Madrid, Spain

Abstract. The main computational cost in Fractal Image Analysis (FIC) comes from the required range-domain full block comparisons. In this work we propose a new algorithm for this comparison, in which actual full block comparison is preceded by a very fast hash–like search of those domains close to a given range block, resulting in a performance linear with respect to the number of pixels. Once the algorithm is detailed, its results will be compared against other state–of–the–art methods in FIC.

1 Introduction

In Fractal Image Compression (FIC) an $N \times N$ gray level image S to be compressed is partioned into a set $\mathcal{R}$ of blocks of $K \times K$ pixels called ranges and for any one R of them a same size image block D taken from a certain codebook set $\mathcal{D}$ is chosen so that $R \simeq D$ in some sense. Typical K values are 16, 8 or 4, while N usually is of the order of 512. To obtain the $\mathcal{D}$ set, baseline FIC first decimates S by averaging every 2×2 block and then somehow selects a set of possibly overlapping $K \times K$ blocks from the decimated image. Several procedures can be used for this; a typical one (and the one used here) is to select all the $K \times K$ blocks with even coordinates of their upper left corner. This basic domain set is finally enlarged with their blocks' isometric images, derived from the 90, 180 and 270 degree rotations and their four symmetries, to arrive at the final domain set $\mathcal{D}$. Now, to compress a given range R_0, a domain D_0 is obtained such that

$$D_0 = argmin_{D \in \mathcal{D}}\{min_{s,o}||R - (sD + o1)||^2\}. \tag{1}$$

The component $sD + o1$ above is the gray level transformation of D, with s the contrast factor and the offset o the luminance shifting. To ensure convergence in the decoding process, s is sometimes limited to the interval $[-1, 1]$. R_0 is then compressed essentially by the triplet (D_0, s_0, o_0), with s_0 and o_0 the minimizing contrast and luminance parameters. In (1) the optimal s_0 and o_0 can be computed quite fast. The $\mathcal{D}$ minimum, however, is very time consuming, as a brute force comparison would require to compare all $|\mathcal{R}| \times |\mathcal{D}|$ blocks, with an overall

---

* With partial support of Spain's CICyT, TIC 01–572 and CAM 02–18.

F.J. Perales et al. (Eds.): IbPRIA 2003, LNCS 2652, pp. 395–402, 2003.

quadratic cost. All the FIC speed up methods try to minimize this block comparison phase. Two basic different approaches for this have been proposed. The first one, classification techniques, first groups the blocks in $\mathcal{R}$ and $\mathcal{D}$ in subsets with common characteristics, and only compares blocks within the same group. On the other hand, in feature vector methods, a certain feature vector is first computed for each block in such a way that full block closeness translates into feature closeness. For a given range, full block comparisons are only perfomed upon the domains in a neighborhood with close features, resulting in a logarithmic time for full domain comparison. The Fisher [1] or Hurtgen [2] schemes are typical classification methods, while Saupe's [5] is the best known feature method. In any case, both approaches are not exclusive and they can be used together (see for instance [4]).

In this work we will present a feature–type approach to FIC acceleration. The key idea is to look at the range–domain matching problem as one of approximate key searching. More precisely, for a given range we have to search in the domain set for one close enough. A naive approach would be to use an entire block as a search key. This is not feasible however, first because an exact range–domain match is highly unlikely, but also because of the very high dimensionality of the key space, in which the domain key subset has a very low density. In this setting, hashing becomes the natural approach to searching and it will be the one followed here. In general terms, once hash keys have been computed for all the domains and these are distributed in a linked hash table, for a given range R to be compressed, an R–dependent ordered hash key subset H_R will be computed and R will be compared only with those domains D whose hash keys $h(D)$ lie in H_R. Moreover, and in order to speed up the search, R will not be compressed in terms of the best matching domain, but we shall use instead one giving a "good enough" match. This domain will, in turn, be moved to the beginning of the hash list, as it is likely to match future ranges. If such a match cannot be obtained, the range R will be then passed to an escape procedure. Here we shall use JPEG DCT on those 8×8 blocks for which at least one 4×4 subblock cannot be compressed. In any case, this clearly degrades compression time, so the escape procedure calls should be quite few.

Besides the usual requirement of a fast computation of the hash function, we also obviously need that closeness of range–domain hash keys translates in relative closeness of actual subblocks. The first requirement can be met by using just a few points of a block B to derive its hash value $h(B)$. These points should be uncorrelated for the hash value to convey a high information content. This is naturally achieved taking the points in the $h(B)$ computation as far as possible within the block. Natural choices are thus the four corner points of the block, to which the center point could be added for a 5–point hash function $h(B)$. In order to meet the second requirement, block closeness, first observe that taking averages and standard errors in the approximation $r_{ij} \simeq s d_{ij} + o$ gives $< r > \simeq s < d > + o$ and $\sigma(r) \simeq |s| \sigma(d)$. Therefore,

$$\frac{r_{ij} - < r >}{\sigma(r)} \simeq \pm \frac{d_{ij} - < d >}{\sigma(d)},$$

which relates approximation parameter estimation to block comparisons. As we shall discuss in the next section, putting these two observations together leads to the hash–like block function $h(B)$ we shall use, namely

$$h(B) = \sum_{h=1}^{H} \left(\left\lfloor \frac{b_{ij}^h - <b>}{\lambda\sigma(b)} + B \right\rfloor \%C \right) C^{h-1} = \sum_{h=1}^{H} b_h C^{h-1}, \qquad (2)$$

where B is a centering parameter and C is taken to cover the range of the fractions in (2). The λ parameter is used to control the spread of the argument of the floor function so that it approximately has a uniform behavior. In other words, (2) should give the base C expansion of $h(B)$ in such a way that the expansion coefficients are approximately uniformly distributed. Concrete choices of B, C and λ will be explained in more detail in the next section, that also describes the algorithm proposed here and its governing parameters, while the third section contains some numerical comparisons between our algorithm and a recent one [4] that combines the well known algorithm of Saupe with mass center features and gives state of the art speed fractal compression. The paper finishes with some conclusions and pointers to further work.

2   Hash Based Block Comparison Algorithm

Assuming that the domain set $\mathcal{D}$ has been fixed, the block hash function (2) is used to distribute the elements in $\mathcal{D}$ in a hash table T, where $T[h]$ points to a linked list containing those $D \in \mathcal{D}$ such that $h(D) = h$. The parameters B and C in (2) are easily established. C is essentially the expected spread of the fraction in (2) while B is chosen to put the modulus operation in the range from 0 to $C - 1$. For instance, if the expected spread is 16, then we take $C = 16$ and $B = 8$. While B and C are not critical, a correct choice of λ is crucial for a good time performance of the algorithm. Recalling the notation

$$b_h = \left\lfloor \frac{b_{ij}^h - <b>}{\lambda\sigma(b)} + B \right\rfloor \%C,$$

notice that if λ is too big, most blocks would give $b_h \simeq B$ values. The resulting hash table would then have just a few, rather long, linked lists, resulting in linear searching times. On the other hand, a too small λ would result in similar domains giving highly different b_h and $h(D)$. Notice that although that should be the desired behavior of an usual hash function, this is not the case here, for we want similar blocks to have similar hash values. On the other hand, as the number of lists is limited, the preceding behavior would result in quite different blocks ending in the same lists. This would result in time consuming full block comparisons between disimilar blocks and lead again to linear searching times. Repeated experiments suggest that general purpose λ values could be 1.5 for 16×16 and 8×8 blocks, and 0.4 for 4×4 blocks.

While a single hash value is computed for each domain, a hash value set H_R will be computed for any range R to be compressed. Notice that an exact match between two values $h(D)$ and $h(R)$ is not likely. The matching domain for R will then be chosen among those D such that $h(D) \in H_R$. The values in the set H_R are given by

$$h_\delta(R) = \sum_{h=1}^{H} \left(\left\lfloor \frac{r_{ij}^h + \delta_h - <r>}{\lambda\sigma(r)} + B \right\rfloor \% C \right) C^{h-1} = \sum_{h=1}^{H} r_h^\delta C^{h-1}, \quad (3)$$

where the displacement $\delta = (\delta_1, \ldots, \delta_H)$ verifies $|\delta_h| \leq \Delta$. The bound Δ also has an impact on the algorithm performance. For instance, it follows from the algorithm below that taking $\Delta = 0$ would result in too many escape calls. On the other hand, a large Δ should obviously increase computation time, while the eventual quality improvements derived from the distant blocks corresponding to large δ would likely be marginal. In any case, our experiments show that Δ and λ are interrelated; in fact, a good choice of λ allows to take $\Delta = 1$. The hash values in H_R are ordered in a spiral like manner. By this we mean that, taking for instance $H = 2$ in (2) and (3), δ would take the values $(0,0), (1,0), (0,1), (-1,0), (0,-1), (1,1), (1,-1)$ and so on.

We can give now the proposed FIC algorithm. We assume the domain set $\mathcal{D}$ given and its hash table T constructed. We also assume that two other parameters d_M and d_C have been set. Let R be the range to be compressed and let $H_R = \{h_1, \ldots, h_M\}$ be its ordered hash set computed according to (3). We define the distance between R and a domain D as

$$dist(R, D) = \sup |r_{ij} - \frac{\sigma(r)}{\sigma(d)}(d_{ij} - <d>) - <r>|$$

where the sup is taken over all the pixels. Since we are forcing a positive contrast factor $\sigma(r)/\sigma(d)$, we shall enlarge the domain set with the negatives of the initial domain blocks. In order to ensure a good decompression, only domains for which $s \leq 1.5$ are considered. The compressing pseudocode is

```
d = infty ; D_R = NULL ;
for i = 1, ..., M :
    for D in T[h_i] :
        d' = dist(R, D) ;
        if d' < d:    D_R = D ; d = d' ;
        if d < d_M:   move D_R to beginning of T[h_i] ;
                      goto end ;
end:
    if d < d_C:   compress R with D_R ;
    else:         escape (R) ;
```

The compression information for a range R consists of an entropy coding of an index to the domain D_R and the parameters s and o; notice that D_R will give a close approximation to R, but not neccessarily an optimal one. On the other hand, R produces a escape call if a close enough domain has not been found.

Fig. 1. Hash (left) and Saupe–MC (right) compressed Lenna images obtained with 1 and 2 seconds execution time repectively. It is arguable that the hash algorithm is "visually" better than MC–Saupe

Following the standard quadtree approach, we will then divide the range in 4 subranges and try to code the subblocks with new domains of suitable size. We shall use this approach in our examples, with 16, 8 and 4 quadtree levels. Notice that a further 2×2 subdivision does not make sense, as the compression code requires by itself about 4 bytes. If a given 4×4 block cannot be compressed, we shall use JPEG DCT on its parent 8×8 block. In any case, these escapes are rare, less than 1 per thousand ranges.

Notice that the preceding code uses two parameters, d_M and d_C, which clearly verify $d_M < d_C$. Ranges are compressed only if the minimal distance d verifies $d < d_C$; a good choice of d_C is about 70% of the full image standard deviation, with 40 being an adequate value. The parameter d_M is critical for the time perfomance of the algorithm, as it stops the time consuming block comparisons as soon as a good enough domain has been found (although, as mentioned before, may be not optimal). Of course, if d_M is too large, it is likely that block comparisons will stop when a not too good domain has been examined. The result will be a fast algorithm but with low quality in the compressed image. On the other hand, a too small d_M will give a good quality for the compressed image (or too many escape calls!) but it will also force possibly too many domains to be examined. A practical estimate is to set d_M to about 70% of the average standard block deviation, with 8 being now an adequate value. We turn next to illustrate the application of hash FIC, comparing its performance with that of the Saupe–MC FIC.

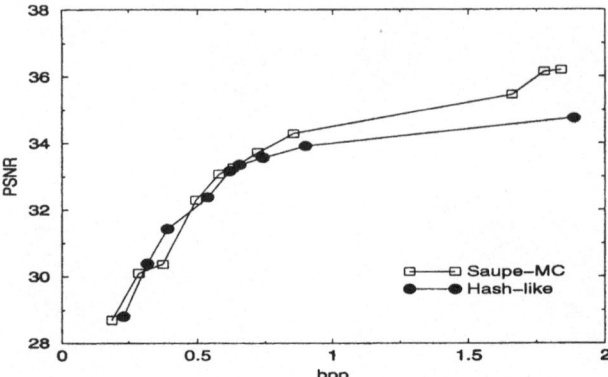

Fig. 2. Rate–distortion curves for the hash (black points) and Saupe–MC algorithms. Both are similar up to 1 bpp, Saupe–MC being better afterwards, because of the earlier saturation of hash FIC (for better comparison, no escape calls have been used)

3   Experimental Results

We will use for our comparisons the well known 512×512 Lenna image whose pixels have a 8 bit gray level. We shall work with a three–level quadtree with range sizes being 16×16, 8×8 and 4×4. When working with, say, 4×4 ranges, we shall use as domains all the 4×4 blocks in the decimated image with even coordinates of their upper left corner. This gives $(128-4+1)^2 \simeq= 15.625$ domains that become 125.000 after isometries are taken into account and 250.000 after adding the negative blocks. The number of hash points H is 5 and the maximum hash key value is thus $16^5 = 2^{20}$, resulting in a hash load factor of about 0.25. As mentioned before, the λ values used are 1.5 for 16×16 and 8×8 blocks, and 0.4 for 4×4 blocks. Other parameters of our hash FIC algorithm are $d_C = 40$, $d_M = 8$, $C = 16$, $B = 8$ and $\Delta = 1$.

There has been much work done to define the "visual quality" of an image in terms of mathematical expressions [3]. We shall not use these measures here, but figure (1), corresponding to 1 second hash and 2 second Saupe–MC execution times, shows that the hash algorithm gives a rather good image quality, arguably better in this case than that of the Saupe–MC algorithm. Anyway, a more quantitative approach to measure the quality of a compression algorithm is to give the evolution with respect to execution time of either the compression rate achieved or the quality of the compressed image. Compresion rate is simply measured by the number of bits per pixel (bpp) in the new image. Image quality is measured by the peak signal to noise ratio PSNR, defined as

$$PSNR = 10 \log_{10} \frac{255^2}{ms\_error}$$

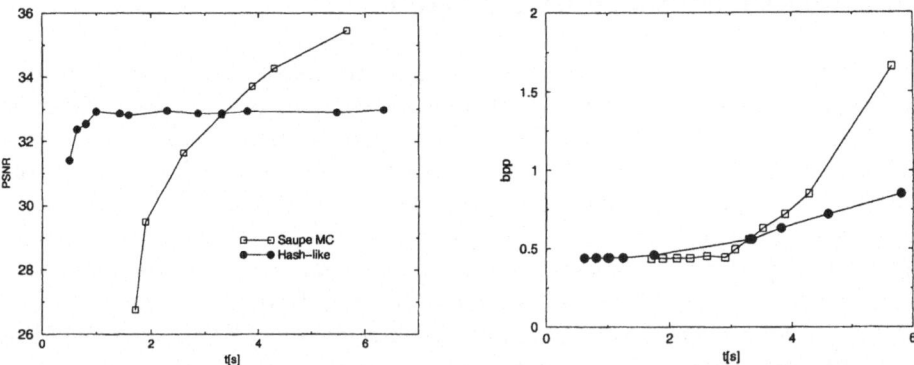

Fig. 3. PSNR and bpp evolutions against execution time for the hash (black points) and Saupe–MC algorithms. Compressions are similar up to 4 seconds with hash giving smaller files after that and Saupe–MC higher PSNR. However the hash algorithm gives better results for small computing times, much better in fact below 2 seconds.

and measured in decibels (dBs). Figure (2) compares the rate–distortion, that is, the PSNR–bpp curves of the hash and Saupe–MC FIC. Clearly the algorithm with a higher curve gives better results. As seen in the figure, both curves are equivalent up to a PSNR of about 33.5. After this value, the Saupe–MC curve is better. In fact, for high image quality compression (and therefore, large comput-ing times), the Saupe–MC algorithm is bound to give somewhat better results. This is due to the fact that Saupe–MC uses an optimal block, while the hash algorithm stops domain searching once a close enough domain has been found. In any case, the well known JPEG algorithm will require smaller compression times than a FIC algorithm for high image quality, so the earlier PSNR satu-ration of the hash algorithm does not have a great practical relevance. Figure (3) gives PSNR and bpp time evolutions of the hash and Saupe–MC algorithms. Execution times are measured in a 800MHz Pentium III machine with 256 MB RAM. A higher PSNR curve is better and it is seen that here again Saupe-MC FIC gives better results in a high quality PSNR range. Notice that, however, be-low 3 seconds (or below a PSNR of 33), the hash PSNR curve is better, keeping in fact the same 33 PSNR down to 1 second. Moreover, while hash PSNR stays above 31 down to 0.5 seconds, Saupe-MC's PSNR drops below 27 even with a 1.5 second execution time. The same figure shows similar compression rates up to 4 seconds. Above 4 seconds hash files are smaller but, as just seen, hash PSNR is lower. It follows from these images that for practical execution times, that is, below 3 seconds, the hash algorithm gives better results than Saupe–MC. Hash results are in fact much better for small execution times and lower quality ranges (as mentioned in [1] low quality image compression may be the most promising image processing area for FIC methods).

4   Conclusions and Further Work

To achieve linear execution time with respect to image size a FIC algorithm should make an average of $O(1)$ full domain comparisons per each range to be compressed. In ordinary key search, hash algorithms can attain this performance and, ideally, the hash FIC method presented here could do so. In our experiments, typical average values for this are 3.9 domain comparisons per range when $PSNR \simeq 33$ and 3.1 comparisons when $PSNR \simeq 27$. The results shown here do support a linear execution time claim, at least in the low PSNR range, where our algorithm can be about 5 times faster than other state of the art acceleration schemes (excluding preparation and I/O times, it could be up to 10 times faster). Recall that as the hash algorithm does not guarantee using optimal domains, it is bound to give lower image quality for longer execution times. It is thus more appropriate to use it in the lower-quality range. There, the time performance of hash FIC makes it feasible to use it in real time compression. Interesting application areas for this could be the compression of images transmitted over mobile phones and even moving image compression, where foreground images would be used for domain codebooks. Another topic being considered is to introduce different block comparisons to get better image quality. In fact, a common problem of FIC algorithms is the presence of visual artifacts in the reconstructed image because of gray level overflows due to the linear nature of their range–domain approximation. This could be improved using non linear, saturating block comparison methods, for which hash FIC is well suited. The price to pay is, of course, longer execution times. With hash FIC, however, a non linear approach could be pursued, given the efficiency of the hash domain search. These and other application areas are currently being researched.

References

[1] Y. Fisher, *Fractal Image Compression–Theory and Application*. New York: Springer–Verlag 1994.
[2] B. Hurtgen and C. Stiller, "Fast hierarchical codebook search for fractal coding of still images", in *Proc. EOS/SPIE Visual Communications PACS Medical Applications '93*, Berlin, Germany, 1993.
[3] M. Miyahara, K. Kotani and V. R. Algazi, "Objective picture quality scale (PQS) for image coding", *IEEE Trans. in Communications*, vol. 46, pp. 1215–1226, 1998.
[4] M. Polvere and M. Nappi, "Speed up in fractal image coding: comparison of methods", *IEEE Trans. Image Processing*, vol. 9, pp. 1002–1009, June 2000.
[5] D. Saupe, "Fractal image compression by multidimensional nearest neighbor search", in Proc. DCC'95 Data Compression Conf., Mar. 1995.

Learning of Stochastic Context-Free Grammars by Means of Estimation Algorithms and Initial Treebank Grammars*

Diego Linares[1], Joan-Andreu Sánchez[2],
José-Miguel Benedí[2], and Francisco Torres[2]

[1] Pontificia Universidad Javeriana - Cali
Calle 18 No. 118-250 Av. Cañasgordas. Cali (Colombia)
[2] Depto. Sistemas Informáticos y Computación, Universidad Politécnica de Valencia
Camino de Vera s/n, 46071 Valencia (Spain)
{dlinares,jandreu,jbenedi,ftgoterr}@dsic.upv.es

Abstract. In this paper we study the problem of learning of Stochastic Context-Free Grammars by means of estimation algorithms. In these algorithms, which are based on a gradient descendent technique, the initial model play an important role. Here we explore the use of initial SCFG obtained from a treebank corpus. Experiments on the UPenn Treebank corpus are reported.

1 Introduction

Over the last few years, there has been increasing interest in Stochastic Context-Free Grammars (SCFGs) for use in different tasks within the framework of Syntactic Pattern Recognition [1, 6, 8] and Computational Linguistics [5]. The reason for this can be found in the capability of SCFGs to model the long-term dependencies established between the different linguistic units of a sentence, and the possibility of incorporating the stochastic information that allows for an adequate modeling of the variability phenomena that are always present in complex problems. Thus, SCFGs have been successfully used on limited-domain tasks of low perplexity. However, the general-purpose SCFGs work poorly on large vocabulary tasks. One of the main obstacles to using these models is the learning of SCFGs for complex real tasks.

Two aspects must be considered with regard to the learning of SCFGs: first, the learning of the structural component, that is, the rules of the grammar, and second, the estimation of the stochastic component, that is, the probabilities of the rules. Although interesting Grammatical Inference techniques have been proposed elsewhere for learning the rules of the grammar, computational restrictions limit their use in complex real tasks. Taking into account the existence of robust techniques for the automatic estimation of the probabilities of the SCFGs

---

* This work has been partially supported by the Spanish CICYT under contract (TIC2002/04103-C03-03)

F.J. Perales et al. (Eds.): IbPRIA 2003, LNCS 2652, pp. 403–410, 2003.

from a sample [1, 6, 9, 12], other possible approaches for the learning of SCFGs by means of a probabilistic estimation process have been explored [11].

All of these estimation algorithms are based on gradient descendent techniques and it is well-known that their behavior depends on the appropriate choice of the initial grammar. When the SCFG is in Chomsky Normal Form, the usual method for obtaining this initial grammar is a heuristic initialization based on an exhaustive ergodic model [6, 9, 11]. This solution is easy to implement but it do not use any structural information of the sample.

When a treebank corpus is available, it is possible to obtain directly an initial SCFG from the syntactic structures which are present in the treebank corpus [3].

In this paper, the underlying conjecture is that the structural component of SCFGs is very important for the learning of stochastic models. In this work, we explore this possibility and we compare the obtained grammar with reestimated ergodic models.

Experiments with the UPenn Treebank Corpus were carried out in order to test the feasibility of this conjecture.

2   Probabilistic Estimation of Stochastic Context-Free Grammars

A *Context-Free Grammar* (CFG) G is a four-tuple (N, Σ, P, S), where N is a finite set of non-terminal symbols, Σ is a finite set of terminal symbols, P is a finite set of rules, and S is the initial symbol. A CFG is in Chomsky Normal Form (CNF) if the rules are of the form $A \to BC$ or $A \to a$ ($A, B, C \in N$ and $a \in \Sigma$). We say that the CFG is in General Format (GF) if no restriction is imposed on the format of the rules.

A *Stochastic Context-Free Grammar* (SCFG) G_s is defined as a pair (G, q), where G is a CFG and $q : P \to]0, 1]$ is a probability function of rule application such that $\forall A \in N: \sum_{\alpha \in (N \cup \Sigma)^+} q(A \to \alpha) = 1$. We define the *probability* of the derivation d_x of the string x, $\Pr(x, d_x \mid G_s)$ as the product of the probability application function of all the rules used in the derivation d_x. We define the *probability* of the string x as: $\Pr(x \mid G_s) = \sum_{\forall d_x} \Pr(x, d_x \mid G_s)$, and the *probability of the best derivation* of the string x as: $\widehat{\Pr}(x \mid G_s) = \max_{\forall d_x} \Pr(x, d_x \mid G_s)$.

Two important problems which are related to SCFG are the calculation of the probability of a string and the estimation of the probabilities of the grammar from a sample. Different algorithms exist for dealing with each problem, and the election of the appropriate algorithm depends on the format of the SCFG. Now, we describe the computation of the probability of a string since this computation is used in the estimation problem.

2.1   Computation of the Probability of a String with a SCFG

When the SCFG is in CNF, the computation of the probability of a string can be solved efficiently using the *inside* algorithm [6]. In addition, this algorithm can be easily modified in order to calculate the probability of the best derivation of a string and the best derivation itself. We call this algorithm the Viterbi algorithm. The time complexity of the *inside* and Viterbi algorithms are $O(|P||x|^3)$, where x is the string to be parsed.

When the grammar is in GF, we can use the Earley algorithm [4]. This algorithm constructs a set of lists $L_0, \ldots L_{|x|}$, where L_i keeps track of all possible derivations that are consistent with the input string until x_i. An *item* is an element of a list and has the form ${}_k^j A \to \lambda \cdot \mu$, where j is the current position in the input and is thereby in the L_j list, k is the position in the input when the item was selected for expanding A, the dot indicates that λ accepts $x_{k+1} \ldots x_j$ and that μ is pending for expansion. This item records the history: $S \overset{*}{\Rightarrow} x_1 x_2 \ldots x_k A \delta \overset{*}{\Rightarrow} x_1 x_2 \ldots x_k \lambda \mu \delta \overset{*}{\Rightarrow} x_1 x_2 \ldots x_k x_{k+1} \ldots x_j \mu \delta$.

The probabilistic version [12] attaches to each item a probability called *inner probability* which is noted as $\gamma({}_i^j A \to \lambda \cdot \mu)$. This value represents the sum of probabilities of all partial derivations that begin with the item ${}_i A \to \cdot \lambda \mu$ and end with the item ${}_i^j A \to \lambda \cdot \mu$ generating the substring $x_{i+1} \ldots x_j$.

An item is added to a list L_j by means of three operations: *predictor, scanner* and *completer*. We propose the following definitions that permit each operation to be applied only once for each list, except for the *completer* that is applied once for each previous item:

$$predictor(L_j) = \{{}_j^j B \to \cdot\sigma \mid B \to \sigma \in P, \ {}_k^j A \to \lambda \cdot C\mu \in L_j, C \overset{*}{\Rightarrow}_L B, 0 \le k \le j\}$$

$$scanner(L_j) = \{{}_k^j A \to \lambda x_j \cdot \mu \mid {}_k^{j-1} A \to \lambda \cdot x_j \mu \in L_{j-1}, \ 0 \le k < j\}$$

$$completer(L_j) = \{{}_k^j A \to \lambda B \cdot \mu \mid {}_k^i A \to \lambda \cdot B\mu \in L_i, {}_i^j C \to \sigma \cdot \in L_j, B \overset{*}{\Rightarrow}_U C, i < j\}$$

where $A \overset{*}{\Rightarrow}_L B$ is the reflexive, transitive closure relation of the left-corner relation $A \to_L B$ and $A \overset{*}{\Rightarrow}_U B$ is the reflexive, transitive closure relation of the unit production relation $A \to_U B$ [12].

To avoid an infinite partial derivation produced by unit productions, the algorithm uses the reflexive transitive closure matrix $R_U(G) = \Pr(A \overset{*}{\Rightarrow}_U B)$ which is computed from the probabilistic unit production relation $P_U(G) = P(A \to B)$, and in such case $R_U(G) = (I - P_U)^{-1}$ when the grammar is consistent [5].

The *inner* probability for each item is calculated using the following recursive definition:

$$\gamma({}_j^j A \to \cdot\mu) = q(A \to \mu), \ 0 \le i < n \ (predictor)$$

$$\gamma({}_k^j A \to \lambda\delta \cdot \mu) = \begin{cases} \gamma({}_k^{j-1} A \to \lambda \cdot \delta\mu) & \text{if } \delta = x_j(scanner) \\ \sum_{i=k}^{j-1} \gamma({}_k^i A \to \lambda \cdot \delta\mu) \sum_C R_U(\delta, C)\gamma({}_i^j C \to \sigma \cdot) & \text{if } \delta \in N(completer) \end{cases}$$

This way, $\Pr(x|G_s) = \gamma({}_0^n \$ \to S\cdot)$, where $\$ \to S$ is a dummy rule which is not in P. The expression $q(\$ \to S)$ is always one and it is used for initialization. The time complexity of the algorithm is $O(|P||x|^3)$ and its spatial complexity is $O(|P||x|^2)$ [12].

The best derivation and its probability (usually called *Viterbi* probability) can be calculated in a way similar to the *inner* probability. The changes necessary for computing this new value are the following: attach to each item a new value in order to accumulate *Viterbi* probability, use maximization instead of sums in the *completer* operation and use $\widehat{R}_U$ matrix instead of R_U matrix. $\widehat{R}_U$ calculates the best partial derivation probability between any pair of non-terminals that are in a unit-production relation and is defined as $\widehat{R}_U(A \overset{*}{\Rightarrow} B) = max(p(A = B), p(A \rightarrow B), max_{\forall C}(p(A \rightarrow C)\widehat{R}_U(C, B)))$. For tree extraction we need to create a new matrix that stores the argument that maximizes $\widehat{R}_U$.

2.2 Probabilistic Estimation of a SCFG

In order to estimate the probabilities of a SCFG, it is necessary to define both a framework to carry out the optimization process and an objective function to be optimized. In this work, we have considered the framework of Growth Transformations [2] in order to optimize the objective function.

In reference to the function to be optimized, we will consider the likelihood of a sample which is defined as: $\Pr(\Omega \mid G_s) = \prod_{x \in \Omega} \Pr(x \mid G_s)$, and the likelihood of the best derivation of a sample which is defined as: $\widehat{\Pr}(\Omega \mid G_s) = \prod_{x \in \Omega} \widehat{\Pr}(x \mid G_s)$, where Ω is a multiset of strings.

Given an initial SCFG G_s and a finite training sample Ω, the iterative application of the following function can be used in order to modify the probabilities $(\forall (A \rightarrow \alpha) \in P)$:

$$q'(A \rightarrow \alpha) = \frac{\sum_{x \in \Omega} \frac{1}{\Pr(x|G_s)} \sum_{\forall d_x} N(A \rightarrow \alpha, d_x)\Pr(x, d_x \mid G_s)}{\sum_{x \in \Omega} \frac{1}{\Pr(x|G_s)} \sum_{\forall d_x} N(A, d_x) \Pr(x, d_x \mid G_s)} . \tag{1}$$

The expression $N(A \rightarrow \alpha, d_x)$ represents the number of times that the rule $A \rightarrow \alpha$ has been used in the derivation d_x, and $N(A, d_x)$ is the number of times that the non-terminal A has been derived in d_x. This transformation optimizes the function $\Pr(\Omega \mid G_s)$. A similar transformation to (1) can be defined in order to optimize the likelihood of the best derivation of the sample. In such case the number of times that each rule has been used in the best parsing is used.

Algorithms which are based on transformation (1) are gradient descendent algorithms and, therefore, the choice of the initial grammar is a fundamental aspect since it affects both the maximum achieved and the convergence process. Different methods have been proposed elsewhere in order to obtain the initial grammar.

When the grammar is in CNF, transformation (1) can be adequately formulated and it becomes the well-known IO algorithm [6]. When the likelihood of the best parse of the sample is optimized, the scores obtained with the Viterbi algorithm can be used (VS algorithm). If a bracketed corpus is available, these algorithms can be adequately modified in order to take advantage of this information [9]. The initial grammar for these estimation algorithms is typically constructed in a heuristic fashion from a set of terminals and a set of non-terminals. The most common way is to construct a model with the maximum number of rules which can be formed with a given number of non-terminals and a given number of terminals [6]. Then, initial probabilities which are randomly generated are attached to the rules. This heuristic has been successfully used for real tasks [11]. However, we think that the number of non-terminals is a critical point which leaves room for improvements.

When the grammar is in GF, transformation (1) can be adequately computed by using an Earley-based algorithm [12]. When the likelihood of the best parse of the sample is being optimized, the Viterbi version of the Earley algorithm (described above) can be used to obtain the scores. In these algorithms, the initial grammar can be obtained from a treebank corpus. Each sentence in the corpus is explored and each syntactic structure is considered as a grammar rule. In addition, the frequency of appearance is adequately maintained and, at the end, these values are conveniently normalized. These initial grammars have been successfully used for real tasks [3], since they allow us to parse real test sets. However, our hypothesis in this work is that these grammars can be conveniently estimated in order to improve their performance

3   Experiments with the UPenn Treebank Corpus

The corpus used in the experiments was UPenn Treebank Corpus[1] [7]. This corpus consists of English texts collected from the Wall Street Journal from editions of the late eighties. It contains approximately one million words distributed in 25 directories. This corpus was automatically labelled, analyzed and manually checked as described in [7]. There are two kinds of labelling: a part of speech (POStag) labelling and a syntactic labelling. The size of the vocabulary is greater than 49,000 different words, the POStag vocabulary is composed of 45 labels[2] and the syntactic vocabulary is composed of 14 labels.

Given the time complexity of the algorithms to be used, we decided to work only with the POStag labelling, since the vocabulary of the original corpus was too·large for the experiments to be carried out. The corpus was divided into sentences according to the bracketing. For the experiments, directories 00 to 20 were used for training but without considering sentences of more than 50 words in the training set. This way, the number of sentences was 41,315 (98.2% over complete training) and the number of words was 959,390 (95.6% over complete training). Directories 23 to 24 were used for testing (3,762 sentences and 89,537 words). The test set perplexity[3] with 3-grams and linear interpolation was 9.39.

In the following section, we experimentally study and compare the performance of the VS estimation algorithm, both stochastically and structurally, for SCFG in CNF and in GF.

3.1   Experiments with SCFG in CNF

The parameters of an initial SCFG in CNF were estimated using the VS algorithm. The initial grammar had the maximum number of rules which can be

---

[1] Release 2 of this data set can be obtained from the Linguistic Data Consortium with Catalogue number LDC94T4B (http://www.ldc.upenn.edu/ldc/noframe.html).

[2] There are 48 labels defined in [7]; however, some of them do not appear in the corpus.

[3] The values were computed using the software tool described in [10] (Release 2.04 is available in http://svr-www.eng.cam.ac.uk/~ prc14/toolkit.html).

Table 1. Test set perplexity (tsp), precision (prec.), recall and size of the estimated grammar obtained when the VS algorithm was used to estimate a SCFG
with a different number of non-terminals ($|N|$)

$|N|$	tsp	prec.	recall	size
14	20.08	27.51	22.70	195
20	20.37	20.61	17.02	255
25	17.62	29.89	24.66	407
30	17.54	27.93	23.05	367
35	16.91	27.51	22.76	600

created with a given number of non-terminal symbols and 45 terminal symbols
(the number of POStags).

In previous works [11], the number of non-terminals was chosen according to
the number of syntactic tags defined in [7]. However, we do not think that this
number of non-terminals is very realistic. Our hypothesis is that better models
can be obtained by increasing the number of non-terminals. In order to test this
hypothesis, we increased this value progressively and the results[4] can be seen in
Table 1.

As we conjectured, the test set perplexity of the model, in general, tended
to decrease as the value of N increased for both estimation algorithms. It is
important to note that time complexity of the estimation algorithms increases
linearly with this value. We can see that the precision and recall were very
bad. This may be due to the fact that this algorithm is very sensitive to the
initialization, and lots of important rules disappeared in the estimation process.
Finally, it can be seen that the size of the final models increased with N.

It is important to remark that other estimation algorithms obtained better
results (the bracketed version of the IO algorithm obtained a test set perplexity of
10.22). This algorithms are more powerful since they consider more information
than the VS algorithm.

3.2   Experiments with Treebank Grammars

We now describe the experiments which were carried out with SCFG in GF.
Given that the UPenn Treebank corpus was used, a treebank grammar was
obtained from the syntactic information. The corpus was adequately filtered in
order to use only the POStags and the syntactic tags defined in [7]. However, 12
additional syntactic labels with high frequency of appearance were found, and
they were also considered. Probabilities were attached to the rules according to
the frequency of each one in the training corpus. This initial grammar was tested
on the test set corpus and the results can be seen in Table 2.

Note that good test set perplexity was obtained and that the precision was
also good. Also note that the number of rules was very large. However, lot of the

---

[4] The precision and recall have been computed using the software developed by
S. Sekine and M. Collins (http://cs.nyu.edu/cs/projects/proteus/evalb).

Table 2. Test set perplexity (tsp), precision (prec.), recall, size of the estimated grammar and number of rejected sentences (rej.) obtained with treebank grammars and estimated grammars.

Absolute	Initial treebank grammar					Reestimated treebank grammar				
frequency	tsp	prec.	recall	size	rej.	tsp	prec.	recall	size	rej.
≥ 1	12.39	76.21	70.55	15,604	0	10.87	74.53	67.67	7,602	5
≥ 2	12.47	75.70	70.77	6,637	4	10.93	73.22	67.62	3,981	4

rules can be deleted without affecting the results [3]. Table 2 shows the results when we deleted the rules with absolute frequency greater than one. We can see that the results were good enough and that the number of rules decreased less than half.

Then, these initial grammars were estimated using the Viterbi version of the Earley algorithm (described above). The results can be seen in Table 2.

There was a significant improvement in the test set perplexity of about 12.3%, which confirms our hypothesis that the initial treebank grammar could be stochastically improved. In addition, there was an important reduction in the size of the model. An interesting aspect to be noted is that the precision and recall decreased slightly. This may be due to the fact that, during the estimation process, some rules disappeared, and the parsing tree of some strings also changed.

Finally, when VS algorithm with SCFG in CNF and the VS algorithm with treebank grammars in GF are compared, there was substantial improvement shown by the latter. This reveals that the initialization step using the first algorithm is not well solved, and more effort should be made in this direction.

4   Conclusions

In conclusion, we can see that in classical SCFG estimation algorithms, the initial model plays a very important role. If the SCFG is in CNF, the results obtained with ergodic models can be substantially improved by choosing an appropriate number of non-terminals. If the SCFG is in GF, the initial grammar can be obtained from treebank corpora. These initial models can be improved by reestimating their probabilities with classical estimation algorithms. The results obtained by these models are very good since they incorporate very rich syntactic information.

For future work, we propose using an estimation algorithm which is similar to the bracketed version of the IO algorithm for SCFG in GF. In addition, we propose studying the use of this sort of models for language modeling in real tasks.

References

[1] J. K. Baker. Trainable grammars for speech recognition. In Klatt and Wolf, editors, *Speech Communications for the 97th Meeting of the Acoustical Society of America*, pages 31–35. Acoustical Society of America, June 1979.

[2] L. E. Baum. An inequality and associated maximization technique in statistical estimation for probabilistic functions of markov processes. *Inequalities*, 3:1–8, 1972.

[3] E. Charniak. Tree-bank grammars. Technical report, Departament of Computer Science, Brown University, Providence, Rhode Island, January 1996.

[4] J. Earley. An efficient context-free parsing algorithm. *Communications of the ACM*, 8(6):451–455, 1970.

[5] F. Jelinek and J. D. Lafferty. Computation of the probability of initial substring generation by stochastic context-free grammars. *Computational Linguistics*, 17(3):315–323, 1991.

[6] K. Lari and S. J. Young. The estimation of stochastic context-free grammars using the inside-outside algorithm. *Computer, Speech and Language*, 4:35–56, 1990.

[7] M. P. Marcus, B. Santorini, and M. A. Marcinkiewicz. Building a large annotated corpus of english: the penn treebank. *Computational Linguistics*, 19(2):313–330, 1993.

[8] H. Ney. Stochastic grammars and pattern recognition. In P. Laface and R. De Mori, editors, *Speech Recognition and Understanding. Recent Advances*, pages 319–344. Springer-Verlag, 1992.

[9] F. Pereira and Y. Schabes. Inside-outside reestimation from partially bracketed corpora. In *Proceedings of the 30th Annual Meeting of the Association for Computational Linguistics*, pages 128–135. University of Delaware, 1992.

[10] R. Rosenfeld. The cmu statistical language modeling toolkit and its use in the 1994 arpa csr evaluation. In *ARPA Spoken Language Technology Workshop*, Austin, Texas, USA, 1995.

[11] J. A. Sánchez and J. M. Benedí. Learning of stochastic context-free grammars by means of estimation algorithms. In *Proc. EUROSPEECH'99*, volume 4, pages 1799–1802, Budapest, Hungary, 1999.

[12] A. Stolcke. An efficient probabilistic context-free parsing algorithm that computes prefix probabilities. *Computational Linguistics*, 21(2):165–200, 1995.

Computer-Aided Prostate Cancer Detection in Ultrasonographic Images*

Rafael Llobet, Alejandro H. Toselli, Juan C. Perez-Cortes, and Alfons Juan

Instituto Tecnologico de Informatica
Universidad Politecnica de Valencia
Camino de Vera, s/n 46071 Valencia Spain
{rllobet,ahector,jcperez,ajuan}@iti.upv.es

Abstract. Prostate cancer is one of the most frequent cancer in men and a major cause of mortality in developed countries. Detection of the prostate carcinoma at an early stage is crucial for a succesfull treatment. In this paper, a method for analysis of transrectal ultrasonography images aimed at computer-aided diagnosis of prostate cancer is presented. Althogh the task is extremely difficult due to a problem of imperfect supervision, we have obtained promising results indicating that valid information for the diagnostic is present in the images. Two classifiers based on k-Nearest Neighbours and Hidden Markov Models are compared.

1 Introduction

Prostate cancer is one of the leading causes of cancer-related mortality in men and a major health issue. Early detection of the prostate carcinoma is extremely important as it is only curable at an early stage.

To distinguish benign prostate diseases from malignant tumors, three diagnostic tests are routinely used in the urology clinic: Digital Rectal Examination (DRE), Prostate Specific Antigen level determination (PSA) and Transrectal Ultrasonography imaging (TRUS). However, the combination of these tests lacks accuracy, especially when early detection of prostate carcinoma is pursued to facilitate treatment. To compensate for this lack of accuracy, it is common practice to perform several TRUS-guided biopsies and histologic analysis of the suspicious tissues. Unfortunately, visual inspection alone of the ultrasonographic image does not help much in the localization of malignant tissue and, in consequence, many painful biopsies are often needed to get reliable results during histologic analysis.

In some cases, even when these diagnostic tests have been carried out and several biopsies have been performed, some incipient cancers are not detected when none of the punctions reaches the precise place where the tumor is present.

---

* This work has been partially supported by the Valencian OCYT under grant CTIDIA/2002/80 and by the Spanish CICYT under grant TIC2000-1703-CO3-01.

A possible way to improve this TRUS-guided biopsying process is to use computer-aided analysis of the ultrasonographic image. In fact, computer analysis of ultrasonographic images has a number of successful precedents in analysis and diagnosis of many pathologies, including liver [13], lung [5] and breast anomalies [9, 14]. The basic idea is to develop a computer-aided tool capable of highlighting the areas most likely to contain cancer cells. The physician would then be able to perform less biopsies while keeping the same risk of a false negative, or carry out the same number of extractions with a lower risk of an actual tumor remaining undetected. Following this idea, limited yet promising qualitative results have been already reported by de la Rosette et. al. [4], using textural features and decision trees in a supervised learning setting.

In this paper, a system for computer-aided, TRUS-based detection of prostate cancer is presented. It was developed in collaboration with the Urology Department of the Hospital "La Fe" in Valencia (Spain), where a corpus of 4944 images was acquired from 1648 biopsy sessions (3 images per session) involving 301 patients (5 to 6 biopsies per patient). During its development, we realized that our task is extremely difficult due to a problem of *imperfect supervision*. Urologists cannot label pixels as positive or negative by analyzing the images at the micro-texture level, and histologic analysis of the extracted tissue can hardly be transformed into a map of pixel labels. Thus we are forced to use a single, imperfect label for all pixels in the biopsied area. Despite this problem, we have obtained very promising results indicating that discrimination between cancerous and non-cancerous tissue is possible to a certain non-negligible degree.

2   Corpus and Protocol

A TRUS-guided biopsy session is routinely carried out at the Hospital "La Fe" for all patients suffering symptoms commonly associated to a prostatic lesion, i.e. a high PSA value and/or anomalous DRE results. A transrectal ultrasonographic probe is inserted to display cross-sectional echographic images of the prostate. When a suspicious area is found, a biopsy needle attached to the probe is triggered for tissue extraction and later histologic analysis. Often, no particularly suspicious areas are found, and a number of biopsies (usually six: three for each lobe) are performed by uniformly scanning the whole gland.

A total of 301 TRUS-guided biopsy sessions were digitally recorded between February 2000 and February 2001, each session involving a different patient and 5 to 6 biopsies. From the set of 301 sessions, 12 with cancer at an advanced stage of development were then discarded, as on the one hand this type of cancer can be easily detected by an urologist by means of traditional tests and on the other hand images with this type of cancer present a different texture than those with incipient cancer (which actually is the one we are interested in) and consequently could increase the uncertainty of the classifier. Finally, a total of 289 sessions involving 1531 biopsies remained.

Five seconds of echographic images before and after each biopsy (puncture) were acquired at a rate of 5 frames per second. Images were acquired at a reso-

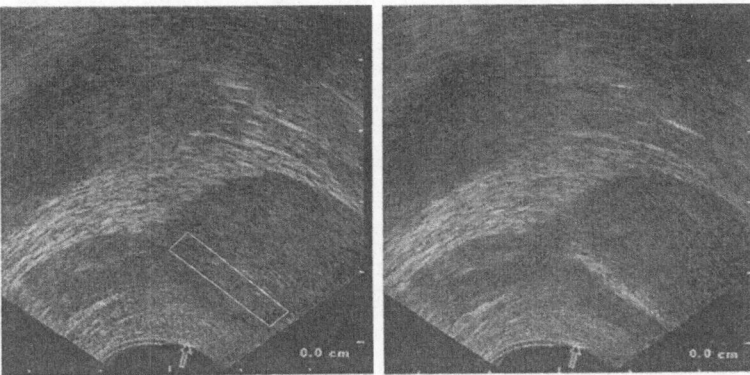

Fig. 1. Images of the same biopsy taken 400ms before puncturing (left) and at the precise moment of puncture (right)

lution of 768×576 pixels and a depth of 8 bits per pixel, using a conventional frame grabber connected to an interlaced video output of a ultrasonograph device. Even-numbered rows and columns were discarded to avoid interlacing artifacts and maintain the original aspect ratio. Therefore, the images actually recorded have a resolution of 384×288 pixels. From the 50 images recorded for each biopsy, 3 of them uniformly distributed in the 2 seconds period previous to the puncture were selected. A total of 1531 individual biopsies were recorded in the 289 sessions, which gives $1531 \cdot 3 = 4593$ images in the corpus.

The two extreme points of the cylinder from where tissue was extracted were manually marked in each biopsy from the first image where the needle completely appears, defining a rectangle. Because of no significant patient movement is produced during de biopsying process, the defined rectangle is employed to label the pixels in the previous images according to the results of the histologic examination. In Figure 1, two images of a biopsy are shown. The image at the left is one of the three stored into the database, along with the coordinates of the polygon delimited by the marked points shown superimposed.

Unfortunately, although the histologic analysis reveals not only if there are malignant cells in the cylinder, but also where they are, it was not possible in our real-world long-term clinical setting to set up a practical and reliable method to physically label the extracted tissue and then map physical labels into pixel labels. Therefore, a large proportion of the pixels labeled as cancerous represent in fact normal tissue that happens to be in the same cylinder as a tumor. However, a pixel labeled as normal always corresponds to non-malignant tissue.

From the whole set of 289 patients, 202 were randomly selected to compose the training set, and the other 87 formed the test set. The selection was performed so that similar *a priori* probabilities were obtained for both sets (13.40% of cancer results in the training set and 12.94% in the test set). This operation was repeated 10 times, which gives 10 different training-test partitions. All the experiments were carried out over the 10 pairs of sets. The average of the resulting values obtained in the different experiments over each set is done as a final result. The number of pixels inside the labelled rectangles of the training sets was around $2,500,000$. In the test sets, the rectangles contained a little more than one million pixels.

3   Approach

3.1   Feature Extraction

Most approaches to tissue segmentation in medical images in the literature use texture descriptors as Spatial Gray Level Dependence Matrices (SGLDM, also known as Coocurrence Matrices) [10], Fractal features [3], and other kinds of textural features [7]. In this work we have tested SGLDM descriptors and also simple gray-map features.

Among the SGLDM descriptors defined in the original work by Haralick et al. [6], we have used the following ones: Angular Second Moment, Contrast, Correlation, Variance, Inverse Difference Moment, Sum Average, Sum Variance, Sum Entropy, Entropy, Difference Variance and Difference Entropy.

A number of different experiments were performed varying the angle and distance parameters, the window size and the number of gray levels on the image (reduced from the original 256 levels by means of vector quantization). In Section 4, the results of the best combinations of parameters are presented in detail.

A more basic kind of features were also tested as a baseline: gray level maps. Each pixel is simply represented by a vector with the gray level values of the nearby pixels as components. Square windows of size $w \times w$ were used as neighborhoods, so each pixel gave rise to a w^2-dimensional vector.

3.2 k-NN Classification

The k-Nearest Neighbor (k-NN) rule is a powerful and robust classification method with well-known theoretical properties and ample experimental success in many pattern recognition tasks. The major drawback often cited for this method is the computational cost. This could be a serious problem in this work due to the huge ammount of pixels (each of them represented in a 30-dimensional space) used in the training set (2.5 million).

In this work, approximate nearest neighbors search in kd-trees has been used to reduce the temporal cost [1].

Instead of classifying each test point according to the most voted class, in our case a confidence criterion function that depends on the distances to the nearest neighbors is used:

$$f_c = \frac{\displaystyle\sum_{i \in s_c} \frac{1}{d(p, n_i)}}{\displaystyle\sum_{i=1}^{k} \frac{1}{d(p, n_i)}},$$

where f_c is the confidence of class c, $d(p, n_i)$ is the distance from the test point to the neighbor i and s_c is the set of sub-indices of the prototypes belonging to class c among the k nearest neighbors found $n_1 \ldots n_k$. Since ours is a two-class problem, only the confidence of one class, *cancer*, is computed. When a threshold T is set, a pixel is considered cancer if that confidence is larger than T. The value of k used in the experiments was empirically set to 50.

3.3   Hidden Markov Model Classification

To avoid the labeling problem pointed out in Section 2, a Hidden Markov Model (HMM) classifier has been used. HMMs and their related algorithms are a powerful tool with high capability of modeling complex (non stationary) phenomena. Particularly, they have been widely used in the field of Pattern Recognition, mainly in Speech Recognition [11] and lately in Handwriting Recognition as well [2].

In order to use HMMs, it is necessary to compute a feature vector as a function of some independent variable. For example, in speech the acoustic signal is divided into a sequence of windows from each of which a feature vector is computed; here the independent variable is clearly the *"time"*. In handwriting recognition, however, the sequence of feature vectors are computed as a function of the *"horizontal position"* along the line of handwritten text.

Based on this idea, and knowing beforehand the path of the biopsy needle when enters each image, we compute a sequence of feature vectors as a function of the pixels along this path.

Continuous density left-to-right HMMs have been used to model both cancer and non-cancer classes, as shown in Figure 2. The HMM cancer class includes three states: non-cancer, cancer and non-cancer. The HMM non-cancer class only includes one non-cancer state. All the non-cancer states of both models are tied (they share the same parameter values).

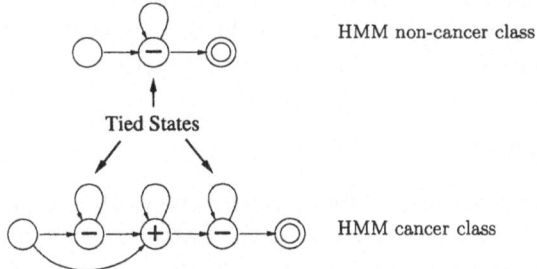

Fig. 2. HMM topologies for non-cancer and cancer classes. Labeled states with "−" model non-cancer tissue and labeled states with "+" model cancer tissue (feature vectors)

These topologies make the implicit assumption that only one cancerous tumor exists in each biopsy image, and that it has a convex shape and a regular growth in all directions.

It is assumed that each HMM state generates feature vectors following an adequate parametric probabilistic law; typically, a *mixture of Gaussian densities*. The required number of densities in the mixture depends, along with many other factors, on the "variability" of feature vectors associated with each state. This number needs to be empirically tuned in each task.

The training process of these models is carried out using the well known instance of the EM algorithm called *backward-forward* or *Baum-Welch* re-estimation [8].

Instead of using the common Viterbi algorithm to classify each test sequence according to the most likely HMM class, it was employed to compute the *a posteriori* probability of cancer class in order to use it as a confidence criterion function f_c in a similar way as the function defined for k-NN classification:

$$f_c = Pp(c|x) = \frac{p_{\text{HMM}_c}(x|c)Pr(c)}{\sum\limits_{\forall c\prime} p_{\text{HMM}_{c\prime}}(x|c')Pr(c')}$$

where $Pp(c|x)$ is the *a posteriori* probability of class c, x is a given sequence of feature vectors, $p_{\text{HMM}_c}(x|c)$ is the computed Viterbi score over HMM_c paths and $Pr(c)$ is the *a priori* probability of class c. Given a computed confidence of cancer class and a threshold T, a biopsy is considered cancerous if that confidence is larger than T.

4   Experiments

A number of experiments were carried out to determine if the feature extraction and the classification scheme proposed could predict the malignancy of a region around a pixel in a TRUS image of a previously unknown patient. As mentioned before, it is a task that trained urologists cannot perform reliably. Our hope was that some local relations among pixels could be represented and recognized better by the algorithms than by the human visual system.

4.1 k-NN Classification

In a first set of experiments, the gray maps of windows of 16×16 to 50×50 pixels around each pixel of the images were extracted. Each resulting vector (of 64 to 625 dimensions) was projected into spaces ranging from 10 to 50 dimensions. The projection basis was computed using Principal Component Analysis (PCA) from a subset of $250,000$ vectors (10%) randomly drawn from the training set. Then a confidence value for each pixel inside the rectangle corresponding to the cylinder analysed was obtained using a k-NN scheme. The confidence value of the biopsy was obtained as the mean of the confidences of each pixel inside the

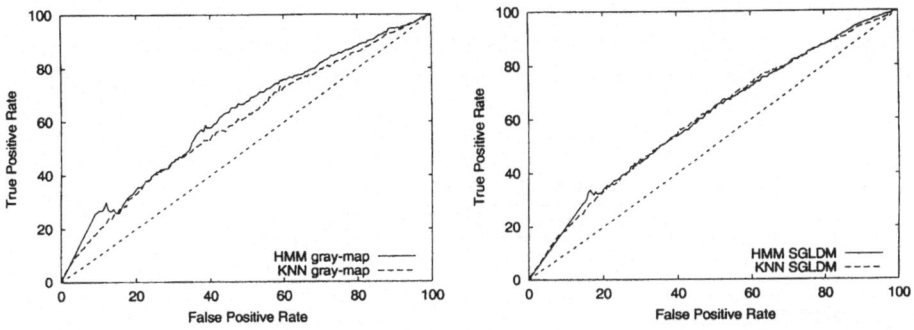

Fig. 3. Receiver Operating Curve (R.O.C.) of the best gray-map (left) and SGLDM (right) settings for k-NN and HMM

rectangle. The best results were obtained with windows of size 30×30 projected into a 30-dimensional space.

In the second set of experiments, SGLDM textural descriptors were computed in windows of 8×8 to 40×40 pixels centered in each pixel of the images. Previously, each image was subject to a standard vector quantization preprocess so as its number of gray-levels was reduced from 256 to exactly 20. The 11 parameters cited in Section 3.1 were extracted from 12 matrices corresponding to four angles $(0, \frac{\pi}{4}, \frac{\pi}{2}$ and $\frac{3\pi}{4})$ and 3 distances (1 to 3 pixels). The parameters obtained were normalized using a basis computed from a subset of the training set, to have a variance of approximately 1.0. Each resulting vector (of 132 dimensions) was then projected into spaces ranging from 10 to 50 dimensions using PCA. The best results were obtained with windows of size 15×15 projected into a 30-dimensional space.

The results for both gray maps and SGLDM, are shown in Figure 3.

4.2   HMM Classification

Similar experiments to those described in Section 4.1 were carried out using a HMM classifier considering different number of gaussians (1 to 1024).

For each number of Gaussian densities, a HMM was trained for each of two classes using the corresponding sequences of feature vectors and six cycles of the Baum-Welch algorithm parameter re-estimation.

Training and test was performed using the well known and widely available standard Hidden Markov Model ToolKit (HTK) [12] for Continuous Speech Recognition.

HMM performed slightly better than k-NN when working with gray maps, however, no significant difference is found between both classifiers when working with SGLDM. In Table 1, the area under R.O.C. for the combination of both classifiers (k-NN and HMM) with both feature extraction scheme (gray map and SGLDM) is done.

Table 1. Area under R.O.C. for the two feature extraction scheme employed (SGLDM and gray maps) tested with the two classifiers (k-NN and HMM)

	KNN	HMM
SGLDM	60.1%	60.0%
Gray map	59.7%	61.6%

5   Conclusions

A system for computer-aided, transrectal ultrasonography-based detection of prostate cancer has been presented. The aim of the system is to help an expert decide where to perform a biopsy.

The results obtained at the biopsy level are very promising, but tests on complete images comparing the decisions of an expert with and without the aid of the system are needed to asses the real clinical value of the model. We hope that the powerful postprocess of the human visual system can make use of the micro-texture-oriented information provided by the system and integrate it with the anatomical and geometrical knowledge of the experts.

References

[1] S. Arya et al. An optimal algorithm for approximate nearest neighbor searching. *Journal of the ACM*, 45:891–923, 1998.

[2] Issam Bazzi, Richard Schwartz, and John Makhoul. An Omnifont Open-Vocabulary OCR System for English and Arabic. *IEEE Trans. Pattern Analysis and Machine Intelligence*, 21(6):495–504, June 1999.

[3] C. Chen, J. Daponte, and M. Fox. Fractal feature analysis and classification in medical imaging, 1989.

[4] J. J. M. C.H de la Rosette et al. Computerized analysis of transrectal ultrasonography images in the detection of prostate carcinoma. *British Journal of Urology*, 75:485–491, 1995.

[5] M. L. Giger et al. Image feature analysis and computer-aided diagnosis in digital radiography. 3. automated detection of nodules in peripheral lung fields. *Medical Physics*, 15:158–166, 1988.

[6] R M Haralick et al. Textural features for image classification. *IEEE Trans. SMC*, 3(6):610–621, 1973.

[7] M. Insana et al. Analysis of ultrasound image texture via generalized rician statistics. *Opt. Eng.*, 25:743–748, 1986.

[8] F. Jelinek. *Statistical Methods for Speech Recognition*. MIT Press, 1998.

[9] S. Lai et al. On techniques for detecting circumscribed masses in mammograms. *IEEE Trans. on Medical Imaging*, 8:377–386, 1989.

[10] G. Landeweerd and E. Gelsema. The use of nuclear texture parameters in the automatic analysis of leukocytes. *Pattern Recognition*, 10:57–61, 1978.

[11] L. R. Rabiner and B. H. Juang. *Fundamentals of Speech Recognition*. Prentice-Hall, Englewood Cliffs, New Jersey, USA, 1993.

[12] S. Young, J. Odell, D. Ollason, V. Valtchev and P. Woodland. *The HTK Book: Hidden Markov Models Toolkit V2.1.* Cambridge Research Laboratory Ltd, March 1997.

[13] E. Schuster, P. Knoflach, and G. Grabner. Local texture analysis: an approach to differentiating liver tissue objectively. *Clin. Ultrasound*, 16:453–461, 1988.

[14] Y. Wu et al. Computerized detection of clustered microcalcifications in digital mammograms: Applications of artificial neural networks. *Medical Physics*, 19:555–560, 1992.

Ultrasound to Magnetic Resonance Volume Registration for Brain Sinking Measurement

David Lloret, Joan Serrat, Antonio M. López, and Juan J. Villanueva

Computer Vision Centre and Dept. d'Informàtica
Universitat Autònoma de Barcelona
08193 Cerdanyola, Spain
{joans,antonio}@cvc.uab.es

Abstract. This paper addresses the registration of ultrasound scans and magnetic resonance (MR) volume datasets of the same patient. During a neurosurgery intervention, pre–operative MR images are often employed as a guide despite the fact that they do not show the actual state of the brain, which sometimes has sunk up to 1 cm. By means of a standard ecographer and a tracker connected to a computer, it is feasible to build on-line an updated picture of the brain. We propose an algorithm which first composes the volume ecography of the brain and registers it to the MR volume. Next, it aligns individual B-scans into the MR volume, thus providing a measure of the suffered deformation.

1 Introduction

The shift of the brain during interventions represents a major source of inaccuracy for any system employing pre-operative imáges. Because the actual position of the brain during the operation differs from the estimation provided by pre-operative images, the information available to neuronavigators will present systematically misregistrations, and thus surgeons will have to deal manually with possible inconsistencies. Several papers trying to quantify the magnitude and direction of the shift have been reported. A simple approach is to monitor the locations of a number of landmarks in the exposed surface of the brain through the operation. Roberts et al. [3] employ for this purpose an operating microscope on a ceiling-mounted robotic platform with tracking capabilities. The statistical analysis of the recorded positions shows displacement on the order of 1 cm, mostly along the gravity axis.

Maurer et al. [4] employ an intraoperative magnetic resonance (MR) device to acquire a number of scannings during the intervention. This procedure is applied to interventions of different type (biopsies, functional and resections), and then images are analyzed to search for volume changes, and also registered with a non-rigid algorithm based on mutual information.

Other papers aim at the registration of pre-operative to intra-operative images. Roche [5] defines for this purpose a new measure, the correlation ratio, and presents results for several phantoms. It is also interesting Xiao's method [6] for imaging the breast accounting for deformations of the tissue.

F.J. Perales et al. (Eds.): IbPRIA 2003, LNCS 2652, pp. 420–427, 2003.

However the proposals in literature are unlikely to be of general use in routine surgery because of their requirements. For instance, those employing intraoperative MR are unavailable to most hospitals due to the cost of a dedicated MR device. Instead of MR , we propose to use ultrasound images for pre-operative image updating. Ultrasound ecography is a popular imaging technique because:

- images are immediately available.
- it is a radiation-free modality.
- the acquisition device is relatively inexpensive and fairly transportable.
- intra-operative ecography devices.

The US acquisition procedure requires the ecography probe to be in physical contact with the surface of the object to be imaged. While the radiologist manipulates the probe along the surface (free-hand scanning), the image displayed in a monitor changes dynamically and he is able to reconstruct mentally the structure underneath the skin. Hard copies of interesting images (individual video frames are called B-scans, $\mathcal{B}$ from here on) are available for a further analysis and measurements.

The free-hand paradigm proposes to track the position of the transducer during the examination, so each $\mathcal{B}$ has a known position and orientation. With this information, the image contents have known spatial location with respect to some external reference system and can be combined to produce a single volume image.

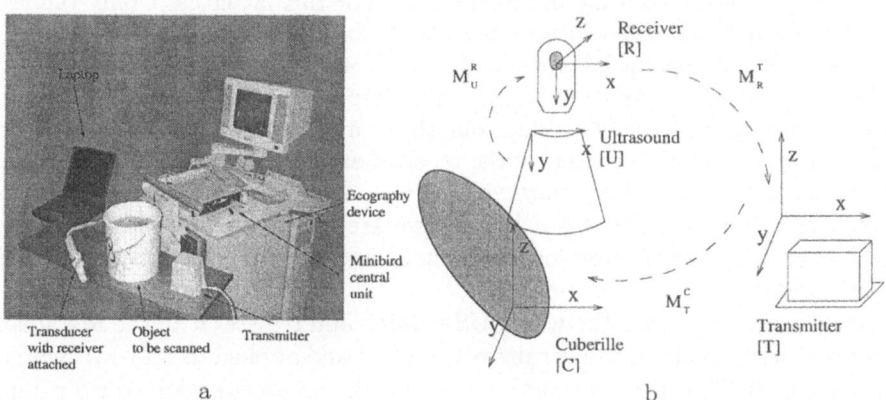

Fig. 1. (a) Picture of the system to acquire and register the US volumes; the laptop (left) would read both the video output of ecography device (top right) and the position from the Minibird tracker (blue box). The transducer was attached with the receiver, while the platform supporting the experiment was metal-free to prevent magnetic interferences. (b) Coordinates systems involved in the free-hand ultrasounding and corresponding transformation matrices : M_U^R from image to receiver, M_R^T receiver to transmitter and M_T^C transmitter to cuberille

Accordingly, we have built a free–hand system, which is able to track the position of the transducer, grab the image acquired at that particular moment and then combine all the information. It consists of the following elements (figure 1a):

- an ultrasound ecographer with video output: Siemens SONOLINE Versa Pro, with three interchangeable probes: 10, 3.5 and 6.5 Mhz.
- a 3-D tracker to measure the position of the ultrasound transducer as accurately as possible: Minibird 800, Ascension Technology, Vermont.
- a device to grab the video frames: Videoport Framegrabber, Transtech systems, Hants, U.K.
- a computer, with two inputs: the ultrasound signal and the tracker position. It is able to store in real time all the incoming data. The computer was a Pentium II working at 366 Mhz and running Microsoft Windows 98.

The data pairs (image, position) can be used to compound a volume image. This volume US image could already be of interest in surgery, since it permits a navigation easier than in the conventional way. But we want to go further: to compare its contents to those of an MR volume, with the final goal of measuring the distances between corresponding features and, eventually, to deform one image according to the other. In this paper we will address only the first part of this goal.

We performed our experiments with an in-vitro adult human brain. This had the advantage to permit the full scan of the surface of the brain, which usually is not feasible during an intervention. For this latter case, only the area immediately below the craniotomy is suitable for scanning. Another advantage was not to depend on the constrains of time of an on-going intervention.

Before proceed on the scanning, the first step was to calibrate the ecography system. Calibration amounts to find out the transformation matrix relating the image coordinate system to that of the receiver and, from there, to the transmitter and the cuberille, an imaginary volume in space where the scanned specimen is contained. For the sake of conciseness, we are not going to develop here this issue. Refer to [7] for an overview of methods and a complete description of the one selected.

Next, we compounded the whole US volume and register it to the MR image (section 2) with an algorithm we already devised and applied to CT –MR volume registration [2]. This first registration step globally aligns the scanned US volume to the usually larger MR one through a rigid transformation. However, it still suffers from the tracker errors, which affect the spatial compounding of the US volume.

But the main cause of misalignment is due to the brain sinking, which is of local nature, and that is precisely what we are interested in. In order to quantify this misalignment, we have proceeded to a second registration step: we have registered individual ecography frames to the MR volume taking as initial position of each B-scan within the MR volume those coordinates given by the global registration transform. As a result we have obtained a preliminary map of deformations similar to those obtained in a real case (section 3), in a form of translation vector to apply to each frame in order to correct the global rigid registration transform.

2   Volume Compounding

After the transducer has been calibrated, the spatial information accompanying each image is used to compound the sequence of video images into a single volume image. To achieve a proper setting of the data, the matrix M_T^C must be chosen carefully to include the area to be imaged. Also, the algorithm must take into account non-scanned voxels and multiply-scanned voxels. For the later case, we have taken the mean value of the pixels with the same final location. Figure 2 shows three orthogonal views of the US volume. Despite the gaps, the features appear fairly constant. We compounded three different volume images of the same in-vitro brain, one for each transducer employed, but we are going to show only images and results for the 10 Mhz transducer, which exhibits the larger depth and field of view.

After building the volume image, the next step was to bring it into alignment with other images. For this purpose, we had taken an MR volume image of the in-vitro brain. The registration did not seem an easy task, as the visual inspection revealed that landmarks were not easy to find in the US volume.

Fortunately, we already had previous experience in similar medical image registration problem [2], and could apply the same algorithm we had employed for CT –MR images. In short, the algorithm has the following characteristics:

- **Feature Space**, this is, the information in the images actually used to compare them. In this case, we segment the contours of the brain, by means of a creaseness-based operator. In effect, sulci (cortical folds) can be seen as valleys in the surface of the brain, and thus can be automatically detected. For a full description, refer to [2]. Achieving a proper segmentation of the sulci is itself a recurrent subject in the literature.
- **Alignment Function.** We take the correlation of the creaseness of the two volumes as the measure of alignment, and consider only rigid transformations.
- **Scheme of Iterative Process.** In order to deal with local maxima, we build a hierarchical structure and iterate the transformations at each level.

We run the algorithm for three compounded US volumes, and successful results did not require any modification of the original algorithm. One can check in figure 2 that the original volumes are visually aligned. Despite the gaps in the image, the shape of the two images is very similar. We have chosen views at the extreme location in the brain to show the most unfavorable case, as misalignments would appear here more clearly. Note that sulci appear much less clearly in the US image than in the MR image. The reason is that small sulci concavities appear as white areas instead of depicting black, empty areas, because the signal is partly reflected back at these points.

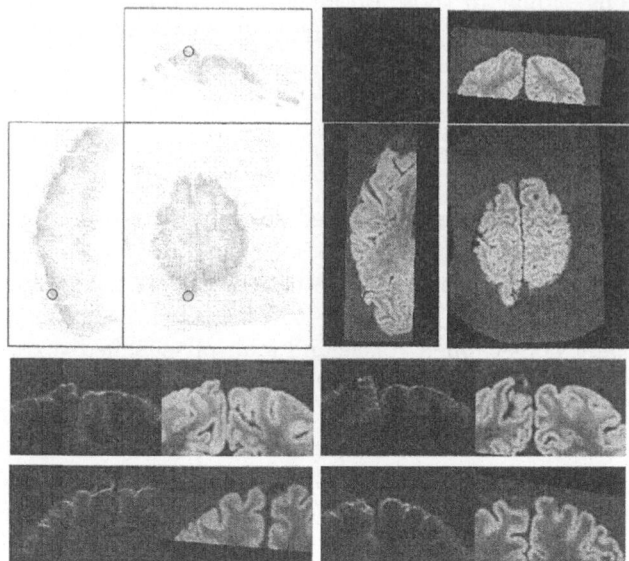

Fig. 2. Top: two corresponding views of US (left) and MR (right) after registering the two volumes. Bottom: B-scan with cutout from registered MR

There is another interesting visualization possibility, which makes use of the whole system of transformations: with the transformation provided by the registration and the matrix M_U^C , it is possible to locate each B-frame into the MR volume, and thus to present its corresponding MR slice. We show corresponding pairs in figure 2. Note that in this slices the alignment seems to be quite good, considering the multiple sources of error and the small size of the image depicted.

3   2D US – 3D US Registration

The registration process performed in the previous section permitted us to relate the coordinates of each video 2–D frame to the MR volume. In a real neurosurgery intervention, there would be some differences between the newly acquired US and the pre–operative MR volume because the tissues would have sunken in some degree. An algorithm could register both images, given the initial estimation of the position provided by volume registration. The resulting transformation would bring locally into alignment the features from both images and would provide an estimation of the deformation needed at that point in order to update the MR volume to the actual features of the brain.

Unfortunately the in-vitro brain could not be employed for this purpose because the tissues were very rigid, and could not be deformed without damage. Yet it is interesting to run a 2D–3D registration with the acquired data, to see whether it can cancel the small positioning errors of the tracking device and,

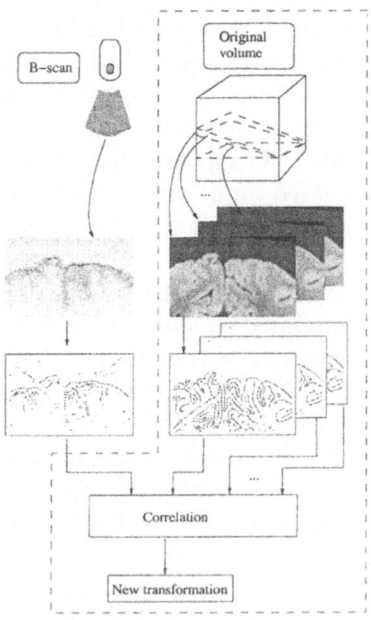

Fig. 3. The iterative part of registration searches new transformations in order to obtain a new cutout more similar to $\mathcal{B}$

more importantly, to correct misalignments due to brain shift. At the same time, the correction vector is a measure of the brain sinking at each frame.

We decided to adapt the creaseness-based algorithm to perform the 2D–3D registration. We modeled the position error as a rigid transformation given by the matrix:

$$M^{ERR} = Trans(T_x, T_y, T_z) \cdot Rot(\phi_x, \phi_y, \phi_z) \tag{1}$$

And we modified the calibration equation (see figure 1b) to include this adjustment:

$$C_{\overline{\mathbf{x}}} = P_{\overline{\mathbf{x}}} \cdot M^{ERR} \cdot M_U^R \cdot M_R^T \cdot M_T^C \cdot M_U^M \tag{2}$$

Recall that M_U^M is the global alignment transform computed in the previous section. We will refer as $\mathcal{C}$ the 2D image in the cuberille, with the coordinates given by the previous equation. M_U^M is the registration matrix computed in the previous section.

The new matrix M^{ERR} measures the error in the position of the slice. We decided to include it in the product before M_U^R because then the units of the transformation would be related to $\mathcal{B}$, i.e., pixels, and not mm as it would be the case had we included it after M_T^C.

The next step was to modify our registration algorithm [7] to run with a 2D–3D scheme. The iterative step could be very similar, the only additional step being the computation of $\mathcal{C}$, i.e. the slice to be compared in the volume. The optimization will modify the values of M^{ERR} , which in turn will change the contents of C , until the desired convergence has been achieved.

But the initial step (exhaustive search in the Fourier domain) had to be redesigned, as the dimensionality of the images was different. This initial step could not be suppressed because otherwise the iteration could get trapped in some local maximum. We took the approach to run the 2D–2D registration with the two initial images, the video frame and the corresponding cutout, and then use the result as the first estimation for the 2D–3D algorithm. This approach is schemed in figure

Figure 4 shows the successful convergence for a few frames. Sometimes, the algorithm fails because the compared creases are too dissimilar. Other times, large artifacts appearing in C mislead the search. Actually, these are the proper results of the creaseness step, only that now the slice is extracted containing the whole surface, instead of a single line as previously. Since the optimization searches the highest correlation value, the search is lead to areas with higher creaseness content. This effect occurs when the initial transformation is poorly estimated because of the lack of reliable landmarks, as it is the case for B depicting border areas of the brain.

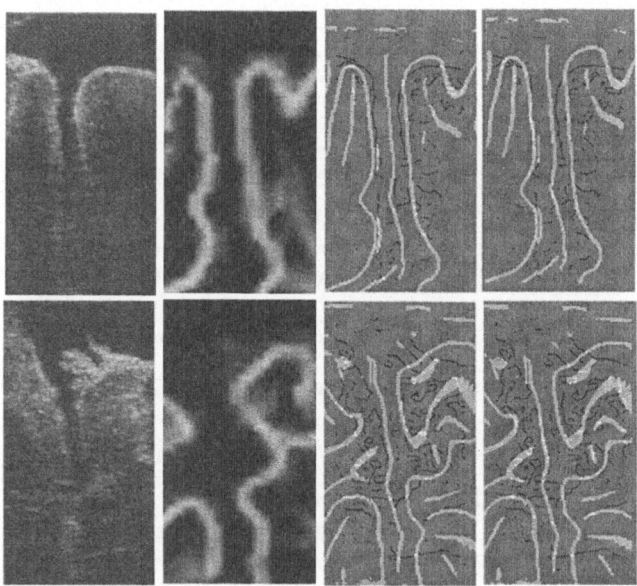

Fig. 4. 2-D to ecography volume registration with the 10 Mhz transducer. First two columns: original B and C . Third column: superimposed creases, drawn in white when they match, before registration. Forth column: same as third, after registration. Note the difficulty to compare images from different modalities and resolutions, which makes the registration process more difficult

4   Conclusions

We have presented an automatic method for the registration of a compounded US volume to an MR image, already employed for other modalities. The algorithm takes the convolutions of the brain as the landmark to align the volumes. This registration is accurate so as to permit the comparison of the $\mathcal{B}$ image to the corresponding cutout in the MR volume. Furthermore, the 2D–3D registration improves accuracy to one or two pixels in the tested volumes, though more quantitative results are needed to support this conclusion.

An immediate application of this registration is measurement of the sinking of the brain during an intervention in neurosurgery. In effect, the features of each $\mathcal{B}$ scan would be matched against the MR volume, and the obtained transformation would be an estimation of the changes for this particular landmark. Since we have applied the algorithm to an undeformable phantom, we have not been able to fully experiment its trade-offs. In our tests, however, the algorithm could correct well the miss-alignment produced by the errors in the position of the transducer provided by the tracking device. Thus, it would presumably be of relevance in original surgery scenario.

Acknowledgments

This paper has been partly funded by the CICYT grants TIC2000–1123 and TIC-1FD97-0667-C02-01. Many thanks to Dr. Derek L.G. Hill from Radiological Sciences at King's College, London and Dr. Donald Farr, Anatomy division, UMDS, London for providing help and support.

References

[1] Prager, R.W., Rohling, R.N., Gee, A.H. and Berman, L.: Automatic calibration for 3–D free-hand ultrasound. Tech. Report CUED/F-INFENG/TR 303, Cambridge University, Department of Engineering (1997)
[2] López, A.M., Lloret, D., Serrat, J. and Villanueva, J.: Multilocal creaseness based on the level set extrinsic curvature. Computer Vision and Image Understanding Vol. 77 (2000) 111–144
[3] Roberts, D., Hartov, A., et al.: Intraoperative brain shift and deformation: A quantitative analysis of cortical displacement in 28 cases. Neurosurgery, Vol. 43, No. 4 (1998) 749–760
[4] Maurer C.R., Hill, D.L.G. et al.: Measurement of intraoperative brain deformation using a 1.5 tesla interventional MR system: Preliminary results. IEEE Transactions on medical imaging, Vol. 17, No. 5 (1998) 817–825
[5] Roche, A., Pennec, X. and Malandain, G.: Rigid registration of 3d ultrasound with mr images: a new approach combining intensity and gradient information. IEEE Transactions on medical imaging, Vol. 20, No. 10 (2001) 1038–1049
[6] Xiao, G., Brady, J.M., and Noble, J.A.: Nonrigid registration of 3d free-hand ultrasound images of the breast. IEEE Transactions on medical imaging, Vol. 21, No. 4 (2002) 405–412
[7] Lloret, D.: Medical image registration based on a creaseness measure. PhD Thesis dissertation. Computer Vision Center, Universitat Autonoma de Barcelona (2001)

Segmentation of Range Images in a Quadtree

Robert E. Loke and Hans du Buf

Vision Laboratory, University of Algarve, 8000-810 Faro, Portugal
tel: +351 289 800900 ext. 7761, fax: +351 289 818560
{loke,dubuf}@ualg.pt http://w3.ualg.pt/~dubuf/vision.html

Abstract. We apply a fast segmenter to planar range images. By segmenting normal vectors of estimated planes in a quadtree, we can analyze very noisy data at high tree levels and guarantee interactivity in visualizing underlying 3D scenes. Techniques to enhance data at the original spatial resolution are given. Results on the ABW range dataset are better than those of several other segmenters.

Keywords: Maximum homogeneity - Edge enhancement - 3D clustering

1 Introduction

Range image data are being obtained by an increasing number of sensors. Their segmentation enables the coding and visualization of structures and objects in scenes. In previous work different segmenters were compared [1, 2]. We have developed an unsupervised, fast and robust segmenter which can be applied to images and 3D data volumes [3] with one-dimensional data, i.e. greyvalue pixels or voxels. By using a quad/octree, this segmenter allows for an interactive processing and visualization of huge datasets. Here we apply this segmenter to range images, using a quadtree with 3D normal vectors at pixel positions.

The paper is organized as follows. First we describe the quadtree framework (Section 2) and the herein performed processing (Section 3). Then we assess its performance on a ground truth set of images (Section 4).

2 Quadtree Representation

Let the original range image of size $dx \times dy$ be tree level 0. Starting at level 0, we add higher levels and compute all pixel values at the higher level L by averaging pixel values in non-overlapping blocks of size 2×2 at level $L - 1$:

$$Z(x, y; L) = \frac{1}{n_4} \sum_{i,j=0}^{1} Z(2x + i, 2y + j; L - 1) \tag{1}$$

where $Z(x, y; L)$ is the pixel value (depth) at position (x, y) of tree level L, $0 \le x < dx$ etc at level L and n_4 is normally 4 (see below). The tree construction

F.J. Perales et al. (Eds.): IbPRIA 2003, LNCS 2652, pp. 428–436, 2003.

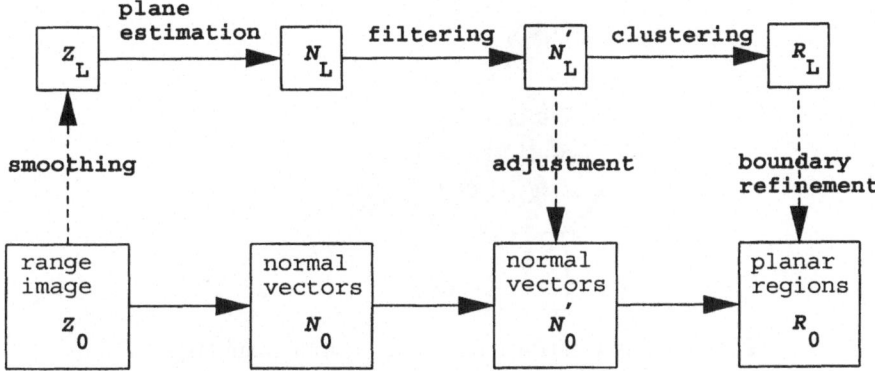

Fig. 1. Processing steps in the quadtree

stops if the highest level consists of one pixel only. The value of this pixel is the mean of all pixels at level 0. Then the tree has height H and counts $H+1$ levels.

We note that there are no constraints on the size of the image: In the case that the image is dyadic ($dx = dy$ being a power of 2), the size of each higher level is 1/4th the size at the previous, lower level, and all parent pixels have exactly four children ($n_4 = 4$). If the image has an arbitrary size, parent pixels do not necessarily have four children ($n_4 \in [1,4]$). However, the spatial resolution in each dimension always reduces with a factor 2. For instance, the size at level 1 is equal to $(dx/2 + dx\%2) \times (dy/2 + dy\%2)$, where / is the integer division operator and % the modulus operator.

The quadtree construction can be adapted to the processing of incomplete images, i.e. images with undefined pixel values (gaps). Although for such images n_4 is not always equal to 4, the resulting data in the tree is about equally smoothed at all positions, with small deviations only at the edges of the image and around gaps at the lowest tree level. In this case, Z in Eq. (1) only denotes available, defined pixel values and $n_4 \in [0,4]$ is the total number of available children at level $L-1$ for a parent pixel at level L. If $n_4 = 0$ for a parent pixel, the undefined pixel value is propagated to the higher level. However, since gaps become smaller, this propagation will stop.

3   Quadtree Processing

Figure 1 shows the processing in the quadtree. First, at a high tree level L, the smoothed range image Z_L is segmented by: (1) Determining a normal vector at each pixel by estimating a plane in the pixel neighborhood. This results in an image of normal vectors N_L. Each normal vector has an x, a y and a z component. (2) Filtering N_L. This results in an image N'_L with an improved homogeneity when compared to N_L. (3) Clustering and classifying N'_L. This results in an image of regions R_L. Each region is characterized by a unique normal vector.

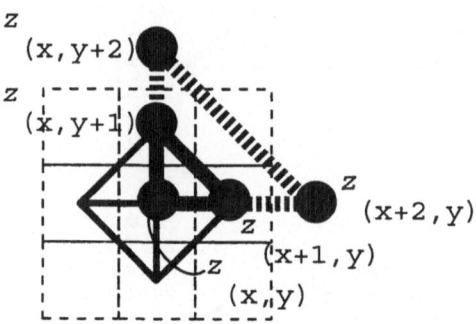

Fig. 2. Plane estimation in one of four pixel triplets

Then, for each lower level M, starting at tree level $L-1$ and ending at level 0, the segmentation is refined by: (A) Again, determining normal vectors, but now using the range data available at the lower level M. (B) Filtering the resulting image of normal vectors N_M. (C) Correcting N_M, using the normal vectors at the higher level $M + 1$. (D) Refining the boundaries of R_{M+1}, using the image of normal vectors N_M. This results in the final segmentation R_M.

We now describe the - totally five - processing steps. All steps are performed locally, in small neighborhoods, except for the clustering. Only in the adjustment and refinement higher level data are used to improve lower level processing.

Plane Estimation The normal vector of a pixel at position (x, y) is determined by first selecting the pixel triplet with the smallest depth difference from the following four pixel triplets: (1) $Z(x, y)$, $Z(x + 1, y)$, $Z(x, y + 1)$, (2) $Z(x, y)$, $Z(x + 1, y)$, $Z(x, y - 1)$, (3) $Z(x, y)$, $Z(x - 1, y)$, $Z(x, y + 1)$, and (4) $Z(x, y)$, $Z(x - 1, y)$, $Z(x, y - 1)$. If the plane estimation is performed at level 0, the two depth values in the direction of each adjacent pixel are averaged; see Fig. 2 (the thick black triangle and the dashed one). This improves the robustness with respect to noise. Then, the normal vector is defined by the plane through the selected triplet. We note that the segmenter is not restricted to this normal vector definition. Other techniques such as least-squares fitting or techniques for estimating curved planes can also be used. However, the estimation must be fast, because, apart from the gaps, it must be done for each pixel in the tree.

Maximum-Homogeneity Filtering Similarly, the filtered normal vector of a pixel at position (x, y) is determined by first selecting the configuration with the smallest variance from nine configurations [4]. The used configurations are shown in Fig. 3. In each configuration, the variance is defined as the sum of the variances of the x, y and z components of N. Then, the filtered normal vector is computed by averaging the x, y and z components of the normal vectors at the pixels indicated by the selected configuration.

Multi-dimensional Local-Centroid Clustering At a certain level L_c ($0 < L_c \leq H$) we cluster the pixels' normal vectors in order to classify the data. Parameter L_c depends on the noise in the data, the number and size of gaps, as well

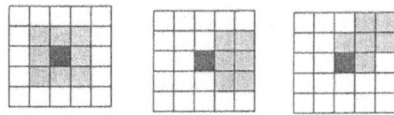

Fig. 3. Maximum-homogeneity filtering. The other six configurations are obtained by projection. Grey denotes filter elements; dark grey the pixel being filtered

as the size of the smallest region targetted at tree level 0. We use unsupervised local-centroid clustering [5] because this algorithm is fast and does not require the number of classes to be known *a priori*. However, any algorithm without spatial connectivity constraints can be used, e.g. fuzzy c-means clustering.

Since we need to classify three-dimensional data, i.e. the x, y and z components of the filtered normal vectors, we had to extend the local-centroid clustering algorithm from one to three dimensions. Therefore, instead of a 1D histogram, which represents greyvalues, we use a 3D one, in order to represent normal vectors. Then, similar to 1D local-centroid clustering, the histogram of the normal vectors is iteratively changed by computing, for each normal vector (i, j, k) with a positive value in the histogram, the centroid, i.e. the weighted sum of all histogram values in a local neighborhood of size $s \times s \times s$ symmetric about (i, j, k). The sum is weighted depending on the distance of the normal vectors to (i, j, k). The sum represents another normal vector to which the histogram value at (i, j, k) is added. The algorithm stops when there are no more changes in the histogram. Then all "voxels" (instead of bins, as in a 1D histogram) with histogram values greater than zero are the clusters. After assigning a unique label to each cluster, we segment level L_c by labeling each normal vector with that of its nearest cluster (minimum-distance classification in which the distances between the x, y and z components of the normal vector and the cluster are added together). The labels can correspond to the actual normal vectors, or can divide the dynamic range $[0, 255]$ into equal intervals.

Data Adjustment The data at the lower levels in the tree need to be adjusted in order to: (A) Maintain, for each normal vector component, the spatial relationship in the quadtree, i.e. every parent pixel is the mean of its child pixels. (B) Enhance the edges. Each component of the new normal vector of a pixel at a lower level is calculated using one of the following four equations:

$$c = f + c - c_\mu, \tag{2}$$

$$c = f_\mu + c - c_\mu, \tag{3}$$

$$c = f + \frac{c - c_\mu}{c_d} \frac{f_{max} - f_{min}}{2}, \tag{4}$$

$$c = f_\mu + \frac{c - c_\mu}{c_d} \frac{f_{max} - f_{min}}{2}, \tag{5}$$

Table 1. Total number of correct regions (%)

set	tree level			norm
	2	**1**	**0**	
training	115 (57)	121 (60)	120 (60)	201 (100)
test	236 (52)	243 (53)	251 (55)	457 (100)

with c being the original value of the normal vector's $(x, y$ or $z)$ component of the pixel, f the value of the $(x, y$ or $z)$ component of the parent of the pixel, c_μ the mean value of the values of the components in an $s_c \times s_c$ neighborhood around the pixel, c_d the maximum deviation about c_μ in this $s_c \times s_c$ neighborhood, f_μ the mean value of the components in an $s_f \times s_f$ neighborhood around the parent of the pixel and f_{max} (f_{min}) the maximum (minimum) value of the components in this $s_f \times s_f$ neighborhood. The equations add the local "contrast" of the child pixel in its neighborhood ($c - c_\mu$) to the (robust) estimation of its "father" at the higher level (f or f_μ). In the latter two equations, the contrast is scaled to the parent values.

Boundary Refinement The boundaries at each lower level are refined using a line filter [3]. Such a filter topology improves the butterfly filter described in [6].

4   Results and Discussion

The range image segmenter was implemented in ANSI C on an SGI Origin 200QC server. CPU time is about 60s per image, using all 4 available processors for the most expensive computation tasks. We note that the Origin has MIPS R10000 processors at 180MHz, and that, apart from any parallellization, a normal Pentium III computer at 733 MHz is faster by a factor of 2.2. Using the latest GHz processors, the total time per image can be reduced to less than 9s.

We applied the segmenter to the ABW range dataset which is divided in a training and test set of 10 and 30 images, all sized 512×512 [1]. All results from the test set which are shown below have been obtained by tuning the above described parameters of the segmenter on the training set. Then the tuned segmenter was applied to the test images. Thus, we assume that with the same parameters good results can be obtained for several images. We note that this is not necessarily true. However, we prefer to follow a robust approach (see also [7] for adaptive segmenter tuning). Table 1 shows the number of correct regions obtained at each level of the quadtree for both the training and test set. Note that the number of correct regions is higher at the lower levels, except for level 0 of the training set. This indicates that the data adjustment improves the spatial relationships in the quadtree and that the boundary refinement improves the final segmentation. The percentage of correct regions per image (55) is higher than the ones (39% and 53%) obtained by the 1D implementation of our algorithm and the PPU algorithm presented in [2]. The other algorithm presented there

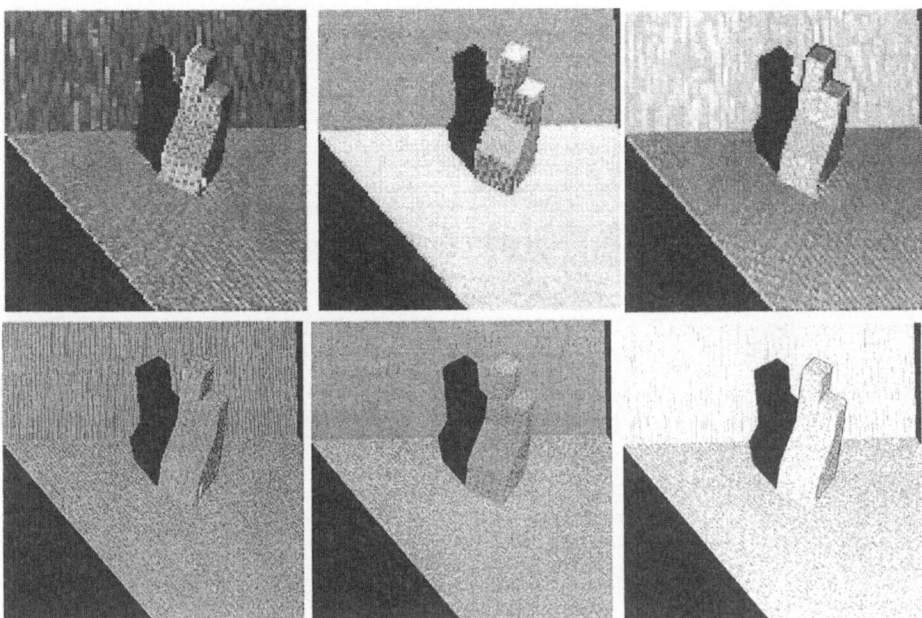

Fig. 4. From left to right: x, y and z components of normal vectors, at tree level 2 (top) and 0 (bottom)

and the four algorithms in [1] are better (percentage ranges from 69 to 89). However, most of these algorithms (except the UB one) are also much slower than our algorithm (one even takes more than one hour per image). We note that although not all regions have been correctly detected according to the methodology in [1], a big part of these regions is still correct, i.e. their surfaces are planar (see Fig. 7: only two regions correspond to non-planar surfaces). Consequently, it will still be possible to improve the analysis and understanding of the underlying scenes, especially if this can be done in an interactive way, by visualizing efficiently-coded surface triangulations at the different tree levels.

Figure 4 shows x, y and z components of normal vectors for one range image. Note that, at the highest tree level, the different components enable the segmentation of different regions and that, at the lowest one, the data are very noisy. Figure 5 shows processed normal vector components, obtained for another range image. The filtering was iterated 4x at tree level 2, 2x at level 1 and 0x at level 0, the adjustment was performed using Eq. (2), and the size of the line filter was 11. Note that: (A) The filtering reduces the noise and improves the region homogeneity. (B) The adjustment improves the coherency in the tree, but causes a blocky effect at tree level 0. Below we will see that by using another adjustment equation this effect can be decreased. However, in the parameter tuning, Eq. (2) was preferred. (C) The refinement improves the quality of the boundaries at tree level 0.

Figure 6 shows components of filtered and adjusted normal vectors at tree level 1 in the case of another range image. Note that the adjustment performs

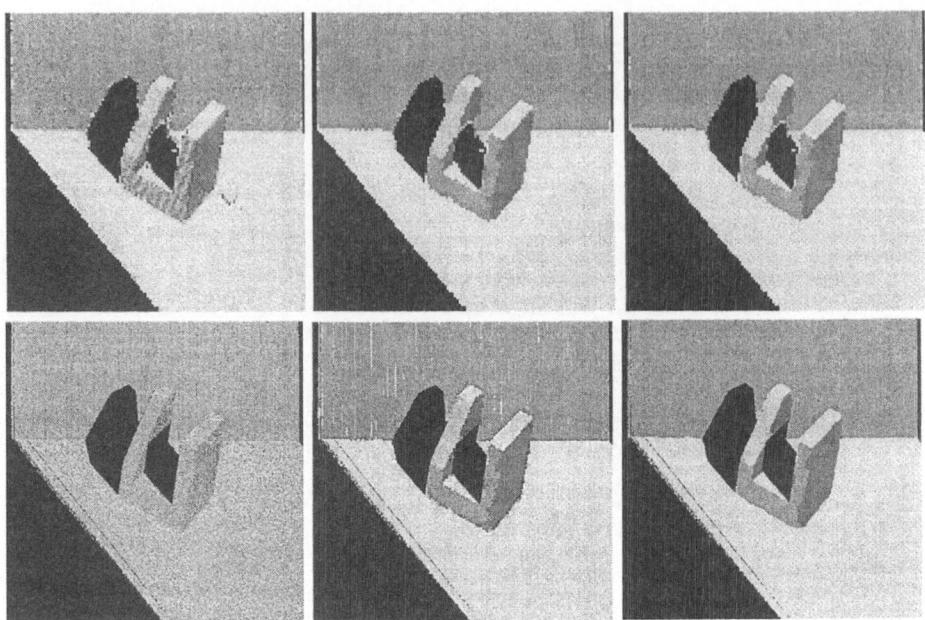

Fig. 5. From left to right: components of estimated, filtered/adjusted and segmented normal vectors, at tree level 2 (top) and 0 (bottom)

well in that it projects higher level regions to the lower level. For example, the regions in the "tower" at the left of the image are only separated after the adjustment. Also note that the boundaries obtained with Eq. (2) are blocky, and that those obtained with Eq. (4) are visually more appealing. However, in the quantization of the segmentation results during the parameter tuning, Eq. (2) was preferred.

Figure 7 shows three segmentations after a connected-component labeling and using the scoring software described in [1]. Note that: (A) Even small and elongated regions were detected. (B) Despite the use of adjustment Eq. (2) the boundaries are *not* blocky at all. This is due to the refinement. (C) Some regions were over-segmented. This may be due to the high level of noise in the original images. (D) Some regions were under-segmented. This is partly due to the fact that these are *adjacent* parallel regions, and such regions have equal normal vectors.

In the future we will further emphasize the use of a simple and fast, but effective, processing embedded in a quadtree, e.g. for estimating curved surfaces. We also plan to use this fast segmenter for the interactive visualization of range images, reconstructing efficiently-coded 3D triangulations of underlying scenes at the different tree levels, with texture mapped and shaded surfaces for an improved analysis and interpretation.

Fig. 6. Normal vector components after filtering, and adjustment with Eqs (2) and (4)

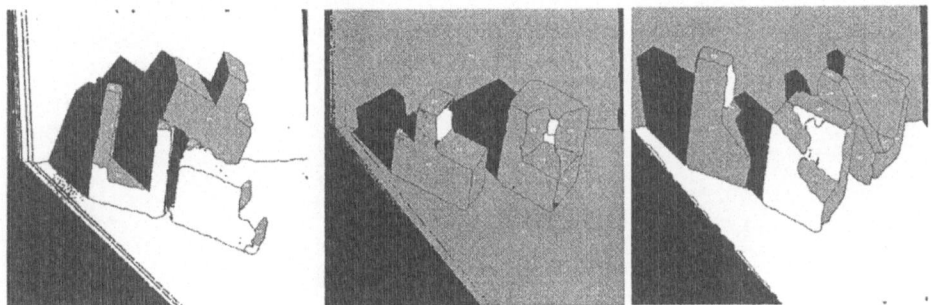

Fig. 7. Final segmentations. Black denotes gaps; grey correct and white over/under-segmented regions

Acknowledgements

The data can be obtained from http://marathon.csee.usf.edu/seg-comp/ SegComp.html/. This work was supported by FCT Programa Operacional Sociedade de Informação (POSI/SRI/34121/1999) in the frame of QCA III. We thank the anonymous reviewers for their suggestions.

References

[1] A. Hoover, G. Jean-Baptiste, X. Jiang, P. Flynn, H.Bunke, D. Goldgof, K. Bowyer, D. Eggert, A. Fitzgibbon, and R. Fisher, "An experimental comparison of range image segmentation algorithms," *IEEE Trans. Pattern Anal. Machine Intell.*, vol. 18, no. 7, pp. 673–689, 1996.

[2] X. Jiang, K. Bowyer, Y. Morioka, S. Hiura, K. Sato, S. Inokuchi, M. Bock, C. Guerra, R. Loke, and J. du Buf, "Some further results of experimental comparison of range image segmentation algorithms," in *Proc. 15th Int. Conf. on Pattern Recogn.*, vol. 4, Barcelona, Spain, Sept. 2000, pp. 877–881.

[3] R. Loke and J. du Buf, "3D data segmentation by means of adaptive boundary refinement in an octree," *Pattern Recognition*, 2002, subm.

[4] J. du Buf and T. Campbell, "A quantitative comparison of edge-preserving smoothing techniques," *Signal Processing*, vol. 21, pp. 289–301, 1990.

[5] R. Wilson and M. Spann, *Image Segmentation and Uncertainty.* Letchworth, England: Research Studies Press Ltd., 1988.

[6] P. Schroeter and J. Bigün, "Hierarchical image segmentation by multi-dimensional clustering and orientation-adaptive boundary refinement," *Pattern Recognition*, vol. 28 (5), pp. 695–709, 1995.

[7] J. Min, "Package of evaluation framework for range image segmentation algorithms," Univ. of South Florida, Tech. Rep. [Online]. Available: http://marathon.csee.usf.edu/seg-comp/SegComp.html

Associative Memory for Early Detection of Breast Cancer

Francisco J. López Aligué, Isabel Acevedo, Carlos Gª Orellana,
Miguel Macías, and Horacio G. Velasco

Department of Electronics and Electromechanical Engineering
Faculty of Sciences, University of Extremadura
Avda. de Elvas, s/n. 06007 - Badajoz, Spain
aligue@unex.es

Abstract. We present a new associative neural network design especially indicated for the early detection of malignant lesions in breast cancer screening. It is a BAM in which we have made some changes to the functioning of its neurons, and for which we have developed an automatic selection algorithm for the prototypes used to calculate the thresholds of the neurons conforming the input layer. The result is a structure that, while considerably reduced, is highly effective in identifying the images that indicate the presence of malignant tumours in screening for breast cancer. We endowed the network with a special pre-processing stage for the treatment of this kind of radiographic image. This pre-processing yields a more detailed analysis of possible signs of tumours.

1   Introduction

Almost from the beginning of their general acceptance by the scientific world, neural networks have been used as a powerful Pattern Recognition tool. Today they form an area of study which has its own identity. This is reflected in numerous examples in the literature, such as those described in [1]. One application of Pattern Recognition that has been receiving a great deal of attention because of its clear interest is the detection of breast cancer. As of now, this task is exclusively one of the human specialist. In the last decade, however, because of the success in other fields of technology, there have been many attempts to incorporate neural networks into the process as an aid to diagnosis.

There is a wide range of possibilities in using neural networks in screening for breast cancer, whether generic [2, 3] or specialized such as in the detection of masses [4, 5] microcalcifications [6, 7] or spiculated lesions [8].

An added problem arises in the real practical application of neural networks to the detection of malignant tumours in that it is necessary, before performing the classification itself, to locate the zones of the mammogram in which there might appear signs of tumours. The recognition of these zones, known as ROI (regions of interest), requires the development of a specific algorithm [9, 10].

We here present an overall solution to these goals using a mixed algorithmic and neural network system based on associative bidirectional memories

F.J. Perales et al. (Eds.): IbPRIA 2003, LNCS 2652, pp. 437–444, 2003.
© Springer-Verlag Berlin Heidelberg 2003

(BAM) [11] and a custom-designed pre-processing unit. We maintain Kosko's classical initial structure, but introduce various changes in the constitutive neurons, in the definition of the weight matrix, and, above all, in the automatic selection of the prototypes used in defining the classes.

With respect to the pre-processing, we set up a division by task, using a generic topological pre-processor (elimination of noise, deformation, scaling, etc.) and another responsible for transforming the (analogical or digital) mammograms into groups of images suitable for treatment by the BAM. The application that we present here formalizes and enlarges on our earlier work on the topic [12].

2   General Structure of the System

Figure 1 shows the general structure of the system with the two aforementioned blocks corresponding to the pre-processor and the associative memory. The former receives the original analogical or digital mammogram and then splits this image (which is usually between 30 MBytes and 50 MBytes in size) up into a set of grid cells which are sent to the topological pre-processor that follows it. As we shall see below, this pre-processor performs certain conventional transformations on the image. Since the result is a certain number of images, this is really a set of BAMs implemented on a multiprocessor network so that they will be able to process the images very quickly. The figure therefore shows them as a network of BAMs.

They are, of course, all constructed and trained identically, and hence form a multiple copy of a single starting associative memory which is executed in the different processors that make up the network, which in our case was developed as a further aspect of the application [13]. In the following sections, we shall analyse separately the functioning of each of these units.

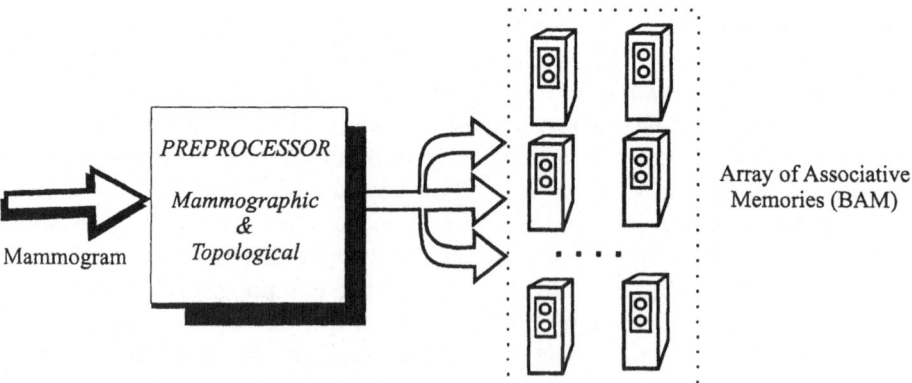

Fig. 1. General block diagram of the mammogram classifier

3   The Pre-processor

As we mentioned above, the pre-processor is responsible for generating from the original mammogram one or more images suitable for submission to the BAM for recognition. Nevertheless, the pre-processor has two clearly differentiated tasks to perform: (i) to generate a medically meaningful image, enhancing and extracting the multiple images that are superposed and mask each other in the original image, and (ii) to eliminate the distortions that are common to all types of image (noise, scaling, etc.). We therefore split the pre-processor into two functionally differentiated units which, by connecting the output of one to the input of the other, provide the overall functioning of the pre-processor system.

3.1   The Mammogram Pre-processor

The mammogram pre-processor consists of two phases. In one, the original image is split into squares of a suitable size for the subsequent processing. A typical initial image has 6 000 x 4 500 pixels and a size of 24 cm x 18 cm, which means 27 Mpixels, i.e., 54 MBytes. From this, we pass to a grid of 432 cells of 1 cm x 1 cm, each of which has 62 500 pixels, i.e., 125 kBytes. Firstly, we eliminate those cells with a null histogram, i.e., those outside the breast, and those of the interior of the breast but lacking contrast. On average, this reduces the number of images by between 20% and 40%, leaving around 300 images to process.

These are grey-scale images, so that there is a strong possibility of overlooking a cancerous lesion because of the masking effect of a background whose intensity is similar to the lesion itself. To avoid this possibility, we generate a set of black and white images from each of these cells using a threshold "window". In particular, we choose a threshold value τ_i and apply the threshold function of Eq. 1

$$f(j) = \begin{cases} 1 \text{ if } \tau_i \leq I(j) \leq \tau_i + \Delta \\ 0 \text{ if } I(j) < \tau_i, \text{ or } I(j) > \tau_i + \Delta \end{cases} \tag{1}$$

where I(j) is the luminosity of the j-th pixel and Δ the "breadth" of the window whose value can be selected arbitrarily.

This means that all those pixels with luminosity greater or less than the specified window will be "darkened", while those whose intensity falls within the window will be "lit". The resulting image will this contain only those pixels with a certain amplitude, eliminating those of greater and lesser luminosity. The new squares allow the visualization of the images whose profile might have been masked by other figures or figure backgrounds.

In sum, we have gone from a grey-scale image of large dimensions and unpredictable mix of outlines, above all difficult for the human eye to distinguish, to a reduced set of binary images much smaller in size, avoiding the difficulty in the detection of the ROI zones that has always been a serious drawback because of the processing speed penalty that its processing involves.

3.2   The Topological Pre-processor

This unit is configured to be an element that modifies the inputs through the following series of topological operations:

⋄ Dispersion
⋄ Calculation of the centre of inertia
⋄ Rotation
⋄ Scaling
⋄ Displacement
⋄ Elimination of noise

Its purpose is to restructure the input image by eliminating all the algorithmically detectable geometric deformations. Its usefulness lies in that the images obtained from the previous subsystem are treated as if they were simply alphanumeric characters, such as handwritten characters, since the problem in this phase is the classification of given images independently of any meaning they might have. Execution begins by calculating the dispersion of the image over the background (pixels that stand out as being part of the body of the "character"). This gives a measure of the area occupied by the character on the total background. Next this character's centre of inertia is found, and the character is rotated around it until reaching a position of minimum moment of rotation. Once appropriately centered, its size is modified to preset appropriate limits (scaling), and is finally displaced until it occupies the centre of the square of the image. At this point, the character already has a suitable form to be taken as a possible input to the BAM.

Lastly, a noise elimination routine is used to eliminate markedly isolated pixels and add others needed to form a coherent image, avoiding gaps inside the character. While the effect is not particularly definitive, it is enough to make the image (that is now ready to send) perfectly classifiable by the BAM.

4   The BAM

In this section we analyse how the associative memory that we have designed functions. As was indicated in Fig.1, there is really a set of memories involved. By means of a suitable mechanism that will depend on each particular application, the different squares will be distributed amongst the various BAMs available in our multiprocessor network. Indeed, the case is simply one of available resources which will condition the relationship between the number of CPUs versus execution time. We shall therefore focus on the design and functioning of the associative memory as a single entity.

One of the most important aspects of the system resides in the design specifications that we introduced into the definition of the BAM. Basically then, this is a two-layer, BAM-type associative memory, in which the inputs of each layer's neurons are totally connected to the outputs of the previous layer's neurons, but there exist no sideways connections within any given layer. The neurons of the first layer (the "input" layer in conventional BAM nomenclature) are defined by the expression

$$y_j = F(I_j) = F(\sum_{i=1}^{N} m_{ji} x_{ki} - \theta_j) \qquad (2)$$

where I_j represents the excitation coming from the second layer's neurons. With respect to the latter, the main difference is that the threshold term "θ_j", does not appear in their function. The significance of this will be seen below. Neither is the function F(.) the same. Whereas for the second layer, the usual sigmoid function or the step function are used, for the first we chose a multi-step function for the reasons that we will present below in discussing the "dead zone".

In order to put forward a reliable classifying system, firstly we use a single prototype to define each of the possible classes of tumour-indicating lesions which the human expert finds meaningful. Following the construction rules of the weight matrix of the BAM, we associate to each of these prototypes a vector that we shall call the class vector V_i that belongs to a canonical structured set with equidistance 2 as in [14], so that one and only one of its components – that which indicates the numeral of the class – is 1 and the rest are 0: $V_1 = (1, 0, \ldots, 0)$, $V_2 = (0, 1, 0, \ldots, 0); \ldots$ We thus have the weight matrix constructed according to its original definition,

$$M = \sum_{i=1}^{N} X_i^T \cdot Y_i = (m_1^T, \ldots, m_N^T), \qquad (3)$$

where N is the class space dimension and P the image vector space dimension, with

$$m_i^T = X_i^T + \sum_{\substack{j=1 \\ j \neq i}}^{N} X_j^{cT}, \qquad (4)$$

where X_j^{cT} is the conjugate vector of X_j^T.

Since the class vector consists of components of value "-1" except that of its own class which is "1", the product will be the sum of the prototypes of the other classes by -1 plus that of its own class multiplied by 1, as is indicated in (3). At this point, suppose that a prototype A_k, is presented at the first layer, and A_k belongs to class "j". The bipolarizer converts A_k into X_k. As one derives from the general formulation of the BAM, if the input images are of dimension P and the number of classes is N, the first layer has N neurons with P inputs each, and each neuron receives an excitation

$$Ij = X_k \cdot m_j = X_k (X_j^T + \sum_{\substack{l=1 \\ l \neq j}}^{Q} X_l^{cT}). \qquad (5)$$

If all these prototypes were completely different from each other, their equivalent bipolar vectors could be identified as a set of orthogonal vectors. Therefore, the excitation of all neurons in the first layer would have all the components negative except the one whose position coincides with that of the class. Consequently, the output from the first layer would be $Y = (y_1, y_2, ..., y_N) = (-1, -1, ..., -1, 1, -1, ..., -1)$ where y_j corresponds to the usual neural function, that is

$$y_j = f(I_j, \theta_j) = f(\sum_{i=1}^{P} w_{ij} \cdot x_i - \theta_j), \tag{6}$$

where "θ_j" is the threshold and with "1" being the output from the position-k neuron in this layer and "-1" the rest. Then, we say that the neural network correctly classifies the input vector A_k. In the general situation of application to real cases, the input vectors are not orthogonal: they present a deal of common, non-representative information.

The consequence is that the neural network is subject to an overlap effect which irrecoverably dilutes the information in the weight matrix. After following the above steps for the vector X_k, one easily sees that if the interference term has an appropriate value, it may cause the neuron to fire in the opposite sense to what was expected generating an output vector that could contain more outputs $y_h = 1$, $h \neq j$. This vector, following the usual BAM mechanism, is sent to the second layer, whose outputs will later substitute the initial input, thus constituting the new input to the first layer. It is possible, however, that (as occurs in the conventional BAM) the process does not generate after a certain number of repetitions an output vector with a single component of "1" and, therefore, the classification of the input will not have been attained.

As a solution to situations of this type, which are very common in the use of BAMs, we propose a method which consists in making use of the threshold θ_j of (6) that is modulated by this overlap noise, so that the neuron becomes insensitive to the interference and is not triggered by the input produced by characters to which it has not been associated. The thresholds are calculated in the "learning phase", when with all the prototypes not belonging to class "j", we have the maximum excitation at the j-neuron as calculated in (5)

$$\text{Max } I_k = \text{Max}(\sum_{i=1}^{N} w_{ij} \cdot x_{ki}), \tag{7}$$

with $X_k \in A_k \neq$ Prototype A_j which means that the maximum of the excitation coming from the prototypes of the class differs from the excitation for the prototypes of the remaining classes by at least a quantity that can be calculated as

$$\varepsilon_j = I_j - \text{Max } I_k. \tag{8}$$

We define now the function of the first layer's neurons as

$$y_j = f(\sum_{i=1}^{N} w_{ij} \cdot x_i - (\text{Max } I_k + \chi)). \tag{9}$$

The term "χ" allows the threshold to be adjusted so that an image not belonging to the class j does not activate the j-th neuron, while all the images that do belong to this class produce sufficient excitation I_j to guarantee the activation of that neuron. Given that this is applied to all the classes, the end result is that the image will be correctly classified.

5   Prototype Selection

One of the most important points in programming the BAM is the correct selection of the prototypes employed to generate the weight matrix defined in (3). One can, however, make a "good enough" selection, given that the optimal choice is often impossible or excessively costly in terms of efficacy. This consists of applying (8) iteratively to the training set that we have chosen. For this purpose, one initially employs for each class any prototype whatever taken from the training set by an absolutely free process (at random, with some fixed criterion, etc.). With this initial set of prototypes, the matrix (3) is calculated with all of them as was indicated above. With this matrix, one determines the value of ε_j for each prototype of the training set. Now, the prototype of each class that generates the greatest value of ε_j will substitute that chosen previously, thereby modifying the weight matrix used before. This process is repeated until either a stable set of prototypes has been generated (the more frequent case) or a pre-set number of iterations has been reached.

6   Results

The system is currently running with a network of 40 Pentium III (1 GHz) processors implementing an associative memory of 400 BAMs with its own operating system developed on Linux. The unit has a mammogram digitalizer so as to accept both digital and analogue images. It also has a complete copy (more than 250 GBytes) of the DDSM (Digital Database for Screening Mammography from the University of South Florida)[15] database with the 4 views of each of the 2620 cases. With respect to the cell images, 100 grey-scale levels are distinguished, and the grey threshold value τ_i and the window Δ can be specified. Away from the context of breast cancer detection, the system has already been tested on the NIST #19 [16] database and on the Display 1 database from the well-known UCI [17] set, with a success rate of 100% and a greater than 40% immunity with respect to noise contamination in all the cases.

Acknowledgment

The authors wish to express their gratitude to the Spanish C.I.C.Y.T. for its support of this work through grant TIC2001-0881.

References

[1] Bishop Ch. M. (2000) (reprint) Neural Networks for Pattern Recognition. Oxford University Press

[2] Wu Y, Giger ML, Doi K, Vyborny CJ, Schmidt RA, Metz CE (1993) Artificial Neural Networks in Mammography: Application to Decision Making in the Diagnosis of Breast Cancer. Radiiology 187 (1):81–87

[3] Aizenberg I, Aizenberg N, Hiltner J, Moraga C, Meyer EB (2001) Cellular neural networks and computational intelligence in medical image processing. Image and Vision Computing 19:177–183

[4] Christoyianni I, Dermatas E, Kokkinakis G (2000) Fast Detection of Masses in Computer-Aided Mammography. IEEE Signal Processing Magazine 17 (1):54–64

[5] Lo S-CB, Li H, Wang Y, Kinnard L, Freedman M (2002) A Multiple Circular path convolution neural network system for detection of mammographic masses. IEEE Trans on Medical Imaging 21 (2):150–158

[6] Chan H-P, Sahiner B, Petrick N, Helvie MA, Lam KL, Adler DD, Goodsitt MM (1997) Computerized classification of malignant and benign microcalcifications on mammograms: texture analysis using an artificial neural network. Phys Med Biol 42:549–567

[7] Yu S, Guan L (2000) A CAD system for the automatic detection of clustered microcalcifications in digitized mammogram films. IEEE Trans on Medical Imaging 19 (2):115–126

[8] Liu S, Babbs ChF, Delp E (2001) Multiresolution detection of spiculate lesions in digital mammograms. IEEE Trans on Image Processing 10 (6):874–884

[9] Privitera CM, Stark LW (2000) Algorithms for defining visual regions-of-interest: comparison with eye fixations. IEEE Trans on PAMI 22 (9):970–981

[10] Zheng L, Chan AK (2001) An artificial intelligent algorithm for tumor detection in screening mammogram. IEEE Trans on Medical Imaging 20 (7):559–567

[11] Kosko B (1988) Bidirectional associative memories. IEEE Trans. on Systems, Man and Cybernetics 18(1):49–60

[12] López-Aligué FJ, Alvarez I, Acevedo I, García-Orellana CJ, Macías MM (2000) Adaptive BAM for pattern classification. Proc. of the IJCNN'2000, 5:529-535

[13] García-Orellana CJ, López-Aligué FJ, González-Velasco HM, Macías MM, Acevedo-Sotoca I (2001) Large neural network: object modeling and parallel simulation. Intl Journal on Artif Intell Tools 3:373–385

[14] Kumar S (2000) Memory anhiliation of structured maps in bidirectional associative memories. IEEE Trans. on Neural Networks 11 (4):1023–1038

[15] Digital Database for Screening Mammography (2002) Available at: http://marathon.csee.usf.edu/Mammography/Database.html

[16] NIST Special Dat Base #19 (1995) Image Processing Group. Advanced Systems Division, National Institute of Standards and Technology

[17] Merz CJ, Murphy PM (1998) UCI Repository of Machine Learning Databases. Available at http://www.ics.uci.edu/~mlearn/MLRepository

Bayesian SPECT Image Reconstruction with Scale Hyperparameter Estimation for Scalable Prior*

Antonio López[1], Rafael Molina[2], and Aggelos K. Katsaggelos[3]

[1] Universidad de Granada. Departamento de Lenguajes y Sistemas Informáticos
18071 Granada, Spain
alopez@ugr.es

[2] Universidad de Granada. Departamento de Ciencias de la Computación e I.A.
18071 Granada, Spain
rms@decsai.ugr.es

[3] Northwestern University. Department of Electrical and Computer Engineering
Evaston, Illinois 60208-3118
aggk@ece.nwu.edu

Abstract. In this work we propose a new method to estimate the scale hyperparameter for convex priors with scalable energy functions in Single Photon Emission Computed Tomography (SPECT) image reconstruction problems. Within the Bayesian paradigm, Evidence Analysis and circulant preconditioners are used to obtain the scale hyperparameter. The proposed method is tested on synthetic SPECT images using Generalized Gaussian Markov Random Fields (GGMRF) as scalable prior distributions.

1 Introduction

SPECT is a technique used in Nuclear Medicine to take projection data by a gamma-camera following an orbit around the patient's body, at regularly spaced angles. A reconstructed SPECT image is the discrete representation of a cross section of the isotope distribution within the patient.

When Bayesian methods are applied to the reconstruction of SPECT images, the parameters of the prior model incorporating the expected structure in the image need to be selected. These parameters are known as hyperparameters and their selection has been a serious limitation to the use of statistical methods in medical reconstruction problems. Therefore, reliable automatic methods for the selection of the hyperparameters are essential to obtain correct reconstructions.

Several works have been published on the hyperparameter estimation problem in SPECT image reconstruction, see [7, 11] and references therein. In [8, 9] we used diagonal preconditioning methods to estimate the unknown hyperparameters. Circulant and shift-variant preconditioners were applied to GGMRF priors in [10], where the best reconstructions and execution times were obtained

---

* This work has been partially supported by CICYT project TIC2000-1275.

F.J. Perales et al. (Eds.): IbPRIA 2003, LNCS 2652, pp. 445–452, 2003.

with a circulant preconditioner. In this paper we propose a new circulant approximation to provide an estimation method of the scale hyperparameter that can be used on any prior with *scalable* energy function (see [3] for a justification on the use of scalable priors).

The rest of the paper is organized as follows. In section 2 we describe the degradation and image models and the Evidence Analysis within the Bayesian paradigm. Section 3 describes the proposed estimation method, as well as, the preconditioning method used. Experimental results are presented in section 4. Section 5 concludes the paper.

2   Hierarchical Bayesian Paradigm and Evidence Analysis

Within the Bayesian paradigm, the reconstruction of the original images X, denoted by $\hat{X}(\theta)$, is selected as:

$$\hat{X}(\theta) = \arg\max_{X} P(Y|X)P(X|\theta) , \tag{1}$$

where θ is a hyperparameter vector, $P(X|\theta)$ is the prior distribution and $P(Y|X)$ models the process to obtain the data Y from the real underlying image X.

The Hierarchical Bayesian paradigm first defines the distributions $P(Y|X)$ and $P(X|\theta)$. Next, a distribution $P(\theta)$ for the hyperparameters is defined and the joint distribution $P(\theta, X, Y)$ is formed. The Evidence Analysis performs then the following steps to estimate the hyperparameter vector and reconstruct the image:

1. $P(\theta, X, Y)$ is integrated over the whole image space X to obtain $P(\theta, Y)$ and

$$\hat{\theta} = \arg\max_{\theta} P(\theta, Y) = \arg\max_{\theta} P(\theta|Y) , \tag{2}$$

   is selected as the hyperparameter vector.
2. The original image X is then obtained as:

$$\hat{X}(\hat{\theta}) = \arg\max_{X} P(Y|X)P(X|\hat{\theta}) . \tag{3}$$

The degradation model for emission tomography is specified as a product of independent Poisson distributions:

$$P(Y|X) = \prod_{i=1}^{M} \frac{(\sum_{j=1}^{N} A_{i,j}x_j)^{y_i} \exp\{-\sum_{j=1}^{N} A_{i,j}x_j\}}{y_i!} , \tag{4}$$

where M is the number of detectors, N is the number of pixels and A is the system matrix. $A_{i,j}$ is the probability that an emitted photon from pixel j reaches detector i.

The prior models we use are convex Markov Random Fields (MRF) with *scalable* energy function. Their density functions have the following form:

$$P(X) = \frac{1}{Z(\sigma, p)} \exp\{-\sum_{i,j\in\mathcal{N}} V(x_i, x_j, \sigma, p)\} = \frac{1}{Z(\sigma, p)} \exp\{-\frac{1}{\sigma} \sum_{i,j\in\mathcal{N}} U(x_i, x_j, p)\} , \tag{5}$$

where V is the potential function which depends on two hyperparameters σ and p, that is, $\theta = (\sigma, p)$, U is the energy function and Z is the partition function. The elements x_i and x_j are neighbouring pixels and $\mathcal{N}$ is the set of all neighbouring pixel pairs. The scale hyperparameter σ determines the overall smoothness of the reconstruction, and p is called the shape parameter. The energy function is *scalable* if for all $X \in \mathcal{R}^N$ and $\alpha > 0$ we have:

$$U(\alpha X, p) = \alpha^p U(X, p). \tag{6}$$

From above it follows that the partition function can be expressed as:

$$Z(\sigma, p) = \sigma^{N/p} Z(1, p). \tag{7}$$

Equation (7) implies that the partition function, for any scalable prior model, is tractable with respect to the scale hyperparamenter σ. Hence, a general method for the estimation of σ can be obtained.

3   Scale Hyperparameter Estimation

We now proceed to estimate the scale hyperparameter for scalable priors in image reconstruction problems. We assume here that $P(\theta) \propto \text{const}$.

In order to solve Eq. (3), we define the following function $M(X, Y|\theta)$:

$$M(X, Y|\theta) = \log P(X|\theta) + \log P(Y|X) =$$

$$-\log Z(\sigma, p) - \frac{1}{\sigma} \sum_{i,j \in \mathcal{N}} U(x_i, x_j, p) + \sum_{i=1}^{M} \left(\sum_{j=1}^{N} (-A_{i,j} x_j) + y_i \log \left[\sum_{j=1}^{N} A_{i,j} x_j \right] \right), \tag{8}$$

and then calculate $P(\theta, Y)$ using

$$P(\theta, Y) \propto P(\theta) \int_X \exp\{M(X, Y|\theta)\} dX . \tag{9}$$

This integral cannot be evaluated analytically and therefore we resort to Gaussian quadrature approximation. Using Taylor series expansion, we expand $M(X, Y|\theta)$ around the MAP estimate, $\hat{X}(\theta)$, up to second order terms. Hence, we have the following approximation of $P(\theta, Y)$:

$$P(\theta, Y) \propto \exp\left[M(\hat{X}(\theta), Y|\theta) \right] \left| G(\hat{X}(\theta)) + \frac{1}{\sigma} F(\hat{X}(\theta)) \right|^{-1/2}, \tag{10}$$

where the (i, j)th elements of the matrices $G(\hat{X}(\theta))$ and $F(\hat{X}(\theta))$ are given by:

$$G_{i,j}(\hat{X}(\theta)) = \sum_{k=1}^{M} y_k \frac{A_{k,i} A_{k,j}}{\left(\sum_{l=1}^{N} A_{k,l} \hat{x}_l(\theta) \right)^2}, \tag{11}$$

$$F_{i,j}(\hat{X}(\theta)) = \begin{cases} \sum_{k \in \mathcal{N}_i} \frac{\partial^2 U(\hat{x}_i(\theta), \hat{x}_k(\theta), p)}{\partial x_i^2} & i = j \\ -\frac{\partial^2 U(\hat{x}_i(\theta), \hat{x}_j(\theta), p)}{\partial x_i \partial x_j} & i \neq j, j \in \mathcal{N}_i \\ 0 & \text{otherwise} . \end{cases} \tag{12}$$

Using Eq. (10) in Eq. (2) we obtain:

$$\sigma = \frac{p}{N} \sum_{i,j \in \mathcal{N}} U(\hat{x}_i(\theta), \hat{x}_j(\theta), p)$$

$$+ \frac{p}{2N} trace \left[\left(G(\hat{X}(\theta)) + \frac{1}{\sigma} F(\hat{X}(\theta)) \right)^{-1} F(\hat{X}(\theta)) \right] . \tag{13}$$

We can now use the following iterative procedure to estimate the reconstruction and the scale hyperparameter. At each step k, we proceed as follows:

1. Given a previously obtained image $\hat{X}^{k-1}$ and a previous estimate of the scale hyperparameter $\hat{\sigma}^{k-1}$, a new value $\hat{\sigma}^k$ is calculated using Eq. (13).
2. A newly estimated image $\hat{X}^k$, is obtained by iterating once a MAP algorithm for $\hat{\sigma}^k$ and $\hat{X}^{k-1}$.

We note that the estimation of σ involves the calculation of $(G(\hat{X}(\theta)) + \frac{1}{\sigma} F(\hat{X}(\theta)))^{-1}$. This inversion is a computationally intensive problem. We use preconditioning to approximate Hessian matrices in order to simplify their inversion.

In this work circulant preconditioning methods are used to approximate the matrix $(G(\hat{X}(\theta)) + \frac{1}{\sigma} F(\hat{X}(\theta)))$. The circulant preconditioner requires the potential function to be convex, symmetric, twice-differentiable with respect to X and have bounded second derivatives (see [10]). This kind of preconditioner improves the approximation of the matrix $(G(\hat{X}(\theta)) + \frac{1}{\sigma} F(\hat{X}(\theta)))$ with diagonal preconditioners and it is of interest since the Discrete Fourier Transform (DFT) can be applied to solve the matrix inversion.

We start by observing that $G(\hat{X}(\theta))$ can be expressed as:

$$G(\hat{X}(\theta)) = A^t W(\hat{X}(\theta)) A , \tag{14}$$

where $W(\hat{X}(\theta))$ is a diagonal matrix with diagonal entries

$$W_{i,i}(\hat{X}(\theta)) = \frac{y_i}{\left(\sum_{l=1}^N A_{i,l} \hat{x}_l(\theta) \right)^2} . \tag{15}$$

We then apply the approximation introduced in [5] to the Fisher information term, which produces:

$$A^t W(\hat{X}(\theta)) A \approx D_{(g)}(\hat{X}(\theta)) A^t A D_{(g)}(\hat{X}(\theta)) , \tag{16}$$

where $D_{(g)}(\hat{X}(\theta))$ is a diagonal matrix with diagonal entries

$$D_{(g)j,j}(\hat{X}(\theta)) = \sqrt{\frac{\sum_{i=1}^M A_{i,j}^2 W_{i,i}(\hat{X}(\theta))}{\sum_{i=1}^M A_{i,j}^2}} . \tag{17}$$

Following [4], the product $A^t A$ is now approximated by a block-circulant matrix G_c. The kernel of G_c is obtained as follows:

1. First we calculate $A^t A \, \epsilon_j$, where ϵ_j represents a unit vector centered with respect to the image.
2. Then, the kernel obtained in the previous step, is approximated by a shift invariant symmetrical blurring function.

We also apply the approximation proposed in [5] to the matrix $F(\hat{X}(\theta))$:

$$F(\hat{X}(\theta)) \approx D_{(f)}(\hat{X}(\theta))(I - \phi C)D_{(f)}(\hat{X}(\theta)) , \tag{18}$$

where the diagonal elements of $D_{(f)}(\hat{X}(\theta))$ have the form:

$$D_{(f)j,j}(\hat{X}(\theta)) = \sqrt{\sum_{k \in \mathcal{N}_j} \frac{\partial^2 U(\hat{x}_j(\theta), \hat{x}_k(\theta), p)}{\partial x_j^2}} , \tag{19}$$

and $(I - \phi C)^{-1}$ is a covariance matrix, with $C_{i,j} = 1$ for two neighbouring pixels and for the 8-point neighborhood system we are using, ϕ is just less than $1/8$).

The matrices $D_{(g)}(\hat{X}(\theta))$ and $D_{(f)}(\hat{X}(\theta))$ are approximated by constant diagonal matrices $\sqrt{\alpha(\hat{X}(\theta))}I$ and $\sqrt{\beta(\hat{X}(\theta))}I$ respectively, where:

$$\sqrt{\alpha(\hat{X}(\theta))} = \frac{1}{N}\sum_{j=1}^{N} D_{(g)j,j}(\hat{X}(\theta)) \text{ and } \sqrt{\beta(\hat{X}(\theta))} = \frac{1}{N}\sum_{j=1}^{N} D_{(f)j,j}(\hat{X}(\theta)) . \tag{20}$$

Using the above approximations we now have,

$$trace\left[\left(G + \frac{1}{\sigma}F\right)^{-1} F\right]$$

$$\approx trace\left[\left(D_{(g)}G_c D_{(g)} + \frac{1}{\sigma}D_{(f)}(I - \phi C)D_{(f)}\right)^{-1} D_{(f)}(I - \phi C)D_{(f)}\right]$$

$$\approx trace\left[\left(\alpha G_c + \frac{1}{\sigma}\beta(I - \phi C)\right)^{-1} \beta(I - \phi C)\right] . \tag{21}$$

where we have removed the dependency of the matrices on $\hat{X}(\theta)$ for simplicity. Finally, using the DFT we obtain the following expression:

$$trace\left[\left(G + \frac{1}{\sigma}F\right)^{-1} F\right] \approx \sum_{i=1}^{N} \frac{\Lambda_i}{\frac{\alpha}{\beta}\Gamma_i + \frac{1}{\sigma}\Lambda_i} , \tag{22}$$

where Γ_i and Λ_i are the (i)th elements of the DFT of G_c and $(I - \phi C)$, respectively.

Now, we use the described estimation method with GGMRF priors [2]. They are scalable and have the form:

$$P(X) = \frac{1}{Z(\sigma, p)} \exp\left\{-\frac{1}{p\sigma^p} \sum_{i,j \in \mathcal{N}} b_{i-j}|x_i - x_j|^p\right\}. \tag{23}$$

The potential function is convex when $p \geq 1$. For $p = 2$ we have the Gaussian distribution. We note that work has been devoted to the estimation of shape parameter p when this class of priors are used on *SPECT* images ([11, 8]). In these papers it was found that the simultaneous estimation of σ and p was not feasible, resulting in values of $p < 1$ for which the potential function is not convex. Based on the literature on *GGMRF* prior distributions, we fixed $p = 1.1$ in our experiments to estimate the scale hyperparameter.

When $p < 2$ the potential function has non bounded second derivative with differences $x_i - x_j = 0$. This is a problem for the circulant approach, since, as we have already mentioned, circulant preconditioner requires the potential function to be convex, symmetric, twice-differentiable with respect to X and have bounded second derivatives [10]. In order to overcome the problem, we have used the approximation suggested in [1] when dealing with wavelet image reconstructions using GGMRF prior models:

$$\sum_{i,j \in \mathcal{N}} b_{i-j}|x_i - x_j|^p \approx \sum_{i,j \in \mathcal{N}} b_{i-j}\left(\left(|x_i - x_j|^2 + \delta\right)^{p/2} - \delta^{p/2}\right), \tag{24}$$

where $\delta > 0$ is a stabilization constant.

Using Eqs. (24) and (22) in Eq. (13), we obtain the following scale hyperparameter estimation:

$$\hat{\sigma}^p = \frac{1}{N} \sum_{i,j \in \mathcal{N}} b_{i-j}|\hat{x}_i - \hat{x}_j|^p + \frac{p}{2N} \sum_{i=1}^{N} \frac{\Lambda_i}{\frac{\hat{\alpha}}{\hat{\beta}}\Gamma_i + \frac{1}{\hat{\sigma}^p}\Lambda_i}, \tag{25}$$

where α and β are obtained from Eq. (20) with:

$$D_{(f)j,j} = \sqrt{\sum_{k \in \mathcal{N}_i} b_{j-k}\left((p/2 - 1)\left(|\hat{x}_j - \hat{x}_k|^2 + \delta\right)^{\frac{p}{2}-2}|\hat{x}_j - \hat{x}_k|^2 + \left(|\hat{x}_j - \hat{x}_k|^2 + \delta\right)^{\frac{p}{2}-1}\right)}$$

4   Experimental Results

We denote by C2 the described estimation method using circulant approximation and GGMRF, the previously proposed estimation methods using diagonal approximation by D1 [8] and C1 the circulant approximation used in [10]. The image update was obtained using the MAP algorithm proposed in [6].

The synthetic image used in the simulations is shown in Fig. 1 (a), with size 128×128 pixels and 128 angles with 128 bins simulated. We have used 8 independent sets of projections. The average estimations provided by the methods are $\hat{\sigma}^{1.1} = 32.4$ (D1), $\hat{\sigma}^{1.1} = 34.3$ (C1) and $\hat{\sigma}^{1.1} = 34.5$ (C2). The reconstructions obtained with these values are visually indistinguishable (Fig. 1 (b) shows the

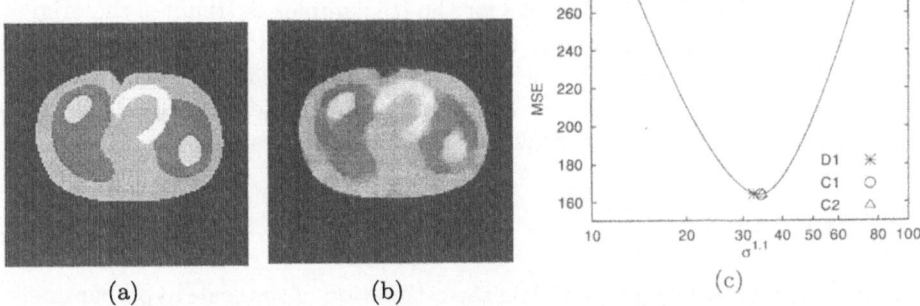

(a)   (b)   (c)

Fig. 1. (a) Original image. (b) Reconstruction. (c) Mean square error as function of $\sigma^{1.1}$. Marked the estimated values of $\sigma^{1.1}$ corresponding to the methods used

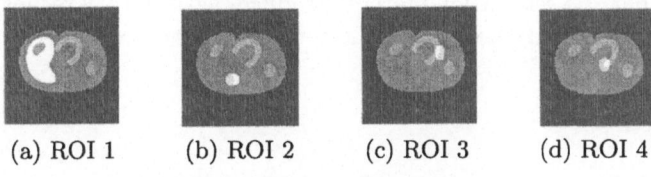

(a) ROI 1   (b) ROI 2   (c) ROI 3   (d) ROI 4

Fig. 2. Regions of Interest

Table 1. $Bias^2 + Variance$

	ROI 1	ROI 2	ROI 3	ROI 4
D1	0.03951	0.03616	0.08670	0.01987
C1	0.03923	0.02959	0.08392	0.01959
C2	0.03917	0.02957	0.08380	0.01958

obtained image with the diagonal approach). The mean squared error of the reconstructed images for different values of $\sigma^{1.1}$ was also calculated. The estimated values of the scale hyperparameter lie within the zone of the minimum of the curve (see Fig. 1 (c)).

Using as stopping criterion $\left|(\hat{\sigma}^{1.1})^k - (\hat{\sigma}^{1.1})^{k-1}\right|/(\hat{\sigma}^{1.1})^k \leq 0.0001$ the average number of iterations needed was: 149 (D1), 122 (C1) and 113 (C2).

We have computed $Bias^2 + Variance$ on Regions of Interest (ROI) to test the quality of the reconstruction. The ROIs are shown in Fig. 2 (the first ROI is uniform and the others include edges). These quantities are defined as:

$$Bias^2 \equiv \frac{1}{ML} \sum_{i=1}^{M} \left(\sum_{l=1}^{L} \frac{\hat{x}_i^l - x_i(true)}{x_i(true)} \right)^2 , \qquad (26)$$

$$Variance \equiv \frac{1}{ML} \sum_{i=1}^{M} \sum_{l=1}^{L} \left(\frac{\hat{x}_i^l - \bar{x}_i}{\bar{x}_i} \right)^2 , \qquad (27)$$

where M is the number of pixels in each ROI, L is de number of samples of y, $\hat{x}_i^l$ is the estimated activity in pixel i for the lth sample, $x_i(true)$ is the original pixel value and $\bar{x}_i$ is the estimated mean activity at pixel i from the L samples. The ROIs are shown in Fig. 2 in white. The obtained $Bias^2 + Variance$ values of with our approximations are shows in Table 1. We observe that C2 is slightly better than D1 and C1 since it provides the smaller values of $Bias^2 + Variance$.

5 Conclusions

In this paper we have concentrated on the estimation of the scale hyperparameter σ for prior models with scalable energy function in SPECT image reconstruction problems. The application of circulant preconditioner to estimate this unknown hyperparameter has been described. Using prior models such as GGMRF, we have found that the estimation method produces satisfactory reconstruction and the circulant preconditioners exhibit a better convergence rate.

References

[1] Belge, M., Kilmer, M. E., Miller, E. L.: Wavelet Domain Image Restoration with Adaptative Edge-Preserving Regularization. IEEE Tr. Im. Proc. **9** (2000) 597–608
[2] Bouman, C. A., Sauer, K.: A Generalized Gaussian Image Model for Edge-Preserving Map Estimation. IEEE Tr. Im. Proc. **2** (1993) 296–310
[3] Brette, S., Idier, J., Mohammad-Djafari, A.: Scale Invariant Markov Models for Bayesian Inversion of Linear Inverse Problems. Maximum Entropy and Bayesian Methods, Kluwer Academic (Skilling, J., Sibisi S., eds.) (1996) 199-212
[4] Clinthorne, N. H., Pan, T., Chiao, P., Rogers, W. L., Starnos, J. A.: Preconditioning Methods for Improved Convergence Rates in Iterative Reconstructions. IEEE Tr. Me. Im. **12** (1993) 78–83
[5] Fessler, J. A., Rogers, W. L.: Spatial Resolution Properties of Penalized-Likelihood Image Reconstruction Methods. IEEE Tr. Im. Proc. **5** (1996) 1346–1358
[6] Hebert, T. J., Leahy, R.: Statistic-Based MAP Image Reconstruction for Poisson Data Using Gibbs Priors. IEEE Tr. on Sig. Proc. **40** (1992) 2290–2303
[7] Lalush, D. S., Frey, E. C., Tsui, B. H.: Fast Maximum Entropy Approximation in SPECT Using the RBI-MAP Algorithm. IEEE Tr. Med. Im. **19** (2000) 286–294
[8] López, A., Molina, R., Katsaggeloss, A. K.: Hyperparamenter Estimation for Emission Computed Tomography Data. Proc. of IEEE Intl. Conf. on Image Processing, Vol. 2 (1999) 667–680
[9] López, A., Vega, M., Molina, R., Katsaggeloss, A. K., Rodríguez, A., López, J. M., Llamas, J. M.: Bayesian Reconstructions of SPECT Images, an Aide in Nuclear Medicine Diagnosis. Submitted to Tr. Med. Im. (2001)
[10] López, Molina, R., Katsaggeloss, A. K.: Scale Hyperparameter Estimation for GGMRF Prior Models with Application to SPECT Images. Proc. of IEEE Intl. Conf. on Digital Signal Processing, Vol. 2 (2002) 521–524
[11] Saquib, S. S., Bouman, C. A., Sauer, K.: Parameter Estimation for Markov Random Fields with Application to Bayesian Tomography. IEEE Tr. Im. Proc. **7** (1998) 445–448

Reducing Training Sets by NCN-based Exploratory Procedures*

M. Lozano, José S. Sánchez, and Filiberto Pla

Dept. Lenguajes y Sistemas Informáticos, Universitat Jaume I
Campus Riu Sec, 12071 Castellón, Spain
{lozano,sanchez,pla}@uji.es

Abstract. In this paper, a new approach to training set size reduction is presented. This scheme basically consists of defining a small number of prototypes that represent all the original instances. Although the ultimate aim of the algorithm proposed here is to obtain a strongly reduced training set, the performance is empirically evaluated over nine real datasets by comparing not only the reduction rate but also the classification accuracy with those of other condensing techniques.

1 Introduction

Currently, in many domains (e.g., in text categorisation, biometrics, and retrieval of multimedia databases) the size of the datasets is so extremely large that real-time systems cannot afford the time and storage requirements to process them. Under these conditions, classifying, understanding or compressing the available information can become a very problematic task. This problem is specially dramatic in the case of using some distance-based learning algorithm, such as the Nearest Neighbour (NN) rule [7]. The basic NN scheme must search through all the available training instances (large memory requirements) to classify a new input sample (slow during classification). On the other hand, since the NN rule stores every prototype in the training set (TS), noisy instances are stored as well, which can considerably degrade classification accuracy.

Among the many proposals to tackle this problem, a traditional method consists of removing some of the training prototypes, so the storage requirements and time necessary for classification are correspondingly reduced. In the Pattern Recognition literature, those methods leading to reduce the TS size are generally referred as to *prototype selection* [9]. Two different families of prototype selection methods can be defined. First, the *condensing* algorithms aim at selecting a sufficiently small subset of prototypes without a significant degradation of classification accuracy. Second, the *editing* approaches eliminate erroneous prototypes from the original TS and "clean" possible overlapping among regions from different classes.

* This work has been supported by grants TIC2000-1703-C03-03 and CPI2001-2956-C02-02 from CICYT Ministerio de Ciencia y Tecnología and project IST-2001-37306 from European Union.

F.J. Perales et al. (Eds.): IbPRIA 2003, LNCS 2652, pp. 453–461, 2003.
© Springer-Verlag Berlin Heidelberg 2003

Wilson introduced the first editing method [13]. Briefly, this consists of using the k-NN rule to estimate the class of each prototype in the TS, and removing those whose class label does not agree with that of the majority of its k-NN. This algorithm tries to eliminate mislabelled prototypes from the TS as well as those close to the decision boundaries. Subsequently, many researchers have addressed the problem of editing by proposing alternative schemes [1, 7, 9, 14].

Within the condensing perspective, the many existing proposals can be categorised into two main groups. First, those schemes that merely select a subset of the original prototypes [1, 8, 10] and second, those that modify the prototypes using a new representation [2, 4, 6]. It has been proven that the former family is partially inferior to the latter [3]. One problem related with using the original instances is that there may not be any vector located at the precise points that would make the most accurate learning algorithm. Thus, prototypes can be artificially generated to exist exactly where they are needed.

This paper focuses on the problem of appropriately reducing the TS size by selecting a subset of prototypes, in such a way that these represent all the instances in the original TS. The primary aim of the proposal presented in this paper is to obtain a considerable size reduction rate, but without an important decrease in classification accuracy.

The structure of the rest of this paper is as follows. Section 2 briefly reviews a set of TS size reduction techniques. The condensing algorithm proposed here is introduced in Section 3. The databases used and the experiments carried out are described in Section 4. Results are shown and discussed in Section 5. Finally, the main conclusions along with further extensions are depicted in Section 6.

2   Training Set Size Reduction Techniques

The problem of prototype selection is primarily related to prototype deletion as irrelevant and harmful prototypes are removed from a TS. This is the case, e.g., of Hart's condensing [10] and MCS scheme of Dasarathy [8], in which only critical prototypes are retained in the TS. On the other hand, some other algorithms artificially generate prototypes in locations accurately determined in order to reduce the TS size, instead of deciding which ones to retain. Within this category, we can find the algorithm presented by Chang [4] and by Chen and Józwik [6].

Hart's [10] algorithm is based on reducing the set size by eliminating prototypes. It is the earliest attempt at minimising the number of prototypes by retaining only a consistent subset of the original TS. A consistent subset, S, of a TS, T, is a subset that correctly classifies every prototype in T using the 1-NN rule. The minimal consistent subset is the most interesting, to minimise the cost of storage and the computing time. Hart's condensing does not guarantee finding the minimal subset as different subsets are given when the TS order is changed.

Chang's algorithm [4] consists of repeatedly attempting to merge the nearest two existing prototypes into a new single one. Two prototypes p and q are merged only if they are from the same class and, after replacing them with prototype z, the consistency property can be guaranteed.

Chen and Józwik [6] proposed an algorithm which consists of dividing the TS into some subsets using the concept of *diameter of a set* (i.e., the distance between the two farthest points). The algorithm starts by partitioning the TS into two subsets by the middle point between the two farthest cases. The next division is performed for the subset that contains a mixture of prototypes from different classes. If more than one subset satisfies this condition, then that with the largest diameter is divided. The number of partitions will be equal to the number of instances initially defined. Finally, each resulting subset is replaced by its centroid, which will assume the same class label as the majority of instances in the corresponding subset.

Recently, Ainslie and Sánchez introduced the family of IRSP algorithms [2], which are based on the idea of Chen's algorithm. The main difference between Chen and IRSP4 is that in the former, any subset containing a mixture of prototypes from different classes could be chosen to be divided. On the contrary, by IRSP4, the subset with the biggest overlapping degree (ratio of the average distance between prototypes belonging to different classes, and the average distance between instances being from the same class) is the one picked to be split. Furthermore, with IRSP4 the splitting process continues until every subset is homogeneous (i.e., all prototypes from a given subset are from a same class).

3   A New Approach to Training Set Size Reduction

The geometrical distribution among prototypes in a TS can become even more important than just the distance between them. In this sense, the so-called *surrounding neighbourhood-based rules* [12] try to obtain more suitable information about prototypes in the TS and specially, for those being close to decision boundaries. This can be achieved by taking into account not only the proximity of prototypes to a given input sample but also their *symmetrical distribution* around it.

Chaudhuri [5] proposed a neighbourhood definition, the Nearest Centroid Neighbourhood (NCN) concept, that can be viewed as a particular realization of the surrounding neighbourhood. Let p be a given point whose k NCN should be found in a TS, $X = \{x_1, \ldots, x_n\}$. These k neighbours can be searched for through an iterative procedure in the following way:

1. The first NCN of p is also its NN, q_1.
2. The i-th NCN, q_i, $i \geq 2$, is such that the centroid of this and previously selected NCN, $q_1, \ldots, q_i$ is the closest to p.

Neighbourhood obtained by this algorithm satisfies some interesting properties that can be further used to reduce the TS size by generating new prototypes. In particular, it is worth mentioning that the NCN search method is incremental and that the prototypes around a given sample have a geometrical distribution that tends to surround the sample, thus compensating the distribution of prototypes around the sample. It is also important to note that the region of influence of the NCN results bigger than that of the NN, as can be seen in Fig. 1.

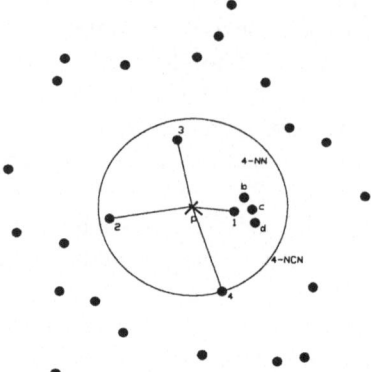

Fig. 1. Example of the NCN concept

3.1 Algorithm Outline

The TS size reduction technique here proposed rests upon the NCN search algorithm. NCN search is used as an exploratory tool to bring out how prototypes
in the data set are geometrically distributed. The use of the NCN of a given
sample can provide local information about what is the shape of the probability
class distribution depending on the nature and class of its NCN, that is, of the
nature of the prototypes in its surrounding area.

The rationale behind it is that prototypes belonging to the same class are
located in a neighbouring area and can be replaced by a single representative
without significantly affecting the original boundaries. The main reason to employ the NCN, instead of the NN, is to benefit from the aforementioned properties
that the NCN covers a bigger region than that of the NN and that they locate
an area of influence around a given sample which is compensated in terms of
their geometrical distribution.

The algorithm attempts to replace a group of neighbouring prototypes that
belong to the same class by a representative. In order to decide which group of
prototypes are to be replaced, we compute the NCN of each prototype p in the
TS until reaching a neighbour with a class label different from that of p.

The prototype with the largest number of neighbours is defined as a representative of its corresponding group, which lie in the area of influence defined by the
NCN distribution and consequently, all its members can be now removed from
the TS. Another possibility is to replace the group by its centroid. In this case,
the reduction of the data set is done by introducing new samples that replace
groups of existing ones.

After this, for each prototype remaining in the set, we update the number
of its neighbours if some was previously eliminated as belonging to the group
of an already existing representative. This is repeated until there is no group of
prototypes to be replaced by a representative. The basic scheme has been here
named *MaxNCN*.

In order to obtain a more important size reduction, a further extension to the idea just described consists of iterating the general process until no more prototypes are removed from the TS. Algorithmically, the iterative version can be written as follows:

Algorithm 1 *Iterative MaxNCN*

---

  while *eliminated_prototypes* > 0 **do**
    for $i = eachprototype$ **do**
      $neighbours\_number[i] = 0$
      $neighbour = next\_neighbour(i)$
      while $neighbour.class == i.class$ **do**
        $neighbours\_vector[i] = Id(neighbour)$
        $neighbours\_number[i] + +$
        $neighbour = next\_neighbour(i)$
      end while
    end for
    while $Max\_neighbours() > 0$ **do**
      $EliminateNeighbours(id\_Max\_neighbours)$
    end while
  end while

---

4   Databases and Experiments

Nine real data sets (see Table 1) have been taken from the UCI Repository [11] to assess the behaviour of the algorithms introduced in the previous section. The experiments have been conducted to compare MaxNCN and iterative MaxNCN with IRSP4, Chen's scheme and Hart's condensing, in terms of both TS size reduction and accuracy rate of the condensed 1-NN classification rule.

Table 1. Data sets used in the experiments

Data set	No. classes	No. features	TS size	Test set size
Cancer	2	9	546	137
Pima	2	6	615	153
Glass	6	9	174	40
Heart	2	13	216	54
Liver	2	6	276	69
Vehicle	4	18	678	168
Vowel	11	10	429	99
Wine	3	13	144	34
Phoneme	2	5	4324	1080

Table 2. Experimental results: 1-NN classification accuracy

	Chen's	IRSP4	Hart's	Iterative	MaxNCN
Cancer	96.78 (1.25)	93,55 (3,70)	94,61 (2,94)	68,60 (3,42)	89,92 (4,61)
Pima	73.64 (2.85)	72,01 (4,52)	73,31 (3,69)	53,26 (5,80)	67,71 (5,45)
Glass	67.18 (3.90)	71,46 (3,13)	67,91 (4,60)	57,19 (9,69)	66,65 (6,28)
Heart	61.93 (5.22)	63,01 (5,11)	62,87 (4,27)	58,16 (7,26)	59,92 (5,53)
Liver	59.58 (5.15)	63,89 (7,73)	62,40 (5,76)	53,31 (8,55)	60,65 (6,74)
Vehicle	58.56 (2.46)	63,47 (1,96)	62,17 (2,16)	55,20 (4,42)	59,33 (2,17)
Vowel	60.16 (9.27)	96,02 (1,77)	90,74 (2,30)	78,63 (5,18)	90,73 (1,78)
Wine	69.31 (7.31)	69,66 (3,47)	71,71 (6,72)	62,50 (6,65)	60,77 (6,19)
Phoneme	70.03 (9.14)	71,60 (8,74)	71,04 (7,90)	65,06 (7,57)	70,00 (8,05)
Average	68.57 (5.17)	73,85 (4,46)	72,97 (4,48)	61,32 (9,95)	69,52 (5,20)

The algorithms proposed in this paper, like in the case of Chen's and IRSP4, need to be applied in practice to overlap-free data sets (that is, there is no overlapping among regions from different classes). Thus, as a general rule and according to previously published results [2, 14], the Wilson's editing has been considered to properly remove possible overlapping between classes. The parameter involved (k) has been obtained in our experiments by performing a five-fold cross-validation experiment using only the TS and computing the average classification accuracies for different values of k and comparing them with the "no editing" option. The best edited set (including the non-edited TS) is thus selected as input for the different condensing schemes.

5   Experimental Results

Table 2 reports the 1-NN accuracy results obtained by using the different condensed sets. Values in brackets correspond to the standard deviation. Analogously, the reduction rates with respect to the edited TS are provided in Table 3. The average values for each method on the nine data sets are also included.

Several comments can be made from the results in these tables. As expected, classification accuracy strongly depends on the number of prototypes in the condensed set. Correspondingly, IRSP4 and Hart's algorithm obtain the highest classification accuracy almost without exception for all the data sets, but they also retain more prototypes than Chen's scheme and the procedures proposed here.

It is important to note that, in terms of reduction rate, the iterative MaxNCN eliminates much more prototypes than any other scheme. Nevertheless, it also obtains the worst classification accuracy. On the contrary, IRSP4 shows the highest accuracy but the lowest reduction percentage. Thus, looking for balancing between accuracy with storage reduction, one can observe that the best options are Hart's, Chen's and the plain MaxNCN approach.

Table 3. Experimental results: set size reduction rate

	Chen's	IRSP4	Hart's	Iterative MaxNCN	MaxNCN
Cancer	98.79	93,72	93,09	99,11	96,10
Pima	90.61	70,03	79,04	95,99	85,35
Glass	67.58	32,71	51,33	73,13	62,15
Heart	85.18	55,80	67,22	92,53	78,35
Liver	82.97	45,41	63,20	91,21	74,83
Vehicle	65.79	35,60	45,98	74,85	56,59
Vowel	79.64	39,54	75,97	84,23	75,09
Wine	86.75	73,13	78,79	89,03	84,83
Phoneme	94.51	69,90	87,91	98,16	90,88
Average	83.54	57,32	71,39	88,69	78,24

In particular, MaxNCN provides an average accuracy of 69.52% (only 4% less than IRSP4, which is the best option in accuracy) with an average reduction rate of 78.24% (approximately 20% higher than that of IRSP4). Results given by Chen's algorithm are similar to those of the MaxNCN procedure, both in accuracy and reduction percentage.

In order to assess the performance relative to these two competing goals simultaneously, Fig. 2 represents the normalised Euclidean distance between each (accuracy, reduction) pair and the origin (0% accuracy, 0% reduction), in such a way that the "best" technique can be deemed as the one that is farthest from the origin. Thus, it is possible to see that the proposed MaxNCN approach along with Hart's and Chen's algorithms represent a good trade-off between accuracy and reduction rate.

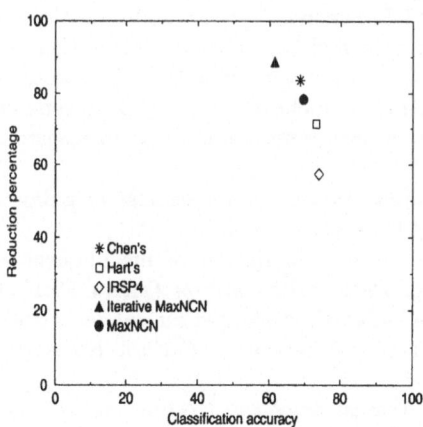

Fig. 2. Averaged accuracy and reduction rates

Finally, it is to be noted that several alternatives to the algorithms here introduced have also been analysed, although all them had a behaviour similar to that of MaxNCN. For example, we defined a simple modification in which, instead of using an original prototype as representative of a neighbouring group, it computes the respective centroid of the NCN. Another alternative consisted of using the NN instead of the NCN, but the corresponding performance was systematically worst than that of MaxNCN.

6   Conclusions

In this paper, a new approach to TS size reduction has been introduced. This algorithm primarily consists of replacing a group of neighbouring prototypes that belong to a same class by a single representative. This group of prototypes is built by using the NCN, instead of the NN, of a given point because in general, those cover a bigger region than the one defined by the NN.

From the experiments carried out, it is apparent that the plain MaxNCN provides a well balanced trade-off between accuracy and TS size reduction rate, in clear contrast to the behaviour of the iterative version, which results in maximum reduction percentage and very poor accuracy performance.

An extension to the algorithms here proposed would consist of including a *consistency test* before removing a prototype from the TS. By this condition, we would try to keep the discriminating power and consequently, to increase the classification accuracy of the resulting condensed set.

References

[1] D. W. Aha, D. Kibler, and M. K. Albert. Instance-based learning algorithms. *Machine Learning*, 6:37–66, 1991.

[2] M. C. Ainslie and J. S. Sánchez. Space partitioning for instance reduction in lazy learning algorithms. In *2nd Workshop on Integration and Collaboration Aspects of Data Mining, Decision Suport and Meta-Learning*, pages 13–18, 2002.

[3] J. C. Bezdek and L. I. Kuncheva. Nearest prototype classifier designs: an experimental study. *International Journal of Intelligent Systems*, 16:1445–1473, 2001.

[4] C. L. Chang. Finding prototypes for nearest neighbor clasifiers. *IEEE Trans. on Computers*, 23:1179–1184, 1974.

[5] B. B. Chaudhuri. A new definition of neighbourhood of a point in multidimensional space. *Pattern Recognition Letters*, 17:11–17, 1996.

[6] C. H. Chen and A. Józwik. A sample set condensation algorithm for the class sensitive artificial neural network. *Pattern Recognition Letters*, 17:819–823, 1996.

[7] B. V. Dasarathy. *Nearest neighbor (NN) norms: NN pattern classification techniques*. IEEE Computer Society Press, Los Alamitos, CA, 1990.

[8] B. V. Dasarathy. Minimal consistent subset (mcs) identification for optimal nearest neighbor decision systems design. *IEEE Trans. on Systems, Man, and Cybernetics*, 24:511–517, 1994.

[9] P. A. Devijver and J. Kittler. *Pattern Recognition: A Statistical Approach.* Prentice Hall, Englewood Cliffs, NJ, 1982.

[10] P. Hart. The condensed nearest neigbor rule. *IEEE Trans on Information Theory*, 14:505–516, 1968.

[11] C. J. Merz and P. M. Murphy. *UCI Repository of Machine Learning Databases.* Dept. of Information and Computer Science, U. of California, Irvine, CA, 1998.

[12] J. S. Sánchez, F. Pla, and F. J. Ferri. On the use of neighbourhood-based non-parametric classifiers. *Pattern Recognition Letters*, 18:1179–1186, 1997.

[13] D. L. Wilson. Asymptotic properties of nearest neigbor rules using edited data sets. *IEEE Trans. on Systems, Man and Cybernetics*, 2:408–421, 1972.

[14] D. R. Wilson and T. R. Martinez. Reduction techniques for instance-based learning algorithms. *Machine Learning*, 38:257–286, 2000.

Probabilistic Observation Models
for Tracking Based on Optical Flow

Manuel J. Lucena[1], José M. Fuertes[1], Nicolas Perez de la Blanca[2],
Antonio Garrido[2], and Nicolás Ruiz[3]

[1] Departamento de Informatica, Escuela Politecnica Superior, Universidad de Jaen
Avda de Madrid 35, 23071 Jaen, Spain
{mlucena,jmf}@ujaen.es
[2] Departamento de Ciencias de la Computacion e Inteligencia Artificial
ETSII. Universidad de Granada
C/ Periodista Daniel Saucedo Aranda s/n
18071 Granada, Spain
{nicolas,agarrido}@ugr.es
[3] Departamento de Electronica, Escuela Universitaria Politecnica
Universidad de Jaen
C/ Alfonso X el Sabio 28, 23700 Linares, Spain
nicolas@ujaen.es

Abstract. In this paper, we present two new observation models based
on optical flow information to track objects using particle filter algorithms. Although optical flow information enables us to know the displacement of objects present in a scene, it cannot be used directly to
displace an object model since flow calculation techniques lack the necessary precision. In view of the fact that probabilistic tracking algorithms
enable imprecise or incomplete information to be handled naturally, these
models have been used as a natural means of incorporating flow information into the tracking.

1 Introduction

The probabilistic models applied to tracking [10, 9, 4, 14] enable us to estimate
the *a posteriori* probability distribution of the set of valid configurations for the
object to be tracked, represented by a vector $\mathbf{X}$, from the set of measurements
$\mathbf{Z}$ taken from the images of the sequence, $p(\mathbf{X}|\mathbf{Z})$. The likelihood in the previous
instant is combined with a dynamical model giving rise to the *a priori* distri-
bution in the current instant, $p(\mathbf{X})$. The relation between these distributions is
given by Bayes' Theorem:

$$p(\mathbf{X}|\mathbf{Z}) \propto p(\mathbf{X}) \cdot p(\mathbf{Z}|\mathbf{X})$$

The distribution $p(\mathbf{Z}|\mathbf{X})$, known as the *observation model*, represents the
probability of the measurements $\mathbf{Z}$ appearing in the images, assuming that a specific configuration of the model in the current instant is known.

In this paper, two observation models are defined based on the optical flow
of the sequence, checking its validity within a scheme of particle filter tracking.

F.J. Perales et al. (Eds.): IbPRIA 2003, LNCS 2652, pp. 462–469, 2003.

2   Optical Flow

The most well-known hypothesis for calculating the optical flow [7] assumes that the local intensity structures found in the image remain approximately constant over time, at least during small intervals of time. This is to say,

$$I_x u + I_y v + I_t = 0 \tag{1}$$

where I_x, I_y, I_t are partial derivatives of the image, and $\mathbf{v} = (u, v)$ represents the flow vector at each point. The problem is ill-posed, since it only has one equation for the calculation of two unknowns, which makes it necessary to use various additional restrictions, in the majority of cases based on smoothness [1, 12].

3   Dynamical Model

The tracking task involves localizing, in each frame of a sequence, the object associated to a state vector that characterizes evidence of the presence of a specific configuration of the model in question. Other authors have successfully used characteristics such as the gradient [2] or intensity distributions [14]. The model which represents the dynamical model of the object will provide an *a priori* distribution on all the possible configurations at the instant t_k, $p(\mathbf{X}(t_k))$, from the estimated distributions in the previous instants of time. In this paper, a second-order dynamical model has been used in which the two previous states of the object model are considered, and this is equivalent to taking a first-order dynamical model with a state vector for the instant t_k of the form [2]

$$\mathcal{X}_{t_k} = [\mathbf{X}_{t_{k-1}}, \ \mathbf{X}_{t_k}]^T$$

The integration of the *a priori* distribution $p(\mathbf{X})$ with the set $\mathbf{Z}$ of the evidences present in each image, in order to obtain the *a posteriori* distribution $p(\mathbf{X}|\mathbf{Z})$, is obtained with Bayes' Theorem. This fusion of information can be performed, if the distributions are Gaussian, by using Kalman's Filter [10]. However, in general, the distributions involved in the process are normally not Gaussian and multimodal [4]. Sampling methods for modelling this type of distribution [6] have shown themselves to be extremely useful, and *particle filter* algorithms [8, 9, 5, 14] based on sets of weighted random samples, enable their propagation to be performed effectively.

4   Observation Models

4.1   Observation Model Based on Intensity Restrictions

In order to build this model, we will use a technique derived from the Lucas-Kanade algorithm[11] taking advantage of knowledge of the position of the flow discontinuities predicted by the object model. Our hypothesis is based on the fact that the point $\mathbf{x}$ of the model outline is situated on the real outline of the object, and therefore we assume that the flow in a neighborhood of $\mathbf{x}$ shall only take two values: one on the inner part of the model, and the other on the outer part.

Let $\mathbf{x} = f(\mathbf{X}_{t_k}; \mathbf{m})$ (where $\mathbf{X}_{t_k}$ defines the specific configuration of the object model, and $\mathbf{m}$ is the parameter vector which associates each point within the model with a point on the image plane), a point belonging to the model outline at the instant t_k. Let S be a neighborhood of $\mathbf{x}$ subdivided in S_i and S_e (corresponding respectively to the parts of the neighborhood which remain towards the interior and exterior of the outline of the object), and $\mathbf{d}(\mathcal{X}_{t_k}, \mathbf{m})$ be calculated using the expression:

$$\mathbf{d}(\mathcal{X}_{t_k}, \mathbf{m}) = f(\mathbf{X}_{t_k}; \mathbf{m}) - f(\mathbf{X}_{t_{k-1}}; \mathbf{m}) \tag{2}$$

The system of equations [11] is therefore solved

$$\begin{bmatrix} \sum_{S_x} (I_x^{(k-1)})^2 & \sum_{S_x} I_x^{(k-1)} I_y^{(k-1)} \\ \sum_{S_x} I_x^{(k-1)} I_y^{(k-1)} & \sum_{S_x} (I_y^{(k-1)})^2 \end{bmatrix} \begin{bmatrix} f_x \\ f_y \end{bmatrix} = \begin{bmatrix} -\sum_{S_x} I_x^{(k-1)} I_t \\ -\sum_{S_x} I_y^{(k-1)} I_t \end{bmatrix} \tag{3}$$

with $I^{(k-1)}$ and $I^{(k)}$ being the images corresponding to the instants of time t_{k-1} and t_k. In order to obtain the flow vector $\mathbf{f}_{S_x} = (f_x, f_y)$, where S_x shall be S_i or S_e, respectively, I_x and I_y are the spatial derivatives of the image and

$$I_t(\mathbf{x}) = I^{(k)}(\mathbf{x} + \mathbf{d}(\mathcal{X}_{t_k}, \mathbf{m})) - I^{(k-1)}(\mathbf{x})$$

In this way, two different flow estimations are obtained, $\mathbf{f}_{S_i}(\mathcal{X}_{t_k}, \mathbf{m})$ and $\mathbf{f}_{S_e}(\mathcal{X}_{t_k}, \mathbf{m})$, corresponding to the inner and outer area of the neighborhood of $\mathbf{x}$, respectively.

The squared norm of the estimated flow vectors are then calculated, which is equivalent to obtaining the quadratic differences with the expected flow, which in this case equals zero:

$$Z_{S_i}(\mathcal{X}_{t_k}, \mathbf{m}) = \|\mathbf{f}_{S_i}(\mathcal{X}_{t_k}, \mathbf{m})\|^2, \qquad Z_{S_e}(\mathcal{X}_{t_k}, \mathbf{m}) = \|\mathbf{f}_{S_e}(\mathcal{X}_{t_k}, \mathbf{m})\|^2 \tag{4}$$

It should be noted that if the point $\mathbf{x}$ is really situated on a flow discontinuity, and the flow in S_i coincides with $\mathbf{d}(\mathcal{X}_{t_k}, \mathbf{m})$, the value of Z_{S_i} must be close to zero and the value of Z_{S_e} must be considerably greater. Using the following expression, these values may be combined and a value of $Z(\mathcal{X}_{t_k}, \mathbf{m})$ may therefore be obtained:

$$Z(\mathcal{X}_{t_k}, \mathbf{m}) = \begin{cases} \dfrac{Z_{S_e}(\mathcal{X}_{t_k}, \mathbf{m})}{Z_{S_e}(\mathcal{X}_{t_k}, \mathbf{m}) + Z_{S_i}(\mathcal{X}_{t_k}, \mathbf{m})} & \text{if } Z_{S_e}(\mathcal{X}_{t_k}, \mathbf{m}) \neq Z_{S_i}(\mathcal{X}_{t_k}, \mathbf{m}) \\ \\ 1/2 & \text{if } Z_{S_e}(\mathcal{X}_{t_k}, \mathbf{m}) = Z_{S_i}(\mathcal{X}_{t_k}, \mathbf{m}) \end{cases} \tag{5}$$

The value of $Z(\mathcal{X}_{t_k}, \mathbf{m})$ satisfies the following properties:

- $0 \leq Z(\mathcal{X}_{t_k}, \mathbf{m}) \leq 1$
- If $Z_{S_e}(\mathcal{X}_{t_k}, \mathbf{m}) \gg Z_{S_i}(\mathcal{X}_{t_k}, \mathbf{m})$, then $Z(\mathcal{X}_{t_k}, \mathbf{m}) \to 1$, which indicates that the adjustment is much better in S_i than it is in S_e, and therefore the point must be situated exactly in a flow discontinuity, in which the inner area coincides with the displacement predicted by the model.
- If $Z_{S_e}(\mathcal{X}_{t_k}, \mathbf{m}) \ll Z_{S_i}(\mathcal{X}_{t_k}, \mathbf{m})$, then $Z(\mathcal{X}_{t_k}, \mathbf{m}) \to 0$. The adjustment is worse in the inner area than it is in the outer area, and therefore the estimated flow does not match the model's prediction.
- If $Z_{S_e}(\mathcal{X}_{t_k}, \mathbf{m}) = Z_{S_i}(\mathcal{X}_{t_k}, \mathbf{m})$, then the adjustment is the same in the inner area as it is in the outer area, and therefore the flow adequately matches the displacement predicted by the model, but it is impossible to guarantee that it is situated on a flow discontinuity. In this case, $Z(\mathcal{X}_{t_k}, \mathbf{m}) = 1/2$.

It is possible that some of the areas S_i or S_e lack enough *structure* to give a good flow estimate. In this paper, we have used the inverse *condition number* [13] of the coefficient matrix in the expression (3), $R = \lambda_{min}/\lambda_{max}$, in order to check the stability of the equation system, so that if it is too small ($< 10^{-10}$), it is necessary to discard the flow values obtained, and therefore $Z(\mathcal{X}_{t_k}, \mathbf{m}) = 1/2$.

We shall consider that the presence probability of the measurements obtained for the image, since they have been caused by the point of the outline corresponding to the vector $\mathbf{m}$ of the sample in question, defined by the vector $\mathcal{X}_{t_k}$, must be proportional to the function $Z(\mathcal{X}_{t_k}, \mathbf{m})$ obtained previously,

$$p(\mathbf{Z}|\mathcal{X}_{t_k}, \mathbf{m}_i) \propto Z(\mathcal{X}_{t_k}, \mathbf{m}_i) \tag{6}$$

and that, given the independence between the different points of the outline,

$$p(\mathbf{Z}|\mathcal{X}_{t_k}) \propto \prod_i Z(\mathcal{X}_{t_k}, \mathbf{m}_i) \tag{7}$$

4.2   Observation Model Based on Similarity Measures

If the prediction which the model makes is good and the intensity maps corresponding to the neighborhood of each point are superimposed, the inner part of the model must fit better than the outer part. In the model defined in this section, in order to estimate the observation probability of each point of the outline, similarity measurements shall be used to quantify the degree to which the inner part fits better than the outer part.

Let $\mathbf{x} = f(\mathbf{X}_{t_k}; \mathbf{m})$ be a point belonging to the model outline at the instant t_k, let S be a neighborhood of $\mathbf{x}$ subdivided in turn into S_i and S_e, let $\mathbf{d}(\mathcal{X}_{t_k}, \mathbf{m})$ be calculated from expression (2), and let $I^{(k-1)}$ and $I^{(k)}$ be images corresponding to the instants of time t_{k-1} and t_k. The quadratic errors are therefore calculated in the following way:

$$Z_{S_i}(\mathbf{X}_{t_k}, \mathbf{m}) = \sum_{S_i} W(\mathbf{x}) \Big(I^{(k-1)}(\mathbf{x}) - I^{(k)}(\mathbf{x} - \mathbf{d}(\mathcal{X}_{t_k}, \mathbf{m})) \Big)^2$$

$$Z_{S_e}(\mathbf{X}_{t_k}, \mathbf{m}) = \sum_{S_e} W(\mathbf{x}) \Big(I^{(k-1)}(\mathbf{x}) - I^{(k)}(\mathbf{x} - \mathbf{d}(\mathcal{X}_{t_k}, \mathbf{m})) \Big)^2 \tag{8}$$

where $W(\mathbf{x})$ is a weighting function. Two non negative magnitudes are obtained, that may be combined using expression (5), in order to obtain a value of $Z(\mathcal{X}_{t_k}, \mathbf{m})$. Since the magnitudes Z_{S_i} and Z_{S_e} are restricted, $Z(\mathcal{X}_{t_k}, \mathbf{m})$ may be considered to be proportional to the observation density $p(\mathbf{Z}|\mathcal{X})$, and therefore we again have:

$$p(\mathbf{Z}|\mathcal{X}_{t_k}, \mathbf{m}_i) \propto Z(\mathcal{X}_{t_k}, \mathbf{m}_i) \tag{9}$$

Supposing the measurements on each point are statistically independent, the following observation model is finally arrived at:

$$p(\mathbf{Z}|\mathcal{X}_{t_k}) \propto \prod_i Z(\mathcal{X}_{t_k}, \mathbf{m}_i) \tag{10}$$

5   Experiments

In order to check the validity of the observation models proposed, they were incorporated into the CONDENSATION algorithm [9], and their performance was compared with that of the observation model based on normals as proposed in [2].

For the experiments, two image sequences were used, lasting 10 seconds, with 25 frames per second, 320×240 pixels, 8 bits per band and pixel, corresponding to the movement of a hand over a background with and without noise. Results can be downloaded from http://wwwdi.ujaen.es/~mlucena/invest.html

5.1   Tracking an Object over a Background without Noise

In order to model the hand, an outline model based on a closed spline with 10 control points and a Euclidean similarity deformation space were used. A second-order dynamical model was used in which the object tended to maintain velocity, and a preliminary tracking was carried out of the hand by using the gradient observation model along the contour normals. With the data obtained, the multidimensional learning method proposed in [3, 2] was used to determine the dynamic parameters.

For the observation model based on contour normals, 20 normals were sketched for each sample. The observation model was applied with parameters $\alpha = 0.025$ and $\sigma = 3$, incorporated into the CONDENSATION algorithm with 200 samples. The initialization was carried out manually, indicating the position of the object in the first frame. Figure 1.a shows the weighted average of the distribution obtained.

The observation model based on intensity restrictions was used on the same 20 points along the outline, defining a neighborhood for each point of 7×7 pixels. In order to calculate the spatial derivatives, each frame was convolved with two Gaussian derivative masks, with vertical and horizontal orientations respectively, with $\sigma = 1.0$. The number of samples was also 200, and the results obtained are shown in Figure 1.b.

In order to apply the observation model based on similarity measures, the same conditions were used as in previous experiments (200 samples and 20 points along the outline, considering a neighborhood of 5×5 pixels for each point). The result obtained is illustrated in Figure 1.c.

5.2   Tracking an Object over a Background with Noise

In this case, the parameters of the dynamic model were adjusted manually for the first 50 frames, and these were used to learn dynamics and to perform an initial tracking of the sequence, using CONDENSATION with the observation model for the contour normals. From the results obtained, and using the same learning method as in the previous experiment, the dynamic parameters were determined.

In order to use the observation model based on contour normals, 18 normals were sketched to each outline. The number of samples was still 200, and the parameters for the observation model in this case were $\sigma = 3$ and $\alpha = 0.055$. The results are shown in Figure 2.a.

The same parameters were used in the observation model based on intensity restrictions as in the previous sequence, that is to say, spatial derivatives from Gaussian derivative masks with $\sigma = 1.0$, and neighborhoods of 7×7 pixels for each point. The results obtained with 200 samples are shown in Figure 2.b.

For the observation model based on similarity measures, neighborhoods of 5×5 pixels and 200 samples for the CONDENSATION algorithm were also used. The results obtained are shown in Figure 2.c.

6   Discussion and Conclusions

The observation model based on contour normals behaves appropriately in the two sequences (Figures 1.a and 2.a). At no time does the tracker lose the object, although it does have problems with noise in the sequence due to the presence of clutter.

For the first sequence, the model based on intensity restrictions, although never completely losing the object, does have problems focusing exactly on its outline. This is due to the absence of texture on the outer part of the object. However, for the second sequence, the presence of a background with a lot of noise is not only irrelevant but also favors the good behavior operation of the observation model.

Due to the fact that there is hardly any texture on the outer part of the object in the first sequence, the observation model based on similarity measures tends to minimize the inner measurement. Nevertheless, a slight deviation occurs at times towards the hand's shadow, since there is actually an ambiguity in the sequence, as the shadow moves jointly with the hand, and by only considering the optical flow, it is impossible to separate them. In the second sequence, there are no significant deviations from the real outline of the object.

The results obtained suggest that the observation models based on optical flow are, in a way, complementary to those based on gradient along normals. The

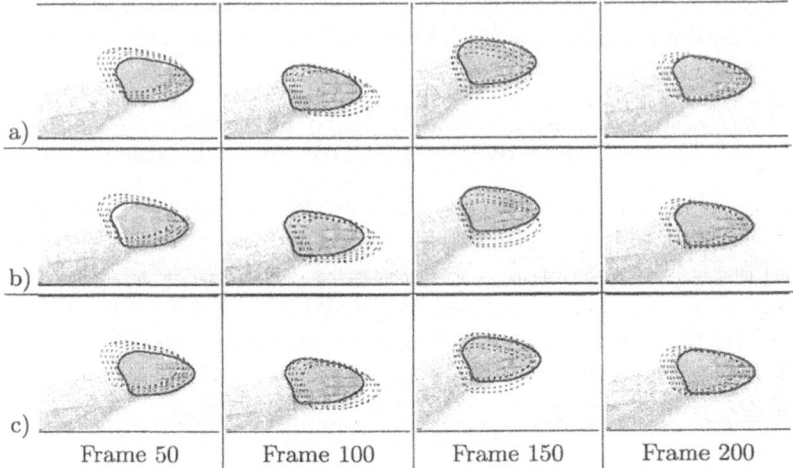

Fig. 1. a) Results obtained with the observation model for the contour normals.
b) Results obtained with the observation model based on intensity restrictions.
c) Results obtained with the observation model based on similarity measures.
The distribution average appears in continuous line in the current frame, and
the averages in some previous frames appear in dotted line

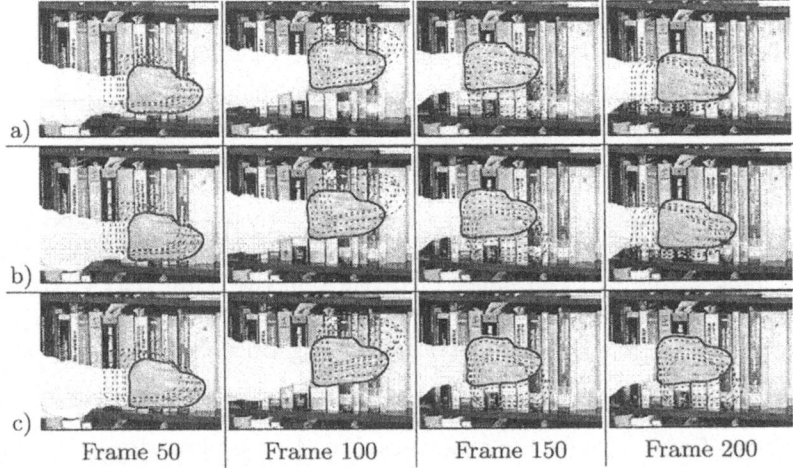

Fig. 2. a) Results obtained with the observation model for the contour normals.
b) Results obtained with the observation model based on intensity restrictions.
c) Results obtained with the observation model based on similarity measures.
The distribution average appears in continuous line in the current frame, and
the averages in some previous frames appear in dotted line

presence of clutter constitutes a source of noise for the first models, while favoring the good behavior operation of models based on flow. In addition, the model based on similarity is more stable numerically than the model based on intensity restrictions, because the former doesn't need to compute image derivatives.

Acknowledgment

This work has been financed by grant TIC-2001-3316 from the Spanish Ministry of Science and Technology.

References

[1] E. H. Adelson and J. R. Bergen. The extraction of spatiotemporal energy in human and machine vision. In *Proceedings of IEEE Workshop on Visual Motion*, pages 151–156, Los Alamitos, CA, 1986. IEEE Computer Society Press.

[2] A. Blake and M. Isard. *Active Contours*. Springer, 1998.

[3] A. Blake, M. Isard, and D. Reynard. Learning to track the visual motion of contours. *Journal of Artificial Intelligence*, 78:101–134, 1995.

[4] J. Deutscher, A. Blake, B. North, and B. Bascle. Tracking through singularities and discontinuities by random sampling. In *Proceedings of International Conference on Computer Vision*, volume 2, pages 1144–1149, 1999.

[5] J. Deutscher, A. Blake, and I. Reid. Articulated body motion capture by annealed particle filtering. In *Proceedings of IEEE Conference on Computer Vision and Pattern Recognition (CVPR)*, 2000.

[6] A. Gelfand and A. Smith. Sampling-based approaches to computing marginal densities. *Journal of the American Statistical Association*, 85(410):398–409, 1990.

[7] Berthold K. P. Horn and Brian G. Schunck. Determining optical flow. *Artificial Intelligence*, 17(1-3):185–203, 1981.

[8] M. Isard and A. Blake. Contour tracking by stochastic propagation of conditional density. In *Proceedings of European Conference on Computer Vision*, pages 343–356, Cambridge, UK, 1996.

[9] M. Isard and A. Blake. Condensation – conditional density propagation for visual tracking. *International Journal on Computer Vision*, 1998.

[10] R. E. Kalman. A new approach to linear filtering and prediction problems. *Transactions of the ASME–Journal of Basic Engineering*, 82(Series D):35–45, 1960.

[11] B. Lucas and T. Kanade. An iterative image registration technique with an application to stereo vision. In *Proceedings of DARPA IU Workshop*, pages 121–130, 1981.

[12] B. McCane, K. Novins, D. Crannitch, and B. Galvin. On benchmarking optical flow. *Computer Vision and Image Understanding*, 84:126–143, 2001.

[13] W. H. Press, S. A. Teulosky, W. T. Vetterling, and B. P. Flannery. *Numerical Recipes in C, Second Edition*. Cambridge University Press, 1992.

[14] J. Sullivan, A. Blake, M. Isard, and J. MacCormick. Bayesian object localisation in images. *International Journal of Computer Vision*, 44(2):111–135, 2001.

Simplified Texture Unit: A New Descriptor of the Local Texture in Gray-Level Images*

Francisco J. Madrid–Cuevas[1], R. Medina Carnicer, M. Prieto Villegas,
N. L. Fernández García, and A. Carmona Poyato

Department of Computing and Numerical Analysis, Córdoba University, 14071
Córdoba, Spain
malmacuf@uco.es

Abstract. In this work we propose a new descriptor of the local texture in gray-level images, named Simplified Texture Unit (STU). This descriptor is a version, with a smaller computational cost as much in its obtaining as in its later use, of the well-known Texture Unit descriptor (TU) [6]. We have carried out a comparative study of the capacity to describe the texture of a region with the capacity provided by the TU descriptor and two other versions of the same one, known as Local Binary Pattern (LBP) and Local Binary Pattern with Contrast (LBP/C) [11]. The results of the experiment allow to affirm that the new descriptor has a greater performance with small region sizes, what makes it suitable for unsupervised texture segmentation since it could allow a greater accuracy in the localization of the frontiers between textured regions.

Keywords: Local texture descriptor, feature distribution, unsupervised texture segmentation.

1 Introduction

The stage of image segmentation is recognized as one of the most complicated in a Computer Vision system [4]. Also, if the characteristic used to segment the regions is the texture, the problem is even more complicated. Many approaches have been used to achieve the segmentation of images using textures [5, 14, 12]. The segmentation can be supervised or not. When the segmentation is supervised, the number of different textures is known. It is often had a model of each one of these textures too, becoming the process of segmenting to a classification process.

When the segmentation is unsupervised, it doesn't have any a priori knowledge on the number and form of the textures that the computer vision system can find. Different methods to carry out unsupervised segmentation of textures have been proposed [3, 13, 8, 15, 17, 10, 7]. A specially effective method has been proposed recently [19, 11]. This method combines the use of a descriptor of the

---

* This work has been supported by the Research Project DPI2002-01013 that is financed by Science and Technology Ministry of Spain and FEDER.

F.J. Perales et al. (Eds.): IbPRIA 2003, LNCS 2652, pp. 470–477, 2003.
© Springer-Verlag Berlin Heidelberg 2003

local texture, generally in a 3×3 neighborhood, together with the distribution of the values of this local descriptor in a region of the image to characterize its texture. Analysis of dissimilarity between two distributions can be used to decide whether two regions of the image are drawn from the same texture class.

The segmentation process will be some version of the split–merge method [16, 9]. First, the non homogeneous regions are split. Next, adjacent region pairs that meet an homogeneity criteria are merged in an iterative way. The merging is repeated until a total merging criterion exceeds a given threshold. At the end of the merging stage, the located regions provide a roughly segmented image. The distributions in these regions will be used as models in the final refinement stage, where the border pixels are relabeled using those models providing the final segmented image. In all these stages, the minimum region size to obtain a distribution that allows to take reliable decisions is a key parameter, since the accuracy in the localization of the frontiers between regions will depend on it.

The texture unit (TU) is a descriptor of the local texture. It was proposed initially by He and Wang [6]. The TU has been shown to be a powerful measure of the local texture by different studies [18, 19].

A major inconvenient of this descriptor is the large range of its possible values (TU $\in [0, 6560]$) at the same time that these values are not correlated, therefore, they can not be grouped. As a consequence, the regions must have a relatively large size to get distributions that allow to compute reliable and stable dissimilarity measures.

Ojala *et al.* [11] have proposed a simplified version of the TU descriptor named Local Binary Pattern (LBP). The LBP reduces the range of its possible values significantly (LBP $\in [0, 255]$). However, this simplification carries with loss of discriminatory power. For this reason, in a later work [16], where they propose a method to carry out unsupervised texture segmentation, the LBP is used in combination with another local feature called Contrast. The joint distribution of both is used as a new descriptor named LBP/C. The range of its values varies in function of how many bins the Contrast has been grouped. Although the number of bins is decreased considerably regarding the TU descriptor, it follows being too large.

In this work we propose a new descriptor of the local texture that consists on a simplification of the TU descriptor. This descriptor, called Simplified Texture Unit (STU), has a more reduced range of values (STU $\in [0, 80]$) without a significant loss of the characterization power. The distributions of this new descriptor will allow to take reliable decisions with smaller region sizes than the above descriptors. This will improve the accuracy of the located frontiers. Other added qualities are the reduction of the requirements memory and computational time.

The paper is organized as follows: The derivation of the studied local texture descriptors is described in Sect.2. The experimental setup is shown in Sect. 3. In Sect. 4 a summary of the experimental results are presented and in Sect.5 the results are discussed concluding the paper.

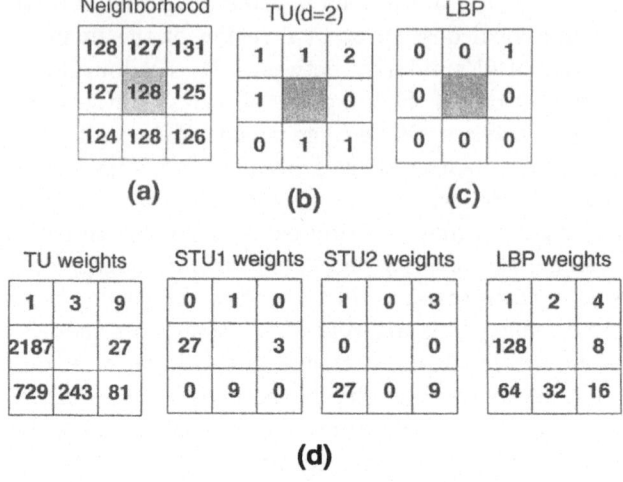

Fig. 1. An example of local neighborhood (a) and the corresponding descriptors: TU with $\Delta = 2$ (b) and LBP (c). The weights for obtaining the N_{TU}, N_{STU_1}, N_{STU_2}, and N_{LBP} are shown in (d)

2   Local Texture Descriptors

The Texture Unit (TU), due originally to He and Wang [6], is a powerful descriptor of the local texture and is defined in a 3×3 neighborhood of a pixel p. Let $V : \{v_0, v_1, \ldots, v_7\}$ the grey-levels of the eight neighbors of the pixel p with gray-level v_p. The Texture Unit, assigned to the position of the pixel p, is defined as the tuple of values TU : $\{e_0, e_1, \ldots, e_7\}$ with

$$e_i = \begin{cases} 0, & \text{if } v_i < (v_p - \Delta), \\ 1, & \text{if } (v_p - \Delta) \leq v_i \leq (v_p + \Delta), \\ 2, & \text{if } v_i > (v_p + \Delta), \end{cases} \tag{1}$$

where v_i is the gray-level of neighbor i and Δ is a tolerance parameter.

The TU descriptor can be represented in a compact way using the Texture Unit Number defined as $N_{\text{TU}} = \sum_{i=0}^{i=7} e_i 3^i$. The range of possible values of N_{TU} is $[0, 6560]$ and, from its definition, it does not make sense to group these values. Figure 1a shows an example of neighborhood. The TU assigned to this neighborhood using (1) with $\Delta = 2$ is shown in Fig. 1b. The corresponding N_{TU}, using the TU weights shown in Fig. 1d, is $N_{\text{TU}} = 1 + 3 + 18 + 81 + 243 + 2187 = 2533$.

Ojala *et al.* [11] have proposed a simplification in the definition of the TU descriptor, named Local Binary Pattern (LBP). This simplification involves thresholding with only one threshold applying the rule:

$$e_i = \begin{cases} 0, & \text{if } v_i \leq v_p, \\ 1, & \text{if } v_i > v_p. \end{cases} \tag{2}$$

The LBP also can be represented in a compact way through the definition of the corresponding $N_{\mathrm{LBP}} = \sum_{i=0}^{i=7} e_i 2^i$. Although the LBP describes the spatial structure of the local texture, it doesn't make the same thing with the contrast. For this reason, Ojala *et al.* use, to carry out unsupervised texture segmentation [16], the LBP combined with a measure of the local contrast C. The local contrast C descriptor is defined as the difference between the averaged gray-level of the pixels with $e_i = 1$ and those that have $e_i = 0$. Figure 1c shows how to obtain the LBP descriptor assigned to a example of neighborhood. The N_{LBP} is 4 where the LBP weights shown in Fig. 1d have been used. The local contrast is $C = 131 - (128 + 127 + 125 + 126 + 128 + 124 + 127)/7 = 5$.

To characterize the texture of a region, the joint grouped distribution of the LBP and C descriptors is used. The joint LBP/C descriptor will have as range of possible values $[0, 256 \times b]$, where b represents the number of bins used to group the contrast. Ojala *et al.* have determined experimentally that a suitable number of bins can be $b = 8$ and, therefore, the minimum region size needed for obtaining a significant histogram of values $N_{\mathrm{LBP/C}}$ can be reduced, regarding the TU descriptor.

The minimum region size can be decreased even more if a new descriptor of the local texture, that is proposed in this work, is used. This new descriptor is defined from the TU descriptor and called Simplified Texture Unit (STU). Only four values of the TU, that is assigned to the studied neighborhood, are involved in. Two versions can be obtained: when using the crosswise neighbors (up, right, down and left neighbors), the version will be named STU_1 and, when using the diagonal neighbors (up–left, up–right, down–right and down–left neighbors), the version will be named STU_2. Again, the STU descriptor will be used in a compact way by using the respective $N_{\mathrm{STU}} = \sum_{i=0}^{i=3} e_i 3^i$. If the STU_1 and STU_2 weights, that are shown in Fig. 1d, are applied to the example of TU shown in Fig. 1b, we get $N_{\mathrm{STU}_1} = 1 + 9 + 27 = 37$ and $N_{\mathrm{STU}_2} = 1 + 6 + 9 = 16$.

3 Experimental Setup

We have carried out a comparative study with the intention of checking whether the new STU descriptor improves or not the characterization power of the textures in an image, regarding the power provided by TU, LBP and LBP/C descriptors. Our experiment is a version (several region sizes are used) of the one carried out by Ojala *et al.* [11] and their results will be used to validate our results.

To carry out the comparative study, a set of fifteen natural textures has been extracted from the Brodatz's album [1]. These textures are easily accessible from Internet. The textures used are: D4, D9, D16, D19, D21, D24, D29, D32, D53, D57, D68, D77, D84, D92 and D93. The images are 640×640 size. Every image has been pre–processed in the following way: a version of the image, processed with a 25×25 median filter, has been subtracted from the original one in order to eliminate the background variations. Finally, a Gaussian match, with mean 127.5 and variance 40.0, has been applied to every image.

We are interested in measuring the performance of the descriptors when the region size has been reduced. The experiment has been carried out using $l \times l$ region sizes with $l \in \{4, 8, 16, 32, 64\}$. For every side l and every image, it has been extracted 100 non overlapping regions.

The TU and STU descriptors have a parameter that is the tolerance Δ. The values used for Δ are: 0, 2, 4, 8, 16 and 32. The LBP/C descriptor has a parameter that is the number of bins b used to group the local contrast. The values used for the parameter b are: 2, 4, 8, 16 and 32. The LBP descriptor has not parameters.

For each descriptor, several sets of grouped distributions have been obtained from the distribution of their values in every region, using the different region sizes and parameter values. Each set has $100 \times 15 = 1500$ distributions. The TU, STU_1 and STU_2 descriptors have $5 \times 6 = 30$ sets each one. The LBP/C descriptor has $5 \times 5 = 25$ sets. The LBP descriptor has 5 sets.

The performance of each descriptor has been evaluated through the miss–classification rate (MCR) of a k nearest neighbors classifier (KNN). The MCR has been obtained using cross–validation for each data set. The KNN classifier has two parameters: the number k of nearest neighbors to be considered and a distance function on the feature space. We have used values for $k \in \{3, 9\}$. Several measures have been proposed to measure the distance, or dissimilarity, between two grouped distributions, standing out the measures [2, 11]: the sum of absolute differences (L_1), the Pearson's statistic (λ) and the logarithmic of the likelihood rate (log–lh).

4   Results

Table 1 shows a ranking of the descriptors using the averaged MCR. To calculate the averaged MCR, the value MCR has been weighted considering the region size, since larger region size more penalized should be a mistake. The weights, for the region sizes with sides 4, 8, 16, 32 and 64, are 1/31, 2/31, 4/31, 8/31 and 16/31 respectively.

Figure 2 shows the performance of each descriptor versus the different region sizes. The parameters in Tab 1 are used for achieving the plotted performances.

The results obtained in the comparative study carried out by Ojala [11] have been used to validate our results. Ojala used in his study a 50×50 region size and

Table 1. Ranking of the evaluated descriptors using their averaged MCR

Descriptor	k	Measure	Parameter	Av. MCR
LBP/C	9	L_1	$b = 4$	0.0698
STU_1	9	λ	$\Delta = 8$	0.0705
STU_2	9	log–lh	$\Delta = 32$	0.0726
TU	9	L_1	$\Delta = 16$	0.0848
LBP	9	λ	$n.a.$	0.0994

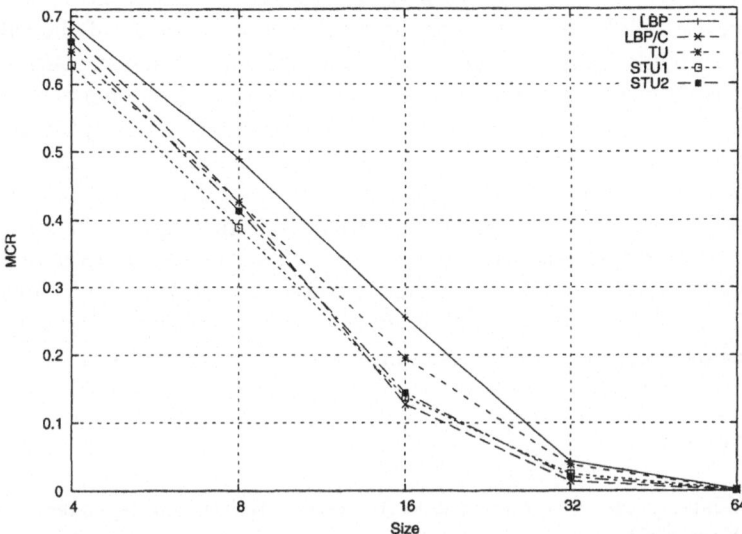

Fig. 2. MCR versus the region size. For each studied descriptor, the shown parameters in Tab. 1 are used

a KNN with $k = 9$. The MCR obtained by the LBP descriptor was 1.98% while we get 2.0%. Using the LBP/C descriptor with $b = 4$, Ojala obtained a MCR of 0.8% and we get the same value. Ojala did not use the TU descriptor in his comparative study.

5   Conclusions

From the averaged MCR shown in the table 1, it can be concluded that the new proposed STU descriptor has a similar performance to the supplied one by the LBP/C descriptor. The version STU_1, that uses the crosswise neighbors, has shown a performance lightly greater than the version STU_2 that uses the diagonal neighbors. Both versions improve the averaged performance provided by the TU descriptor. This demonstrates that the TU descriptor introduces redundancy. The LBP descriptor has shown the worse performance between the studied descriptors.

When large size regions (larger than 32×32) are used, all the descriptors have a low MCR with small differences between them. When small size regions (less than 16×16) are used, the new proposed STU descriptor has a greater performance. It is worth noting the LBP/C descriptor with $b = 4$ has $256 \times 4 = 1024$ bins while the STU descriptor has 81 bins only.

We are in agreement with Ojala *et al.* [11] since a significant difference between the used distance measures is not found. Therefore, if we keep in mind the *computational time*, the measure to be used should be the L_1 metric. However, the λ statistic can be accompanied together with the value of the achieved significance level (ASL) of a χ^2 statistical homogeneity test. The ASL provides an index of the reliability when a decision is taken in function of the calculated statistic. We should be careful when using the ASL since the distributions of the values of the descriptor are not selected in a random and independent way.

It is justified, in our opinion, the use of the new STU descriptor in spite of being simpler than the original TU. The carried out simplification does not imply any significant loss of its characterization power of texture when a large region size is used. When a small region size is used, it improves the characterization power of TU, LBP/C and LBP descriptors. This greater performance, when small region sizes are used, could mean a greater accuracy in the localization of frontiers between textured regions. Also, the carried out simplification reduces, in a significant way, the requirements in memory and computational time.

References

[1] P. Brodatz. *Texture: A Photografyc Album for Artists and Designers*. Reinhold, New York, 1968.

[2] R. Brunelli and O. Mich. Histograms analysis for image retrieval. *Pattern Recognition*, 34:1625-1637, 2001.

[3] P. C. Chen and T. Pavlidis. Segmentation by texture using a co-ocurrence matrix and a split-and-merge algorithm. *CVGIP*, 26:172-180, 1979.

[4] R. C. González and R. E. Woods. *Digital Image Procesing*. Addison-Wesley Publishing Company Inc., 1992.

[5] R. M. Haralick and L. G. Shapiro. Image segmentation techniques. *Computer Vision, Graphics and Image Processing*, 29:100-132, 1985.

[6] D-C. He and L. Wang. Texture unit, texture spectrum and texture analysis. *IEEE Trans. Geoscience Remote Sensing*, 28(4):509-512, 1990.

[7] A. K. Jain and F. Farrokhnia. Unsupervised texture segmentation using gabor filters. *Pattern Recognition*, 24(12):1167-1186, 1991.

[8] A. Mitiche L. S. Davis and Mites. A model driven, iterative texture segmentation algorithm. *CVGIP*, 19:95-110, 1982.

[9] F. J. Madrid-Cuevas, R. Medina, M. Prieto, and A. Carmona. Coarse-to-fine unsupervised texture segmentation using texture unit distributions. In Asociación Española de Reconocimiento de Formas y Análisis de Imágenes, editor, *Proc. IX Symposium Nacional de Reconocimiento de Formas y Análisis de Imágenes*, pages 157-162(Vol. II), Benicasim (Castellón), España, 2001.

[10] J. Mao and A. K. Jain. Texture classification and segmentation using multiresolution simultaneous autoregressive models. *Pattern Recogniton*, 25:173-188, 1992.

[11] T. Ojala. A comparative study of texture measures with classification based on feature distributions. Technical report, University of Maryland, Center for Automatic Research., ftp://ftp.cfar.umd.edu/TRs/CVL-Reports-1996/TR3731-ojala.ps.gz, 1996.

[12] N. R. Pal and S. K. Pal. A review on image segmentation techniques. *Patter Recognition*, 26(9):1277-1294, 1993.

[13] Pietikäinen and A. Rosenfeld. Image segmentation by texture using pyramid node linking. *IEEE trans. SMC* 11:822-825, 1981.

[14] T. R. Reed and J. M. H. du Buf. A review of recent texture segmentation and feature extraction techniques. *CVGIP: Image Understanding*, 57(3):359-372, 1993.

[15] M. Spann and R. Wilson. A quad-tree aproach to image segmentation wich combines statistical and spatial information. *Pattern Recogniton*, 18:257-269, 1985.

[16] M. Pietikäinen T. Ojala. Unsupervised texture segmentationu using feature distributions. *Pattern Recogniton*, 32:477-486, 1999.

[17] M. Unser and M. Eden. Multiresolution feature extraction and selection for texture segmentation. *IEEE PAMI*, 11:717-728, 1989.

[18] L. Wang and D-C. He. Texture clasification using texture spectrum. *Pattern Recognition*, 23:905-910, 1990.

[19] L. Wang and D-C. He. A new statistical approach for texture analysis. *Photogrammetic Eng. Remote Sensing*, 56(1):61-66, 1991.

Active Region Segmentation of Mammographic Masses Based on Texture, Contour and Shape Features

Joan Martí, Jordi Freixenet, Xavier Muñoz, and Arnau Oliver

Institute of Informatics and Applications, University of Girona
Campus de Montilivi s/n 17071 Girona, Spain
{joanm,jordif,xmunoz,aoliver}@eia.udg.es

Abstract. In this paper we propose a supervised method for the segmentation of masses in mammographic images. The algorithm starts with a selected pixel inside the mass, which has been manually selected by an expert radiologist. Based on the active region approach, an energy function is defined which integrates texture, contour and shape information. Then, pixels are aggregated or eliminated to the region by optimizing this function allowing to obtain an accurate segmentation. Moreover, a texture feature selection process, performed before the segmentation, ensures a reliable subset of features. Experimental results prove the validity of the proposed method.

1 Introduction

Breast cancer is considered a major health problem in western countries, and indeed it constitutes the most common cancer among women. Recent studies [1] show that in the European Community, for example, breast cancer represents 19% of cancer deaths and fully 24% of all cancer cases. In absolute terms, this data means that approximately 10% of women will develop breast cancer during the course of their lives. Mammographic screening is the main method to identify early breast cancer, because it allow identification of tumour when it is not yet palpable. However, of all lesions previously diagnosed as suspicion and sent to biopsy, approximately 25% were confirmed malignant lesions, and approximately 75% were diagnosed benign lesions. This high false-positive rate is related with the difficulty in obtaining an accurate diagnosis [2]. In this sense, computerized image analysis are going to play an important role in improving the issued diagnosis. The effort in such computerized schemes have been carried out for detection of two major signs of malignancy, named clustered microcalcifications and masses.

In this sense, in a previous work we proposed the use of selected shape-based features in order to classify clustered microcalcifications between benign and malignant [3]. The computerized analysis of microcalcifications was divided into four steps: 1) digitization of mammograms and enhancement of images; 2) detection and localization of suspicious areas using a region growing segmentation

F.J. Perales et al. (Eds.): IbPRIA 2003, LNCS 2652, pp. 478–485, 2003.
© Springer-Verlag Berlin Heidelberg 2003

algorithm based on Shen proposal [4]; 3) extraction of shape-based features for every segmented microcalcification; and 4) analysis of the features using Case-Based Reasoning techniques. More recently, we have studied how to characterise clusters of microcalcifications, due to its demonstrated relevance for issuing a diagnosis [5]. It has been observed, in a great number of malignant diagnosed mammograms, that the only indicator used to issue a diagnosis was the number of microcalcifications and their distribution inside every cluster.

On the other hand, masses also contain important signs of breast cancer and are hard to detect as they often occur in dense glandular tissue. In this sense, a number of researchers consider the computer analysis of masses to be more challenging as compared to that microcalcifications because masses are normally indistinguishable from the surrounding tissues [6].

Sahiner et al. [7] analysed and summarized a whole set of mass segmentation methods. Several works are focused on the use of texture and shape features. For instance, Kilday et al. [8] applied seven morphological features, while Petrosian et al. [9] investigated the usefulness of texture features based on spatial gray-level dependence matrices. Rangayyan et al. [10] used an adaptive method of edge profile acutance, and shape measures of compactness, Fourier descriptor, and moment based measure. On the other hand, Wu et al. [11] selected 14 features from a total of 43 for classification of malignant and benign masses and applied artificial neural network.

In this paper we propose a novel method for masses segmentation based on the principle of active region that takes into account texture, contours, and shape features. A set of 80 texture features are extracted and then selected according its homogeneity behaviour in order to choose an appropriated subset for the segmentation. Furthermore, an energy function is then defined which integrates all these sources of information. Then, the active region starts to grow optimizing this function in order to segment the mass region. The remainder of this paper is structured as follows: Section 2 describes the proposed segmentation approach detailing the selection of the texture features as well as the segmentation process based on the active region model. Experimental results proving the validity of our proposal appear in Section 3. Finally, conclusions are given in Section 4.

2   Proposed Segmentation Method

The method is grounded on the observations: 1) that masses in mammographic images have approximately uniform textures across their interiors, 2) the mass edges coincide with maxima in the magnitude of the gray level gradient, and 3) that changes in masse profile shape are small.

Taking these observations into account our proposal is based on the definition of an energy function, which integrates all these sources of information. Roughly speaking, the method starts from a connected set of pixels known to occupy the mass interior, which have been provided by the user (expert radiologist). Then, the algorithm is composed by two basic stages. Firstly, best texture features to segment the mass are selected; and secondly, the region grows by optimizing the energy function, which ensures the homogeneity inside the region, the presence of edges at its boundary, and the similarity of the region shape with those of previously-determined regions.

Furthermore, our proposal is based on the active region model, which has been recently introduced as a way to combine region and boundary information. This model is a considerable extension on the active contour model since it incorporates region-based information with the aim of finding a partition where the interior and the exterior of the region preserve the desired image properties. The underlying idea is that the region moves through the image (shrinking or expanding) in order to contain a single, whole region. The works of Chakraborty et al. [12], Hibbard [13] and Sahiner et al. [7] are good examples of active regions applied to the segmentation in medical images.

2.1   Texture Features Selection

One of major problems of texture segmentation is the selection of adequate texture features to model the homogeneity of regions, which are able to provide us the information required to perform the segmentation. In order to solve this difficulty, we use the knowledge provided by the user selecting an area of the image which is known of belonging to the region, and features which are homogeneous in this neighbourhood are selected.

Co-occurrence matrices proposed by Haralick et al. [14] are used in this work. Some of the most typical features, contrast, energy, entropy and homogeneity, are computed for distances from one to five and for $0°, 45°, 90°$ and $135°$ orientations, providing a set of 80 features. Then, the homogeneity of each feature inside the initial region is tested by measuring its match with a normal distribution using a skewness and kurtosis test, which many authors recommend by its simplicity [15]. Hence, a small subset of k texture features which present an homogeneous behaviour inside the region are selected for the next step of the segmentation process.

2.2   Active Region Segmentation

The combination of region, edge and shape information represents more accurately boundaries in medical images than either region growing or edge detection alone was compellingly argued by Chakraborty al. [12]. With the aim of integrating all these kinds of information in an optimal segmentation, the global energy is defined with three basic terms. Region terms measures the homogeneity in the interior of the region by the probability that these pixels belong to the region. Boundary term measures the probability that boundary pixels are really edge pixels. And finally, shape term measures the similarity of the contour shape with those of previously determined cases.

Some complementary definitions are required: let $\rho(R)$ be a partition of the image into two non-overlapping regions, where R_0 is the region corresponding to the background region and R_1 corresponds to the mass region. Let ∂R_1 be the current region boundaries of the growing region R_1. The energy function is then defined as

$$E(\rho(R)) = \alpha \sum_{i=0}^{1} - \log P_{Region}(j : j \epsilon R_i | R_i) + \beta(- \log P_{Boundary}(j : j \epsilon \partial R_1))$$
$$+(1 - \alpha - \beta)(- \log P_{Shape}(R_i))$$

$$(1)$$

where α is a model parameter weighting the region term and β weights the boundary term. The influence of these parameters on the segmentation results will be analised in Section 3.

Region Information

The region term measures the homogeneity of the pixels into a texture region which is modelled by a multivariate Gaussian distribution. Hence, the probability of a pixel j characterized by the selected texture features $\vec{x_j}$ of belonging to the region R_1 is

$$P_{Region}(\vec{x_j}|R_1) = \frac{1}{\sqrt{(2\pi)^k|\Sigma_1|}} \exp\{-\frac{1}{2}(\vec{x_j} - \vec{\mu_1})^T \Sigma_1^{-1}(\vec{x_j} - \vec{\mu_1})\} \qquad (2)$$

where $\vec{\mu_1}$ is the mean vector of the region and Σ_1 its covariance matrix. The background is treated as a single region having uniform probability distribution P_0.

Boundary Information

The second term in equation 1 depends on the coincidence of the region boundary with the image edges appearing as coherent features in the scalar gradient of the gray levels. Hence, we can consider $P_{Boundary}(j)$ as directly proportional to the value of the magnitude gradient of the pixel j.

Shape Information

Region shape is specified from Fourier descriptors, which use the Fourier transform over the points that define the contour of the region, where each point (x, y) is defined as a complex number $(x + jy)$. Thus, we have a sequence of complex numbers that represent the region contour. Nevertheless, the Fourier transform algorithm requires an input array whose length is an integral power of 2. So, if the number of points of the contour does not satisfy this condition, we need to follow the contour until the condition is true. Due to the periodic rate of the Fourier transform, this will have no effect on the result. There are other changes that must be applied to the Fourier descriptors to eliminate their dependence on position, size, orientation and starting point of the contour. A change in the position of the contour alters only the first descriptor, so we initialize this descriptor to null. A change of size only requires multiplying by a constant.

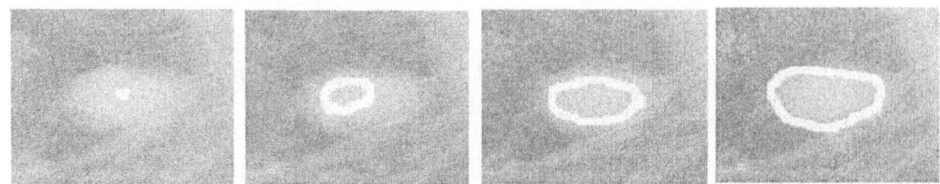

Fig. 1. Sequence of the region growth. The region starts to grow from the interior area selected by the user, competing for the image pixels in order the segment the whole mass

A rotation on the region requires multiplying each coordinate by $\exp(j\phi)$ where ϕ is the rotation angle.

$$NFD(k) = \begin{cases} 0 & k = 0 \\ \frac{A(k)}{A(1)} & k = 1, 2, ..., N/2 \\ \frac{A(k+N)}{A(1)} & k = -1, -2, ..., -N/2 + 1 \end{cases} \tag{3}$$

With these Fourier descriptors we achieve a set of points that characterizes the region. However, a solely value would be advisable. In this sense, we use the measure defined by Shen [4] that gives a single descriptor for each region.

$$FF = \frac{\sum_{k=-\frac{N}{2}+1}^{N/2} \frac{\|NFD(k)\|}{|k|}}{\sum_{k=-\frac{N}{2}+1}^{N/2} \| NFD(k) \|} \tag{4}$$

Hence, the match of the region shape and the model shape, which is related to previously determined cases, is given by the difference between their corresponding FF descriptors.

Optimization

The energy function is then optimized by a region competition algorithm [16] which takes the neighbouring pixels to the current region boundary ∂R_1 into account to determine the next movement. Specifically, the region aggregates a neighbouring pixel when this new classification decreases the energy of the segmentation. Intuitively, the region begin to move and grow, competing for the pixels of the image until an energy minimum is reached. A sequence of the region growth is shown in Figure 1.

3   Experimental Results

Twenty mammographic images including sixteen circumscribed-benign and four circumscribed-malignant were selected from the Mammographic Image Analysis Society (MIAS, UK) database. The spatial resolution of the image is 50μm x

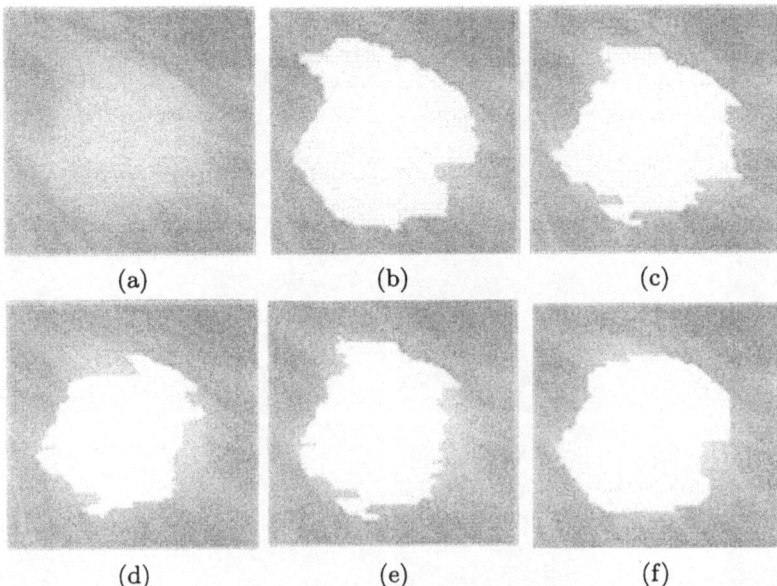

(a)   (b)   (c)

(d)   (e)   (f)

Fig. 2. Segmentations results using different weights (α) and (β) on the terms of the energy function. (a) Original mass, and segmentations obtained considering (b) texture, (c) contour, (d) texture and shape, (e) contour and shape, and (f) all three terms

50μm. The optical density is linear in the range $0 - 3.2$ and quantized to 8 bits. The boundary of each mass was traced by an expert radiologist specialized on mammography and were used as the basis for visual evaluation of the segmented results obtained by the proposed mass detection algorithm.

The influence of the three terms which are considered in the energy function (region, boundary and shape) was analised. Figure 2 shows segmentation results obtained with different weights of these terms. As is stated, all sources provide us useful information to perform the segmentation. However, best results have been achieved considering all three terms together.

An expert radiologist was the responsible to provide an initial placement inside the mass to segment. Some segmentation results obtained then by our proposal are shown in Figure 3. As is stated, the technique allows to correctly segment the masses and results have been considered very positive for radiologists.

4   Conclusions and Further Work

This paper has presented a segmentation method for the identification of masses in mammographic images. The technique is based on the integration of texture, *contour and shape information* in the segmentation process. Hence, an energy function which considers all these sources together has been defined. Then, the

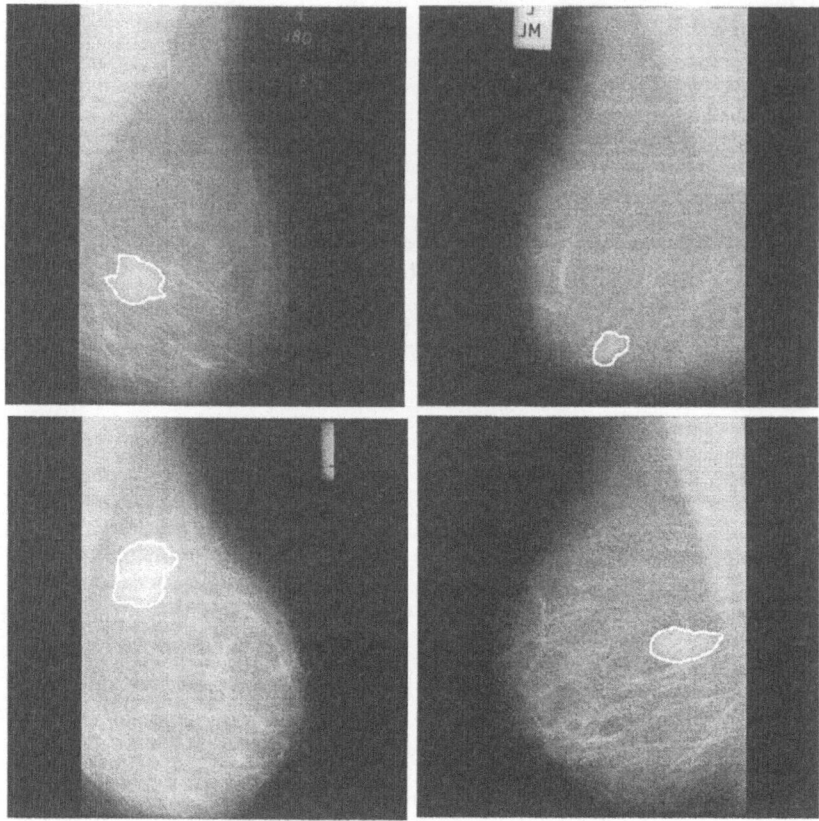

Fig. 3. Mass segmentation results

growing of the region by optimizing this function allows to obtain an accurate segmentation. Furthermore, the a-priori selection of the most adequate texture features to segment the mass has been described.

Experimental results over 20 images from the Mammographic Image Analysis Society database demonstrate the effectiveness of the proposed algorithm in estimating mass regions and their boundaries with high accuracy.

Further work is focused on two different directions. First, the inclusion of an automatic module of mass detection and seed placement in order to perform an unsupervised segmentation. And second, the extension of our proposal to deal with spicular masses.

References

[1] J. Esteve, A. Kricker, J. Ferlay, and D. Parkin. Facts and figures of cancer in the european community. Technical report, International Agency for Research on Cancer, Lyon, France, 1993.

[2] L. Basset and R. Gold. *Breast Cancer Detection: Mammograms and Other Methods in Breast Imaging*. Grune & Stratton, New York, 1987.

[3] J. Martí, J. Español, E. Golabardes, J. Freixenet, R. García, and M. Salamó. Classification of microcalcifications in digital mammograms using case-based reasoning. In *International Workshop on Digital Mammography*, pages 285–294, Toronto, Canada, June 2000.

[4] L. Shen, R. M. Rangayyan, and J. E. L. Desautels. Application of shape analysis to mammographic calcifications. *IEEE Transactions on Medical Imaging*, 13:263–274, June 1994.

[5] J. Freixenet, P. Planiol, J. Martí, R. García, J. Batlle, and R. Bassaganyas. Cluster-shape characterization of microcalcifications. In *IEE Proceedings of Medical Applications of Signal Processing*, pages 5/1–5/5, London, UK, October 2002.

[6] H. Li, M. Kallergi, L. Clarke, V. Jain, and R. Clark. Markov random field for tumor detection in digital mammography. *IEEE Transactions on Medical Imaging*, 14(3):565–576, September 1995.

[7] B. Sahiner, N. Petrick, H. Chan, L. M. Hadjiiski, C. Paramagul, M. A. Helvie, and M. N. Gurcan. Computer-aided characterization of mammographic masses: Accuracy of mass segmentation and its effects on characterization. *IEEE Transactions on Medical Imaging*, 20(12):1275–1284, December 2001.

[8] J. Kilday, F. Palmieri, and M. D. Fox. Classifying mammographic lesions using computer-aided image analysis. *IEEE Transactions on Medical Imaging*, 12:664–669, December 1993.

[9] A. Petrosian, H. P. Chan, N. Petrick, D. Wei, M. A. Helvie, D. D. Adler, and M. M. Goodsit. Computer-aided diagnosis in mammography: classification of mass and normal tissue by texture analysis. *Physics in Medicine and Biology*, 39:2273–2288, 1994.

[10] R. M. Rangayyan, N. M. El-Faramawy, J. E. L. Desautels, and O. A. Alim. Discrimination between benign and malignant breast tumors using a region-based measure of edge profile acutance. In *International Workshop on Digital Mammography*, pages 213–218, 1996.

[11] Y. Wu, M. L. Giger, K. Doi, C. J. Vyborny, R. A. Schmidt, and C. E. Metz. Artificial neural networks in mammography: application to decision making in the diagnosis of breast cancer. *Radiology*, 187(1):81–87, 1993.

[12] A. Chakraborty, L. H. Staib, and J. S. Duncan. Deformable boundary finding in medical images by integrating gradient and region information. *IEEE Transactions on Medical Imaging*, 15:859–870, 1996.

[13] L. S. Hibbard. Maximum a posteriori segmentation for medical visualization. In *IEEE Workshop on Biomedical Image Analysis*, pages 93–102, Santa Barbara, California, June 1998.

[14] R. M. Haralick, K. Shanmugan, and I. Dinstein. Texture features for image classification. *IEEE Transactions on Systems, Man, and Cybernetics*, 3(6):610–621, November 1973.

[15] L. Wilkinson. Statistical methods in psychology journals. *American Psychologist*, 54(8):594–604, 1999.

[16] S. C. Zhu and A. Yuille. Region competition: Unifying snakes, region growing, and bayes/mdl for multi-band image segmentation. *IEEE Transactions on Pattern Analysis and Machine Intelligence*, 18(9):884–900, September 1996.

Refining 3D Recovering by Carving through View Interpolation and Stereovision

Enric Martin, Joan Aranda, and Antonio Martinez

Department of Automatic Control and Computer Engineering
Universitat Politècnica de Catalunya
08028 Barcelona, Spain
{emartin,aranda,abmv}@esaii.upc.es

Abstract. In this paper, we present a method for obtaining accurate 3D models by merging the carving and stereo-matching algorithms. Multiple views of an object are taken from known camera poses. Object images, when segmented, are used to carve a rough 3D model of the object. View synthesis results are compared with real object views in order to validate the recovered model. When errors are detected, commonly due to occlusions and/or concavities, a fine stereo-matching algorithm is applied. Obtained depth map updates the inconsistent areas of the object model. Performed tests show the reached improvements in the accuracy of the model.

1 Introduction

Nowadays 3D shape reconstruction is a fundamental problem for computer vision researchers. Several groups are obtaining encouraging results applying different approaches: the use of multiple-view stereo matching techniques [1], mathematical approaches [2] or a plenoptic modeling from multiple images [3]. Real time 3D inference from scene views needs algorithm improvements, hardware acceleration and the integration of different techniques with the aim to be reliable.

Space carving methods are good enough recovering 3D structure with a minimal set of constraints [4]. However, these methods fail when dealing with concavities or partial occlusions. Stereo matching techniques can help in these cases, but these cases must be detected. A measure of error in the model construction is needed.

View synthesis [5] can be a proper tool to find failures in the carved 3D recovering of an object. As the synthesis procedures need some three-dimensional information, the used synthesis algorithm will propagate existing errors in the model.

The main idea of this paper is to merge 3D carving and stereo matching, searching a balance between the reliable but coarse carving algorithm and the slow and smart stereovision process. Next chapters will explain the basic features of the proposed method.

F.J. Perales et al. (Eds.): IbPRIA 2003, LNCS 2652, pp. 486–493, 2003.

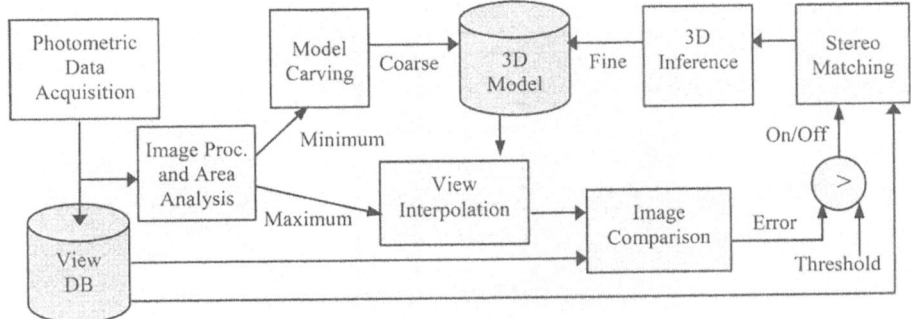

Fig. 1. Process scheme. An overview of the several algorithms involved

2   Process Description

The process consists of several steps, each one involving classical computer vision algorithms (see figure 1). The photometric data acquisition step comprises image capture, filtering, segmentation and area analysis of the segmented objects; allowing the creation of a dense view database. A carving process creates a rough three-dimensional recovering of the object, where some errors due to concavities or occlusions could appear. Next step is the synthesis of interpolated views from captured images and the obtained 3D information. Interpolated views are compared with the real views saved in the database. If the error is greater than a threshold value, a stereo matching process will infer a smoother 3D data to correct the carved object model.

3   Carving Process

The main goal of this step is to obtain a rough 3D description of an object. As the system is fully calibrated (see a system snapshot on figure 2, left), is possible to carve a voxel volume assuming the limitations of the method due to concavities or occlusions. Other authors use similar structures for 3D recovering from multiple photographs [4]. In the proposed implementation, to increase process speed, the views used for carving are selected by a minimum object projection area criterion.

3.1   Object Segmentation

First step of carving process consists in segmenting the object of interest from the background of the scene. A chroma-keying environment has been used and binarization is made by Hue component. Then a labeling of the background is performed and resulting blobs are filtered by area. Those background blobs which area was below a threshold are considered as part of the object. Finally, the view is saved in the image database. For each view, the saved data is: image pixels, camera pose and object (foreground) area. Figure 2, center, shows the process results.

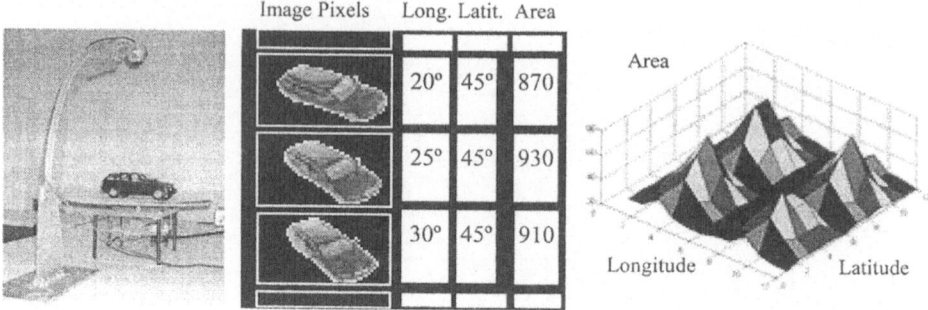

Image Pixels	Long.	Latit.	Area
	20°	45°	870
	25°	45°	930
	30°	45°	910

Fig. 2. Acquisition system snapshot, captured data in database and area analysis function

3.2   View Set Selection

From saved data, area of the object projection for every camera pose is read. Local minimums and maximums are found (see Figure 2, right). The minimum-area views are used to carve a 3D volume, like the raise, plant and section views in architecture. Performed experiments show that minimum-area views carve the maximum in the voxel mesh. Meanwhile, the maximum-area views will be used later for view interpolation.

3.3   Carving

The carving process is based on the drilling of a voxel volume according to view pixels belonging to the background. Initially, a 512x512x512 voxel volume is set to logical value true. When a pixel of a view belongs to the background, all the voxels in its projection cone are cleared. This procedure is repeated for all background pixels in all the preselected views. A lot of time is saved using only minimum-area views for carving. Figure 3 shows the carving scheme and a result example.

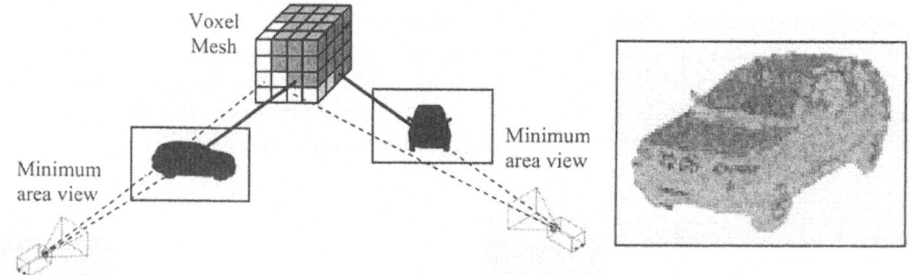

Fig. 3. Carving Scheme and OpenGL projection of a recovered 3D object

4   View Interpolation Step

With the obtained photometric data and view disparity information that can be deduced from the carved model, is possible to interpolate intermediate views, and compare it with those real views saved in the view database.

4.1   View Synthesis Overview

Several authors work in view synthesis algorithms under different perspectives:

Using a previously known 3D model of the scene. Then, the photometric information given by the cameras will be used to render the new images, texturing the surfaces projected by the 3D model. The group of [1] in the Carnegie-Mellon University is using this method, under the generic name of virtualized reality.

Inferring the 3D structure from the images. Using stereovision techniques is possible to reconstruct dynamically the 3D structure of the scene and re-project the new view. A research group in France [6] has created special representation structures to optimally generate the new views.

Dealing directly with the images, without using explicitly the three-dimensional information. Employing epipolar geometry properties and the photometric data, it is possible to interpolate directly the pixels of the new image with the pixels of the captured ones [7].

Our work infers the 3D structure from images with a fast carving algorithm and then refine it with a fine stereo matching algorithm.

4.2   View Rectifications and Interpolation

When a pair of views with local area maximums is selected a view interpolation algorithm begins. The process requires the rectification of the two given views and the one to be interpolated, to obtain common epipolar lines. This algorithm is named three-view rectification [5]. Then, the disparity maps are calculated for the pair of images using the information collected in the model, and the new view is interpolated by solving a simple linear equation. Finally the interpolated view must be derectified. Figure 4 shows an interpolation example.

5   Image Comparisons and Error Analysis

Interpolated images must be tested to evaluate the quality of the recovered model. As in the acquisition step intermediate views have been densely captured, the interpolated view and the real view for the same camera position can be compared. The image interpolation algorithm errors are dependent of the disparity map calculation errors [5], and the disparity map errors are related to the 3D model accuracy, so the results of the comparison will evaluate the quality of the 3D recovering.

Fig. 4. View Interpolation example, form left to right: left object view, rectified left view, interpolated view, rectified right view and right view

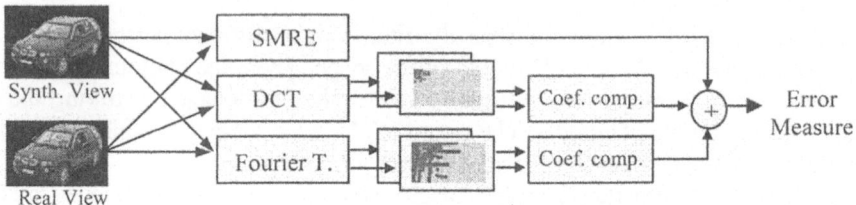

Fig. 5. Synthetic view error measure calculation scheme

From several quality evaluators [8] three have been selected: RMSE (root medium square error) to directly compare pixels color intensity, Fourier transform coefficients comparison to detect frequency perturbations (related to object focusing) and DCT (discrete cosine transform) coefficient comparison to detect spatial distortion. If the result of the three evaluators numerical average is greater than a threshold (see figure 5) a stereo matching algorithm will be used to refine the 3D model.

6   Stereo Matching

Once a pair of images has been rectified so that epipolar lines are horizontal scan lines, a pair of homologue edges can be searched for only within the same horizontal line.

The main difficulty in passive stereo vision is the matching between homologue points from left and right images, so that, given the camera model, the depth can be computed by triangulation. In edge-based stereo techniques, edges in the images are used as the elements to be match.

The method presented here uses the edges of previously segmented regions as points to be matched. Images are segmented using a region growing technique based on color and depth information [9].

We have developed a matching procedure inspired by the approach proposed by Ohta and Kanade [10]. The edges are matched by finding a path through a 2D search plane whose axes are the left and right segmented lines (see figure 6). A dynamic programming technique can handle this search efficiently.

In this plane, the vertical lines represent the position of the edges from the left image, and the horizontal lines represent the position of the right image edges. The intersections between these lines correspond to the nodes where a decision has to be made in order to select an optimal path to that node. The examination of the correspondences between two edges is performed sequentially from the left to the right of each line; so, the final path goes from the upper left to the lower right corners monotonically. This is equivalent to the non reversal constraint in edge correspondence. Also the search in the lower left half plane (the darkest area in figure 6) is omitted due to the positive disparity constraint between left and right images.

The procedure searches the elementary paths between two successive intersections by means of an error index that indicates the quality of the matches. From the current intersection that represents the last matched edges, only three elementary paths are possible: horizontal (to the right), vertical (down) or diagonal shifting. The best elementary shifting is the one that yields the minimum error index. The new intersection becomes the current intersection and the matching process is iterated until it reaches the end of the left image.

In this search, an horizontal elementary path corresponds to the case in which a visible interval in the left image is occluded in the right image (as interval *d* in fig. 6). Similarly, a vertical elementary path corresponds to the case in which a visible interval in the right image is occluded in the left image (as interval *F* in fig. 6). Only diagonal elementary paths correspond to matched intervals. Three different costs have been assigned to these paths.

Let H_l and H_r be the mean of color values of two given intervals from left and right images. Let L_l and L_r be the lengths of these intervals. Then, the cost for an elementary diagonal path that matches these two intervals is defined as follows:

$$C = (H_l - H_r)^2 \cdot \max(L_l, L_r) \qquad \text{(Eq. 1)}$$

By using this metric, it should be noted that an elementary path actually corresponds to matching of the segmented intervals delimited by edges rather than a matching of the edges themselves.

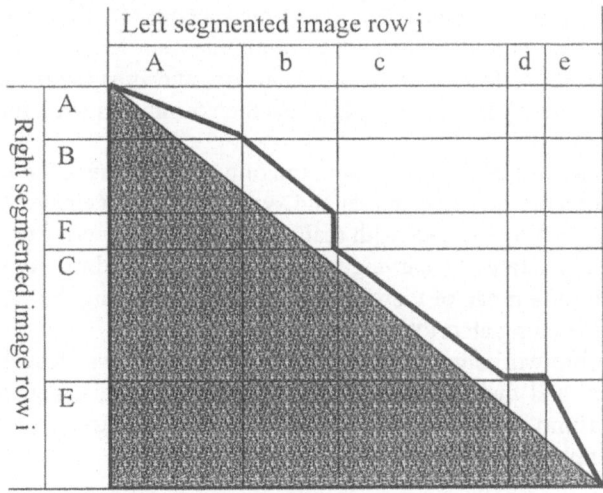

Fig. 6. 2D search plane for solving the correspondence problem between segmented intervals from left and right images. Interval sequence abcde from the left image row is matched with interval sequence ABFCE from the right image row, so that, a→A, b→B, c→C and e→E. F is an occluded interval in the left image and d is an occluded interval in the right image, so they are not matched

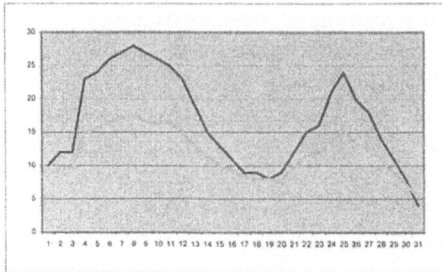 

Fig. 7. Calculated error for a range of 32 interpolated views (they cover a object rotation of 45 degrees). The dark values show error before stereo matching model correction (left). OpenGL projection of a CAD made recovered object (right)

The cost for an horizontal or vertical elementary path corresponding to an occluded interval of length L, is defined as: $C = K \cdot L$. Where K is a constant value used as a threshold in order to help diagonal paths over any vertical-horizontal (or horizontal-vertical) sequence path.

Once the matches between segmented intervals from left and right images have been assigned, the disparity of boundary pixels is calculated and depth is computed by triangulation from camera geometry.

7   Results

As a test bed, positioner consisting on a rotational table to turn the objects with an arch to change the tilt angle of the camera has been built (Figure 2, left). The table allows an accuracy of one degree. The camera has a 640x480 RGB CCD. Illumination has been controlled with 30 white light ultra luminescent LEDs. One PC Pentium III at 800 Mhz controls both the table and the camera, and runs the presented 3D recovering algorithm. The whole process takes less than 5 minutes even for complex shape objects.

When no model of the object is given, the only way to check the robustness of the method is the comparison between real and synthetic views generated from recovered model of the object. Several tests with real objects show how error decreases when refining the model generated by carving with the stereo algorithm. Figure 7, left, shows error calculation for a range of views, before and after refining the carved voxel mesh with the stereo matching algorithm.

However, before working with real objects, the method was tested with CAD volumes as objects, and their 2D projections as images. In this scenario, the volume-recovering algorithm obtains correct results, as expected. Figure 7, right, shows a 3D recover of a complex CAD object.

8   Conclusions and Further Work

The presented method shows that the combination of a carving process and a stereo matching algorithm allows the refinement of a 3D recovering. The comparison between real images and interpolated synthetic ones has been proved to be a good and fast checker in order to evaluate errors in the generated model.

Applications like augmented reality [11] can take advantage of this method since it gives a complete view description together with a fine 3D model of an object. In this way, registration between real world images and the synthetic object will be more accurate.

As a further work our priorities include:
- To segment the object from any background.
- To improve carving process speed.
- To implement by hardware some parts of the process, as carving, image comparison, view synthesis and stereo matching [12].

References

[1] Takeo Kanade, Research Group in Computer Science, Carnegie Mellon Univ., Virtualized Reality Home Page: http://www.cs.cmu.edu/~virtualized~reality/
[2] Faugeras, O.D., Keriven, R. : Variation Principles, surface evolution, pde's level set methods and the stereo problem. IEEE Trans. Image Processing (7) pps 336-344. 1998
[3] Steven M. Seitz, Kiriakos N. Kutulakos: Plenoptic Image Editing. International Journal of Computer Vision 48. pps. 115-129. Kluwer Academic Press 2002
[4] Kiriakos N. Kutulakos, Steven M. Seitz. A theory of Shape by Space Carving. International Journal of Computer Vision 38. pps. 199-218. Kluwer Academic Press, 2000
[5] Daniel Scharstein, View Synthesis Using Stereo Vision. Ed. Springer-Verlag, Berlin 1999. ISSN 0302-9743
[6] Stéphane Laveau, Olivier Faugeras, Oriented projective geometry for Computer Vision, Tech. Report INRIA Sophia-Antipolis, 1997
[7] Takeshi Naemura, Hiroshi Harashima, The University of Tokyo, Japan: The Ray-Based Approach to Augmented Spatial Communication and Mixed Reality, from the book Mixed Reality, merging Real and Virtual Worlds, edited by Y. Ohta, H. Tamura, Ed. Ohmsha, Ltd. Tokyo 1999
[8] A. J. Ahumada Jr. Computational image quality metrics: a review. Research Report. NASA Ames Research Center. 1993
[9] J. Fernandez and J. Aranda, Image Segmentation Combining Region Depth and Object Features, Int. Conf. On Pattern Recognition ICPR'00. Barcelona. Spain. Pp. 618-621. September 2000
[10] Y. Otha and T. Kanade, Stereo by intra and inter-scanline search using dynamic programming, IEEE Trans. PAMI, vol. 7, n. 2, pp. 139-154. 1985
[11] Antonio Martínez, J.P. Arboleda, E.X. Martín. Mixed Reality in traffic Scenes in Entertainment Computing, Technologies and Applications, chapter 5, Ed. Kluwer, 2003. ISBN 1402073607
[12] J. Aranda, J. Climent, A. Grau "Low Cost Architecture for Structure Measure Distance Computation", Intern. Conf. on Pattern Recognition, ICPR 1998, Brisbane, Australia, pp. 1592-1594

Chromosome Classification Using Continuous Hidden Markov Models*

César Martínez[1], Héctor García[2], Alfons Juan[3], and Francisco Casacuberta[3]

[1] Facultad de Ingeniería, Universidad Nacional de Entre Ríos
Ruta 11, Km. 10. CP 3100 Paraná, Entre Ríos (Argentina)
cmartinez@fi.uner.edu.ar
[2] Instituto Valenciano de Investigaciones Económicas (IVIE)
46020 Valencia (Spain)
hector.garcia@ivie.es
[3] DSIC/ITI, Universitat Politècnica de València
Camí de Vera s/n, E-46071 València (Spain)
{ajuan,fcn}@iti.upv.es

Abstract. Up-to-date results on the application of Markov models to chromosome analysis are presented. On the one hand, this means using *continuous Hidden Markov Models (HMMs)* instead of discrete models. On the other hand, this also means to conduct empirical tests on the same large chromosome datasets that are currently used to evaluate state-of-the-art classifiers. It is shown that the use of *continuous HMMs* allows to obtain error rates that are very close to those provided by the most accurate classifiers.

1 Introduction

A common task in cytogenetics is the *karyotye analysis of a cell*. It consists of labelling each chromosome of the cell with its class label, in order to have the genetic constitution of individuals. This analysis provides important information about number and shape of the chromosomes, which serves as a basis to study the possible abnormalities the individual could have.

In a normal, nucleated human cell there are 46 chromosomes. The *karyogram* is a standard format which shows the complete set organized into 22 classes (each one consisting of a matching pair of two *homologous* chromosomes), ordered by decreasing length, and two sex chromosomes, *XX* in females or *XY* in males.

The first attempts to automate this task were made in the early 1960s, motivated by the fact that manual analysis is very tedious and labour-intensive. Since then, many classification techniques have been tried, including both statistical and structural approaches. Most of them, however, are conventional, statistical

---

* Work supported by the Valencian "Oficina de Ciència i Tecnologia" under grant CTIDIA/2002/80, the Spanish "Ministerio de Ciencia y Tecnología" under grant TIC2000-1703-CO3-01 and the Argentinian "Ministerio de Educación de la Nación" under fellowship FOMEC 1108.

F.J. Perales et al. (Eds.): IbPRIA 2003, LNCS 2652, pp. 494–501, 2003.

classification techniques in the sense that they reduce each chromosome image to a point in some multi-dimensional feature space [6]. Instead, the use of structurally richer approaches has been rare and focused mainly on *discrete Markov models* [3, 7].

The aim of this paper is to provide up-to-date results on the application of Markov models to chromosome analysis. On the one hand, this means using *continuous Hidden Markov Models (HMMs)* instead of discrete models. On the other hand, this also means to conduct empirical tests on the same large chromosome datasets that are currently used to evaluate state-of-the-art classifiers [6]. It is worth noting that this is a new application of standard Speech Recognition technology and, in particular, a new application of the well-known and widely available standard *HMM Tool Kit (HTK)* [8]. However, this is not a straightforward application of HTK since we also have to take care of preprocessing, feature extraction and HMM topology design. These aspects are covered in the next section. Empirical results and the main conclusions drawn are given in sections 3 and 4, respectively.

2   The Approach

The basic steps of our HTK-based approach are illustrated in Figure 1. They are described in what follows.

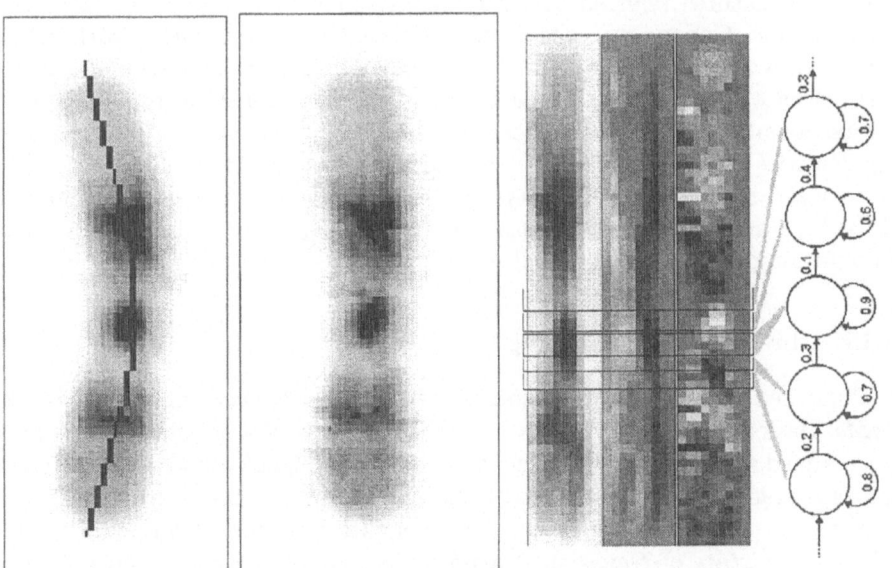

Fig. 1. Basic steps of our HTK-based approach. From left to right: computation of the longitudinal axis, unfolding, feature extraction and HMM modelling

Computation of the Longitudinal Axis and Unfolding

The computation of the longitudinal axis of a chromosome is a standard pre-processing step in chromosome analysis. However, no precise definition has been widely accepted and, in fact, it is a matter of current research [6]. In our case, we have used a rather standard procedure that includes the classical Hilditch's thinning algorithm for *medial axis* computation and some refinements [2].

Once the longitudinal axis has been computed, it is traversed at unit speed and a perpendicular slice is cut at each sampled axis point to obtain an unfolded, straight version of the chromosome. After this *chromosome unfolding*, feature extraction reduces to compute an appropriate set of features from each image row.

Feature Extraction

Feature extraction for *local* characterization of chromosomes is an interesting, open problem. Based on our previous experience [5] and some informal tests, we have considered the following four types of features:

- **9p:** grey densities
- **D:** horizontal derivative
- **A:** horizontal acceleration
- **V:** vertical derivative

The set of features referred to as 9p corresponds to 9 equidistant Gaussian-filtered points. Concretely, each point was filtered by convolution with a 5×5 filter mask with weights: 16 in the center, 2 at a 1-pixel distance and 1 at a 2-pixel distance. Derivatives and acceleration were computed from successive 9p vectors. As an example, the sequence of feature vectors shown Fig. 1 comprises grey densities plus horizontal and vertical derivatives (9p+D+V).

It must be noted that these types of features come from previous work on HTK-based handwriting recognition. Please see [1, 4] for more details on the computation of these types of features.

HMM Chromosome Modeling

As illustrated in Fig. 1, chromosomes are modelled by *continuous left-to-right HMMs*. Basically, an HMM for a chromosome class is a stochastic finite-state device aimed at modelling the succession, along the longitudinal axis, of feature vectors extracted from instances of the chromosome class. Each HMM state generates feature vectors following an adequate parametric probabilistic law; typically a *mixture of Gaussian densities*. The number of states and number of densities per state that are appropriate to model each chromosome class depend on the class variability and the amount of training data available. So, these numbers need some empirical tuning. The training process is carried out with the HTK toolkit, using conventional re-estimation formulas [8].

3   Experiments

The data set used in the experiments was the Cpa, a corrected version of the Cpr corpus (the complete *Copenhagen* data set) [6]. The corpus contains the segmented chromosome images of 2804 human cells, 1344 of which are female and 1460 are male.

3.1   Context-Free Classification

The usual method for classifying a test chromosome is to find the HMM with the highest probability in the Viterbi decoding. This is the so-called *context-free* classification, because each chromosome is classified with independence of each other. The experiments reported in this subsection were done under this context-free framework.

As discussed before, one of the two basic parameters characterising continuous left-to-right HMMs is the number of states chosen for each class-conditional HMM M_i. This number has been computed as $s_i = \frac{f_i}{k}$, where f_i is the average length of the sequence of vectors used to train M_i, and k is a design parameter measuring the average number of feature vectors modelled per state. This rule of setting up s_i attempts to balance modelling effort across states and also captures important discriminative information about the typical length of each chromosome class. Following this rule, a first series of experiments was carried out on a partition involving $2400 + 400$ training and testing cells. We used the 9p feature set and the values of k: 1.5, 2, 2.5, 3 and 4. For each value of k, the number of Gaussian densities per state was varied as $1, 2, 4, ldots$ until reaching a minimum classification error rate. The results obtained, which are omitted here for brevity, showed a degradation of the error rate as the value of k increases. So, in accordance with these results, a value of $k = 1.5$ was fixed for the remaining experiments.

After deciding on the value of k, a second series of experiments was conducted on the same data partition to study the classifier performance as a function of the number of Gaussian densities per state, and for several feature sets. The results are shown in Fig. 2. From these results, it is clear that an appropriate feature set consist of using grey densities plus horizontal and vertical derivatives (9p+D+V). Also, 64 seems to be an adequate number of Gaussian densities per state.

Although the results obtained up to this point were satisfactory, we decided to do further experiments using windows of feature vectors instead of single vectors. This was done as as an attempt to reproduce the behaviour of the input layer of Recurrent Neural Networks, in which a small moving-window of feature frames is processed at each time and this seems to be very effective in improving classification results [5]. Fig. 3 shows the classification error rate (estimated as before) for varying Gaussian densities per state and several window sizes. As expected, the use of windows of feature vectors helps in improving classification error and, in fact, the best result (5.6%) was obtained with a window of 3 feature vectors (and 64 Gaussian densities per state).

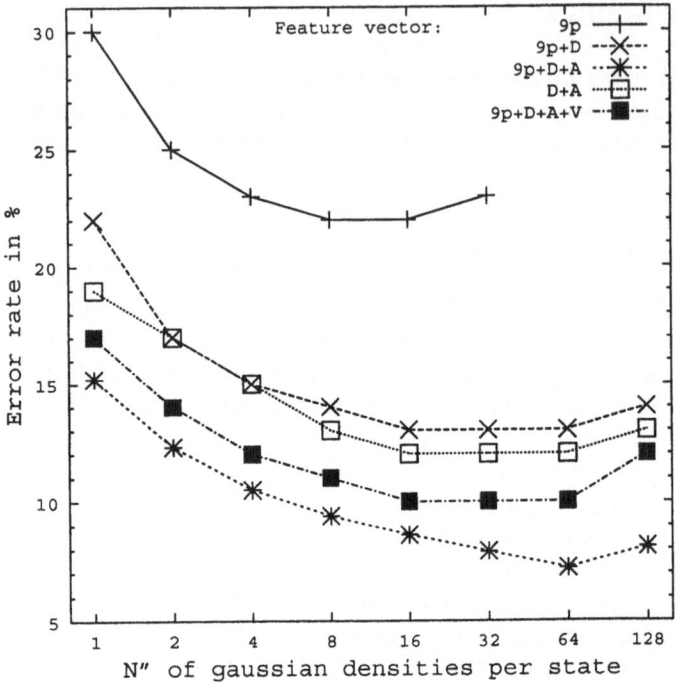

Fig. 2. Classification error rate as a function of the number of Gaussian densities per state, and for several feature sets

All the experiments reported so far were carried out using a single partition of the complete corpus. In order to obtain more precise results, the classification error rate was also estimated using a 7-fold cross-validation procedure in which the blocks were chosen to have 400 cells each. It is given in Table 3.1 as a function of the number of Gaussian densities per state (the remaining parameters were set to the values that provided a 5.6% of error). The best result for the cross-validation method, again obtained with 64 Gaussian densities, is 7.5%.

3.2   Context-Dependent Classification

The classification error rate can be reduced by taking into account the fact that the normal karyotype consists of 22 pairs of autosomes and a pair of sex chromosomes. This knowledge imposes a constraint that penalizes, e.g., the allocation of more than two chromosomes to one class and less than two chromosomes to other class. This is the called *context-dependent* classification.

An iterative algorithm was formulated to restrict the isolated chromosome classification by including the contextual cell information. The algorithm receives as input, for each chromosome of a cell, the output probabilities of each HMM. Then, in successive iterations, the algorithm classifies pairs of chromosomes for each class using *solved classes*; i.e., classes with only two chromosomes having

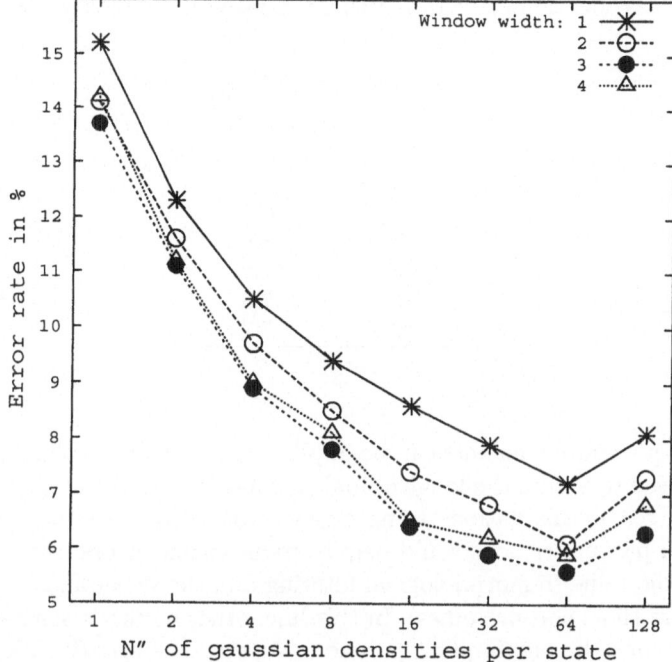

Fig. 3. Classification error rate as a function of the number of Gaussian densities per state, and for window widths

the highest probability for that class, and both probabilities greater than a lower bound. After that, the probabilities of solved classes are crossed-out for the remaining chromosomes, whose probabilities are renormalized and the process is repeated until the complete cell is classified.

In order to complete the experiments reported in the preceding subsection, the context-dependent classification algorithm discussed above was applied to the best classifier found under the context-free framework. The classification error rate was again estimated using the 7-fold cross-validation procedure and, as expected, it was reduced from 7.5% up to 4.6%. This figure is close to those provided by the most accurate classifiers [6].

4   Conclusions

We have provided up-to-date results on the application of Markov models to chromosome analysis. It has been shown that the use of *continuous Hidden Markov Models (HMMs)* allows to obtain error rates that are very close to those provided by the most accurate classifiers. As in the case of handwriting recognition, the main advantage of using HMMs is that they can be easily integrated into systems based on finite-state technology [4].

Table 1. Classification error rate estimated using a 7-fold cross-validation procedure

N° of G. D.	error rate
1	15.7
2	12.5
4	10.4
8	9.3
16	8.4
32	7.9
64	7.5
128	7.7

A number of improvements can be applied to the entire system. The skeleton technique used to obtain the longitudinal axis has the disadvantage of being non-parametric, so approximations using eigenvectors have to be used to calculate the slices. A parametric axis could help to reduce some errors introduced by the current method due to morphological filtering and the skeletonization algorithm (especially in short chromosomes). In this line, other methods are being studied: polynomial curve-fitting, implicit polynomials, etc. The iterative algorithm that implements the *context-dependent* classification could be improved by dynamic programming, allowing a more detailed analysis for finding the *solved classes*.

Acknowledgements

The authors wish to thank Dr. Gunter Ritter (*Fakultät für Mathematik und Informatik, Universität Passau, Passau, Germany*) for kindly providing the database of chromosome images Cpa used in this work.

References

[1] J. Doménech, A. H. Toselli, A. Juan, E. Vidal, and F. Casacuberta. An off-line HTK-based OCR, system for isolated handwritten lowercase letters. In *Proc. of the IX Spanish Symposium on Pattern Recognition and Image Analysis*, volume II, pages 49-54, Benicàssim (Spain), May 2001.

[2] H. García. Preproceso y extracción de características (sintáctica) para el diseño de clasificadores de cromosomas humanos. Master's thesis, Faculty of Computer Science, Polytechnic University of Valencia, 1999.

[3] J. Gregor and M. G. Thomason. A Disagreement Count Scheme for Inference of Constrained Markov Networks. In L. Miclet and C. de la Higuera, editors, *Grammatical Inference: Learning Syntax from Sentences*, volume 1147 of *Lecture Notes in Computer Science*, pages 168-178. Springer, 1996.

[4] A. Juan et al. Integrated Handwriting Recognition and Interpretation via FiniteState Models. Technical Report ITI-ITE-01/1, Institut Tecnològic d'Informàtica, Valencia (Spain), July 2001.

[5] César Martínez, Alfons Juan, and Francisco Casacuberta. Using Recurrent Neural Networks for Automatic Chromosome Classification. In *Proc. of the Int. Conf. on Artificial Neural Networks ICANN 2002*, volume 2415 of *Lecture Notes in Computer Science*, pages 565-570, Madrid (Spain), August 2002. Springer-Verlag.

[6] G. Bitter and G. Schreib. Using dominant points and variants for profile extraction from chromosomes. *Pattern Recognition*, 34:923-938, 2001.

[7] M. G. Thomason and E. Granum. Dynamic Programming Inference of Markov Networks from Finite Sets of Sample Strings. *IEEE Trans. on PAMI*, PAMI-8(4):491501, 1986.

[8] S.J. Young et al. HTK: Hidden Markov Model Toolkit. Technical report, Entropic Research Laboratories Inc., 1997.

Generalized k-Medians Clustering for Strings*

Carlos D. Martínez-Hinarejos, Alfons Juan, and Francisco Casacuberta

Institut Tecnològic d'Informàtica, Dep. de Sistemes Informàtics i Computació
Universitat Politècnica de València, Camí de Vera s/n, 46022, València, Spain
{cmartine,ajuan,fcn}@iti.upv.es

Abstract. Clustering methods are used in pattern recognition to obtain natural groups from a data set in the framework of unsupervised learning as well as for obtaining clusters of data from a known class. In sets of strings, the concept of set median string can be extended to the *(set) k-medians problem*. The solution of the k-medians problem can be viewed as a clustering method, where each cluster is generated by each of the k strings of that solution. A concept which is related to set median string is the (generalized) median string, which is an NP-Hard problem. However, different algorithms have been proposed to find approximations to the (generalized) median string. We propose extending the (generalized) median string problem to k strings, resulting in the *generalized k-medians problem*, which can also be viewed as a clustering technique. This new technique is applied to a corpus of chromosomes represented by strings and compared to the conventional k-medians technique.

1 Introduction

One of the classical problems in pattern recognition is the clustering problem. Clustering attempts to obtain natural groups of data (named *clusters*) from a whole data set, based on the similarities among the data. This similarity is usually based on the definition of *distance* between the patterns which represent the data. When data is represented by vectors in a metric space, a natural dissimilarity measure is the Euclidean distance. When data is represented by strings [1], several dissimilarity measures can be defined. The most popular one is the *edit distance* [2], but other distances are also used, such as the *normalized edit distance* [3].

From a set of points in a metric space, the median is defined as the point in the set which minimizes the sum of distances to each point of the set. The problem of finding the median can be generalized to finding a subset of k points (known as *representatives*) from a data set. This subset minimizes the sum of distances from the rest of the points to their closest representative. This problem is known as the *k-medians problem*. Solving the k-medians problem defines a partition in the data set: each point in the data set pertains to the cluster represented by its closest representative.

---

* Work partially supported by the Spanish CICYT under grant TIC2000-1703-C03-01 and by the Valencian OCYT under grant CTIDIA/2002/80.

F.J. Perales et al. (Eds.): IbPRIA 2003, LNCS 2652, pp. 502–509, 2003.

For string-coded data, the search for the median is equivalent to computing the *set median string* [4]. This problem is easily extended, as in the case of a metric space, to the *(set) k-medians problem*. The solution of the (set) k-medians problem also defines a partition in the string data set, and it has been the most widely used clustering technique for data represented by strings.

A concept which is related to the set median string is the *(generalized) median string*. This is the string of all the possible strings which minimizes the sum of distances to all the strings of the set. This problem is an NP-Hard problem [5] and only approximations can be obtained in reasonable time. The concept of (generalized) median string can also be extended to finding the k string representatives which minimize the sum of distances to the set of strings. We call this problem the *generalized k-medians problem*, and its solution also defines a set of clusters in the data set.

In this work, both (set) k-medians clustering and the new generalized k-medians clustering are applied to a corpus of chromosomes represented by strings. The results will demonstrate that this new proposal outperforms the k-medians clustering under certain conditions (and is equivalent in the other cases). In Section 2, the median string is defined and its approximation algorithm is described. In Section 3, the new generalized k-medians clustering procedure is formulated by means of a modification of the k-medians process. In Section 4, the data used is described and results are presented. In Section 5, some conclusions and final remarks are provided.

2   Median String

Given an alphabet Σ, Σ^* represents the free monoid over Σ (the set of all the strings of finite length over Σ). Given a set of strings $T \subseteq \Sigma^*$, the *(generalized) median string* [4] of T is given by the string $s \in \Sigma^*$ which minimizes the following expression:

$$z(s) = \sum_{t \in T} d(s, t) \tag{1}$$

where d represents the distance used to compare two strings (edit distance [2], normalized edit distance [3]...).

The problem of finding the median string is known to be an NP-Hard problem [5]. Therefore, only approximations can be achieved in reasonable time. The most popular approximation is the *set median string* of T [4], where the string is constrained to pertain to the set T. This string can be obtained in polynomial time with a time complexity of $O(l^2 \cdot |T|^2)$ when the distance computation presents a time complexity of $O(l^2)$, where l is the maximum length of the strings in T.

It is clear that the set median string is a rough approximation to the median string of T. Other heuristic methods for obtaining more approximated strings have been proposed in the literature. In [6], a greedy method was proposed to build an approximation to median string based on adding a symbol in each iteration until a stop criterion ocurrs. The main drawback of this algorithm is that it can only be applied when using the edit distance (it cannot be employed when using the normalized edit distance).

A more general algorithm was proposed in [7]. This algorithm consists of making successive perturbations to the current string. Over each position of the current string, all possible substitutions, insertions and deletions are performed, and the best among the altered strings and the current string (i.e., the string which presents less accumulated distance to the set of strings) is taken for the next position. The process is applied until there is no change in any position of the current string. Clearly, an initial string is necessary at the beginning of the process. This initial string is usually the set median string of the set, but it could be any other string of Σ^*.

The results presented in [7] demonstrate that the approximation produced by this algorithm provides better results in classification tasks than the set median. This algorithm can be applied to any distance function defined and presents a time complexity of $O(l^3 \cdot |T| \cdot |\Sigma|)$ per main iteration when the time complexity of the distance computation is also $O(l^2)$.

3   The Generalized k-Medians Algorithm

Clearly, the concept of (generalized) median string can be extended to, say, k strings just like the concept of mean and set median have been extended to k-means and (set) k-medians, respectively [8, 9]. We call such an extension *generalized k-medians*[1]. Formally, a generalized k-medians of a given training set $T \subseteq \Sigma^*$ is simply a set S of k strings in Σ^* with minimum:

$$z(S) = \sum_{t \in T} \min_{s \in S} d(s, t) \tag{2}$$

Compare Eq. (2) with Eq. (1). In Eq. (1), a single string is forced to be the only representative for every training string. In contrast, in Eq. (2) the task of representing T is divided among k string representatives and each training string is assigned to (the group or cluster of) its most similar representative.

As in the particular case of $k = 1$, we are interested in devising heuristics to obtain good approximate solutions in reasonable time. To this end, a direct approach is to use heuristics for the *(set) k-medians problem*, i.e., that of minimizing Eq.(2) over all sets of k representatives drawn only from the training set T. Note that the only difference with respect to the generalized problem is that representatives cannot be drawn from the entire string space Σ^*, only from T. Although this constraint entails a huge reduction of the set of feasible solutions, the (set) k-medians problem is still a difficult, NP-Hard problem [10]. In contrast to its generalized version, however, it has been extensively studied as a model for facility location and pattern clustering [9, 11].

---

[1] We use this denomination following Kohonen's nomenclature (*generalized median*) and to avoid confusion with k-means technique.

Algorithm generalized k-medians
Input: T, d, k, S^0 /* Strings, distance, num. clusters, initial representatives */
Output: $S = \{s_1, s_2, \ldots, s_k\}$ /* Final set of representatives */
Function: $s = \text{median\_string}(S', s, d)$ /* Median string computation */
Method:
$S = S^0$
for $i = 1$ **to** k **do** $C_i = \{t \in T : i = \arg\min_{j=1,\ldots,k} d(t, s_j)\}$ **endfor**   /* Initial clusters */
repeat
    $interchange = false$
    for $i = 1$ **to** k **do**   /* For each cluster compute new representative */
        $aux = s_i$
        $s_i = \text{median\_string}(C_i, s_i, d)$ /* New representative: approx. median string */
        if $s_i \neq aux$ **then** $interchange = true$ **endif**   /* The representative changed */
    endfor
    $\forall t \in T$ **do**   /* Cluster reorganization */
        let $i : t \in C_i$ /* i is the current cluster for t */
        $i' = \arg\min_{j=1,\ldots,k} d(t, s_j)$ /* i' is the cluster of the nearest representative to t */
        if $i' \neq i$ **then** $C_i = C_i - \{t\}$; $C_{i'} = C_{i'} \cup \{t\}$ **endif**   /* Exchanges t */
    end$\forall$
until not $interchange$

Fig. 1. Generalized k-medians algorithm. The parameters for the median_string function are a set of strings S', an initial string s and a distance function d

A good and efficient heuristic for the k-medians problem is, precisely, the technique known as *k-medians algorithm* [12, 11]. This technique is best described as a clustering method in which both the set of k (cluster) representatives and its associated training set partition are iteratively updated. The basic updating rule is a necessary optimality condition: each representative of an optimal set must be a set median of its cluster; otherwise, an improved set of representatives can be obtained by interchanging each representative with a set median of its cluster. This updating rule is actually the first of the two basic steps that are carried out in each iteration of the algorithm. The second step is simply to update the current partition of the training set in accordance with the (new) set of representatives obtained in the first step. These two basic steps are repeated until no change of representatives occurs. For more details about the k-medians algorithm, including the aspects of computing efficiency and initialization, see [12, 11].

Although the k-medians algorithm can effectively provide good approximate solutions to the generalized problem, we think that significantly better solutions can be obtained using *ad-hoc* optimization methods. With this idea, we propose here to generalize the k-medians algorithm so that is works with arbitrary strings as cluster representatives, not just with strings included in the training set. More precisely, we propose using the "perturbation" method described in Section 2 in order to attempt to improve the generalized representative of each cluster. See

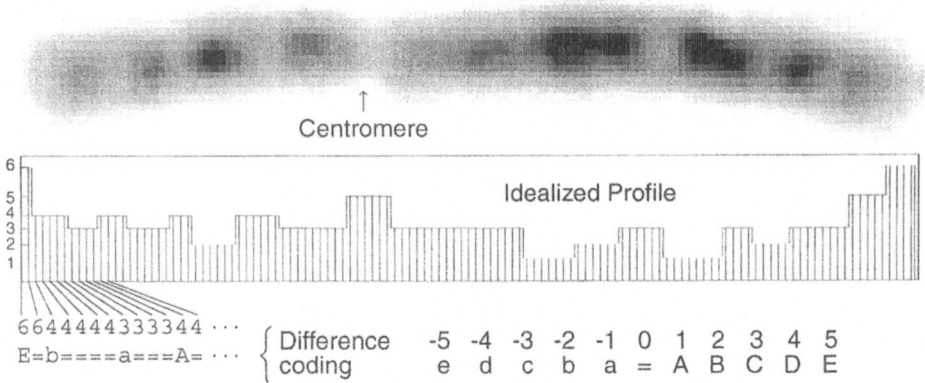

Fig. 2. Chromosome preprocessing. Each digitized chromosome image is transformed into a string by first computing an idealized, one-dimensional density profile and then difference-coding successive density values

Fig. 1 for a detailed algorithmic description of this new *generalized k-medians algorithm*. The time complexity of this algorithm (per iteration) depends mainly on the approximated median string computation for each cluster. Therefore, the time complexity is proportional to $O(l^3 \cdot |T| \cdot |\Sigma|)$. A straightforward approach to initializing this algorithm consists of using the solution given by the conventional method.

4   Experiments and Results

The data used in the experiments, known as the *Copenhagen* corpus, was extracted from a database of approximately $7,000$ chromosomes that were classified by cytogenetic experts [13]. Each digitized chromosome image was automatically transformed into a string by using the procedure illustrated in Fig. 2. This procedure starts by obtaining an idealized, one-dimensional density profile that emphasizes the band pattern along the chromosome. The idealized profile is then mapped into a string composed of symbols from the alphabet $\{1, 2, 3, 4, 5, 6\}$. Then this string is difference coded to represent signed differences of successive symbols, using the alphabet $\Sigma = \{e, d, c, b, a, =, A, B, C, D, E\}$ ("$=$" for a difference of 0; "A" for +1; "a" for -1; etc.). See [14] for a detailed description of this procedure.

The chromosome dataset actually used in the experiments comprises 200 string samples for each of the 22 non-sex chromosome types, i.e. a total of 4400 samples. The standard classification procedure to estimate the error rate of a classifier for this data is a 2-fold cross-validation in which both sets are chosen to have 100 samples of each of the 22 non-sex chromosomes types. Following this procedure, recently an error rate around 4% was achieved by using the *k*-Nearest

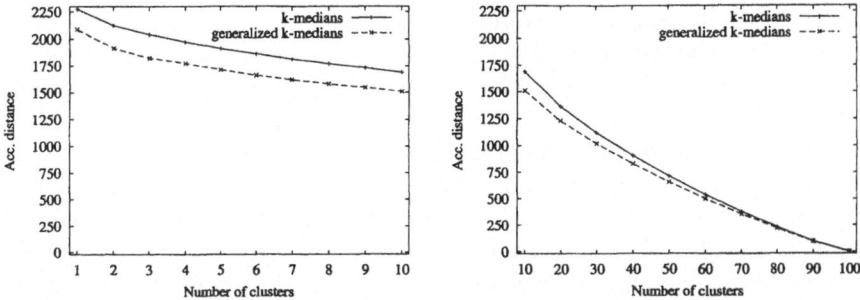

Fig. 3. Accumulated distance for the conventional k-medians and the generalized k-medians algorithms as a function of k (number of clusters)

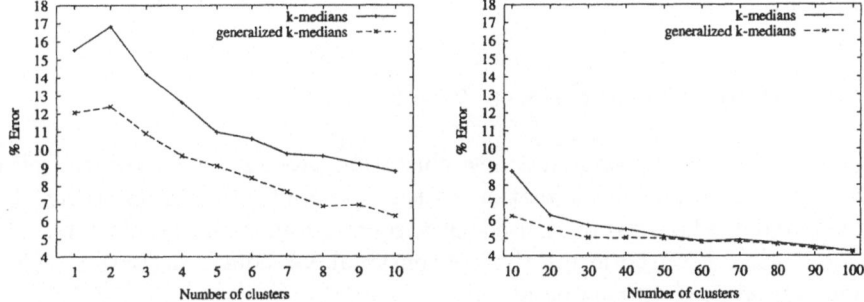

Fig. 4. Classification error for the conventional k-medians and the generalized k-medians algorithms as a function of k (number of clusters). The base classifier is a 3-NN classifier built from the k string prototypes of each class

Neighbour classifier (k-NN) with $k \geq 3$ and a (properly) weighted normalized edit distance [7].

In this work, the above-mentioned estimation procedure was repeated using a 3-NN classifier built from k string prototypes of each class. Both the conventional k-medians algorithm and its generalized version were used to compute the k string prototypes of each class. The idea is to measure to what extent our new technique improves on the conventional algorithm to obtain accurate yet compact models of string sets. To this end, the classification error rate for each algorithm was computed as a function of k (number of clusters per class), and also the accumulated distance (i.e., the value of the objective function (2)). See Figs. 3 and 4.

As expected, the results shown in Figs. 3 and 4 indicate that the generalized k-medians algorithm gives more accurate representatives than the conventional k-medians algorithm, both in terms of accumulated distance and in terms of classification error rate. Generally speaking, it can be said that the accuracy gained is not very significant when the desired number of clusters (representatives) is large in comparison to the size of the training set (e.g., more than, say,

10 clusters in our chromosome task). On the contrary, when only a small number of representatives is to be computed, we can get significant improvements in accuracy by using generalized medians instead of set medians. An example of this is given in the left panel of Fig. 4, where a relative error rate reduction of around 30% is reported for $k \leq 10$.

It must be noted that, for the experiments conducted here, we have used a simple initialization procedure. On the one hand, in order to compute an initial solution for the conventional algorithm, we simply use the set of representatives returned by the $(k-1)$-medians algorithm plus the string sample whose closest representative is the farthest away. On the other hand, to obtain an initial solution for the generalized algorithm, we directly use the k representatives given by the conventional k-medians algorithm. Of course, this is not the only procedure we can use for initialization purposes and, in fact, there are several initialization techniques for the conventional algorithm that could be generalized to work with arbitrary strings [11].

5 Conclusions and Future Work

In this work, we have proposed a new clustering process, called generalized k-medians, based on an approximation to the (generalized) median string. The approximated median string is used as a representative of the clusters. This alternative clearly outperforms the conventional k-medians algorithm, whose solution is used as a starting point.

Future work is directed towards exploring other combinations of both set median and approximated median string in the clustering. One possibility could be to use the approximated median string in the initialization process (i.e., not to use the k-medians result as initialization, but rather to use the generalized k-medians result). Exploring different initializations in the computation of the approximated median string (and not only the current cluster representative) is another interesting option.

Acknowledgements

The authors wish to thank Dr. Jens Gregor for providing the preprocessed chromosome data used in this work.

References

[1] K. S. Fu *Syntactic Pattern Recognition*. Prentice-Hall, 1982.
[2] R. Wagner and M. Fisher. The string-to-string correction problem. *Journal of the ACM*, 21:168–178, 1974.
[3] A. Marzal and E. Vidal. Computation of normalized edit distance and applications. *IEEE Trans. on Pattern Analysis and Machine Intelligence*, 15(9):926–932, sep 1993.

[4] T. Kohonen. Median strings. *Pattern Recognition Letters*, 3:309–313, 1985.

[5] C. de la Higuera and F. Casacuberta. Topology of strings: Median string is np-complete. *Theoretical Computer Science*, 230:39–48, 2000.

[6] F. Casacuberta and M. de Antonio. A greedy algorithm for computing approximate median strings. In *Proceedings of the VII Simposium Nacional de Reconocimiento de Formas y Análisis de Imágenes*, pages 193–198, Bellaterra, April 1997.

[7] C. D. Martínez Hinarejos, A. Juan, and F. Casacuberta. Median strings for k-nearest neighbour classification. *Pattern Recognition Letters*, 24(1-3):173–181, 2003.

[8] R. O. Duda, P. Hart, and D. G. Stork. *Pattern Classification.* John Wiley, 2001.

[9] Mirchandani P. B. and Francis R. L. editors *Discrete Location Theory.* Wiley, 1990.

[10] O. Kariv and S. L. Hakimi. An algorithmic approach to network location problems. II: the p-medians. *SIAM Journal on Applied Math*, 37(3):539–560, 1979.

[11] A. Juan and E. Vidal Comparison of Four Initialization Techniques for the K-Medians Clustering Algorithm In *Lecture Notes in Computer Science 1876, Proc. of Joint IAPR Int. Workshops SSPR and SPR 2000*, 842–852, Springer Verlag, 2000.

[12] A. Juan and E. Vidal. Fast k-means-like clustering in metric spaces. *Pattern Recognition Letters*, 15(1):19-25, 1994.

[13] C. Lundsteen, J. Philip and E. Granum. Quantitative Analysis of 6895 Digitized Trypsin G-banded Human Metaphase Chromosomes *Clinical Genetics*, 18, 355–370, 1980.

[14] E. Granum and M. Thomason. Automatically Inferred Markov Network Models for Classification of Chromosomal Band Pattern Structures. *Cytometry*, 11, 26–39, 1990.

A Quadtree-Based Unsupervised Segmentation Algorithm for Fruit Visual Inspection*

Adolfo Martínez Usó

Filiberto Pla, Pedro García-Sevilla, Universidad Jaume I
Sos Baynat s/n, Castellón, 12071, Spain
auso@lsi.uji.es

Abstract. Many segmentation techniques are available in the literature and some of them have been widely used in different application problems. Most of these segmentation techniques were motivated by specific application purposes. In this article we present the preliminary results of an unsupervised segmentation algorithm through a multiresolution method using color information for fruit inspection tasks. The use of a Quadtree structure simplifies the combination of a multiresolution approach with the chosen strategy for the segmentation process and speeds up the whole procedure. The algorithm has been tested in fruit images in order to segment the different zones of the fruit surface. Due to the unsupervised nature of the procedure, it can adapt to the huge variability of color and shape of regions in fruit inspection applications.

1 Introduction

Image segmentation has had a large attention since the very beginning in computer vision. There exist many different approaches for image segmentation [5], which mainly differ in the criterion used to measure the similarity of two regions and in the strategy applied to guide the segmentation process. Most of these image segmentation techniques are application oriented and have been developed from specific purposes. There are also different segmentation methods in the literature that try to solve the segmentation problem from a general point of view [1, 12]. These segmentation techniques can be applied to a wide range of particular problems. However, each application usually has specific requirements that makes appropriate the development and use of application-oriented approaches, in order to take advantage of the characteristics of each particular application.

In the image segmentation framework, we can distinguish two main approaches to solve the problem. The first one takes a criterion as the basis for the whole segmentation process and this criterion guides all the algorithm steps [4]. On the other hand, a particular strategy can be established as the basis for the segmentation process. In this

---

* This work has been partly supported by grants CPI2001-2956-C02-02 from Spanish CICYT and IST-2001-37306 from the European Union.

F.J. Perales et al. (Eds.): IbPRIA 2003, LNCS 2652, pp. 510-517, 2003.

case, a more o less general strategy is used to address the problem in a structural way and different criteria can be used to particularize the method for a certain type of segmentation problem [1]. The work presented here can be included in the later case.

The main motivation of the developed work has been to obtain a method able to segment images of fruits for their classification in visual inspection processes. There exist some approaches in this particular application domain [2, 7]. Most of them use supervised techniques to address the problem [6].

Due to the nature of the fruit inspection problem, the following requirements for the image segmentation of fruits should be accomplished:

- An unsupervised method would be needed, due to manifold variables and the huge variability of situations which can arise in the images of fruits. Thus, any prior knowledge should be avoided for the segmentation procedure.
- The segmentation method has to be mainly based in color criteria.
- Edge information should be included in the process, in order to define the segmented region boundaries as accurately as possible. In this sense, not only gray level information should be used in order to segment color regions due to hue/saturation variations.
- The algorithm has to be computationally efficient to be implemented due to the time requirements of the application in industrial environments.

In order to meet the above mentioned requirements, an adequate image data representation should be used that can support those required features. In this case, a Quadtree (QT) structure has been chosen to support the method developed. Quadtree is commonly used to decompose a given frame into blocks of different sizes, since it enables an efficient representation of the resulting decomposition. Furthermore, well-known algorithms are available for searching and neighbouring operations over these sort of trees.

It is quite obvious that, from the described requirements, color would be the particular criterion to be used in the segmentation procedure. Apart from the decision of which is the color space to best represent a given problem [13], the main point to be fixed is the segmentation strategy to be followed. This strategy will be conditioned and orientated by the image representation adopted, that is, by the QT.

Other unsupervised segmentation algorithms can be found in the literature. Some of them do not use edge information [12]. Other can be computationally expensive for some applications when the process attempts to consider many of the possible image variables [9]. Finally, there are some algorithms that do not use the color information to separate the regions in the image [1].

The rest of the paper is structured as follows. In section 2, we introduce the QT structure and explain what kind of criterion has been used to allow the construction of the QT. In section 3, we explain the segmentation strategy and discuss some of the preliminary attempts to solve the problem. In section 4, we formulate the problem of using color information and propose the method to solve it. In section 5 some results on fruit images for inspection purposes are shown. Finally, some conclusions are described in section 6.

2   Generating an Image Quadtree

The QT data structure is used to successively decompose the image into blocks until fulfilling a certain criterion as shown in Figure 1. It enables an efficient representation of the resulting decomposition. QT has been adopted as the supporting data representation of the segmentation process and, therefore, it is intimately related to our segmentation strategy and must be combined together with the segmentation criteria.

This data structure allows to divide the image within a complete tree representation, including neighbouring information. This spatial information can be further used by a merging strategy which joins the QT leaves using color information.

To calculate the QT representation of an image, the procedure starts considering the whole image in the root node. If the segmentation criterion is not fulfilled in the region representing the node, then the region is divided into four children regions. The criterion is recursively applied to each subregion (children nodes) until the criterion for a node is accomplished (see Figure 1). Obviously, this process will produce subregions of different sizes represented in a tree structure, the subregions may vary from pixel size to the complete image.

This structure has been extensively used in works such as the one by Wilson and Spann in [14]. One of the most recent applications of this data structure can be found in [1] where, through a methodology of multiresolution based on a QT, information of borders is combined with a region growing strategy to obtain the image segmentation on grey images. A similar strategy has been used in this work but using a different criterion to compare two regions and extending its application to a color environment. Moreover, the algorithms described in Samet [10] have been used in the QT structure for the implementation of the neighbourhood operations.

3   The Segmentation Process

As it was mentioned in the introduction, the segmentation method here proposed is based on a segmentation strategy, supported by a QT data representation of the image, and the use of color information as particular criteria in the segmentation strategy.

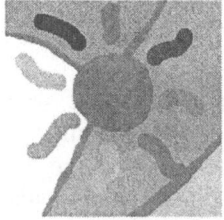 

Fig. 1. Quadtree structure of a synthetic image using an homogeneity color criterion

3.1   Segmentation Strategy

Taking as a starting point the construction of the QT structure, the first step of the procedure consists of building an oversegmented representation of the image, the QT is developed until every square region is homogeneus according to the homogeneity criteria. The simplest homogeneity criteria is that all pixels in the Quatree leaf have the same color. This will lead to a significant expanded QT. Other softer homogeneity criteria would lead to a compacter initial QT without affecting the final segmentation.

The oversegmented representation is input to the algorithm that starts pruning the QT by recursively merging neighbouring leaves based on a color criterion. This criterion stablishes a threshold tolerance for merging leaves representing smooth regions. This stage is aimed at compacting the QT in order to increase the accuracy and efficiency of the final process.

A further step will consist of a merging strategy which looks for leaves in the pruned QT structure that belong to the same region in the image. These regions (clusters of nodes) will be represented as sets of leaves in the QT that meet some spatial constraints.

In this phase of the procedure, edge information is added in the merging criterion in order to find accurate region borders at the same time as looking for consistent image regions.

During the fusion process the following premises are respected:

-    Regions are arranged according to their size, giving more importance to the bigger regions and facilitating the merging of small regions with the big ones.
-    Only regions with a common boundary can be merged. This will represent the spatial constraint in the merging process.

Figure 2 shows the outline of the segmentation strategy used, which is basically an iterative process. In the iterative loop, each cluster is compared to all its neighboring clusters and, when the segmentation criterion is satisfied, the clusters are merged. Candidate merging clusters are searched through a list of clusters ordered by size, beginning with the biggest clusters, favoring initially the merging and formation of bigger regions that will act as seeds to further collect smaller regions. This clustering process stops when no other merging can be performed.

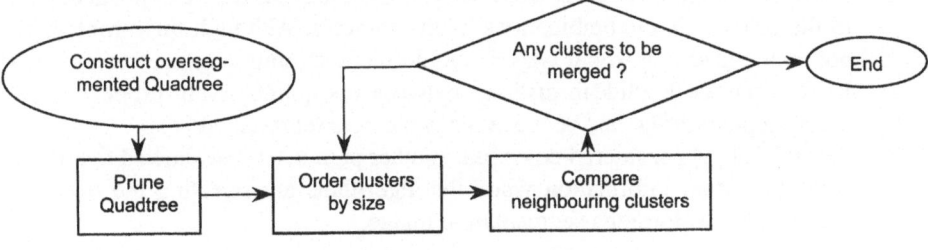

Fig. 2. Segmentation process flow chart

3.2   Algorithm

The process described can be summarized in the following algorithm:

1. Generate the L*a*b* color space of the image.
2. Construct an oversegmented representation of the image using a color similarity criterion. The most restrictive one may be that each region has all its pixels with the same color.
3. Prune the QT merging neighboring leaves with the same parent node using a color criterion less restrictive than the one used in the first step. This merging process is not iterative. The aim is to achieve a compacter QT representation to speed-up the rest of the process.
4. Consider each leave from the pruned tree as an initial cluster and create an ordered list according to their size.
5. Look for the first pair of neighbouring clusters in the list that can be merged according to the color merging criterion. The search is done beginning by the biggest cluster in decreasing size order. Merging bigger regions first is aimed at looking for significant clusters supported by as much pixels as possible that act as seeds that grow by further collecting smaller neighbour clusters.
6. If any clusters are merged, reorder the list of clusters.
7. Repeat steps 5 and 6 until regions became stable. This part of the process correspond to an iterative sequence that may be seen as a coarse-to-fine segmentation process.

At the end of the procedure, every cluster in the list is represented by a set of leaves of the QT, which are labeled as a single resulting region.

4   Use of Color Information

Although many authors in the literature use partial information of a particular color space [8], it is evident that ignoring some color component causes a loss of information that can be very important.

Thus, we have decided to use all color information but taking into account that:

1. There exist problems in the RGB scale. RGB scale has a HW dependency due to the infinite CCD combinations of the cameras. Although this problem can not be avoided in a trivial way, it should be taken into account. Moreover, in RGB space the Euclidean distance between two points is not proportional to the perceptual difference between the two colors represented [11].
2. Pal and Pal [5] considered color like another parameter and showed that it provides important information when the algorithms are selecting the definitive regions that conform the segmentation image.

Therefore, the approach here presented uses the three planes simultaneously in a L*a*b* color space. In this color space the distances between two colors is approximately proportional to the human perceptual difference between those two colors.

We assume that the pixels in each region (clusters of leaves in the QT) follow a Normal distribution. The color average μ and standard deviation σ are calculated. For each region, when the algorithm must decide if two regions are merged, it calculates the Probability Density function of the Normal distribution of both regions and the common area between them is computed. If the difference is lower than a threshold then these two region are merged.

Let us assume that $N_A(\mu_A, \sigma^2_A)$ and $N_B(\mu_B, \sigma^2_B)$ are two normal distributions for neighbouring regions A and B respectively. To calculate the output of the color criterion, the next expression is evaluated in each plane of L*a*b* color space:

$$| N_A(\mu_A, \sigma^2_A) - N_B(\mu_B, \sigma^2_B) | < \text{Threshold}$$

If this difference, in each color component, is below the threshold, the process allows regions A and B to be merged. This is the simpler version of the merging criterion that has been used in the preliminary tests carried out in this work. This criterion can be completed and improved adding some color border information.

5   Experiments and Results

Such as it was mentioned in the introduction, the segmentation method here presented has been aimed at characterizing images of fruits in visual inspection applications. The segmentation of fruit images are used as input in a further process to characterize and classify each region in the fruit surface to identify and detect different types of defects and parts of the fruit.

There exist a great variability of situations and color regions that can arise in fruit images. Thus, the use of an unsupervised color segmentation process like the one presented here is very appealing for such a problem. The proposed algorithm has been tested in different types of fruit images. Images obtained from a RGB color camera were transformed into L*a*b* color space. The results presented here were obtained applying the algorithm over 256x256 images.

Figure 3 shows some examples of the results of the segmentation on different types of fruits and situations to be characterized. Note how the segmentation process has adapted to the regions of each image due to its unsupervised nature. For instance, in Figures 3a and 3e there are different type of stains in the fruit surface. Figures 3b and 3f show their corresponding segmentations and how the different stains have been quite accurately clustered and separated from the rest of the fruit parts.

Figure 3c show an example of fruit image where there are many different parts to be identified and separated. Figure 3d shows the result of the proposed algorithm that has been able to satisfactorily segment the different type of regions and parts of the fruit, providing a quite accurate definition of the regions corresponding to the seed and stains of different nature. It is important to note how the regions found by the proposed method fit and adapt to the contour of regions in an accurate way, characterizing the shape of the regions.

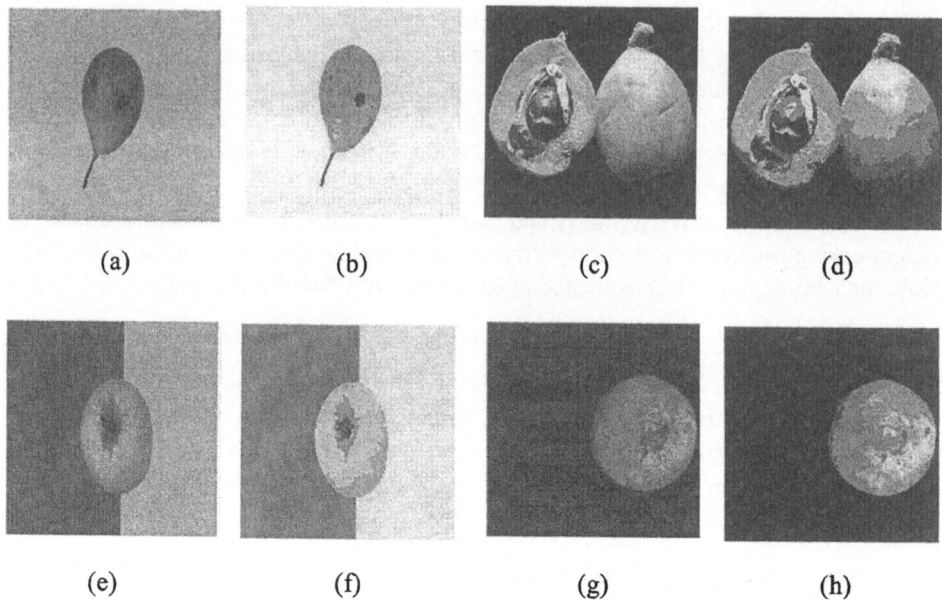

(a)   (b)   (c)   (d)

(e)   (f)   (g)   (h)

Fig. 3. Segmentation results in fruit images

Figure 3g shows an example of fruit with various stains produced by effect of rot and how the segmentation obtained, Figure 3h, has found the different variations of the stains of the rotten zone. This will allow the extraction of region descriptors in a more appropriate way for their identification and classification.

6   Conclusions and Future Work

In this work, some preliminary results of an unsupervised color segmentation algorithm have been presented. The method has been applied to fruit images in order to characterize the variety of regions appearing on the fruit surfaces for a further classification in fruit inspection tasks.

The results obtained show how the algorithm can adapt to the different situations and variability of color regions, being able to segment areas of the fruit surfaces locating the borders quite accurately, which can facilitate the extraction of region descriptors for further classification purposes.

The use of color information combined with a QT representation of the image is the base of an unsupervised segmentation strategy that can locate color regions finding their contours in a satisfactory way.

Future and current work being carried out is directed to add color edge information to the segmentation process. The use of color edge information will allow to obtain even more accurate results in defining the border of the regions obtained in the segmentation.

The method here presented is also being extended to be applied in multispectral images, extending the concept of color borders to multispectral borders and the color criteria to multispectral criteria in the algorithm.

References

[1]   Bhalerao, A., Wilson, R.: Unsupervised Image Segmentation Combining Region and Boundary Estimation. In Image and Vision Computing. Vol. 19, Num. 6, (2001) 353–386

[2]   Chen, Y., Mhori, K., Namba, K.: Image Analysis of Bruised Oorin Apples. Proceedings of V Symphosium on Fruit, Nut and Vegetable Production Engineering. Davis, CA, USA (1997)

[3]   Di Zenzo, S.: A Note on the Gradient of a Multi-Image. Computer Vision, Graphics and Image Processing 33. (1986) 116-128

[4]   García, P., Pla, F., Gracia, I.: Detecting edges in colour images using dichromatic differences. 7th International Conference on Image Processing and its Applications, IEEE. ISBN: 0-85296-717-9. Manchester (UK). (1999) 363-367

[5]   Pal, N.R., Pal, K.P.: A Review on Image Segmentation Techniques. Pattern Recognition, 26(9): (1993) 1277–1294

[6]   Power, W., Clist, R.S.: Comparison of supervised learning techniques applied to colour segmentation of fruit images. SPIE vol. 2904. Boston (1996) 370-381

[7]   Rigney, M.P., Brusewitz, G.H., Krauzler, G.A.: Asparaus Defect Inspection with Machine Vision. Transactions of the ASAE. vol. 35(6) (1992) 1873-1878

[8]   Robinson, G.S.: Color edge detection. Optical Engineering, 16(5): (1977) 479-484

[9]   Saber, E., Murat, A., Bozdagi, G.: Fusion of Color and Edge Information for Improved Segmentation and Edge Linking. IVC, vol.15 (1995) 769-780

[10]   Samet, H.: Applications of Spatial Data Structures: Computer Graphics, Image Processing and GIS. Addison-Wesley, (1990)

[11]   Schettini, R.: A segmentation algorithm for color images. Pattern Recognition Letters, vol 14. (1993) 499-506

[12]   Sharon, E., Brandt, A., Basri, R.: Fast Multiscale Image Segmentation. Computer Vision and Pattern Recognition, 2000. Proceedings. IEEE Conference on. vol.1 (2000) 70–77

[13]   Singh, M., Markou, M., Singh, S.: Colour Image Texture Analysis: Dependence on Colour Spaces. ICPR. Quebec (2002)

[14]   Wilson, R.G., Spann, M.: Finite Prolate Spheroidal Sequences and their Applications II: Image Feature Description and Segmentation. IEEE Transactions on Pattern Analysis and Machine Intelligence, 10(2) (1988) 193-203

Shape Deformation Models Using Non-uniform Objects in Multimedia Applications*

Miquel Mascaró Portells, Arnau Mir, and Francisco Perales

Departament de Matemàtiques i Informàtica
Unitat de Gràfics i Visió
Universitat de les Illes Balears
Crta. de Valldemossa, Km. 7,5
07071 Palma de Mallorca
http://dmi.uib.es/research/GV

Abstract. In this paper we describe a system to generate in an interactive way and thinking in multimedia applications, realistic simulation of a 3D deformable object's. The physically elastic deformation techniques are actually an important and challenging feature in applications where three-dimensional object interaction and behaviour is considered or explored. Also, in multimedia environments we need a rapid computation of deformations with a good visual realism. In this paper we present a prototype of a system for the animation and simulation of elastic objects in an interactive system and under real-time conditions. The approach makes use of the finite elements method (F.E.M) and Elasticity Theory. Using picking node selection the user can interactively apply forces to objects causing their deformation. The deformations computed with our approach have a physical interpretation based on the mathematical model defined. In particular we extend our original system to non-homogeneous regions. This property is very important to able simulations with material that have deferents density functions. Finally, a set of results are presented which demonstrate this capability. All programs are written in C++ using POO, VRML and Open Invertor tools.

Keywords: Elastic Deformation, Finite Elements Method, Elasticity Theory, Computer Animation, Physical Models, VRML, Non-homogeneous objects.

1 Introduction and Related Work

Obviously, flexible and deformable objects are inherently more difficult to model and animate in computer graphics than rigid objects. Until recent years, the computer graphic methods proposed were limited to modelling rigid objects. However, recent advances in algorithms and computer graphics hardware support the processing of flexible objects. Today, there is a great need in many

---

* This work is partially subsidized by CICYT under grant TIC2001-0931 and by UE under grant Humodan-IST-2001-32202.

F.J. Perales et al. (Eds.): IbPRIA 2003, LNCS 2652, pp. 518–529, 2003.

engineering and medical applications to be able to simulate the material and geometrical behaviour of 3D objects under real forces. In general, different modelling techniques are usually classified into three categories: geometrical, physical and hybrid:

Geometrical Techniques. Geometrical models do not consider the physical properties of objects.

Physical Techniques. In this group of techniques, the objects are modelled as a triangular or rectangular grid in 2D or voxeled volumed in 3D. Each joint or node in the grid can be affected by forces and the global grid is governed by the interaction of physical forces on each node considered.

Hybrid Techniques. Finally, we can combine physical and geometrical methods to avoid problems and improve efficiency.
See [7] for more details.

In particular, the growth in hardware graphics can overcome the time consuming restrictions of physically based methods. So in this paper we present our extended system to deal with non-homogeneous objects. It is based on Finite Element Methods (F.E.M) and uses the Elasticity Theory. As we know, the solid theory used guarantees the robustness of the system and is actually widely used by other researchers [4]. Thus, we are principally interested in designing a new system that can run in real or near real time systems. We believe that in Virtual Reality systems the time in interaction and feedback is very critical. In this case, the efficiency of implementation is very important and results must be checked to reach this condition. In some cases, an initial off-line process can be introduced to improve efficiency.

This paper is organized in several sections. The second section includes a biref introduction of the mathematical model proposed. The third section is dedicated to presenting the F.E.M implemented. The fourth section includes the extension to non-homogeneous simulations, presenting the new extended model and some intereting results. Finally, we conclude with some considerations about parallelization, efficiency and computational cost. The paper also includes the conclusions, future work and related bibliography.

2 Mathematical Model Proposed

Let Ω be an enclosed and connected solid in $\mathbb{R}^3$. Let us assume that the boundary of Ω, Γ, is C^1 piecewise. We divide Γ into two parts, Γ_0 and Γ_1, where Γ_1 is the part of the boundary which receives external forces and Γ_0 is the fixed part of the boundary whose size we assume to be strictly positive. Note that boundary Γ does not necessarily need to be connected, which will enable us to simulate deformations of objects with holes.

The aim of this work is to study and analyse the computational cost of the evolution of Ω under the action of external forces f on the inside and external sources g on the boundary Γ_1.

The position of the object is defined by the function $u(t, x)$. Our problem is, therefore, reduced, given the functions u_0 (initial position of the object) and u_1 (initial speed), to finding the position $u(t, x) = (u_1, \ldots, u_3)$ of these in the domain $Q_T = \Omega \times (0 \times T)$ which will verify the following evolution system in time:

$$
\begin{cases}
\rho \frac{\delta^2 u_i}{\partial t^2} - \sum_{j=1}^{3} \frac{\partial}{\partial x_j} \sigma_{ij} = f_i, \, i = 1, 2, 3 \, \text{en} \, Q_T, \\
u_i = 0, \, i = 1, 2, 3 \, \text{en} \, \Gamma_0 \times (0, T), \\
\sum_{j=1}^{3} \sigma_{ij} n_j = g_i, \, i = 1, 2, 3 \, \text{en} \, \Gamma_1 \times (0, T), \\
u_i(\cdot, 0) = u_{0,i}, \, i = 1, 2, 3 \, \text{en} \, \Omega, \\
\frac{\partial u_i}{\partial t}(\cdot, 0) = u_{1,i}, \, i = 1, 2, 3 \, \text{en} \, \Omega.
\end{cases}
\tag{1}
$$

where functions σ_{ij} are the components of the tension tensor, n_j are the components of the normal vector at a point on the surface of the domain $\Gamma_1 \times (0, T)$ and ρ is the density of the object.

The resolution of the above problem is carried out by variational formulation. The solution of a discrete approximation u_h of the above formulation gives us the approximate solution to our problem.

Specifically, we consider a subspace V_h with a finite dimension $I = I(h)$ of Hilbert's space H defined by $H = \left\{ v \in \left(H^1(\Omega) \right)^3, \text{tal}, \text{que } v = 0 \, \text{sobre} \, \Gamma_0 \right\}$.

Our problem is reduced to finding a function u_h defined in Q_T solution to the following differential system:

$$
\begin{cases}
\forall v_h \in V_h, \, \rho \frac{d^2}{dt^2} (u_h(t), v_h) + a(u_h(t), \underline{m} v_h) = L(v_h), \\
u_h(0) = u_{0,h}, \\
\frac{du_h}{dt}(0) = u_{1,h},
\end{cases}
\tag{2}
$$

where the expression $a(\cdot, \cdot)$ is the bilinear continous form defined by $a(u, v) = \sum_{i,j=1}^{3} \int_\Omega \sigma_{i,j}(u) \varepsilon_{ij}(v) \, dx$, $(\cdot, \cdot)$ is the following scale product defined for functions defined in Q_T: $(u, v) = \sum_{i=1}^{3} \int_\Omega u_i(x) v_i(x) \, dx$ and $L(v)$ is the following continuous linear form on V_h: $L(v) = \sum_{i=1}^{3} \int_\Omega f_i v_i dx + \int_{\partial\Omega} g_i v_i d\sigma$.

Let φ_i be a V_h base of functions. If we write the solution to look for u_h as, $u_h(t) = \sum_{i=1}^{I} \xi_i(t) \varphi_i$, the components ξ_i verify the next differential system:

$$
\rho \sum_{i=1}^{I} \xi_i''(t) (\varphi_i, \varphi_j) + \gamma \sum_{i=1}^{I} \xi_i'(t) (\varphi_i, \varphi_j) + \sum_{i=1}^{I} a(\varphi_i, \varphi_j) \xi_i(t) = L(\varphi_j).
\tag{3}
$$

In the above system we have added a new term $(\gamma \sum_{i=1}^{I} \xi'(t)(\varphi_i, \varphi_j))$ to simulate a damping effect of the object. The above system, written in a matrix form, is:

$$\rho M \xi'' + \gamma M \xi' + K \xi = L, \tag{4}$$

with M and K as the mass and tension matrices respectively:

$M = ((\varphi_i, \varphi_j)) \ i, j = 1, \ldots, I$

$K = (a(\varphi_i, \varphi_j)) \ i, j = 1, \ldots, I$.

By discretizing in time this last equation:

$$M \left(\tfrac{\rho}{\Delta t^2} + \tfrac{\gamma}{2\Delta t} \right) \xi(t + \Delta t) =$$
$$= L + \tfrac{\rho M}{\Delta t^2} (2\xi(t) - \xi(t - \Delta t)) + \tfrac{\gamma M}{2\Delta t} \xi(t - \Delta t) - K\xi(t). \tag{5}$$

The simulation of different physical phenomena such as instantaneous blows, constant forces, waves, etc. are implicit in the expression of vector L.

3 F.E.M and K, M, L. Definition

In order to choose the type of finite elements to use we will base our decision on two basic criteria: the type of finite element to be used must correctly transmit the propagation of the tensions in the direction perpendicular to each face of the finite element and the type of finite elements to be used must possibility a real time computational process.

This is why finite elements of a rectangular prism type will be chosen. This kind of finite element makes a right transmition of the propagation of the tensions in the direction perpendicular to each face of the finite element and gets a low computational cost.

Note that by means of the type of finite elements chosen it is possible to define uniform grids (grids which possess all the finite elements of an identical length), and non-uniform grids. This second type of grid let us make an approach of the boundary of Ω.

First of all, we will define the fundamental tool which will allow us to work with the finite elements: domain with a pair of points.

Let i and j be two arbitrary nodes of the grid of finite elements of the object. Let sup φ_i be the set $\mathbb{R}^3$ where $\varphi_i \neq 0$.

$\Omega_{i,j}$ is defined as the integration domain of a pair of points (i, j) such as

$$\Omega_{i,j} = \text{sup } \varphi_i \cap \text{sup } \varphi_i.$$

3.1 Base Functions

In the three-dimensional model, there are three types of base functions:

$$\varphi_i^{(1)} = (\varphi_i, 0, 0) \ , \varphi_i^{(2)} = (0, \varphi_i, 0) \ , \varphi_i^{(3)} = (0, 0, \varphi_i) \ . \tag{6}$$

The expression of φ_i is the same in each base function: it is that function which has a value of 1 in the i-th node and 0 in the other nodes.

3.2   Deformations Tensor

The deformations tensor is defined by the following expression:

$$\varepsilon_{ij}\left(v\right) = \frac{1}{2}\left(\frac{\partial v_i}{\partial x_j} + \frac{\partial v_j}{\partial x_i}\right), \ 1 \le i, j \le n. \tag{7}$$

3.3   The Tension Matrix K

The internal bonds of the object can be seen in tension matrix K. The compo-
nents of matrix K are: $K_{ij} = K(\varphi_i^{(k)}, \varphi_j^{(k)})$, where $\varphi_i^{(k)}$ and $\varphi_j^{(k)}$ are the base
functions defined in (6) and the expression of $K(u, v)$ is the following where u
and v are any H functions:

$$K\left(u, v\right) = \lambda \int_\Omega \left(\sum_{k=1}^n \frac{\partial u_k}{\partial x_k}\right)\left(\sum_{k=1}^n \frac{\partial v_k}{\partial x_k}\right) dx_1 dx_2 dx_3$$

$$+ 2\mu \sum_{i,j=1}^n \int_\Omega \varepsilon_{ij}\left(u\right)\varepsilon_{ij}\left(v\right) dx_1 dx_2 dx_3, \quad \forall u, v \in H. \tag{8}$$

The expression of matrix K is the following:

$$K = \begin{pmatrix} K\left(\varphi_i^{(1)}, \varphi_j^{(1)}\right) & K\left(\varphi_i^{(1)}, \varphi_j^{(2)}\right) & K\left(\varphi_i^{(1)}, \varphi_j^{(3)}\right) \\ K\left(\varphi_i^{(2)}, \varphi_j^{(1)}\right) & K\left(\varphi_i^{(2)}, \varphi_j^{(2)}\right) & K\left(\varphi_i^{(2)}, \varphi_j^{(3)}\right) \\ K\left(\varphi_i^{(3)}, \varphi_j^{(1)}\right) & K\left(\varphi_i^{(3)}, \varphi_j^{(2)}\right) & K\left(\varphi_i^{(3)}, \varphi_j^{(3)}\right) \end{pmatrix}. \tag{9}$$

The space of functions we consider is that generated by the polynomials $\mathbb{R}^3$
$< 1, x_1, x_2, x_3, x_1 \cdot x_2, x_1 \cdot x_3, x_2 \cdot x_3, x_1 \cdot x_2 \cdot x_3 >$. Therefore, the function φ_i will
have a linear combination of these polynomials.

The calculation of $\int\int\int_{Q_s} \frac{\partial\varphi_i'}{\partial x_i}\frac{\partial\varphi_j'}{\partial x_j} dx_1' dx_2' dx_3'$ is quite simple as we are working with a standard cube.

In this way, the 64 possible values $K_{ij}^{(k)}$ can be obtained. It can be seen that
there are only 8 different values.

3.4   The Mass Matrix M

The mass matrix M will be made up of nine sub-matrices whose expression is
the following:

$$M = \begin{pmatrix} \left(\varphi_i^{(1)}, \varphi_j^{(1)}\right) & 0 & 0 \\ 0 & \left(\varphi_i^{(2)}, \varphi_j^{(2)}\right) & 0 \\ 0 & 0 & \left(\varphi_i^{(3)}, \varphi_j^{(3)}\right) \end{pmatrix}, \text{ where:}$$

$$\left(\varphi_i^{(1)}, \varphi_j^{(1)}\right) = \left(\varphi_i^{(2)}, \varphi_j^{(2)}\right) = \left(\varphi_i^{(3)}, \varphi_j^{(3)}\right) \ne 0 \text{ si } \Omega_{ij} \ne \emptyset.$$

In order to calculate (φ_i, φ_j) in an effective way, we will use a method of approximate integration using the vertices of the finite elements as nodes. That is, using: $\left(\varphi_i^{(1)}, \varphi_j^{(1)}\right) = \sum_{k|Q_k \subset \Omega_{ij}} \int_{Q_k} \varphi_i(x)\varphi_j(x)dx$, we approximate the integration as:

$$\int_{Q_k} \varphi_i(x)\varphi_j(x)dx \approx \sum_{l=1}^{8} A_i \varphi_i(P_l)\varphi_j(P_l), \tag{10}$$

where P_l are the vertices of the finite element Q_k and A_i are the coefficients of the approximate integration formula.

In this way, we manage to make the mass matrix M diagonal since $\varphi_i(P_l) = \delta_{il}$. Furthermore, since the numerical integration error is less than the error we make in the variational approximation of the problem which is in the order of h^3 where h is the maximum length of the sides Q_k (see [7]), the use of the integration method does not increase the overall error in the approximation.

3.5   The External Force Vector L

The external force vector L will be of the type:

$L = \left(L\left(\varphi_i^{(1)}\right), L\left(\varphi_i^{(2)}\right), L\left(\varphi_i^{(3)}\right)\right)^\top$, where $L\left(\varphi_i^{(k)}\right)$, $k = 1, 2, 3$, are dimension vectors N with N as the number of nodes of the grid of finite elements which does not belong to Γ_0, that is, non fixed nodes.

The expressions of the vectors $L(\varphi_i)$, $L(\varphi'_i)$ and $L(\varphi''_i)$ are the following:

$$L\left(\varphi_i^{(k)}\right) = \int_{\sup \varphi_i} f_k(x)\varphi_i(x)dx + \int_{\partial\Omega \cap \sup \varphi_i} g_k(x)\varphi_i(x)d\sigma,$$

where $k = 1, 2, 3$.

In all the experiments carried out, we have assumed that $f = 0$. Therefore, the first term in the above expressions will be null.

If the external forces g applied on the boundary are constant, the above expressions are reduced to: $L\left(\varphi_i^{(k)}\right) = g_k \int_{\partial\Omega \cap \sup \varphi_i} \varphi_i(x)d\sigma$.

Our problem is, therefore, reduced to finding $\int_{\partial\Omega \cap \sup \varphi_i} \varphi_i(x)d\sigma$.

We will assume that the boundary of Ω is approximated by square prism type finite elements. Therefore, we have the case in which the integration domain $\partial\Omega \cap \sup \varphi_i$ will be: $\partial\Omega \cap \sup \varphi_i = \cup\Pi_{ik}$, where Π_{ik} are flat rectangles situated on a plane $x_i =$ constant.

We have, therefore, the case in which the value of the above integral can be calculated as: $\int_{\partial\Omega \cap \sup \varphi_i} \varphi_i(x)d\sigma = \sum_k \int_{\Pi_{ik}} \varphi_i(x)d\sigma$

The above integral $\int_{\Pi_{ik}} \varphi_i(x)d\sigma$ can be reduced by the variable change adapted to a double integral on the standard square $[0, 1] \times [0, 1]$.

For more details about Mahtematical Model, Dynamic Solution System, Parallelization and Computational Cost you canrefers to [7].

4   Non-homogeneous Objects Simulation

In this section we introduce our new proposal, to simulate objetcs with differents F.E. with more than one dentsity value.

Two important points in the simulation of elastic deformations in a three-dimensional solid object made of a certain material, such as the precise definition of the objects boundary and the application of forces on a precise region of the boundary, require a greater precision in the definition of the object. This precision can be obtained in a very simple way: by decreasing the size of the elements of the grid defining the deformable object. This would be a good solution if the use of the application was aimed at animation techniques, but not at virtual reality environments, where the desired real time computation would cease to be feasible, since, by griding the object with a greater quantity of elements, the increase in memory and computation time required to attain a solution are too high for such a purpose.

One possible solution to the problem would be to use a progressive grid, where the areas of the object that need a greater definition are grided with finer finite elements, whereas the rest of the object can be made up of elements with a greater dimension. This simple solution is not applicable to the model represented here for two fundamental reasons:

- The progressive grid can only partly solve the problem of the increase in the matrices in the system and the computation time of the final solution.
- On the other hand, the model presented here does not allow for the use of a group of elements which do not have, at least, one of the faces which are identical, which in part makes the progressive grid impossible.

All of this leads us to look for the solution to the problem in another direction, since in our model, it is only possible to refine the boundary of the object to a certain point. Thus, the solution could be to use the elements of the grid which have a behaviour capable of defining the boundary of the object in a precise and accurate way. That is, using finite elements which do not represent a uniform behaviour throughout their whole domain. In this way, it would be feasible to represent boundaries of any kind, since a cutting funtion can be defined which would divide the finite element in two, where each of them would have a material with different characteristics. In figure 1 we can see the definition of a 2D object using a uniform grid with non-uniform finite elements. On the other hand, the joint use of non-uniform grids and non-uniform finite elements, as far as the characteristics of the material is concerned, would make it possible to define a whole range of objects made up of different materials (layers, blocks, etc).

5   Objects with Grid Elements Made of Different Materials

This type of grid would enable us to define obejcts made up of layers of different materials.

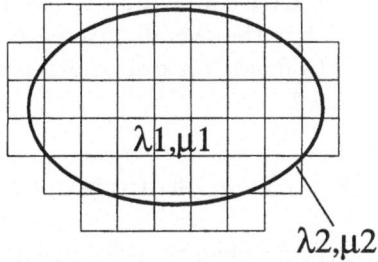

Fig. 1. Object where the spare part of the grid elements would be made up of a very weak material or of one with little resistence to an external force

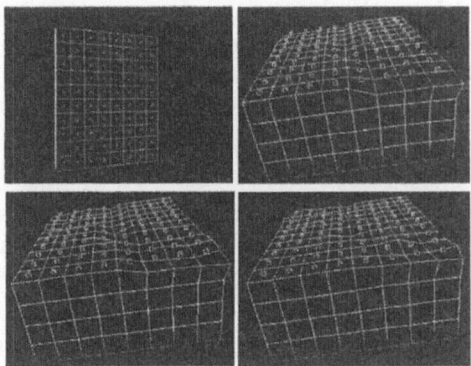

Fig. 2. Sequences of the deformation of an object with finite elements of two different materials. The time instants represented from left to right and top to bottom are: 0, 4, 6 and 10 seconds of the simulation

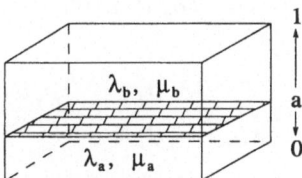

Fig. 3. Non-homogeneous finite element with two areas made of a different material

As an example of how well this model works with this type of elements, we will take an object made of two types of materials: hard rubber and soft rubber. In figure 2 it can be observed that the object is made up of hard rubber (green) but it has a series of zones at the top made up of another type of softer rubber (blue). The object is fixed at the bottom and an external force defined by p = (0,100,0) Pa is applied to its upper face (blue cubes in figure 2). This pressure is applied for the ten seconds the simulation lasts. The initial result expected is that in the elements which have softer rubber, the incidence of the external forces will be much greater, but the overall coherence of the behaviour of the object must be maintained. In figure 2 it can be observed that the result of the simulation is what we expected.

6   Objects which Have Non-homogeneous Finite Elements

With the aim of simplifying the problem, we will simulate deformations in objects which have non-homogeneous finite elements as far as their Young Module and Poisson Coefficient are concerned.

With the purpose of checking the validity of the strategy, we opted for the use of elements with a cut in the Y plane of the elements domain and where each part of this will be made up of a different material. In figure 3, a non-homogeneous element of this type can be seen.

6.1   Changes in the Model

The general equation of the dynamic system (5) does not change at all, what will change is the value of some of its components. Since the elasticity conditions are the only ones to change, the only value of (equation 5) to undergo modifications is tension matrix K. To obtain the values of matrix K: Taking into account the fact that, in non-homogeneous elements, the parameters lambda and mu are not constant throughout the whole of the integration domain; the expression of the terms $K\left(\varphi_i, \varphi_j\right)$ of tension matrix K would be as follows, the rest would be calculated in an analogous way:

$$K\left(\varphi_i, \varphi_j\right) = \left(\lambda_a + 2\mu_a\right) \int_{\Omega_a} \frac{\partial \varphi_i}{\partial x_1} \frac{\partial \varphi_j}{\partial x_1} \, dx_1 dx_2 dx_3$$

$$+ \mu_a \int_{\Omega_a} \frac{\partial \varphi_i}{\partial x_2} \frac{\partial \varphi_j}{\partial x_2} + \frac{\partial \varphi_i}{\partial x_3} \frac{\partial \varphi_j}{\partial x_3} \, dx_1 dx_2 dx_3 \; + \qquad (11)$$

$$\left(\lambda_b + 2\mu_b\right) \int_{\Omega_b} \frac{\partial \varphi_i}{\partial x_1} \frac{\partial \varphi_j}{\partial x_1} \, dx_1 dx_2 dx_3$$

$$+ \mu_b \int_{\Omega_b} \frac{\partial \varphi_i}{\partial x_2} \frac{\partial \varphi_j}{\partial x_2} + \frac{\partial \varphi_i}{\partial x_3} \frac{\partial \varphi_j}{\partial x_3} \, dx_1 dx_2 dx_3 \; ,$$

In this expression, the terms Ω_a and Ω_b correspond to the integration domains of the two existing parts in a non-homogeneous finite element.

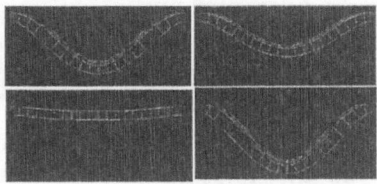

Fig. 4. The time instants corresponding to 10, 20, 30 and 40 seconds of the simulation of the deformation in a homogeneous rod are represented from left to right and from top to bottom

7   Results and Experiments

7.1   An Elastic Non-homogeneous Simulation Example

The experiment will be carried out initially with a rubber-band type of material with the aim of defining the base behaviour of this so as, in later experiments, to introduce into the object some parts made of plywood material and to observe the changes that are produced.

a) Simulation in an Homogeneous Rod For this experiment, we take a rod such as that in figure 5 and fix its ends. The rod is subjected to the action of the normal gravitational field and its behaviour is observed over 40 seconds. We can see the result of the simulation in figure 4. The material used to carry out the simulation has the following physical parameters:

- Density: $960 \, kg/m^3$.
- Damping: $1 \, s^{-1}$.
- Young's Module: $0.35 \, MPa$.
- Poisson Coefficient: 0.45.

b) Simulation in a Half Rubber, Half Plywood Rod For this experiment, we take a rod similar to the one in the above experiment, as far as its shape and situation are concerned, but modifying the material it is made of, in such a way that the left hand side of the rod is made of plywood (hypothetically high density) and its right hand side of rubber. The rod is subjected to the action of the normal gravitational field and its behaviour is observed over 40 seconds. The materials used to carry out the simulation for both halves are:

$Left\,side\,(plywood)$	$right\,side\,(rubber)$
$Density: 960 \, kg/m^3$	$Density: 960 \, kg/m^3$
$Damping: 1 \, s^{-1}$	$Amortiguación: 1 \, s^{-1}$
$Young's Module: 1800 \, MPa$	$Young's Module: 0.35 \, MPa$
$Poisson Coefficient: 0.32$	$Poisson Coefficient: 0.45$

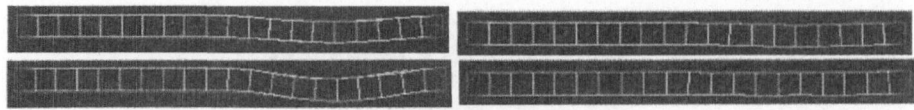

Fig. 5. Rod with two halves made of different materials. The time instants corresponding to 10, 20, 30 and 40 seconds of the simulation are represented from left to right and top to bottom

In figure 5, we can observe the instants corresponding to 10, 20, 30 and 40 seconds of the simulation of the deformation, obtained after 260 seconds of computation. In figure 5, it can be appreciated that, while the left hand side behaves like plywood, the right hand side behaves like rubber. This would be the case of an object made up of homogeneous finite elements of two types of different materials.

8   Conclusions and Future Work

In this work we have implemented a 3D deformation dynamic model based on the Theory of Elasticity which is capable of simulating deformations in three-dimensional objects with non-homogeneous finite elements and of automatically generating animations of such simulations. The capacities of this model make it suitable for virtual reality uses where it is important to attain a solution in real time, which is managed through the use of parallel programming techniques and heuristics which simplify the computational cost associated to attaining the solution of the model. This model uses a rectangular parallepiped grid of finite elements that lets us make pre-computation values of matrices M & K. The main contributions can be summed up in the following points:

- An application of deformations which implements a model of physical deformations has been obtained. The application is capable of generating by itself simulations of objects from a few initial parameters introduced by the user. What is more, all the software used in the development of the application is of free use (public domain software) which, together with the fact that it is based on the use of multiplatform libraries and on object oriented programming techniques, make it a free, portable, modern system.
- We have posed and developed a new technique and implemented an application of deformations which uses non-homogeneous finite elements, which will make it possible in the future to adapt the model in order to simulate deformations in objects with a complex geometry and material properties without the need to increase the data load involved in the calculation.

The possibilities afforded by the work carried out as regards future lines of research and development in the field of animation and virtual reality are varied. Although it is true that in the near future it is worth highlighting the following:

- By introducing collision detection techniques in the model, it will be possible to simulate elastic deformations in scenes made up of different objects.
- To increase the capacities of the model in order to simulate rips/tears by incorporating techniques which enable us to control the rip/tear tension in the materials used to represent the objects, which opens the doors to the automatic generation of a wide range of visual effects.
- To adapt the model implemented in order to generate deformations in parts of the human body with the aim of producing realistic animations in this in an automatic way.

References

[1] Aono, M. A. Wrinkle Propagation Model for Cloth. Proc. CG. Int'l, Springer-Verlag, 95-115, 1990.
[2] Faloutsos, P. and M. van de Panne. And Demetri Terzopo ulos. Dynamic Animation Sinthesis with Free-Form Deformations. IEEE Transaction on Visualization and Computer Graphics, vol 3, n. 3, 1997.
[3] González, M., Mascaró, M., Mir, M., Palmer, P., Perales, F. *Modeling and animating deformable objects.* AERFAI. Publicacions de la Universitat Jaume I. Volumen: 1. Número: 6. Sèries: Treballs d'informàtica i tecnologia", pages 279-290. Alicant, Espanya. 2001.
[4] Gibson, S. F. F. and Mirtch, B. A Survey of Deformable Mod elling in Computer Graphics. Technical Report, Mitsubishi Electrical Research, 1997.
[5] Hagenlocke, M., Fujimura, K. CFFD: a tool for designing flexible shapes. The Visual Computer (1998) 14:271-287, Springer-Verlag 1998.
[6] Mascaró, M., Mir, A., Perales, F. Elastic Deformations Using Finite Element Methods in Computer Graphic Applications. AMDO 2000, pp. 38-47, 2000. Springer-Verlag Berlin Heidelberg 2000.
[7] Mascaró, M., Mir, A., Perales, F. P3DMA: A Physical 3D Deformable Modelling and Animation System. AMDO 2002, pp. 68-79, 2002. Springer-Verlag Berlin Heidelberg 2002.
[8] McInerney, T., Terzopoulos, D. Medical image segmentation using topologically adaptable surfaces. Dept. of Computer Science , University of Toronto, Canada. Published in the Proc. CVRMed'97, Grenoble, France, march, 1997.
[9] Metaxas, D. N. Physics-Based Deformable Models. University of Pensylvania, USA. KluwerAcademic Publishers, 1997.
[10] Palmer, P., Mir, A., González, M. *Stability and Complexity Study of Animated Elastically Deformable Objects.* AMDO 2000, pp. 58-71, 2000. Springer-Verlag Berlin Heidelberg 2000.
[11] Thalmann, N. M., Carion, S., Courchesne, M., Vol ino, P., Wu, Y. Virtual Clothes, Hair and Skin for Beutiful Top Models. MIRAlab, University of Geneva, 1998.
[12] Zabaras, N. Srikanth, A. An Object-Oriented Programming Approach to the Lagrangian FEM Analysis of Large Inelastic Deformations and Metal-Forming Processes. International Journal for Numerical Methods in Engineering. Int. J. Numer. Meth. Engng. 45, 399-445 (1999).

An Experimental Comparison of Dimensionality Reduction for Face Verification Methods*

David Masip and Jordi Vitrià

Computer Vision Center-Dept. Informàtica
Universitat Autònoma de Barcelona
08193 Bellaterra, Barcelona, Spain
{davidm,jordi}@cvc.uab.es

Abstract. Two different approaches to dimensionality reduction techniques are analysed and evaluated, Locally Linear Embedding and a modification of Nonparametric Discriminant Analysis. Both are considered in order to be used in a face verification problem, as a previous step to nearest neighbor classification. LLE is focused in reducing the dimensionality of the space finding the nonlinear manifold underlying the data, while the goal of NDA is to find the most discriminative linear features of the input data that improve the classification rate (without making any prior assumption on the distribution).

1 Introduction

Many problems in Computer Vision often use dimensionality reduction techniques to obtain more compact representations of the input data. The advantages of dimensionality reduction are the compression of the data, and the fact of simplifying decisions making in a higher dimensional level (reducing the amount of parameters to estimate in a classifier, etc..). Dimensionality reduction can be faced under two points of view: focusing the algorithm to find a low dimensional space to embed the data, or focusing the method to find the most discriminative features and reduce dimensionality at the same time. In this paper we will compare two different techniques which belong to these two classes, LLE and NDA, in order to be applied to a face verification scheme.

Reduction of data dimensionality applied to face classification has been subject of deep research in the last years. Some of the most spread out techniques are Principal Component Analysis and eigenfaces ([1, 2]), where the goal is to find the low dimensional representation that preserves the maximum amount of input data variance. In the same way Linear Discriminant Analysis (LDA [3]) tries to find the most discriminative features in the dimensionality reduction, but it has some limitations, basically LDA assumes Gaussian densities and the resulting dimensionality is upper bounded by the number of classes. These algorithms are linear projections of the input data in low dimensional spaces,

---

* This work is supported by Ministerio de Ciencia y Tecnologia grant TIC2000-0399-C02-01.

F.J. Perales et al. (Eds.): IbPRIA 2003, LNCS 2652, pp. 530–537, 2003.

but sometimes they are not completely efficient for the classification of complex structures. Last years, some nonlinear techniques have appeared, like Isomap [4] or LLE ([5, 6]). Isomap technique takes into account the geodesic distances between input points to improve the data embedding. The scope of LLE will be explained in next section with more detail. In section 3 we will introduce the Nonparametric Discriminant Analysis approach, and a modification of the original algorithm. In section 4 we will show the experiments in face verification, to compare both techniques (LLE and NDA). The final conclusions will we exposed in section 5.

2   Dimensionality Reduction Techniques

2.1   Locally Linear Embedding (LLE)

The goal of LLE is to find a mapping from a high dimensional space to a low dimensional one. Sometimes the high dimensional data lies in a nonlinear manifold which can be represented using less dimensions than the dimensionality of the original points. To reach this objective, LLE takes into account the restriction that neighborhood points in the high dimensional space must remain in the same neighborhood in the low dimensional space, and placed in a similar relative spatial situation (it doesn't change the local structure of the nearest neighbors of each point).

Algorithm Let's suppose that we have N $n \times m$ training images, the inputs to the LLE algorithm will be N d-dimensional vectors, X_i ($d = n \times m$). So the LLE algorithm is divided in 3 steps. In the first step, the nearest neighbors of each point are found. In the second step the goal is to capture the local geometry of the input data, using a set of **W** coefficients per each point, corresponding to the weights that best reconstruct the vector from its K nearest neighbors (usually using Euclidean distance). So the weights W_{ij} must minimize the error reconstruction equation:

$$\varepsilon(W) = \sum_{i=1}^{N} |\vec{X_i} - \sum_{j=1}^{K} W_{ij}\vec{X_j}|^2 \tag{1}$$

To find the vectors that minimize this equation, a least-squares problem must be solved. For more details see [6].

In the last step the coordinates of each point in the low dimensional space $d' \ll d$ are computed as the vectors Y_i that best minimize the equation:

$$\theta(Y) = \sum_{i=1}^{N} |\vec{Y_i} - \sum_{j=1}^{K} W_{ij}\vec{Y_j}|^2 \tag{2}$$

Here the weights found during the previous stage are constant, and we want to find the low dimensional outputs $\vec{Y_i}$ that best reconstruct each vector using its K nearest neighbors and the weights of the second step, which capture the local geometric properties of each point in the original space. So the equation to find the output vectors is independent of the input vectors $\vec{X}$ in the final step. To find efficiently the vectors $\vec{Y_i}$ an eigenvector problem must be solved. A new sparse matrix $\mathbf{M}$ is created and defined as:

$$M_{ij} = \delta_{ij} - W_{ij} - W_{ji} + \sum_{k=1}^{K} W_{ki} W_{kj} \tag{3}$$

It can be proved that the output vectors $\vec{Y_i}$ are the $d' + 1$ eigenvectors of the matrix $\mathbf{M}$ associated to the lowest eigenvalues (see [6, 5] for more details).

2.2 Projections of the Test Vectors

As it has been shown, the LLE algorithm is a globally nonlinear technique. This property has some advantages when finding the underlaying manifolds, but there's an important drawback when a new point $\vec{u}$ is entered as a new input to the system. An approximation of the mapping is necessary in order to avoid rerunning the algorithm each time (solving the expensive eigenvector problem each time). Parametric (probabilistic) and non-parametric models have been used to solve this problem (see [6, 5]).

What we propose here is to use a neural network approach to learn the mapping, using a multilayer perceptron network to solve the regression problem. The idea is to run the LLE algorithm with a set $\vec{X}$ of N training vectors (so the network must have N inputs), in order to obtain their projection $\vec{Y}$ in the low dimensional space. Then we train the MLP using X as inputs and $\vec{Y}$ as desired outputs. As a previous step all the vectors must be normalized to the range [-1,1]. The intrinsic characteristics of the neural network can depend on the problem, but in our experiments we have seen that a MLP with 2 hidden layers (with 15 and 10 neurons each one) is enough to capture the nonlinear dimensionality reduction. The projection of new input vectors in the low dimensional space becomes easy, it's only necessary to run a forward step in the multilayer perceptron in order to obtain the reduced vector.

3   NDA

As we have seen LLE can be considered a dimensionality reduction method that preserves the local neighborhood structure of points. NDA (Nonparametric discriminant analysis) algorithm also tries to find a low dimensional space of the input data, but it takes into account labels too, so the main goal of NDA is to perform a dimensionality reduction focused on getting the most discriminative features. We propose a modification of the classic NDA (as is presented by Fukunaga [8]). In the next sections, we will introduce the basis of discriminant analysis and classic NDA, and our modification of the original algorithm (designed to improve the Nearest Neighbor performance).

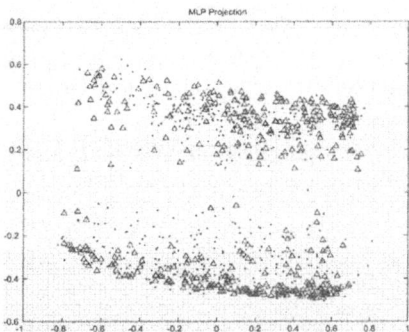

Fig. 1. Example of MLP projection in a 2-class problem (the results of LLE are two clouds of points corresponding to each class). 500 points were used to train LLE and the MLP (plotted as dots). Other different 500 points were projected using the MLP (plotted as triangles). As can be seen, the MLP reaches a good approximation of LLE projection

3.1 Linear Discriminant Analysis

In Linear Discriminant Analysis (see [3]) the goal is to find the linear transformation W to project the input data $\vec{X}$ (N d-dimensional vectors) in a low dimensional space d', and find the features that best separate the data in different classes. To reach it, two matrices are needed, the scatter of the vectors between different classes S_b, and within class S_w. The algorithm to project the original data to the reduced space consist of three steps:

- First, the data is whitened with respect to S_w projecting the sample vectors with the matrix $\Lambda^{-1/2}\Phi^T$, where Φ is the eigenvector matrix of S_w and Λ the corresponding eigenvalues.
- Then the S_b matrix is computed using the whitened data. A new matrix $\Psi_{d'} = [\psi_1, \ldots, \psi_{d'}]$ is created with the d' eigenvectors of largest eigenvalue of the matrix S_b.
- The final linear transform to project the input data, is refined as $A = \Psi_M^T \Lambda^{-1/2}\Phi^T$.

The main limitation of LDA is that it assumes gaussianity on the class-conditional distributions, so the efficiency of the algorithm decreases when the problem requires to classify complex non gaussian structures.

3.2 Nonparametric Discriminant Analysis

To solve this problem, NDA uses a nonparametric between-class scatter matrix not based in differences among class means. This matrix is constructed using vectors that point locally to another class.

- For each sample $\mathbf{x}$ its extraclass nearest neighbor is defined as $\mathbf{x}^E = \{\mathbf{x}' \in \overline{L_c}/\|\mathbf{x}' - \mathbf{x}\| \le \|\mathbf{x_k} - \mathbf{x}\|, \forall \mathbf{x_k} \in \overline{L_c}\}$. The intraclass nearest neighbors are defined in similar way $\mathbf{x}^I = \{\mathbf{x}' \in L_c/\|\mathbf{x}' - \mathbf{x}\| \le \|\mathbf{x_k} - \mathbf{x}\|, \forall \mathbf{x_k} \in L_c\}$.
- The next step is define the extra-class and intra-class differences as: $\mathbf{x}^E$ $\Delta^E = \mathbf{x} - \mathbf{x}^E$ and $\Delta^I = \mathbf{x} - \mathbf{x}^I$.
- The non-parametric between-class matrix is defined as:

$$S_b = \frac{1}{N} \sum_{n=1}^{N} w_n (\Delta_n^E)(\Delta_n^E)^T \tag{4}$$

where Δ_n^E is the extraclass difference of the sample n, and W_n is a sample weight that deemphasizes samples which are far from the boundaries.

$$w_n = \frac{\min\{\|\Delta^E\|^\alpha, \|\Delta^I\|^\alpha\}}{\|\Delta^E\|^\alpha + \|\Delta^I\|^\alpha} \tag{5}$$

where $\alpha \in (0, \infty)$ is a control parameter to adjust how fast the sample weights will fall from 0.5 to 0, according to the distance of the sample to the boundary.
- The within-class scatter matrix is chosen in the same way as in LDA:

$$S_w = \frac{1}{C} \sum_{c=1}^{C} \Sigma_c \tag{6}$$

Finally, sample data is projected in the same way as in LDA algorithm.

Our modification of classic NDA ([9])suggest to use a different within-class scatter matrix, in a nonparametric form too (while between-class scatter matrix remains the same as (4)):

$$S_w = \sum_{n=1}^{N} \Delta_n^I \Delta_n^{I\,T} \tag{7}$$

In our experiments we've seen that this modification in the whitening of the data improves the nearest neighbor classification with respect to classic NDA, because second-order statistics measuring the mean distance to the mean, fail to represent classes with complex distributions.

4   Experiments

4.1   Acquisition Protocol

Our experimental data consist of a set of 3000 face images of 50 different people, acquired in a fixed location of the Computer Vision Center building (in the principal access). There were no restrictions in users pose or illumination conditions (images were taken all day long). Images where captured in a natural and non controlled environment: they were taken during different days, subject to strong light changes, there were not the same number of faces of each person and faces can be slightly rotated, smiling, and other similar gesture effects. Each

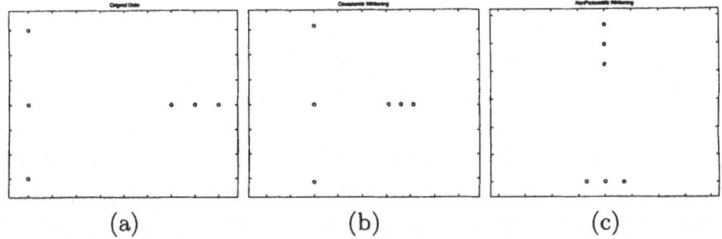

Fig. 2. (a)Original data from a toy dataset (b)Whitened data using covariance matrix (c)Whitened data using our nonparametric modification. As can be seen in (c) the distribution of the intra-class nearest neighbor distances are normalized, while the whitening using (6) fails to reach this goal

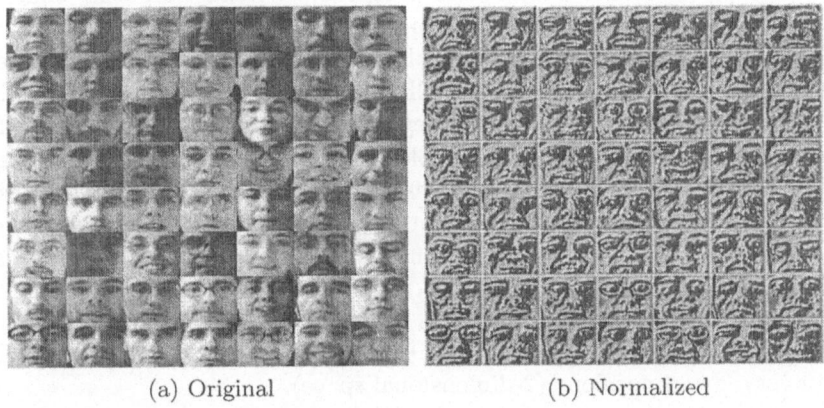

(a) Original   (b) Normalized

Fig. 3. (a) Example of 56 capture samples eye-centered (b) The same samples after light normalization

image was preprocessed by a face detector, which aligns and centers the eyes of each face image, and scales the image to a normalized size. Light normalization consisting of ridges and valleys detection is performed. The resulting image is scaled and cropped to a 64×64 picture, which is reshaped to a 4096-dimensional vector.

4.2 Training the System

The set of 3000 images is divided in two subsets of 1000 train images and 2000 test images. The train set is composed of 250 images from the same person (subject of verification) and 750 images randomly selected, and the test set is composed of 200 images from the same person and the remaining 1800 images.

Our experiments use a LLE projection to a low dimensional space, a NDA projection and a standard PCA (see [1] for more details). To project the test points onto the LLE space a MLP Neural Network (as it was described in previous sections) has been used.

4.3   Tests

Our goal is to find the best dimensionality reduction technique to use in the problem of verification of face images. In this kind of problems there are two different ratios to determine the efficiency of the system: the percentage of faces wrongly accepted as the target person (so incorrectly authorized), called false acceptance, and the percentage of faces incorrectly rejected (false rejection). In the experiments we have analyzed both ratios as a function of the final dimension. Once each image vector has been projected onto the reduced space, we have used the nearest neighbor as the classification procedure to get the labels of the test data. The use of the NN classification is justified because we have a lot of images of each person, and both algorithms tested are designed to work well using NN.

As can be seen in Fig. 4 both techniques improve the PCA results. LLE ratios are slightly better than NDA in false acceptance (where we obtain 93.54 percent using nearest neighbor in the original space), what suggests that nonlinear techniques are more appropriate to deal with this kind of problems, where images often have gesture, rotations, and illumination. The main drawback of NDA is that it usually decreases the accuracy when the number of different classes increases (more than 50 different people have been used in the experiments). Another important drawback of NDA is that it is not very robust in presence of noise in the images. This inconvenient can be solved applying a preprocessing step, typically a PCA, to eliminate the noise. In our experiments the dimensionality has been reduced (using PCA) from 4096 to 1000 before the application of the discriminant analysis.

An important advantage of LLE is that it reaches good recognition scores, even in very low dimensions (2-dimensional space).

The results in false rejection are very similar in both techniques, and remain very close to Euclidean distance classification in the original space (99.7 percent).

5   Conclusions

In this paper two different approaches to dimensionality reduction have been shown (LLE focused on preserving the spatial relation between points in the embedding and NDA focused on finding the best discriminative features). As we have seen, LLE can be a good candidate algorithm for face verification problems. The fact that LLE is able to reach almost the best ratios at very low dimensional space, allows additional advantages, if a more sophisticated classifier is used (Bayesian classifier), because the number of parameters to estimate decreases drastically. Another interesting application is the easy visualization of input data, in a 2-3 dimensional space (losing not much information).

The results obtained with LLE suggest that other techniques could be combined with LLE to improve the ratios, and to be applied to the problem of face verification, where the ratios of false acceptance should be as close to 0 as possible. Boosting algorithms are been studied in order to reach this goal.

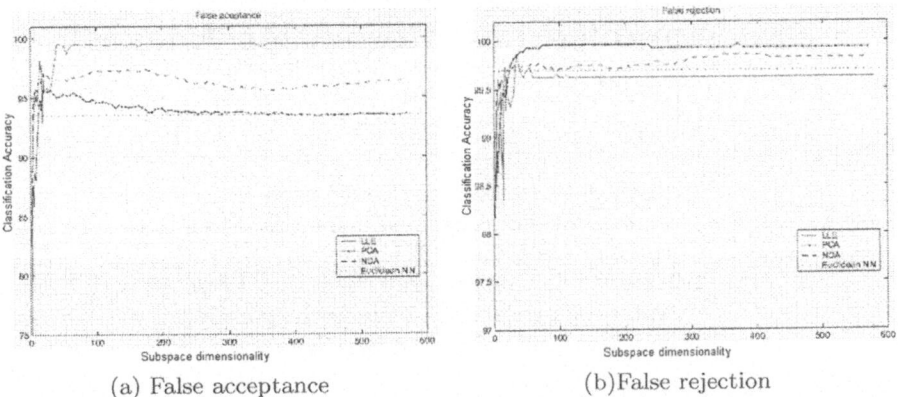

(a) False acceptance   (b) False rejection

Fig. 4. (a) False acceptance as a function of dimensionality reduction (we reach the maximum ratio at 99.5 percent using LLE) (b) False rejection as a function of dimensionality reduction (using PCA we reach the maximum at 99.96 percent)

On the other side, we have showed that our improvement of Nonparametric Discriminant Analysis improves the classic PCA algorithm, and can be very useful in finding the most discriminative features.

References

[1] Matthew Turk and Alex Pentland. Eigenfaces for recognition. Journal of Cognitive Neuroscience, 3(1), 1991.
[2] M. Kirby and L. Sirovich. Application of the Karhunen-Loève Procedure for the characterization of human faces. IEEE Transactions on Pattern Analysis and Machine Inelligence, 12(1) 1990.
[3] R. Fisher. The use of multiple measurements in taxonomic problems, Ann Eugenics 7 (1936) 179-188.
[4] Joshua B. Tenenbaum, Vin de Silva, John C. Langford. A Global Geometric Framework for Nonlinear Dimensionality Reduction, Science, 290:2319-2323, 2000.
[5] Roweis Sam T., Saul Lawrence K. Nonlinear DImensionality Reduction by Locally Linear Embedding Science, 290:2323-2326, 2000.
[6] Saul Lawrence K.,Roweis Sam T. Think Globally, Fit Locally: Unsupervised Learning of Nonlinear Manifolds. Technical Report MS CIS-02-18, University of Pennsylvania.
[7] Christopher M. Bishop. Neural Networks for Pattern Recognition. Oxford University Press,1995.
[8] K. Fukunaga, J. Mantock. Nonparametric discriminant analysis, IEEE Transactions on PAMI 5 (1983) 671-678.
[9] Marco Bressan, Jordi Vitria. Nonparametric Discriminant Analysis and Nearest Neighbor Classification, CVC Technical report.

Bayesian Image Estimation
from an Incomplete Set of Blurred,
Undersampled Low Resolution Images*

Javier Mateos[1], Miguel Vega[2], Rafael Molina[1], and Aggelos K. Katsaggelos[3]

[1] Dpto. de Ciencias de la Computación e I.A.
Universidad de Granada, 18071 Granada, Spain
[2] Dpto. de Lenguajes y Sistemas Informáticos
Universidad de Granada, 18071 Granada, Spain
[3] Dept. of Electrical and Computer Engineering
Northwestern University, Evanston, IL 60208-3118

Abstract. This paper deals with the problem of reconstructing a high-resolution image from an incomplete set of undersampled, blurred and noisy images shifted with subpixel displacement. We derive mathematical expressions for the calculation of the maximum a posteriori estimate of the high resolution image and the estimation of the parameters involved in the model. We also examine the role played by the prior model when this incomplete set of low resolution images is used. The performance of the method is tested experimentally.

1 Introduction

High resolution images can, in some cases, be obtained directly from high precision optics and charge coupled devices (CCDs). However, due to hardware and cost limitations, imaging systems often provide us with only multiple low resolution images. In addition, there is a lower limit as to how small each CCD can be, due to the presence of shot noise [1] and the fact that the associated signal to noise ratio (SNR) is proportional to the size of the detector [16].

Over the last two decades research has been devoted to the problem of reconstructing a high-resolution image from multiple undersampled, shifted, degraded frames with subpixel displacement errors (see [3] for a review). Most of the reported work addresses the problem of estimating an $LM \times LN$ high resolution image from at least $L \times L$ low resolution images of size $M \times N$, that is, when the number of available low resolution images is at least equal to L^2, where L is the magnifying factor. In Molina et al. [12] a method for simultaneously estimating the high resolution image and the associated parameters within the Bayesian model is presented. Kim et al. [9] explore the conditions the shifts of the $L \times L$ low resolution images have to satisfy in order to solve the high resolution problem, at least from the least squares perspective. Elad and Feuer [6]

---

* This work has been partially supported by the "Comisión Nacional de Ciencia y Tecnología" under contract TIC2000-1275.

F.J. Perales et al. (Eds.): IbPRIA 2003, LNCS 2652, pp. 538–546, 2003.
© Springer-Verlag Berlin Heidelberg 2003

study the same problem when combining Bayesian, Projection onto Convex Sets and Maximum Likelihood methodologies on high resolution problems. Baker and Kanade [2] also examine the impact of increasing the number of low resolution images, when proposing an alternative approach to the super resolution problem. However, not much work has been reported on the role played by the prior model when the system is incomplete, that is, when we have less than $L \times L$ low resolution images or when the shifts do not satisfy the conditions in [9] or [6]. In our previous work [10] we proposed a new method to solve the high resolution problem from an incomplete set of low resolution images when no blurring was present in the observation process. The method was based on the general framework for frequency domain multi-channel signal processing developed by Katsaggelos et al. in [8] (a formulation that was also later obtained by Bose and Boo [4] for the high resolution problem).

In this paper we extend the approach in [10] by considering that the low resolution images are also blurred, a case that frequently appears in Astronomy (see [11] for instance) and remote sensing. We also propose a method for estimating the high resolution image and the parameters associated to the model when blurring is present in the low resolution observations. The method performs well even when very few low resolution blurred images are available and they have different noise characteristics. Finally, we examine how the prior model compensates for the lack of information in the incomplete noisy and blurred low resolution observation set.

The rest of the paper is organized as follows. The problem formulation is described in section 2. In section 3 the degradation and image models used in the Bayesian paradigm are described. The application of the Bayesian paradigm to calculate the MAP high resolution image and estimate the hyperparameters is described in section 4. Experimental results are described in section 5. Finally, section 6 concludes the paper.

2   Problem Formulation

Consider a camera sensor with $N_1 \times N_2$ pixels and assume that we have a set of q shifted images, $1 \leq q \leq L \times L$. Our aim is to reconstruct an $M_1 \times M_2$ high resolution image with $M_1 = L \times N_1$ and $M_2 = L \times N_2$, from the set of low-resolution observed images.

The low resolution sensors are shifted with respect to each other by a value proportional to $T_1/L \times T_2/L$, where $T_1 \times T_2$ is the size of each sensing element (note that if the sensors are shifted by values proportional to $T_1 \times T_2$ or $q < L \times L$, the high-resolution image reconstruction problem becomes singular). In this paper we assume that the normalized horizontal and vertical displacements are known (see [4, 13] for details). When the displacements are unknown see, for instance, [7] and [17] for their estimations.

Let $g_{l1,l2}$ be the $(N_1 \times N_2) \times 1$ observed low resolution image acquired by the $(l1, l2)$ sensor. Our goal is to reconstruct f, the $(M_1 \times M_2) \times 1$ high resolution image, from a set of q low resolution images $g_{l1,l2}$, with $1 \leq q \leq L^2$. We will denote by $\mathcal{I}$, the set of indices of the available low resolution images.

The process to obtain the observed low resolution image by the $(l1, l2)$ sensor, $g_{l1,l2}$, from f can be modeled as a two stages process as follows. In the first stage, the optical distortion in the observation process is represented by $B_{l1,l2}$, the $(M_1 \times M_2) \times (M_1 \times M_2)$ point spread function defining a systematic blur, assumed to be known, due , for example, to motion or out of focus blurring, defects in the camera optics, etc. The second stage models the CCD pixel resolution. Let $H_{l1,l2}$ be an $(M_1 \times M_2) \times (M_1 \times M_2)$ integrating matrix that represents the way a set of pixels in the high resolution image affects each low resolution pixel. In this paper we use an $H_{l1,l2}$ representing a linear space-invariant blurring system with impulse response

$$h_{l1,l2}(u, v) = \begin{cases} \frac{1}{L^2} & u, v = -(L-1), \ldots, 0 \\ 0 & \text{otherwise} \end{cases}. \tag{1}$$

Let now D_{l1} and D_{l2} be the 1-D downsampling matrices defined by

$$D_{l1} = I_{N_1} \otimes e_l^t, \qquad D_{l2} = I_{N_2} \otimes e_l^t, \tag{2}$$

where I_{N_i} is the $N_i \times N_i$ identity matrix, e_l is the $L \times 1$ unit vector whose nonzero element is in the l-th position and $\otimes$ denotes the Kronecker product operator.

Then for each sensor the discrete low-resolution observed image $g_{l1,l2}$ can be written as

$$g_{l1,l2} = D_{l1,l2} H_{l1,l2} B_{l1,l2} f + n_{l1,l2} = W_{l1,l2} B_{l1,l2} f + n_{l1,l2}, \tag{3}$$

where $D_{l1,l2} = D_{l1} \otimes D_{l2}$, denotes the $(N_1 \times N_2) \times (M_1 \times M_2)$ 2D downsampling matrix and $n_{l1,l2}$ is modeled as independent white noise with variance $\beta_{l1,l2}^{-1}$. We denote by g the sum of the upsampled low resolution images, that is,

$$g = \sum_{u,v \in \mathcal{I}} D_{u,v}^t g_{u,v}. \tag{4}$$

Note that the only, but important, difference between the model in equation 3 and the one used in [10] is the presence of additional blurring in the observation process.

3   Degradation and Image Models

From Eq. 3, the probability density function of $g_{l1,l2}$, the $(l1, l2)$ low resolution image, with f the 'true' high resolution image, is given by

$$p(g_{l1,l2} | f, \beta_{l1,l2}) \propto \frac{1}{Z(\beta_{l1,l2})} \exp\left[-\frac{\beta_{l1,l2}}{2} \| g_{l1,l2} - W_{l1,l2} B_{l1,l2} f \|^2 \right], \tag{5}$$

where $Z(\beta_{l1,l2}) = (2\pi/\beta_{l1,l2})^{(N_1 \times N_2)/2}$ and $\beta_{l1,l2}$ the inverse of the noise variance.

Since we have multiple low resolution images, the probability density function of g given f is

$$p(g|f,\underline{\beta}) = \prod_{(l1,l2)\in\mathcal{I}} p(g_{l1,l2}|f,\beta_{l1,l2})$$

$$\propto \frac{1}{Z_{noise}(\underline{\beta})} \exp\left[-\frac{1}{2}\sum_{(l1,l2)\in\mathcal{I}} \beta_{l1,l2} \parallel g_{l1,l2} - W_{l1,l2}B_{l1,l2}f \parallel^2\right], (6)$$

where $\underline{\beta} = (\beta_{l1,l2}|(l1,l2)\in\mathcal{I})$, and $Z_{noise}(\underline{\beta}) = \prod_{(l1,l2)\in\mathcal{I}} Z(\beta_{l1,l2})$.

As prior model for f we use a simultaneous autoregression (SAR) [15], that is

$$p(f|\alpha) = \frac{1}{Z_{prior}(\alpha)} \exp\{-\frac{1}{2}\alpha f^t C^t C f\}, \tag{7}$$

where the parameter α measures the smoothness of the 'true' image, $Z_{prior}(\alpha) = (\prod_{i,j} \lambda_{ij}^2)^{-1/2}(2\pi/\alpha)^{(M_1\times M_2)/2}$ and $\lambda_{ij} = 1 - 2\phi(\cos(2\pi i/M_1) + \cos(2\pi j/M_2))$, $i = 1,2,\ldots,M_1$, $j = 1,2,\ldots,M_2$ and C is the Laplacian operator.

4 Bayesian Analysis

Having defined the degradation and image models, the Bayesian analysis is performed to estimate the hyperparameters, α and β, and the high-resolution image. In this paper we use the following two steps:

Step I: Estimation of the hyperparameters

$\hat{\alpha}$ and $\hat{\underline{\beta}} = (\hat{\beta}_{l1,l2}|(l1,l2)\in\mathcal{I})$ are first selected as

$$\hat{\alpha},\hat{\underline{\beta}} = \arg\max_{\alpha,\underline{\beta}} \mathcal{L}_g(\alpha,\underline{\beta}) = \arg\max_{\alpha,\underline{\beta}} \log p(g|\alpha,\underline{\beta}), \tag{8}$$

where $p(g|\alpha,\underline{\beta}) = \int_f p(f|\alpha)p(g|f,\underline{\beta})df$.

The solution to this equation is obtained with the EM-algorithm with $\mathcal{X}^t = (f^t, g^t)$ and $\mathcal{Y} = g = [0 \; I]^t\mathcal{X}$.

Note that although different methods have been proposed for the estimation of the parameters in high resolution problems (see, for instance, [14, 5]), those works assume the same noise variance for all the low resolution observations. In the framework we are proposing, these variances may be different.

Step II: Estimation of the high-resolution image

Once the hyperparameters have been estimated, the estimation of the high-resolution image, $f_{(\hat{\alpha},\hat{\underline{\beta}})}$, is selected to minimize

$$\hat{\alpha} \parallel Cf \parallel^2 + \sum_{(l1,l2)\in\mathcal{I}} \hat{\beta}_{l1,l2} \parallel g_{l1,l2} - W_{l1,l2}B_{l1,l2}f \parallel^2, \tag{9}$$

which results in

$$f_{(\hat{\alpha},\hat{\beta})} = Q\left(\hat{\alpha},\hat{\underline{\beta}}\right)^{-1} \sum_{(l1,l2)\in\mathcal{I}} \hat{\beta}_{l1,l2} B_{l1,l2}^t W_{l1,l2}^t g_{l1,l2}, \qquad (10)$$

where $Q(\hat{\alpha},\hat{\beta}) = \hat{\alpha} C^t C + \sum_{(l1,l2)\in\mathcal{I}} \hat{\beta}_{l1,l2} B_{l1,l2}^t W_{l1,l2}^t W_{l1,l2} B_{l1,l2}$.

Note that the prior model in Eq. 7 plays an important role in the estimation of the high-resolution image and the hyperparameters. If we examine the matrix $Q(\alpha,\beta)$ in Eq. 10 we note that when fewer than $L \times L$ low resolution observations are available or when the shifts in those low resolution images do not satisfy the conditions in [9] and [6] this matrix would not be invertible without the presence of C. It is therefore important to examine the quality of the reconstruction and also the accuracy of the estimated hyperparameters as a function of the number of low resolution observations, q. This is done experimentally, as described in detail in the next section.

It is important to note that the calculations involved in finding $\hat{\alpha}, \hat{\beta}$ and $f_{(\hat{\alpha},\hat{\beta})}$ can be performed using the general framework for frequency domain multi-channel signal processing developed in [8].

5   Experimental Results

A number of experiments were performed with the proposed algorithm over a set of images to evaluate its behavior as a function of the number of available low resolution images. Results are presented in Fig.1.

The performance of the proposed algorithm was evaluated by measuring the peak signal-to-noise ratio (PSNR) defined as PSNR$= 10 \times \log_{10}[M_1 \times M_2 \times 255^2/ \parallel f - f_{(\hat{\alpha},\hat{\beta})} \parallel^2]$, where f and $f_{(\hat{\alpha},\hat{\beta})}$ are the original and estimated high resolution images, respectively.

According to Eq. 3 the high resolution image in Fig. 1a was blurred using a motion blur of length 10. Then, the integrating function in Eq. 1 was applied to the blurred image obtaining $u = HBf$. This high resolution image, u, was downsampled with $L = 4$, thus obtaining a set of 16 low resolution images, $u_{l1,l2}(x,y) = u(L_1 x + l1, L_2 y + l2)$, $x,y = 0,\ldots,\frac{M_1}{L} - 1$, $l1,l2 = 0,\ldots,3$. Gaussian noise was added to each low resolution image to obtain three sets of sixteen low resolution images, $g_{l1,l2}$, with 20, 30 and 40dB SNR. The noise variances for the 30dB set of images are shown in Table 1.

In order to test the performance of the proposed algorithm we ran it on different sets of q randomly chosen low resolution images with $1 \leq q \leq 16$. For comparison purposes, Fig. 1b depicts the zero-order hold upsampled image of $g_{0,0}$ for 30dB SNR (PSNR=13.68dB) while the bilinear interpolation of $g_{0,0}$ is shown Fig. 1c (PSNR=14.22dB). The estimated high-resolution images using 1, 2, 4, 6 and 16 low resolution images are depicted in Fig. 1d–h, respectively. A visual inspection of the resulting images shows that the proposed method clearly outperforms zero-order hold and bilinear interpolation even when only one low resolution input image is used and the quality of the high resolution estimated

Table 1. Noise variances for the low resolution image set with SNR of 30dB

$\beta_{l1,l2}^{-1}$	0	1	2	3
0	3.44	3.44	3.45	3.46
1	3.44	3.44	3.45	3.46
2	3.42	3.42	3.43	3.43
3	3.42	4.42	3.43	3.43

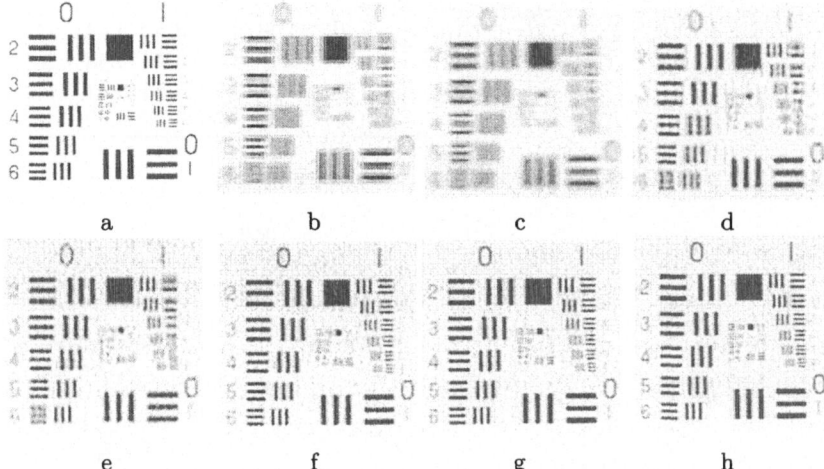

Fig. 1. (a) original image (b) zero order hold, (c) bilinear interpolation, (d)-(h) results with the proposed method using 1, 2, 4, 6, and 16 low resolution images

image increases with the number of images. Note also that the visual quality of the estimated high resolution images obtained using 6 and 16 low resolution input images (depicted in Fig. 1g and h, respectively) are almost indistinguishable, which means that the prior model assists in accurately recovering the high resolution image even when we have little information.

The estimated noise parameters, $\hat{\beta}$, using the proposed algorithm on the 30dB low resolution image set are shown in Table 2. From our experiments we conclude that the proposed method produces accurate estimations for all low resolution image noise variances especially when the number of input images is high. The proposed algorithm also provides good results when only a few input images are considered, even when only one low resolution input image is used.

PSNR evolution against the number of low resolution input images is shown in Fig. 2 for all the 20, 30 and 40dB low resolution images sets. Numerical results show that the proposed method provides a clear improvement even in the case when severe noise is present, although higher improvements are obtained as the noise decreases. Note that the proposed algorithm always outperforms bilinear interpolation even when only one image is used. For example, for the 30dB SNR low resolution images set, the PSNR for the reconstructed image using just one

Table 2. Estimated noise variances for the low resolution image set with SNR of 30 dB

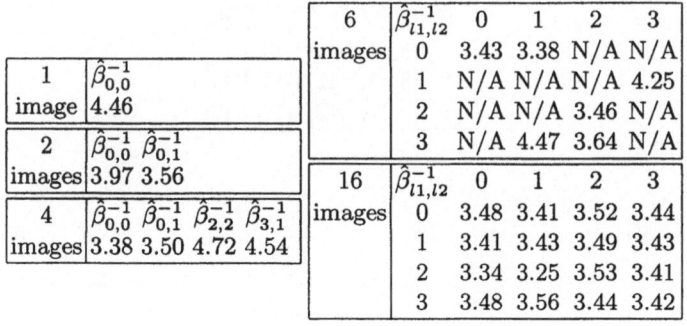

1 image	$\hat{\beta}_{0,0}^{-1}$
	4.46

2 images	$\hat{\beta}_{0,0}^{-1}$	$\hat{\beta}_{0,1}^{-1}$
	3.97	3.56

4 images	$\hat{\beta}_{0,0}^{-1}$	$\hat{\beta}_{0,1}^{-1}$	$\hat{\beta}_{2,2}^{-1}$	$\hat{\beta}_{3,1}^{-1}$
	3.38	3.50	4.72	4.54

6 images	$\hat{\beta}_{l1,l2}^{-1}$	0	1	2	3
	0	3.43	3.38	N/A	N/A
	1	N/A	N/A	N/A	4.25
	2	N/A	N/A	3.46	N/A
	3	N/A	4.47	3.64	N/A

16 images	$\hat{\beta}_{l1,l2}^{-1}$	0	1	2	3
	0	3.48	3.41	3.52	3.44
	1	3.41	3.43	3.49	3.43
	2	3.34	3.25	3.53	3.41
	3	3.48	3.56	3.44	3.42

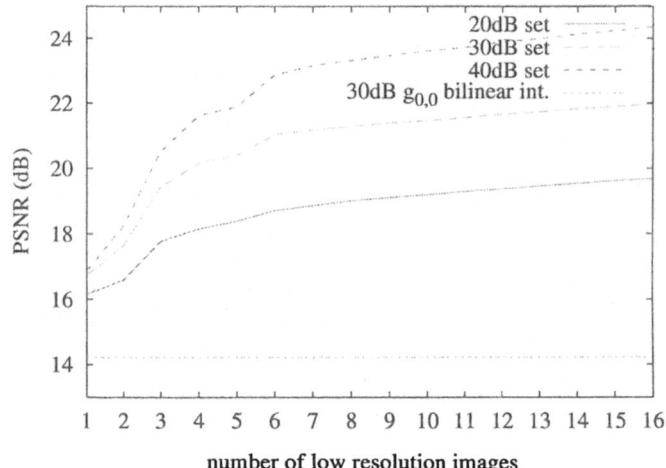

Fig. 2. PSNR evolution with the number of low resolution images

low resolution input image is equal to 16.74dB (see Fig. 1d), and it increases monotonically to 21.96dB with the number of images. Note also that most of the improvement is achieved when a low number of input images is used. This makes clear the importance of the prior model in the information recovering process.

6   Conclusions

A new method to estimate a high resolution image from an incomplete set of blurred, undersampled low resolution images has been proposed. The approach followed can be used with any number of low resolution images from 1 to L^2, since the prior model accurately recovers the high resolution image even in the case where just one or very few input images are provided. The proposed method has been validated experimentally.

References

[1] K. Aizawa, T. Komatsu, and T. Saito. A scheme for acquiring very high resolution images using multiple cameras. In *IEEE Conference on Audio, Speech and Signal Proc.*, volume 3, pages 289–292, 1992.

[2] S. Baker and T. Kanade. Limits on super-resolution and how to break them. *IEEE Transactions on Pattern Analysis and Machine Intelligence*, 24(9), 2002.

[3] S. Borman and R. Stevenson. Spatial resolution enhancement of low-resolution image sequences. A comprehensive review with directions for future research. Technical report, Laboratory for Image and Signal Analysis, University of Notre Dame, 1998.

[4] N. K. Bose and K. J. Boo. High-resolution image reconstruction with multisensors. *Int. Journ. Imaging Systems and Technology*, 9:141–163, 1998.

[5] N. K. Bose, S. Lertrattanapanich, and J. Koo. Advances in superresolution using L-curve. *IEEE International Symposium on Circuits and Systems*, 2:433–436, 2001.

[6] M. Elad and A. Feuer. Restoration of a single super-resolution image from several blurred, noisy, and undersampled measured images. *IEEE Trans. on Image Proc.*, 6:1646–1658, 1997.

[7] M. Irani and S. Peleg. Motion analysis for image enhancement: Resolution, occlusion, and transparency. *J. of Visual Comm. and Image Representation*, 4(4):324–335, 1993.

[8] A. K. Katsaggelos, K. T. Lay, and N. P. Galatsanos. A general framework for frequency domain multi-channel signal processing. *IEEE Image Proc.*, 2(3):417–420, 1993.

[9] S. P. Kim, N. K. Bose, and H. M. Valenzuela. Recursive reconstruction of high resolution image from noisy undersampled multiframes. *IEEE Trans. on Acoustics, Speech and Signal Proc.*, 38(6):1013–1027, 1990.

[10] J. Mateos, R. Molina, and A. K. Katsaggelos. Bayesian high resolution image reconstruction with incomplete multisensor low resolution systems. To appear in Proc. International Conference on Acoustic, Speech and Signal Proc., 2003.

[11] R. Molina, J. Núñez, F. Cortijo, and J. Mateos. Image restoration in Astronomy. A Bayesian review. *IEEE Signal Proc. Magazine*, 18:11–29, 2001.

[12] R. Molina, M. Vega, J. Abad, and A. K. Katsaggelos. Parameter estimation in Bayesian high-resolution image reconstruction with multisensors. *Submitted to IEEE Trans. Image Proc.*, 2002.

[13] M. K. Ng and A. M. Yip. A fast MAP algorithm for high-resolution image reconstruction with multisensors. *Multidim. Systems and Signal Proc.*, 12:143–164, 2001.

[14] N. Nguyen, P. Milanfar, and G. Golub. A computationally efficient superresolution image reconstruction algorithm. *IEEE Trans. on Image Proc.*, 10(4):573–583, 2001.

[15] B. D. Ripley. *Spatial Statistics*. John Wiley, 1981.

[16] H. Stark and P. Oskoui. High-resolution image recovery from image-plane arrays, using convex projections. *Journal of the Optical Society A*, 6(11):1715–1726, 1989.

[17] B. C. Tom, N. P. Galatsanos, and A. K. Katsaggelos. Reconstruction of a high resolution image from multiple low resolution images. In S. Chaudhuri, editor, *Super-Resolution Imaging*, chapter 4, pages 73–105. Kluwer Academic Publishers, 2001.

A Procedure for Biological Sensitive Pattern Matching in Protein Sequences

Juan Méndez, Antonio Falcón, and Javier Lorenzo

Intelligent Systems Institute. IUSIANI
Univ. Las Palmas de Gran Canaria, Spain
{jmendez,afalcon,jlorenzo}@dis.ulpgc.es

Abstract. A Procedure for fast pattern matching in protein sequences is presented. It uses a biological metric, based on the substitution matrices as PAM or BLOSUM, to compute the matching. Biological sensitive pattern matching does pattern detection according to the available empirical data about similarity and affinity relations between amino acids in protein sequences. Sequence alignments is a string matching procedure used in Genomic; it includes insert/delete operators and dynamic programming techniques; it provides more sophisticate results that other pattern matching procedures but with higher computational cost. Heuristic procedures for local alignments as FASTA or BLAST are used to reduce this cost. They are based on some successive tasks; the first one uses a pattern matching procedure with very short sequences, also named k-tuples. This paper shows how using the L_1 metric this matching task can be efficiently computed by using SIMD instructions. To design this procedure, a table that maps the substitution matrices is needed. This table defines a representation of each amino acid residue in a n-dimensional space of lower dimensionality as possible; this is accomplished by using techniques of Multidimensional Scaling used in Pattern Recognition and Machine Learning for dimensionality reduction. Based on the experimental tests, the proposed procedure provides a favorable ration of cost vs matching quality.

Keyword: Pattern Matching, Biological Pattern Analysis, Sequence Alignments, Multidimensional Scaling, SIMD Processing.

1 Introduction

The fast growing of information contained in the biological databases[2] requires more efficient processing systems to find functionality and meaning in the DNA and protein sequences. More efficient systems are obtained by hardware and architectural improvements, and also by defining more efficient computational procedures. Artificial Intelligence, Pattern Recognition and Machine Learning techniques can provide additional approaches to allow better computational performances in Gemomic related systems[14]. This paper uses Pattern Recognition and Machine Learning techniques applied in Bioinformatics[4] to define a matching procedure to get some architectural improvements in alignment procedures of

F.J. Perales et al. (Eds.): IbPRIA 2003, LNCS 2652, pp. 547–555, 2003.
© Springer-Verlag Berlin Heidelberg 2003

biological sequences. These architectural improvements are initially introduced for multimedia and information retrieval applications, but by means of special software design they can also be used in genomic related computations.

Single Instruction Multiple Data(SIMD) instructions are included in most microprocessors of low cost computer systems, as Intel and AMD. They can be used to speed up workstations and servers in Genomic, but special designs are needed because available compilers do not take advantage of these instructions for general software. Modern computer items as cache hierarchy, memory access and SIMD processing upgrade the performance of generic software, but additional increase of the power in genomic based procedures can be obtained if they are designed according to the above processor characteristics[6]. Some works have dealt with the use of parallel computation for sequence analysis[13, 24], and also with the use of SIMD instructions in the improvements of local alignments[20, 19]. However, this work presents a process for the first stages of some local alignment procedures. The proposal requires the computation of some tables to map the amino acid residues in a n-dimensional space according to the biological properties represented in the score or substitution matrices, as PAM[8] and BLOSUM[11].

The search of local alignment between biological sequences is one of the most used tools in discovering the functional and evolutionary similarities. The Smith-Waterman procedure[23], based on dynamic programming, has the highest biological significance. However, its computational cost is greater than other heuristics procedures as FASTA[18] and BLAST[1] which have lower computational cost having a high level of biological significance. The first stage of both FASTA and BLAST is the searching of very short pre-coded sequences, named k-tuples, in the sequences included in the biological databases. The matching of k-tuples, named ktup in FASTA and w-mers in BLAST, between a query sequence and the database can be efficiently computed by information retrieval procedures.

However instead of naive ASCII code matching, a n-dimensional code matching based on the biological information contained in the score or substitution matrices is proposed in this paper. The information retrieval procedure takes advantage of two architectural improvements of modern microprocessors: parallel computation with multiple data processing units, and sequential memory access which increases the cache throughput. This paper present the process to map the amino acid residues in a virtual meaning less n-dimensional space. This is accomplished by non-linear dimensionality reduction methods used in Multidimensional Scaling(MDS)[9, 10, 15, 3, 22] which are mainly used in Pattern Recognition and Machine Learning for feature selection and also for visualization of high dimensional data sets.

2   Pattern Matching of k-Tuples

An efficient procedure for pattern matching of k-tuples is proposed. The distance $D(U, V)$ between two vector U and V in $\mathbf{R}^M$ based on the L_1 norm is defined as:

$$D(U, V) = \sum_{i=1}^{M} \mid U_i - V_i \mid \qquad (1)$$

The Intel IA-32 computer architecture includes an instruction to compute this distance with $M = 8$ in a single system clock cycle. The norm for $M = 8 \times m$ also can be fast computed from the previous. The continuous increasing of microprocessor clock frequency provides a powerful method to speed up many of data processing tasks which can be re-formulated to fit in a L_1 norm. This instruction is part of the MMX instruction set included to improve the performance of multimedia, text retrieval and signal processing applications. Most of problems related with sequence analysis are based on score matrices to model the amino acid distances and similarities; this is not an efficient choice to use the power that current hardware provides. If $\mathcal{A}$ is the amino acid symbols set, instead of using a score matrix $s(a, b); a, b \in \mathcal{A}$, a distance based on norm L_1 can be required:

$$D_X(a, b) = \sum_{i=1}^{n} \mid X_i(a) - X_i(b) \mid \qquad (2)$$

where $\mathbf{X}(a)$ is a n-dimensional vector which is the representation of the amino acid, and $D_X(a, b)$ is the desired distance. In raw text searching of query sequence in a biological database, this vector is the 1-dimensional ASCII code of the residue symbol. However, this is a too simplistic representation of the amino acid properties which ignores the biological meaning and the affinity relations. The similarity relations of amino acid require the introduction of a representation in a multidimensional space with the lowest dimensionality as possible. This representation must contain the biological information of similarity which is gathered in the substitution matrices. PAM and BLOSUM matrices are defined from statistical properties related with residues substitutions from evolutionary or blocks alignments. They are nor distance neither similarity functions. They are score factors which verifies: $s(a, b) = s(b, a)$ and also generally: $s(a, a) \geq s(a, b)$. From a score matrix several distance functions, $d(a, b)$, can be proposed; the considered in this paper is:

$$d(a, b) = s(a, a) + s(b, b) - 2s(a, b) \qquad (3)$$

This verifies the symmetrical property: $d(a, b) = d(b, a)$, is lower bounded: $d(a, b) \geq 0$ and also verifies: $d(a, a) = 0$, but is not a metric. When is verified that $s(a, a) > s(a, b)$, it is also verified that if $d(a, b) = 0$ it must be: $a \equiv b$. The triangular properties is not verified in the general case, thus the proposed function is a distance, but not a metric one. This distance has also a probabilistic expression when is computed from the PAM and BLOSUM substitution matrices. Both are obtained by means of a probabilistic ratio obtained from different

empirical environments. In these cases, the score matrix and the distance are
defined as:

$$s(a,b) = \frac{1}{\lambda} \log \frac{p(a,b)}{p_a p_b} \qquad d(a,b) = -\frac{2}{\lambda} \log \frac{p(a,b)}{\sqrt{p(a,a)p(b,b)}} \qquad (4)$$

where $p(a,b)$ is the probability of substitution between two residues, p_a term is
defined from the $p(a,b)$, and λ is a suitable parameter. The score of a k-tuple
of two sequences U and V is computed in the alignment procedures[23, 16] by
using substitution matrices as:

$$s(U,V) = \sum_{j=1}^{k} s(u_j, v_j) \qquad (5)$$

where $u(j)$ and $v(j)$ correspond to the amino acid in the k-tuple. If the distance
of this k-tuple, $d(U,V)$, is defined as: $d(U,V) = s(U,U) + s(V,V) - 2s(U,V)$, it
can be computed as:

$$d(U,V) = \sum_{j=1}^{k} d(u_j, v_j) \simeq D_X(U,V) = \sum_{j=1}^{k} \sum_{i=1}^{n} \mid X_i(u_j) - X_i(v_j) \mid \qquad (6)$$

If $d(a,b)$ can be computed by $D_X(a,b)$ with a reduced error. This last is a L_1
norm with $M = n \times k$. Due to hardware constraints, the optimal computation
can be achieved when $n \times k = 8 \times m$. The high k value reduces the sensibility
whereas the low k value implies a lower significative; BLAST uses $k = 3, 4, 5$, to
compute the hits or initial alignment clues. The k-tuple matching between two
sequences is computed in this paper as:

$$T(h,l) = \sum_{j=1}^{k} \sum_{i=1}^{n} \mid X_i(u_{h+j-1}) - X_i(v_{l+j-1}) \mid \qquad (7)$$

2.1 Multidimensional Scaling

A problem which must be solved is how compute $D_X(a,b)$ as a good approxima-
tion of $d(a,b)$; this requires the computing of the vector set: $\mathbf{X}(a), a \in \mathcal{A}$. The
Sammon method [21] is used to achieve this goal; it provides a good ratio of re-
sult quality to computational complexity[15, 3, 22]. It maps a distance function
to a reduced dimensionality space based on the minimization of an objective
function assigning to each amino acid tentative coordinates. These coordinates
are meaning less, and they are useful only to compute the distance. The Sammon
method is based on the minimization of a non-lineal goal function related with
the error between the original distances and the tentative ones, consequently
several solutions can be obtained if some local minimum exists. The procedure
requires the minimization of the goal function $S(X)$ which can be assimilated
to a relative error of the mapping process:

$$\min_{X} S(X) = \frac{\sum_a \sum_{b<a} \frac{[D_X(a,b) - d(a,b)]^2}{d(a,b)}}{\sum_a \sum_{b<a} d(a,b)} \qquad (8)$$

while the relative error is compute as:

$$E(X) = \frac{2}{N(N-1)} \sum_a \sum_{b<a} \frac{[D_X(a,b) - d(a,b)]^2}{d^2(a,b)} \tag{9}$$

where N is the amino acid number. The $\mathbf{X}$ solution is not unique due to the geometrical transformations that preserve the distance D_X. For the L_1 metric the freedom degrees are less that in euclidean or L_2 metric, because the rotation group is finite dimensional in the first case instead of infinite dimensional of the second case. The vector $\mathbf{X}(a)$ provided by the optimization procedure is transformed to the $\mathbf{Y}(a)$ vector in the byte values range $[0, 255]$ by geometrical transformations of translation and scaling. Table 1 contains the second coordinate type for 1,2,4 and 8-dimensional mapping. Due to the hardware restrictions these dimensional values are the most useful for practical proposes. The translation to the origin of coordinates does not modify the distances, whereas the scaling to fit the $[0, 255]$ range modifies the distance with a constant factor ρ related with the scaling transformation. The relation between the distances computed by mean of the two vector type is:

$$D_X(a,b) = \rho D_Y(a,b) \tag{10}$$

3   Results

Both Genetic and Gradient optimization methods can be used to achieve the minimization of the goal function. Gradient procedures have better convergence around local minima, while Genetic procedures allow a better global optimization by considering several local minima. Many solutions are expected in the proposed problem, covering a wide range of both local minimum due to non-linearity and also due to geometrical transformations.

A Genetic Algorithm is used to obtain a solution which is afterward refined by applying a Gradient procedure based on Quasi-Newton algorithm. Genetic algorithm are good to jump far of tentative local minima. However, in practice after a number of iterations the genetic algorithm is mainly working in the refinement of a local minimum, but for this task the gradient procedures are more efficient. The minimum of several trial cases of genetic and gradient procedures is chosen as the solution. GAOT[12] is a public domain Genetic Toolbox that is used for the first stage and the MATLAB Optimization Toolbox[7] for the second one. Figure 1 shows the graphical representation of the value $S(X)$ of the Sammon function and the relative error $E(X)$ vs the dimensionality n of the mapping space. Table 1 contains the obtained $\mathbf{Y}$ coordinates for 1,2,4, and 8-dimensionality.

To illustrate the pattern matching procedure an example with two protein sequences is used. These proteins have the entry names GTH2_TOBAC and GTH1_MAIZE in SWISS-PROT database; both are related proteins, member of the Glutathione S-transferases family[17], included in the GST_C entry of the Pfam protein families database[5].

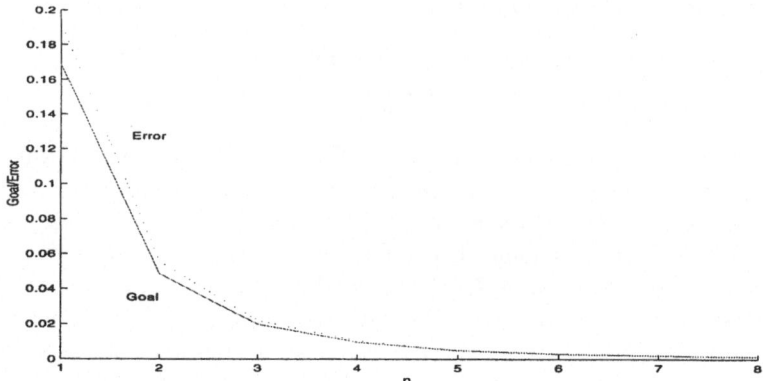

Fig. 1. Goal function $S(X)$ and error $E(X)$ vs the mapping space dimensionality n

Table 1. Mapping coordinates for 1,2,4 and 8-dimensionality of BLOSUM62 transformed to integer $[0,255]$ range for use in fast matching procedures

Amino Acid	$n=1$	$n=2$		$n=4$				$n=8$							
	Y_1	Y_1	Y_2	Y_1	Y_2	Y_3	Y_4	Y_1	Y_2	Y_3	Y_4	Y_5	Y_6	Y_7	Y_8
A	140	100	180	182	94	68	49	31	66	120	85	139	105	98	40
R	180	161	113	181	16	108	79	24	89	105	38	0	97	77	24
N	203	198	191	244	26	73	71	94	83	35	46	63	89	90	41
D	216	227	168	255	59	51	98	117	62	82	66	64	175	84	72
C	31	0	166	154	191	61	56	31	87	149	114	100	0	178	63
Q	164	184	146	173	10	65	100	34	68	88	35	36	129	43	50
E	190	177	175	205	36	54	110	13	66	87	53	49	176	85	46
G	228	148	233	230	105	101	61	88	67	88	70	175	63	71	11
H	239	207	92	193	0	0	66	25	67	0	69	40	81	73	126
I	97	63	142	157	65	50	8	36	34	158	17	115	103	115	80
L	89	76	124	154	50	70	0	22	24	144	4	101	88	106	66
K	173	170	134	181	42	88	123	24	121	109	42	63	132	73	25
M	115	95	127	151	33	81	23	28	41	149	0	95	98	50	56
F	59	91	76	97	52	37	45	0	20	207	61	88	78	75	96
P	255	129	255	167	65	164	97	37	34	56	167	107	150	69	25
S	154	139	171	199	76	74	76	69	77	102	81	88	107	86	47
T	131	113	198	142	85	73	89	54	30	101	61	77	107	150	34
W	0	121	0	0	46	82	61	33	0	255	69	52	44	0	0
Y	71	129	62	117	44	8	63	37	10	184	74	40	79	71	122
V	105	70	153	163	70	55	16	37	34	157	35	121	116	115	64
ρ	0.1444	0.1036		0.0802				0.0421							

Figure 2 at left shows the standard dotplot representation of both proteins. The dotplot is the simplest matching procedure, it is a 1-tuple matching. In this figure each point means a score value greater that a threshold. In this case

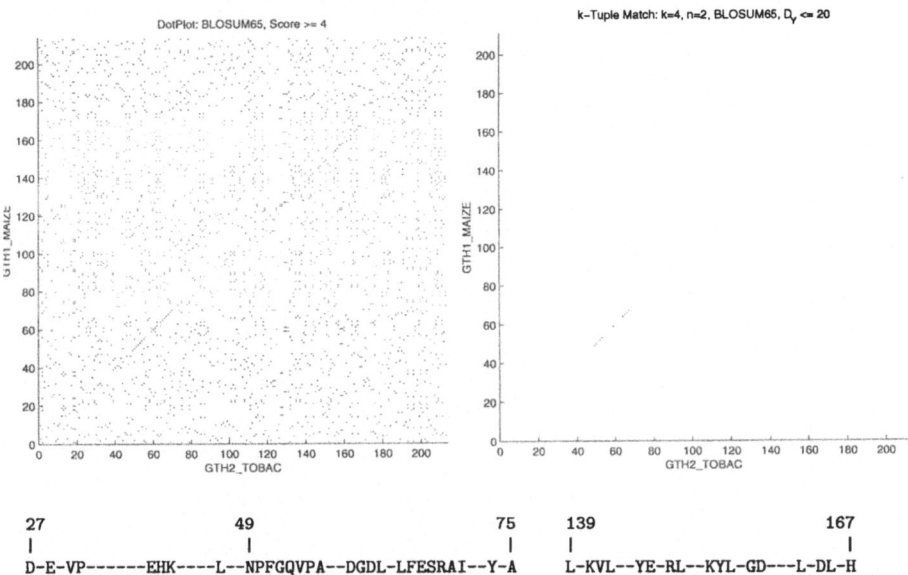

Fig. 2. At left, Dotplot representation between two proteins, GTH2_TOBAC and GTH1_MAIZE. Both are related proteins members of the Glutathione S-transferases family. Each point has a score $s(a, b) \geq 4$ using the BLOSUM62 substitution matrix. The two local alignments between the proteins are shown below with the position in the sequence. Each amino acid symbol means exact match, while the - symbol means mismatch. The stronger similarity is in the 49-75 region, also very week alignments are detected in the 27-48 and 139-167 regions. At right, k-Tuple matching representation between both proteins by using a tuple size $k = 4$ and a mapping dimensionality $n = 2$ of the BLOSUM65 matrix. Shown points have a tuple distance $D_Y(U, V) \leq 10$

$s(a, b) \geq 4$ according with the BLOSUM65 matrix. The previous alignment of both sequence shows a significative match in the 49-75 region. Other matches are too weak to be considered. Also, Figure 2 at right shows the solution of the matching procedure with tuple size $k = 4$, the mapping dimensionality $n = 2$, by using a threshold $D_Y(U, V) \leq 20$. As shown the significative region is detected as can be supplied to next stages of heuristics procedures as FASTA or BLAST.

Figure 3 shows a comparative evaluation of the computational time of some matching procedures. The sequence of the protein GTH1_MAIZE is matched with some randomly chosen sequences in the SWISS-PROT database. The length of the GTH1_MAIZE sequence is 213 amino acids, the figure shows the computational cost in msec. of each protein match vs the sequence length. To avoid the noise produced by the operating system interruptions and services, no other user task was running and each represented value is the mean over a thousand cases. The computation of the dotplot is compared with the computation of the

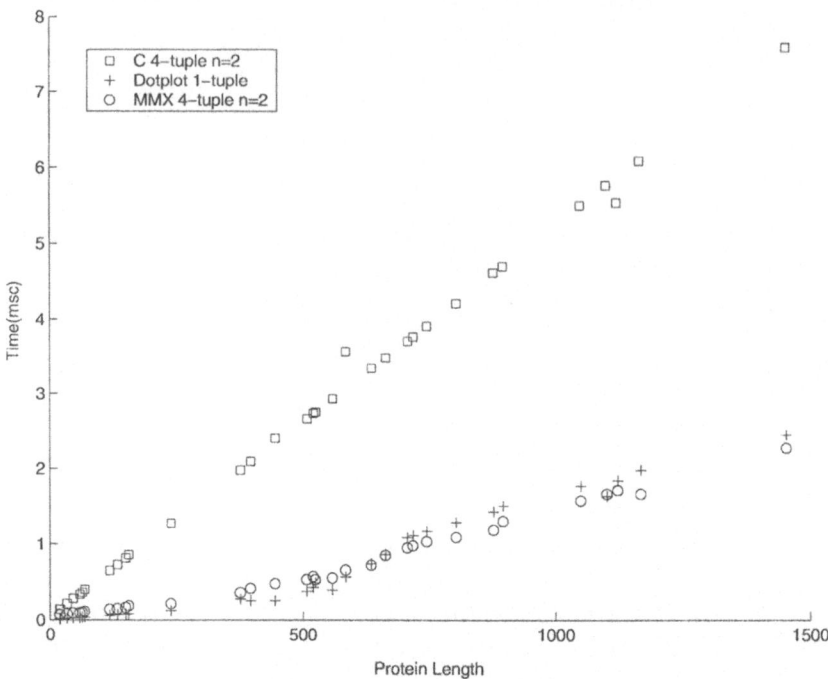

Fig. 3.   Computational time in msec. of matching procedures between the GTH1_MAIZE and some randomly chosen protein sequences vs the protein length. Included Procedures are Dotplot, which is an 1-tuple, C and MMX implementations of matching 4-tuple with a mapping dimensionality $n = 2$. MMX implementation has a similar computational cost that Dotplot that is the simplest k-tuple procedure, while it allows a high quality detection of preliminary regions of local alignments

matching procedure defined in equation (7) with $k = 4$ and $n = 2$; the latter is computed by coding in C language and also by using the MMX instruction set in assembler language. The processor used is a Intel Pentium IV at 2Ghz. It is concluded that the 4-tuple matching coded in MMX has similar cost that the dotplot, but the quality of results is better as shown in Figure 2. The MMX procedure is slight faster than the dotplot in long sequence and also slight slower in short sequences. In all case the 4-tuple matching in C is the slower option.

References

[1] S. F. Altschul, W. Gish, W. Miller, E. W. Myers, and D. J. Lipman. Basic local aligment search tool. *Jor. Mol. Biol.*, 215:403–410, 1990.

[2] T. K. Attwood and D. J. Parry-Smith. *Introduction to Bioinformatics*. Prentice-Hall, 1999.

[3] S. De Backer, A. Naud, and P. Scheunders. Nonlinear dimensionality reduction techniques for unsupervised feature extraction. *Pattern Recognition Letters*, 19:711–720, 1998.

[4] P Baldi and S. Brunak. *Bioinformatics, The Machine Learning Approach.* MIT Press, 2001.

[5] Alex Bateman, Ewan Birney, Richard Durbin, Sean R. Eddy, Kevin L. Howe, and Erik L. Sonnhammer. The pfam protein families database. *Nucleic Acids Research*, 28:263–266, 2000.

[6] A. Bik, M. Girkar, P. Grey, and X. Tian. Efficient exploitation of parallelism on pentium III and pentium 4 processor-based systems. *Intel Technology Journal Q1*, pages 1–9, 2001.

[7] T. Coleman, M. A. Branch, and A. Gracce. *Optimization Toolbox User's Guide.* Mathworks Inc., 1999.

[8] M. O. Dayhoff, R. M. Schwartz, and B. C. Orcutt. *Atlas of Protein Sequence and Structure*, volume 5. Nat. Biomed. Res. Found., 1978.

[9] O. de Vel, S. Li, and D. Coomans. *Learning from Data: AI and Statistics*, chapter Non-Linear Dimensionality Reduction: A Comparative Performance Analysis, pages 323–331. Springer-Verlag, 1996.

[10] R. O. Duda, P. E. Hart, and D. G. Stork. *Pattern Classification.* John Wiley and Sons, 2001.

[11] S. Henikoff and J. G. Henikoff. Amino acid substitution matrices from protein blocks. *Proc. Natl. Acad. Sci.*, 89:10915–10919, November 1992.

[12] C. R. Houck, J. A. Joines, and M. G. Kay. A genetic algoritm for function optimization: A matlab implementation. Technical report, NCSU, 1995.

[13] R. Hughey. Parallel hardware for sequence comparison and alignment. *CABIOS*, 12(6):473–479, December 1996.

[14] L. Hunter. *Artificial Intelligence and Mollecular Biology.* MIT Press, 1993.

[15] S. Li, O. de Vel, and D. Coomans. Comparative performance analysis of nonlinear dimensionality reduction methods. Technical report, James Cook Univ., 1995.

[16] S. B. Needleman and C. D. Wunsch. A general method applicable to the search for similarities in amino acid sequences of two proteins. *Jor. Mol. Biol.*, 48:443–453, 1970.

[17] William R. Pearson. Protein sequence comparison and protein evolution. Technical report, Dept. Biochemistry and Molecular Genetics. Unv. Virginia, 2001.

[18] W. R. Pearson and D. J. Lipman. Improved tools for biological sequence comparation. *Proc. Natl. Acad. Sci.*, 85(8):2444–2448, April 1988.

[19] T. Rognes. Paralign: a parallel sequence algorithm for rapid and sensitive databases searches. *Nucleic Acids Research*, 29(7):1647–1652, 2001.

[20] T. Rognes and E. Seeberg. Six-fold speed-up of smith-waterman sequence database searches using parallel processing on common microprocessors. *Bioinformatics*, 16(8):699–706, 2000.

[21] J. W. Sammon. A nonlinear mapping for data structure analysis. *IEEE Trans. Computers*, 18:401–409, 1969.

[22] P. Scheunders, S. De Backer, and A. Naud. Non-linear mapping for feature extraction. *Lecture notes in computer science*, 1451:823–830, 1998.

[23] T. F. Smith and M. S. Waterman. Identification of common molecular subsequences. *Jor. Mol. Biol.*, 147:195–197, 1981.

[24] T. K. Yap, O. Frieder, and R. L. Martino. Parallel computation in biological sequence analysis. *IEEE Trans. on Parall. and Distr. Syst.*, 9(3):1–12, 1998.

An Algebra for the Treatment of Multivalued Information Systems

Margaret Miró-Julià and Gabriel Fiol-Roig

Departament de Ciències Matemàtiques i Informàtica
Universitat de les Illes Balears
07122 Palma de Mallorca, SPAIN
{margaret.miro,biel.fiol}@uib.es

Abstract. Descriptive knowledge about an Information System can be expressed in declarative form by means of a binary Boolean based language.

This paper presents a contribution to the study of an arbitrary multivalued Information System structure by introducing an algebra (not binary) that allows the treatment of multiple valued data tables with systematic algebraic techniques.

Elements $|t_i|$ and $||t_p||$, called arrays and co-arrays, are defined, operations $\sim$, $\ddagger$ and $\circ$ are described. The proposed methodology allows multivalued algebraic expressions describing a multivalued Information System (multivalued Object Attribute Table).

Furthermore, the same Information System can be described by several distinct, but equivalent, algebraic expressions. Among these, the prime-ar expression is singled out. The usefulness of the described algebra to represent an Information System is shown.

1 Introduction

Scientific and engineering disciplines are developing daily. This progress is strongly connected to complex techniques and methods. However, it is surprising to observe that the majority of Information Systems considered are binary and, of course, the methods and techniques used are binary based.

Much of the knowledge one has about its environment is descriptive and can be expressed in declarative form by means of a language. A first level declaration or itemized description describes one object. A second level declaration or declarative description refers to subsets of objects not in terms of the elements of the subset but in terms of the attributes and the values these attributes take. Thus, declarative expressions describe aspects of the reality in terms of subsets of objects characterized by their attribute values.

The transfer of knowledge from the declarative level to the itemized level is very simple, since every one of the elements of the subset inherits the properties assigned to the subset in the declaration. On the other hand the construction of a true declarative sentence describing a given subset of objects is not a simple matter. In general the problem is not trivial because it may have multiple solutions.

F.J. Perales et al. (Eds.): IbPRIA 2003, LNCS 2652, pp. 556–563, 2003.
© Springer-Verlag Berlin Heidelberg 2003

The need to establish computer programs that determine declarations has brought the problem back to the surface and several groups have designed approaches to it. Directly or indirectly, work by Michalski [1], Quinlan [2], Pawlak [3], Miró [4], Wille [5] and Fiol [6] has to do with this problem. However, their efforts are mainly directed to binary descriptions.

Definition 1. *Let $D = \{d_1, d_2, \ldots, d_i, \ldots, d_m\}$ be an ordered set called domain, of elements d_i representing the m objects, let $R = \{r_g, \ldots, r_c, \ldots, r_a\}$ be a set of the g attributes or properties of the objects. The set of values of attribute c is represented by $C = \{[c_{n_c}], \ldots, [c_j], \ldots, [c_1]\}$. The elements of set C, $[c_j]$, are called 1-spec-sets since the elements are defined by means of one specification. An Object Attribute Table (OAT) is a table whose rows represent the objects, and whose columns represent the attributes of these objects. Each element $[c_i]$ represents the value of attribute r_c that corresponds to object d_i.*

In order to handle the multivalued OAT a new mathematical tool is needed: a multivalued language.

2 Multivalued Language

2.1 Symbolic Representation of a Subset

The initial objective of the multivalued language is to offer a general and compact symbolic representation of an arbitrary subset $C_h \subseteq C$ and of the set operations between subsets.

The set of all subsets of a given set C (the power set of C), $\rho(C)$, forms a Boolean algebra $< \rho(C), \cup, \cap, \hat{\,}, \emptyset, C >$. There is a parallel Boolean algebra $< \mathcal{S}_c, +, \cdot, \hat{\,}, \vee_c, \wedge_c >$ defined on the set $\mathcal{S}_c$ of all possible symbols representing subsets of C. Throughout this paper, the symbol $\rightsquigarrow$ may be read as: "is described by". Therefore, $C_h \rightsquigarrow c_h$ expresses: "subset C_h is described by symbol c_h". The symbolic representations of regular set operations complement ($\hat{\,}$), union ($\cup$) and intersection ($\cap$) are: $\widehat{C_h} \rightsquigarrow \hat{c}_h$, $\quad C_h \cup C_k \rightsquigarrow c_h + c_k$, $\quad C_h \cap C_k \rightsquigarrow c_h \cdot c_k$.

This symbolic representation has been carefully studied in [7]. Also, tables for operations $\hat{\,}$, $+$ and $\cdot$ in octal representation are provided.

2.2 Fundamental Concepts

All the concepts and operations introduced above make reference to only one set, that is, one attribute. A multivalued OAT has more than one attribute.

Let $R = \{r_c, r_b, r_a\}$ be a set of 3 attributes whose attribute values are $C = \{[c_{n_c}], \ldots, [c_2], [c_1]\}$, $B = \{[b_{n_b}], \ldots, [b_2], [b_1]\}$ and $A = \{[a_{n_a}], \ldots, [a_2], [a_1]\}$. The elements of sets C, B, A are 1-spec-sets (one specification). A 3-spec-set, $[c_k, b_j, a_i]$, is a chain ordered description of 3 specifications, one from set C, one from set B and one from set A. Each spec-set represents itself and all possible permutations: $[c_k, b_j, a_i] = [c_k, a_i, b_j] = [b_j, c_k, a_i] = [b_j, a_i, c_k] = [a_i, c_k, b_j] = [a_i, b_j, c_k]$.

This idea can be generalized for g attributes. In all definitions that follow, $R = \{r_g, \ldots, r_b, r_a\}$ is the set of g attributes whose attribute values are given by non-empty sets $G, \ldots, B, A$ respectively.

Definition 2. *The cross product $G \otimes \cdots \otimes B \otimes A$ is the set of all possible g-spec-sets formed by one element of G, ..., one element of B and one element of A.*

$$G \otimes \cdots \otimes B \otimes A = \{[g_x, \ldots, b_j, a_i] \mid [g_x] \in G, \ldots, [b_j] \in B, [a_i] \in A\}$$

It is important to mention that the cross product is not the cartesian product. A g-spec-set represents itself and all possible permutations whereas the elements of the cartesian product are different if the order in which there are written varies. The basis T is an ordered chain which establishes the sequential order in which the spec-sets are always written. In this paper $T = < G, \ldots, B, A >$.

The set of all possible g-spec-sets induced by sets $G, \ldots, B, A$ is called the **universe** U and every subset of the universe, $U_i \subseteq U$, is called a **subuniverse**.

Definition 3. *Let $G_i \subseteq G$, ..., $B_i \subseteq B$, $A_i \subseteq A$, an array $|t_i| = |g_i, \ldots, b_i, a_i|$ is the symbolic representation of the cross product $G_i \otimes \ldots \otimes B_i \otimes A_i$ where $G_i \rightsquigarrow g_i$, ..., $B_i \rightsquigarrow b_i$, and $A_i \rightsquigarrow a_i$.*

$$G_i \otimes \cdots \otimes B_i \otimes A_i \rightsquigarrow |t_i| = |g_i, \ldots, b_i, a_i|$$

An array $|t_y^E|$ is called an elementary array if it describes a subuniverse formed by only one g-spec-set.

Definition 4. *Let $G_p \subseteq G$, ..., $B_p \subseteq B$, $A_p \subseteq A$, the symbolic representation of the complement (in the universe) of the cross product of subsets $\hat{G}_p \otimes \ldots \otimes \hat{B}_p \otimes \hat{A}_p$ where $G_p \rightsquigarrow g_p$, ..., $B_p \rightsquigarrow b_p$, and $A_p \rightsquigarrow a_p$ is called a co-array $\|t_p\| = \|g_p, \ldots, b_p, a_p\|$.*

$$\sim (\hat{G}_p \otimes \ldots \otimes \hat{B}_p \otimes \hat{A}_p) \rightsquigarrow \|t_p\| = \|g_p, \ldots, b_p, a_p\|$$

Arrays and co-arrays are symbolic representations of subuniverses, 2-dimensional (two attributes) arrays and co-arrays can be represented graphically as shown in Fig. 1.

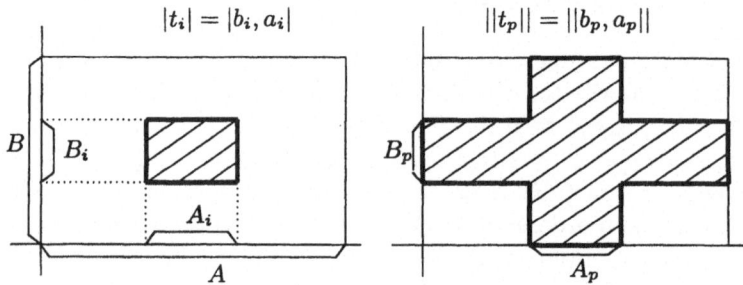

Fig. 1. Arrays and co-arrays in 2 dimensions

Definition 5. *If* $|t_i| = ||t_i||$, *then* $|t_i|$ *is called a degenerate array or a degenerate co-array.*

Degenerate arrays deserve special consideration and have been studied in [7]. There are three types of degenerate arrays:

1. The identity array (co-array) $\bigwedge$, which describes the universe: $U \rightsquigarrow \bigwedge = |\wedge_g, \ldots, \wedge_b, \wedge_a| = ||\wedge_g, \ldots, \wedge_b, \wedge_a||$.
2. The zero array (co-array) $\bigvee$, describing the empty universe: $\emptyset \rightsquigarrow \bigvee = |\vee_g, \ldots, \vee_b, \vee_a| = ||\vee_g, \ldots, \vee_b, \vee_a||$.
3. Arrays of the form $|t_i| = |\wedge_g, \ldots, d_i, \ldots, \wedge_b, \wedge_a| = ||\vee_g, \ldots, d_i, \ldots, \vee_b, \vee_a||$.

The arrays and the co-arrays describe subuniverses, therefore regular set operations may be performed with them. Let $|t_i| = |g_i, \ldots, b_i, a_i|$ and $|t_j| = |g_j, \ldots, b_j, a_j|$ be two arrays, the following operations between arrays are introduced:

1. $\sim$ complement respect to $\bigwedge$: $\sim (G_i \otimes \cdots \otimes B_i \otimes A_i) \rightsquigarrow \sim |t_i|$.
2. $\ddagger$ sum of arrays: $(G_i \otimes \cdots \otimes B_i \otimes A_i) \cup (G_j \otimes \cdots \otimes B_j \otimes A_j) \rightsquigarrow |t_i| \ddagger |t_j| = |g_i, \ldots, b_i, a_i| \ddagger |g_j, \ldots, b_j, a_j|$.
3. $\circ$ product of arrays: $(G_i \otimes \cdots \otimes B_i \otimes A_i) \cap (G_j \otimes \cdots \otimes B_j \otimes A_j) \rightsquigarrow |t_i| \circ |t_j| = |g_i, \ldots, b_i, a_i| \circ |g_j, \ldots, b_j, a_j| = |g_i \cdot g_j, \ldots, b_i \cdot b_j, a_i \cdot a_j|$.
   The $\circ$ product is a closed operation in the set of all arrays.

Let $||t_p|| = ||g_p, \ldots, b_p, a_p||$ and $||t_q|| = ||g_q, \ldots, b_q, a_q||$ be two co-arrays, the following operations between co-arrays are introduced:

1. $\sim$ complement respect to $\bigwedge$: $\sim [\sim (\hat{G}_p \otimes \cdots \otimes \hat{B}_p \otimes \hat{A}_p)] \rightsquigarrow \sim ||t_p|| = |\hat{g}_p, \ldots, \hat{b}_p, \hat{a}_p|$.
2. $\ddagger$ sum of co-arrays: $\sim (\hat{G}_p \otimes \cdots \otimes \hat{B}_p \otimes \hat{A}_p) \cup \sim (\hat{G}_q \otimes \cdots \otimes \hat{B}_q \otimes \hat{A}_q) \rightsquigarrow ||t_p|| \ddagger ||t_q|| = ||g_p, \ldots, b_p, a_p|| \ddagger ||g_q, \ldots, b_q, a_q|| = ||g_p + g_q, \ldots, b_p + b_q, a_p + a_q||$.
   The $\ddagger$ sum is a closed operation in the set of all co-arrays.
3. $\circ$ product of co-arrays: $\sim (\hat{G}_p \otimes \cdots \otimes \hat{B}_p \otimes \hat{A}_p) \cap \sim (\hat{G}_q \otimes \cdots \otimes \hat{B}_q \otimes \hat{A}_q) \rightsquigarrow ||t_p|| \circ ||t_q|| = ||g_p, \ldots, b_p, a_p|| \circ ||g_q, \ldots, b_q, a_q||$.

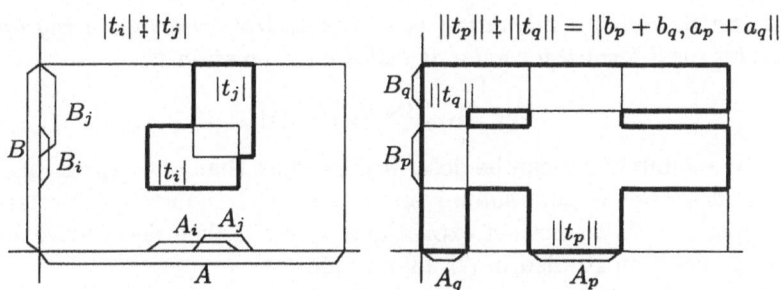

Fig. 2. $\ddagger$ sum of arrays and co-arrays

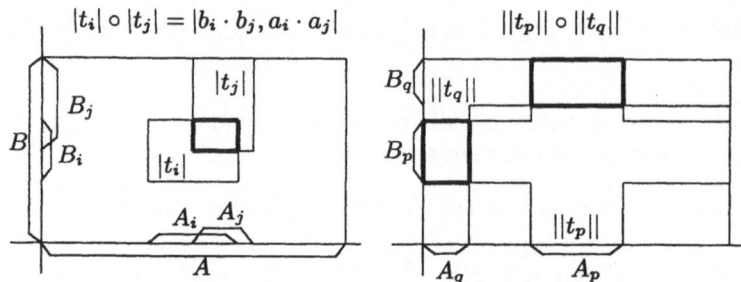

Fig. 3. ∘ product of arrays and co-arrays

All the results obtained by use of operations $\sim$, $\ddagger$ and ∘ on arrays or co-arrays are symbolic representations of subuniverses. If only two attributes are considered, these operations can be represented graphically as shown in Figures 2 and 3.

3   Algebraic Results

The multivalued language provides us with expressions, such as the $\ddagger$ sum of arrays or the ∘ product of co-arrays, that have only a symbolic value without being computable. The use of degenerate arrays allows: a) to express an array as a ∘ product of co-arrays; b) to express a co-array as a $\ddagger$ sum of arrays; c) to perform mixed operations between arrays and co-arrays; and d) to calculate complements.

All these results have been proven in [7]. Even though only the ∘ product of arrays and the $\ddagger$ sum of co-arrays are closed operations, expressions involving the ∘ product of co-arrays or the $\ddagger$ sum of arrays have been obtained.

4   Expressions

Subuniverses can be described by algebraic expressions of arrays and/or co-arrays. An expression is a symbolic representation of a subuniverse, an expression represents the reality described by an OAT.

Definition 6. *Every combination of arrays and/or co-arrays using operations* $\sim$, $\ddagger$ *and* ∘ *(well formed formula) is called an expression* E_i.

$$E_i = |t_i| \ddagger (\sim |t_j|) \circ ||t_k|| \ldots$$

Generally, a subuniverse can be described by more than one expression. Expressions that describe the same subuniverse are said to be equivalent (declaratively). The comparison of two distinct expressions, as far as their declarative describing capability, has been studied in [7], [8] and [9].

Expressions represent subuniverses, therefore an order relation equivalent to set inclusion may be introduced: $U_i \subseteq U_j \rightsquigarrow E_i \preceq E_j$. This order relation has been studied in [7] and has been used to find simplified equivalent expressions.

$$E_i = |t_1| \updownarrow |t_2| \updownarrow |t_3| \qquad\qquad E_p = ||t_1|| \circ ||t_2|| \circ ||t_3||$$

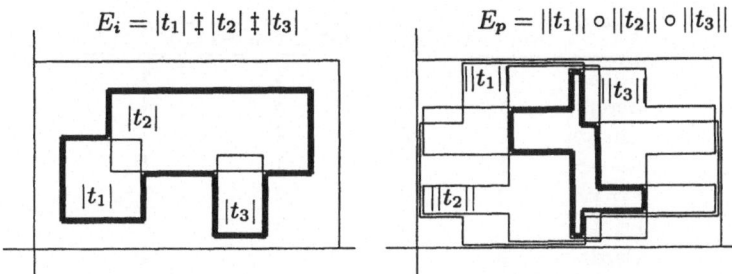

Fig. 4. 2-dimensional array and co-array expressions

Definition 7. *An expression E_i is called an array expression if it is written as a $\updownarrow$ sum of arrays: $E_i = |t_z| \updownarrow \cdots \updownarrow |t_y| \updownarrow \cdots \updownarrow |t_x|$.*

An expression E_i is called a co-array expression if it is written as a $\circ$ product of co-arrays: $E_i = ||t_p|| \circ \cdots \circ ||t_q|| \circ \cdots \circ ||t_r||$.

Fig. 4 displays 2-dimensional array and co-array expressions.

An array expression is called elementary if each of the arrays in the $\updownarrow$ sum is an elementary array: $E_i^E = |t_z^E| \updownarrow \cdots \updownarrow |t_y^E| \updownarrow \cdots \updownarrow |t_x^E|$.

5   All-Prime-Ar Expression

So far, concepts and procedures come as couples of dual statements. From now on only the array expressions will be considered.

Definition 8. *Let $E_i = |t_z| \updownarrow \cdots \updownarrow |t_y| \updownarrow \cdots \updownarrow |t_x|$, an array $|t_y|$ is a prime-ar (prime array) of E_i if there is no other array $|t_j|$ such that $|t_y| \preceq |t_j| \preceq E_i$. A prime-ar is a "largest" array contained in E_i.*

Consider the array expression given in Fig. 4. Both $|t_1|$ and $|t_2|$ are prime-ars, however $|t_3|$ is not a prime-ar.

Definition 9. *The $\updownarrow$ sum of all the prime-ars of an expression E_i is called the all-prime-ar expression of E_i.*

The same subuniverse can be described by more than one prime-ar expression. How can the equivalency between expressions be studied? This question was originally proposed in [8] and further studied in [10]. Two prime-ar expressions are equivalent if their all-prime-ar expressions are equal. Even though the all-prime-ar expression is a unique expression, the number of prime-ars in the expression may not be minimal.

The following table, studied in [7], represents the general grades on conduct (r_d), diligence (r_c), attentiveness (r_b) and orderliness(r_a) given to a class at the Ludwig-Georgs-Gymnasium. The data base represents a file of students together with the grades received. The grades (attributes) are numerical values, conduct and attentiveness take values from 1 (best grade) to 3 (worst grade), whereas diligence and orderliness take values from 1 (best grade) to 4 (worst grade).

	conduct	diligence	attentiveness	orderliness
Anna	3	4	3	4
Berend	3	4	3	4
Christa	2	2	2	2
Dieter	1	1	1	1
Ernst	2	2	2	2
Fritz	2	1	2	2
Gerda	2	2	2	3
Horst	2	2	2	3
Ingolf	2	3	3	2
Jurgen	2	2	3	2
Karl	2	3	2	2
Linda	2	1	2	2
Manfred	2	2	2	2
Norbert	3	3	2	2
Olga	1	1	2	2
Paul	1	1	1	1
Quax	2	2	2	2
Rudolf	3	4	3	3
Stefan	1	1	1	1
Till	1	1	1	1
Uta	1	1	2	2
Volker	2	2	3	2
Walter	3	4	3	4
Xaver	1	1	1	1
Zora	2	2	2	2

The basis is $T = < D, C, B, A >$ with $D = \{3, 2, 1\}$, $C = \{4, 3, 2, 1\}$, $B = \{3, 2, 1\}$ and $A = \{4, 3, 2, 1\}$. This data is first traslated into octal representation, and using algebraic techniques it is transformed into an elementary array expression. Then the all-prime-ar expression describing the data is found.

$$E = | 1, \ 01, \ 1, \ 01| \ddagger | \ 4, \ 04, \ 2, \ 04| \ddagger | \ 4, \ 10, \ 4, \ 04| \ddagger | \ 2, \ 02, \ 2, \ 06| \ddagger$$
$$\ddagger | \ 3, \ 01, \ 2, \ 02| \ddagger | \ 2, \ 07, \ 2, \ 02| \ddagger | \ 2, \ 06, \ 6, \ 02|$$

The proposed array algebra allows a simple description of the data provided. The all-prime-ar expression allows for notation economy and forsees ways of joining expressions (information systems) or finding common descriptions between two or more expressions (information systems).

6   Conclusion

The proposed array algebra does not handle raw data, it handles declarative descriptions of the data. Declarative expressions from a multivalued information system can be obtained using arrays and/or co-arrays and declarative expressions can be transformed by application of the algebraic techniques.

The algebra of arrays allows the description of an arbitrary information system by means of an array expression describing the same partial reality. These array expressions are not unique. In order to find a unique array expression the concept of prime-ar is introduced. The ‡ sum of all prime-ars is a unique expression, although it is not necessarily minimum in the number of prime-ars.

The introduction of the array algebra vastly improves time efficiency when comparing two sources of information. Furthermore, the technique developed here is independent of the number of attributes and the number of values of each attribute. Multivalued and binary information systems are treated similarly.

Finally, it should be mentioned that this array algebra has a dual version, the co-array algebra that has been introduced in [7] and should be further studied.

Acknowledgements

This work has been supported by the Universitat de les Illes Balears through the UIB 2003/11 project.

References

[1] Michalski, R. S.: A Theory and Methodology of Inductive Learning. Artificial Intelligence **20** (1983) 111–161.

[2] Quinlan, J. R.: Induction of Decision Trees. Machine Learning **1** (1986) 81–106.

[3] Pawlak, Z.: Rough Sets: Theoretical Aspects of Reasoning About Data. Kluwer Academic Publisher (1991).

[4] Miró, J. and Miró-Julià, J.: Uncertainty and Inference through Approximate Sets. Uncertainty in Intelligent Systems. North Holland (1993) 203–214.

[5] Ganter, B. and Wille, R.: Formal Concept Analysis. Mathematical Foundations. Springer-Verlag (1999).

[6] Fiol, Gabriel and Miró Nicolau, José and Miró-Julià, José: A New Perspective in the Inductive Acquisition of Knowledge from Examples. Lecture Notes in Computer Science **682** (1992) 219–228.

[7] Miró-Julià, M.: A Contribution to Multivalued Systems. Ph.D. thesis. Universitat de les Illes Balears (2000).

[8] Miró, J. and Miró-Julià, M.: Equality of Functions in CAST. Lecture Notes in Computer Science **1030** (1995) 129–136.

[9] Miró, J. and Miró-Julià, M.: A Numerical Computation for Declarative Expressions. Lecture Notes in Computer Science **1333** (1997) 236–251.

[10] Miró-Julià, M. and Miró, J.: Transformation of Array Expressions. Proceedings of the Second IASTED International Conference. Artificial Intelligence and Applications (2002) 273–278.

Adaptive Learning for String Classification*

Ramón A. Mollineda, Enrique Vidal, and Carlos Martínez-Hinarejos

Instituto Tecnológico de Informática
Universidad Politécnica de Valencia, Camino de Vera s/n, 46071 Valencia, Spain
{rmollin,evidal,cmartine}@iti.upv.es

Abstract. A new LVQ-inspired adaptive method is introduced to optimize strings for the 1-NN classifier. The updating rule relies on the edit distance. Given an initial number of string prototypes and a training set, the algorithm builds supervised clusters by attaching training samples to prototypes. A prototype is then rewarded to get it closer to the members of its cluster. To this end, the prototype is updated according to the most frequent edit operations resulting from edit distance computations to all members of its cluster. The process reorganizes training samples into new clusters and continues until the convergence of prototypes is achieved. A series of learning/classification experiments is presented which show a better 1-NN performance of the new prototypes with respect to the initial ones, that were originally good for classification.

Keywords: Adaptive learning, structural pattern analysis, string matching, nearest neighbor, nonparametric classifier, self-organization.

1 Introduction

The 1-*Nearest Neighbor* (1-NN) rule is a simple and, under certain conditions, a close-to-optimal classifier. Given a (large) training set of labeled patterns and a new pattern x with an unknown label, the 1-NN rule attaches to x the label of its closest training pattern according to some metric. In spite of its simplicity, it performs well for large training sets. In fact, its recognition rates tend to be asymptotically better as the number of (representative) training patterns increases [1]. This worthwhile theoretic result comes into conflict with the feasibility of the 1-NN implementation procedure, which needs to compute distances (given a metric) between x and all known patterns from the training set. This amount of computation becomes prohibitive for large data sets, specially for structural pattern recognition in (non-vectorial) spaces where metrics are usually complex algorithms, for example, in graph or string matching.

This computational drawback can be overcome with *condensing* methods [2, 3, 4, 5], which aims at find a reduced set of training prototypes from the original training set, as a trade-off between minimal cardinality and maximum classification accuracy. Apart from reducing the size of the training set, these methods

* This work has been partially supported by the grant CTIDIA/2002/80 of Valencian OCYT and by the grant TIC2000-1703-CO3-01 of Spanish CICYT.

F.J. Perales et al. (Eds.): IbPRIA 2003, LNCS 2652, pp. 564–571, 2003.

aim to optimize the 1-NN rule performance for an optimum classification of the original training samples.

One of these most effective scheme for nonparametric classifier design is the one known as *Learning Vector Quantization* (LVQ) [3, 6]. It consists of a simple adaptive optimization procedure based on competitive learning rules to adjust an initially given set of prototypes with respect to a training set. The algorithm rewards or punishes a wining prototype depending on some 1-NN based rule at classifying a reference training pattern. The reward/punishment strategy relies on the Euclidean metric which makes sense only in vectorial spaces.

This paper introduces a novel adaptive method to learn strings as reference prototypes for 1-NN classification. The algorithm starts from an initial set of string prototypes, and organizes the training samples into supervised clusters based on a 1-NN criterion. It continuously optimizes prototypes according to the most frequent local differences with respect to the members of their clusters. The clusters are reorganized after each iteration. The process finishes when prototypes converge to a stable configuration.

2   The Learning Vector Quantization Strategy

Given a training data set T of labeled samples, the LVQ scheme is a nonparametric algorithm which optimizes a number of labeled vectors (prototypes) to classify T with the 1-NN rule. These vectors are initialized by setting initial locations, and their labels are computed from simple majority vote of training samples in T that have each vector as their closest prototype.

The learning procedure consists of a gradient search strategy. The basic LVQ algorithm searches the closest vector v to a specific training sample s. If the label associated with s and the label of v agree, the vector v is moved in the direction of s (*reward*). On the contrary, if they disagree then the vector v is moved away from s (*punishment*). The process iterates until all the vectors converge.

Later versions of LVQ [3] search two vectors (instead of just the closest one) according to some 1-NN based rule, applying a reward/punishment scheme to update them. A generic LVQ model is shown in Fig. 1.

3   An Adaptive Learning Scheme for String Classification

The previous LVQ strategy is based on the following issues:

- a *metric* δ to compute distances which also defines the update rules
- a 1-NN criterion C to obtain *winner* prototypes
- a δ-based update rule φ to *reward* a prototype
- a δ-based update rule ϑ to *punish* a prototype

A new LVQ-inspired adaptive algorithm is introduced to learn string prototypes for 1-NN classification. The method starts from a training set T of labeled strings and another set of labeled prototypes which are the strings to be "optimized" with respect to T. The learning strategy is based on the edit distance computation [7]. A preliminary skeleton of this method could be:

> *Input:*   a training set T, an initial set of labeled prototypes P
>
> a nonincreasing series of positive learning rates $\{\alpha_t\}$
>
> an *Euclidean*-based update rule $\varphi(\alpha_t)$ to *reward* a prototype
>
> an *Euclidean*-based update rule $\vartheta(\alpha_t)$ to *punish* a prototype
>
> a 1-NN criterion $\mathcal{C}$ to obtain *winner* prototypes
>
> *Output:*   the final set of adapted prototypes P
>
> *Method:*
>
> **repeat**
>
> **for all** $s \in T$ **do**
>
> Let $W = \mathcal{C}(s, P)$ be a subset of prototypes to be rewarded
>
> Let $L = \mathcal{C}(s, P)$ be a subset of prototypes to be punished
>
> **for all** $p_t \in W$ **do** $p_{t+1} = \varphi(p_t, \alpha_t, s)$
>
> **for all** $q_t \in L$ **do** $q_{t+1} = \vartheta(q_t, \alpha_t, s)$
>
> **end-do**
>
> **until** convergence of all prototypes in P

Fig. 1. A generic description of a LVQ scheme

- the *metric* is the *Edit Distance* (*ED*)
- training strings are organized in supervised clusters defined by prototypes, which are the *winner prototypes* with respect to their cluster members
- the *ED*-based reward rule φ consists of applying to each prototype the most frequent local transformations (in terms of edit operations) obtained from *ED* computations between the prototype and the strings in its cluster
- none of prototypes is punished

Once all prototypes are updated, a reorganization of training samples into new clusters is carried out. The process continues until the convergence of prototypes is achieved. The following sections present a detailed description of each part of the method.

3.1   The Edit Distance: A Collection of Local Differences

The *edit distance* [7] is a metric which evaluates the extent in which two strings differ. It measures the total difference between two strings of symbols regarding a sequence of local differences. They are known as *edit operations* because they *operates* over a source string x by actively changing (*editing*) it into a target string y. The edit distance is formally defined as the total cost (weight) of a minimum-cost sequence of weighted edit operations that *transforms* x into y.

Let Σ be an alphabet and let Σ^* be the set of all finite-length strings over Σ. Let ϵ denote the empty symbol. An *edit operation* is an ordered pair $(x_i, y_j) \in$

$(\Sigma \cup \{\epsilon\}) \times (\Sigma \cup \{\epsilon\}), (x_i, y_j) \neq (\epsilon, \epsilon)$, denoted by $x_i \rightarrow y_j$. The basic edit operations and the local editions they perform on x are:

- *substitute* operation $x_i \rightarrow y_j$, that *replaces* the symbol x_i in x by y_j of y
- *delete* operation $x_i \rightarrow \epsilon$, that *removes* the symbol x_i from x
- *insert* operation $\epsilon \rightarrow y_j$, that *inserts* in a position in x the symbol y_j of y

As a by-product of the edit distance computation, a corresponding sequence of edit operations can be obtained [7]. Each edit operation is a local difference that can be used to locally edit x to make it most similar to y. This fact can be trivially stated as follows.

Lemma 1. *Given two strings x and y and an edit sequence $s = e_1 e_2 \ldots e_m$ obtained from $\delta(x, y)$ computation, the edition of x according to any edit operation e_i in s produces a string x^* such that $\delta(x, y) \geq \delta(x^*, y)$.*

Proof. This intuitive result can be proved from splitting s into $s_p = e_1 \ldots e_{i-1}, e_i$ and $s_s = e_{i+1} \ldots e_m$, being s_p the dynamic programming subsequence [7] that transforms with minimum cost a prefix of x into a prefix of y, and s_s, the optimum subsequence that transform a suffix of x into a suffix of y. The edition of e_i in x removes a possible local difference without modifying s_p and s_s.

As many edit operations we perform as much the source string x approaches the target string y. The application of all edit operations on x completely transform x into y.

3.2   Supervised Clustering Based on a 1-NN Criterion

A training set T of classified strings is used to adapt a different set P of labeled string prototypes for an optimized 1-NN classifier with respect to T. A preliminary organization of training data into supervised clusters associated to prototypes is performed. For each training string $s \in T$, the clustering procedure searches the same-class nearest prototype $p_= \in P$ and the different-class nearest prototype $p_{\neq} \in P$. The string s is added to the cluster of $p_=$ if it is the (absolute) nearest prototype to s or if $\delta(p_=, s)$ is "approximately" equal to $\delta(p_{\neq}, s)$ given a similarity degree β. This 1-NN based rule could be formally stated as follows:

$$\delta(s, p_=) < \delta(s, p_{\neq}) \quad \text{or} \quad \frac{\delta(p_{\neq}, s)}{\delta(p_=, s)} > \beta, \ 0 < \beta < 1 \ . \tag{1}$$

A cluster is then defined by a prototype that is close enough to a number of same-class training strings which are attached to it. The update rule "optimizes" each (*winner*) prototype with respect to its cluster members. Once all prototypes are updated, training strings are reorganized into new clusters and prototypes are rewarded again. The process finishes when no prototype is modified after a complete update iteration.

3.3   An δ-Based Reward Rule

The *ED*-based reward rule φ consists of performing on each prototype the most frequent edit operations obtained from the edit distance computation between the prototype and the strings members of its cluster.

Let p be a prototype to be optimized and let T_p, the set of all training strings currently associated to p (its cluster). The reward process computes edit distances between p and all $s \in T_p$. Apart from distance measures, a collection of sequences of edit operations that transforms p into any member of T_p is also obtained. Because all edit operations from any sequence edit p, many of them appear repeatedly. The number of occurrences of each edit operation are counted and they are ranked from most to least frequent in an ordered list $\mathcal{L}$.

The reward rule edits p with the "most voted" edit operations, those whose frequencies are greater than a specific threshold η. This parameter can be interpreted as the minimum number of members of T_p whose edit sequences must include an edit operation to be selected among the most frequent ones.

An example of the reward rule operation is commented. Given a prototype p, the strings x_i members of T_p, the distances $\delta(p, x_i)$ and their edit sequences:

p	T_p	$\delta(p, x_i)$	edit sequences	$\bar{\delta} = \frac{1}{3} \sum \delta(p, x_i)$
	$x_1 = abab$	0	$\{a \to a, b \to b, a \to a, b \to b\}$	
$abab$	$x_2 = baab$	2	$\{a \to b, b \to a, a \to a, b \to b\}$	1,33
	$x_3 = bbaa$	2	$\{a \to b, b \to b, a \to a, b \to a\}$	

The reward rule ranks all edit operations of previous sequences in the list $\mathcal{L}$, considering each edit operation as a structure in the form (*edit operation, position in p from* 0, *frequency*). The ordered list is $\mathcal{L} = \{(a \to a, 2, 3), (a \to b, 0, 2), (b \to b, 1, 2), (b \to b, 3, 2), (a \to a, 0, 1), (b \to a, 1, 1), (b \to a, 3, 1)\}$. For any $1 \le \eta < 2$, the reward rule edits p with only the first four edit operations which have frequencies greater than η. The updated prototype is $p^* = bbab$ and distances from p^* to x_i are now $\delta(p^*, x_1) = 1$, $\delta(p^*, x_2) = 1$, $\delta(p^*, x_3) = 1$. The new average distance $\bar{\delta}$ from p^* to $x_i \in T_p$ has been reduced from 1,33 to 1.

4   The Learning Algorithm

The integration of previous components leads to the algorithm of Fig. 2. The increasing series of positive learning rates $\{\alpha\}$, $0 \le \alpha \le 1$, are relative minimum frequencies to perform an edit operation, which are common for all β-clusters in each iteration t regardless of their sizes. The convergence is stated in the following lemma.

Lemma 2. *Given an increasing series of positive learning rates $\{\alpha_i\}$, $0 \le \alpha_i \le 1$, the algorithm of Fig. 2 converge if $\alpha_i \to 1$ when i increases.*

Proof. An increasing series of $\{\alpha_i\}$ guarantees a progressive reduction of prototype modifications. When α_i is close enough to 1 for some i, no edit operation

---

Input: a training set T of strings, an initial set of labelled string prototypes P

let δ be the edit distance

an *increasing* series of positive learning rates $\{\alpha_t\}$, $0 \leq \alpha_t \leq 1$

an *edit distance*-based update rule $\varphi(\alpha_t)$ to *reward* a string

a similarity degree β to build clusters according to rule (1)

Output: the final set of adapted string prototypes P

Method:

Organize all $s \in T$ into β-clusters T_p attached to $p \in P$

repeat

for all $p_t \in P$ do

Get the ordered list $\mathcal{L}$ of edit operations from $\delta(p_t, s)$ for all $s \in T_{p_t}$

$\eta_t = \alpha_t * |T_{p_t}|$, the minimum frequency to performe an edit operation

$p_{t+1} = \varphi(p_t, \eta_t, \mathcal{L})$

end-do

Re-organize all $s \in T$ into *new* β-clusters $T_{p_{t+1}}$ attached to $p_{t+1} \in P$

until convergence of all prototypes in P

Fig. 2. The learning algorithm to adapt strings for the 1-NN classification

will have a frequency greater than its $|T_p|$, and no modifications of prototypes will be accomplished.

5 Experimental Results

A Chromosome Data Set. The first data set is a part of a larger one which has 6895 chromosome images [8]. Each digitized image was transformed into a string of codes (from an alphabet of 11 codes) representing differences between adjacent density values from a one-dimensional density profile built from the image [9]. A total of 4400 samples were collected, 200 of each of the 22 non-sex chromosomes types. Two different random sets (for training and test) with 2200 strings each one were obtained keeping uniform distributions among the 22 classes. The metric used was the edit distance post-normalized by the sum of lengths of the two strings and the weights of the edit operations are those reported in [9]. The training set was divided into 10, 20, up to 90 clusters per class and, for each clustering, a corresponding set of 10, 20 up to 90 prototypes (one per cluster) were computed (from a minimum distance criterion) as median strings of the members of each cluster [9]. As a result, 9 sets of 220, 440, 660, 880, 1100, 1320, 1540, 1760, 1980 median strings of clusters were used as the original prototypes to be updated by the learning algorithm. The parameters used (after

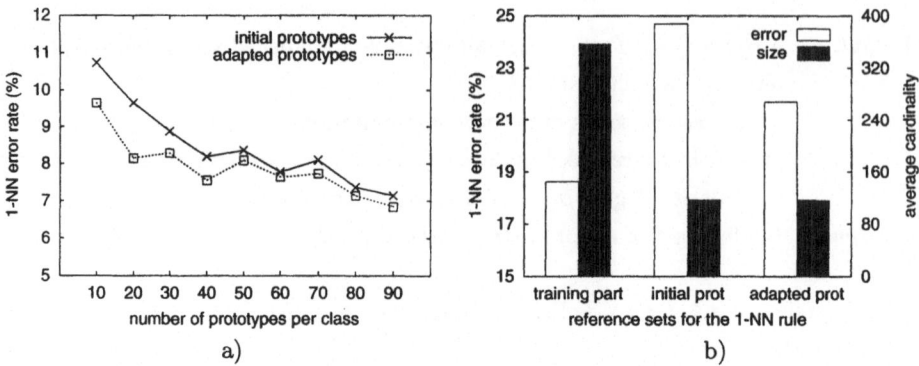

Fig. 3. **a) Results on chromosomes data:** the error rates of the 1-NN rule at classifying the test set as a function of the number of initial and adapted prototypes. **b) Results on chicken pieces data:** error rates of the 1-NN rule on test partitions and average cardinalities of training partitions and the sets of prototypes

a few tries) were $\beta = 0.75$ and as $\{\alpha_t\}$, a geometric series starting at 0.5 with a ratio 1.1. Figure 3a) illustrates the error rates of the 1-NN rule at classifying the test set as a function of the number of initial and adapted prototypes. A clear (but slight) improvement of the 1-NN generalization performance of all sets of prototypes is achieved. The 1-NN error rate using the whole training set is 6.55.

A Chicken Pieces Data Set. A second experiment uses a set of chain-code contours describing silhouettes of chicken parts. A set composed by 446 images from chicken pieces was used [10], each image containing a silhouette from a particular piece. Each piece belongs to one of five categories (different parts of the chicken): wing (117 samples), back (76), drumstick (96), thigh and back (61), and breast (96). All images were adequately clipped and scaled into 64x64 pixels images. A standard 8-direction chain-encoding procedure was applied to obtain a contour string associated to each silhouette. The metric used was the same post-normalized edit distance, and weights of edit operations were 0 for identical substitutions (matching) and 1 for the others.

A 5-fold cross validation experiment was carried out. The average number of samples of the training partitions was 357 and, using them as reference sets, the accumulated error of the 1-NN classification on test partitions was 18.6%. Each training partition was condensed by the GMCA method [5], which can be used to *select* a subset of good prototypes that classify without errors the initial set. The average cardinality of condensed sets was 117 and when used as reference sets, the 1-NN error rate at classifying test sets was 24.7%. Finally, condensed sets were used as initial sets of prototypes to be *adapted* by the learning scheme of Fig. 2 with respect to their original training partitions. The parameters selected (after a few tries) were $\beta = 0.65$ and as $\{\alpha_t\}$, a geometric series starting at 0.5 with a ratio 1.05. The 1-NN error rate considering the optimized set of prototypes is

21.7%. These results are shown in Fig. 3b). The error rate obtained from adapted prototypes is notably lower than that of initial prototypes (which classify without errors the training partitions). The adapted solution is then a trade-off between cardinality (the average number of prototypes is the third part of the average cardinality of training partitions) and classification performance, which is not as good as that obtained from training partitions.

6 Conclusions and Further Work

A new LVQ-inspired adaptive algorithm is introduced to learn string prototypes for 1-NN classification. The learning strategy is based on the edit distance computation [7], and the update rule consists of performing on each prototype the most frequent edit operations with respect to a number of close training samples. The process iterates until prototypes converge. Experiments were intended for the improvement of initial prototypes which were already good for classification, what made the task more difficult. Results show a clear trend to obtain adapted prototypes with a better 1-NN performance. A natural extension could involve the definition of a punishment rule to "move" prototypes away from samples of different classes. Another future line of work could be an integrated approach to adapt both prototypes and weights of edit operations.

References

[1] Dasarathy, B.V., ed.: Nearest Neighbor (NN) Norms: NN Pattern Classification Techniques. IEEE Computer Society Press, Los Alamitos, CA (1991)

[2] Hart, P.E.: The condensed nearest neighbor rule. IEEE Transactions on Information Theory 14 (1968) 515–516

[3] Kohonen, T.: Improved versions of learning vector quantization. In: Proc. of the Int. Conf. on Neural Networks. Volume 1., San Diego, CA (1990) 545–550

[4] Bezdek, J.C., Reichherzer, T.R., Lim, G.S., Attikiouzel, Y.: Multiple-prototype classifier design. IEEE Trans. on System, Man and Cybernetics 28 (1998) 67–79

[5] Mollineda, R., Ferri, F., Vidal, E.: An efficient prototype merging strategy for the condensed 1-nn rule through class conditional hierarchical clustering. Pattern Recognition 35 (2002) 2771–2782

[6] Kohonen, T., Barna, G., Chrisley, R.: Statistical pattern recognition with neural networks: Benchmarking studies. In: Proc. IJCNN. Volume I., San Diego, CA, IEEE Computer Soc. Press (1988) 61–68

[7] Wagner, R.A., Fischer, M.J.: The string-to-string correction problem. J. Assoc. Comput. Machinery 21 (1974) 168–173

[8] Lundsteen, C., Philip, J., Granum, E.: Quantitative analysis of 6895 digitized trypsin g-banded human chromosomes. Clinic Genetics 18 (1980) 355–370

[9] Martínez-Hinarejos, C.D., Juan, A., Casacuberta, F.: Median strings for k-nearest neighbour classification. Pattern Recognition Letters (2003)

[10] Andreu, G., Crespo, A., Valiente, J.M.: Selecting the toroidal self-organizing feature maps (TSOFM) best organized to object recognition. In: Proceedings of ICNN97. Volume 2., Houston, Texas (USA), IEEE (1997) 1341–1346

Multiple Segmentation of Moving Objects by Quasi-simultaneous Parametric Motion Estimation

Raúl Montoliu and Filiberto Pla

Dept. Lenguajes y Sistemas Informáticos
Jaume I Univerisity, Campus Riu Sec s/n 12071 Castellón, Spain
{montoliu,pla}@uji.es
http://www.vision.uji.es

Abstract. This paper presents a new framework for the motion segmentation and estimation task on sequences of two grey images without a priori information of the number of moving regions present in the sequence. The proposed algorithm combines temporal information, by using an accurate Generalized Least-Squares Motion Estimation process and spatial information by using an inlier/outlier classification process which classifies regions of pixels, in a first step, and the pixels directly, in a second step, into the different motion models present in the sequence. The performance of the algorithm has been tested on synthetic and real images with multiple objects undergoing different types of motion.

1 Introduction

Segmentation of moving objects in a video sequence is basic task for several applications of computer vision, e.g. a video monitoring system, intelligent-highway system, tracking, airport safety, surveillance tasks and so on. In this paper, Motion Segmentation, also called spatial-temporal segmentation, refers to labelling pixels which are associated with different coherently moving objects or regions in a sequence of two images. Motion Estimation refers to assigning a motion vector to each region (or pixel) in an image.

Although the Motion Segmentation and Estimation problem can be formulated in many different ways ([4], [10], [5], [2]), we choose to approach this problem as a multi-structural parametric fitting problem. In this context, the segmentation problem is similar to robust statistical regression. The main difference is that robust statistical regression usually involves statistics for data having one target distribution and corrupted with random outliers. Motion segmentation problems usually have more than one population with distinct distributions and not necessarily with a population having absolute majority.

The problem of fitting an a priori known model to a set of noisy data (with random outliers) was studied in the statistical community for a number of decades. One important contribution was the Least Median of Squares (LMedS) robust estimator but it has the break down point of 50%. This means

F.J. Perales et al. (Eds.): IbPRIA 2003, LNCS 2652, pp. 572–579, 2003.

that LMedS technique needs the population recovered to have at least a majority of 50% (plus 1). Other robust estimators have been developed in order to overcome this problem, which is frequently encountered in different computer vision tasks. They are Adaptive Least k-th Order residual (ALKS) [6] and Minimum Unbiased Scale Estimator (MUSE) [7]. These techniques minimize the k-th order statistic of the square residuals where the optimum value for the k is determined from the data. The problem of both techniques is the estimation of the correct value of k suffers high computation effort. Bab-Hadiashar and Suter presented a method named Selective Statistical Estimator (SSE) [1] which is a variation of the Least K-th order statistic data regression where the user proposes the value k as the lower limit of the size populations one is interested in. All the Motion Segmentation LKS-based algorithms start selecting an initial model using random sampling, and classifying all the pixels into this model using a scale measure. With the remaining pixels the process is repeated until all the pixel have been classified. The main problem of these algorithms is that there are frequently pixels that can be more suitable to belong to a model but they have been classified in an earlier model.

Danuser and Stricker [3] presented a similar framework for parametric model fitting. Their algorithm has a fitting step that is one component of the algorithm which also collect model inliers, detects data outliers and determines the a priori unknown total number of meaningful models in the data. They apply a quasi simultaneous application of a general Least Squares fitting while classifying observations in the different parametric data models. They applied their algorithm to multiple lines and planes fitting tasks. The most important advantages with respect to LKS-based algorithms are the use of an exchange step, that permits change of observations among models, and the use of a inliers/outliers classification process, which increases the accuracy of the segmentation.

In [8] a quasi-simultaneous motion segmentation and estimation method based on a parametric model fitting algorithm was presented. The method accurately estimates the affine motion parameters using a generalized least squares fitting process. It also classifies the pixels into the motion models present in two consecutive frames. This algorithm uses each pixel of the image as observation. It suffers from problems of isolated points because it does not use neighbourhood information and need given good initial models to obtain the final motion segmentation. Nevertheless, it indicates that the quasi-simultaneous application of the inliers/outliers classification algorithm and the accurate motion estimator can be useful to be applied in Motion Segmentation tasks.

This paper presents a Motion Segmentation and Estimation algorithm that, in a first step uses regions of pixels as observations in order to obtain good initial models that in a second step will be improved using each pixel as observation. The use of regions in the first step makes the segmentation more spatial consistent. In addition, the algorithm uses neighbourhood constraints to collect new inliers to the model, only regions (or pixels) that are neighbour of the model are considered to be inliers. This algorithm overcomes the need of a good enough previous segmentation of the models (they are obtained in the first step) and allows extracting the models without a priori information of the number of moving regions present in the sequence.

The rest of the paper is organized as follows: Section 2 explains the complete Motion Segmentation and Estimation algorithm. Section 3 presents a set of experiments in order to verify the results obtained with our approach. Finally, some conclusions drawn from this work are described.

2   Algorithm Outline

In this paper we use the term **Model** as a structure with two elements, the first is a parametric motion vector and the second is a list of regions of the image that support the parametric motion vector. We refer as **Region** to a set of pixels with grey-level coherence.

The input of the algorithm are two consecutive images of a sequence, the first one I_1 captured at time t and the second one I_2 captured at time $t + 1$. The output of the algorithm are a motion-based segmentated image I_s and a list of motion parameters corresponding at each region in I_s. For the sake of clarity, we describe the first part of the proposed algorithm in 6 steps:

1. **Preliminaries**: In this step, I_2 is segmented using a given grey level segmentation algorithm. The regions obtained are used as input of the algorithm. An adjacency graph of the previous segmentation is created. In addition the spatial derivates of the images I_1 and I_2 are estimated.
    The purpose of the grey-level segmentation process is to classify the pixels into regions. Our Motion Segmentation algorithm requires that each segmented region should not have pixels belonging to more than one final motion models. Any grey level segmentation algorithm that wherever possible tries to fulfil the previous constraint can be used.
2. **Get Initial Model**: The aim of this process is find the best possible start point to the global Motion Segmentation and Estimation algorithm. A good initial model is make up of a set of regions that have a high likelihood to belong to the same model. The process starts selecting a region randomly. A model with this region and its neighbours is formed. The motion is estimated for this model using the process in subsection 2.1. A goodness measure GM is calculated for this model. The previous step is repeated q times. The model with the best goodness measure is selected as the initial model.
    The goodness measure is calculated using the following expression: $GM = ((1 - l_{avg}) * 2 + (l_{best} - l_{worst}))$ where l_{avg} is the average of the likelihood $L_{M_n}(R)$ for each region R using the motion model M_n (see point 3), l_{best} is the highest likelihood of the regions and l_{worst} is the lowest likelihood of the regions. Therefore, the best initial model is the one which has the less GM.
3. **Improve the Model**: An iterative classification process is started in order to find the inliers and to reject outliers between the k regions that make up the initial model. With the set of resulting regions, we start another

classification process with the neighbours of the last inserted regions not yet processed. This process continues until there are not more new neighbour regions to be processed.

The loop of the inliers/outliers classification consists of:

(a) Estimate the motion parameters using all the pixels belonging the regions of the model (see subsection 2.1).

(b) Look for outliers into the regions of the model, if there are outliers, improve the motion parameters. A region R is considered outlier (with respect to model M_n) if the likelihood of region R belonging to a model M_n is lower than a threshold.

(c) Test each outlier if it can be now considered inlier according the new estimated parameters. If there are new inliers, the parameters are improved again. A region R is considered inlier (with respect to model M_n) if the likelihood of the region R belonging to a model M_n is higher than a threshold.

(d) Go to step b and repeat until there are not changes in the set of regions of the model.

In order to estimate a likelihood of a region R belonging to a model M_n, the next expressions are used:

$$L_{M_n}(R) = (\sum_{p_i \in R} L_{M_n}(p_i))/N_R$$

$$L_{M_n}(p_i) = e^{-0.5*\frac{F^2_{M_n}(p_i)}{\sigma_2}}$$

$$(1)$$

where N_R is the number of pixels of the region R. For each pixel p_i belonging to the region R the likelihood $L_{M_n}(p_i)$ of the pixel belonging to a model M_n is calculated. This likelihood ([2]) has been modelled as a Gaussian like function where $F_{M_n}(p_i)$ is the residual for the pixel p_i of the objective function using the motion parametric vector of the model M_m.

4. **Exchange of Regions**: If a valid model M_n has been extracted, then a region exchange procedure is started. The goal of this procedure is to reclassify regions that have been captured by an early model M_m where $m < n$. A region is moved if it lies closer to the new extracted model and there is a neighbour relationship between the region and the new model. If all the regions of the model M_m lie closer to the new Model M_n then the model M_m is deleted. When for each region of model M_m we can not decide if it lies closer to the model M_m or to the model M_n, then the models are merged, that is, it is considered both models have similar motion parameters.

5. **Repeat**: Go to step 2 and repeat the same process with another initial model if any. If there is any problem estimating the motion of some model, e.g. not enough texture information, not enough number of observations, etc., the regions of this model are moved to a set called *regions with problems* (RWP).

6. **End**: When all possible models have been extracted, the models that only have one region are tested in order to try to merge them with their neighbour

models. In addition, each region in the RWP set is tested in order to move it into some of the models in its neighbourhood.

At the end of the first part of the algorithm, a set of NM motion models have been extracted. Each motion model is made up of a vector of parametric motion models and a set of regions which support the motion. Our Motion Segmentation algorithm requires that each region from the given grey-level segmentation should not have pixels belonging to more than one final motion model. It is very likely that some regions will not fulfill this constraint. The second part of the algorithm is performed in order to improve motion segmentation in these regions. In this step, instead of using a region of pixels as observation, each pixel is considered as observation. This process consists of:

1. **Find Outliers**: For each extracted model M_n $(n = 1 \ldots NM)$, find all the pixels that can be considered as outliers. They are the pixels p_i which their likelihood respect to the model M_n, $L_{M_n}(p_i)$ is less than a threshold. All the outlier pixels are included in a set, together with the pixels belonging to the region which have been considered outliers in the previous part.
2. **Improve Parameters**: The motion parameters for the motion models that have new outliers are improved (see subsection 2.1).
3. **Find Inliers**: For each outlier, test if it can be included in some of the motion models. A pixel p_i will be included in the model with the greatest likelihood $L_{M_n}(p_i)$, $n = 1 \ldots NM$, if it is bigger than a threshold and there is a neighbourhood relationship between the pixel p_i and the model M_n.
4. **Improve Parameters**: The motion parameters for the motion models that have new inliers are improved (see subsection 2.1).
5. **Repeat**: Repeat 1 to 4 while there are changes in the set of pixels.

At the end of the two parts of the algorithm the pixels have been classified into the different motion models corresponding to the moving objects in the scene. The pixels that could not be included in any model will be considered as outliers.

2.1   Motion Estimation

The Generalized Least Squares (GLS) algorithm is used in order to obtain the motion parameters of a model. The GLS algorithm [3] is based on minimizing an objective function O over a set S of r observation vectors, $S = \{L_1, \ldots, L_r\}$.

$$O = \sum_{L_i \in S} (F_i(\chi, L_i))^2 \qquad (2)$$

where $\chi = (\chi^1, \ldots, \chi^p)$ is a vector of p motion parameters and L_i is a vector of n observation $L_i = (L_i^1, \ldots, L_i^n)$, $i = 1 \ldots r$.

The equation (2) is non-linear, but it can be linearized using the Taylor expansion and neglecting higher order terms. This implies that an iterative solution has to be found. At each iteration, the algorithm estimates $\Delta\chi$, that improves the parameters as follows: $\chi_{t+1} = \chi_t + \Delta\chi$. The increment $\Delta\chi$ is calculated (see [3]) using the following expressions:

$$\Delta X = \left(A^T(BB^T)^{-1}A\right)^{-1} A^T(BB^T)^{-1}W$$

$$B = \begin{pmatrix} B_1 & 0 & 0 & 0 \\ 0 & B_2 & 0 & 0 \\ \cdots & \cdots & \cdots & \cdots \\ 0 & 0 & 0 & B_r \end{pmatrix}_{(r\times(r\times n))}$$

$$A = \begin{pmatrix} A_1 \\ A_2 \\ \cdots \\ A_r \end{pmatrix}_{(r\times p)} \qquad W = \begin{pmatrix} w_1 \\ w_2 \\ \cdots \\ w_r \end{pmatrix}_{(r\times 1)} \tag{3}$$

$$B_i = \left(\frac{\partial F_i(\chi_t, L_i)}{\partial L_i^1}, \frac{\partial F_i(\chi_t, L_i)}{\partial L_i^2}, \cdots, \frac{\partial F_i(\chi_t, L_i)}{\partial L_i^n} \right)_{(1\times n)}$$

$$A_i = \left(\frac{\partial F_i(\chi_t, L_i)}{\partial \chi^1}, \frac{\partial F_i(\chi_t, L_i)}{\partial \chi^2}, \cdots, \frac{\partial F_i(\chi_t, L_i)}{\partial \chi^p} \right)_{(1\times p)}$$

$$w_i = -F_i(\chi_t, L_i)$$

In motion estimation problems ([9]) the objective function is based on the assumption that the grey level of all the pixels of a region remains constant between two consecutive images. The motion parameters vector, χ, depends on the motion model being used. For each point i, the vector of observation L_i has three elements: column, row and grey level of second image at these coordinates. The objective function is expressed as follows:

$$O = \sum_{L_i \in S} (F_i(\chi, L_i))^2 = \sum_{L_i \in S} (I_1(x_i', y_i') - I_2(x_i, y_i))^2 \tag{4}$$

where $I_1(x_i', y_i')$ is the grey level of the first image in the sequence at the transformed point x_i', y_i', and $I_2(x_i, y_i)$ are the grey level of the second image in the sequence at point x_i, y_i. Here, $L_i = (x_i, y_i, I_2(x_i, y_i))$.

The affine motion model is used in this work, which is able to cope with translations, scaling, rotation and shear of images and is defined with a vector of $\chi = (a_1, b_1, c_1, a_2, b_2, c_2)$.

3   Experimental Results

In order to show the performance of the approach presented, two types of experiments have been carry out. In the first experiment, synthetic sequences have been used, where the final motion segmentation and the motion parameters of each model are known. In the second experiment real scenes are used, where the final motion segmentation and the motion parameters are unknown.

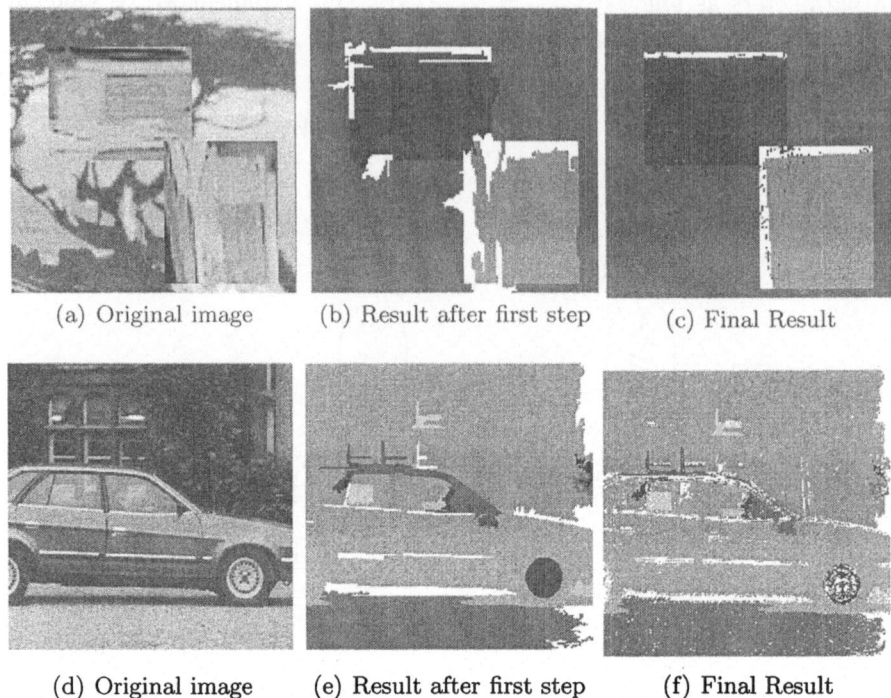

(a) Original image   (b) Result after first step   (c) Final Result

(d) Original image   (e) Result after first step   (f) Final Result

Fig. 1. Second Image and Results obtained with synthetic and real sequences

Figure 1a shows the second image of an example of synthetic sequence. In this synthetic sequence three different motion models can be found. The first one is the background, which performs a null-motion. The second motion model performs a change of scale and the third one corresponds to a rotational motion. Figure 1d shows the second image of an example of real sequence.

Figures 1b,c,e,f show the result after the first step of the algorithm and the final results for both sequences. The white pixels in figures 1b and 1e, are the ones that have not been classified in any model. These regions correspond mainly to areas that include pixels from different models.

Figures 1c and 1f show the segmentation performed after the second step showing how segmentation has been improved in previous regions. Now, white pixels are the ones considered as outliers. They are mainly pixels belonging to occluded areas due to the motion and pixels where our algorithm could not estimate the motion due to lack of texture or to the presence of too large motions.

4   Conclusions

In this paper, a motion segmentation and estimation algorithm has been presented, which can extract different moving regions present in the scene quasi-simultaneously and without a priori information of the number of moving objects. The main properties of our approach are:

- A GLS Motion Estimation is used, which produces accurate estimation of the motion parameters.
- A classification process which collects inliers, rejects outliers and exchanges regions among models allows to improve motion segmentation.
- It uses, in the first step, regions of pixels and neighbourhood information, that improves the spatial consistency and provides a good initial point to start the second step of the algorithm, which using pixels as observations improves the segmentation in the regions.
- The pixels considered as outliers are mainly pixels belonging to occluded areas due to the motion, thus, detection of outliers provides valuable information about occluded areas.

Future work must study hierarchical techniques in order to improve the speed of the algorithm and to cope with larger motion. The possibility of using sequences with more than two images will be also studied.

References

[1] Alireza Bad-Hadiashar and David Suter. Robust motion segmentation using rank ordering estimators. In *Third Asian Coference on Computer Vision ACCV98, Honk Kong*, 1998.
[2] M. Bober and J. V. Kittler. Estimation of complex multimodal motion: An approach based on robust statistics and hough transform. *IVC*, 12(10):661–668, December 1994.
[3] G. Danuser and M. Stricker. Parametric model-fitting: From inlier characterization to outlier detection. *PAMI*, 20(3):263–280, March 1998.
[4] M. Irani, B. Rousso, and S. Peleg. Computing occluding and transparent motion. *IJVC*, 12(1):5–16, February 1994.
[5] Jong Bae Kim and Hang Joon Kim. Effient region-based motion segmentation for a video monitoring system. *Pattern Recognition Letters*, 24:113–128, 2003.
[6] Kil-Moo Lee, Peter Meer, and Rae-Hong Park. Robust adaptive segmentation of range images. *IEEE Transactions on Pattern Analysis and Machine Intelligence*, 20(2):200–205, 1998.
[7] James V. Miller and Charles V. Stewart. Muse: Robust surface fitting using unbiased scale estimates. In *Computer Vision and Pattern Recognition 1996*, pages 300–306, 1996.
[8] R. Montoliu and F. Pla. Multiple parametric motion model estimation and segmentation. In *ICIP01, 2001 International Conference on Image Processing*, volume II, pages 933–936, October 2001.
[9] R. Montoliu, V. J. Traver, and F. Pla. Log-polar mapping in generalized least-squares motion estimation. In *Proccedings of 2002 IASTED International Conference on Visualization, Imaging, and Image Processing (VIIP'2002)*, pages 656–661, September 2002.
[10] F. Odone, A. Fusiello, and E. Trucco. Robust motion segmentation for content-based video coding. In *RIAO 2000 6th Conference on Content-Based Multimedia Information Access*, pages 594–601, 2000.

Fusion of Color and Shape for Object Tracking under Varying Illumination

Francesc Moreno-Noguer, Juan Andrade-Cetto, and Alberto Sanfeliu

Institut de Robòtica Industrial, Universitat Politècnica de Catalunya
Llorens Artigas 4-6, 08028, Barcelona, Spain
{fmoreno,cetto,asanfeliu}@iri.upc.es

Abstract. In this paper a new technique to perform tracking in cluttered scenarios with varying illumination conditions is presented. The robustness of the approach lies in the integration of appearance and structural information of the object. The fusion is done using the CONDENSATION algorithm that formulates multiple hypothesis about the estimation of the object's color distribution and validates them taking into account the contour information of the object.

1 Introduction

Color represents a visual feature commonly used for object detection and tracking systems, specially in the field of human-computer interaction [1][5]. For such cases in which the environment is relatively simple, with controlled lighting conditions and an uncluttered background, color can be considered a robust cue. The problem appears when we are dealing with scenes with varying illumination conditions and confusing background. For example, in the upper row of Fig. 1 we can see some frames from a motion sequence of a Lambertian surface, in which the object of interest revolves around the light source. In the lower row, we show the corresponding color distributions, (in RGB color space) that belong to the reddish rectangle. Last image shows the path followed by the color distribution for the entire sequence.

Thus, an important challenge for any color tracking system to work in real unconstrained environments, is the ability to accommodate variations in the amount of source light reflected from the tracked surface.

The choice of different color spaces like HSL, normalized color rgb ([10],[7]), or the color space $(B - G, G - R, R + G + B)$, can give some robustness against varying illumination, highlights, interreflections or changes in surface orientation (see [2] for an analysis of different color spaces). But none of these transformations is general enough to cope with arbitrary changes in illumination.

Instead of searching for color constancy, other approaches try to adapt the color distribution over time. In [6], for example, Gaussian mixtures models are used to estimate densities of color, and under the assumption that lighting conditions change smoothly over time, the models are recursively adapted. In [8], the color distribution is parameterized as a random vector and a second order

F.J. Perales et al. (Eds.): IbPRIA 2003, LNCS 2652, pp. 580–588, 2003.
© Springer-Verlag Berlin Heidelberg 2003

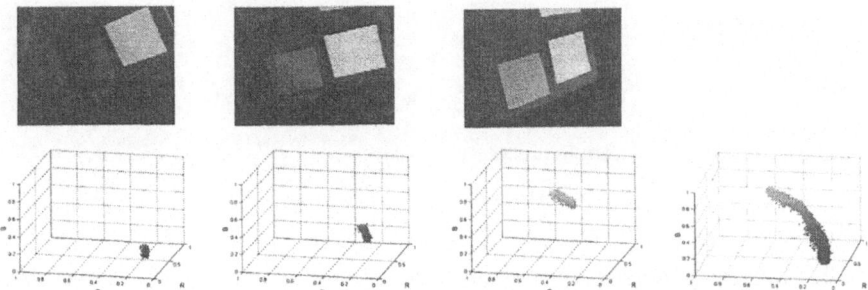

Fig. 1. Example frames of a time-varying color illuminant

Markov model is used to predict the evolution of the corresponding color histogram. These techniques perform much better than the mere change of color space representation, but have the drawback that they do not check for the goodness of the adaptation, which can lead to a failure.

The fusion of several visual modules using different criteria offers more reliability than methods that only use one feature. In this sense, the real-time head tracking system presented in [1], models the head of a person by an ellipse and uses intensity gradients and color histograms to update the head position over time. In [5], color histograms are fused with stereovision information in order to dynamically adapt the size of the tracked head. These real time applications are constrained to tracking of elliptical shapes.

In this paper, we present a new methodology that addresses the problems presented by the approaches described above, that results in a robust tracking system able to cope with cluttered scenes and varying illumination conditions. The robustness of our method lies in the fusion of color and shape information, which are iteratively adapted using the CONDENSATION algorithm [3].

Section 2 presents the main features of our method and the advantages of fusing color and shape. In Section 3 a detailed description of the method is given. Results and conclusions are presented in Sections 4 and 5, respectively.

2   Overview

Before entering into a detailed description of the proposed method we give a short glimpse of its main features:

- **Integration of Color and Shape Information:**fusion of both vision modules makes our method appropriate to work in cluttered scenes. In Fig. 2 we can see an example of the power of this fusion in the tracking of a snail shell. Fig. 2b illustrates the clutter of the scene difficulting the tracking procedure when only using edge information. If the color distribution of the shell is known, the image can be segmented via color histograms [9] (see Fig. 2c), and use this information to discriminate many false edges (Fig. 2d).

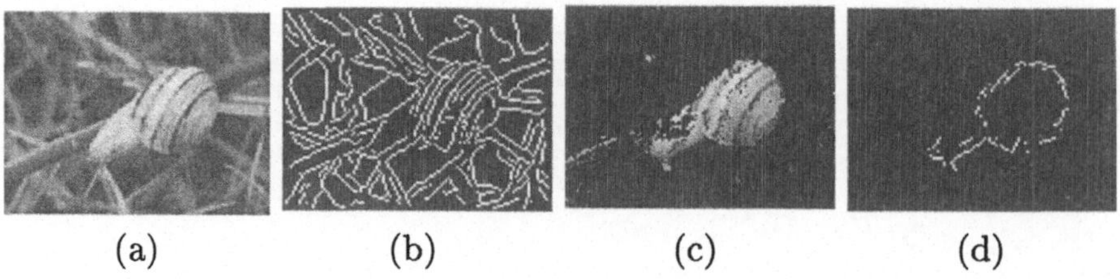

(a)   (b)   (c)   (d)

Fig. 2. Clutter in edge-map is reduced using the information from the object's color

- **Ability to Adapt Shape Deformation and Varying Illumination:** accommodation to varying illuminating conditions is needed to get a good color segmentation of the tracked object. As shown above (Fig. 2d), color segmentation is used to eliminate many false edges from the region of interest, simplifying a final stage of adapting a snake (maintaining affinity) to the contour of the object (assuming that the set of possible shapes of image contours do indeed form affine spaces). We introduce a restriction to the classical snake minimization procedure [4], to obtain affine deformations only. This feature makes our system robust to partial occlusions of the target.
- **Fusion of Color and Shape in a Probabilistic Framework:** the CON- DENSATION algorithm offers the appropriate framework to integrate both color and contour information, and to perform tracking of the object color distribution in color space, and that of the object contour in image space, both simultaneously. That is, using the predictive filter, multiple estimates of the object color distribution are formulated at each iteration. These estimates are weighted and updated taking into account the object shape, enabling the rejection of objects with similar color but different shape than the target. Finally, the best color distribution is used to segment the image and refine the object's contour.

3   The Tracking Algorithm

In this section a detailed description of the steps used in the method is presented. For ease of explanation these steps are divided as in the CONDENSATION algorithm (Fig. 3 shows the one dimensional case):

3.1   Parameterization and *pdf* of Color Distribution

It has been pointed out that an interesting feature of the presented method is that tracking is performed simultaneously in both color and image spaces. In fact, the element being directly tracked by the filter is the object color distribution C, that at time t is the collection of all image pixel color values I_t that belong to the target, i.e, $C_t = \{(R_i, G_i, B_i) \mid i = 1, \ldots, M_t\}$, where M_t is the number

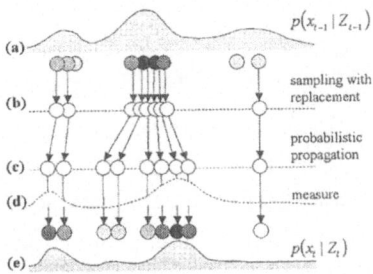

Fig. 3. One iteration of the CONDENSATION algorithm for the one-dimensional case. The weight of each sample is represented by its gray level

of object points at time t, and $0 \le R_i, G_i, B_i \le 1$ (we assume without loss of generality, that the color space is RGB, but it is extensible to any color space). As the set of object points can be arbitrarily high, the state vector $\mathbf{x}_t$ will be a parameterization of C_t with components (adapted from [8]) $\mathbf{x}_t = \left[\mathbf{m}_t^\mathsf{T}, \boldsymbol{\lambda}_t^\mathsf{T}, \theta_t, \phi_t\right]^\mathsf{T}$, where $\mathbf{m}_t = \left[\bar{R}, \bar{G}, \bar{B}\right]^\mathsf{T}$ is the centroid of C_t , $\boldsymbol{\lambda}_t = [\lambda_1, \lambda_2, \lambda_3]^\mathsf{T}$ are the magnitudes of the principal components of C_t; and θ_t, ϕ_t are the angles centered at $\mathbf{m}_t$ that align the two most significant principal components of C_t with respect to the principal components of C_{t-1} (see Fig. 4).

At time t, a set of N samples $\mathbf{s}_{t-1}^{(n)}$ $(n = 1, \ldots, N)$ of the form of $\mathbf{x}$, parameterizing N color distributions $C_{t-1}^{(n)}$ are available (step (a) from Fig. 3). Each distribution has an associated weight $\pi_{t-1}^{(n)}$. The whole set represents an approximation of the *a posteriori* density function $p\left(\mathbf{x}_{t-1}|\mathcal{Z}_{t-1}\right)$ (see Fig. 5), where $\mathcal{Z}_{t-1} = \{z_0, \ldots, z_{t-1}\}$ is the history of measurements.

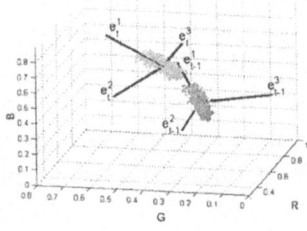

Fig. 4. Principal directions of two consecutive color distributions. The parameter θ_t is the angle that aligns $\mathbf{e}_{t-1}^1$ with respect to $\mathbf{e}_t^1$. The parameter ϕ_t is the angle that aligns $\mathbf{e}_{t-1}^2$ with respect to $\mathbf{e}_t^2$ after having rotated $\mathbf{e}_{t-1}^2$ an angle θ_t around the axis $\mathbf{e}_{t-1}^1 \times \mathbf{e}_t^1$

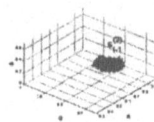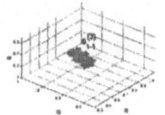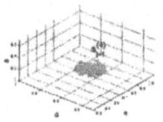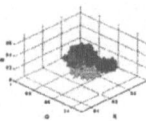

Fig. 5. Four samples of color distribution from the set $\left\{ s_{t-1}^{(n)} \right\}$ (in the last image, samples are shown together). Gray level is proportional to the sample weights. The set of all these distributions approximates the *a posteriori pdf* $p\left(\mathbf{x}_{t-1} | \mathcal{Z}_{t-1} \right)$

3.2 Sampling from $p\left(\mathbf{x}_{t-1} | \mathcal{Z}_{t-1} \right)$

The next step in the estimation of $p\left(\mathbf{x}_t | \mathcal{Z}_t \right)$ consists of sampling with replacement N times the set $\left\{ s_{t-1}^{(n)} \right\}$, where each element has probability $\pi_{t-1}^{(n)}$ of being chosen (step (b) from Fig. 3). This, will give us a new set $\left\{ s'^{(n)}_t \right\}$ of color distribution parameterizations. Those distributions having higher weights may be chosen several times, so the new set can have identical copies of elements. On the other hand, those distributions having lower weights may not be chosen (see Fig. 6a).

3.3 Probabilistic Propagation of Samples

Each sample $s'^{(n)}_t$ of the set is propagated (see Fig. 3c and Fig. 6a) according to the following dynamic model:

$$s_t^{(n)} = As'^{(n)}_t + B\mathbf{w}_t^{(n)}$$

where A is the deterministic part, assigned as a first order model describing the movement of an object with constant velocity. $B\mathbf{w}_t^{(n)}$ is the stochastic component, with $\mathbf{w}_t^{(n)}$ a vector of standard normal random variables with unit standard deviation, and BB^{T} is the process noise covariance. The parameters A and B are estimated a priori from a training sequence.

Each predicted sample $s_t^{(i)}$ represents the set of parameters defining the rigid transformations that will be used to warp the color distribution $\mathcal{C}'^{(i)}_t$ associated with the sample $s'^{(i)}_t$, in order to obtain the new estimated distribution $\mathcal{C}_t^{(i)}$ (with parameters $s_t^{(i)}$).

3.4 Measure and Weight

In this step, each element $s_t^{(n)}$ has to be weighted according to some measured features, and is precisely at this point where we integrate the structural information of the object's contour. From the propagated color distributions $\mathcal{C}_t^{(n)}$, we

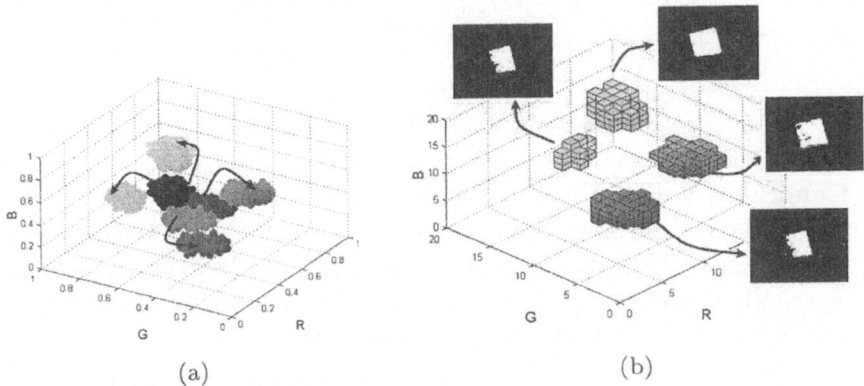

(a)   (b)

Fig. 6. (a) Sampling and probabilistic propagation from color distributions $C_t^{(n)}$, of Fig. 5. Observe that the sample having the highest weight has been chosen two times, while another sample with lower weight has not been chosen. (b) Construction of the histograms $\mathcal{H}_t^{(n)}$ and results of the corresponding segmentations $S_t^{(n)}$

construct the color histograms $\mathcal{H}_t^{(n)}$ with $\mathcal{R} \cdot \mathcal{G} \cdot \mathcal{B}$ bins:

$$\mathcal{H}_t^{(n)}(r,g,b) = \#\left\{(R,G,B) \in C_t^{(n)} \mid \frac{r-1}{\mathcal{R}} < R \leq \frac{r}{\mathcal{R}}, \frac{g-1}{\mathcal{G}} < G \leq \frac{g}{\mathcal{G}}, \frac{b-1}{\mathcal{B}} < B \leq \frac{b}{\mathcal{B}}\right\}$$

and where $r = [1,\ldots,\mathcal{R}]$, $g = [1,\ldots,\mathcal{G}]$, $b = [1,\ldots,\mathcal{B}]$, with $\{r,g,b,\mathcal{R},\mathcal{G},\mathcal{B}\} \in \mathbb{N}$. This histogram is used to generate a segmentation $S_t^{(n)}$ from the entire image I_t. That is, given a pixel $I_t(u,v)$ with color value (R,G,B) the corresponding value of the segmented image $S_t^{(n)}(u,v)$ will be assigned a value 1 if $H_t^{(n)}(r,g,b) > 0$, where $r = \lfloor R \cdot \mathcal{R} \rfloor$, $g = \lfloor G \cdot \mathcal{G} \rfloor$ and $b = \lfloor B \cdot \mathcal{B} \rfloor$ (Fig. 6b).

The goal is to assign higher weights to the samples $s_t^{(n)}$ generating "better" segmentations of the tracked object. To this end, simple morphological operations are performed on $S_t^{(n)}$ to extract a blob corresponding to the segmented object (Fig. 7a). After adjusting a snake along the contour of this blob, the weight assigned to $s_t^{(n)}$ is computed according to the function:

$$\pi_t^{(n)} = e^{-\frac{\rho^2}{2\sigma^2}}$$

and $\rho = \mu_1(1 - \Phi_{affine}) + \mu_2(1 - \Phi_{area}) + \mu_3(1 - \Phi_{quality})$.

Functions Φ_{affine}, Φ_{area} and $\Phi_{quality}$ return a value in the range $[0,1]$ and represent a measure of the following features:

- **Affine Similarity**: let $\nabla S_t^{(n)}$ be a binary image of the edges of $S_t^{(n)}$, and r_{t-1} a collection of image points along the snake adjusted to the contour of the object in the iteration $t-1$. r_{t-1} is used as initialization of an affine snake $r_t^{(n)}$

that is adjusted to $\nabla S_t^{(n)}$. Φ_{affine}, measures the similarity between $r_t^{(n)} = (u_t^{i,(n)}, v_t^{i,(n)})$ $(i = 1, ..., N_r)$, and $\nabla S_t^{(n)}$:

$$\Phi_{affine} = \frac{1}{N_r} \sum_{i=1}^{N_r} \nabla S_t^{(n)} \left(u_t^{i,(n)}, v_t^{i,(n)} \right)$$

- **Congruent Value of Area**: another factor to take into account when evaluating the goodness of the segmentation $S_t^{(n)}$ is how close is the area $Area_t^{(n)}$ of the snake $r_t^{(n)}$ to the predicted area $\widetilde{Area}_t = Area_{t-1} + \mu(Area_{t-1} - Area_{t-2})$, where $Area_{t-i}$ is the area of the refined snake at iteration $t - i$ (see Sect. 3.5). This is considered in the function:

$$\Phi_{area} = |\widetilde{Area}_t - Area_t^{(n)}| / \max \left\{ \widetilde{Area}_t, Area_t^{(n)} \right\}$$

- **Quality of the Segmentation**: the function $\Phi_{quality}$ is introduced to penalize those segmentations of "low" quality that present some holes into the area of the segmented object. $\Phi_{quality}$ is a linear function of the Euler number of the processed $S_t^{(n)}$.

Finally, the set of N weights $\pi_t^{(n)}$ associated to each of the samples $s_t^{(n)}$, represents an approximation to the *a posteriori* density function $p(\mathbf{x}_t | \mathcal{Z}_t)$.

3.5   Contour Updating

The last step of our algorithm, consists in refining the fitting of the object boundary, in order to obtain r_t. This is done by taking the contour of the segmented image corresponding to the best sample ($\nabla S_t^{(i)} \mid \pi_t^{(i)} \geq \pi_t^{(j)} \forall j \neq i, 1 \leq j \leq N$), and instead of adjusting the snake r_{t-1} to $\nabla S_t^{(i)}$, it is adjusted

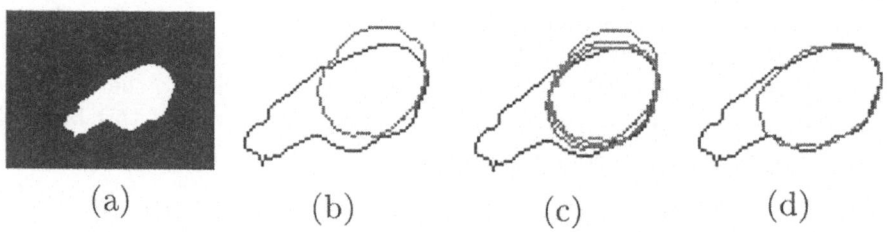

(a)   (b)   (c)   (d)

Fig. 7. (a) Segmented image $S_t^{(n)}$ after postprocessing operations (the example from Fig. 2) (b) The red curve is the initial snake (r_{t-1}). The black curve is the boundary ($\nabla S_t^{(n)}$) of the segmented image. (c) Intermediate steps of the affine snake fitting. (d) Final result of the snake fitting ($r_t^{(n)}$). Observe that if the deformations were not affine, the snake may have erroneously evolved to encompass the neck of the snail

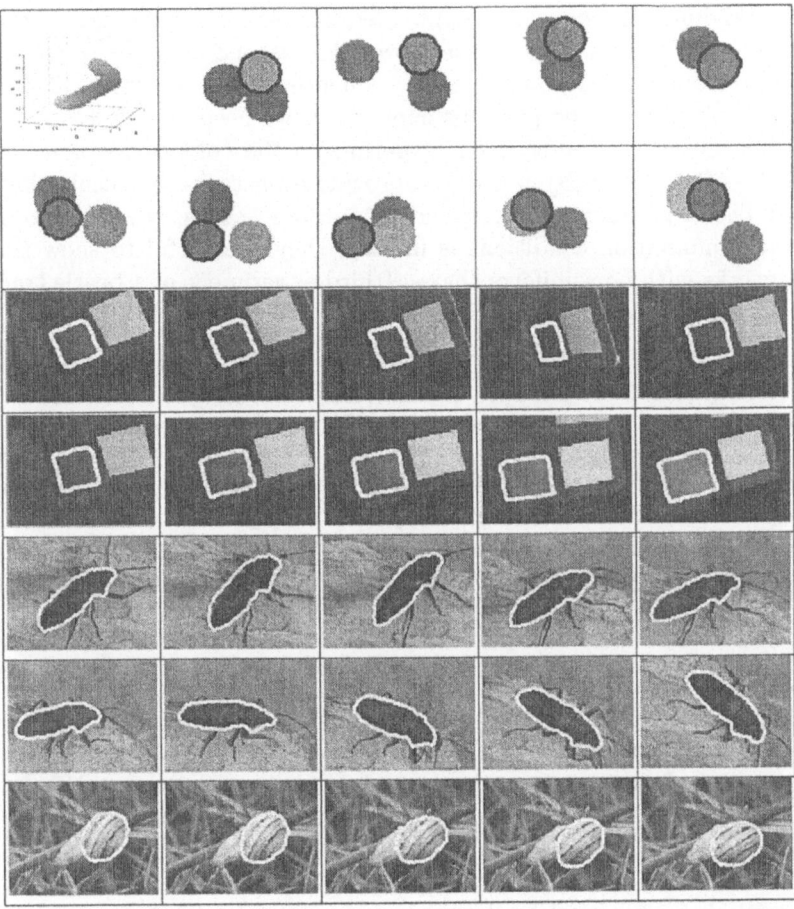

Fig. 8. Results of the 4 experiments

to $\nabla I_t^* = \nabla I_t \cdot dil(\nabla S_t^{(i)})$, where ∇I_t is the gradient of I_t, and the function $dil(\cdot)$, refers to a morphological dilate operation. ∇I_t^* is in fact the original edge image, from which all the clutter and disturbing edges have been eliminated (see Fig. 2).

4 Experimental Results

In this Section four sets of sequence results are presented (summarized in Fig. 8) to illustrate the robustness of our system under different conditions. As the algorithm has been implemented in an interpretative language (MATLAB), speed results will not be analyzed. Attention will be focused on the effectiveness of the method. In the first experiment we show how our system is able to accommodate color by applying it over a synthetic sequence of circles moving around and changing randomly its color. In the upper left image of Fig. 8 the path of the color distributions for the tracked circle is shown. The second experiment (tracking of a colored rectangle) corresponds to the sequence introduced in Fig 2. It has to be pointed out that in the previous experiment we used the RGB color space, but in the present and subsequent experiments the color space used was the $(B - G, G - R, R + G + B)$ in order to provide robustness to specular higlights. The last two experiments, correspond to outdoor scenes, where although the change in illumination conditions is limited, they are useful to show that our method works with non-uniform shapes (third experiment of a beatle tracking), and in cluttered scenarios (fourth experiment of a snail tracking).

5   Conclusions

In this paper we have presented a new approach to the color object tracking under cluttered and varying illumination environments that dynamically accommodates the color distribution and shape of the object. The robustness of the method lies in the fusion of both modules in the probabilistic framework provided by the CONDENSATION algorithm. Results demonstrate the reliability of the tracking system in several experiments.

Acknowledgements

This work was supported by CICYT projects DPI2001-2223 and DPI2000-1352-C02-01, and by a fellowship from the Spanish Ministry of Science and Technology.

References

1. Birchfield, S.: Elliptical head tracking using intensity gradients and color histograms. CVPR. (1998), 232–237.
2. Gevers, T., Smeulders A.: Color Based Object Recognition. Pattern Recognition. (1999), 32, 453–464.
3. Isard, M., Blake, A.: Condensation-Conditional Density Propagation for Visual Tracking. Int. J. Computer Vision. (1998), 28(1), 5–28.
4. Kass, M., Witkin, A., Terzopoulos, D.: Snakes: Active Contour Models. Int. J. Computer Vision. (1987), 1(4), 321–331.
5. Moreno, F., Tarrida, A., Andrade-Cetto, J., Sanfeliu, A.: 3D Real-Time Head Tracking Fusing Color Histograms and Stereovision. ICPR. (2002), 368–371.
6. Raja, Y., Mckenna, S. J., Gong, S.: Tracking and Segmenting People in Varying Lighting Conditions using Colour. AFG. (1998), 228–233.
7. Schwerdt, K., Crowley, J.: Robust Face Tracking using Color. AFG. (2000), 90–95.
8. Sigal, L., Sclaroff, S., Athitsos, V.: Estimation and Prediction of Evolving Color Distributions for Skin Segmentation Under Varying Illumination. CVPR. (2000).
9. Swain, M., Ballard, D.: Color Indexing. Int. J. Computer Vision. (1991), 7(1), 11–32.
10. Yang, J., Lu, W., Waibel, A.: Skin-color Modeling and Adaption. ACCV. (1997), 687–694.

Extending Fast Nearest Neighbour Search Algorithms for Approximate k-NN Classification

Francisco Moreno-Seco, Luisa Micó, and Jose Oncina*

Dept. Lenguajes y Sistemas Informáticos
Universdad de Alicante, E-03071 Alicante, Spain
{paco,mico,oncina}@dlsi.ua.es

Abstract. The nearest neighbour (NN) and k-nearest neighbour (k-NN) classification rules have been widely used in pattern recognition due to its simplicity and good behaviour. Exhaustive nearest neighbour search can become unpractical when facing large training sets, high dimensional data or expensive similarity measures. In the last years a lot of NN search algorithms have been developed to overcome those problems, and many of them are based on traversing a data structure (usually a tree) and selecting several candidates until the nearest neighbour is found.

In this paper we propose a new classification rule that makes use of those selected (and usually discarded) prototypes. Several fast and widely known NN search algorithms have been extended with this rule obtaining classification results similar to those of a k-NN classifier without extra computational overhead.

Keywords: Nearest Neighbour, Classification Rule, Pattern Recognition.

1 Introduction

The nearest neighbour (NN) rule classifies an unknown sample into the class of its nearest neighbour according to some similarity measure (a *distance*). Despite its simplicity, classification accuracy is usually enough for many tasks. However, some tasks may require finding the k nearest neighbours in order to improve classification, thus the NN rule has been generalized to the k-NN rule [3]. Many classification tasks represent data as vectors and use one of the Minkowsky metrics as the distance, usually the L_2 (Euclidean distance). However, there are other tasks where a vector representation is not natural, and thus other distance measures are used: string distance, tree distance, etc.

Although initially used in pattern recognition, the NN rules have been also of interest for other fields such as data mining and information retrieval, which

---

* The authors wish to thank the Spanish CICyT for partial support of this work through project TIC2000–1703-CO3-02.

F.J. Perales et al. (Eds.): IbPRIA 2003, LNCS 2652, pp. 589–597, 2003.

usually involves searching in very large databases and facing with high dimensionality data. Whenever the classification task requires large training sets, expensive distance measures or high dimensionality, the simple exhaustive search for the NN becomes unpractical. To overcome some of these problems, a large number of fast NN search algorithms [5, 4, 18, 16, 2, 14] have been developed, and most of them can be easily extended to find the k-NN. However, the requirement of finding exactly the k-NN involves higher computing effort (dependent on the value of k).

Recently developed algorithms are suitable for any kind of representation which allows to define a distance that holds the properties of a metric, that is, they do not make use of the coordinates of the prototype. Several fast NN search algorithms are based on or can be viewed in an approximation and elimination framework [15]: a training prototype is selected as the current nearest neighbour, and then it is used to prune the training set and find the next candidate to nearest neighbour, until the training set is completely traversed or pruned. Then, the current candidate to nearest neighbour is actually the nearest neighbor.

The structure of the paper is as follows: in the next section we shall briefly describe the new classification rule. Then, we will show the results of this rule when applied to various NN search algorithms in experiments with synthetic and real data. Finally, we will conclude and outline some future work.

2   The k-NSN Classification Rule

In this paper we propose a simple but powerful extension for any approximation-elimination based NN search algorithm: when looking for the nearest neighbour, a number of candidates to nearest neighbour are selected until the actual nearest neighbour is found. We store the k nearest selected neighbours (k-NSN); at the end, the sample is classified by majority voting using these neighbours (which include the nearest neighbour). This technique can be considered a new classification rule which requires very little computational effort over a NN search (storing the k nearest selected neighbours). In addition, as we shall see in the next section, this rule achieves classification results very similar to those of the k-NN rule. Obviously, if this rule is applied to an exhaustive NN search it yields to the k-NN rule. This rule raises up as an extension of our previous work on the LAESA algorithm [13, 11].

Approximation and elimination search algorithms are usually based on the following idea: during preprocessing, a data structure is built to allow pruning of the training set. During classification, a candidate to nearest neighbour is selected and stored, and its distance to the sample is computed. This distance is used to prune the training set (using the data structure) and maybe to select a new candidate. This process ends when all the training set has been pruned or selected. Extending such an algorithm to find the k-NN is usually simple: the distance used to prune the training set is the distance to the kth nearest neighbour found so far. This involves less pruning and more distances to compute,

Table 1. Fast NN search algorithms which have been extended with the k-NSN rule

ALGORITHM	Author(s)
kd-tree	Friedman *et al.*[4]
FN75	Fukunaga and Narendra [5]
vp-tree	Yianilos [18]
AESA	Vidal [16]
LAESA	Micó *et al.* [13]
TLAESA	Micó *et al.* [12]
GNAT	Brin [2]

which derives in an additional computational overhead, always dependent on the value of k.

The k-NSN rule does not involve more significant overhead[1] than a typical NN search, and usually achieves similar results as a k-NN search. Of course, there is a drawback in our approach: the value of k may not be augmented indefinitely to improve classification rates; beyond a certain (big) value of k the rates start to worsen.

3   Experiments

We have performed several series of experiments in order to test the application of the k-NSN rule to some fast NN search algorithms (see table 1). All these algorithms fit in an approximation and elimination framework, and all are suited for general metric spaces except kd-tree, which requires point coordinates. The algorithms of AESA family (AESA, LAESA, TLAESA) focus on reducing the number of distance computations, thus are best suitable for expensive distances. The vp-tree and GNAT were developed to face large training sets and/or high dimensionality of data, and thus the number of distance computations is important but it is not its main goal.

Two sets of experiments have been performed: first, a set of synthetic data experiments to test the performance of the rule in a widely known environment. Then, some tests have been performed with several real data tasks. In both cases our main goal was to study the error rates of these algorithms using the k-NSN rule and to compare them with the k-NN error rates.

---

[1] The simplest implementation is to keep sorted an array of k elements each time a distance is computed. The extra time complexity over the NN search is $O(ck)$, where c is the number of computed distances. Although it is possible to reduce this time complexity with a heap, this overhead is almost negligible when compared to the overhead of computing c distances.

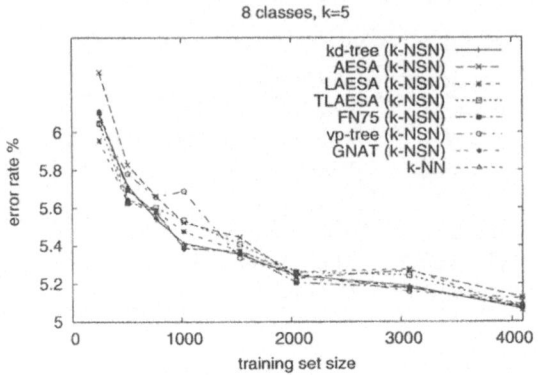

Fig. 1. Comparison between k-NN and k-NSN classifiers, for $k = 5$

3.1   Experiments with Synthetic Data

For these experiments we have generated Gaussian data from 4 and 8 classes of dimensionality 10 using the algorithm for generating clustered data in [8]. Tests have been performed for several values of k: 5, 11 and 17, and with training sets of growing size (from 256 to 4096). Test set had always 1024 prototypes. Also, 16 different train/test sets of each size were generated in order to obtain more sound results.

Figure 1 shows the error rates of these classifiers with data from 8 classes for $k = 5$ (results for 4 classes data were similar), and figure 2 plots the same results for $k = 17$ but including the NN error rate just to show the difference with respect to k-NN and k-NSN rates. These results show that the differences in error rates are negligible for k-NSN and k-NN classifiers, and are better than those of an NN classifier.

In order to study the behaviour of the k-NSN rule as the value of k increases another experiment was performed keeping the train and test sizes to 2048 and 1024 respectively. All the algorithms were run with 16 different train/test sets, and the average results are shown in figure 3. As can be seen in that figure, even for high values of k most of the k-NSN classifiers still obtain classification rates comparable to those of the k-NN classifier. Algorithms from AESA family seem to be very sensitive to an increase in the value of k. This may be due to the fact that they compute very few distances with respect to the others (i.e. they select less candidates to nearest neighbour). However, this question should be studied more carefully and we plan to do it in the future. Finally, note that with (almost) the same computational effort of finding the nearest neighbour, the error rates obtained with k-NSN are much better than NN rates and comparable to those of a k-NN classifier.

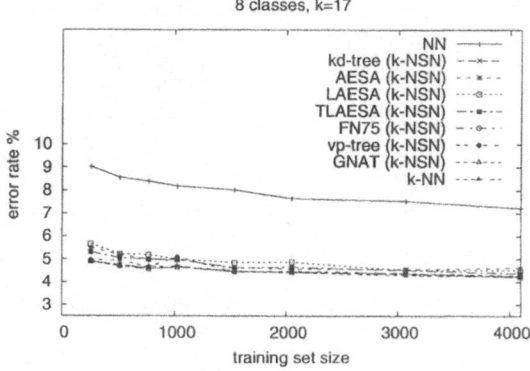

Fig. 2. Nearest neighbour error rate compared to k-NN and k-NSN

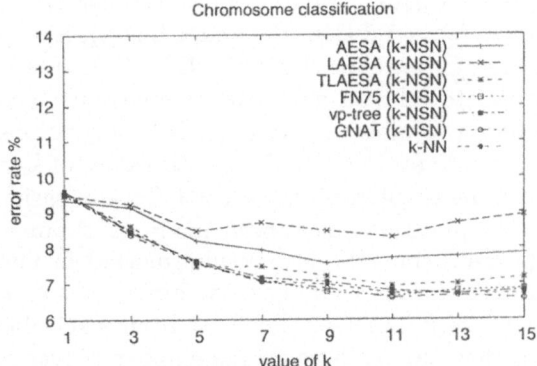

Fig. 3. Comparison between k-NN and k-NSN classifiers as k increases

3.2 Experiments with Real Data

We have performed experiments with two different data sets: first we have tested our rule with chromosome data [9, 7, 6] and then with the PHONEME database from the ROARS ESPRIT project [1].

The chromosome database contains 4400 samples coded as strings, and we have chosen to use the Levenshtein distance [17, 19] for this task (the kd-tree has not been tested with this database due to this feature). The database has been divided into two sets of 2200 samples each, and two experiments have been performed using one of them for training and the other one for test. Figure 4 shows the average error rates of k-NN and k-NSN classifiers as the value of k increases. There is a parameter for LAESA and TLAESA (see [13, 12] for more details), the number of *base prototypes*, which has been set to 40, which it is not probably its optimal value. However, the search for this optimal value is

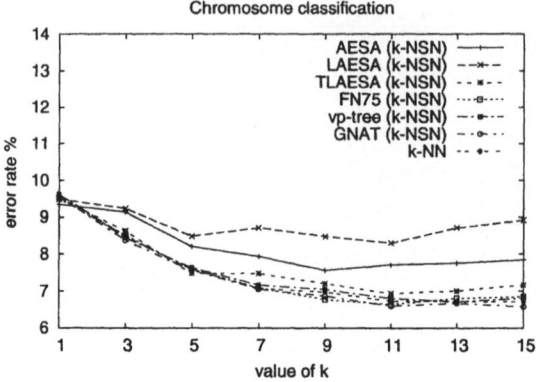

Fig. 4. Error rate comparison in chromosome classification

beyond the scope of this paper. Table 2 shows the average classification time per sample in seconds (on a 1.5 GHz PC under Linux); it is also shown in this table the average time for an extension of LAESA to find the k-NN, named k-LAESA [10], in order to allow a more fair comparison than with exhaustive search k-NN classifier. The value of k for the k-NSN algorithms does not appear because the average times are very similar for all values of k (as expected).

The PHONEME database consists of 5404 five-dimension vectors from 2 classes. Five different partitions have been made to obtain train/test sets of 4300/1000 samples approximately. The results plotted in figure 5 are the average of the five different runs, and show the error rates of k-NN and k-NSN classifiers as the value of k increases. The best results are obtained by LAESA and TLAESA. This may happen because the number of *base prototypes* was set to 40, which probably is higher than the optimum. Both LAESA and TLAESA compute more distances than all other algorithms.

Table 2. Ordered table of average classification time of chromosomes

Algorithm/rule	Time (secs.)
AESA (k-NSN)	0.024
TLAESA (k-NSN)	0.029
LAESA (k-NSN)	0.029
k-LAESA (k=5)	0.044
GNAT (k-NSN)	0.044
FN75 (k-NSN)	0.045
k-LAESA (k=15)	0.048
vp-tree (k-NSN)	0.060
k-NN (exhaustive)	0.091

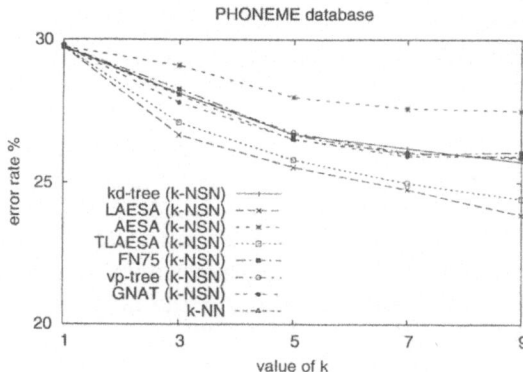

Fig. 5. Error rate comparison in phoneme classification

From this two sets of experiments we can conclude that for low values of k (the most often used) the error rates of the k-NSN rule are always better than those of a NN with the same computational cost, and it nearly reaches or even improves the k-NN error rate for some tasks. Thus, this new rule may be interesting for some real tasks because it may obtain better results than k-NN classifiers and improves NN error rates with (almost) no extra computational effort.

4   Conclusions and Future Work

A new NN based classification rule (the k-NSN rule) has been developed. Our experiments show that classification results similar to those of the k-NN rule are obtained using this rule with very little extra computational effort with respect to a NN classifier. The k-NSN rule is applicable to any approximation-elimination NN search algorithm. Whenever a fast approximation-elimination NN search algorithm is applicable, it may be easily modified to classify using the k-NSN rule and thus it may obtain error rates lower than those of NN, without the extra overhead of searching for the k-NN. Moreover, the time performance of k-NSN classifiers does not depend on the value of k. We have tested this rule with various well known NN fast search algorithms: kd-tree, Fukunaga and Narendra's, vp-tree, GNAT. We have also tested the rule with the algorithms of AESA family, which compute a very low number of distances.

There is still a lot of work to do to explore the possibilities and range of application of the k-NSN rule. As for the future, we plan to:

- study the evolution of k-NSN error rates as the value of k become higher than those tested in this work, and compare them with k-NN,
- extend the NN search algorithms we have implemented to find the k-NN, and then make a comparison with k-NSN rule studying error rates and time performance,

- test the performance of the k-NSN rule as the dimensionality or the number of classes increase, and
- apply the k-NSN rule to other approximation-elimination NN search algorithms.

Acknowledgments

The authors wish to thank Juan S. Sánchez and Alfons Juan for providing us the PHONEME database and the chromosomes database, respectively. We also would like to thank José Manuel Iñesta and the anonymous referees for their valuable comments.

References

[1] Alinat, P.: Periodic progress report 4, ROARS project ESPRIT II - Number 5516. Thomson Technical Report TS ASM 93/S/EGS/NC/079 (1993)

[2] Brin, S.: Near Neighbor Search in Large Metric Spaces. Proceedings of the 21st VLDB Conference (1995) 574–584

[3] Duda, R., Hart, P.: Pattern Classification and Scene Analysis. Wiley (1973)

[4] Friedman, J. H., Bentley, J. L., Finkel, R. A.: An algorithm for finding best matches in logarithmic expected time. ACM Transactions on Mathematical Software (1977) **3** 209–226

[5] Fukunaga, K., Narendra, M.: A branch and bound algorithm for computing k-nearest neighbors. IEEE Trans. Computing (1975) **24** 750–753

[6] Granum, E., Thomason, M. G.: Automatically inferred Markov network models for classification of chromosomal band pattern structures. Cytometry (1990) **11** 26–39

[7] Granum, E., Thomason, M. G., Gregor, J.: On the use of automatically inferred Markov networks for chromosome analysis. In Automation of Cytogenetics, C. Lundsteen and J. Piper, eds., Springer-Verlag (1989) 233–251

[8] Jain, A. K., Dubes, R. C.: Algorithms for clustering data. Prentice-Hall (1988)

[9] Lundsteen, C., Phillip, J., Granum, E.: Quantitative analysis of 6985 digitized trypsin G-banded human metaphase chromosomes. Clinical Genetics (1980) **18** 355–370

[10] Moreno-Seco, F., Micó, L., Oncina, J.: Extending LAESA fast nearest neighbour algorithm to find the k nearest neighbours. Structural, Syntactic, and Statistical Pattern Recognition. Lecture Notes in Computer Science, T. Caelly et al (Eds.) vol. 2396, Springer-Verlag (2002) 691–699

[11] Moreno-Seco, F., Micó, L., Oncina, J.: A modification of the LAESA algorithm for approximated k-NN classification. Pattern Recognition Letters (2003) **24** (1-3) 47–53

[12] Micó, L., Oncina, J., Carrasco, R. C.: A fast branch and bound nearest neighbour classifier in metric spaces. Pattern Recognition Letters (1996) **17** 731–739

[13] Micó, L., Oncina, J., Vidal, E.: A new version of the nearest neighbour approximating and eliminating search algorithm (AESA) with linear preprocessing-time and memory requirements. Pattern Recognition Letters (1994) **15** 9–17

[14] Nene, S., Nayar, S.: A Simple Algorithm for Nearest Neighbor Search in High Dimensions. IEEE Transactions on Pattern Analysis and Machine Intelligence (1997) **19**(9) 989–1003

[15] Ramasubramanian, R., Paliwal, K. K.: Fast nearest-neighbor search algorithms based on approximation-elimination search. Pattern Recognition **33** (2000) 1497–1510

[16] Vidal, E.: New formulation and improvements of the Nearest-Neighbour Approximating and Eliminating Search Algorithm (AESA). Pattern Recognition Letters (1994) **15** 1–7

[17] Wagner, R. A., Fischer, M. J.: The String-to-String Correction Problem. Journal of the Association for Computing Machinery (1974) **21**(1) 168–173

[18] Yianilos, P. N.: Data Structures and Algorithms for Nearest Neighbor Search in General Metric Spaces. ACM-SIAM Symposium on Discrete Algorithms (1993) 311–321

[19] Zhang, K., Shasha, D.: Simple fast algorithms for the editing distance between trees and related problems. SIAM Journal of Computing (1989) **18** 1245–1262

ART-VENA: Retinal Vascular Caliber Measurement

Antonio Mosquera[1], Raquel Dosil[1], Víctor Leborán[1], Fernando Pardo[1],
Francisco Gómez-Ulla[2,3], Bashir Hayik[3], Antonio Pose[4] and Marta Rodríguez[4]

[1] Grupo de Visión Artificial, Departamento de Electrónica e Computación, Universidade de Santiago de Compostela. Campus Universitario Sur s/n, 15706 Santiago de Compostela, Spain.
mosquera@dec.usc.es, {rdosil,nelbla,fpardo}@usc.es
[2] Departamento de Cirugía, Universidad de Santiago de Compostela.
San Francisco s/n, 15705 Santiago de Compostela, Spain.
ciulla@usc.es
[3] Servicio de Oftalmología, Hospital de Conxo, Complejo Hospitalario Universitario de Santiago de Compostela; Conxo, 15706 Santiago de Compostela, Spain.
[4] Servicio de Medicina Interna, Hospital de Conxo, Complejo Hospitalario Universitario de Santiago de Compostela; Conxo, 15706 Santiago de Compostela, Spain.

Abstract. The size of retinal vascular caliber in eye fundus images is a fundamental diagnosis parameter in the study of systemic vascular pathologies, like arterial hypertension or arteriosclerosis. ART-VENA is a semiautomatic system to measure the retinal vascular caliber. From the medical point of view, its repeatability (coefficients of variation under 1.5%) turns it into a reliable tool to objectify vascular changes which previously depended on the observer's subjectivity.

1 Introduction

The automatic computerized analysis of blood vessels from medical images has played, in the last years, an important role in many clinical and research studies on a large number of diseases. The presence of noise, the variability of the anatomical fundus and the low and changing contrast of vessels in many image modalities make the reliable vessel detection a difficult task. Therefore, automatic detection becomes a key starting point. Particularly, retinal vascular caliber is a fundamental parameter in the study of systemic vascular pathologies, like arterial hypertension or arteriosclerosis. Vessels present in the eye are the first to manifest the symptoms of the arterial hypertension [1]. The abnormalities in the retinal vascularization can reflect the degree of damage provoked by these diseases, an aspect that decisively influences the development of brain and cardiovascular complications.

Before the analysis of the alterations in the retinal vascular caliber due to these systemic diseases, it is necessary to study the variations caused by age in normal patients. This is a controversial topic in the medical field. Several classic authors have observed that old age is directly related to arteriolar caliber alterations in normal patients, though there is not an agreement on the causes of this relation [2, 3, 4]. On

F.J. Perales et al. (Eds.): IbPRIA 2003, LNCS 2652, pp. 598-605, 2003.
© Springer-Verlag Berlin Heidelberg 2003

the contrary, other authors do not find retinal vascular caliber changes in old patients [5, 6, 7]. It has to be taken into account that these descriptions are highly subjective.

It would be very useful, therefore, to develop an effective and reproducible method to objectively evaluate the retinal vascular caliber. This objective measure could definitively determine whether observed alterations are related to age in normal patients, and, in case that this relation exists, it could distinguish between these changes and those originated by general diseases, like arterial hypertension or arteriosclerosis.

1.1 Retinal Vascular Caliber Measurement

Retinal vascular caliber measurement has been a widely studied subject in the area of Ophthalmology. In the middle of the 20th century many works begin to be carried out with the aim of predicting, from these measures, the state and prognosis of diseases like arterial hypertension or arteriosclerosis.

In a first stage, from the 50's to the 80's, vascular width measurement from eye fundus photographs was manually made by means of retinal image projections [8, 9, 10, 11, 12, 13]. Several works prove that these measures can be performed with an error inferior to $3\mu m$ at the retina level [11, 14]. Obtained results turned out to be contradictory in many cases, probably as a result of the high subjectivity of the analysis and the lack of statistical studies on the acquired data. Brinchmann-Hansen and col. realized the first studies statistically analyzed [15]. They found the caliber of three arteries and three veins, achieving a coefficient of variation of 3.6 %. Posterior studies reach a decrease in the coefficient of variation down to 2.3% [16, 17].

At the end of the 80's decade, computerized vessel measurement techniques appeared. In the main, these techniques use the computer just to visualize and store the data. The spotting of blood vessel boundary points is made manually by the specialist. Some works reached coefficients of variation between 0.6% and 4.0%, with mean value around 2.2% [18, 19, 20]. Especially important are the works of Polak and col. on the reproducibility and sensitivity of the Zeiss' analyzer of retinal vessels (Zeiss RVA) [21]. In size measurements of arteries and veins they obtained coefficients of variation values of 1.3% and 2.6% respectively. These data place the Zeiss' vessel analyzer among the reference commercial instruments in this area.

1.2 Vessel Detection

Automatic detection of vessels has involved much research in the field of digital image processing during the last years. Many works in the literature address the problem of automatic detection of blood vessels in various domains.

Tracking of vessels has been one of the more studied techniques in recent years [22, 23]. In general, given a starting vessel contour point and one search direction, vessel tracking involves exploring the image to find other contour points. The criterion to define boundary points is based on the analysis of the pixel gray level values on a section that is orthogonal to the tracking direction. More sophisticated versions of this idea transform the problem of vessel contour detection in that of graph optimal path search [24]. Other artificial intelligence or computer vision methods have been also proposed to obtain a complete automation of the detection procedure, exploiting in a more exhaustive way the available anatomical knowledge [25, 26].

The majority of the developed methods adopt boundary detection as the basic tool for vessel detection. Since vessel contours are usually smooth and fuzzy and the fundus is noisy, a number of authors have applied, as an initial strategy, the maximization of vessel enhancement. Some approaches are based on rotation invariant operators or linear morphological operators of suitable size and orientation, which are applied to the image to minimize noise [25, 27]. Alternative approaches involve image convolution with multiple filters per model, each of them designed to detect vessels of given size and orientation [28]. The main drawback to these methods is their high computational cost, which renders them practically unusable for on-line diagnosis assistance systems or systems requiring relatively short response times. Zana and Klein developed a vessel bifurcation detection method as a previous step to image registration [29]. Quek and Kirbas carried out a method for vessel extraction from angiographies based on wave propagation [30].

2 Retinal Vascular Caliber Measurement

The measurement method developed in this work is nearly completely automatic. The operator is initially required just to mark the optic nerve, though high accuracy is not necessary. Once this initial reference is set, the automatic sequence of detection and measurement of the vessels on the image starts. The method output is a list of the structures identified as vessels and their widths, ready to be analyzed by the expert.

As the fundus vascular structures are inherently radial, the width measurement of retinal vessels will be performed over various circumferences centered at the optic nerve, at distances that are multiple of the optic disk radius, depicted by the operator (a common procedure in Ophthalmology). Using a polar coordinate space, a linear representation of the gray level profiles is obtained for each of the analyzed circumferences, as shown in left side of Fig. 1. The gray level profile along each circumference is characterized by the presence of valleys, which are potential vessels. They are placed over the noise of the anatomical fundus that is nearly uniformly distributed. Before its detection, a preprocessing stage is needed to minimize noise effects.

The employed filter for noise reduction must not modify the location of the profile transition regions, which determine vessel widths in the measurement phase. To minimize noise, a median filter has been chosen. It permits to remove gray level values that differ too much from the surrounding values. This filtering reduces the detection of valleys caused by noise perturbations induced by the anatomical fundus. The median filter used in this work has a window size of 11 pixels centered at the pixel under analysis. One important property of this filter is that it does not alter the magnitude of the gray level gradient and, therefore, respects the position of transitions. The right side of Fig. 1 shows the profile obtained after the filtering process.

Although the median filter eliminates many noise valleys, some of them, produced by illumination variations and the presence of fundus anatomical structures other than vessels, still remain, together with the blood vessel valleys. For that reason, the simple detection of filtered sequence minima does not warranty correct identification of

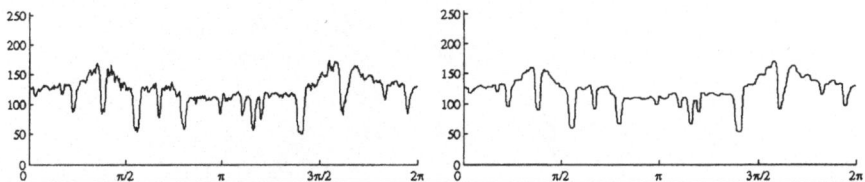

Fig. 1. Left: Gray level profile along one circumference centered at the optic nerve. Right: Gray level profile after median filter application.

vessels. The definitive detection of blood vessels valleys is established as a function of their 1D and 2D morphology. In this work the hypothesis that the traversal vessel profiles are deep is assumed (1D model), i.e., their gray levels are much smaller than the surrounding fundus ones. Consequently, the intensity differences between vessel valleys and fundus are greater than those of noise valleys. Moreover, the vessel valley structure is stable in the radial direction regarding the optic disk (2D model).

Fig. 2 shows the 1D vessel model. Points x_1, x_2 and x_3 correspond respectively to the sites of the previous maximum, the minimum and the posterior maximum on the valley structure. Parameters y_1, y_2 and y_3 are the profile heights (gray levels) measured at x_1, x_2 and x_3 respectively. Using the three height parameters, a valley quality measure reflecting relative depth is established. This measure is given by the expression

$$Q = 1 - \frac{2y_2}{y_1 + y_3}. \tag{1}$$

Valleys with Q values greater than 0.06 are considered candidates to form blood vessels. This process is realized individually over 2n+1 circumferences, with n positive integer and with their radius differing in one pixel, being the innermost circumference radius selected by the specialist. The n value, which can be modified by the operator, is recommended to be set between 5 and 9. Smaller values do not warranty the straight vessel hypothesis which will be applied in the width measurement stage. These data are the input to the 2D modeling phase. For a region to be considered a true vessel, a valley must appear in 2/3 of the analyzed circumferences. In addition, the angular distance between valleys associated to consecutive circumferences must be lesser than 0.089 radians. In the top left hand side of Fig. 3, a sequence of 11 valleys (n=5) can be observed, which verifies the 1D and 2D imposed conditions, so that they determine the existence of a blood.

When the vessel positions are located, the next step is width measurement. This task is

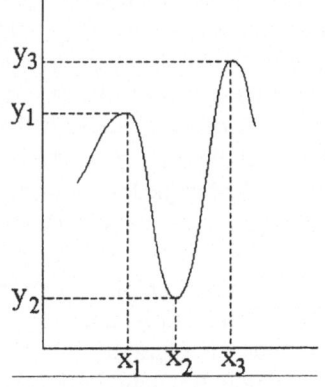

Fig. 2. Vessel model

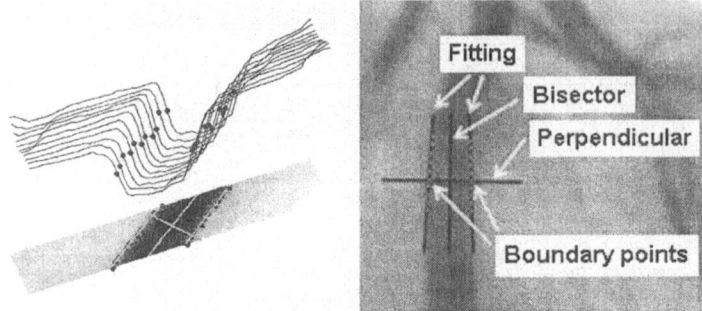

Fig. 3. Left: Sequence of profiles verifying 1D and 2D modeling conditions. Right: Geometric calculus of the straight line that is used to determine de the blood vessel width.

accomplished by locating the extremes of the gray level derivative along the angular direction, i.e., along the profiles. Hence, positions of vessel walls are set at the maximum transition points of the intensity profile. These extreme points are obtained by means of quadratic interpolation (fit to a parabola) of the derivative values, to obtain subpixel accuracy. In this way, potential image quantization ambiguities are avoided and results are better assessed. Assuming the hypothesis of the analyzed vessel segment is straight, the available points can be fitted to a straight line, as shown on the bottom left hand side and on the right hand side images in Fig. 3. Caliber is finally estimated over a line perpendicular to the bisector of the lines fitted to both vessel borders, as can be seen in Fig. 3.

3   Results

In order to validate the developed procedure, a reproducibility/reliability study has been designed in three stages. These phases are intended to evaluate the reproducibility/reliability of the method against diverse factors that can influence the study. These factors include variability on the measurements made by an observer, variability among different observers and variability due to the patient under study.

Once the goals of this experience were explained to the volunteers, chosen from the companion of the patients that came to the Servicio de Urgencias de Oftalmología of the Complejo Hospitalario Universitario de Santiago de Compostela (Spain) and after they had signed the informed consent to proceed with pupil dilation and an ophthalmologic exam, the volunteer pupil was dilated using an instillation of two drips of tropicamide and two drips of phenylephrine. After a period of 20 to 30 minutes, an eye fundus photograph was taken from both eyes of each subject at 50 degrees, with aneritra light (540 nanometers) and centered at the papilla. The camera used to take the fundus photographs was the Topcon TRC-50 IA connected to the IMAGEnet 1024 Digital Imaging Systems by Topcon Instruments, Paramus, NJ. All captured images were directly stored in optical disks and displayed on a high resolution monitor (1280x1024 pixels) for their visualization and posterior analysis. The direct digitalization of the captured image was made by means of a digital camera connected to the aforementioned fundus camera. The elimination of the intermediate step, usually included in many other procedures, avoids the introduction of error factors [31].

To achieve the objectives of this work, a basic population sample was formed by 120 normotensive volunteers (240 fundus images), without any known vascular pathologies. A subject is classified as normotensive in the absence of a previous diagnosis of arterial hypertension and the presence of PAS/PAD quantities under 140/90, following the procedures of the American National Committee of HBP [32]. Subject ages ranged from 10 to 69 years, with a 1:1 ratio between sexes. Each age group (10-19; 20-29; 30-39; 40-49; 50-59; 60-69) is constituted by 20 individuals, 10 males and 10 females. In all cases the volunteers had transparent media in both eyes and a refractive defect inferior to 3 diopters of hypermetropia, myopia and astigmatism.

Table 1 shows the results obtained for the coefficient of variation over the individual measures and the Pearson's momentum correlation coefficient (p<0.001) over the global measures. The intraobserver reproducibility indicates agreement in measurements made by the same observer when repeating the measure over the same set of images. To analyze this factor, one single observer evaluated 40 images corresponding to 40 eyes of 20 individuals (20 left eyes and 20 right eyes) two times, separated from each other by an interval of 24 hours, without knowing nor the results neither the measurement points in the previous attempt. The interobserver reproducibility indicates agreement in measurements realized independently by two different observers. In this case, two observers evaluated, without information exchange, 30 images corresponding to 30 eyes of 15 individuals (15 left eyes and 15 right eyes). Intraindividual reproducibility indicates concordance in measurements, realized in a blind fashion, by the same observer over images of the same subject and same eye taken with a difference in some time interval. To analyze this factor, one single observer evaluated two images of the same eye, separated by a time period of one month, repeating the process for 30 eyes of 15 individuals (15 left eyes and 15 right eyes), without knowing nor the results neither the measurement points in the previous trial.

Table 1. Coefficient of variation (CV) and Pearson's momentum correlation coefficient (r) obtained in the various planted experiments.

	CV (r)			C
	Intraobserver	Interobserver	Intraindividual	Polak, 2000
Artery	1.10 % (0.96)	1.30 % (0.94)	1.08 % (0.93)	1.3 %
Vein	0.98 % (0.91)	1.47 % (0.86)	1.12 % (0.93)	2.6 %
Arteriovenous index	0.50 % (0.99)	0.99 % (0.95)	0.40 % (0.99)	

4 Discussion

Reproducibility of measurement methods is a crucial aspect in Medicine [31]. For this reason, the first planted goal in this work is to demonstrate that repeated vascular caliber measurements over the same photograph without knowing the reference points bring the same results. As a second objective, it has been proposed to demonstrate that the same thing happens when one certain photograph is measured by two different observers. As a third objective, to demonstrate also that vascular caliber measurements from two photographs of the same individual with a time difference of one month do not present significant variations.

Intraobserver, interobserver and intraindividual variabilities are small in our method and the measurement reproducibility in the three groups presents a very high degree of concordance, with a Pearson's momentum correlation coefficient (equivalent to the intraclass correlation coefficient) over 0.86 and a coefficient of variation inferior to 1.47% in all cases, while Polak et col. obtained coefficient of variation values between 1.3% and 2.6% in their work with the Zeiss' retinal vessel analyzer (Zeiss RVA) [21]. In particular, this coefficient of variation superior bound is the best obtained by the whole of the previously commented methods. These results render the presented method a secure tool to objectify microvascular changes which previously depended on the observer's subjectivity.

The research project "Desarrollo y Validación de un Método de Medida del Calibre Microvascular Retiniano en la Población Normal" carried out using ART-VENA (inscribed in the Spanish IP Register, with number 2001/15/934) was prized with the Premio de Investigación Academia Médico-Quirúrgica /Consellería de Sanidade of the Xunta de Galicia (Spain).

References

1. EYEfacts, *"Systemic Disease and the Eye"*, UIC Eye Center, University of Illinois at Chicago (2002)
2. Ballantyne, A.J., Trans. Ophthalmol. Soc. UK., 57, 301-318 (1937)
3. Vogelius, H. and Bechgaard, P., *"The Ophthalmoscopical Appearance of the Fundus Oculi in Elderly Persons with Arteriosclerosis and Normal Blood Pressure"*, Br. J. Ophthalmol., 34, 404-408 (1950)
4. Leishman, R., *"The Eye in General Vascular Disease: Hypertension and Arteriosclerosis"*, Br. J. Ophthalmol., 41, 641-701 (1957)
5. Kagan, A., Aurell, E. and Dobree, J.A., *"A Note of Signs in the Fundus Oculi and Arterial Hypertension Conventional Assessment and Significance"*, Bull. World Health Organ., 34, 955-960 (1966)
6. Aoki, N., Horibe, H. and col., *"Epidemiological Evaluation of Funduscopic Findings in Cerebrovascular Diseases III: Observer Variability and Reproducibility for Funduscopic Findings"*, Jpn. Circ. J., 41, 11-17 (1977)
7. Dimmitt, S.B., West, J.N. and col., *"Usefulness of ophthalmoscopy in mild to moderate hypertension"*, Lancet, 1, 1103-1106 (1989)
8. Boyd, T.A.S. and de Margerie, J., *"Caliber of Retinal Arterioles in Hypertension"*, Trans. Can. Ophthalmol. Soc., 23, 65-76 (1960)
9. Hill, D.W. and Dollery, C.T., *"Caliber Changes in Retinal Arterioles"*, Trans. Ophthal. Soc. UK., 83, 61-70 (1963)
10. Michaelson, I.C., The Ocular Circulation in Health and Disease, Can. J. S., Ed. Kimpton, London (1969)
11. Hodge, J.V., Parr, J.C. and Spears, S., *"Comparison of Methods of Measuring Vessel Widths on Retinal Photographs and the Effect of Fluorescein Injection on Apparent Retinal Vessel Calibers"*, Am. J. Ophthalmol., 68, 1060-1068 (1969)

12.Sanchéz-Salorio, M., Retinopatías Vasculares., Ed. Grafinsa (1971)

13.Parr, J.C. and Spears, G.F.S., *"General Caliber of the Retinal Arteries Expressed as the Equivalent Width of the Central Retinal Artery"*, Am. J. Ophthalmol., 77, 472-477 (1974)

14.Parr, J. C., *"Hypertensive Generalized Narrowing of Retinal Arteries"*, Trans. Ophthalmol. Soc. NZ, 26, 55-60 (1974)

15.Brinchmann-Hansen, O. and Heier, H., *"The Apparent and the True Width of the Blood Column in Retinal Vessels"*, Acta Ophthalmologica, Supplement 179. 64, 29-32 (1986)

16.Delori, F.C., Fitch, K.A. and col., *"Evaluation of Micrometric and Microdensitometric Methods for Measuring the Width of Retinal Vessels Images on Fundus Photographs"*, Graefe's Archive for Clinical and Experimental Ophthalmology, 226, 393-399 (1988)

17.Stanton, A.V., Mullaney, P. and col., *"A Method of Quantifying Retinal Microvascular Alterations Associated with Blood Pressure and Age"*, J. Hypertens., 13, 41-48 (1995)

18.Meehan, R.T., Taylor, G.R. and col., *"An Automated Method of Quantifying Retinal Vascular Response during Exposure to Novel Environmental Conditions"*, Ophthalmology, 97, 875-881 (1990)

19.Rassam, S.M.B., Patel, V. and Col, *"Accurate Vessel Width Measurement from Fundus Photographs: A New Concept"*, Br. J. of Ophthalmology, 78, 24-29 (1994)

20.Pedersen, L., Grunkin, M. and col., *"Quantitative Measurement of Changes in Retinal Vessel Diameter in Ocular Fundus Images"*, Pattern Recognit. Lett., 21, 1215-1223 (2000)

21.Polak, K., Dorner, G. and col., *"Evaluation of the Zeiss Retinal Vessel Analyser"*, Br. J. Ophthalmol., 84, 1285-1290 (2000)

22.Liu, I. and Sun, Y., *"Recursive Tracking of Vascular Networks in Angiograms based on the Detection-Deletion Scheme"*, IEEE Trans. Med. Imaging, 12, 2, 334-341 (1993)

23.Miles, F.P. and Nuttall, A.L., *"Matched Filter Estimation of Serial Blood Vessels Diameters from Video Images"*, IEEE Trans. Med. Imaging, 12, 2, 147-152 (1993)

24.Sonka, M., Wilbricht, C.J. and col., *"Simultaneous Detection of both Coronary Borders"*, IEEE Trans. Med. Imaging, 12, 3, 588-599 (1993)

25.Xia, W. and Lü, W., *"Correspondence Analysis for Regional Tracking in Coronary Arteriograms"*, IEEE Trans. Med. Imaging, 11, 2, 153-160 (1992)

26.Coppini, M., Demi, M. and col., *"An Artificial Vision System for X-ray Images of Human Coronary Trees"*, IEEE Trans. Pattern Anal. Mach. Intell., 15, 2, 156-162 (1993)

27.Thackray, B.D. and Nelson, A.C., *"Semi-automatic Segmentation of Vascular Network Images using a Rotation Structuring Element (ROSE) with Mathematical Morphology and Dual Feature Thresholding"*, IEEE Trans. Med. Imaging, 12, 3, 835-392 (1993)

28.Gerig, G., Koller, G. Th. and col., *"Segmentation and Symbolic Description of Cerebral Vessel Structure Based on MR Angiography Volume Data"*, Computer Assisted Radiology CAR`93, Lemke, H. U., Inamura, K., Jaffe, C.C. and Félix, R., editors, 359-365 (1993)

29.Zana, F. and Klein, J.C., *"A Multimodal Registration Algorithm of Eye Fundus Images using Vessels Detection and Hough Transform"*, IEEE Trans. Med. Imaging, 18, 5, 419-428 (2001)

30.Quek, F.K.H. and Kirbas, C., *"Vessel Extraction in Medical Images by Wave-Propagation and Traceback"*, IEEE Trans. Med. Imaging, 20, 2, 117-131 (2001)

31.Couper, D.J., Klein, R. and col., *"Reliability of Retinal Photography in the Assessment of Retinal Microvascular Characteristics: The Arteriosclerosis Risk in Communities Study"*, Am. J. Ophthalmol., 133, 78-88 (2002)

32.Joint National Committee on the Prevention, Detection, Evaluation, and Treatment of High Blood Pressure, Sixth Report Arch. Intern. Med., 157, 21, 2413-2446 (1997)

Use of Band Ratioing for Color Texture Classification

Rubén Muñiz and José Antonio Corrales

Department of Informatics
University of Oviedo, Gijón, Spain
{rubenms,ja}@lsi.uniovi.es

Abstract. In the recent years, many authors have begun to exploit the extra information provided by color images to solve many computer vision problems. Among these problems, we find the texture classification field, which traditionally has used grayscale images, primarily due to the high hardware and processing costs.

In this paper, a new approach for enhancing classical texture analysis methods is presented. By means of the band ratioing technique, we can extend any feature extraction algorithm to take advantage of color information and achieve higher classification rates. To prove this extreme, three standard techniques has been selected: Gabor filters, Wavelets and Cooccurrence Matrices.

For testing purposes, 30 color textures have been selected from the Vistex database. We will perform a number of experiments on that texture set, combining different ways of adapting the former algorithms to process color textures and extract features from them.

1 Introduction

Texture classification is a key field in many computer vision applications, ranging from quality control to remote sensing. Briefly described, there is a finite number of texture classes we have to learn to recognize. In the first stage of the development of such kind of systems, we extract useful information (features) from a set of digital images, known as the training set, containing the textures we are studying. Once this task has been done, we proceed to classify any unknown texture into one of the known classes.

Since the earlier approaches to the problem, grayscale images has been widely used, primarily due to acquisition hardware limitations and/or limited processing power. In the near past, much effort has been done to develop new feature extraction algorithms (also known as texture analysis algorithms) to take advantage of the extra information contained in color images. On the other hand, many classical grayscale algorithms has been extended to process color textures [1, 2, 3].

Texture analysis algorithms can be divided into statistical and spectral ones. The former methods extract a set of statistical properties from the spatial distribution of intensities of a texture. Common examples of this approach are the

F.J. Perales et al. (Eds.): IbPRIA 2003, LNCS 2652, pp. 606–615, 2003.
© Springer-Verlag Berlin Heidelberg 2003

histogram method and the family of algorithms based on cooccurrence matrices [4, 5]. The latter techniques, on the other hand, compute a number of features obtained from the analysis of the local spectrum of the texture. In the following sections we will give an overview of two spectral methods (Gabor filters and Wavelets) and a statistical one (Cooccurrence matrices).

2   Gabor Filters

Gabor filters have been extensively used for texture classification and segmentation of grayscale and color textures [6, 1, 3, 7, 8]. These filters are optimally localized in both space and spatial frequency and allow us to get a set of filtered images which correspond to a specific scale and orientation component of the original texture. There are two major approaches to texture analysis using Gabor filters. First, one can look for specific narrowband filters to describe a given texture class, while the other option is to apply a bank of Gabor filters over the image and process its outputs to obtain the features that describe the texture class.

2.1   2D Gabor Filterbank

The Gabor filter bank used in this work is defined in the spatial domain as follows:

$$f_{mn}(x,y) = \frac{1}{2\pi\sigma_m^2} \exp\left[-\frac{x^2+y^2}{2\sigma_m^2}\right] \cdot \cos 2\pi(u_m x \cos\theta + u_m y \sin\theta) \ . \qquad (1)$$

where m and n are the indexes for the scale and the orientation, respectively, for a given Gabor filter. Depending on these parameters, the texture will be analyzed (filtered) at a specific detail level and direction.

As in [1], we define a filterbank with three scales and four orientations. The bandwidth B_θ [6] is taken to be 40° in order to maximize the coverage of the frequency domain and minimize the overlap between the filters.

2.2   Gabor Features

To obtain texture features we must filter the texture images using the generated FIRs. This is achieved by convolution on the frequency domain (2), due to the size of the filters used. For each filtered image, we extract a single feature μ_{mn} which represents its energy, as shown below.

$$G_{mn}(x,y) = I(x,y) * f_{mn} \ . \qquad (2)$$

$$\mu_{mn}(x,y) = \sqrt{\sum_{x,y}(G_{mn}(x,y))^2} \ . \qquad (3)$$

This approach is only valid when grayscale images are used. If we want to filter a color image, we have to preprocess it before this method can be applied. The more obvious solution for this problem is to transform the image by a weighted average of the three color bands.

Using this transformation, different colors can give the same grayscale intensity, so color information is lost. To overcome this obstacle, (2) can be applied on each of the RGB color bands of the image to obtain unichrome features [1]. With this approach, we obtain a set of energies from each spectral band, so the information extracted from textures, grows by a factor of three. Another disadvantage of this technique is that color information is not correlated because it is simply concatenated. A good idea to solve this independency was proposed by Palm et al. in [3]. They convert the RGB image to HSV, discarding the intensity value, and taking the Hue and Saturation to form a complex number, which can be used to compute the convolution between the image and the gabor filter by means of a complex FFT.

3   Wavelets

3.1   Introduction

The name "Wavelets" was first introduced by Morlet, a French geophysicists, in the early 80's. The kind of data he was studying couldn't be properly analyzed by Fourier analysis, due to the fast change of their frequency contents. For this reason, he looked for a family of functions suitable for the analysis of that kind of signals and he found the wavelets.

A wavelet family is a set of functions derived from a single function with special features, named the *mother* wavelet, by means of two parameters a and b:

$$\psi_{a,b}(t) = \frac{1}{\sqrt{a}}\psi\left(\frac{t-b}{a}\right) .$$

(4)

The parameter a represents the dilation (which is inversely proportional to frequency) and b the displacement (time localization).

Wavelets are rather complex and we would require a complete book [9] to deal with them. In the following lines we will show only the basics of this kind of analysis, focused on texture feature extraction.

3.2   2D Discrete Wavelet Transform and Multiscale Analysis

Wavelets allow to study a signal at different levels of detail. In the case of 2D signals, this can be interpreted as analyzing the images at different resolutions or scales. There are more than a single wavelet transform. For this work we will focus on a non-redundant representation using quadrature mirror filters (QMF), which consist in two decomposition filters, named $\tilde{h}$ and $\tilde{g}$, and their mirrors h and g for signal reconstruction. In Figure 1 we can see an schema of the decomposition stage. In each filtering step, a *low resolution* image L_{j+1} and

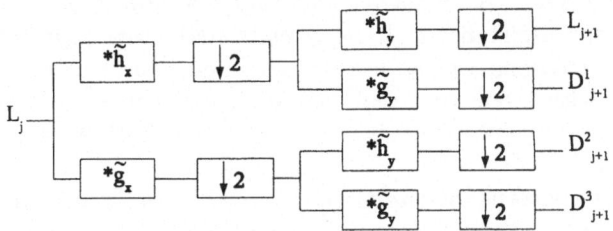

Fig. 1. 2D DWT using FIR filters

three *detail images* are produced. The detail images $D_j^{1...3}$ contain the details (high frequency components) extracted from D_j that are not present in $D_j + 1$. This scheme can be applied recursively until a given depth is reached.

3.3   Wavelet Features

Detail images obtained by applying 2D DWT can be used as a source for extracting texture features. Since those images contain essentially edge information at a specific direction (horizontal, vertical and diagonal), its energy is a very good texture feature. It is defined as follows:

$$E_{ij}(x,y) = \sqrt{\sum_{x,y} (D_{ij}(x,y))^2} \ . \tag{5}$$

where $i = 1 \ldots 3$ and $j = 0 \ldots depth - 1$.

As in the case of Gabor filters, we need some mechanism to be able to process color images, such as grayscale conversion and independent color band feature extraction. In this particular case we can use a set of correlation measures [2], known as *wavelet covariance signatures*, which are defined as follows:

$$C_{ij}^{B_k B_l}(x,y) = \sum_{x,y} D_{ij}^{B_l} D_{ij}^{B_k} \ . \tag{6}$$

where B_k and B_l represent a color band, and $k, l = 1, 2, 3, k \le l$.

Covariance signatures are, by definition, proportional to the energies. To get rid of the redundant information, we can define a new set of measures, called *wavelet correlation signatures*, defined as follows:

$$\widetilde{C}_{ni}^{B_k, B_l} = \begin{cases} E_{ni}^{B_k} & k = l \\ \dfrac{C_{ni}^{B_k, B_l}}{E_{ni}^{B_k} E_{ni}^{B_l}} & k \ne l \end{cases} \ . \tag{7}$$

4   Gray Level Cooccurrence Matrices

4.1   Introduction

Gray level cooccurrence matrices (GLCM) were introduced for the first time by Haralick [4] in the early 70's. A GLCM is a matrix where each cell i, j contains the number of times a point having intensity i occurs in a position j located at an angle θ and a distance d. If we want to make this approach not sensible to orientation variations, we can use the neighbourhood located at a distance d from the pixel with intensity i. Only the first quadrant of that neighbourhood need to be explored, which is equivalent to take $\theta = 0, 45, 90$ simultaneously for the same matrix.

A final topic concerns the size of the GLCM. If we directly use the 256 gray levels available in a image, the resulting matrix will be huge, so a mechanism to reduce its dimensions is needed. There are some options to do this. In this paper, we have used two different preprocessing tasks:

1. Use Sobel filters to detect the edges of the image. The resulting image will have five different values: horizontal edge, vertical edge, diagonal edge, secondary diagonal edge, and no edge. The resulting matrix belongs to a class of matrices known as Cooccurrence Generalized Matrices (CGM).
2. Reduce the gray levels to 16 using some quantization algorithm such as IGS. In this case, the resulting matrices are named Spatial Gray Level-Dependent Matrices (SGLDM).

4.2   Feature Extraction

From a cooccurrence matrix, a number of second order statistics can be computed. The most popular ones are those known as *Haralick features* [4], followed by the set of measures introduced by Conners et al. [5].

Obviously, a GLCM cannot be computed directly from a color image, but from a grayscale one, so a modification is needed to be able to process that kind of images. There are three ways for doing this:

1. Convert the color image to monochrome. This is straightforward, but it discards the chromatic information from the images.
2. Process each RGB band separately. With this approach, a GLCM is computed from each color band and the resulting feature vector f_v is the concatenation of three feature vectors f_R, f_G, f_B, obtained from each matrix separately. The main disadvantage is that the computational cost increases considerably and the obtained information is not correlated.
3. Use cross-cooccurrence matrices [10]. This technique follows to extend the cooccurrence idea explained before to color images. The process consists in, given a pixel from a color band B_1 with intensity i, we will look for the intensity of a pixel located in another color band B_2 at a distance d and orientation θ. As before, we can use three angles at the same time to compute a single matrix. Obviously, if $B_1 = B_2$ then we are computing a conventional GCLM. The main advantage of this class of matrices is that features extracted from them contain color information, because color planes are processed in pairs, but the feature vector length is increased by a factor of six.

5   Band Ratioing

In the previous sections, we have given a brief introduction to three of the most commonly used feature extraction algorithms, and we have seen the way many authors are extending them to process color textures. In this section, we will show a novel approach to do that, obtaining in many cases the highest classifier performance, while keeping a low number of features.

5.1   Introduction

Band ratioing is a enhancement technique mainly used in the field of remote sensing. It is usually applied to process LANDSAT TM images[1] to enhance details such as vegetation, grass, soil, etc. It is defined as follows:

$$I(x,y) = \frac{B_1(x,y)}{B_2(x,y)} \ . \tag{8}$$

where $B_1(x,y)$ and $B_2(x,y)$ are two different spectral bands of the color image. Its computation is extremely easy, but the bands involved must be processed to avoid the case when $B_2(x,y) = 0$. To accomplish this, we only have to increase every pixel from both bands by 1. Theoretically, ratios will be in the interval (0,256], but in practice most values will be rather small. For this reason, it is advisable to use logarithm compression to enhance small ratios over larger ones, so (8) can be rewritten as follows.

$$I'(x,y) = \log\left(\frac{B_1(x,y)}{B_2(x,y)}\right) \ . \tag{9}$$

It can be easily seen that this technique tends to enhance what is different in two spectral bands, and as it will be seen in the following section, its output is suitable for feature extraction.

5.2   Feature Extraction from Rationed Color Textures

In the previous section, we saw that Band Ratioing enhances what is different in two color bands. If a pixel contains a grayscale value ($R = G = B$), its ratio will be 1, but if at least two color components are not equal, the band ratio will encode the color information in a single value. This is very interesting for feature extraction from color textures, since we can directly use any grayscale feature extraction method available. In the following lines, we will show the way to enhance the Gabor filtering method using band ratioing.

To apply Gabor filtering on a rationed image, we can combine (9) and (2) to get the following expression:

$$G'_{mn}(x,y) = \log\left(\frac{B_1(x,y)}{B_2(x,y)}\right) * f_{mn}(x,y) \ . \tag{10}$$

---

[1] http://rst.gsfc.nasa.gov/Sect1/Sect1_15.html

Note that (10) directly convolves the band ratios with the Gabor filter, so it is not necessary to scale the ratios to fit in a byte value.

A very interesting topic is about the implementation of the previous scheme. When we compute a band ratio, the operands are both eight-bit numbers, i.e, ranging from $0 \ldots 255$, but the result will be a real number. There are two different ways to deal with this value:

1. Adjust the result to fit in a byte value (some information is lost).
2. Use the real ratio directly as input to the FFT.

It is easy to see that the second approach is much better since no information is lost. In our experiments, we have observed a 10% of performance increase compared to the case when byte values are used. Nevertheless, this option is only applicable to feature extraction algorithms that make use of the FFT, since we can not use real numbers to compute cooccurrence matrices, for example.

6 Experiments

For testing the performance of the band ratioing technique combined with the three feature extraction algorithms presented before, we have used the texture set defined in [2] which is composed of 30 color textures taken from the Vistex database[2] (Fig. 2). As in [3] we divide each 512x512 image into 64 disjunct images of 64x64 pixels each, which give us a total of 1920 texture samples. For each texture class, we randomly select a 80% of the samples for training, and the rest for testing purposes (hold-out method).

We have performed a number of experiments, applying different color processing techniques to be able to process color images. The tables showed in the next section, gather the classifier performance in all cases.

7 Results

For evaluating the performance of the feature sets obtained in each case, we have used a Knn classifier, taking $K = 5$. To measure the distance between two feature vectors in $\mathbb{R}^n$, the 1-norm is used. To be able to compare the computational efficiency of each color processing technique, we provide execution time (in seconds), measured in a PC powered by an AMD Athlon XP 1800+, which is a very common configuration nowadays. This time obviously depends on the implementation of each algorithm, which may be more or less optimized, but it will serve us to have a general idea in terms of performance.

---

[2] http://www-white.media.mit.edu/vismod/imagery/VisionTexture/vistex.html

Fig. 2. 30 color textures: Bark0, Bark4, Bark6, Bark8, Bark9, Brick1, Brick4, Brick5, Fabric0, Fabric4, Fabric7, Fabric9, Fabric11, Fabric13, Fabric16, Fabric17, Fabric18, Food0, Food2, Food5, Food8, Grass1, Sand0, Stone4, Tile1, Tile3, Tile7, Water6, Wood1, Wood2 (left/right,top/bottom)

7.1 Gabor Results

Gabor features were extracted by filtering the textures at 3 scales and 4 different orientations. This give us a total of 12 gabor energies for each texture sample. As it can be seen in Table 1, the best performance is achieved by the concatenation of two band ratios. These results are not only interesting for this topic, but for the reduced number of features used. If we look at the RGB row, we see that by using raw color information, 36 features are extracted and the performance is worse. It is also remarkable the fact that using band ratios, we can even improve the performance of the *Complex Gabor Features* introduced in [3], not only in terms of classification success, but in execution time, due to the higher processing requirements of the complex FFT.

7.2 Wavelet Results

For Wavelet features we have set the analysis depth at 4, which produces a total number of 12 features for each texture sample. The wavelet functions used for this analysis were the biorthogonal Wavelets *Bior6.8* available in MatLAB v6.5. In this case, the performance of the concatenation of two band ratios is not the best at all, but the classification success is only 1.67% less than the case when correlation signatures are used, computing three times less features, so classifier performance is better.

7.3   Cooccurrence Matrices Results

GLCM features were obtained by computing two coocurrence matrices at distances 2 and 4. For each matrix, we have calculated Haralick features $f_1 \ldots f_{12}$ that give us a total number of 24 texture measures for each sample. The overall performance in this case is worse than for the case where spectral methods are used, but we still see a performance increase when band ratios are involved. It is remarkable to notice how the concatenation of two band ratios still providing the best results while keeping the number of used features low. In this case, we only provide the execution time for the SGLDM data, since it is proportional to the CGM case.

Table 1. Classification rates for Gabor & Wavelet data

Preprocessing algorithm	Feat. #	Hits Gabor (exec. time)	Hits Wavelets (exec. time)
Grayscale	12	89.05% (72.59 s)	88.10% (30.47 s)
Red band	12	89.52% (67.1 s)	90.48% (29.44 s)
Green band	12	90.24% (67.1 s)	85.24% (29.44 s)
Blue band	12	87.38% (67.1 s)	86.19% (29.44 s)
R+G+B	12 × 3	93.5 % (201.3 s)	91.19% (88.32 s)
Ratio R/G	12	86.67% (60.7 s)	83.33% (31.53 s)
Ratio R/B	12	90.24% (60.7 s)	87.62% (31.53 s)
Ratio G/B	12	85.48% (60.7 s)	80.95% (31.53 s)
Rat. R/G & R/B	12 × 2	95.24% (121.4 s)	93.57% (62.86 s)
Rat. R/G, R/B & G/B	12 × 3	95.24% (182.1 s)	93.81% (94.59 s)
Complex color features	24	94,05% (605.94 s)	N/A
Correlation signatures	72	N/A	95.24% (89.45 s)

Table 2. Classification rates for CGM and SGLDM data

Preprocessing algorithm	Feature #	Hits CGM	Hits SGLDM (execution time)
Grayscale	24	77.62%	81.43% (104.34 s)
Red band	24	78.57%	83.10% (91.39 s)
Green band	24	79.29%	84.05% (91.39 s)
Blue band	24	79.05%	85.24% (91.39 s)
R+G+B	24 × 3	84.76%	93.1% (274.17 s)
Ratio R/G	24	72.38%	74.76% (130.51 s)
Ratio R/B	24	70.24%	76.43% (130.51 s)
Ratio G/B	24	64.29%	70% (130.51 s)
Ratios R/G & R/B	24 × 2	85.24%	89.28% (274.17 s)
Ratios R/G, R/B & G/B	24 × 3	85.71%	91.67% (391.53 s)
Cross-coocurrence	24 × 3	81.19%	90.24% (274.17 s)

8   Conclusions

In this paper, a new method for extracting color texture features has been presented. Using band ratioing technique, we have combined RGB color bands to produce monochromatic images suitable to use as input to any feature extraction algorithm currently available. From an implementation point of view, feature extraction algorithms that can use real images are preferred since no information is lost from band ratios. The most important conclusion is the fact that this technique allows us to compress textural color information which leads to higher classification performance while keeping the number of features low. It is interesting to see how the use of three band ratios does not lead to better performance (or very little increase) than the case where only two ratios are involved. This is obvious since the third one is a linear combination of the other two, so the extra features do not contain additional information.

References

[1] Jain, A., Healy, G.: A multiscale representation including opponent color features for texture recognition. IEEE Transactions on Image Processing **7(1)** (1998) 124–128

[2] de Wouver, G. V.: Wavelets for Multiscale Texture Analysis. PhD thesis, University of Antwerp (Belgium) (1998)

[3] Palm, C., Keysers, D., Lehmann, T., Spitzer, K.: Gabor filtering of complex hue/saturation images for color texture classification. In: Proceedings of 5th Joint Conference on Information Science (JCIS2000), Atlantic City, USA. Volume 2. (2000) 45–49

[4] Haralick, R., Shanmugam, K., Dinstein, I.: Textural features for image classification. IEEE Transactions on Systems, Man, and Cybernetics **3(6)** (1973) 610–621

[5] Conners, R., McMillin, C.: Identifying and locating surface defects in wood: Part of an automated lumber processing system. IEEE Transactions on Pattern Analysis and Machine Intelligence **5** (1983) 573–584

[6] Bovik, A., Clark, M.: Multichannel texture analysis using localized spatial filters. IEEE Transactions on Pattern Analysis and Machine Inteligence **12(1)** (1990) 55–73

[7] Kruizinga, P., Petkov, N., Grigorescu, S.: Comparison of texture features based on gabor filters. In: Proceedings of the 10th International Conference on Image Analysis and Processing, Venice, Italy. (1999) 142–147

[8] Dunn, D., Higgings, W., Wakeley, J.: Texture segmentation using 2-d gabor elementary functions. IEEE Transactions on Pattern Analysis and Machine Intelligence **16** (1994) 130–149

[9] Mallat, S.: A Wavelet Tour of Signal Processing. Academic Press (1999)

[10] Palm, C., Metzler, V., Lehmann, T., Spitzer, K.: Color texture classification by within and cross-cooccurence matrices. In: Proceedings of 15th International Conference on Pattern Recognition, Barcelona, Spain. (2000)

Does Independent Component Analysis Play a Role in Unmixing Hyperspectral Data?*

José M. P. Nascimento[1] and José M. B. Dias[2]

[1] Instituto Superior de Engenharia de Lisboa and Instituto de Telecomunicações
R. Conselheiro Emídio Navarro N 1, edifício 5, 1949-014 Lisboa Portugal
zen@isel.pt
Tel.: +351.21.8317237, Fax: +351.21.8317114
[2] Instituto Superior Técnico and Instituto de Telecomunicações
Av. Rovisco Pais, Torre Norte, Piso 10, 1049-001 Lisboa Portugal
bioucas@lx.it.pt
Tel.: +351.21.8418466, Fax: +351.21.841472

Abstract. Independent Component Analysis (ICA) have recently been proposed as a tool to unmix hyperspectral data. ICA is founded on two assumptions: i) The observed data vector is a linear mixture of the sources (abundance fractions); ii) sources are independent. Concerning hyperspectral data, the first assumption is valid whenever the constituent substances are surface distributed. The second assumption, however, is violated, since the sum of abundance fractions associated to each pixel is constant due to physical constraints in the data acquisition process. Thus, sources cannot be independent.

This paper gives evidence that ICA, at least in its canonical form, is not suited to unmix hyperspectral data. We arrive to this conclusion by minimizing the mutual information of simulated hyperspectral mixtures. The hyperspectral data model includes signature variability, abundance perturbation, sensor Point Spread Function (PSF), abundance constraint and electronic noise. Mutual information computation is based on fitting mixtures of Gaussians to the observed data.

1 Introduction

The development of high spatial resolution airborne and satellite sensors have improved the capability of ground-based data collection in the fields of agriculture, geography, geology, mineral identification, and detection and classification of targets activities [1], [2].

Hyperspectral sensors use many contiguous bands of high spectral resolution in optical and infrared spectra [3], [4]. The signal read by the sensor on a given band at a given pixel is a mixture of substances reflected energy (on the same band) presented in the respective pixel spatial coverage.

---

* This work was supported by the Fundação para a ciência e Tecnologia, under the project POSI/34071/CPS/2000

F.J. Perales et al. (Eds.): IbPRIA 2003, LNCS 2652, pp. 616–625, 2003.

Hyperspectral unmixing is the decomposition of the pixel spectra into constituent ground cover substances, also called endmembers, and their corresponding fractional abundances.

Depending on the substance distribution at each pixel, the observed mixture is either linear or non-linear. Linear mixing model assumes that substances are surface distributed in the scene and the incident solar radiation is scattered by surface through a single bounce. Non-linear model assumes that substances are volume distributed in the scene and the incident solar radiation is scattered by scene through multiple bounces [5].

Under the linear mixing model, and assuming that the number of substances and their reflectance spectrum are known, hyperspectral unmixing is a simple linear problem, which can be addressed, for example, under the maximum likelihood setup. In practice this knowledge is very difficult, if not impossible, to obtain. Hyperspectral unmixing falls, therefore, into the class of blind source separation problems [6].

Recently, blind source separation, feature extraction, and unsupervised recognition has been addressed under the Independent Component Analysis (ICA) framework [7]. ICA consists in finding a linear decomposition of observed data into independent components.

Given that hyperspectral data are, in given circumstances, linear mixtures, ICA come to mind as a possible tool to unmix this class of data. In fact the application of ICA to hyperspectral data has been proposed in [8], [9], [10], [11]. However, ICA is based on the assumption of mutually independent sources, which is not the case of hyperspectral data, since the sum of abundance fractions is constant, implying dependence among abundances. These dependence compromises ICA applicability to hyperspectral images.

This paper address hyperspectral data source dependence and its impact on ICA performance. The study is based on mutual information minimization. Hyperspectral observations are obtained by a generative model. This model takes into account the degradation mechanisms normally found in hyperspectral applications, namely signature variability, abundance perturbation, abundance constraint and system noise. Mutual information is computed based on mixture of Gaussians whose parameters (number of components, means, covariances and weights) are inferred using the Minimum Description Length (MDL) based algorithm [12]. We study the behaviour of the mutual information as function of the unmixing matrix. The conclusion is that the unmixing matrix minimizing the mutual information might be very far from the true unmixing matrix.

The computation of mutual information is based on simulated sample data because the analytical determination of mutual information is very hard, if not impossible, even though we know the probability density functions of the sources (they are simulated).

This paper is organized as follows. Section 2 formulates the mixed pixel classification problem as a linear mixture model and introduces a model accounting for data dependence, signature variability, and abundance perturbation. Section 3 presents a brief resume of ICA. In Section 4 performance analysis of ICA on

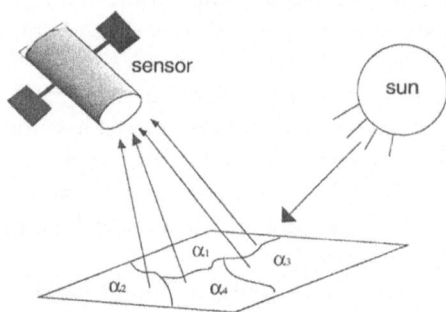

Fig. 1. Surface distributed substances in spatial cover area

hiperspectral data are studied based on simulations results. Section 5 concludes with some remarks.

2   Linear Spectral Mixture Model

Linear mixture model considers that substances present in the scene are surface distributed according to their abundance fractions (see Figure 1). Thus, each mixed pixel vector is a linear mixture of endmember spectra presented in the covered area. Let r_j be the sensor received signal at the jth frequency and $h(x, y)$ the point spread function (PSF) of the sensor. Then, r_j at the origin is

$$r_j = \int_A m_j(x, y) h(-x, -y) \, dx dy, \tag{1}$$

where $m_j(x, y)$ is the backscattered signal at jth frequency of a point with coordinates (x, y) in the spatial cover area of the sensor denoted by A. Assuming that

$$m_j(x, y) = m_{ji}, \qquad (x, y) \in A_i, \tag{2}$$

where A_i is the area occupied by the ith endmember, we then have

$$r_j = \sum_i \int_{A_i} m_{ji} h(-x, -y) \, dx dy, \tag{3}$$

since m_{ji} does not depend on the surface coordinates (x, y). Assuming that $h(x, y) = 1$ in the covered area, it follows that

$$r_j = \sum_i m_{ji} A_i. \tag{4}$$

If PSF is not a constant then expression (4) should be replaced by

$$r_j = \sum_i m_{ji} \beta_i A_i, \tag{5}$$

where

$$\beta_i = \frac{\int_{A_i} h(-x, -y) \, dx dy}{A_i}.$$ (6)

Denoting $\alpha_i \equiv \beta_i A_i$, it follows that

$$\sum_i \alpha_i = \int_A h(-x, -y) \, dx dy = c,$$ (7)

where c is a constant.

Let $\mathbf{r}$ be an $L \times 1$ vector where L is the total number of bands and $\mathbf{m}_i = [m_{1i}, m_{2i}, \ldots, m_{Li}]^T$ is the so-called signature of the ith endmember. Equation (5) can be written as

$$\mathbf{r} = \mathbf{M}\alpha,$$ (8)

where $\mathbf{M} = [\mathbf{m}_1, \mathbf{m}_2, \ldots, \mathbf{m}_p]$ is a matrix with signatures of the endmembers present in spatial cover area and $\alpha = [\alpha_1, \alpha_2, \ldots, \alpha_p]^T$. The notation $(\cdot)^T$ indicates vector transposed.

In hyperspectral applications endmembers signature may vary from pixel to pixel. These perturbations has been studied and accounted for in the unmixing algorithms [13], [14], [15]. In this paper we model signature variability by

$$\mathbf{m}_i = \theta_i * \mathbf{m}_i^o + \mathbf{n}_i,$$ (9)

where $\mathbf{m}_i^o$ is a reference endmember signature, θ_i is a scale parameter centered about one and $\mathbf{n}_i$ a zero-mean white random vector. Model (9) does not describe all the possible variations of endmember signatures. Nevertheless, by choosing θ_i with a small variance and a unitary mean and an appropriate variance for the components of random vector $\mathbf{n}_i$, we can approximate many real signature variations.

Illumination may vary from pixel to pixel and affect all bands equally. We model this by a random variable γ according to

$$\mathbf{r} = \mathbf{M}\underbrace{\gamma\theta\alpha}_{s} + \mathbf{n}.$$ (10)

where θ is a $p \times p$ diagonal matrix and $\mathbf{n}$ is additive white Gaussian noise with zero-mean and covariance matrix $\sigma^2 \mathbf{I}$ ($\mathbf{I}$ is the identity matrix) resulting from electronic noise and signature variability.

Apart from noise vector $\mathbf{n}$, model (10) has a canonical mixture form, i.e., $\mathbf{r} = \mathbf{M}\mathbf{s}$, where $\mathbf{s} = \gamma\theta\alpha$.

A spectral linear unmixing method estimates the unknown sources $\mathbf{s}$. If $\mathbf{M}$ is known, estimation of $\mathbf{s}$ is an ordinary linear problem. If $\mathbf{M}$ is unknown the problem is more difficult, and has been addressed under ICA framework in [16], [17], [18].

3   Independent Component Analysis

ICA [7] is an unsupervised source separation process, which has been successfully applied to blind separation problems [19], [20], [21]. Let $\mathbf{x}$ be an $L \times 1$ observation column vector, such as

$$\mathbf{x} = \mathbf{Ms}, \tag{11}$$

where $\mathbf{M}$ is an unknown $L \times p$ ($L \geq p$) mixing matrix and $\mathbf{s} = [s_1 \ s_2 \ ... \ s_p]^T$ an unknown random data vector of mutually independent components and unknown distributions, although at most one α_i might be Gaussian distributed. ICA finds a $p \times L$ separating matrix $\mathbf{W}$, such that

$$\mathbf{y} = \mathbf{Wx} = \mathbf{PCs}, \tag{12}$$

where $\mathbf{y}$ is a vector of independent components, and $\mathbf{P}$ and $\mathbf{C}$ are permutation a scale matrices, respectively.

Separating matrix $\mathbf{W}$ minimizes the mutual information of $\mathbf{y}$ given by

$$I(y_1, y_2, \ldots, y_p) = \sum_i H(y_i) - H(\mathbf{y}), \tag{13}$$

where $H(\mathbf{y})$ is the entropy (see, e.g., [19], [20]). The *Negentropy* (see, e.g., [21]), an entity close related with the mutual information, is also used as objective function to obtain $\mathbf{y}$.

In applying ICA to hyperspectral data, one is faced with the following differences with respect to model (11):

− Presence of noise $\mathbf{n}$;
− Source dependence due to the constraint,

$$\sum_{k=1}^{p} s_k = c, \tag{14}$$

where c is a constant. In spite of this, ICA has recently been applied to hyperspectral imagery (see [8], [9], [10], [11]).

In what follows, we give evidence that constraint (14) compromises the application of ICA to hyperspectral data.

Positivity and normalization constraints (see Eq.14) of the abundance fractions are incorporated as priors in [22], where the authors propose a unsupervised Bayesian approach to unmix hyperspectral data.

3.1   Minimization of Mutual Information

Given a matrix $\mathbf{W}$, the entropy of $\mathbf{y} = \mathbf{Wx}$ is $H(\mathbf{y}) = H(\mathbf{x}) + \log(\mathbf{W})$. The mutual information, as function of $\mathbf{W}$, is then given by

$$I(y_1, y_2, \ldots, y_p, \mathbf{W}) = \sum_i H(y_i) - H(\mathbf{x}) - \log|\mathbf{W}|. \tag{15}$$

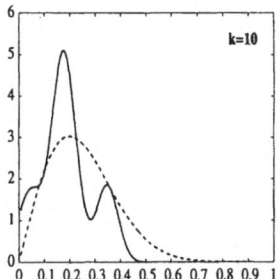 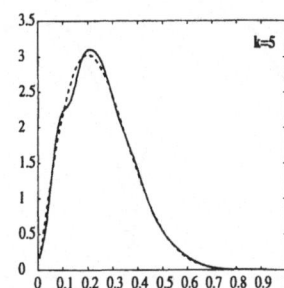 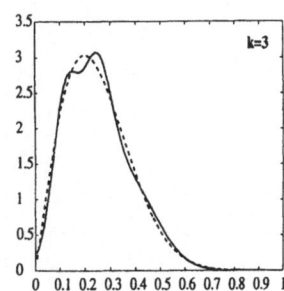

Fig. 2. Rayleigh probability density function (dashed line) fitted with a Gaussian mixture (solid line). Left: Initial Gaussian modes parameters (ten Gaussian modes). Center: solution of [12] with five Gaussian modes. Right: Solution of [12] constrained to three Gaussian modes

Assuming $|\mathbf{W}|$ constant, the mutual information minimization reduces to finding

$$\widehat{\mathbf{W}} = \arg \min_{\mathbf{W}} I(y_1, y_2, \dots, y_p, \mathbf{W}) = \min_{\mathbf{W}} \sum_i H(y_i), \qquad (16)$$

where

$$H(y_i) = -\int_{-\infty}^{+\infty} f_{y_i}(u) \log f_{y_i}(u) du \qquad (17)$$

To compute (17), we need to know f_{y_i}, the source probability density function of y_i. To obtain an estimate of f_{y_i}, we fit sample data with a mixture of Gaussians [23]. The number of Gaussians modes and respective parameters (means, covariances and weights) are calculated by the MDL-EM algorithm [12]. The entropy (17) is computed via numerical integration.

Figure 2, shows an example of a Rayleigh probability density function fitted with a Gaussian mixture using algorithm [12]. On the left, center, and right are presented probability density functions obtained with, respectively, the initial parameters, the solution, and the solution constrained to three Gaussian modes.

Various authors [21], [24] have referred to that maximum of $I(y_1, y_2, \dots, y_p, \mathbf{W})$ is not very sensitive to the shape of f_{y_i}. For example [24] uses only three Gaussian modes to fit whatever density shape. Herein, however, we use all modes given by the MDL-EM algorithm [12], as we are interested, not only in the separting matrix $\mathbf{W}$, but also in computing the mutual information $I(y_1, y_2, \dots, y_p, \mathbf{W})$ as function of $\mathbf{W}$.

4   Experimental Results

In the next five experiments, we study the behavior of the mutual information $I(y_1, y_2, \dots, y_p, \mathbf{W})$, for $\mathbf{W}$ in the neighborhood of the true unmixing matrix. In

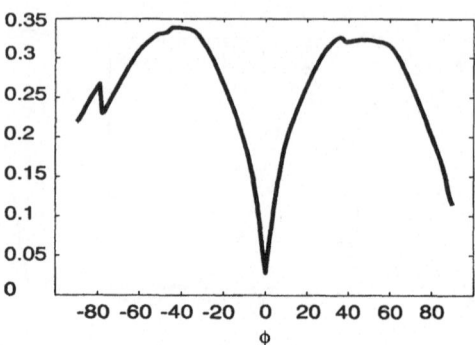

Fig. 3. Mutual information as function of the rotation angle ϕ for independent sources

all experiments we assume that **W** is a rotation matrix. This is always possible by spherizing the observed data [21].

Experiment I The first experiment consider independent sources with uniform distribution to test our setup under canonical mixing conditions. This experiment assume $p = 2$ (number of sources), $L = 2$ (number of bands), $\mathbf{M} = \mathbf{I}$, $\theta = \mathbf{I}$, $\gamma = 1$ and $\mathbf{n} = \mathbf{0}^T$.

Figure 3 shows the mutual information as function of the rotation angle ϕ in the interval $[-\pi/2, \pi/2]$. The minimum is global in this interval and occurs for $\phi = 0$, i.e., $\mathbf{W} = \mathbf{I}$. As expected the true unmixing matrix was recovered.

Experiment II Second experiment is similar to the previous one. It takes now three independent sources with uniform distribution and parameters $p = 3$, $L = 3$, $\mathbf{M} = \mathbf{I}$ $\theta = \mathbf{I}$, $\gamma = 1$, and $\mathbf{n} = \mathbf{0}^T$.

Figure 4 (top left) shows the Mutual information as function of ϕ_1 (azimuth angle) and ϕ_2 (elevation angle) in a gray scale. The minimum is global and occurs for $\phi_1 = 0$ and $\phi_2 = 0$, i.e., $\mathbf{W} = \mathbf{I}$.

As mentioned above abundance fractions in hyperspectral data are not independent. In order to test ICA with these constraints, we choose for the following experiments a Dirichlet distribution parameterized by $\mu_1 = 1$, $\mu_2 = 1$ and $\mu_3 = 1$ (μ_i is the expected value) for the sources. Such distribution constraints sources to $0 \le \alpha_i \le 1$ and $\sum \alpha_i = 1$.

Experiment III In this experiment, we assume that $p = 3$, $\mathbf{M} = \mathbf{I}$, $\theta = \mathbf{I}$, $\gamma = 1$, $\mathbf{n} = \mathbf{0}^T$.

In Figure 4 (top right) we present the mutual information as function of angles ϕ_1 and ϕ_2. It shows that ICA do not separate the original dependent data correctly. We obtain $(\hat{\phi}_1 = -\pi/4, \hat{\phi}_2 = -\pi/5)$, far from the true unmixing matrix ($\phi_1 = 0$, $\phi_2 = 0$).

Experiment IV In this experiment the sources are dependent and Dirichlet distributed ($\mu_1 = 1$, $\mu_2 = 1$, $\mu_3 = 1$). The remaining parameters are $\mathbf{M} = \mathbf{I}$, $\mathbf{n} = \mathbf{0}^T$, θ_i uniformly distributed with in the interval [0.9 1.1] and γ Beta distributed ($\sigma_1 = 1$, $\sigma_2 = 0.8$).

Figure 4 (bottom left) presents the mutual information as function of angles ϕ_1 and ϕ_2. Although there is a local minimum at $\phi_1 = 0$ and $\phi_2 = 0$, the absolute minimum occurs at $\hat{\phi}_1 = -\pi/4$ and $\hat{\phi}_2 = -\pi/5$.

Experiment V Last simulation is similar to experiment IV, but now we add white Gaussian noise with zero means and variance $\sigma^2 = 0.03$.

Figure 4 (Bottom right) shows the obtained mutual information. Image exhibits a more random pattern than top right and bottom left ones. The absolute minimum occurs at $\hat{\phi}_1 = 7\pi/18$, $\hat{\phi}_2 = \pi/36$, again far from ($\phi_1 = 0$, $\phi_2 = 0$).

The pattern of behaviour described in experiment III, IV, and V was systematically observed in an array of experiments with differ source distributions (different shapes and parameters).

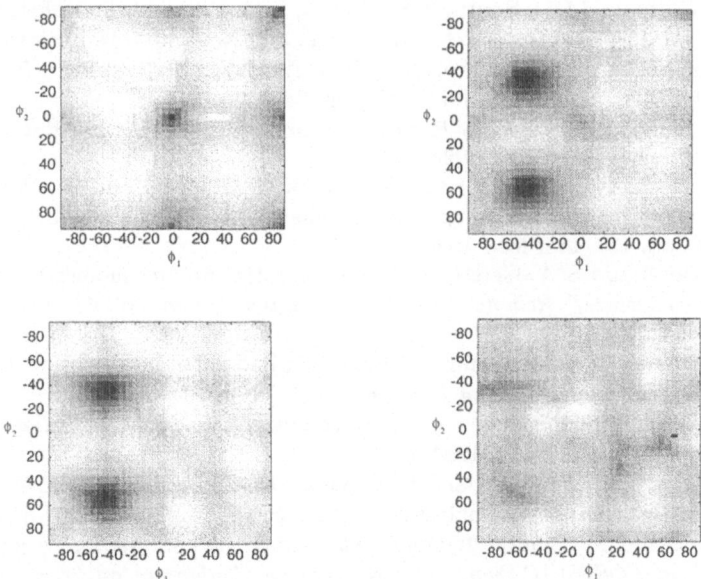

Fig. 4. Mutual information in function of parameters ϕ_1 and ϕ_2. Top left: three independent sources; Top right: Sources are dependent; Bottom left: Sources are dependent and parameters γ and θ are considered; Bottom right: Noise was added

5 Concluding Remarks

We have studied the applicability of Independent component Analysis (ICA) to hyperspectral imagery. Results reveals that ICA in its canonical form is not well suited to unmix hyperspectral sources (abundance fractions). Dependence due to physical constraint and noise due to signature variability are the main violations of ICA assumption.

Acknowledgement

The authors acknowledge Dr. Mario A. T. Figueiredo for providing the MDL-EM code.

References

[1] M. O. Smith, P. E. Johnson, and J. B. Adams, "Quantitative determination of mineral types and abundances from reflectance spectra using principal component analysis," in *Proc. 15th Lunar and Planetary Sci. Conf., Part 2, Geophys. Res.*, vol. 90, Feb. 1985, pp. C797–C804.

[2] A. R. Gillespie, M. O. Smith, J. B. Adams, S. C. Willis, A. F. Fisher, and D. E. Sabol, "Interpretation of residual images: Spectral mixture analysis of aviris images, owens valley, california," in *Proc 2nd AVIRIS Workshop, R. O. Green, Ed., Jpl Publ.*, vol. 90-54, June 1990, pp. 243–270.

[3] T. Lillesand and R. Kiefer, *Remote Sensing and Image Interpretation*, 3rd ed. John Wiley & Sons, Inc., 1994.

[4] G. Vane, R. Green, T. Chrien, H. Enmark, E. Hansen, and W. Porter, "The airborne visible/infrared imaging spectrometer (aviris)," *Remote Sens. Environ.*, vol. 44, pp. 127–143, May 1993.

[5] C. C. Borel and S. A. Gerstl, "Nonlinear spectral mixing models for vegetative and soils surface," *Remote Sensing of the Environment*, vol. 47, no. 2, pp. 403–416, 1994.

[6] P. Common, C. Jutten, and J. Herault, "Blind separation of sources, part ii: Problem statement," *Signal Processing*, vol. 24, pp. 11–20, 1991.

[7] P. Common, "Independent component analysis: A new concept," *Signal Processing*, vol. 36, pp. 287–314, 1994.

[8] J. Bayliss, J. A. Gualtieri, and R. Cromp, "Analysing hyperspectral data with independent component analysis," in *Proc. SPIE*, vol. 3240, 1997, pp. 133–143.

[9] C. Chen and X. Zhang, "Independent component analysis for remote sensing study," in *EOS/SPIE Symp. Remote Sensing Conference on Image and Signal Processing for Remote Sensing V*, vol. 3871, Sept. 20-24 1999, pp. 150–158.

[10] T. M. Tu, "Unsupervised signature extraction and separation in hyperspectral images: A noise-adjusted fast independent component analysis approach," *Opt. Eng./SPIE*, vol. 39, no. 4, pp. 897–906, April 2000.

[11] S.-S. Chiang, C.-I. Chang, and I. W. Ginsberg, "Unsupervised hyperspectral image analysis using independent component analysis," in *Proc. IEEE Int. Geoscience and Remote Sensing Symp*, July 24-28 2000.

[12] M. A. T. Figueiredo and A. K. Jain, "Unsupervised learning of finite mixture models," *IEEE Trans. Pattern Anal. Machine Intell.*, vol. 44, no. 3, pp. 381–396, Mar. 2002.

[13] C. Bateson, G. Asner, and C. Wessman, "Endmember bundles: A new approach to incorporating endmember variability into spectral mixture analysis," *IEEE Trans. Geosci. Remote Sensing*, vol. 38, pp. 1083–1094, Mar. 2000.

[14] F. Kruse, "Spectral identification of image endmembers determined from aviris data," in *Summaries of the VII JPL Airborne Earth Science Workshop*, 1998.

[15] J. Boardman and F. Kruse, "Automated spectral analysis: a geological example using aviris data, northern grapevine mountains, nevada," in *Proc. 10th Thematic Conference, Geologic Remote Sensing*, 1994.

[16] C. Brumbley and C.-I. Chang, "An unsupervised vector quantization-based target signature subspace projection approach to classification and detection in unknown background," *Pattern Recognition*, vol. 32, pp. 1161–1174, July 1999.

[17] H. Ren and C.-I. Chang, "A generalized orthogonal subspace projection approach to unsupervised multispectral image classification," *IEEE Trans. Geosci. Remote Sensing*, vol. 38, no. 6, pp. 2515–2528, Nov. 2000.

[18] C.-I. Chang and D. Heinz, "Subpixel spectral detection for remotely sensed images," *IEEE Trans. Geosci. Remote Sensing*, vol. 38, no. 3, pp. 1144–1159, May 2000.

[19] A. J. Bell and T. J. Sejnowski, "An information-maximization approach to blind separation and blind deconvolution," *Neural Computation*, vol. 10, pp. 215–234, 1995.

[20] J. Cardoso, "Infomax and maximum likelihood of source separation," *IEEE Signal Processing Lett.*, vol. 4, no. 4, pp. 112–114, Apr 1997.

[21] A. Hyvarinen and E. Oja, "Independent component analysis: Algorithms and applications," *Neural Networks*, vol. 13, no. 4-5, pp. 411–430, 2000.

[22] L. Parra, K.-R. Mueller, C. Spence, A. Ziehe, and P. Sajda, "Unmixing hyperspectral data," *Advances in Neural Information Processing Systems*, vol. 12, pp. 942–948, 2000.

[23] G. McLachlan and D. Peel, *Finite Mixture Models*. John Wiley & Sons, Inc., 2000.

[24] H. Attias, "Independent factor analysis," *Neural Computation*, vol. 11, no. 4, pp. 803–851, 1999.

Vertex Component Analysis:
A Fast Algorithm to Extract Endmembers
Spectra from Hyperspectral Data*

José M. P. Nascimento[1] and José M. B. Dias[2]

[1] Instituto Superior de Engenharia de Lisboa and Instituto de Telecomunicações
R. Conselheiro Emídio Navarro N 1, edifício 5, 1949-014 Lisboa Portugal
zen@isel.pt
Tel.: +351.21.8317237, Fax: +351.21.8317114
[2] Instituto Superior Técnico and Instituto de Telecomunicações
Av. Rovisco Pais, Torre Norte, Piso 10, 1049-001 Lisboa Portugal
bioucas@lx.it.pt
Tel.: +351.21.8418466, Fax: +351.21.841472

Abstract. Linear spectral mixture analysis, or linear unmixing, has proven to be a useful tool in hyperspectral remote sensing applications. It aims at estimating the number of reference substances, also called endmembers, their spectral signature and abundance fractions, using only the observed data (mixed pixels).
This paper presents new method that performs unsupervised endmember extraction from hyperspectral data. The algorithm exploits a simple geometric fact: endmembers are vertices of a simplex. The algorithm complexity, measured in floating points operations, is $O(n)$, where n is the sample size. The effectiveness of the proposed scheme is illustrated using simulated data.

1 Introduction

Hyperspectral remote sensing exploits the fact that all substances scatter electromagnetic energy, at specific wavelengths, in distinctive patterns related to their molecular composition [1], [2]. Hyperspectral sensors have been developed to sample the scattered portion of the electromagnetic spectrum that extends from the visible region through the near-infrared and mid-infrared, in hundreds of narrow contiguous bands [3], [4]. The number and variety of potential civilian and military applications for hyperspectral remote sensing is enormous [5], [6].

One of the most challenging task underlying many hyperspectral imagery applications is the spectral unmixing, which decompose a mixed pixel into a collection of reflectance spectra, called endmember signatures, and a set corresponding abundance fractions [7], [8], [9].

---

* This work was supported by the Fundação para a ciência e Tecnologia, under the project POSI/34071/CPS/2000.

Due to the spatial resolution of the hyperspectral sensors, a single pixel in a image is as a mixture of the substances present in the corresponding resolution cell [3]. Depending on the substance distribution at each pixel, the observed mixture is either linear or non-linear. Linear mixing model assumes that substances are surface distributed in the scene and the incident solar radiation is scattered by surface through a single bounce. Non-linear model assumes that substances are volume distributed in the scene and the incident solar radiation is scattered by the scene through multiple bounces [10]. Linear spectral unmixing is one of the most important approaches for the analysis of hyperspectral data [11]. It considers that a mixed pixel is a linear combination of endmembers signatures weighted by correspondent abundance fractions. Linear unmixing approach require the determination of endmember signatures. Once these spectra are found, hyperspectral data can be unmixed into the abundance fractions of each material at each pixel.

Different endmember determination algorithms based on the notion of spectral mixture model have been proposed [12], [13], [14]. One of the most successful approach is the pixel purity index (PPI) [13], [15], which is based on the geometry of convex sets [16]. several recent efforts pursue the fully automated identification of endmembers in hyperspectral data sets without dimensionality reduction [17]. The N-FINDR algorithm [18] is based on the fact that in N spectral dimensions, the N-volume contained by a simplex formed by the purest pixels is larger than any other volume formed from any other combination of pixels. This algorithm finds the set of pixels with the largest volume by "inflating" a simplex inside the data. Other works take into account endmember variability in unmixing process using extensive libraries [19], multiple endmembers [20] or use spatial and spectral information [21].

Independent Component Analysis (ICA) have also recently been proposed as a tool to unmix hyperspectral data [22], [23], [24], [25]. ICA is based on the assumption of mutually independent sources, which is not the case of hyperspectral data, since the sum of abundance fractions is constant, implying dependence among abundances. These dependence compromises ICA applicability to hyperspectral images [26].

In this paper we introduce the *vertex component analysis* (VCA) to unmix linear mixtures of hyperspectral sources. The algorithm is unsupervised and exploits the fact that endmembers occupy vertices of a simplex.

This communication is structured as follows. Section 2 describes fundamental principles in the proposed method. In Section 3 proposed method is evaluated with simulated data. Section 4 ends the paper by presenting some concluding remarks.

2   Vertex Component Analysis Algorithm

Assuming the linear mixture scenario, each pixel is a linear combination of endmember spectra present in the covered area.

Let **r** be an $L \times 1$ vector, where L is the total number of bands, and $\mathbf{m}_i$ the so-called signature of the ith endmember. Thus

$$\mathbf{r} = \mathbf{M}\boldsymbol{\alpha}, \tag{1}$$

where $\mathbf{M} = [\mathbf{m}_1, \mathbf{m}_2, \dots, \mathbf{m}_p]$, $\boldsymbol{\alpha} = [\alpha_1, \alpha_2, \dots, \alpha_p]^T$ is the abundance fractions of each endmember, and p is the number of endmembers present in spatial cover area. The notation $(\cdot)^T$ stands for vector transposed.

Due to physical constraints [11], abundance fractions satisfy

$$0 \leq \alpha_k \leq 1, \tag{2}$$

$$\sum_{k=1}^{p} \alpha_k = 1. \tag{3}$$

Each pixel can be viewed as a vector in an L-dimensional Euclidean space, where each channel is assigned to one axis of space, all being mutually orthogonal. Due to constraints (2) and (3) the observed vector **r** belongs to a simplex with pure pixels in the vertices. For instance, Figure 1 (left) illustrates a projection of a simplex defined by a mixture of three endmembers into a plane defined by two bands. As result we have a triangle whose vertices are the endmembers projections on the same plane.

The pseudo-code for the VCA algorithm is shown in Algorithm 1. Symbols $[\widehat{\mathbf{M}}]_{:,j}$ and $[\widehat{\mathbf{M}}]_{:,i:k}$ stands for the jth column of $\widehat{\mathbf{M}}$ and the columns i to k of $\widehat{\mathbf{M}}$, respectively. Symbol $\widehat{\mathbf{M}}$ stands for the estimated mixing matrix and $[\mathbf{z}]_{:,k}$ is the kth column of matrix **z**.

Assume that there exists at least one pure pixel of each endmember in the input sample $\mathbf{z} \equiv [\mathbf{r}_1, \mathbf{r}_2, \dots, \mathbf{r}_n]$. In this case, each time the loop *for* is executed, a vector **f** orthonormal to $\widehat{\mathbf{M}}$ is generated and all input sample **z** are projected onto **f**. Since we assume that pure endmembers occupy the vertices of a simplex, then $a \leq \mathbf{f}^T \mathbf{r}_i \leq b$, where values a and b correspond to and only to pure pixels.

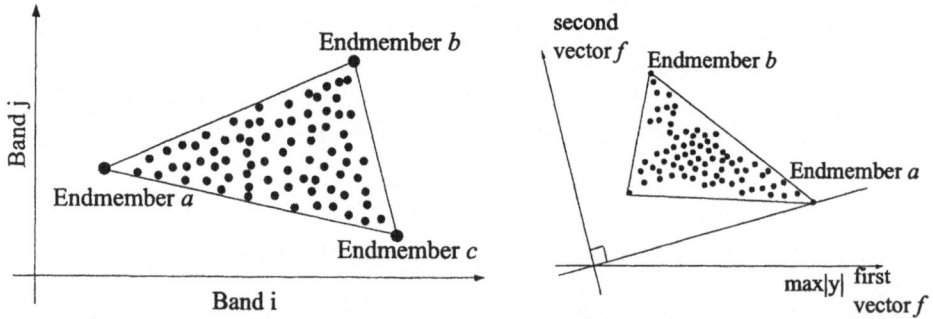

Fig. 1. Left: Scatter-plot of 2-D spectral data illustrating a mixture model based on endmembers. Right: Illustration of the VCA algorithm

Algorithm 1 Vertex Component Analysis

INPUT: p and $\mathbf{z} \equiv [\mathbf{r}_1, \mathbf{r}_2, \ldots, \mathbf{r}_n]$

$\widehat{\mathbf{M}} := 0 \ \{L \times p \text{ estimated mixing matrix}\}$;

$\mathbf{f} := \underbrace{[1, 0, \ldots, 0]}_{L}{}^T$;

for $i := 1$ to p **do**

$\quad \mathbf{y} := \mathbf{f}^T \mathbf{z}$;

$\quad k := \arg \max_{j=1,\ldots,n} \|y(j)\|$;

$\quad [\widehat{\mathbf{M}}]_{:,i} := [\mathbf{z}]_{:,k}$;

$\quad \{\text{generate a vector } f \text{ orthonormal to span} \left([\widehat{\mathbf{M}}]_{:,1:i} \right) \}$

$\quad \mathbf{f} := \text{orthonormal}([\widehat{\mathbf{M}}]_{:,1:i})$;

end for

We store the endmember signature corresponding to $\max(\|a\|, \|b\|)$. The next time loop *for* is executed, $\mathbf{f}$ is orthogonal to the space spanned by the signatures already determined. Figure 1 (right) shows the input samples $\mathbf{z}$ and the first chosen pure pixel, after the projection $y = \mathbf{f}^T \mathbf{z}$. Then a second vector $\mathbf{f}$ orthonormal to the endmember a is generated, and the second endmember is stored.

3   Evaluation of VCA Algorithm

In this section we evaluate the performance of the proposed algorithm by using simulated data based on laboratory spectra from the U.S. geological survey (USGS) digital spectral library [27].

A 30×30 pixel hyperspectral scene have been generated using three selected signatures ($p = 3$ and $L = 224$). This scene has nine regions, each one, of 10×10 pixel, with different abundance fractions for each endmember (see Fig. 2).

In order to determine the accuracy of our method, we compare the estimated abundances to the true abundances. Figure 3 (top), shows the abundance frac-

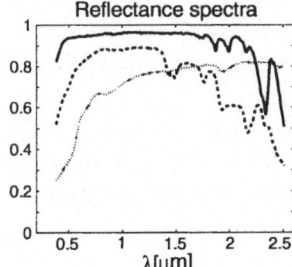

$\alpha_1 = 0.3$	$\alpha_1 = 0.5$	$\alpha_1 = 1.0$
$\alpha_2 = 0.3$	$\alpha_2 = 0.5$	$\alpha_2 = 0.0$
$\alpha_3 = 0.4$	$\alpha_3 = 0.0$	$\alpha_3 = 0.0$
$\alpha_1 = 0.0$	$\alpha_1 = 0.4$	$\alpha_1 = 0.3$
$\alpha_2 = 0.5$	$\alpha_2 = 0.3$	$\alpha_2 = 0.4$
$\alpha_3 = 0.5$	$\alpha_3 = 0.3$	$\alpha_3 = 0.3$
$\alpha_1 = 0.0$	$\alpha_1 = 0.5$	$\alpha_1 = 0.0$
$\alpha_2 = 1.0$	$\alpha_2 = 0.0$	$\alpha_2 = 0.0$
$\alpha_3 = 0.0$	$\alpha_3 = 0.5$	$\alpha_3 = 1.0$

Simulated Scene

Fig. 2. Left: Reflectances spectra used to generate simulated scene. Right: Regions with endmembers abundances in simulated scene

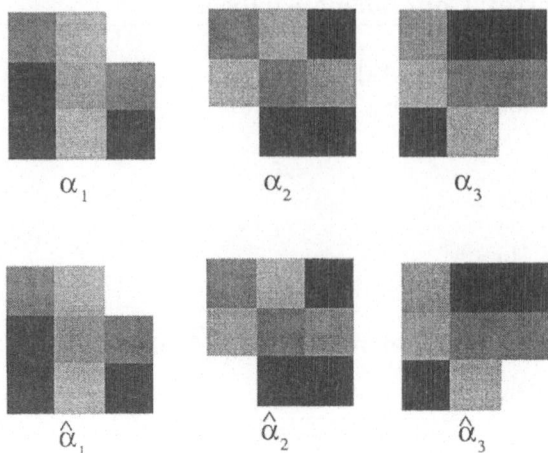

Fig. 3. Top: Abundance fractions of three endmembers. Bottom: Estimated abundance fractions

tions of the three endmembers in a gray scale. The same figure (bottom) presents the estimated abundance fractions by the algorithm. As we see, all regions have the correct abundance values.

Based on the same signatures (see Fig. 2), two other experiments were made, where abundance fractions follow the Dirichlet distribution with parameters $\mu_1 = 1$, $\mu_2 = 1$, and $\mu_3 = 1$, for the first experiment and $\mu_1 = 1$, $\mu_2 = 1$, and $\mu_3 = .3$ for the second (μ_i is the expected value). This choice takes into account the constraints (2) and (3).

In order to illustrate the noise impact on the algorithm performance, several experiments were made with different levels of signal-to-noise ratio (SNR), which is defined as

$$SNR = 10 \log \frac{\Sigma_{ji}\|m_{ji}\|^2/L}{\sigma^2},$$ (4)

where σ^2 is the noise variance of each band. Figure 4 (left), presents a scatter-plot of data without noise in bands $\lambda = 470nm$ and $\lambda = 2070nm$. It is also plotted a triangle whose vertices represent the real endmembers (solid line) and a triangle whose vertices represent the estimated endmembers (dashed line). Figure 4 (right) presents a scatter-plot of data with noise ($SNR = 30dB$), in the same bands.

A comparison of the proposed algorithm with PPI and N-FINDR algorithms is shown in Figure 5, with different levels of noise, and different Dirichlet distributions to the abundance fractions. To evaluate the performance of the three algorithms we adopt the mixing matrix error ϵ_M and the mean square recon-

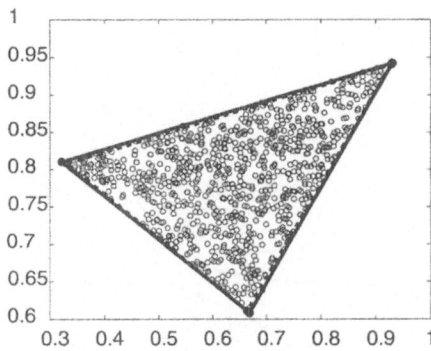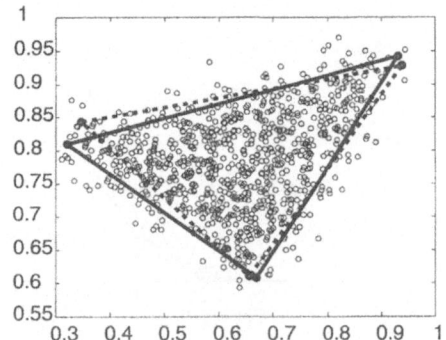

Fig. 4. Scatter-plot of data in bands $\lambda = 470nm$ and $\lambda = 2070nm$, triangle based on real endmembers (solid line) triangle based on estimated endmembers (dashed line) Left: Without noise. Right: With noise

struction error ϵ_α [28], given by:

$$\epsilon_M = \left(\frac{1}{L^2 - L}\sum_{i \neq j=1}^{L} \mathbf{J}_{ij}^2\right)\left(\frac{1}{L}\sum_{i=1}^{L} \mathbf{J}_{ii}^2\right)^{-1}, \tag{5}$$

$$\epsilon_\alpha = \frac{1}{L}\sum_{i=1}^{L} E(\hat{\alpha}_i - \alpha_i)^2, \tag{6}$$

where $\mathbf{J} = \hat{\mathbf{M}}^\sharp \mathbf{M}$, $\hat{\mathbf{M}}$ is the estimated endmember signatures and $\hat{\alpha}_i$ the abundance estimation of the ith endmember. The notation $(\cdot)^\sharp$ stands for the pseudoinverse matrix. This figure illustrates that in a noiseless scenario all the algorithms can extract the true endmembers. The presence of noise in data degrades the performance the algorithms. For SNR levels inferior than $15dB$, the average mean square error of the abundances is larger than 0.035. Figure 5 (Bottom) present the results for abundance fractions with Dirichlet distribution ($\mu_1 = 1$, $\mu_2 = 1$, and $\mu_3 = .3$). We conclude that the mean square reconstruction error is worse in this case. PPI algorithm is the most sensible to the distribution of the abundance fractions. This is explained by the fact of one of the endmembers does not have pure pixels.

In order to illustrate how the algorithm performance depends with the size of the spatial covered area, several experiments were made with different number of pixels. For this experiments we assume the signatures presented in Figure 2, and the abundances fractions follow the Dirichlet distribution with parameters $\mu_1 = 1$, $\mu_2 = 1$, and $\mu_3 = 1$, for the first set of experiments and $\mu_1 = 1$, $\mu_2 = 1$, and $\mu_3 = .3$ for the second one. Figure 6 (top left) shows that VCA, PPI and N-FINDR algorithm have identical performance, i.e., the mixing matrix error is better as the number of pixels grows. Only with ten pixels the result for N-FINDR algorithm is worse. When we change the distribution (see Fig. 6 top right) PPI algorithm is better, but the main difference occurs when we have few

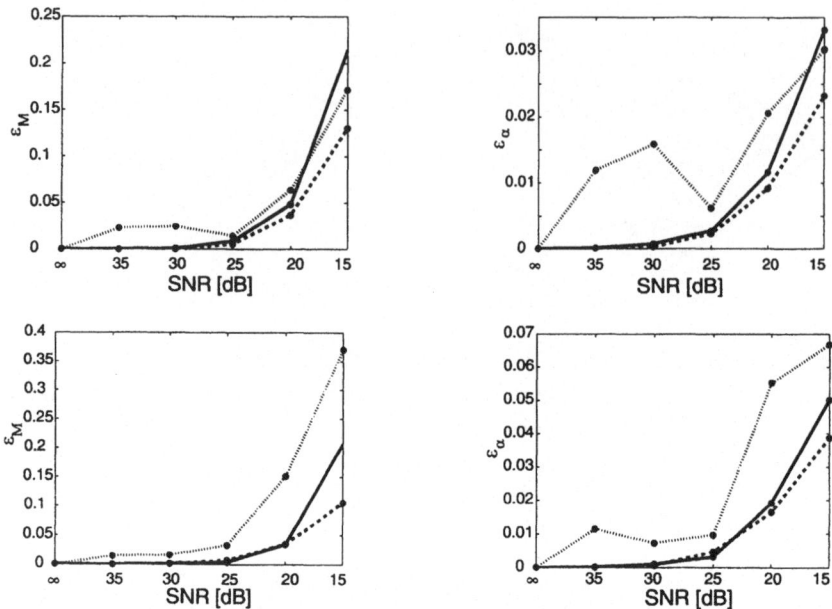

Fig. 5. VCA algorithm (solid line) N-FINDR algorithm (dashed line) PPI algorithm (dot line). Top left: Mixing matrix error, sources with Dirichlet distribution ($\mu_1 = 1$, $\mu_2 = 1$, and $\mu_3 = 1$) ; Top Right: Mean square reconstruction error, sources with Dirichlet distribution ($\mu_1 = 1$, $\mu_2 = 1$, and $\mu_3 = 1$); Bottom left: Mixing matrix error, sources with Dirichlet distribution ($\mu_1 = 1$, $\mu_2 = 1$, and $\mu_3 = .3$); Bottom Right: Mean square reconstruction error, sources with Dirichlet distribution ($\mu_1 = 1$, $\mu_2 = 1$, and $\mu_3 = .3$)

pixels. The same experiments where made with noise ($SNR = 30dB$, see Fig. 6 Bottom). In those experiments, the PPI algorithm have the worse result, VCA and N-FINDR algorithms are comparable.

Finally, we measured the number of floating point operation, in order to compare the complexity of VCA, PPI, and N-FINDR algorithms. Table 1 presents the result when the number of pixels in the image were 100, 1000, and 10000. The VCA algorithm complexity is much lower than the other ones. In fact, N-FINDR algorithm computes several times the determinant of a matrix (number of pixel × number of endmembers), and PPI algorithm make several projections of data into "skewers". Another reason for PPI and N-FINDR have such complexity, is the need to spherize data.

4   Conclusions

In this paper, we have proposed an algorithm to unmix linear mixtures of hyperspectral sources. The algorithm is unsupervised and exploits the fact that

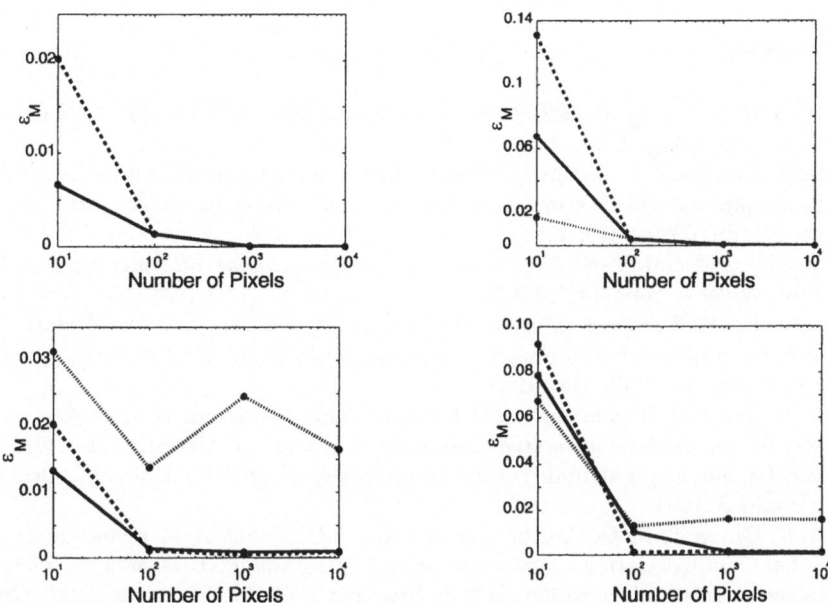

Fig. 6. Mixing matris error for VCA algorithm (solid line) N-FINDR algorithm (dashed line) PPI algorithm (dot line). Top left: Dirichlet distribution ($\mu_1 = 1$, $\mu_2 = 1$, and $\mu_3 = 1$) without noise ; Right: Dirichlet distribution ($\mu_1 = 1$, $\mu_2 = 1$, and $\mu_3 = .3$) without noise; Bottom left: Dirichlet distribution ($\mu_1 = 1$, $\mu_2 = 1$, and $\mu_3 = 1$) with $SNR = 30dB$; Bottom right: Dirichlet distribution ($\mu_1 = 1$, $\mu_2 = 1$, and $\mu_3 = .3$) with $SNR = 30dB$

Table 1. Floating point operations for VCA and N-FINDR algorithms with 100, 1000, and 10 000 pixels

	100 pixels	1000 pixels	10 000 pixels
VCA	1 040 259	2 249 859	14 345 859
N-FINDR	109 095 369	200 367 011	1 116 791 923
PPI	208 861 351	796 126 721	6 671 079 586

endmembers occupy the vertices of a simplex. In the performed tests, the PPI and N-FINDR algorithms have a complexity four hundred and seventy times higher than VCA algorithm, respectively, for a similar performance.

References

[1] B. Hapke, *Theory of Reflectance and Emmittance Spectroscopy*. Cambridge, U. K.: Cambridge Univ. Press, 1993.

[2] R. N. Clark and T. L. Roush, "Reflectance spectroscopy: Quantitative analysis techniques for remote sensing applications," *J. of Geophysical Research*, vol. 89, no. B7, pp. 6329–6340, 1984.

[3] T. Lillesand and R. Kiefer, *Remote Sensing and Image Interpretation*, 3rd ed. John Wiley & Sons, Inc., 1994.

[4] G. Vane, R. Green, T. Chrien, H. Enmark, E. Hansen, and W. Porter, "The airborne visible/infrared imaging spectrometer (aviris)," *Remote Sens. Environ.*, vol. 44, pp. 127–143, May 1993.

[5] M. O. Smith, J. B. Adams, and D. E. Sabol, *Spectral mixture analysis-New strategies for the analysis of multispectral data*, J. Hill and J. Mergier, Eds. Brussels and Luxemburg, Belgium: Image Spectrometry-A Tool for Environmental Observations, 1994.

[6] A. R. Gillespie, M. O. Smith, J. B. Adams, S. C. Willis, A. F. Fisher, and D. E. Sabol, "Interpretation of residual images: Spectral mixture analysis of aviris images, owens valley, california," in *Proc 2nd AVIRIS Workshop, R. O. Green, Ed., Jpl Publ.*, vol. 90-54, June 1990, pp. 243–270.

[7] J. J. Settle, "On the relationship between spectral unmixing and subspace projection," *IEEE Trans. Geosci. Remote Sensing*, vol. 34, pp. 1045–1046, July 1996.

[8] Y. H. Hu, H. B. Lee, and F. L. Scarpace, "Optimal linear spectral unmixing," *IEEE Trans. Geosci. Remote Sensing*, vol. 37, pp. 639–644, Jan. 1999.

[9] M. Petrou and P. G. Foschi, "Confidence in linear spectral unmixing of single pixels," *IEEE Trans. Geosci. Remote Sensing*, vol. 37, pp. 624–626, Jan. 1999.

[10] C. C. Borel and S. A. Gerstl, "Nonlinear spectral mixing models for vegetative and soils surface," *Remote Sensing of the Environment*, vol. 47, no. 2, pp. 403–416, 1994.

[11] D. Manolakis, C. Siracusa, and G. Shaw, "Hyperspectral subpixel target detection using linear mixing model," *IEEE Trans. Geosci. Remote Sensing*, vol. 39, no. 7, pp. 1392–1409, July 2001.

[12] A. Ifarraguerri and C.-I. Chang, "Multispectral and hyperspectral image analysis with convex cones," *IEEE Trans. Geosci. Remote Sensing*, vol. 37, no. 2, pp. 756–770, Mar. 1999.

[13] J. Boardman, "Automating spectral unmixing of aviris data using convex geometry concepts," in *Summaries of the Fourth Annual JPL Airborne Geoscience Workshop, JPL Pub. 93-26, AVIRIS Workshop.*, vol. 1, 1993, pp. 11–14.

[14] M. D. Craig, "Minimum-volume transforms for remotely sensed data," *IEEE Trans. Geosci. Remote Sensing*, vol. 32, pp. 99–109, 1994.

[15] J. Theiler, D. Lavenier, N. Harvey, S. Perkins, and J. Szymanski, "Using blocks of skewers for faster computation of pixel purity index," in *Proc. SPIE Int. Conf. Optical Science and Technology*, 2000.

[16] S. R. Lay, *Convex Sets and Their Applications*. New York: John Wiley & Sons, Inc., 1982.

[17] K. Staenz, T. Szeredi, and J. Schwarz, "Isdas - a system for processing/analysing hyperspectral data," *Can. J. of Remote Sensing*, vol. 24, pp. 99–113, 1998.

[18] M. E. Winter, "N-findr: an algorithm for fast autonomous spectral end-member determination in hyperspectral data," in *Proc. SPIE Imaging Spectrometry V*, 1999, pp. 266–275.

[19] D. Roberts, M. Gardener, J. Regelbrugge, D. Pedreros, and S. Ustin, "Mapping the distribution of wildfire fuels using aviris in the santa monica mountains," in *Summaries of the VIII JPL Airborne Earth Science Workshop*, 1998.

[20] C. Bateson, G. Asner, and C. Wessman, "Endmember bundles: A new approach to incorporating endmember variability into spectral mixture analysis," *IEEE Trans. Geosci. Remote Sensing*, vol. 38, pp. 1083–1094, Mar. 2000.

[21] A. Plaza, P. Martinez, R. Perez, and J. Plaza, "Spatial/spectral endmember extraction by multidimensional morphological operations," *IEEE Trans. Geosci. Remote Sensing*, vol. 40, no. 9, pp. 2025–2041, Sep. 2002.

[22] J. Bayliss, J. A. Gualtieri, and R. Cromp, "Analysing hyperspectral data with independent component analysis," in *Proc. SPIE*, vol. 3240, 1997, pp. 133–143.

[23] C. Chen and X. Zhang, "Independent component analysis for remote sensing study," in *EOS/SPIE Symp. Remote Sensing Conference on Image and Signal Processing for Remote Sensing V*, vol. 3871, Sept. 20-24 1999, pp. 150–158.

[24] T. M. Tu, "Unsupervised signature extraction and separation in hyperspectral images: A noise-adjusted fast independent component analysis approach," *Opt. Eng./SPIE*, vol. 39, no. 4, pp. 897–906, April 2000.

[25] S.-S. Chiang, C.-I. Chang, and I. W. Ginsberg, "Unsupervised hyperspectral image analysis using independent component analysis," in *Proc. IEEE Int. Geoscience and Remote Sensing Symp*, July 24-28 2000.

[26] J. M. P. Nascimento and J. M. B. Dias, "Does independent component analysis play a role in unmixing hyperspectral data?" in *IbPRIA'03*, Sep. 2003, to be published.

[27] R. N. Clark, G. A. Swayze, A. Gallagher, T. V. King, and W. M. Calvin, "The u.s. geological survey digital spectral library: Version 1: 0.2 to 3.0 μm," U. S. Geological Survey," Open File Report 93-592, 1993.

[28] H. Attias, "Independent factor analysis," *Neural Computation*, vol. 11, no. 4, pp. 803–851, 1999.

On the Relationship between Classification Error Bounds and Training Criteria in Statistical Pattern Recognition

Hermann Ney

Lehrstuhl für Informatik VI – Computer Science Department
RWTH Aachen – University of Technology, 52056 Aachen, Germany
ney@informatik.rwth-aachen.de

Abstract. We present two novel bounds for the classification error that, at the same time, can be used as practical training criteria. Unlike the bounds reported in the literature so far, these novel bounds are based on a strict distinction between the true but unknown distribution and the model distribution, which is used in the decision rule. The two bounds we derive are the squared distance and the Kullback-Leibler distance, where in both cases the distance is computed between the true distribution and the model distribution. In terms of practical training criteria, these bounds result in the squared error criterion and the mutual information (or equivocation) criterion, respectively.

1 Introduction

The classification error is the most important performance criterion in any pattern recognition task. The goal of this work to establish a direct relationship between practical training criteria and exact upper bounds for the classification error. There are three novel contributions of this paper:

- All the considerations will be based on the model-based classification error as opposed to the Bayes classification error. The Bayes error is only of theoretical value, because it requires the true but unknown distribution. Instead, we will use the model distribution in the decision rule whose parameters have to be learned from training data.
- Since the classification error is difficult to handle, we will derive two upper bounds that are more convenient for mathematical analysis.
- Using these bounds, we derive two practical training criteria which are well known in pattern recognition and show that they are related to upper bounds of the model-based classification error.

The concept of using the classification error directly as training criterion is widely known in pattern recognition [7, pp.46/47], [9, pp.106/107]. However, these studies always use the Bayes classification error. In addition, upper bounds are reported, but again only for the Bayes classification error [7, pp.46/47], [10]. In [6], the model-based classification error is studied, but only for two-class

F.J. Perales et al. (Eds.): IbPRIA 2003, LNCS 2652, pp. 636–645, 2003.
© Springer-Verlag Berlin Heidelberg 2003

problems. Vapnik's framework of empirical risk minimization [6, pp. 187],[18] is more concerned with statistical fluctuations from one sample set to another sample set, and the reference error rate is *not* the Bayes classification error. To the best of our knowledge, the exact mathematical dependence between the model-based classification error and the possible training criteria has not been studied before.

2   Model-Based Decision Rule and Classification Error

2.1   Classification Task and True Distribution

In statistical pattern recognition, we consider the observation (or feature) vector $x \in \mathcal{X} \subset \mathbb{R}^D$ and the class index $c = 1, ..., C$ to be random variables with a joint distribution:

$$\text{pair of random variables:} \quad (x, c)$$
$$\text{with true distribution:} \quad pr(x, c) = pr(x)\, pr(c|x) \qquad (1)$$

The classification task is to determine for each observation vector x the associated class index c. For such a task, the minimum classification error is obtained for the Bayes decision rule in which the class posterior distribution $pr(c|x)$ plays a crucial role. We will refer to it simply as the true distribution.

2.2   Model Distribution and Associated Decision Rule

In all practical applications, the true distribution $pr(c|x)$ is not known, and we can use only a so-called model distribution $p_\vartheta(c|x)$ instead. For such a model distribution, the functional dependence of the class index c on the observation vector x is fully specified using some unknown parameter set ϑ. The choice of this functional dependence is very much application specific. A large number of widely used techniques in pattern recognition fit into this interpretation. Examples are artificial neural networks or any type of discriminant functions, decision tree (CART) approaches, the single Gaussian and Gaussian mixture classifiers and maximum entropy (or log-linear) models. In case of observation vectors over a time axis, Hidden Markov models are typically used.

To be more exact, the model distribution $p_\vartheta(c|x)$ is a posterior distribution over the classes $c = 1, ..., C$:

$$\text{model distribution:} \quad p_\vartheta(c|x)$$
$$\text{with:} \quad 0 \leq p_\vartheta(c|x) \qquad \sum_c p_\vartheta(c|x) = 1 \qquad (2)$$

We interpret it as the score of the hypothesis that the observation x has been generated by the class c, and thus it is a natural requirement to normalize these scores in such a way that, for each observation x, they sum up to unity. Note that, for non-negative scores $p_\vartheta(c, x)$, we can always satisfy this constraint by simple re-normalization.

To find the unknown class identity of an observation x, we define the model-based decision rule:

$$\text{decision rule } c_\vartheta(\cdot): \quad c_\vartheta : \mathcal{X} \to \{1, ..., C\}$$

$$x \to c_\vartheta(x) := \arg\max_c \left\{ p_\vartheta(c|x) \right\} \qquad (3)$$

In order to avoid an awkward notation, we use only the parameter ϑ as index on the decision rule to express the dependence on the *full* model distribution $p_\vartheta(c|x)$. We use the attribute *model-based* to distinguish this decision rule from the *Bayes* decision rule where the true but unknown distribution $pr(c|x)$ is needed. In the following, the goal will be to study whether and how the classification error of the model-based decision rule will get close to the minimum classification error.

2.3   Model-Based Classification Error

When using such a decision rule $x \to c_\vartheta(x)$, we have a classification error count $e(x, c)$ for a joint event (x, c):

$$e(x, c) := 1 - \delta(c_\vartheta(x), c) \qquad (4)$$

where $\delta(\cdot, \cdot)$ denotes the Kronecker delta. The *local* classification error $E_\vartheta\{e|x\}$ is the x-conditional expectation of $e(x, c)$, which is obtained by using the true class posterior distribution $pr(c|x)$ in the point x of the observation space:

$$E_\vartheta\{e|x\} := \sum_c pr(c|x) \cdot \left[1 - \delta(c_\vartheta(x), c) \right]$$

$$= 1 - pr(c_\vartheta(x)|x) \qquad (5)$$

The *global* classification error $E_\vartheta\{e\}$ is obtained by integrating over the whole space of observations x:

$$E_\vartheta\{e\} = \int_x dx \, pr(x) \, E_\vartheta\{e|x\} \qquad (6)$$

Ideally, we would like to directly minimize this classification error in order to learn the unknown parameter set ϑ. However, the direct solution to this optimization problem is extremely difficult for two reasons: First, there are two extreme nonlinearities, namely the maximum operations and the Kronecker delta. Second, we have to compute the expectation over the true distribution $pr(x)$ which however is unknown and for which only a training sample is available.

3   Bounds for Local Classification Error

In this section, we will derive bounds for the local classification error when the decision rule Eq.(3) is used with *any type* of model $p_\vartheta(c|x)$. We will start with the x-conditional, i.e. *local*, classification error and consider the global classification error later.

3.1   Principle

It is well known that the global minimum of the error rate is obtained by the Bayes decision rule:

$$x \to c_*(x) := \arg\max_c \left\{ pr(c|x) \right\} \tag{7}$$

i.e. when the true (but unknown) posterior distribution $pr(c|x)$ is used as model distribution $p_\vartheta(c|x)$. The associated local Bayes classification error $E_*\{e|x\}$ is:

$$E_*\{e|x\} = 1 - pr(c_*(x)|x) \tag{8}$$

Therefore, the Bayes error is also the absolute minimum of *any* model $p_\vartheta(c|x)$ (for a *fixed* type of observations x), and we will consider the *difference* between the model-based classification error $E_\vartheta(e|x)$ and the Bayes classification error $E_*\{e|x\}$. In the following, we will derive an inequality of the form:

$$E_\vartheta\{e|x\} - E_*\{e|x\} \le \alpha \cdot \left\| pr(\cdot|x) - p_\vartheta(\cdot|x) \right\| \tag{9}$$

where we have a positive constant α and we use a suitable norm $\|\cdot\|$ of a C-dimensional difference vector between the true distribution $pr(c|x)$ and the model distribution $p_\vartheta(c|x)$. Depending on the type of norm $\|\cdot\|$, we will refer to these bounds as l_1, l_2 and l_∞ bounds.

3.2   Basic Inequality

Using the basic definitions introduced so far, we can write down the following sequence of equations and inequalities:

$$
\begin{aligned}
E_\vartheta\{e|x\} - E_*\{e|x\} &:= \\
&:= \left[1 - pr(c_\vartheta(x)|x) \right] - \left[1 - pr(c_*(x)|x) \right] \\
&= pr(c_*(x)|x) - pr(c_\vartheta(x)|x) \\
&\le pr(c_*(x)|x) - pr(c_\vartheta(x)|x) + p_\vartheta(c_\vartheta(x)|x) - p_\vartheta(c_*(x)|x) \\
&= \left[pr(c_*(x)|x) - p_\vartheta(c_*(x)|x) \right] + \left[p_\vartheta(c_\vartheta(x)|x) - pr(c_\vartheta(x)|x) \right] \\
&\le \left| pr(c_*(x)|x) - p_\vartheta(c_*(x)|x) \right| + \left| pr(c_\vartheta(x)|x) - p_\vartheta(c_\vartheta(x)|x) \right|
\end{aligned}
$$

$$(10)$$
$$(11)$$

Here, the first inequality Eq.(10) is true because, by the definition of the model-based decision rule $x \to c_\vartheta(x)$, we must have for any class c:

$$p_\vartheta(c|x) \le \max_{\tilde{c}} \left\{ p_\vartheta(\tilde{c}|x) \right\} \equiv p_\vartheta(c_\vartheta(x)|x) \tag{12}$$

The second inequality Eq.(11) results simply from the application of the triangle inequality.

3.3   Local Bounds

From the inequality Eq.(11), we immediately obtain what will be referred to as l_1 bound:

$$E_\vartheta\{e|x\} - E_*\{e|x\} \le \sum_c |pr(c|x) - p_\vartheta(c|x)| \tag{13}$$

It is easy to verify that this bound is also correct in the special case: $c_\vartheta(x) = c_*(x)$. In addition, we can also immediately establish the l_∞ bound (or maximum bound) and the l_2 bound:

$$E_\vartheta\{e|x\} - E_*\{e|x\} \le 2 \cdot \max_c \left\{ |pr(c|x) - p_\vartheta(c|x)| \right\} \tag{14}$$

$$\le 2 \cdot \sqrt{\sum_c [pr(c|x) - p_\vartheta(c|x)]^2} \tag{15}$$

We would like to emphasize that each of these three *local* bounds is tight in the following sense. When the model distribution $p_\vartheta(c|x)$ approaches the true distribution $pr(c|x)$, the bound goes to zero so that the model-based classification error $E_\vartheta\{e|x\}$ approaches the Bayes classification error $E_*\{e|x\}$.

4   Bounds for Global Classification Error

In this section, we will establish bounds for the *global* classification error that have similar properties as the bounds for the local classification error.

4.1   From Local to Global Bounds

We consider the difference between the model-based classification error $E_\vartheta\{e|x\}$ and the Bayes classification error $E_*\{e|x\}$:

$$E_\vartheta\{e|x\} - E_*\{e|x\} \le g(x)$$

where $g(x)$ stands for one of the local bounds derived so far. We move from local to global bounds by integrating over the whole space of observations using the true probability (density) distribution $pr(x)$:

$$E_\vartheta\{e\} - E_*\{e\} = \int dx\, pr(x) \left(E_\vartheta\{e|x\} - E_*\{e|x\} \right)$$

$$\le \int dx\, pr(x)\, g(x) \tag{16}$$

In carrying out the integration, the local inequality is preserved and we obtain a global inequality. Now it turns out that, in order to arrive at useful bounds, it is helpful to consider the *squared* difference:

$$\left(E_\vartheta\{e\} - E_*\{e\} \right)^2 \le \left(\int dx\, pr(x)\, g(x) \right)^2$$

$$\le \int dx\, pr(x)\, g^2(x) \tag{17}$$

The second inequality is true because for any function $x \rightarrow g(x)$ we have the inequality:

$$\left(\int dx \, pr(x) \, g(x) \right)^2 \leq \int dx \, pr(x) \, g^2(x) \tag{18}$$

since:
$$0 \leq Var\{g(x)\} := E\{[g(x) - E\{g(x)\}]^2\}$$
$$= E\{g^2(x)\} - E^2\{g(x)\}$$

where $E\{\cdot\}$ denotes the statistical expectation using the distribution $pr(x)$. The ultimate justification for considering the *squared* difference in the classification error will be the usefulness of the practical training criteria to be presented in Section 5.

4.2 Squared Distance Bound

We start with the local bound Eq.(15) and immediately obtain the global bound using Eq.(17):

$$\left(E_\vartheta\{e\} - E_*\{e\} \right)^2 \leq 4 \cdot \int dx \, pr(x) \sum_c [pr(c|x) - p_\vartheta(c|x)]^2 \tag{19}$$

This global bound will be called squared error bound because it is based on the squared difference between the true distribution $pr(c|x)$ and the model distribution $p_\vartheta(c|x)$.

4.3 Kullback-Leibler Bound

To derive this bound, we make use of the Pinsker inequality for two probability distributions p_c and q_c (with normalization $\sum_c p_c = \sum_c q_c = 1$) [5, p. 300],[17]:

$$\frac{1}{2} \left(\sum_c |p_c - q_c| \right)^2 \leq - \sum_c p_c \log \frac{q_c}{p_c} \tag{20}$$

The term on the right-hand side of this inequality is known as the Kullback-Leibler distance (or relative entropy) between the two distributions p_c and q_c [5, p. 18]. It was originally introduced in the context of statistics and information theory *without* any link to the classification error rate. We use the Kullback-Leibler distance as a distance between the true distribution $pr(c|x)$ and the model distribution $p_\vartheta(c|x)$.

Inserting the local bound Eq.(13) into Eq.(17), we obtain the global bound:

$$\left(E_\vartheta\{e\} - E_*\{e\} \right)^2 \leq \int dx \, pr(x) \left(\sum_c |pr(c|x) - p_\vartheta(c|x)| \right)^2$$

$$\leq - 2 \cdot \int dx \, pr(x) \sum_c pr(c|x) \log \frac{p_\vartheta(c|x)}{pr(c|x)} \tag{21}$$

Each of the two global bounds Eqs.(19) and (21) is *tight*: When the model distribution approaches the true distribution, the bound goes to zero, and so does the difference between model-based classification error and Bayes classification error.

5   Empirical Training Criteria

In this section, we will show how each of the global bounds can be used *directly* as training criterion to learn the unknown parameter set ϑ from a set of training data.

5.1   From Error Bounds to Empirical Training Criteria

The approach is based on re-writing the inequality for each of the classification error bounds in the form:

$$\left(E_\vartheta\{e\} - E_*\{e\}\right)^2 \leq \int dx \sum_c pr(x, c)\, h_\vartheta(x, c) \tag{22}$$

with a suitable function $h_\vartheta(x, c)$. To obtain a practical training criterion, we apply two steps:

- For the classification error $E_\vartheta\{e\}$ to approach the Bayes error $E_*\{e\}$, we tighten the bound on the right-hand side by minimizing it over the unknown parameter set ϑ.
- Now, of course, the true distribution $pr(x, c)$ is not known, and we have only access to a *representative sample*, i.e. a set of labelled observations from the task for which we want to design our pattern classification system:

$$(x_n, c_n), \ n = 1, ..., N$$

i.e. observation x_n with class label c_n. Using this set of labelled training data, we define the *empirical* distribution

$$pr(x, c) = \frac{1}{N} \sum_{n=1}^{N} \delta(x, x_n)\, \delta(c, c_n)$$

where, for continuous-valued observations x, $\delta(x, x_n)$ is the Dirac delta function rather than the Kronecker delta.

The training criterion for determining the optimum parameter set $\hat{\vartheta}$ can now be written as:

$$\hat{\vartheta} := \arg\min_\vartheta \left\{ \int dx \sum_c pr(x, c)\, h_\vartheta(x, c) \right\}$$

$$= \arg\min_\vartheta \left\{ \frac{1}{N} \sum_{n=1}^{N} h_\vartheta(x_n, c_n) \right\} = \arg\min_\vartheta \left\{ \sum_{n=1}^{N} h_\vartheta(x_n, c_n) \right\} \tag{23}$$

If, in addition to determining the optimum parameter set $\hat{\vartheta}$, we want to estimate the classification error using this method, we have to be careful and avoid too optimistic an estimate [8, p. 248]. In other words, the approach presented here does not address the problem of *overfitting*.

5.2   Squared Error Criterion

To derive the squared error criterion, we use the following identity [13]:

$$\sum_c [pr(c|x) - p_\vartheta(c|x)]^2 =$$

$$= \sum_c pr(c|x) \sum_{c'} [p_\vartheta(c'|x) - \delta(c',c)]^2 - \left(1 - \sum_c pr^2(c|x)\right) \quad (24)$$

This identity has been re-discovered several times in the context of statistical pattern recognition and artificial neural networks. The earliest reference (using a different framework of notation) we know is [15]. Inserting this identity into Eq.(19) and dropping the terms independent of ϑ, we arrive at the following training criterion for the unknown parameter set ϑ:

$$\hat{\vartheta} = \arg\min_\vartheta \left\{ \sum_{n=1}^N \sum_{c'} [p_\vartheta(c'|x_n) - \delta(c',c_n)]^2 \right\} \quad (25)$$

This is the standard training criterion used for neural networks and other types of discriminant functions, namely the sum of the squared differences between the actual network output and the desired output for each output node [7, p. 290]. If the model distribution is non-parametric, i.e. has enough degrees of freedom, the global optimum can be really attained (on the training data), and the model distribution is then identical to the true distribution. This is the case for decision trees [3] with a non-parametric model distribution for the discrete-valued observations x. The minimum values of the training criterion is then the second term (with a positive sign) on the right-hand side of Eq.(24), which is referred to as Gini criterion.

5.3   Kullback-Leibler Criterion

From the Kullback-Leibler bound, we obtain the practical training criterion by simply separating the model distribution $p_\vartheta(c|x)$ and dropping the constant terms:

$$\hat{\vartheta} = \arg\max_\vartheta \left\{ \sum_{n=1}^N \log p_\vartheta(c_n|x_n) \right\} \quad (26)$$

This is the general form of a maximum likelihood criterion. Here, we have the likelihood of the class posterior distribution $p_\vartheta(c|x)$ as opposed to the class conditional distribution $p_\vartheta(x|c)$. This criterion has become popular in the context of so-called discriminative training and is referred to under different names: *conditional maximum likelihood* [4, 12] and *maximum mutual information* [1, 14]. In the framework of information theory, the training criterion can be interpreted as the empirical expectation of the model-based equivocation, which, in the special case of constant class probabilities, is equivalent to mutual information. In the context of decision trees [3], the criterion is called *entropy* criterion.

6   Discussion

We have derived two novel bounds for the model-based classification error: the squared distance bound and the Kullback-Leibler bound, both of which result in widely used practical training criteria. Although both these quantities have been used before in statistical pattern recognition, they were not known to provide *strict bounds* for the model-based classification error.

It is interesting to note that, in a Bayesian framework independent of the classification error, some authors [2, pp.67-81] have analyzed criteria for estimating unknown probability distributions and have considered two specific criteria that have attractive properties. These two criteria are identical to the two training criteria that we have derived here. They are referred to as the *quadratic* and the *logarithmic* scoring function.

The bounds we have presented are based on the *square* of the difference between the model-based classification error and the Bayes classification error. The open question is how this is related to approaches where the smoothed classification error is used directly as training criterion [11, 16].

Acknowledgment

Part of this work was done when the author was a visiting scientist at the UP of Valencia in 2002. In particular, the author would like to thank Francisco Casacuberta, Alfons Juan and Enrique Vidal for many helpful discussions.

References

[1] L. R. Bahl, P. F. Brown, P. V. de Souza, R. L. Mercer: Maximum Mutual Information Estimation of Hidden Markov Model Parameters. IEEE Int. Conf. on Acoustics, Speech and Signal Processing, Tokyo, April, 1986.

[2] J. M. Bernardo, A. F. M. Smith: Bayesian Theory. J. Wiley & Sons, Chichester 1994.

[3] L. Breiman, J. H. Friedman, R. A. Ohlsen, C. J. Stone: Classification And Regression Trees. Wadsworth, Belmont, CA, 1984.

[4] F. Casacuberta: Maximum Mutual Information and Conditional Maximum Likelihood Estimation of Stochastic Regular Syntax-Directed Translation Schemes. Int. Coll. on Grammatical Inference, Montpellier, France, Sep. 1996, pp. 282-291 in L. Miclet, C. de la Higuera (eds.), Lecture Notes in Computer Science, Springer, Berlin 1996.

[5] T. M. Cover, J. A. Thomas: Elements of Information Theory. John Wiley & Sons, New York, NY, 1991.

[6] L. Devroye, J. Györfi, G. Lugosi: A Probabilistic Theory of Pattern Recognition. Springer, New York, 1996.

[7] R. O. Duda, P. E. Hart, D. G. Stork: Pattern Classification. 2nd ed., J. Wiley & Sons, New York, NY, 2001.

[8] B. Efron, R. J. Tibshirani: An Introduction to the Bootstrap. Chapman & Hall, New York, 1993.

[9] K. Fukunaga: Introduction to Statistical Pattern Recognition. Academic Press, New York, 1972.

[10] M. E. Hellman, J. Raviv: Probability of Errors, Equivocation and the Chernoff Bound. IEEE Trans. on Information Theory, Vol. IT-16, No. 4, pp. 368-372, July 1970.

[11] B.-H. Juang, S. Katagiri: Discriminative Learning for Minimum Error Classification. IEEE Transactions on Signal Processing, Vol. 40, No. 12, pp. 3043-3054, Dec. 1992.

[12] A. Nadas, D. Nahamoo, M. Picheny: On a Model-Robust Training Method for Speech Recognition. IEEE Trans. on Acoustics, Speech and Signal Processing, Vol. 36, No. 9, pp. 1432-1435, Sep. 1988.

[13] H. Ney: On the Probabilistic Interpretation of Neural Net Classifiers and Discriminative Training Criteria. IEEE Trans. on Pattern Analysis and Machine Intelligence, Vol. PAMI-17, No. 2, pp. 107-119, Feb. 1995.

[14] Y. Normandin, R. Cardin, R. De Mori: High-Performance Connected Digit Recognition Using Maximum Mutual Information Estimation. IEEE Trans. on Speech and Audio Processing, vol. 2, no. 2, pp. 299-311, April 1994.

[15] J. D. Patterson, B. F. Womack: An Adaptive Pattern Classification Scheme. IEEE Trans. on Systems, Science and Cybernetics, Vol.SSC-2, pp.62-67, Aug. 1966.

[16] R. Schlüter, H. Ney: Model-based MCE Bound to the True Bayes' Error. IEEE Signal Processing Letters, Vol. 8, No. 5, pp. 131-133, May 2001.

[17] F. Topsoe: Some Inequalities for Information Divergence and Related Measures of Discrimination. IEEE Trans. on Information Theory, to appear, 2003.

[18] A. N. Vapnik, V. Y. Chervonenkis: On the Uniform Convergence of Relative Frequencies of Events to their Probabilities. Theory of Probability and Its Applications, Vol. 16, pp. 264-280, 1971.

Application of Multinomial Mixture Model to Text Classification

Jana Novovičová and Antonín Malík

Department of Pattern Recognition, Institute of Information Theory and Automation
Academy of Sciences of the Czech Republic, Prague, Czech Republic
{novovic,amalik}@utia.cas.cz

Abstract. The goal of text document classification is to assign a new document into one class from the predefined classes based on its contents. In this paper, a mixture of multinomial distributions is proposed as a model for class-conditional distributions in document classification task. A bag-of-words approach to vector document representation is employed. It is shown, that the accuracy of the Bayes document classifier can be improved by the proposed model in comparison with the Bayes classifiers based on the multivariate Bernoulli model, the multinomial model as well as the multivariate Bernoulli mixture model. Experimental results on the Reuters and the Newsgroups data sets indicate the effectiveness of the multinomial mixture model. Furthermore, an increase in classification accuracy is achieved for small training data sets, when multiclass Bhattacharyya distance is used instead of average mutual information as a feature selection criterion.

1 Introduction

The goal of document classification is to assign a new document to one of the predefined classes based on its contents. This concept implies the existence of a labelled training set, representation of the documents, and a statistical classifier learned using the chosen representation of the training set.

Document classification is a domain in which obtaining labelled data is expensive. A large number of parameters often must be estimated from a small amount of labelled data. When little training data is being used to estimate the parameters for a large number of features, it is often best to use simple learning methods. In such cases, there is not enough data to estimate feature correlations and other complex interactions. One such simple classification method that performs surprisingly well is the *naive Bayes* classifier. While the naive Bayes classifier often performs document classification very well (see e.g. [5, 3, 7]), the class-conditional independence assumption calls for developing better alternatives.

We suggest to use mixtures of multinomial distributions (*multinomial mixture* model) for class-conditional probability function. Maximum-likelihood estimation of multinomial mixture parameters is done by the well-known expectation-maximization (EM) algorithm. Preliminary experimental results on the Reuters

F.J. Perales et al. (Eds.): IbPRIA 2003, LNCS 2652, pp. 646–653, 2003.

and on the Newsgroups data sets indicate the effectiveness of proposed multinomial mixture model. An increase in classification accuracy is achieved in comparison with standard models [5] as well as multivariate Bernoulli mixture model investigated by Juan and Vidal [4].

Feature selection (FS) is a very important step in text classification, because irrelevant and redundant features often degrade the performance of classification algorithms both in speed and prediction accuracy.

We proposed to use the *multiclass Bhattacharrya distance* (MBD) [11] as FS criterion. An increase in classification accuracy was achieved for small training data sets, when MBD was used instead of *average mutual information* (AMI) [5, 12].

2   Probabilistic Framework for Text Classification

We approach classification of the text document to one class from the set of classes $C = \{c_1, ..., c_{|C|}\}$ in a Bayesian learning framework with a bag-of-words document representation. In this representation, each document d_i is described by a feature vector consisting of one feature variable for each word w_t in the vocabulary $V = \{w_1, ..., w_{|V|}\}$. The data generation procedure for a document d_i can be understood as selecting a mixture component (a class) according to the mixture weights - *class prior probabilities*, $P(c_j|\theta)$, then having the corresponding mixture component generate a document according to its own parameters with *class-conditional probability function* (p.f.) $P(d_i|c_j; \theta_j)$. The *unconditional probability function* of generating document d_i independent of its class is given by

$$P(d_i; \theta) = \sum_{j=1}^{|C|} P(c_j|\theta)P(d_i|c_j; \theta_j) \tag{1}$$

where the mixture weights, written $\theta_{c_j} = P(c_j|\theta)$, $0 \leq \theta_{c_j} \leq 1$, $\sum_{j=1}^{|C|} \theta_{c_j} = 1$ indicate the probabilities of selecting the different class mixture components, $P(d_i|c_j; \theta_j)$. The number of mixtures components $|C|$ is fixed and known. Each class is modelled by a single component $P(d_i|c_j; \theta_j)$. Clearly, $\theta = \{(\theta_{c_j}, \theta_j) : j = 1, ..., |C|\}$ is an unknown parameter set.

There are two common models in the representation of text documents (see e.g. [5]). The Bernoulli model represents each document by a vector of binary feature variables B_{it}, indicating whether or not a certain word w_t occurs in the document. In the *multinomial* model, the document d_i is represented by a feature vector, each feature variable N_{it} is the number of times certain word w_t occurs in that document. In this model each document is drawn from a multinomial distribution over the set of all words in V with as many independent trials as the length $|d_i|$ (the number of words from V occurring in the document). The order of the words is lost, however the number of occurrences is captured. This representation has been found superior to the Bernoulli model [5]. A set of class-labelled training data is used to estimate a complete set of model parameters θ.

The estimates for Bernoulli and multinomial models can be found in [5]. The tested document is classified by maximum posterior probability.

3   Finite Mixture Models

Finite mixture models have become increasingly popular both from theoretical and practical point of view as a model in statistical pattern recognition (see e.g. [6, 11]). The reason behind this is that mixture models are able to represent arbitrarily complex probability function. This makes mixtures also suited for representing complex class-conditional p.f. in classification task.

Our approach to learning on text document is based on the fact that documents are often mixtures of multiple topics. In mixture approach to document classification the jth class-conditional probability $P(d_i|c_j; \theta_j)$ is modelled as a finite mixture of the same M probabilities with its own parameters. It can be expressed as

$$P(d_i|c_j; \theta_j) = \sum_{m=1}^{M} \alpha_{jm} P_m(d_i|s_{jm}; \theta_{jm}) . \tag{2}$$

Here M denotes the number of subclasses, say s_{jm}, in each class c_j, α_{jm} is the mixing proportion of the mth model component s_{jm} in jth class c_j, $\alpha_{jm} \geq 0$, $\sum_{m=1}^{M} \alpha_{jm} = 1$, $j = 1, ..., |C|$. $P_m(d_i|s_{jm}; \theta_{jm})$ denotes the probability of d_i in the mth subclass within the class c_j.

3.1   Multinomial Mixture Model

We propose to use the mixture of multinomial distributions as a model for document classification. It means that the probability

$$P(d_i|c_j; \theta_j) = \sum_{m=1}^{M} \alpha_{jm} \frac{|d_i|!}{\prod_{t=1}^{|V|} N_{it}!} \prod_{t=1}^{|V|} \theta_{t|jm}^{N_{it}} . \tag{3}$$

Here associated with each subclass s_{jm} is a word probability written $\theta_{t|jm} = P(w_t|s_{jm}; \theta_{jm})$ for all words in the vocabulary $|V|$, $0 \leq \theta_{t|jm} \leq 1$. The parameter set $\theta_j = \{(\alpha_{jm}, \theta_{jm}) : m = 1, ..., M\}$, $j = 1, ..., |C|$ with $\theta_{jm} = (\theta_{1|jm}, ..., \theta_{|V||jm})$, $\sum_{t=1}^{|V|} \theta_{t|jm} = 1$ is unknown.

3.2   Model Fitting with the EM Algorithm

Let $\mathcal{D}_j = \{d_1, ..., d_{|\mathcal{D}_j|}\}$ be a set of $|\mathcal{D}_j|$ independent and identically distributed training documents from class $c_j \in C$. We find out the parameters of $P(d_i|c_j; \theta_j)$ by maximizing the log-likelihood function

$$L(\theta_j) = \sum_{i=1}^{|\mathcal{D}_j|} \log \left[\sum_{m=1}^{M} \alpha_{jm} P_m(d_i|s_{jm}; \theta_{jm}) \right] . \tag{4}$$

We are excluding the number M of class-conditional components from the estimation procedure.

The estimate $\hat{\theta}_j$ cannot be found analytically. A possible approach is the *expectation-maximization* (EM) algorithm [1]. From this point of view, an observed document d_i can be regarded as being incomplete where the missing part is the true subclass labelling. The EM algorithm alternates two steps: (1) E-step (an expectation step) where posterior probabilities are computed for the latent subclass variables, based on current estimates of the parameters, (2) M-step (maximization step) where parameters are updated based on so called expected complete data log-likelihood which depends on the posterior probabilities computed in the E-step.

The EM algorithm for model (3) takes the following form [9]:

E-Step: $j = 1, ... |C|,\ m = 1, ..., M,\ i = 1, ..., |\mathcal{D}_j|,\ k = 0, 1...$

$$p^{(k)}(s_{jm}|d_i) = \frac{\alpha_{jm}^{(k)} \prod_{t=1}^{|V|} \left(\theta_{t|jm}^{(k)}\right)^{N_{it}}}{\sum_{r=1}^{M} \alpha_{jr}^{(k)} \prod_{t=1}^{|V|} \left(\theta_{t|jr}^{(k)}\right)^{N_{it}}}. \tag{5}$$

M-Step: $j = 1, ... |C|,\ m = 1, ..., M,\ t = 1, ..., |V|$

$$\alpha_{jm}^{(k+1)} = \frac{1}{|\mathcal{D}_j|} \sum_{i=1}^{|\mathcal{D}_j|} p^{(k)}(s_{jm}|d_i) \tag{6}$$

and

$$\theta_{t|jm}^{(k+1)} = \frac{\sum_{i=1}^{|\mathcal{D}_j|} N_{it}\, p^{(k)}(s_{jm}|d_i)}{\sum_{r=1}^{|V|} \sum_{i=1}^{|\mathcal{D}_j|} N_{ir}\, p^{(k)}(s_{jm}|d_i)}. \tag{7}$$

The class priors can be estimated as

$$\hat{\theta}_{c_j} = \frac{|\mathcal{D}_j|}{|\mathcal{D}|} \tag{8}$$

where $|\mathcal{D}| = \sum_{j=1}^{|C|} |\mathcal{D}_j|$. An initial value for the parameters is required to start the EM algorithm. For the experiments reported in Section 5.1 we used random initialization for parameters $\theta_{t|jm}$ and $\alpha_{jm}^{(0)} = 1/M$ for both Bernoulli mixture and multinomial mixture models.

4   Feature Selection

Feature selection methods for text document classification use some evaluation function that is applied to a single feature. All features are independently evaluated, a score is assigned to each of them and the features are sorted according to the assigned score. Then, a predefined number of the best features is taken to form the best feature subset.

Scoring of individual features can be performed using some of the measures, for instance, *document frequency, term frequency, mutual information, information gain (average mutual information),* χ^2 *statistic,* and *term strength.* Yang and Pedersen [12] give experimental comparison of the above mentioned measures in text classification. The average mutual information were reported to work well on text data.

We propose to use the multiclass Bhattacharrya distance for multinomial model as a FS criterion to measure the ability of feature subsets in discriminating between classes and to take into consideration how features work together (opposed to AMI). We calculated MBD explicitly for a multinomial distribution in [9]:

$$J_B(d) = -|d| \sum_{j=1}^{|C|-1} \sum_{k=j+1}^{|C|} \theta_{c_j} \theta_{c_k} \log \sum_{t=1}^{|V|} \sqrt{\theta_{t|j} \theta_{t|k}} \tag{9}$$

where $\theta_{t|j}$ and $\theta_{t|k}$ are the probabilities of the word w_t in class c_j and c_k, respectively.

5   Experimental Results

This section provides two empirical evidences. First, the mixture models (Bernoulli mixture and the multinomial mixture) perform better than the corresponding standard models (Bernoulli and multinomial). Second, the multiclass Bhattacharyya distance criterion achieves higher accuracy than average mutual information on very small training sets. All experiments were tested on the Reuters data set and the Newsgroups data set.

The Reuters data set[1] was used by various authors (e.g. [12, 5, 7, 10]) as a test set for different methods of text classification. Since the aim is classification, in which each document has an unique class, we discarded documents with no label or with multiple labels. The classes with less than 20 documents were removed. The resulting data set had 9159 documents in 33 classes. The vocabulary was constructed by removing stop words and too infrequent words (words that had less than 4 occurrences per document). The Porter stemming algorithm[2] was used. This resulted in 7425 words.

In addition, the Newsgroups data set[3] was used. After removing very short documents (less than 4 words), the resulting data set had 19958 documents in 20 classes. The vocabulary was constructed by removing stop words, too infrequent words (words that had less than 5 occurrences per document) and by using the Porter stemming algorithm, similarly to the Reuters data set. This resulted in the vocabulary of 21951 words.

Following a traditional FS techniques for text classification, non-discriminative words were removed in accordance to the AMI [5]. It was com-

---

[1] http://www.daviddlewis.com/resources/testcollections/reuters21578.
[2] http://www.tartarus.org/~martin/PorterStemmer.
[3] http://www.cs.cmu.edu/~textlearning.

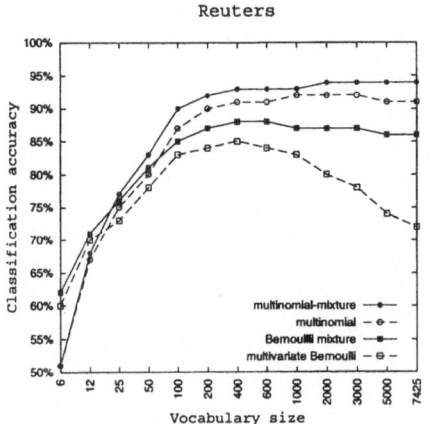

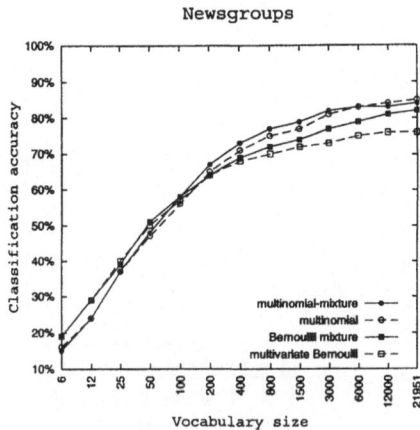

Fig. 1. Classification accuracy of the standard and the mixture models on the Reuters data set

Fig. 2. Classification accuracy of the standard and the mixture models on the Newsgroups data set

puted from the training set for each word. Several values of $|V|$ were considered in the experiments. We randomly split the data set into two-third training set and one-third testing set. We repeated this random split twenty times on the Reuters data set and ten times on the Newsgroups data set. The effectiveness of Bayes classifier was measured by classification accuracy estimated as $accuracy = (N_c/N_{test})100\%$, where N_c is the number of correctly classified documents from testing set and N_{test} is the total number of documents in the testing set. The average classification accuracy was computed over all testing sets.

5.1 Standard Models versus Mixture Models

Figure 1 shows the performance of both the standard and the mixture models for several vocabulary sizes on the Reuters data set. We can see that the multinomial model performs better than the Bernoulli model. Good behavior of the Bernoulli model is observed for dimensions equal or smaller than 400, after this point the performance of the classifier degrades with an increase in vocabulary size. Accuracy of multinomial model improves monotonically.

The Bernoulli mixture is found to be better than the Bernoulli model on average of 5%. The multinomial mixture achieves the highest accuracy 94,9% and is on average 2% better than multinomial model and on average 4% better than Bernoulli mixture. The multinomial mixture performs the best results over all vocabulary sizes, except on very small number of words.

Figure 2 shows the behavior of the standard and the mixture models on the Newsgroups data set. The Bernoulli mixture achieves on average 2.1% the higher accuracy than Bernoulli model. The multinomial mixture performs slightly better than the standard multinomial model (on average 0.6%).

Reuters

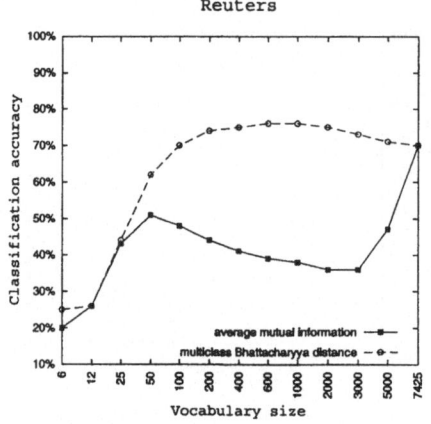

Newsgroups

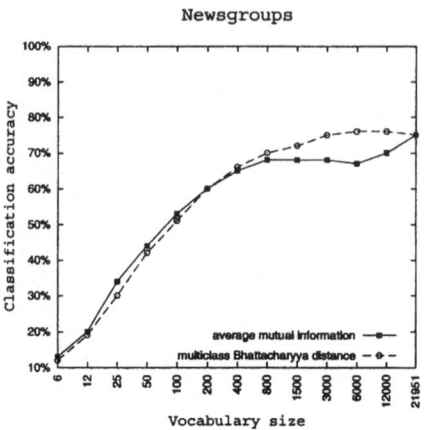

Fig. 3. Classification accuracy of the multinomial model using AMI and MBD on the Reuters data set

Fig. 4. Classification accuracy of the multinomial model using AMI and MBD on the Newsgroups data set

The number of components for each class-conditional mixture also has an important impact on performance. Good behavior was observed with three components per class for both mixture models on the Reuters data set. Six components per class for multinomial mixture and three components for the mixture Bernoulli model were used on the Newsgroups data set. The methods for learning classifier based on finite mixtures for class-conditional p.f. are computationally more demanding than methods based on standard models (because of EM algorithm).

5.2   Feature Selection on Small Training Data Set

Two criteria were used to obtain the subset of features representing the document using the multinomial model. AMI criterion was used with *Best Individual Features* search procedure [2] and MBD (9) was used with *Sequential Forward Selection* search algorithm [2]. This criterion can be computed recursively.

The performance of FS on small training sets was observed. We used a few documents for training the multinomial model; ten documents from each class of the Reuters data set and hundred documents from each class of the Newsgroups data set. The rest of documents was employed for testing.

Figure 3 shows difference between MBD and AMI on the Reuters data set. The behavior of both methods is similar on an extremely small number of documents (less than 25) but after this point the classification accuracy of MBD is considerably higher. When compare the MBD with AMI feature selection methods an increase in classification accuracy of about 21% is achieved.

Figure 4 shows the difference between MBD and AMI on the Newsgroups data set. AMI performs equally or slightly better than MBD on small number of documents (less than 400), behind this point the classification accuracy of MBD is again higher. MBD has achieved on average 2% higher accuracy than AMI.

6 Conclusions and Future Work

The following conclusions are reached from this paper: An observation of the performance of Bayes classifier for text classification on the Reuters and the Newsgroups data sets suggests that learning methods based on mixture models for class-conditional probabilities of the documents perform better than the standard models. The multinomial mixture is a promising model for class-conditional distributions in the document classification. The experimental results show that this model performs better than the Bernoulli mixture.

Many areas of future work remain. Ongoing work includes: Design of a new model for text document modelling based on a modification of distribution mixtures of factorized components [8] to be able to solve simultaneously the problem of the optimal feature subset and the optimal number of mixture components.

Acknowledgements

The work has been supported by grants the Grant Agency of the Academy of Sciences of the Czech Republic No A2075302 and the Complex research project of the Academy of Sciences of the Czech Republic K1019101.

References

[1] Dempster, A. P., Laird, N. M., Rubin, D. B.: Maximum Likelihood from Incomplete Data via the EM Algorithm. *J. Royal Stat. Soc.*, 39 (1977) 1-38
[2] Jain, A. K., Duin, R. P. W., Mao, J.: Statistical Pattern Recognition: A Review. *IEEE Trans. on Pattern Analysis and Machine Intelligence* (2000) 22(2): 4–37
[3] Joachims, T.: Text Categorization with Support Vector Machines: Learning with Many Relevant Features. *Proc. of the ECML'98* (1998) 137-142
[4] Juan, A., Vidal, E.: On the Use of Bernoulli Mixture Models for Text Clasification. *Pattern Recognition*, 35 (2002) 2705–2710
[5] McCallum, A., Nigam, K.: A Comparison of Event Models for Naive Bayes Text Classification. *Proc. of the AAAI-98 workshop on Learning for Text Categorization* (1998)
[6] McLachlan, G. J., Peel, D.: *Finite Mixture Models*. John Wiley, New York (2000)
[7] Nigam, K., McCallum, A. K., Thrun, S., Mitchell, T.: Text Classification from Labeled and Unlabeled Documents Using EM. *Mach. Learning* 39 (2000) 103-134
[8] Novovičová, J., Pudil, P., Kittler, J.: Divergence Based Feature Selection for Multimodal Class Densities. *IEEE Trans. on PAMI* 18 (1996) 218–223
[9] Novovičová, J., Malík, A.: Text Document Classification Using Finite Mixtures. *Research Report ÚTIA AVČR*, (2002) No 2063
[10] Torkkola, K.: Discriminative Features for Document Classification. *Proc. of the 16th International Conference on Pattern Recognition ICPR'2002* (2002) Canada
[11] Webb, A.: *Statistical Pattern Recognition*. Arnold London, (1999)
[12] Yang, Y., Pedersen, J. O.: A Comparative Study on Feature Selection in Text Categorization. *Proc. of the 14th ICML97* (1997) 412-420

An Empirical Comparison of Stack-Based Decoding Algorithms for Statistical Machine Translation*

Daniel Ortiz[1], Ismael García Varea[1], and Francisco Casacuberta[2]

[1] Dpto. de Inf.
Univ. de Castilla-La Mancha, 02071 Albacete, Spain
ivarea@info-ab.uclm.es
[2] Inst. Tecnológico de Inf.
Univ. Politécnica de Valencia, 46071 Valencia, Spain

Abstract. Unlike other heuristic search algorithms, stack-based decoders have been proved theoretically to guarantee the avoidance of search errors in the decoding phase of a statistical machine translation (SMT) system. The disadvantage of the stack-based decoders are the high computational requirements. Therefore, to make the decoding problem feasible for SMT, some heuristic optimizations have to be performed. However, this yields unavoidable search errors. In this paper, we describe, study, and implement the state of the art stack-based decoding algorithms for SMT making an empirical comparison which focuses specifically on the optimization problems, computational time, and translation results. Results are also presented for two well known task, the TOURIST Task and the HANSARDS task.

1 Introduction

The goal of the translation process in SMT can be formulated as follows: a source language string $\mathbf{f} = f_1^J = f_1 \ldots f_J$ is to be translated into a target language string $\mathbf{e} = e_1^I = e_1 \ldots e_I$. Each target string is regarded as a possible translation for the source language string with maximum a-posteriori probability $Pr(\mathbf{e}|\mathbf{f})$. According to Bayes' decision rule, we have to choose the target string that maximizes the product of both the target language model $Pr(\mathbf{e})$ and the string translation model $Pr(\mathbf{f}|\mathbf{e})$. Alignment models for structuring the translation model are introduced in [2]. In statistical alignment models, $Pr(\mathbf{f}, \mathbf{a}|\mathbf{e})$, the alignment $\mathbf{a} = a_1^J$ is introduced as a hidden variable, and the alignment mapping is $j \rightarrow i = a_j$ from source position j to target position $i = a_j$.

Typically, the search is performed using the so-called maximum approximation:

$$\hat{\mathbf{e}} = \arg\max_{\mathbf{e}} \{Pr(\mathbf{e}) \cdot \sum_{\mathbf{a}} Pr(\mathbf{f}, \mathbf{a}|\mathbf{e})\} \approx \arg\max_{\mathbf{e}} \{Pr(\mathbf{e}) \cdot \max_{\mathbf{a}} Pr(\mathbf{f}, \mathbf{a}|\mathbf{e})\} \quad (1)$$

* Work partially supported by Spanish CICYT under grant TIC2000-1599-C02-01.

F.J. Perales et al. (Eds.): IbPRIA 2003, LNCS 2652, pp. 654–663, 2003.

Many works [1, 6, 3, 5] have adopted different types of stack-based algorithms to solve the global search optimization problem stated above. All these works make their own optimizations in order to make the use of stack decoders feasible. Here, we pay special attention to some optimization problems which are not addressed in previous works, and we propose some possible solutions.

In this paper we show how to perform the global search optimization problem following the different types of stack-based decoding algorithms proposed so far. Then, we describe, study, and implement the state of the art stack-based decoding algorithms for SMT making an empirical comparison which focuses specifically on the optimizations problems, computational time, and translation results.

2   Stack-Based Decoding

The stack decoding algorithm, also called A^* algorithm, was introduced by F. Jelinek in [4] the first time. The stack decoding algorithm attempts to generate partial solutions, called *hypotheses*, until a complete sentence is found; these hypotheses are stored in a stack and ordered by their *score*. In our case, this measure is a probability value given by both the translation and the language model introduced in section 1. The decoder follows a sequence of steps for achieving an optimal hypothesis:

1. Initialize the stack with an empty hypothesis.
2. Iterate
   (a) Pop h (the best hypothesis) off the stack.
   (b) If h is a complete sentence, output h and terminate.
   (c) Expand h.
   (d) Go to step 2a.

The search is started from a null string and obtains new hypotheses after an expansion process (step 2c) which is executed at each iteration. The expansion process consists of the application of a set of operators over the best hypothesis in the stack. Thus, the design of stack decoding algorithms involves defining a set of operators to be applied over every hypothesis as well as the way in which they are combined in the expansion process. Both the operators and the expansion algorithm depend on the translation model that we use. In our case, we used IBM Model 3 and IBM Model 4.

The operators we used in our implementation for IBM Model 3 and IBM Model 4 are those defined in [1] and [3], that we describe below:

- *add*: adds a new target word and aligns a single source word to it.
- *extend*: aligns an additional source word to the last generated target word.
- *addZfert*: adds two new target words: the first has fertility zero, and the second is aligned to a single source word.
- *addNull*: aligns a source word with the target $NULL = e_0$ word.

Algorithm 1.1 Expansion_algorithm_for_IBM_Model_3(*hip*)

---

for all not(*covered_position_j_in*(*hip*) **do**
  if *hip.is_opened*() **then**
    hip' = *hip*
    hip'.extend(); *push*(*hip'*) {opened extension}
    hip'.close(); *push*(*hip'*) {closed extension}
  else
    f =obtain_*j*-th_source_word(*j*)
    for all *e* word_of_source_vocabulary **do**
      if *e* <> *NULL* **then**
        hip' = *hip*
        hip'.add(*e*, *j*); *push*(*hip'*) {add}
        hip'.close(); *push*(*hip'*) {add + close()}
        for all *ze* word_of_source_vocabulary **do**
          hip' = *hip*
          hip'.addZfert(*ze*, *e*, *j*); *push*(*hip'*) {addZfert}
          hip'.close(); *push*(*hip'*) {addZfert + close()}
        end for
      else {Connect j with *NULL*}
        if *hip.phi0* < *m*/2 **then**
          hip' = *hip*
          hip'.addNull(*j*; *push*(*hip'*)) {addnNull}
        end if
      end if
    end for
  end if
end for

The expansion algorithm we have implemented is strongly inspired on the one given in [1] for IBM Model 3, (see Algorithm 1.1 for details). This algorithm was adapted to use IBM Model 4.

Basically, there are two different stack-based algorithms depending on the number of stacks used in the decoding process (one or several). The first type of algorithm is the *A* algorithm* which uses a single stack and its basic operating mode was described in the previous section; in this case the stack will store all the hypotheses ranked by their score. The second type of algorithm are the *Multi-stack algorithms* where those hypotheses with different subsets of source aligned words are stored in different stacks. All the search steps given for *A** algorithm can also be applied here, except step 2a. This is due to the fact that multiple stacks are used instead of only one. In this case another distinction can be made according to the criterion of hypotheses selection:

- *Multi-stack algorithms.* They select the best hypothesis or the *N*-best hypotheses that are stored in the queues.
- *Multi-stack algorithm with threshold.* In this case all stacks are explored, and a numeric *threshold* value is calculated and associated to each stack. Only those hypotheses whose scores are greater than the threshold of the stack

can be candidates to be selected within the expansion process. The definition of a function to compute the threshold is needed in order to characterize the algorithm. A specific example of a thresholding function is given in [1].

3   Optimizations and Related Search Errors

Stack decoding has a remarkable advantage: under certain conditions, the optimality of the search process can be guaranteed. However, it has an important disadvantage: the search process requires a high computational complexity.

Let $\hat{e}$ be the optimal reference translation of a source sentence f and let e be the translation that the decoder returns. If $e = \hat{e}$, we say that a translation **hit** has occurred. In contrast, a **search error** occurs when $e \neq \hat{e}$ and $Pr(e \mid f) < Pr(\hat{e} \mid f)$. There exists another possibility, if $e \neq \hat{e}$ and $Pr(e \mid f) > Pr(\hat{e} \mid f)$, then we say that the error is due to the translation and/or language models.

In the following, we describe the possible optimizations (proposed in [3, 5]) to be applied in order to reduce the search space and the corresponding associated search errors. In all cases, the description is corroborated by empirical results. To establish a compromise between efficiency and effectiveness, we carried out some experiments[1] corresponding to a test set of 100 input sentences of length 8 from the TOURIST task. As in previous works, we used IBM Model 4 as translation model and 3-grams as a language model.

The following optimizations do not require further explanation, but note that the search errors can be avoided by using their maximum values, which always involves a substantial increment in the computational time:

- *Reduce the number of possible source word translations* (W) from the size of the target vocabulary to a prioritized candidate list as defined in [3]. From $W = 1$ to $W = 12$ we reduce the search errors from 82 errors to 18 errors, but the secs. per sentence are increased (on average) from 14 secs. to 31 secs. Higher values of W do no pay off.
- *Reduce the number of possible zero fertility words* (Z), that is, consider only a certain number of zero fertility target words of a prioritized list. A similar experiment was done varying Z from 1 to 50 reducing search errors from 79 to 13 errors but increasing the secs. per sentence from 2.7 secs. to 98 secs.
- *Stack length limitation* (S). The number of possible partial hypotheses to be stored during the search can be huge. Then, in order to avoid memory overflow problems, the maximum number of hypotheses that a stack may store has to be limited. It is important to note that for a partial hypotheses, the higher the aligned source words, the worse score. These partial hypotheses will be discarded sooner when an A^* search algorithm is used due to the possible effect of the S parameter. This cannot occur if a multi-stack algorithm is used, because only hypotheses with the same number of covered positions can compete with each other.

---

[1] Experiments were done on a Pentium III machine at 600 MHz.

– *Restrict the number of source position to be aligned per expansion* (*A*) for every position yet uncovered of the source sentence. Then the amount of hypotheses generated in every expansion can be reduced by setting the maximum value to *A*. This is specially important for dealing with long sentences. Furthermore, in the experiments, we obtained 67% of search errors for $A = 1$, and 18% for $A = 8$ (the length of the sentences). No improvements were obtained for higher values of $A = 4$.

However, the optimization of the *reduction of addZfert comlexity* proposed in [3] cannot avoid search errors. This optimization is based on the fact that the *addZfert* operation should not be systematically applied but applied only when the probability of a partial hypothesis is increased. That is, the *addZfert* operation can yield a better hypothesis than the *add* operation if it increases the language model probability more than it decreases the translation model probability. This is because *addZfert* adds a single contribution to the translation model probability consisting of the fertility term of the zero fertility word added. We have observed that this optimization can cause search errors if a trigram language model is used, this was not observed in [3]. Let us suppose that, during the expansion process, the *addZfert* operation is not applied because of the optimization condition. In the next iteration, the uninserted zero fertility word might substantially increase the language model probability, thus yielding a much better partial hypothesis than the one obtained without applying the *addZfert* operation. The immediate solution to this problem could be to use a bigram instead of a trigram. However, this solution will degrade the translation quality as has been shown in other works. The solution we propose is to postpone the decision to discard the *addZfert* operation (and obviously the associated hypothesis) to the next iteration when all history for the trigram language model is known. Table 1 shows that the *addZfert* optimization (as proposed in [3]) has, in effect, created search errors, which could be avoided by using our solution. The 18% of search errors are due to the other optimizations. As expected a substantial decrease in computational time is achieved.

In the experimentation process we carried out, we observed a special phenomenon which was not mentioned in previous works. In a relatively high number of sentences, the optimal translation of a given source sentence had two or more consecutive zero fertility words, or the sentence ended with a zero fertility word. According to the proposed operators in the literature, the decoders will not be

Table 1. Experiments with *addZfert* optimizations

	Without opt.	Heuristic opt.	Postponed opt.
secs. per sent.	48.5	7.6	26.4
Hits	43	38	43
Model errors	39	39	39
Search errors	18	23	18

Table 2. $add2Zfert$ and $reverseAddZfert$ test

	$addZfert$	$add2Zfert$	$reverseAddZfert$
Secs. per sent.	15.4	26.4	33.8
Hits	32	43	45
Model errors	30	39	38
Search errors	38	18	17

able to yield the optimal hypothesis because there does not exist a sequence of operators to avoid this phenomenon. We have called these errors as *algorithm-inherent search errors*. We propose introducing two new operators in order to reduce the algorithm-inherent search errors:

- *add2Zfert*: this works like the *addZfert* operator, but one more word with zero fertility is added. This operator allows the algorithm to produce two consecutive words with zero fertility.
- *reverseAddZfert*: this is similar to the *addZfert* operator, but the word with zero fertility is added after the word whichd has a fertility greater than zero. The *reverseAddZfert* can also yield hypotheses in which the last word has zero fertility.

Table 2 shows an experiment which shows the reduction of search errors due to these two new operators. The experiment was carried out maintaining the other optimizations parameters at the same value. In spite of this, a total of 8 search errors occurred due to the fact that there were more than two consecutive zero fertility words. Thus, the definition of a new $addNZfert$ $(N > 2)$ operation is needed in order to completely avoid search errors. Obviously, the secs. per sentence are increased in all cases.

We also implemented two optimizations proposed in [5] which do not provoke any search errors and involve a substantial speed up. The first optimization is *hypotheses Recombination* which can discard hypotheses which cannot be distinguished by their language model state or by the translation model state, the second optimization is the *use of admissible heuristic functions* which estimates the cost of completing a partial hypothesis. A heuristic function is called admissible if it never underestimates the probability of a completion of a partial hypothesis. Here we used T, TF and TFL. These functions take into account the probabilities of the lexicon model, the fertility model, and the language model respectively, in order to calculate the heuristic value. The sentence cost is significantly reduced from 26 secs. without any heuristic function to 11 secs. if we use TFL heuristic.

For the rest of the experiments, we adopted the compromise to use: $W = 12$, $Z = 24$, $A = 5$, TFL and $S(A^*) = 10000$, $S(Mstack) = 1000$, for the TOURIST task. Similar experimentation was carried for the HANSARDS task yielding the following values: $W = 8$, $Z = 8$, $A = 3$, TF(due to the extremely huge cost of calculating the language model probabilities required by TFL heuristic). These

Table 3. Complexity per iteration with and without optimizations

Algorithm	Without optimizations	With optimizations
A^*	$m\lvert\mathcal{E}\rvert^2 \cdot 2\log(x)$	$AWZ \cdot 2\log(S_{Stack})$
M-stack	$N2^m + m\lvert\mathcal{E}\rvert^2 \cdot 2(g(2^m) + \log(x))$	$N2^m + AWZ \cdot 2(g(2^m) + \log(S_{Mstack}))$
M-stack + thr	$2^m f() + m\lvert\mathcal{E}\rvert^2 \cdot 2(g(2^m) + \log(x))$	$2^m f() + AWZ \cdot 2(g(2^m) + \log(S_{Mstack}))$

values allowed for a reasonable computation time without quantitatively degrading the translation quality.

4   Complexity per Iteration

A study of the complexity per iteration for the worst case has allowed us to understand more about the effects of the optimizations. See Table 3 for a study of the complexity of the algorithms with and without optimizations (the complexity is expressed in terms of m). The symbols used are:

- m: number of words of the source sentence.
- $\lvert\mathcal{E}\rvert$: cardinality of the target vocabulary.
- $f()$: complexity of the function that calculates the threshold.
- $g()$: complexity of retrieving the appropriate stack for inserting the given hypothesis into it (only for multiple-stack algorithms). If we use a hash table, the mean cost of this operation is considered constant.
- x: the number of hypotheses in the stack. Without optimizations, this value is not bounded, and with optimizations, it is fixed to the values of S.

If no optimization is applied, the complexity will be prohibitive, specially for multiple-stack algorithms, where we have to iterate over all the stacks in order to select the hypotheses that will be expanded later. This task introduces an exponential term in the complexity. On the contrary, if we apply the optimizations, the complexity per iteration will be reduced.

5   Efficiency of Stack-Based Decoders

In order to compare the three different stack decoders introduced in section 2, a simple experiment for the TOURIST task was carried out. The results are shown in Table 4. The threshold algorithm obtained the worst results. The thresholding function used here consisted of taking the best hypothesis of each stack for expansion. Such a strategy requires many more iterations than the approaches without threshold. Further work must be done with algorithms of this kind. On the contrary, we have similar costs for A^* and multi-stack (without threshold) algorithms. However, we expected the A^* algorithm to have better results due to its lower complexity. A more detailed study is shown in Table 5 where we have processed five different test corpora of sentences with a fixed length.

Table 4. Algorithm influence using a test set of 100 sentences of length 8

	A^*	multi-stack	threshold
Secs. per sent.	28.2	26.4	557.2
Hits	43	43	43
Model errors	39	39	39
Search errors	18	18	18

Table 5. Comparison between A^* and multi-stack algorithms

	Sent. length	4	6	8	10	12
A^*	Secs. per sent.	0.64	3.90	28.22	62.32	300.84
	Expansion time (secs.)	0.63	3.87	28.10	62.12	300.15
	Select hyp. time (secs.)	0	0	0	0	0
	μ-secs. per push op.	16	18	23	26	32
	Discarded hyps due to S	0	0	169K	624K	4.8M
multi-stack	Secs. per sent.	0.59	3.63	27.00	64.50	374.77
	Expansion time	0.57	3.59	26.45	62.02	330.43
	Select hyp. time	0.01	0.04	0.46	2.24	43.30
	μ-secs. per push op.	17	25	26	27	31
	Discarded hyps due to S	228	8.9K	202K	496K	3.5M

As we expected, the decoding cost increases in relation to the length of the sentence. However, if we use a single stack algorithm, no time is spent on selecting the best hypothesis for the expansion. On the contrary, multi-stack algorithms spend a significant part of their decoding time doing this for long sentences. In any case, the value of the parameter S and its effect on the amount of discarded hypotheses seems to be more important than the importance of the hypotheses selection. Note that the value of S is closely related to the algorithm type, and theoretically, can be lower for multiple-stack algorithms than for the $A*$ algorithm. Further work must be done in order to set the minimum values of the parameters for each algorithm. Finally, the cost of the push operation is very similar for all the different algorithms. This result is in accordance with the theoretical complexity due to the logarithmic factor used in the expression.

6   Translation Results

The experimental results were carried out using two different tasks:

- The TOURIST task consists of a semi-automatically generated Spanish–English corpus. The domain of the corpus consists of a human-to-human communication situation at a reception desk of a hotel. The corpus consist of 10,000 random sentence pairs for training purposes from the above corpus. The input and output vocabulary sizes were 689 and 514, respectively.

Table 6. Translation quality for the TOURIST and HANSARDS tasks for different test sentence lengths and different values of $S(S = 10K$ and $S = 100K$, left and right columns respectively; "-" means equal value). In all cases, 100 test sentence were translated, by using the A^* algorithm

	TOURIST task								HANSARDS task							
Sent. length	6		8		10		12		6		8		10		12	
WER	16.9	-	11.3	-	6.6	-	10.0	-	51.6	-	52.9	53.2	63.8	64.8	63.9	63.8
PER	16.6	-	11.3	-	6.5	-	9.8	-	50.9	-	50	50	61.5	61.7	57.3	58.3
SER	56	-	57	-	50	-	63	-	89	-	84	84	100	100	98	97
Secs×sent.	2.10	2.26	10.3	12.6	20.2	24.7	88.3	104	28.2	34.8	141	273	374	1335	912	4569

- The French-English HANSARDS task consists of debates in the Canadian Parliament. This task has a very large vocabulary of about 100,000 French words and 80,000 English words. A sub-corpus of 128,000 sentences was selected for training purposes.

For both tasks, the training of the different translation models was carried out using GIZA++ software (`http://www-i6.informatik.rwth-aachen.de/ och`). One hundred sentences (disjointly from the training corpus) of length up to 12 were selected for testing. A 3-gram language model was used, which was trained with the English counterparts of both tasks.

To evaluate the translation quality, three different error criteria were used: WER (Word Error Rate) computed as the minimum number of substitution, insertion and deletion operations that have to be performed to convert the generated string into a reference target string; PER (Position independent Error Rate) similar to WER but the order of the words is not taken into account; and SER (Sentence Error Rate) defined as the number of times that the translation generated by the decoder is not identical to the reference sentence.

The translation quality for both the TOURIST task and the HANSARDS task is shown, in Table 6. For the TOURIST task, the effects of the heuristic optimizations produced significant error rates. Further work must be done in order to improve the training stage, including a preprocessing of the corpus. On the other hand, the HANSARDS task is much more complex than the TOURIST task, so it has higher error rates. The results are shown for two different values of the parameter S. Note the small influence of this parameter on the translation quality, and the great reduction in the processing time.

7   Conclusions

An empirical and theoretical study of stack-based algorithms has been done, paying special attention to those optimization problems that were not discussed in previous works. According to the experimental results we can conclude that:

- Stack-based decoders cannot yield optimal translations with a reasonable temporal cost per sentence. Even if we do not apply any optimization, the

way the operators are defined produces algorithm inherent search errors. We propose $addNZfert$-like operations to deal with such errors. In our opinion, errors of this kind could also be reduced by using better trained or better translation models.
- The main source of search errors seems to be the zero fertility words and their related optimizations. A possible solution is also proposed.
- The model errors that we obtained were always higher than the search errors. For a complex task like HANSARDS, this problem is much more important. Further work must be done on the statistical model if we want to improve the translation quality.
- Multi-stack algorithms have the negative property of spending significant amounts of time in selecting the hypotheses to be expanded. In contrast, for the A^* algorithm, it is not possible to reduce the S parameter, as much as in the multi-stack case, in order to speed up the search without loss of translation quality.

For future work, we plan to investigate in detail the specific effect of the S parameter on the different algorithms as well as the use of different thresholding functions for multi-stack algorithms. We also plan to make a more exhaustive comparison paying particular attention to the influence of the optimizations.

We have just started to apply these algorithms to translation assistant applications where the prediction of short partial hypotheses is used instead of whole sentence translations. These are offering very promising results.

References

[1] Adam L. Berger, Peter F. Brown, Stephen A. Della Pietra, Vincent J. Della Pietra, John R. Gillett, A. S. Kehler, and R. L. Mercer. Language translation apparatus and method of using context-based translation models. United States Patent, No. 5510981, April 1996.

[2] Peter F. Brown, Stephen A. Della Pietra, Vincent J. Della Pietra, and R. L. Mercer. The mathematics of statistical machine translation: Parameter estimation. *Computational Linguistics*, 19(2):263–311, 1993.

[3] Ulrich Germann, Michael Jahr, Kevin Knight, Daniel Marcu, and Kenji Yamada. Fast decoding and optimal decoding for machine translation. In *Proc. of the 39th Annual Meeting of the ACL*, pages 228–235, Toulouse, France, July 2001.

[4] F. Jelinek. A fast sequential decoding algorithm using a stack. *IBM Journal of Research and Development*, 13:675–685, 1969.

[5] Franz J. Och, Nicola Ueffing, and Hermann Ney. An efficient A* search algorithm for statistical machine translation. In *Data-Driven MT Workshop*, pages 55–62, Toulouse France, July 2001.

[6] Ye-Yi Wang and Alex Waibel. Fast decoding for statistical machine translation. In *Proc. of the ICSLP*, pages 1357–1363, Sydney, Australia, November 1998.

Detection of Colour Channels Uncoupling for Curvature-Insensitive Segmentation*

Alberto Ortiz and Gabriel Oliver

Mathematics and Computer Science Department
University of the Balearic Islands, Spain
{alberto.ortiz,goliver}@uib.es

Abstract. A segmentation method based on a physics-based model of image formation is presented in this paper. This model predicts that, in image areas of uniform reflectance, colour channels keep coupled in the sense that they are not free to take any intensity value, but they depend on the values taken by other colour channels. This coupling property is, however, broken at reflectance transition locations. Surface material changes (i.e. reflectance changes) can, thus, be found by looking for violations of the coupling properties. If edges are defined at points breaking the coupling and connected image areas not including edges are found, the set of resultant regions are guaranteed not to contain a material change. If, besides, edges are added to the most similar adjacent region, a first partition of the image can be obtained. Finally, a merging stage is executed to remove the probably low degree of oversegmentation which can result.

1 Introduction

Generally speaking, irradiance values measured at pixel locations are a combination of several scene factors which interact with each other: the illumination distribution, the reflection properties of scene objects —which determine their colour—, the objects geometry, the propagation medium and the performance of the imaging sensor. Leaving aside the propagation medium and the characteristics of the camera, an image encodes, thus, the lighting conditions and the curvature and reflectance properties of the surfaces of the scene.

When shading is hardly noticeable in the image, as well as specularities and other optical phenomena such as inter-reflections, areas of the scene of uniform reflectance appear as regions of more or less constant colour if shadows are avoided. Throughout the years, many segmentation and edge detection algorithms have exploited this model of image formation to find areas of uniform reflectance (i.e. uniform colour) in the image.

Nevertheless, when curved objects are imaged, the scene curvature and the objects glossiness, among others, give rise to noticeable changes in image intensity not necessarily related to object boundaries. In those situations, the simplified model of a noisy piecewise constant bidimensional function is not enough

---

* This study has been partially supported by project CICYT-DPI2001-2311-C03-02 and FEDER fundings.

F.J. Perales et al. (Eds.): IbPRIA 2003, LNCS 2652, pp. 664–672, 2003.

detailed so as to guarantee, at least theoretically, finding regions of uniform reflectance in the image. However, embedding a physics-based model of image formation into the segmentation algorithm allows coping with the aforementioned effects in a more suitable way.

Early work in physics-based vision dates from the 1970s, when Berthold Horn at MIT first applied optical laws to supplement the traditional geometric analysis in the process of automatic visual interpretation [1]. Since then, a lot of research has been published mainly in the areas of shape recovery and colour image understanding [2]. However, little effort has been devoted to applying the physics of image formation to the segmentation of an image with respect to the effort invested in traditional segmentation. Among the several physics-based segmentation strategies which have been proposed, some of them are based on estimating directly the reflectance of the surfaces present in the scene (see for instance [3]), others look for certain configurations of clusters in colour space, as it is predicted by the Dichromatic Reflection Model proposed by Shafer [4] (by way of example, see [5, 6]), and, finally, others use photometric invariants in their different forms ([7, 8], among others).

The segmentation method proposed in this paper is also based on the Dichromatic Reflection Model, but it does not use any of the approaches mentioned above. Its main point, which is the most important contribution of the paper, is based on the fact that, in uniform reflectance areas, colour channels are coupled by the reflectance of the surface material, while, in reflectance transition zones, such coupling can be broken in a number of ways. Consequently, material changes can be found by looking for violations of the coupling properties, which allows computing an edge map from which a first partition of the image can be obtained. A region merging stage follows next, in order to remove the probably low, but not generally zero, degree of oversegmentation which can result.

The rest of the paper is organized as follows: section 2 describes the image formation model considered in this work, and comment on the properties of uniform reflectance areas according to that model; section 3 presents the segmentation algorithm; section 4 presents some segmentation results for real images; and, finally, conclusions appear in section 5.

2   Image Formation Model

2.1   General Description

In general, when light interacts with matter, two reflection components must be taken into account [4]: the interface or specular reflection, and the body or diffuse reflection. The former is originated at the interface between air and the surface medium and is due to the difference between both indexes of refraction. On the other hand, body reflection is caused by light which finally penetrates into the surface and undergoes scattering due to multiple light-material interactions. It is generally accepted that final reflection is an additive composition of the body and interface components, as it is expressed by equation 1:

$$L_x(\lambda) = \overbrace{m_b(x)\left[E_x(\lambda)\rho_{bx}(\lambda)\right]}^{L_{bx}(\lambda)} + \overbrace{m_i(x)\left[E_x(\lambda)\rho_{ix}(\lambda)\right]}^{L_{ix}(\lambda)} \tag{1}$$

where $L_x(\lambda)$ is the light reflected by the surface at a given surface point x and for a certain wavelength λ, and L_{bx} and L_{ix} are, respectively, the body and interface components of the radiance. With a reasonable degree of accuracy [4], each component $L_{jx}(j \in \{b,i\})$ can be modeled as the product of two terms: $C_j(\lambda) = E_x(\lambda)\rho_{jx}(\lambda)$, expressing the fraction of the incoming light $E_x(\lambda)$ which is conveyed by that reflection component due to the body/interface reflectance $0 \leq \rho_{jx}(\lambda) \leq 1$; and $m_j(x) \in [0,1]$, which is a geometrical factor depending on the surface geometry at point x.

The final pixel value given by a camera can be expressed as:

$$I^k(u,v) = p_0^k \int_\Lambda E_{u,v}(\lambda)\tau^k(\lambda)s(\lambda)d\lambda \tag{2}$$

where $I^k(u,v)$ is the intensity of the k colour channel at image cell (u,v), Λ represents the set of wavelengths in the visible spectrum, p_0^k is a scaling factor, $E_{u,v}(\lambda)$ is the incoming light at image cell (u,v), $\tau^k(\lambda)$ is the filter transmitance for the k colour channel, and $s(\lambda)$ is the spectral responsivity of the sensor [9]. In a typical RGB camera, $k \in \{r,g,b\}$, while $\tau(\lambda) = 1$ in a monochrome camera.

After some considerations, which are not included here due to lack of space (see [10] for the details), the image formation model turns out to be:

$$I^k(u,v) = m_b(u,v)I_b^k(u,v) + m_i(u,v)I_i^k(u,v) \tag{3}$$

where I_b^k and I_i^k are, respectively, the so-called body and interface composite reflectances, representing the joint contribution of lighting and material reflectance to the corresponding reflection component.

To finish, notice that, within an image area whose pixels correspond to scene points belonging to the same material, the body and interface colours are constant if the light distribution is also uniform throughout the area. In a noiseless environment, colour changes between image locations are, thus, only due to changes in the geometrical factors m_b and m_i. This fact is exploited in the next two sections to introduce three properties of the image formation model, which result very useful for the purpose of partitioning images into the different materials present in the scene.

2.2 Properties of the Image Formation Model For Non-glossy Pixels

If the illumination is uniform throughout the scene, within an area not containing a material change, colour channels keep coupled as follows if the pixels involved do not show interface reflection: (See [10] for the formal proofs.)

Property 1. *For any pair of colour channels k_1 and k_2 and any two image locations (u_1, v_1) and (u_2, v_2) not showing interface reflection and coming from the same scene material,*

$$(1) \; I^{k_1}(u_1, v_1) \geq I^{k_2}(u_1, v_1) \Leftrightarrow I^{k_1}(u_2, v_2) \geq I^{k_2}(u_2, v_2)$$

$$(2) \; I^{k_1}(u_1, v_1) \leq I^{k_2}(u_1, v_1) \Leftrightarrow I^{k_1}(u_2, v_2) \leq I^{k_2}(u_2, v_2)$$

Property 2. *For any pair of colour channels k_1 and k_2, any image location (u, v) not showing interface reflection and not corresponding to a material change, and any direction ξ over the image plane,*

$$(1) \; \left(\frac{dI^{k_1}(u, v)}{d\xi} \right) \geq 0 \Leftrightarrow \left(\frac{dI^{k_2}(u, v)}{d\xi} \right) \geq 0$$

$$(2) \; \left(\frac{dI^{k_1}(u, v)}{d\xi} \right) \leq 0 \Leftrightarrow \left(\frac{dI^{k_2}(u, v)}{d\xi} \right) \leq 0$$

Property 3. *For any pair of colour channels k_1 and k_2 and any two image locations (u_1, v_1) and (u_2, v_2) not showing interface reflection and coming from the same scene material,*

$$(1) \quad I^{k_1}(u_1, v_1) \geq I^{k_1}(u_2, v_2) \text{ and } I^{k_1}(u_1, v_1) \geq I^{k_2}(u_1, v_1), \text{ or}$$
$$I^{k_1}(u_1, v_1) \leq I^{k_1}(u_2, v_2) \text{ and } I^{k_1}(u_1, v_1) \leq I^{k_2}(u_1, v_1)$$
$$\Leftrightarrow I^{k_1}(u_1, v_1) - I^{k_2}(u_1, v_1) \geq I^{k_1}(u_2, v_2) - I^{k_2}(u_2, v_2)$$

$$(2) \quad I^{k_1}(u_1, v_1) \geq I^{k_1}(u_2, v_2) \text{ and } I^{k_1}(u_1, v_1) \leq I^{k_2}(u_1, v_1), \text{ or}$$
$$I^{k_1}(u_1, v_1) \leq I^{k_1}(u_2, v_2) \text{ and } I^{k_1}(u_1, v_1) \geq I^{k_2}(u_1, v_1)$$
$$\Leftrightarrow I^{k_1}(u_1, v_1) - I^{k_2}(u_1, v_1) \leq I^{k_1}(u_2, v_2) - I^{k_2}(u_2, v_2)$$

Property 1 means that colour channels do not cross each other in an area of uniform body reflectance. On the other hand, property 2 means that, in an area of uniform body reflectance, colour channels vary in a coordinated way: when one changes, so do the others, and in the same sense, all increase or all decrease. This result extends to the fact that, given two image locations (u_1, v_1) and (u_2, v_2), if $I^{k_1}(u_1, v_1) \geq I^{k_1}(u_2, v_2)$, then $I^{k_2}(u_1, v_1) \geq I^{k_2}(u_2, v_2)$, and the same applies for '$\leq$'. Finally, property 3 means that, as the intensity in one channel decreases, so does the difference between colour channel intensities; the opposite happens when the intensity in one channel increases.

3   Segmentation Algorithm

In general, segmenting an image consists in grouping pixels in homogeneous regions, generally according to a certain perceptually-based homogeneity criterion.

Most times, one is interested in the image regions corresponding to the same perceptual colour. In physical terms, this means grouping pixels in uniform body reflectance areas.

In those areas, colour channels keep coupled according to the properties introduced in section 2.2. When a reflectance change takes place, colour channels evolve so as to adopt the configuration corresponding to the new body reflectance (i.e. they are coupled in a different way, see figure 1), giving rise to the violation of at least one of the properties at the corresponding image locations. Therefore, it is proposed to look for those locations to build an edge map where body reflectance transitions are indicated.

As looking for regions satisfying the homogeneity criterion and looking for the region borders are, at least theoretically, complementary problems, at the next step of the segmentation process, non-edge pixels are grouped and the resultant connected regions give rise to a first partition of the image, although not yet complete. It is completed by adding edge pixels to the most similar adjacent region. Finally, as it is discussed in section 3.1, a certain (low) number of false positive edges can be expected, mostly due to image noise, and therefore a certain (low) degree of oversegmentation can result. In order to remove it, a region merging stage is executed next.

3.1   Edge Map Computation Process

The edge map is built by checking, at every pixel, all three properties. If the pixel under consideration belongs to a closed 1D interval over the image plane $[(u_1, v_1), (u_2, v_2)]$ such that (u_1, v_1) and (u_2, v_2) do not satisfy at least one property, then an edge is registered at the corresponding map location. Although a reflectance transition should theoretically involve just two pixels, in real images they tend to span along several image cells because of real cameras' aliasing. As a consequence, the edge map must in general be expected to consist of thick edges.

By checking those three properties, a broad spectrum of body reflectance transitions is covered. On the one hand, if property 1 is infringed, it is because at least one colour channel crosses one another (*channel crossing* edge (CHC), see figure 1(a)). Otherwise, at that image pixel, colour channels do not cross one another, but, still, property 2 can be violated. In such a case, at least two colour channels diverge in the sense that, while in one channel the intensity increases, at the other one decreases (*non-coinciding derivative* edge (NCD), see figure 1(b)). In case the intensity at all colour channels vary in a coordinated way —all increase or all decrease—, it can so happen that property 3 is not fulfilled; that is to say, when intensity decreases in both channels, the difference between them increases instead of decreasing, or vice versa (*non-decreasing difference* edge (NDD), see figure 1(c)).

With this procedure, only those transitions whose effects on the colour channel signals do not violate any of properties 1-3 are left undetected. For instance, reflectance transitions where both body reflectances have approximately the same direction but different magnitude, e.g. light red against dark red, satisfy all

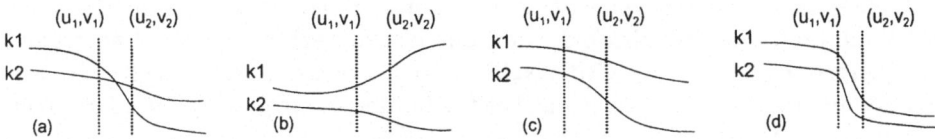

Fig. 1. Examples of body reflectance transitions dectected and corresponding edges: (a) CHC edge; (b) NCD edge; (c) NDD edge; (d) GRD edge

three properties —notice that reflectances can be seen as n-dimensional vectors, with n = 3 for an RGB camera. In those cases, the algorithm resorts to gradient information (edge of type GRD, see figure 1(d)).

Given the fact that the properties formulated in section 2.2 require pixels not to show interface reflection, pixels around specularities are expected to be labelled as edges. Although not always edges of type CHC, NCD or NDD are found near specularities, edges of type GRD will clearly be found, except for "smooth" specularities.

From the implementation point of view, edges are found by checking the coupling properties on 1-dimensional neighbourhoods centered at the pixel under consideration and oriented in a number of directions. Finally, in order to get thinner edges, the final map is obtained after removing edges not coinciding with LOG zero crossings of any magnitude (see [10] for a discussion about the usefulness of second-order derivative operators for curvature-dominated images).

3.2 Region Growing Strategy

Once the edge map has been computed, connected components not including edge pixels are found. The resultant groups correspond to regions satisfying all three properties everywhere, and, therefore, body reflectance is uniform within all of them. As it is predicted by the Dichromatic Reflection Model, pixels coming from the same scene material lie in a hyperplane in colour space, spanned by the body and the interface reflectances, and constituted by a linear or point cluster corresponding to the matte pixels and another, more or less, linear cluster corresponding to the glossy pixels. As the edge map is expected to separate glossy pixels from matte pixels, the corresponding regions are expected to be describable by linear or point clusters in colour space. Using Principal Component Analysis, the line or point best characterizing the cluster corresponding to every region is found. Next, edge pixels join the most similar adjacent region. In this context, the orthogonal distance to the cluster descriptors has been used as the similarity measure. As a result of this step, an initial partition of the image is obtained.

3.3 Region Merging

Because thick edges can still appear in the edge map and due to the treatment given to specularities, it is expected that some regions of uniform reflectance appear separated into several parts. In order to remove this oversegmentation, all three properties are checked again but just at region borders. Two regions are merged if edges of type CHC, NCD or NDD are not found along its common border and there is at least one pixel at the border whose gradient at all channels is below an adaptive threshold: $\epsilon_1 \overline{\frac{dI^k}{d\xi}} + \epsilon_2$, where ξ is any direction connecting both regions, $\overline{x}$ is the average operator over a 1D neighbourhood centered at the pixel, and (ϵ_1, ϵ_2) are parameters of the algorithm.

As for specularities, they are characterized as small regions with a colour average above a certain intensity level in at least one colour channel (parameters N_{sp} and I_{sp}). Moreover, to be joined with an adjacent region, the compound cluster in colour space must be fitted by a plane with a low fitting error (below a parameter σ_{sp}). Using such criteria, adjacent regions are again considered to be merged, giving rise to the final segmentation.

4   Experimental Results and Discussion

To prove experimentally the usefulness of the segmentation method proposed, several results for real curvature-dominated images are given below. All the test images were captured with gamma correction γ set to 1. Results for standard images are not given because they were not captured with a linear camera ($\gamma \neq 1$) and they do not generally consist of curved objects. Moreover, different surface materials were included in the different scenes (plastics, ceramics, clothing, paper, wood, etc.).

As for parameters, 1D neighbourhoods used to check properties fulfillment were oriented horizontally, vertically and diagonally (both diagonals), and their length was set to 10×2+1 pixels. For the rest of parameters, the following values were used for all the images presented here: (1) the standard deviation for LOG, σ_{LOG}, was set to 1; (2) $\epsilon_1 = 1$ and $\epsilon_2 = 2$; (3) $N_{sp} = 200$, $I_{sp} = 200$ and $\sigma_{sp} = 5$.

For the segmentation results, see figures 2 and 3. On the one hand, for comparison purposes between a physics-based and a non-physics-based approach, figure 2(right) shows the result obtained, using the undersegmentation option, from the recognized mean-shift based segmentation algorithm by Comaniciu and Meer [11] [1], for the original image corresponding to figure 2(left). The edge map obtained from our method is given in figure 2(center), while the original image with the corresponding region contours overimposed in white appears in figure 2(left). On the other hand, figure 3 presents more segmentation results for a varied set of scenes containing different sorts of materials and glossy curved objects. More experimental results and a more detailed discussion about them and the algorithm parameters, which are not included here due to lack of space, can be found in [10].

---

[1] Its code is available in the web at URL:
http://www.caip.rutgers.edu/riul/research/papers/abstract/feature.html.

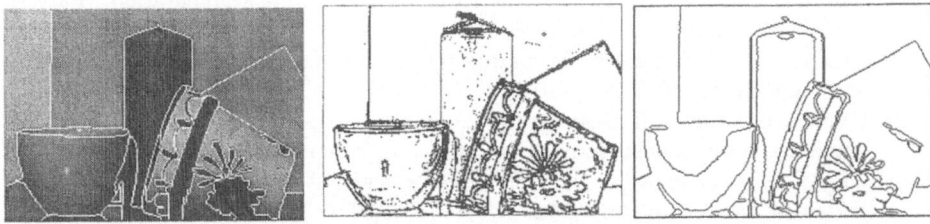

Fig. 2. (left) original image with region contours overimposed; (center) edge map; (right) contours resultant from the mean-shift based approach

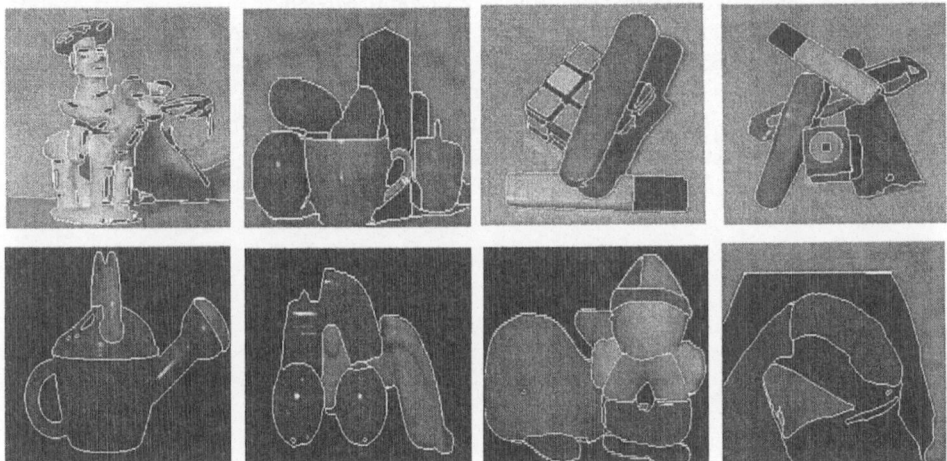

Fig. 3. Segmentation results for different types of surface materials: plastics, ceramics, clothing, paper, wood, etc.

5   Conclusions

A curvature-insensitive segmentation method, based on a physics-based image formation model, has been proposed. The method uses the coupling between colour channels in uniform reflectance areas to locate image locations where colour channels turn out to be uncoupled because of a reflectance transition arising there. Experiments with real images have been presented, showing the power of the approach for dealing with scenes with glossy curved objects and different surface materials.

References

[1] Horn, B. K.: Shape from shading: a method for obtaining the shape of a smooth opaque object from one view. PhD thesis, MIT, Dep. of Elec. Eng (1970)
[2] Healey, G. E., Shafer, S. A., Wolff, L. B., eds.: Physics-based vision: principles and practice. Jones and Bartlett Publishers (1992) (series consisting of three volumes)

[3] Lee, C. H., Rosenfeld, A.: Albedo estimation for scene segmentation. Pattern Recognition Letters **1** (1983) 155–160

[4] Shafer, S. A.: Using color to separate reflection components. COLOR Research and Application **10** (1985) 210–218

[5] Klinker, G., Shafer, S., Kanade, T.: A physical approach to color image understanding. International Journal of Computer Vision **4** (1990) 7–38

[6] Ong, C. K., Matsuyama, T.: Robust color segmentation using the dichromatic reflection model. In: Proc. 14th ICPR. (1998) 780–784

[7] Healey, G. E.: Using color for geometry-insensitive segmentation. Journal of the Optical Society of America A **6** (1989) 920–937

[8] Gevers, T.: Adaptive image segmentation by combining photometric invariant region and edge information. PAMI **24** (2002) 848–852

[9] Novak, C., Shafer, S.: Color vision. In: Encyclopedia of Artificial Intelligence. J. Wiley and Sons (1992) 192–202

[10] Ortiz, A., Oliver, G.: Segmentation of images based on the detection of reflectance transitions. Technical Report A-3-2003, Departament de Matemàtiques i Informàtica (Universitat de les Illes Balears) (2003)

[11] Comaniciu, D., Meer, P.: Mean-shift analysis and applications. In: Proc. ICCV. (1999)

Analyzing Periodic Motion Classification

Xavier Orriols and Xavier Binefa*

Computer Vision Center
Universitat Autònoma de Barcelona, Barcelona, Spain, 08193 Bellaterra
{xevi,xavierb}@cvc.uab.es
http://www.cvc.uab.es/~xevi

Abstract. In this paper, we present a new technique for separating different types of periodic motions in a video sequence. We consider different motions those that have different periodic patterns with one or many fundamental frequencies. We select the temporal Fourier Transform for each pixel to be the representation space for a sequence of images. The classification is performed using Non-Negative Matrix Factorization (NNMF) over the power spectra data set. The paper we present can be applied on a wide range of applications for video sequences analysis, such as: background subtraction on non-static backgrounds framework, object segmentation and classification. We point out the fact that no registration technique is applied in the method that we introduce. Nevertheless, this method can be used as a cooperative tool for the existing techniques based on camera motion models (motion segmentation, layer classification, tracking of moving objects, etc).

1 Introduction

The aim of finding periodicities in image sequences goes back to the beginnings of Computer Vision. Many biological reasons support the idea of dealing with this specific issue. Periodic motion detection is a strong cue for object and action recognition in human motion perception [3, 4]. Actually, studies on recognizing moving light displays show the ability of human perception for recognizing biological motion [3, 4]. Even when dealing with very low resolution image sequences, humans are capable of recognizing periodic movements [2].

As it has been pointed out in [11, 7, 10], periodicity is striking in that it can be detected without taking into account the structure of objects in a scene (rigid and non-rigid objects are accounted for), and, at the same time, techniques for periodic motion detection, segmentation and classification can assist in many applications requiring object and activity recognition and representation [6, 1].

Recent analysis that categorize the existing methods for periodic motion recognition and segmentation can be found in [2], and can be summarized into: *Fourier based* methods [10, 7, 2], *Point correspondences* based methods [11], *Linear Dynamic models* methods [1], fitting spatio-temporal surfaces [8], and

---

* This work was supported by CICYT TEL 99-1206-C02-02.

F.J. Perales et al. (Eds.): IbPRIA 2003, LNCS 2652, pp. 673–680, 2003.
© Springer-Verlag Berlin Heidelberg 2003

Flow-based methods [9]. Many of them use spatio-temporal alignment, background subtraction and tracking techniques for targeting periodic patterns. The work we present in this paper is certainly compatible with these techniques, even though, for the purpose of this paper, they are not the main point of discussion.

1.1 Contribution

We present a novel technique to deal with a new and interesting problem, which can be stated as follows: How many different types of periodic movements are in a specific scene? Is it possible segmenting different objects from their motion when: a) there are occlusions in the scene across time and b) the same object has disconnected parts? Both questions have an answer when studying the global behavior of a sequence that contains different objects moving with different periodic movements. The algorithm we propose yields a manner for detecting in each frame : i) which pixels correspond to a specific object? and ii) which are the fundamental frequencies that contribute to its motion? The referenced works were about detecting periodicity and segmenting a particular region where periodic movements occur, however no classification for different periodic movements in the same scene was proposed.

The technique we present can be used when dealing simultaneously with moving objects plus moving backgrounds such as: waterfalls, waves, smoke, etc. Typically, this sort of backgrounds are considered video textures. The main problem, in this case, is when approaching them with either background subtraction or spatio-temporal alignment techniques, since the collection of pixels belonging to the background do not correspond to a pure camera transformation and they are not static in their pixel value (gray, color). We treat the background with no particular distinction among the rest of pixels.

1.2 Outline

First, we build a model for one-dimensional images in order to analyze the different contributions of shape, motion and frame-rate to the Fourier power spectra. In section 3, we present a brief study on the reliability of periodic motion classification and power spectrum factorization. The segmentation of multiple periodic moving objects in video sequences is based on the formulation presented in section 4. The algorithm is shown in section 5. Section 6 presents a set of experiments in order to show the algorithm's performance. Finally, the conclusions are presented in section 7.

2 Periodic Motion Analysis

In this section, we justify how the fundamental frequency can be extracted from a set of observed images. To this end, we show an example that deals with one dimensional images. It can be directly extended to 2-D images.

Let $I(x)$ be an one dimensional image with d pixels, where x indicates the pixel position. The following example shows an oscillating spot of length L and amplitude A across time. Therefore, the observation is a set of N images with the spot at different positions. The frequency of oscillation is $\omega_0 = 2\pi/T_0$, and we consider those cases where $T_0 < N$. For each pixel position, there is a 1-D periodic signal which consists of a pattern of bars with amplitude s and intra-bar separation a.

The size of the object L and the frequency of oscillation determine the behavior of s and a at each height x location. The oscillation model corresponds to the domain defined by the two following boundary signals:

$$f_1(t) = A \, \cos(\omega_0 t) + \frac{L}{2} \tag{1}$$

$$f_2(t) = A \, \cos(\omega_0 t) - \frac{L}{2} \tag{2}$$

We can see that the length of the object for image in the sequence is $f_1(t) - f_2(t) = L$, with $L \geq 0$. For a specific pixel position x within the oscillation amplitude interval, there is a 1-D signal that corresponds to the intersection of x with each of the two boundaries (eqs. (1) and (2)): $x = A \, \cos(\omega_0 t_1) + \frac{L}{2}$ and $x = A \, \cos(\omega_0 t_1) - \frac{L}{2}$. Therefore, x intersects at t_1 and t_2 yielding the bar width $s =\mid t_2 - t_1 \mid$:

$$s(x, A, L, \omega_0) = \frac{1}{\omega_0} \left| \cos^{-1}\left(\frac{x + \frac{L}{2}}{A}\right) - \cos^{-1}\left(\frac{x - \frac{L}{2}}{A}\right) \right| \tag{3}$$

The intra-bar separation a can be written in terms of (x, A, L, ω_0):

$$a(x) = \frac{1}{\omega_0} \left| 2\pi - 2\cos^{-1}\left(\frac{x + \frac{L}{2}}{A}\right) - \cos^{-1}\left(\frac{x - \frac{L}{2}}{A}\right) \right| \tag{4}$$

For each pixel location x, there is a temporal periodic signal with $(a, s, T_0 = \frac{2\pi}{\omega_0})$. Let $Q_a(t)$ be defined as a step function defined as follows:

$$Q_s(t) = \begin{cases} 1 & \text{if } 0 \leq t \leq s(x) \\ 0 & \text{else} \end{cases} \tag{5}$$

The temporal signal for a specific pixel location x can be defined as follows:

$$f(t) = \sum_n Q_{s(x)}(t - nT_0) + \sum_n Q_{s(x)}(t - nT_0 - a(x)) \tag{6}$$

Assuming a frame-rate sufficiently fast to capture the periodicity, the power spectrum at x can be written as follows:

$$S(\omega, x) = 16 \sum_n \delta(\omega - \omega_0 n) \frac{1}{\omega_0^2 n^2} U_n(\omega_0 a(x)) U_n(\omega_0 s(x)) \tag{7}$$

where $U_n(z) = [1 + \cos(nz)]^2$ has been defined for notation simplicity. From equations (4) and (3) we note that $U_n(\omega_0 a(x))$ and $U_n(\omega_0 s(x))$ do not actually depend on the fundamental frequency ω_0. This implies that the power spectrum consist of the contribution of two terms of different nature: i) one corresponding to the sampling effect due to the fundamental frequency ω_0, and ii) another term corresponding to the contribution of the pixel location x and the object's shape parameters:

$$S(\omega, x) = \sum_n \delta(\omega - \omega_0 n) H_n(A, L, x) \qquad (8)$$

Moreover, the discretization effect due to the number of frames in the sequence makes equation (8) to be re-written approximately as follows:

$$S(\omega, x) \approx \sum_{k=0}^{N-1} \delta(\omega - k) \sum_{n=0}^{T_0} \delta(\omega - \frac{N}{T_0} n) H_n(x) \qquad (9)$$

This is just an approximation of a sum of exponentials, however, for our range analysis we will further show that is very useful since it allows to study the influence of $H_n(x)$ on the spectra obtained from the observations. It is worth to note that when T_0 approaches to N, i.e., the ratio $\frac{N}{T_0} \to 1$, no information about the fundamental frequency can be extracted from the observations. The corresponding spectra miss the common property that allows to identify them as the result of the same motion origin.

3   Variance

The purpose of this section is to study the possibility of classifying different spectra belonging to different types of periodic motions. Consider a sequence of two moving objects with fundamental frequencies ω_1 and ω_2. The resulting spectra for each pixel position are:

$$S_1(\omega, x) \approx \sum_{k=0}^{N-1} \delta(\omega - k) \sum_{n=0}^{T_1} \delta(\omega - \frac{N}{T_1} n) H_n^1(x)$$

$$S_2(\omega, x) \approx \sum_{k=0}^{N-1} \delta(\omega - k) \sum_{n=0}^{T_2} \delta(\omega - \frac{N}{T_2} n) H_n^2(x)$$

The aim of this example is to analyze the variance due to the pixel position in comparison with the average difference between the two types of spectra. Let us call *intra-class* difference to the variance due to the pixel position (and object's shape), and *inter-class* difference to the average difference between the two spectra.

A symmetrical measure that express the inter/intra-class ratio variance can be the geometrical mean of the ratios: $d(S_1, S_2)/ < \Delta S_1 >$ and $d(S_1, S_2)/ < \Delta S_2 >$, which is expressed in terms of the periods T_1 and T_2 as follows:

$$R_{S_1, S_2} = 4\sqrt{\left(1 + \frac{T_1^4}{T_2^4}\right)\left(1 + \frac{T_2^4}{T_1^4}\right)} \tag{10}$$

The bigger is the ratio between the two periods T_1/T_2 the bigger is the variance R_{S_1, S_2}, and therefore, the most distinguishable are the two types of motion. For instance, consider T_1 being twice T_2, therefore, $R_{S_1, S_2} \approx 16$ times between intra-class and inter-class. This yields to study the possibility of applying statistical techniques to segment the different types of periodic movements that occur in an image sequence.

4   Segmenting Different Periodic Motions

The fact that two different motions are sampled different, the distance between them is much bigger, than the differences due to shape and pixel location of different spectra originated by the same periodic motion as it is shown in equation (10). Therefore, the fact of factoring the power spectra does not block the possibility of segmenting different types of periodic motions:

$$S(\omega, x) = \sum_{n=1}^{T_0} W_n(\omega) H_n(x) \approx \bar{W}(\omega)\bar{H}(x) \tag{11}$$

This approximation is the central point for analyzing the segmentation of periodic motions. Since the contribution of shape has been minimized through this approximation, we can see that the method can deal with non rigid objects (no assumption based on rigidity has been made).

For a model that assumes different periodic moving objects, the idea is that the power spectrum at each pixel location x factorizes as follows:

$$S(\omega, x) = \sum_{k=1}^{q} \bar{W}_k(\omega)\bar{H}_k(x) \tag{12}$$

where q different types of movements have been assumed. Further, we embed this model into a Bayesian framework in order to select from data the number of possible different types of motion automatically. In order to analyze the linear superposition assumption in the spectra, we refer to the linear property of the Fourier transform, and the fact the interferences when computing the power spectra are taken into account in the variance analysis (intra and inter class).

The parameter estimation has to take into account the fact that $S(\omega, x)$, $\bar{W}_k(\omega)$ and $\bar{H}_k(x)$ are non negative. To this end, we base our method on the technique presented in [5]. The error function to minimize takes into account both the reconstruction error and a prior function over $\bar{H}_k(x)$ in order to automatically control the effective number of sufficient parameters (number of possible moving objects q). Therefore, a set of hyper-parameters $\{\alpha_1, \ldots, \alpha_q\}$ is introduced in order to behave as switchers; activating or deactivating the components $\bar{H}_k(x)$. For large values of α_k the corresponding component will tend to be small, and therefore, such component will be neglected.

$$\mathcal{E} = \frac{1}{\sigma^2} \sum_x \sum_\omega \left| S(\omega, x) - \sum_{k=1}^q \bar{W}_k(\omega)\bar{H}_k(x) \right|^2 + \sum_{k=1}^q \alpha_k \sum_x \bar{H}_k(x) \tag{13}$$

The update rules that take into account non-negativity are:

$$\bar{H}_k(x)^{t+1} = \bar{H}_k(x)^t \left\{ \frac{\sum_\omega S(\omega, x)\bar{W}_k(\omega)}{\sum_\omega \bar{W}_k(\omega) \sum_{i=1}^q \bar{W}_i(\omega)\bar{H}_i(x)^t + \sigma^2 \sum_{i=1}^q \delta_{ik}\alpha_i\bar{H}_i(x)^t} \right\} \tag{14}$$

with unity constraints. The computation for the noise variance σ^2 and the model selectors α_k can be performed as follows:

$$\sigma^2 = \frac{1}{V_x V_\omega} \sum_x \sum_\omega \left| S(\omega, x) - \sum_{k=1}^q \bar{W}_k(\omega)\bar{H}_k(x) \right|^2 \tag{15}$$

and

$$\alpha_k = \frac{V_x}{\sum_x \bar{H}_k(x)} \tag{16}$$

where V_x and V_ω are the number of pixel locations and frequencies respectively. The idea, here, was to show the manner the factors are estimated avoiding masking the procedure with extra mathematical formalisms.

5   Algorithm and Examples

Two sequences of images are used in order to show the performance of the algorithm. The first one is a synthetic generated sequence with the purpose of studying the manner the algorithm deals with occlusions. Three moving objects are in the scene: two of them evolving according to a translational motion, and a third one according to a zoom operation. The three moving objects have different frequencies. Figure 2 shows 25 frames of a 100 frames sequence - in 1 out of 4 order-. Optical flow-based techniques are often used to estimate the motion of objects in image sequences. The main weakness of those techniques is their reliance on texture. In this specific sequence, we selected the objects to have no texture.

A second sequence consists of natural images with two main periodic motions: a moving face with lower frequency than a moving hand. In this case, occlusion is also a notable factor to be concerned when tackling this problem with local approaches. Moreover, in this sequence, there is a third issue to be analyzed: "non-rigid objects". We can consider the hand to be a non-rigid object,

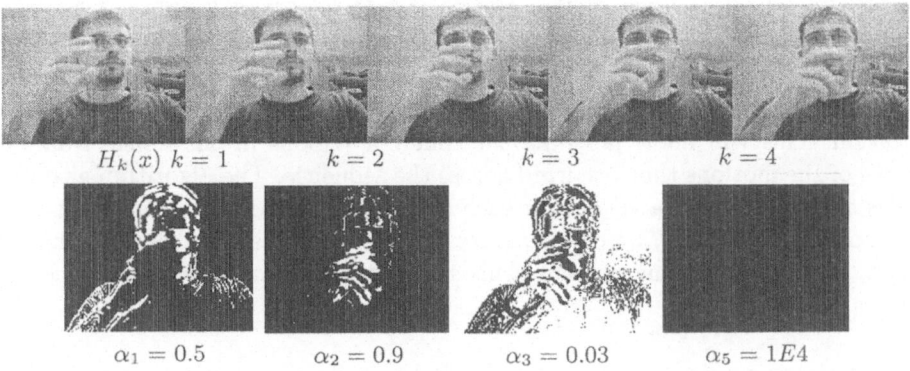

Fig. 1. Top row: Some frames of the face sequence. Bottom row: Components indicating the contribution of each type of periodic movement to each pixel location x. A large value of α_k indicates negligible component

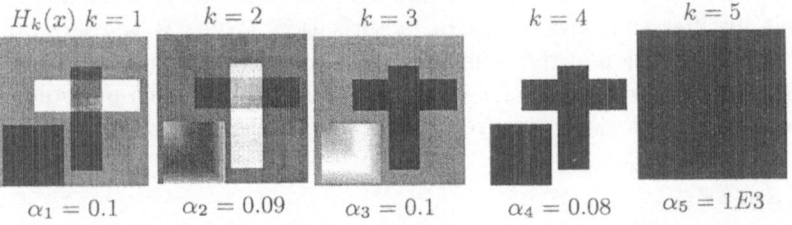

Fig. 2. Components indicating the contribution of each type of periodic movement to each pixel location x. A large value of α_k indicates negligible component

or, more properly, an articulated object - for the purpose it does not matter -. The fact is that, techniques based on parametric motion estimation lack of enough flexibility to deal with the segmentation of this moving hand (see fig. 1). Parametric techniques are either too restrictive or not enough general to be applied in a variety of situations. The technique we present is able, instead, to deal with non-rigid objects with the same approach applied in the first sequence.

In both sequences, few first compute the time Fourier transform for each pixel location x, and therefore, their corresponding power spectra. After, this first step, its necessary to assign an initial guess to the number of different periodic motions, which are supposed to be in the scene. It is recommendable to assume that there are many motions in the scene, since the Bayesian approach of this algorithm will explain how many true different motions are in the scene. For the synthetic sequence we chose 5 different motions as initial guess. In the other one we select 4 as initial guess. Having the power spectra for each sequence, we run the estimation process described in the previous section. After convergence, the hyper parameters α_k will explain in each case the number of sufficient different motions to be considered as shown in figures 2 and 1.

The algorithm provides a "location mask" $H_k(x)$ for each different detected motion. Since for each pixel location $\bar{H}_k(x)$ is normalized to the unity with respect to the motion model components k, the $\bar{H}_k(x)$ values indicate the contribution in terms of probabilities of each single segmented motion in each pixel location. This will allow labelling the different regions in the image frame in terms of the motions that occurred across the sequence. The algorithm also provides the power spectra $W_k(\omega)$ for each different detected movement. Using the components separately, we can generate synthetic video sequences with the different segmented moving objects. This segmentation is performed in space and time at the same time.

6   Conclusions

We have presented a technique that classifies the different periodic motions that can be present in a video sequence. We have firstly built a model in order to show the different effects that contribute to the temporal Fourier spectra, such as: shape, motion and frame-rate. Moreover, we have shown a reliability analysis that justifies the power spectra factorization, which is the key point for a spectral classification of the different pixels in an image sequence. This analysis permits dealing with occlusions, non-rigid objects and quasi-periodic moving backgrounds such as video textures (waterfalls, smoke, sea, waves etc.).

References

[1] C. Cohen, L. Conway, and D. Koditschek. Dynamical system representation, generation, and recognition of basic oscillatory motion gestures. In *Int. Conf. Auto. Face and Gesture Recognition*, volume 1, pages 60–65, 1996.

[2] R. Cutler and L. Davis. Real-time periodic motion detection, analysis, and applications. In *Computer Vision and Pattern Recognition*, volume 1, pages 326–332, 1999.

[3] N. Goddard. The interpretation of visual motion: Recognizing moving lights. In *In IEEE Worshop on Motion*, volume 1, pages 212–220, 1989.

[4] G. Johansson. Visual motion perception. *Scientific American*, 232:75–88, 1976.

[5] D. D. Lee and H. S. Seung. Learning the parts of objects with nonnegative matrix factorization. *Nature*, 401:788–791, July 1999.

[6] J. Little and J. Boyd. Recognizing people by their gate: the shape of motion. In *Videre*, volume 1, pages –, 1998.

[7] F. Liu and R. Picard. Finding periodicity in space and time. In *International Conference on Computer Vision*, volume 1, pages 376–383, 1998.

[8] S. Niyogi and E. Adelson. Analyzing and recognizing walking figures in xyt. In *Computer Vision and Pattern Recognition*, volume 1, pages 469–474, 1994.

[9] R. Polana and R. Nelson. Low level recognition of human motion. In *In IEEE Worshop on Motion of Non-rigid and Articulated Objects*, volume 1, pages 77–82, 1994.

[10] R. Polana and R. Nelson. Detection and recognition of periodic, non-rigid motion. *International Journal of Computer Vision*, 23:261–282, 1997.

[11] S. Seitz and C. Dyer. View-invariant analysis of cyclic motion. *International Journal of Computer Vision*, 25:1–23, 1997.

Finding Breaking Curves in 3D Surfaces

Xavier Orriols and Xavier Binefa*

Computer Vision Center
Universitat Autònoma de Barcelona, Barcelona, Spain, 08193 Bellaterra
{xevi,xavierb}@cvc.uab.es
http://www.cvc.uab.es/~xevi

Abstract. In this paper we present a recursive least squares technique for extracting the *breaking curve* of a $3D$ range open surface. Unlike differential operators-based methods, the algorithm we propose is robust to noise and is applied to unorganized point sets. No assumptions such as smoothness and/or continuity on the boundary's shape are performed. The method we present deals with large amount of data under a low computational cost, since no local computation is performed. A global approach is given to the technique in order to make it more robust, faster and simpler than individual point plus neighbours approaches.

1   Introduction

Many problems are associated with extracting the boundaries of noisy $3D$ surfaces: segmentation [8], object recognition, perceptual organization [3], applications to archaeology pottery reconstruction [4, 5], sherds classification, the $3D$ puzzle problem, etc. These applications deal usually with broken pieces and patches which can be characterized by their *breaking curves*. This type of curves can characterize the $3D$ spatial organization of a set of broken sherds in order to reconstruct the original object.

Breaking curves are a particular case of 3D edges; they are the boundaries corresponding to a 2D surface embedded in a 3D space. Actually, the points belonging to a 2D surface are considered to be *edge points* since there is a discontinuity in at least one direction of the first derivatives ($3D$ gradient). Much work has been done on 3D edge detection through differential operators [7, 2]. The main drawback is that neighboring-based operations are highly expensive in terms of computational cost. Other local approaches are either based on computations that require a previous data ordering -triangular meshes- [8, 6] or *boundary following*-like algorithms [9]. Techniques based on local computations -such as partial differential equations- suffer from extreme sensitiveness to noise.

1.1   Contribution

We propose a new method that is based on global computations, and, which : *i)* is fast in very large data sets, *ii)* is robust to noise, and *iii)* does not need

---

* This work was supported by CICYT TEL 99-1206-C02-02.

F.J. Perales et al. (Eds.): IbPRIA 2003, LNCS 2652, pp. 681–688, 2003.

data to be organized. This method is based on a recursive algorithm that starts fitting a plane to the surface and in each iteration increases the number of planes by splitting the previous estimated ones. In each estimation the boundaries for each plane are computed. The boundaries of each sub-portion fitted by a plane must be consistent with the whole data set. This means that only the plane boundaries points consistent with the surface boundaries are taken as "true" boundary points. The procedure can be described as a tree structure, where each level contains information on the sherd's boundary at a certain scale. Once, the algorithm is at the lowest level of the tree-structure, all the consistent boundary points are collected from all the branches and leaves. These points are the sherd's *boundary points*. As it is shown in the experiments, the more levels are investigated, more accuracy is obtained for describing the breaking curve. Issues such as: "how many levels are needed?", and "when it is necessary to stop the splitting?" are answered as well. Moreover, from a computational point of view, we show that the algorithm is initialization independent. The manner it is formulated avoids implicitly ill-conditioning problems without being forced to add ad hoc numerical treatments.

1.2   Outline

he paper first introduces the mathematical framework where the algorithm is based on. Afterwards, the algorithm is presented. In section 4 some experiments are shown. Finally, in section 5, we present the conclusions.

2   Background

In this section, we introduce the mathematical framework and the main geometrical idea behind the algorithm. Before beginning with the formulation, an issue to be considered is that a $2D$ surface can be approximated by $2D$ planar patches. Ideally, an infinite number of these planar patches would reconstruct the surface exactly.

2.1   Fitting a Plane to a Distribution of Points

The first and easiest sort of surface to start with is a planar surface described by a few number of points. This type of surfaces can be represented by a specific set of coordinate orthogonal axes adapted to the points spatial distribution. These are obtained by means of a linear regression that fits a $2D$ plane minimizing the orthogonal distance to the mentioned plane. A plane, actually, can be described by just two degrees of freedom that locate any point belonging to it. These two degrees of freedom are scalar values that measure the distance of a point along each of the axes.

The estimation of the principal axes is performing through Principal Component Analysis (hereafter PCA) [1]. The result of applying PCA on set of $3D$ points is a set of 3 unitary vectors and 3 scalar values. The unitary vectors are known as *eigenvectors*, and the scalar values as *eigenvalues*. The eigenvalues give a notion of the importance of a specific axis with respect to the others. This importance measure is actually the variance -in statistical terms- of the data along each axis. This means that an axis with large variance associated has the data distributed in a larger portion of space, than another axis with lower variance associated. In other words, when it comes to fit a plane to a planar distribution of points, there is an axis with negligible variance, which determines the noise of the planar distribution. The larger is the amount of variance in that direction, the lower is the likelihood of the point distribution to be a plane. PCA algorithm is coordinate free, which means that results are adapted to the nature of the data distribution but to the frame of reference where data is represented. This makes the technique independent of the absolute position, which is quite useful when dealing with pottery (pieces in general) scans.

Let us analyze some useful consequences of computing the principal axes of a noisy planar distribution of points. Firstly, the study of the projections along each of the two principal axes gives a manner of start investigating the surface dimensions. We can consider as a rough approximation the surface's shape to be a rectangle. Under this coarse way of studying the surface's dimensions, we can notice that the limits are defined in each of the two principal directions, i.e., the orthogonal projections onto each of the eigenaxis (fig. 1).

This approximation permits finding a bounding box to the planar surface. There are at least four interesting points for a general contour shape of a planar distribution of points. Each of these four points are the contact points with the bounding box, and each one corresponds to be the limit point projection in each eigenaxis direction. It is interesting to note that the fewer number of points are in the planar distribution, the simpler is the object's shape and therefore, better approximated by the mentioned bounding box. This reasoning plays a crucial role when attempting to describe a complex surface by means of assembling simpler structures.

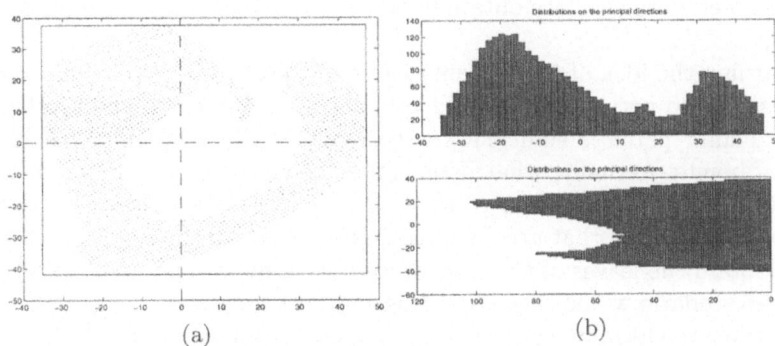

(a)   (b)

Fig. 1. (a) Planar surface approximation and principal directions. This distribution can be bounded by a rectangle defined by (b) the orthogonal projections onto each of the two principal axis

2.2   Recursive Splitting

When approximating a $2D$ surface through a plane, the error might be higher than a certain degree of tolerance. In that case, it is necessary performing a more complex modeling. After a first approximation through one plane, the second step is to consider two planar surfaces to fit the original distribution of points. Typically, when a simple model does not fit well data is because the data has to be explained through more complex models, or, through a combination of simple sub-models, which is more practical. In the case we consider, given the geometrical nature of the observed data, that the point distribution can be approximated by higher number of planar patches (a combination of simple models).

Given the principal directions $W = \{e_1, e_2\}$ and the sample mean μ there are some ways of dividing data into sub-portions. A manner of dividing data into two sets is along on of the principal direction, for instance, the one with the largest variance e_1. The splitting in this case would be selecting all those points that are left to the sample mean in the e_1 and the other set all those which are right to μ. More explicitly, one sub-set $\mathcal{P}_1^1$, will consist of points whose projection onto e_1 is :

$$e_1'(\boldsymbol{p}_{n_1} - \mu) \leq 0$$

and another set $\mathcal{P}_2^1$, will be formed by those points whose projection is:

$$e_1'(\boldsymbol{p}_{n_2} - \mu) > 0$$

The same reasoning can be applied to the e_2 direction. However for the sake of notation, we now just consider a division into two sub-sets. The notation that has been used for the two sub-sets is described as follows: for $\mathcal{P}_1^1$, the upper-index means that is, in this case, the first division applied to the data set $\mathcal{P}$. The sub-index is sub-portion index, in this specific case we have two sub-sets : $\mathcal{P}_1^1$ and $\mathcal{P}_2^1$.

The point here is that the same technique can be applied to each of the sub-sets. Therefore, what we obtain finally is a tree structure of sub-sets decompositions.

Regarding the idea of the certain degree of tolerance for splitting, there will be nodes that do not need to be split up. These usually correspond to flat areas where a planar patch is sufficient to represent locally a specific spatial distribution of points. Actually, what determines the stop-splitting is the mentioned degree of tolerance. When the considered area is sufficient flat, the algorithm decides not to split on that area, and therefore, when all the branches stop splitting we obtain the leaves of the tree. Since the number of points N is finite, the worst case scenario would mean splitting $\log_2(N)$ times.

According to the main subject in the paper, the algorithm has to find in each step the *breaking curve points* or boundary points. Finding the first four contact points before division is a coarse estimation of the boundaries of the surface. After division, the process of finding contact points has to be repeated for each sub-set of points.

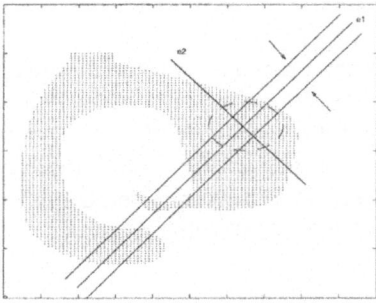

Fig. 2. Boundary analysis of a sub-set; projection onto the 2 principal axes

Figure 2 shows the way the boundary points are determined. First, select one of the two principal directions, for instance e_1. Therefore, project onto e_1 only the points that satisfy:

$$p_n \text{ such that } |e_2'(p_n - \mu)| < \epsilon \tag{1}$$

The same way a certain degree of tolerance was necessary to determine when a set should be divided into two sub-sets, the algorithm needs for a for an amplitude ϵ tolerance. These are the only two tuning parameters of the technique we present. Further, we show the effect of these values on the final segmentation. This ϵ parameter makes possible to deal with complex contour shapes. Figure 2 shows geometrically the idea of the condition expressed in eq. (1). From these projections, the only points we can select are those which belong to the data sub-set (the points inside the ellipse in figure 2), the rest of points belonging to the whole data set are just to check if the *boundary* point belonging to the subset is a "true" *boundary* point. Formally, the condition to be safitied by a boundary point of a sub-set $\mathcal{P}_n^L$ is:

$$p_k \in \mathcal{P}_n^L \text{is boundary if} \begin{cases} e_1'(p_k - \mu) \geq e_1'(p_i - \mu)\forall i \text{ and } p_i \in \mathcal{P} \\ \\ \text{or} \\ \\ e_1'(p_k - \mu) \leq e_1'(p_i - \mu)\forall i \text{ and } p_i \in \mathcal{P} \end{cases} \tag{2}$$

where $\mathcal{P}$ is the whole set of points. Note that the symbols "$\geq$" and "$\leq$" are taking into account the fact that a point belonging to the sub-set also belongs to $\mathcal{P}$. Also notice that no point outside the subset $\mathcal{P}_n^L$ is considered, at this step, to be a boundary point since we are just dealing with projections, there is no security of finding a "true" boundary point which does not belong to $\mathcal{P}_n^L$ from this projection.

3   The Algorithm

This section summarizes the procedure for finding *breaking curves*. The recursive function that computes the boundary points has four arguments: the set of $3D$ points $\mathcal{P}$, the subset of points corresponding to a specific surface patch $\mathcal{P}_{\text{subset}}$, and the tuning tolerances stop-splitting τ and amplitude control ϵ. For a given data set $\mathcal{P} = \{p_1, \ldots, p_N\}$, the initial considered sub-set is the same data set $\mathcal{P}$. The function is described in the following steps:

function b = computeBoundaryPoints($\mathcal{P}$,$\mathcal{P}_{\text{subset}}$,$\tau$,$\epsilon$)

- Find the principal components (e_1, e_2) and compute the sample mean μ for $\mathcal{P}_{\text{subset}}$.
- Compute the boundary points b_0 for $\mathcal{P}_{\text{subset}}$ the using $\mathcal{P}$, ϵ and the conditions eq. (1) and eq.(2).
- Stop-splitting condition:
  - **If** the error fitting the sub-set $\mathcal{P}_{\text{subset}}$ to a plane defined by (e_1, e_2) and μ is bigger than τ, then split

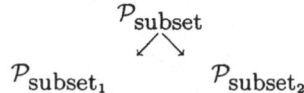

$$\mathcal{P}_{\text{subset}}$$
$$\swarrow \quad \searrow$$
$$\mathcal{P}_{\text{subset}_1} \qquad \mathcal{P}_{\text{subset}_2}$$

  - $*$ b_1 = computeBoundaryPoints($\mathcal{P}$,$\mathcal{P}_{\text{subset}_1}$,$\tau$,$\epsilon$)
  - $*$ b_2 = computeBoundaryPoints($\mathcal{P}$,$\mathcal{P}_{\text{subset}_2}$,$\tau$,$\epsilon$)
  and concatenate the resulting boundary points into $b = \text{cat}(b_0, b_1, b_2)$. Therefore, **return** b.
  - **else return** $b = b_0$.

The function calls itself twice, according to the split along the first principal direction e_1. However, there are many possible combinations, such as splitting according to the first and the second principal direction (e_1, e_2), which implies calling four times the function computeBoundaryPoints, and therefore, spanning a tree of four branches each time. We have described only a partition into two subsets in order to follow the previous section's description, and for sake of notation. Anyhow, in the experiments we performed a four times splitting.

4   Experiments

In this section, we present some results obtained from real archaeological (2000 years old) pieces. Figure 3 shows four pieces and their breaking curves. The first point we like to emphasize is the fact that three of them have high curvature regions. When applying differential operators, and local techniques to this type

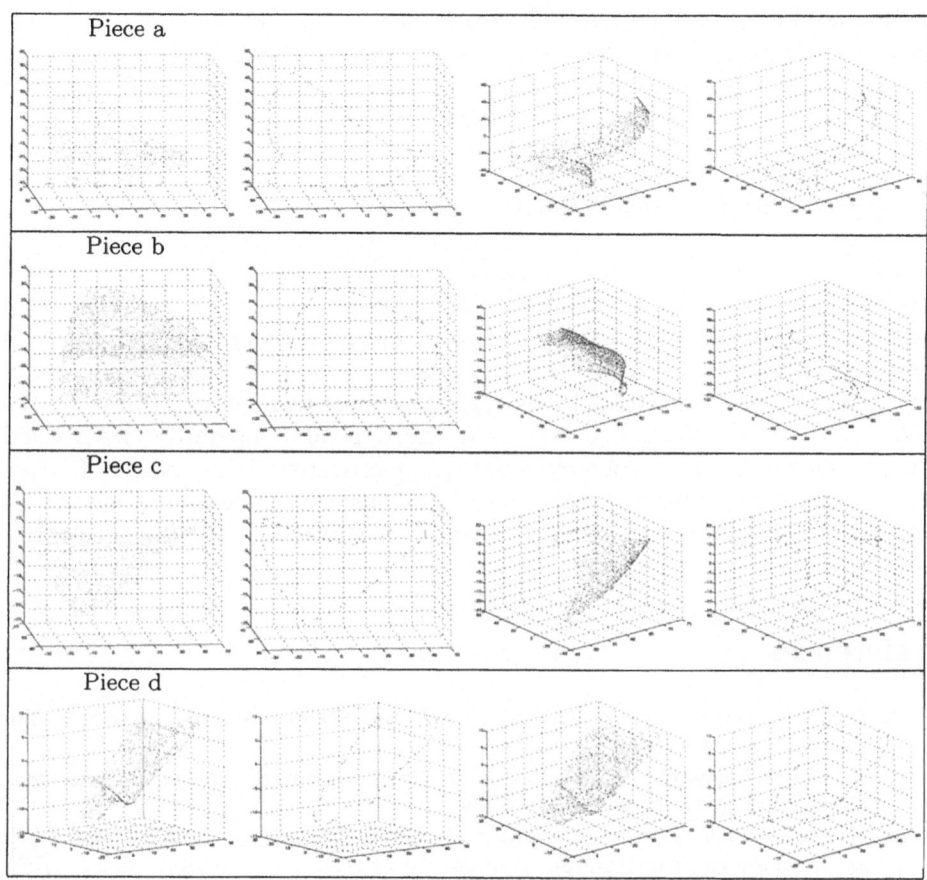

Fig. 3. Different views of four pieces and their extracted breaking curves

of surfaces with high curvature regions, they can yield to misleading results. The algorithm we have presented clearly overcomes this sort of regions, since data has been treated under a global approach. Actually, this is exactly the role played by the tuning parameter ϵ, which controlled the amplitude for checking "true" boundary points. Actually, the higher is ϵ value, the larger is the number of point to be analyzed through equation (2), the likelihood of selecting a boundary point

Table 1. Time consumed for a computation using $\tau = 0.001$ and $\epsilon = 0.01$

Piece	Number of Points	Consumed Time (Matlab)
a	18979	2.01s
b	18495	1.97s
c	12072	1.37s
d	18471	2.15s

at that level is lower. The role of τ parameter is to control the number of splits to be carried out. Finally, the table 1 shows the employed time corresponding to each piece. The tuning parameters were the same for all the pieces since their scanning resolution was practically the same in all cases.

5   Conclusions and Future Work

In this paper, we have presented a technique computes the breaking curves of $2D$ open surfaces from unorganized sets of $3D$ points. The formulation takes into account the spatial distribution of data. The more complex is the surface in terms of curvatures, the more time is necessary to invest in the computation of the breaking curve since more levels of the tree must be explored. Unlike partial differential equations techniques, or local scale depending-operators, the method we have introduced relies on only two tuning parameters. It's a matter of future work to study the empirical/analytical relation between these tuning parameters and the surface geometrical features such as curvature and the average density of points (scanning resolution).

References

[1] D. Bartholomew. *Latent Variable Models and Factor Analysis*. Charles Griffin and Co. Ltd., 1987.

[2] P. Bhattacharya and D. Wild. A new edge detector for gray volumetric data. *Comput. Biol. Med.*, 26:315–328, 1996.

[3] R. Bolle and D. Cooper. On optimally combining pieces of information, with applications to estimating 3d complex-object position from range data. *IEEE Transactions on Pattern Analysis and Machine Intelligence, 8(5):619–638*, 1986.

[4] D. Cooper. et al. Bayesian virtual pot-assembly from fragments as problems in perceptual-grouping and geometric-learning. In *Proceedings of the International Conference on Pattern Recognition (ICPR'02), Quebec City, Canada IEEE Computer Society Press.*, 2002.

[5] D. B.Cooper. et al. Assembling virtual pots from 3d measurements of their fragments. In *Proceedings of the International Symposium on Virtual Reality, Archaeology and Cultural Heritage (VAST2001)*, 2001.

[6] M. Garcia and L. Basanez. Fast extraction of surface primitives from range images. *13th IAPR International Conference on Pattern Recognition, Vienna, Austria*, 1996.

[7] J. F.Canny. A computational approach to edge detection. *IEEE trans. Pattern Analisys and Machine Intell.*, 8(6):679–698, 1986.

[8] A. Lejeune and F. P. Ferrie. Finding the parts of objects in range images. *Computer Vision and Image Understanding: CVIU*, 64(2):230–247, 1996.

[9] T. Pavlidis. Algorithms for graphics and image processing. *New York:Springer*, 1982.

Robust Segmentation and Decoding
of a Grid Pattern for Structured Light

Jordi Pagès, Joaquim Salvi, and Carles Matabosch

University of Girona, Institute of Informatics and Applications
av. Lluís Santaló s/n, 17071 Girona, Spain

Abstract. This paper describes the implementation details of a coded
structured light system useful for one-shot measurements of a surface.
Since a unique pattern is projected, the technique is useful for measuring
moving surfaces. A pattern based on grid structure is used. The main
advantage of such structure is that redundant codification is applied to
the cross-points. Since both pattern axis are coded, decoding errors can
be corrected thanks to the proposed algorithm. Moreover, not only the
cross-points of the grid can be reconstructed but also the pixels belonging
to vertical and horizontal slits. A description of the segmentation and
decoding stage is given in order to take profit of the advantages of the
pattern codification.

1 Introduction

Structured light systems appeared in order to ease the correspondence problem of
stereovision systems. Such techniques are based on replacing one of the cameras
by a light source. Then, projecting a set of known patterns onto the measuring
scene and grabbing images with the remaining camera(s), the correspondence
problem is solved by all those points where the patterns have been projected on.
The former systems projected patterns consisting of simple geometric primitives
like points or lines. Later, more complex patterns were developed, including
some kind of codification in order to distinguish different parts of the pattern
and increasing the number of correspondences in every projection. Such approach
has been known as coded structured light.

A large number of 3D points are recovered if multiple patterns can be projected. However, when measuring dynamic surfaces, techniques based on a unique
pattern must be used. Nevertheless, the resolution decreases since the codification must be condensed in a single pattern [1].

The most used coding strategy to generate such patterns is based on spatial
neighborhood codification. This approach consists of identifying a set of points
of the pattern with the information contained in a small neighborhood nearby.
Then, a set of well distributed pixels on the image can be reconstructed with
a single projection.

This paper presents the implementation of a low-cost coded structured light
technique based on spatial neighborhood codification. The technique permits

F.J. Perales et al. (Eds.): IbPRIA 2003, LNCS 2652, pp. 689–696, 2003.

to obtain the shape of an unknown surface even if it is moving. Besides, since the proposed pattern has a grid structure, both row and column codification is included into the crossing points. With such redundancy some interesting features are obtained: high accuracy in the reconstruction of the cross points, possibility to reconstruct both vertical and horizontal slits, and error detection and correction when decoding the cross points.

The main drawback of most part of techniques based on a unique pattern is their inability to reconstruct surfaces containing discontinuities correctly. In this paper it is demonstrated that encoding both pattern axis such limitation can be eliminated.

The paper is structured as follows: first, the codification principle of the pattern is detailed in section 2. The image processing involved in the segmentation of the pattern and the proposed algorithm for robust decodification are presented in section 3. Afterwards, in section 4 some examples of surface reconstruction using the implemented technique are shown. The paper ends with conclusions.

2   Pattern Design

The proposed coded structured light has been designed in order to use low-cost devices such a LCD projector to project the pattern, a color video camera, a frame-grabber and a standard PC.

The codification principle of the pattern used for the current implementation was proposed by Salvi et al. [2]. The structure of the projected pattern is defined as a grid composed of vertical and horizontal colored slits of a certain thickness over black background. In order to choose the sequence of colors that is assigned to the horizontal and vertical slits, a De Bruijn sequence is used. De Bruijn sequences have been used by several authors with the aim of defining patterns without periodicity. Concretely, the most exploited patterns coded with De Bruijn sequences consists of parallel slits, i.e. the one proposed by Monks et al. [3].

A De Bruijn sequence of order m over an alphabet of n symbols is a circular string of length n^m that contains each substring of length m exactly once. Such characteristic is called window property. For example, given the De Bruijn sequence of eq. 1, if every element of the alphabet $\{0, 1, 2\}$ is mapped to a certain color, a total of $3^3 = 27$ parallel slits of a pattern can be colored by mapping such sequence. The given sequence has length 29 due to its circular property.

$$22021020012011010002212111222 \tag{1}$$

Since the given De Bruijn sequence has a window property of 3, every three consecutive slits in the pattern will be uniquely identified by the codeword formed by their three colors. Another author who took profit of this coding strategy was Zhang et al. [4] proposing a coded pattern containing 125 vertical slits with a De Bruijn sequence of order 3 and 5 colors.

Other pattern structures coded with De Bruijn sequences have been proposed. For example, Griffin et al. used an array of colored dots such that every window of 3 × 3 dots in the pattern was unique [5]. The dot representation requires to locate the mass centers of all the imaged spots in order to triangulate them. Nevertheless, all those spots that appear partially occluded in the camera image must be discarded since their mass center might not be well segmented.

The work by Salvi et al. [2] proposed to design a grid pattern instead of a single sequence of parallel slits or a dot array. By selecting the colors of both vertical and horizontal slits with the same De Bruijn sequence, both axis are coded. The set of colors used to encode vertical and horizontal slits is different in order to differentiate both kind of slits. All the pixels belonging to a vertical or horizontal slit have a codeword which indicates the position of the slit in the pattern. All the imaged pixels belonging to the slits can be reconstructed by intersecting the equation of the camera 3D line which contains the image pixel and the equation of the 3D plain corresponding to the slit. Moreover, the cross points of slits in the grid have two codewords. Therefore, cross points can be reconstructed more accurately by intersecting the equations of two 3D lines. Another advantage of this pattern structure is that redundancy in the coding is included since two codewords are defined for every cross point. This fact permits to detect and even correct errors in the decoding stage of the imaged pattern.

The colors used for the horizontal slits are red, green and blue, while yellow, cyan and magenta are used for the vertical slits. The resulting pattern can be observed in figure 1a. Lavoie et al., a year later, proposed a similar pattern [6].

3   Pattern Segmentation and Decodification

Once the pattern is projected onto the measuring surface, an image must be grabbed with the camera. Then, for all those cross points of the grid that can be identified and decoded, the correspondence problem between camera and projector can be solved and, therefore, the corresponding 3D points can be triangulated.

In order to segment the grid in the image, a stage of image processing must be fulfilled. Then, the decoding stage must obtain the codewords of every visible cross point of the grid. This stage must be robust against errors since some parts of the projected grid can be occluded from the camera point of view.

The implemented algorithm has been structured in the following steps: first the segmentation of the grid, then, the cross points detection, and finally, the decodification of the detected cross points. Hereafter, all three steps are detailed.

3.1   Segmentation of the Grid

For correctly segment the projected grid it is necessary to clearly distinguish the 6 primary colors used. In order to success, a color calibration procedure is made only once, when installing the system in the working area, by projecting the grid onto a color-neutral surface and calibrating the gains for every projected color. The camera iris is also adjusted to perceive basically only the projected grid.

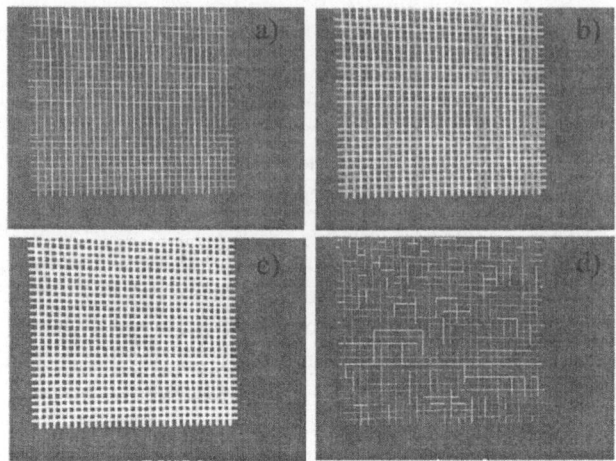

Fig. 1. Pattern segmentation. a) original 24-bit. b) image after edge detection, conversion to 8-bit and 3 Close iterations. c) binarization. d) thinning until skeleton

The first step of the segmentation algorithm consists of applying a Sobel operator to the camera image in order to detect the edges of the projected grid. The resulting image is converted to 8-bit greyscale. Afterwards, three Close morphological operators are applied in order to merge the parallel edges that appear using Sobel filter. Then, the obtained image is binarized with a low threshold in order to get thick slits. Finally, a thinning algorithm must be applied until the skeleton of the image is obtained. The sequence of operations can be observed in figure 1.

3.2   Cross Points Detection

Once the camera image has been processed in order to enhance and to segment the grid skeleton, the cross points between horizontal and vertical slits can be located. The set of masks shown in figure 2 are convolved with the image containing the skeleton of the grid.

$$\begin{pmatrix} 0 & 0 & 1 & 0 & 0 \\ 0 & 0 & 1 & 0 & 0 \\ 1 & 1 & 1 & 1 & 1 \\ 0 & 0 & 1 & 0 & 0 \\ 0 & 0 & 1 & 0 & 0 \end{pmatrix} \begin{pmatrix} 0 & 1 & 0 & 0 & 0 \\ 0 & 1 & 0 & 0 & 0 \\ 1 & 1 & 1 & 1 & 1 \\ 0 & 0 & 1 & 0 & 0 \\ 0 & 0 & 1 & 0 & 0 \end{pmatrix} \begin{pmatrix} 0 & 0 & 0 & 1 & 0 \\ 0 & 0 & 0 & 1 & 0 \\ 1 & 1 & 1 & 1 & 1 \\ 0 & 0 & 1 & 0 & 0 \\ 0 & 0 & 1 & 0 & 0 \end{pmatrix} \begin{pmatrix} 0 & 0 & 1 & 0 & 0 \\ 1 & 1 & 1 & 0 & 0 \\ 0 & 0 & 1 & 1 & 1 \\ 0 & 0 & 1 & 0 & 0 \\ 0 & 0 & 1 & 0 & 0 \end{pmatrix} \begin{pmatrix} 0 & 0 & 1 & 0 & 0 \\ 0 & 0 & 1 & 1 & 1 \\ 1 & 1 & 1 & 0 & 0 \\ 0 & 0 & 1 & 0 & 0 \\ 0 & 0 & 1 & 0 & 0 \end{pmatrix} \cdots$$

Fig. 2. Samples of the binary masks used to detect grid cross points

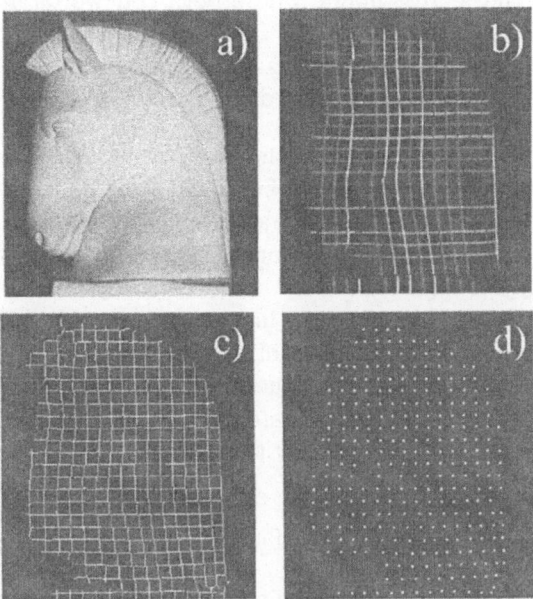

Fig. 3. Cross points detection. a) A horse statue. b) the pattern projected. c) the extracted skeleton of the grid. d) the detected cross points

For every position of the image where the convolution result is greater than 6 for any of the masks, the pixel is considered to be a cross point of the grid. All these masks must be used since the thinning operation to obtain the grid skeleton not always leads to perfect intersections.

An example of the cross-point detection process can be seen in figure 3, where the pattern has been projected onto a horse statue.

3.3   Decoding the Detected Cross Points

The projected grid is colored so that every cross point has two codewords. The first codeword is formed by the colors of the vertical slit containing the cross point and the colors of both adjacent vertical slits. The second is generated in the same way but with the horizontal slits. Both codewords are unique for every cross point (window property), so there is a direct mapping from both codewords to the cross point coordinates in the pattern.

In the previous subsection the process to detect cross points in the camera image has been explained. In order to decode the maximum number of cross points the following algorithm is applied:

- Generation of the cross points adjacency graph
- Obtaining the horizontal and vertical slits colors corresponding to every cross point

- Decoding all those cross-points whose both codewords have been found by using the adjacency graph
- Transfer of codewords to neighbors not decoded
- Correction of inconsistent codewords

To generate the adjacency graph is necessary to start from the coordinates of every cross point and track the edges of the grid skeleton towards four directions in order to find the neighbors. Since the skeleton has thickness of 1 pixel, windows of dimensions 1×3 and 3×1 are enough for tracking vertical and horizontal edges respectively.

The colors of the slits intersecting in every cross point are recovered during the tracking process. The mean Hue of every tracked edge is used to identify the original color projected. Let define the neighborhood of a cross-point as the grouping of its two codewords. Therefore, the neighborhood of a cross-point whose position in the grid is the y row the x column is defined as a vector like

$$neighborhood(crosspoint(y,x)) = [c_x \quad r_y \quad c_{x-1} \quad r_{y-1} \quad c_{x+1} \quad r_{y+1}] \quad (2)$$

Where c_i and r_j are the colors of column number i and row number j respectively. The graphic interpretation of the neighborhood of a cross-point can be seen in figure 4. Note that thanks to the De Bruijn codification, the neighborhood of a cross-point uniquely identifies its position in the projected grid.

Once the adjacency graph is constructed, the neighborhoods of all the detected cross-points in the camera image can be obtained. Firstly, only the cross-points whose complete neighborhood has been recovered are decoded. Otherwise, the cross point remains undecoded. The decodification of a detected cross-point consists of searching in the original pattern in which coordinates there is a cross-point with the same neighborhood. Then, the correspondence between both camera pixel and projector pixel is solved.

The following step tries to decode such cross points not decoded in the previous step by choosing the proposed pattern coordinates most voted by all the available decoded neighbors. For example, the cross-point occupying the x column and the y row in fig. 4, will propose the following coordinates to its four

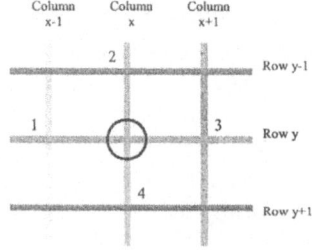

Fig. 4. Neighborhood of a cross-point

Fig. 5. Side view of the horse reconstruction

neighbors 1, 2, 3 and 4 respectively: $(x - 1, y)$, $(x, y - 1)$, $(x + 1, y)$, $(x, y + 1)$. The transfer step is repeated until no changes occur.

The final step of the algorithm consists of comparing the decoded pattern coordinates of every cross points with the coordinates that its neighbors would propose. Then, if the decoded pattern coordinates of a cross point do not coincide with the most voted coordinates proposed by its neighbors, such most voted coordinates are accepted as the correct ones. The last step of the algorithm is also repeated until no changes in the decoded coordinates occur.

4   Experimental Results

The hardware setup used for the experiments consists of a Mitsubishi XL1 video projector, a Sony 3 CCD camera, a Matrox Meteor-II frame grabber and a standard PC. The resolution of the projected pattern is 1024×768 pixels, while the camera images are digitized at 768×576 pixels, width a depth of 24 bits per pixel.

The rendered surface corresponding to the 3D reconstruction of the horse statue from figure 3a can be observed in figure 5 from different points of view.

As a second example, a human hand has been reconstructed to demonstrate the robustness of our technique against surfaces containing discontinuities. The cloud of 3D points obtained after applying the technique is presented in figure 6. The fingers of the hand are difficult to reconstruct since their small surface does not permit to contain large neighborhoods of cross-points, so none can be decoded directly. However, thanks to the transfer and correction steps of the designed decoding stage such constraint is removed.

5   Conclusions

The implementation of a coded structured light technique based on the projection of a unique grid pattern has been detailed. The paper has focused on the design of a robust decoding stage.

696   Jordi Pagès et al.

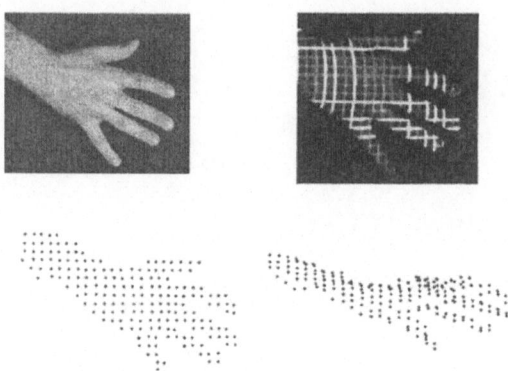

Fig. 6. Human hand reconstruction

The grid structure of the used pattern improves other pattern representations proposed in the bibliography. The different set of colors used for vertical and horizontal slits permit to be distinguished easily. Since both axis of the pattern are coded, cross points of the grid are redundantly coded, leading to a more accurate triangulation. Redundancy also permits to detect and correct errors in the cross points decodification.

The resolution of the technique can be increased by enlarging the number of slits and, therefore, the length of the De Bruijn sequence used to encode the grid. Moreover, since the pixels belonging to the horizontal and vertical slits are also coded with respect to a single axis, they can also be reconstructed producing a denser surface.

References

[1] J. Batlle, E. Mouaddib, J. Salvi, Recent progress in coded structured light as a technique to solve the correspondence problem: a survey, Pattern Recognition 31 (7) (1998) 963–982.
[2] J. Salvi, J. Batlle, E. Mouaddib, A robust-coded pattern projection for dynamic 3d scene measurement, Pattern Recognition Letters (19) (1998) 1055–1065.
[3] T. P. Monks, J. N. Carter, C. H. Shadle, Colour-encoded structured light for digitisation of real-time 3D data, in: International Conference on Image Processing, 1992, pp. 327–30.
[4] L. Zhang, B. Curless, S. M. Seitz, Rapid shape acquisition using color structured light and multi-pass dynamic programming, in: Int. Symposium on 3D Data Processing Visualization and Transmission, Padova, Italy, 2002.
[5] P. Griffin, L. Narasimhan, S. Yee, Generation of uniquely encoded light patterns for range data acquisition, Pattern Recognition 25 (6) (1992) 609–616.
[6] P. Lavoie, D. Ionescu, E. Petriu, A high precision 3D object reconstruction method using a color coded grid and nurbs, in: Proceedings of the International Conference on Image Analysis and Processing, Venice, Italy, 1999, pp. 370–375.

A New Reference Point Detection Algorithm Based on Orientation Pattern Labeling in Fingerprint Images

Chul-Hyun Park, Sang-Keun Oh, Dong-Min Kwak, Bum-Soo Kim, Young-Chul Song, and Kil-Houm Park

School of Electrical Engineering and Computer Science
Kyungpook National University, Daegu, Korea
{nagne,taesa,imis,bskim}@palgong.knu.ac.kr
{songyc03,khpark}@ee.knu.ac.kr

Abstract. Most fingerprint-based biometric systems establish a reference point in a fingerprint, then extract features based on this reference point. As such, the consistency and accuracy of the reference point location considerably affects the overall system performance. Accordingly, this paper presents an accurate and consistent reference point detection algorithm based on orientation pattern labeling. Experimental results demonstrate that the proposed method can produce a better performance in terms of accuracy and speed than Poincaré index or sine map-based methods.

1 Introduction

In most fingerprint-based verification or identification systems, a reference point is established and used to extract fingerprint features robust to translation or rotation. Generally, a core point, one of the singularities of a fingerprint, is used as such a reference point. A core point can be defined as the topmost or bottommost point on the innermost recurving ridgeline. The orientation pattern in a small local neighborhood around a core point has semi-circular tendency [1]. The number of core points differs according to the type of fingerprint [2], [3]. Tented arch (TA), left loop (LL), and right loop (RL) -type fingerprints have one core point, while twin loop (TL) and whorl (W) -type fingerprints have two core points. Arch (A) -type fingerprint images are known as having no core point. Therefore, in order to use a core point as a reference point, additional reference point detection method is required for arch-type fingerprints. In the case of fingerprints with two core points, the upper core point is normally used, which exists in all types of fingerprints, except for arch-type.

A core point detection method based on a Poincaré index analysis is one of the most commonly used techniques [1], [2], [3]. This method is simple and relatively fast compared to other methods, however, it is unable to detect a core point in most arch-type fingerprints, plus if the image quality is poor, the performance is severely deteriorated. Thus, to detect core points in low quality fingerprint

F.J. Perales et al. (Eds.): IbPRIA 2003, LNCS 2652, pp. 697–703, 2003.

images, the sine map-based method was developed [4]. This method is able to detect a reference point in the case of arch-type or low quality fingerprint images, yet it requires much processing time. Accordingly, this paper presents a new reference point location algorithm that can rapidly detect a reference point in all types of fingerprint images using orientation pattern labeling. The following section describes the proposed reference point detection algorithm in detail.

2   Reference Point Detection Algorithm

In non-singular regions, a fingerprint has a smooth and parallel flow of ridges, while in singular regions, the direction of the ridge flow changes abruptly. In particular, there is a big difference between the ridge directions of the upper and lower regions of a core point, as shown in Fig. 1.

The proposed algorithm exploits the fact that the ridges of the upper region of a core point generally have a quantized direction of 0°. First, the local ridge direction is calculated, then the regions with a quantized direction of 0° are detected. Among these regions, the upper part maximum region is found using connected component labeling. Thereafter, the position of the core point is determined using information on the lowest block line of the detected upper part maximum region.

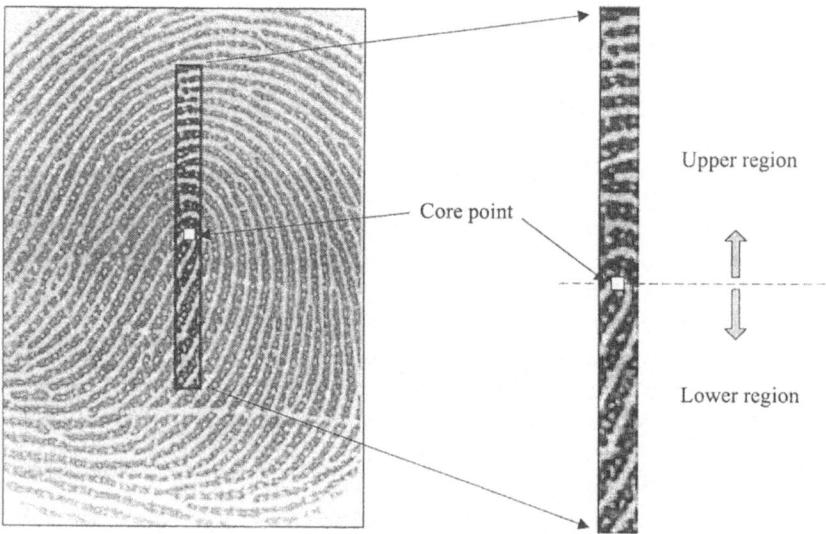

Fig. 1. Ridge distribution in neighborhood of core point

2.1 Calculation of Orientation Pattern

The orientation pattern is calculated using a least mean square orientation estimation algorithm [5] with the following procedure:

1) Divide the image into sub-blocks of size $w \times w$. A block size of 5×5 was used in the current experiment.
2) Compute the x and y direction gradients G_x, G_y for each pixel in block using 3×3 Sobel operators.
3) Calculate the orientation, $O(i,j)$, at the center pixel (i,j) of each block using the equation below:

$$O(i,j) = \frac{1}{2} \tan^{-1} \left[\frac{\sum_{u=i-w/2}^{i+w/2} \sum_{v=j-w/2}^{j+w/2} 2G_x(u,v)G_y(u,v)}{\sum_{u=i-w/2}^{i+w/2} \sum_{v=j-w/2}^{j+w/2} \left(G_x^2(u,v) - G_y^2(u,v)\right)} \right]. \quad (1)$$

2.2 Smoothing of Orientation Pattern

The resulting orientation pattern includes a lot of noise, therefore, the orientation field is smoothed by converting it into a vector form, i.e. $(\cos(2O(i,j)))$, $\sin(2O(i,j)))$, then averaging the two components of the vectors separately. Thereafter, the smoothed vector is transformed again into a direction [3]. In our experiment, a 5×5 mean filter was employed.

2.3 Labeling of Smoothed Orientation Pattern

An orientation pattern image is binarized by making all the blocks with a quantized direction of $0°$ a binary 1 and all other blocks a binary 0. Generally, two big regions with a quantized direction of $0°$ exist in the binarized image as shown in Fig. 2(d). The upper part maximum region is detected by labeling the binarized image. The reference point is determined from the upper part maximum region. The procedure for detecting a reference point is as follows:

1) Quantize the orientations into 8 directions: $0°$, $22.5°$, $45°$, $67.5°$, $90°$, $112.5°$, $135°$, and $157.5°$.
2) Binarize the quantized orientation pattern image by making all the blocks with a quantized direction of $0°$ a binary 1 and all other blocks a binary 0.
3) Perform connected component labeling [6] on the binarized image.
4) Extract the region with the maximum area from the upper part of the labeled image.
5) Find the lowest block line in the upper maximum region obtained in 4), then determine the position of the reference point. The block located one block below the center block of the lowest block line is determined as the reference block, as shown in Fig. 3. The center point of the reference block is then determined as the reference point.

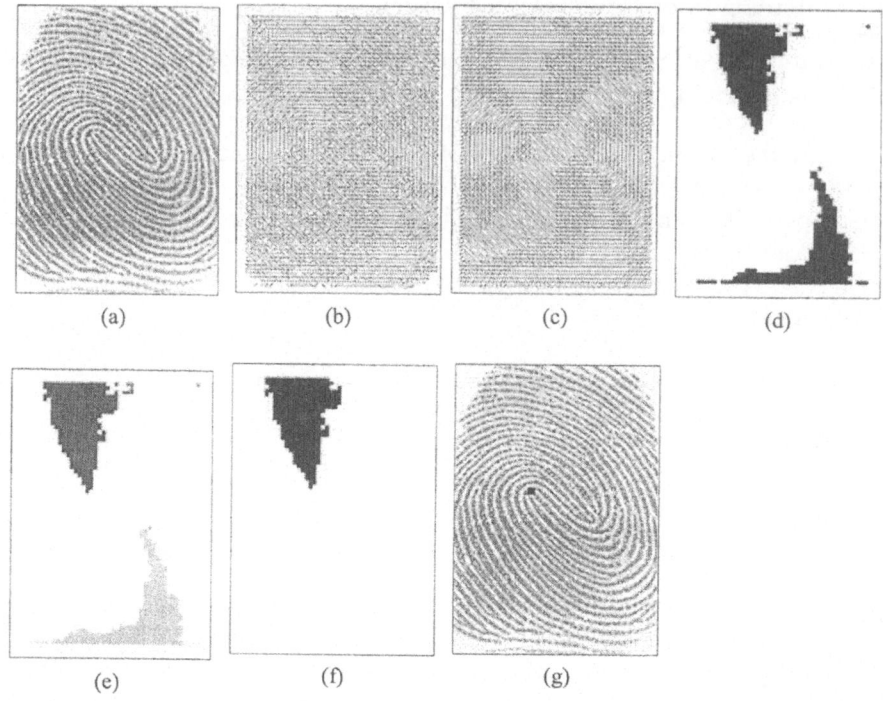

Fig. 2. Procedure for reference point detection. (a) Original image, (b) orientation pattern, (c) smoothed orientation pattern, (d) region with quantized direction of 0°, (e) labeled image, (f) upper part maximum region, and (g) detected reference point

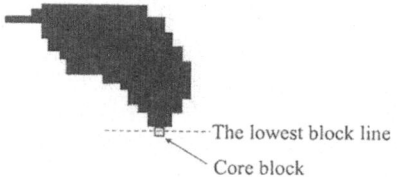

Fig. 3. Location of reference block

2.4   Re-labeling

In some fingerprint images, when labeling regions with a quantized direction of 0°, the upper part maximum region can be connected with the lower part maximum region, as shown in Fig. 4(d). In this case, the reference point can not be correctly detected by only one labeling. Therefore, to solve this problem, the proposed method changes the quantization ranges by a certain angle ($\pm n\Delta°$) and performs the labeling again. The quantization range shift is iteratively made increasing the extent of the shift until the upper and lower maximum regions are separated. The procedure for reference point detection by re-labeling is as follows:

1) If the extent of a quantization range shift is $-(n-1)\Delta°$ in the previous step, shift the quantization ranges by $+(n-1)\Delta°$, else if the extent of a quantization range shift is $+(n-1)\Delta°$ in the previous step, $-n\Delta°$. Here $n = 1, 2, 3, \ldots, N$.
2) Perform labeling on the binarized image to which the shift quantization ranges have been applied, and then go to step 3).
3) If the lowest block line of the detected upper maximum region is located at the bottom of the image, go to step 1), otherwise, determine the reference point according to the condition of step 5) of Section 2.3.

If the lowest block line of the upper maximum region is still located at the bottom of the image though all the specified quantization range shifts are tested, the proposed method fails in detecting a reference point. In this work, we set Δ to 3.

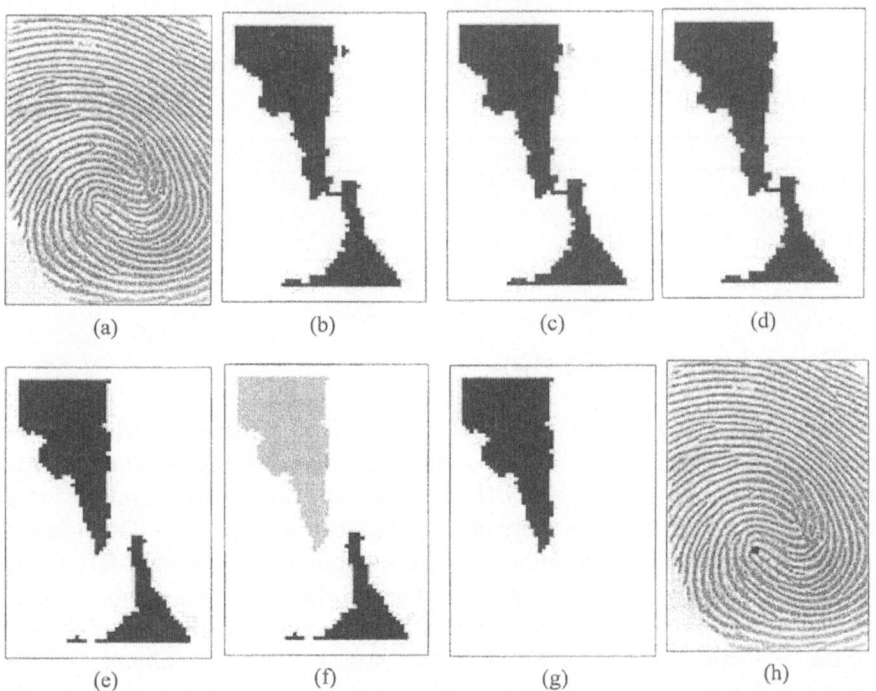

Fig. 4. Procedure for reference point detection by re-labeling. (a) Original image, (b) region with quantized orientation of $0°$, (c) labeled image of (b), (d) upper maximum region of (c), (e) region with quantized orientation of $0°$ after shifting the quantization range by $-3°$, (f) labeled image of (e), (g) upper maximum region of (f), and (h) detected core point

Table 1. Distribution of fingerprint classes

	A	TA	LL	RL	TL	W	Total
Number	30	5	140	105	185	235	700

Table 2. Processing time for each method (msec)

	A	TA	LL	RL	TL	W	Total
Poincaré	6.2	6.6	6.7	11.0	10.4	6.9	8.4
Sine map	141.9	146.0	144.0	154.4	140.2	145.2	144.9
Proposed	5.9	5.4	5.7	6.7	6.2	6.6	6.3

Table 3. Detection rate for each method (%)

	A	TA	LL	RL	TL	W	Total
Poincaré	0.0	100.0	92.4	92.4	98.8	95.2	91.1
Sine map	53.5	100.0	90.5	93.3	98.8	94.3	92.9
Proposed	46.7	100.0	95.2	96.2	98.8	95.2	94.3

Table 4. Performance comparison in terms of speed, robustness to rotation, low quality, arch type

	Speed	Rotation	Low quality	Arch type
Poincaré	High	High	Low	Low
Sine map	Low	Low	High	Medium
Proposed	High	Medium	Medium	Medium

3 Experimental Results

To acquire fingerprint images for experiments, a capacitive fingerprint capture device was used and a total of 700 fingerprint images were obtained from 140 fingers. Five fingerprint images with different rotations were acquired for each finger. The fingerprint images were all 256 grayscale images 364 × 256 in size. The experiments were conducted on a personal computer using a 700-MHz Pentium III processor. To evaluate the proposed method, its performance was compared with that of the Poincaré index-based method and sine map-based method.

The determination of correct detection was performed manually by visual inspection. Cases where no reference point was detected or the position of the reference point was considered as wrong by an observer were determined as misdetections. The extent of translation between the fingerprint images from the same finger was also reflected in the determination. Table 1 shows the distribution of the fingerprint classes in the database. The processing time and detection rate for each method are shown in Tables 2 and 3, respectively. The proposed method produced a faster performance than the other two methods for all types of fingerprints and a better detection rate than the other two methods for most types of fingerprint images. For arch-type fingerprints, the detection rate with the proposed method was inferior to that with the sine map-based method, however, the proposed method had a much better detection rate than the Poincaré index-based method.

The proposed method was able to accurately detect a reference point of the moderately rotated fingerprint image, however in case that the fingerprint was rotated much, the detected reference point had a tendency to deviate from the true location. The Poincaré index-based method well detects a reference point regardless of the extent of rotation, while this method fails to correctly detect a reference point in poor quality fingerprints. For the sine map-based method, since the reference point determination is based on multiresolution analysis of the orientation pattern, it has good performance even in case of fingerprint images with poor quality, whereas it requires much processing time. The performances are approximately compared in terms of speed, robustness to rotation, low quality, arch type in Table 4.

4   Conclusion

A new and effective reference point detection method was proposed based on labeling the orientation pattern. Experimental results showed that the proposed method could effectively detect a reference point in an arch-type fingerprint, which can not be detected based on a Poincaré index analysis, and produced a better performance in terms of accuracy and speed than Poincaré index-based method or sine map-based method.

References

[1] Hong, L., Jain, A. K.: Classification of Fingerprint Images. Proc. 11th Scandinavian Conf. on Image Analysis (1999)

[2] Kawagoe, M., Tojo, A.: Fingerprint Pattern Classification. Pattern Recognition **17** (1984) 295–303

[3] Karu, K., Jain, A. K.: Fingerprint Classification. Pattern Recognition **29** (1996) 389–404

[4] Jain, A. K., Prabhakar, S., Hong, L., Pankanti, S.: Filterbank-Based Fingerprint Matching. IEEE Trans. Image Processing **9** (2000) 849–859

[5] Rao, A.: A Taxonomy for Texture Description and Identification. New York, NY: Springer-Verlag (1990)

[6] Haralick, R. M., Shapiro, L. G.: Computer and Robot Vision. Addison Wesley **1** (1992) 28–48

Global Motion Estimation in Sprite Generation by Eliminating Local Object Motions

Sungchan Park[1], Miyoung Kim[2], and Gueesang Lee[1]*

[1] Department of Computer Science, Chonnam National University
300 Youngbong-dong, Buk-gu, Gwangju, 500-757, Korea
schpark@multimedia.chonnam.ac.kr
gslee@chonnam.ac.kr
[2] School of Internet & Information Technology, Provincial College of Damyang
262 Hanggyo-Ri, Damyang-Gun, Chonnam-Province, 517-802, Korea
kimmee@damyang.ac.kr

Abstract. In this paper, a new feature point selection method for the global motion estimation(GME) in sprite generation is proposed. GME for the sprite generation presented in this paper consists of two stages, feature selection and global motion estimation with selected blocks. First, local object motions are distinguished from the static background. Blocks with local motions are excluded in the subsequent procedure because local object motions would not be helpful to GME and often are even harmful to the exact motion estimation. Note that sprite generation mainly concerns the generation of the static background for a sequence of image frames. To identify local motions, conventional block-based motion estimation is performed for the blocks in the current frame. If it has a greater residual error than a threshold, this block is considered to have an object with local motions and is excluded in the subsequent procedure. Note that a large residual error of a block implies a change in the shape of the object and the block image could not be a part of the static background. The second stage extracts edges in the image excluding blocks selected in the first step and they are used for GME. Experiments show the proposed algorithm performs faster in selected images than existing methods with improved objective/subjective quality.

1 Introduction

A sprite, also referred to a mosaic, is an image composed of pixels belonging to a video object visible throughout a video sequence[1]. An obvious example of a sprite is a background sprite, also referred to as background mosaic [2], which consists of all the pixels belonging to the background of a scene during camera-panning recording.

Broadly speaking, sprite-based coding can be categorized into two main types, sprite generation and sprite image coding. First, the sprite generation concerns how to quickly produce a sprite with high quality. The most important

---

* Corresponding author

F.J. Perales et al. (Eds.): IbPRIA 2003, LNCS 2652, pp. 704–711, 2003.

operation is the GME, where the differential errors need to be calculated at all pixels of a frame[3, 4] or feature-based selected pixels of a frame [5, 6, 10] to obtain motion parameters. Since GME is a time-consuming task, there have been many studies to accelerate the sprite generation. The verification model(VM) of MPEG-4 employs the Levenberg-Marquardt algorithm as a tool for GME[7]. Secondly, for the compression of a sprite image, MPEG-4 object-based coding has been developed, where the sprite image is dealt with as a single INTRA VOP with arbitrary shape[8] and there are other new coding techniques using padding techniques[9].

This paper concerns the first issue of efficient generation of a sprite. The main idea of the feature selection is to mask out the blocks with local motions which are not helpful and even sometimes harmful to the exact GME for the static background. Local motion estimation is performed for the reduced image of each block in the current frame. If it has a greater residual error than a threshold, this block is considered as an object with local motions and is excluded in the subsequent procedure. Note that a large residual error of a block implies a change in the shape of the object, possibly with abrupt motions, and the block could not be a part of the static background. Excluding the blocks with local motions, edges are extracted in the image and they are used for the final motion estimation.

This paper is organized as follows. GME adopted in MPEG-4 VM and feature-based GME are explained in section 2. Section 3 describes the proposed method and experiment results are shown in section 4. The last part contains conclusions.

2   GME in MPEG-4 VM and Feature-Based GME

This section examines GME adopted in MPEG-4 VM and feature-based GME. First, the GME in MPEG-4 VM includes all pixels of the current frame except pixels of foreground segmentation[3, 4]. Second, feature-based pixel selections[5, 6, 10] use a feature such as edges or Hessian images instead of considering all the pixels in the image to reduce computations.

3   Proposed Algorithm

In this section, the proposed feature selection algorithm for sprite generation is explained. The proposed algorithm distinguishes local object motions from static background because local object motion would not be reliable and even harmful to the GME.

Generally, a sprite image is generated from a sequence of image frames with the foreground segmentation masked out as shown in Fig.1. But there could be many local object motions in the background such as spectators (in dotted rectangle of Fig.1). These local object motions are not helpful or even harmful for the GME.

To identify local object motions, block-based motion estimation is performed for each block first and the residual error result from the motion estimation

Fig. 1. General segmentation information

Fig. 2. Local motion vectors

is used. Since motion vectors are not enough to distinguish blocks with local motions from static background, the residual error should be considered. Note that, motion vectors of blocks in a frame are sometimes very similar without respect to the type of objects. One can observe that, however, if a residual is large enough, it could be the indication of locally moving objects because large residual errors imply the change of shapes of the objects with abrupt movements. Fig. 2 shows that motion vectors are very similar in blocks belonging static background or foreground objects as well as local motion objects(spectators). Detailed flow of the proposed algorithm is described in Fig. 3.

3.1 Computation of Residual Errors

In order to reduce the computational complexity, a low-pass image pyramid is used. Both the length and the width of the top level image are 4 times smaller than the corresponding image in the bottom level of the pyramid, and block-based motion estimation is performed in each 8 by 8 block in the top image of the current frame with respect to the previous frame. For block-based motion estimation the three step search algorithm is employed in this paper for simplicity. The residual image is generated by subtracting the motion compensated

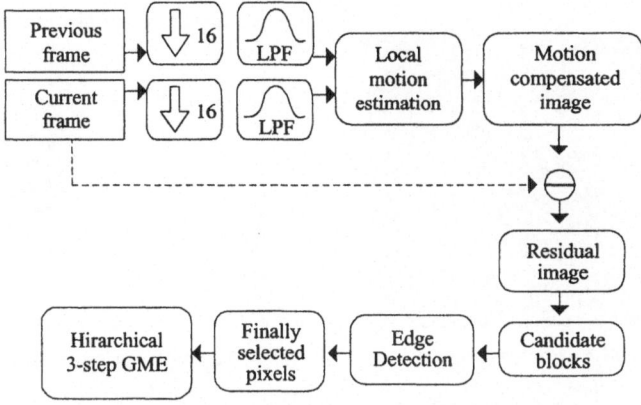

Fig. 3. Proposed feature point selection scheme

image from the current image. Local object motions would have greater residual errors than static parts. Fig. 4 shows residual error of the 6th frame of the Stefan sequence and we can notice that parts of the spectators have greater residuals than other parts of the frame.

3.2   Selection of Candidate Blocks for Edge-Based GME

Threshold for the identification of blocks with local motions has been set by the average of the residuals in the frame. Any blocks with residual errors larger than the average are considered as a block with local motions. First, the residual image is divided into 8 by 8 blocks.

$a.$ Compute $Avg = \dfrac{1}{k} \sum_{1}^{k} residual(i)$

$b.$ If $residual(i)$ is greater than Avg, the block contains local motions

Fig. 4. Residual image

 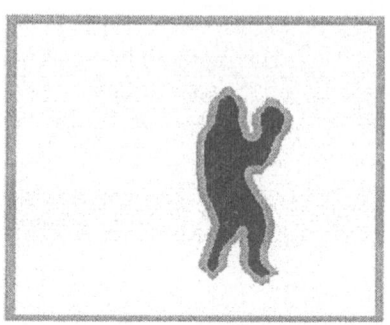

(a) Newly appeared areas   (b) Outlier rejection areas

Fig. 5. Outlier rejection areas

where $residual(i)$ denotes the residual of the ith block.

Note that blocks within the threshold in the residual are the candidate blocks for the subsequent GME procedure.

3.3   Edge-Based Feature Selection

In order to further reduce the number of pixels involved in the GME, the edge-based feature is used with candidate blocks selected in the first stage. Edges are detected using Sobel operator in this paper.

3.4   Outlier Rejection

As the camera moves (panning and zooming) and foreground objects move, new regions that did not exist in the previous frame appear in the current frame. Fig. 5 shows the 6th frame in the Stefan sequence. Dotted rectangle area in Fig. 5(a) represent newly visible region and grey areas(boundary of the foreground and the outer boundary rectangle) in Fig. 5(b) are excluded for the GME. Fig. 6 shows an example image of feature points selected by proposed method.

Table 1. Comparison of the objective quality of the reconstructed frames using VM and proposed method

Sequence & Time	MPEG-4 VM PSNR	MPEG-4 VM+Edge PSNR	Proposed Method PSNR
Stefan	18.62	18.83	19.31
Time	914735	574916	577832

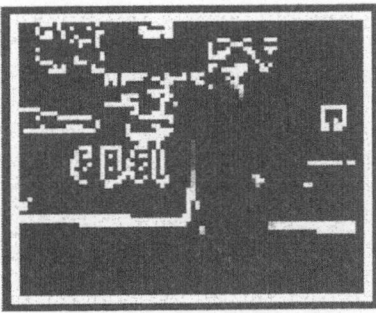

Fig. 6. Selected feature points

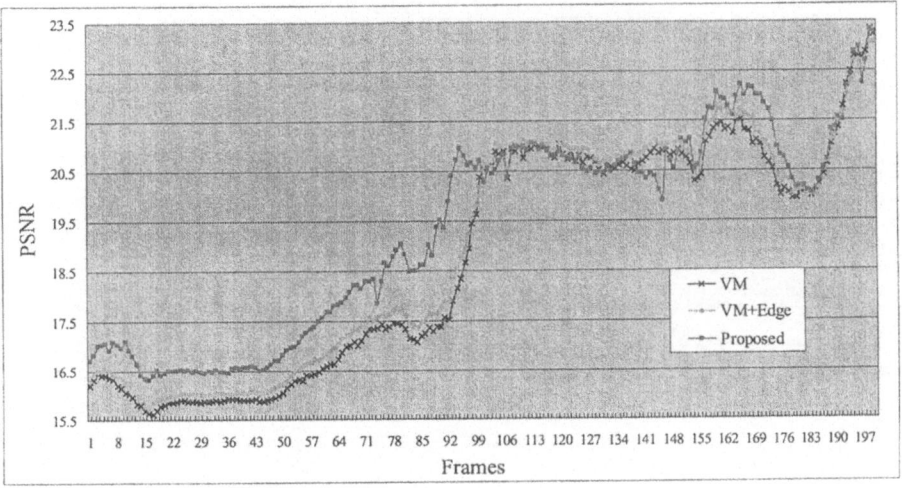

Fig. 7. PSNR-Y of Stefan sequence

4   Experimental Results

This section describes simulation results using the proposed technique with the comparison to the GME in MPEG-4 VM and edge-based GME. Simulations have been carried out using Stefan YUV files with corresponding segmentation files. The test sequence is of 200 frames in CIF (352*288) format. Table 1 shows the average PSNR-Y (dB) of Stefan test sequence as an example. The proposed method is about 1.6 times faster than MPEG-4 VM and better quality than MPEG-4 VM or MPEG-4 VM with edge-based GME. Note that the proposed method is slightly slower than MPEG-4 VM with edge-based GME because of the block-based motion estimation performed in the proposed approach.

Fig. 7 shows PSNR-Y comparison of test sequences. Fig. 8 and 9 show the generated images by proposed method for subjective comparison.

(a) Sprite image by VM method

(b) Sprite image by proposed method

Fig. 8. Comparison of the subjective quality

(a) VM method   (b) Proposed method

Fig. 9. Comparison of the subjective quality of enlarged image

5   Conclusions

In this paper, a new feature selection method for the GME in the sprite generation was proposed. GME for the sprite generation in this paper consists of two stages. The first step distinguishes local object motions from static background because local object motion could be often harmful in GME.

The second stage extracts edges for the final motion estimation excluding the blocks with local motions detected in the first stage.

Since this algorithm excludes local object motions that are not helpful for the GME, high quality sprite image is generated. Experiments show the proposed algorithm is about 1.6 times faster than the algorithm in MPEG-4 VM with improved quality.

Acknowledgement

This work was supported by grant No. R05-2000-000-00280-0 from the Korea Science & Engineering Foundation.

References

[1] T. Sikora.: The MPEG-4 video standard verification model. IEEE Trans. Circuits Systems and Video Technology. 5 (1997) 19–31
[2] F. Dufaux and F. Moscheni.: Background Mosaicking for Low Bitrate Video Coding. Proceedings of the International Conference on Image Processing(ICIP). (1996) 673–676
[3] MPEG Video Group.: The MPEG-4 Video Standard Verification Model 18.0. ISO/IEC JTC1/SC29/WG11 N3908. (2001)
[4] M. C. Lee, W. G. Chen, C. L. B. Lin, C. Gu, T. Markoc, S. I. Zabinsky, and R. Szeliski.: A layered video object coding system using sprite and affine motion model. IEEE Transactions on Circuits and Systems for Video Technology. 7(1) (1997)
[5] Frederic Dufaux and Janusz Konrad.: Efficient, Robust, and Fast Global Motion Estimation for Video Coding. IEEE Transactions on Image Processing. 9(3) (2000)
[6] H. K. Cheung and W. C. Siu.: Fast Global Motion Estimation for Sprite Generation. IEEE International Symposium on Circuits and Systems(ISCAS02). (2002) III-1 – III-4
[7] S. Fukunaga, Y. Nakaya, S. H. Son, and T. Nagumo.: MPEG-4 Video Verification Model version 14.2. Coding of Moving Pictures and Audio, International Organization for standarization, Maui. (1999)
[8] ISO/IEC JTC1.: Generic coding of audiovisual objects-part 2 : visual. ISO/IEC 14496-2, version 3. (2001)
[9] Yan Lu, Wen Gao, and Feng Wu.: High efficient sprite coding with directional spatial prediction. IEEE International Conference on Image Processing (ICIP'2002). (2002)
[10] Yan Lu, Sen Gao, and Feng Wu.: Fast and robust sprite generation for MPEG-4 video coding. IEEE Pacific-Rim Conference on Multimedia(PCM2001). (2001) 118–125

Automatic Inspection of Wooden Pallets Using Contextual Segmentation Methods

Miguel Ángel Patricio[1] and Darío Maravall[2]

[1] Departamento de Informática, Universidad Carlos III de Madrid
mpatrici@inf.uc3m.es
[2] Department of Artificial Intelligence, Faculty of Computer Science
Universidad Politécnica de Madrid, Campus de Montegancedo, 28660 Madrid, Spain
dmaravall@fi.upm.es

Abstract. This paper presents a comparative study of several well-known and thoroughly tested techniques for the segmentation of textured images, including two algorithms belonging to the adaptive Bayesian family of restoration and segmentation methods, a probabilistic relaxation process, and a novel approach based on the recently introduced concept of the frequency histogram of connected elements. The application domain chosen for comparison purposes is the problem of detecting very thin cracks -around 1 mm width- in the wooden boards of used pallets, where a tricky balance between the crack detection and false alarm ratios must be guaranteed. After a brief description of each segmentation method and their respective application to the problem at hand, the paper discusses the comparative results, showing the excellent performance achieved with the frequency histogram of connected elements, which can be considered an attractive and versatile novel instrument for the analysis and recognition of textured images.

1 Introduction

The authors have been working for several years on the development of automated wooden pallet inspection systems using computer vision techniques. One of the hardest problems in the automatic inspection of wooden boards, like the ones employed in pallets, is the detection of very thin cracks -around 1 mm range width-, in which a really tricky balance must be guaranteed between the crack detection ratio and the false alarms generated by wood veins, paint remains, shadows created by the lighting system etc.

Although bidimensional histograms, computed from the co-occurrence matrices ([1] and [2]), provide useful information about the spatial distribution (actually, about a specific two-point spatial relationship) of the particular discriminant variable at hand, which is obviously relevant information as far as texture analysis and recognition are concerned, they have two serious disadvantages: their excessive computational burden and, in particular, the curse of dimensionality that produces a considerable amount of irrelevant information and noise. On the contrary, unidimensional histograms, which are computationally speaking very

F.J. Perales et al. (Eds.): IbPRIA 2003, LNCS 2652, pp. 712–721, 2003.
© Springer-Verlag Berlin Heidelberg 2003

attractive and discriminant enough to efficiently solve the segmentation problem in many applications, do not provide as much discriminant information, in
particular spatial and textural information, as the bidimensional histograms.

As a result of our work on practical automatic quality inspection based on vision systems, we have recently introduced a novel idea for image segmentation:
the so-called frequency histogram of connected elements (FHCE), [3] and [4].
Being a conventional unidimensional histogram, the FHCE incorporates all the
computational advantages, in terms of both simplicity and speed, inherent to the
histogram-based segmentation methods. Simultaneously, it includes information
about the spatial distribution of the specific discriminant feature in the digital
image, as bidimensional histograms also do. The FHCE concept has an additional
advantage in comparison to bidimensional histograms, as it is based on a much
more powerful spatial function than the simple two-point relationships, typical
of bidimensional histograms and co-occurrence matrices, which is the concept of
structuring element or spatial predicate. This spatial predicate is somewhat, but
not entirely, related to the structuring element concept used in morphological
image processing [7]. Furthermore, the FHCE has yet another interesting advantage as compared with the conventional unidimensional histogram. This is its
flexibility with regard to the range of values of the discriminant variable -which,
in conventional unidimensional histograms, is absolutely rigid- and which provides an interesting degree of freedom, what we have called *connectivity level*,
for texture analysis and recognition.

The paper has been organized in two parts. In the first part, a brief description is given of the techniques for the segmentation of textures used in our
comparative study. In the second part, we describe the results of applying these
techniques to the problem of detecting thin cracks in the wooden boards of used
pallets.

2   Contextual Segmentation Methods: Adaptive Bayesian Segmentation and Probabilistic Relaxation Processes

The objective of detecting thin cracks in wood can be modeled as a biclass
pattern recognition problem, as the computer vision system has to discriminate between pixels belonging to the crack class and to the sound wood class.
By exploiting the empirical evidence that both classes or patterns have different grayscale intensity distributions, an automatic thresholding process can, in
principle, be applied in order to obtain a first approximation of the real distribution of both classes in the particular image under analysis. Afterwards, a more
specialized local segmentation process can be activated to take into account the
spatial dependencies -i.e. the texture distributions- within the image.

In this paper, we have selected three well-known of this kind of local/global or
hybrid methods: (1) the majority vote filter, (2) the iterated conditional modes
(ICM) algorithm and (3) a probabilistic relaxation process. The first two methods are instances of the adaptive Bayesian segmentation approach and are among
the most popular within the adaptive or contextual family of image restora-

tion and segmentation techniques [5], whereas relaxation processes, along with Markovian random fields, are powerful and widely used segmentation methods for textured images [6].

2.1   Adaptive Bayesian Segmentation

Let us begin with a brief description of the basic functioning of the two Bayesian methods chosen for comparison purposes. Both methods are based on a previous conventional global Bayesian segmentation. As a result of this preliminary global segmentation, all the pixels in the image are labeled –i.e. segmented-. Afterwards, a local, spatial segmentation process is activated, which in the case of the ICM algorithm is as follows, where the image –or the region of interest, ROI- under analysis has been denoted $\{I(i,j)\}_{NxM} = \{I(i,j)\}_{0 \leq i \leq N-1; 0 \leq j \leq M-1}$ and the two existing classes or patterns, α_1 and α_2. The following description of the ICM algorithm is basically taken from [5].

1. Compute the two class averages, $\hat{m}_1(l)$ and $\hat{m}_2(l)$, and the between-class variance at the generic iteration l:

$$\hat{m}_1(l) = \frac{1}{N_1} \sum_{\forall I(i,j) \in \alpha_1} I(i,j) \; ; \quad \hat{m}_2(l) = \frac{1}{N_2} \sum_{\forall I(i,j) \in \alpha_2} I(i,j)$$

$$\hat{\sigma}^2 = \frac{1}{NxM} \sum_{i=0}^{N-1} \sum_{j=0}^{M-1} [I(i,j) - \hat{m}(i,j)]^2 = \frac{N_1 \hat{\sigma}_1^2 + N_2 \hat{\sigma}_2^2}{N_1 + N_2} \tag{1}$$

where $N_1 + N_2 = NxM$ is the total number of pixels labeled or segmented as class α_1 and class α_2, respectively.

2. Re-label every pixel $I(i,j)$ as class α_1 or class α_2 recursively according to the following rule:

$$[I(i,j) - \hat{m}_1(l)]^2 - \beta \hat{\sigma}^2(l) N_1(i,j) \underset{\alpha_2}{\overset{\alpha_1}{\lessgtr}} [I(i,j) - \hat{m}_2(l)]^2 - \beta \hat{\sigma}^2(l) N_2(i,j) \tag{2}$$

where $N_1(i,j)$ and $N_2(i,j)$ are the number of pixels labeled as α_1 and α_2, respectively, in a certain neighborhood of the generic pixel $I(i,j)$ under re-segmentation. The size and shape of this neighborhood and the parameter β have to be carefully designed for each particular application. This re-segmentation process is equivalent to the application of a new optimum threshold $\tau_0(l+1)$:

$$\tau_0(l+1) = \frac{\hat{m}_1(l) + \hat{m}_2(l)}{2} + \frac{\beta \hat{\sigma}^2(l) [N_1(i,j) - N_2(i,j)]}{2 [\hat{m}_1(l) - \hat{m}_2(l)]} \tag{3}$$

3. **If** $\tau_0(l+1) \neq \tau_0(l)$, **then** repeat steps 2 and 3, **else** end segmentation process.

Majority vote filtering has a similar, although slightly simpler, structure as step 2 is reduced to a re-labeling based on the dominant label at the respective neighborhood.

2.2   Relaxation Processes

When applying the relaxation process to the segmentation problem, the task of labeling -i.e. classifying- the generic pixel (i, j) as belonging to a certain class α_m can be expressed as

$$P_{\alpha_m}[(i, j)] \quad / \quad m = 1, 2, \ldots S \; ; \; 0 \leq i \leq N - 1 \; ; \; 0 \leq j \, M - 1 \qquad (4)$$

Obviously, the probabilities are normalized to unity:

$$\sum_{m=1}^{S} P_{\alpha_m}[(i, j)] = 1 \quad ; \quad \forall i, j \qquad (5)$$

The next step is to introduce a compatibility function for the pixel's neighborhood, with the intention of capturing the spatial information relevant to the segmentation process. First of all, a specific neighborhood spatial function $N[(i, j)]$ has to be defined and, afterwards, the respective compatibility function C can be expressed as follows:

$$C \triangleq \{ C_{\alpha_m, \alpha_n}[(i, j), (k, l)] \} \quad / \quad 0 \leq m, n \leq S \; ; \; (k, l) \in N[(i, j)] \qquad (6)$$

which represents the compatibility between the fact that pixel (i, j) *belongs to* class α_m and that the neighboring pixel (k, l) *belongs to* class α_n.

Let us now describe the adaptive spatial segmentation process based on the above ideas. As a matter of fact, an iterative process for updating the probabilities of labelling a certain generic pixel (i, j) as belonging to one of the possible classes can be established as follows:

$$p_{\alpha_m}^{r+1}[(i, j)] = \frac{p_{\alpha_m}^{r}[(i, j)] \, c_{\alpha_m}^{r}[(i, j), (k, l)]}{\sum\limits_{n=1}^{S} p_{\alpha_n}^{r}[(i, j)] \, c_{\alpha_n}^{r}[(i, j), (k, l)]} \quad ; \quad m = 1, 2, \ldots S \qquad (7)$$

where the superindex r stands for the iteration order in the segmentation process. For the current iteration, the compatibility function is given by:

$$c_{\alpha_m}^{r}[(i, j), (k, l)] = \frac{1}{Card[N(i, j)]} \sum_{n=1}^{S} p_{\alpha_m / \alpha_n}[(i, j)/(k, l)] \, p_{\alpha_n}^{r}[(k, l)] \qquad (8)$$

$$m = 1, 2, \ldots S \; ; \forall (k, l) \in N[(i, j)]$$

3   The Frequency Histogram of Connected Elements

Let us now proceed with a brief exposition of the theoretical foundation of the FHCE.

Fig. 1. Two test images for crack detection

Definition 1 (The Neighborhood Concept). *Let $\{I(i,j)\}_{N x M}$ be a digital image. If we denote the coordinates of a generic pixel as (i,j), the neighborhood of this pixel is defined as follows:*

$$v = \{\varphi_{i,j}, (i,j) \in I\}$$
$$\varphi_{i,j} = \{(k,l) \in I/D((k,l),(i,j)) \text{ is true}\} \tag{9}$$

where D is a predicate defined by a distance-based condition. For instance, a valid definition of the neighborhood of a pixel $I(i,j)$ can be given by the set:

$$\varphi_{i,j}^{r,s} = \{(k,l) \in I/\|k-i\| \leq r \text{ and } \|l-j\| \leq s\}; r,s \in \mathbb{N} \tag{10}$$

which indicates that the neighborhood of the pixel is formed by a set of pixels whose distances are not greater than two integer values r and s, respectively.

Definition 2 (The Connected Element Concept).
   A connected element is:

$$C_{i,j}(T) = \{\varphi_{i,j}^{r,s} \ / \ I(k,l) \subset [T-\varepsilon, T+\varepsilon] \ , \ \forall (k,l) \in \varphi_{i,j}^{r,s}\} \tag{11}$$

where I is the grayscale intensity or brightness of pixel (k,l). In other words, a connected element is any neighborhood unit whose pixels have a grayscale level close to a given grayscale level T.

Definition 3 (The Frequency Histogram of Connected Elements). *We define the FHCE as:*
$$H(T) = \sum_{\forall (i,j) \in I} C_{i,j}(T) \tag{12}$$

$$0 \leq T \leq I_{max} - 1$$

That is to say, $H(T)$ approximates a density function for a random event occurring in a digital image $\{I(i,j)\}_{N x M}$. This event is related to the idea of connected element, which in turn is related to the pseudo-random structure of the grayscale intensity distribution of a particular texture. Obviously, there is no universal connected element valid for any domain application. In the design leading to the FHCE, there is a critical and domain-dependent step, which is *responsible for selecting the parameters defining the optimum connected element. These parameters are: (1) the morphological parameter and (2) the connectivity level. See [4] for a general discussion of these parameters and paragraph 4.3 for the particularities of the digital images under analysis.*

4   Detecting Thin Cracks in Wood

For the comparative study, we have chosen two rather difficult cases, in which the cracks to be detected have some hidden parts and, at the same time, the apparently sound wood regions present special textures that can be mistaken for cracks as well. Figure 1 shows the two different examples for the comparative analysis.

4.1   Adaptive Bayesian Segmentation

The application of the two adaptive Bayesian methods described in paragraph 2.1 is straightforward. Figure 2 shows the results obtained with the mayority vote filter and the ICM algorithm.

For the first case, notice that the final results are not entirely satisfactory, since part of the crack has been lost. However, both techniques perform extremely well for regions of the image with a clear difference in the grayscale intensity distributions of each pattern. Concerning the second and much more difficult case, both algorithms perform very poorly as almost half of the wood board has been classified as cracked.

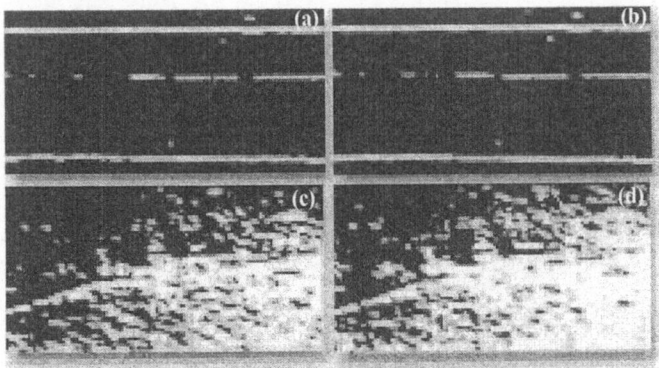

Fig. 2. Segmentation results achieved with the ICM algorithm (a and c) and the mayority vote filter (b and d), for the two wood boards appearing in Figure 1

4.2   Relaxation Processes

The key element in a relaxation process lies in the choice of the local distribution of neighbor dependency. More specifically, the crucial point is the correct choice of the compatibility function. The individual coefficients c_{α_1/α_1} , c_{α_1/α_2}, c_{α_2/α_1} and c_{α_2/α_2} have to be established, as there are two classes α_1 *(sound wood)* and α_2 *(crack)* in our wooden board segmentation problem. In fact, as the following relations hold:

$$c_{\alpha_m/\alpha_m}\left[(i,j),(k,l)\right] = 1 - c_{\alpha_m/\alpha_n}\left[(i,j),(k,l)\right]$$

$$m = 1,2 \; ; \; n = 1,2$$

(13)

only two compatibility coefficients have to be introduced. A neighborhood spatial function has to be settled to complete the definition of the compatibility functions. Let us consider an omnidirectional 3x3 neighborhood function -see Figure 3-. Because of the diagonality of the cracks in the particular wooden boards considered in our comparison, an omnidirectional neighborhood spatial restriction does not seem to be the best choice. However, unless all the possible existing cracks in the wooden boards had the same diagonal orientation, an omnidirectional spatial restriction would be preferable, as it is the least biased *a priori*. In conclusion, we can establish the following compatibility coefficients:

$$c_{\alpha_1/\alpha_1}\left[(i,j),(k,l)\right] = 0.9 \quad \leftrightarrow \quad c_{\alpha_1/\alpha_2} = 0.1$$
$$c_{\alpha_2/\alpha_1}\left[(i,j),(k,l)\right] = 0.2 \quad \leftrightarrow \quad c_{\alpha_2/\alpha_2} = 0.8$$

(14)

$$0 \le i \le N-1 \; ; \; 0 \le j \le M-1 \; ; \; \forall (k,l) \in N\left[(i,j)\right]$$

Note that the sound wood pixels have different compatibility coefficients to the crack pixels, due to the fact that cracks are thin and elongated whereas the sound wood regions are much larger and their pixels are much more homogenous. Figure 3 shows the respective neighborhood function and the compatibility coefficients.

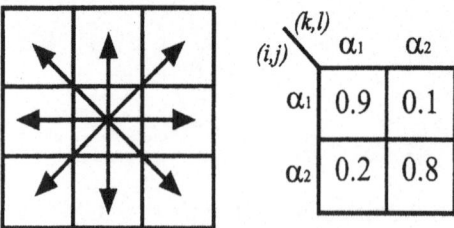

Fig. 3. The neighborhood spatial function and the compatibility matrix discussed in the text

Fig. 4. Segmentation results for the application of a relaxation process to (a) Figure 1a and (b) Figure 1b

Figure 4 shows the segmentation results achieved with this type of probabilistic relaxation process for the two test images. Although crack detection has improved quite appreciably for the first case -Figure 4a-, there are still some losses and some false alarms. Regarding the second case -Figure 4b-, the results are just as poor as for the Bayesian methods.

4.3 The Frequency Histogram of Connected Elements

As for any other contextual segmentation procedure aimed at exploiting the local or spatial information of the image under analysis, the key issue when applying the FHCE concept is a correct selection of the scanning window size. As is well known, the basic idea in textured images is to apply a window whose size is big enough to capture the essential structure of any texture present in the image. In our particular application to detect thin cracks, we have found that a window of 40x30 pixels seems to be optimum in most cases.

After exhaustive experimentation with a plethora of digital images of sound and defective wood boards we have selected the neighborhood function for the connected element event defined by a 5x3 window. This function is the so-called morphological parameter of the FHCE. As we can see, there are more horizontal pixels than vertical pixels, the reason being founded on the a priori knowledge available about the problem at hand. In fact, there is empirical evidence that cracks in a piece of wood tend to appear in the same direction as the wood grain. As computer vision inspection is performed horizontally from the wood boards standpoint, the shape of the selected neighborhood function is easily deduced.

To complete the connected element concept definition, we need to select the connectivity level that a particular neighborhood should possess to be considered as such. The FHCE is computed for each image portion by shifting through all the pixels in a window of the same 5x3 shape as the neighborhood. This scanning process is performed by means of a top-bottom and left-right movement and by computing, at each pixel, the maximum and the minimum gray level within its neighborhood. Each pixel's neighborhood is classified as a connected element if and only if the difference between the maximum and the minimum values is small as compared with the dynamic range of the histogram in the whole window. After some experimental work, we have chosen a 10% ratio, which is

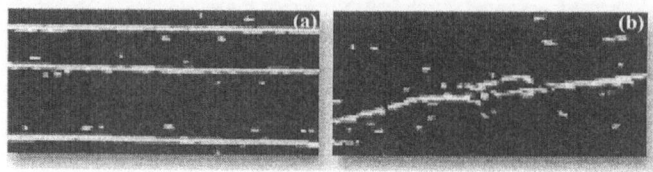

Fig. 5. Results of the segmentation process by applying the FHCE concept to (a) Figure 1a and (b) Figure 1b. In both cases, note the efficiency in segmenting the cracks appearing in the two boards

a good compromise between wooden portions in good and in bad conditions. Therefore, the following condition has to hold for a neighborhood to be labeled as connected element: $((i_{max} - i_{min})/(I_{max} - I_{min})) \leq 0.1$,where I_{min} and I_{max} are the maximum and the minimum values of the window –i.e. the dynamic range of the window's histogram–, and i_{min} and i_{max} are the maximum and the minimum grayscale intensity levels of the neighborhood. Therefore, if the gray-level variability of a particular neighborhood is less than ten percent of the dynamic range of the global window, the pixel in question is a connected element and the FHCE will compute a new event valued T = $(i_{min} + i_{max})/2$.

Figure 5 shows the result obtained with the FHCE method for the two test images. Note the excellent segmentation of the cracks as compared with the Bayesian and relaxation methods applied to the same images, in particular for the second and hardest case -Figure 5b- in which the thin hidden crack has been successfully detected.

5   Conclusions

A comparative study of several well-known and thoroughly tested contextual techniques for the segmentation of textured images -i.e. two adaptive Bayesian methods and a probabilistic relaxation process- and the recently introduced concept of connected elements histogram has been presented. For comparison purposes, the detection of very thin cracks -around 1 mm width- in the wooden boards of used pallets has been considered, in which the false alarm ratio is the main obstacle to the performance of any segmentation method. The experimental results obtained have demonstrated the excellent performance obtained with the FHCE method, which can be considered an attractive and versatile novel instrument for the analysis and recognition of textured images.

References

[1] Walker, R. F., Jackway, P. T., Longstaff, I. D.: Recent Developments in the Use of the Co-occurrence Matrix for Texture Recognition. In Proceedings of the IEEE Int. Conf. on Digital Signal Processing, Vol. 1, (1997) 63–65.

[2] Clausi, D. A. and Zhao, Y.: Rapid Extraction of Image Texture by Co-occurrence Using a Hybrid Data Structure. Computers & Geosciences, 28(6), Elsevier Science, (2002), 763–774.

[3] Patricio, M. A., Maravall, D.: Wood Texture Analysis by Combining the Connected Elements Histogram and Artificial Neural Networks. In J. Mira, A. Prieto (Eds). Bio-inspired Applications of Connectionism, LNCS 2085, Springer, Berlin, (2001) 160–167.

[4] Maravall, D., Patricio, M. A.: Image Segmentation and Pattern Recognition: A Novel Concept, the Histogram of Connected Elements. In D. Chen and X. Cheng (Eds). Pattern Recognition and String Matching, Kluwer Academic Publishers, (2002).

[5] Glasbey, C. A., Horgan, G. W.: Image Analysis for the Biological Sciences. John Wiley and Sons, New York, (1995).

[6] Kitler, J.: Probabilistic Relaxation and the Hough Transform. Pattern Recogniton 33, (2000) 705–714.

[7] Soille, P.: Morphological Image Analysis. 2nd Ed, Springer, Berlin, (2003).

Gabor Wavelets and Auto-organised Structures for Directional Primitive Extraction

Marta Penas[1], María J. Carreira[2], and Manuel G. Penedo[1]

[1] Dpto. Computación, Fac. Informática
Universidade da Coruña, 15071 A Coruña, Spain
{infmpc00,cipenedo}@dc.fi.udc.es
[2] Dpto. Electrónica e Computación
Universidade de Santiago de Compostela, 15782 Santiago de Compostela, Spain
mjose@dec.usc.es

Abstract. This paper describes a computational framework developed for the extraction of low-level directional primitives present in an image, and subsequent organization using the laws of perceptual grouping. The system is divided in two stages. The first one consists on the extraction of the direction of pixels in the image, through an efficient implementation of Gabor wavelet decomposition. The second one consists on the reduction of these high dimensionality results by means of an auto-organized structure. For this second stage, three different auto-organized structures have been studied: self-organized maps (SOM), growing cell structures (GCS) and growing neural gas (GNG). Results have showed that GCS is the most appropriate structure in the context of this work.

Keywords: perceptual primitives, Gabor wavelets, self-organized structures, growing cell structures, growing neural gas, chromaticity diagram.

1 Introduction

In human vision, perceptual organization refers to the human visual system basic capability to derive relevant groupings and structures from an scene without prior knowledge of its contents. In computer vision, perceptual organization is the study of how features are clustered prior to object recognition.

The main goal of perceptual organization is object recognition, which is basically a searching problem. Perceptual organization will be crucial for reducing the size of this search. In this frame, the most important functions of perceptual organization are [1]: segmentation, or division of the image into sets of related features; three-space inference, as perceptual organization results in the formation of two-dimensional relations between image features that can lead to specific three dimensional interpretation; and indexing of world knowledge, as in large databases a very important factor determining the size of the searching space is the selection of the appropriate object from the set of possibilities.

The final goal of our work is developing a computational framework that integrates the relationships offered by Gestalt psychology (parallelism, continuity, similarity, symmetry, common region and closure) among extended tokens

F.J. Perales et al. (Eds.): IbPRIA 2003, LNCS 2652, pp. 722–732, 2003.

to form larger groups, as the significance of large organizations is higher than a small organized form. All the approaches to this goal [2, 3] are based on the results extracted from traditional edge detectors. Opposite to this, our goal is to detect perceptual primitives through the use of the directional properties that Gabor filters provide, as an alternative to classical edge detectors. As stated in a previous paper [4], the introduction of the computationally expensive process of Gabor wavelet decomposition can improve the final system's performance as: the results obtained by this process provide global information about the orientation of the pixels in the image, instead of the local information provided by traditional edge detectors. And they are independent of the kind of images to process, as opposed to classical edge detectors which need parameter tuning dependent of the kind and quality of the images. Besides these advantages, we have implemented an approximation to Gabor wavelets that reduces the computation time through the use of a pyramidal multi-scale Gabor wavelet transform in the spatial domain, which is faster than conventional frequency domain implementations.

Once that Gabor components for various frequencies and orientations have been computed, the image intensity information has been transformed into a high-dimensional Gabor components space. All this information must be organized in order to extract the directional primitives present in the image. A reduction of this input space dimensionality is also necessary in order to fix an objective criterion to perform feature grouping that work well with any kind of image to process. Auto-organized structures seem to be a suitable instrument to achieve this dimensionality reduction, as the output space generated must maintain the topology of the input Gabor space, being faithful to existent characteristics. In this work, three different structures have been investigated: self-organized maps, growing cell structures and growing neural gas.

2   Gabor Wavelet Decomposition

Gabor wavelets are complex exponential signals modulated by gaussians. There is evidence that visual cortical cells in mammals closely resemble this configuration, and maybe the most important property they have is that their conjoint resolution in spatial and frequency domain is optimized [5]. These properties make them good edge detectors with optimum localization of edges in space. An additional advantage of Gabor wavelets with respect to traditional edge detectors, like Canny or Sobel, is that they do not use any image-dependent parameters.

The main drawback of Gabor wavelet decomposition is its high complexity both in memory and computational time. This is the reason why, in a previous paper [4], we developed a multiresolution spatial domain implementation of the 2D Gabor wavelet decomposition at two main frequencies $(\frac{1}{4}, \frac{1}{8})$ and eight main orientations $(\frac{k\pi}{8}, k = 0..7)$. Multi-resolution implementations are based on the fact that reducing an image to half its size and convolving it with a Gabor filter centered at a determined frequency is analogous to convolve the original image with a filter centered at half the previous frequency. Thus, in that case, the filters for second frequency channel will be the same than those for first frequency channel, but applied to an image half the size of the original one. Later on, when the integration of both channels takes place, the results for this channel must be expanded to double their size in order to have same size results for both frequency channels.

In [4], Gabor wavelets were used for the extraction of the directional primitives present in an image. In particular a bank of 16 filters, distributed over 2 frequency channels and 8 main orientations in each frequency channel, will be employed. The result of this decomposition has been though a set of 16 images. The application of Gabor wavelet decomposition has mapped the original image to a high dimensional space. First of all, the input to these auto-organized structures must be determined, as the following step in our perceptual grouping process was the reduction of this high space dimensionality through the use of auto-organized structures. This input is a nine component vector generated this way: an eight component vector $H^i(x, y)$ was assigned to each pixel (x, y) in the original image for each frequency channel i, where each component corresponded to the value of the Gabor decomposition centered at a main orientation; and a ninth component, called response, was added to each gaborjet in order to determine the presence of a directional feature and reduce inter-image and inter-frequency variability:

$$response_i(x, y) = 0.5 + \frac{\arctan\left(\frac{(|H^i(x,y)| - |\bar{H}^i|)}{|\bar{H}^i|}\right)}{\pi} \tag{1}$$

where $i = 0, 1$ represents each frequency channel. The response in pixel (x, y) for frequency channel i was obtained from the modulus of the $H^i(x, y)$ vector normalized to zero mean and unit variance through the modulus of the mean and standard deviation of the H^i vectors over the whole image. Then this expression was bounded to the range $[0, 1]$ through the application of a sigmoid function using eq. 1. High response values determine the presence of an important component in one of the main orientations considered. The first eight components in $H^i(x, y)$ were scaled such that their modulus was equal to the response, reducing inter-image and inter-frequency variability (as low-level frequency filters tend to produce a greater range of values). As previously mentioned, these nine component vectors constitute the input to the following step in the process just described.

The main drawback for the implementation proposed in [4] is the high thickness of the edges detected, as can be seen in the middle image of fig. 1. This happens because this implementation is based on that described in [6], which was developed for image compression and restoration, and not for edge detection. The problem is that, as previously stated, this method employed only the modulus of the odd part of the wavelet. The thickness of the edges comes from the 1D filter masks of 11 components. This is the reason why a new implementation, based on that exposed in [7], has been developed. In this new implementation, for each main orientation, the exact position of the edges were detected as the

Fig. 1. Left: Corridor original image. Middle: Response (9th component of the gaborjet) for Gabor decomposition using only the modulus of the odd part. Right: Response (9th component of gaborjet) for Gabor decomposition taking the edges around the maximum modulus with a zero-crossing in the even or odd part of the Gabor result

conjunction between a maximum in the modulus and a zero-crossing in the even or the odd part of the Gabor result. Only these positions and their direct neighbors have been considered edgels, and the rest of pixels were assigned a zero value. This way, we are using the important property of Gabor filters of good localization. Once computed the initial gaborjet this way, the last step is the calculus of the response (eq. 1). Result can be seen in fig. 1 right .

3   Auto-organized Structures for Dimensionality Reduction

As previously mentioned, Gabor wavelet decomposition result is a set of gabor-jets, one for each frequency channel (centered at $\frac{1}{4}$ and $\frac{1}{8}$) and composed of 9 components: first eight for the orientations considered ($\frac{k\pi}{8}, k = 0..7$) and the last for response (eq. 1). A reduction of the dimensionality of this input space is necessary in order to fix an objective criterion to perform a feature grouping that work well with any kind of images to process. To this end, auto-organized structures based on artificial neural networks will be employed. The election of such structures is mainly based on their properties, as they are suitable for solving clustering problems, allowing simultaneously a reduction of the input space and the projection of the topological ordering in the input space to the output structure [8]. We have focused our attention in three of such structures: self-organized maps (SOM) [9], growing cell structures (GCS) [10] and growing neural gas (GNG) [11].

The process followed consisted of studying the results obtained from these auto-organized structures for the first frequency channel. From these analysis, the structure that produced the best results will be chosen for its application in the second frequency channel and also in the integration of both channels.

These auto-organized structures are artificial neural networks with a number of processing elements ($\#pe$) over which a neighborhood relation is established. This relation determines a topology in the structure. For SOM, $\#pe$ is established a priori, while for GNG and GCS the own structures fix this number during the learning process. The difference between GCS and GNG is that the first structure maintains the topology defined at the beginning of the training process while the second has a free topology.

The input to each network is a vector I projected over each processing element pe_k of the structure through a weight vector w_k assigned to it. This weight vector represents the center of the cluster associated to the processing element.

The adjustment of these structures is based on an unsupervised training process. This means that the structures are trained based only on a set of input vectors called training set. The objective of the training is to determine the parameters that define the structure of the network. For SOM, these parameters are the weight vectors assigned to each processing element. For GCS and GNG, these parameters are the weights and the final number of processing elements. For the last two structures, in order to determine these variables, a parameter called *resource value* (rv_k) is assigned to each processing element pe_k. This parameter indicates where new processing elements must be inserted in order to satisfy a merit function. GNG also has another parameter called *age* (t_{ij}) assigned to each connection between processing elements pe_i and pe_j that measures the degree of vicinity between them. The value of this parameter determines if the connection can be broken, giving each processing element a greater degree of freedom to locate their weights through the training process.

Once the structures are trained, each processing element pe_k represents a cluster associated to the input vectors, and its weights corresponds to the center of that cluster. The topological order, which implies that two neighboring processing elements must have similar weighting vectors, is obtained through the established neighboring relations. This topological order is crucial for a right dimensionality reduction between the input and the output space.

Two different controls make auto-organization possible: the activity control, based on the competition between processing elements for the opportunity of winning and learning, and the plasticity control, that enables the weight modification of the processing elements belonging to the interest region S_w centered on the winning processing element pe_w. The degree of weight modification for a processing element pe_k depends on its proximity to the winning processing element pe_w in base to the neighborhood relation defined through a function $h(k, w)$. For GNG and GCS this relation is restricted to the direct neighbors.

For all the structures, the training process begins by fixing the topology and, for SOM, the number of processing elements and the interest region. After this, the weights of the structure are randomly initialized, the function h that defines the weight's update is fixed and also a parameter called learning rate is specified. Last, for SOM, the times the training set will be input to the net must be fixed, and for GCS and GNG a merit function to satisfy (that usually depends on the resource value) will also be fixed in order to achieve a right training.

3.1   Analysis of Auto-organization Results

At this point, it was necessary to think about an adequate way of representing the results graphically. We decided to use a colormap, where each processing element was assigned a different color that represented in some way the distance between processing elements. Thus, if a main cluster is assigned a determined color, then the elements around must have similar colors.

Assigning colors to processing elements in SOM was not complicated due to the rectangular and static neighborhood relation between processing elements. The assignation result is a color graduation proportional to the size of the map and shown in fig. 2 left. For GCS and GNG, the assignation of colors was more complicated, due to the dynamic nature of these structures. The objective was the selection of 8 equidistant colors representing the 8 main orientations in such a way that the combination of two neighboring colors could not be other selected color. For this purpose, we have recurred to the chromaticity diagram [12]. Our objective was computing the parameters that define a circle centered at white color in chromaticity diagram, in order to draw 8 equidistant points on its perimeter as shown in fig. 2 right. Once these points were calculated, they were transformed into RGB coordinates.

Different kind of images have been used to compare the results from different auto-organized structures. Rows in fig. 3 show original and results from a synthetic image containing two concentric circles, where all possible orientations are present, a corridor indoor image and an plane outdoor image, respectively.

Results obtained from test images in the first column of fig. 3 for first frequency channel and using the colormaps previously exposed, are depicted in the following columns of fig. 3. Second column corresponds to a rectangular 12 × 12

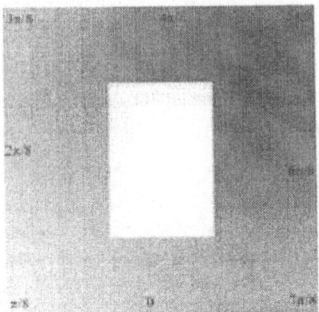
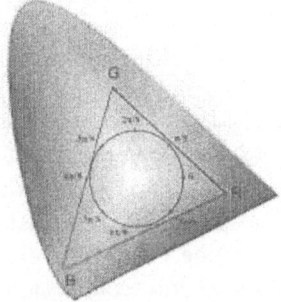

Fig. 2. Left: Graduation of colors for processing elements in a 12 × 12 SOM. Colors are smoothly variated from left to right and up to bottom from the 4 corners (red, green, cyan and magenta). Right: Chromaticity diagram with RGB triangle inside. The maximum circumscribed circle centered on white color is divided in 8 equidistant points. Points around this circle show color graduation assigned to processing elements in GCS. For both figures, background is assigned white color

Fig. 3. First column shows the original images. Columns from second to fourth show the results using SOM, GCS and GNG respectively for first frequency channel. Last column shows the results from GCS analysis for second frequency channel

SOM, where noise presence is relevant and some directional features are not detected by the map. These results are due to the insufficient separation between the processing elements assigned to main orientations and background. Some pixels that should be assigned to the background are assigned to another orientation motivating the noise presence, while pixels belonging to an intermediate orientation or a weak edge are assigned the background color motivating the lost of some directional features. Third column shows the results obtained with a GCS composed of 200 processing elements and implementing the *resource value* as a local counter that contains the number of input vectors assigned to the processing element. These images show an important noise reduction and a better detection of perceptual directional primitives. These results are due to the formation of a set of clusters with a similar number of processing elements around winning processing elements for each main orientation and background, with a limited interconnection between them. When the gaborjet assigned to a pixel is not close enough to the gaborjet that represents one of the eight main directions, it is assigned the background color. This happens, for example, with noisy pixels that produce soft values in some of the eight main orientations. These gaborjets are not close enough to a main orientation to be colored. Fourth column shows results obtained with a GNG composed of 100 processing elements and implementing *resource value* as an accumulator of the error between the processing element's weights and the input vectors assigned to it. In these images noise presence is almost null but some directional primitives are not detected by the map. This lost of information is related to the low generalization capacity of the net, motivated by the excessive separation between the clusters in the final structure. When a pixel belongs to an edge in a determined orientation, but the edge is not strong or the orientation is intermediate between two main orientations, it is assigned to the background and the directional information it contains is lost.

As a conclusion, GCS is the structure that best fits the objectives of our implementation for first frequency channel and so it will be employed for the analysis of the second frequency channel and the integration of both frequency channels. As results for second frequency channel are half the size of the original image, due to the multi-resolution spatial domain implementation of the Gabor decomposition exposed in previous section, these results must be expanded to double their size. This expansion motivates a diffusion effect (see fifth column of fig. 3) coherent with the low-pass nature of the set of filters employed.

One could think that first frequency could be enough to detect directional features, but results from images like the plane show that second frequency channel (last column of fig. 3) provides very useful information in images where background contains a great quantity of information (in this case the wood's texture) that is not as important as the foreground image. Second frequency channel discards this information and enforces the main shape.

3.2   Integration of Both Frequency Channels

The last step is the integration of information from both frequency channels by means of GCS, as earlier stated. This integration process will take as input the RGB output from each individual map, and produce an unique RGB result containing relevant information from previous ones.

As for individual frequency channels, the first step was the input space definition: each pixel was assigned a six component vector, the first three components represented the RGB output for the first frequency channel and the last three components the RGB output for the second frequency channel, both normalized to interval $[0, 1]$. Training set for GCS was generated from a set of artificial images containing almost the same proportion of lines in each main orientation. Background was included in the same proportion as the rest of orientations. The final goal was the generation of a set of clusters with a similar proportion of processing units assigned to each main orientation and background. The final map structure was the same as for individual frequency channel results.

Results for images in fig. 3 are depicted in fig. 4. As for individual frequency channels, in order to show the results graphically, a color has been assigned to each processing element using the chromaticity diagram and the following set or rules: If any of the RGB components of the processing element weights correspond to background color (white), the processing element is assigned the RGB color defined by the other three components. If these also correspond to background color, the processing element is assigned the white color. In any other case, the RGB color is computed by means of the chromaticity diagram as the

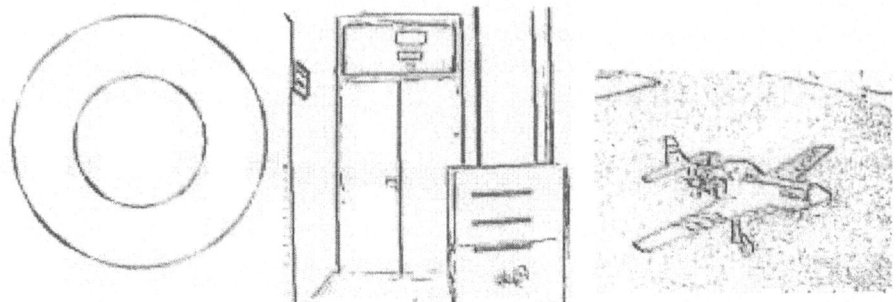

Fig. 4. Integration of both frequencies for images in fig. 3 using GCS

Fig. 5. Results from GCS analysis applied to different kind of images

arithmetical media of the original colors transformed to a RGB color belonging to the chromaticity diagram.

4 Results

Fig. 5 shows the final results obtained by the system with a set of different kinds of images. As can be observed in these images, GCS results contain the most important directional features in the image. Each orientation has the same color assigned in each of the images, which will be crucial for the next stage. This stage will consist on the detection of the segments that the image contains. All the results have been obtained from the same set of parameters, defined in sec. 3, a priori fixed without intervention of the final user.

5 Discussion and Conclusions

In this paper, the directional perceptual primitives of an image have been extracted by means of an efficient multi-resolution spatial-domain implementation of Gabor wavelet decomposition, centered at 2 frequency channels and 8 orientations. Frequency channels analyzed have been those centered at $\frac{1}{4}$ and $\frac{1}{8}$, this is, high and intermediate frequencies respectively, as those are the channels where most important image features are localized. Good localization of edges was achieved through an implementation that uses information from the even part, the odd part and the modulus of the wavelet.

Later on, these primitives have been organized and grouped by means of growing-cell structures (GCS) in a two layer hierarchy. The first layer organizes the information from different orientations in each frequency channel. The second layer integrates the organizations from different frequency channels so as to have an unique result where information from different frequency channels complement each other. This result has been a RGB image containing the most important directional features in it. For most images, first frequency channel could be enough, but for images with textured background, such as the plane in fig. 3, the second frequency channel is necessary to obtain right results.

The next step will be the analysis of this RGB image in order to detect the segments contained in the image. The result of this process will be a list of segments which, later on, will be organized into larger groups in order to select those low-level features that belong to a single object. This is, the directional features extracted from Gabor decomposition will be used as the primitives of a perceptual organization process.

Acknowledgements

This work has been partly supported by Xunta de Galicia though grant PGiDT01PXI10502PR.

References

[1] D.G. Lowe. Perceptual organisation in computer vision: A review and a proposal for a classificatory structure. *IEEE Transactions on Systems Man and Cybernetics*, 23(2):382-399, 1993.

[2] S. Sarkar and K.L. Boyer. *Computing Perceptual Organization in Computer Vision*. World Scientific, 1994.

[3] S. Sarkar and P. Soundararajan. Supervised learning of large perceptual organization: Graph spectral partitioning and learning automata. *IEEE Transactions on Pattern Analysis and Machine Intelligence*, 22(3):504-517, 2000.

[4] M.J. Carreira, M. Mirmehdi, B.T. Thomas, and M. Penas. Perceptual primitives from an extended 4D Hough transform. *Image and Vision Computing*, 20(13-14):969-980, 2002.

[5] J.G. Daugman. Uncertainty relation for resolution in space, spatial frequency, and orientation optimized by two-dimensional visual cortical filters. *Journal of the Optical Society of America*, 2(7):1160-1169, 1985.

[6] O. Nestares, R. Navarro, J. Portilla, and A. Tabernero. Efficient spatial-domain implementation of a multiscale image representation based on gabor functions. *Journal of Electronic Imaging*, 7:166-173, 1998.

[7] J.H. Van Deemter and J. M. H. Du Buf. Simultaneous detection of lines and edges using compound gabor filters. *International Journal of Pattern Recognition and Artificial Intelligence*, 14(4):757-777, 2000.

[8] B. Fritzke. Growing cell structures - a self-organizing network for unsupervised and supervised learning. *Neural Networks*, 7(9):1441-1460, 1994.

[9] T. Kohonen. Self-organised formation of topologically correct feature maps. *Biological Cybernetics*, 43:267-273, 1982.

[10] B. Fritzke. Growing self-organising networks - why? In *Proceedings of the $4^t h$ European Symposium on Artificial Neural Networks*, ESANN, pages 61-72, 1996.

[11] T. Martinetz and K. Schulten. A 'neural-gas' network learns topologies. In *Proceedings of the 1991 International Conference*, ICANN-91, pages 397-402, 1991.

[12] J.D. Foley. *Computer Graphics. Principles and Practice*. Addison-Wesley, 1990.

A Colour Tracking Procedure for Low-Cost Face Desktop Applications

F.J. Perales, R. Mas, M. Mascaró, P. Palmer, A. Igelmo, and A. Ramírez

Computer Graphics and Vision Group
Department of Computer Science, Universitat de les Illes Balears (UIB)
{paco.perales,ramon.mas,mascport}@uib.es
{pere.palmer,angel.ingelmo}@uib.es

Abstract. In this paper we present an environment for the tracking of a human face obtained from a real video sequence. We will describe the system and discuss the advantages and disadvantages of our approximation. We mainly focus on the situation of the main attributes of the human face (eyes, eyebrows, nose and moth). The tracking algorithm and the ulterior animation of the synthetic model must guarantee the real time response without the need of any additional markup of the actor. Due to the complexity of the process, we make an initial selection of the facial attributes involved without any efficiency or robustness loss. We define a probabilistic model of skin face area and we would like to track this region in the sequence of images. In parallel we propose additional criteria to search inside this tracked area main features in human face (as lisp, eyes, eyebrows, nose, etc..). The tracking algorithm is based in a efficient implementation of continuously adaptive mean shift procedure (CAMSHIFT) and this process is improved also with the second step with feature detections. In this paper only we present the whole process, the tracking background criteria and lips detection procedure. The synthesis phase is out scope of this paper and we generate the facial animations parameters (FAP) as input to a compliant MPEG-4 facial animation engine (FAE). This system is designed as a computer interface for controlling commercial computer applications which include avatar or clones in real time.

1 Introduction

A lot of work has been devoted in the literature to the tracking of human face and which somehow contribute in the approach we present in this paper [1,2]. Having in mind the existing previous work, we want to perform a realistic animation of a synthetic actor from a real sequence of images captured using a low-cost low-performance video camera. We have mainly focused in the main attributes of the human face although we have also included additional information like blobs, templates and a relational graph of visual entities.

F.J. Perales et al. (Eds.): IbPRIA 2003, LNCS 2652, pp. 733-739, 2003.
© Springer-Verlag Berlin Heidelberg 2003

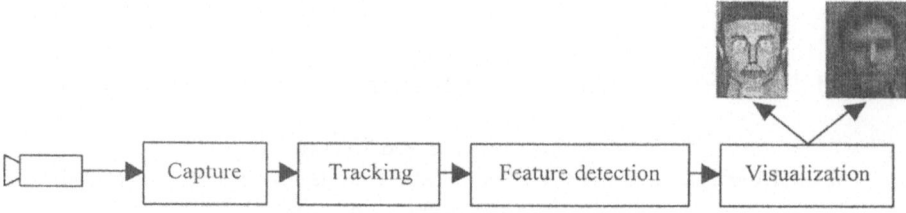

Fig. 1. The system architecture

The tracking and animation techniques for the facial model must guarantee the real time requirement with the constraint of not using any kind of additional markup for the human actor being tracked. However, we impose some constrains also to the kind of allowed occlusions of the regions of interest (ROI) as can be the hair on the eyebrows, the glasses or the beard. Due to the initial complexity of the problem we have used a previous manual selection (only in the first frame) of the face attributes involved without any noticeable loss of neither efficiency nor robustness of the system. We plan in future to do automatically this initialization step.

In the next sections we describe the architecture of our system and their different modules. Finally we conclude our work with some examples of face tracking and axis visualization.

2   System Architecture

Figure 1 shows a global view of the system, where we can see each of the different modules and tasks interacting. The union nexus is a simple but easy-to-use and fully functional user interface. The interface mainly allows the visualizing and the capture of the real actor and the animation of the virtual avatar.

Each module is intended to have the greatest possible degree of autonomy to minimize the influence of local algorithm modifications. The main modules are:

- the capture and visualization of real images module
- the geometrical characteristics recognition and tracking module
- the synthetic visualization module

The first module takes the input of both video and audio from a low-cost video camera (USB interfaced, IEEE 1934, etc.) We have also tried a medium-cost SONY EVI-D31 Pan/Tilt Zoom camera to test the validity of the approximation. The capture and visualization module provides the input to the second module at the same time than visualizes the input sequence. Both processes must be fully synchronized. The second module is the kernel of detection, tracking and recognition process. We have implemented a tracking method based on basic visual entities. At the same time, we have designed a tracking algorithm for the shape of the human actor based on color information using the HSL (hue, saturation and luminance) model although images are captured in RGB. The theoretical model is statistic; the symmetry axis and inertial moments are computed over the color distribution (hue) in order to be able to identify in every moment, the precise position and orientation of the human face. There are some constraints affecting the position and orientation of the face respect to the camera but when the system detects a loss of tracking it asks for a recovery position. We assume that the person is in a frontal plane respect to the camera.

The module for the visualization of the synthetic model represents the motion of the tracked points and regions. An easy and practical extension in order to make an open system would be to code the resulting motion using the FAT (facial animation tables) of the MPEG-4 standard. The synthetic actor or clone uses the information extracted by the geometrical characteristics computation and tracking module from the real images to automatically reproduce the motion of the real actor. The clone can be easily used as a videoconferencing low-band interlocutor. Only few points are needed to update the clone modification between frames.

To minimize the errors in the segmentation and in the tracking of the face, the registration process takes place in a controlled illumination background. The camera is supposed to be in near front view and the variations in the orientation of the human actor with respect to the image plane must be moderate (less than 5 degrees). In case a high variation is produced, the tracking algorithm can gather position and orientation errors, which can drive the system to an erroneous state. This constraint is constantly controlled using a predefined threshold.

3   The Tracking Module

One important step of the system is the tracking of the ROI in the face of the person. To get real time tracking we have to solve multiple problems as the solutions can not be as computationally expensive as those usually used in the face recognition systems. One of the main troubles deals with the great variety in the physical appearance of the studied subjects: skin color, eyes color, beard, glasses, hair and many other variables. Moreover, the facial attributes can be totally or partially occluded or in shadows which make the edges of the features indistinguishable. All this set of complications lead to an increase in the difficulty to recognize the face and the ulterior tracking of the ROI considered.

To minimize the effect of those problems in our system, the key points considered and their associated information are manually identified in an initialization or learning process. The initialization process is trivial and adjustable depending on the level of precision required by the application. We can select areas in the tracked attributes (the face, the nose, the moth, the eyes and the eyebrows). We have stored a logical structure between face attributes which allows the validation of the initialization phase to help the tracking and recognition. Once the areas have been identified using boxes, the system captures the color and edges characteristics of the regions.

The tracking subsystem is divided in several phases according to the primitives or attributes considered. The main consideration of the tracking system is that the face has an homogeneous color distribution (skin distribution). To take profit of this fact we can define robust parameters and probabilistic distributions which have the necessary properties to allow efficient and noise tolerant in the adjustment process. The algorithm implemented is based in a robust non-parametric technique (Mean shift) which augments the gradients density to find the nearest dominant mode [1].

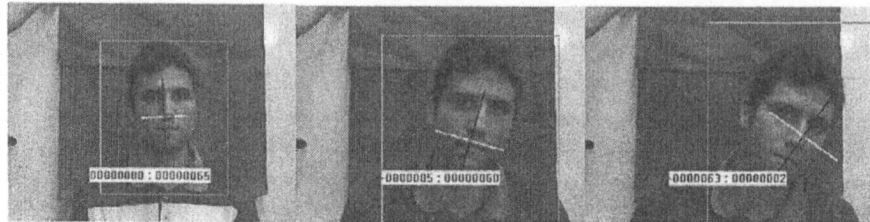

Fig. 2. Three steps of the tracking process: moving the face laterally

We have detected that the algorithm works well when we have a near constant illumination and the color of the face occupies most of the images with no similar colors in its neighborhood. Although not useful for the tracking of the attributes of the face themselves, the algorithm has provided to be good for a global positioning and orientation of the face, as can be seen in the results shown in figure 2. Notice in green colour the dynamic window used, and the centroid and axis on the face.

To track the moth, the eyes and the eyebrows we have had to adapt the color distribution to match the particularities of the minor regions. The synthetic essays have shown to be encouraging. In the real images we experience relatively frequent losses of the goal, if a hand or similar skin region move over face region. But the system recover the main region after this overlapping state. Moreover we would like to recognize the facial features on face so we need additional control criteria. Let see how we deal with the moth. We have some procedures for eyes and eyes browns but are not yet fully tested. So we concentrate in this paper in lips study.

3.1   Detection of the Mouth

The mouth is one of the most difficult facial attributes to analyze and track. Its shape is very versatile and multiple facial muscles take part in its motion. As an added problem, the beard, moustache, tongue and teeth can be disturbing appearing and disappearing properties. To simplify this casuistic we will make the assumption that no beard nor moustache are present and we may include structural information about the anatomy of the person. Lets consider that:

1. The upper teeth are fixed in the skull and than its relative position is constant.
2. The lower teeth move downwards from its initial position following the rotation of the lower mandible.
3. The shape of the moth depends on the lower maxilar motion.
4. Facial muscles can contribute to the shape of the moth.

The initial selection of the main areas of the tracked features makes the initial control points or lines more easier. With this consideration in mind, the detection of the moth must take into account the detection of each of its parts and their partial occlusions. So we base our algorithm in the following main points:

1. ROI selection in the initialization process.
2. Filtering and space color translation (RGB to HSL).
3. Lips edges detection.

4. Lips center line detection. Minimum luminance.
5. Detection of the corners of the mouth. Finding of the mean point and of the Cupid point.
6. Determination of the equivalent lower point.
7. Interpolation using a spline to get the full curve of the lips.
8. Finding the best elements combination to adjust the found edges. Initially, mouth closed.
9. Definition of the similitude function from the candidates and the obtained image. Maximize this function.

The main idea is to compute the edges of the vertical transitions of a line from the nose to the chin. We sample several lines and we verify the computed edges. Simultaneously we consider the HUE as in some cases the edge of the lower lip is difficult to detect. The final comparison is based in the three generated curves, which provides added robustness to the matching process, and considering the variation of the length of the moth in each basic position (closed or open). This can be seen in the figure 2.

The computed data are temporarily stored in the face structure. We are now working in a mouth database to create a model to allow better initial position detection. The model of the open mouth can be seen in the figure 4. When the mouth is closed, points 17 and 30, 20 and 27, 23 and 24 all superpose. From these characteristics the vertical curve will have a different shape depending on the status of the mouth:

1) Open mouth: the central contour is strong and the edges corresponding to the upper and lower lips are less pronounced respect to the skin of the face. Teeth are not visible.
2) Closed moth: the teeth are visible, contours are more visible in the lip-teeth and teeth-lip unions. The extern transitions lip-face are softer. In some cases, some of the intern transitions are not detectable when the lip occludes teeth.

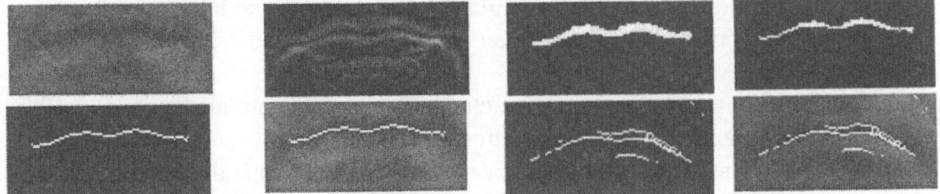

Fig. 3. Original image, edges and mean line recognized of the mouth

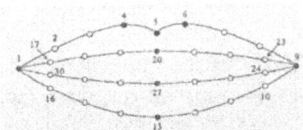

Fig. 4. The model of the mouth

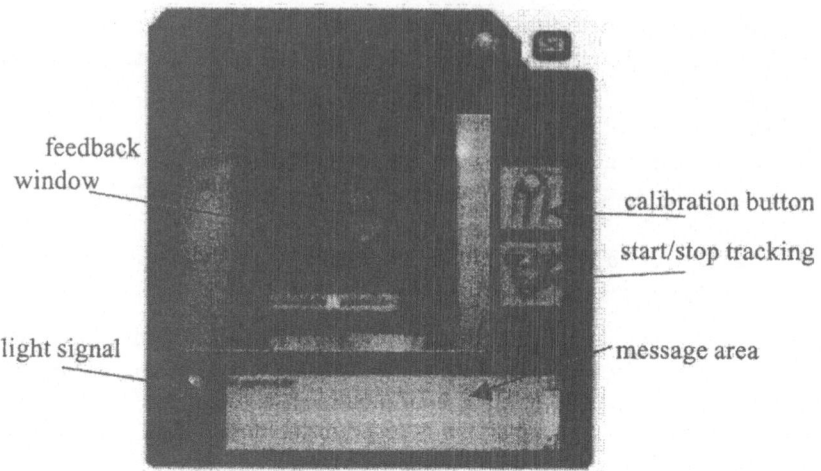

feedback window

calibration button

start/stop tracking

light signal

message area

Fig. 5. the main interaction window

We use fourteen points for both, the model of the open mouth and of the closed mouth despite some of them may superpose when closing the mouth. The relative distance between the coincident points determine the degree of opening of the mouth.

4   The Interaction Module

Even though the main part of this project is the tracking of the human face, it is necessary to design a graphical user interface in order to provide an efficient interaction with the system. The most important parts are (see figure 4):

- A window where the user face got from the camera will be shown. On this window the key points will be displayed, giving an easy to handle feedback.
- A system with which the user can manually select and adjust the key points considered.
- Some button where the user can activate the manual calibration, start and stop the tracking and finish the application.
- A message area where the system can show information and give indications to the user. Also with a light signal mechanism with which to mark the general situation.

The user interface must be as simple as possible, only the valid actions are available. The message area is the only one with text. The other parts follow the icon-based paradigm to avoid the complexity. The aspect is closer to the multimedia systems actually in use. The whole interface is configurable using skinning techniques. Before to use the system it is necessary select an image source from the list of all capture devices detected by the operating system; the user can select one of them from a list in a modal window. After this first step the main window appears. The message area shows a welcome text and the user image obtained from the selected camera is displayed in the feedback window. The only action the user can do at this time is calibrating the system. The calibration requires another auxiliary window where the user can select one by one the different areas to fit in the feedback window Once the user has picked over one area, he can select over his own face the corresponding region. The user image keeps static during this procedure in order to make an easy selection. The areas of interest are: the whole face, eyes, mouth and nose.

After this step, when all areas have been selected and correctly marked over the user image, the light signal changes to green colour if the areas are valid or to red colour if there is an invalid area. When the calibration window is closed the user image becomes dynamic once again and before the start the tracking procedure the user should fit his face over the areas defined in the calibration procedure.

5   Conclusions and Future Work

In this paper we have presented a new approach of human face tracking and facial feature detection. We would like to reach all the process in near real time. The tracking process is based on an improved version of CAMSHIFT procedure and feature detection is considered on eyes, eyebrows and lips. Due to space, we only present the lips procedure and some initial results. Also the tracking procedure is presented and fully tested. Also, our system is completed with an interactive procedure interface for non experts end users. Our future goal is to extend the system, to cope with the analysis of all of the facial features. Also, at the moment we export the points detected to a FAE MPEG-4 compliant animation engine. We are working in a stereo version to improve the errors in Z measurement.

References

[1]   Computer Vision Face Tracking for Use in a Perceptual User Interface. Gary R. Bradsky. Microcomputer Research Lab, Intel Corporation. 2001.Robust object location detection – Automatic head contour detection. Multimedia communications research laboratory. Bell Labs. 2000.Rapid Design of MPEG-4 Compliant Animated Faces and Bodies. Erich Haratsch.Technical University of Munich. 1997.Intel © Image Processing Library & Open Source Computer Vision Library. Reference Manuals. Intel Corporation. 2001.ISO/IEC JTC1/WG11 N1902.Text for CD 14496-2 Visual Fribourg meeting,   ovember1997.

Local Motion Estimation from Stereo Image Sequences

N. Pérez de la Blanca[1], J. M. Fuertes[2], M. Lucena[2,] and A. Garrido[1]

[1] Department of Computer Science and Artificial Intelligence
ETSII, University of Granada, 18071 Granada, Spain
nicolas@ugr.es
agarrido@decsai.ugr.es
[2] Departmento de Informática, Escuela Politécnica Superior
Universidad de Jaén, Avenida de Madrid 35, 23071 Jaén, Spain
{jmf,mlucena}@ujaen.es

Abstract. This paper proposes a method for representing local temporal deformations of a 3D flexible surface in an orthogonal space from a sequence of stereo images. The approach uses a disparity space as the main space in order to represent all the 3D information. The local motions are estimated removing the rigid motions from the global motion in the disparity space. A robust algorithm based on the RANSAC approach is used to estimate the rigid motions through the image sequence. An incremental SVD algorithm is used to estimate the representation space of the local motions as data is received. The approach presented in this paper is valid for any type of camera.

1   Introduction

This paper proposes a technique for representing the instantaneous motions of a 3D deformable surface in a linear space from its projections in a sequence of stereo images. To date, many efforts have been made to study the problem of static surface reconstructions from features extracted from monocular or stereo images [10,12,13,15]. However, little attention has been paid to the case of deformable surfaces [1,6,11]. The main inconvenience when deformable surfaces are studied is the impossibility of predicting the location of their projection on the images in the absence of a geometrical restriction on the 3D motion of the points. In order to constrain and regularize the motion parameter estimation problem in this situation, different approaches have been proposed in the case of monocular image sequences.

The most successful approach to date is to fit a 3D template into the projected data and move this template according to the tracked motions of a set of landmark points on the image [2,6,9,14]. Although effective in many situations, the shortcoming of this approach is that it requires a 3D template of the surface. Another more general approach, based only on the coordinates of a set of image points tracked through the image sequence, defines an object model as a linear combination of the deformation axes. The estimation process of these axes and the shape coefficients associated to each instant only needed the knowledge of the point coordinates [3,5]. Interesting

F.J. Perales et al. (Eds.): IbPRIA 2003, LNCS 2652, pp. 740–747, 2003.
© Springer-Verlag Berlin Heidelberg 2003

results have been found in the case of parallel projection cameras, although the general analytical solution has been shown to be extremely complex [3]. To the best of our knowledge, the solution for general perspective cameras still remains open.

Since we are interested in studying the 3D deformations of objects near the camera, we use the general perspective camera model in order to analyze our images. An important instance of this situation appears in the 3D videoconferencing system, where the 3D shape of the head and face of each participant must be refreshed in each instant of time, and the usual short distance between cameras and surfaces introduces strong perspective effects. The problem of iteratively estimating an orthogonal linear space, which characterizes all deformations is also of great interest, since once we have learned this space, the new observations could be auto-coded by the coefficients of their projection in this space.

In this paper, the disparity space from stereo images is used to solve the instantaneous reconstruction problem from deformable surfaces, and at the same to estimate 3D rigid motions. In order to define a reconstruction linear space and to adapt it to each new observation, we propose that an incremental SVD algorithm be used which will allow us to adapt the base of the space when the new observations appear. In Section 2, we introduce the geometrical concepts of the disparity space. In Section 3, we study the rigid motion estimation in the disparity space. In Section 4, we approach the local deformation estimation by proposing the use of an incremental algorithm for adapting the base of the reconstruction space. In Section 5, simulation experiments carried out on synthetic data are shown. Finally, in Section 6, discussions and conclusions are presented.

2   Stereo Images

Let us consider a calibrated rectified stereo rig, *i.e.* the epipolar lines are parallel to the x-axis. It is not a loss of generality since it is possible to rectify the images of a stereo rig once the epipolar geometry is known [10]. We also assume that both cameras of the rectified stereo rig have known and similar internal parameters.

Stereo reconstruction has been studied for years, and is now a standard topic in computer vision. Let us consider a rectified image pair, and let (x,y) and (x',y') be two corresponding points in that image pair. Since the corresponding points must lie on the epipolar line, the relation between the two points is

$$x' = x - d$$
$$y' = y \tag{1}$$

where d is defined as the disparity of the point (x,y). From rectified stereo images, we can define representation spaces based on the projected coordinates that are equivalent to a 3D reconstruction of the points up to a homography of the 3D space [8]. These spaces are known as *disparity spaces*. The equations relating the 3D coordinates (X,Y,Z) with the disparity coordinates in the case of oriented and rectified cameras are [13]:

$$
\begin{pmatrix} X \\ Y \\ Z \end{pmatrix} = \frac{B}{\bar{x} - \bar{x}'} \begin{pmatrix} \bar{x} \\ \bar{y} \\ 1 \end{pmatrix} \qquad \bar{x} = \frac{x - x_0}{\alpha}, \quad \bar{y} = \frac{y - y_0}{\alpha}, \quad \bar{x}' = \frac{x' - x'_0}{\alpha'} \tag{2}
$$

where x_0, y_0, x'_0 are the principal point coordinates of the left and right image, respectively, α and α' are the focal distance of the left and right cameras, respectively and B is the baseline of the stereo-rig. All image coordinates in are expressed in terms of pixels.

In this paper, we use the disparity space defined by the triple (x,y,d). From expression (2), taking $\alpha = \alpha'$ the homographic relationship between the 3D coordinates of a point $X = (X,Y,Z)^T$ and its associated disparity vector $(\bar{x}, \bar{y}, d)^T$ can be expressed as,

$$
Z \begin{bmatrix} \bar{x} \\ \bar{y} \\ d \\ 1 \end{bmatrix} = \begin{bmatrix} \alpha & 0 & 0 & 0 \\ 0 & \alpha & 0 & 0 \\ 0 & 0 & 0 & \alpha B \\ 0 & 0 & 1 & 0 \end{bmatrix} \begin{bmatrix} X \\ Y \\ Z \\ 1 \end{bmatrix} \tag{3}
$$

or in a shorter way as

$$
\begin{pmatrix} \tau \\ 1 \end{pmatrix} \cong H_B \begin{pmatrix} X \\ 1 \end{pmatrix} \qquad , \quad \tau = (\bar{x}, \bar{y}, d)^T \tag{4}
$$

From equation (3), it is clear that in the case of non-calibrated cameras each pair of rectified stereo images provides us with the reconstruction of the surface being imaged up to projectivity. From the intrinsic parameters of the stereo rig, the projective reconstruction can be upgraded to metric.

3   Rigid Motions in the Disparity Space

Let us apply a rigid motion on the 3D data. If X and X' represent the 3D coordinates of a point before and after the motion, we have

$$
\begin{pmatrix} X' \\ 1 \end{pmatrix} = \begin{pmatrix} R & T \\ 0^T & 1 \end{pmatrix} \begin{pmatrix} X \\ 1 \end{pmatrix} \tag{5}
$$

From expressions (4) and (5) we obtain

$$
\lambda \begin{pmatrix} \tau' \\ 1 \end{pmatrix} = H_B \begin{pmatrix} R & T \\ 0^T & 1 \end{pmatrix} H_B^{-1} \begin{pmatrix} \tau \\ 1 \end{pmatrix} = \Gamma \begin{pmatrix} \tau \\ 1 \end{pmatrix} \tag{6}
$$

Equation (6) describes the 3D homography Γ relating the disparity homogeneous coordinates of a point before and after the motion.

3.1   Noise on the Data

An important feature of the disparity space is that the noise associated to the data vectors $(\bar{x}, \bar{y}, d)^T$ under some assumptions can be considered isotropic and homogeneous. The $\bar{x}, \bar{y}$ disparity coordinates are affected by the noise produced by the discretization effect and without additional information can be assumed equal for all pixels. The noise on d is associated to the change in the gray level of the pixels in the stereo matching process and could be estimated from this process. So, we can assume that the noises associated to $\bar{x}, \bar{y}$ and d are independent. If we assume that the variance of d is of the same magnitude as the variance of the discretization error the covariance matrix of the noise on each point of our disparity space is $\Omega = \sigma^2 \mathbf{I}_{3x3}$.

In our case, apart from the above measurement errors, we also assume that in our scene there are points in motion. All the correspondences associated with these moving points are therefore potentially erroneous. In order to select point correspondences not affected by the moving points, we use the RANSAC algorithm to select subset of point correspondences that are free of this contamination.

3.2   Rigid Motion Estimation

Let (τ_i, τ'_i) be a set of point correspondences. The problem of estimating the rigid motion parameters $(\mathbf{R}, \mathbf{T})$ from the set of points (τ_i, τ'_i) amounts to minimizing the error

$$E^2 = \sum_i d(\tau'_i, \Gamma\tau_i)^2, \quad d(\tau'_i, \Gamma\tau_i)^2 = (\tau'_i - \tau'^{\Gamma}_i)^T \Omega^{-1}(\tau'_i - \tau'^{\Gamma}_i) \tag{7}$$

where $\tau'^{\Gamma}_i = (\tau'^{\Gamma}_{i1}/\tau'^{\Gamma}_{i4} \quad \tau'^{\Gamma}_{i2}/\tau'^{\Gamma}_{i4} \quad \tau'^{\Gamma}_{i3}/\tau'^{\Gamma}_{i4})$ is the estimated Euclidean coordinate vector for τ'_i from (6), and Ω is the covariance matrix of the disparity vectors. Here we assume an i.i.d noise model. Equation (6) shows that this error function is not linear in the parameters for $(\mathbf{R}, \mathbf{T})$, so a non-linear method has been used to estimate the vector of six unknowns by parameterizing the rigid motion.   Here we are interested in the case of small rotations (< 5 degree), so the rotation matrix can be expressed as $\mathbf{R} = \mathbf{I} + [\omega]_x$, where I is the identity matrix and $[\omega]_x$ represents the skew-symmetric matrix associated to the vector ω In order to estimate the solution vector $(\omega, \mathbf{T})^T$ a quasi-linear iterative algorithm has been used on the normalized image coordinated [7]. An initial solution for the vector $(\omega, \mathbf{T})^T$ can be calculated from equation (6), solving the linear system   that appear considering the equations associated to Euclidean coordinates of the all points τ and τ' and assuming all $\lambda = 1$. In the next iteration we recalculate the value of λ from the above solution and solve again the equation (6) for a new solution. We iterate until the convergence of the vector $(\omega, \mathbf{T})^T$. In our experience three of our iterations are enough.

4   Local Deformations

Now we are interested in learning an orthogonal linear space for representing all local motions on the 3D surface. This space is estimated from the residual vectors of the points observed in the disparity space after the rigid motion component has been removed. This residual shall of course be contaminated with noise associated mainly to the matching point and rigid motion registration processes.

Let $\hat{\mathbf{R}}_i$ and $\hat{\mathbf{t}}_i$ denote the rotation and translation estimation from the $(i\text{-}1)$-th to the i-th images. Let $\mathbf{X}_{in}$ denote the 3D coordinates of the i-th scene point in the instant $n>0$. The 3D local deformation vector associated to this point is therefore calculated by

$$\hat{\mathbf{D}}_{in} = \hat{\mathbf{R}}_1^T \times \cdots \times \hat{\mathbf{R}}_n^T \left(\mathbf{X}_{in} - \hat{\mathbf{T}}_i \right) - \mathbf{X}_{i0} \ , \quad \hat{\mathbf{T}}_i = \hat{\mathbf{R}}_i \hat{\mathbf{T}}_{i-1} + \hat{\mathbf{t}}_i \ , \quad \hat{\mathbf{T}}_0 = \mathbf{0} \qquad (8)$$

From (5) and (8), there is a homography Γ_n mapping the disparity vectors of the n-th image to those of the initial image plus the present local deformation

$$\begin{pmatrix} \tau_{in} \\ 1 \end{pmatrix} \cong \Gamma_n \begin{pmatrix} \tau_{i0} + \tau_{D_{in}} \\ 1 \end{pmatrix}, \qquad \Gamma_n = \mathbf{H}_B \begin{pmatrix} \hat{\mathbf{R}}_n \cdots \hat{\mathbf{R}}_1 & \hat{\mathbf{T}}_n \\ \mathbf{0}^T & 1 \end{pmatrix} \mathbf{H}_B^{-1} \qquad (9)$$

Since the vectors τ_{i0} are fixed and the matrix Γ_n can be calculated from the rigid motion estimate, we can estimate the vectors $\tau_{D_{in}}$ iteratively from (9) once the corresponding parameters $(\mathbf{R}_n, \mathbf{T}_n)$ have been estimated. Assuming all 3D points are present in all images, for each stereo-image j we concatenate all its local deformations disparity vectors $\tau_{D_{ij}}$ in a single column vector τ_{D_j}. We also assume, without loss of generality, that the local deformations are mainly defined by cyclic patterns. Then the set of vectors $\tau_{\mathbf{D}} = \{ \tau_{D_j}, j{=}1,\dots,n \}$ can be embedded, for n sufficiently large, in a orthogonal linear space using a Singular Value Decomposition (SVD) algorithm. In order to estimate this orthogonal space and update it iteratively, we applied an incremental SVD algorithm to the sequence of disparity vectors $\{ \tau_{D_j}, j{=}1,\dots,n \}$ [4].

If $\tau_{\mathbf{D}} = \mathbf{UDV}^T$ denote the SVD of $\tau_{\mathbf{D}}$, the orthogonal matrix $\mathbf{U}$ is considered the basis for our local deformation space.

5   Simulation Experiments

Experiments with simulated data were carried out in order to compare the quality of the approach. A 3D scene defined by 243 points on two orthogonal planes, was used; see Figure 1(a). This scene was projected onto the stereo images, before and after a rigid motion of the scene, using a virtual stereo rig. We assume that the intrinsic parameters of the stereo rig ($B{=}3$, $\alpha'{=}\alpha{=}549$) are known. The distance between the scene and the stereo rig was four times the height of the scene. Gaussian noise with variable standard deviation ($\sigma{=}0$ to 1.4 pixel) was added to the image coordinates. In our case, a fixed percentage, of scene points, is free to move its 3D location during the global rigid motion.

5.1 Rigid Motion Estimation

A set of point correspondences was used to estimate the rigid motion. In order to avoid point correspondences associated to moving points, a RANSAC algorithm was used from 50 random samples of two disparity vector correspondences, since two vectors provided us with six restrictions to estimate the six parameters. The accuracy of the estimate was measured in terms of the relative error of the quadratic norm of the residual. Figure 1(b) shows the average evolution of 500 simulations for increasing values of noise in the case of small motions (rotation angle < 5 degree and a maximum translation of 0.5 units on each axe).

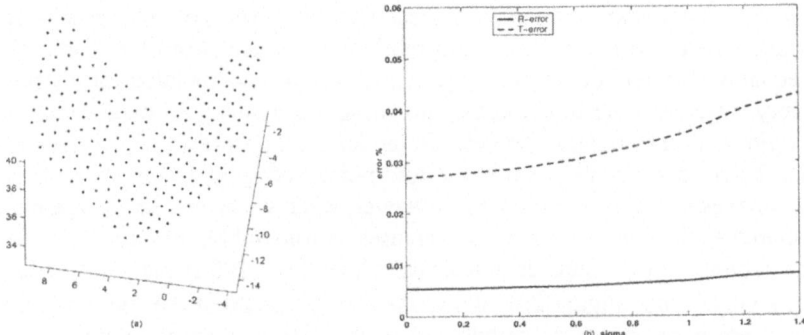

Fig. 1. a) 3D scene used in the simulation experiments, b) Estimation of the relative rotation and translation errors for small motions

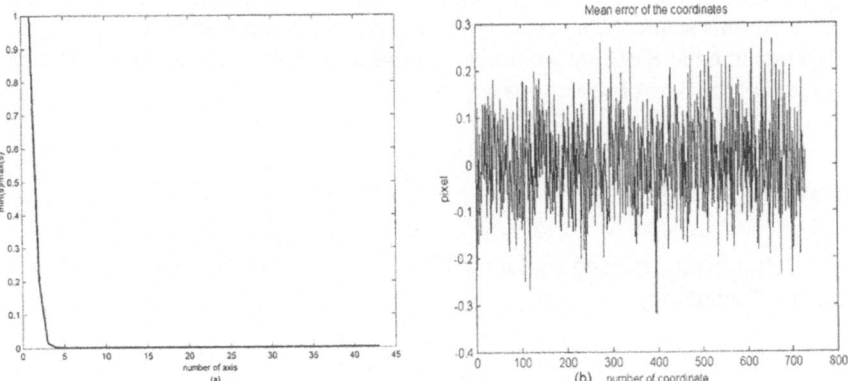

Fig. 2. a) Average curve of the learning curves from 100 sequences of 100 images with 40% of moving points in the scene, b) Average vector of the orthogonal components to the subspace spanned by **U** from 200 simulations with sigma=0.5

5.2   Linear Space Estimation

To analyze the evolution of the dimensionality of the space with the complexity of the local motions, we have applied random rigid motions to our scene and we have calculated the associated sequence of vectors τ_D. The 3D moving points follow a periodic affine motion on each plane in our scene. The translation and scale parameters of the affine transformation were modulated with a periodic function along the sequence. As criteria for stopping the updating process we fixed a superior threshold ($< 10^{-4}$) on the ratio between the minimum and maximum singular values.

6   Discussion and Conclusions

Figure 1(b) shows how the rotation and translation estimate between two images is very accurate even for high level of noise. The algorithm we use is fast enough since no more than 3-4 linear iterations are needed for convergence. This result allows us to use this method to remove the rigid motion component from the disparity vector using equation (9). Of course, for large sequences the accumulated error could come to be very large. In order to avoid this situation, more than two images must be used in the rigid motion estimation process. In the learning process, the proposed stopping criterion behaves adequately since for low noise and global non-rigid motions the number of axes is as low as expected. However, when we have a very large number of local motions, the number of axes increases considerably. Figure 2(a) shows the average evolution of the number of axes calculated from 100 sequences of 100 images of our moving scene. Figure 2(b) shows the average graph of the vectors $(\mathbf{I}-\mathbf{U}\mathbf{U}^T)\tau_D$, that is the components of τ_D orthogonal to the subspace spanned by U. From the experimental simulations can be established that the estimated space U represents quite well the full sequence of vectors τ_D even with high level of noise on the observations.

This paper has presented a technique to estimate 3D local motions as vector in orthogonal space. The rigid motion fitting on the disparity space has been the key point, since in this space the errors can be considered isotropic and homogeneous. The use of an incremental SVD algorithm has allows us to update the representation space at the time that the new observations appear.

Acknowledgments

This work, has been financed by Grant IT-2001-3316 from the Spanish Ministry of Science and Technology

References

[1]   Bascle, B., and Blake, A.: Separability of pose and expression in facial tracking and animation. In Proc. Int. Conf. Computer Vision. 1998.

[2]   Basu, S., Oliver, N., Pentland A.: 3D modelling and tracking of human lip motions, ICCV'98, 1998.

[3]   Brand, M. : 3D Morphable models from video. In Proc. CVPR'01. 2001.

[4]   Brand, M.: Incremental singular value decomposition of uncertain data with missing value. In Proc. Europ. Conf. Computer Vision, ECCV-2002, LNCS-2350, 707-720.

[5]   Bregler, C., Hertzmann, A., Biermann, H.: Recovering non-rigid 3D shape from image streams. In   Proc. IEEE Conf. Computer Vision and Pattern Recognition (CVPR'00). 2000.

[6]   Decarlo,D., and Metaxas, D.: Optical flow constraints on deformable models with application to face tracking. International Journal of Computer Vision, 38(2),99-127, 2000.

[7]   Demirdjian, D., and Darell, T.,: Motion estimation from disparity images, In Proc. ICCV01, Vancouver Canada, 2001, vol-II, 628-635.

[8]   Devernay,F. and Faugeras.O.: From projective to Euclidean reconstruction. In Proceedings Computer Vision and Pattern Recognition, 264-269,1996.

[9]   Fua, P,: Regularized bundle-adjustment to models heads from image sequences without calibration data, International Journal of Computer Vision, 38(2), 2000.

[10]   Hartley, R. Zisserman A.,: Multiple View geometry in computer vision. CUP, 2002.

[11]   Lanitis, A., Taylor, C.J., Cootes, T.F. and Ahmed, T.: Automatic interpretation of human faces and hand gestures using flexible models. In Int. Workshop on Autom. Face-and-Gesture Recognition, 1995.

[12]   Pollefeys, M., Van Gool, L., Zisserman, A., and Fitzgibbon, A: 3D Structure from images – SMILE 2000, Lecture Notes in Computer Science 2018, Springer, 2000.

[13]   Tarel, J.P.,: Global 3D Planar Reconstruction with Uncalibrated Cameras a Rectified Stereo Geometry, Machine Graphics & Vision Journal, vol-6, 4, 1997, 393-418.

[14]   Valente.S., and Dugelay, J.L.: A visual analysis/synthesis feedback loop for accurate face tracking, Signal Processing Image Communications, 16, 2001, 585-608.

[15]   Zhang, Z., Faugeras, O.: 3D Dynamic Scene Analysis,: A stereo based approach. Springer series in Information Science, 27, Springer-Verlag, 1992.

A Change Validation System for Aerial Images Based on a Probabilistic Latent Variable Model

Fernando Pérez Nava

Departamento de Estadística, Investigación Operativa y Computación
Universidad de la Laguna. Islas Canarias. 38271 Spain
fdoperez@ull.es

Abstract. Change detection is an important part of image interpretation and automated geographical data collection. In this paper, we show a quality control system for the verification of image changes detected by a human operator. The system is based on a probabilistic system that learns the operator behaviour and tests the founded changes. Maximum likelihood estimators for the model are presented and their derivation is shown. Computational results are given with real image data that show the performance of the system.

1 Introduction

Change detection on the terrestrial surface from aerial images is an important problem in the update and maintenance of digital cartographic maps. This is one of the working areas of the company GrafCan S.A. (www.grafcan.com) located in the Autonomous Community of the Canary Islands (Spain). The company is dedicated to Geographical Information Systems (GIS), a field of increasing importance in the last years due to the importance of its applications: house census, environmental planning, verification of city-planning norms, etc. These applications are of importance to organisms that need a massive processing of geographical information.

One of the main costs associated to GIS is the information maintenance cost, since geographical information changes temporally. One way to detect these variations is the use of pairs of images of the same area at different times. A human operator then detects changes by means of the visual analysis of images. Human visual analysis is favoured by the implicit incorporation of intelligent processing associated to the operator. However, and also due to the explicit intervention of the operator, this analysis is not free of disadvantages due to operator fatigue, operator inconsistencies or operator costs.

In this paper, we present a quality control system for the verification of the changes detected by a human operator in pairs of images. The systems checks if each change can be explained by the operator global behavior and eventually select a subset of the changes for revision. The learning system is based on a probabilistic latent variable

F.J. Perales et al. (Eds.): IbPRIA 2003, LNCS 2652, pp. 748-757, 2003.
© Springer-Verlag Berlin Heidelberg 2003

model whose parameters are estimated from the set of changes detected by the operator.

To propose a model for changes, a crucial aspect is the definition of features to carry out the comparison. At the present moment, two different strategies are widely employed: techniques based on a pixel level comparison of images and techniques based on scene model definition and matching. Methods based on pixel-to-pixel analysis of images are of relatively simple implementation, they usually show high sensitivity and low semantic information. On the other hand, the comparison of multitemporal images based on high-level models is less prone to changes not directly related to the structural content of the scene. Nevertheless model definition and matching is a very complex computational problem.

To analyse the aerial images provided by GrafCan where content is variable and where changes are generated by a great variety of sources, we have employed a multispectral pixel-to-pixel analysis. From the first studies in [1], the development of techniques of change detection based on the analysis of multispectral data has undergone a continuous evolution and several approaches have been developed: Image differencing [2], Image quotient [3], Vegetation Index Difference [4], Image regression [5], Principal component Analysis (PCA) [6], Change Vector [7], and Iterative Principal Component Analysis (IPCA) [8]. In this paper we propose a mixed model from Reduced Rank Regression [9] and Probabilistic Principal Component Analysis (PPCA) [10].

2   Probabilistic Learning of Image Changes

In this section, we propose an initial model for image change and show how to estimate its parameters from the operator behaviour. Given an image I_1 captured at time t_1 and its corresponding image I_2 of the same region but taken at time t_2, we select image patches Ix from image I_1 and Iy from image I_2. They are selected small enough so that it can be approximately assumed that entirely they belong to the 'Change' (CH) class or 'No Change' (NC) class. We will build a vector from the pixels of the patches obtaining two d-dimensional vectors x and y. The proposed model for y is:

$$y = \mu + At + Cu + \varepsilon, \quad t = Bx, \quad u \sim N(0, I), \quad \varepsilon \sim N(0, \sigma^2 I), \tag{1}$$

where t is an r dimensional random variable, u is q dimensional random variable and t, u, ε are independently distributed. The dimension of matrix A is $d \times r$, the dimension of matrix B is $r \times d$ and both matrices have rank r. The dimension of matrix C is $d \times q$ and its rank is q.

Therefore we can express the d dimensional variable y in terms of two latent variables t and u of dimensions r and q where usually $d \gg r + q$. The proposed model then states that image patch y is related to:

- Latent variable t, that linearly depends on image patch x. The term $At = ABx$ can be interpreted as a reduced rank regression [9] of y over x.
- Latent variable u, that accounts for those aspects in y not explained by t. This term is related to probabilistic principal component analysis (PPCA) [10].
- An overall mean μ.
- Random variable ε, that expresses an isotropic noise model.

2.1   Model Parameter Estimation

The use of an isotropic Gaussian noise model in (1) implies that the conditional distribution over y can be written as:

$$y \mid x, u \sim N(\mu + ABx + Cu, \sigma^2 I). \tag{2}$$

Integrating out u, we have:

$$y \mid x \sim N(\mu + ABx, M), \quad M = CC^T + \sigma^2 I. \tag{3}$$

Then, given a learning set $H = \{(y_1, x_1), (y_2, x_2), \ldots, (y_N, x_N)\}$, the Maximum Likelihood Estimators (MLE) for the model are (see the Appendix):

$$\hat{\mu} = \hat{\mu}_y - \hat{A}\hat{B}\hat{\mu}_x, \quad \hat{A} = V_r, \quad \hat{B} = V_r^T S_{yx} S_{xx}^{-1}, \text{ with:}$$

$$\hat{\mu}_x = \frac{1}{N}\sum_{i=1}^{N} x_n, \quad \hat{\mu}_y = \frac{1}{N}\sum_{i=1}^{N} y_n \tag{4}$$

$$S_{yx} = \frac{1}{N}\sum_{i=1}^{N}(y_n - \hat{\mu}_y)(x_n - \hat{\mu}_x)^T, S_{xx} = \frac{1}{N}\sum_{i=1}^{N}(x_n - \hat{\mu}_x)(x_n - \hat{\mu}_x)^T,$$

and where V_r is the eigenvector matrix corresponding to the r largest eigenvalues of the matrix $S_{yx} S_{xx}^{-1} S_{xy}$. To calculate the MLE estimators for C, σ^2 we must define:

$$S = \frac{1}{N}\sum_{i=1}^{N}(y_n - \hat{\mu} - \hat{A}\hat{B}x_n)(y_n - \hat{\mu} - \hat{A}\hat{B}x_n)^T, \text{ then:}$$

$$\hat{C} = U_q(\Lambda_q - \hat{\sigma}^2 I)^{1/2} R, \quad \hat{\sigma}^2 = \frac{1}{d-q}\sum_{j=q+1}^{d}\lambda_j, \tag{5}$$

where the q column vectors in the $d \times q$ matrix U_q are the eigenvectors of S, with corresponding eigenvalues in order of decreasing magnitude in the $q \times q$ diagonal matrix Λ_q, and R is an arbitrary $q \times q$ orthogonal matrix.

To classify as NC or CH a new pair of image patches Ix and Iy, we will assume $p(x \mid NC) = p(x \mid CH)$ and apply the optimal bayesian rule [11]:

$$p(x, y \mid NC) / p(x, y \mid CH) = p(y \mid x, NC) / p(y \mid x, CH) > (<) bias \tag{6}$$

2.2   The Learning Set

This set is given by the operator's work and consist in a set of point locations in the image where she observes a change. Then, for each detected change, an image patch around this location is generated. This provides the learning set for the 'Change' class to the classification algorithm.

After an operator processes an image, there are not examples for the 'No Change' class. To provide a set of examples for this class we randomly sample locations from the image except in a neighborhood of the locations in the 'Change' class. The image patches generated from these locations are the learning set for the 'No Change' class. In Figure 1, we can see two examples from the learning set.

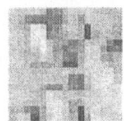     

Fig. 1. Image patches from the learning set of the 'Change' class (left) and 'No Change' class (right)

2.3   A Mixture Model

A reasonable criticism for the model in (1) arises from the task we want to achieve (to validate the operator's work) and from the learning set. The main objection consists in that we are estimating the parameters in the model assuming that the samples from the 'Change' class that are given by the operator in fact belong to this class. This will result in a biased estimation. The same problem arises in the 'No Change' class since we can't be completely sure that these samples belong to that class. In this section, we show a mixture model to solve this problem.

In the mixture model, it is assumed that the distribution for all the image patches is:

$$p(y \mid x) = p(y \mid x, NC)\pi_{NC} + p(y \mid x, CH)\pi_{CH}. \tag{7}$$

Then, we have to estimate the parameters for the probability distribution and the mixing parameters π_i, $i=CH$, NC from the learning set. These parameters are estimated (see Appendix) through a variation of the iterative Expectation Maximization (EM) algorithm as follows: Given previous values for the parameters in the probability distribution, the responsibilities $R_{n,i}$ are computed:

$$R_{n,i} = \frac{p(y \mid x, i)\pi_i}{p(y \mid x)}, \quad i = NC, CH \tag{8}$$

and the parameters are reestimated using:

$$\tilde{\pi}_i = \frac{1}{N}\sum_{i=1}^{N} R_{n,i}, \quad i = NC, CH$$

$$\tilde{\mu}_i = \left(\tilde{\mu}_{y,i} - \tilde{A}\tilde{B}\tilde{\mu}_{x,i}\right), \quad \tilde{\mu}_{y,i} = \frac{\sum_{n=1}^{N} R_{n,i} y_n}{N\tilde{\pi}_i}, \quad \tilde{\mu}_{x,i} = \frac{\sum_{n=1}^{N} R_{n,i} x_n}{N\tilde{\pi}_i},$$

$$\tilde{A}_i = V_{r_i,i}, \quad \tilde{B} = V_{r_i,i}^{\mathrm{T}} \tilde{S}_{yx,i}\tilde{S}_{xx,i}^{-1}, \quad \tilde{C}_i = U_{q_i,i}(A_{q_i,i} - \tilde{\sigma}_i^2 I),$$

$$\tilde{\sigma}_i^2 = \frac{1}{d-q_i}\sum_{j=q_i+1}^{d} \lambda_{j,i} \tag{9}$$

$$\tilde{S}_{yx,i} = \frac{\sum_{n=1}^{N} R_{n,i}\left(y - \tilde{\mu}_{y,i}\right)\left(x - \tilde{\mu}_{x,i}\right)^{\mathrm{T}}}{N\tilde{\pi}_i}, \tilde{S}_{xx,i} = \frac{\sum_{n=1}^{N} R_{n,i}\left(x - \tilde{\mu}_{x,i}\right)\left(x - \tilde{\mu}_{x,i}\right)^{\mathrm{T}}}{N\tilde{\pi}_i}$$

$$\tilde{S}_i = \frac{\sum_{n=1}^{N} R_{n,i}\left(y_n - \tilde{\mu}_i - \tilde{A}_i\tilde{B}_i x_n\right)\left(y_n - \tilde{\mu}_i - \tilde{A}_i\tilde{B}_i x_n\right)^{\mathrm{T}}}{N\tilde{\pi}_i},$$

where the r_i column vectors in the $d \times r_i$ matrix $V_{r_i,i}$ are the eigenvectors corresponding to the r_i largest eigenvalues of $\tilde{S}_{yx,i}\tilde{S}_{xx,i}^{-1}\tilde{S}_{xy,i}$ and where the q_i column vectors in the $d \times q_i$ matrix U_{q_i} are the q_i leading eigenvectors from $\tilde{S}_i$.

3   Computational Results

We show now some computational results from the mixture model. In Figure 2 we show an aerial image from the island of Gran Canaria (Spain) in black and white. The learning set extracted from this image comprised 493 changes detected by the operator. Image patches were taken with size 15×15 pixels, hence $d = 225$. After a cross-validation step values for r and q were $r_{CH} = 0$, $q_{CH} = 1$, $r_{NC} = 1$, $q_{CH} = 16$, showing a great information reduction. The percentage of points where the probabilistic model and the operator agreed started at 84% in the first iteration of the EM algorithm and converged to 88% after 6 iterations. In the left image of Figure 3 the log-likelihood of change is shown. Whiter regions denote a greater probability of change. In the right image of Figure 3 coincidences between the operator and the system are shown with circles and differences with squares.

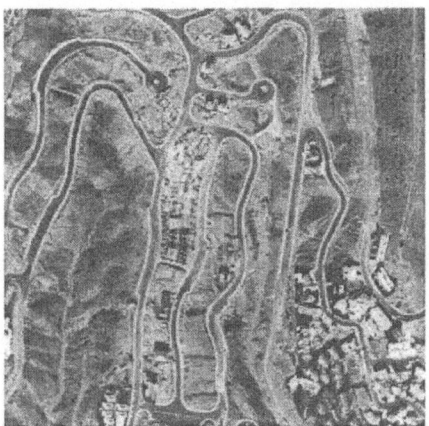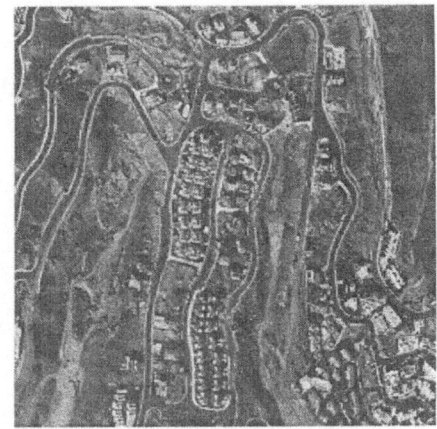

Fig. 2. Detail of one pair of the image from the experiments

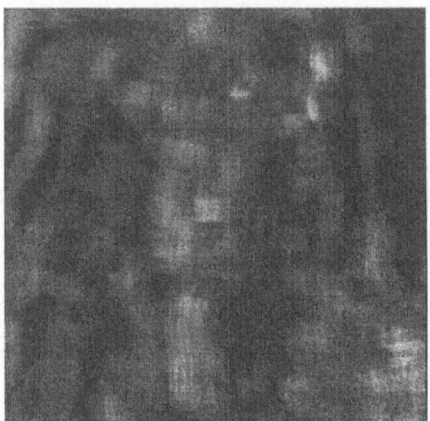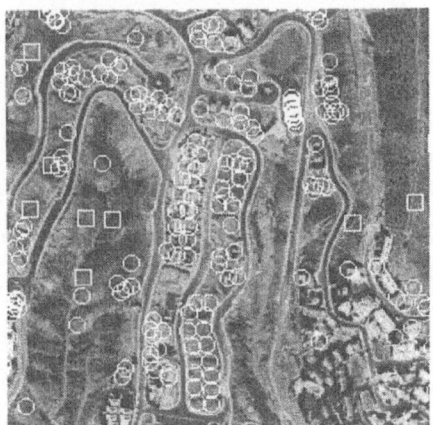

Fig. 3. Left: Log-likelihood of change. Right: Coincidences of the operator and the system are denoted with circles and differences with squares.

4   Conclusions

Change detection is an important part of image interpretation and automated GIS data collection. In this paper, we have presented a probabilistic model for change validation in aerial images. This model uses a latent variable representation whose parameters are estimated by maximum likelihood. Computational results are given that show the validity of the results.

Acknowledgments

The author would like to than all the facilities and support provided by GrafCan.

Appendix

First we show that the MLE estimators of the model (1) are those given in (4), (5). Suppose we have a learning set $H=\{(y_1, x_1), (y_2, x_2), ...,(y_N, x_N)$. Collect $Y=[y_1, y_2, ..., y_N]$ and $X=[x_1, x_2, ..., x_N]$. The MLE estimators for the model are obtained maximizing the log-likelihood L:

$$L = -N/2\left(d\ln(2\pi)+\ln|M|+trace(M^{-1}S)\right),$$

$$S = \frac{1}{N}(Y-\mu\mathbf{1}^{\mathrm{T}}-ABX)^{\mathrm{T}}(Y-\mu\mathbf{1}^{\mathrm{T}}-ABX), M = CC^{\mathrm{T}}+\sigma^2 I. \tag{10}$$

Assuming that μ, A and B are fixed the maximum likelihood estimator for C is [10]:

$$\hat{C} = U_q(\Lambda_q-\hat{\sigma}^2 I)^{1/2}R, \tag{11}$$

where the q column vectors in the $d \times q$ matrix U_q are the eigenvectors of S, with corresponding eigenvalues in order of decreasing magnitude in the $q \times q$ diagonal matrix Λ_q, and R is an arbitrary $q \times q$ orthogonal matrix. We define $\hat{\sigma}^2$ as the MLE estimator of σ^2:

$$\hat{\sigma}^2 = \frac{1}{d-q}\sum_{j=q+1}^{d}\lambda_j, \tag{12}$$

where $\lambda_{q+1,...,}\lambda_d$ are the smallest eigenvalues of S. Then, substituting these values into the log-likelihood (10) we have:

$$L = -N/2\left(d\ln(2\pi)+\ln|\Lambda|+d\right), \tag{13}$$

where Λ is a $d \times d$ diagonal matrix with the eigenvalues of S. Therefore, we have to minimize $\log|\Lambda|$ with respect to A, B, μ. Then, taking :

$$\hat{A} = V_r, \quad \hat{B} = V_r^{\mathrm{T}}S_{yx}S_{xx}^{-1}, \quad \hat{\mu} = \hat{\mu}_y - \hat{A}\hat{B}\hat{\mu}_x, \tag{14}$$

where the r column vectors in the $d \times r$ matrix V_r are the eigenvectors corresponding to the r largest eigenvalues of $S_{yx}S_{xx}^{-1}S_{xy}$, all the eigenvalues of Λ are simultaneously minimized [12], hence the result follows.

To establish the results for the mixture model we suppose again that we have the learning set $H=\{(y_1, x_1), (y_2, x_2), ...,(y_N, x_N)\}$ of all samples and define the variables:

$$z_{n,i} = \begin{cases} 1 & \text{if the pair } (y_n, x_n) \text{ comes from the } i \text{ class} \\ 0 & \text{if the pair } (y_n, x_n) \text{ does not come from the } i \text{ class} \end{cases} \quad i = CH, NC \quad (15)$$

then we can write the log-likelihood as:

$$L = \sum_{n=1}^{N} z_{n,CH} \ln(\pi_{CH} p(y_n \mid x_n, CH)) + z_{n,NC} \ln(\pi_{NC} p(y_n \mid x_n, NC)). \quad (16)$$

Assuming the component labels $z_{n,CH}$ and $z_{n,NC}$ as missing data, we can consider the corresponding expected complete data log-likelihood given by:

$$\hat{L} = \sum_{n=1}^{N} R_{n,CH} \ln(\pi_{CH} p(y_n \mid x_n, CH)) + R_{n,NC} \ln(\pi_{NC} p(y_n \mid x_n, NC)) \quad (17)$$

where $R_{n,CH}$ and $R_{n,NC}$ represent the posterior probabilities and are given by:

$$R_{n,i} = \frac{p(y \mid x, i) \pi_i}{p(y \mid x)}, \quad i = NC, CH \quad (18)$$

maximization of (17) with respect to π_{CH}, π_{NC} gives:

$$\tilde{\pi}_i = \frac{1}{N} \sum_{i=1}^{N} R_{n,i}, \quad i = NC, CH \quad (19)$$

similarly, maximization of (17) with respect to μ, A, B gives:

$$\tilde{\mu}_i = \left(\tilde{\mu}_{y,i} - \tilde{A} \tilde{B} \tilde{\mu}_{x,i} \right), \quad \tilde{\mu}_{y,i} = \frac{\sum\limits_{n=1}^{N} R_{n,i} y_n}{N \tilde{\pi}_i}, \quad \tilde{\mu}_{x,i} = \frac{\sum\limits_{n=1}^{N} R_{n,i} x_n}{N \tilde{\pi}_i},$$

$$\tilde{A}_i = V_{r_i,i}, \quad \tilde{B} = V_{r_i,i}^{\mathrm{T}} \tilde{S}_{yx,i} \tilde{S}_{xx,i}^{-1}, \quad (20)$$

$$\tilde{S}_{yx,i} = \frac{\sum\limits_{n=1}^{N} R_{n,i} (y - \tilde{\mu}_{y,i})(x - \tilde{\mu}_{x,i})^{\mathrm{T}}}{N \tilde{\pi}_i}, \quad \tilde{S}_{xx,i} = \frac{\sum\limits_{n=1}^{N} R_{n,i} (x - \tilde{\mu}_{x,i})(x - \tilde{\mu}_{x,i})^{\mathrm{T}}}{N \tilde{\pi}_i}$$

and where the r_i column vectors in the $d \times r_i$ matrix $V_{r_i,i}$ are the eigenvectors corresponding to the r_i largest eigenvalues of $\tilde{S}_{yx,i} \tilde{S}_{xx,i}^{-1} \tilde{S}_{xy,i}$, $i = NC, CH$

In order to update C_i, σ_i^2 we will follow [10]. We will use:

$$\widetilde{S}_i = \frac{\sum_{n=1}^{N} R_{n,i}\left(y_n - \widetilde{\mu}_i - \widetilde{A}_i\widetilde{B}_i x_n\right)\left(y_n - \widetilde{\mu}_i - \widetilde{A}_i\widetilde{B}_i x_n\right)^{\mathrm{T}}}{N\widetilde{\pi}_i}, \widetilde{C}_i = U_{q_i,i}(\Lambda_{q_i,i} - \widetilde{\sigma}_i^2 I) \quad (21)$$

where the q_i column vectors in the $d \times q_i$ matrix U_{q_i} are the eigenvectors of $\widetilde{S}_i$, with corresponding eigenvalues in order of decreasing magnitude in the $q_i \times q_i$ diagonal matrix Λ_{q_i}, and R is an arbitrary $q_i \times q_i$ orthogonal matrix and $\widetilde{\sigma}_i^2$ is defined as:

$$\widetilde{\sigma}_i^2 = \frac{1}{d - q_i} \sum_{j=q_i+1}^{d} \lambda_{j,i} \quad (22)$$

where $\lambda_{q_i+1,i}, ..., \lambda_{d,i}$ are the smallest eigenvalues of $\widetilde{S}_i$. This guarantees an increase in the likelihood [10] and the algorithm continues in an iterative fashion.

References

[1] H. Lillestrand (1972). Techniques for Change Detection. IEEE Transactions on Computers, Vol. 7, pp. 654-659.
[2] D.L. Williams y M.L. Stauffer (1978). Monitoring Gypsy Moth Defoliation by Applying Change Detection Techniques to Landsat Imagery. Processings of the Symposium for Vegetation Damage Assessment, American Society for Photogrammetry , pp. 221-229.
[3] P.J. Howarth and G.M. Wickware (1981). Procedures for Change Detection Using Landsat Digital Data. International Journal of Remote Sensing, Vol. 2, pp. 277-291.
[4] R.F. Nelson (1982). Detecting Forest Canopy Change Due to Insect Activity Using Landsat MSS. Photogrammetric Engineering and Remote Sensing, Vol. 49, pp.1303-1314.
[5] K. Ingram, E. Knapp and J.W. Robinson (1981). Change detection technique development for improved urbanized area delineation, Technical memorandum CSC/TM-81/6087, Computer Sciences Corporation, Silver Springs, Maryland, USA.
[6] G.F. Byrne, P.F. Crapper, and K.K. Mayo (1980). Monitoring Land Cover Change by Principal Component Analysis of Multitemporal Landsat Data. Remote Sensing of Environment, Vol. 10, pp. 175-184.
[7] W.A. Malila (1980). Change Vector Analysis: An Approach for Detecting Forest Change with Landsat. Processings Annual Symposium on Machine Processing of Remotely Sensed Data, IEEE, pp. 326-336.

[8] R. Wiemker, A. Speck, D. Kulbach, H. Spitzer and J. Bienlein (1997). Unsupervised Robust Change Detection on Multispectral Imagery Using Spectral and Spatial Features. Proceedings of the Third International Airborne Remote Sensing Conference and Exhibition, Copenhague, Denmark.
http://kogs-www.informatik.uni-hamburg.de/projects/Censis.html.

[9] G. C. Reinsel and R.P. Velu. (1998) Multivariate Reduced Rank Regression: Theory and Applications. New- York. Springer-Verlag.

[10] M. Tipping and Christopher Bishop. (1997). Mixtures of probabilistic principal component analyzers. Technical Report NCRG/97/003, Neural Computing Research Group, Aston University,
http://citeseer.nj.nec.com/tipping98mixtures.html.

[11] R. O. Duda, P. E. Hart and D. G. Stork, (2001) Pattern Classification, John Wiley & Sons.

[12] C. R. Rao. (1979). Separation theorems for singular values of matrices and their applications in multivariate analysis. J. Multivariate Analysis, 3, pp. 141-160.

Petrographic Classification at the Macroscopic Scale Using a Mathematical Morphology Based Approach

Pedro Pina and Teresa Barata

CVRM / Geo-Systems Centre, Instituto Superior Técnico
Av. Rovisco Pais, 1049-001 Lisboa, Portugal
{ppina,tbarata}@alfa.ist.utl.pt

Abstract. A novel methodology for the automatic classification of the different textural classes that constitute a rock at the macroscopic scale is presented in this paper. The methodology starts with the segmentation of elementary textural units of the image followed by their classification, whose feature space partition results from the geometric modelling of the training sets. This approach uses mainly mathematical morphology operators and is tested with images of macroscopic polished surfaces of 14 types of portuguese grey granites.

1   Introduction

Quantitative assessment of petrography is an essential task in geosciences as it provides fundamental information to the successful interpretation of the genesis of a rock. In the basis of petrography is the determination of mineral phases that normally are associated to other features of spatial and structural nature. Classic manual techniques have been used intensively for petrographic quantifications for years, but the limitation and subjectivity introduced by the expert/operator in interpreting the information extracted has not allowed, in most of the cases, to obtain important statistics of the rocks. The possibility of disposing of an automatic way of performing this routinous work has always been waited with expectation, specially when the possibility of digitising images resulting from the great development of informatics in the 1960-70 decades has given to birth and has strongly pushed the development of several digital analysis methods in its theoretical concepts. Its early application in proposing several solutions in geosciences (in porous media [7], for computing grain size distributions [5] or in the characterisation of iron ores [11], just to name a few examples)), has created a false expectation, suggesting that solutions to the problems would not be difficult tasks to accomplish within a short period of time. But the intrinsic complexity of "geological" images, allied to the fact that only binary (black and white) images (in the 1960s) or grey level images (in the 1970s) with low spatial discretisation could be processed by that time, has shown a rather different picture. Only a few years later, in the 1980s, with the possibility of acquiring digital images with higher spatial and spectral resolutions, the easier access to computers and, mainly, due to some maturity

F.J. Perales et al. (Eds.): IbPRIA 2003, LNCS 2652, pp. 758-765, 2003.
© Springer-Verlag Berlin Heidelberg 2003

reached by the digital image analysis methods in its theoretical formalisms [11][12], an inversion of this tendency has occurred. As referred by Fortey [4] and Russ [11], image analysis started to be used for petrographic studies with a certain frequency mainly in microscopic analysis (in optical microscopy but specially in scanning microscopy associated to microprobe analysis) for diverse applications with different degrees of success, existing abundant publications on the subject (good review on [9]). On the contrary, the quantitative assessment at hand-specimen size has not received great attention. Some recent studies have proposed some methodologies to classify mineral phases in igneous rocks [6] with very interesting results but also with evident difficulties of generalisation. The possibility of quantifying automatically other features, after the identification of its components, namely the ones related to neighbourhood aspects (to quantify for instance the contacts between different mineral phases), orientation or dispersion of phases (important issue, for instance, in marbles) or structural aspects exhibited by several rocks are also open fields waiting for important scientific contributions.

2   Proposed Methodological Approach

Mathematical Morphology is a theory used in digital image analysis that was created in the middle 1960's by Georges Matheron and Jean Serra in the École des Mines de Paris. Although its initial purpose was related to an application in porous media [7], the further developments since then have permitted to construct a solid theoretical framework [11] acting and contributing to the several chapters of digital image analysis and used in several application fields (a recent review can be consulted in [12]). In particular, in segmentation procedures emerge, among others, the watershed and the top-hat transforms, original creations of S. Beucher/Ch. Lantuéjoul [2] and F. Meyer [8], respectively. The direct use of these transforms together with the construction of other more elaborated ones using morphological elementary operators has shown to be a good option to exploit when geometrical or textural features of images are to be considered, like several published studies in several application areas have demonstrated.

The developed methodological approach is mainly based on mathematical morphology operators and is performed within two main phases: in the first one the elementary units of the image are defined by morphological texture segmentation, while in the second one a minerals class is assigned to these segmented units.

2.1   Segmentation of Elementary Textural Units

The watershed transform, by considering a grey level image as a topographic surface, consists of identifying the catchment basins that are associated to each grey level minimum. This transform has been enriched with several contributions over the years (major contributions described in [3] and good synthesis in [12]) that has become a powerful and popular segmentation tool. Anyhow, the success of its application is, in the majority of situations, directly linked to the choice of good markers, i.e., to the selection of markers that indicate the regions of interest to delineate.

The sequence used to segment the elementary textural units of the granites follows a quite standard procedure: the markers associated to each catchment basin are obtained on the gradient image and are used to compute the watershed transform, not over the gradient image itself but over the initial one. The markers X consist of the minima *min* of the gradient *grad* of the initial image f, since these are the regions of the image without transitions between the mineralogical phases, whether the darkness or lightness degree exhibited. This sequence is summed up in the following equation:

$$X = WSH_{\min(grad(f))}(f) \tag{1}$$

An example is presented in figure 1 applied to the intensity image of a sample of *COR-Branco Coral* granite, where an initial smoothing by median was previously performed to filter the small dimension peaks/valleys. The catchment basins obtained constitute now the elementary textural units to classify.

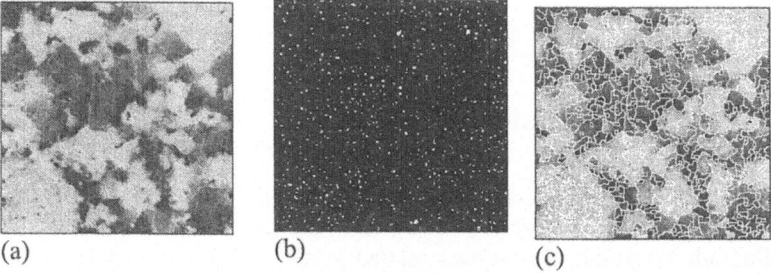

(a)   (b)   (c)

Fig. 1. Segmentation sequence of elementary textural elements: (a) intensity image of *COR-Branco Coral* granite; (b) minima of the gradient and (c) watershed lines superimposed to initial image

2.2   Classification of the Segmented Textural Elements

In this process guided by the segmentation, the basins detected by the watershed transform are going to be used as the points of the clouds of the training sets for the classification procedure. Therefore, each catchment basin is considered as an elementary textural unit of the image and is represented by the average value of the points of the variable contained within it.

For this case study on Portuguese granites, their colourless type permits to work with a reduced number of variables. Some previous empirical tests have shown that it is possible to work with only two variables: between the several possible combinations of RGB and HIS channels, the variables intensity (I) and hue (H) were the ones chosen, since they have shown a higher discriminator power. The catchment basins obtained in figure 1, are now represented for hue and intensity images, by the average grey level value of the pixels contained inside them (see figure 2).

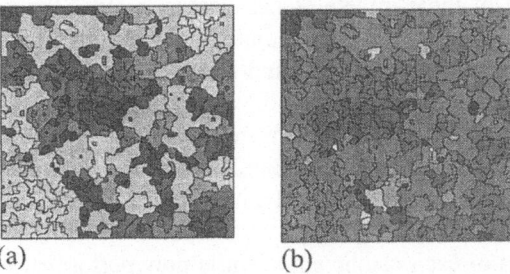

(a)   (b)

Fig. 2. Average attribute of each basin for: (a) intensity and (b) hue images

The definition of the training sets of points for each mineralogical class is based on these images. Since the delimitation of the regions corresponding to each mineralogical class is already done, the manual analysis by the user/expert allows classifying each catchment basin, whose projection is performed in the I-H feature space. The granites are igneous rocks compulsory constituted by quartz and feldspars and also by other ancillary minerals, very often by micas (biotite or/and muscovite) among other less common minerals. The quartz and feldspar minerals occur in large quantities, the micas in much smaller quantities while the other minerals in very low percentages. For the types and samples of granites under study, from a previous analysis it was decided to consider only three mineralogical classes: feldspar, quartz and biotite. Thus, the projection in I-H feature space for each class is presented in figure 3a-c. Although, there exists an important separability between the different classes there exists also a certain degree of overlapping. It was decided to model the geometry of these clouds of points before classifying the elementary textural units.

The methodology used here follows the one previous developed to classify several land-use classes in multispectral satellite images [1], where a significant increase in the classification rates, compared to traditional approaches, was obtained. It consists on modelling the geometry of the training sets in feature space, obtaining at the end of the procedure decision regions that respect the geometric features, namely, size, shape and orientation, of the initial training sets. The methodology that can be consulted in [1] for the details, is summed up in the following six main steps:

(i)   Construction of strong nucleus for each class in feature space;

(ii) Construction of structuring elements that summarise the features of each class (size, shape and orientation);

(iii) Construction of individual distance functions with the structuring elements;

(iv) Construction of a global distance function for all classes;

(v)   Computation of the watershed transform over the global distance function using the nuclei of the classes as markers: the watershed lines obtained correspond to the borders of the decision regions between the different classes;

(vi) Classification of the elementary textural elements of the images into one of the classes previously defined.

The illustration of its application is shown with the same type of granite (COR-Branco Coral). Each basin resulting from the image of the watershed is then classified by an expert in one of three mineralogical classes: biotite (the darker one), feldspar (the lighter one) and quartz (the intermediate one). The training sets of these classes were constructed with the intensity (I) and hue (H) images, being each basin of the watershed in both images substituted by the average grey level of the points that constitute it. This way, three training sets were constructed: biotite (figure 3a), quartz (figure 3b) and feldspar (figure 3c). The creation of strong nuclei (step (i)) by alternate closings and openings is presented in figure 3d. The resulting space partition (steps (ii) to (vi)) is obtained in figure 3e.

The classification of each catchment basin is now performed in one of the classes according to the decision region where its point falls in the feature space. The classification of the elements of the image that has been used as example in this paper is presented in figure 4a. The watershed or crest lines are after that assigned to the most frequent class in its neighbourhood (figure 4b).

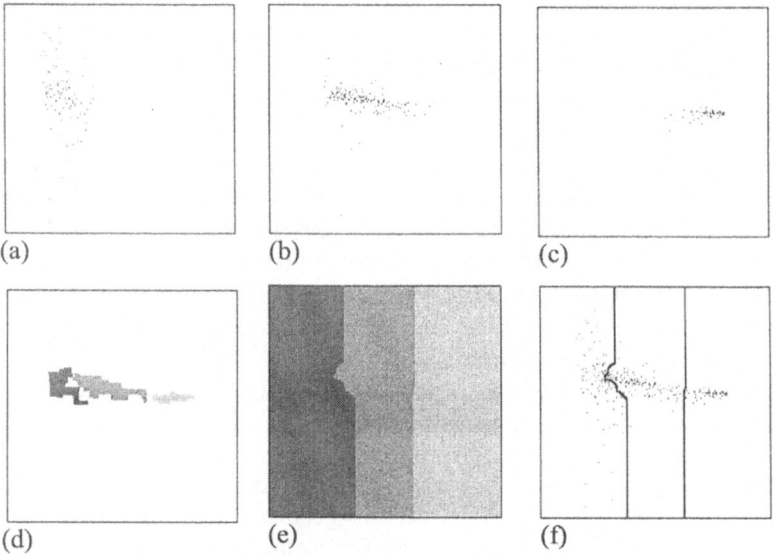

Fig. 3. Geometric modelling in intensity (horizontal axis)-hue (vertical axis) feature space (the origin is located at the bottom left corner): (a) biotite training set; (b) quartz training set; (c) feldspar training set; (d) strong clusters; (e) decision regions; (f) decision region borders and initial training sets

3   Application to Granites at the Macroscopic Scale

The developed process was applied to a set of 14 types of portuguese grey granites. Although this commercial label includes the real grey types, it also includes other similar colourless types (bluish, whitish and yellowish).

The methodology was applied to several samples of each type of granite (the slabs of 15 cm x 15 cm were digitized with a spatial resolution of 150 dpi): 25% of them were chosen as training sets while 15% as testing sets. The segmentation of unitary elements and their respective classification by the proposed methodology (examples for each type of granite studied are presented in Fig. 5) has lead to very good results, which are presented in Table 1. The novel approach is indicated by MM and the results refer to average values obtained from the study of several samples. Simultaneously, the same samples were classified with other common methods (minimum distance (MD) and maximum likelihood (ML)) whose results are also presented in Table 1.

The main conclusions to retain are the following:

- MM is the method that clearly gives the best classification results for all the types of granites;

Although the choice of points to create the clouds of the training sets is, like many authors defend, a crucial factor for obtaining good classification rates, the posterior shape modelling of the training sets introduces an evident improvement.

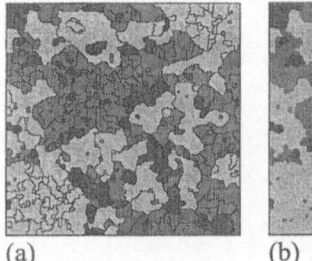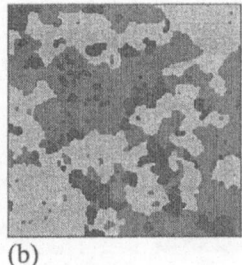

(a)   (b)

Fig. 4. Classified image: (a) with watershed lines (in black) and (b) with watershed lines assigned to one of the mineralogical classes

Table 1. Global classification rates (% of well classified textural elements, weighted by their area) using the methods: MD-Minimum distance; ML-Maximum Likelihood; MM-Mathematical Morphology

Type of granite	Classification Method		
	MD	ML	MM
ALM (Branco Almeida)	76.29	31.12	96.88
ANT (Branco Antas)	46.48	40.89	94.79
ARI (Branco Ariz)	73.82	55.12	96.87
ARIC (Cinzento Ariz)	43.64	44.30	97.86
AZU (Azulália)	08.37	27.21	97.67
CAR (Branco Caravela)	37.89	17.82	95.03
COR (Branco Coral)	59.60	33.72	97.44
EUL (Cinzento Sta. Eulália)	63.04	50.24	98.87
EVO (Cinzento Évora)	51.99	36.00	97.74
FAV (Favaco)	48.51	48.30	97.17
JAN (Jané)	07.69	21.80	96.73
SAL (Pedras Salgadas)	07.64	62.65	97.54
SPI (SPI)	36.40	47.73	96.10
VIM (Branco Vimieiro)	78.05	87.57	97.63

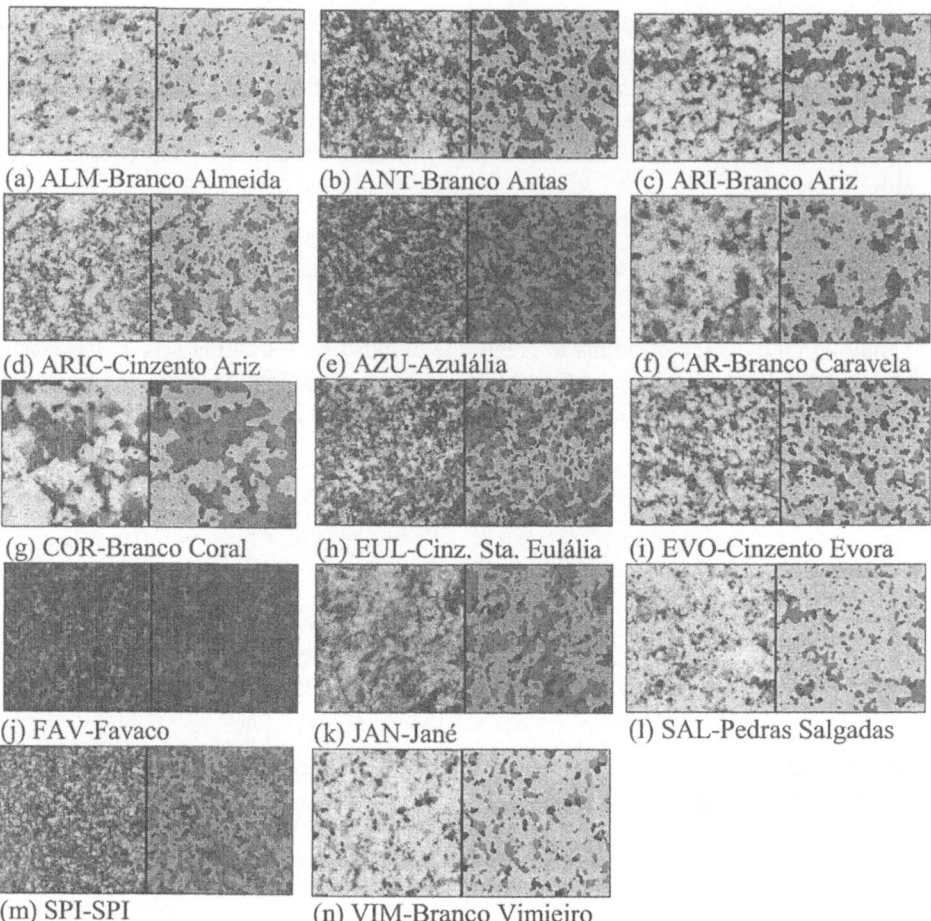

Fig. 5. Classification of the 14 types of granites (each pair represents the initial (left) and classified (right) images)

4   Conclusions

A mathematical morphology based methodology is applied in this paper to the segmentation/classification of mineralogical phases of ornamental stones at the macroscopic scale with success. These results are very important for the description of the granites, as it provide a better and more accurate characterisation, namely, through their size, shape, contact and neighbourhood features. The possibility of extracting these parameters in an automatic way gives the possibility to construct the variation intervals of the aesthetic features of an ornamental stone in an objective (quantitative) way. Moreover, these parameters will have a valuable contribution to the development of methodologies to simulate textures since it is possible to quantify the variation of textural aesthetic features within the same type of stone.

Acknowledgements

This paper has been developed in the frame of the project "Simulation of ornamental stones textures using granulometrical features (SILEX)" (POCTI/ECM/37998/2001) funded by *FCT – Fundação para a Ciência e a Tecnologia*.

References

[1] Barata, T., Pina, P.: Construction of decision region borders by geometric modelling of the training sets. Application to land cover classes in remotely sensed images. In: Talbot, H. & Beare, R. (eds.), Mathematical Morphology, CSIRO Publishing, Sydney (2002) 147-156

[2] Beucher, S., Lantuéjoul, Ch.: Use of watersheds in contour detection, Proc. Int. Work. Image Processing, Real Time Edge & Motion Detection-Estimation, Rennes (1979) 12 pp

[3] Beucher S., Meyer F.: The morphological approach to segmentation: The watershed transformation, In: Dougherty, E. (ed): Mathematical morphology in image processing, Marcel Dekker, New York (1993) 433-482

[4] Fortey, N.: Image analysis in mineralogy and petrology, Mineral. Mag., 59(395) (1995) 177-179

[5] Haas A., Matheron, G., Serra, J.: Morphologie mathématique et granulometries en place, Annales des Mines XI (1967) 734-753

[6] Marschallinger, R.: Automatic mineral classification in the macroscopic scale, Computers & Geosciences, 23(1) (1997) 119-26

[7] Matheron, G.: Éléments pour une théorie des milieux poreux, Masson, Paris (1967)

[8] Meyer, F.,: Cytologie quantitative et morphologie mathématique, Thèse de doctorat, ENSMP, Paris (1979)

[9] Russ, J.C.: Computer-assisted microscopy-The measurement and analysis of images, Plenum Press, NYC (1990)

[10] Russ, J.C.: The handbook of image processing, CRC Press & Springer, Boca Raton & Heildelberg (1999)

[11] Serra, J.: Image analysis and mathematical morphology, Academic Press, London (1982)

[12] Soille, P.: Morphological image analysis. Principles and applications, 2nd edition, Springer, Berlin (2003)

On the Efficiency of Luminance-Based Palette Reordering of Color-Quantized Images

Armando J. Pinho[1] and António J. R. Neves[2]

[1] Dep. Electrónica e Telecomunicações
IEETA, University of Aveiro
3810–193 Aveiro, Portugal
ap@det.ua.pt
[2] IEETA, University of Aveiro
3810–193 Aveiro, Portugal
an@ieeta.pt

Abstract. Luminance-based palette reordering is often considered less efficient than other more complex approaches, in what concerns improving the compression of color-indexed images. In this paper, we provide experimental evidence that, for color-quantized natural images, this may not be always the case. In fact, we show that, for dithered images with 128 colors or more, luminance-based reordering outperforms other more complex methods.

1 Introduction

Traditionally, most color-quantized images have been encoded according to the well-known and widely used Graphical Interchange Format[1] (GIF). As part of this format there is a coding engine based on the Lempel-Ziv-Welch (LZW) compression algorithm [1], a variant of one of the seminal algorithms developed by Ziv and Lempel [2], commonly known as LZ78. LZW is intrinsically a compression technique for one-dimensional sequences of symbols and, therefore, might not be particularly tailored for exploiting the two-dimensional dependencies that characterize image data.

Two-dimensional approaches specifically designed for coding color-indexed images have been proposed. Among them we find methods such as PWC [3], EIDAC [4], RAPP [5] or the method recently proposed by Chen *et al.* [6]. On the other hand, it is frequently convenient to address the problem of coding color-quantized images under the framework of general purpose coding techniques, such as JPEG-LS [7, 8] or lossless JPEG 2000 [9, 10].

Color-indexed images are represented by a matrix of indexes (the index image) and by a color-map or palette. The indexes in the matrix point to positions in the color-map and, therefore, establish the colors of the corresponding pixels. For a particular image, the mapping between index values and colors (typically, RGB triplets) is not unique — it can be arbitrarily permuted, as long

---

[1] http://pds-geophys.wustl.edu/info/gif.txt.

F.J. Perales et al. (Eds.): IbPRIA 2003, LNCS 2652, pp. 766–772, 2003.

as the corresponding index image is changed accordingly. However, for most continuous-tone image coding techniques these alternative representations are generally not equivalent, having sometimes a dramatic impact on the compression performance.

With the aim of minimizing this drawback several preprocessing techniques have been proposed. Basically, they rely on finding a suitable reordering of the color table in such a way that the corresponding image of indexes becomes more amenable to compression. These preprocessing techniques have the advantage of not requiring post-processing and of being cost-less in terms of side information. However, if the optimal configuration is sought, then the computational complexity involved can be high (for M colors, $M!$ configurations have to be tested). Clearly, exhaustive search is impractical for most of the interesting cases, which motivated several sub-optimal, lower complexity, proposals.

In this paper, we provide a comparison of three palette reordering methods in what concerns their ability to improve compression rates. Two standard image compression techniques are used to perform this evaluation: JPEG-LS and lossless JPEG 2000. Our study addresses a particular class of images (color-quantized natural images, with and without dithering), and intends to show that, for this class of color-indexed images, a simple luminance-based palette reordering approach can provide comparable or better results than other more complex approaches.

2   Palette Reordering for Improving Compression

The problem of reordering a color map for better fitting the coding model of general purpose image coding techniques is not a trivial task, due to the combinatorial nature of the problem [11]. Several sub-optimal solutions have been proposed, based on approximated solutions to the traveling salesman problem [12, 13], on the maximization of the compression performance through a greedy index assignment [14], on greedy pairwise merging heuristics [11], or on color reordering by luminance [15].

In this paper, we compare the performance of three of these methods in what concerns their ability to improve compression: (1) the pairwise merging heuristic proposed by Memon *et al.*, (2) the greedy index assignment proposed by Zeng *et al.* and (3) luminance-based reordering.

The method proposed by Zeng *et al.* [14] starts by finding the symbol that is most frequently located adjacent to other symbols ($S_{\max}$), i.e., the symbol that most contributes to transitions. This symbol is put into a symbol pool and, right next to it, the symbol that is most frequently found adjacent to $S_{\max}$. New symbols are added to the symbol pool only from the left or right end position. A particular symbol S_i is chosen to integrate the pool if it is the one among the unassigned symbols that maximizes

$$D_i = \sum_{j=0}^{n-1} w_{n,j} C(S_i, L_j)$$

where $C(S_i, S_j)$ denotes the number of occurrences, measured on the initial index image, corresponding to pixels with symbol S_i spatially adjacent to pixels with symbol S_j, and where $w_{n,j}$ are some appropriate weights. The summation is performed over all symbols L_j already located in the symbol pool. Moreover, it is suggested in [14] that setting

$$w_{n,j} = \log_2(1 + 1/d_{n,j})$$

is usually a good choice, where $d_{n,j}$ corresponds to the physical distance between the current end position of the pool and the position of symbol L_j.

Memon et al. formulated the problem of palette reordering under the framework of linear predictive coding [11]. In that context, the objective is to minimize the zero-order entropy of the prediction residuals, a goal that can be very difficult to achieve. However, they noticed that, for image data, the prediction residuals are usually well modeled by a Laplacian distribution and that, in this case, minimizing the absolute sum of the of the prediction residuals leads to the minimization of the zero-order entropy. For the case of a first-order prediction scheme, the absolute sum of the prediction residuals reduces to

$$E = \sum_{i=0}^{M-1} \sum_{j=0}^{M-1} N(i,j)|i - j|$$

where $N(i, j)$ denotes the number of times index i is used as the predicted value for a pixel whose color is indexed by j (note that, according to this definition, generally we have $N(i, j) \neq N(j, i)$), and M denotes the number of colors of the image. The problem of finding the bijection that minimizes E can be formulated as the optimization version of the optimal linear ordering problem, which is known to be NP-complete [11].

One of the heuristics proposed by Memon et al. for finding good solutions to the above stated problem is the so-called pairwise merge heuristic. Essentially, it is based on repeatedly merging ordered sets of colors until obtaining a single (reordered) set. Initially, each color is assigned to a different set. Then, the two sets, S_a and S_b, maximizing

$$\sum_{i \in S_a} \sum_{j \in S_b} (N(i,j) + N(j,i))|i - j|$$

are merged together. This procedure should be repeated until having a single set. To alleviate the computational burden involved in selecting the best way of merging the two sets, only a limited number of possibilities are generally tested [11].

Palette reordering based on luminance [15] is the simplest of the three methods addressed in this paper, since it only requires sorting the colors according to its luminance. Luminance is usually computed according to

$$Y = 0.299R + 0.587G + 0.114B,$$

where Y denotes the luminance, and R, G and B the intensities of the red, green and blue components, respectively.

3   Experimental Results

In this section, we present experimental results based on the set of the 23 "kodak" color images[2]. These are 768 × 512 true color images from which we generated additional sets with resolutions 384 × 256 and 192 × 128. Color quantization was then applied, both with and without Floyd-Steinberg color dithering, creating images with 256, 128 and 64 colors. Image manipulations have been performed using version 1.2.3 of the "*Gimp*" program.[3]

Table 1. Each row of this table shows average JPEG 2000 lossless compression results, in bits per pixel, concerning a particular instance of the "kodak" image set. Compression results obtained directly from the unsorted index images and obtained using the GIF format are also given for reference. The best values are shown in **boldface**

JPEG 2000

Image size	Colors	Dither	GIF	Unsorted	Zeng	Memon	Luminance
192 × 128	64	No	3.965	4.826	**3.819**	3.896	4.002
	128		5.100	6.032	**4.864**	4.905	4.993
	256		6.402	7.280	6.138	6.089	**6.086**
	64	Yes	4.371	5.306	**4.242**	4.311	4.316
	128		5.565	6.445	5.314	5.416	**5.254**
	256		6.880	7.609	6.491	6.488	**6.282**
384 × 256	64	No	3.498	4.476	**3.389**	3.457	3.674
	128		4.528	5.657	**4.422**	4.457	4.608
	256		5.695	6.824	5.574	**5.540**	5.611
	64	Yes	**3.924**	5.016	3.934	4.001	4.034
	128		4.994	6.129	4.955	4.966	**4.902**
	256		6.194	7.212	6.021	5.917	**5.833**
768 × 512	64	No	3.270	4.208	**3.147**	3.203	3.400
	128		4.277	5.359	4.203	**4.144**	4.309
	256		5.386	6.575	5.281	**5.229**	5.275
	64	Yes	**3.730**	4.845	3.808	3.892	3.816
	128		4.746	5.902	4.755	4.770	**4.650**
	256		5.941	7.035	5.835	5.709	**5.538**

---

[2] These images can be obtained from http://www.cipr.rpi.edu/resource/stills/kodak.html.

[3] http://www.gimp.org.

Table 2. Each row of this table shows average JPEG-LS lossless compression results, in bits per pixel, concerning a particular instance of the "kodak" image set. Compression results obtained directly from the unsorted index images and obtained using the GIF format are also given for reference. The best values are shown in **boldface**

JPEG-LS

Image size	Colors	Dither	GIF	Unsorted	Zeng	Memon	Luminance
192 × 128	64	No	3.965	4.219	**3.346**	3.363	3.496
	128		5.100	5.488	4.421	**4.371**	4.509
	256		6.402	6.769	5.672	**5.526**	5.599
	64	Yes	4.371	4.899	**3.901**	3.943	3.945
	128		5.565	6.104	5.013	5.037	**4.902**
	256		6.880	7.330	6.177	6.045	**5.919**
384 × 256	64	No	3.498	3.899	**2.997**	3.009	3.229
	128		4.528	5.090	4.000	**3.983**	4.160
	256		5.695	6.286	5.138	**5.015**	5.161
	64	Yes	3.924	4.666	**3.655**	3.677	3.731
	128		4.994	5.805	4.682	4.646	**4.602**
	256		6.194	6.906	5.724	5.548	**5.520**
768 × 512	64	No	3.270	3.661	**2.804**	2.812	3.002
	128		4.277	4.839	3.844	**3.722**	3.926
	256		5.386	6.078	4.908	**4.765**	4.898
	64	Yes	3.730	4.532	3.591	3.624	**3.556**
	128		4.746	5.621	4.537	4.501	**4.399**
	256		5.941	6.765	5.596	5.389	**5.289**

Table 1 shows JPEG 2000 lossless compression[4] results of the reordered index images, using Zeng's method[5], Memon's method[6] and the luminance-based approach. Table 2 displays the corresponding results when a JPEG-LS codec is used[7]

Each row of the tables shows average compression results, in bits per pixel, concerning a particular instance of the "kodak" image set. Besides the size of the encoded index image, the (uncompressed) size of the color table is also accounted in the results shown. For reference, we also include compression results using directly the (unsorted) index images and also the GIF file format.

Observing Tables 1 and 2 it can be seen that, for images with dithering and 128 or more colors, the luminance-based palette reordering technique provides

---

[4] Compression was obtained using the JasPer 1.700.2 JPEG 2000 codec (http://www.ece.uvic.ca/~mdadams/jasper).

[5] The implementation of this algorithm was provided by the authors.

[6] We used an implementation of this technique included in a software package developed by Battiato *et al.*

[7] Compression was obtained using the SPMG / JPEG-LS V.2.2 codec (ftp://spmg.ece.ubc.ca/pub/jpeg-ls/ver-2.2/).

the best results, being the second best in a number of other situations. It can also be observed that Memon's method generally provides better results in images with 128 colors or more, whereas Zeng's method seems to work better for images with 128 colors or less.

4 Conclusions

Palette reordering is a very effective approach for improving the compression performance of general purpose image coding techniques, such as lossless JPEG 2000 or JPEG-LS, on color-indexed images. In this paper, we provided experimental results showing the compression improvements provided by three palette reordering approaches — Zeng's method, Memon's method and the luminance-based method — under the context of color-quantized natural images with and without dithering.

Luminance-based palette reordering is often considered inefficient, when compared to other more complex approaches. However, we provided experimental evidence showing that this may not be always the case. In fact, for dithered images with 128 or more colors it outperforms the other more complex methods, being very competitive in a number of other cases, specially if we take into account its simplicity. The remaining cases are divided almost evenly among Zeng's and Memon's methods, with a tendency for a better performance of Zeng's method in images having 128 colors or less, and for Memon's method in images with 128 colors or more.

Acknowledgement

The authors would like to thank Dr. W. Zeng and Dr. S. Battiato for providing software which was a great help for performing the experimental part of this work.

References

[1] T. A. Welch, A technique for high-performance data compression, IEEE Computer 17 (6) (1984) 8–19.

[2] J. Ziv, A. Lempel, Compression of individual sequences via variable-rate coding, IEEE Trans. on Information Theory 24 (5) (1978) 530–536.

[3] P. J. Ausbeck Jr., The piecewise-constant image model, Proceedings of the IEEE 88 (11) (2000) 1779–1789.

[4] Y. Yoo, Y. G. Kwon, A. Ortega, Embedded image-domain compression using context models, in: Proc. of the 6th IEEE Int. Conf. on Image Processing, ICIP-99, Vol. I, Kobe, Japan, 1999, pp. 477–481.

[5] V. Ratnakar, RAPP: Lossless image compression with runs of adaptive pixel patterns, in: Proc. of the 32nd Asilomar Conf. on Signals, Systems, and Computers, 1998, Vol. 2, 1998, pp. 1251–1255.

[6] X. Chen, S. Kwong, J.-F. Feng, A new compression scheme for color-quantized images, IEEE Trans. on Circuits and Systems for Video Technology 12 (10) (2002) 904–908.

[7] ISO/IEC 14495–1 and ITU Recommendation T.87, Information technology - Lossless and near-lossless compression of continuous-tone still images (1999).

[8] M. J. Weinberger, G. Seroussi, G. Sapiro, The LOCO-I lossless image compression algorithm: principles and standardization into JPEG-LS, IEEE Trans. on Image Processing 9 (8) (2000) 1309–1324.

[9] ISO/IEC International Standard 15444–1, ITU-T Recommendation T.800, Information technology - JPEG 2000 image coding system (2000).

[10] A. Skodras, C. Christopoulos, T. Ebrahimi, The JPEG 2000 still image compression standard, IEEE Signal Processing Magazine 18 (5) (2001) 36–58.

[11] N. D. Memon, A. Venkateswaran, On ordering color maps for lossless predictive coding, IEEE Trans. on Image Processing 5 (5) (1996) 1522–1527.

[12] S. Battiato, G. Gallo, G. Impoco, F. Stanco, A color reindexing algorithm for lossless compression of digital images, in: Proc. of the IEEE Spring Conf. on Computer Graphics, Budmerice, Slovakia, 2001, pp. 104–108.

[13] A. Spira, D. Malah, Improved lossless compression of color-mapped images by an approximate solution of the traveling salesman problem, in: Proc. of the IEEE Int. Conf. on Acoustics, Speech, and Signal Processing, ICASSP-2001, Vol. III, Salt Lake City, UT, 2001, pp. 1797–1800.

[14] W. Zeng, J. Li, S. Lei, An efficient color re-indexing scheme for palette-based compression, in: Proc. of the 7th IEEE Int. Conf. on Image Processing, ICIP-2000, Vol. III, Vancouver, Canada, 2000, pp. 476–479.

[15] A. Zaccarin, B. Liu, A novel approach for coding color quantized images, IEEE Trans. on Image Processing 2 (4) (1993) 442–453.

Feature-Driven Recognition of Music Styles

Pedro J. Ponce de León and José M. Iñesta

Departamento de Lenguajes y Sistemas Informáticos
Universidad de Alicante
Ap. 99, E-03080 Alicante, Spain
{pierre,inesta}@dlsi.ua.es

Abstract. In this paper the capability of using self-organising neural maps (SOM) as music style classifiers of musical fragments is studied. From MIDI files, the monophonic melody track is extracted and cut into fragments of equal length. From these sequences, melodic, harmonic, and rhythmic numerical descriptors are computed and presented to the SOM. Their performance is analysed in terms of separability in different music classes from the activations of the map, obtaining different degrees of success for classical and jazz music. This scheme has a number of applications like indexing and selecting musical databases or the evaluation of style-specific automatic composition systems.

Keywords: Multimedia applications, computer music, self-organising maps, feature selection, content-based information retrieval.

1 Introduction

The automatic machine learning and pattern recognition techniques, successfully employed in other fields, can be also applied in music analysis. One of the tasks that can be posed is the modelization of the music style. Immediate applications are the classification, indexation and content-based search in digital music libraries, where digitised (MP3), sequenced (MIDI) or structurally represented (XML) music can be found. The computer could be trained in the user musical taste in order to look for that kind of music over large musical databases. Such a model could also be used in cooperation with automatic composition algorithms to guide this process according to a stylistic profile provided by the user.

Our aim is to develop a system able to distinguish musical styles from a symbolic representation of a melody using musicological features: melodic, harmonic and rhytmic ones. Our working hypothesis is that melodies from a same musical genre may share some common features that permits to assign a musical style to them. For testing our approach, we have initially chosen two music styles, jazz and classical, for our experiments. We will also investigate whether such a representation by itself has enough information to achieve this goal or, on the contrary, also timbric information has to be included for that purpose.

The key point of this work is to test the ability of self-organising maps (SOM) [1], to automatically perform this task. SOM are neural methods able to

F.J. Perales et al. (Eds.): IbPRIA 2003, LNCS 2652, pp. 773–781, 2003.

obtain approximate projections of high-dimensional data distributions in low-dimensional spaces, usually bidimensional. With the map, different clusters in the input data can be located. These clusters can be usually semantically labelled to characterise the training data and also hopefully future new inputs.

1.1   Related Work

A number of recent papers explore the capabilities of SOM to analyse and classify music data. Rauber and Frühwirth [2] pose the problem of organising music digital libraries according to sound features of musical themes, in such a way that similar themes are clustered, performing a content-based classification of the sounds. Whitman and Flake [3] present a system based on neural nets and support vector machines, able to classify an audio fragment into a given list of sources or artists. Also in [4], the authors describe a neural system to recognise music types from sound inputs. In [5] the authors present a hierarchical SOM able to analyse time series of musical events and then discriminate those events in a different musical context. In the work by Thom [6] pitch histograms (measured in semitones relative to the tonal pitch and independent of the octave) are used to describe blues fragments of the saxophonist Charlie Parker. The pitch frequencies are used to train a SOM. Also pitch histograms and SOM are used in [7] for musicological analysis of folk songs.

These works pose the problem of music analysis and recognition using either digital sound files or symbolic representations as input. The approach we propose here is to use the symbolic representation of music that will be analysed to provide melodic, harmonic and rhythmic descriptors as input to the SOM (see Fig. 1) for classification of musical fragments into a, initially reduced, set of styles. We use standard MIDI files as the source of monophonic melodies.

2   Methodology

The monophonic melodies are isolated from the rest of the musical content in the MIDI files. This way we get a sequence of musical events that can be either notes or silences. Other kind of MIDI events are filtered out. Each note can take a value from 0 to 127 (the pitch) and the duration is the distance in pulses from the event that onsets the sound of a note to the finishing event.

Here we will deal only with melodies written in 4/4. In order to have more restricted data, fragments of 8 bars are taken (enough to get a good sense of the melodic phrase in the context of a 4/4 signature). For this, each melody sequence has been cut into fragments of such duration.

We have chosen a vector of musical descriptors of the melodies as the input for the SOM, instead of the explicit representation of the melodies. Thus, a description model is needed. Firstly, three groups of features are extracted: melodic, harmonic and rhythmic properties. Then, from this initial set of features a selection procedure will be performed based on their values for the weight vectors

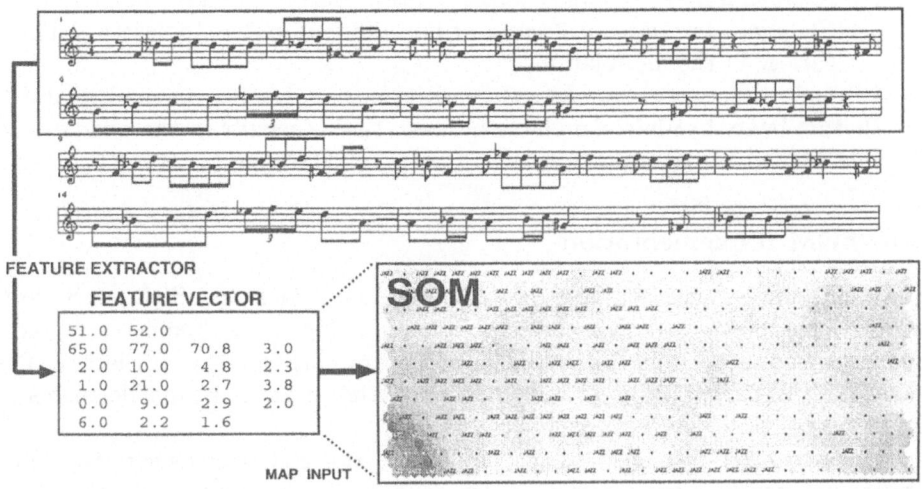

Fig. 1. Structure of the system: musical descriptors are computed from a window 8-bar wide and provided to the SOM for training and classification. Once trained, a style label is assigned to the units. During classification, the label of the winning unit provides the style to which the music fragment belongs to. This example is based on the Charlie Parker's jazz piece "Dexterity"

of the trained SOM. This way, some reduced models have been constructed and their classification ability tested.

The features are computed using a time resolution of $Q = 48$ pulses per bar[1]. The initial set of 22 musical descriptors is:

- Overall descriptors:
  - Number of notes and number of silences in the fragment.
- Pitch descriptors:
  - Lowest, highest (provide information about the pitch range of the melody), average, and standard deviation (provide information about how the notes are distributed in the score).
- Note duration descriptors (these descriptors are measured in pulses):
  - Minimum, maximum, average, and standard deviation.
- Silence duration descriptors (in pulses):
  - Minimum, maximum, average, and standard deviation.
- Interval descriptors (distance in pitch between two consecutive notes):
  - Minimum, maximum, average, and standard deviation.
- Harmonic descriptors:
  - *Number of non diatonic notes.* An indication of frequent excursions outside tonality (extracted from the MIDI file) or modulations.

---

[1] This is call quantisation. $Q = 48$ means that if a bar is composed of 4 times, each time can be divided, at most, into 12 pulses.

- *Average degree[2] of non diatonic notes*. Describes the kind of excursions.
- *Standard deviation of degrees of non diatonic notes*. Indicates a higher variety in the modulations.
- Rhytmic descriptor: *number of syncopations*: notes not beginning at the rhythm beats but in some places between them (usually in the middle) and that extend across beats.

2.1 SOM Implementation

For SOM implementation and graphic representations the SOM_PAK software [8] has been used. For the experiments, a hexagonal geometry for unit connections and a bubble neighbourhood for training have been selected. The value for this neighbourhood is equal for all the units in it and decreases as a function of time.

The maps are displayed using the U-map representation, where the units are represented by hexagons with a dot or label in their centre. The grey level of unlabelled hexagons represents the distance between neighbour units (the clearer the closer they are). For the labelled units is an average of the neighbour distances. This way, clear zones are clusters of units, sharing similar weight vectors. The labels are a result of calibrating the map with a series of test samples and indicate the class of samples that activates more times each unit.

2.2 Feature Selection Procedure

The utilized features have been designed according to those used in musicological studies but there is no theoretical support for them. We have devised a selection procedure in order to keep those descriptors that actually contribute to make the classification. The procedure is based on the values for the features in the weight vectors of the trained SOMs. The maps are trained and labelled (calibrated) in an unsupervised manner (see Fig 2-a for an example. We try to find which descriptors provide more useful information for the classification. Some descriptor values for the weight vectors correlate better than others with the label distribution in the map. It is reasonable to consider that these descriptors contribute more to achieve a good separation between classes. See Fig. 2-b and 2-c for descriptor planes that correlate and that do not with the class labels.

Consider that the N descriptors are random variables $\{x_i\}_{i=1}^N$ that corresponds to the weight vector components for each of the M units in the map. We drop the subindex i for clarity, because all the discussion is related to each descriptor. We will divide the set of M values for each descriptor into two subsets: $\{x_j^C\}_{j=1}^{M_C}$ are the descriptor values for the units labelled with the classical style and $\{x_j^J\}_{j=1}^{M_J}$ are those for the jazz units, being M_C and M_J the number of units labelled with classical and jazz labels, respectively. We want to know whether these two set of values follow the same distribution or not. If false, it is an indication that there is a clear separation between the values of this descriptor for

---

[2] Measured in distance in pitch from the key note of the diatonic scale.

the two classes, so it is a good feature for classification and should be kept in the model and otherwise it does not seem to provide separability to the classes.

We have considered that both sets of values hold normality conditions and the following statistical for sample separation has been applied:

$$z = \frac{|\bar{x}_C - \bar{x}_J|}{\sqrt{\frac{s_C^2}{M_C} + \frac{s_J^2}{M_J}}} \quad , \qquad (1)$$

where $\bar{x}_C$ and $\bar{x}_J$ are the means, and s_C^2 and s_J^2 the variances for the descriptor values for both classes. The larger the z value is, the higher the separation between both sets of values is for that descriptor. This value permits to order the descriptors according to their separation ability and a threshold can be established to determine which descriptors are suitable for the model. This threshold, computed from a t-student distribution with infinite degrees of freedom and a 99.5% confidence interval, is $z = 2.81$.

Fig. 2. Contribution to classification: (a:left) callibrated map ('X' and 'O' are the labels for both styles); (b:center) weight space plane for a feature that correlates with the areas; (c:right) plane for a feature that does not correlate

3   Experiments and Results

As stated above, we have chosen two given music styles: jazz and classical for testing our approach. The jazz samples were taken from jazz standards from different jazz styles like be-bop, hard-bop, big-band swing, etc., and the melodies were sequenced in real time. Classical tunes were collected from a number of styles like baroque, romantic, renaissance, impressionism, etc.

From the MIDI files, 430 jazz and 522 classical melodic samples have been extracted, all of them made up of 8 bars. From them, the 22 descriptors were computed. Two different SOM sizes have been used. Their parameters are displayed in the table below. Those maps have been trained with different subsets of descriptors.

| map | coarse training | | | fine training | | |
size	iterations	neighb.rad.	learn.rate	iterations	neighb.rad.	learn.rate
16 × 8	3,000	12	0.1	30,000	4	0.05
30 × 12	10,000	20	0.1	100,000	6	0.05

After training and labelling, maps like that in figure 3 have been obtained. It is observed how the labelling process has located the jazz labels mainly on the left zone, and those corresponding to classical melodies on the right. Some units can be labelled for both music styles if they are activated by fragments from

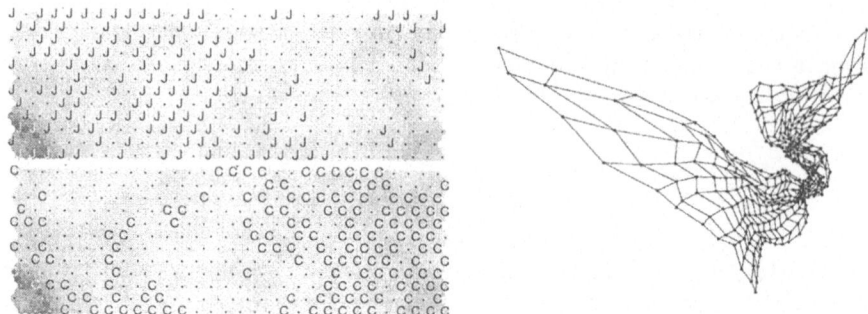

Fig. 3. Left: SOM map after being labeled with jazz (top) and classical (down) melodies. Note how both classes are clearly separated. Right: Sammon projection of the SOM, a way to display in 3D the organisation of the weight vector space

both styles. In these cases there is always a winner label (the one displayed) according to the number of activations. The proportion of units with both labels is the overlapping degree, that for the presented map was very low (8.0 %), allowing a clear distinction between styles.

In the Sammon projection of the map in figure 3 a knot separates two zones in the map. The zone at the left of the knot has a majority presence of units labelled with the jazz label and the zone at the right is mainly classical.

3.1 Feature Selection Results

Firstly we have trained the maps with the whole set of 22 features. This way a reference performance for the system is obtained. In addition, we have trained other maps using just melodic descriptors and also melodic and harmonic ones. We get a set of five trained maps in order to study the values of the weight space planes, using the method described in 2.2. This number of experiments has been considered enough due to the repetitivity of the obtained results. For each experiment we have ordered the descriptors according to their value for z_i (see eq. 1). In table 1 the feature selection results are displayed, including what descriptors have been considered for each model according to those results. Each model number denotes the number of descriptors included in that model. We have chosen four reduced model sizes: 6, 7, 10 and 13 descriptors. Descriptors with no entry in the order column are those having a z_i value under the threshold. Entries marked with a 'x' are not considered in that experiment.

3.2 Classification

For obtaining reliable results a scheme based on *leave-k-out* has been carried out. In our case $k = 10\%$ of the size of the whole database. This way, 10 sub-experiments were performed for each experiment and the results have been averaged. In each experiment the training set was made of a different 90% of the

Table 1. Feature selection results. For each descriptor the ordered position according to the statistical z_i for all the experiments and the average position are displayed. In the rightmost column, the models in which each descriptor is included are also presented

descriptor	order in experiments					avg. order	models
Syncopation	x	x	1	x	1	1.0	7+10+13
Highest pitch	2	1	2	1	2	1.6	6+7+10+13
Max. interval	1	3	5	4	3	3.2	6+7+10+13
Dev. note duration	6	4	4	3	5	4.4	6+7+10+13
Max. note duration	7	5	3	5	4	4.8	6+7+10+13
Dev. pitch	3	2	6	7	7	5.0	6+7+10+13
Avg. note duration	4	7	7	2	6	5.2	6+7+10+13
Avg. pitch	9	8	8	8	8	8.2	10+13
Dev. interval	5	6	10	11	9	8.2	10+13
number of notes	8	9	9	6	10	8.4	10+13
number of silences	10	10	11	10	12	10.6	13
Min. note duration	11	11	12	9	–	10.8	
Min. silence duration	–	–	–	–	11	11.0	
Min. interval	12	12	13	12	13	12.4	13
Avg. interval	–	13	–	–	–	13.0	
Dev. non-diatonic degrees	–	–	14	x	–	14.0	
Num. non-diatonic notes	13	14	16	x	14	14.3	13
Lowest pitch	–	–	15	13	15	14.3	
Max. silence duration	–	–	–	–	–	–	
Avg. silence duration	–	–	–	–	–	–	
Dev. silence duration	–	–	–	–	–	–	
Avg. non-diatonic degrees	–	–	–	x	–	–	

total database and the other 10% was kept for testing. The results are presented in table 2. The results in the table are those obtained in the next experiments:

- All descriptors: all the 22 melodic, harmonic and rhythmic features.
- 6 descriptors: max.pitch, max.interval, note number std.deviation, note number max., pitch std.deviation, and note number mean.
- 7 descriptors: all above plus syncopation.
- 10 descriptors: all above plus pitch mean, interval std.dev. and note number.
- 13 descriptors: all above plus silence number, min.interval, non-diatonic num.

The data presented in the table are successful classification rates for jazz and classical. Each model has been evaluated with the two different size SOM, and in each case the best partition and the average results for the 10 partitions of the leave-k-out experiment are displayed.

The best average performances were consistently obtained with the smaller map, with a success classification rate around 80 %. The best average results were obtained for that map when using the 7-descriptor model (84.2 %). It is observed that 6-descriptor model performance are systematically improved when syncopation is included in the 7-descriptor model. In some experiments even a 98.0 % of success (96.0 % for both styles) has been achieved. The inclusion of more descriptors in the model worsens the results and the worst case is when all of them are used (76.1 % and 66.0 %).

Table 2. Classification results (success rates are in percentages). "Best" results are not neccesarely with the same map. "Best" results for "Both" styles are averaged for jazz and classical styles with a particular map

	JAZZ				CLAS				BOTH			
	16x8		30x12		16x8		30x12		16x8		30x12	
Descr.	BEST	AVG.	BEST	AVG.	BEST	AVG.	BEST	AVG.	BEST	AVG.	BEST	AVG.
All	89.8	72.7	87.8	61.2	93.2	79.6	85.1	70.8	90.8	76.1	80.7	66.0
6	98.0	79.4	81.6	68.4	95.2	82.1	90.5	**89.3**	92.5	80.8	78.3	73.3
7	96.0	**81.8**	83.7	74.1	97.3	86.5	97.3	76.6	96.0	**84.2**	85.1	75.4
10	98.0	78.8	87.8	63.3	96.0	82.7	90.5	74.6	88.8	80.7	89.2	68.9
13	87.8	72.0	89.8	67.1	97.3	82.6	85.1	68.8	84.4	77.3	78.0	68.0

4   Conclusions and Future Works

We have shown the ability of SOM to map symbolic representations of melodies into a set of musical styles using melodic, harmonic and rhythmic descriptions. The best recognition rate has been found with a 7-descriptor model where syncopation, note duration, and pitch have an important role. The overlapping degree does not seem to be a key point when assessing the quality of a map.

Some of the misclassifications can be caused by the lack of a smart method for melody segmentation. The music samples have been arbitrarily restricted to 8 bars, getting just fragments with no relation to musical motives. This fact can introduce artifacts in the descriptors leading to less quality mappings. The main goal was to test the feasibility of the approach, and average recognition rates above 80% have been achieved, that is very encouraging keeping in mind these limitations and others like the lack of valuable information for this task like timbre.

A number of possibilities are yet to be explored, like the development and study of new descriptors. It is very likely that the descriptor subset models are highly dependent on the styles to be discriminated. To achieve this goal a large music database has to be compiled and tested using our system for multiple different style recognition in order to draw significant conclusions.

Acknowledgements

Thanks to the Spanish CICyT project TAR, code: TIC2000–1703–CO3–02, and to the CICyT TIC2001-5057-E pattern recognition thematic network.

References

[1] T. Kohonen. Self-organizing map. *Proceedings IEEE*, 78(9):1464–1480, 1990.
[2] A. Rauber and M. Frühwirth. *Automatically analyzing and organizing music archives*, pages 4–8. 5th European Conference on Research and Advanced Technology for Digital Libraries (ECDL 2001). Springer, Darmstadt, Sep 2001.

[3] Brian Whitman, Gary Flake, and Steve Lawrence. Artist detection in music with minnowmatch. In *Proceedings of the 2001 IEEE Workshop on Neural Networks for Signal Processing*, pages 559–568. Falmouth, Massachusetts, September 10–12 2001.

[4] Hagen Soltau, Tanja Schultz, Martin Westphal, and Alex Waibel. Recognition of music types. In *Proceedings of the IEEE International Conference on Acoustics, Speech, and Signal Processing (ICASSP-1998)*. Seattle, Washington, May 1998.

[5] O. A. S. Carpinteiro. A self-organizing map model for analysis of musical time series. In A. de Padua Braga and T. B. Ludermir, editors, *Proceedings 5th Brazilian Symposium on Neural Networks*, pages 140–5. IEEE Comput. Soc, 1998.

[6] Belinda Thom. Unsupervised learning and interactive jazz/blues improvisation. In *Proceedings of the AAAI2000*, pages 652–657, 2000.

[7] Petri Toiviainen and Tuomas Eerola. Method for comparative analysis of folk music based on musical feature extraction and neural networks. In *III International Conference on Cognitive Musicology*, pages 41–45, Jyvskyl, Finland, 2001.

[8] T. Kohonen, J. Hynninen, J. Kangas, and J. Laaksonen. Som_pak, the self-organizing map program package, v:3.1. Lab. of Computer and Information Science, Helsinki University of Technology, Finland, April, 1995. http://www.cis.hut.fi/research/som_pak.

Multiple Model Approach to Deformable Shape Tracking

Daniel Ponsa and Xavier Roca

Centre de Visió per Computador
Universitat Autònoma de Barcelona
08193 Bellaterra (Barcelona), Spain
daniel@cvc.uab.es

Abstract. This paper describes a new proposal for tracking deformable objects in video sequences using multiple shape models of heterogeneous dimensionality. This models are generated unsupervisedly from a training sequence, and used to estimate the shape of an object along time by means of a novel tracking framework proposed. This framework is based in estimate the rigid and non-rigid shape transformations in two separated but related processes. The advantage of proceed in that way is that the a priori knowledge contained in the learned models is better exploited, resulting in a more reliable tracking performance. The Condensation algorithm is used to estimate the rigid transformation of the shape, while the non-rigid shape deformation is determined by combining the response of several Kalman Filters. The proposal is evaluated tracking a synthetic form, and the silhouette of a pedestrian.

1 Introduction

Many approaches to shape tracking pose this problem as determining the parameters of a deformable curve from measures obtained in image frames. One popular technique applied in this task is known as Active Contour or Active Shape Estimation [1, 2]. This is a model based approach that applies methods developed in estimation theory (mainly Kalman and Particle Filters) to estimate the parameters of a model which encapsulates the shape variability of the object to be tracked. Usually this model is linear, determined from the Principal Component Analysis(PCA) of a training set. This model is also complemented with a constraint model delimiting the valid parameterizations of the model [3, 4, 5]. The use of both models by estimation filters brings to quite robust tracking performances. However, if the shape to be modeled changes abruptly over time, the accuracy of the linear shape model diminishes, while the complexity of the constraint in the space of valid shape parameters increases (requires a model of higher order). Realizing that, our recent past research has focused in studying the benefits of using several models in this modeling task. The natural following step has been defining a tracking strategy that takes advantage of the multiple models to achieve robust tracking performances.

F.J. Perales et al. (Eds.): IbPRIA 2003, LNCS 2652, pp. 782–792, 2003.
© Springer-Verlag Berlin Heidelberg 2003

In this paper we propose a novel tracking framework that manages multiple models to track a deformable shape over time. Section 2 briefly describes our modelisation strategy, which determines unsupervisedly a collection of models from a training sequence. Next, section 3 details how complement this models to consider, beside the learned deformations, the common rigid transformations that suffer objects in common tracking applications (translations, change of scale, ...). Section 4 discusses the difficulties in the estimation of the parameters of the proposed models, and proposes a two-phase tracking framework which takes advantage of the implicit a-priori information contained in the models. Section 5 evaluates the performance of the proposal in synthetic and real sequences. The paper ends with a brief summary and some conclusions.

2   Unsupervised Multiple Model Generation

Given a training set of aligned curve parameterizations $\mathbf{Q} = \{Q_1, \ldots, Q_n\}$ that represent the object to be modeled, common approaches make a PCA to determine a low-dimensional linear shape model. This model is defined by the matrix of principal eigenvectors W of the distribution of $\mathbf{Q}$, and its corresponding mean $\bar{Q}$. The elements in the training set Q_k can be approximately recovered using equation 1, being X_k^D the projection of Q_k in the *shape space* W.

$$Q_k = WX_k^D + \bar{Q}, \quad k \in \{1, \ldots, n\} \tag{1}$$

The feasible values of X_k^D are constrained to lay in a specific region, in order to generate only curve parameterizations similar to the ones in $\mathbf{Q}$. This constrain region, denoted as Subspace of Valid Shapes (SVS), is usually represented with a Gaussian Mixture Model(GMM). This mixture of Gaussian models the distribution of $\mathbf{X^D}$ (the projection of $\mathbf{Q}$ onto the shape space W) and is characterized by its amount of components K and their corresponding parameters $\Phi = \{(P_1, \mu_1, \Sigma_1), \ldots, (P_K, \mu_K, \Sigma_K)\}$.

$$p(X_k^D) = \sum_{i=1}^{K} p(X_k^D | \mu_i, \Sigma_i) P_i \tag{2}$$

To determine an appropriate parameterization several different proposals can be found in the literature [6, 7, 8]. Each GMM component delimits an hiperellipsoid in the W-space, where projects a subset of elements in $\mathbf{Q}$ whose shape variability can be delimited by a Gaussian distribution. This fact suggests us to replace this linear model constrained by a GMM with a set of linear models, each one constrained by a single Gaussian. First each projected training sample X_k^D is assigned to the component j that maximizes its likelihood. This allow us to define K subsets $\mathbf{Q}^i$ in the training sequence $\mathbf{Q}$, where

$$\mathbf{Q}^i = \cup\{Q_j\} \,\forall X_j^D \mid i = \arg \max_{k=1}^{K} p(X_j^D, k) P(k) \ . \tag{3}$$

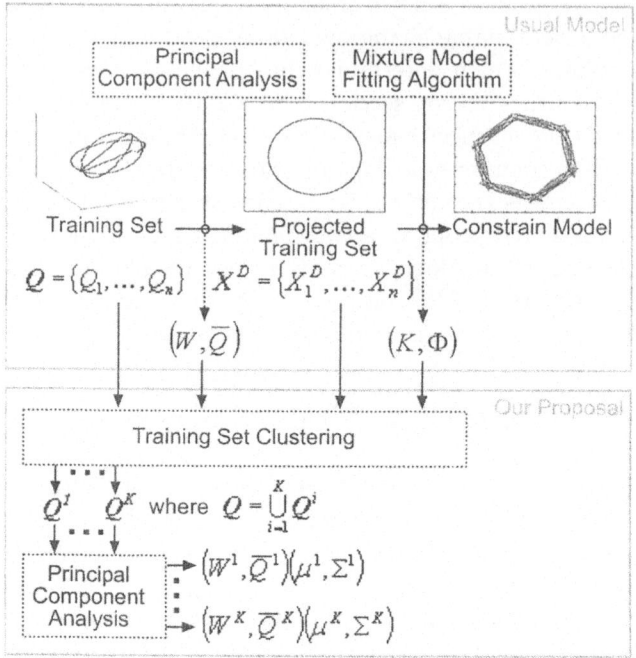

Fig. 1. Unsupervised construction of a collection of Gaussian-constrained shape models

This procedure clusters the training set in groups similar in shape. We propose to define an specific linear shape model for each of them, constraining its respective SVS with a single Gaussian. Figure 1 summarizes the overall procedure.

As elements in $\mathbf{Q}^i \subset \mathbf{Q}$ present a high degree of similarity, a linear model W^i of dimensionality lower than W is expected to be determined. We determine the specific model dimension d^i by the minimal one which obtains a mean squared reconstruction error lower that the one obtained with W. That is,

$$\min \ d^i \mid \sum_{Q_j \in \mathbf{Q}^i} \left(Q_j - (W^i X_j^{Di} + \bar{Q}^i)\right)^2 \leq \sum_{Q_j \in \mathbf{Q}^i} \left(Q_j - (W X_j^D + \bar{Q})\right)^2 \ , \quad (4)$$

where X_j^{Di} is the projection of Q_j onto the W^i space. We found that the most important benefit of proceed in that way, more than the gain of accuracy (that is set at a feasible minimum), is the reduction in dimensionality of shape spaces. This fact reduces the computational load of tracking algorithms, which favors to obtain more robust performances (allow a better temporal sampling of sequences, considering more sofisticated image measurement, etc). Also, having a lower dimensionality supposes implicitly a gain in the SVS constraint, as the degrees of freedom of the shape parameterizations are reduced. Moreover, the Gaussian constraint of each model can be elegantly applied in a tracking algorithm by assuming a constrained Brownian motion for the dynamics of shape parameters (see [1] for a description). Our experiments show than in practical problems, the constrained multiple model approach improves the traditional approach in terms of the Minimum Description Length criterion. For a more detailed description and study of this modelisation proposal, the reader may refer to [9].

For an efficient use of this collection of models in tracking applications, a dynamical model of the transitions between the different models is required. If the training set $\mathbf{Q}$ contains an ordered sequence of the typical deformation cycle of the modeled object, a Model Transition Matrix MTM can be constructed by histograming the pair of model identifiers (M_i, M_{i+1}) assigned to each consecutive pair of elements in $\mathbf{Q}$. Figure 2 show an schematic of this process.

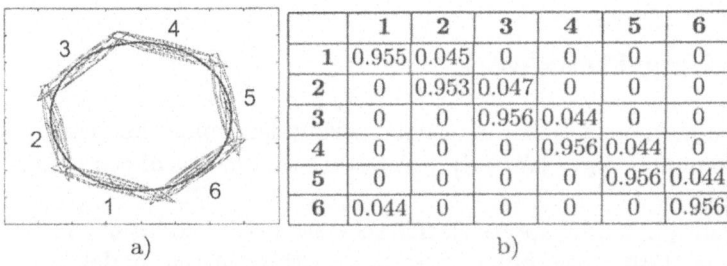

	1	2	3	4	5	6
1	0.955	0.045	0	0	0	0
2	0	0.953	0.047	0	0	0
3	0	0	0.956	0.044	0	0
4	0	0	0	0.956	0.044	0
5	0	0	0	0	0.956	0.044
6	0.044	0	0	0	0	0.956

a)   b)

Fig. 2. Dynamic learning process of a Markov Chain model, for a synthetic training set. a) A GMM models the SVS. b) The MTM computed from a training sequence, using the procedure described in [4]

3   Rigid Transformations Extension

The models described in the previous section encapsulate the non rigid transformations present in the training set. However, beside shape deformations, objects in tracking applications mainly present translations, changes of scale, and other transformations that affect globally the shape of the object. To take this transformations into account, the learned models have to be complemented with new parameters X^R, which describe the global transformation affecting the whole object. Assuming that this global transformation is linear, curve parameters Q are determined by means of the following expression:

$$Q = W_{X^R} \left(W^i X^D + \bar{Q}^i \right) + T_{X^R} \ . \tag{5}$$

For Euclidean transformations, $X^R = \{s, \theta, t_x, t_y\}$. W_{X^R} is a scaling-rotation matrix whose elements depend on the parameters s(scale) and θ (angle), and T_{X^R} is an appropriate translation vector constructed from t_x and t_y.

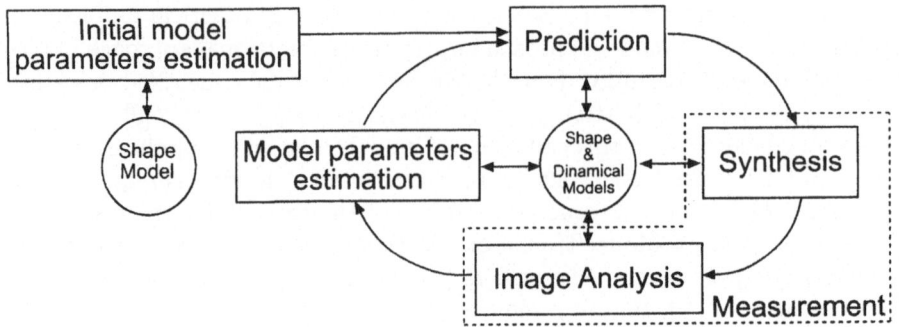

Fig. 3. Block diagram of a model based tracking application

4   Tracking Framework

Estimation methods applied in visual tracking determine the distribution of the model parameters $X_t = \{X_t^R, X_t^D\}$ at instant t by means of the iterative process shown in figure 3.

In a multiple model approach this scheme is still valid, but requires to complement the state of the object with an identifier of the model i_t active at instant t. Therefore the state of the object becomes $X_t = \{X_t^R, X_t^D, i_t\}$. Moreover, the algorithm at each iteration has to consider multiple state hypothesis $\mathbf{H} = \{X_{t_{h1}}, \ldots, X_{t_{hn}}\}$. From the estimation at the previous instant X_{t-1}, the prediction module uses the Model Transition Matrix with the value of i_{t-1} to predict a subset of posible active models $\mathbf{i_H} = \{i_{h_1} \ldots i_{h_n}\}$ in the current instant. All this models share a common predicted rigid transformation, and have its specific deformation parameters. After all this hypothesis are evaluated, we consider the one which better explain the observed measures as the estimate of the state at instant t.

Estimate X_t^R and X_t^D for each hypothesis is difficult, because the effect of each parameter is observed combined in the measurements. However, doing some assumptions, their corresponding effect can be isolated, and this can be used to take more profit of the a priori information in the models. The following sections describe a proposal to estimate the elements $\{X_t^R, X_t^D\}$ separately, which allow a more precise estimation of each of them, achieving a more robust tracking performance. Then, the criterion to choose the more likely hypothesis is detailed.

4.1 X_t^R Estimation

We apply an adaption of the CONDENSATION algorithm [10] to estimate X_t^R, which makes use of the multiple models hypothesized. At time $t-1$ we have a population of samples $\{X_{t-1_i}^R\}$ $i = 1 \ldots n$ representing the probability density function of X^R, conditioned with the history until $t-1$. We propagate the sample set to instant t, assuming a constant velocity model for translation parameters, and a constrained Brownian motion for scale and rotation parameters. Then, each sample $X_{t_i}^R$ is evaluated, determining its fitness to observations π_i from the combination of the likelihood of the multiple hypothesized models.

$$\pi_i = \sum_{i_{h_j} \in H} p(Z_t | X_{t_i}^R, i_{h_j}) \tag{6}$$

In that way we emulate in a particle filter the procedure of a simplified generalized pseudo-Bayesian estimator of first order for managing multiple hypothesis [11]. After the normalization of the π_i values, X_t^R is determined from the weighted linear combination of the predicted sample set $X_t^R = \sum_{i=1}^n \pi_i X_{t_i}^R$.

As equation 6 shows, the basis to apply this reasoning is obtaining measurements Z_t that do not depend on the value of $X_{t_i}^D$. To achieve this, we define for each model a submodel R^k, which is a rigid template corresponding to the zone in the model less affected by deformations. First we project the variance Σ_k of the model's SVS constraint into a space of samples along the modeled contour, with expression

$$\Sigma_{samples}^k = B^T W^{k^T} \Sigma_k W^k B \ . \tag{7}$$

B is a matrix that projects a vector of control points Q into a predefined sampling of its corresponding curve. From $\Sigma_{samples}^k$ the position covariance $\Sigma_{s_i}^k$ of each sample point s_i in the curve is obtained. The samples which suffer less deformation are identified, and selected to define R^k (see figure 4).

To estimate X_t^R, measurements Z_t are obtained applying an edge detector along lines perpendicular to the contour regions in R^k. The likelihood $p(Z_t | X_{t_i}^R, i_{h_j})$ is defined as proposed in [10].

4.2 X_t^D Estimation

Having determined the more likely value of X_t^R, now we can apply this rigid transformation to the hypothesized models and focus just on the estimation of X_t^D. We do that applying a Kalman Filter for each hypothesized model.

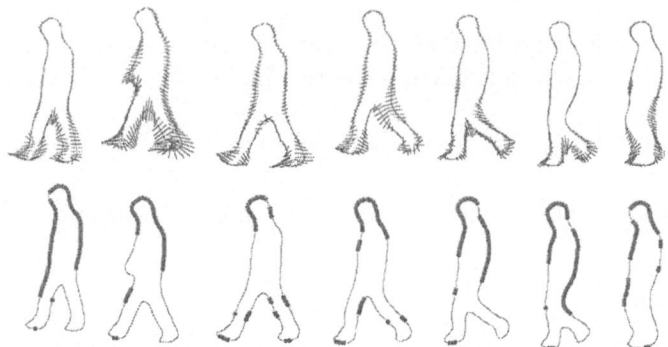

Fig. 4. Example for a pedestrian tracking application. Deformation associated to the learned contours, and the zone determined to estimate X_t^R

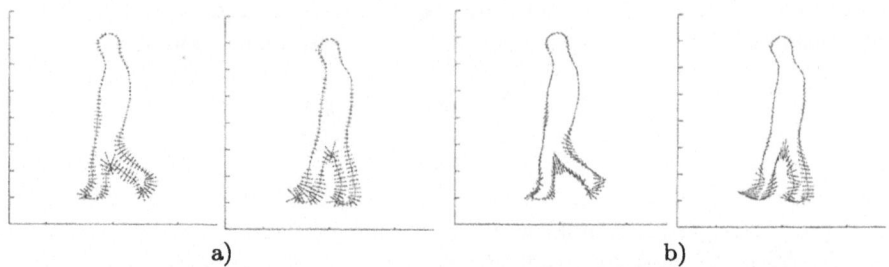

a)   b)

Fig. 5. Example in a pedestrian tracking application. a) Measurements perpendicular to the contour(the common approach). b) Measurements in the more probable direction of deformation. For each pose, one can agree that it corresponds to the logical direction of deformation

First, each model predicts its deformation at the current instant using a constrained Brownian motion model, with parameters determined from the parameters (μ_k, Σ_k) of its corresponding constrain region.

$$X_t^D - \mu_k = A\ (X_{t-1}^D - \mu_k) + \omega_k \ . \tag{8}$$

Matrix A corresponds to aI (with $a = 0.9$) and ω_k is a vector of d^k independent random variables $\mathcal{N}(0, \epsilon\Sigma_k)$, where $\epsilon = 1 - a^2$. For the hypothesis $i_{h_j} \neq i_{t-1}$ the value of X_{t-1}^D is established as μ_j. This dynamical model guarantees that the predicted deformation lay inside its constrain region. Then, to estimate X_t^D, new measurements Z_t are extracted from the image, profiting by the fact that now the rigid transformation is already estimated. This allow to define a more coherent measurement process, measuring along lines oriented toward the more probable direction of shape deformation (see [12] for details). As shows figure 5 in a real example, the measurements obtained in this direction will reflect more confidently the deformation suffered by the object.

4.3   Final X_t Estimation

From the multiple hypothesis **H**, we select the one that better fits the image using expression 9, which is taken to be the final estimation of X_t.

$$X_t = \{X_{t_{h_k}}^D, X_t^R, i_{h_k}\} \mid h_k = \arg \max_{i_{h_j} \in H} p(Z_t | X_{t_{h_j}}^D, X_t^R, i_{h_j}) \tag{9}$$

Figure 6 shows an schematic of the overall process proposed

5   Results

In order to measure the performance of the tracking proposal, we have reproduced the experiment proposed in [13]. First we have generated a collection of models from a binary sequence showing the deformation period of a synthetic

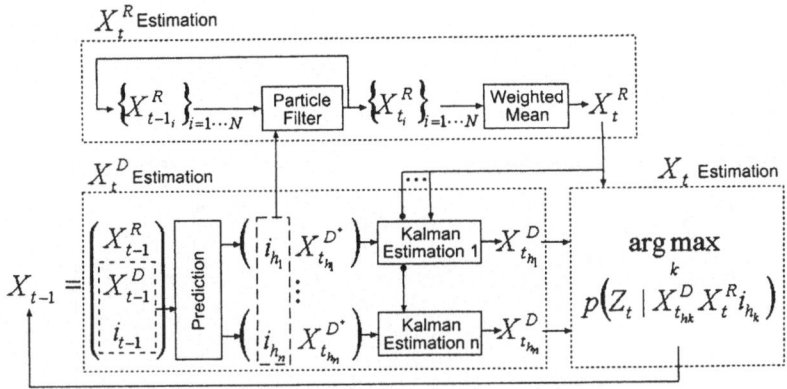

Fig. 6. Block diagram of the proposed tracking strategy

shape. Then we have used this models to track a test sequence, showing the learned shape suffering oscillatory changes of position, rotation, and scale (see Figure 7). Different degrees of noise have been added to the test sequence, in order to check the robustness of the proposal.

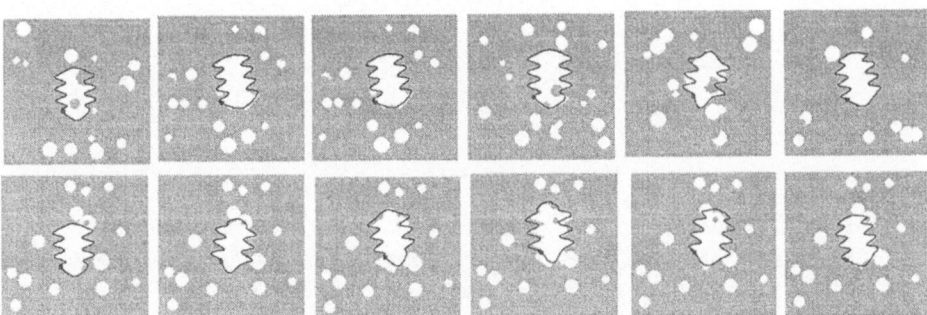

Fig. 7. Some results in frames corresponding to a Signal-to-Noise (SNR) ratio around 6 dB. *Top*: uncorrelated noise. *Bottom*: correlated noise

Our algorithm tracks robustly the shape, even when a high number of artifacts corrupts the test sequence (see Figure 8). For uncorrelated artifacts, the tracking is fairly robust when noise is over 4 dB. For correlated noise, its behavior is acceptable when noise is around 6 dB. An output SNR less than 7.5 dB results when the system fails to track more than 25% of the sequence.

We have also tested the proposal in a pedestrian tracking application. Good results have been obtained in several test sequences showing different people walking sideways, even when the initial parameterization of the tracker was vague. Pedestrians location and scale its correctly estimated, while its outline is recovered accurately in the 78.5% of the frames.

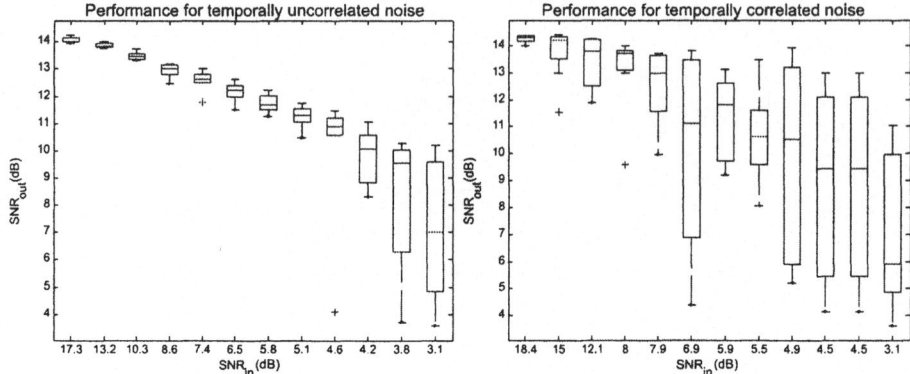

Fig. 8. Tracking statistics for the proposed method

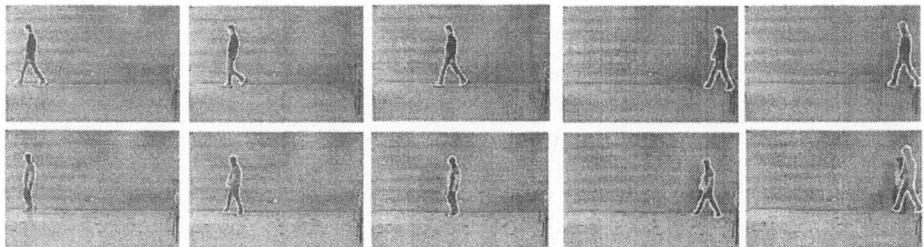

Fig. 9. From *right* to *left*, some results in a pedestrian tracking application. Despite the inaccurate initialization of the tracker, it succeeds in recovering the pedestrian outline

6   Summary and Conclusions

This papers describes an unsupervised method to determine a collection of shape models from a training set, and presents a novel two-phase algorithm that uses them for the robust tracking of objects. The proposal estimates sequentially the rigid and non-rigid object transformations in two different processes. The rigid transformation is determined evaluating several rigid template models in a particle filter. For the sake of efficiency, the object's non-rigid deformations is obtained analytically by evaluating the response of several kalman filters, each of them checking a concrete space of object deformations. Using a particle filter for locating the object makes our algorithm robust to clutter, and allow to recover for temporal miss-track. Deformation parameters are estimated by Kalman filters, as its priors and dynamics are Gaussian, and assuming a Gaussian observation density is not critical, provided the effect of clutter is already considered in the object localization.

Acknowledgments

This work has been partially supported by TIC2000-0382, Spain.

References

[1] Blake, A., Isard, M.: Active Contours. Springer-Verlag (1998)
[2] Cootes, T., Taylor, C.: Statistical moedls of appearance for computer vision. Technical report, Wolfson Image Analysis Unit, Imaging Science and Biomedical Engineering, University of Manchester (2001)
[3] Heap, A., Hogg, D.: Improving specificity in pdms using a hierarchical approach. In: British Machine Vision Conference. (1997)
[4] Heap, T., Hogg, D.: Wormholes in shape space: Tracking through discontinuous changes in shape. In: Sixth International Conference on Computer Vision. (1998) 344–349
[5] Cootes, T., Taylor, C.: A mixture model for representing shape variation. Image and Vision Computing 17 (1999) 567–574
[6] Richardson, S., Green, P.: On Bayesian analysis of mixtures with an unknown number of components. Journal of the Royal Statistical Society (Series B) 59 (1997) 731–758
[7] Roberts, S., Husmeier, D., Rezek, I., Penny, W.: Bayesian Approaches To Gaussian Mixture Modelling. IEEE Transaction on Pattern Analysis and Machine Intelligence 20 (1998) 1133–1142
[8] Ponsa, D., Roca, X.: Unsupervised parameterisation of gaussian mixture models. LNAI: Topics in Artificial Intelligence 2504 (2002) 388–398
[9] Ponsa, D., X.Roca: A novel approach to generate multiple shape models for tracking applications. LNCS: Articulated Motion and Deformable Objects 2492 (2002) 80–91
[10] Isard, M., Blake, A.: Condensation – conditional density propagation for visual tracking. International Journal of Computer Vision 1 (1998) 5–28

[11] Bar-Shalom, Y., Li, S., Kirubarajan, T.: Estimation with Applications to Tracking and Navigation. Wiley-Interscience (2001)
[12] Baumberg, A.: Hierarchical shape fitting using an iterated linear filter. In: British Machine Vision Conference. Volume 1. (1996) 313–322
[13] Baumberg, A.: Learning Deformable Models for Tracking Human Motion. PhD thesis, School of Computer Studies. University of Leeds (1995)

Pixel-Based Texture Classification by Integration of Multiple Texture Feature Evaluation Windows

Domènec Puig   Miguel Angel García

Intelligent Robotics and Computer Vision Group
Department of Computer Science and Mathematics
Rovira i Virgili University
Av. Països Catalans 26, 43007 Tarragona, Spain
{dpuig, magarcia}@etse.urv.es

Abstract

A wide variety of texture feature extraction methods have been proposed for texture based image classification and segmentation. These methods are typically evaluated over windows of the same size, the latter being usually chosen for each particular method on an experimental basis. This paper shows that pixel-based texture classification can be significantly improved by evaluating a given texture method over multiple windows of different size and then by integrating the results through a classical Bayesian scheme. The proposed technique has been applied to well-known families of texture methods that are frequently utilized for feature extraction from textured images. Experiments show that the integration of multi-sized windows yields lower classification errors than when optimal single-sized windows are considered.

1 Introduction

A wide variety of *texture feature extraction methods* (*texture methods* in short) have been proposed in the computer vision and image processing literature in order to characterize different texture patterns (e.g., [7][10][14][16][17]). A texture method is a process that can be applied to a pixel of a given image in order to generate a measure (*feature*) related to the texture pattern to which that pixel and its neighbors belong. The performance of the different families of texture methods basically depends on the type of processing they apply, the neighborhood of pixels over which they are evaluated (*evaluation window*) and the texture content.

Traditionally, texture methods have been evaluated over windows of a single size, the latter being commonly defined on an experimental basis. The role played by both the shape and size of evaluation windows was studied in [6], showing that texture characterization is much more influenced by the window size than by its shape, although no hints on optimal sizes were provided.

Although many studies regarding the performance of the different families of texture feature extraction methods have been carried out in the past (e.g., [4][11][14]), only a few have dealt with the issue of determining optimal window sizes. The majority of those works find out optimal sizes for specific texture methods (e.g., [2][10]). In the scope of pixel-based texture classification, [12] presents a tech-

---

This work has been partially supported by the Government of Spain under the CICYT project DPI2001-2094-C03-02.

F.J. Perales et al. (Eds.): IbPRIA 2003, LNCS 2652, pp. 793–801, 2003.

nique for determining the window size that leads to the maximum separability among texture models, given an arbitrary texture method and a set of texture models of interest.

Following a different approach, this paper shows that by integrating the features obtained after the evaluation of a texture method over multiple windows of different size, classification rates are significantly larger than when the same method is applied over windows of the same size, even if this size is optimal under some criterion, such as separability [12]. The paper is organized as follows. Section 2 describes how texture methods are evaluated over multisized windows. Section 3 presents the proposed scheme for integrating multiple evaluation windows. Section 4 shows experimental results obtained with the proposed technique when applied to texture feature extraction methods that are widely used for texture classification, as well as a comparison with a well-known texture classification framework (*MeasTex* [9]). Conclusions and further improvements are finally given in section 5

2   Evaluation of Texture Methods over Multisized Windows

Let $\{\tau_1, \ldots, \tau_T\}$ be a set of T texture models of interest. Each model τ_k is described by a sample image $\mathbf{I}_k$ that contains a pattern of that texture. Let $\mathbf{I}$ be a two dimensional test image of $R \times C$ pixels that contains several regions of uniform texture. The usual way of classifying each pixel $\mathbf{I}(x, y)$ consists of computing a texture feature f obtained by applying a texture feature extraction method μ to the pixels contained in a neighborhood of $\mathbf{I}(x, y) : f = \mu(x, y)$. That neighborhood is usually a square window centered at $\mathbf{I}(x, y)$ whose size is experimentally set for each method. The computed feature is then fed into a pattern classifier in order to determine the texture model corresponding to $\mathbf{I}(x, y)$.

Instead of using a single window, we propose the evaluation of the given texture method μ over N square windows, $\{w_1, \ldots, w_N\}$, with each window having a different size. Every window w_j is considered to contain $s_j \times s_j$ pixels, with $s_j = 2^j + 1$. Hence, every texture method μ generates a feature vector F with N texture features for every pixel to which the method is applied.

We consider that whenever an evaluation window is not totally contained in the given image, the texture method cannot be evaluated, since it would generate a value based on a fraction of the texture pattern. This means that the strip of pixels that belong to the boundary of $\mathbf{I}$ will not be classified, as no window centered at them will entirely fit into the image. Let W, $W \le N$, be the number of windows that do entirely fit into the image for a specific pixel $\mathbf{I}(x, y)$. In this case, μ generates a vector F of W features: $F = (f_1, \ldots, f_W)$.

3   Pixel-Based Texture Classification Using Multisized Windows

Given an image $\mathbf{I}$ and a texture feature extraction method μ, which generates a feature vector F when it is evaluated in the neighborhood of pixel $\mathbf{I}(x, y)$ by using a set of W windows of different size, $\{s_1 \times s_1, \ldots, s_W \times s_W\}$, this section presents a technique for integrating the W texture features of F in order to determine whether pixel $\mathbf{I}(x, y)$ can be classified into one of T given texture models $\{\tau_1, \ldots, \tau_T\}$.

The first stage of the proposed technique applies a supervised training scheme in order to obtain a set of frequency tables (histograms). Each histogram models the behavior of texture method μ when it is applied to all the pixels of the sample image corresponding to one of the given texture models by using one of the chosen window sizes. Each of those histograms will allow to compute the likelihood of pixel $\mathbf{I}(x, y)$ according to method μ, window size $s_j \times s_j$ and texture model τ_k. Such basic likelihood functions are denoted as $P_j(\mathbf{I}(x, y)|\tau_k)$. Thus, given a texture method μ, $W \times T$ frequency tables and, hence, basic likelihood functions are computed.

In the second stage, the W basic likelihood functions corresponding to the different window sizes $s_j \times s_j$ are integrated, for each texture model τ_k, obtaining a new subset of T intermediate likelihood functions, $P(\mathbf{I}(x, y)|\tau_k)$. Finally, in the last stage, the $P(\mathbf{I}(x, y)|\tau_k)$ likelihood functions obtained above are combined through the Bayes rule in order to obtain the posterior probability that pixel $\mathbf{I}(x, y)$ belongs to texture model τ_k according to texture method μ, $P(\tau_k|\mathbf{I}(x, y))$. Pixel $\mathbf{I}(x, y)$ will be classified to the texture model with the maximum posterior probability.

The three stages of the proposed technique are further described below.

3.1   Supervised Training Stage

Let μ_j be a texture feature extraction method μ evaluated over a window of size $s_j \times s_j$. When μ_j is applied to a pixel $\mathbf{I}(x, y)$, it generates a value $\mu_j(x, y)$ that represents a feature of the texture pattern to which $\mathbf{I}(x, y)$ belongs. Every known texture model τ_k is associated with an image $\mathbf{I}_k$ that contains an example of its pattern. For instance, Fig. 2(*top*) shows eight texture models belonging to the *Brodatz album* [3].

By evaluating method μ_j at each of the pixels contained in $\mathbf{I}_k$, it is possible to determine the probability distribution P_{jk} associated with the feature values generated by μ when applied to τ_k with a window size $s_j \times s_j$. In practice, P_{jk} is approximated by a frequency table (histogram) with θ bins (e.g., $\theta = 256$). The feature values computed by μ_j will range in a specific real interval:

$$\mu_j : \mathbf{I}_k \rightarrow [MIN_{jk}, MAX_{jk}] \subset \mathbf{R} \tag{1}$$

The basic likelihood function $P_j(\mathbf{I}(x, y)|\tau_k)$ is then defined as:

$$P_j(\mathbf{I}(x, y)|\tau_k) = P_{jk}(\mu_j(x, y) \in [MIN_{jk}, MAX_{jk}]) \tag{2}$$

$P_j(\mathbf{I}(x, y)|\tau_k)$ can be interpreted as the likelihood that pixel $\mathbf{I}(x, y)$ belongs to texture τ_k according to method μ when it is evaluated on a window of size $s_j \times s_j$.

3.2   Integration of Multiple Window Sizes

Given a texture method μ and its corresponding set of $W \times T$ basic likelihood functions P_j defined in the supervised training stage (2), the objective now is to integrate the likelihoods corresponding to the W window sizes associated with each texture model: $\{P_1(\mathbf{I}(x, y)|\tau_k), ..., P_W(\mathbf{I}(x, y)|\tau_k)\}$. The result will be a set of T combined likelihood functions: $P(\mathbf{I}(x, y)|\tau_k)$.

The likelihood functions corresponding to the evaluation of a texture method over different windows centered at the same pixel of a textured image are assumed to be statistically independent. The reason is that each window captures a subimage of a particular size, which is constituted by pixels that have independently captured the reflectivity of one or several microtextured surfaces that are intrinsically noisy by nature. Therefore, a same texture method may produce significantly different values when it is applied to a small window or to a large one, although both windows are centered at the same pixel. This implies that the corresponding likelihoods may also be different and uncorrelated.

The combination of different basic likelihood functions can be modeled as a *linear opinion pool* [1]:

$$P(\mathbf{I}(x, y)|\tau_k) = \sum_{j=1}^{W} w_{jk}\, P_j(\mathbf{I}(x, y)|\tau_k) \tag{3}$$

The weights w_{jk} are computed as the normalized average of the *Kullback J-divergence* [8] between τ_k and the other texture models:

$$w_{jk} = d_{jk} / \sum_{r=1}^{W} d_{rk} \qquad d_{jk} = \frac{1}{T-1} \sum_{l=1, l \neq k}^{T} KJ_j(\tau_l, \tau_k) \tag{4}$$

The *Kullback J-divergence* measures the separability between two classes (texture models in this context) as:

$$KJ_j(\tau_a, \tau_b) = \sum_{\forall u, v} (A - B)\log(A/B) \tag{5}$$

with A and B being obtained in our context from the histograms computed during the supervised training stage (1): $A = P_{ja}(u \in [MIN_{ja}, MAX_{ja}])$ and $B = P_{jb}(v \in [MIN_{jb}, MAX_{jb}])$.

3.3   Maximum a Posteriori Estimation

Given a set of T likelihood functions $P(\mathbf{I}(x, y)|\tau_k)$ (3), the posterior probabilities $P(\tau_k|\mathbf{I}(x, y))$ are finally computed by applying the Bayes rule:

$$P(\tau_k|\mathbf{I}(x, y)) = \frac{P(\mathbf{I}(x, y)|\tau_k)P(\tau_k)}{\sum_{l=1}^{T} P(\mathbf{I}(x, y)|\tau_l)P(\tau_l)} \tag{6}$$

with the prior probability corresponding to each texture model being defined as:

$$P(\tau_k) = \sum_{j=1}^{W} w_{jk} \left(\sum_{l=1}^{T} \sum_{j=1}^{W} w_{jl} \right)^{-1} \tag{7}$$

At this point, T posterior probabilities have been generated: $\{P(\tau_1|\mathbf{I}(x, y)), ..., P(\tau_T|\mathbf{I}(x, y))\}$, one per texture model.

Finally, pixel $\mathbf{I}(x, y)$ will be considered to belong to texture class τ_k iff $P(\tau_k|\mathbf{I}(x, y)) > P(\tau_l|\mathbf{I}(x, y))$, $\forall l \neq k$, which is generally known as the *maximum a*

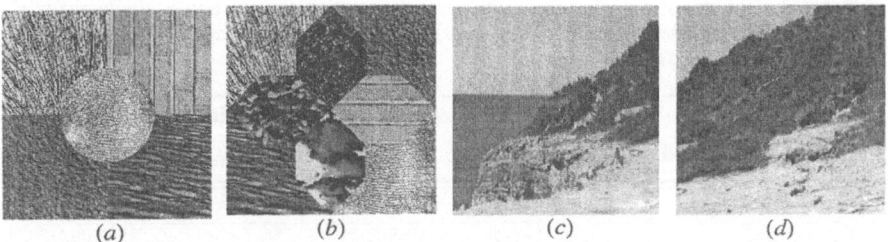

Fig. 1. Test images with portions of Brodatz texture patterns: (*a*),(*b*). Test images with real outdoor scenes: (*c*),(*d*)

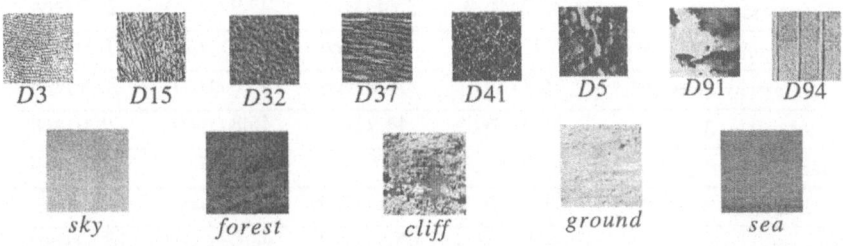

Fig. 2. Detail of texture models τ_k from (*top*) the Brodatz album and (*bottom*) real outdoor scenes

posteriori (MAP) estimation. This process is iteratively applied to all the pixels in **I**.

4   Experimental Results

Taking recent surveys into account [14][16], several widely-used texture feature extraction methods have been chosen to validate the proposed technique: four *Laws filter masks* (*R5R5, E5L5, E5E5, R5S5*), two *wavelet transforms* (*Daubechies-4, Haar*), four *Gabor filters* with different wavelengths (8, 4) and orientations (0°, 45°, 90°, 135°), two *first-order statistics* (*variance, skewness*), a *second-order statistic* (*homogeneity*) based on *co-occurrence matrices* and the *fractal dimension*.

The proposed technique has been tested on a set of composite Brodatz images [3], Fig. 1(*a*)(*b*), and on real outdoor images, Fig. 1(*c*)(*d*). Fig. 2(*top*) shows eight Brodatz texture patterns utilized as models for the training stage. Each pattern belongs to one of the eight texture categories proposed by Rao and Loshe [15] as representatives of the variability of natural textures according to human perception. Fig. 2(*bottom*) shows five outdoor texture patterns.

In the first set of experiments, each texture method was evaluated over a single window size at a time. Six window sizes were considered in turn: {3x3, 5x5, 9x9, 17x17, 33x33, 65x65}. For every test image, texture method and window size, the classification rate after just applying the MAP estimation stage was obtained. Table 1 shows the largest classification rates obtained for every texture method when applied to the test images presented in Fig. 1. The window sizes that led to such largest rates are considered to be optimal for each method and test image, and are also

Table 1. Classification rates (%) with the proposed technique and a single texture method, by considering a single (optimal) window size per image and method (the optimal window size is also shown)

Texture Feature Extraction Method	Optimal Single Window			
	Fig. 1(*a*)	Fig. 1(*b*)	Fig. 1(*c*)	Fig. 1(*d*)
Laws R5R5	55.3 *(9x9)*	55.7 *(17x17)*	50.5 *(9x9)*	23.7 *(9x9)*
Laws E5L5	64.1 *(9x9)*	40.5 *(9x9)*	56.7 *(9x9)*	35.7 *(9x9)*
Laws E5E5	58.3 *(17x17)*	43.5 *(9x9)*	58.3 *(9x9)*	35.2 *(9x9)*
Laws R5S5	66.6 *(17x17)*	48.7 *(9x9)*	58.2 *(9x9)*	28.0 *(17x17)*
Variance	59.4 *(9x9)*	46.0 *(9x9)*	55.6 *(9x9)*	19.8 *(17x17)*
Skewness	37.2 *(65x65)*	35.4 *(33x33)*	23.9 *(33x33)*	25.5 *(9x9)*
Homogeneity (5, 45°)	7.8 *(33x33)*	11.1 *(9x9)*	61.4 *(9x9)*	67.0 *(17x17)*
Gabor (wav 4,ori 45°)	56.7 *(17x17)*	44.0 *(9x9)*	46.0 *(33x33)*	27.9 *(9x9)*
Gabor (wav 8,ori 0°)	56.6 *(17x17)*	44.9 *(9x9)*	46.8 *(33x33)*	29.0 *(9x9)*
Gabor (wav 4,ori 90°)	56.0 *(17x17)*	43.6 *(9x9)*	45.8 *(33x33)*	26.8 *(9x9)*
Gabor (wav 8,ori 135°)	56.2 *(17x17)*	43.1 *(17x17)*	46.1 *(33x33)*	28.5 *(9x9)*
Fractal	48.8 *(65x65)*	45.5 *(33x33)*	48.0 *(33x33)*	18.2 *(17x17)*
Wavelet Daubechies 4	49.7 *(17x17)*	44.8 *(17x17)*	66.5 *(9x9)*	60.7 *(9x9)*
Wavelet Haar	56.2 *(17x17)*	55.4 *(9x9)*	65.3 *(9x9)*	62.4 *(9x9)*

shown in the table.

According to these experiments, it is important to point out that, in practice, a single texture method usually has different optimal window sizes depending on the image contents. Therefore, a window size considered to be optimal from a theoretical standpoint [12] does not necessarily lead to optimal classification in practice, given an arbitrary test image.

In order to determine the benefits of integrating multiple windows of different size, the second set of experiments tested the proposed technique by evaluating every texture method over windows of the aforementioned sizes.

Table 2 shows the pixel classification rates obtained for each texture method and test image in Fig. 1 when multiple windows are integrated. By comparing Table 1 and Table 2, it can be noticed that the classification rates corresponding to the integration of multiple windows are significantly larger than the rates associated with single optimal windows in the majority of experiments. Those cases in which a single optimal window was superior are also highlighted.

The proposed technique has also been compared to MeasTex [9], a widely recognized texture classification framework. MeasTex provides a set of texture classifiers based on the combination of a texture method (e.g., Gabor, Markov, Fractal, Grey-Level Co-occurrence Matrices) evaluated over single-sized windows and a pattern classification algorithm (e.g., Multivariate Gaussian Bayes [MVG], K-Nearest Neighbors [KNN]). MeasTex was utilized to classify every pixel of the test images given a subimage of 33x33 pixels centered at that pixel —33x33 is the default win-

Table 2. Classification rates (%) with the proposed technique applied to each texture method. Multiple window sizes are integrated per method. Shadowed cells correspond to the only experiments in which optimal single window sizes (Table 1) led to better classification rates than multiple sizes

Texture Feature Extraction Method	Multiple Windows			
	Fig. 1(a)	Fig. 1(b)	Fig. 1(c)	Fig. 1(d)
Laws R5R5	59.0	56.7	54.1	29.8
Laws E5L5	65.8	42.0	59.8	31.7
Laws E5E5	56.8	51.4	70.3	52.6
Laws R5S5	75.1	61.6	60.5	37.7
Variance	62.2	51.8	62.7	23.6
Skewness	36.9	41.1	35.4	33.8
Homogeneity (5, 45°)	8.9	11.5	61.4	64.0
Gabor (wav 4,ori 45°)	68.1	54.4	57.1	42.9
Gabor (wav 8,ori 0°)	69.0	53.4	58.0	49.9
Gabor (wav 4,ori 90°)	70.0	54.7	56.3	41.4
Gabor (wav 8,ori 135°)	69.7	54.4	56.9	42.5
Fractal	51.1	53.7	44.7	23.6
Wavelet Daubechies 4	55.0	51.8	61.0	58.0
Wavelet Haar	56.3	59.2	65.8	66.5

dow size used by MeasTex [9]. The sample images utilized for the proposed classifier (Fig. 2) were also used as the training dataset for MeasTex.

Table 3 shows the classification rates obtained by applying the previous procedure, by considering four Gabor filters as texture methods and two classification algorithms currently supported by MeasTex (MVG, KNN). In all cases, MeasTex yielded lower classification rates than the proposed technique. In some cases (e.g., Gabor wav 4, ori 45°), the difference in favor of the proposed technique was rather significant. Furthermore, the best result obtained with MeasTex for each test image was achieved by using a different type of Gabor filter and classifier.

Fig. 3 shows qualitative results for the test image shown in Fig. 1(c) corresponding to the evaluation of Gabor (wav 8, ori 0°), which is the texture method that produced the best result for that test image with MeasTex. Fig. 3(a) shows the original image. Fig. 3(b) is the corresponding ground-truth classification. Fig. 3(c) presents the result of applying the proposed multiwindow technique according to Table 2. Fig. 3(d) shows the same technique by using a single optimal window size (33x33 according to Table 1), instead of multiwindow integration. Fig. 3(e) shows the result obtained with MeasTex according to Table 3.

5 Conclusions

This paper shows that pixel-based image classification can be both quantitatively and qualitatively improved by utilizing texture methods evaluated over multiple windows of different size. The proposed technique has been applied to different well-known families of texture methods, showing better classification rates than when a

Table 3. Classification rates (%) for the test images shown in Fig. 1 and different configurations of the MeasTex texture classifier (considering a single 33x33 window size)

Texture Feature Extraction Method and Classifier	Single Window (33x33)			
	Fig. 1(a)	Fig. 1(b)	Fig. 1(c)	Fig. 1(d)
Gabor (MVG,wav 4,ori 45°)	45.5	38.4	46.4	35.6
Gabor (MVG,wav 8,ori 0°)	30.6	20.8	51.3	41.7
Gabor (MVG,wav 4,ori 90°)	48.3	41.1	50.2	37.3
Gabor (MVG,wav 8,ori 135°)	37.3	27.0	41.5	34.8
Gabor (5-NN,wav 4,ori 45°)	49.2	39.8	48.5	36.9
Gabor (5-NN,wav 8,ori 0°)	35.3	24.9	54.0	43.8
Gabor (5-NN,wav 4,ori 90°)	51.1	42.2	52.3	38.1
Gabor (5-NN,wav 8,ori 135°)	40.3	29.3	45.5	37.2

single window size is utilized per method, as it has been traditionally done. Results also show that, in practice, it is not feasible to determine a unique window size that allows optimal discrimination for an arbitrary textured image and texture method.

Further work will consist of the combination of the proposed technique with the pixel-based classifier presented in [5][13], which integrates different texture methods. The goal is to obtain a pixel-based texture classifier based on the integration of multiple texture methods, each evaluated over multiple windows of different size. This classifier is to be applied to real-world problems involving the identification of specific texture patterns in digital images, such as specific kinds of tissue in medical imagery, or terrain in aerial images.

References

[1] J. Berger. *Statistical Decision Theory and Bayesian Analysis*. Springer-Verlag, 1985.

[2] D. Blostein and N. Ahuja. Shape from Texture: Integrating Texture-Element Surface Estimation. *IEEE Trans. PAMI*, 2(12): 1233-1251, 1989.

[3] P. Brodatz. *Textures: A Photographic Album for Artists and Designers*. Dover & Greer Publishing Company, 1999.

[4] K.I. Chang, K.W. Bowyer and M. Sivagurunath. Evaluation of Texture Segmentation Algorithms. *Proc. IEEE CVPR*, Fort Collins (USA), 1999.

[5] M.A. García and D. Puig. Improving Texture Pattern Recognition by Integration of Multiple Texture Feature Extraction Methods. *16th IAPR Int. Conf. on Pattern Recognition*, vol. 3, pp 7-10, Quebec, Canada, 2002.

[6] P. García-Sevilla and M. Petrou. Analysis of Irregularly Shaped Texture Regions: A Comparative Study. *15th IAPR Int. Conf. on Pat. Recog.*, 1080-1083, Barcelona, 2000.

[7] R.M. Haralick, K. Shanmugam and I. Distein. Textural Features for Image Classification. *IEEE Trans. SMC*, 6(3): 610-622, 1973.

[8] J. Kittler. Feature Selection and Extraction. *Handbook of Pattern Recognition and*

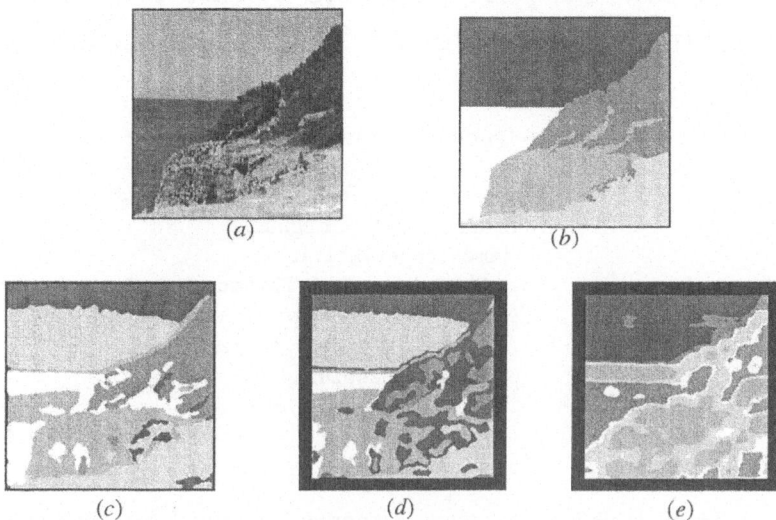

Fig. 3. Texture classification results corresponding to Fig. 1(c) with Gabor (wav 8, ori 0°). (a) Original image; (b) Ground-truth classification; (c) Proposed technique (58%); (d) MAP estimation upon single optimal window size 33x33 (46.8%); (e) Best MeasTex result (Gabor, 5-NN, 33x33): 54%.

Image Processing, T.Y. Young, K.S. Fu, editors. Academic Press, pp. 60-81, 1986.

[9] MeasTex Image Texture Database and Test Suite. *http://www.cssip.uq.edu.au/ staff/meastex/meastex.html.*

[10] S.Novianto et al. Multiwindowed Approach to the Optimum Estimation of the Local Fractal Dimension for Natural Image Segmentation. *Int. Conf. Im. Proc.,* Japan, 1999.

[11] T. Ojala, M. Pietikäinen and D. Harwood. A Comparative Study of Texture Measures with Classification Based on Feature Distributions. *Pattern Recognition,* 29(1), pp. 51-59, 1996.

[12] D. Puig and M.A. García. Determining Optimal Window Size for Texture Feature Extraction Methods. *IX Spanish Symposium on Pattern Recognition and Image Analysis,* vol. 2, pp 237-242, Castello, Spain, 2001.

[13] D. Puig and M.A. García. Recognizing Specific Texture Patterns by Integration of Multiple Texture Methods. *IEEE Int. Conf. on Image Processing,* vol. 1, pp 125-128, Rochester, USA, 2002.

[14] T. Randen and J.H. Husoy. Filtering for Texture Classification: A Comparative Study. *IEEE Trans. PAMI,* 21(4): 291-310, 1999.

[15] A.R. Rao and G.L. Lohse. Towards a Texture Naming System: Identifying Relevant Dimensions of Texture. *Vision Research,* 36(11), pp. 1649-1669, 1996.

[16] T.R. Reed and J.M. Hans du Buf. A Review of Recent Texture Segmentation and Feature Extraction Techniques. *CVGIP: Image Underst.,* 57(3): 359-372, 1993.

[17] J.C. Weszka, C.R. Dyler and A. Rosenfeld. A Comparative Study of Texture Measures for Terrain Classification. *IEEE Trans. SMC,* 6: 269-285, 1976.

Vessel Segmentation and Branching Detection using an Adaptive Profile Kalman Filter in Retinal Blood Vessel Structure Analysis

Pedro Quelhas[1,2] and James Boyce[1]

[1] King's College London, Department of Physics
Strand, London, England
james.boyce@kcl.ac.uk
http://www.kcl.ac.uk/Physics
[2] IDIAP - Dalle Molle Institute for Perceptual Artificial Intelligence
Rue Du Simplon 4, Martigny, Switzerland
pedro.quelhas@idiap.ch
http://www.idiap.ch

Abstract. This paper presents an improved tracking based method for retinal vessel segmentation that uses blood vessel morphology to adapt the tracking parameters. The method includes branching detection and avoidance methods. A bi-level threshold method, based on local vessel information, is used for segmentation. Tracking is based on Kalman filtering. The results are compared with existing ground truth. It is concluded that ground truth segmentation is not easily comparable.

1 Introduction

Several diseases affect blood vessels in the human body, making blood vessel appearance an important indicator for many diagnoses [1]. The retina is one place in the human body where the network of blood vessels can be viewed directly in vivo and examined for pathological changes [2]. The structure of the blood vessels in the retina can in this way be used in the grading of disease severity [3].

Retinal analysis in done through image collection. At present the analysis of these images can only be made by qualified medical staff, but there is a shortage of personnel to perform such examinations. An automated method to analyze the images from the retina would be a precious tool. There are two types of images that can be collected of the retinal blood vessels: retinal angiograms and retinal fundus images. Fundus images were used in this work because, although having lower contrast, they are captured by a non-invasive technique and hence are preferred by the medical community.

Two strategies have been employed in the past for the automatic detection of the retinal blood vessels [4]: scanning [5–7] and tracking [4,8,9]. Scanning is normally a two-pass operation. First feature points are enhanced, followed by a threshold to obtain a binary image. Chaining centerline midpoints is then

F.J. Perales et al. (Eds.): IbPRIA 2003, LNCS 2652, pp. 802–809, 2003.
© Springer-Verlag Berlin Heidelberg 2003

used to recognize the vessel structure while excluding isolated points. Tracking is a single-pass operation that starts from a given position and extracts image features, gathering structural information, while proceeding using the continuity properties of the vessel. Scanning methods always provide total image segmentation but result in difficult to extract and normally incomplete structural data. Tracking methods easily gather structural information but require vessel continuity for stable operation, and a selected starting point. Scanning methods are more computationally intensive than tracking based methods [4].

We chose to use a tracking method for its computational efficiency and ease of structural information extraction. Kalman filter [11] based tracking was chosen since it has proven itself to be adequate in this type of application [4, 9, 10].

Retinal structure tracking methods must segment the image into vessel/non-vessel pixels. Three approaches exist: amplitude segmentation [8, 9], template matching [4–6, 12] and parametric model fitting [10, 15]. Thresholding is always needed, either on the filter response (matching) or on the segmentation level (amplitude segmentation/model fitting).

Tracking methods segment the vessel based on its image intensity transverse section (profile). The profile is normally modelled as deriving from a Gaussian shape, caused by the reflection curve from the outer layer of a cylindrical column. In some vessels, due to light refraction on the column of blood within the vessel's wall, light is reflected to the camera causing a 'dip' at the top of the Gaussian shape [14]. Gao et al. [13] analyzed several models and concluded that the best model for blood vessel profiles in retinal fundus images where the 'dip' effect occurs is the difference of two Gaussian functions.

2 Methods

Based on accepted biological properties the following assumptions have been made concerning the appearance of vessels on retinal fundus images:

Piece-Wise Linear Structure: Piece-wise linear, i.e. small curvature, has been assumed in all previous tracking processes [4, 9, 10]. This assumption enables the setting of an upper limit for the curvature of the vessel, so that we can constrain the Kalman filter to a more stable operation point.

Binary Branching Tree: The binary nature of the vessel branching tree can be easily recognized in retinal images. Thus, there can only be two vessels emanating from a branching point [2].

Constant Vessel Width Between Branching Points: The average width variation in interbranch sections of the vessel can be ignored, in low pathology incidence. Useful in the detection and avoidance of pathologies and crossing, improving the tracking stability.

Used in past literature without proof [8, 9], this property was here verified by observed results. A total of 520 vessel profiles were gathered from linear sections of several different vessels with different widths. The variation of those vessels' width was measured. Using the Kolmogorov-Smirnov statistical the estimate for the average width variation is 0 ± 0.32 pixels with a confidence of 95%.

2.1 Blood Vessel Tracking

The Kalman filter implements a predictor-corrector type estimator that is optimal in the sense that it minimizes the estimated error covariance in optimal conditions. Though the conditions necessary for optimality rarely exist the filter works well for many applications [16].

The case of Kalman filter tracking of blood vessels deserves special attention since the filter applied to the tracking process is modified so that the calculations become simpler.

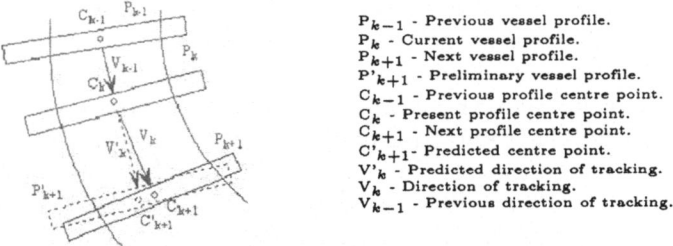

P_{k-1} - Previous vessel profile.
P_k - Current vessel profile.
P_{k+1} - Next vessel profile.
P'_{k+1} - Preliminary vessel profile.
C_{k-1} - Previous profile centre point.
C_k - Present profile centre point.
C_{k+1} - Next profile centre point.
C'_{k+1}- Predicted centre point.
V'_k - Predicted direction of tracking.
V_k - Direction of tracking.
V_{k-1} - Previous direction of tracking.

Fig. 1. Tracking algorithm schematics.

Fig. 1 shows the spatial schematics for the used Kalman filter. The algorithm uses the previous and current profile's center to predict the vessel's trajectory. Measurement is done and a new profile is obtained giving the correct vessel's trajectory.

$$\hat{px}(k+1) = \phi \times px(k) \quad (1)$$

$$p = \left[\begin{pmatrix} x \\ vx \\ ax \end{pmatrix}, \begin{pmatrix} y \\ vy \\ ay \end{pmatrix} \right] \quad (2)$$

$$\phi = \left\{ \begin{matrix} 1 & T & \frac{1}{2}T^2 \\ 0 & 1 & T \\ 0 & 0 & 1 \end{matrix} \right\} \quad (3)$$

$$px(k+1) = \hat{px}(k+1) + \beta \times P(k) \quad (4)$$

$$P(k) = \left\{ \begin{matrix} Z(k) \\ \frac{1}{T}\left(\frac{3}{2}Z(k) - 2Z(k-1) + \frac{1}{2}Z(k-2) \right) \\ \frac{1}{T^2}\left(Z(k) - 2Z(k-1) + Z(k-2) \right) \end{matrix} \right\} \quad (5)$$

Equations 1-5 give the applied Kalman filter mathematical structure, where T is the tracking step size, $px(k)$ is the state vector, $\hat{px}(k)$ is the predicted state vector, $Z(k)$ is the measurement from the image, β is the filter mixing gain and k is the current tracking step. In literature the gain β is normally one, giving absolute confidence to the measurements [9, 10]. Some authors try to assess a value depending on the assumed errors in each of the model's variables [4].

$$\beta = \begin{cases} 0, \text{current width variation} > 2 \times \text{standard deviation} \\ 1, \text{current width variation} < 2 \times \text{standard deviation} \end{cases} \quad (6)$$

We here introduce a novel tracking gain that varies as a function of the vessel's width. Based on the constant width principle introduced in Section 2 we assume that if the width doesn't vary the vessel is being followed correctly and so we keep the gain high. Significant changes in width occur only in branch points, crossings or pathology, in those cases the filter's gain is reduced, thus causing the tracking to follow the predicted path without deviation. Gain variation was implemented according to the rules presented in equation 6.

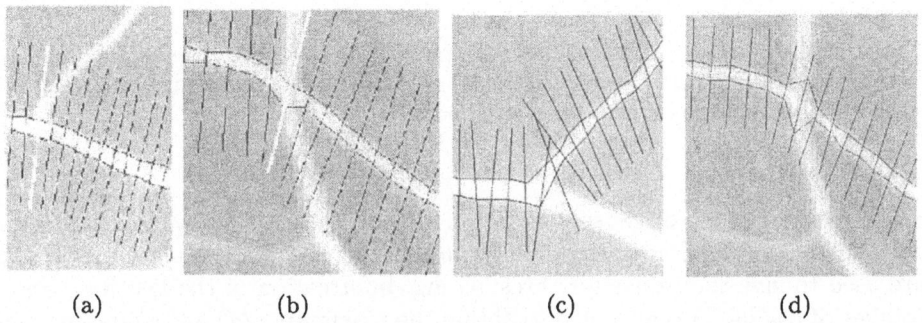

| (a) | (b) | (c) | (d) |

Fig. 2. Tracking examples: (a) and (b) show correct tracking resulting from variable gain usage (white line marks the profile where gain was varied), contrary to these results, fixed gain produced the erroneous results in images (c) and (d).

Fig. 2 shows the results from the developed tracking method. Comparing the results in (a) and (b) with (c), respectively, and (d) its is easy to see that fixed gain methods can cause both trajectory (c) and measurement errors (d).

Often, after branching or crossing, several vessels will be detected vessel. The problem of choosing from the several possible vessels is solved based on similarity with the previously tracked vessel. Similarity is measured by euclidian distance in a two dimensional feature space based on width difference and trajectory deviation. The choice is constrained to smaller vessel than the one previously tracked since resulting vessels are always thinner [2]. If no vessel can be found that fits the requirements tracking is terminated and pathology is reported.

2.2 Vessel Segmentation

The objective of this work is the analysis of the retinal vessel structure so an accurate method for vessel segmentation is needed. Matching is known to have low accuracy [12]. Parameterized model techniques presented in [10, 15] were incapable of providing good results in the presence of low contrast or very thin vessels. Single-level direct segmentation [8, 9] was tested using half-height threshold, the results were unsatisfactory since it is more prone to produce sub-division of wider vessel and false positives, as can be seen in Fig. 3 (b).

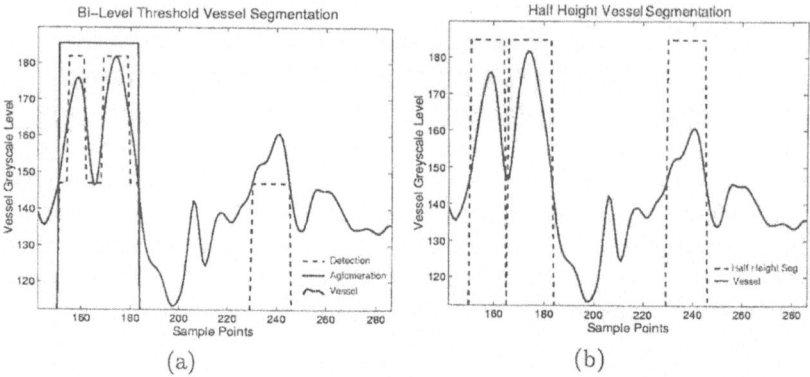

Fig. 3. Bi-Level versus half height segmentation: (a) shows the results from the bi-level thresholding method developed in this work, (b) shows the result from a normal half-height thresholding method as presented in [9].

Here we present a direct segmentation method based on bi-level segmentation with subsequent agglomeration. The values gathered from the previous profiles are used to give the values for thresholding. Information of the last four vessel profiles (if available) is averaged to obtain the maximum (M) and minimum (m) levels used to set the thresholds. Thresholds are set by equation 7.

$$\begin{cases} t1 = m + 0.33 * (M - m) \\ t2 = m + 0.66 * (M - m) \end{cases} \tag{7}$$

Any pixel having intensity above t2 is classified as vessel (condition 1) and all points above t1 that have a neighbor above t2 are also classified vessel (condition 2). This is repeated until there are no more vessel in condition 2. Fig. 3 (a) show the final result of this method.

In literature great importance is placed upon the reproduction of ground-truth data [5, 12]. This is logical since we are trying to replace the human interpretation of the retinal images.

It was found that, in existing data [5], ground-truth segmentation levels are asymmetric, as can be observed in Fig. 4 (b). Since the used segmentation method produces a symmetric segmentation, ground truth was impossible to reproduce with the presented method. Fig. 4 (a) shows the ROC curves for a symmetric and asymmetric ground-truth blood vessel respectively. In Fig. 4 (a) the point of operation of a simple half-height segmentation method on a symmetric ground-truth blood vessel is marked by a plus sign.

It is believed that the human observer tends to bias its segmentation based on the illumination of the vessel. The flash light used to take the images produces shadow on one of the vessel's side and not in the other due to the spherical geometry of the retina. This makes the ground truth segmentation complex.

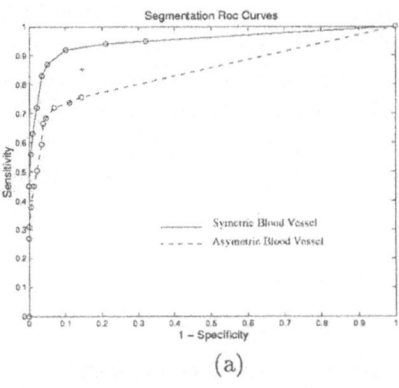 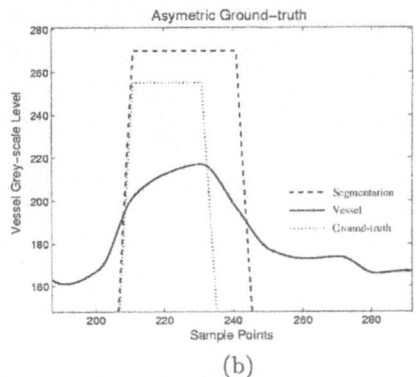

(a)   (b)

Fig. 4. Ground-truth comparison results: (a) shows the resulting ROC curves from symmetric and asymmetric ground-truth blood vessels, (b) shows an example of asymmetric ground-truth blood vessel segmentation.

2.3   Branching Detection

Most of the tracking methods existing in literature [9, 10] ignore branching of vessels or base detection on the local curvature of the vessel [4]. The first option gives reliable results only during linear sections of the vessel; the second ignores all the small vessels that can branch off the main vessel.

Currently there is no strategy that fully solves this problem: this is because branching is highly irregular and branching rules are not easily gathered from images [2].

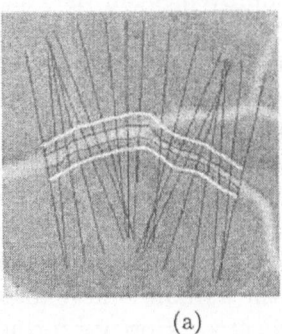 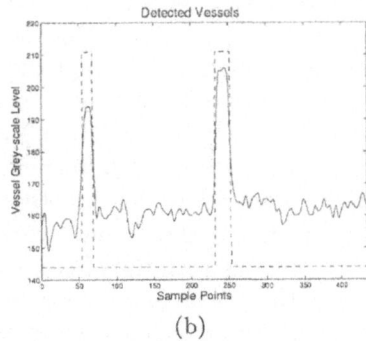

(a)   (b)

Fig. 5. Branching Detection Method. (a) shows the tracking of the vessel with two white lines at each side of the vessel, this is where the branching vessels are going to be searched, (b) shows the gathered pixel values and detected vessels in the left side line.

Although the tracking method presented here detects branching points which would perturb the tracking so that they can be compensated, there are some vessels that are either too small to perturb the tracking or are missed because they exist between profile samples. To solve the problem we propose the collection of the grey levels in two lines parallel to each side of the vessel, this allows searching for branching vessels using the bi-level threshold used in the main vessel. Fig. 5 shows results of branch detection.

The detected branches can then be used as seed points for the main tracking algorithm.

3   Results

The performance of the variable gain tracker when in presence of branches or crossings was proven to be effective in the available set of images, as can be observed in Fig. 2. This allowed for a better quality in the acquired structural data.

The introduced blood vessel bi-level threshold detection method was found to be more effective than the normally used half-height method [9, 8] as can be seen in Fig. 3 (a). It can be seen that in the presence of symmetric ground-truth this method has higher segmentation quality.

The assumption that blood vessels don't change width between branching points was found to be correct by statistical inference and consequential results.

4   Discussion

The strategy used to develop this algorithm was found to be adequate for retinal blood vessel segmentation. Tracking was shown to allow the integration of local statistical information, effectively allowing for improvement in the tracker efficiency. The variable gain allowed for the avoidance of singularities that otherwise might disturb tracking and corrupt the structural data.

The bi-level threshold technique enabled the correct detection of the vessel even in presence of significant 'dip' effects and nearby smaller vessels.

The proposed method for branching detection gave promising results and is believed to be a good base for a method capable of complete segmentation.

The asymmetry of the ground truth made the reproduction of human segmentation impossible with the presented method. If the proposed dependency of the ground-truth data on illumination is proven, the authors believe that correct segmentation may by possible even in asymmetric cases. However further study is needed.

5   Acknowledgements

This work was the result of the dissertation work for the M.Res. in Image and X-Ray Physics at King's College London, founded by EPSRC. Retinal images were supplied as a part of a collaboration with St. George's Hospital, Tooting.

This work was done with the financial support of the Portuguese Foundation for Science and Technology (FCT) and the European Social Fund (FSE) through the scholarship SFRH/BM/8054/2002.

The authors acknowledge financial support provided by the Swiss National Center of Competence in Research (NCCR) on Interactive Multimodal Information Management (IM)2. The NCCR is managed by the Swiss National Science Foundation on behalf of the Federal Authorities.

References

1. American Academy of Ophthalmology: Ophthalmic Pathology. Basic and Clinical Science Courses, Section 11,179,(1991).
2. M. Martinez-Perez: Computer Analysis of the Geometry of the Retinal Vasculature. PhD. thesis of the University of London, Imperial College, November 2000.
3. M. Figueiredo, and J. Leitao: A Nonsmmoothing Approach to the Estimation of the Vessel Contours in Angiograms. IEEE Trans. in Med. Imag., V. 14, 162-172, 1995.
4. O. Chutatape, L. Zheng, and S. Krishnan: Retinal Blood Vessel Detection and Tracking by Matched Gaussian and Kalman Filters. 20th Annual International Conference of the IEEE Engineering in Medicine and Biology Society, Hong Kong, 29 October - 1 November 1998,3144-3149.
5. A. Hoover, V. Kouznetsova, and M. Goldbaum: Locating Blood Vessels in Retinal Images by Piecewise Threshold Probing of a Matched Filter Response. IEEE Transaction on Medical Image, V. 19, N. 3, 203-210, 2000.
6. S. Chaudhuri, S. Chatterjee, N. Katz, M. Nelson, and M. Goldbaum: Detection of blood vessels in retinal images using two-dimensional matched filters. IEEE Trans. on Medical Imaging, V. 8, N. 3, 263-269, September 1989.
7. B. Cote, W. Hart, M. Goldbaum, P. Kude, and M. Nelson: Classification of blood vessels in ocular fundus images. Computer Science and Engineering Department University of California, San Diego, Technical Report, 1994.
8. Y. Tolias, and M. Panas: A fuzzy vessel tracking algorithm for retinal images based on fuzzy clustering. IEEE Trans. on Medical Imaging, V. 17, N. 2, 263-273, 1998.
9. Y. Sun: Automated Identification of Vessel Contours in Coronary Arteriograms by an Adaptive Tracking Algorithm. IEEE Trans. on Med. Imag., V. 8, N. 1,1989.
10. A. Zhou, M. Rzeszotarski, and L. Singerman: The detection and quantification of retinopathy using digital angiograms. IEEE Trans. on Med. Imag., V. 13, N. 4, 1994.
11. R. Kalman: A New Approach to Linear Filtering and Prediction Problems. Transaction of the ASMEJournal of Basic Engineering, 82, Series D, 35-45, 1960.
12. L. Gang, O. Chutatape, and S. Krishnan: Detection and Measurement of Retinal Vessels in Fundus Images Using Amplitude Modified Second-Order Gaussian Filter. IEEE Trans. on Biomedical Engineering, V. 49, N. 2, February 2002.
13. X. Gao, A. Bharath, A. Stanton, A. Hughes, N. Chapman, and S. Thom: Towards retinal vessel parameterisation. SPIE conference on medial imaging, 1997.
14. O. Brinchman-Hansen, and H. Heier: Theoretical Relations between Light Streak Characteristics and Optical Properties of Retinal Vessels. Acta Ophthalmologica, Supplement 179, 33, 1986.
15. X. Gao, A. Bharath, A. Stanton, A. Hughes, N. Chapman, and S. Thom: Measurement of Vessel Diameters on Retinal Images for Cardiovascular Studies. Department of Clinical Pharmacology, Imperial College School of Medicine, London, UK, 2001.
16. G. Bishop, G. Welch: An Introduction to the Kalman Filter. University of North Carolina, Department of Computer Science, Course 8, SIGGRAPH 2001,.

Reconstruction of Quadrics
from Two Polarization Views

Stefan Rahmann

Institute for Pattern Recognition and Image Processing
Computer Science Department, University of Freiburg
Georges-Koehler-Allee 52, 79110 Freiburg, Germany
rahmann@informatik.uni-freiburg.de

Abstract. This paper addresses the problem of reconstructing texture-less objects of quadric like shape. It is known that a quadric can be uniquely recovered from its apparent contours in three views. But, in the case of only two views the reconstruction is a one parameter family of quadrics.

Polarization imaging provides additional geometric information compared to simple intensity based imaging. The polarization image encodes the projection of the surface normals onto the image and therefore provides constraints on the surface geometry.

In this paper it is proven that two polarization views of a quadric contain sufficient information for a complete determination of its shape. The proof itself is constructive leading to a closed-form solution for the quadric. Additionally, an indirect algorithm is presented which uses both polarization and apparent contours. By experiments it is shown that the presented algorithm produces accurate reconstruction results.

1 Introduction

Quadrics in 3D space and conics in 2D space, besides points, lines and planes, are basic geometric entities, which are widely used and have been extensively studied in the domain of computer vision. This paper focuses on the problem of the recovery of texture-less objects of quadric shape from the information available in two views. As no texture on the quadric surface is present, no point correspondences can be used to reconstruct the surface via triangulation of point features. Hence, the only available information is the apparent contour or the outline of the quadric. It has been shown that a quadric can be uniquely recovered from its outlines in three views [2, 7, 6]. The problem can be solved in a linear way deploying dual-space geometry. But, from two views the reconstruction is ambiguous and a one parameter family of quadrics will project onto the same apparent contours in the images. A second challenge is the recovery of quadrics under circumstances where the outlines are not or only partially available, for example due to occlusion.

Polarization imaging analyzes the state of polarization of reflected light. In a polarization image the projection of the underlying surface normals is encoded

F.J. Perales et al. (Eds.): IbPRIA 2003, LNCS 2652, pp. 810–820, 2003.
© Springer-Verlag Berlin Heidelberg 2003

and constraints on the surface geometry can be derived. This fact was first deployed by Wolff in [11] where the orientation of a plane was determined based on two polarization images. Recently, it was shown that polarization imaging can be used for the reconstruction of specular surfaces [9] and in photometric stereo [3, 4].

In this paper it is shown that using two polarization views a quadric can be determined uniquely. It is proven that solely the polarization information (without the apparent contours) provides in general a unique solution for the quadric shape (In some exceptional cases the shape is recovered only up to a scale factor.). The proof is constructive and a closed-form solution for the quadric can be derived. But, it is shown that for real images the linear algorithm is not the first choice. Instead, we propose a non-linear algorithm. This indirect optimization scheme has the advantage that information available from the apparent contours can be easily incorporated. We show experiments on real images and access the quality of the results for both solely polarization and polarization plus apparent contours.

2   Polarization Imaging

Polarization analysis is the determination of the complete state of polarization of the light. In the case of partial linear polarized light, the polarization image is equivalent to a set of three images encoding the intensity (that is what a normal camera would see), the degree of polarization and the orientation of polarization (see figure 2). The orientation of polarization is encoded in the so called phase image.

The two basic assumptions for a geometric scene interpretation using polarization imaging are, that the object under investigation exhibits a microscopically smooth surface structure and that the light illuminating the scene is not polarized. The assumption of unpolarized lighting results in phase images being invariant with respect to the intensity of the illumination and therefore becoming a characteristic entity of the object's shape, which is clearly shown in figure 2. Even though this assumption is not strictly fulfilled, as in real environments reflected light is slightly polarized, good reconstruction results can be achieved.

3   Polarization Imaging and Orthographic Projection

For a proper polarization analysis the incoming light has to pass orthogonally through the polarizing filter. Therefore, the scaled orthographic projection, see eg. [5], is the appropriate camera model: 3D world points $\mathbf{X} = (X, Y, Z)^T$ project onto 2D image points $\mathbf{x}^i = (x^i, y^i)^T$ in the i-th camera, having squared pixels and no skew. Rotation and translation between world and camera coordinate system are given as $\mathbf{R}^{i^T} = (\mathbf{R}_1^i, \mathbf{R}_2^i, \mathbf{R}_3^i)$ and $\mathbf{t}^{i^T} = (t_1^i, t_2^i, t_3^i)$ respectively. Be $\tilde{\mathbf{X}}$ and $\tilde{\mathbf{x}}$ the projective extension of $\mathbf{X}$ respectively $\mathbf{x}$, we can write in homogeneous coordinates:

$$\lambda \tilde{\mathbf{x}}^i = \begin{pmatrix} \alpha & 0 & \alpha t_1^i + x_0 \\ 0 & \alpha & \alpha t_2^i + y_0 \\ 0 & 0 & 1 \end{pmatrix} \begin{pmatrix} 1\,0\,0\,0 \\ 0\,1\,0\,0 \\ 0\,0\,0\,1 \end{pmatrix} \begin{pmatrix} \mathbf{R}^i & \mathbf{0}_3 \\ \mathbf{0}_3^T & 1 \end{pmatrix} \tilde{\mathbf{X}} = \mathbf{K}^i \mathbf{P}_{\|} \mathbf{T}^i \tilde{\mathbf{X}} \quad, \quad (1)$$

where $\alpha = \frac{f}{Z_{ave}^i}$ is the quotient of the focal length and the average depth. As the experimental setup is fully calibrated and the average depths Z_{ave}^i can be computed from the image data, the camera matrices $\mathbf{K}^i$ are known as well. Therefore, image points $\tilde{\mathbf{x}}^i$ can be substituted with their normalized counterpart $(\mathbf{K}^i)^{-1}\tilde{\mathbf{x}}^i$, which finally yields:

$$\lambda \tilde{\mathbf{x}}^i = \mathbf{P}_{\|} \mathbf{T}^i \tilde{\mathbf{X}} \quad. \tag{2}$$

4   Level Curves as the Projection of Surface Profiles

In the context of polarization imaging the notion of level curves was first introduced in [8]. Level curves are the projection of surface profiles where the surface profiles are the intersections of the surface and planes parallel to the image plane. It was shown that level curves can be computed based solely on the phase image. In figure 1 the case of a quadric surface is shown. The polarization based reconstruction problem can then be formulated as follows: given a set of level curves the corresponding surface profiles are known as well, up to their depth. Can two sets of level curves computed from two polarization images provide a unique solution for the quadratic surface shape?

5   Quadric Surfaces and Conic Surface Profiles

5.1   Definition of a Quadric, Coordinate Transformation and the Power Substitution

The equation of a quadric in homogeneous coordinates is $\tilde{\mathbf{X}}^T \mathbf{Q} \tilde{\mathbf{X}} = 0$, with a symmetric matrix $\mathbf{Q}$.

Let us define a vector $[\tilde{\mathbf{X}}]^2$ as $[\tilde{\mathbf{X}}]^2 = (X^2, XY, XZ, Y^2, YZ, Z^2, X, Y, Z, 1)^T = (([\mathbf{X}]^2)^T, \mathbf{X}^T, 1)^T$; $[\tilde{\mathbf{X}}]^2$ is called the second power of $\tilde{\mathbf{X}}$. Then, an alternative formulation of a quadric is to write the implicit polynomial as the scalar product of a coefficient vector $\mathbf{C}$ and $[\tilde{\mathbf{X}}]^2$:

$$\mathbf{C}^T [\tilde{\mathbf{X}}]^2 = 0 \quad. \tag{3}$$

The coefficient vector can be decomposed into blocks referring to elements of the power vector of the same degree: we define $\mathbf{C}^T = (\mathbf{C}_2^T, \mathbf{C}_1^T, C_0)$, which gives $\mathbf{C}^T [\tilde{\mathbf{X}}]^2 = \mathbf{C}_2^T [\mathbf{X}]^2 + \mathbf{C}_1^T \mathbf{X} + C_0$.

Be $\mathbf{T}$ a general invertible transformation mapping $\tilde{\mathbf{X}}$ onto $\tilde{\mathbf{X}}'$: $\tilde{\mathbf{X}}' = \mathbf{T}\tilde{\mathbf{X}}$. There exist a linear transformation $[\mathbf{T}]^2$ mapping $[\tilde{\mathbf{X}}]^2$ onto $[\mathbf{T}\tilde{\mathbf{X}}]^2$: $[\mathbf{T}\mathbf{X}]^2 =:$

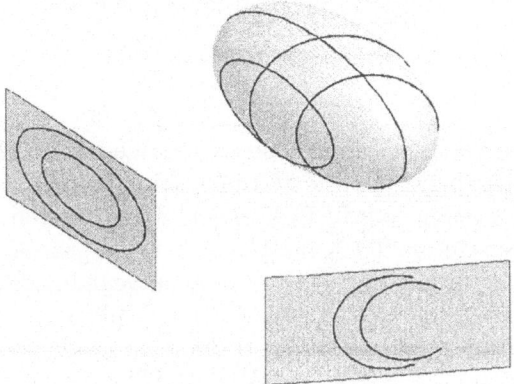

Fig. 1. Level curves are the projection of surface profiles, which are parallel to the image plane. Surface profiles and level curves of a quadric are conics. Two calibrated images with two level curves each are sufficient to determine the shape of the quadric

$[\mathbf{T}]^2[\tilde{\mathbf{X}}]^2$. $[\mathbf{T}]^2$ is called the second power substitution of $\mathbf{T}$. The original publication presenting the general n-degree power substitution is [10]. An overview over the properties of the power substitution and an application to image analysis and recognition can be found in [1]. Equipped with the concept of the power substitution a coordinate transformation in equation (3) results in: $\mathbf{C}^T[\tilde{\mathbf{X}}]^2 = \mathbf{C}^T[\mathbf{T}^{-1}]^2[\mathbf{T}]^2[\tilde{\mathbf{X}}]^2 = \mathbf{C}^T[\mathbf{T}^{-1}]^2[\tilde{\mathbf{X}}']^2 = \mathbf{C}'^T[\tilde{\mathbf{X}}']^2 = 0$. Here, we see a very nice advantage of the power substitution: the transformation of the coefficient vector is a simple linear mapping in contrast to a left- and right-hand side matrix multiplication in the case of the quadratic matrix formulation.

5.2 Surface Profiles

Assuming the Z-axis to be the direction of (parallel) projection and the quadric given in the camera coordinate system. As it was explained already, surface profiles parallel to the X/Y-plane can be computed from the phase image. The profiles have constant depth values resulting in $\tilde{\mathbf{X}} = (X, Y, Z_0, 1)^T$. Equation (3) will then transform into

$$\mathbf{C}^T[\tilde{\mathbf{X}}]^2{}_{|Z=Z_0} =$$
$$(C_1, C_2, C_4, C_3 Z_0 + C_7, C_5 Z_0 + C_8, C_6 Z_0^2 + C_9 Z_0 + C_{10})(X^2, XY, Y^2, X, Y, 1)^T$$
$$\Rightarrow \quad \mathbf{C}^T[\tilde{\mathbf{X}}]^2{}_{|Z=Z_0} = \mathbf{C}^T \mathbf{Z}_0[\tilde{\mathbf{x}}]^2 = \mathbf{c}^T[\tilde{\mathbf{x}}]^2 = 0 \quad ,\text{where} \quad \tilde{\mathbf{x}} = (X, Y, 1)^T \quad .$$
$$(4)$$

Surface profiles of a quadric, as an intersection with a plane parallel to the image plane, will project onto the image plane as conics. The following homogeneous equation holds:

$$\mathbf{c} \sim \mathbf{Z}_0^T \mathbf{C} \ . \tag{5}$$

Here, the sign $\sim$ means equality up to a non zero scale factor. The 10×6 matrix $\mathbf{Z}_0$, as a function of Z_0, plays the role of a projection matrix.

Points in the i-th camera coordinates system $\tilde{\mathbf{X}}^i$ are related to world coordinates $\tilde{\mathbf{X}}$ by the transformation $\mathbf{T}^i$: $\tilde{\mathbf{X}}^i = \mathbf{T}^i \tilde{\mathbf{X}}$. Then, the general equation for the projection of a quadric surface onto the j-th level curve in image i, corresponding to the depth $Z_0^{i,j}$, is:

$$\mathbf{c}^{i,j} \sim (\mathbf{Z}_0^{i,j})^T ([\mathbf{T}^i]^2)^{-T} \mathbf{C} \ . \tag{6}$$

As it was stated in equation (1) the transformation is a simple rotation. Hence, $[\mathbf{T}^i]^2$ and its inverse $([\mathbf{T}^i]^2)^{-1}$ exhibit a block-diagonal structure: $diag(\, ([\mathbf{T}^i]^2)^{-1}\,) = (\, ([\mathbf{R}^i]^2)^{-1}, (\mathbf{R}^i)^{-1}, 1\,)$. The individual blocks of the transformation matrix can be written explicitly as: $([\mathbf{R}^i]^2)^{-1} = (\mathbf{r}_1^i, \ldots, \mathbf{r}_6^i)$ and $(\mathbf{R}^i)^{-1} = (\mathbf{r}_7^i, \mathbf{r}_8^i, \mathbf{r}_9^i)$. Now, equation (6) can be separated into quadratic, linear and constant terms:

$$(\mathbf{r}_1^i, \mathbf{r}_2^i, \mathbf{r}_4^i)^T \mathbf{C}_2 \qquad\qquad\qquad = \lambda^i\, \mathbf{c}_2^{i,j} \ , \tag{7}$$

$$Z_0^{i,j}\, (\mathbf{r}_3^i, \mathbf{r}_5^i)^T \mathbf{C}_2 \ + \quad (\mathbf{r}_7^i, \mathbf{r}_8^i)^T \mathbf{C}_1 \qquad = \lambda^i\, \mathbf{c}_1^{i,j} \ , \tag{8}$$

$$Z_0^{i,j\,2}\, (\mathbf{r}_6^i)^T \mathbf{C}_2 \ + \ Z_0^{i,j}\, (\mathbf{r}_9^i)^T \mathbf{C}_1 \ + \ C_0 = \lambda^i\, c_0^{i,j} \ . \tag{9}$$

The λ^i is a scaling factor which is constant for all the different profiles j in one image i. This is because the quadratic term does not change for different depth $Z_0^{i,j}$, see (7). Assumed that two conics $\mathbf{c}^{i,1}$ and $\mathbf{c}^{i,2}$ have been computed from the phase image. After normalization by the norm $|\mathbf{c}_2^{i,j}|$ it holds: $\mathbf{c}_2^{i,1} = \mathbf{c}_2^{i,2}$.

6   Recovery of the Quadric

6.1   Calculating the Quadratic Term

According to (7) one level curve in each image provides six equations in seven parameters (six in $\mathbf{C}_2$ and, for example, one for λ^1 while setting $\lambda^2 = 1$). Furthermore, the matrix $(\mathbf{r}_1^1, \mathbf{r}_2^1, \mathbf{r}_4^1, \mathbf{r}_1^2, \mathbf{r}_2^2, \mathbf{r}_4^2)$ is rank deficient. Hence, not enough constraints for the calculation of $\mathbf{C}_2$ are provided. Fortunately, more than one level curve in each phase image can be computed. Taking the difference in (8) for two different level curves yields:

$$(\mathbf{r}_3^i, \mathbf{r}_5^i)^T \mathbf{C}_2 \ = \ \frac{\lambda^i}{(Z_0^{i,1} - Z_0^{i,2})}\, (\mathbf{c}_1^{i,1} - \mathbf{c}_1^{i,2}) \ = \ \delta^i\, \Delta \mathbf{c}_1^i \ . \tag{10}$$

As the difference in depth $(Z_0^{i,1} - Z_0^{i,2})$ is not known a new scaling factor δ^i is introduced. Combining (7) and (10) in a single system yields:

$$
\begin{pmatrix}
(\mathbf{r}_1^1, \mathbf{r}_2^1, \mathbf{r}_4^1)^T & -\mathbf{c}_2^{1,1} & \mathbf{0}_3 & \mathbf{0}_3 & \mathbf{0}_3 \\
(\mathbf{r}_3^1, \mathbf{r}_5^1)^T & \mathbf{0}_2 & -\Delta\mathbf{c}^1 & \mathbf{0}_2 & \mathbf{0}_2 \\
(\mathbf{r}_1^2, \mathbf{r}_2^2, \mathbf{r}_4^2)^T & \mathbf{0}_3 & \mathbf{0}_3 & -\mathbf{c}_2^{2,1} & \mathbf{0}_3 \\
(\mathbf{r}_3^2, \mathbf{r}_5^2)^T & \mathbf{0}_2 & \mathbf{0}_2 & \mathbf{0}_2 & -\Delta\mathbf{c}^2
\end{pmatrix}
\begin{pmatrix}
\mathbf{C}_2 \\
\lambda^1 \\
\delta^1 \\
\lambda^2 \\
\delta^2
\end{pmatrix}
= \mathbf{0}_{10} \quad . \tag{11}
$$

Writing the above equation shortly as: $\mathbf{My} = (\mathbf{M_r}, \mathbf{M_c})\mathbf{y} = \mathbf{0}$. The solution vector $\mathbf{y}$ is the null space of the matrix $\mathbf{M}$. Therefore, the rank of $\mathbf{M}$ has to be investigated in order to categorize the solution in $\mathbf{y}$.

6.2   General Solution and Degeneracy

General Quadrics By general quadric it is understood that the matrix $\mathbf{Q}$ has full rank, i.e. the quadric is a sphere or a hyperboloid of one sheet (up to any projective transformation). In this case the quadratic vectors $\mathbf{c}_2^{i,j}$ do not vanish. Furthermore, assuming the $\Delta\mathbf{c}_1^i$ not to be both zero. Then, it can be proven that the matrix $\mathbf{M}$ has rank 9 and, what is important for a unique solution in $\mathbf{C}_2$, $\mathbf{M_r}$ has rank 6. The solution in $\mathbf{y}$ is unique and a unique solution in $\mathbf{C}$ and all the depth $Z_0^{i,j}$ can be derived as well (which will be shown in the next section).

General Quadrics Viewed from Principal Axes If the quadric is viewed from a principal axis, the elements C_3 and C_5 in equation (4) are zero. Therefore, $\Delta\mathbf{c}_1^i$ is a zero vector and two distinct level curves $\mathbf{c}^{i,1}$ and $\mathbf{c}^{i,2}$ differ only in the last element $c_0^{i,j}$. Assuming that both images are taken from principal axes. Then, both columns in $\mathbf{M}$ containing $\Delta\mathbf{c}_1^i$ can be discarded resulting in a 8 element solution vector $\mathbf{y}^T = (\mathbf{C}_2^T, \lambda^1, \lambda^2)$. Then, it can be proven that $\mathbf{M}$ has rank 7 and a unique solution in $\mathbf{y}$ exists. But, as (δ^1, δ^2) can not be calculated the depths $Z_0^{i,j}$ can be derived only up to a scalar factor. This implies that the shape of the quadric can be determined up to a scalar factor too. This is, for example, the case if the quadric is a sphere: all spheres with the same origin but arbitrary radius will result in identical phase images. At least one viewing direction must not be a principal axis in order to uniquely determine the quadric.

Degenerated Quadrics A quadric is called degenerated if the rank of $\mathbf{Q}$ is three or less. Quadrics of rank three are cones or all different sorts of cylinders (elliptic, hyperbolic or parabolic). Looking onto a cylinder from a direction normal to its major axis, level curves are pairs of lines, i.e. a degenerated conics. If all viewing directions, two or more, are such that the resulting level curves are degenerated, then the shape of the quadric can not be determined.

6.3   Calculating the Linear and Constant Term

The scheme for the calculation of the linear term is quite similar to that for the calculation of the quadratic term. It can been seen, that using (8) for one level curve each in two images provides only four equations in five unknowns. Because of (10), considering more than one level curve will not help to calculate $\mathbf{C}_1$. So, the difference in (9) for two different level curves is taken which yields:

$$\mathbf{C}_2^T \mathbf{r}_6^i \left(Z_0^{i,1} + Z_0^{i,2} \right) + \mathbf{C}_1^T \mathbf{r}_9^i = \delta^i \, \Delta c_0^i \ . \tag{12}$$

Combining equation (8) and (12) for two views yields:

$$
\begin{pmatrix}
2(\mathbf{r}_7^1, \mathbf{r}_8^1)^T & (\mathbf{r}_3^1, \mathbf{r}_5^1)^T \mathbf{C}_2 & \mathbf{0} \\
(\mathbf{r}_9^1)^T & (\mathbf{r}_6^1)^T \mathbf{C}_2 & \mathbf{0} \\
2(\mathbf{r}_7^2, \mathbf{r}_8^2)^T & \mathbf{0} & (\mathbf{r}_3^2, \mathbf{r}_5^2)^T \mathbf{C}_2 \\
(\mathbf{r}_9^2)^T & \mathbf{0} & (\mathbf{r}_6^2)^T \mathbf{C}_2
\end{pmatrix}
\begin{pmatrix}
{}^1\mathbf{C} \\
Z_0^{1,1} + Z_0^{1,2} \\
Z_0^{2,1} + Z_0^{2,2}
\end{pmatrix}
=
\begin{pmatrix}
\lambda^1(c_1^{1,1} + c_1^{1,2}) \\
\delta^1 \Delta c_0^1 \\
\lambda^2(c_1^{2,1} + c_1^{2,2}) \\
\delta^2 \Delta c_0^2
\end{pmatrix} . \tag{13}
$$

The system provides six equations for five unknowns. Generally, the matrix has rank five and a unique solution exists. But, as it was shown previously, the situation is different if viewing directions are parallel to principal axes of the quadric. In this case the δ^i can not be determined in (11) and the entry $(\mathbf{r}_3^i, \mathbf{r}_5^i)^T \mathbf{C}_2$ is identical to the zero vector. Thus, the corresponding column and equation line has to be discarded, and the depth $Z_0^{i,1} + Z_0^{i,2}$ can not be calculated. As the matrix $(\mathbf{r}_7^1, \mathbf{r}_8^1, \mathbf{r}_7^2, \mathbf{r}_8^2)$ has rank three, there are in any cases enough independent equations for unique solution in $\mathbf{C}_1$.

If at least one viewing direction i is not parallel to a principal axis, the δ^i can be calculated in (11) followed by the calculation of $Z_0^{i,1} + Z_0^{i,2}$ in (13). Knowing the depths $Z_0^{i,j}$ the constant term C_0 can be derived from (9). In the case the second viewing direction is a principal axis there exist two solutions in the depths $Z_0^{2,j}$.

If both viewing directions are principal axes the depths $Z_0^{i,j}$ are functions of the unknown coefficients C_0 (including a twofold ambiguity).

7 Reconstruction Based on Level Curves

The proof, presented in section 6, is of constructive type. Hence, it describes a direct algorithm for the computation of a quadric based on two or more level curves computed in each of both phase images. We carried out synthetic experiments and by this means the proof could be verified.

But, in practice, we encountered two problems. First, the computation of the level curves is not accurate enough. This is due to image noise and to the fact that the required area of valid phase information can be quite small (see the cylinder in figure 2). The second problem is the limitation of the scaled orthographic projection model. This goes along with difficulties in the estimation of the average depth for equation (1), which is sometimes not accurate enough for a precise reconstruction of the quadric.

8 Reconstruction Using Phase Images

Instead of the above outlined direct reconstruction scheme based on few level curves we favor an indirect scheme which takes into account the complete phase

Table 1. Numerical reconstruction results: the sphere is recovered quite accurately (Using only phase information, the sphere can be recovered only up to scale; therefore, the global scaling of the principal axes is of no importance.). Using solely phase information the cylinder is approximated by an ellipsoid; using phase information plus outlines it is approximated by a hyperboloid (indicated by the $j = \sqrt{-1}$). The z-component of the origin is dropped, because it has no meaning here

	Origin	Principal axes
	Sphere	
Phase image	-3.27 , -0.25 , 2.58	2.20 , 2.13 , 2.10
Phase image + outlines	-3.42 , -0.27 , 2.76	1.93 , 1.90 , 1.89
	Cylinder	
Phase image	-3.50 , -0.66 , —	2.1 , 2.5 , 5.0
Phase image + outlines	-3.44 , -0.26 , —	2.13 , 1.83 , 5.72j

image. A similar idea is presented in [9]: the optimal surface reconstruction has to produce phase images very close to the actual captured phase images. A global optimization scheme produces accurate results because all available phase values are used and a general camera model can be applied.

Denoting by Φ_i the original phase image and by $\hat{\Phi}_i(\hat{\mathbf{C}}, \mathbf{P}_i)$ the phase image generated by the estimated quadric $\hat{\mathbf{C}}$. The projection matrix is $\mathbf{P}_i$, which can be a general perspective projection matrix. Assuming perfect data the quadric $\hat{\mathbf{C}}$ is identical to the real underlying quadric $\mathbf{C}$ if $\hat{\Phi}_i = \Phi_i$. A suitable error function can be stated as follows:

$$e = \sum_{i=1,2} \left(\hat{\Phi}_i(\hat{\mathbf{C}}, \mathbf{P}_i) - \Phi_i \right)^2 \tag{14}$$

There is a one-to-one equivalence between the set of level curves and the phase image: the phase image uniquely defines the level curves, and a complete set of level curves uniquely defines the phase image. Hence, an optimization based directly on the phase images should converge to the unique solution of the quadric. As initial solution an ellipsoid is computed from the centroids and the general shape of the regions, where phase information is available in both images. The optimization is carried out using the Levenberg-Marquardt algorithm and the numerical results are shown in table 8. The shape of the sphere is estimated with 2.5% accuracy (maximum of the relative error of the principal axes). It has to be stressed that the cylinder is quite short; therefore, it is not surprising that the estimation of the shape is poor.

Fig. 2. A pair of polarization images showing a billiard ball placed on top of a cylinder: intensity images in the upper line and phase images in the lower line (The phase images are zoomed, to better perceive the phase information.). The gray-values in the phase image encode the orientation of polarized light: the range of orientation angles $[-\frac{\pi}{2}, \frac{\pi}{2}]$ maps onto the range $[0, 1]$ of gray-values, where the zero angle encodes the vertical direction

9   Reconstruction Using Phase Images and Apparent Contours

As it is shown for example in [2], the dual $\mathbf{Q}^{-1}$ of the quadric $\mathbf{Q}$ projects onto the dual of the apparent contour $\mathbf{C}_{\text{out}}^{-1}$ as $\mathbf{C}_{\text{out}}^{-1} \sim \mathbf{P}\mathbf{Q}^{-1}\mathbf{P}^T$. The condition for image points $\mathbf{x}_{\text{out}}$ to lie on the conic outline defined by the vector $\mathbf{c}_{\text{out}}$ is $\mathbf{c}_{\text{out}}^T[\tilde{\mathbf{x}}_{\text{out}}]^2 = 0$. The error function incorporating the information of the phase image and the apparent contours is:

$$e = \sum_{i=1,2} \left(\hat{\Phi}_i(\hat{\mathbf{C}}, \mathbf{P}_i) - \Phi_i \right)^2 + \lambda \sum_{i=1,2} \sum_{\forall \mathbf{x}_{\text{out},i}} \left(\hat{\mathbf{c}}_{\text{out},i}^T[\tilde{\mathbf{x}}_{\text{out},i}]^2 \right)^2 \quad , \quad (15)$$

where λ is a weighting factor which has to be chosen appropriately. It has been observed that in general the convergence of the optimization is fast. In table 8 the results are presented. It can be seen that using both phase images and apparent

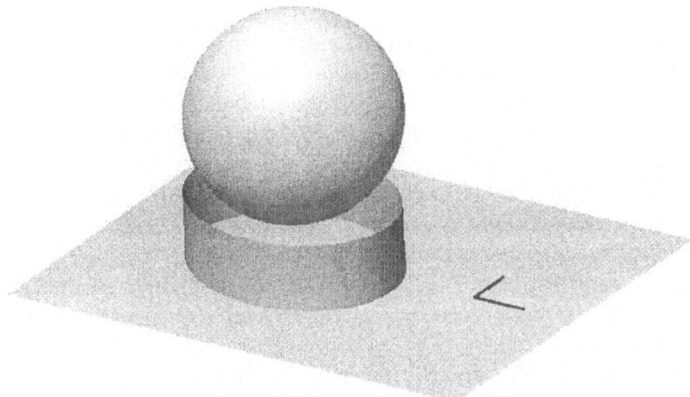

Fig. 3. Visualization of the reconstruction result. The origin and the orientation of the reference calibration grid are indicated

contours the reconstruction is accurate. The principal axes of the sphere are estimated with an accuracy of 1% (maximum of the relative error of the principal axes). Even though the numerical results for the cylinder seem not to be accurate, the visualization of the reconstructed part, see figure 3, shows the cylinder like shape.

10   Conclusion

A method for the reconstruction of quadrics using polarization imaging has been presented. It was proven that, in general, already two views provide a unique solution. The method can be applied in cases where the contour generators of the quadric are not or only partially visible in the images, for example due to occlusion: in these cases purely intensity based imaging algorithm would fail. Using both polarization information and apparent contours, in general, a unique solution in the quadric can be derived. A global optimization scheme has been presented, producing accurate reconstruction results.

The method can be extended to implicit surfaces of a degree greater than two. Using more than just two images, it can be expected that more complicated shapes can be recovered accurately.

Acknowledgments

This work was supported by the "Deutsche Forschungsgemeinschaft (DFG)".

References

[1] N. Canterakis. 3d zernike moments and zernike affine invariants for 3d image analysis and recognition. In *Scandinavian Conf. on Image Analysis (SCIA)*, 1999.

[2] Geoff Cross and Andrew Zisserman. Quadric surface reconstruction from dual-space geometry. In *Proc. of Intl. Conf. on Computer Vision (ICCV)*, pages 25–34, 1998.

[3] O. Drbóhlav and R. Sara. Unambiguous determination of shape from photometric stereo with unknown light sources. In *Proc. of Intl. Conf. on Computer Vision (ICCV)*, volume 1, pages 581–586, 2001.

[4] O. Drbohlav and R. Sara. Specularities reduce ambiguity of uncalibrated photometric stereo. In *Proc. of European Conf. on Computer Vision (ECCV)*, volume 2, pages 46–62, 2002.

[5] R. Hartley and A. Zisserman. *Multiple View Geometry in Computer Vision*. Cambridge University Press, Cambridge, UK, 2000.

[6] W.C. Karl, G.C. Verghese, and A.S. Willsky. Reconstructing ellipsoids from projections. *Computer Vision, Graphics and Image Processing*, 56(2):124–139, March 1994.

[7] S.D. Ma and L. Li. Ellipsoid reconstruction from three perspective views. In *Proc. of Intl. Conf. on Pattern Recognition (ICPR)*, pages 344–348, 1996.

[8] S. Rahmann. Polarization images: a geometric interpretation for shape analysis. In *Proc. of Intl. Conf. on Pattern Recognition (ICPR)*, volume 3, pages 542–546, 2000.

[9] S. Rahmann and N. Canterakis. Reconstruction of specular surfaces using polarization imaging. In *Proc. of IEEE Conf. on Computer Vision and Pattern Recognition (CVPR)*, volume 1, pages 149–155, 2001.

[10] I. Schur. *Vorlesungen über Invariantentheorie*. Springer, 1968.

[11] L.B. Wolff. Surface orientation from two camera stereo with polarizers. In *Optics, Illumination, Image Sensing for Machine Vision IV*, volume 1194 of *SPIE Proceedings*, pages 287–297, 1989.

Some Results
about the Use of Tree/String Edit Distances
in a Nearest Neighbour Classification Task

Juan Ramón Rico-Juan and Luisa Micó *

Dept. Lenguajes y Sistemas Informáticos, Universdad de Alicante
E-03071 Alicante, Spain
{juanra, mico}@dlsi.ua.es

Abstract. In pattern recognition there is a variety of applications where the patterns are classified using edit distance. In this paper we present some results comparing the use of tree and string edit distances in a handwritten character recognition task. Some experiments with different number of classes and of classifiers are done.

Keywords: nearest neighbour, handwritten character recognition, edit-distance; metric space.

1 Introduction

One of the most useful and simplest techniques in Statistical Pattern Recognition that can be used in a wide range of applications of computer science and technology is the Nearest Neighbour (NN) rule. In this rule, an input pattern is assigned to the class of the nearest prototype pattern. Many times, each class is a set of prototype patterns and a k-NN rule is used: the input pattern is assigned to the class containing the larger fraction of the k nearest prototypes.

A variety of applications can be developed using the NN rule. Some of them are directly related with Pattern Recognition (as the handwritten recognition task), but also in data compression [1], data mining [2] or information retrieval [3].

When patterns may be represented as strings or trees, conventional methods based on a vector representation can not be used. In this case methods that only use a distance (and the metric properties of the distance) and an adequate data structure can be used to perform the classification. Some algorithms as **AESA** [4] and **LAESA** are focused on the reduction in the number of distance computations [5][1]. Others such as Fukunaga [6] are focused on the reduction of the temporal overhead using a tree structure. Recently, a new algorithm based on

---

* Work partially supported by the spanish CICYT TIC2000-1599-C02 and TIC2000-1703-CO3-02.

[1] These methods are adequate when the computational cost of the distance is very expensive.

F.J. Perales et al. (Eds.): IbPRIA 2003, LNCS 2652, pp. 821–828, 2003.
© Springer-Verlag Berlin Heidelberg 2003

approaching spatially the searched objects and called sa-tree (spatial approximation tree) was proposed [7].

Given a particular representation, the edit distance between two objects is defined as the number of insertions, deletions and substitutions needed to transform one representation into the other. In the case of a string representation, insertions, deletions and substitutions are made on the individual symbols of the strings. In the case of a tree representation, insertions, deletions and substitutions are made on the nodes of the tree.

In previous works as [8] the experiments were done using digits (10 classes). In this work, some additional experiments are done using characters (26 classes) to have a better knowledge of the behaviour of two fast search algorithms (**AESA** and **LAESA**) when two different (string and tree) edit distances are used in a handwritten character recognition task.

2   String and Tree Representation of Characters

Two different representations of handwritten characters are done. In both cases, the mathematical morphology opening transformation are used to avoid noisy pixel and to smooth the shapes of characters.

2.1   Tree Code

The Nagendraprasad-Wang-Gupta thinning algorithm modified as in [9] was applied (figure 1b). The result image is transformed into a tree representation using the following steps:

1. The first up and left pixel, r, is marked and assigned the tree root with a special label "0". Two empty pixel sets C and G and created.
2. $C \Leftarrow \{r\}$
3. If $C = \emptyset$ go to the end (step 8).
4. For all elements $t \in C$ collect in set G every unmarked pixels into the window (size 11) centred in the pixel associate to t (figure 1c). Follow connected pixels until a below criteria was true:
   (a) the branch has the maximum fixed parameter size (see figure 1b);
   (b) the pixel has no unmarked neighbours (terminal pixel);
   (c) the pixel has more than one unmarked neighbour (intersection pixel).
5. Create the new branches: branch(t, g) : $g \in G$. The label is assigned to the branch depending on the final pixel, g, relative position to the starting one[2], t.
6. $C \Leftarrow G$ and erase all elements from G.
7. Go to step 3.
8. End.

A complete process showing this feature extraction with character 'F' is presented in figure 1.

---

[2] The 2D space is divided in 8 regions (figure 2).

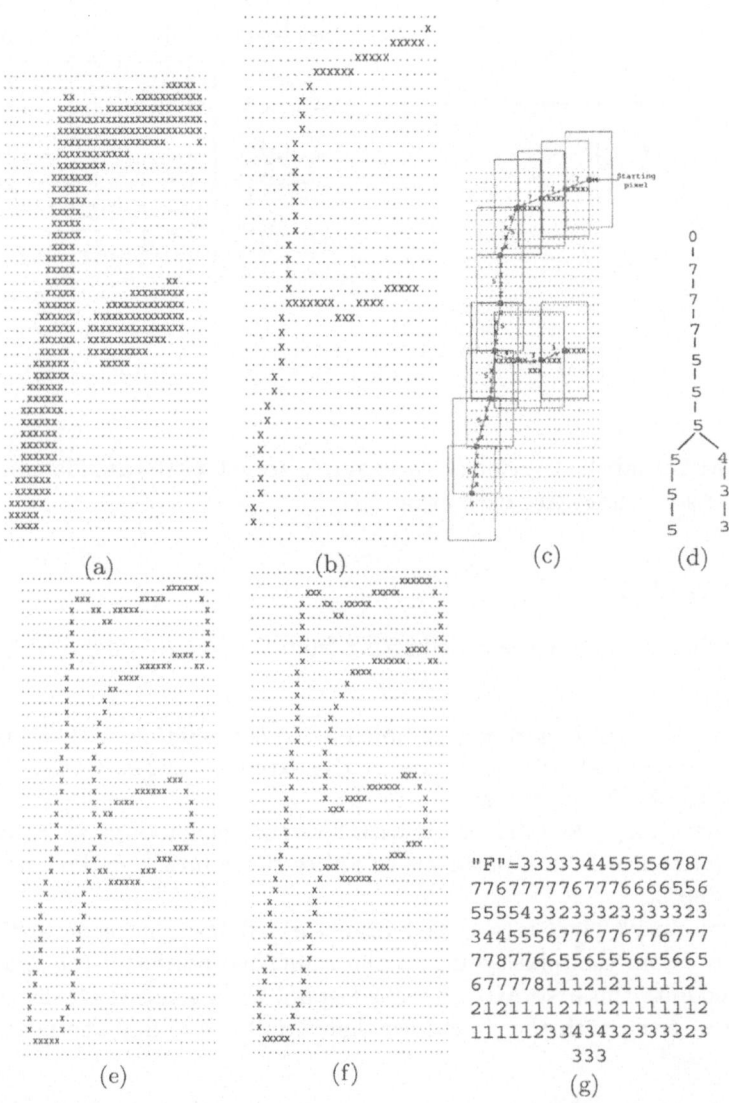

Fig. 1. Example of character "F" (a) original image; (b) thinned image; (c) tree labelling process; (d) final labelled as a tree; (e) problem image to extract the contour string; (f) image right formed to extract contour string; (g) coded string

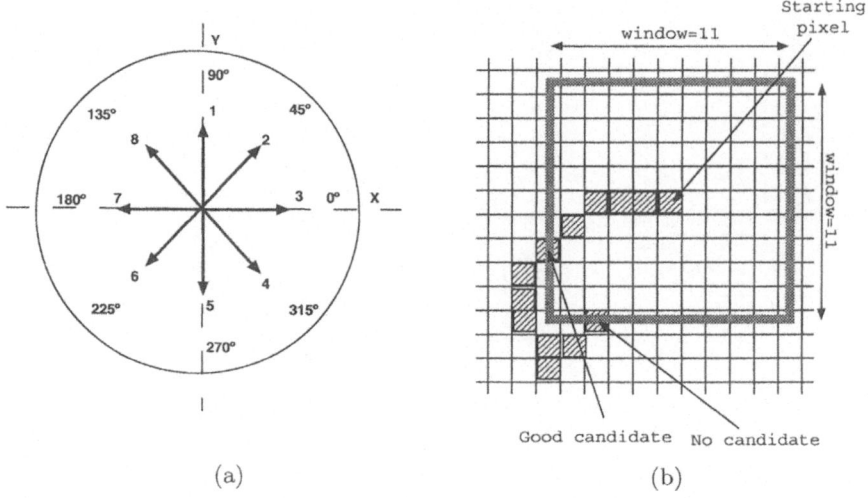

(a)   (b)

Fig. 2. (a) 2D labelled regions; (b) example to get next candidates to create branches in structured tree extraction

2.2 String Code

The algorithm to extract the coded string from the image is detailed below:

1. Assign $i = 1$.
2. The mathematical morphology opening transformation with i pixels was applied and the algorithm to extract the external contour of the characters is used to obtain the patterns from the images.
3. If the new image contains pixels with 3 o more neighbours, as in figure 1e), the algorithm will have problems to follow the contour, so do $i = i + 1$ and go to step 2.
4. The first black pixel is searched from the left-to-right scan starting from the top. From this pixel going to the right, the border of the character is followed until this first pixel is reached again. During this route the algorithm builds a string with the directions that it follows to find the next pixel of the border[3].

---

[3] There are eight neighbouring pixels that can be found after a given pixel (figure 1f and 1g), therefore, only eight symbols can appear in this chain-code (see figure 2a).

3   Edit Distances

3.1   The Tree Edit Distance

A general tree edit distance is described in [10]. The distance between two ordered trees is considered to be the weighted number of edit operations (insertion, deletion and substitution) to transform one tree into another.

A dynamic programming algorithm is implemented to compute the distance between two trees, T_1 and T_2 whose complexity is in space $O\left(|T_1| \times |T_2|\right)$ and time $O(|T_1| \times |T_2| \times \min(\text{depth}(T_1),\ \text{leaves}(T_1)) \times \min(\text{depth}(T_2),\ \text{leaves}(T_2)))$.

Each basic operation has an associated weight. Substitution weights w_{ij} are $\min\left(|i-j|, 8-|i-j|\right)$. Both insertion and deletion have a weight $w_I = w_D = 2$. This distance is finally normalised with the sum of the number of nodes in each tree.

3.2   The String Edit Distance

The string edit distance is defined as the minimum-cost set of transformations to turn a string into the other. The basic transformations are deletion, insertion and substitution of a single symbol in the string. The cost values are equal as those used in tree edit distance. The string edit distance can be computed in time in $O(|x|, |y|)$ using a standard dynamic-programming technique [11]. As in the tree edit distance, this final measure is normalised, in this case by the sum of the lengths of the strings.

4   Experiments

Two fast approximating-eliminating search algorithms have been used in this work: AESA and LAESA. These algorithms has been applied in a handwritten character recognition task using the NIST SPECIAL DATABASE 3 of the National Institute of Standards and Technology. Some results using only digits from this data set have been presented in a recent work [8]. In this work new experiments are made using the upper handwritten characters. The increasing-size training samples for the experiments were built by taking 500 writers and selecting the samples randomly. The figures show the results averaged for all combinations.

A first set of experiments using AESA were made to compare the average error rate between the string and the tree edit distances. In these experiments (see figure 3), different number of classes have been used: one set with 26 classes representing all the alphabet, and two different sets of 10 classes (the first 10 characters of the alphabet and the 10 more frequently used characters). In all the cases the use of strings allow to have a better accuracy in the recognition task. However, as figure 4 shows, the average number of distance computations is higher that in the tree representation. Moreover, the computation of the string distance is more expensive than the tree edit distance in average, because the number of symbols in the strings is higher than the number of nodes in the tree.

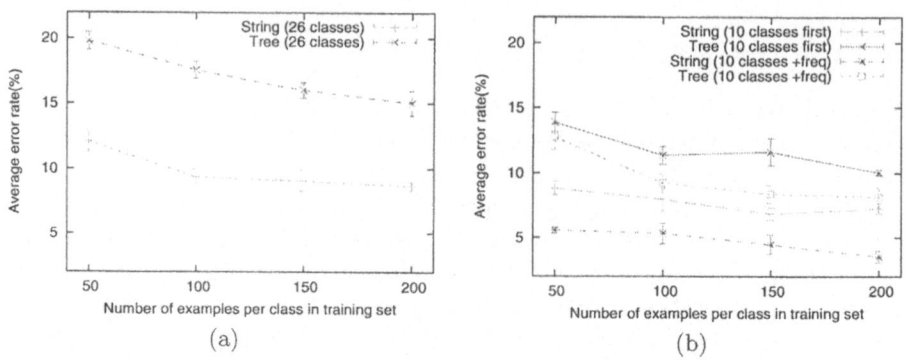

Fig. 3. Average error rate as a function of the different training examples size: (a) 26 character classes (b) two different sets of 10 character classes

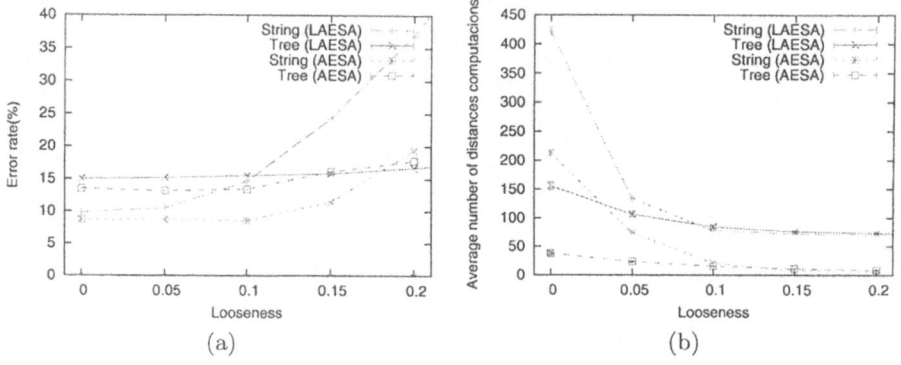

Fig. 4. Results applying **AESA** and **LAESA** algorithms as a function of looseness using 5200 prototypes belonging to 26 character classes: (a) average error rate; (b) average number of distance computations

The application of the **AESA** and **LAESA** algorithms in previous works, as [12] and [13], shows that the "looseness" H in the triangle inequality can be used to reduce the number of distance computations[4].

The performance of both algorithms is compared evaluating the average error rate and the average number of distance computations as a function of the

---

[4] Given a representation space E, the *looseness* is defined for each $x, y, z \in E$ as $h(x, y, z) = d(x, y) + d(y, z) - d(x, z)$. If a histogram of the distribution of $h(x, y, z)$ is computed, this histogram can be used to estimate of the probability that the triangle inequality is satisfied with a *looseness* smaller than H [14].

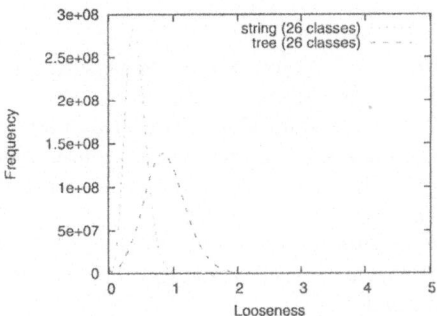

Fig. 5. Histograms from looseness using normalised edit distance

"looseness" [5] (see figure 4). This experiment reveals that the "looseness" is not a critical parameter when the tree representation is used. For any value of H between 0 and 0.2, the error rate in the classification and the average number of distance computations have a slight variation for the tree representation. However, in the case of the string representation there is a large variation. It will be necessary to use a higher value of H to reduce significantly the average number of distance computations in the tree case. The problem is that in this case the average error increases dramatically.

The histograms of the looseness can help to understand the last statement[6]. The figure 5 shows that the smallest looseness is observed for strings. For this reason, the error rate increases for smaller values of H for strings than for trees.

5   Conclusions

In this paper we have done some experiments comparing the performance and the accuracy of a handwritten recognition task using two different representations. Our experiments show that the tree edit distance is a suitable choice as opossed to the string edit distance. Although the error rate is higher for the tree representation when no looseness is used, this difference dissapears when the looseness is applied to speed up the classification.

---

[5] The size of the set of base prototypes, B is selected to minimise the number of computed distances per sample, so is 70 and 140 for trees and strings, respectively.

[6] The triangle inequality is almost always satisfied for both representations and the distribution is reasonably normal-like.

References

[1] Allen Gersho and Robert M. Gray. *Vector quantization and signal compression.* Kluwer Academic Publishers, 1991.

[2] T. Hastie and 1996. R. Tibshirani. Classification by pairwise coupling. Technical report, Stanford University and University of Toronto, 1996.

[3] G. Salton and M. J. McGill. *Introduction to Modern Information Retrieval.* McGraw Hill, New York, 1983.

[4] Enrique Vidal. New formulation and improvements of the Nearest-Neighbour approximating and eliminating search algorithm(AESA). *Pattern Recognition Letters*, 15(1):1–7, January 1994.

[5] L. Micó, J. Oncina, and E. Vidal. A new version of the nearest-neighbour approximating and eliminating searh algorithm with linear preprocessing-time and memory requirements. *Pattern Recognition Letters*, 15:9–17, 1994.

[6] K. Fukunaga and P. M. Narendra. A branch and bound algorithm for computing k-nearest neighbours. *IEEE Transactions on Computers*, 24(7):750–753, 1975.

[7] Gonzalo Navarro. In *String Processing and Information Retrieval Symposium and International Workshop on Groupware*, pages 141–148. IEEE Press, 1999.

[8] J. R. Rico-Juan and L. Micó. Comparison of AESA and LAESA search algorithms using string and tree edit distances. *Pattern Recognition Letters*, 24(9):1427–1436, 2003.

[9] R. C. Carrasco and M. L. Forcada. A note on the Nagendraprasad-Wang-Gupta thinning algorithm. *Pattern Recognition Letters*, 16:539–541, 1995.

[10] K. Zhang and D. Shasha. Simple fast algorithms for the editing distance between trees and related problems. *SIAM Journal of Computing*, 18:1245–1262, 1989.

[11] R. A. Wagner and M. J. Fischer. The string-to-string correction problem. *J. ACM*, 21:168–173, 1974.

[12] E. Vidal and M. J. Lloret. Fast speaker independent DTW recognition of isolated words using a metric-space search algorithm (AESA). *Speech Communication*, 7:417–422, 1988.

[13] L. Micó and J. Oncina. Comparison of fast nearest neighbour classifiers for handwritten character recognition. *Pattern Recognition Letters*, 19:351–356, 1998.

[14] Enrique Vidal, Francisco Casacuberta, and H. Rulot. Is the DTW distance really a metric? an algorithm reducing the number of dtw comparisons in isolated words. *Speech Communication*, 4:333–344, 1985.

Line Detection Using Ridgelets Transform for Graphic Symbol Representation

Oriol Ramos Terrades* and Ernest Valveny**

Centre de Visió per Computador,
Edifici O, Campus UAB,
Bellaterra 08193, Spain
{oriolrt,ernest}@cvc.uab.es
http://cvc.uab.es

Abstract. Retrieval and recognition of symbols in graphic images requires good symbol representation, able to identify those features providing the most relevant information about shape and visual appearance of symbols. In this work we have introduced Ridgelets transform as it permits to detect lineal singularities in an image, which are the most important source of information in graphic images. Sparsity is one of the most important properties of Ridgelets transform, which will permit us to extract a set of descriptors based on the angle and the distance to the origin of every straight line. We show how this representation can be normalized to make it invariant on traslation, rotation and scaling of the symbol. We present some preliminary results showing the usefulness of this representation with a set of architectural symbols.

1 Introduction

Symbol representation is the basis for a lot of applications working with graphic images, such as indexation and content-based retrieval in databases of document images, graphic web navigation or symbol recognition. As graphic images are basically composed of lines, any symbol representation should be based on information about lines. Vectorization[8] has usually been used to extract lines in graphic images. These methods usually work only with local information and are very noise sensitive and dependent on accurate tuning of a set of parameters. As different symbols have different number of lines, it is difficult to find an homogeneous representation easy to compare and to use in retrieval operations. In this work we explore another way to identify and represent line information applying a global transformation - Ridgelets transform - to the image which will provide an homogenous representation for all symbols. Similar approaches have been recently reported using the Hough[5] and the Radon[7, 9] transforms.

From a visual image analysis we see that graphic symbols use to be very structured, with only few particular features - lines and arcs - allowing to describe them. In addition, if we consider such lines being of zero-width, we can

---

* Supported by DURSI. Generalitat de Catalunya.
** Partially supported by CICYT TIC2000-0382, Spain.

F.J. Perales et al. (Eds.): IbPRIA 2003, LNCS 2652, pp. 829–837, 2003.

observe that this kind of images are zero almost everywhere, except for a small set corresponding to lines. So, all relevant information is concentrated in a small set of "singularities" where the image is non-zero, usually one in binary images. Therefore, this global transformation should convert these singularities in original images into characteristic points in the transformed image. In this way, we will introduce Ridgelets transform[2, 3] to extract a set of features describing symbol lines. This transform belongs to the non-separated wavelet family and it is specially suited to detect linear singularities in two dimensional spaces. Ridgelets transform -better than Radon and Hough transform- localizes straight lines in any orientation and distance to the origin. Then, we will use the Ridgelets coefficients to to build up a feature vector representing the longest symbol lines.

We briefly resume Ridgelets transform and its properties in section 2. We discuss the choice of the parameters and how we extract the set of features representing the symbols. Then, in section 3, we will present a set of invariant features built up from the original set of features. Finally, in sections 4 and 5, we discuss some experiments and state some conclusions.

2   Ridgelets Transform

The Ridgelets transform was first defined by Candès[2]. It is a family of non-separated wavelets defined as follows. Let ψ be a wavelet. For each positive a, any $t \in \mathbb{R}$ and $\theta \in [0, 2\pi)$, we define $\psi_{a,t,\theta} : \mathbb{R}^2 \to \mathbb{R}^2$ as:

$$\psi_{a,t,\theta}(x, y) = a^{-1/2}\psi((x\cos\theta + y\sin\theta - t)/a).$$

This function is constant along lines $x\cos\theta + \sin\theta = t$ and transverse to the "ridges" - lines -, it is a wavelet. Then, the continuous Ridgelets transform of a function f is defined as:

$$\mathcal{R}f_\psi(a, t, \theta) = \int f(x, y)\bar{\psi}_{a,t,\theta}(x, y)dxdy \qquad (1)$$

This transform has good properties such as coefficient sparsity and the existence of orthonormal basis[3]. Moreover, higher coefficients will be concentred around the parameters θ and t corresponding to longer lines. Thus, sparsity permits us to localize and to separate line singularities into the parameter space. This is the main property that distinguish this wavelet from usual separate wavelets (Haar, Daubechies, Meyer,...)[6].

We compute the Ridgelets coefficients using a modified Flesia et al. algorithm[4]. Essentially, Ridgelets coefficients of an image $f(x, y)$ are Wavelets coefficients of f's Radon transform, $Rf(t, \theta)$[1]. In the original algorithm, the dimension of the space parameter corresponding to the orthonormal Ridgelets is five, due to the two dimensional wavelets decomposition. However, in our implementation, our dimension of the space parameter is only three: the scale a, and the line parameters t and θ. The reason is that we only do, for each angle θ, a 1D-wavelet decomposition in t parameter.

2.1   Feature Extraction

We want to represent linear symbols by the parameters of their longest lines. We will use the Ridgelets decomposition to extract the position of lines, (t, θ)) and the Radon transform to extract the length of the lines. Higher coefficients in the Ridgelets transform will denote the position of the longest lines. The ability to accurately detect the longest lines depends on two parameters: the scale a used to compute the Ridgelets transform, and the threshold applied to select the highest coefficients. At each scale, only singularities with value above the threshold value will be taken into account. Therefore, the threshold value must be independent to scale.

As we want to detect lines whose length is longer than some pre-fixed value, we propose to define the threshold value as $L_{min}\alpha$, where L_{min} is the minimal line length and $\alpha = 0.65$ is a real value, obtained experimentally from the analysis, at different scales, of the response of the theoretical Ridgelets transform to a line of length 1.

To choose a, the scale parameter, we have used the Radon transform properties explained in section 3 and the analytic expression of the square Radon transform. In this way, we are able to compute the continuous Radon transform of any gray image, with such precision as we want. This continuous Radon transform permits us to study with precision the a's choice. We have found, experimentally, that scale parameters ranging from $a = 1$ to $a = 8$ are the best suited for our problem. Lower values for a are sensible to the square Radon transform singularities[1], and do not detect lines in arbitrary directions. In other words, small scales see pixels but not the drawing that they compose. Higher values loose precision to localize lines.

Thus, we compute the Ridglets transform for each scale, having, for each value of a, an image of Ridgelets coefficients. We apply the threshold to these images and add them, using the resulting image as a mask. Because of Ridgelets sparsity, it is composed of clouds of points that are dense around lines' position. Moreover, if we haven't chosen high a values, these clouds will be separated.

Finally, we must group each cloud, applying morphological operations to get a blob for every line. Then, we can extract the gravidity center of each blob, (t_n, θ_n), which will correspond to the position of each line. The number of blobs tells us how many line are in the image. Vertical lines present some difficulties. They have their Ridgelets coefficients near 0 and π angle. (t, θ) and $(-t, \theta + \pi)$ represent the same straight line. According to this symmetry, we extend the Radon transform to angles $[-\pi/2, 3\pi/2)$. In that way we duplicate blobs near 0 and π keeping lines with angle in $[0, \pi)$ and, therefore, unifying representation for vertical lines.

Figure 2.1 shows an example of this feature extraction procedure. We can see the original image with its main lines, the Radon transform of this image, the Ridgelet transform at scale 4, and the mask obtained after applying the threshold to the Ridgelets coefficient. We can see the blobs corresponding to line locations.

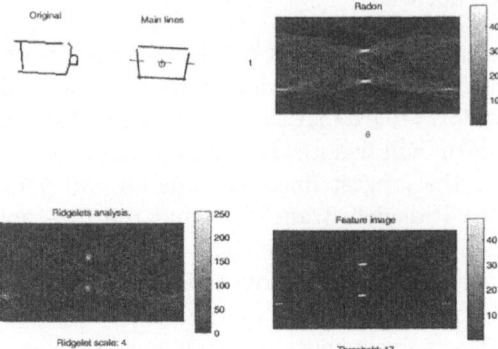

Fig. 1. Feature extraction using the Ridgelets transform

Using this procedure, for a given symbol s, we can just build up a feature vector, whose dimension, $nlin$ denote the number of lines detected and where each component is a structure with three fields: t and θ Let us denote $t_s(n)$ and $\theta_s(n)$ the position and angle of the n-th line of the symbol s.

3   Similarity Invariance

If we want to recognize similar symbols, we need feature vectors invariant to affine transformations (traslation, rotation and scaling). As ridgelets coefficients are the wavelets coefficients of the image's Radon transform, we can build up these similarity invariant vectors using some properties of the Radon transform:

- **Rotation** Let G_α be the rotation of angle α, which is applied to an image $f(x)$:

$$R\left(f \circ G_\alpha(x)\right)(t,\theta) = Rf(t, \theta + \alpha).$$

- **Shift** Let $T_v(x) = x + v$, $v \in \mathbb{R}^2$, be the traslation of an image:

$$R\left(f \circ T_v(x)\right)(t,\theta) = Rf(t + t'(\theta), \theta),$$

where $t'(\theta) = v_1 \cos(\theta) + v_2 \sin(\theta)$.
- **Scale** Let $H_a(x) = ax$, $a > 0$, be the scaling of an image:

$$R\left(f \circ H_a(x)\right)(t,\theta) = \frac{1}{a} Rf(at, \theta),$$

Suppose we have detected $nlin$ representative lines in a symbol s. We can define the gravidity center of s, glc_s, as the point:

$$glc_s = \frac{1}{nlin} \sum_{n=1}^{nlin} t_s(n) e^{i\theta_s(n)} \tag{2}$$

If we displace s by a vector $v = (v_x, v_y)$, we get a new symbol $\tilde{s}$ whose gravidity center, $glc_{\tilde{s}}$, can be computed using the traslation property of the Radon transform:

$$glc_{\tilde{s}} = glc_s + \frac{1}{nlin} \sum_{n=1}^{nlin} (v_x \cos\theta_s(n) + v_y \sin\theta_s(n)) e^{i\theta_s(n)} \qquad (3)$$

Given a traslated symbol $\tilde{s}$ and making $glc_{\tilde{s}} = 0$ we can find an easy 2×2 linear system whose solution is vector v, which will usually be (but not always) the vector displacement. Therefore, we can correct shift effects by subtracting to each line the term $v_x \cos\theta_s(n) - v_y \sin\theta_s(n)$.

We will correct rotation by computing the inertia angle, α from the feature vector. We compute this angle by using the usual moments formula :

$$\alpha = \frac{1}{2} \arctan(\frac{2\mu_{11}}{\mu_{20} - \mu_{02}}) \qquad (4)$$

For each line we take two points in computing the inertia angle: $t_s(n)e^{i\theta_s(n)}$ and $(t_s(n) + i\lambda_s(n))e^{i\theta_s(n)}$, the middle point and one ending point. This formula give us an angle, $\alpha \in [0, \pi)$, which permit us to correct the orientation by subtracting α, modulus π, to each line, using the rotation property of the Radon transform. However, we can't distinguish among rotations which change symbol sense (α and $\alpha + \pi$). In some cases, we can solve it by multiplying t_s by the mean t_s's sign.

Finally, we get scale invariance from the scaling property of the Radon transform. The Second order moments compose a symmetric, semi-defined positive matrix. Computing its largest eigenvalues we can estimate the scale factor. Using the square root of the largest eigenvalue we can correct scale effects.

4   Experiments and Discussion

We have used a set of seven different linear symbols to test the validity of the Ridgelets transform to represent them. Figure 2 shows these symbols and the lines detected by the Ridgelets transform that will describe every symbol. We can see how all lines, except very short lines, have been detected with position and length close to the original ones. We could distinguish two different groups of symbols. The first one is composed of figures containing a rectangle and some linear structures added to it: symbols 1,2,3 and 4. The second group is a collection of arrow symbols. Differences among the elements on this group are minima.

In order to measure the power of Ridgelet transform in capturing symbol similarities and differences we have defined a distance d. Let us denote s_l our symbol collection, $l = 1, \ldots, 7$, and $s_l(j)$ the j-th line's of symbol l. The Radon transform's parameter space is $\mathbb{R} \times [0, 2\pi)$ but we will only use half space, $\mathbb{R} \times [0, \pi)$ because points (t, θ) and $(-t, \theta + \pi)$ have the same Radon transform value. This property originates some problems for lines near the horizontal because points $(t, 0)$ and $(-t, 0)$ correspond to the same line. This fact can be modelled using

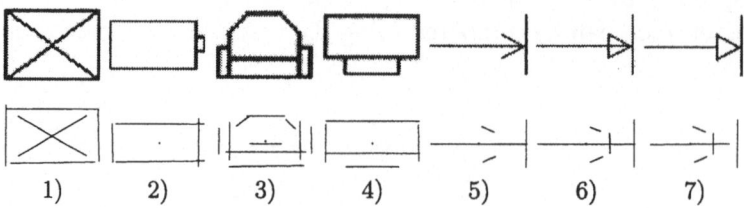

Fig. 2. Symbols used in our experiments and their main lines

a Moëbius strip and defining the distance d taking into account the geometry of the Moëbius strip. As a preliminary approach we project each point of the Radon parameter space into the Moëbius strip using a parametrization of the Moëbius strip, ϕ, $s_n(j) = \phi(t_n(j), \theta_n(j))$. Then we define a "non-symmetric distance" between two symbols $d(n, m)$ taking the distance in the 3-D space as:

$$d(n, m) = \frac{1}{N_m} \sum_{j=1}^{N_m} \min_{i=1,\ldots,N_n} \{\|s_n(i) - s_m(j)\|\} \qquad (5)$$

where N_l is the number of representative lines for symbol s_l. However, if we want to test similarity between symbols, we need a symmetric distance D, defined as $D(s_n, s_m) = \frac{1}{2}(d_{n,m} + d_{m,n})$:

Figure 3 shows the matrix of symmetric distances among all the symbols. This distances have been normalized in the range $[0, 100]$. We can see how the symbols in group one have lower distances among them than with symbols in group two. This is due to the fact that all symbols in this group share a common structure around a rectangle. Inside this group of symbols, the lowest distance is between symbols 2 and 4, which corresponds to the visual evidence of similarity between them. We also observe how distances among symbols in group 2 are the lowest, corresponding to the fact that their similar appearance is very similar.

	⊠	▭	⌂	⊟	→┤	→┤	→┤
⊠	0.00	21.48	18.08	16.31	62.74	63.81	63.74
▭	21.48	0.00	28.63	5.29	100.00	95.27	95.24
⌂	18.08	28.63	0.00	21.16	72.21	66.15	66.28
⊟	16.31	5.29	21.16	0.00	77.43	69.58	69.56
→┤	62.74	100.00	72.21	77.43	0.00	2.00	1.99
→┤	63.81	95.27	66.15	69.58	2.00	0.00	0.03
→┤	63.74	95.24	66.28	69.56	1.99	0.03	0.00

Fig. 3. Distance matrix between symbols

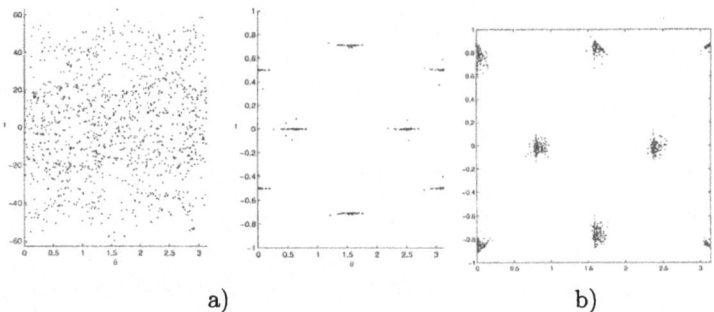

a)   b)

Fig. 4. Ridgelets coefficients of symbol 1 under transformations. (a) Normalized coefficients for rotation and traslation. (b) Distribution of coefficients for deformed images

To test the invariance of the features defined in section 3, we have built 200 images of each symbol using random rotations and traslations. For each symbol, we have plotted all images features before and after normalization. In figure 4(a) we can see the result for symbol 1. After normalization, feature values are grouped around normalized line location. The variability in the parameter θ is due to the fact that we have to take one ending line point when computing the inertia angle. However, if we only take the middle point of every line, we could not compute the inertia angle when we only have two lines in the symbol. In figure 4(b) we show the behavior of ridgelet coefficients under shape distortions. We have generated 100 distorted images of symbol 1 -figure 5(b)- where we see how features have grouped around symbol model features showing the robustness to symbol distortions.

An important factor which can introduce some distortions in the invariant representation of a symbol is the number of lines detected by the feature extraction procedure. In some cases such as arrow symbols, short lines near the threshold value cant't be detected in some orientations due to discretization problems, as we are working with one-pixel width lines. Then, as we can see in figure 5 normalized representation of the symbol can be distorted. This problem should disappear when working with wider lines.

5   Conclusions and Future Work

Having a good representation of images, able to capture the most relevant information, is the basis for any application concerning matching, retrieval, browsing or recognition. In this work we have explored the possibilities of the Ridgelets transform to get such representation in images of lineal graphic symbols.

We have seen that the Ridgelets transform is a global transform where higher coefficients have a clear geometric sense that permit us to accurately detect and localize lines. As a global transform, it presents robustness to distortion and noise, except in cases where lines are short (with respect to image size) or thin

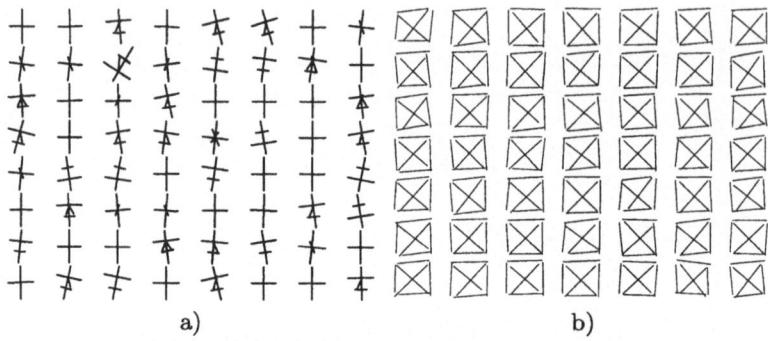

a)   b)

Fig. 5. (a) Symbol 7's Normalized representation. (b) Some symbol 1's distortions

(one or two pixels) and then the coefficients value is near the threshold value. We have studied the effect of the scale parameter in feature extraction and we propose to use scales in the range $[1, 8]$. We have also defined a set of invariant features, computed from the properties of the Radon transform, and a distance to test the ability of this representation to capture the similarity between symbols.

These results must be taken as a preliminary study in the way of getting a general representation model for symbols. We have seen how the application of the distance give results which correspond with our visual evidence. However further studies must be carried on taking a wider set of symbols and images and testing different distance definitions. Moreover, we also need to study the effects of noise and distortion to number of lines detected in order to improve the problems in the normalization of the feature vectors.

References

[1] R. N. Bracewell. *Two-Dimensional Imaging.* Prentice Hall International, Englewood, New Jersey, 1995.
[2] E. J. Candès and D. L. Donoho. Ridgelets: a key to higher-dimensional intermittency? *Phil. Trans. R. Soc. Lond. A*, 357:2495–2509, 1999.
[3] D. L. Donoho. Orthonormal ridgelets and linear singularities. 2001.
[4] A. G. Flesia, H. Hel-Or, A. Averbuch, E. J. Candès, R. R. Coifman, and D. L. Donoho. Digital implementation of ridgelet packets. *Beyond Wavelets*, 1–33, 2001.
[5] P. Fränti, A. Mednonogov, V. Kyrki, and H. Kalviainen. Content-based matching of line-drawing images using the hough transform. *IJDAR*, 3:117–124, 2000.
[6] S. Mallat. *A Wavelet Tour of Signal Processing.* Academic Press, 1999.
[7] S. Tabbone and L. Wendling. Technical symbols recognition using the two-dimensional radon transform. In *Proceedings of the 16th International Conference on Pattern Recognition*, volume 3, pages 200–203, August 2002. Montreal, Canada.

[8] K. Tombre, C. Ah-Soon, P. Dosch, G. Masini, and S. Tabonne. Stable and robust vectorization: How to make the right choices. In A. Chhabra and D. Dori, editors, *Graphics Recognition: Recent Advances*, pages 3–18. Springer-Verlag, Berlin, 2000. Vol. 1941 of Lecture Notes in Computer Science.

[9] O. Ramos, E. Valveny. Radon Transform for Lineal Representation. *To appear:* ICDAR2003 proceedings.

Tree-Structured Representation of Musical Information

David Rizo, José Manuel Iñesta, and Francisco Moreno-Seco

Departamento de Lenguajes y Sistemas Informáticos, Universidad de Alicante
Ap. 99, E-03080 Alicante, Spain
{drizo,inesta,paco}@dlsi.ua.es

Abstract. The success of the Internet has filled the net with lots of symbolic representations of music works. Two kinds of problems arise to the user: content-based search of music and the identification of similar works. Both belong to the pattern recognition domain. In contrast to most of the existing approaches, we pose a non-linear representation of a melody, based on trees that express the metric and rhythm of music in a natural way. This representation provide a number of advantages: more musical significance, more compact representation and others. Here we have worked on the comparison of melodies for identification.

Keywords: Multimedia applications, computer music, structural recognition.

1   Introduction

There are lots of symbolic representations of music works in the Internet (for example, in standard MIDI file format). Two kinds of problems arise to the user: content-based search of music and the identification of similar works. Both belong to the pattern recognition domain. The applications range from the study and analysis tasks in musicology to the detection of plagiarism, useful to protect copyrights in the music record industry.

Traditionally music has been represented by means of a set of tuple strings, where each tuple, in diverse ways, usually contains information on pitch, duration and onset time. Both the retrieval and the comparison have been tackled with structural pattern matching techniques in strings [4]. There are some other approaches, seldom applied, like the geometric one, which transforms the melody into a plot obtained tracing a line between the successive notes in the staves. This way, the melody comparison problem is converted into a geometric one [2].

In this paper, we use a nonlinear representation of melody: by means of trees that express the metric and rhythm of music in a natural way. The approach to tree construction is based on the fact that the different music notation figures are designed on a logarithmic scale: a whole note lasts twice a half note, whose length is the double of a quarter note, etc. This representation provides us with a richness of possibilities that the strings never will: implicit description of rhythm and more musical meaning and automatic emphasising of relevant

F.J. Perales et al. (Eds.): IbPRIA 2003, LNCS 2652, pp. 838–846, 2003.

notes, for example. Moreover, the way in which a string representation is coded strongly conditions the outcome of the string processing algorithms [6].

In this work, we have dealt with the comparison of melodic lines and compared the performance to that with string representations. Although tree comparison algorithms have higher complexity than the existing methods for strings, the results improve the ones in the same way using strings. This preliminary results open a promising new field for experimentation in a number of applications on the symbolic representation of music.

Firstly, the method for tree construction is presented and how it deals with the notation problems that may appear. Secondly, a procedure for tree pruning and labelling is described in order to deal with the complexity above described. Then, the method for comparison and the results are presented, and finally conclusions are stated.

2   Tree Construction Method

As described above, the tree construction method is based on the logarithmic relation among duration of the different figures. A sub-tree is assigned to each measure, so the root of this sub-tree represents the length in time of the whole measure. If just a whole note is found in the measure, the tree will consist of just the root, but if there were two half notes, this node would split into two children nodes. Thus, recursively, each node of the tree will split into two until representing the notes actually found in a measure (see Fig. 1).

For the representation of a melody, each leaf node represents a note or silence. Different kind of labels can be used to represent a note, but we have used five of them: 1) the absolute pitch (the name and octave of each note); 2) the pitch name (same as before but without octave); 3) the contour (three possible labels: +1 if the pitch of the note is higher than that of the one before, −1 if is lower and 0 if is the same); 4) the high-definition contour (same as before but also including +2 and −2 if the pitch differences exceed ±4 semitones) [10]; and 5) intervals: the difference in semitones between a note and the one before. Silences are represented with a special label. Each node has an implicit duration

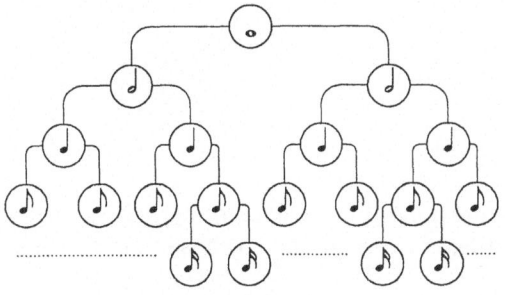

Fig. 1. Duration hierarchy

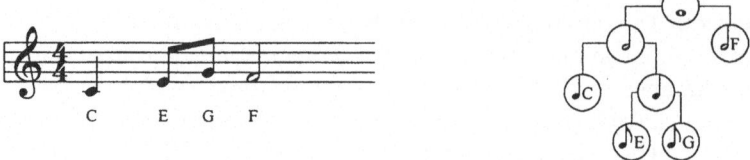

Fig. 2. Simple example of tree construction

according to the level of the tree in which it appears. In addition to the duration of the notes, the left to right ordering of the leaves also establish the time in the measure in which they begin to play. Initially, only the leaf nodes will contain a label value, but then a bottom-up propagation of these labels is performed to fully label the tree nodes. The rules for this propagation will be described later.

An example of this scheme is presented in Fig. 2 with pitch labels. The left child of the root has been splitted into two subtrees to represent the quarter note C. This one lasts the time represented by the leaf node in which it is: one beat in the measure. In order to represent the durations of the two eighth notes it will be necessary to unfold one more level. The half note F onsets at the third beat and, as it lasts two beats, its position is in the second level of the tree.

In some occasions the situation can be more complicated. For example, if the duration of a note is greater than that of the half corresponding subdivision, like happens for dotted or tied notes (see Fig. 3). In this situation, a note can not be represented only by the complete subtree in which it onsets. It is well known that the ear does not perceive in a very different way a whole C note from two half C notes played one after the other, even more if the interpreter play them *legato* [9]. Thus, when a note exceeds the proper duration, we will subdivide it in order to complete the time of the note by means of nodes in sub-trees enough to complete the duration of the note with smaller Also, tied notes, are represented in the same way, breaking the tie in the tree representation. In Fig. 3 an example of these situations is presented and how they are represented in this scheme.

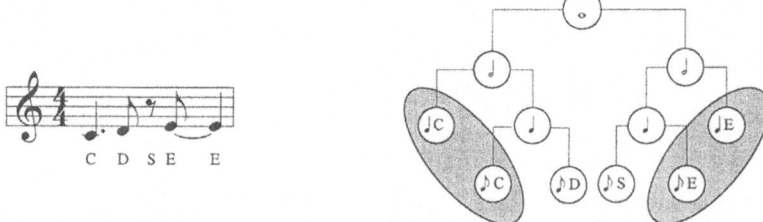

Fig. 3. Tree representations of notes exceeding their notation length: dotted and tied notes. Rounded leaves correspond to those notes. 'S' stands for "silence"

Other music notation events, like other rhythm meters, non-binary structures, compound meters, adornment notes, trills, etc., can appear, but the described method can be extended without difficulty to cope with all these situations [8].

Once each measure has been represented by a single sub-tree, joining all of them is needed to build the tree for the complete melody. For this, a method for grouping the sub-trees is required. Initially we could group them by adjacent pairs, hierarchically, repeating this operation bottom-up with the new nodes until a single tree is obtained. Nevertheless, trees would grow in height very quickly this way and this would make the tree edit distance computation algorithms very time consuming. We have chosen to build a tree with a root for the whole melody and each measure is a child of the root (Fig. 4). Thus, the level of the tree for the whole melody only grows in one with respect to the measure's sub-tree. This is like having a forest but linked to a common root node that represents the whole melody.

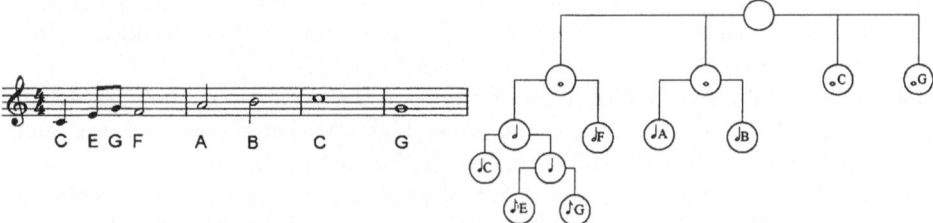

Fig. 4. All the measures of a melody are represented by a single tree

3 Bottom-Up Propagation of Labels and Pruning

The tree edit distance algorithms need all the nodes to have a label [1]. We will use a set of rules for the propagation of labels from the leaves to the root according to musicology criteria (see below). The propagation of a label upwards implies that the note in that node is more important than that of the sibling node. The propagation criteria proposed here are based on the fact that, in a melody, there are notes that contribute more than others to its identity.

In addition, the resulting trees can be very complex if the rhythmical structure does not agree exactly with the successive subdivisions of the binary tree, for example in real-time sequenced MIDI files. This implies a greater time and space overhead in the algorithms [1] and makes it more difficult to match equivalent notes between two different interpretations of the same score. Our goal is to represent melodies in a reduced format able to keep the main features of the melody. For this, the trees need to be pruned.

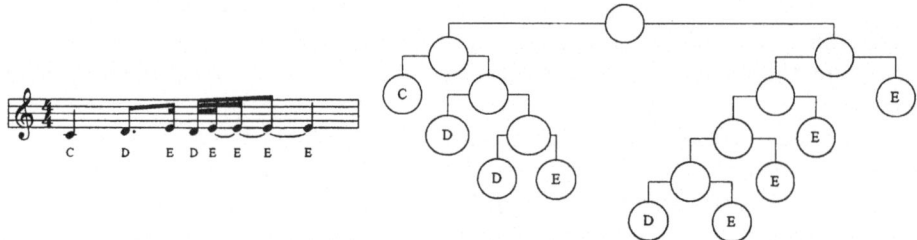

Fig. 5. One measure-melody and its tree representation with pitch labels (only in the leaves now) before pruning and label propagation

If a maximum tree depth level is established, when a label is upgraded from children that are below that level, then those children nodes are pruned in addition to the label propagation.

These are the propagation (and pruning when applicable) rules:

R1 Given a node with two children, if one of those children contains the same label as the brother of the father node, the other child is promoted. Thus, more melodic richness is represented with less tree depth.

R2 In case that all the children of a node have the same label, they are deleted and its label is placed in the father node. Thus, two equal notes are equivalent to just one with double duration (see [3] for justification).

R3 If one of the brothers is the result of applying R3 three or more times (it had originally at least one eighth of the duration of the other brothers, then the brother of greater original duration is chosen. Thus we avoid very short notes (adornment notes) having more importance than longer notes[1].

R4 When various nodes are equivalent in original duration or when promoting a note implies losing the other, the label of the left node is upgraded.

R5 Silences never have greater precedence than notes.

R6 In case that there is only one child (either because of the tree construction or by propagation) it is automatically upgraded.

We will illustrate how these rules perform in an example of a melody. In Fig. 5-left one measure with some notes with different durations is presented, and Fig. 5-right, shows the tree originally built for its representation.

In Fig. 6-left it can be observed how the propagation rules apply and prune the tree. In the first half of the melody, the labels E and A ascend by the rule R1. The second part shows how an adornment note is deleted by the application of the rules. The resulting tree corresponds to the score displayed in Fig. 6-right, that retains the perceptually important features of the melody. Once the tree has been pruned, the labels are propagated upwards, applying the same rules, without deleting nodes, until the roof in order to achieve a fully labelled tree.

---

[1] the difference of one eighth of the duration has been established in an empirical way

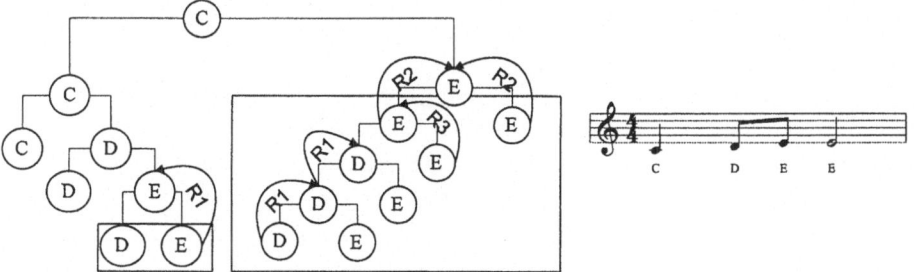

Fig. 6. Propagation of the leaf labels using the rules. The nodes into the rectangles disappear after pruning. The resulting melody is displayed in a score on the right

4   Tree Edit Distance

We can define the edit distance between two trees like the minimum cost of the sequence of operations that transforms a tree into the other [1]. The edit operations are the same as those used in the string edition: deletion of a node, insertion, and substitution of the label of a node. In the insertion, a new node is added to the tree in a given point. The children of the node where the new node is inserted will become children of the new node. In the deletion, the children of the deleted node will become children of their previous grandfather node. The more similar the structure of the trees are, the less operations of deletion and insertion have to be done, and the smaller distance between them is achieved.

The deletion and insertion of nodes in a tree are not trivial matters, and it is necessary to understand the musical meaning of those actions. The important point is to note that the tree structure is closely related to the rhythmical structure of the melody.

5   Experiments and Results

In our experiments the influence of different pitch representations on classification rates has been explored. Also, the application of prune rules and label propagation has been studied in relation with performance and error rates.

Three corpora made up with monophonic melodies have been used in our tests (in all cases only 8 measures have been taken from the melody start):

Real: built from 110 MIDI files fetched from Internet, it has 12 different classes (musical themes) from classic, jazz and pop/rock. The track containing the melody and the initial measure have been manually selected.

Latin: a synthetic database built from latin jazz melodies previously normalised which have been distorted with simulated human-made mistakes to obtain 3 more melodies of each. These melody distortions are based on small changes in both the note onset time and small errors in the pitch (e.g. errors like

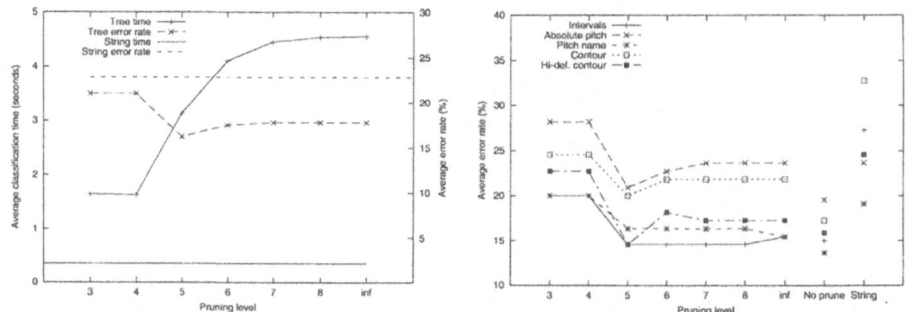

Fig. 7. Classification times and errors with different representations: (left) evolution of time and error rate versus tree pruning level (averaged for all the different labels). References for strings are plotted as horizontal lines. (right) error rates for the trees with the different labels. Errors for non-pruned trees and for strings are also displayed

pressing the adjacent key instead of the right one in a keyboard). The original set had 40 melodies, and with the distorted melodies added we have obtained 160 melodies.

Classical: another synthetical database built using the same technique as above. The original set had 99 melodies, and the hole set has 393 melodies.

The weights used for the edit distance have (in all experiments) been set to 1 for insertion and deletion. For substitution, the weight is 0 if the interval/note is the same and 1 otherwise. Other tested weights did not improve the results.

The experiments with the three corpora have been made using the nearest neighbour rule and a leave-one-out scheme. Figure 7 shows the average error rates and time for the three corpora (tested separately). Experiments were run on a 750 MHz PC under Linux.

The performances for the five different kind of labels and for maximum tree levels ranging from 3 to 8, and without maximum level restriction (inf. in the graphs) were tested. Other experiments were to apply propagation without any pruning and the comparative performance of strings, coding both pitch and pitch plus duration sequences, as a reference.

The best error rate has been obtained with non pruned trees (see Table 1), but the high complexity of the distance calculation makes it very slow (38 s per sample in the 'real' corpus), making it unpractical. So we have focused in how much can we prune the trees keeping the error rates in a good level, always better that those for strings (see Fig. 7-left). A maximum level of 5 seems to be a good compromise between error and time.

In Fig. 7-right, the performance for the five codification labels is compared. The average errors for all the corpora are plotted for each kind of label. Note that the best results, apart from those obtained without pruning are obtained again for maximum level 5. Note also that trees perform better than strings.

Table 1. Best tree classification error rates (in percentage) obtained for all the experiments, compared to those obtained for non pruned trees and strings

Kind of labels	Pruned trees	Corpus	Non pruned trees	Strings
Absolute pitch	1.25	Latin	1.25	3.75
Pitch name	1.25	Latin	1.25	3.75
Contour	13.64	Real	11.87	12.48
Hi-def. contour	14.37	Latin	11.87	12.46
Interval	9.38	Latin	10.0	12.42

6 Discussion and Conclusions

Our results show that tree coding of melodies allows for better results than string coding. The addition of rhythmic information to string coding in order to improve classification rates is difficult, while tree coding naturally represents that information in its hierarchical structure.

Tree pruning has proved to be a good option in order to overcome the high time overhead of the tree edit distance, without significantly loosing classification accuracy. A maximum depth of 5 for pruning seems to be a good choice.

Preliminar experiments have been developed using polyphonic melodies and the results are promising, even better than those reported in this paper. We also plan to make use of the whole melody (not only 8 measures), developing some new methods for automatic extraction and segmentation of melodies.

Acknowledgements

This work has been funded by the Spanish CICYT project TAR; code TIC2000–1703–CO3–02.

References

[1] Shasha S., Zhang K. Approximate Tree Pattern Matching. Pattern Matching Algorithms (1997) 341–371, Oxford University Press
[2] Ó Maidin, D. A geometrical algorithm melodic difference. Computing in Musicology (1998) 65–72, MIT Press
[3] Mongeau M., Sankoff D. Comparison of musical sequences. Computers and the Humanities **24** (1990) 161–175.
[4] Smith L. A., McNab R. J., Witten I. H. Sequence-Based Melodic Comparison: A Dynamic-Programming Approach. Melodic Similarity. Concepts, Procedures, and Applications (1998) 1001–117. MIT Press and Center for Computing in the Humanities (CCARH), Stanford University
[5] Lerdahl F. , Jackendoff R. A Generative Theory of Tonal Music (1983) MITP Cambridge, Massachusetts

[6] Cruz-Alcázar P. P., Vidal-Ruiz E., Learning Regular Grammars to Model Musical Style: Comparing Different Coding Schemes. Proceedings of the 4th International Colloquium on Grammatical Inference (ICGI-98) LNAI **1433** (1998) 211-222.

[7] Mitzenmacher M., Owen S. Estimating Resemblance of MIDI Documents. ALENEX (2001) 79–90.

[8] Rizo D., Iñesta J. M. Tree-structured representation of melodies for comparison and retrieval Proc. of the Int. Workshop on Pattern Recognition in the Information Society (2002), 140–155.

[9] Uitdenbogerd A. L., Zobel J. Manipulation of music for melody matching. In B. Smith and W. Eelsberg, editors, Proc. ACM International Multimedia Conference, Bristol, UK (1998) 235–240.

[10] Kim Y. E., Chai W., Garcia R., Vercoe B. Analysis Of A Contour-Based Representation For Melody. Proc. International Symposium on Music Information Retrieval (2000).

Comparative Study of the Baum-Welch and Viterbi Training Algorithms Applied to Read and Spontaneous Speech Recognition

Luis Javier Rodríguez and Inés Torres*

Departamento de Electricidad y Electrónica (Facultad de Ciencias)
Universidad del País Vasco, Apartado 644, 48080 Bilbao, Spain
luisja@we.lc.ehu.es

Abstract. In this paper we compare the performance of acoustic HMMs obtained through Viterbi training with that of acoustic HMMs obtained through the Baum-Welch algorithm. We present recognition results for discrete and continuous HMMs, for read and spontaneous speech databases, acquired at 8 and 16 kHz. We also present results for a combination of Viterbi and Baum-Welch training, intended as a trade-off solution. Though Viterbi training yields a good performance in most cases, sometimes it leads to suboptimal models, specially when using discrete HMMs to model spontaneous speech. In these cases, Baum-Welch shows more robust than both Viterbi training and the combined approach, compensating for its high computational cost. The proposed combination of Viterbi and Baum-Welch only outperforms Viterbi training in the case of read speech at 8 kHz. Finally, when using continuous HMMs, Viterbi training reveals as good as Baum-Welch at a much lower cost.

1 Introduction

Most speech recognition systems use Hidden Markov Models (HMM) to represent the acoustic content of phone-like units and words. Though other criteria may be applied, the reestimation of HMM parameters is commonly done according to the the *Maximum Likelihood Estimation* (MLE) criterion, i.e. maximizing the probability of the training samples with regard to the model. This is done by applying the *Expectation-Maximization* (EM) algorithm [1], which relies on maximizing the log-likelihood from incomplete data, by iteratively maximizing the expectation of log-likelihood from complete data. As shown in [2], this leads to the *Baum-Welch* reestimation formulas.

The MLE criterion can be approximated by maximizing the probability of the best HMM state sequence for each training sample, given the model, which is known as *segmental k-means* [3] or *Viterbi training*. Viterbi training involves

* This work was partially supported by the Basque Country University, under a generic grant for research groups, and the Spanish MCYT, under projects TIC2001-2812-C05-03 and TIC2002-04103-C03-02.

F.J. Perales et al. (Eds.): IbPRIA 2003, LNCS 2652, pp. 847–857, 2003.
© Springer-Verlag Berlin Heidelberg 2003

much less computational effort than Baum-Welch, still providing the same — or slightly worse— performance, so it is a common choice among designers of speech recognition systems.

However, the Baum-Welch algorithm shows very interesting properties: (1) in the case of discrete HMMs it does not need *any* model initialization, but just non-zero random values verifying the stochastic constraints; (2) in the case of continuous HMMs, a suitable initialization can be done with the output distribution parameters of discrete HMMs, on the one hand, and the means and variances of acoustic prototypes obtained by vector quantization, on the other —though other strategies have been successfully applied [4]; and (3) it exhaustively uses all the available data to produce robust and optimal estimates. With regard to Viterbi training, (1) it is shown that even in the case of discrete HMMs, it requires some reasonable initialization, either by using the models obtained for other databases, or by training initial models on a hand-labelled subset of the training database; and (2) it makes a limited use of the training data, since only observations inside the segments corresponding to a given HMM state are used to reestimate the parameters of that state, resulting in sharper but less robust models. It will depend on the the amount of available data whether or not Viterbi training produces robust enough estimates. Though the segmentation implicitly done by Viterbi training will not exactly match the right one —i.e. that produced by an expert— they overlap to a great extent, as shown in a previous work [5]. When the amount of training data is large enough, segmentation errors will cancel each other, and the right observations —i.e. the relevant features that identify an HMM state— will stand out.

The rest of the paper is organized as follows: Sections 2 and 3 briefly review the Baum-Welch and Viterbi training algorithms; Section 4 presents a combination of Viterbi segmentation and Baum-Welch reestimation, intended as a trade-off solution; Section 5 compares the amount of training data used to estimate HMM parameters for the three training algorithms; Section 6 defines a measure of segmentation quality based on hand-labelled segmentations generated by experts; Section 7 describes the experimental framework, and presents and discusses phonetic recognition results for read and spontaneous speech databases; finally, conclusions are given in Section 8.

2   The Baum-Welch Algorithm: Single vs. Embedded Model Reestimation

The Baum-Welch algorithm is based on the computation of two functions, known as *Forward* and *Backward* probabilities, $\alpha(i,t)$ and $\beta(i,t)$, for each state $i \in [1, N]$ of an HMM and each frame $t \in [1, T]$ of an observation sequence $O = O_1, O_2, \ldots, O_T$. Computing these functions yields a complexity of order $O(N^2 T)$. Once computed, *Forward* and *Backward* probabilities are used to weight the contributions of each observation O_t to the HMM parameters. Reestimation formulas can be found in [2]. Note that *each* observation O_t contributes to the reestimation of *all* the HMM parameters.

If L observation sequences $O^{(l)} = O_1^{(l)}, O_2^{(l)}, \ldots, O_{T_l}^{(l)}$, with $l = 1, 2, \ldots, L$, are explicitly available for an HMM, the resulting procedure is known as *single model Baum-Welch* reestimation [6]. This procedure is typically applied for training a word HMM starting from speech samples of that word, or for initializing phone HMMs starting from explicit hand-labelled phone segments. For each observation sequence $O^{(l)}$, the *Forward* and *Backward* probabilities must be computed, and then various contributions and norms accumulated, which yields a computational complexity of order $O(3N^2T_l + NT_l + NT_lRC)$ for discrete HMMs, and $O(3N^2T_l + NT_l + NT_lMD)$ for continuous HMMs, where R is the number of acoustic streams or representations, C the number of symbols in the discrete output distributions, M the number of gaussian components in the mixtures used to represent the output distributions in continuous HMMs, and $D = \sum_{i=1}^{R} d_i$ —with d_i the dimension of the acoustic stream i— the total number of components of acoustic vectors in the continuous case. In the most common configurations, the last term of the summation is dominant. Summing for all the training sequences and all the phone HMMs, we get complexities of order $O(NTRC)$ and $O(NTMD)$, respectively, where T is the length of the training database.

However, usually only a small fraction of the speech databases is hand-labelled, so phone HMMs must be jointly trained starting from phonetic transcriptions of speech utterances. This is known as *embedded model Baum-Welch* reestimation [6]. For each training sequence $O^{(l)}$ a large HMM $\Lambda_{train}(O^{(l)})$ is built by concatenating the phone HMMs corresponding to the transcription of $O^{(l)}$. If no phone skips are allowed in training, the possible state transitions reduce to those ocurring inside a phone HMM or between two consecutive phone HMMs. This results in that both the *Forward* and *Backward* procedures yield complexities of order $O(N^2T_lF_l)$, where F_l is the length of the phonetic transcription of $O^{(l)}$. Not only the *Forward* and *Backward* procedures, but also their contributions to the HMM parameters must be computed, resulting a complexity of order $O(5NT_lF_l + 3N^2T_lF_l + NT_lF_lRC)$ in the discrete case, and $O(5NT_lF_l + 3N^2T_lF_l + NT_lF_lMD)$ in the continuous case. Again, the last term is dominant, so these complexities can be approximated by $O(NT_lF_lRC)$ and $O(NT_lF_lMD)$, respectively. Defining $\mathcal{F} = \frac{1}{T}\sum_{l=1}^{L} T_lF_l$, and summing for all the training utterances, we get complexities of order $O(NT\mathcal{F}RC)$ and $O(NT\mathcal{F}MD)$, respectively. So the *embedded model Baum-Welch* reestimation is approximately $\mathcal{F}$ times more expensive than the *single model Baum-Welch* reestimation.

3   The Viterbi Training Algorithm

The Viterbi algorithm [7] can be applied to get the most likely state sequence $\hat{S}^{(l)}$ in the training sequence HMM $\Lambda_{train}(O^{(l)})$. This is sometimes called *forced alignment*, and takes a computational complexity of order $O((NF_l)^2T_l)$. Viterbi reestimation is based on maximizing the likelihood of $\hat{S}^{(l)}$, given the observation sequence $O^{(l)}$ and the model $\Lambda_{train}(O^{(l)})$. It uses the most likely state sequence

$\hat{S}^{(l)}$ to estimate the HMM parameters, so each observation $O_t^{(l)}$ *only* contributes to reestimate the parameters of the most likely state at time t, $s_t^{(l)}$. Reestimation formulas can be found in [3]. Without phone skips, the possible state transitions in $\Lambda_{train}(O^{(l)})$ reduce to those ocurring inside a phone HMM or between two consecutive phone HMMs. So the computational complexity of the algorithm reduces to $O(N^2 F_l T_l)$. On the other hand, for each observation sequence, contributions to the estimation of HMM parameters must be computed, which yields a complexity of order $O(T_l R C)$ in the discrete case, and $O(T_l M D)$ in the continuous case. Summing for all the training utterances, we get complexities of order $O(N^2 \mathcal{T} \mathcal{F} + \mathcal{T} R C)$ and $O(N^2 \mathcal{T} \mathcal{F} + \mathcal{T} M D)$, respectively. In practice, these complexities are between one and two orders of magnitude lower than those of the *embedded model Baum-Welch* algorithm.

The sharpness of Viterbi estimates becomes a problem in the case of discrete HMMs, since some symbols not seen in training for a particular output distribution, may appear in an independent test corpus, thus leading to zero probability and breaking the search. So a kind of smoothing must be applied to the output distribution parameters. The simplest technique —which we apply in our implementation— consists of changing only values under a certain threshold τ, by assigning them the value τ and renormalizing the distribution to verify the stochastic constraints. Threshold smoothing only guarantees that the search will not crash, and more sophisticated techniques can be found in the literature. However, such techniques make assumptions —which might not be true— about the underlying distributions. On the other hand, the *embedded model* Baum-Welch reestimation provide smooth and robust parameters in a more natural way —at the expense of higher computational costs.

4   Combining Viterbi Segmentation and Single Model Baum-Welch Reestimation

We propose the following methodology:

1. For each training sequence $O^{(l)}$, the Viterbi algorithm is applied to find the most likely state sequence $\hat{S}^{(l)}$ in the training sequence HMM $\Lambda_{train}(O^{(l)})$.
2. The single model Baum-Welch reestimation formulas are used to update the parameters of each phone HMM, starting from the phone segments obtained after step (1) over $\Omega = \{O^{(l)} | l = 1, 2, \ldots, L\}$.
3. Steps (1) and (2) are repeated until convergence.

This is a sort of tradeoff between the Baum-Welch and Viterbi training algorithms, the most likely phone segmentation —corresponding to the most likely state sequence— playing the role of a hand-labelled segmentation in *single model Baum-Welch* reestimation. On the one hand, this algorithm requires less computational effort than the *embedded model Baum-Welch* algorithm: summing for all the training utterances, complexity is of order $O(N^2 \mathcal{T} \mathcal{F} + N \mathcal{T} R C)$ in the discrete case, and $O(N^2 \mathcal{T} \mathcal{F} + N \mathcal{T} M D)$ in the continuous case, which is slightly higher than that of Viterbi reestimation. On the other hand, the resulting estimates are expected to be more robust than Viterbi estimates, since all the state sequences inside phone segments —instead of just the most likely state sequence— are considered.

5   Counting Effective Training Data

The Baum-Welch and Viterbi training algorithms differ in the use of the data. Whereas Viterbi uses each observation vector O_t to reestimate the parameters of just *one specific* HMM state, Baum-Welch uses it to reestimate the parameters of *all* the HMM states. In other words, Baum-Welch estimates are obtained from much more data than Viterbi estimates. To evaluate these differences, we next count the number of observation vectors *effectively* used to estimate HMM parameters for the three training algorithms.

In the case of *embedded model* Baum-Welch, assuming no phone skips in the training model $\Lambda_{train}(O^{(l)})$ of an observation sequence $O^{(l)}$, the function $\alpha^{(l)}(i,t)$ is zero for the first i/N frames, and in the same way the function $\beta^{(l)}(i,t)$ is zero for the last $F_l - i/N - 1$ frames. So for each given state i of $\Lambda_{train}(O^{(l)})$, there are $F_l - 1$ frames for which the corresponding contributions to the HMM parameters are zero. Summing for all the states of phone HMMs in $\Lambda_{train}(O^{(l)})$ and for all the training utterances, we find that the number of *effective* training observations is $\sum_{l=1}^{L}\sum_{f=1}^{F_l}\sum_{e=1}^{N}(T_l - F_l + 1) = N\sum_{l=1}^{L}[T_lF_l - F_l^2 + F_l] = NT\mathcal{F} - NL(\bar{F^2} - \bar{F})$, where $\bar{F^2} = \frac{1}{L}\sum_{l=1}^{L}F_l^2$ and $\bar{F} = \frac{1}{L}\sum_{l=1}^{L}F_l$.

In the case of Viterbi training, each observation sequence $O^{(l)}$ is divided into F_l segments, and each observation vector in those segments is assigned to a specific state in $\Lambda_{train}(O^{(l)})$. Let $n^{(l)}(f,i)$ be the number of observation vectors assigned to state i of the phone HMM f. Then, summing for all the states of phone HMMs in $\Lambda_{train}(O^{(l)})$ and for all the training utterances, the number of *effective* training vectors is $\sum_{l=1}^{L}\sum_{f=1}^{F_l}\sum_{i=1}^{N}n^{(l)}(f,i) = \sum_{l=1}^{L}T_l = \mathcal{T}$.

In the case of combined Viterbi segmentation + *single model* Baum-Welch reestimation, segmentation is done only at the phone level, and the parameters of each HMM state are trained with *all* the observation vectors assigned to the corresponding phone. Let $n^{(l)}(f)$ be the number of observation vectors assigned to the phone HMM f in $\Lambda_{train}(O^{(l)})$. Then, the number of *effective* training vectors for the entire training database is $\sum_{l=1}^{L}\sum_{f=1}^{F_l}\sum_{e=1}^{N}n^{(l)}(f) = N\sum_{l=1}^{L}\sum_{f=1}^{F_l}n^{(l)}(f) = N\sum_{l=1}^{L}T_l = N\mathcal{T}$.

This means that the *embedded model* Baum-Welch algorithm uses $\mathcal{F} - \frac{L}{T}(\bar{F^2} - \bar{F})$ times more data than the combined approach, which, on the other hand, uses N times more data than Viterbi training.

6   Measuring Segmentation Quality

Viterbi training depends on the quality of the segmentation implicitly associated to the most likely state sequence, so we set out to evaluate automatic segmentations. A subset of the training utterances may be hand labelled and segmented. Then, hand-labelled segments may be compared with those automatically produced by forced alignment —based on a given set of HMMs. Let n_r be the number of frames assigned by forced alignment to the same phone than experts, and n_w the number of frames assigned to the *wrong* phones. Then $S = \frac{n_r}{n_r+n_w} * 100$ is the percentage of frames correctly classified. If the HMMs used in forced alignment were obtained through Viterbi training, S can be interpreted as the amount of acoustic information *correctly* used to estimate the parameters of such models.

7 Phonetic Recognition Experiments

Experiments were carried out over four different databases, whose main features are shown in Table 1.

The mel-scale cepstral coefficients (MFCC) and energy (E) —computed in frames of 25 milliseconds, taken each 10 milliseconds— were used as acoustic features. The first and second derivatives of the MFCCs and the first derivatives of E were also computed. Four acoustic streams were defined ($R = 4$): MFCC, ΔMFCC, Δ^2MFCC and (E,ΔE). In the discrete case, vector quantization was applied to get four codebooks, each one consisting of 256 centroids ($C = 256$) minimizing the distortion in coding the training data. The set of sublexical units consisted of 23 context-independent phones and two auxiliary units: *silence* and

Table 1. Speech databases used in phonetic recognition experiments

	SENGLAR16	SENGLAR08	INFOTREN	CORLEC-EHU-1
Sampling rate (kHz)	16	8	8	16
Speech modality	read	read	spontaneous	spontaneous
Recording conditions	microphone laboratory	telephone simulated laboratory	telephone office	analog tape all environments
Other design issues	phonetically balanced	phonetically balanced	task specific	generic, noisy
Speakers (training/test)	109/37	109/29	63/12	79/37 73/43 80/36
Utterances (training/test)	1529/700	1529/493	1349/308	1414/723 1433/704 1427/710
Frames (training/test)	469620/244026	469626/179762	703719/182722	1357783/681601 1355586/683698 1365399/673985
Phones (training/test)	60399/32034	60399/23607	62729/13683	189108/90596 187331/92373 182969/96735
$\mathcal{F}$	47.93	47.93	82.88	323.25 338.25 335.06
$\mathcal{F} - \frac{L}{T}(\bar{F}^2 - \bar{F})$	41.74	41.74	75.18	278.98 292.23 290.75

Table 2. Recognition rates using discrete HMMs. Numbers in parentheses indicate the iteration for which the maximum rate was found

	$w = 1.0$			$w = 1/H$		
	emBW	**Vit**	**Vit +** **smBW**	**emBW**	**Vit**	**Vit +** **smBW**
SENGLAR16	65.67 (8)	65.66 (10)	65.64 (9)	65.28 (8)	65.36 (3)	65.35 (7)
SENGLAR08	63.12 (8)	57.71 (12)	59.55 (11)	62.70 (7)	57.70 (10)	59.15 (8)
INFOTREN	50.70 (19)	49.63 (19)	49.48 (8)	52.53 (20)	51.50 (11)	50.97 (19)
CORLEC-EHU-1(1)	42.27 (40)	29.98 (16)	29.74 (8)	42.06 (40)	30.07 (17)	30.44 (16)
CORLEC-EHU-1(2)	44.45 (20)	43.71 (20)	43.98 (20)	44.85 (20)	44.33 (20)	44.68 (20)
CORLEC-EHU-1(3)	46.10 (17)	45.27 (17)	45.45 (18)	46.29 (17)	45.70 (16)	45.95 (14)
CORLEC-EHU-1 **(average)**	44.27	39.65	39.72	44.40	40.03	40.36

filler, this latter used only with spontaneous speech. Each sublexical unit was represented with a left-right HMM consisting of three states ($N = 3$) with self-loops but no skips, the first state being initial and the last one final. The output probability at each time t was computed as the non-weighted product of the probabilities obtained for the four acoustic streams. No phonological restrictions were applied. Instead, transitions between sublexical HMMs in the recognition model were given a fixed weight w —sometimes called *insertion penalty*. Only the most common values were applied, namely $w = 1.0$ and $w = 1/H$, H being the number of phone HMMs.

When using discrete HMMs to model read speech at 16 kHz, all the algorithms yielded almost the same performance. This reveals that applying threshold smoothing to Viterbi estimates is enough to handle independent data in recognition. However, with read speech at 8 kHz significant differences were found, as shown in Table 2. The *embedded model* Baum-Welch algorithm gave the best result (63.12%, with $w = 1.0$), more than 5 points better than that obtained through Viterbi (57.71% with $w = 1.0$) and more than 3 points better than that obtained through the combined approach (59.55% with $w = 1.0$). Note also that including insertion penalties ($w = 1/H$) did not improve the performance.

Do these differences come from a poor segmentation at 8 kHz? Table 3 shows the value of the parameter S defined in Section 6, computed for a hand-labelled part of the training database —the same for SENGLAR16 and SENGLAR08–, consisting of 162 utterances. It reveals that the *quality* of automatic segmentations produced with Viterbi HMMs reduces from almost 90% at 16 kHz to less than 60% at 8 kHz. On the other hand, all the training approaches yielded similar S values at 16 kHz, whereas remarkable differences were observed at 8 kHz, specially between Viterbi HMMs and *embedded model* Baum-Welch HMMs. However, since these latter were not trained based on *that* segmentation but instead on *all* the possible state sequences, the resulting parameters were smoother and more robust than those obtained through Viterbi. This demonstrates that

Table 3. *Quality* of automatic segmentations obtained with the best discrete HMMs for SENGLAR16 and SENGLAR08

	Vit	Vit+smBW	emBW
SENGLAR16	89.72	89.64	87.98
SENGLAR08	58.86	55.03	41.67

the best HMMs —in terms of recognition rates— might not provide the best segmentations, and vice versa.

Things were quite different when using discrete HMMs to model spontaneous speech. First, as shown in Table 2, recognition rates were much lower: more than 10 points lower than those obtained for SENGLAR08 in the case of IN-FOTREN, and more than 20 points lower than those obtained for SENGLAR16 in the case of CORLEC-EHU-1. Second, the *embedded model* Baum-Welch algorithm yielded the best results in all the cases. Third, the combined approach slightly outperformed Viterbi training in the case of CORLEC-EHU-1, but it led to slightly worse results in the case of INFOTREN. Fourth, both Viterbi and the combined approach might lead to very suboptimal models, as in the case of CORLEC-EHU-1(1), where the recognition rate for the *embedded model* Baum-Welch algorithm was 12 points higher than those obtained for the other approaches. This may be due (1) to very inaccurate segmentations in the training corpus, (2) to a great mismatch between the training corpus and the test corpus, either because of speaker features or because noise conditions, and (3) to the increased acoustic variability of spontaneous speech, which may require a more sophisticated smoothing technique for Viterbi estimates. Finally, insertion penalties did almost always improve performance, more clearly in the case of INFOTREN. This may reveal the presence of silences and spontaneous speech events like filled pauses or lengthened vowels, lasting more than the average and implying the insertion of short phones in recognition.

Attending to the asymptotic complexities given in Sections 2, 3 and 4, the *embedded model* Baum-Welch algorithm should be 100 times more expensive than Viterbi training for SENGLAR16 and SENGLAR08, 144 times more expensive for INFOTREN, and 254 times more expensive for CORLEC-EHU-1. However, attending to the experiments, the *embedded model* Baum-Welch algorithm took between 13 and 23 times the time of Viterbi training. This may be due to the fact that the *Forward* and *Backward* functions were zero much more times than expected and the corresponding contributions to the HMM parameters were not really computed. This is an important result, since the *embedded model* Baum-Welch algorithm, in practice, seems to be *only* one order of magnitude more expensive than Viterbi training. Regarding the combined approach, it was in practice (with $N = 3$) around 2 times more expensive than Viterbi training, which is coherent with their asymptotic complexities.

As shown in Table 4, when using continuous HMMs to model read speech, all the training algorithms yielded similar rates. Again, insertion penalties did not improve performance for read speech. Among the mixture sizes tested, $M =$

Table 4. Recognition rates using continuous HMMs with various mixture sizes (M = 8, 16, 32 and 64), over the read speech databases SENGLAR16 and SENGLAR08

	M	w = 1.0			w = 1/H		
		emBW	Vit	Vit+smBW	emBW	Vit	Vit+smBW
SENGLAR16	8	70.24 (12)	70.26 (12)	70.43 (12)	69.79 (12)	70.01 (12)	69.82 (10)
	16	71.76 (12)	71.91 (12)	71.83 (12)	71.36 (10)	71.56 (12)	71.45 (12)
	32	72.72 (12)	72.72 (10)	72.72 (11)	72.47 (11)	72.37 (12)	72.42 (11)
	64	73.18 (6)	73.16 (6)	73.15 (6)	72.88 (7)	72.85 (11)	72.90 (11)
SENGLAR08	8	65.82 (12)	66.01 (12)	65.91 (12)	65.71 (12)	65.86 (12)	65.77 (12)
	16	67.26 (12)	67.35 (11)	67.28 (12)	67.12 (12)	67.10 (11)	67.13 (12)
	32	68.37 (12)	68.32 (12)	68.30 (12)	68.30 (12)	68.54 (11)	68.21 (12)
	64	68.65 (12)	68.73 (9)	68.76 (11)	68.67 (12)	68.60 (9)	68.60 (7)

Table 5. *Quality* of automatic segmentations obtained with the best continuous HMMs for SENGLAR16 and SENGLAR08

	Vit	Vit+smBW	emBW
SENGLAR16	88.05	88.00	87.95
SENGLAR08	53.57	53.52	53.41

32 revealed as the best choice, yielding a good balance between recognition rate and computational cost. However, the best rates were found for $M = 64$, outperforming discrete HMMs in more than 7 points for SENGLAR16, and in more than 5 points for SENGLAR08.

Does this mean that Viterbi segmentation improves when using continuous HMMs? The answer is *no*. In fact, as shown in Table 5, except for the *embedded model* Baum-Welch HMMs for SENGLAR08, the quality of segmentations obtained with continuous HMMs is worse than that obtained with discrete HMMs. The improvement must be claimed for the continuous representation of the output distributions, which in the case of Viterbi training compensates for the sharpness of the estimates. So Viterbi training reveals as the best choice for continuous HMMs, since it yields the same rates as *embedded model* Baum-Welch at a much lower cost.

According to the asymptotic complexities obtained above, using the *embedded model* Baum-Welch algorithm to train continuous HMMs with 8, 16, 32 and 64 gaussians per mixture, should be approximately 60, 85, 105 and 120 times more expensive than using Viterbi training, for SENGLAR16 and SENGLAR08. In practice, the *embedded model* Baum-Welch algorithm was only between 15 and 30 times more expensive than Viterbi training. On the other hand, according to the experiments —and as expected from the asymptotic complexities—, using the combined approach to train continuous HMMs for SENGLAR16 and SENGLAR08, was again around 2 times more expensive than using Viterbi.

8   Conclusions

In this paper we showed the robustness of the *embedded model* Baum-Welch reestimation of discrete HMMs, compared to Viterbi training, for both read and spontaneous speech. In the case of spontaneous speech, the presence of noises, filled pauses, silences, lengthenings and other *long-lasting* events —revealed by the need for insertion penalties in recognition—, could seriously degrade the performance of Viterbi training, whereas Baum-Welch estimates kept robust to those phenomena. Experiments showed that Baum-Welch reestimation was *only* an order of magnitude more expensive than Viterbi training. The combination of Viterbi segmentation and *single model* Baum-Welch reestimation only outperformed Viterbi training in the case of read speech at 8 kHz, but still yielding lower rates than the *embedded model* Baum-Welch reestimation.

On the other hand, it was shown that the best models in terms of recognition accuracy may not provide the best segmentations. The best models in terms of segmentation quality were always obtained through Viterbi training, which is coherent, since Viterbi training aims to maximize the probability of the most likely state sequence, given the model and the sample. When using discrete HMMs, Viterbi training led to worse estimates than Baum-Welch. This may be explained either by a strong dependence on segmentation quality, by a great mismatch between training and test data, or by the increased acoustic variability of spontaneous speech, which may require a more sophisticated smoothing technique for Viterbi estimates.

With regard to continuous HMMs, all the training approaches yielded the same performance, so Viterbi training —the cheapest approach— revealed as the best choice. It was shown that continuous HMMs did not yield better segmentations than discrete HMMs, so —as expected— the performance of Viterbi training did not only depend on the quality of segmentations but also on the *acoustic resolution* of HMMs, which is drastically increased with the continuous representation of output distributions. Finally, phonetic recognition experiments with continuous HMMs are currently in progress for the spontaneous speech databases INFOTREN and CORLEC-EHU-1, applying only Viterbi training.

References

[1] A. P. Dempster, N. M. Laird and D. B. Rubin. *"Maximum likelihood from incomplete data via the EM algorithm"* Journal of the Royal Statistical Society, Series B, Vol. 39, no. 1, pp. 1-38, 1977.

[2] X. D. Huang, Y. Ariki and M. A. Jack. *"Hidden Markov Models for Speech Recognition"* Edinburgh University Press, 1990.

[3] B. H. Juang and L. R. Rabiner. *"The segmental k-means algorithm for estimating parameters of Hidden Markov Models"* IEEE Transactions on Acoustics, Speech and Signal Processing, Vol. 38, no. 9, pp. 1639-1641, September 1990.

[4] L. R. Rabiner, J. G. Wilpon and B. H. Juang. *"A segmental k-means training procedure for connected word recognition"*. AT&T Technical Journal, Vol. 65, no. 3, pp. 21-31, May-June 1986.

[5] I. Torres, A. Varona and F. Casacuberta. *"Automatic segmentation and phone model initialization in continuous speech recognition"*. Proceedings of the CRIM/FORWISS Workshop on Progress and Prospects of Speech Research and Technology, pp. 286-289, Munich, Germany, 5-7 September, 1994.

[6] S. Young, D. Kershaw, J. Odell, D. Ollason, V. Valtchev and P. Woodland. *"The HTK Book (version 2.2)"* Entropic Speech Technology, January 1999.

[7] G. D. Forney. *"The Viterbi algorithm"* Proceedings of the IEEE, Vol. 61, pp. 268-278, March 1973.

Skin Lesions Diagnosis Based on Fluorescence Image Processing: Simple Parameters Scanning

E. Ros[1], M. M. Rodriguez[2], S. Mota[1], J. L. Bernier[1], I. Rojas[1],
C. G. Puntonet[1], and E. W. Lang[3]

[1] Departamento de Arquitectura y Tecnología de Computadores
Universidad de Granada, E-18071, Granada, Spain
{eros,smota,jbernier,irojas,carlos}@atc.ugr.es
[2] Unidad de Investigación, Hospital Virgen de las Nieves, Granada, Spain
[3] Institute of Biophysics, University of Regensburg
D-93040 Regensburg, Germany

Abstract. This paper studies the viability of a skin lesion diagnosis scheme based on fluorescence images. Three kinds of skin lesions are considered: actinitic keratosis, basal cell carcinoma and psoriasis. A wide and diverse set of simple parameters have been extracted and their discrimination potential is evaluated through an automatic diagnosis scheme based on the k-nearest neighbours. We use a sequential scanning technique that automatically selects the most relevant parameters for the addressed problem.

1   Introduction

The skin lesion diagnosis through image processing has a strong motivation due to the development of telemedicine, i.e. images can be sent through Internet easily and fast to highly specialized centres where a fast diagnosis, can be done, advising a biopsy if necessary. In this way, areas far away from these specialists can get a fast and preliminary diagnosis of these kind of lesions.

The fluorescence technique [1] has been used to obtain images of three different skin lesions (see Fig. 1):

- Actinitic keratosis. The UV radiation is considered the main factor causing this lesion. About 15 % of the population will develop Actinitic keratosis during their lifetime. It is considered a pre-cancerous skin condition (10-20% of the cases develop skin cancer). It only affects the skin surface, and therefore its elimination process is easy. Being sun exposition its main development factor, this drives the body regions in which it is normally found. It appears normally on body areas that suffer of important sun exposition Localization, colour and tactile characteristics are the main hints for its diagnosis and a skin biopsy is done when suspected.

F.J. Perales et al. (Eds.): IbPRIA 2003, LNCS 2652, pp. 858-867, 2003.

- Basal Cell Carcinoma. It is the most common form of malignant skin cancer. It grows fast but less than 1% of the cases metastasise in other parts of the body. It appears normally on body regions that suffer of important sun exposition. It can affect different sizes and depths and it has to be removed completely. Localization, size evolution and colours are the main hints that lead to its diagnosis, and always a skin biopsy must be done when suspected.
- Psoriasis. It is a benign, chronic skin disease that affects approximately 2% of the population. It is characterized by hyperkeratosis and inflammation. It usually appears on the extensor surfaces of knees and elbows. The localization of affected regions in the body is a very important factor for its diagnosis. Topic treatment is normally applied.

Many of the parameters defined in Section 2 may seem naive but the purpose of this work is to check out a wide number a diverse parameters, therefore we do not want to discard them a priori. Furthermore, other parameters, could be also be integrated easily in the study since the diagnosis scheme used in section 3 is modular. We will use the Automatic Diagnosis Scheme described in Section 3 to focus on the most relevant ones for the goal discrimination function. The unknown scale of the images is an important handicap for some parameters that are clearly scale-dependent, but we let the automatic parameter selection scheme choose the most robust ones among the whole set. A future stage of the study could address the definition and test of more specific scale-independent parameters for this concrete diagnosis application.

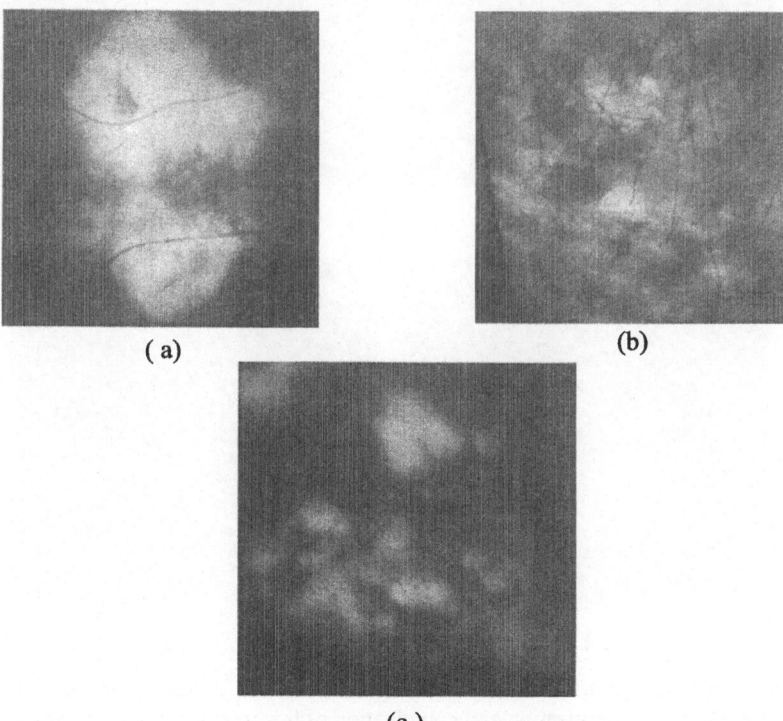

(a)   (b)

(c)

Fig. 1. (a) Actinitic Keratosis. (b) Basal Cell Carcinoma. (c) Psoriasis

Section 2 describes briefly the different types of parameters extracted from the images. Section 3 presents an automatic parameter scanning scheme based on the K-nearest neighbours classifier. Finally, Section 4 presents the classification results.

2   Methods: Database Description and Parameters Extraction

The database is composed by 61 cases of actinic keratosis, 51 of basal cell carcinoma and 66 cases of psoriasis. We have a single fluorescence image of each case with a resolution of 256x256 and 8 bit depth. The scale (skin area) of the images is not known and therefore size-related parameters are not expected to be good but some of them have been defined. Each image has been processed to extract a total of 115 parameters, but after a redundancy study only 65 of them have been selected. A brief description of the different parameters (P_1, ... , P_{65}) that have been considered in this paper is summarized.

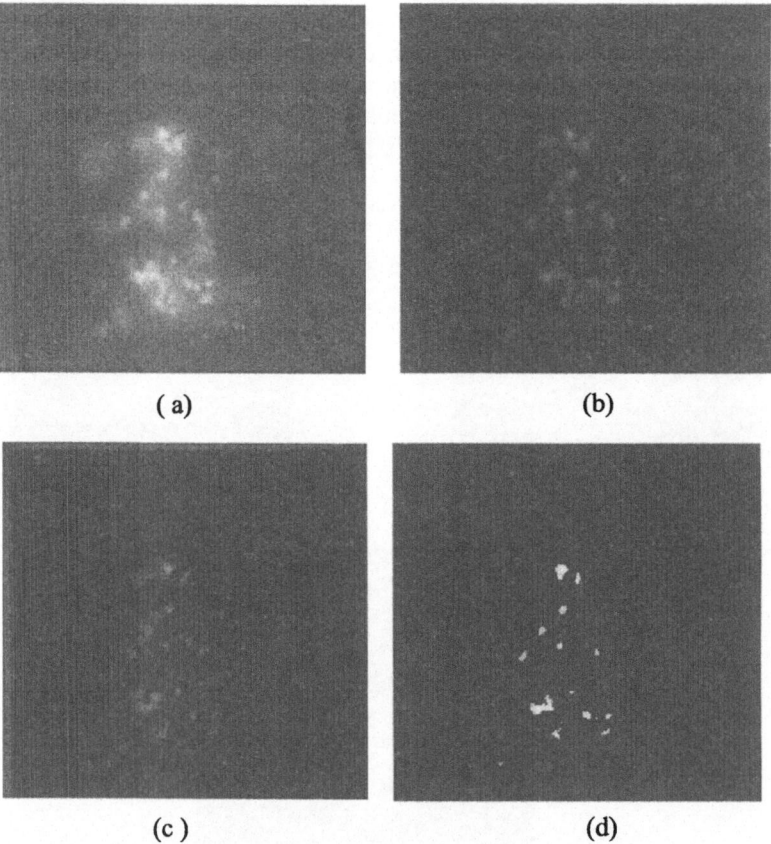

(a)   (b)

(c)   (d)

Fig. 2. a) Original image. b) Result after the top-hat transform. c) Result after the DoG filter. d) Final result after the digitization and combination of the previous characteristics through a conditional enlargement operator

2.1   Morphologic Filters [2]

We define a number of parameters based on groups of granular zones of the image with similar grey levels. We calculate the top-hat transform (h1) of the image (Fig. 2.b) taking as structure element a circle of 13 pixels of diameter. With this process we enhance the image characteristics with a size smaller than the structure element. On the other hand, the original image is filtered with a DoG kernel obtaining h2 (Fig. 2.b) These two images are digitized with a threshold and finally combined with a conditional enlargement operator. In this way the points detected with the gaussian filters are extended until the borders defined by the top-hat characteristics (Fig. 2.d).

The parameters defined based on these morphologic filtered images are:

P_1.- Number of separated spots.
P_2.- Average of the area of the detected spots.
P_3.- Standard deviation of the area of the detected spots.
P_4.- Average of the perimeter of the detected spots.
P_5.- Average of the median grey levels of the detected spots.
P_6.- Standard deviation of the median grey levels of the detected spots.
P_7.- Average of the standard deviation of the grey levels of the detected spots.
P_8.- Standard deviation of the standard deviation of the grey levels of the detected spots.

2.2   Digitization

We threshold the image (Threshold=128), to obtain some parameters.

P_9.- Euler Number [3]. Based on the borders detected in the binary images we compute the expression (1).

$$N_{Euler} = N_{objects} - N_{holes} \tag{1}$$

Being the objects closed contours and the holes well defined areas within these contours with high contrast with respect to its surrounding object. These pigmentation contrasts are characteristic of tumour images.

P_{10}.- Total segmented area of the binary image.
P_{11}.- Number of segmented spots.
P_{12}.- Irregularity Index [4]. This parameter tries to represent the contour irregularities of the segmented objects in the binary image. It is calculated using the expression (2).

$$I = \frac{Peri^2}{4 \cdot \pi \cdot A} \tag{2}$$

Where *Peri* is the perimeter and *A* is the area.

2.3   Closed Contours

The image is represented in 10 grey levels. Under this modality we have defined the ten parameters (P_{13} to P_{22}) representing the number of closed contours in each of these grey levels.

2.4   Histogram

The histogram H(k) of a grey image is the number of pixels with a particular grey value.

P_{23}.- Most frequent grey level (k value of $H_{max}(k)$).
P_{24}.- Standard deviation of the grey values, (Std(H(k)).
P_{25}.- Average of the 25 most frequent grey values (25 highest peaks in H(k)).
P_{26}.- Standard deviation of the 25 most frequent grey values (25 highest peaks in   H(k)).
P_{27} - to P_{36} are the ten most frequent grey values, highest peaks in H(k). P_{27} is the tenth most frequent grey value and P_{36} is the most frequent one.

2.5   Fourier Transform

We calculate the one dimensional Fourier transform of each row (and column) of the image and we define a global configuration parameter as the maximum of the whole image (F_{max}). We divide the frequency axes into several intervals, and we calculate the average value (F_i) for each interval. The final parameters are the number of intervals whose (F_i) are higher than a percentage of F_{max} in all the rows (and columns). Therefore each parameter of this kind is configured with the axes in which the transform is computed, the number of intervals in which the frequency domain is divided and the percentage of the maximum that is taken as threshold. A wide and diverse set of this kind of parameters has been considered (70, 80 and 90 percentages, with 5,10 and 15 frequency pool intervals) to scan the whole input space, but only three of them have finally been selected as non redundant parameters.

P_{37}.- x axes, 5 intervals, 70%.
P_{38}.- y axes, 5 intervals, 70%.
P_{39}.- y axes, 5 intervals, 90%.

2.6   Square Cells Board

With these kind of parameters we attempt to look for global contrast. In a first step, we divide the image with a grid in square cells, and we define a global configuration parameter as the maximum intensity of the whole image (I_{max}) and the minimum (I_{min}). In a second step, the intensity average is calculated in each spatial cell (I_c). Finally we count the number of cells (N_{sc}) that fulfil the following conditions:

Table 1. Square cell board parameter configurations. The different parameters are obtained with different cell sizes

Parameters	Modality: condition	Configuration percentage
P_{40} to P_{44}	$N_{sc}\{\ I_c > P_\%(I_{max})\ \}$	% (70, 80 and 90)
P_{45} to P_{47}	$N_{sc}\ \{I_c < P_\%(I_{min})\}$	% (30, 20 and 10)
P_{48} to P_{65}	$N_{sc}\ \{I_c > P_{1,\%}(I_{max})\} - N_{sc}$ $\{I_c < P_{2,\%}(I_{min})\}$	%, Combinations of the above values

Therefore, each of the parameters defined with this technique has to be configured under a modality (Max, Min or Max - Min), the size of the cell and with a particular percentage value, i.e. N_{sc}(Modality, Cell size, %) where the modality can be Max, Min or Max-Min, the cell size can be 4, 8, 16 or 32, and the percentages used are 70, 80 and 90 (with respect to the maximum) or 30, 20 and 10 (with respect to the minimum).

We extracted parameters of this kind with a different range of percentages, but they showed up to be redundant, and therefore we selected only some configurations shown in the Table 1.

3   Automatic Diagnosis Scheme

The diagnosis application addressed in this work has been divided into two classification tasks, motivated by the different ways of actuating in the presence of the goal lesion:

- **Easy Task:** Detection of cancerous or pre-cancerous lesions (Actinitic keratosis and Basal Cell Carcinoma cases) among the whole database. The goal class is composed by cases of Actinitic keratosis and Basal Cell Carcinoma. A positive detection of this kind of lesion would advise a confirming biopsy.
- **Difficult Task:** Detection of Basal Cell Carcinoma within a database composed by the cases of Basal Cell Carcinoma and Actinitic keratosis. This task has less medical interest because in both cases a biopsy is required to confirm any diagnosis. Nevertheless a positive detection of this kind of lesion would encourage urgency in the biopsy process.

It has to be pointed out that the diagnosis application can achieve better classification results if other parameters such as colour, tactile texture, localization, etc, (not available from these images) are also used. The incorporation of parameters extracted from other sources, into the diagnosis system would be straightforward, because the classification scheme described here is modular.

After extracting the parameters, each case is characterized by a 65 component vector $(P_1, ..., P_{65})$. A modular classification algorithm based on the nearest K-neighbours has been used for this application. The labelled vectors work as references of the classification system. For each new non-labelled vector, the Euclidean distances to the labelled vectors are calculated. The labels of the K nearest neighbours are consulted and the final label is calculated through a voting scheme as the label of the majority of the K-neighbours. In this way the classification algorithm is modular, new parameters can be added easily, only the dimension considered in the Euclidean distance calculation step has to be modified. The modularity of the classification algorithm enables the parameter scanning techniques described below.

Instead of doing an exhaustive statistical study of the discrimination power of the different parameters, we have used a sequential parameter scanning technique [5] to select the parameters that lead to better classification results. With two methods:

- **Forward Method.** In a first step an uni-parametric classifier is used (trying, one by one, with all the parameters). The parameter that leads to a better classification performance is selected. In a second step, the classifier is used with the selected parameter and a new one (trying combinations with all but the already selected parameter). The second parameter leading to a better result is also selected. In this way the parameter set in which the classifier is based grows up by the addition of a single parameter in each cycle until all the parameters are considered. The performance curve, obtained as the parameter set grows, increases for the first parameters and decreases when too many parameters are taken into account. The best parameter set is finally selected, i.e. the minimum parameter set with the maximum classification performance.

- **Backward Method.** In a first step all the parameters are used in the classifier. In a second step one of the parameters is dropped out (trying with all the parameters individually). The parameter set that reaches a better classification is maintained. In this way, a different parameter is dropped out in each cycle. The final parameter set is again the one that maximizes the classification performance with a minimum size.

The presented scanning technique [5] is a well known searching method already used successfully for diagnosis problems optimisation [6]. But other approaches, such as genetic algorithms can also be used in the context of automatic multi-path searching technique for parameter selection in diagnosis problems [7], and in fact, this represents a future approach to be addressed elsewhere.

4   Experimental Results

For biomedical diagnosis applications, the final diagnostic of a specific disease for a patient can be **ill** (suffering of a certain pathology) or **healthy** (free of this concrete pathology). This means that the classification result:

True Positive (TP). The algorithm detects the goal pathology in a real patient.
True Negative (TN). The algorithm classifies a healthy subject as healthy.
False Positive (FP). The algorithm classifies as ill patient a healthy subject
False Negative (FN). The algorithm classifies as healthy subject a patient suffering the goal pathology.

Table 2. Easy task with forward and backward method: Cancerous or pre-cancerous cases among the whole database

Forward Method						
Number of neighbours	Training results			Test results		
	Class. rate	Sensitivity	Specificity	Class. rate	Sensitivity	Specificity
1	100±0	100±0	100±0	99.4±1.0	100±0	98.3±2.9
3	99.5±0.9	100±0	98.6±2.5	98.2±1.8	99.1±1.6	96.7±2.9
5	100±0	100±0	100±0	97.0±2.7	97.2±2.8	96.7±5.8
7	100±0	100±0	100±0	98.2±1.8	97.2±2.8	100±0
9	100±0	100±0	100±0	98.8±2.1	98.2±3.2	100±0
Backward Method						
1	99.5±0.5	99.6±0.7	99.3±1.3	97.0±3.7	96.3±4.2	98.3±2.9
3	99.7±0.5	100±0	99.3±1.3	98.8±1.0	99.1±1.6	98.3±2.9
5	98.9±1.2	98.8±1.3	99.3±1.3	98.8±1.0	99.1±1.6	98.3±2.9
7	99.5±0.9	99.2±1.4	100±0	96.4±1.0	98.2±3.2	93.3±5.8
9	98.4±1.4	97.5±2.2	100±0	97.6±1.0	97.2±1.0	98.3±2.9

With these cases, different functions of interest can be defined (3): *Classification rate* (CR), *Sensitivity* (SE) and *Specificity* (SP).

$$CR = \frac{TP + TN}{TP + TN + FP + FN} \; ; \; SE = \frac{TP}{TP + FN} \; ; \; SP = \frac{TN}{TN + FP} \qquad (3)$$

Note that the *Sensitivity* represents the ratio between the detected ill patients and the total ill patients. While the *Specificity* represents the ration between the detected healthy subjects and the total healthy subjects.

In order to obtain classification results, the database has been divided into two subsets:

- **Training Set:** composed by 70 % of the cases of each class in the database. This is used to configure the classifier to focus on some parameters following the forward of backward method.
- **Test Set:** composed by 30 % of the cases of each class in the database. This set is only used at the end to extract the classification result on new data (not showed during the configuration process).

We have obtained three training sets, and three complementary test sets to calculate average results. The classification results of the training sets have been obtained using the leaving-one-out method [8].

The diagnosis of the easy task seems to be very accurate (Table 2) obtaining classification rates around 99% even with the test set. The best results are obtained following the forward method. We can now have a look to the specific parameters that lead to these results. With the three data subsets and 5 neighbourhood configurations we obtain a total of 15 solutions. The solutions obtained by this scanning process are based most frequently on the following parameters: 12 solutions include P_{11}, 10 solutions include P_5, and 7 solutions include P_1. P_1 and P_5 are based on morphologic filters and P_{11} is based on the digitized image. Other frequently used parameters are: P_6 (present in 6 solutions), P_{13} (present in 4 solutions) and P_{37} (present in 5 solutions). P_6 is also a morphologic parameter, P_{13} is a closed contour parameter and P_{37} is a Fourier transform parameter.

These parameters are enough to achieve good classification results (any combination of three of these parameters would represent a very valid solution), but other parameters may also lead to similar performances. An exhaustive parameter study would be necessary to assess the discrimination potential of each individual parameter.

In the case of the difficult task, poor classification results are obtained (Table 3) indicating that the parameters described in this paper are not sufficient to achieve good results, more sophisticated parameters [9, 10] may lead to better results.

5   Conclusions

In this paper we have addressed a skin lesion diagnosis scheme based on fluorescence images. The purpose of this contribution is double, on one hand to assess the validity of this kind of images for the described diagnosis tasks, and ,on the other hand, to scan the parameters that include enough information to achieve good diagnosis results.

Table 3. Difficult task with the forward and backward: Basal Cell Carcinoma detection among the database composed by the Actinitic Keratosis and Basal Cell Carcinoma cases

Forward Method					
Number of neigh-bours	Training results			Test results		
	Class. rate	Sensitivity	Specificity	Class. rate	Sensitivity	Specificity
1	58.8±3.3	38.6±26.5	77.0±18.5	63.9±8.3	88.2±10.2	42.1±24.1
3	64.6±5.8	60.5±9.5	68.3±3.6	58.3±2.8	58.8±10.2	57.9±10.5
5	65.8±2.6	61.4±8.0	69.8±9.0	54.6±11.2	51.0±9.0	57.9±13.9
7	63.8±2.2	60.5±11.5	66.7±6.3	58.3±2.8	58.8±5.9	57.9±9.1
9	69.6±1.4	66.7±5.5	72.2±3.6	62.0±11.6	74.5±23.8	50.9±16.9
Backward Method						
1	57.9±1.9	51.7±6.6	63.5±2.8	58.3±5.6	62.8±6.8	54.4±6.1
3	64.6±0.7	56.1±8.5	72.2±7.3	55.6±13.9	56.9±18.0	54.4±11.0
5	64.2±2.6	60.5±7.0	67.5±1.4	51.8±4.2	56.9±3.4	47.4±5.3
7	66.7±5.1	63.2±12.1	69.8±3.6	54.6±12.5	54.9±18.0	54.4±8.0
9	64.6±2.6	69.3±6.1	60.3±1.4	46.3±4.2	39.2±6.8	52.6±5.3

We have seen that the fluorescence technique is very valid for the easy task, the discrimination of tumour lesions (Basal Cell Carcinoma and Actinitic Keratosis) against Psoriasis, even using simple parameters as the ones described in this paper. A wide variety of parameters haven been proved to be good for this diagnosis problem: parameters based on morphologic filters, parameters based on simple image binarization, parameters base on closed contours and Fourier Transforms.

On the other hand, the parameters described in this paper achieved very poor classification results when addressing the difficult task. Therefore they are not sufficient to assess the validity of the fluorescence technique to discriminate between Basal Cell Carcinoma (Malignant tumour) and Actinitic Keratorisis (Pre-cancerous state).

Acknowledgments

We would like to acknowledge José Piñero and Alexis Toledo for the work carried out for this contribution. We would also like to thank its useful help to C. Bauer.

References

[1]   Ackermann, G.: Photophysikalische Grundlagen zur Fluoreszenzdiagnostik von Tumoren der Haut. PhD. Dissertation, University of Regensburg, 2001.

[2]   Serra. J.: Image analysis and Mathematical Morphology. Vol. II, Theoretical Advances. Academic Press, London, 1988.

[3]   Zhang, Z.; Stoecker, W.V.; Moss, R.H.: Border Detection on Digitized Skin Tumor Images, IEEE Transactions on Medical Imaging, Vol. 19, N. 11, 2000.

[4]   IEEE Transactions on Medical Imaging: Vol 41, No 9, September 1994

[5]   Narendra, P.M. & Fukunaga, K.: A branch and bound algorithm for feature subset selection", IEEE Transactions on Computers, Vol. 26, pp. 917-922, 1977.

[6]   Ros E., Mota S., Toro, F.J., Díaz A.F., Fernández F.J.: Paroxysmal Atrial Fibrillation: Automatic Diagnosis Algorithm based on not Fibrillating ECGs. (BSI2002), pp. 251-254.

[7]   F. de Toro; E. Ros, S. Mota, J. Ortega: Multiobjective Optimization Evolutionary Algorithms applied to Paroxismal Atrial Fibrillation diagnosis based on the k-nearest neighbours classifier. 8 th Iberoamerican Conference on Artificial Intelligence, Seville, November 2002 (In Press)

[8]   Hand, D.: Discrimination and Classification. Wiley & Sons, New York. 1981.

[9]   Mies, C.; Bauer, C., Ackermann, G. ; Bäumler, W.; Abels, C.; Puntonet, C.G.; Alvarez, M.R.; Lang, E.W.: Can ICA Help Classify Skin Cancer and Benign Lesions? LNCS 2085, pp. 328-335, 2001.

[10]   Bauer, C. : Independent Component Analysis of Biomedical Signals. PhD. Dissertation, University of Regensburg, 2001.

Incrementally Assessing Cluster Tendencies
with a Maximum Variance Cluster Algorithm

Krzysztof Rządca[1] and Francesc J. Ferri[2,*,**]

[1] Institute of Computer Science, Warsaw University of Technology, Poland
krzadca@elka.pw.edu.pl
[2] Dept. Informàtica. Universitat de València. 46100 Burjassot, Spain
ferri@uv.es

Abstract. A straightforward and efficient way to discover clustering tendencies in data using a recently proposed Maximum Variance Clustering algorithm is proposed. The approach shares the benefits of the plain clustering algorithm with regard to other approaches for clustering. Experiments using both synthetic and real data have been performed in order to evaluate the differences between the proposed methodology and the plain use of the Maximum Variance algorithm. According to the results obtained, the proposal constitutes an efficient and accurate alternative.

1 Introduction

Clustering can be defined as the task of partitioning a given data set into groups based on *similarity*. Intuitively, members of each group should be more similar to each other than to the members of other groups. It is possible to view clustering as assigning labels to (unlabeled) data. Clustering is very important in a number of domains as document or text categorization, perceptual grouping, image segmentation and other applications in which is not possible or very difficult to assign appropriate labels to each object.

There is a variety of clustering algorithms and families [5]. On one hand, *hierarchical* approaches produce a hierarchy of possible clusters at each stage. On the other hand, *partitional* approaches usually deliver only one solution based on a certain criterion. In terms of the criterion used and the kind of representation used, clustering algorithms can be divided into *square error algorithms*, *graph theoretic, mixture resolving, mode seeking* and *nearest neighbors*. Additionally, the same search space can be scanned in a number of ways (deterministic, stochastic, using genetic algorithms, simulated annealing, neural networks etc.). Finally, the algorithms can be classified as *hard/crisp* or *fuzzy* according to the way the membership of objects to clusters is dealt with [1].

More formally, let $X = \{x_1, x_2, \ldots, x_N\}$ be a set of $N = |X|$ data points in a p-dimensional space. Clustering consists of finding the set of clusters $C =$

---

* Work partially supported by Spanish CICYT TIC2000-1703-C03-03.
** Contacting author

F.J. Perales et al. (Eds.): IbPRIA 2003, LNCS 2652, pp. 868–875, 2003.
© Springer-Verlag Berlin Heidelberg 2003

$\{C_1, C_2, \ldots, C_M\}$ which minimizes a given criterion with given X and, usually but not necessarily, given M.

One of the simplest and most used methods to measure the quality of clustering is the square-error criterion:

$$J_e = \frac{\sum_{i=1}^{M} H(C_i)}{N} \tag{1}$$

where

$$H(Y) = \sum_{x \in Y} dist(x, \mu(Y))$$

is the cluster error (*dist* is a distance measure function, e.g. Euclidean distance) and $\mu(Y) = \frac{1}{|Y|} \sum_{x \in Y} x$ is the cluster mean.

The straight minimization of equation 1 produces a trivial clustering where each data member is in its own cluster. Consequently, some constraints should be used in order to obtain meaningful results as in the (well-known) case of the k-means algorithm [6] in which the number of clusters, M, is fixed as a constraint. There are a number of algorithms [5, 3] that share this feature with the k-means and all of them suffer from a common drawback: the difficulty of determining in advance the number of clusters. Most of the algorithms require trying different number of clusters and take a further stage to validate or assess which is the best result. The fact that the criterion used at each step cannot be used for validation makes the problem difficult [4, 7].

2   Maximum Variance Cluster Algorithm

A straightforward clustering algorithm using a constraint based on variances of each cluster has been recently proposed [8]. This approach has a number of advantages. First, knowing cluster variances can be easier than the final number of clusters in some applications. Secondly, the same criterion can be used for the cluster validation. Additionally, as the number of clusters is modified, the algorithm seems to deal with outliers in a more natural way.

The so-called Maximum Variance Cluster (MVC) algorithm [8] requires that the variance of the union of any two clusters be greater than a given limit, σ_{max}^2:

$$\forall C_i, C_j, i \neq j : Var(C_i \cup C_j) \geq \sigma_{max}^2 \tag{2}$$

where $Var(Y) = \frac{H(Y)}{|Y|}$. Clusters produced with such a constraint generally (but not necessarily) have variances below σ_{max}^2.

The way in which such a result is searched for consists of a stochastic optimization procedure in which the square error criterion in (1) is minimized (thus minimizing distances from the cluster centroids to cluster points) while holding the constraint on the cluster variance in (2). At each step, the algorithm moves points between neighboring clusters. In order to do this in an efficient way, the concepts of *inner* and *outer* borders of a cluster are introduced.

For a given point x, the qth order inner border, G_x, is a set of q furthest points belonging to the same cluster. The kth order outer border, F_x, is a set of k nearest points belonging to other clusters. The qth order inner border and kth order outer border of a cluster C_a can then be defined as the union of inner (outer) borders of all points in C_a,

$$I_a = \bigcup_{x \in C_a} G_x \quad \text{and} \quad B_a = \bigcup_{x \in C_a} F_x$$

respectively. Borders defined in a such a way grow when clusters grow and the algorithm never ends up with empty borders.

The MVC algorithm starts with a cluster per data point and then repeats iterations in which the inner and outer borders of each cluster are the candidates to be moved from and to other clusters. To speed up the algorithm, only random subsets of sizes $i_a < |I_a|$ and $b_a < |B_a|$ are considered instead of the whole inner and outer borders, respectively. In particular, one of the three following operators is applied to each cluster (taken in random order) at each iteration:

- *isolation*: if the variance of the current cluster is higher than the predefined maximum, σ^2_{max}, the cluster is divided by isolating (in a new cluster) the furthest point (with regard to the cluster mean) among the i_a taken from the inner border.
- *union*: if the variance constraint is satisfied, the algorithm checks if the cluster can unite with one of the neighboring clusters which are found by looking at the b_a points taken from the outer border. Cluster union is performed only if the joint variance is lower than σ^2_{max}.
- *perturbation*: if none of the previous operators can be applied, the algorithm identifies the best candidate among the b_a taken from the outer border to be added to the cluster in terms of the gain this produces in the criterion J_e. The candidate is added to the cluster if the gain is positive. Otherwise, there is a small probability P_d (occasional defect) of adding the candidate regardless of the gain produced.

The algorithm in this form does not necessarily converge and a limited number of iterations E_{max} needs to be established in order to get a convenient result. After E_{max} iterations, isolation is no longer allowed and the probability P_d is set to 0. The clustering is considered as a final result when there is no change in the cluster arrangement for a certain number of iterations.

3   Cluster Tendency Assessing Using Maximum Variance

The cluster tendency refers to looking for possible cluster structures in raw data. In the particular case of the MVC algorithm, it is possible to assess cluster tendency while finding the appropriate values of the maximum variance parameter σ^2_{max} in (2). In order to do this, one possibility is to construct curves [8] showing the mean square error as a function of the maximum variance. *Plateaus* in this curve can be defined as the regions where the square error does not change while the maximum variance increases. The *strength* of the plateau ranging from σ_A^2 to σ_B^2 is defined as the ratio between both variances, $\frac{\sigma_B^2}{\sigma_A^2}$. A plateau is considered as *significant* if its strength is roughly above 2. This heuristic comes from the fact that the average distance to the new mean when two clusters are joined has to increase about 2 times in the worst case if one starts with two *real* clusters [8]. The significant plateaus in the mean square error curve have corresponding plateaus (with the same variance values) if the number of clusters, M, is plotted as a function of σ_{max}^2.

The most important drawback of directly using MVC to discover significant plateaus is the computational burden. One has to select the starting point and step size in order to be able to compute the curve in terms of σ_{max}^2. Moreover, the accurate detection of plateaus may depend on the above extra parameters of the algorithm. At the end, the MVC algorithm needs to be run hundreds or even thousand times in order to obtain the corresponding results.

4   Incrementally Assessing the Cluster Tendency

One of the properties of MVC is that it converges very quickly. Usually after less than 10 iterations the algorithm is able to find a solution very close to the finally obtained one. This happens because the algorithm works mainly by *uniting* clusters. For every value of σ_{max}^2, it starts by joining one-point clusters into groups of about 3 elements. Then it continues uniting such groups until the variance constraint is no longer satisfied. Isolation is performed occasionally and perturbation usually concerns a very limited number of points.

This behavior suggests a new strategy to discover significant plateaus without having to run MVC for each possible value of σ_{max}^2.

Let us suppose that we have a *stable* solution (i.e. a cluster-data points assignment) obtained by running the MVC with a value σ_A^2 which corresponds to the beginning of a plateau. The goal consists of directly finding the value σ_B^2 which corresponds to the end of the same plateau. Let us suppose that we know the value σ_B^2 and we run the MVC algorithm with it, starting with the previous cluster assignment. As a consequence, we would not obtain any new isolation (if there was any, it would have occurred with the previous value σ_A^2 and the initial solution would have been unstable). Perturbation would not occur neither, because it depends only on the error criterion. The only operator which could make profit from that increase is union which directly depends on σ_{max}^2.

Consequently, we can assume that the minimum value σ_B^2 which leads to changes in the cluster assignment is the minimum value required to join any 2 clusters in the assignment corresponding to σ_A^2.

To directly obtain σ_B^2 once σ_A^2 is given, any two neighboring clusters (in terms of their outer borders) are tentatively merged and the corresponding joint variances are computed. The smallest joint variance is taken as σ_B^2. Three different cases are then possible:

1. If the MVC algorithm with variance σ_B^2 converges to a solution with exactly one cluster less, we can conclude that the previous assumptions were correct. The value σ_B^2 is the starting point of a new plateau and its corresponding cluster assignment can be used without having to fully run MVC starting with singletons.

2. If the MVC algorithm with variance σ_B^2 converges to a solution with more than one cluster less, this implies that the true end of the plateau is smaller than σ_B^2. In such a case, our proposal runs again the MVC algorithm with σ_A^2 but using the cluster assignment obtained for σ_B^2. With very high probability, the algorithm will increase the number of clusters but with an assignment different from the one originally obtained with σ_A^2. This newly obtained stable solution can be used as explained above to compute the end of the sought plateau. It may happen that this produces an infinite loop if the original assignment is arrived at again. The proposed solution in this easily detectable case is to mark the whole zone as an unstable plateau and proceed from σ_B^2.

3. It is strictly possible but very unlikely that the MVC algorithm with variance σ_B^2 converges to a solution with the same (or even bigger) number of clusters. In this case, we proceed with the algorithm from this starting point but the whole zone has to be marked as unstable (in this case, even the σ_B^2 value cannot belong to any significant plateau).

The above introduced procedure which starts from a small value for σ_A^2 and proceeds by obtaining the corresponding ends of plateaus, will be referred to in this work as Incremental Maximum Variance Clustering (IMVC) algorithm. This procedure, obtains a list of variance values, $\{\sigma_i^2\}$ where some of them are marked as unstable. The algorithm always runs the original MVC algorithm with σ_i^2 starting from the cluster assignment obtained at σ_{i-1}^2. The corresponding computational burden is then certainly bounded by the cost of one run of the MVC algorithm times the number of plateaus.

5   Experiments and Results

Basically the same experiments reported in [8] using synthetic and real data have been repeated using MVC and the methodology of cluster validation and tendency assessment proposed in this work. The Euclidean distance has been used in the mean square criterion which implies that hiperspherical clusters are implicitly considered. The parameter setting for the basic algorithm is also the same: The number of points randomly selected from the inner and outer borders are fixed as the square root of the corresponding border sizes. The number of no change iterations needed to consider a cluster assignment as stable for the MVC algorithm is set to 10.

In particular, 3 artificial data sets (shown in Figure 1) consisting of spherically shaped bivariate Gaussian clusters have been considered. The R15 data set consists of 15 clusters of 40 points each positioned in two rings (7 each) around

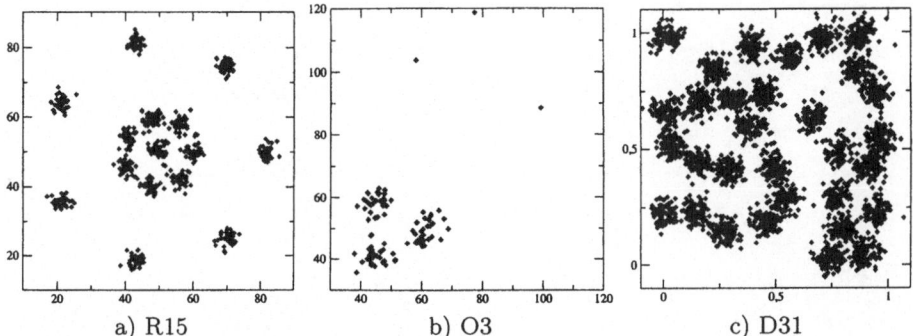

a) R15   b) O3   c) D31

Fig. 1. Scatter plot of the three synthetic data sets used in the experiments

a central cluster. Two possible clustering results are possible: one with the 15 clusters, and the other with the 8 central clusters united in one big cluster. The O3 data set consists of 3 clusters of 30 points plus three outliers. A good solution for O3 consists of finding the three true clusters and isolate the outliers. The D31 data set consists of 31 randomly placed (non overlapping) clusters. As there are 100 points in each cluster, this can be considered as a large-scale clustering problem with regard to the previous ones.

Also the well-known Iris data set has been considered [2]. This consists of three dimensional data corresponding to three different classes of iris flowers. The goal consists of identifying these three classes in an unsupervised way.

The cluster tendency plots corresponding to the plain MVC and the incremental version are shown in Figure 2. In all cases the solid and dashed lines show the results obtained (number of clusters and squared error, respectively) by running the MVC using a fixed step size for the maximum variance parameter, σ^2_{max}. The algorithm has been run 10 times for each value of σ^2_{max} and the corresponding average value is plotted. Significant plateaus are identified by looking for approximately constant regions in this plots which are usually surrounded by oscillations. The standard deviations (not shown in the figures) are negligible at the plateaus and are relatively small in the transition zones.

The circles and diamonds show the exact values of σ^2_{max} used (once) by the IMVC algorithm. Horizontal wide grey lines represent the corresponding induced plateaus identified by the algorithm.

In the case of the R15 data set in Figure 2a, there is a significant plateau discovered by both approaches ([6.23 . . . 22.47]) with strength 3.60 which corresponds to 15 clusters. The next plateau discovered by IMVC is located at [96.14 . . . 185.62] (8 clusters) with strength 1.93. In this case the plateau identified by MVC is slightly smaller but still is the second most important. In general, the plots induced by the IMVC algorithm closely follow the ones obtained directly with MVC for σ^2_{max} values below 150.

In the Figure 2b corresponding to the O3 data set, there is a significant plateau (strength 3.91) at [21.12 . . . 82.61] with 6 clusters discovered by both

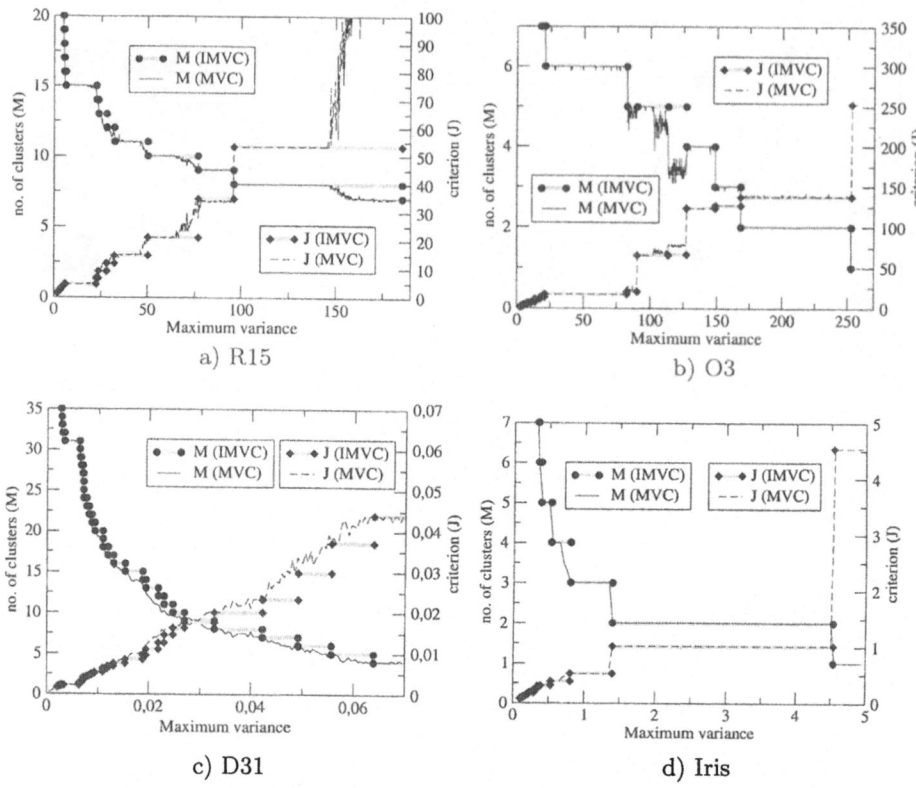

a) R15

b) O3

c) D31

d) Iris

Fig. 2. Number of clusters, M, and criterion value, J_e, as a function of the maximum variance, σ^2_{max}, using the MVC algorithm and the incremental procedure IMVC

approaches. However, the plateau induced by IMVC at $[90.58\ldots113.77]$ corresponds to a region of big instabilities (switching among solutions with 5, 4 and 3 clusters) and consequently is not taken into account (This plateau is the only one marked as unstable in the presented figures). The only zone in which the plots induced by IMVC are different from the MVC plots is the above mentioned plateau. It is worth noting that besides this difference the IMVC algorithm does not identifies any significant plateau in the unstable zones.

The plots corresponding to D31 data set in Figure 2c has the most significant plateau (strength 1.87) identified by both approaches at $[0.0033\ldots0.0063]$ with 31 clusters. Apart from this, the MVC plots show a very unstable behavior and the plots induced by the IMVC differ significantly from them. From $\sigma^2_{max} = 0.02$, the IMVC produces one more cluster in average than the MVC which roughly corresponds to the standard deviation (in 10 runs) measured for the MVC curve in these regions. The IMVC results can be seen as an upper approximation (in terms of number of clusters) of the results obtained by MVC.

The Iris data set in Figure 2d gives rise to two most significant plateaus found by both approaches at $[0.80\ldots1.40]$ and $[1.40\ldots4.54]$ with strengths 1.74 and 3.25, respectively. In this case, the whole plots obtained by both approaches are very similar.

6   Concluding Remarks and Further Work

A straightforward and efficient way to discover appropriate values of the maximum variance parameter for the recently proposed MVC algorithm has been presented. One of the major benefits of this algorithm is the possibility of using it for exploratory data analysis by looking for cluster tendencies. The algorithm presented constitutes an efficient and accurate alternative to the plain and exhaustive use of the MVC as proposed in [8].

We have found evidence about the ability of our proposal to quickly find the right clustering results. Only when the original algorithm exhibits severe instabilities (which means there is no real clustering result there) the approximation given by the proposed approach is not tight.

In our opinion, more experimentation is needed to properly assess the benefits of the original MVC algorithm with regard to other clustering approaches (which has been partially done in [8]) and also to fully test our approach to discover cluster tendencies in real data corresponding to challenging and nontrivial clustering problems. Nevertheless, the preliminary results obtained in this work give enough evidence to see the proposed methodology as very promising both because the good results obtained and the relatively small computational burden.

References

[1] J. C. Bezdek. *Pattern Recognition with Fuzzy Objective Function Algorithms.* Plenum Press, 1981.
[2] C. L. Blake and C. J. Merz. UCI repository of machine learning databases, 1998.
[3] L. O. Hall, B. Ozyurt, and J. C. Bezdek. Clustering with a genetically optimized approach. *IEEE Transactions on Evolutionary Computation,* 3(2):103–112, 1999.
[4] A. K. Jain and R. C. Dubes. *Algorithms for Clustering Data.* Prentice Hall, 1988.
[5] A. K. Jain, M. N. Murty, and P. J. Flynn. Data clustering: A review. *ACM Computing Surveys,* 31(3):265–323, 1999.
[6] J. MacQueen. Some methods for classification and analysis of multivariate observations. In L. M. Le Cam and J. Neyman, editors, *Proc. Fifth Berkeley Symp. Math. Statistics and Probability,* volume 1, pages 281–297, 1967.
[7] G. Schwarz. Estimating the dimension of a model. *The Annals of Statistics,* 6, 1978.
[8] Cor J. Veenman, Marcel J. T. Reinders, and Eric Backer. A maximum variance cluster algorithm. *IEEE Transactions on Pattern Analysis and Machine Intelligence,* 24(9):1273–1280, 2002.

Musical Style Recognition by Detection of Compass

F. J. Salcedo, J. E. Díaz-Verdejo, and J. C. Segura

Department of Architecture and Computers Technology
University of Granada, 18071 Granada , Spain
{jedv,segura}@ugr.es

Abstract. The present paper describes a method for the automatic classification of musical styles from the musical signal. This method can be used for searching and indexing purposes in musical databases, which constitutes one of the applications of MPEG-7. The method is based on applying HMM models to detect the compass in a way very similar to what is done for continuous speech recognition. The experiments demonstrate the kindness of the HMMs applied to the recognition of musical styles.

1 Introduction

The increase in the amount of audiovisual information stored in very different formats -videotapes, CDs, DVDs, digital storage, etc.- makes necessary the automatic handling of this information, in order to classify, search and retrieve it in a fast and easy way. Although the computers already carry many of these tasks out in an efficient manner, to increase their potential they should be nearer to the human understanding in order to allow information handling by its contents. One of the challenges of MPEG-7 is to describe the content of a multimedia piece of information in an automatic way.

Among many other applications of the standard related to sound are those related to music. Its author, composition date, title, etc. can classify a musical piece. According to its context, it can be classified by the musical type it belongs to (Waltz, Samba, Tango, etc.), its movement (Slow, Allegro, etc.) or even by the feeling perceived when listening (sad, cheerful, relaxing, etc.).

The present work is centered in the classification of songs by their musical style. Some timid efforts have been made in order to accomplish this task automatically. Among them we can mention some studies based on Stochastic Grammar Inference [1], which have shown good discriminative properties (up to 90,1% of correct classification), but that have only been applied to 3 styles of monophonic music. Another approach described in the bibliography is the classification based on statistical features obtained using different transforms, which are applied to a classifier [2]. This method has also shown good results (up to 91.7%) but against that they have only been applied to three very generic types of music: Rock, Piano and Jazz. Time modeling Neural Networks has been applied to the classification of 4 music types in [3] with a capacity of discrimination of 86%.

F.J. Perales et al. (Eds.): IbPRIA 2003, LNCS 2652, pp. 876-883, 2003.

In our opinion, all these mentioned methods also present another disadvantage so that to be really effective and it is that they don't incorporate any information about the musical structure. For analogy with continuous speech recognition, these approaches would be similar in some way to trying to recognize words without keeping in mind their phonetic structure. Using explicit knowledge about subjacent structures has proven significant improvements in speech recognition. We expect this statement to be applicable to music.

The present work will use the Markov models as proposed in [3] as the starting point and will show the power of the Hidden Markov Models (HMMs) when applied to music style classification by modifying the base system in two different ways: improving the parameterization of samples and applying the HMMs to recognize and classify the music compasses instead of recognizing the music segment as a whole.

In the following section we will explain the basis of using the compass as a discriminator of music types. Section 3 will explain the use of HMMs for this task. Experiment design is explained in section 4, while sections 5 and 6 are devoted to experimental results and conclusions, respectively.

2   The Compass as a Musical Characteristic

The compass is a grouping of temporary segment with the same length and is itself an amorphous continent. Its content depends on the rhythm, that is to say, on the sequence of musical notes that integrate it. Each compass can be occupied by a single or several notes whose configuration determines the rhythm of the song that nevertheless is enclosed and measured by oneself pulsation of time. Therefore, each compass contains the basic periodicity elements and can be considered as the fundamental component of the rhythm of a song. For analogy with the human language, the different compasses are to the music like the letters of the alphabet, they allow to facilitating the understanding and the control of the rhythm. Therefore, it is deduced that any song can be written as a succession of compasses.

The notation of the compasses has fraction form, in which the numerator indicates the total duration of the compass in figures (white, quarter note, quaver, etc.) and the denominator the unit of time of the compass also in figures. This way for example, the compass 3/4 indicates that the unit of time is the quarter note and that they fit three quarter notes in the compass.

The compasses are divided in two main groups: the simple ones and the compounds that are distinguished to each other because in the first ones the figure unit of time is always a divisible value in two equal parts, while in the compounds it is a divisible value in three same parts.

Most of the classic dances have a rhythmic formulation based on the succession of oneself simple compass. For example, a Waltz is composed by a succession of compasses 3/4 and a Tango of compasses 2/4. Four classic dances have been chosen with three different compasses to test the system. The dances are: the Tango, the Waltz, the Rumba (a Spanish dance) and the Mambo. As is shown in fig. 1, the Mambo and the Rumba share the same compass although they present a different rhythmic formula or characteristic sequence of notes. This election has been made this way in order to be able to determine the discriminative power of the method proposed in this article.

Fig. 1. Classic dances used and their compasses and rhythm formulas

3   Design of Experiments

Four different experiments have been carried out. Two experiments use the HMMs for recognition of the music style by considering the song segment as a whole (in an isolated-word-like approach), while the other two experiments try to detect and recognize compasses.

The database consists on 120 samples of 30 seconds each one of the 4 types of selected music, that is to say, there are 30 samples per style. All the samples have been extracted from CDs, sampled at 16 kHz in monaural mode and low-pass filtered at 8 kHz.

In order to improve the statistical validity of the results the leave-one-out method has been used by splitting the set of samples 5 in disjointed sets each one composed by 96 samples for training and 24 samples for testing.

3.1   Feature Extraction Improvements

The reference system has been established according to [3], using the same HHM topology, feature extraction and training procedure. Anyway, it is possible to archive some improvement in the performance of the system without any changes in the number of states in the HMM nor in the transition structure of the HHM. In order to select a good parameterization for the music it is necessary to take into account that the musical signal is, at every time, the sum of the signals from several instruments, occasionally, the voice of the singer or singers. The complexity of this kind of signal requires a parameterization that minimizes the loss of information during the process.

The proposed feature extraction is based in two main concerns:

1) To have parameter vectors close enough in time so as not to loss the rhythm information. It is necessary to keep in mind that there are compasses that can last around 3 seconds and that can contain up to 9 different notes (as in Rumba). This establishes a ratio of 30 msec per note.

2) To include more cepstrum coefficients and their time derivatives, that is to say, delta coefficients and acceleration. These parameters help to improve the time evolution modeling of the samples and, therefore, the discriminative power of the HMMs.

The segments of the samples has been made by applying them a 20 msec Hamming window and obtaining a parameter vector each 10 msec. A pre-emphasis filter has been used with a coefficient of 0.97. Each parameter vector is composed by 14 cepstrum coefficients, the energy and their corresponding first and second derivatives. Therefore, each parameter vectors has a total of 45 components. Finally, an energy normalization procedure has been applied in order to avoid the variability introduced due to different recording conditions.

3.2   Detection of Compasses

To be able to use the HMMs in the continuous detection of compasses, it is necessary to extract an exact number of compasses from the samples for embedded training purposes in order to avoid misalignments in the transcriptions and the use of incomplete compasses. To accomplish this requirement a manual segmentation of the samples, by choosing the initial and ending point of the sequence of compasses in a sample and the number of compasses in the sequence, is needed. Obviously, basic knowledge of music is needed to carry out this extraction and labeling. Once segmented, the samples are transcribed in terms of compasses and used for training.

We have chosen a left-to-right topology for the HMMs (fig. 2) instead of the structure proposed in [3]. In order to select the number of states in each HMM some experiments have been carried out using different number of states and different number of gaussians to characterize the emission probabilities. From fig. 3 it is deduced that the best results are obtained by using 11 states and 3 gaussians (per state).

The used grammar is adapted to the music types to classify. As mentioned in the second section, it consists on an uncertain succession of same compasses for each sample.

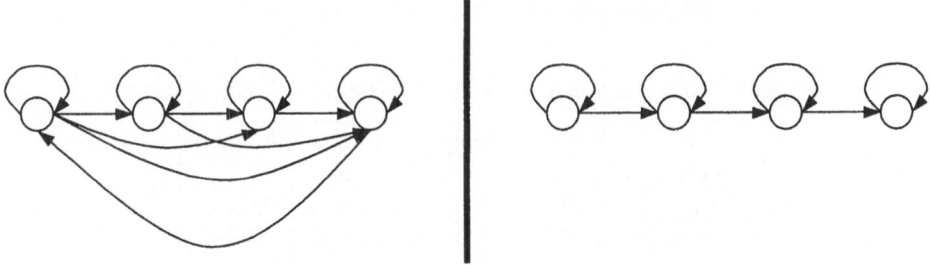

Fig. 2. HMM topology used in [1] (left) and in this paper (right)

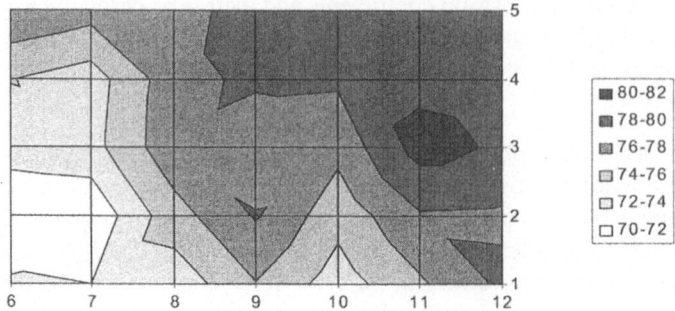

Fig. 3. Correct alignment percentage vs. Number of states in HMMs (x's axis) and number of gaussians (y's axis)

4   Experimental Results

4.1   Isolated Recognition of Samples

In the first experiment the parameterization has been used according to that proposed in [3]. Four HMMs, one for each music type, have been trained. All the models are initialized with one gaussian and during the training, the number of gaussians is increased each three iterations. The recognition began after 9 training iterations. The results on the used database give a 79.25% recognition rate (table 1). This result is the same to that obtained in [3] for the database of samples of Rock, Pop, Techno and Classic.

Applying the improved parameterization exposed in the section 3.1 a recognition rate of 86.7% is obtained (table 2), which supposes a substantial improvement regarding the previous one. This result demonstrates the importance that has the parameterization of the musical samples to train the HMMs, and to take the maximum yield out of these in the recognition. It has been demonstrated that a sensitive information loss is obtained with the parameterization made in the first.

Table 1. Confussion matrix for the first experiment (reference system)

S/R[1]	Waltz	Tango	Rumba	Mambo
Waltz	93.3%	3.3%	0%	3.3%
Tango	3.3%	80%	0%	16.7%
Rumba	0%	10%	76.7%	13.3%
Mambo	0%	16.6%	16.6%	66.6%

---

[1] Stimulus/response: entry of row i column j is the rate how many samples from type i was classified as type j

Table 2. Confussion matrix when using the improved parametrization

S/R	Waltz	Tango	Rumba	Mambo
Waltz	96.7%	3.3%	0%	0%
Tango	10%	83.3%	0%	6.7%
Rumba	0%	3.3%	76.7%	3.3%
Mambo	6.7%	3.3%	16.7%	73.3%

4.2   Continuous Recognition of the Compass

In this case the HMMs than have been used are the ones defined suitable for the characterization of the compass, as justified in the section 3.2. The analysis and parameterization of the samples is the same as for experiment 2 (improved parameterization). The difference rests in that previously a HMM represented a musical type as a whole and is trained using a single sample. Now, when applying continuous compasses, each sample represents a group of identical compasses. During training, the corresponding HMM is trained several times by the same sample (as many as the number of compasses in the sample).

The grammar model used for recognition is shown in fig. 4. As shown in these figure, a sample is supposed to be a sequence of identical compasses. The recognition process will provide the class of the sample and the alignment of the compasses that constitutes it.

The result obtained for this method is a 94.2% recognition rate, increasing in a 7.5% the discriminative power of the best of the isolated models. As shown in table 3, the level of minimum recognition is of 90% and the biggest number of confusions takes place between the Rumba and the Mambo (10%) and in smaller amount between the Waltz and the Tango (6.7%). This is owed in the first case to that these types share the same compass 4/4 although they possess different rhythmic formula. On the other hand, the confusions between the Waltz and the Tango can be due to the similarity of the compasses 2/4 and 3/4.

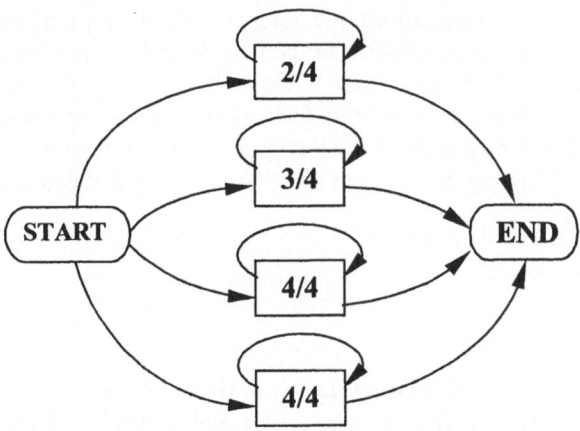

Fig. 4. Grammar model used for continuous recognition of compasses

Table 3. Confussion matrix for recognition of compasses

S/R	Waltz	Tango	Rumba	Mambo
Waltz	100%	0%	0%	0%
Tango	6,7%	90%	0%	3.3%
Rumba	0%	0%	96.7%	3.3%
Mambo	0%	3.3%	6.7%	90%

Table 4. Confussion matrix for an experiment with different compasses

S/R	Waltz	Tango	Rumba
Waltz	100%	0%	0%
Tango	3.3%	96.7%	0%
Rumba	0%	0%	100%

To check the power of the method in the recognition of the compass another experiment in which the Mambos have been eliminated has been carried out. This way the three remaining types possess all different compass type. The results are shown in table 4.

The results of the recognition of musical pieces with different compass type demonstrate that modeling of the compass is getting through the HMMs. If these results are compared with the previous ones it can be proven that even HMM are distinguishing among different rhythmic formulas that use the same compass. This is what happens in the case of the Mambo and the Rumba in which there is only a 10% of error in the recognition among them.

5   Conclusions

Present work has shown the potential that have the HMMs applied to the recognition of music types modeling songs of unique compass. The incorporation of information on the musical structure (the compass) to the HMMs and the grammar, together with an appropriate parameterization allow a recognition power that oscillates among 94.2% when common compasses exist, to 99% when all the compasses are different.

The future work will be guided to modeling more compass types, as well as to relax the used grammar, allowing the recognition of music types that possess successions of different compasses.

References

[1]   Cruz-Alcázar, P.P. and Vidal-Ruiz, E.: A Study of Grammatical Inference Algorithms in Automatic Music Composition and Musical Style Recognition, Proceedings of the 14th International Conference on Machine Learning (ICML-97), Nashville, USA (July 1997)

[2]   Lambrou, T., Kudumakis, P., Speller, R., Sandler, M. and Linney, A.: Classification of Audio Signals Using Statistical Features on Time and Wavelet Transform Domains, Proceedings of IEEE ICASSP 98, Seattle, USA (May 1998)

[3]   Soltau, H., Schultz, T., Westphal, M. and Waibel:, A. Recognition of Music Types, Proceedings of IEEE ICASSP 98, Seattle, USA (May 1998)

[4]   De Pedro, D.: Teoría Completa de la Música, (Vol.2), Ed. Real Musical, Madrid, Spain (1992)

Subtexture Components for Texture Description

Anna Salvatella, Maria Vanrell, and Ramon Baldrich

Computer Vision Center, Edifici O, campus UAB
08193 Bellaterra, Spain
{annasg,maria,ramon}@cvc.uab.es
http://www.cvc.uab.es

Abstract. In this paper the problem of texture description for image browsing or annotation is approached. Previous works in this direction have proposed solutions that have shown to be limited due to the high degree of complexity natural textures can achieve. This problem is solved here by defining textures as a combination of several subtexture components, whose description is simpler since they only have one characteristic element. A computational method based on multiscale filtering with Laplacian of Gaussian is presented to identify the subtexture components of a texture, and a texture description based on these subtexture components attributes is given.

1 Introduction

Texture is an important visual cue for image understanding that still lacks of a standard and general definition in Computer Vision. Texture is necessary for many machine vision applications, and thus several computational approaches to build texture representations have been presented[1] In most cases the representations obtained were directed by specific taks such as image classification [2],image retrieval [3]or image segmentation [4],however psychophysical studies on human texture perception have been the motivation for others [5]. Some texture spaces have been derived from these studies, but for the moment none of the approaches leads to a general texture representation space.

A texture description in textual terms and related to how textures are perceived by human beings is necessary for image browsing or image annotation. In this scope, the MPEG-7 standard, devoted to provide a set of standardized tools to describe multimedia content, proposes a perceptual browsing descriptor (PBC) [6]. In this paper we present a new approach to texture description based on perceptual considerations. We try to extend the PBC descriptor so that it comprehends all the texture information and a wider and adaptable description is obtained.

To this end, the paper is organised as follows. Section 2 sets the background and section 3 defines the concept of subtexture component giving the computational details on how to obtain them. The texture description based on the subtexture components is presented in section 4. Some results are shown in section 5 and finally section 6 presents the conclusions and further work.

F.J. Perales et al. (Eds.): IbPRIA 2003, LNCS 2652, pp. 884–892, 2003.

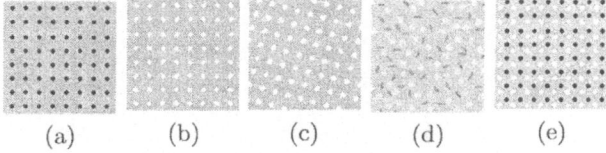

(a)   (b)   (c)   (d)   (e)

Fig. 1. Examples of simple textures

2   Background

As mentioned in the introduction, texture does not have a standard definition in Computer Vision. In this paper, a grey-level image is considered to be a texture if it presents homogeneity in its grey-level distribution along the image which is given by the repetition of basic primitives across the image. We will consider an image as a texture when at least four non-overlapped windows can be taken from the image sharing the same texture properties.

Any approach to texture description should be based on how human beings perceive and describe textures. To this end, let us analyse the results that have been obtained in psychophysics on texture perception. Two approaches are confronted as being the basis for an internal visual representation of texture. On one hand, local feature extraction processes have received a hard support from the Julesz's [7] texton theory, and on the other hand, a global spatial analysis has been demonstrated to be necessary by Beck [8]. Examples in figure 1 show that both methods form part of the process by which the human visual system deals with texture: textures in images (a) and (b) are segregable due to differences in the blob contrast, i.e. local features, whereas images (b) and (c) are segregable because of the orientation of the patterns emerging from the texture image. Therefore, not only global methods but also local properties should be taken into account when dealing with texture description.

It can be shown that if textures are regarded as blobs and emergent patterns, the complexity level of textures, both natural and synthetised, is unlimited, like textures in figure 1 (d) and (e), which are made out of combination of different simpler textures, i.e. (e) is obtained by combining (a) and (b). Despite this wide range of complexity degrees in texture, in previous texture descriptors all textures are described with the same number of features. However, if human subjects are asked to describe more complex textures, they will use more words or features than they use for simpler textures.

Another advantage of considering textures as a combination of properties from blobs and emergent patterns is the ability to build objective descriptors. Most of the experiments that have been done to derive the dimensions of the texture space have been based on texture comparison or segregation. Therefore, the results that are obtained might not be suitable for texture description, but for texture comparison. Rao et al, in [9], presented a serie of psychophyiscal experiments concluding there are three main dimensions for texture, namely structure or regularity, scale, and directionality, nonetheless these concepts can

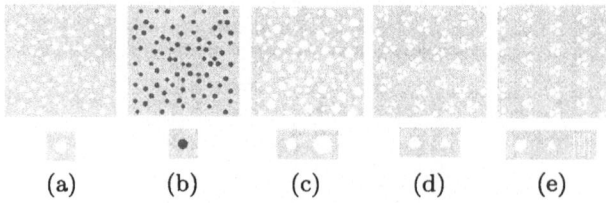

(a)   (b)   (c)   (d)   (e)

Fig. 2. Textures having different number of subtexture components which are defined by the property presented below each image

not be clear and objective enough for description when both regular and random patterns appear in a texture at the same time. The foregoing discussion makes us consider that a texture descriptor willing to be general and meaningful should fulfil two conditions: (i) different texture degrees of complexity must be taken into account and (ii) textures have to be represented by attributes of their own characteristic elements, and not only by comparison to other textures. These considerations have motivated the introduction of the concept of subtexture component, which is defined in the following section.

3   Subtexture Components

Previous considerations lead us to define a subtexture component of a texture image as a *set of blobs or emergent patterns sharing a common property all over the image*. Then, a texture image will be formed by several subtexture components, each one characterized by only one kind of blobs or emergent patterns. In figure 2 textures with different number of subtexture components are shown. The texture in image (a) has only one subtexture component defined by bright blobs randomly positioned, the image in (c) has two components due to the different size of the bright blobs and in (d) there are also two subtexture components, since there are bright blobs but also triangles emerging from the blobs grouping. Finally, texture in (e) has three subtexture components, since the triangles are positioned forming a stripped emergent pattern.

The fact that textures are understood as a combination of components allows to describe textures in terms of the attributes of their components, instead of describing the whole texture. This approach to texture description fulfils the aforesaid conditions: (i) a texture can be made out of as many subtexture components as necessary, and thus the adaptation to different degrees of complexity is assured, and (ii) the subtexture components can be described in terms of the attributes of its own blobs or emergent patterns, and not by comparison with other textures.

Once this concept has been defined and explained, now the goal is to define a computational approach to automatically extract them since it will be the base of the texture descriptor presented in the following section.

We propose a multiscale filtering approach to obtain the subtexture components, since it allows detecting blobs and emergent patterns with different sizes. The images will be smoothed by a gaussian filter, so that at higher scales the details disappear and only global structures of the image remain. For each scale, blobs will be detected and subtexture components are obtained by gathering those sets of blobs having the same contrast. In [10] the laplacian of gaussian filter was used to detect blobs in texture images; in this case the method will be extended by varying the size of the filter. Filtering with the laplacian of gaussian presents several advantages: (i) if no threshold is considered, the zero-crossings are closed, and thus its duals can be interpreted as blobs, (ii) the multiscale filtering permits tunning with different blob sizes and (iii) the sign of the pixels in the filtered image gives its contrast with the neighbouring pixels, which will be used to determine the contrast of the blobs.

Thus, the first step to obtain the subtexture components is to find the blobs or emergent patterns for a given scale. For a given texture image I, for each scale σ, the smoothed version of the image, S_σ and its Laplacian, L_σ, are calculated:

$$S_\sigma(I) = I * G_\sigma \; ; \; L_\sigma = \nabla^2(I * G_\sigma) = I * (\nabla^2 G_\sigma) = I * LoG_\sigma \qquad (1)$$

where G_σ is a gaussian filter with standard deviation ,σ, which takes p values within the range $[\sigma_{min}, \sigma_{max}]$. The zero-crossings of L_σ are the closed edges of the smoothed image; therefore, its duals can be considered as blobs. The following step consits on classifying the blobs according to their contrast [11], which is given by the grey-level values of L_σ in each blob : bright blobs are those verifying $L_\sigma < 0$ and dark blobs those where $L_\sigma > 0$.

At this point, the blobs of an image S_{σ_i} having the same contrast form a subtexture component if they appear uniformly through all the image. Otherwise, it is supposed that the blobs are not characteristic elements of the texture and therefore they are rejected. Thus, for an image I we obtain n subtexture components $\{S^i\}_{i=1,...n}$ where $n \leq 2p$.

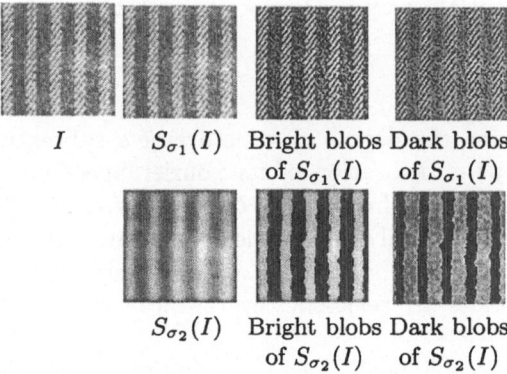

$$I \qquad S_{\sigma_1}(I) \qquad \text{Bright blobs} \quad \text{Dark blobs}$$
$$\text{of } S_{\sigma_1}(I) \quad \text{of } S_{\sigma_1}(I)$$

$$S_{\sigma_2}(I) \qquad \text{Bright blobs} \quad \text{Dark blobs}$$
$$\text{of } S_{\sigma_2}(I) \quad \text{of } S_{\sigma_2}(I)$$

Fig. 3. Extraction of subtexture components by multiscale filtering

The images in figure 3 show different steps to obtain subtexture components. The original image I, the smoothed image and the subtexture components for bright and dark blobs are shown for two different scales, $\sigma_1 = 0.75$ and $\sigma_2 = 3$.

4   Texture Description

Once we have outlined the method to obtain the subtexture components of a texture, let us present the texture descriptor based on their attributes. In [12] the PBC descriptor for a texture image is given by the regularity, two predominant directions and two predominant scales. In our case, we propose to describe a subtexture component $\mathcal{S}^i(I)$ of a texture I by

$$\mathcal{D}(\mathcal{S}^i(I)) = [c, sc, st, d_1, d_2, d_3, d_4] \tag{2}$$

where the meaning of the 7 components is the following:

- c gives the contrast of the blobs, b for bright blobs and d for dark blobs
- sc represents the scale, ranging from 1 (*small*) to 5 (*large*).
- st is the structure, ranging from 1 (*completely random*) to 5 (*structured*).
- d_1, d_2, d_3 and d_4 are the orientations of the predominant directions.

Let us define the steps to compute the subtexture attributes.

Contrast and Scale
In previous section it has been stated that the contrast and scale of the blobs or emergent patterns forming a subtexture component are the attributes that identify it. As it has been shown, the contrast of the blobs has been derived from L_σ, and the scale is directly given by corresponding filter.

In order to estimate the remaining features of the subtexture components we have chosen to calculate the Fourier Spectrum, which has already been used for texture feature extraction [14]. Moreover, there are psychophysical evidences that support frequential analysis plays an important role in human perception of textures [13].

Degree of Structure
In order to determine the degree of structure of a subtexture component, we will study the shape and location of its Fourier Spectrum peaks. Firstly, we will estimate a measure of the stability of them by gradually thresholding the spectrum. Afterwards, we will evaluate the alignement of the peaks by computing a modified Hough transform of the maxima, since only the lines which have been voted by several points are selected. Several measures are extracted from this analysis:

- sp : number of stable peaks (i.e. appearing in 3 or 4 thresholds)
- vsp : number of very stable peaks (i.e. appearing in 5 or more thresholds)
- l : number of straight lines

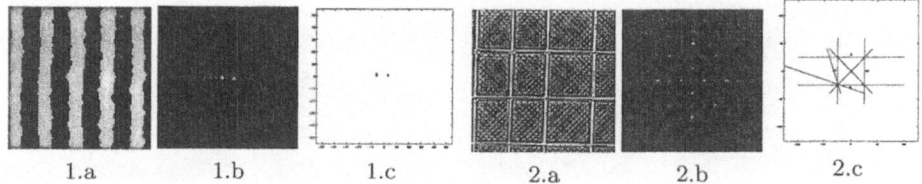

1.a   1.b   1.c   2.a   2.b   2.c

Fig. 4. Examples of subtexture components analysis for the evaluation of the degree of structure: images 1.a and 2.a are the subtexture components, their spectrums are shown in 1.b and 2.b respectively, and 1.c and 2.c illustrate the maxima and the straight lines obtained from the analysis

The calculation of the degree of structure is then given by a weighted sum of these parameters:

$$st = \alpha \times l + \beta \times sp + \gamma \times vsp \tag{3}$$

The values for $[\alpha, \beta, \gamma]$ have been estimated to be $[0.2, 0.3, 0.5]$ from a preliminar psychophysical experiment where 16 subjects were asked to describe textures in terms of their subtexture components features.

Predominant Orientations

The predominant orientations of the subtexture components are easily detected in the spectrum, since they also appear as predominant orientations in the frequency domain. The spectrum is transformed to polar coordinates and a histogram of the orientations with 8 equally distributed bins is computed. The predominant orientations of the subtexture component are those having more than 20% of the points. This value has also been deduced from the psychophysical experiment mentioned above. The descriptor will take into account up to 4 orientations, since it is difficult to find subtextures with more predominant directions.

Building the Global Texture Descriptor

Since the presented computational approach can extract more than one component representing the same subtexture, we will firstly apply a selective step that removes redundant subtexture components. This redundancy is easily removed by doing a similarity test. We will denote the number of relevant subtexture components as k.

The texture global descriptor, $\mathcal{GD}(I)$ is a matrix whose rows are the description of the relevant subtextures:

$$\mathcal{GD}(I) = (\mathcal{D}(S^i(I)), \ldots, \mathcal{D}(S^k(I)))^T \tag{4}$$

As it can be seen, the number of rows of the texture descriptor depends on the texture complexity. In next section some examples of texture descriptions are given.

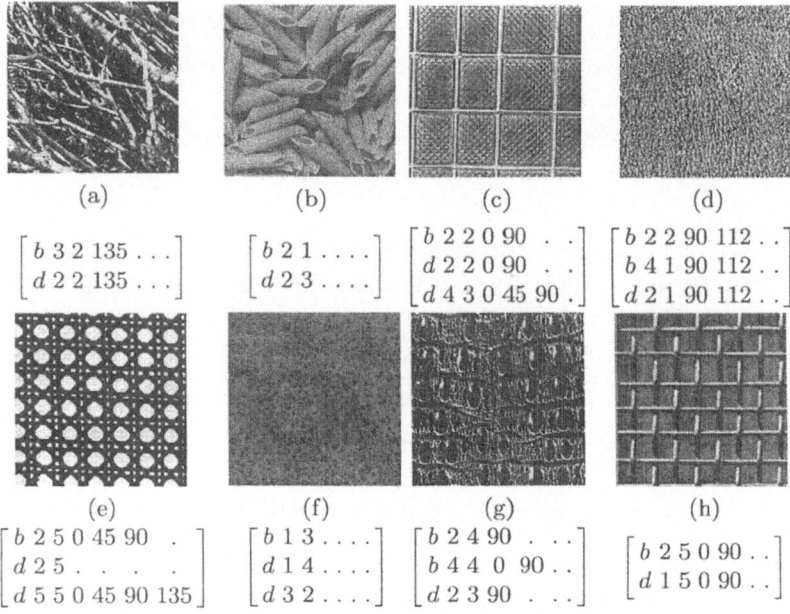

Fig. 5. Examples of texture descriptions

5 Results

The description of several textures is presented in figure 5, under every image I the corresponding global descriptor $\mathcal{GD}(I)$ is given. For example, image (a) is formed by two subtextures, one made out of bright blobs of medium scale ($sc = 3$) with an almost random structure ($st = 2$) and a predominant orientation of 135°, and another one made out of small dark blobs with the same structure and predominant orientation. On one hand it can be seen that the number of subtexture components that are obtained matches the complexity the texture, images (c) and (e) which can be considered complex textures are described by three components and images (a) and (h), which are much simpler, are described by two components only. On the other hand, we can see that the contrast, degree of structure and orientations of the subtexture components are quite well detected in most cases, whereas the scale needs to be improved. Finally, it can be seen from the examples that the presented texture description is enriched by the fact that subtexture components are treated separately. For instance, in image (g) the horizontal orientation due to the emergent pattern is only detected for a high scale, while the vertical orientation due to small elongated blobs appears at smaller scales.

6   Conclusions and Further Work

This paper has mainly two contributions. Firstly, the concept of subtexture component has been introduced, which allows a texture description that can be interesting both from a computational and a perceptual point of view. Secondly, we have presented a first approach to a computational texture descriptor which is shown to be general enough to give the description of any natural texture.

The fact that the number of subtexture components can vary makes this approach suitable to all levels of texture complexity, which is very important for Computer Vision applications where all types of images can be found. The presented texture descriptor is based on perceivable characteristics of the image without the need of comparison. This is indispensable for applications such as image browsing where images have to be described in terms of its own properties and in a way that makes it easy to go from natural language to computational representations. Further work will be focused on the improvement of the scale detection and on the introduction of more complex information such as the shape of the emergent patterns.

Acknowledgements

We want to thank Prof. Manjunath for the interesting discussions about this work and his excellent suggestions. This work has been partially supported by the project TIC 2000-0382 of the Spanish government and the grant BE 2002 from the Catalan government.

References

[1] Tuceryan, M., Jain, A. K.: *Handbook of Pattern Recognition and Computer Vision*, chapter Texture Analysis, pages 235–276. World Scientific, 1993.

[2] Ojala, T., Pietikainen, M., Harwood, D.: A comparative study of texture measures with classification based on feature distributions. *PR*, 29(1):51–59, 1996.

[3] Manjunath, B. S., Ma, W. Y.: Texture features for browsing and retrieval of image data. *IEEE-PAMI*, 18(8), 1996.

[4] Boyer,K., Sarkar, S. editors: *Perceptual organitzation for artificial vision systems*, chapter 9, pages 139–172. Kluwer Academic Publishers, 2000.

[5] Malik, J., Perona,P.: Preattentive texture discrimination with early vision mechanisms. *JOSA*, 7:923–932, 1990.

[6] Manjunath, Salembier, and Sikora, editors. *Introduction to MPEG-7.Multimedia Content Description Interface*. John Wiley and Sons, 2002.

[7] Julesz, B., Bergen, J. R.: Textons, the fundamental elements in preattentive vision and perception of textures. *Bell Systems Techn. Journal*, 62:1619–1645, 1983.

[8] Beck, J.,Sutter, A.Ivry, R.: Spatial frequency channels and perceptual grouping in texture segregation. *CVGIP*, 37:299–325, 1987.

[9] Rao,A. R. ,Lohse, G. L.: Towards a texture naming system: Identifying relevant dimensions of texture. *Vision Research*, 36:1649–1669, 1996.

[10] Voorhees, H., Poggio,T.: Detecting textons and texture boundaries in natural images. In *First ICCV*, pages 250–258, 1987.

[11] Syeda-Mahmood, T. F.: Detecting perceptually salient texture regions in images. *Computer Vision and Image Understanding*, 76(1):93–108, 1999.

[12] Wu,P. ,Manjunath, B. S., Newsam,S. Shin, H. D.: A texture descriptor for browsing and similarity retrieval. *Journal of Signal Processing: Image Communication*, 16:33–43, 2000.

[13] Harvey, L.,Gervais, M.: Visual texture perception and Fourier analysis. *Perception and Psychophysics*, 24(6):534–542, 1978.

[14] Liu, F., Picard R. W.: Periodicity, directionality, and randomness: Wold features for image modelling and retrieval. *IEEE Trans. on PAMI*, 18(7):722–733, 1996.

A 3D Ultrasound System for Medical Diagnosis*

João Sanches[1], Jorge S. Marques[1], Fausto Pinto[2], and Paulo J. Ferreira[3]

[1] Instituto Superior Técnico, Instituto de Sistemas e Robótica
Torre Norte, Av. Rovisco Pais, 1049 Lisbon, Portugal
[2] Faculty of Medicine, University of Lisbon, Portugal
[3] University of Aveiro, IEETA, Aveiro

Abstract. This paper presents a system for 3D ultrasound which aims to reconstruct a volume of interest from a set of ultrasound images. A Bayesian reconstruction algorithm has been recently proposed to perform this task. However, it is too slow to be useful in practice. This paper describes several techniques to improve the efficiency of the reconstruction procedure based multi-scale principles and based on the expansion of the likelihood function in a Taylor series. This allows the use of sufficient statistics which avoid processing all the images in each iteration and leads to a space-varying recursive filter designed according to the statistical properties of the data. Experimental results are provided to assess the performance of the proposed algorithms in medical diagnosis.

1 Introduction

Ultrasound is a non ionizing, non invasive and cheap medical imaging technology. Current systems, operating in B-scan mode, allow real time observation of cross sections of the human body. Several attempts have been made to extend ultrasound techniques in order to compute and visualize 3D representations of the human organs leading to three dimensional ultrasound systems [1].

Three dimensional ultrasound has several advantages with respect to classic ultrasound systems. First it provides new visual information since it allows the observation of the organs surface, as well as cross sections of the human body which can not be observed in B-scan mode, due to physical constrains. Second it provides quantitative measurements of volumes which can not be accurately obtained using standard B-scan mode. Both issues are important for medical diagnosis.

Three dimensional ultrasound can be performed either by using special types of probes, e.g. mechanical scanners which automatically sweep a region of interest by varying the inspection plane in a predefined way, or by using free hand scanning systems [1]. Mechanical scanners are simpler but they are more expensive and can only reconstruct small regions of the human body, while free hand scanners can be be used to reconstruct larger regions. They require complex reconstruction algorithms though.

---

* This work was partially supported by FCT in the scope of project POSI/33726/CPS/2000.

F.J. Perales et al. (Eds.): IbPRIA 2003, LNCS 2652, pp. 893–901, 2003.
© Springer-Verlag Berlin Heidelberg 2003

This paper describes a free-hand 3D ultrasound system. This system allows the estimation of a volume of data from a sequence of ultrasound images, corresponding to non parallel cross sections of the human body. This is a difficult task since we have to estimate the whole volume from a finite number of noisy images, corrupted by speckle noise. The system must be able to perform noise reduction, to interpolate the data in regions which are not observed and also to compensate for the geometric deformations of the human organs during the data aquisition process. Bayesian techniques have been recently proposed to address these problems in a principled way but they are very time consuming [8] and can not be directly used in practice.

This paper describes several techniques to improve the efficiency of the reconstruction procedure based on multi-scale principles and on the expansion of the likelihood function in a Taylor series. This allows the use of sufficient statistics which avoid processing all the images in each iteration, leading to a space-varying recursive filter designed according to the statistical properties of the data. Experimental results are provided to assess the performance of the proposed algorithms in medical applications.

2   System Overview

This paper aims to reconstruct a volume of interest from a sequence of ultrasound images. The data acquisition system adopted in this work has three main components (see Fig.1),

- a medical ultrasound equipment with an ultrasound probe operating at 1.7 MHz.
- a spatial location system used for real time measurement of the probe position and orientation.
- a personal computer to capture the probe positions and ultrasound images at 25Hz rate, and reconstruct the volume.

During a medical exam a sequence of ultrasound images is provided, corresponding to non parallel cross sections of the human body. The probe position and orientation, associated to each image, are also available. This allows to estimate the position of each pixel in 3D space, provided that we know the geometric transformation from the image coordinates into the probe coordinate system. This is estimated by a calibration procedure, similar to the single-wall calibration described in [13].

The volume of interest is reconstructed from the pixel intensities and positions, using a Bayesian reconstruction algorithm which is briefly described in section 3. This algorithm manages to interpolate the observed data, filling the gaps, and combines multiple observations to reduce the speckle noise. This is performed by adopting a parametric model for the function to be estimated, which depends on a large number of coefficients (many thousands), estimated using Bayesian techniques.

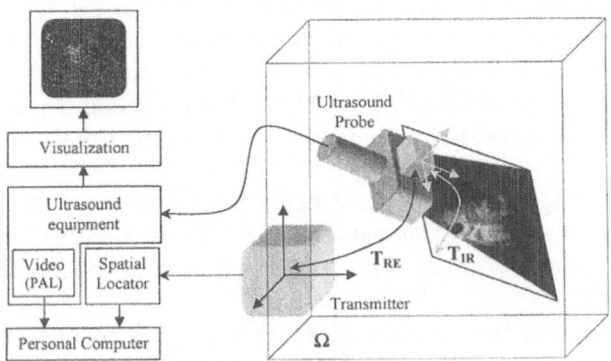

Fig. 1. Acquisition system

Visualization techniques (re-splicing, ray casting and thresholding) are used to display the results of the 3D reconstruction algorithm. All the software modules (data acquisition, sensor calibration, reconstruction and visualization) were developed in C++ in a Windows 2000 platform.

3   3D Reconstruction

Let $V = \{(x, y)_i\}$ the observed data after calibration, i.e., after the estimation of the transformation that relates the image coordinate system with the patient coordinate system. Each element of the vector V, contains the intensity, y_i and the corresponding 3D position, x_i, of each observed pixel from all images that form the sequence. This observed data is used to reconstruct the volume.

Let consider the region to be estimated $\Omega \in R^3$ formed by a set of cubic cells called voxels.

The scalar function $f(x)$, describing the acoustic properties of the volume of interest, is obtained, inside each voxel, by interpolating the values of its vertices, i.e.,

$$f(x) = \Phi(x)^T U \tag{1}$$

where $\Phi(x) = \{\phi_1(x), \phi_2(x), ...\phi_n(x)\}$ is a vector of interpolation functions and $U = \{u_1, u_2, ..., u_n\}$ a vector of intensity values associated to the grid nodes. The estimation of the volume is performed by estimating the vector U.

Each interpolation function is a separable function of the form $\phi_i(x) = \phi_i^1(x)\phi_i^2(x)\phi_i^3(x)$ where

$$\phi_i^j(x^j) = \begin{cases} (1 - \frac{d_i^j(x)}{\Delta}) & d_i^j(x) \leq \Delta \\ 0 & \text{otherwise} \end{cases} \tag{2}$$

Using the MAP method, the estimation of U is obtained by minimizing an energy function, i.e.

$$\hat{U} = arg \min_U E(Y, X) \tag{3}$$

where $E(Y, X) = -l(V, U) - \log(p(U))$. $l(V, U) = log(p(V|U))$ is the log likelihood function and $p(U)$ is the prior associated to the vector of nodes to estimate. The prior plays two important roles. First it allows to interpolate the data in points which were not observed, i.e., which do not belong to any observation plane. Second it improves the numerical stability of the iterative reconstruction algorithm.

Ultrasound images are very noisy being corrupted by multiplicative noise. A Rayleigh model is used in this paper to describe the observations. This noise, called *speckle*, is usually observed in process involving coherent radiation like LASER or SAAR.

It is assumed that the elements of Y are i.i.d. (independent and identically distributed) random variables with Rayleigh distribution ([2]),

$$p(y_i) = \frac{y_i}{f(x_i)} e^{-\frac{y_i^2}{2f(x_i)}} \tag{4}$$

where y_i denotes the amplitude of i-th pixel and $f(x_i)$ is the value of the function f computed at position x_i. The likelihood functions is generated by

$$l(V, U) = \sum_i \{\log [\frac{y_i}{f(x_i)}] - \frac{y_i^2}{f(x_i)}\} \tag{5}$$

The statistical independence of all elements of V is assumed ([3]), despite the PSF (point spread function) of the image acquisition system be, in general, larger than the inter-pixel distance. In fact, it is not easy to estimate the PSF of the acquisition system. This function depends, not only on the impulsive response of the ultrasound probe and the associated electronics, but also on the image processing performed by ultrasound equipment. In particular, the filtering procedure that smoothes the original raw data by converting the polar grid of the RF signal to grid the image in cartesian coordinates introduces correlation among the pixels which is difficult to model. Furthermore, the improvement achieved in the reconstruction results by considering the statistical dependence among the pixels of the image is not relevant when compared with the computational complexity introduced in the algorithm, as noted by [4].

To derive $p(U)$ let us consider X as being a Markov random field. According the Hammersley-Clifford theorem, $p(U)$ is a Gibbs distribution. In this paper a Gibbs distribution with quadratic potential function is used

$$p(U) = \frac{1}{Z} e^{-\frac{\alpha}{N_v/2} \sum_{g,s} (u_g - u_g^s)^2} \tag{6}$$

where Z is a partition function, N_v is the number of neighbors of u_g, α is a parameter and u_g^s is the s-th neighbor of u_g (see details [7]). A 6-neighborhood system is considered in this paper. Note, that only half of the neighbors are considered in this summation to guarantee that each clique appears only once.

Using (5) and (6) leads to

$$E(V, U) = -\sum_i \{\log [\frac{y_i}{f(x_i)}] - \frac{y_i^2}{f(x_i)}\} + \frac{\alpha}{N_v/2} \sum_{g,s} (u_g - u_g^s)^2 \tag{7}$$

The minimization of (7) with respect of U is a difficult task. The number of coefficients to estimate is of order of a million and $E(V, U)$ is a non convex function. To solve (3) the ICM algorithm, proposed by Besag is used [5]. In each iteration, the ICM algorithm minimizes the energy function with respect to only one variable, keeping all the others constant. To optimize (7) with respect to the variable u_n the following condition must be met

$$\frac{\partial E(V, U)}{\partial u_n} = 0 \tag{8}$$

which leads to

$$\frac{1}{2} \sum_i \frac{y_i^2 - 2f(x_i)}{f^2(x_i)} \phi_n(x_i) + 2\alpha N_v(u_n - \bar{u}_n) = 0 \tag{9}$$

where N_v is the number of neighbors of u_n, $\phi_n(x)$ is the interpolation function associated to the n-th node and $\bar{u}_n = \frac{1}{N_v} \sum_{j=1}^{N_v} (u_n)_j$ is the average value of the neighboring nodes of u_n.

This equation can be solved using the fixed point method leading to the next recursion expression

$$\hat{u}_n = \frac{1}{2\alpha N_v} \sum_i \frac{y_i^2 - 2f(x_i)}{f^2(x_i)} \phi_n(x_i) + \bar{u}_n \tag{10}$$

The solution of (3) using the ICM method leads to a set of non-linear equations, (9) which requires processing the pixels of the whole image sequence. Therefore, the reconstruction algorithm is computationally demanding and slow. To speed up the reconstruction process, several measures can be taken. In the next section three methods are proposed to simplify and speed up the solution of (10): i) a multi-scale approach, ii) the linearization of (10) allowing sufficient statistics and iii) a IIR filter to efficiently compute the MAP estimation of the volume.

4   Fast Algorithms

Three methods are considered to speed-up the reconstruction process. Detailed descriptions of these methods are published in [9, 10, 12].

Multi-scale The propagation of the information along the lattice due the prior is one of the main factors that slows down the convergence rate of the algorithm described in section 3. To overcome this difficulty, a multi-scale version is used. In this approach, coarse grids are used in the initial iterations being progressively refined until the final resolution is achieved. In this way, the long range interactions propagate fast in the first iterations speeding up the global convergence rate. In the last iterations the algorithm only performs small local adjustments. In this method the estimated volume obtained in a given iteration is used as starting point for the next iteration, and the resolution is doubled in consecutive iterations [9].

Linearization It is not possible to compute sufficient statistics associated to eqn (10) since he can not factorize the pdf. To obtain sufficient statistics a linearization of the likelihood function in the vicinity of the maximum likelihood estimate is performed. With this method, a small set of statistics computed in the initialization stage of the reconstruction algorithm and used along the whole optimization process. Therefore, the observations only have to be read from the disk and processed at the beginning. The observed data, compressed into a smaller number of coefficients, speeds up the processing time by more than one orders of magnitude [10]. The resulting equations are

$$\hat{u}_n = (1 - k_n)u_n^{ML} + k_n \bar{u}_n \tag{11}$$

$$u_n^{ML} = \frac{\sum_i y_i^2 \phi_n(x_i)}{\sum_i \phi_n(x_i)} \tag{12}$$

$$k_n = \frac{1}{1 + \frac{1}{4\alpha} \frac{\sum_i \phi_n(x_i)}{(u_n^{ML})^2}} \tag{13}$$

Filtering Equation (13) defines an IIR filter. This filter is not wedge supported [11]. Each output depends on past and future outputs since it depends on $\bar{u}_p$. Therefore, it is not possible to recursively compute the output in a single iteration. To overcome this difficulty we consider a set of eight wedge supported filters (see details on [12]), which can be recursively computed. The reconstructed volume is obtained by averaging the outputs of the eight wedge supported filters. This approach allows to improve the reconstruction time exploiting the computational efficiency of the recursive processing. With this methodology, reduction up to 25 times in the processing time can be achieved.

In this paper these three methods are used and combined into five different reconstruction strategies. They will be compared, using three figures of merit: the number of iterations, the processing time and the likelihood function. In the case of experiments using synthetic data a fourth figure of merit is also used: the signal to noise ratio. The methods considered in the experiments are

i)   NLMAP-SS   Non multi-scale and non linear base algorithm.
ii) NLMAP-MS   Multi-scale and non linear base algorithm.
iii) LMAP-SS   Non multi-scale and linear algorithm.
vi) LMAP-MS   Multi-scale and linear algorithm.
v)   IIRMAP   Recursive algorithm.

5   Experimental Results

Experimental tests were carried out to evaluate performance of the five reconstruction techniques with synthetic and medical data using several figures of merit. Two examples are described in this section to illustrate the performance

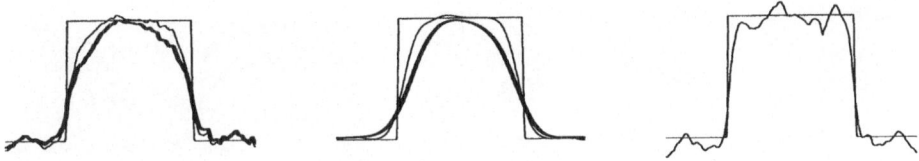

Fig. 2. Intensity profiles of the original and reconstructed volumes using i) NLMAP-SS and NLMAP-MS (bold); ii) LMAP-SS and LMAP-MS (bold); iii) IIRMAP

of the system with synthetic and medical data. More tests were performed but can not be included here due to space restrictions.

Synthetic Data This example considers the reconstruction of a binary function f defined as follows: $f(x) = A, if x \in [-.5, .5]^3$, $f(x) = B$, otherwise. Volume reconstruction is obtained from a set of 100 parallel cross-sections of the region $[-1, 1]^3$ corrupted by Rayleigh noise according to (4).

Figure 2 shows the intensity profiles of the original and reconstructed volumes along a given line. It is concluded that all the methods manage to estimate the original object reasonably well, showing some distortion at the transitions (blurring). The best transitions are obtained with the IIRMAP algorithm although this algorithm has the worst performance in stationary regions.

Table 1 shows four figures of merit which allow an objective comparison of several techniques in terms of SNR, final energy, iterations and computational effort. All methods manage to minimize the energy function and provide similar SNR results, except LMAP-MS which achieves worse results. The computational time is strongly dependent on the reconstruction method, the fastest reconstructions being achieved by the IIRMAP algorithm. The multi-scale approaches also achieve significant savings with respect to the single scale methods since they reduce the number of iterations. The fast algorithms reduce the computational effort of the NLMAP algorithm by 70 times (almost two orders of magnitude).

Table 1. Results with synthetic and medical data

Method	Synthetic Data				Medical data		
	SNR (dB)	E ($\times 10^3$)	Time (s)	iterations	E ($\times 19^3$)	Time (s)	iterations
NLMAP-SS	20.1	8000.8	1534.53	64	8990.5	1893.4	96
NLMAP-MS	18.2	7999.5	403.32	17	8983.0	737.7	37
LMAP-SS	19.2	8000.8	298.17	36	9013.4	263.7	59
LMAP-MS	16.6	8002.5	113.63	9	8982.9	216.8	38
IIRMAP	20.4	8020.1	22.44	8	9156.3	21.4	8

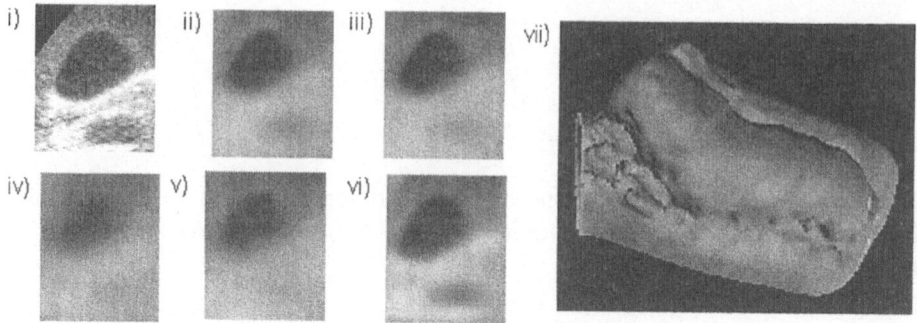

Fig. 3. Results with medical data: original cross section (i) and reconstructed cross sections obtained with ii) NLMAP-SS; iii) NLMAP-MS: iv) LMAP-SS; v) LMAP-MS; vi) IIRMAP; vii)Surface rendering of the gall bladder

Medical Data Reconstruction tests were performed using the experimental setup described in section 2. This example shows the reconstruction of a gall blader from a set of 100 images corresponding to non parallel cross sections of the human body.

Figure 3 shows a cross section of the human body and the reconstructed results obtained by the five algorithms. These results are achieved by computing f along the inspection plane. Acceptable reconstruction results are obtained by all the algorithms. Table 1 shows the figures of merit associated to all the algorithms. Similar energy functions are obtained by all the methods, the best results being obtained by NLMAP-MS method.

Significant computational savings are achieved by using the fast algorithms, the fastest reconstruction being obtained by the IIRMAP method. The IIRMAP is 90 faster than the NLMAP algorithm. This can also be concluded from fig. 4 which displays the evolution of the energy during the optimization process as a function of the number of iterations. The surface of the gall bladder obtained with etdips 2.0 package is shown in Fig. 3.vii).

6   Conclusions

This paper considers the reconstruction of human organs from a set of ultrasound images, using five algorithms. A Bayesian approach is adopted in all these algorithms, leading to the optimization of an energy function which depends on a large number of variables (typically, a million variables). Two key ideas were explored: i) the use of multi-scale techniques which use coarse grids in the first iterations and finer grids afterwards and ii) a second order approximation of the energy function using the Taylor series. The Taylor series approach allows to reconstruct the volume of interest by low pass filtering the data with a space variant IIR filter, reducing the computational effort by almost two orders of magnitude. The best results were obtained by the IIRMAP method which provides a good trade off between accuracy and computational time.

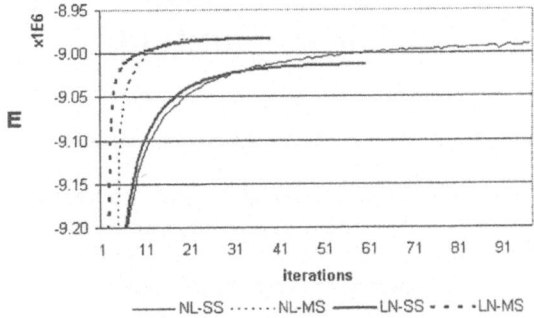

Fig. 4. Convergence 3D reconstruction methods i) NLMAP-SS; ii) NLMAP-MS: iii) LMAP-SS; iv) LMAP-MS; v) IIRMAP

References

[1] T. Nelson, D. Downey, D. Pretorius, A. Fenster, Three-Dimensional Ultrasound, Lippincott, 1999.

[2] Burckhardt C., Speckle in Ultrasound B-Mode Scans, IEEE Trans. on Sonics and Ultrsonics, vol. SU-25, no.1, pp.1-6, January 1978.

[3] Dias J. and Leitão J., Wall position and thickness estimation from sequences of echocardiograms images, IEEE Transactions on Medical Imaging, vol.15, pp.25-38, February 1996.

[4] E. Rignot and R. Chelappa, Segmentation of polarimetric sunthetic aperture radar data, IEEE Trans. Image Processing, vol.1, no.1, pp. 281-300, 1992.

[5] J. Besag, On the Statistical Analysis of Dirty Pictures, J. R. Statist. Soc. B, vol.48, no. 3, pp. 259-302, 1986.

[6] R. W. Prager, R. N. Rohling, A. H. Gee and L. Berman. Rapid calibration for 3-D freehand ultrasound. Ultrasound in Medicine and Biology, 24(6):855-869, July 1998.

[7] J. Sanches and J. S. Marques, A Rayleigh reconstruction/interpolation algorithm for 3D ultrasound, Pattern Recognition Letters, 21, pp. 917-926, 2000.

[8] J. Sanches and J. S. Marques, Joint Image Registration and Volume Reconstruction for 3D Ultrasound, Special Issue on 3D Ultrasound, Pattern Recognition Letters (Aceite).

[9] J. Sanches and J. S. Marques, A Multi-Scale Algorithm for three dimensional Free Hand Ultrasound, Ultrasound in medicine and biology, Elsevier (Aceite).

[10] J. Sanches and J. S. Marques, A Fast MAP Algorithm for 3D Ultrasound, Proceedings Third International Workshop on Energy Minimization Methods in Computer Vision and Pattern Recognition, Sophia Antipolis, France, pp. 63-74, September 2001.

[11] Jae. S. Lim, Two-Dimensional Signal and Image Processing, PTR Prentice Hall, Englewood Cliffs, New Jersey.

[12] J. Sanches and J. S. Marques, A MAP Filter for 3D Ultrasound, Proceedings IEEE International Conference on Image Processing, Rochester-NY, USA, September 2002 (Aceite).

[13] R. W. Prager, R. N. Rohling, A. H. Gee and L. Berman, Automatic Calibration for 3-D Free-Hand Ultrasound, Cambridge University, CUED/F-INFENG/TR 303, September 1997.

Shot Segmentation
Using a Coupled Markov Chains Representation
of Video Contents

Juan M. Sánchez and Xavier Binefa*

Computer Vision Center and Dept. d'Informàtica
Edifici O, Universitat Autònoma de Barcelona
08193, Bellaterra, Barcelona, Spain.
{juanma,xavierb}@cvc.uab.es

Abstract. We present a shot segmentation method based on the representation of visual contents in video using a coupled Markov chains approach. This representation allows us to combine different image features and to keep information about all the images since the beginning of the shot, instead of simply comparing adjacent frames. We also define an adaptive detection threshold that depends on the distance measures that are obtained, instead of trying to find a fixed threshold. Results show that the combination of color and motion image features in the same representation provides a more robust detection of shot boundaries than using each feature separately.

1 Introduction

Shot boundary detection is the basic first step for indexing and organizing digital video assets. Most of the algorithms found in the literature follow the same paradigm [3]. They obtain a certain feature of each frame, and then a distance between the features of adjacent frames is computed. When this distance exceeds a certain pre-defined threshold, a shot boundary is detected. This approach has been used either on compressed and uncompressed video. The feature that has been reported to provide better results is the global intensity or color histogram, and using the cosine distance [7].

This kind of algorithms have two main problems. First, the selection of a pre-defined threshold is extremely difficult. A fixed threshold depends on the domain of the contents (sports, news, commercials, ...). O'Toole et al. proposed in [4] a semi-automatic selection of the threshold depending on the domain of video, which must be known a priori. However, even within the same domain, threshold selection requires a trade-off between recall and precision that depends on the target application. Usually, a small number of false detections is harmless, while a missed boundary can be dramatic. However, a threshold tailored to avoid missing true boundaries can report an overwhelming number of false shots.

---

* Work supported by CICYT grant TEL99-1206-C02-02. Partial funding from Visual Century Research.

F.J. Perales et al. (Eds.): IbPRIA 2003, LNCS 2652, pp. 902–909, 2003.

(a) Single Markov chain   (b) Coupled Markov chain

Fig. 1. Graphical representations of the single and coupled Markov chain models

Second, the frame-to-frame approach works well with abrupt transitions, also known as cuts. However, it is not appropriate for gradual transitions [2]. Particularly, the variation of a global intensity or color histogram between adjacent frames in a gradual transition is very subtle and difficult to detect. Zabih et al. developed in [9] an interesting approach to gradual transitions detection based on the analysis of intensity edges. This method also has limitations due to the edge detection process. Boreczky and Rowe argue in [1] that a combination of features might produce better results than each of them individually. Sánchez et al. extended Zabih's approach in [6] by combining edges and color information.

In this paper, we present a shot segmentation method based on the representation of visual contents in video using coupled Markov chains from [5]. This method has the several advantages. It allows us to combine multiple features in the same representation. Also, information from all the frames since the beginning of the shot is kept in the representation, instead of using a simple frame-to-frame comparison. Finally, we define an adaptative threshold that only depends on the distance measures obtained during the process.

2   Description of Visual Contents in Video

A discrete Markov chain (MC) is a sequence of random variables X_t, $t \in [1, m]$, taking values in state space $S = \{1, \ldots, n\}$, which fulfills the Markov property:

$$P(X_t|X_{t-1}, \ldots, X_1) = P(X_t|X_{t-1}) \tag{1}$$

Figure 1(a) shows a graphical representation of this model. The MC is characterized by the n^2-matrix of state transition probabilities T, where $T_{ij} = P(X_t = j|X_{t-1} = i)$. Following its definition, T fulfills $\sum_{j \in S} T_{ij} = 1$, $\forall i \in S$.

The likelihood of a realization $x = \{x_1, \ldots, x_m\}$, $x_i \in S$, of a MC with respect to a MC model Ψ is given by:

$$P(x|\Psi) = P(x_1|\Psi) \prod_{t=2}^{m} P(x_t|x_{t-1}, \Psi) \tag{2}$$

To simplify, we will omit the conditioning of the probabilities to the model Ψ, unless it may lead to confusion. The likelihood can be also expressed as:

$$P(x) = P(x_1) \prod_{(i,j) \in S^2} T_{ij}^{C_{ij}} \tag{3}$$

where C_{ij} is the number of times that state j follows state i in the MC, i.e. the temporal cooccurrence of states i and j. We can take logarithms for simplicity and efficiency:

$$P(x) = P(x_1) \exp \left[\sum_{(i,j) \in S^2} C_{ij} \log T_{ij} \right] \qquad (4)$$

Clearly, a MC is the particular case of a 1-dimensional causal Markov random field (MRF). In order to apply this model to the representation of visual contents in a video sequence, we consider the video as a 3-dimensional MRF. Given a sequence of L images of size $M \times N$, the set of sites of the MRF is X_{uvt}, $(u, v, t) \in M \times N \times L$. The state of each site is given by the quantization of a scalar measure on a particular image feature. The set of cliques is formed by every pair of sites with the same spatial position and consecutive time instants. In this way, a global model of the temporal behavior of the feature is obtained.

The parameters of the model are obtained from a training sequence as relative frequencies of transitions. Particularly, the maximum likelihood (ML) estimate is computed from the state cooccurrence matrix C:

$$T_{ij} = \frac{C_{ij}}{\sum_{j \in S} C_{ij}}, \quad \forall i \in S \qquad (5)$$

Our goal is to extend the MC model in order to include information about a set of image features $F = \{1, \ldots, f\}$. A straightforward way to do this is by considering one independent MC for each image feature, which become a set of independent MRF's in the case of video contents representation. The likelihood of a realization is then computed as:

$$P(x) = P(x^1, \ldots, x^f) = \prod_{i \in F} P(x^i) \qquad (6)$$

where x^i are the observations of feature i, and $P(x^i)$ is computed as in eq. (2). The assumption of independence between features is not necessarily true. A more realistic approach should consider interactions that may exist between different features.

We propose a representation of the dependencies between multiple image features by coupling their corresponding MC's. In this way, the random variable of one feature at time t, not only depends on the value of the same feature at $t-1$, but also on the values of other features at $t - 1$. This structure of dependencies is graphically shown in fig. 1(b). The causality of the model has the particular advantage that the likelihood of a realization can be expressed as a product of conditional likelihoods:

$$P(x) = \prod_{i \in F} P(x_1^i) \prod_{t=2}^{m} P(x_t^i | \{x_{t-1}^j, \forall j \in F\}) \qquad (7)$$

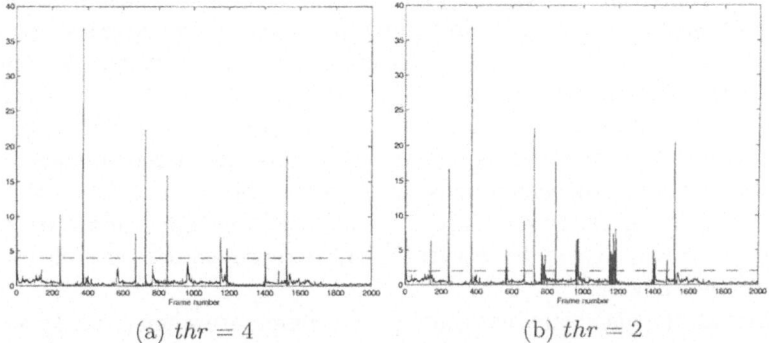

(a) $thr = 4$ (b) $thr = 2$

Fig. 2. Selection of a fixed detection threshold. A high threshold (a) misses some boundaries, while a low one (b) reports too many false detections. The threshold is shown as a dashed line.

The likelihood of a CMC can also be expressed as a Gibbs distribution similar to eq. (4), and its ML parameters can be estimated as well from the cooccurrence matrix in a similar way as in eq. (5). For video contents representation, this model becomes a set of coupled 3-dimensional MRF's with dependencies between their sites.

This representation allows us to compare two distributions with parameters Ψ_1 and Ψ_2 obtained from two observed image sequences S_1 and S_2 in different ways. For example, we can use the Kullback-Leibler distance (KLD):

$$KLD(\Psi_1||\Psi_2) = \log \frac{P(S_1|\Psi_1)}{P(S_1|\Psi_2)} \tag{8}$$

KLD, also known as relative entropy, is a measure of the loss of accuracy to represent the image sequence S_1 if we used the distribution with parameters Ψ_2 instead of the real distribution given by Ψ_1. Note that it is not symmetric.

3   Shot Segmentation

A change of shot is characterized by a change of the contents in the images (either sudden or gradual). Given the representation of visual contents in an image sequence briefly discussed above, we can define a shot segmentation scheme that checks the consistency of the transition into a new image with respect to the images already contained in the representation. That is, we can compute how well the observations attached to the next step in the image sequence fit a probability distribution obtained from the previous images. This can be expressed as:

$$D_{t+1} = P(I_t \rightarrow I_{t+1}|I_1 \rightarrow I_2 \rightarrow I_3 \cdots I_{t-2} \rightarrow I_{t-1} \rightarrow I_t) \tag{9}$$

where $I_i \rightarrow I_j$ represents the image feature transitions between images i and j in the sequence. If the transition from I_t to I_{t+1} fits the probability distribution, then it is included in the representation. Otherwise, a shot change is detected. The KLD measure from eq. (8) can be used by defining the image sequences $S_1 = \{I_t, I_{t+1}\}$ and $S_2 = \{I_1, \ldots, I_t\}$, and computing the parameters Ψ_1 and Ψ_2 of their corresponding distributions.

The main advantages of our approach with respect to most shot segmentation algorithms found in the literature are: (1) we are not based on the degree of correlation between adjacent frames. In our case, the contents of all the images from the beginning of the shot are considered in the representation. And (2), multiple features can easily be integrated in the representation in order to obtain a more robust detection.

Besides all the disadvantages that we can enumerate when a fixed pre-defined threshold is used, the selection of a detection threshold is particularly difficult in our case. The probability distribution that represents the images in the shot gets more accurate as the number of images considered grows. When the number of observations is large, we obtain a better estimation of the parameters. At the beginning of the shot, we may have a less accurate estimation and the distances computed can be higher than when the estimation is correct. For this reason, a fixed threshold can not be used in order to detect shot boundaries and we have defined an adaptive threshold. If we compute the mean μ and standard deviation σ of the distribution of distance measures from the beginning of the shot, μ will tend to a value that depends on the contents, and σ will tend to 0, as the distribution representing video contents gets more accurate. The adaptive threshold can be established, for instance, at $thr = \mu + 3\sigma$, so that distance values that do not correspond to expected values will be detected. Note that this threshold only depends on the contents, and that no model is defined on, for example, shot duration like in [8].

4   Experimental Results

We have focused our experiments on a short sequence of 2000 frames from a news video. This sequence was particularly selected in order to analyze two main things: (1) the selection of a fixed pre-defined detection threshold vs. the use of an adaptive one, and (2) the improvement achieved by coupling multiple image features in the model with respect to the use of individual features alone. The interest of our test sequence is found in the variety of transition effects in it: 8 cuts and 5 gradual transitions (4 wipes and 1 dissolve). The location and type of these transitions are detailed in table 1. Besides, there are two complex computer-generated sequences that mark the beginning and the end of the news summary (see fig. 4(a)).

The image features considered in our experiments were color and motion. Many shot segmentation methods have been based on these two features. In our case, the color feature is the hue component from the HSV color model, while the motion feature is the normal flow. Each feature is computed for every non-overlapping 16×16 image block. Both features were quantized in 8 levels.

Table 1. Location and type of the shot transitions in our test sequence

Frame number	Transition	Frame number	Transition	Frame number	Transition
246	Cut	767	Wipe	1154	Cut
374	Cut	850	Cut	1187	Wipe
568	Wipe	938	Cut	1405	Dissolve
671	Cut	964	Wipe	1527	Cut
727	Cut				

The problems of a fixed pre-defined detection threshold are shown in fig. 2. The plots show the distance measure defined combining eqs. (8) and (9) as a solid line, and the threshold value as a dashed line. All plots in this test were obtained using the coupled motion and color model. When the threshold selected is too high ($thr = 4$ in fig. 2(a)), false positive detections are avoided, but some actual transitions are missed. Particularly, wipes around frames 568, 767 and 964 were not detected. Moreover, the cut at frame 938 was not detected either. On the other hand, when the threshold is too low ($thr = 2$ in fig. 2(b)), gradual transitions can be correctly detected, but we obtain 20 false positive detections. Furthermore, the cut at frame 938 is still not detected. This means that the threshold should be even lower, and more false positive detections would be reported. We can conclude that a fixed threshold is very difficult to define, and in many cases there will not exist an appropriate threshold. The results obtained with the adaptative threshold are shown in fig. 3. All the transitions in the sequence were correctly reported, with only 3 false positive detections at frames 1158, 1191 and 1482. Note that the probability distribution representing shot contents is initialized every time a shot boundary is detected. For this reason, a fixed threshold may report several detections during a gradual transition. The adaptative threshold minimizes these false detections because it depends on the distance measures, so that the threshold is high when distances are high too.

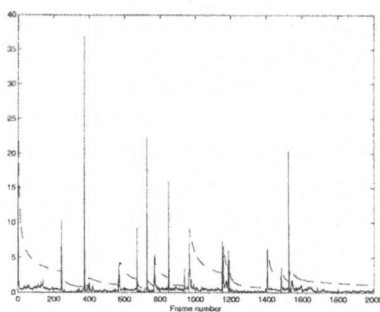

Fig. 3. Shot segmentation results using the coupled model of motion and color features and the adaptative threshold, shown as a dashed line

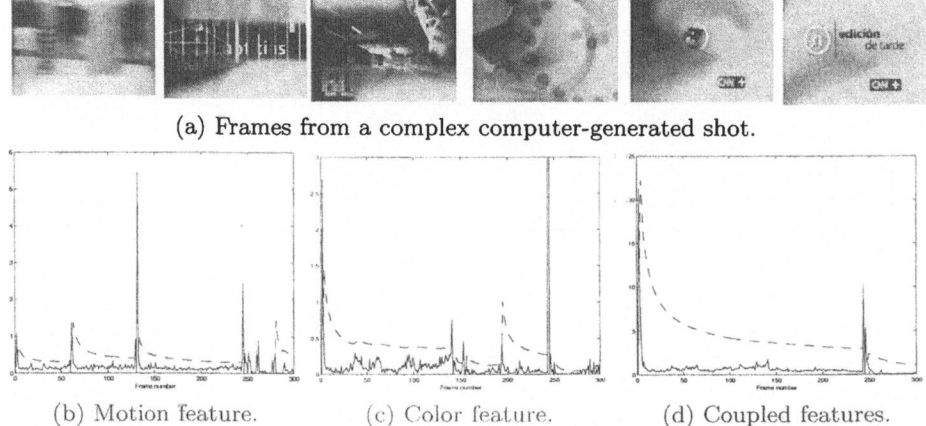

(a) Frames from a complex computer-generated shot.

(b) Motion feature.   (c) Color feature.   (d) Coupled features.

Fig. 4. (a) Frames from a complex computer-generated sequence (frames 1-245 of our test sequence). (b) Motion and (c) color features individually do a poor job and report false positives. (d) When they are coupled, one compensates the errors of the other. The adaptive threshold is shown as a dashed line

Table 2. Summary of results using single-feature and multiple-feature models on our short test sequence

Feature	Correct	Missed	False	Precision	Recall
Motion	11	2	22	.33	.85
Color	13	0	21	.38	1
Coupled	13	0	3	.81	1

One of the computer-generated shots in the sequence spans from frame 1 to 245 (1 of every 40 frames are shown in fig. 4(a)). Figures 4(b) and (c) show detection results using single-feature motion and color models respectively. These plots are very noisy, specially with color. Several false positive detections are reported during the shot (2 with motion, 3 with color). On the other hand, when both features are coupled (fig. 4(d)), the plot is much smoother and no false positives are reported. Errors caused by one feature are compensated by the other one. Both features thus cooperate in order to better determine when a real shot boundary is found and the behavior of both color and motion change, and also when we are still in the same shot and one of the features may have changed but the other keeps the same behavior. Considering the full video sequence, we obtain the results summarized in table 2. Single-feature models have good recall, i.e. most actual transitions are correctly detected. However, they are quite unstable in the sense that the variations in the distance measures are too significant and many false positive detections are reported. That is, their precision is low. The combination of multiple features in the model shows higher precision. In other words, the detection is more robust and less noisy.

5 Conclusions

We have presented a shot segmentation method based on the representation of visual contents in video using a coupled Markov chains approach, with the following advantages: (1) multiple image features can be easily combined in the same representation, and (2) information from all the images since the beginning of the shot is kept in the representation, so that not only adjacent frames are compared. Experimental results have lead us to the following conclusions:

- The selection of a fixed pre-defined detection threshold is usually difficult, and many times it is not appropriate for the video contents we are dealing with.
- An adaptative threshold that depends on the distance values that are computed is more appropriate in order to allow the method to work correctly on different video contents.
- The combination of different image features in the same model provides a more robust representation than each of them individually. In our case, color and motion features cooperate in order to better detect actual shot boundaries and avoid false detections.
- Both abrupt and gradual transitions are detected by our method with high recall and precision.

References

[1] J. S. Boreczky and L. A. Rowe. Comparison of video shot boundary detection techniques. In I. Sethi and R. Jain, editors, *Proc. Storage and Retrieval for Image and Video Databases IV, SPIE*, volume 2670, pages 170–179, 1996.

[2] U. Gargi, R. Kasturi, and S. H. Strayer. Performance characterization of video-shot-change detection methods. *IEEE Transactions on Circuits and Systems for Video Technology*, 10(1), February 2000.

[3] I. Koprinska and S. Carrato. Temporal video segmentation: A survey. *Signal Processing: Image Communication*, 16:477–500, 2001.

[4] C. O'Toole, A. Smeaton, N. Murphy, and S. Marlow. Evaluation of automatic shot boundary detection on a large video test suite. In *Proc. Challenge of Image Retrieval, 2nd UK Conf. on Image Retrieval (CIR'99)*, Newcastle, UK, February 1999.

[5] J. M. Sánchez, X. Binefa, and J. R. Kender. Coupled Markov chains for video contents characterization. In *Proc. International Conference on Pattern Recognition*, Quebec, Canada, August 2002.

[6] J. M. Sánchez, X. Binefa, and J. Vitrià. Shot partitioning based recognition of TV commercials. *Multimedia Tools and Applications*, 18:233–247, 2002.

[7] X. Ubiergo Cabedo and S. K. Bhattacharjee. Shot detection tools in digital video. In *Proc. Noblesse Workshop on Non-linear Model Based Image Analysis (NMBIA'98)*, pages 231–236, Glasgow, Scotland, July 1998.

[8] N. Vasconcelos and A. Lippman. Statistical models of video structure for content analysis and characterization. *IEEE Transactions on Image Processing*, 9(1):3–19, January 2000.

[9] R. Zabih, J. Miller, and K. Mai. A feature-based algorithm for detecting and classifying scene breaks. In *ACM Conference on Multimedia*, San Francisco, California, November 1995.

Estimating Confidence Measures
for Speech Recognition Verification
Using a Smoothed Naive Bayes Model*

Alberto Sanchis, Alfons Juan, and Enrique Vidal

Institut Tecnològic d'Informàtica
Departament de Sistemes Informàtics i Computació
Universitat Politècnica de València
46071 València (Spain)
{asanchis,ajuan,evidal}@iti.upv.es
http://www.iti.upv.es/~prhlt

Abstract. Verification in speech recognition systems can be seen as a conventional pattern classification problem in which each hypothesized word is to be transformed into a feature vector and then classified as either correct or incorrect. Thus, our basic problems are to find appropriate pattern features and to design an accurate pattern classifier. In this paper, we present a new feature and a smoothed naive Bayes classification model. Experimental results are reported comparing the new feature with a set of well-known features. The best performance is obtained using the new feature in combination with *Acoustic Stability*.

Keywords: Utterance verification, confidence measures, naive Bayes, smoothing.

1 Introduction

Current speech recognition systems are not error-free, and in consequence it is desirable for many applications to predict the reliability of each hypothesized word. From our point of view, this can be seen as a conventional pattern recognition problem in which each hypothesized word is to be transformed into a feature vector and then classified as either correct or incorrect [1]. Thus, our basic problems are to find appropriate pattern features and to design an accurate pattern classifier.

The problem of finding appropriate (pattern) features has been extensively studied by several authors. Some of them have noticed that correctly recognized words are often among the most probable hypotheses. Accordingly, they suggest the use of features derived from n-best lists [2, 3] or word graphs [4, 6]. Other authors have found that incorrectly recognized words are especially sensitive to the *Grammar Scale Factor* (GSF), i.e. a weighting between acoustic and language

---

* This work was partially supported by the EU project "TT2" (IST-2001-32091).

F.J. Perales et al. (Eds.): IbPRIA 2003, LNCS 2652, pp. 910–918, 2003.

model scores [7]. In section 2, we combine these two ideas to derive a new feature that is referred to as *Word Trellis Stability* (WTS).

To design an accurate pattern classifier, we first consider a *word-dependent* naive Bayes model in which the estimation of class posteriors is carried out using conventional relative frequencies (we assume that features are discrete). Due to the lack of training data, this model underestimates the true probabilities involving rare words and the incorrect class. To deal with this problem of data spareness, our basic model is smoothed with a generalized, *word-independent* naive Bayes model. The details are given in section 3.

In section 4, we present some experimental results comparing the WTS with a set of well-known features suggested in the literature. The best performance achieved using a naive Bayes combination of different features is also presented.

2 *Word Trellis Stability* Feature

The motivation of the *Word Trellis Stability* feature (WTS) comes from the following observations: a word is most probably correct if it appears, within approximately the same time interval, in the majority of the most probable hypotheses; and, on the other hand, incorrect words are more sensitive to variations of the GSF.

Let us assume that, during the recognition stage, we maintain all the partial hypotheses that survived the pruning process for each time frame t. For our propose, only those partial hypotheses which end in a word-level final state are considered. We also store, for these hypotheses, the boundaries between the words obtained through Viterbi segmentation. Following these assumptions, in general, a hypothesis h of k words can be represented as: $h = \{(w_1, t_{s_1}, t_{e_1}), \ldots, (w_k, t_{s_k}, t_{e_k})\}$; where t_{s_i} corresponds to the starting time and t_{e_i} the ending time of word w_i, for all $i = 1, \ldots, k$. Obviously, $t_{s_i} - 1 = t_{e_{i-1}}$ for all $i = 2, \ldots, k$; and t_{e_k} corresponds to the last time frame.

Given a sequence of feature vectors $\Theta_1^n = \{\Theta_1, \ldots, \Theta_n\}$, the path score for a partial hypothesis h of k words is computes as:

$$Sc(h) = \alpha \cdot P_{LM}(h) + P_{AC}(h) \tag{1}$$

where α is the GSF, and $P_{LM}(h)$ and $P_{AC}(h)$ denotes the N-gram language model log probability and the acoustic log-score, respectively, for partial hypothesis h.

Clearly, equation (1) is a function of the GSF value; that is, a partial hypothesis can be most probable or not depending on the value α (see figure 1). In the calculation of the WTS feature, we consider the word-boundary partial hypotheses that are the best-first for any interval of α values within a fixed range.

Let $h = \{(w_1, t_{s_1}, t_{e_1}), \ldots, (w_k, t_{s_k}, t_{e_k})\}$ be a first-best partial hypothesis for the interval $[\alpha_i \ldots \alpha_f]$ at time frame t. The interval size $\delta(h) = (\alpha_f - \alpha_i)$ for which the hypothesis h is the most probable can be considered as a measure of

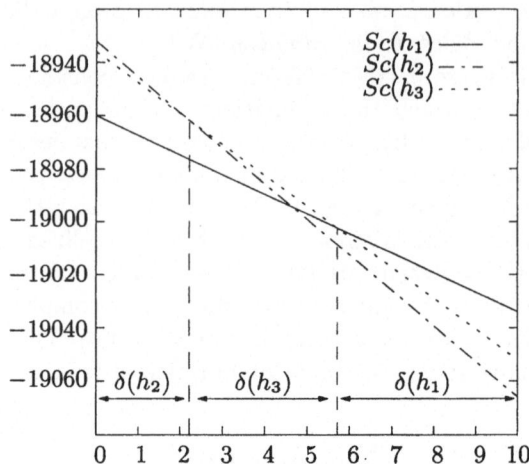

Fig. 1. Path scores of three competing partial hypotheses, as a function of the GSF value. The range of GSF values is restricted to interval $[0, 10]$

the hypothesis stability. In a first step, we accumulate the value $\delta(h)$ for each hypothesized word, at each time frame t' within its boundaries; that is:

$$C(w_i, t') = C(w_i, t') + \delta(h) \tag{2}$$

for all $i = 1, \ldots, k$ and $t_{s_i} \leq t' \leq t_{e_i}$.

This is calculated for all word-boundary hypotheses that are the most probable for any valid interval of the GSF, at every time frame of the recognition process.

In a second step, when the recognized sentence is obtained, we compute the WTS feature for each hypothesized word w_i as:

$$WTS(w_i) = \frac{1}{t_{e_i} - t_{s_i} + 1} \sum_{t'=t_{s_i}}^{t_{e_i}} \frac{C(w_i, t')}{C(t')}$$

where $C(t')$ is the total sum of interval size values contributed by all first-best partial hypotheses for the frame t'.

Note that the WTS feature can take values in the interval $[0, 1]$. Figure 2 shows the frequency histograms of WTS values for correct and incorrect class. These histograms, obtained using the training corpus described in section 4.1, show that words with a lower WTS value are more likely to be incorrect.

3   Smoothed Naive Bayes Model

We denote the class variable by c; $c = 0$ for correct and $c = 1$ for incorrect. Given a hypothesized word w and a D-dimensional vector of (discrete) features $\boldsymbol{x}$, the class posteriors can be calculated via the Bayes' rule as

$$P(c|\boldsymbol{x}, w) = \frac{P(c|w)\, P(\boldsymbol{x}|c, w)}{\sum_{c'} P(c'|w)\, P(\boldsymbol{x}|c', w)} \tag{3}$$

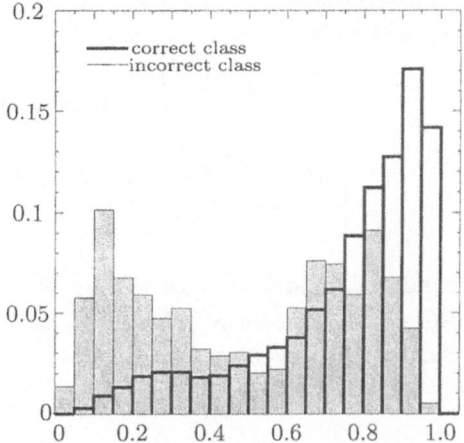

Fig. 2. Distribution of WTS values for correct and incorrect class

Therefore, our basic problem is to estimate $P(c|w)$ for each word and $P(\boldsymbol{x}|c, w)$ for each class-word pair. For simplicity, we make the naive Bayes assumption that the features are mutually independent given a class-word pair,

$$P(\boldsymbol{x}|c, w) = \prod_{d=1}^{D} P(x_d|c, w) \tag{4}$$

Given N training samples $\{(\boldsymbol{x}_n, c_n, w_n)\}_{n=1}^{N}$, we can estimate the unknown probabilities using the conventional frequencies

$$P(c|w) = \frac{N(c, w)}{N(w)} \tag{5}$$

$$P(x_d|c, w) = \frac{N(x_d, c, w)}{N(c, w)} \qquad d = 1, \ldots, D \tag{6}$$

where the $N(\cdot)$ are suitably defined event counts; i.e., the events are (c, w) pairs in (5) and (x_d, c, w) triplets in (6).

Unfortunately, these frequencies often underestimate the true probabilities involving rare words and the incorrect class. To circumvent this problem, we have considered an *absolute discounting* smoothing model imported from statistical language modelling [8]. The idea is to discount a small constant $b \in (0, 1)$ to every positive count and then distribute the gained probability mass among the null counts (unseen events). Thus, for each word w, if $N(c, w) = 0$ for $c = 1$ (or $c = 0$), (5) is replaced by

$$P(c|w) = \begin{cases} \dfrac{N(c, w) - b}{N(w)} & \text{if } N(c, w) > 0 \\[2mm] \dfrac{b}{N(w)} & \text{if } N(c, w) = 0 \end{cases} \tag{7}$$

Similarly, for each (c, w), if $N(x_d, c, w) = 0$ for one or more possible values of x_d, the probability function (6) becomes

$$P(x_d|c, w) = \begin{cases} \dfrac{N(x_d, c, w) - b}{N(c, w)} & \text{if } N(x_d, c, w) > 0 \\[3mm] M \dfrac{P(x_d|c)}{\sum\limits_{x_d' : N(x_d', c, w) = 0} P(x_d'|c)} & \text{if } N(x_d, c, w) = 0 \end{cases} \tag{8}$$

where M denotes the gained probability mass ($\frac{b}{N(c,w)}$ times the number of seen events). Note that $P(x_d|c)$ is used as a *generalized distribution* to divide M among the unseen events. To prevent null estimates, it is also smoothed by absolute discounting (with a uniform backoff)

$$P(x_d|c) = \begin{cases} \dfrac{N(x_d, c) - b}{N(c)} & \text{if } N(x_d, c) > 0 \\[3mm] \dfrac{b}{N(c)} \dfrac{\sum\limits_{x_d' : N(x_d', c) > 0} 1}{\sum\limits_{x_d' : N(x_d', c) = 0} 1} & \text{if } N(x_d, c) = 0 \end{cases} \tag{9}$$

In practice, there are many (c, w) pairs for which nearly all $N(x_d, c, w)$ counts are null and, therefore, even the smoothed model (8) gives inaccurate estimates. To deal with these extreme cases, we have defined a global threshold for the $N(c, w)$ counts. For those (c, w) pairs with counts below this threshold, the generalized model (9) is used instead of (8). Similarly, if a word w does not occur in the training data, $P(c|w)$ is approximated by $P(c)$.

Using the models trained as explained above, in the test phase, utterance verification is performed by classifying a word as incorrect if $P(c = 1 \mid x, w)$ is greater that a certain threshold τ (cf. section 4.2).

4   Experiments

4.1   Experimental Setup

For the experimental study we have used a speech corpus composed of 4 subcorpus with the following characteristics:

			Speakers	
Subcorpus	Utterances	Words	Male	Female
A	1,530	10,700	4	5
B	1,249	10,960	8	8
C	330	2,768	2	2
D	396	3,390	6	6

The subcorpus A was designed to contain a representative sample of all the Spanish phonemes for acoustic training purposes.

The subcorpus *B*, *C* and *D* are part of the so-called *Traveler Task*, a speech recognition task involving communication situations at the reception desk of a hotel, with a vocabulary size of 683 Spanish words, acquired within the EU-TRANS project [9]. All the utterances have been processed to obtain, every 10 milliseconds, 10 cepstral coefficients of a Mel-filter bank plus the energy and the corresponding first and second derivatives.

A bigram language model has been estimated using the whole training *text* corpus of the *Traveler Task* [9]. Each one of 24 context-independent Spanish phonemes has been modeled by a continuous-density hidden Markov model (HMM) with three emitting states, a left-to-right topology with loops in the emitting states, and a emission distribution in each state which is a mixture with a maximum of 32 Gaussian distributions. These HMMs have been estimated using the subcorpus *A* and *B*. The final HMMs have a total of 2,174 Gaussian distributions.

Finally, a conventional continuous speech recognizer based on Viterbi beam search has been run using this bigram language model and HMMs. The word features to estimate the smoothed model parameters were obtained with the subcorpus *B* and *C*. The classification results presented were achieved using the subcorpus *D*. The speakers of the subcorpus *D* are a subset of the speakers of the subcorpus *B* but the utterances differ. The test-set Word Error Rate of the speech recognizer using the same bigram and HMMs with the subcorpus D is 5.5 %.

4.2 Experimental Results

In evaluating verification systems, two measures are of interest: the *True Rejection Rate* (TRR, the number of words that are incorrect and are classified as incorrect divided by the number of words that are incorrect) and the *False Rejection Rate* (FRR, the number of words that are correct and are classified as incorrect divided by the number of words that are correct). The trade-off between TRR and FRR values depends on a decision threshold τ (see section 3). A *Receiver Operating Characteristic* (ROC) curve represents TRR against FRR for different values of τ. The area under a ROC curve divided by the area of a worst-case diagonal ROC curve, provides an adequate overall estimation of the classification accuracy. We denote this area ratio as AROC. Note that an AROC value of 2.0 would indicate that all words can be correctly classified. We have used both ROC curves and the AROC measure to conveniently evaluate and compare the classification accuracy for different feature combinations.

For the experimental study, we chose a set of well-known alternative features:

- *Acoustic stability* (AS): Number (or the percentage) of times that a hypothesized word appears at the same position (as computed by Levenshtein alignment) in K alternative outputs of the speech recognizer obtained using different values of the GSF [7].
- *LMProb*: Language model probability [2].

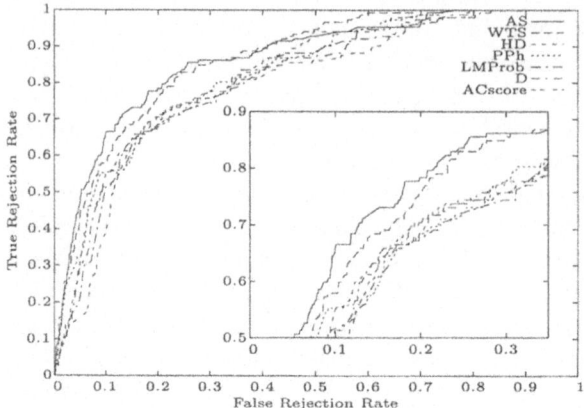

Fig. 3. ROC curves for each individual feature

- *PercPh* (PPh): The percentage of hypothesized word phones that match the phones obtained in a "phone-only" decoding [2].
- *Hypothesis density* (HD): The average number of the active hypotheses within the hypothesized word boundaries [4].
- *Duration* (D): The word duration in frames divided by its number of phones [2].
- *ACscore*: The acoustic log-score of the word divided by its number of phones [5].

Figure 3 represents the ROC curves obtained through the (single-feature) smoothed model (eq. 3). It can be observed that AS is the best performing feature, which confirms previous works results [7, 2, 4]. On the other hand, the newly introduced WTS feature significantly outperforms all the other traditional features but, in general, does not improve AS performance. Table 1 shows the AROC values.

To further exploit the usefulness of the features, the smoothed naive Bayes model presented in section 3 was used to combine different features in the classification process. The best performance was achieved through the combination

Table 1. AROC value for each individual feature

Feature	AROC
AS	1.73
WTS	1.73
HD	1.65
PercPh	1.65
LMProb	1.62
Duration	1.62
ACscore	1.59

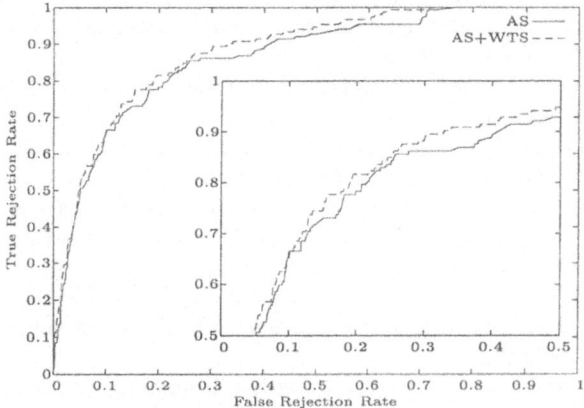

Fig. 4. The comparative ROC curves for the single best feature (AS) versus the best feature combination (AS+WTS)

of the two best features: AS and WTS. Figure 4 shows that, in general, the combination of these two features slightly (but consistently) outperforms the AS-only performance. The AROC value obtained for this combination was 1.77. We confirmed that to add one or more features to this combination does not produce significantly better classification accuracy. Also, in general, the combination of one or more features with only one of these two best features just outperformed insignificantly the best single-feature performance. On the other hand, combinations without AS or WTS features did not improve the best single-feature performance. For all the experiments, different values for the discounting constant were tested without significantly affecting the classification accuracy.

5   Conclusions

This paper has presented a smoothed naive Bayes model along with a new feature for speech recognition verification. Smoothing is based on traditional techniques applied in the context of statistical language modelling for speech recognition. The results show that the new feature improves the single-feature performance of a set of well-known features but, in general, it is not better than another useful feature: the *Acoustic Stability* [7]. Nevertheless, the best performance was achieved through the (naive Bayes) combination of these two features.

References

[1] A. Sanchis, V. Jiménez, and E. Vidal, "Efficient Use of the Grammar Scale Factor to Classify Incorrect Words in Speech Recognition Verification," in *ICPR*, 2000, vol. 3, pp. 278–281.
[2] L. Chase, *Error-responsive feedback mechanisms for speech recognizers*, Ph.D. thesis, School of Computer Science, Carnegie Mellon University, USA, 1997.

[3] T. J. Hazen, T. Burianek, J. Polifroni, and S. Seneff, "Recognition confidence scoring for use in speech understanding systems," *Computer Speech and Language*, vol. 16, no. 1, pp. 49–67, 2002.

[4] T. Kemp and T. Schaaf, "Estimating confidence using word lattices," in *EUROSPEECH*, 1997, pp. 827–830.

[5] T. Schaaf and T. Kemp, "Confidence measures for spontaneous speech recognition," in *ICASSP*, 1997, pp. 875–878.

[6] F. Wessel, R. Schlüter, K. Macherey, and H. Ney, "Confidence measures for large vocabulary continuous speech recognition," *IEEE Transactions on Speech and Audio Processing*, vol. 9, no. 3, pp. 288–298, 2001.

[7] T. Zepenfeld, M. Finke, K. Ries, M. Westphal, and A. Waibel, "Recognition of conversational telephone speech using the JANUS speech engine," in *ICASSP*, 1997, pp. 1815–1818.

[8] H. Ney, S. Martin, and F. Wessel, "Statistical language modeling using leaving-one-out," *Young, S. and Bloothoft, G., editors, Corpus Based Methods in Language and Speech Processing*, pp. 174–207, 1997.

[9] J. C. Amengual, J. M. Benedí, F. Casacuberta, M. A. Castaño, A. Castellanos, V. M. Jiménez, D. Llorens, A. Marzal, M. Pastor, F. Prat, E. Vidal, and J. M. Vilar, "The EuTrans-I speech translation system," *Machine Translation*, vol. 15, pp. 75–103, 2000.

A New Wavelets Image Fusion Strategy

M. Santos, G. Pajares, M. Portela, J.M de la Cruz

Dpto. Arquitectura de Computadores y Automática. Facultad de CC. Físicas.
Universidad Complutense de Madrid. 28040-Madrid, Spain
msantos@dacya.ucm.es

Abstract. The aim of image fusion is to combine information from multiple images of the same scene. The result of image fusion is a new image, which is more suitable for human and machine perception or further image-processing tasks such as segmentation, feature extraction and object recognition. Different fusion methods have been proposed in the literature. This paper presents new methods based on the computation of local and global gradient. A comparative analysis is carried out against other existing strategies. The results are encouraging.

1   Introduction

Pixel-level fusion serves to increase the useful information content of an image so that the performance of image-processing tasks such as segmentation, feature extraction and object recognition can be improved [1, 2]. This paper presents a new pixel-level wavelet fusion approach based on the gradient concept. The gradient concept exploits the relevant information derived from the grey level variation in the images, particularly around the edges. Initially for each pixel location a gradient matrix is computed. Then taking into account neighbourhood gradient interactions through non-overlapping or overlapping areas, such matrix is modified by a relaxation procedure.

Therefore, we propose a new strategy based on the gradient, where two processes are involved: local and global. The use of the local and global gradient approaches in image fusion makes up the main findings of this paper. As our method is based on the gradient, it is suitable for images where edges are abundant, such as indoor environments.

This paper is organised as follows. Section 2 presents an overview about wavelet decomposition and fusion merging methods. In section 3 we propose new merging methods based on the gradient computation. Section 4 presents some experimental results that have been satisfactory compared to other classical existing methods. Finally section 5 summarizes the conclusions.

F.J. Perales et al. (Eds.): IbPRIA 2003, LNCS 2652, pp. 919-926, 2003.

2   Overview: Wavelet Decomposition and Merging Fusion Methods

Many researchers recognised that multi-scale transforms are very useful for image fusion [3, 4, 5]. Nowadays the wavelet mathematical theory has received special attention for multi-scale representations. This is because using *Discrete Wavelets Transform* (DWT) it is possible to reach the desired decomposition level preserving the image information [2].

In order to achieve the fused image (i.e. the improved image), a sequence of operations is required. Figure 1 summarises them as a block diagram. Two original *input* images are to be fused. The DWT is applied to each one, and the result of this transformation is a *Multi-scale* image at different resolution levels. As we will see in the next section, this transformation produces the called frequency bands. From the multi-scale images a *Select and Merging* (*S&M*) method is applied to achieve a *Fused Multi-scale* image. Then, by applying the *Inverse Discrete Wavelets Transform* (IDWT) the final fused image is obtained, which contains the best information from the two incoming images. This paper is only concerned with the *S&M* strategy. The DWT and IDWT operations are called analysis and synthesis respectively.

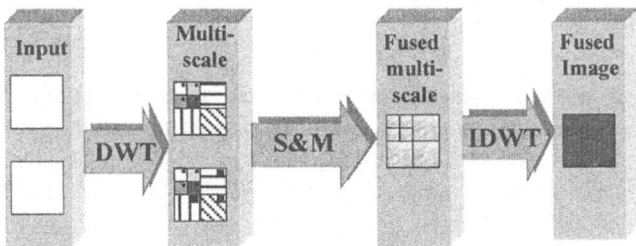

Fig. 1. Fusion Scheme

2.1   Discrete Wavelet Transform (DWT)

According to [6, 7, 8, 9, 10], the 2-D wavelet analysis operation consists in filtering and down-sampling horizontally using the 1-D lowpass filter L and the highpass filter H to each row in the image $I(x,y)$, producing the coefficient matrices $I_L(x,y)$ and $I_H(x,y)$. In this paper, we have used the Haar filters. Vertically filtering and down-sampling follows, using the lowpass and highpass filters L and H to each column in $I_L(x,y)$ and $I_H(x,y)$, and produces four subimages $I_{LL}(x,y)$, $I_{LH}(x,y)$, $I_{HL}(x,y)$ and $I_{HH}(x,y)$ for one level of decomposition. $I_{LL}(x,y)$ is a smooth subimage corresponding to the low frequency band of the multi-scale decomposition and can be considered as a smoothed and subsampled version of the original image $I(x,y)$, i.e. it represents the coarse approximation of $I(x,y)$. $I_{LH}(x,y)$, $I_{HL}(x,y)$ and $I_{HH}(x,y)$ are detail subimages, which represent the horizontal, vertical and diagonal directions of the image $I(x,y)$. They are respectively low-high, high-low and high-high frequency bands. Details about the implementation of the DWT and IDWT can be found in [6, 11]. Figure 2 shows a representation of a two level image decomposition. We can notice that there is only one low frequency band, I_{LL1} in the two-level decomposition. The rest of bands are high-frequency bands. This can be extended to any *K-level* where only a low frequency band is available, $I_{LL(K-1)}$.

Fig. 2. A representation of a two-level image decomposition and an example

2.2   Select and Merging Strategy (S&M)

In figure 1, the *Multi-scale* block shows the 2-D structures of a multi-scale transform with two decomposition levels. A given textured square corresponds to the same decomposition level in the two images. The black small squares in different frequency bands correspond to the same group of pixels, which indicate the spatial localisation of the transform. These are the pixels to be fused. Hence, only the fusion at the same resolution level is allowed through the called fusion rule [1].

Generally an image I has its multi-scale decomposition representation denoted as D_I. Given two inputs images X and Y, a fusion rule can be defined in order to obtain the resulting combination Z. Consider the following example, assume that images X and Y have been two-level decomposed, this means that we can fuse for example X_{LL1} and Y_{LL1} obtaining Z_{LL1} . They should be represented as D^X_{LLk}, D^Y_{LLk} and D^Z_{LLk} respectively. With simplification purposes, for the first decomposition level, i.e. $k = 0$, we do not use the sub-index k. Some merging strategies can be found in [1], such as:

$$\text{Maximum: } D^Z_{ijk}(p) = max\left(\left|D^X_{ijk}(p)\right|,\left|D^Y_{ijk}(p)\right|\right),$$

$$\text{Arithmetic average combination } D^Z_{ijk}(p) = w_X(p)D^X_{ijk}(p) + w_Y(p)D^Y_{ijk}(p)$$

$$\text{Geometric average combination } D^Z_{ijk}(p) = \sqrt{D^X_{ijk}(p)D^Y_{ijk}(p)} + b$$

where w_X, w_Y are weighting coefficients, p denotes the pixel position and b is an arbitrary constant. The fact that the above magnitudes are functions of p means that they can vary according to the pixel position.

In the next section, a new fusion merging strategy based on the gradient is introduced, which takes into account grey level differences at each position p. Also the position concept p is extended, so that it includes p and an area surrounding p. Different approaches are analysed and studied.

3   Gradient Merging Based Methods

This section analyses new strategies based on the gradient concept at each location p, which is computed considering a region R surrounding p as follows,

$$G_{ijk}^h(p) = \sum_{\substack{q \in A \\ q \neq p}} \left(D_{ijk}^h(q) - D_{ijk}^h(p) \right) \tag{1}$$

where ij represents a frequency band LL, LH, HL or HH; k is the decomposition level; h is a given input image X or Y; A is the area surrounding p and q is a location in A.

From fig. 1 and equation (1), the following algorithm LGM (Local Gradient Method) performs the fusion process:

1. Initialisation: define the area size A which will be used around each location p and the decomposition level K. Set $k = -1$.

2. Inputs: images X and Y; set $U = X$ and $V = Y$

3. Multi-scale wavelets decomposition: obtain the transformed subimages.
    $k = k+1; U,V \rightarrow \mathrm{DWT} \rightarrow D_{LLk}^{U,V}, D_{LHk}^{U,V}, D_{HLk}^{U,V}, D_{HHk}^{U,V}$

4. Fused image: *Select*: for each location p at (x,y) in the transformed subimages compute the following gradient values using equation (1):

    $$G_{ijk}^U(p) \, ; \, G_{ijk}^V(p) \text{ with ij = LL, LH, HL and HH}$$

    Merge: for each location p compute the following values

    $$g_{ijk}(p) = max \left\{ \left| G_{ijk}^U(p) \right|, \left| G_{ijk}^V(p) \right| \right\} \text{ with ij = LL, LH, HL and HH}$$

    $$D_{ijk}^W(p) = D_{ijk}^U(p) \text{ if } g_{ijk}(p) \text{ comes from U else } D_{ijk}^W(p) = D_{ijk}^V(p)$$

5. Check for the end of the multi-scale decomposition:

    if $k < K$ then set $U = D_{LLk}^U$, $V = D_{LLk}^V$ and go to 3; else go to 6

6. While $k \neq -1$

    apply IDWT to D_{LLk}^W, D_{LHk}^W, D_{HLk}^W and D_{HHk}^W obtaining $D_{LL(k-1)}^W$; $k = k-1$

7. Output: fused image $Z = D_{LLk}^W$

In this paper $k = 0$, i.e., a unique decomposition level is used without lack of generalisation.

We have carried out our experiments with the two images in Figure 3. They are multifocus images where depending on the image the same area appears defocused or focused. The goal is to choose the best area from each image, so that the resulting image is a perfect focused image. Our gradient method is motivated by the fact that the blurred effect is more evident around the edges and the degree of blurring can be measured by the gradient.

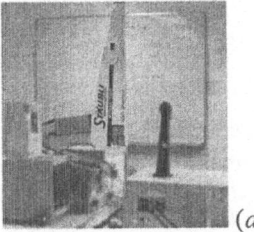 

(a)　　　　　　　　　　　　　　　　　　　*(b)*

Fig. 3. Input images: (a) image 1 (focus on far); (b) image 2 (focus on close)

We have verified that the results obtained with the above algorithm LGM, when applying the local gradient straightforward, are satisfactory if comparing them to other methods, although they can be improved. With such purpose we have studied and analysed different approaches derived from this algorithm. As expected, some mistakes appear around the edges. Hence, we have focused on the behaviour of our method near the edges. Within the different methods we have implemented, the following three alternatives have been analysed in deep: 1) *Local gradient applied to the I_{HH} subimage*; 2) *Local gradient applied to a region*, and 3) *Global gradient*.

3.1   Local Gradient Applied to the I_{HH} Subimage

In the step 4 of our algorithm, the different $D_{ijk}^{W}(p)$ are obtained for the four subimages. This could result in, for example, two values are selected from image X and the other two from image Y. To avoid this, the four coefficients are selected from the same image by choosing the most significant subimage, the I_{HH} which contains high frequency structures. The original algorithm should be modified in step 4 as follows:

Compute $g_{ijk}(p) = max\left\{\left|G_{ijk}^{U}(p)\right|, \left|G_{ijk}^{V}(p)\right|\right\}$ with ij = HH

If the maximum $g_{HHk}(p)$ value comes from U, then $D_{HHk}^{W}(p) = G_{HHk}^{U}(p)$ and the remainder $D_{ijk}^{W}(p)$ with *ij = LL, HL* and *LH* are also selected from U, otherwise from V. This step is repeated for each p of the HH subimages coming from X and Y.

3.2   Local Gradient Applied to a Region

Instead of using the gradient at each location p we consider a region around p. That allows considering more information. We compute the gradient average value in a region and use the following criterion, which alters the step 4 of the algorithm as follows. Compute (2),

$$g_{ijk}(p) = \max\left\{\left|\frac{1}{n_R}\sum_{q_h\in\Re}G_{ijk}^U(q_h)\right|,\left|\frac{1}{n_R}\sum_{q_h\in\Re}G_{ijk}^V(q_h)\right|\right\} \qquad (2)$$

where $\Re$ is a rectangular region of size $n{\times}m$, q_h are the coefficients belonging to $\Re$ and $n_R = n{\times}m$ is the number of coefficients in $\Re$. Select W = U in $D_{ijk}^W(p)$ if $g_{ijk}(p)$ comes from U, otherwise W = V. The size of the region is defined by the user. In our approach the region has size 3×3 around p, hence $n = 9$. As before, if the maximum value comes from U, then the remainder $D_{ijk}^W(p)$ with $ij = LL, LH$ and HL are selected from U, otherwise from V.

3.3   Global Gradient

3.3.1   Version 1

Instead of using only the I_{HHk} subimage, we have used the three subimages that contain some high-pass filtering, namely: I_{LHk}, I_{HLk} and I_{HHk}. Now the step 4 is,

$$g_{ijk}(p) = \max\left\{\left|\sum_{ij=S}\frac{1}{n_R}\sum_{q_h\in\Re}G_{ijk}^U(q_h)\right|,\left|\sum_{ij=S}\frac{1}{n_R}\sum_{q_h\in\Re}G_{ijk}^V(q_h)\right|\right\} \qquad (3)$$

where $S = \{LH, HL, HH\}$ and $ij = LL, LH, HL$ and HH. If the maximum $g_{ijk}(p)$ value comes from U, then $D_{ijk}^W(p) = G_{ijk}^U(p)$, otherwise W = V.

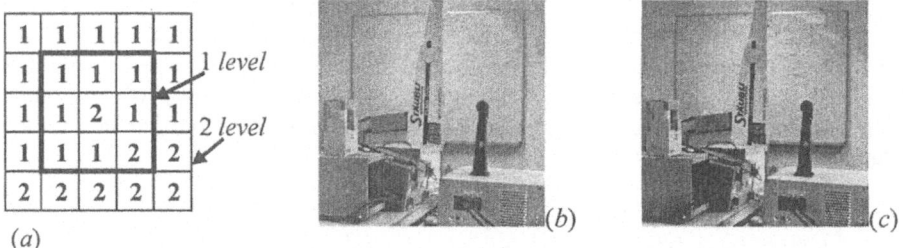

Fig. 4. Fused image obtained through global gradient (Version1)

So, each of the regions of the fused image is taken from one of the input images following that criterion, as it is represented in Figure 8. Assume $N{\times}M$ the U and V sizes, we build that global matrix of size $\frac{N}{n}{\times}\frac{M}{m}$ in which each element is labelled as "1" or "2" depending on if the selection comes from U or V respectively. That matrix is called the global matrix. Now we start a relaxation process to modify the global matrix values. We define a region and its labels are modified according to a majority criterion. In this way, for the example shown in figure 4(a), the central element, labelled with 2, can be expected to be a mistake, as it is surrounded by regions that will be taken from the other input image. So, it would be exchanged for "1". This process continues until no modifications appear. After this, we select the $D_{ijk}^{W}(p)$ coefficients according to the final labels in the global matrix.

The number of elements of the global matrix under consideration can be increased, to apply the relaxation process taking into account more information. For example, a second level can be considered (Figure 4a), and that could vary the final results.

3.3.2 Version 2

We compute the eight values of the gradient surrounding the central one at position p:

$$g_{ij}^{T} = \left| \sum_{q_h \in \mathfrak{R}} G_{ijk}^{T}(q_h) \right| \quad \text{for ij = LL, LH, HL and HH; and T = U, V}.$$

If the majority of maximum g_{ij} values come from U, the corresponding global matrix element is labelled as "1" otherwise as "2". The relaxation process is executed as in version 1.

3.3.3 Version 3

In this version, the global matrix is built as in version 1, but we introduce an additional constraint in its updating process. Indeed, a label "1" in the global matrix is changed if most of the labels in its neighbourhood are "2" as in version 1, and also if $d_U > d_V$, new in version 3, equation (4). And vice versa for labels "2".

$$d_T = \left| \sum_{ij=S} \sum_{q_h \in \mathfrak{R}} D_{ijk}^{T}(q_h) \right| \quad \text{where } T = \{U, V\} \tag{4}$$

That refers to the fact that the element which has the highest absolute value of the gradient has more information about the details of the image.

3.3.4 Version 4

Until now, we have split the input images into non-overlapping regions. This version considers four overlapping areas surrounding the central region.

4   Experimental Results

In order to verify the performance of the proposed local and global gradient methods, we compare different merging methods including classical ones: Maximum (MAX); Arithmetic (AAV) and Geometric average (GAV); Local Gradient Method (LGM), Local gradient applied to the I_{HH} (LGI) and to a region (LGR); Global Gradient Version 1 (GG1), Version 2 (GG2), Version 3 (GG3) and Version 4 (GG4). As a quality measure we use an objective fidelity criterion: the root-mean-square error e_{rms}. This comparison is carried out against the benchmark image in figure 4(b).

Table 1. Root-mean-squared error for different methods

Methods	MAX	AAV	GAV	LGM	LGI	LGR	GG1	GG2	GG3	GG4
e_{rms}	4.6012	5.0870	7.3385	2.5656	2.1943	1.7196	1.3555	1.6222	1.4525	1.3767

From the results in table 1: 1) As expected, the best results are achieved with our proposed gradient global strategies, as a relaxation process always improves the local results; 2) The best performance is achieved with version 1 (Figure 4c). This is because such method uses all subimages containing high frequency information. Therefore, we can point out that the errors come from the edges and it is embedded in the gradient. This assertion can be verified also with the results obtained in version 3 which are slightly worst than those obtained in version 1, i.e. additional information out of the gradient does not improve the results. The use of overlapping regions (version 4) improves the results of version 3, where non-overlapping regions are used.

5   Conclusion

We have developed several gradient based methods with fusion merging purposes. We have found its performance against other methods, with encouraging results. We have verified that the best performance is achieved applying gradient based strategies, particularly with the global ones. This means that the gradient appears as a good strategy in image fusion applications using wavelets.

References

[1]   Z. Zhang and R.S. Blum, A categorization of Multiscale-Decomposition-Based Image Fusion Schemes with a Performance Study for a Digital Camera Application, Proceedings of the IEEE 87(8) (1999) 1315-1326.
[2]   H. Li, B.S. Manjunath, S.K. Mitra, Multisensor Image Fusion Using the Wavelet Transform, Graphical Models and Image Processing 57(3) (1995) 235-245.
[3]   P.J. Burt, E. Adelson, The Laplacian pyramid as a compact image code, IEEE Trans. Commun. 31 (1983) 532-540.
[4]   E. H. Adelson, C.H. Anderson, J.R. Bergen, P.J. Burt, J. Ogden, Pyramid methods in image processing, RCA Engineer, 29(6) (1984) 33-41.
[5]   T. Lindeberg, Scale-Space Theory in Computer Vision, Kluwer, Norwell: MA, 1994.
[6]   S. Mallat, A Wavelet Tour of Signal Processing, Academic Press, 2nd ed, 1999.
[7]   E.J. Stollnitz, T.D. DeRose, D.H. Salesin, Wavelets for Computer Graphics: A Primer, Part 1, IEEE Computer Graphics and Applications 15(3) (1995) 76-84.
[8]   I. Daubechies, Ten Lectures on Wavelets, SIAM, Philadelphia, 1992.
[9]   I. Daubechies, Orthonormal Bases of Compactly Supported Wavelets, Comm. Pure Applied Mathematics 41 (1988) 909-996.
[10]   J.L. Starck, F. Murtagh, A. Bijaoui, Image Processing and Data Analysis: The multiscale approach. Cambridge, University Press, 2000.
[11]   G. Pajares, J. M. de la Cruz, Visión por Computador: Imágenes Digitales y Aplicaciones, RA-MA: Madrid, 2001.

Quality Assessment of Manufactured Roof-Tiles Using Digital Sound Processing

Vasco C. F. Santos[1], Miguel F. M. Sousa[1], and Aníbal J. S. Ferreira[2]

[1] INESC Porto, Porto, Portugal
{vsantos,mfalcao}@inescporto.pt
[2] FEUP / INESC Porto, Porto, Portugal
emailajf@fe.up.pt

Abstract. This paper describes a method for automatically assessing the quality of manufactured roof-tiles using digital audio signal processing and pattern recognition techniques. A prototype system has been developed that is based on a mixed PC/DSP platform, where the real-time constraint is one of the main key issues.

The suitability of the classification process for implementation in an industrial environment is also addressed.

1 Introduction

Ceramic industries have a long tradition within the Iberic Peninsula and, although they have benefited from significant technological improvements of the production process, quality-control procedures have basically been the same for many centuries. It generally consists of a manual procedure, conducted by human experts, who apply a non-destructive stroke on the ceramic pieces, using a metallic object. The structural quality of the pieces is directly assessed through the resulting audio impulse response heard by the expert. Obviously, this is a physically and psychologically agressive task that frequently leads to classification mistakes, which bring additional costs to the production flow. As a result, this quality control procedure is typically applied to only a few samples of the whole production (e.g. red-bricks, roof-tiles, mosaics, etc.) output.

This paper presents an efficient computational method for the automatic classification of the structural integrity and quality of ceramic roof-tiles, based on the digital processing of their acoustical response to a mechanical stimulus.

Throughout this paper, the simple case of a binary GOOD/BAD classification scheme is considered.

The feasibility of the idea has been demonstrated by preliminary research studies involving red-bricks [1].

This paper is organized as follows. The various parts of the system are described in Section 2, as well as the kind of technologies and algorithms used. Results are presented in Section 3, where the influence of noise in the classification system is also analyzed. Finally, some relevant conclusions about the experiments and topics for future developments are presented in Section 4.

F.J. Perales et al. (Eds.): IbPRIA 2003, LNCS 2652, pp. 927–934, 2003.

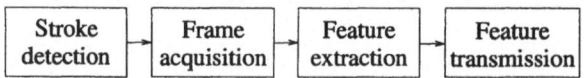

Fig. 1. Basic processing tasks of the DSP algorithm

2 System Modules

The framework for this project is basically a laboratory prototype composed of three basic modules: a stimulation module responsible for the task of applying a stroke on the piece to be analyzed; a signal acquisition and analysis module that captures the acoustic signal produced at the stimulation stage, that analyzes it and that extracts relevant signal features; and a classification module that provides a final binary GOOD/BAD decision, based upon the features that were collected by the signal acquisition and analysis module. A more detailed description of each of these modules as well as of the interactions between them is presented in the next sections.

2.1 The Stimulation Module

This module is composed of a metallic arm with a spherical tip (hammer), which moves by the influence of a pneumatic actuator. In order to avoid stroke rebounds, so as to obtain a good impulse response estimate, the spherical tip was made mechanically flexible by using a spring. This is all supported by a metallic structure, which also holds the ceramic piece to be analyzed. A view of the system can be seen at **http://telecom.inescn.pt/research/audio/tiles/**. The orders to the pneumatic actuator are given by a PC, which also plays an important role in the classification stage.

2.2 The Signal Acquisition and Analysis Module

The signal acquisition is implemented by using a set of two measurement microphones. There are two main reasons for using more than one microphone for capturing the impulse response of the piece. On one hand, the acoustical energy emitted by the piece varies along its structure. Therefore, it is reasonable to put more than one microphone in carefully selected spots, namely near the *hot spots*, as are the edges of the piece. On the other hand, critical reflections and other perturbances related with the propagation of sound may influence the analysis process. Considering more than one capture spot creates a diversity that somewhat compensates this problem.

The sound captured by the microphones is digitized and analyzed by a DSP platform. Samples are taken at 44.1 kHz with 16-bit resolution. After having extracted the relevant features of the acquired signal, the DSP board transmits them to the PC via serial port, using the RS232 protocol.

The algorithm executed by the DSP is illustrated in Fig. 1. The different processing steps are explained next.

Stroke Detection. This stage consists on a transient detector capable of identifying acoustic pulses existing in the signal captured by the microphones. These pulses correspond, with high probability, to the impulse responses that one intends to store and analyze in this module.

The implemented transient detector works by searching relevant changes on the energy of the output of a 5th order inverse LP filter, applied over the 128 newest samples ($\sim$2.9 ms) of the input signal[1], as detailed in [2, 3].

Frame Acquisition. This stage is triggered once a relevant transient period has been detected in the captured signal. Basically, this stage is in charge of acquiring a per-channel 4864-point length signal frame (including the first 128 points already used in the transient detector), representing approximately 95 ms of audio content. All samples are stored in memory for the subsequent processing stages.

Feature Extraction. Direct inspection of time or frequency information of the captured signals does not permit to accurately assess on whether the piece under analysis is a GOOD or a BAD one. Therefore, the used analysis scheme follows a mixed time-frequency approach. It basically consists in the inspection of the evolution of certain spectral characteristics through time. For that, sixteen 1024-point FFTs are computed, overlapping with each other by 75%. The hanning window function is used in the segmentation of the audio signal.

The spectral content (512 points) is partitioned in 4 non-uniform frequency bands as detailed in [2], and all features are obtained through the analysis of the evolution of the energy within each band through time. The energy contained within each band is computed using the expression

$$E_b(s) = 10 \log_{10} \left\{ \frac{1}{N_b} \sum_{k=\text{start}_b}^{\text{start}_b + N_b - 1} [X_s(k)]^2 \right\}, \tag{1}$$

where $b = 1, 2, 3, 4$ is the frequency band, start_b and N_b are, respectively, the start bin and number of bins of the corresponding band b, $s = 1, 2, \ldots, 16$ is the time segment, and $X(k)$ represents the FFT value at the k-th frequency bin.

The number of obtained features is 6, which gives a total of 12 available features (considering both input channels). They are presented next.

Persistence (energy decay per band) - $\mathcal{F}_1$ to $\mathcal{F}_4$. Comparing the typical audio impulse responses of both GOOD and BAD kinds of pieces, one can see that the former kind has a longer, thus more persistent, response. Four features, one per each band, are extracted as

$$\mathcal{F}_b = \sum_{s=1}^{16} |\max[E_b(\cdot)] - E_b(s)|, \quad b = 1, 2, 3, 4. \tag{2}$$

---

[1] Notice that the energy is calculated within 128-sample periods.

Stability (energy decay regularity) - $\mathcal{F}_5$. Analysing the energy decay within each frequency band, it is seen that the logarithmic value of the energy evolves in an approximately linear way. However, for the BAD pieces, this evolution is more unstable. The 5th feature is obtained through the standard deviation of the energy differences between consecutive time segments of the signal, and computed as

$$\mathcal{F}_5 = \frac{1}{4} \sum_{b=1}^{4} \sqrt{\frac{1}{15} \sum_{s=1}^{15} \left\{ \Delta_E^b(s) - \text{avg}\left[\Delta_E^b(\cdot)\right] \right\}^2}, \tag{3}$$

where

$$\Delta_E^j(i) = E_j(i) - E_j(i+1) \tag{4}$$

is the energy difference between the i-th segment and its subsequent one, given the frequency band j.

Dispersion (spectral evolution profile) - $\mathcal{F}_6$. From a subjective analysis, it can be seen [2] that there are differences in the timbres of the two kinds of pieces, although they are not structured in an evident way. From here, another relevant feature can be extracted, that evaluates the spectral balance of the response of the piece under analysis.

From the existing 4 frequency bands, the 3 most consistent ones are selected, which have been found to correspond to the first 3 bands. From these bands, an average value of their energy for each time segment s, is calculated:

$$A(s) = \frac{1}{3} \sum_{b=1}^{3} E_b(s), \quad s = 1, 2, \ldots, 16. \tag{5}$$

To obtain $\mathcal{F}_6$, the Euclidean distances between all $E_b(s)$ and $A(s)$ are used, as can be seen in the expression

$$\mathcal{F}_6 = \frac{1}{16} \sum_{s=1}^{16} \sqrt{\sum_{b=1}^{4} [E_b(s) - A(s)]^2}. \tag{6}$$

The value of $\mathcal{F}_6$ from Eq. 6 represents a measure of the syntony or spectral openness through time.

Figure 2 illustrates the class separation obtained using these features for a set of 17 GOOD and 17 BAD roof-tiles which have been previously classified by human experts. Also, as the histograms of the features can be modeled by Gaussian functions, the plots presented in the figure refer to the Gaussian distributions obtained through the mean and standard deviation values, as estimated from data pertaining to each one of the two classes.

Feature Transmission. This stage is responsible for transmitting the 12 features calculated in the precedent processing stage to the PC, one by one, as soon as they are calculated. The RS232 serial protocol is used.

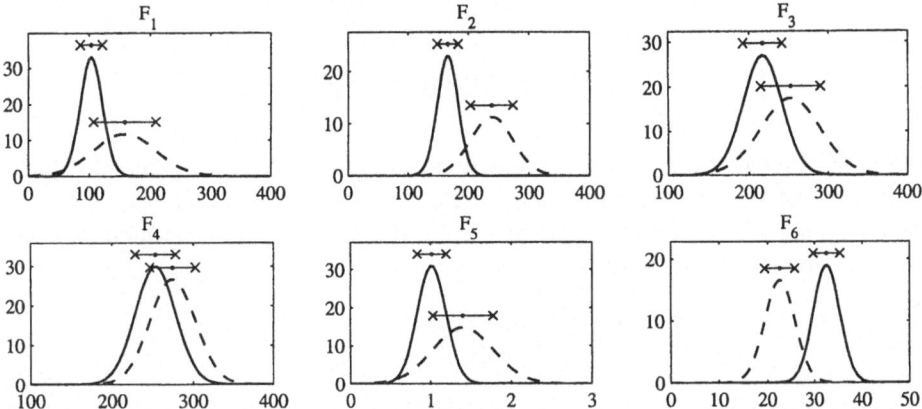

Fig. 2. Plots of the Gaussian functions that represent the probability distributions for each extracted feature for only one audio channel, denoting their contribution for class separation within the analyzed set of ceramic pieces. Class GOOD is represented by solid lines, while class BAD is plotted by dashed curves

2.3   The Classification Module

This module consists of a MATLAB application running on a PC. This application has a graphical user interface capable of providing flexibility, interactivity and ease of use.

In the current implementation of the system, the command activating the stroke to be applied to the ceramic piece (which will trigger the whole classification algorithm) is given by the user from the user-interface application[2]. The command is transmitted to the pneumatic actuator through the parallel I/O port of the PC.

After having received the processed signal features from the serial I/O port, the user-interface application will provide the final classification result. This result, as well as the received features, are displayed on the computer screen.

Several pattern recognition techniques were implemented, including the *Fisher Linear Discriminant* function (FLD), *k–Nearest-Neighbor* estimation (*k*NN), *Learning Vector Quantization* (LVQ), and *Gaudio* techniques [2].

The Gaudio Classifying Technique. This technique corresponds to a supervised, parametric classifying method [2]. The classifier has a non-linear behaviour and assumes that the probability density function of each feature follows a Gaussian distribution. For the simple case of a two-class problem and given the input

---

[2] Note that, in the final implemented system, it is intended that the stroke orders be given automatically upon detection of the presence of a piece.

vector $x = [x_1, x_2, \ldots, x_M]$, the output of the classifier will be

$$C_x = \sum_{i=1}^{M} W_i \cdot \max\left[0, \min\left[1, \frac{x_i - \mu_i^A}{\mu_i^B - \mu_i^A}\right]\right], \tag{7}$$

where W_i is a weighting factor for feature i, and μ_i^α represents the mean value of the distribution of class α for feature i. The output of the classifier is limited in the interval $[0, 1]$, which requires that $\sum_{i=1}^{M} W_i = 1$. The final decision is taken through the use of the following rule:

$$x \in \begin{cases} \text{class } A, \text{ if } C_x \leq 0.5 \\ \text{class } B, \text{ if } C_x > 0.5 \end{cases}. \tag{8}$$

The weighting factors are obtained by calculating the point that intersects both distributions, which is

$$\theta_i = \frac{\mu_i^B - \mu_i^A}{\sigma_i^B + \sigma_i^A}, \tag{9}$$

where σ_i^α are the standard deviations of the class distributions. The weights are then found by [2]

$$W_i = \frac{\theta_i}{\sum_{m=1}^{M} \theta_m}. \tag{10}$$

LVQ-Based Experiments. A series of experiments using this kind of technology were made, and meaningful results have been achieved. The $N \times M$ cells network is initialized using the *Self-Organizing Map* (SOM) algorithm [4]. The training process is accomplished using OLVQ1 and LVQ2 [2, 4].

Automatic Feature Selection. Not all 12 features have good discrimination properties, as they may even somewhat confuse the training process. Besides that, their ability to separate the classes varies with different training sets. Moreover, for practical reasons, one surely prefers an as-simple-as-possible classifier.

The selected algorithm for the task of selecting the subset of K most discriminant features is the *Forward Sequential Search* algorithm [5], following a *wrapper* strategy [6], which means that the final classifier itself is used in every iteration. The inputs of the algorithm are the training examples and the number of desired features, K. The outputs are only the K features selected by the algorithm. Several values of K have been specified for evaluation purposes, as detailed next.

3   Results

A set of 34 roof-tiles (17 GOOD, 17 BAD) was used in the experiments. They were all obtained from the same manufacturer and are all of the same type. As the available set is short, and because the differences on the results obtained for different strokes on the same piece are somewhat considerable, 10 strokes

Table 1. Some results obtained for each of the experimented classifying techniques

Technique	FLD			kNN ($k = 1$)			kNN ($k = 3$)			*Gaudio*		
Number of features	4	6	12	4	6	12	4	6	12	4	6	12
Performance (error %)	2.1%	1.8%	2.6%	1.5%	2.1%	1.8%	2.1%	2.1%	2.4%	1.8%	1.2%	1.5%
Technique	LVQ (2 × 4 cells)			LVQ (3 × 3 cells)			LVQ (4 × 5 cells)			LVQ (5 × 5 cells)		
Number of features	4	6	12	4	6	12	4	6	12	4	6	12
Performance (error %)	4.1%	2.4%	3.8%	3.8%	2.6%	4.4%	3.5%	2.4%	4.7%	4.7%	4.4%	4.7%

were applied to each one of the pieces, giving a total of 170 examples for each class. The whole set of 340 examples is divided into 10 equally sized subsets, and a cross-validation scheme is used. So, 9 subsets are used for training, while the remainder is used for performance measure. All combinations are executed, and the final performance measure is the average of the performances of each of the combinations[3].

Some of the most interesting results obtained, regarding the variation of the number of features used for each technique, are presented in Table 1. In particular, the *Gaudio* classifier exhibits a remarkable performance. In fact, the lowest error percentage obtained is 1.2%, which is a good result. As a parametric classifier, its suitability for real-time implementation is obvious, and is a strong candidate for the final implementation of this system. On the other hand, the use of the weighting factors W_i permits the classifier to be more independent with respect to the dimension of the input feature vectors, which adds flexibility to the process. The FLD and the kNN classifiers present also good results, but the former lacks a bit on flexibility and the latter lacks on computational simplicity. The LVQ presents less good results but should not be ignored because, as many neural network classifiers, it is very flexible. Also, it exhibited error percentages as low as 2.4%, which is comparable to the results of the other techniques.

3.1 Analysis of the Influence of Noise

The performance of the system was also tested in an industrial environment which, for this kind of industry, is rather hostile for an application based on sound analysis. Several minutes of the noise present in the production unit were recorded and digitally stored on a DAT tape. The classifying system was tested in the laboratory, with the help of a DAT player. The speaker was directed to the system prototype and the sound volume set to 80 dB SPL, which is a typical

---

[3] Note that for the kNN technique this does not apply, since the *Leave-one-out* strategy [7] is used instead.

value of the sound intensity in the factory. The *Gaudio* classifier was chosen and all 12 available features present to the input of the classifier. There were no errors using the referred set of example pieces. It is only when the noise intensity exceeds 90 dB SPL (which corresponds to an SNR of about 5 dB) that mistakes start to appear, as well as undetected strokes.

4 Conclusions and Future Work

As can be seen in Table 1, good results may be achieved by using the methods described in this paper. The *Gaudio* classifier, that has been derived in an empirical way [2], appears to be capable of a particularly interesting performance. Considering the low representativeness of the set of examples used in the experiments, one cannot assume that the LVQ classifier is not suitable in this context. In general, all the techniques presented here exhibit a satisfactory performance, which somehow indicates that the success of the classification process depends primarily on an appropriate choice of the signal features and associated discrimination power.

The influence of noise was shown to be low, despite the fact that the system does not have any noise cancellation scheme implemented yet.

In summary, one can conclude that this system is suitable for integration in an industrial roof-tile production flow.

Topics for future work include: the inclusion of an active noise cancellation scheme; the study of other kinds of features extracted from more sophisticated analyses (like *wavelets*, for example); experiments with other classifying technologies; and adaptation of the mechanical sub-system to the continuous flow of roof-tiles in a production line.

References

[1] Sousa, M., Vieira, J., Ferreira, A.: Classificação Automática de Tijolos. 4.º Encontro Nacional do Colégio de Engenharia Electrotécnica, Portugal (1999)
[2] Sousa, M.: Caracterização Semântica de Sinais Acústicos: Aplicação à Classificação Automática de Peças Cerâmicas. Master's thesis. Faculdade de Engenharia da Universidade do Porto, Portugal (2002) – http://www.inescporto.pt/gaudio
[3] Ferreira, A.: Spectral Coding and Post-Processing of High Quality Audio. PhD thesis. Faculdade de Engenharia da Universidade do Porto, Portugal (1998) – http://telecom.inescn.pt/doc/phd_en.html
[4] Kohonen, T.: Self-Organizing Maps. 3rd edn. Springer-Verlag (2000)
[5] Devijver, P., Kitler, J.: Pattern Recognition: A Statistical Approach. Prentice-Hall, Englewood Cliff, NJ (1982)
[6] John, G., Kohavi, R., Pfleger, K.: Irrelevant Features and the Subset Selection Problem. Machine Learning: Proceedings of the Eleventh International Conference (1994) 121–129
[7] Marques de Sá, J. P.: Pattern Recognition: Concepts, Methods, and Applications. Springer-Verlag (2001)

Graph Representations
for Web Document Clustering

Adam Schenker[1], Mark Last[2], Horst Bunke[3], and Abraham Kandel[1]

[1] University of South Florida, Department of Computer Science and Engineering,
4202 E. Fowler Ave. ENB 118, Tampa, FL, 33620, USA
{aschenke,kandel}@csee.usf.edu
[2] Ben-Gurion University of the Negev
Department of Information Systems Engineering
Beer-Sheva 84105, Israel
mlast@bgumail.bgu.ac.il
[3] University of Bern, Department of Computer Science
Neubrückstrasse 10, CH-3012 Bern, Switzerland
bunke@iam.unibe.ch

Abstract. In this paper we describe clustering of web documents represented by graphs rather than vectors. We present a novel method for clustering graph-based data using the standard k-means algorithm and compare its performance to the conventional vector-model approach using cosine similarity. The proposed method is evaluated when using five different graph representations under two different clustering performance indices. The experiments are performed on two separate web document collections.

1 Introduction

Clustering is an active area of research that has been applied in many domains. With clustering the goal is to partition a given group of data items into *clusters* such that items in the same cluster are similar to each other and dissimilar to the items in other clusters. When representing data items for clustering, a numerical vector representation is often used. This model is simple and allows the use of numerical techniques that deal with real-valued feature vectors in a Euclidean space. However, using a vector representation potentially discards useful structural information that is inherent in the original data items, such as web documents. By keeping information such as term ordering and location, which is lost when using a vector representation of web documents, we could possibly improve clustering performance. Traditional clustering methods require the computation of distances between data items or the calculation of cluster representatives, both of which are easily accomplished in a Euclidean space.

In order to overcome this problem, we have introduced an extension of classical clustering methods that allows us to work with graphs as fundamental data structures instead of being limited to vectors of numeric values [8]. Our approach has two main benefits: (1) it allows us to keep the inherent structure

F.J. Perales et al. (Eds.): IbPRIA 2003, LNCS 2652, pp. 935–942, 2003.

Inputs:	the set of n data items and a parameter, k, defining the number of clusters to create
Outputs:	the centroids of the clusters and for each data item the cluster (an integer in $[1,k]$) it belongs to
Step 1.	Assign each data item randomly to a cluster (from 1 to k).
Step 2.	Using the initial assignment, determine the centroids of each cluster.
Step 3.	Given the new centroids, assign each data item to be in the cluster of its closest centroid.
Step 4.	Re-compute the centroids as in Step 2. Repeat Steps 3 and 4 until the centroids do not change.

Fig. 1. The basic k-means clustering algorithm

of the original data items by modeling each as a graph instead of a vector, and (2) we can apply straightforward extensions to existing clustering algorithms, such as k-means, rather than having to create new algorithms from scratch.

In this paper we will address comparison of different graph representations of web documents in the context of document clustering performance. We will use the k-means clustering algorithm to cluster two web document collections. The web documents will be modeled using five different graph representations in order to compare and evaluate the performance of each representation. Clustering of web documents is an important problem for two major reasons: (1) clustering a document collection into categories enables it to be more easily browsed, and (2) clustering can improve the performance of search and retrieval on a document collection. Clustering with graphs is well established. However in those methods the entire clustering problem is treated as a graph: nodes represent the items to be clustered and weights on edges connecting two nodes indicate the distance between the objects the nodes represent. The usual procedure is to create a minimal spanning tree of the graph and then remove the remaining edges with the largest weight until the number of desired clusters is achieved [11].

This paper is organized as follows. In Sect. 2, we briefly describe our extension of the k-means algorithm that allows the use of graphs instead of numerical vectors. In Sect. 3, we propose several graph representations of web documents. Experimental results comparing clustering using alternative representations with respect to ground truth under two performance measures are given in Sect. 4. Conclusions are provided in Sect. 5.

2 k-Means with Graphs

The k-means clustering algorithm is a simple and straightforward method for clustering data [5]. The basic algorithm is given in Fig. 1. The common paradigm is to represent each data item, which consists of m numeric values, as a vector in the space $\Re^m$. The distance measure used by the algorithm is usually the Euclidean distance, however in vector-based models for information retrieval the cosine similarity measure is often used due to its length invariance property.

If methods of computing distances between graphs and determining a representative of a set of graphs are available, then it is possible to extend many clustering methods to work directly on graphs instead of vectors. First, any distance calculations between data items to be clustered, which are now represented by graphs and not vectors, is accomplished with a graph-theoretical distance measure. Second, since it is necessary to compute the distance between data items and cluster centers, it follows that the cluster centers (centroids) must also be graphs. Therefore, we compute the representative "centroid" of a cluster as the *median graph* of the set of graphs in that cluster. The graphs we use in this paper are the regular directed graphs with labeled nodes and edges.

A method for computing the distance between two graphs using the maximum common subgraph has been proposed:

$$dist(G_1, G_2) = 1 - \frac{|mcs(G_1, G_2)|}{max(|G_1|, |G_2|)} \qquad (1)$$

where G_1 and G_2 are graphs, $mcs(G_1, G_2)$ is their maximum common subgraph, $max(\ldots)$ is the standard numerical maximum operation, and $|\ldots|$ denotes the size of the graph [1]. For our application of clustering web documents, the size of a graph will usually be defined as the number of nodes and edges in the graph (i.e. $|G| = |V| + |E|$). Other distance measures which are also based on the maximum common subgraph have been suggested [3][10]. However, the distance measure of Eq. (1) has the advantage that it requires the least number of computations when compared to the other two distance measures we mentioned above. In the general case the computation of mcs is NP-Complete [4], but for our graph representations the computation of mcs is polynomial time due to the existence of unique node labels in the graph representations (i.e. we can just look at the intersection of the nodes and edges, since each node is unique).

Finally, as a cluster representative we use the median of a set of graphs, which is defined as that graph from a set of graphs which has the minimum average distance to all the other graphs in the set. Here the distance to every other graph is computed (with Eq. (1)) and the sum of those distances is divided by the number of graphs in the set. Note that the computation of the median requires only $O(n^2)$ graph distance computations and then finding the minimum among those distances.

3   Graph Representations

In this section we will detail the five methods we will use to represent web documents using graphs instead of vectors, which are called the *standard*, *simple*, *n-distance*, *n-simple distance*, and *frequency* representations. First, we have the *standard* representation. This representation, and all the others presented here, are based on the adjacency of terms in a web document. Under the standard method, we represent each document as a graph as follows. First, each term (word) appearing in the document, except for *stop words* such as "the", "of",

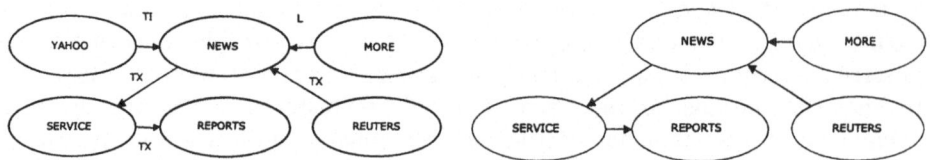

Fig. 2. Example of *standard* (left) and *simple* (right) graph representations of a document

and "and" which convey little information, becomes a vertex in the graph representing that document. This is accomplished by labeling each node with the term it represents. Note that we create only a single vertex for each word even if a word appears more than once in the text. Thus each vertex in the graph represents a unique word and is labeled with a unique term not used to label any other node. Second, if word a immediately precedes word b somewhere in a "section" s of the document, then there is a directed edge from the vertex corresponding to a to the vertex corresponding to b with an edge label s. We take into account certain punctuation (such as periods) and do not create an edge when these are present between two words. Sections we have defined are: *title*, which contains the text related to the documents title and any provided keywords (meta-data); *link*, which is text that appears in clickable hyper-links on the document; and *text*, which comprises any of the readable text in the document (this includes link text but not title and keyword text). Next, we apply a simple stemming method and conflate terms to the most frequently occurring form by re-labeling nodes and updating edges as needed. Finally, we remove the most infrequently occurring words on each document, leaving at most m nodes per graph (m being a user provided parameter). This is similar to the dimensionality reduction process for vector representations [7]. An example of this type of graph representation is given in Fig. 2 (left side). The ovals indicate nodes and their corresponding term labels. The edges are labeled according to title (TI), link (L), or text (TX). The document represented by the example graph has the title "YAHOO NEWS", a link whose text reads "MORE NEWS", and text containing "REUTERS NEWS SERVICE REPORTS". Note there is no restriction on the form of the graph and that cycles are allowed.

The second type of graph representation we will look at is what we call the *simple* representation. It is basically the same as the standard representation, except that we look at only the visible text on the page (no title or meta-data is examined) and we do not label the edges. An example of this type of representation is given in Fig. 2 (right side).

The third type of representation is called the *n-distance* representation. Under this model, there is a user-provided parameter, n. Instead of just looking to see what term immediately follows a given term in a web document, we look up to n terms ahead and connect the terms with an edge that is labeled with the distance between them. For example, if we had the following text on a web page, "AAA BBB CCC DDD", then we would have an edge from term AAA to term

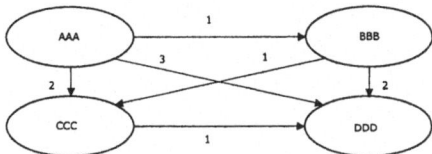

Fig. 3. Example of an *n-distance* graph representation

BBB labeled with a 1, an edge from term AAA to term CCC labeled 2, and so on. The complete graph is shown in Fig. 3. Similar to *n*-distance, we also have the fourth graph representation, *n-simple distance*. Under this representation, any two words separated by *n* terms or less are connected by an unlabeled edge.

Finally, the fifth graph representation is what we call the *frequency* representation. This is similar to the simple representation, but each node and edge has associated with it a frequency measure. For nodes this indicates how many times the associated term appeared in the web document; for edges, this indicates the number of times the two connected terms appeared adjacent to each other in the specified order. For this representation the graph size is defined as the total of the node frequencies added to the total of the edge frequencies. Further, when we compute the maximum common subgraph we take the minimum frequency element (either node or edge) as the value for the *mcs*.

4   Experimental Results

Our experiments were performed on two different collections of documents, called the *F-series* and the *J-series*. The data sets are available under these names at ftp://ftp.cs.umn.edu/dept/users/boley/PDDPdata/. Each collection contains web documents in HTML format. The F-series originally contained 98 documents assigned to one or more of 17 sub-categories of four major category areas. Since there are multiple and sometimes conflicting sub-category classifications, we have reduced the categories to just the four major ones in order to simplify the problem. There were five documents that had conflicting classifications (i.e., they were classified to belong to two or more of the four major categories) which we removed, leaving 93 total documents. The J-series contains 185 documents and ten classes; we have not modified this document collection.

There are already several pre-created term–document matrices available for our vector model experiments (from the above site). For the F-series documents there are 332 dimensions (terms) used, while the J-series has 474 dimensions. With the vector model experiments we used a distance based on the cosine similarity [7]. For both approaches we repeated the same experiment ten times and took the average in order to account for the variance between runs due to the random initialization of the clustering algorithm. Our graph-based experiments used the graph representations described above in Sect. 3. For the distance related graph representations, *n*-distance and *n*-simple distance, we used $n = 5$

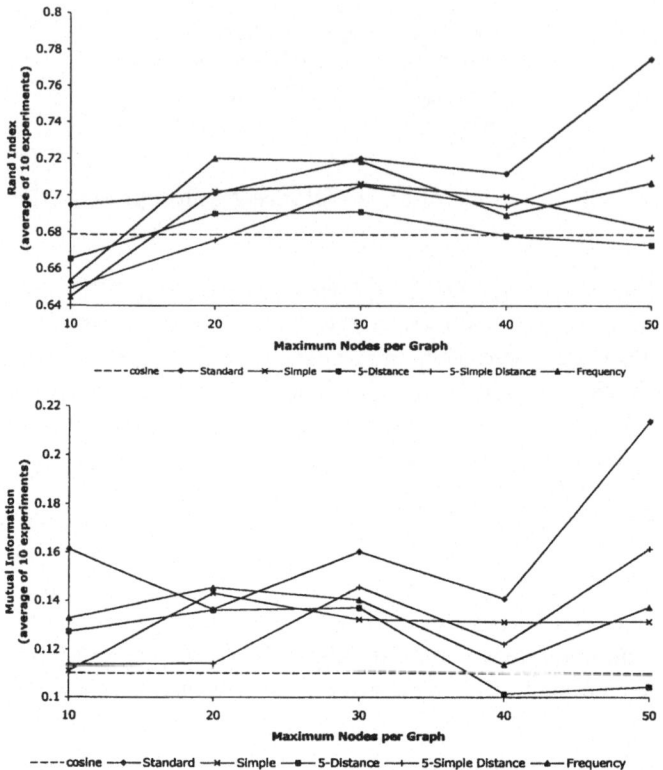

Fig. 4. Experimental results for F-series data set: Rand index (top); mutual information (bottom)

(i.e. 5-distance and 5-simple distance). We have evaluated performance using two clustering performance measures which measure the matching of obtained clusters to the "ground truth" clusters. The first performance index is the *Rand index* [6], which is computed by examining the produced clustering and checking how closely it matches the ground truth clustering. It produces a value in the interval [0, 1], with 1 representing a clustering that perfectly matches ground truth. The second performance index we use is *mutual information* [2][9], which is an information-theoretic measure that compares the overall degree of agreement between the clustering under consideration and ground truth, with a preference for clusters that have high purity. Higher values of mutual information indicate better performance.

From our experimental results, which are presented in Figs. 4 and 5 as a function of the maximum number of nodes allowed in a graph for the F-series and the J-series, respectively, we see that the various graph representations can perform as well or better than the conventional vector model approach in terms of clustering accuracy. The F-series showed good results for the graph representations, but the J-series was not quite as good, especially for representations

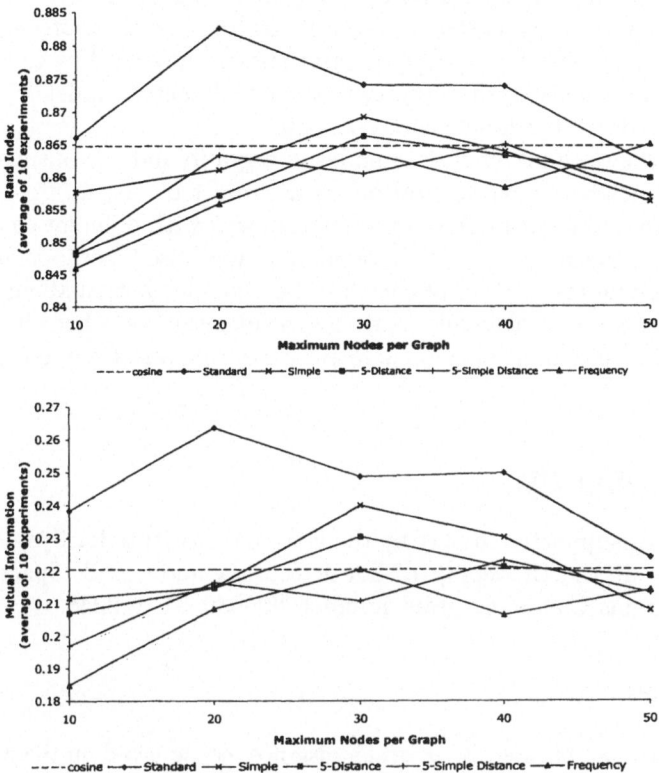

Fig. 5. Experimental results for J-series data set: Rand index (top); mutual information (bottom)

other than standard. In terms of ranking the various graph representations, the results do not show a clear ordering that is consistent for both data sets with the exception that the standard representation is generally the best performing and it outperformed the vector representation in nearly all cases for both data sets. The effect of the maximum graph size (number of nodes) on the clustering performance is not obvious: in the J-series, the accuracy is steadily decreasing after reaching its maximum at 20 nodes for standard, while in the F-series we see a sharp increase in accuracy between 40 and 50 nodes. We intend to further study the effect of graph size in our future work.

5 Conclusions

In this paper we have compared the performance of several graph representations for web documents, which are used during clustering instead of the traditional vector representation. The graph representations were used in the k-means clustering algorithm by employing a graph-theoretical distance measure and the concept of median graphs instead of the typical distance measure and centroid calculation, respectively. Our experimental results show an improvement in clustering performance with graph representations, as measured by the Rand index and mutual information, over the typical case of vector model representation, especially for our "standard" representation.

Finding the optimal number of nodes in a graph and the optimal value of n for our distance-based representations is a subject of our future research. We also intend to apply our method to other data sets with different characteristics. Other avenues to explore include developing graph-based methods for automatically determining the number of clusters when no information about the number of actual categories is available, and the modification of other clustering algorithms, such as hierarchical agglomerative clustering and fuzzy c-means, for use with graphs.

Acknowledgments

This work was supported in part by the National Institute for Systems Test and Productivity at the University of South Florida under U.S. Space and Naval Warfare Systems Command grant number N00039-01-1-2248.

References

[1] Bunke, H. and Shearer, K.: A graph distance metric based on the maximal common subgraph. Pattern Recognition Letters 19 (1998) 255–259
[2] Cover, T. M. and Thomas, J. A.: Elements of Information Theory. Wiley (1991)
[3] Fernández, M.-L. and Valiente, G.: A graph distance metric combining maximum common subgraph and minimum common supergraph. Pattern Recognition Letters 22 (2001) 753–758
[4] Messmer, B. T. and Bunke, H.: A new algorithm for error-tolerant subgraph isomorphism detection. IEEE Transactions on Pattern Analysis and Machine Intelligence 20 (1998) 493–504
[5] Mitchell, T. M.: Machine Learning. McGraw-Hill, Boston (1997)
[6] Rand, W. M.: Objective criteria for the evaluation of clustering methods. Journal of the American Statistical Association 66 (1971) 846–850
[7] Salton, G.: Automatic Text Processing: the Transformation, Analysis, and Retrieval of Information by Computer. Addison-Wesley, Reading (1989)
[8] Schenker, A., Last, M., Bunke, H., and Kandel, A.: Clustering of web documents using a graph model. Web Document Analysis: Challenges and Opportunities, Antonacopoulos, A. and Hu, J. (Eds.). To appear
[9] Strehl, A., Ghosh, J. and Mooney, R.: Impact of similarity measures on web-page clustering. AAAI-2000: Workshop of Artificial Intelligence for Web Search (2000) 58–64
[10] Wallis, W. D., Shoubridge, P., Kraetz, M. and Ray, D.: Graph distances using graph union. Pattern Recognition Letters 22 (2001) 701–704
[11] Zahn, C. T.: Graph-theoretical methods for detecting and describing gestalt structures. IEEE Transactions on Computers C-20 (1971) 68–86

Learning Decision Trees and Tree Automata for a Syntactic Pattern Recognition Task*

José M. Sempere and Damián López

Departamento de Sistemas Informáticos y Computación
Universidad Politécnica de Valencia, Valencia (Spain)
{jsempere,dlopez}@dsic.upv.es

Abstract. Decision trees have been widely used for different tasks in artificial intelligence and data mining. Tree automata have been used in pattern recognition tasks to represent some features of objects to be classified. Here we propose a method that combines both approaches to solve a classical problem in pattern recognition such as Optical Character Recognition. We propose a method which is organized in two stages: (1) we use a grammatical inference technique to represent some structural features of the characters and, (2) we obtain edit distances between characters in order to design a decision tree. The combination of both methods benefits from their individual characteristics and is formulated as a coherent unifying strategy.

1 Introduction

Syntactic Pattern Recognition is a well known research area from Artificial Intelligence in which the target task is to recognize objects from the real world (speech, image, medical signals, ...) which are represented as formal languages [HU79]. Mainly, the most common representations in these tasks have been some families of string languages (regular, context-free, ...), some families of tree languages (regular ones) or some families of graph languages (graphs based on vertex substitutions or hypergraphs with edge replacement). So, the goal in any syntactic pattern recognition learning task is to guess the hidden formal language from examples (strings, trees or graphs).

By the other hand, decision trees [Qu93] can be considered as tree-like representations of finite sets of *if-then-else* rules. This representation allows to take some decisions for the analysis of a set of attributes of a given concept. Mainly, the decision can be applied to a classification task, a predictive task or an advisement task (i.e. expert systems). During the last years, decision trees have been applied in the very promising area of *data mining* [MBK98] to extract knowledge from large databases.

In this work, we combine these two different approaches to the learning problem in order to construct a system to solve an Optical Character Recognition (OCR) task. Here, we will work only with handwritten isolated digits from 0

---

* Work supported by the Spanish CICYT under contract TIC2000-1153.

F.J. Perales et al. (Eds.): IbPRIA 2003, LNCS 2652, pp. 943–950, 2003.
© Springer-Verlag Berlin Heidelberg 2003

to 9. Our solution is based on a two stages system. First, the system learns a set of tree automata (one per digit) by using an error-correcting technique based on a grammatical inference method. Basic concepts and methods on grammatical inference can be viewed in [AS83, Sa97]. Then, the system obtains a set of edit distances of every digit to every tree automaton. In the last stage, the system learns a decision tree from the last set of distances that will classify any digit according to a set of rules based on distances.

The structure of this work is as follows: First, we will explain the OCR task that the method attempts to solve. We will explain the learning methods on every phase (i.e. learning of tree automata and learning of decision trees). Finally, we will show some preliminary results from an experimentation using our approach and we will give some research guidelines for future works.

2   The Problem: Optical Character Recognition

The target problem of this work is related to the working area of Handwritten Recognition. Here, the general goal is to construct a robust system which be able to recognize any phrase or text that has been previously handwritten by a human being. This task has not yet completely solved. So, some subproblems are involved to solve this task. For example, there exists an increasing area that attempts to construct good segmentation rules in order to factorize any phrase in words an any word in letters or digits. Other researchers have focused their interest on constructing good language models for task-oriented systems (for example, some systems are focused on medical writings, or mathematics writings and so on). We will focus on another task which consists on isolated digits recognition. The solution to this task is important to construct more sophisticated systems. Here, the task is quite simple given that phrase and word segmentation tasks are avoided. This is the problem that we try to solve with a syntactic pattern recognition approach.

2.1   Representation of the Digits

First, we will consider how the real world objects will be represented. Let us observe in Figure 1 a digit 2 that has been obtained from a handwriting scanning.

Under our approach, the first stage to represent any digit is to obtain a *quad tree* (*qtree*) [HS79] from its digital image. A qtree can be constructed by drawing a square window around the digit and splitting the window in four windows of the same size recursively up to a predefined depth. In Figure 2 we can observe how the window of digit 2 is recursively split.

Once the system obtains the windows of the digit, then it assigns a label to every window of the smallest size. The systems assigns one label to every window depending on the grey scale (black, white or grey). So, every smallest window is represented by a label of a three symbols alphabet (i.e. $\{a, b, c\}$). The relationships between windows can be represented by a tree by using an up-down and left-to-right scanning of the qtree. In Figure 3 we can observe the tree

Fig. 1. Handwritten digit 2

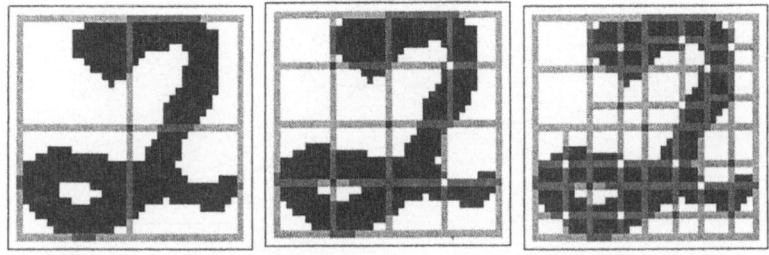

Fig. 2. Constructing a qtree for digit 2

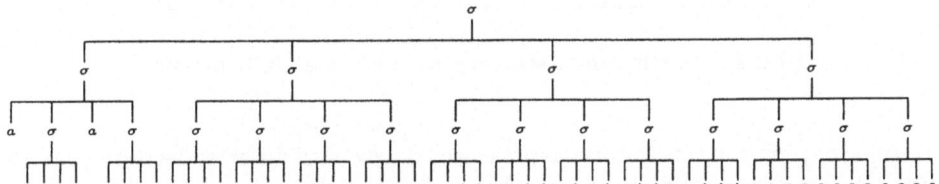

Fig. 3. Handwritten digit qtree with a depth that equals to 3. Label a corresponds to a at least 75% white square, label b corresponds to a at least 75% black square, and label c corresponds to a grey square

obtained for digit 2 by using a depth that equals to 3 while constructing the qtree. From now on, we will use this tree representation.

3   Learning Methods

We will use two different learning paradigms to solve the learning stage of the previously defined problem. First, we will use grammatical inference methods to construct a tree automaton from every set of trees representing the same digit. Then, we will go to a second learning stage to obtain a different representation of the digit based on distances of every digit (every tree) to every concept (every

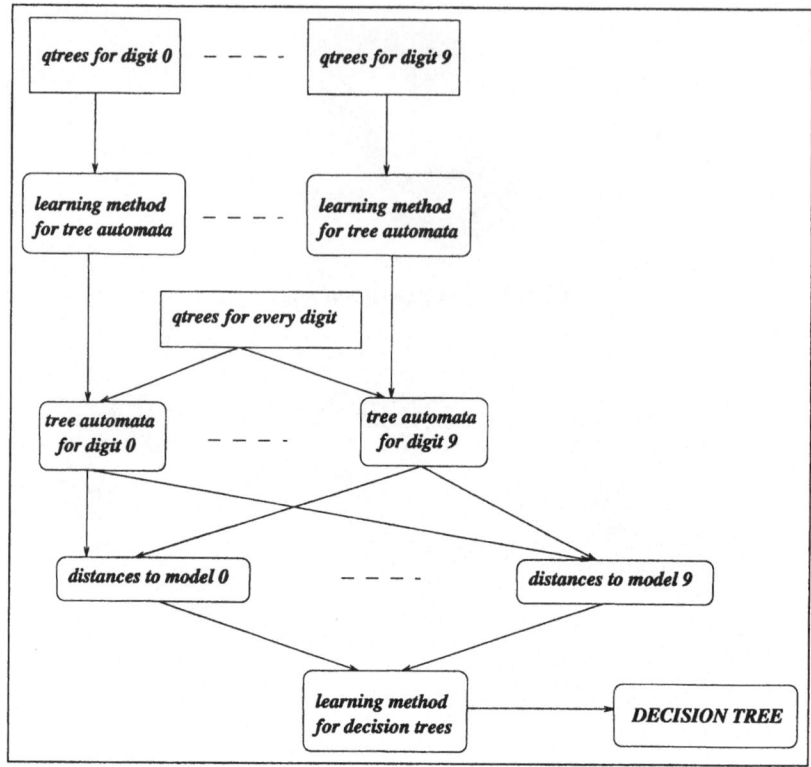

Fig. 4. Our learning strategy to solve the OCR problem

automaton). From this second representation we will infer a decision tree by using standard methods based on the entropy of the examples and distances. The learning scheme is showed in Figure 4.

Now we will explain the different methods that we have used at every learning stage.

3.1   Grammatical Inference of Error-Correcting Tree Automata

The first stage of our learning approach is based on a grammatical inference method for tree languages. Grammatical inference [AS83, Sa97] is an inductive approach to the learning problem based on the representation of concepts as formal languages. Here, as previously explained, we use trees to represent the digits for the OCR task.

Several methods have been proposed to infer tree languages from examples [Ga93, GO93, Sa92]. We will apply a method based on error-correcting distances from trees to tree automata. The definition of such distance is based on classical editing distances for strings to finite string automata [LSG00]. Once, the distance has been defined then, the learning method is an error-correcting grammatical inference technique [LE02].

3.2   C4.5 Learning Algorithm

Learning decision trees is a classical topic on machine learning. A decision tree is a representation of a finite set of *if-then-else* rules. The main characteristics of decision trees are the following:

1. The examples can be defined as a set of numerical and symbolic attributes.
2. The examples can be incomplete or contain noisy data.
3. The main learning algorithms work under *Occam's razor principle* and *Minimum Description Length* approaches.

The main learning algorithms for decision trees have been proposed by Quinlan [Qu93]. First, Quinlan defined $ID3$ algorithm based on the *information gain* principle. This criterion is performed by calculating the entropy that produces every attribute of the examples and by selecting the attributes that save more decisions in information terms. Later, Quinlan defined $C4.5$ algorithm [Qu93] which is an evolution of $ID3$ algorithm. We will use $C4.5$ algorithm for the second learning phase. The main characteristics of $C4.5$ are the following:

1. The algorithm can works with continuous attributes (i.e. real data).
2. Information gain is not the only learning criterion.
3. The trees can be post-pruned in order to refine the desired output.

4   Experiments and Results

We have performed two experiments in order to carry out a first evaluation of our learning strategy. The digits that we have used for training and test is a subset from the data set "NIST SPECIAL DATABASE 3, NIST Binary Images of Handwritten Segmented Characters" [Ga94].

The protocol that we have performed in both experiments is the following one: First, we obtain the *qtree* representations of every digit in the data set. Then, we divide this set in two disjoint subsets (Set 1 and Set 2) and we apply to Set 1 the Error-Correcting inference technique in order to obtain a tree automaton for every digit. We calculate the distance of every digit to every automaton (so, every digit has ten attributes that represent the distances to every model). Then, we calculate the distances of every digit in Set 2 to every tree automaton.

From Set 1 and Set 2 we perform a learning plus testing phase for decision trees. We have used an implementation of $C4.5$ algorithm in C which is available from internet at J.R. Quinlan's Home Page [QuHTTP]. Observe that for every digit at Set 1 there is at least one distance with value 0, while this is not true in general for digits of Set 2.

Experiment 1

We have selected 3000 digits for Set 1 (300 samples for every digit) and 1000 digits for Set 2 (100 samples for every digit). We have performed three rounds on $C4.5$ algorithm in order to use different samples with or without distance 0. The results of this experiment are showed in Figure 5.

Round 1
Evaluation on training data (2666 items)

Before Pruning	After Pruning		
Size	Errors	Size	Errors	Estimate
189	44(1.7 %)	173	48(1.8 %)	5.8 %

Round 2
Evaluation on training data (2667 items)

Before Pruning	After Pruning		
Size	Errors	Size	Errors	Estimate
167	54(2.0%)	159	55(2.1%)	(5.7%)

Evaluation on test data (1334 items)

Before Pruning	After Pruning		
Size	Errors	Size	Errors	Estimate
189	122(9.1%)	173	120(9.0%)	5.8%

Evaluation on test data (1333 items)

Before Pruning	After Pruning		
Size	Errors	Size	Errors	Estimate
167	116(8.7%)	159	114(8.6%)	(5.7%)

Round 3
Evaluation on training data (2667 items)

Before Pruning	After Pruning		
Size	Errors	Size	Errors	Estimate
205	56(2.1%)	187	60(2.2%)	6.5%

Evaluation on test data (1333 items)

Before Pruning	After Pruning		
Size	Errors	Size	Errors	Estimate
205	87(6.5%)	187	86(6.5%)	6.5%

Fig. 5. Results for the first experiment

Experiment 2

We have selected 3000 digits for Set 1 (300 samples for every digit) and 2000 digits for Set 2 (200 samples for every digit). We have performed three rounds on $C4.5$ algorithm in order to use different samples with or without distance 0. The results of this experiment are showed in Figure 6.

Conclusions

It can be observed that, for every round that we have carried out on the experiments, the error median in training data is less than the one in test data. This is a trivial result that all learning methods would hold.

After, the pruning of the decision trees the median error decreases. It implies that some rules that $C4.5$ obtains are not useful for the classification task.

The results on the first experiment are better than in the second. Here, the input sample defines how the rules are extracted. In the first experiment, there is a number of examples with distance 0 to any tree automata which is three times those examples whose distances to every tree automata is not equal to 0. So, the input sample for constructing the tree automata is very important to obtain not only the distances but the decision tree.

Round 1

Evaluation on training data (3333 items)

Before Pruning	After Pruning		
Size Errors	Size	Errors	Estimate
315 88(2.6%)	293	93(2.8%)	8.1 %

Evaluation on test data (1667 items)

Before Pruning	After Pruning		
Size Errors	Size	Errors	Estimate
315 189(11.3%)	293	185(11.1%)	8.1%

Round 2

Evaluation on training data (3333 items)

Before Pruning	After Pruning		
Size Errors	Size	Errors	Estimate
305 86(2.6%)	281	93(2.8%)	7.9%

Evaluation on test data (1667 items)

Before Pruning	After Pruning		
Size Errors	Size	Errors	Estimate
305 186(11.2%)	281	185(11.1%)	7.9%

Round 3

Evaluation on training data (3334 items)

Before Pruning	After Pruning		
Size Errors	Size	Errors	Estimate
323 88(2.6%)	289	97(2.9%)	8.1%

Evaluation on test data (1666 items)

Before Pruning	After Pruning		
Size Errors	Size	Errors	Estimate
323 207(12.4%)	289	208(12.5%)	8.1%

Fig. 6. Results for the second experiment

Finally, an important remark is that the method has a better performance than some other methods that uses only a grammatical inference approach [LE02]. Furthermore, if we compare this method with some other methods based on geometrical approaches then, the differences between median errors can be balanced with the complexity behaviors (i.e. geometrical methods have a worst behavior than our approach under time and space complexities).

5 Future Works

From the initial results that we have obtained, our approach to the OCR problem has showed itself as a promising one. Anyway, we can point out to the following research guidelines in order to improve this work.

- We should enrich the attributes of every digit by including not only the distances but some other structural features.
- The criteria for decision tree learning could be change in order to take into account the distribution of the distances obtained from tree automata.
- Finally, we should apply this method to other pattern recognition tasks.

References

[AS83]   D. Angluin, C. Smith. *Inductive Inference : Theory and Methods*. Computing Surveys, vol. 15. No. 3, pp 237-269. 1983.

[Ga93]   P. García. *Learning k-testable tree sets from positive data*. Technical Report DSIC II/46/1993. Departamento de Sistemas Informáticos y Computación. Universidad Politécnica de Valencia. 1993.

[GO93]   P. García and J. Oncina. *Inference of recognizable tree sets.* Technical Report DSIC II/47/1993. Departamento de Sistemas Informáticos y Computación. Universidad Politécnica de Valencia. 1993.

[Ga94]   M. D. Garris. *Design and Collection of a handwriting sample image database.* Encycl. of Comp. Sci. & Tech. Marcel Dekker, N. Y. Vol 31, Supp. 16, pp 189-214. 1994.

[HU79]   J. Hopcroft, J. Ullman. *Introduction to Automata Theory, Languages and Computation.* Addison-Wesley Publishing Co. 1979.

[HS79]   G. M. Hunter and K. Steiglitz. *Operations on images using quad trees.* IEEE Transactions on Pattern Analysis and Machine Intelligence Vol. 1, No. 2, pp 145-153. 1979.

[LSG00]   D. López, J. M. Sempere, P. García. *Error Correcting Analysis for Tree Languages.* International Journal on Pattern Recognition and Artificial Intelligence, Vol. 14, No.3, pp 357-368. 2000.

[LE02]   D. López, S. España. *Error-correcting tree language inference.* Pattern Recognition Letters 23, pp 1-12. 2002.

[MBK98]   R. Michalski, I. Bratko and M. Kubat. *Machine Learning and Data Mining. Methods and Applications.* John Wiley and Sons LTD. 1998.

[Qu93]   J. R. Quinlan. *C 4.5: programs for machine learning.* Morgan Kaufmann. 1993.

[QuHTTP]   R. Quinlan's Home Page **http://www.cse.unsw.edu.au/~quinlan/**

[Sa92]   Y. Sakakibara. *Efficient learning of context-free grammars from positive structural examples.* Information and Computation 97, pp 23-60. 1992.

[Sa97]   Y. Sakakibara. *Recent advances of grammatical inference.* Theoretical Computer Science 185, pp 15-45. 1997.

MOTRICO Project – Geometric Construction and Mesh Generation of Blood Vessels by Means of the Fusion of Angiograms and IVUS

Francisco J. Seron, Elsa Garcia, and Jorge del Pico

Engineering Research Institute of Aragon,
Grupo de Informatica Grafica Avanzada, Centro Politecnico Superior
Universidad de Zaragoza, Maria de Luna 1,
50018 Zaragoza, Spain
seron@posta.unizar.es, http://giga.cps.unizar.es

Abstract. The MOTRICO project plans the development of an advanced environment that will offer computer assistance for cardiac therapy and diagnosis, which would be useful in the hemodynamics units of those hospitals that have access to the instrumental techniques of Angiography and Intravascular Ultrasounds. The work presented in this paper will describe modeling and finite element mesh generation of an anatomically realistic model of the human left coronary artery bifurcation. The computational geometric model has been developed on the basis of real anatomical information and it has a coronary vessel segment developed on the basis of the information obtained by means of the fusion of angiograms and intravascular ultrasound images(IVUS).

1 Introduction

The MOTRICO project plans the development of an advanced environment that will offer computer assistance:

- For constructing an anatomically realistic model of segments of the human vascular system. This three-dimensional geometric model is generated on the basis of the information obtained by means of the fusion of angiograms and intravascular ultrasound images(IVUS).
- For simulating blood flow through arteries in order to calculate the wall shear stress distribution in these arteries.
- For allowing the user to interact with the system as friendly, quickly and intuitively as possible using virtual and augmented reality techniques for the visualisation of 3D data.

The aim of this paper is to describe the modeling and finite element mesh generation of an anatomically realistic model of the human left coronary artery bifurcation. The structure of this paper is organized as follows: Geometric Model Construction of the Left Coronary Bifurcation, Finite Element Mesh Generation, The Problem of Bifurcations, Geometric Model and Meshes Obtained. Mesh Quality Assessment and Conclusions and Future Work.

F.J. Perales et al. (Eds.): IbPRIA 2003, LNCS 2652, pp. 951–961, 2003.

2   Geometric Model Construction of the Left Coronary Bifurcation

2.1   Geometry and Morphology

The root of the Left Coronary Tree is the left main coronary artery (LM or LMCA). This artery arises from the aortic sinus of Valaslva and it covers around 1 cm before it branches into two slightly smaller arteries: the left anterior descending coronary artery(LAD) and the left circumflex coronary artery(LCX). As far as morphology is concerned, there is a large body of literature that deals with quantification of coronary diameters using angiography and IVUS images [1] [2]. Moreover, Zamir and Chee (1987) carried out measurements of lengths and diameters in a total of 1614 vessel segments in two human hearts [3]. Regarding branching characteristics, two principles suffice to model the human coronary network and to determine diameters of child vessels and branch angles: the principle of minimum pumping power and the principle of minimum volume [4] [5]. In addition, there are several studies on coronary branching sites [6] [7] [8].Finally, it is important to mention that the blood vessel wall consists of three layers: the intima, the media and the adventitia. The intima is the innermost layer, the media is the middle one and the adventitia is the outermost layer. The thickness of the media layer is between two and three times the thickness of the adventitia.

Dimensions in Lengths, Diameters, Branching Angles and Thickness of the Bifurcation Model. According to the geometry information described in this section, an idealized geometric model of the LM-LAD-LCX bifurcation is modeled (See figure 5) on the following dimensions: The lengths are 0.9 cm, 2.7 cm and 1.06 cm for the LM, LAD and LCX, respectively. The vessel of the LM artery has an average diameter of 3.8 mm. The LAD and LCX vessels have 3.1 mm and 2.7 mm for initial diameters and 2 mm and 2.3 mm for final diameters, respectively. The total branch angle is 76 degrees and the angles between the LM-LAD and the LM-LCX are 116 and 168 degrees. It is easy to observe that these dimensions in angles and diameters are in keeping with the principles cited in this section. The thicknesses are 0.1 mm, 0.3 mm for the adventitia and media layers, respectively. The thickness of the intima layer is considered null because it consists only of the endothelium.

2.2   Idealized 3D Construction of the LM-LAD-LCX Bifurcation

The following operations have been performed in order to construct the idealized bifurcation geometric model :

- A semi-circle with the LMCA's diameter is created and the bifurcation trajectory is described using three cubic NURBS curves.
- Three NURBS surfaces are created by extruding the semi-circle along each of the NURBS curves.

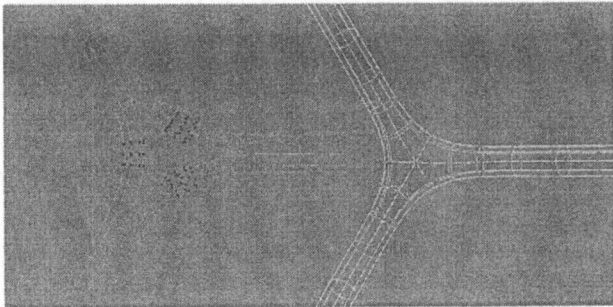

Fig. 1. The snap of three NURBS surfaces created using the techniques "snap to grid" and "snap to point"

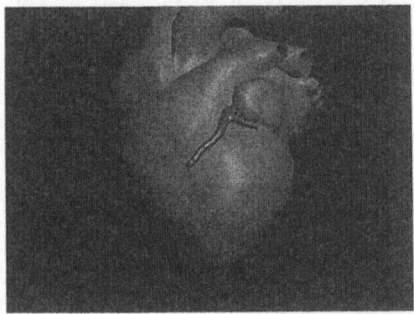

Fig. 2. The model of the Left Coronary Bifurcation placed in a heart model

- In order to eliminate the hole formed where the three surfaces meet in a complex way, they must meet at a point. However, this can pose a problem, because simply joining them at the central point causes overlapping edges. To solve the problem, knots of multiplicity 3 are created. The multiknots produce a discontinuity that helps align the surfaces, so continuity is maintained across the multiknot curves as if they were junctions.
- Similar points in each curve are aligned (See figure 1) by activating the techniques called "snap to grid" and "snap to point" [9].
- In order to perform the adjustment of the vessel diameters, the control points related to each section are scaled according to the diameters cited in the section Sect. 2.1.
- Branching angles are also modified according to the angles cited in the section Sect. 2.1. The adjustment of branching angles are made in two steps. The first step is to create a set of thin and long reference objects and to place them in space according to the correct orientation and the second one is to align the control points of each branch with their corresponding reference object.

The following operations have been performed in order to construct the geometric model of the vessel segments of the idealized arteries: [10]

- The two semi-circular curves of the final cross section in each branch are extruded along a NURB curve that the trajectory of each artery describes in space.
- Cross section diameters are modified according to each individual artery.
- The NURBS surfaces of each branch are deformed with the purpose of obtaining the correct curvature. For this reason, the curvature of the surface of heart is applied to each branch. A 3D model of a heart is obtained. The constructed model is placed into the heart model and the adjustment of the surface over the heart surface is made by rotating and traslating each control point until it touchs the heart surface (See figure 2).

These operations have been performed for each of the surfaces that separate vessel wall layers with different diameters. All surface patches are saved as IGES surfaces. Afterwards, different subvolumes required for mesh techniques are composed from these IGES surfaces using boolean operations. Finally, the four models (bifurcation and three vessels) are joined as a single model.

2.3   Real 3D Reconstruction of a LAD Vessel Segment

In the idealized bifurcation model, a LAD vessel segment has been replaced with a real 3D reconstruction of the same segment (See figure 5). This segment has an average length of 1.35 cm. This reconstruction of the LAD segment has been obtained from the sequence of IVUS images and angiographies. Both methods (IVUS and angiogram) provide a lot of information on the internal and the external shape of the coronary vessels.

The vessel model is reconstructed using deformable models and compounding methods (See figure 3). Deformable models are very well suited for lumen and vessel wall detection, as they allow modeling of the vessel via an elastic dynamic

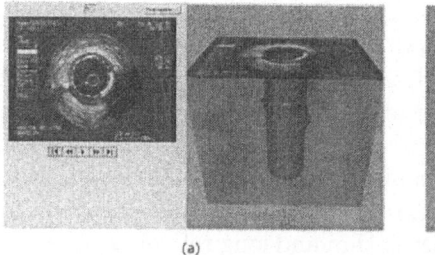

(a)   (b)

Fig. 3. 3D Reconstruction of a Vessel Segment. (a) The reconstruction using deformable models and compounding methods. (b) The correspondence between IVUS and angiogram data. The photos are courtesy of P. Radeva and D. Rotger

model that adjusts to the image features for reconstructing the vessel. Once the vessel boundaries have been detected, compounding methods are used to interpolate IVUS data [11]. This technique is complemented by a 3D reconstruction of the vessel using biplane angiography support (See figure 3). IVUS images are located in space thnaks to a 3D reconstruction of the catheter trajectory on the basis of the registration of the catheter in two views of angiograms before and after the pullback of the IVUS catheter. Note that this spatial curve represents the trace of the centers of the IVUS images. Each IVUS plane is placed in space in order to allow later reconstruction of vessel tortuosity [12].

3   Finite Element Mesh Generation

Coronary vessels could be defined using their cross sections and the trajectory they describe in space. This is the reason that they could be considered to be sweepable volumes, that is, a blood vessel could be meshed using sweeping algorithms. The sweeping algorithms take the 2-D quadrilateral mesh from one cross section surface (source) and project it through the vessel to another cross section surface (target).

3.1   Mesh Generation of Blood Vessels

In the first place, it is necessary to subdivide the vessel into subregions with different physical characteristics suitable for finite element analysis. The vessel decomposition has as many subvolumes as materials (adventitia, media and intima layers and lumen of the artery). As far as the geometry is concerned, it is possible to distinguish two types of subvolumes:

Ring-Shaped. This type ranges the adventitia, media and intima layers of the artery wall. The method employed for meshing the source surface of this type of subvolumes is called *Hole* (See figure 4). A polar coordinate-like mesh with the singularity removed is produced with this method [13].

Cylinder-Shaped. This ranges the lumen of the artery. The technique used to obtain an unstructured mesh on the 2D cross section of this type of subvolumes is called *Paving* (See figure 4). The Paving technique introduced by Blacker and Stephenson presents a method for forming complete rows of elements starting from the boundary and working inward [14].

3.2   Mesh Generation of Bifurcations

A bifurcation is not a sweepable volume because its volume has two sweep directions, one for the trunk and another for its branch. This constraint has been lifted by decompositing the initial volume into sweepable subvolumes. Therefore, the main difference between meshing an isolated vessel and a bifurcation is, in essence, the initial decomposition of the volume. The bifurcation model

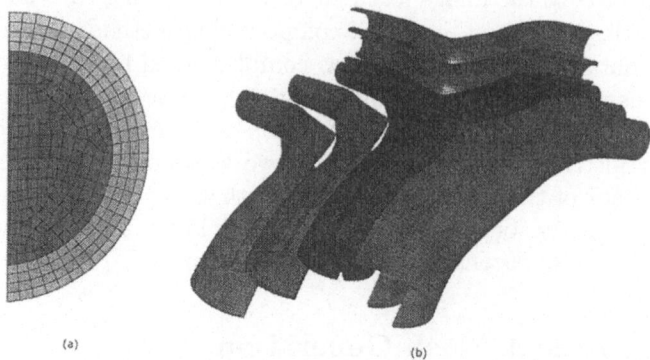

Fig. 4. Mesh Generation of the LM-LAD-LCX bifurcation.(a) Generated bidimensional paving and hole meshes for the source surface of the cross section of each of three subvolumes.(b) Tridimensional meshes of each of three subvolumes

Fig. 5. Geometric model of the human left coronary artery bifurcation.(a) The tridimensional model of the LAD vessel segment developed by means of angiograms and IVUS. (b) The idealized geometric model with the 3D reconstruction of the LAD vessel segment

has been subdivided into three subvolumes according to the surfaces that contain the bifurcation axis and are perpendicular to the bifurcation plane. After that, each of the subvolumes is decomposed by different materials such as blood vessels (See figure 4). The mesh generation techniques employed in each of the three subvolumes have been *Hole* and *Paving* for meshing the source surface of the cross section of adventitia and media layers and of the artery lumen, respectively and *Sweeping* to generate the three-dimensional mesh by projecting the 2D paving and hole meshes through each of the three subvolumes. Finally, the three submeshes of domains with the same material are joined adequately as a single mesh has been generated.

4   The Problem of Bifurcations

Both the geometric model and the finite element meshes entail certain constraints and problems.

4.1   Constraints Related to Geometric Modeling

Surface Continuity of Geometric Models. An important characteristic of the geometry of coronary arteries is the absence of corners and peaks on their surfaces, so the main constraint related to geometric modeling of coronary vessels is the smoothness and continuity of the boundary surfaces. A frequently used branch-modeling method is to construct the geometric models of trunk and branch separately and to intersect them afterwards. This method was dismissed because of the corners resulting from such intersection.

Initial Decomposition of the Domain. Some constraints related to the later descomposition of the domain have been assessed before geometric modeling of the bifurcation, in order to model the bifurcation surfaces already divided into as many parts as necessary. Such constraints are mainly related to the quality of the mesh elements. In keeping with this, several possibilities of bifurcation modeling were considered. One of them was to preserve the triangular-shaped hole formed where the three semicylinder-shaped surfaces meet (See Sect. 2.2) and to mesh it as another subvolume. But this option was dismissed because of the low quality of the mesh produced for this subvolume.

4.2   Constraints Related to Mesh Generation Techniques

Hole. In this method, the number of intervals in the azimuthal direction is controlled by setting the number of intervals on the inner and outer bounding loops of the surface. The number of intervals must be the same on each loop. There are usually problems with the correspondance between mesh nodes on the inner and outer boundaries [13].

Paving. The paving boundary must always contain an even number of nodes. This is a necessary condition when generating an all-quadrilateral mesh [14].

Sweeping. To maintain the structured mesh in the sweep direction, sweeping algorithms require that the linking surfaces (those that connect the source to the target) be mappable or submappable. This constraint limits the number of solids that can be meshed with these algorithms. They specifically exclude solids with imprints or protrusions on the linking surfaces as bifurcations. There is an algorithm called grafting that lifts this constraint on linking surfaces. This algorithm has three major steps: meshing of the trunk, modification of the base surface mesh at the graft surface, and meshing of the branch. However, it is not

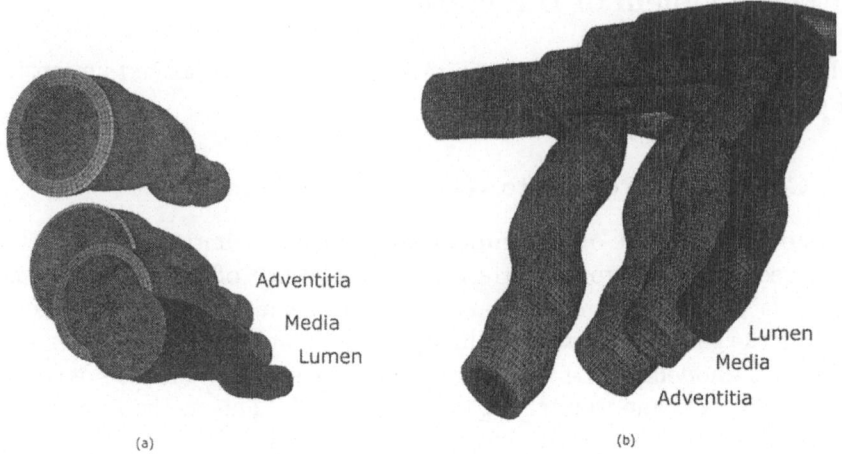

Fig. 6. The finite element meshes.(a) Meshes obtained for the tridimensional reconstruction of the LAD vessel segment.(b) Meshes obtained for the geometric model of the left coronary bifurcation

employed in this case because of the decomposition of materials required by the finite element method and because the solids that generally benefit from the grafting algorithm have one major sweep direction which is perpendicular to the other one, that is, solids with corners [15].

5   Geometric Model and Meshes Obtained – Mesh Quality Assessment

A geometric model of the human left coronary artery bifurcation have been produced. The computational geometric model has been developed on the basis of real anatomical information. In this idealized bifurcation model, a LAD vessel segment has been replaced with a real 3D reconstruction of the same segment. This reconstruction has been developed on the basis of the information obtained by the fusion of angiograms and intravascular ultrasound images (See figure 5). A total of amount of 244844 mesh nodes has been created for the geometric model of the human left coronary artery bifurcation (See figure 6). Five meshes have been generated for this model:

- The first mesh contains the adventitia layer, which is formed using Hole and Sweeping mesh techniques and is an hexahedral mesh.
- The second one is a bidimensional mesh of quadrilateral elements produced when the first mesh is generated. It covers the outermost surface of the adventitia layer.
- The third mesh contains the media layer and is generated in the same way as the first one.

Fig. 7. The inside view of the lumen surface mesh of the left coronary bifurcation model

- The fourth one is a quadrilateral mesh produced as a result of generating the third mesh. It covers the intima layer.
- The fifth one is the lumen mesh of the bifurcation. The paving method is employed to generate the quadrilateral mesh of the cross section surfaces and sweeping to form the hexahedral mesh through the lumen (See figure 7).

The quality of all the generated finite element meshes has been assessed using a variety of verification algorithms [16]. The individual characteristics of each element are verified by calculating common metrics like aspect ratio or jacobian, depending on the element type. For each metric, the minimum, maximum, average, and standard deviation have been tracked. For example, the shear metric measures element skew and ranges between zero and one, with a value of zero signifying a non-convex element, and a value of one being a "perfect" element. Therefore, the average of the shear metric of the finite element meshes generated is 0.8986957, the standard deviation is 0.11968, the minimum value is 0.3954066 and the maximum value is 0.9999164.

On the other hand, hexahedral elements and quadrilateral elements are checked to see if any faces of hexahedral elements or quadrilateral element share three nodes with another face of a hexahedral or quadrilateral element. The topology and the exterior surface of the mesh are carefully analyzed too, looking for any defects in the mesh connectivity or continuity that would invalidate the mesh.

6   Conclusions and Future Work

A geometric model and five finite element meshes of the human left coronary artery bifurcation have been produced. In this paper, the idealized construction of the bifurcation, the modification of this model with a real 3D reconstruction of the LAD vessel segment and the finite element mesh generation of the definitive model have been described. Moreover, the quality of the geometric model and the finite element meshes obtained has been assessed using verification algorithms. As part of future work, coronary atheromas are planned to be modeled and to generate a finite element mesh in an attempt to seek the validation of the hypothesis that relates the shear stress with the development of the atherosclerosis.

Acknowledgement

This work has been partly financed by the Spanish "Ministerio de Ciencia y Tecnologia" (contracts number TIC 2000-1635-C04-01).

References

[1] Nissen, S. E., Gurley, J. C., Grines, C. L., et al.: Intravascular Ultrasound Assessment of Lumen Size and Wall Morphology in Normal Subjects and Patients with Coronary Artery Disease. Circulation, Vol. 84.(1991) 1087–1099

[2] De Sheerder, I., De Man, F., Herregods M. C., et al.: Intravascular Ultrasound versus Angiography for Measurement of Lumen Diameters in Normal and Diseased Coronary Arteries. Am. Heart J., Vol. 127.(1994) 243–251

[3] Zamir, M., Chee, H.: Segment Analysis of Human Coronary Arteries. Blood Vessels, Vol. 24.(1987) 76–84

[4] Changizi, M. A., Cherniak, C.: Modeling the Large-Scale Geometry of Human Coronary Arteries. Can. J. Physiol. Pharmacol., Vol. 78.(2000) 603–611

[5] Murray, C. D.: The Physiological Principle of Minimum Work applied to the Angle of Branching Arteries. J. Gen. Physiol., Vol. 9.(1926) 835–841

[6] Brinkman, A. M., Baker, P. B., Newman, W. P., Vigorito, R., Friedman, M. H.: Variability of Human Coronary Artery Geometry: An Angiographic Study of the Left Anterior Descending Arteries of 30 Autopsy Hearts. Can. J. Physiol. Pharmacol., Vol. 22.(1994) 34–44

[7] Zamir, M., Chee, H.: Branching Characteristics of Human Coronary Arteries. Can. J. Physiol. Pharmacol., Vol. 64.(1986) 661–668

[8] Hutchins, G. M., Miner, M. M., Boitnott, J. K.: Vessel Caliber and Branch-Angle of Human Coronary Artery Branch-Points. Circulation Research, Vol. 38.(1976) 573–576

[9] Bayne, J., et al.: SOFTIMAGE XSI version 2.0, Modeling and Deformations. Avid Technology (2001)

[10] Seron, F. J., Garcia, E., Sobreviela, E. J., del Pico, J.: Proyecto Motrico. El Problema de la Generacion de Mallas. Actas, XX Congreso Anual de la Sociedad Espaniola de Ingenieria Biomedica, Zaragoza, Spain (2002) 301–304

[11] Pujol, 0., Radeva, P.: Lumen Detection in Ivus Images using Snakes in a Statistical Framework. Actas, XX Congreso Anual de la Sociedad Espaniola de Ingenieria Biomedica, Zaragoza, Spain (2002) 129–132

[12] Rotger, D., Radeva, P., Mauri, J., Fernandez-Nofrerias, E.: Internal and External Coronary Vessels Images Registration. Lecture Notes in Artificial Intelligence, Vol. 2504, Springer-Verlag, Castelló de la Plana (2002) 408–418

[13] Blacker, T. D., et al.: CUBIT Mesh Generation Environment, vol. 1: User's Manual. SAND94-1100, Sandia National Laboratories, Albuquerque, New Mexico (1994)

[14] Blacker, T. D., Stephenson, M. B.: Paving: A New Approach To Automated Quadrilateral Mesh Generation. International Journal For Numerical Methods in Engineering, Vol. 32.(1991) 811–847

[15] Jankovich, S. R., Benzley, S. E., Shepherd, J. F., Mitchell, S. A.: The Graft Tool: An All-Hexahedral Transition Algorithm for Creating a Multi-Directional Swept Volume Mesh. Proceedings, 8th International Meshing Roundtable, South Lake Tahoe, CA, U. S. A. (1999) 387–392

[16] Merkley, K. G., Meyers, R. J., Stimpson, C., Ernst, C.: Verde Users Manual Version 2.6. SAND94-1100, Sandia National Laboratories, Albuquerque, New Mexico (2002)

Skipping Fisher's Criterion

A. Sierra[1] and A. Echeverría[2]

[1] Escuela Politécnica Superior, Universidad Autónoma de Madrid
28049 Madrid, Spain
Alejandro.Sierra@ii.uam.es
[2] Departamento de Inteligencia Artificial, Universidad Europea de Madrid
28670 Madrid, Spain
aerey@dinar.esi.uem.es

Abstract. A new version of Fisher's discriminant analysis (FDA) is introduced in this paper. Our algorithm searches also for a reduced space in which patterns can be discriminated. However, no intermediate class separability criterion (such as Fisher's mean distance divided by variance) is used whatsoever. Classification performance is optimized directly. Since no statistical hypothesis are made, the method is of general applicability. Our evolutionary approach for optimization makes the number of projections and classes independent of each other. Even different numbers of projections, not necessarily the means, can be used for each class. As a proof of concept, the UCI thyroid problem (three classes) is solved in one dimension instead of two with state of the art performance and making use of only three of the 21 original features.

1 Introduction

Classical FDA [1, 2] is originally a supervised dimensionality reduction technique which allows to plot patterns in a dimension equal to the number of classes minus one. A clever class separability criterion is maximized leading to an elegant analytical solution. It is quite common to use this solution for classification by distance to projected means. Our proposal consists in constructing the projection by maximizing classification performance directly, thus addressing some side effects due to separability criteria. For instance, the number of projections and classes are independent which is very helpful in problems with more than three classes. Besides, since no scatter matrices are used all rank deficiency problems are bypassed.

In order to do this a multilevel evolutionary approach is used. The first level is a genetic algorithm (GA) [3] searching for relevant subsets of features. Starting from individual features, the GA selects and combines subsets based on the classification performance of the projections found for each subset. Finding the actual projections and the classification error involved is the task accomplished by the second level: a simple evolution strategy (ES) [4]. It is this breaking of the task into two pieces what makes our approach powerful. To prove this point we use the two simplest available algorithms and apply them to a difficult UCI problem: the thyroid set.

F.J. Perales et al. (Eds.): IbPRIA 2003, LNCS 2652, pp. 962–969, 2003.
© Springer-Verlag Berlin Heidelberg 2003

This problem consists in determining whether a patient referred to a clinic is hypothyroid. There are 7200 patients in the database each characterized by 21 attributes, 15 binary (from x_2 to x_{16}) and 6 continuous (x_1, x_{17}, x_{18}, x_{19}, x_{20}, x_{21}). The categories are three: normal (2.1%), hyperfunction (5.2%) and subnormal functioning (92.7%). The error incurred by assigning patterns to the majority class is 7%. We will be using thyroid2, a distribution of the original patterns into training (3600 patterns), validation (1800) and test sets (1800), prepared by Prechelt [5].

The organization of the paper is as follows. Section 2 reviews briefly the classical algorithm and its performance on our benchmark. The inner piece of our algorithm is introduced in Section 3 and later applied to the UCI thyroid problem showing improvement over classical FDA but demanding further work. Section 4 puts the two pieces together and shows how powerful this combination turns to be. Finally, the conclusions can be found in Section 5.

2   Fisher's Discriminant Analysis

Let us review briefly classical discriminant analysis. Suppose we have a set of patterns each characterized by d features and classified as belonging to one of c different classes. Fisher's classical algorithm looks for a projection $\mathbf{W}$ from d to d' dimensions (d' to be specified later) maximizing the class separability criterion

$$J(\mathbf{W}) = \frac{|\mathbf{W}'\mathbf{S}_b\mathbf{W}|}{|\mathbf{W}'\mathbf{S}_w\mathbf{W}|} \tag{1}$$

where $\mathbf{S}_b$ is the between-class scatter matrix and $\mathbf{S}_w$ is the within-class scatter matrix. The optimization leads to the following generalized eigenvector problem

$$\mathbf{S}_b\mathbf{w}_i = \lambda_i\mathbf{S}_w\mathbf{w}_i. \tag{2}$$

The output dimension d' is upper bounded by $c - 1$ because at most $c - 1$ of the eigenvalues λ_i are different from zero. This is due to the rank limitation of matrix $\mathbf{S}_b$, which is constructed as the sum of c matrices whose rank is 1 at most. The corresponding eigenvectors form the $c - 1$ columns of the optimal projection $\mathbf{W}$.

The space expanded by the two non-zero eigenvectors of the training set of the thyroid2 problem works poorly: the error rates are 21.53%, 22.67% and 22.00% for the training, validation and test sets, respectively. More specifically, the classification matrix on the test set is the following:

$$C_{(x_1,...,x_{21})} = \begin{bmatrix} 22 & 18 & 0 \\ 1 & 64 & 25 \\ 3 & 349 & 1318 \end{bmatrix} \tag{3}$$

where element C_{ij} represents the number of patterns of class i actually classified as belonging to class j. It is clear from this matrix that class 1 is not confused with class 3. The confusion comes mainly from the overlapping between the other two pairs of classes. This poor performance is due to the mixture of binary and continuous features as well as to the noise introduced by some of the features as their removal proves. We have shown elsewhere [6] that FDA can benefit enormously from feature selection. Here a further step is taken by giving up intermediate criteria and minimizing classification error directly as explained next.

3   A (1+1) Evolution Strategy as Discriminant

We report in this section about the prospects of using the arguably simplest evolutionary algorithm, a (1+1) evolution strategy [4], to optimize classification performance directly. A (1+1) ES is an optimization procedure which in our case follows these steps:

- The dimension for the projected space is fixed (here one for notational simplicity).
- An initial projection $\mathbf{w} = (w_1, \ldots, w_{21})$ is chosen at random and the following steps are repeated for a prescribed number of times:
  - The weight vector is mutated by adding independent random variables $\sigma_i \in N(0, 1)$ to each component

$$\mathbf{w} = (w_1, \ldots, w_{21}) \rightarrow \mathbf{w'} = (w_1 + \sigma_1, \ldots, w_{21} + \sigma_{21}) \qquad (4)$$

  - The classification error $\epsilon_{w'}$ associated to projection $\mathbf{w'}$ is calculated as shown below.
  - The weight $\mathbf{w}$ is replaced by $\mathbf{w'}$ when $\epsilon_{w'} < \epsilon_w$.
- The classification matrix on the independent test set is calculated for the current weight vector.

Errors are calculated by classifying patterns as belonging to the class of the closest mean as follows:

- The means of each class are projected according to the weights. These means are calculated out of the training patterns exclusively.
- The patterns of both training and validation sets are projected and assigned to the class of the closest mean. Excluding validation patterns from the calculation of means tends to control overfitting.
- The error on the training and validation sets is summed into a single figure $\epsilon(w_1, \ldots, w_{21})$.

Figure 1 shows that this simplest procedure can work properly if applied to a good set of features. The figure shows test error rate versus number of generations for two (1+1) evolution strategies: one making use of the whole set of features $(x_1, \ldots, x_{21})$ and the other using only the subset (x_3, x_8, x_{17}), which we know contains essentially all of the relevant information. It is clear from the

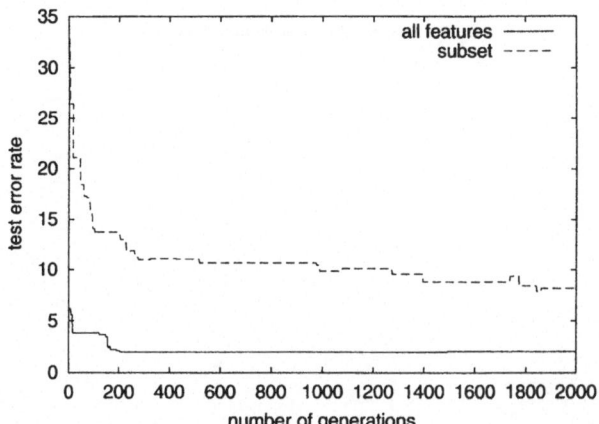

Fig. 1. Test error rate versus number of generations for two runs of a simple (1+1) evolution strategy applied to the thyroid problem: one makes use of the whole set of features and the other benefits from the subset (x_3, x_8, x_{17})

figure that the ES can do the job if we provide it with the right set of features. The classification matrix on the test set for subset (x_3, x_8, x_{17}) is

$$C_{(x_3, x_8, x_{17})} = \begin{bmatrix} 19 & 21 & 0 \\ 2 & 88 & 0 \\ 3 & 10 & 1657 \end{bmatrix} \tag{5}$$

which shows an important reduction in the overlapping between the second and third classes. The error rate is 2% while the rate reached by FDA applied to this subset is 11%. We next show how we have actually found this subset of features.

4   A Wrapped Evolution Strategy

Previous section's main lesson is that the simplest of the strategies is enough if combined with selection of features. That is why we propose using a wrapper genetic algorithm in combination with the strategy as a two level evolutionary solution (see Figure 2):

– The first level is a genetic algorithm evolving a population of binary chromosomes coding subsets of features. The fitness of each subset is calculated by running the second level (1+1) evolution strategy.
– The second level ES evolves the projection weights as in previous section but using only the features of the subset.

Thus the GA is in charge of discovering which features are relevant based on what the ES is capable of doing with them. Breaking the process into these two

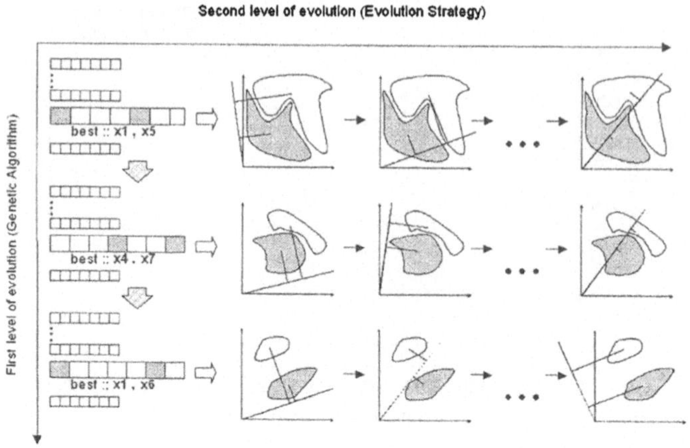

Fig. 2. Two levels of evolution: the genetic algorithm evolves a population of subsets of features and the evolution strategy evolves the projection weights for each of these subsets

steps allows us to use the simplest available algorithms without finetuning of the parameters. The power is not in each level since we use very simple algorithms, but in the combination. The simple genetic algorithm works like this:

- The dimension for the projected space is fixed as before.
- The initial population is formed by 21 binary chromosomes (one for each feature)

$$(1, 0, 0, \ldots, 0) \rightarrow x_1 \quad (0, 1, 0, \ldots, 0) \rightarrow x_2 \quad \ldots \quad (0, 0, 0, \ldots, 1) \rightarrow x_{21} \quad (6)$$

representing the 21 one dimensional subsets.
- The following points are iterated for a prescribed number of generations:
  - The fitness of each chromosome is calculated by running the ES described in previous section but applied to the selected features only.
  - A new population is constructed by selecting individuals proportional to their fitness (see below) and combining them by one-point crossover and mutation [3].
- The best subset is used to calculate the classification matrix on the test set.

Fitness is calculated combining error and complexity. For instance, the subset (x_3, x_8, x_{17}) is assigned the following fitness

$$\text{Fitness}(x_3, x_8, x_{17}) = \epsilon(x_3, x_8, x_{17}) + \alpha(3/21) \quad (7)$$

where $\epsilon(x_3, x_8, x_{17})$ is the sum of training and validation classification errors incurred by the evolution strategy, and the second term is a complexity penalizing

Table 1. Evolution on the thyroid2 data set. Training, validation and test error rates are shown for the successive improvements in fitness. Column 1 shows the generation in which each discriminant is found. The last column shows the features actually used to construct the discriminant

Gen.	Tr. %	Val. %	Te. %	Subset
0	53.31	53.50	53.00	x_1
0	9.06	8.11	9.17	x_9
0	4.78	4.17	3.89	x_{17}
1	3.94	3.67	3.89	$x_{10}\ x_{17}$
1	3.83	3.56	3.56	$x_9\ x_{17}$
6	3.39	3.33	3.00	$x_3\ x_{10}\ x_{17}\ x_{19}$
7	2.36	2.50	2.11	$x_3\ x_{17}$
14	2.22	2.33	2.00	$x_3\ x_8\ x_{17}$

term proportional to the percentage of input features used. Constant α combines numerically both objectives giving priority to classification accuracy ($\alpha = 0.01$).

Table 1 shows a typical evolution on the thyroid2 problem. Training, validation and test error rates of the successive improvements in fitness are shown. The generation in which the individual is found is shown in the first column. Thanks to the initial genetic population, simple models are tried first and noisy or irrelevant features are discarded quickly. Only 200 generations are run for each strategy what further penalizes complex models. The GA stopping criterion is such that it terminates when no fitness increase is found after 50 generations.

Our evolutionary discriminants have state of the art performance as the comparison of Table 2 shows. The GA+ES figure corresponds to the mean performance of 10 runs of our algorithm. The non-linear neural network slightly outperforms our algorithm but involves searching for the right architecture by hand [5]. Besides, our approach ends up with a subset of significant features apart from the model itself. It is most surprising what a simple linear projection can do when no statistical hypothesis are made. Notice that the linear neural network results are far from the error rate reached by our linear projection. We are currently working on the extension of these results to non-linear projections.

5   Conclusions

A new supervised dimensionality reduction algorithm is introduced in this paper. It shares with classical FDA its target free nature: the algorithm does not try to learn artificially assigned output codings but to project patterns closer to their own mean than to the rest of means. The main difference with respect to classical FDA is that classification error is optimized directly without any intermediate class separability criteria. This gives rise to a number of advantages such as:

- No statistical hypothesis are made and therefore the method is of general applicability.

Table 2. Classical discriminant analysis versus its evolutionary counterpart applied to the UCI thyroid2 problem. The average training, validation and test error rates are shown for the thyroid data permutation. Column 5 shows the average number of features used by the evolved projections

	Training error rate %	Validation error rate %	Test error rate %	Number of features
Classical Fisher's discriminant	21.53	22.67	22.00	21
Linear Neural Networks	-	-	6.56	21
Non-linear Neural Networks	-	-	1.86	21
GA+ES discriminant	2.27	2.38	2.02	2.8

- The number of projections is not dependent on the number of classes. Here we can generate one or two dimensional projections even with hundreds of classes. This can be very helpful for visualization purposes.
- Although classical FDA requires that the input dimension be at least equal to the number of classes minus one, our algorithm can use as few input features as one, whatever the number of classes may be. In fact evolution is started from a population of minimal discriminants in order to discard redundant features.
- The constructive nature of the algorithm and its complexity penalizing term gives rise to astonishingly simple models as the thyroid problem shows.

We are currently generalizing the algorithm for it to be capable of finding projections which are not necessarily means, even several projections per class. This is an easy way of addressing non-linear problems while keeping the original algorithm. We hope to report soon on this work.

Acknowledgments

This paper has been sponsored by the Spanish Interdepartmental Commission of Science and Technology (CICYT), project number TIC2001-0572-C02-02.

References

[1] Fisher, R. A.: The Use of Multiple Measurements in Taxonomic Problems. Annals of Eugenics **7** (1936) 179–188

[2] Rao, C. R.: The Utilization of Multiple Measurements in Problems of Biological Classification (with Discussion). Journal of the Royal Statistical Society series B **10** (1948) 159–203

[3] Goldberg, D. E.: Genetic Algorithms in Search, Optimization and Machine Learning. Addison-Wesley, Reading MA (1989)

[4] Beyer, H. G., Schwefel, H. P.: Evolution Strategies. A Comprehensive Introduction Natural Computing **1** (2002) 3–52

[5] Prechelt, L.: Some Notes on Neural Learning Algorithm Benchmarking. Neurocomputing **9** (3) (1995) 343–347

[6] Sierra, A.: High Order Fisher's Discriminants. Pattern Recognition **35** (2002) 1291–1302

New Class of Filters for Impulsive Noise Removal in Color Images

Bogdan Smolka*

Department of Automatic Control, Silesian University of Technology,
Akademicka 16, 44-101, Gliwice, Poland

Abstract. In this paper a novel approach to the problem of impulsive noise reduction in color images based on the nonparametric density estimation is presented. The basic idea behind the new image filtering technique is the maximization of the similarities between pixels in a predefined filtering window. The new method is faster than the standard vector median filter and better preserves edges and fine image details. Simulation results show that the proposed method outperforms standard algorithms of the reduction of impulsive noise in color images.

1 Introduction

A number of nonlinear, multichannel filters, which utilize correlation among multivariate vectors using various distance measures has been proposed [1-6]. The most popular nonlinear, multichannel filters are based on the ordering of vectors in a predefined moving window. The output of these filters is defined as the lowest ranked vector according to a specific vector ordering technique.

All standard filters detect and replace well noisy pixels, but their property of preserving pixels which were not corrupted by the noise process is far from the ideal. In this paper we show the construction of a simple, efficient and fast filter which removes noisy pixels, but has the ability of preserving original image pixel values.

Let $\mathbf{F}(x)$ represents a multichannel image and let W be a window of finite size $n + 1$ (filter length). The noisy image vectors inside the filtering window W are denoted as $\mathbf{F}_j$, $j = 0, 1, ..., n$. If the distance between two vectors $\mathbf{F}_i, \mathbf{F}_j$ is denoted as $\rho(\mathbf{F}_i, \mathbf{F}_j)$ then the scalar quantity $R_i = \sum_{j=0}^{n} \rho(\mathbf{F}_i, \mathbf{F}_j)$ is the distance associated with the noisy vector $\mathbf{F}_i$. The ordering of the R_i's: $R_{(0)} \leq R_{(1)} \leq ... \leq R_{(n)}$, implies the same ordering to the corresponding vectors $\mathbf{F}_i$: $\mathbf{F}_{(0)} \leq \mathbf{F}_{(1)} \leq ... \leq \mathbf{F}_{(n)}$. Nonlinear ranked type multichannel estimators define the vector $\mathbf{F}_{(0)}$ as the filter output. However, the concept of input ordering, initially applied to scalar quantities is not easily extended to multichannel data, since there is no universal way to define ordering in vector spaces. To overcome this problem, distance functions are often utilized to order vectors, [1-3].

* Supported by KBN Grant 7T11A01021.

F.J. Perales et al. (Eds.): IbPRIA 2003, LNCS 2652, pp. 970–978, 2003.
© Springer-Verlag Berlin Heidelberg 2003

2   Proposed Algorithm

2.1   Gray-Scale Images

Let us assume a filtering window W containing $n + 1$ image pixels, $\{F_0, F_1, \ldots, F_n\}$, where n is the number of neighbors of the central pixel F_0, and let us define the similarity function $\mu : [0; \infty) \rightarrow \mathbf{R}$ which is non-ascending in $[0; \infty)$, convex in $[0; \infty)$ and satisfies $\mu(0) = 1$, $\mu(\infty) = 0$. The similarity between two pixels of the same intensity should be 1, and the similarity between pixels with far distant gray scale values should be very close to 0. The function $\mu(F_i, F_j)$ defined as $\mu(F_i, F_j) = \mu(|F_i - F_j|)$ satisfies the three above conditions.

Let us additionally define the cumulated sum M of similarities between the pixel F_k and all its neighbors. For the central pixel we have M_0 and for the neighbors of F_0 we define M_k as

$$M_0 = \sum_{j=1}^{n} \mu(F_0, F_j), \quad M_k = \sum_{\substack{j=1 \\ j \neq k}}^{n} \mu(F_k, F_j), \tag{1}$$

which means that for F_k which are neighbors of F_0 we do not take into account the similarity between F_k and F_0, which is the main idea behind the new algorithm. The omission of the similarity $\mu(F_k, F_0)$ privileges the central pixel, as in the calculation of M_0 we have n similarities $\mu(F_0, F_k)$, $k = 1, 2, \ldots, n$ and for M_k, $k > 0$ we have $n - 1$ similarity values, as the central pixel F_0 is excluded from the sum M_k.

In the construction of the new filter the reference pixel F_0 in the window W is replaced by one of its neighbors if $M_0 < M_k$, $k = 1, \ldots, n$. If this is the case, then F_0 is replaced by that F_i for which $i = \arg\max M_i$, $i = 1, \ldots, n$. In other words F_0 is detected as being corrupted if $M_0 < M_k$, $k = 1, \ldots, n$ and is replaced by its neighbors F_i which maximizes the sum of similarities M between all its neighbors excluding the central pixel. This is illustrated in Figs. 1 and 2.

Our basic assumption is that a new pixel must be taken from the window W (introducing pixels which do not occur in the image is prohibited like in the VMF and VDF). For this purpose μ must be convex, which means that in order to find a maximum of the sum of similarity functions M it is sufficient to calculate the values of M only in points $F_0, F_1, \ldots, F_n$, [6].

2.2   Color Images

The presented approach can be applied in a straightforward way to color images. We use the similarity function defined by $\mu\{\mathbf{F}_i, \mathbf{F}_j\} = \mu(\|\mathbf{F}_i - \mathbf{F}_j)\|$ where $\|\cdot\|$ denotes the specific vector norm. Now in exactly the same way we maximize the total similarity function M for the vector case.

We have checked several convex functions in order to compare our approach with the standard filters used in color image processing presented in Tab. 1a) and we have obtained the best results (Tab. 1b) when applying the following similarity functions, which can be treated as kernels of nonparametric density estimation, [7]

$$\mu_0(x) = \exp\left\{-\left(\frac{x}{h}\right)^2\right\}, \mu_1(x) = \exp\left\{-\frac{x}{h},\right\}, \mu_2(x) = \frac{1}{1+x/h}, h \in (0;\infty),$$

$$\mu_3(x) = \frac{1}{(1+x)^h}, \mu_4(x) = 1 - \frac{2}{\pi}\arctan\left(\frac{x}{h}\right), \mu_5(x) = \frac{2}{1+\exp\left\{\frac{x}{h}\right\}}, h \in (0;\infty)$$

$$\mu_6(x) = \frac{1}{1+x^h}, \quad \mu_7(x) = \begin{cases} 1 - x/h & \text{if } x \le h, \\ 0 & \text{if } x > h, \end{cases} \quad h \in (0;\infty).$$

It is interesting to note, that the best results were achieved for the simplest similarity function $\mu_7(x)$, which allows to construct a fast noise reduction algorithm. In the multichannel case, we have

$$M_0 = \sum_{j=1}^{n} \mu(\mathbf{F}_0, \mathbf{F}_j), \quad M_k = \sum_{\substack{j=1 \\ j \ne k}}^{n} \mu(\mathbf{F}_k, \mathbf{F}_j) \tag{2}$$

where $\rho\{\mathbf{F}_i, \mathbf{F}_k\} = ||\mathbf{F}_k - \mathbf{F}_l)||$ and $|| \cdot ||$ is the L_2 vector norm, as it yields the best results, (Tab. 1c). Applying the linear similarity function μ_7 we obtain

$$\mu(\mathbf{F}_i, \mathbf{F}_k) = \begin{cases} 1 - \rho(\mathbf{F}_i, \mathbf{F}_k)/h & \text{for } \rho(\mathbf{F}_i, \mathbf{F}_k) < h \\ 0 & \text{otherwise} \end{cases} \tag{3}$$

Then we have from (1)

$$M_0 = n - \frac{1}{h}\sum_{j=1}^{n}\rho(F_0, F_j) \text{ and}$$

$$M_k = \sum_{\substack{j=1, \\ j \ne k}}^{n}\left(1 - \frac{\rho(F_k, F_j)}{h}\right) = n - 1 - \frac{1}{h}\sum_{j=1}^{n}\rho(F_k, F_j) \tag{4}$$

In this way the difference between M_0 and M_k is

$$M_0 - M_k = n - \frac{1}{h}\sum_{j=1}^{n}\rho(F_0, F_j) - \left[n - 1 - \frac{1}{h}\sum_{j=1}^{n}\rho(F_k, F_j)\right]$$

$$= 1 - \frac{1}{h}\sum_{j=1}^{n}[\rho(F_0, F_j) - \rho(F_k, F_j)] \tag{5}$$

$$M_0 - M_k > 0 \text{ if } h > \sum_{j=1}^{n}[\rho(F_0, F_j) - \rho(F_k, F_j)] \tag{6}$$

If this condition is satisfied, then the central pixel is considered as not disturbed by the noise process, otherwise the pixel $\mathbf{F}_i$ for which the cumulative similarity value achieves maximum, replaces the central noisy pixel. In this way the filter replaces the central pixel only when it is really noisy and preserves the original undistorted image structures. The parameter h can be set experimentally (Fig. 5a) or can be determined adaptively using the technique described in [6].

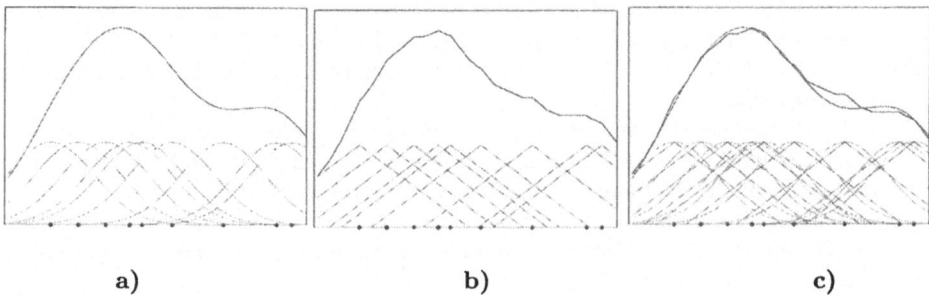

a)   b)   c)

Fig. 1. Cumulative similarity values dependence on the pixel gray scale value for a window containing a set of pixels with intensities $\{15, 24, 33, 41, 45, 55, 72, 90, 95\}$, (see Fig. 2), using the μ_0 function (a) and μ_7 function (b). Plot (c) shows the comparison of the total similarity functions M_0 when using two different kernels

3   Results and Conclusions

For evaluation purposes, the color test image *LENA* was corrupted with impulsive noise defined by $\mathbf{x}_{ij} = \mathbf{v}_{ij}$ with probability p, where i, j define a pixel position, p describes the intensity of the noise process, $\mathbf{x}_{ij}$ denotes the original image pixel and $\mathbf{v}_{ij}$ denotes a pixel corrupted by the noise process $\mathbf{v}_{ij} = \{\nu_R, \nu_G, \nu_B\}$, where ν_R, ν_G, ν_B are random integer variables from the interval $[0, 255]$ updated for each corrupted pixel.

The root of the mean squared error (RMSE), peak signal to noise ratio (PSNR), normalized mean square error (NMSE) [1,2] were used for the analysis. The comparison shows that the new filter outperforms by far the standard vector median filter, which can be treated as a reference filter, and other filters listed in Tab. 1a). The efficiency of the new filtering technique is shown in Tab. 1b), in Figs. 3, 4 and also in Fig. 5b) and 5c).

The new algorithm presented in this paper can be seen as a fast modification and improvement of the Vector Median Filter. The comparison with standard color image processing filters, (Tab. 1b, Fig. 3-5) shows that the new filter outperforms the standard procedures used in color image processing. Another advantage of the proposed filtering class is its lower computational complexity compared to the VMF, which makes the new filter class interesting for real-time applications

References

[1] I. Pitas, A. N. Venetsanopoulos, 'Nonlinear Digital Filters : Principles and Applications', Kluwer Academic Publishers, Boston, MA, (1990)

[2] K. N. Plataniotis, A. N. Venetsanopoulos, 'Color Image Processing and Applications', Springer Verlag, (June 2000)

[3] I. Pitas, P. Tsakalides, Multivariate ordering in color image processing, IEEE Trans. on Circuits and Systems for Video Technology, 1, 3, 247-256, (1991)

[4] J. Astola, P. Haavisto, Y. Neuovo, Vector median filters, IEEE Proceedings, 78, 678-689, (1990)

[5] K. N. Plataniotis, D. Androutsos, A. N. Venetsanopoulos, Colour Image Processing Using Fuzzy Vector Directional Filters, Proceedings of the IEEE Workshop on Nonlinear Signal/Image Processing, Greece, 535-538, (1995)

[6] B. Smolka, A. Chydzinski, K. Wojciechowski, K. Plataniotis, A. N. Venetsanopoulos, On the reduction of impulsive noise in multichannel image processing, Optical Engineering, vol. 40, no. 6, pp. 902-908, 2001.

[7] D. W. Scott, "Multivariate Density Estimation", New York, John Wiley, 1992

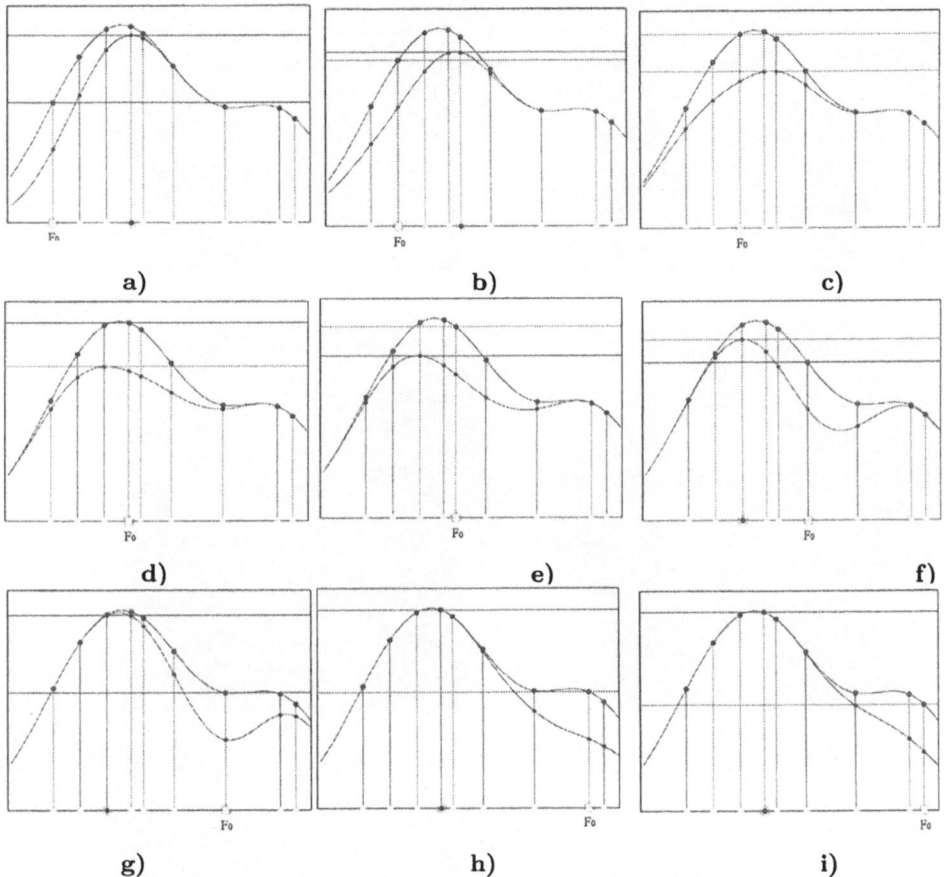

Fig. 2. Illustration of the new filter construction using the Gaussian kernel. The supporting window W of size 3×3 contains 9 pixels of intensities $\{15, 24, 33, 41, 45, 55, 72, 90, 95\}$, (see Fig. 1). Each of the graphs from **a)** to **i)** shows the dependence of M_0 and $M_{/0}$, $(M_{/0} < M_0)$, where $M_{/0}$ denotes the cumulative similarity value with rejected central pixel F_0 on the pixel gray scale value. Graph **a)** shows the plot of M_0 and $M_{/0}$ for $F_0 = 15$, plot **b)** for $F_0 = 24$ and so on till plot plot **i)** which shows the graphs of M_0 and $M_{/0}$ for $F_0 = 95$. The arrangement of pixels surrounding the central pixel F_0 is not relevant. The central pixel will be replaced in cases: (**a**), (**b**), (**f**)- (**i**), as in those cases there exists a pixel F_i for which $M_0 < M_i$

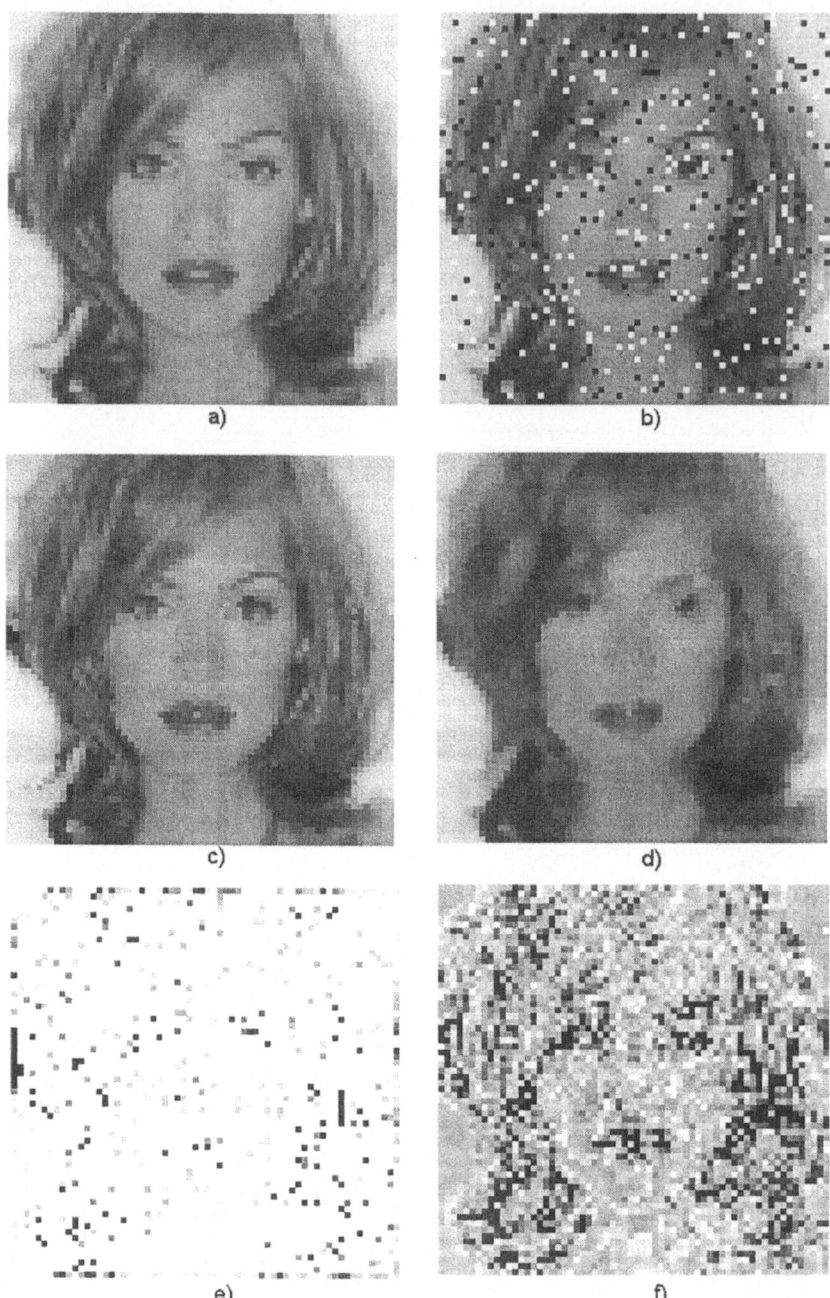

Fig. 3. Illustration of the efficiency of the new algorithm of impulsive noise reduction in gray scale images: **a)** test image, **b)** image corrupted by 4% impulsive *salt&pepper* noise, **c)** new filter output, **d)** effect of median filtering (3×3 mask), **e)** and **f)** the difference between the original and restored images

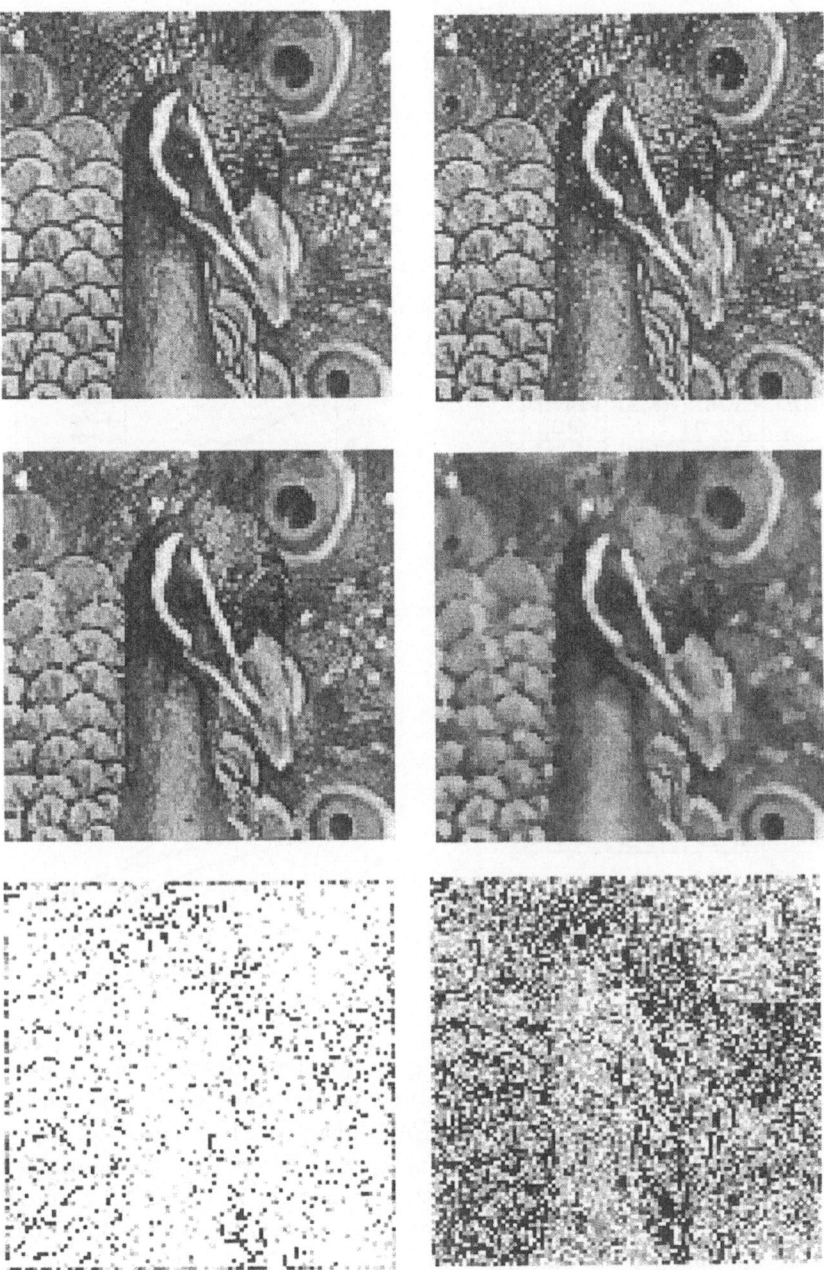

Fig. 4. Illustration of the efficiency of the new algorithm of impulsive noise reduction in color images: **a**) test image, **b**) image corrupted by 4% impulsive *salt&pepper* noise, **c**) new filter output, **d**) effect of median filtering (3×3 mask), **e**) and **f**) the difference between the original and restored images

Notation	Filters [1-2]
AMF	Arithmetic Mean
VMF	Vector Median
ANNF	Adaptive Nearest Neighbor
BVDF	Basic Vector Directional
HDF	Hybrid Directional
AHDF	Adaptive Hybrid Directional
DDF	Directional-Distance
FVDF	Fuzzy Vector Directional

a)

METHOD	NMSE $[10^{-4}]$	RMSE	PSNR [dB]
NONE	514.95	32.165	17.983
AMF	82.863	12.903	25.917
VMF	23.304	6.842	31.427
ANNF	31.271	7.926	30.149
BVDF	29,074	7.643	30.466
HDF	22.845	6.775	31.513
AHDF	22,603	6,739	31.559
DDF	24.003	6.944	31,288
FVDF	26.755	7.331	30.827
FILTERING KERNELS			
$\mu_0(x)$	5.056	3.103	38.137
$\mu_1(x)$	4.959	3.157	38.145
$\mu_2(x)$	5.398	3.294	37.776
$\mu_3(x)$	9.574	4.387	35.288
$\mu_4(x)$	5.064	3.190	38.054
$\mu_5(x)$	4.777	3.099	38.307
$\mu_6(x)$	11.024	4.707	34.675
$\mu_7(x)$	**4.693**	**3.072**	**38.384**

b)

	L_1	L_2	L_3	L_∞
$\mu_1(x)$	3,615	**3,157**	3,172	3,462
$\mu_5(x)$	3,579	**3,099**	3,167	3,694
$\mu_7(x)$	3,838	**3,072**	3,138	3,752

c)

Table 1. Filters taken for comparison **a)**, comparison of the new algorithm based on different kernel functions with the standard techniques, using the *LENA* color image contaminated by 4% of impulsive noise **b)** and evaluation of the efficiency of the new algorithm in terms of RMSE using different vector norms **c)**

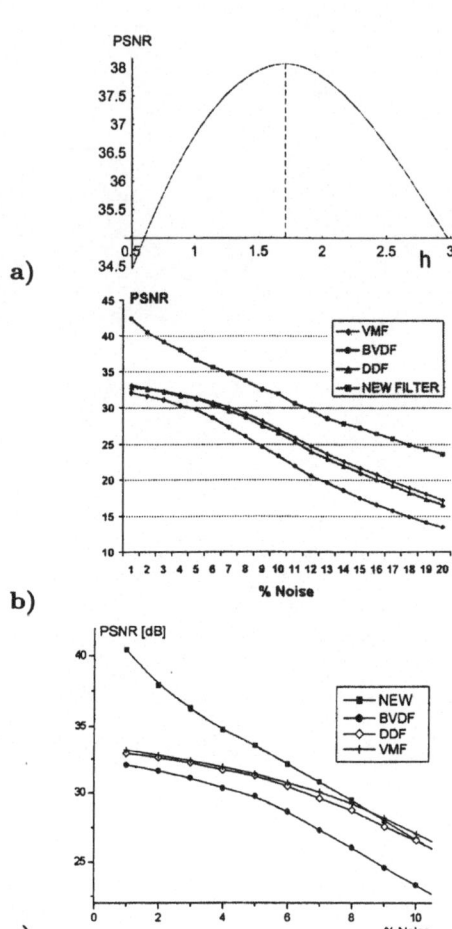

a)

b)

c)

Fig. 5. a) Dependence of the the filtering results on the h parameter, *LENA* image with 12% of corrupted pixels. **b)** Efficiency of the new algorithm in terms of PSNR in comparison with standard filters. The color image *LENA* has been contaminated by impulsive noise with p from 1% to 20% and independently on each channel with p from 1% to 10%, **c)**

On the Nonparametric Impulsive Noise Reduction in Multichannel Images

Bogdan Smolka*

Department of Automatic Control,
Silesian University of Technology,
Akademicka 16, 44-101, Gliwice, Poland

Abstract. This paper presents a new filtering scheme for the removal of impulsive noise in multichannel images. It is based on estimating the probability density function for image pixels in a filtering window by means of the kernel density estimation method. The filtering algorithm itself is based on the comparison of pixels with their neighborhood in a sliding filter window. The quality of noise suppression and detail preservation of the new filter is measured quantitatively in terms of the standard image quality criteria. The filtering results obtained with the new filter show its excellent ability to reduce noise while simultaneously preserving fine image details.

1 Introduction

The reduction of noise in multichannel images has been the subject of extensive research during the last years, primarily due to its importance to color image processing. In order to achieve optimal filtering results, the knowledge of the underlying statistical distribution of the signal and noise are needed. These distributions are often unknown and must be estimated from the data to prevent unrealistic assumptions that deteriorate the filter performance. If no information on the shape of the density distribution is known, non-parametric density estimation can be used, [1, 2]. The filter proposed in this paper is based on the non-parametric technique of *Parzen* or *Kernel Density Estimation* (KDE), [3], which is widely used in the field of pattern recognition and classification.

2 New Filter Design

Let the mapping: $Z^l \rightarrow Z^q$ represents a multichannel image, where l is an image dimension and q characterizes a number of channels ($q = 3$ for color images). Let $W = \{\mathbf{x}_i \in Z^l; i = 0, 1, \ldots, n\}$ represents the samples in the filter window, Fig. 1. Each input vector $\mathbf{x}_i$ can be associated with the cumulative distance measure D_i given by $D_i = \sum_{j=0}^{n} \|\mathbf{x}_i - \mathbf{x}_j\|, i = 0, \ldots, n$, where $\mathbf{x}_i = (x_{i_1}, \ldots, x_{i_q})$ and $\mathbf{x}_j = (x_{j_1}, \ldots, x_{j_q})$ characterize two q-dimensional vectors and $\| \cdot \|$ denotes

---

* Supported by KBN Grant 7T11A01021.

F.J. Perales et al. (Eds.): IbPRIA 2003, LNCS 2652, pp. 979–985, 2003.
© Springer-Verlag Berlin Heidelberg 2003

a chosen vector norm. Since $D_0, D_1, \ldots, D_n$ are scalar values, their ordered set can be written simply as $D_0 \leq D_1 \leq \ldots \leq D_n$. If the same ordering is implied to the input set $\mathbf{x}_0, \ldots, \mathbf{x}_n$, the ordered input set is described as $\mathbf{x}_{(0)}, \mathbf{x}_{(1)}, \ldots, \mathbf{x}_{(n)}$ and the vector median filter (VMF) output is given by the sample $\mathbf{x}_{(0)}$ from the input set that minimizes the sum of vector distances with other vectors, [4].

Density Estimation describes the process of modelling the probability density function $f(x)$ of a given sequence of sample values drawn from an unknown density distribution. The simplest form of density estimation is the histogram: sample space is first divided into a grid, then the density at the center of the grid cells is approximated by the number of sample values that fall into one bin divided by the width of one grid cell. The main disadvantage of the histogram is the strong dependence of the histogram's shape on the chosen bin-width and the origin of the grid.

Kernel Density Estimation, (KDE) avoids this disadvantage by placing a kernel function on every sample value in the sample space and then summing the values of all functions for every point in the sample space. This results in a smooth density estimates that are not affected by an arbitrarily chosen partition of the sample space, Fig. 2.

The multivariate kernel density estimator in the q-dimensional case is defined as [1, 2]

$$\hat{f}_{\mathbf{h}}(\mathbf{x}) = \frac{1}{N} \sum_{i=0}^{n} \frac{1}{h_1 \ldots h_q} \mathcal{K}\left(\frac{x_{i_1} - x_1}{h_1}, \ldots, \frac{x_{i_q} - x_q}{h_q}\right), \tag{1}$$

with $\mathcal{K}$ denoting a multidimensional kernel function $\mathcal{K} \colon \mathbb{R}^q \to \mathbb{R}$ and $h_1, \ldots, h_q$ denoting bandwidths for each dimension and $N = n + 1$ is the number of samples in W. A common approach to build multidimensional kernel functions is to use a *product kernel* $\mathcal{K}(u_1, \ldots, u_q) = \prod_{i=1}^{q} K(u_i)$, where K is a one-dimensional kernel function. Intuitively, the kernel function determines the shape of the 'bumps' placed around the sample values and the bandwidths $h_1, \ldots, h_q$ their width in each dimension. In case bandwidth is equal for all dimensions, multivariate radial-symmetric kernel functions can be used. Equation (1) then changes to

$$\hat{f}_h(\mathbf{x}) = \frac{1}{nh^q} \sum_{i=1}^{n} K\left(\frac{\|\mathbf{x}_i - \mathbf{x}\|}{h}\right). \tag{2}$$

The shape of the approximated density function depends heavily on the bandwidth chosen for the density estimation. Small values of h lead to spiky density estimates showing spurious features. On the other hand too big values of h produce over-smoothed estimates that hide structural features.

The unknown density function is assumed to be the standard normal distribution re-scaled to have the same variance as the sample values. Choosing the Gaussian kernel function for K, the optimal bandwidth is in the one-dimensional case, [2]: $h_{opt} = 1.06\hat{\sigma}n^{-\frac{1}{5}}$, where $\hat{\sigma}$ denotes the standard deviation, and for the q-dimensional case

$$h_{opt} = (4/(q+2))^{\frac{1}{q+4}} \hat{\sigma}\, n^{-\frac{1}{q+4}}. \tag{3}$$

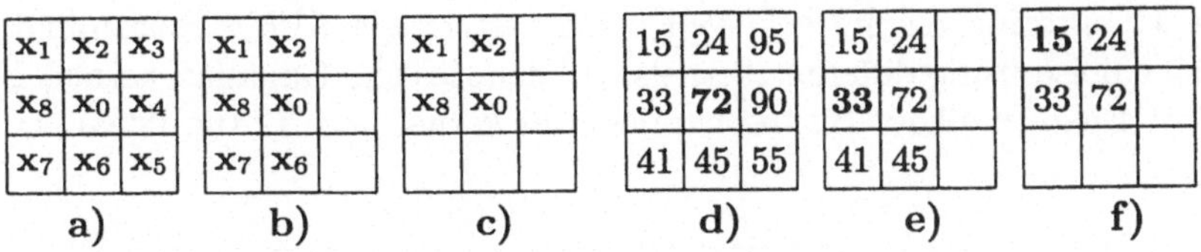

a)

x_1	x_2	x_3
x_8	x_0	x_4
x_7	x_6	x_5

b)

x_1	x_2
x_8	x_0
x_7	x_6

c)

x_1	x_2
x_8	x_0

d)

15	24	95
33	**72**	90
41	45	55

e)

15	24
33	72
41	45

f)

15	24
33	72

Fig. 1. Illustration of the adjacency concept: **a)** the central pixel x_0 has 8 neighbors belonging to the filtering window, **b)** the pixel x_8 has then 5 adjacent neighbors and the pixel x_1 has only three adjacent neighbors contained in W, **(c)**. Below an example of the filtering window with gray scale intensities related to Fig. 3 is shown, **(d - f)**

The proposed filter is based on the idea of comparing image pixels contained in a filter window with their adjacent pixels. The filter output is that pixel in the filter window that is most similar to its neighborhood. The estimated probability density function therefore serves as a measure of similarity in the chosen color space, [5, 6]. If a pixel is similar to its neighborhood, the density estimation for that pixel results in a relatively large value. Noisy pixels on the other hand are almost always outliers from the cluster formed by adjacent pixels. Hence the density estimation for that pixels results in very small values.

Given a set W of noisy image samples $x_0, x_1, ..., x_n$ from the filter window W let $\sim$ denotes the adjacency relation between two pixels contained in W. Assuming the 8-neighborhood system, the central pixel will have 8 adjacent neighbors, the pixels in the corners will have 3 adjacent neighbors and the remaining pixels in W will have 5 adjacent neighbors determined by the $\sim$ relation, (see Fig. 1).

The probability density for sample x_i is then estimated as

$$\hat{f}_h(x_i) = \sum_{x_j \sim x_i} K\left(\frac{||x_j - x_i||}{h}\right). \tag{4}$$

The filter output is defined as that x_i for which $\hat{f}_h$ is maximal, (see Fig. 3). In contrast to Eq. (2) the probability density is not normalized to bandwidth and number of sample values. The reason is that the values of $\hat{f}_h$ for different x_i are only used for comparison among each other and omission of normalization results in a significant performance gain as it privileges the central sample, which has the largest number of neighbors, (Fig. 1 a, d).

The bandwidth is determined according to Eq. (3) and hence depends on the standard deviation $\hat{\sigma}$. Since $\hat{\sigma}$ is computed using only a few pixels from the filter window, the bandwidth is sensitive to noise and may vary over a big range of values. As an option an experimentally chosen fixed value can be used as bandwidth to avoid this effect, (Fig. 4).

3 Filtering Results

For evaluation purposes, the color test image *LENA* was corrupted with 1 to 10 percent impulsive noise defined by $x_{ij} = v_{ij}$ with probability p, where i, j define

Table 1. Filtering results achieved using test image *LENA* contaminated by impulsive noise using different kernels, (*G* denotes the Gaussian kernel, *Ep* the kernel of Epanechnikov, *Ex* the exponential kernel and *Tr* the linear, triangle kernel)

Noise p [%]	0.05	0.05	0.05	0.10	0.10	0.10
Criterion	MAE	MSE	NCD	MAE	MSE	NCD
Noisy	2.54	393.3	0.0415	5.10	790.2	0.0838
VMF	**3.27**	**31.2**	**0.0387**	**3.42**	**34.2**	**0.0400**
BVDF	3.81	39.8	0.0400	3.95	44.2	0.0412
DDF	3.39	32.8	0.0389	3.51	35.4	0.0400
HDF	3.42	31.2	0.0399	3.55	33.9	0.0412
G, L_2, ad.	0.79	11.5	0.0093	0.98	20.2	0.0125
G, $h = 55$	0.42	11.8	0.0051	0.79	20.8	0.0100
G, L_1, ad.	0.82	14.8	0.0101	1.16	24.9	0.0149
Ep, L_2, ad.	1.17	15.3	0.0138	1.23	21.7	0.0151
Ex, L_2, ad.	0.43	10.59	0.0055	0.84	34.16	0.0128
Tr, L_2, ad.	0.45	14.01	0.0063	0.96	50.79	0.0159

a pixel position, p describes the intensity of the noise process, x_{ij} denotes the original image pixel and v_{ij} denotes a pixel corrupted by the noise process $v_{ij} = \{\nu_R, \nu_G, \nu_B\}$, where ν_R, ν_G, ν_B are random integer variables from the interval $[0, 255]$ updated for each corrupted pixel.

The filter quality is measured using the *Mean Absolute Error* (MAE), *Mean Square Error* (MSE) and *Normalized Color Difference* (NCD), [7]. In general, these criteria reflect the filter capabilities of the signal detail preservation (MAE), the noise suppression (MSE) and the color chromaticity preservation (NCD).

Tab. 1 and Fig. 5 show the results of a quantitative comparison between the new filter scheme and the Vector Median Filter as well as the Basic Vector Directional Filter (BVDF), Hybrid Directional Filter (HDF) and the Directional Distance Filter (DDF), [7].

For experiments with fixed bandwidth an experimental value of $h = 55$ was chosen, which brought subjectively good but not optimal results, (Fig. 4). As can be seen from Tab. 1 the noise reduction capability depends on the choice of the filter kernel. Apart from the sometimes up to a few times lower MAE and NCD values compared with the vector median, the new filter shows enormous improvements in detail preservation for every used filter structure. The remarkably good results for the density estimation with fixed bandwidth indicate that the presented method of adaptive bandwidth selection does not work well enough and further research on this problem is needed.

4   Conclusions

The experimental results show that the biggest advantage of the new filter is its excellent image detail preservation (Fig. 6). The always very low values of

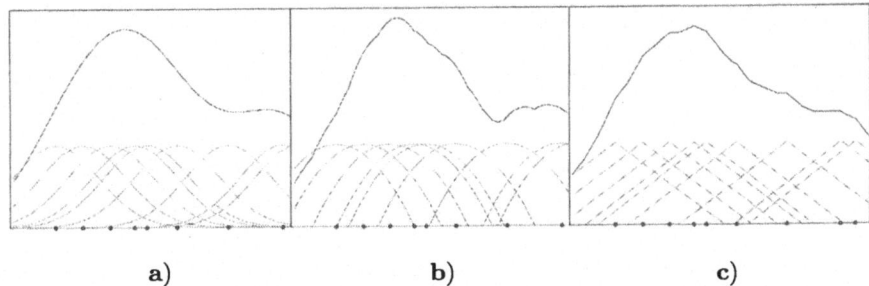

a)   b)   c)

Fig. 2. Illustration of the concept of nonparametric kernel density estimation using the sample values from Fig. 1 d). Figure **a)** shows the density estimation for the sample set $\{15, 24, 33, 41, 45, 55, 72, 90, 95\}$ using the Gaussian kernel: $(\sqrt{2\pi})^{-1} \exp\{-x^2/2\}$, using the kernel of Epanechnikov: $(3/4)(1 - x^2)$ for $h \leq 1$, and Fig. **c)** shows the estimation using the linear (triangular) kernel

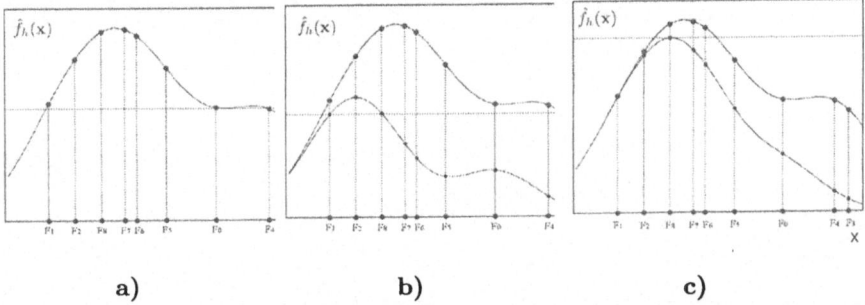

a)   b)   c)

Fig. 3. Density estimation plot for in case of a filtering window consisting of pixels shown in Fig. 1, **a)** and additional plots of the kernel density estimation algorithm using the $\sim$ neighborhood concept for F_1, **b)** and F_8 **c)**. As can be seen the highest value of the density estimation is obtained for F_8 and this pixel will replace the central noisy pixel F_0

MAE and NCD show that the new filter is clearly superior to VMF, BVDF and DDF in terms of detail preservation for all applied filter settings. Further, the comparison of different filter settings shows that the problem of choosing the bandwidth adaptive to the sample data is not yet completely solved and should be investigated in the future work.

Another advantage of the proposed filtering class is its low computational complexity compared to the VMF. For the VMF filtering the calculation of 36 distances between pixels are needed, whereas the new filter structure with fixed bandwidth requires only 20 different distances, which makes the new filter class interesting for real-time applications

984   Bogdan Smolka

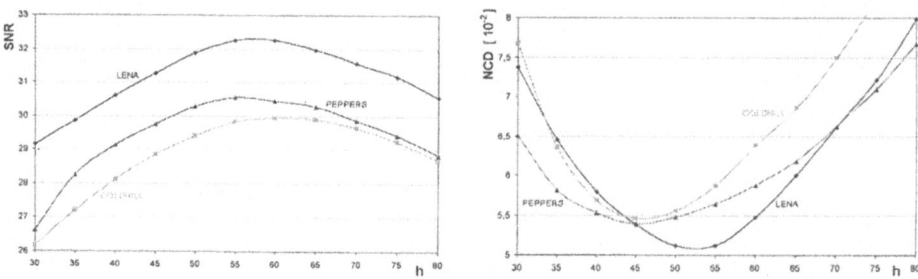

Fig. 4. Dependence of the filter efficiency (SNR and NCD) on the global, constant bandwidth of the Gaussian kernel, for test images *LENA, PEPPERS, GOLDHILL* contaminated by 5% impulsive noise. The value of $h = 55$ was used for the comparison with standard filtering techniques shown in Tab. 1

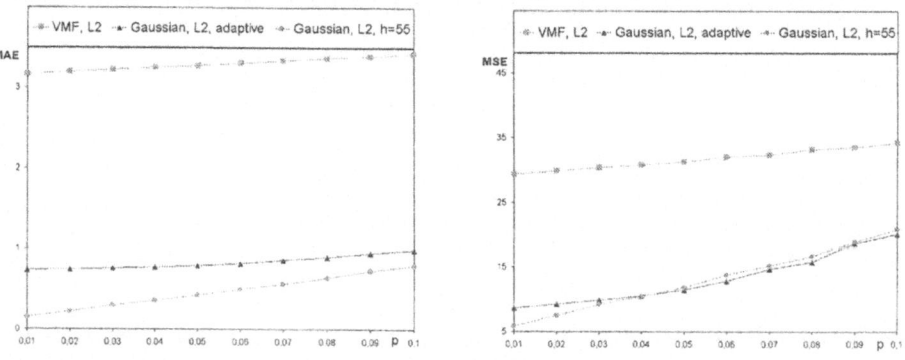

Fig. 5. Results obtained with the new filtering technique in terms of MAE and MSE. The plots show the new filter performance in comparison with the vector median filter

References

[1] B. W. Silverman, "Density Estimation for Statistics and Data Analysis", London, Chapman and Hall, 1986
[2] D. W. Scott, "Multivariate Density Estimation", New York, John Wiley, 1992
[3] E. Parzen, On estimation of a probability density function and mode, Ann. Math. Stat., Vol. 33, 1065-1076, 1962
[4] J. Astola, P. Haavisto, Y. Neuovo, Vector median filters, IEEE Proc. 78, 678-689, 1990
[5] A. Fotinos, N. Laskaris, G. Economou, S. Fotopoulos, Multidimensional fuzzy filtering using statistical parameters, Multidimensional Systems and Signal Processing, 10, 415-424, 1999
[6] D. Sindoukas, N. Laskaris, S. Fotopoulos., Algorithms for color image edge enhancement using potential functions, IEEE Signal Processing Letters, Vol. 4, No. 9, September 1997
[7] K. N. Plataniotis, A. N. Venetsanopoulos, "Color Image Processing and Applications", Springer Verlag, August 2000

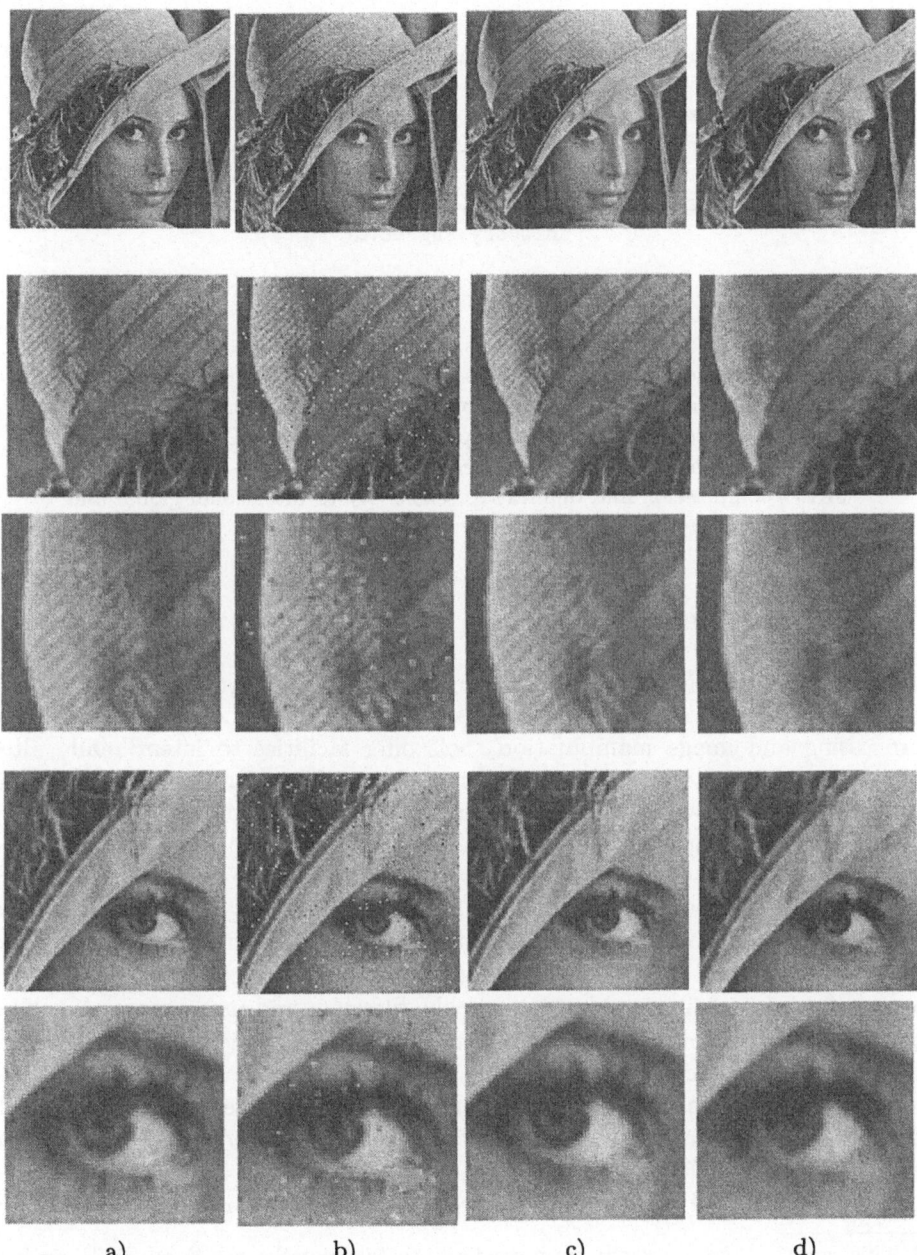

a)   b)   c)   d)

Fig. 6. Illustration of the efficiency of the new filter in comparison with the VMF: **a)** parts of the test image *LENA*, **b)** test images corrupted by impulsive noise with $p = 0.05$, **c)** new filter output using the Gaussian kernel and the adaptive scheme, **d)** VMF output

Robust Hash Functions for Visual Data: An Experimental Comparison*

Champskud J. Skrepth[1][**] and Andreas Uhl[1,2]

[1] Carinthia Tech Institute, School of Telematics & Network Engineering
Primoschgasse 8, A-9020 Klagenfurt, Austria
[2] Salzburg University, Department of Scientific Computing
Jakob-Haringerstr.2, A-5020 Salzburg, Austria
uhl@cosy.sbg.ac.at

Abstract. Robust hash functions for visual data need a feature extraction mechanism to rely on. We experimentally compare spatial and transform domain feature extraction techniques and identify the global DCT combined with the cryptographic hash function MD-5 to be suited for visual hashing. This scheme offers robustness against JPEG2000 and JPEG compression and qualitative sensitivity to intentional global and local image alterations.

1 Introduction

The widespread availability of multimedia data in digital form has opened a wide range of possibilities to manipulate visual media. In particular, digital image processing and image manipulation tools offer facilities to intentionally alter image content without leaving perceptual traces. Therefore, it is necessary to provide ways of ensuring integrity other than human vision.

Classical cryptographic tools to check for data integrity like the cryptographic hash functions MD-5 or SHA are designed to be strongly dependent on every single bit of the input data. While this is desirable for a big class of digital data (e.g. executables, compressed data, text), manipulations to visual data that do not affect the visual content are very common and often necessary. This includes lossy compression, image enhancement like filtering, and many more. All these operations do of course change the bits of the data while leaving the image perception unaltered.

To account for this property of visual data new techniques are required which do not assure the integrity of the digital representation of visual data but its visual appearance. In the area of multimedia security two types of approaches have been proposed to satisfy those requirements in recent years: semi-fragile

---

* This work has been partially supported by the Austrian Science Fund FWF, project no. P15170.
** This artificial name represents a group of students working on this project in the framework of the multimedia 1 laboratory (winterterm 2001/2002).

F.J. Perales et al. (Eds.): IbPRIA 2003, LNCS 2652, pp. 986–993, 2003.

watermarking and robust multimedia hashes (see [1, 2, 3, 6] for some examples of the latter approach).

Main advantages of semi-fragile watermarking schemes are that watermarks are inserted into the image and become integral part of it and that image manipulations may be localized in most schemes. The main advantage of hashing schemes is that image data is not altered and not degraded at all.

In this work we focus onto robust visual hash functions to provide a means to protect visual integrity of image data. In particular, we propose to combine the extraction of robust visual features with the application of a classical cryptographic hash function to result in a robust visual hash procedure. In section 2 we first discuss requirements of a robust visual hashing scheme. Subsequently, we introduce several possibilities to extract perceptually relevant visual features in the spatial and transform domain. In section 3, we experimentally evaluate robustness against JPEG 2000 and JPEG compression and sensitivity towards intentional image modification of visual hashing schemes based on the feature extraction techniques proposed in section 2 and the cryptographic hash function MD-5. Section 4 concludes our paper and provides an outlook to future work in this direction.

2   Approaches to Robust Visual Hashing

Robust hash functions for image authentication have to satisfy 2 major requirements. First, for perceptually identical images, the hash values should be identical. Second, for perceptually different images, the hash values should be different. This requirement also implies that given an image, it is almost impossible to find a visually different image with identical hash value. In other words, it should be impossible to create a forgery which results in the same hash value as the original image.

In addition to these two requirements there is another often requested property. There should exist a metric between the hash values of two images under consideration which could serve as a measure of similarity between those images, i.e. should give a quantitative result instead of the qualitative result of a cryptographic hash function. Although desirable from the applications viewpoint, this property excludes cryptographic hash functions as possible components of such schemes. As a consequence, several visual hashing schemes with increased functionality in the abovementioned sense but at least questionable security properties have been suggested.

Our approach investigated in this work therefore basically consists of two steps:

- First, features robust to common (non-hostile) image processing operations (we especially focus onto compression) but sensitive to malicious modifications are extracted from the image.
- Subsequently, a classical hash function is applied to those features.

In the following subsections, we introduce the types of feature extraction techniques which are experimentally compared for their robustness against compression and sensitivity towards intentional image modifications in this study. Note that for simplicity we assume 512×512 pixels images with 8 bit/pixel (bpp).

2.1 Spatial Domain Feature Extraction Techniques

Multiresolution Pyramids As a first step we construct a quater-sized version of the image ("approximation") using a 4-pixel average (AV), a 4-pixel median (ME), or subsampling by 2 in each direction (DS). Subsequently, the construction of the approximation is iterated to construct smaller versions. An approximation of specific size is used as feature. Whereas the bitdepth is not influenced by these operations (AV is rounded to integer) we only obtain a limited number of differently sized approximations the hash function may be applied to: 256^2 values for one iteration, 128^2 values after two iterations, ..., and $16^2 = 256$ values after five iterations which is the maximal number of iterations we consider.

Bitplanes We consider the 8bpp data in the form of 8 bitplanes, each bitplane associated with a position in the binary representation of the pixels. The feature extraction approach is to consider a subset of the bitplanes only, starting with the bitplane containing the MSB of the pixels. Each possible subset of bitplanes may be chosen as feature, however, it makes sense to stick to the order predefined by the significance of the binary representation. After having chosen a particular subset of bitplanes, the hash function is applied to pixel values which have been computed using the target bitplanes only. Note that the smallest amount of data the hashing may be applied to (i.e. one bitplane) corresponds to 32768 pixels in this case (1/8 of the total number of pixels in the image). Note also that this feature extraction technique BP comes for free from a computational point of view.

2.2 Transform Domain Feature Extraction Techniques

In contrast to spatial domain methods the feature extraction operation (i.e. the transform) increases the bitdepth of the data significantly. To obtain comparability to the spatial domain techniques, the range of coefficients is mapped to the interval [0,255] and subsequently rounded to integer values.

DCT The DCT is well known to extract global image characteristics efficiently and is used for watermarking applications for these reasons (see e.g. Cox's scheme). We use the DCT in two flavours: as full frame DCT (DCT1) and as DCT applied to 8×8 pixels blocks (DCT2) due to complexity reasons. Following the zig-zag scan order (compare e.g. JPEG) we apply the hash-function to a certain number of coefficients or a certain number of coefficients from each block, respectively. Given a 512×512 pixels image and using DCT2, the lowest number of coefficients the hash function may be applied to is 4096 (i.e. the DC coefficient is hashed only for each block), whereas the number of coefficients subjected to hashing may be set almost arbitrarily with DCT1.

Wavelet Transform In many applications wavelet transforms (WT) compete with and even replace the DCT due to their improved localization properties (e.g., the WT is used in many watermarking schemes). We use the Haar transform due to complexity and sensitivity reasons. Equivalently to the Multiresolution pyramids, the decomposition depth is a parameter for this method, in case of WT the hash function is applied to the approximation subband only. As it is the case for Multiresolution pyramids, we only obtain a limited number of differently sized approximation subbands the hash function may be applied to. Note that the data subject to hashing resulting from applying the WT is equivalent in principle to that obtained by the Multiresolution pyramid AV.

3 Experiments

The aim of the experimental section is to investigate whether the introduced visual hashing schemes are

- indeed robust to JPEG and JPEG2000 compression and
- sensitive to intentional image modifications (i.e. attacks).

3.1 Experimental Settings

We use the classical 8bpp, 512×512 pixels Lena and Escher grayscale images (see Fig. 2.a for the latter) as testimages. In order to investigate the robustness of the visual hashing schemes, we subject the image Lena to JPEG 2000 (J2K) and JPEG compression with different compression ratios (Cr). The sensitivity to intentional and/or malicious image modifications is assessed by conducting a couple of local and global image alterations:

- Adding a small artificial birthmark to Lenas upper lip (Fig. 1.a, "augmented Lena") - local
- Applying Stirmark [4] attack options b and i (Fig. 1.b and Fig. 1.c) - global
- Increase or decrease the luminance of each pixel of the image Lena by a value of 5 - global
- Addition of an alternating dark/light pattern in a door arch in Eschers painting (Fig. 2.b) - local

All feature extraction schemes are implemented using MATLAB®, as hash function we use the well known MD-5 [5] system giving 128 output hashbits. Note that MD-5 may be applied to a certain number of feature values given in full 8bpp precision ("Full") or to feature values with reduced bitdepth by simply ignoring the bits of lower significance (where e.g. 3 BP stands for three bitplanes and MSB for the use of the most significant bitplane only).

(a) Augmented Lena   (b) Stirmark attack b=20   (c) Stirmark attack i=20

Fig. 1. Local and global attacks against Lena

3.2 Experimental Results

In table 1 we display the minimal number of feature values required to detect global attacks against the Lena image using multiresolution pyramids AV, ME, and DS. Note that the smallest number considered is $16^2 = 256$ which corresponds to 5 iterations of constructing approximations to the image. A larger entry in the table corresponds to higher robustness against the type of attack (desired or not) as indicated in the leftmost column. In this table we consider only the three most significant bitplanes.

We notice robustness to a certain extent against JPEG 2000 and JPEG compression. For example, J2K compression is not detected using 16^2 features

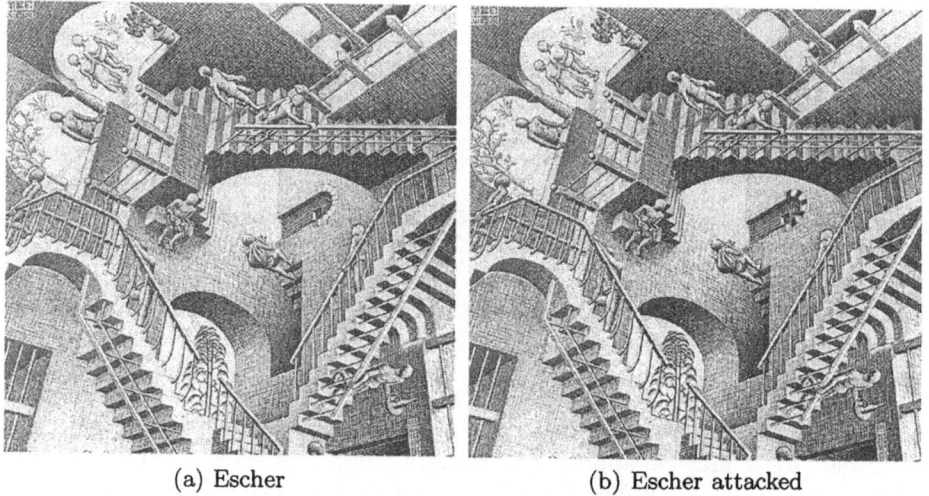

(a) Escher   (b) Escher attacked

Fig. 2. Local attack against a painting by Escher

Table 1. Minimal number of feature values required to detect the global attacks: Multiresolution pyramids

Attack	AV			ME			DS		
	3 BP	2 BP	MSB	3 BP	2 BP	MSB	3 BP	2 BP	MSB
J2K Cr 2	16^2	32^2	64^2	16^2	16^2	64^2	16^2	16^2	64^2
J2K Cr 6	16^2	32^2	32^2	16^2	16^2	32^2	16^2	16^2	16^2
J2K Cr 14	16^2	16^2	32^2	16^2	16^2	16^2	16^2	16^2	16^2
JPEG Cr 1.7	64^2	64^2	64^2	16^2	32^2	32^2	32^2	32^2	32^2
JPEG Cr 2.9	64^2	64^2	64^2	16^2	16^2	16^2	16^2	16^2	16^2
JPEG Cr 7.6	32^2	32^2	32^2	16^2	16^2	16^2	16^2	16^2	16^2
Fig. 1.b b=2	16^2	16^2	16^2	16^2	16^2	16^2	16^2	16^2	16^2
Fig. 1.c i=2	16^2	16^2	16^2	16^2	16^2	16^2	16^2	16^2	16^2
Lum +5	16^2	16^2	16^2	16^2	16^2	16^2	16^2	16^2	16^2
Lum -5	16^2	16^2	16^2	16^2	16^2	16^2	16^2	16^2	16^2

up to Cr 6 using 2 bitplanes and up to Cr 14 using the MSB only when employing AV. JPEG compression is not even detected using 32^2 features up to Cr 3 and 16^2 features up to Cr 7.6 even when employing three bitplanes and AV. ME and DS are less robust against compression as compared to AV.

Now let us consider malicious modifications. On the one hand, sensitivity against Stirmark attacks and luminance modifications is high as being desired. For example, choosing AV as multiresolution pyramid and selecting the MSB of 16^2 feature values (i.e. 5 decompositions) is robust against all compression settings considered and reveals all global attacks discussed.

On the other hand, the situation changes when we investigate the sensitivity against local attacks as displayed in table 2.

Especially in case of the augmented Lena image we notice extremely low sensitivity against this attack. Choosing again AV as multiresolution pyramid and selecting the MSB of 16^2 feature values there is no way to detect this attack (even when using 4 bitplanes we already require 32^2 feature values to detect it). The situation is even worse regarding ME and DS. In case of the Escher image the result is not that bad but the sensitivity of multiresolution pyramid based hashing is comparable to that against compression which is of course not desirable.

Table 2. Minimal number of feature values required to detect the local attacks: Multiresolution pyramids

Figure	Fig. 1.a			Fig. 2.b		
	AV	ME	DS	AV	ME	DS
Full	16^2	32^2	128^2	16^2	16^2	32^2
4 BP	32^2	256^2	128^2	16^2	16^2	32^2

Table 3. Minimal number of feature values required to detect the attacks: DCT1

Attack	Full	7 BP	6 BP	5 BP	4 BP	3 BP	2 BP	MSB
J2K Cr 2	40	40	54	54	>200	>200	>200	>200
J2K Cr 10	40	40	40	40	162	>200	>200	>200
J2K Cr 14	40	40	40	40	79	79	174	>200
JPEG Cr 1.7	55	65	131	>200	>200	>200	>200	>200
JPEG Cr 6.1	54	54	65	65	65	>200	>200	>200
JPEG Cr 13	40	40	40	65	65	174	174	175
Fig. 1.a	40	40	40	43	43	72	**72**	175
Fig. 1.b b=2	4	4	4	4	4	4	4	4
Fig. 1.c i=2	40	40	40	41	41	41	41	54
Lum +5	2	2	2	2	2	2	2	2
Lum -5	2	2	2	2	2	2	2	2
Fig. 2.b	4	4	4	4	4	4	4	65

When turning to bitplanes as a means to feature extraction it turns out immediately that there is no way to make such a scheme robust to compression at all. Even the slightest degradation is propagated to some extent to the MSB information causing the hash function to identify the compressed image as being tampered with.

Now we turn to the transform domain. In table 3 we display the results concerning the full frame DCT (DCT1). In contrast to the multiresolution pyramids, the number of feature values may be varied continously. Even when using full 8bpp precision for the feature values we still require 40 values to detect a J2K compression with Cr 14, the same is true for JPEG compression with Cr 13. Consequently we may state that robustness against compression may be achieved.

Sensitivity against intentional attacks, on the other hand, is satisfactory for all types of attacks. Especially for luminance modification, but also for most settings regarding Stirmark attack b and the modified Escher image the alterations are detected using 4 feature values or even less. Also for the remaining attacks sensitivity is always higher as against the strongest compression considered. As a consequence, we may define DCT1 based visual hash functions which are sensitive to all attacks considered but robust to moderate compression. As a concrete example, we could use 2 bitplanes of 80 feature values. In this case the number of feature values to detect J2K and JPEG compression is significantly higher (174 in either case of maximal compression) and therefore this hash function is also robust against even more severe compression. On the other hand, all considered attacks are revealed including the augmented Lena which is detected using 72 feature values (displayed boldface in the table).

Contrasting to the visual hash function based on DCT1, we could not achieve any robustness against compression for DCT2. Therefore, as it is the case for the bitplane approach, it makes no sense to investigate the sensitivity against intentional tampering. Note that both techniques, bitplanes and DCT2, produce a much higher number of feature values (even using their lowest parameter, i.e. MSB or one coefficient per block, respectively) as compared to the other schemes which definitely is the reason for their higher responsiveness.

Finally we focus onto the wavelet transform. Due to the equivalence to the Multiresolution pyramid AV (see previous section), the results are almost identical to this method and are therefore not discussed further.

4   Conclusion

We have found that global DCT seems to be the most suitable feature extraction approach to base a robust visual hash function upon if robustness against moderate compression is a prerequisite for such a scheme. Although the computationally most demanding approach, the robustness against JPEG2000 and JPEG compression and the responsiveness to intentional global and local image alterations exhibited by the DCT based system are by far superior as compared to the competing wavelet transform and multiresolution pyramid based schemes. Visual hash functions based on block-based DCT and selective bitplane hashing have failed to provide robustness against compression.

References

[1] Jiri Fridrich and Miroslav Goljan. Robust hash functions for digital watermarking. In *Proceedings of the IEEE International Conference on Information Technology: Coding and Computing*, Las Vegas, NV, USA, March 2000.

[2] T. Kalker, J. T. Oostveen, and J. Haitsma. Visual hashing of digital video: applications and techniques. In A. G. Tescher, editor, *Applications of Digital Image Processing XXIV*, volume 4472 of *Proceedings of SPIE*, San Diego, CA, USA, July 2001.

[3] M. Kivanc Mihcak and Ramarathnan Venkatesan. A tool for robust audio information hiding: a perceptual audio hashing algorithm. In *Proceedings of the 4th Information Hiding Workshop '01*, Portland, OR, USA, April 2001.

[4] Fabien A. P. Petitcolas, Caroline Fontaine, Jana Dittmann, Martin Steinebach, and Nazim Fatès. Public automated web-based evaluation service for watermarking schemes: Stirmark benchmark. In *Proceedings of SPIE, Security and Watermarking of Multimedia Contents III*, volume 4314, San Jose, CA, USA, January 2001.

[5] B. Schneier. *Applied cryptography (2nd edition): protocols, algorithms and source code in C*. Wiley Publishers, 1996.

[6] Ramarathnam Venkatesan, S.-M. Koon, Mariusz H. Jakubowski, and Pierre Moulin. Robust image hashing. In *Proceedings of the IEEE International Conference on Image Processing, ICIP '00*, Vancouver, Canada, September 2000.

Error Concealment Using Discontinuity Features

NamRye Son and GueeSang Lee*

Department of Computer Science, Chonnam National University
300 Youngbong-dong, Buk-gu, Gwangju 500-757, Korea
{nrson,gslee}@chonnam.ac.kr

Abstract. In transmitting compressed video bit-stream over Internet, packet loss causes error propagation in both spatial and temporal domain, which in turn leads to severe degradation in image quality. In this paper, a new error concealment algorithm is proposed to repair damaged portions of the video frames in the receiver. Conventional BMA(Boundary Matching Algorithm) assumes that the pixels on the boundary of the missing block and its neighboring blocks are very similar, but has no consideration of edges across the boundary. In our approach, the edges are detected across the boundary of the lost or erroneous block. Once the orientation of each edge is found, only the pixel difference along the expected edges across the boundary is measured instead of the calculation of differences between all adjacent pixels on the boundary. Therefore, the proposed approach needs very few computations and the experiment shows an improvement of the performance over the conventional BMA in terms of both subjective and objective quality of video sequences.

1 Introduction

Hybrid block based MC/DPCM/DCT algorithm has been adopted in several international video coding standards such as the ITU-T H.261, H.263, MPEG-1,2,4,7[1, 2]. Typical applications include video conferencing, video phone and digital TV. For most of these applications, the bitstream will be transmitted over a communication channel where bit error or packet loss sometimes is inevitable. In recognizing the need to provide reliable video communications, error concealment methods have been developed and they play an important role as we find more and more applications of digital video over packet networks and wireless channels.

Due to the coding structure of the hybrid block based MC/DPCM/DCT coding algorithms, Motion Vectors(MVs) is crucial in reconstructing the predicted frames. For example, if one block's variable length coded motion vector is lost by a burst error, the error propagates until a new resynchronization is occurred. These prevalent video coding schemes use a row of MBs(macroblocks), called slice(in MPEG-2) or GOB(in H.26x), as the minimal resynchronization unit. Thus the effect of one erroneous block is spread out to the end of underlying

---

* Corresponding author

F.J. Perales et al. (Eds.): IbPRIA 2003, LNCS 2652, pp. 994–1002, 2003.

slice in spatial domain. In addition, a motion compensation scheme employs the images in the previous frame, an erroneous block has an influence on afterward frames until the next new Intracoded frame(I-picture) appears.

Among many robust video coding schemes, the error concealment technique is considered as one of the most effective ways to give error resiliency to the system, which is used either in sole or together with other robust video coding approaches. In most cases, existing error concealment algorithms fall into two categories. The first one is the technique in which the DCT coefficients, partially lost or erroneously, are recovered[3]. Secondly, lost MBs are compensated by the recovered motion vector based on the boundary matching criterion[4].

In this paper, we propose a new error concealment method which recovers the MV of lost or corrupted MBs in inter-frame. Once a MV is recovered, the image in the previous frame(motion compensated image) is taken to replace the corrupted MB[7, 8].

BMA has been proved to be one of the most effective solutions to the problem, in which a fixed number of candidate MVs are examined and the one which results in the minimum pixel variations at the boundaries of the lost block and the neighboring blocks is selected[4]. Since it assumes the adjacent pixels are highly correlated, it provides a good performance when the edges are horizontally or vertically oriented along the boundaries of the erroneous MB. However, it may perform poorly with edges of arbitrary orientations. To deal with such problems, a modified BMA has been proposed[5]. But, it requires very high computations and more than that, it assumes that all edges across a MB boundary has same directions, which may not be true in many cases. We propose algorithms for the detection of edges across the boundaries of the erroneous MB and the decision of edge directions which are used in measuring distortions of the image found by the candidate MV.

In section 2, the ideas in the conventional BMA and the modified BMA are briefly overviewed and the proposed algorithms are given in section 3. Experimental results are shown in section 4 and conclusions follow.

2   Related Works

2.1   Boundary Matching Algorithm (BMA)

Boundary Matching Algorithm aims that the corrupted block is replaced by the most feasible block of the previous frame by means of strong correlations among the neighboring pixels[3]. This concept basically can be explained by the smoothness constraint measure[6]. Let the top-left pixel (p, q) denote the first pixel of $N \times N$ MB X in Fig. 1, and assume that the Variable Length Coded(VLC) data for MB X is confused by a random bit error or burst error. Thus some macro blocks after MB X are lost until the next synchronization codeword is occurred. To recover each corrupted MB, the missing block is replaced by an image block from the previous frame which is found by a candidate MV and the distortion d_S is computed as shown in equation (1).

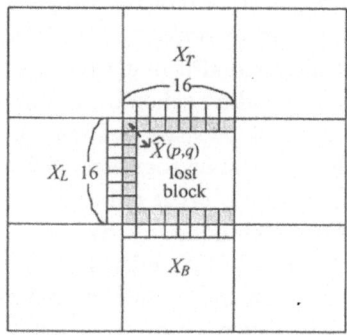

Fig. 1. BMA(Boundary Matching Algorithm)

$$d_L = \sum_{i=0}^{N-1} \left[\hat{X}(p,i) - X_L(p-1,i) \right]^2$$

$$d_T = \sum_{i=0}^{N-1} \left[\hat{X}(i,q) - X_T(i,q-1) \right]^2$$

$$d_B = \sum_{i=0}^{N-1} \left[\hat{X}(i,q+N-1) - X_B(i,q+N) \right]^2$$

$$d_S = d_L + d_T + d_B \tag{1}$$

The set of candidate MVs are usually composed of the MV of :

1) The same block in the previous frame
2) Neighboring blocks available (Top, Left and Bottom blocks)
3) Median of the available neighboring blocks
4) Average of the available neighboring blocks
5) The ZERO MV

In this candidate set, a MV which results in the minimum error d_S is finally selected as the MV for the lost MB.

2.2 A Modified BMA

Since the differences of the neighboring pixels are computed along the boundary of the erroneous MB for the distortion measure, BMA works well when there are no specific edges across the boundary or there are edges vertically located across the boundary. However, in most cases diagonal or anti-diagonal edges exist across the boundary and the computation of errors on the boundary in BMA may deviate severely from the exact distortion measure. To solve this problem, a modified BMA(MBMA) is proposed which considers different edge orientations in computing the boundary difference[5]. One of the three edge orientations, diagonal, anti-diagonal and horizontal(vertical), is decided by equation (2), by which pixel differences along the boundary are computed. For example, if E_{Ld} produces the highest value in equation (2), left diagonal edges dominate over other edge orientations on the boundary of the erroneous MB. Now the pixel differences are computed between pixels located left-diagonal across the boundary as shown in Fig. 2.

$$E_{Ld} = \frac{1}{N-1} \sum_{i=0}^{N-2} [X_L(p+i, q-1) - X_L(p+i+1, q-2)]^2$$

$$E_{La} = \frac{1}{N-1} \sum_{i=0}^{N-1} [X_L(p+i, q-1) - X_L(p+i-1, q-2)]^2$$

$$E_{Lh} = \frac{1}{N-1} \sum_{i=0}^{N-1} [X_L(p+i, q-1) - X_L(p+i, q-2)]^2 \qquad (2)$$

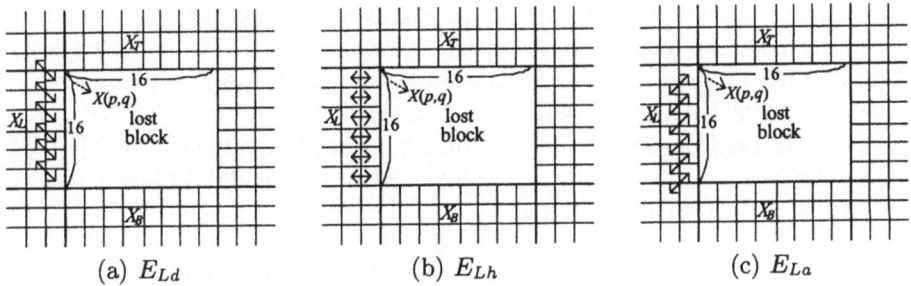

(a) E_{Ld} (b) E_{Lh} (c) E_{La}

Fig. 2. Decision of edge orientations at the boundary

3 Proposed Approach

MBMA requires high computations and more than that, it assumes that all edges across a MB boundary has same directions or at least one of the edge orientation dominates over others, which may not be true in many cases. We propose a simple algorithm for the detection of every edge across the boundaries of the erroneous MB. When the orientation is decided for each edge, the pixel difference between pixels which lie across the boundary along the detected orientation is computed and added to the total distortion of the candidate image block. In this way, each edge is considered separately along the boundary and only the pixel differences along the edges are added to the distortion, leading to very few computations. Details of our proposed approach for reconstructing the lost block in interframe(P-frame) are described as follows.

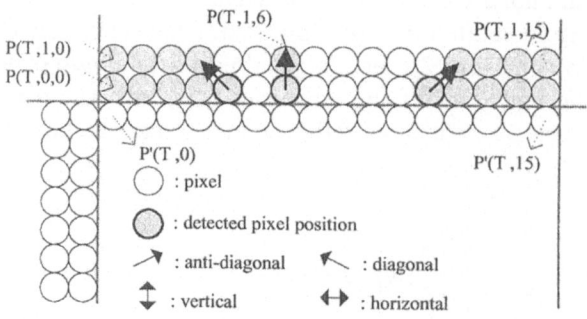

Fig. 3. Detection Method of edge

Step 1) Boundary Selection: Select a boundary of the erroneous or lost MB. If all the boundaries between a normal MB and the lost MB have been considered, the algorithm terminates.

Step 2) Edge detection: Scanning the pixels just outside of the boundary, calculate the difference between adjacent pixels on the boundary of the neighboring block as in eq. 3 and shown Fig. 3. If the difference is greater than a *threshold*, we assume that an edge is detected. $P(K,p,q)$ denotes the pixel value of the $[p,q]$ th pixel in the 32 pixels outside of the lost MB in the direction of K, where K=T(Top), L(Left) or B(Bottom). Note that K has been selected in step 1). P'(K,q) denotes the pixel value of the $[q]$ th pixel in the 16 pixels just inside of the lost MB in the candidate image as shown in Fig. 3.

$$diff = |P(k,0,q-1) - P(k,0.q)|, \; q = 0,15 \qquad (3)$$

Step 3) Decision of edge orientations across the boundary: Now if a candidate image is presented by a candidate motion vector, the distortion value is calculated along the edge direction detected in step 2) using eq. 4. Fig 4. shows the edge orientations detected. If there are more boundaries to be selected go to step 1).

$$\text{(a)direction} : |P(K,p+1,q-1) - P(K,p,q)|$$
$$\text{(b)direction} : |P(K,p+1,q) - P(K,p,q)|$$
$$\text{(c)direction} : |P(K,p+1,q+1) - P(K,p,q)| \qquad (4)$$

Step 4) Measuring distortion: Assuming that the lost or erroneous MB is replaced by an image block from the previous frame by a candidate MV, the difference between pixel $P(K,p,q)$ in Fig. 4 and the pixel P'(K,q) inside the lost MB located along the edge orientation is computed, which is added to the total distortion.

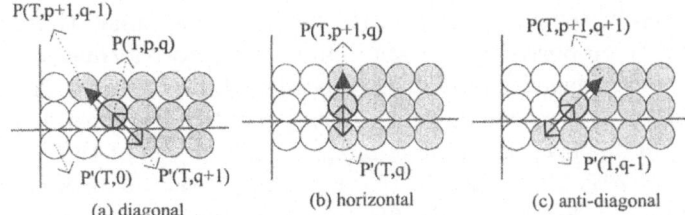

Fig. 4. Decision of edge direction and distortion

Step 5) Measuring edge misalignment: To improve the accuracy of the measurement of edge distortion, the amount of edge misalignment is computed as shown in Fig. 5. When the edge is not placed correctly in the candidate image, the edge is further searched to measure the displacement d which is the amount of misalignment. To accomplish this step, the edge in the candidate image should be traced until the desired edge is detected. In the real implementation, only a few neighboring pixels are searched for simplicity. For example, in Fig. 5(b), the displacement of the detected edge in the candidate image is measured to the left of the expected edge position. The weighted amount of the misalignment d is added to the distortion measure.

Step 6) If the pixel is not the last pixel on the boundary of the lost MB, goto step 4). Otherwise, terminate.

Step 1) through step 3) is carried out for the detection of edges and their orientations. Step 4) through step 6) is applied to measure the distortion for each candidate MV. The candidate MV which results in the smallest distortion measure will be selected for the recovery of the lost MB.

4 Simulation Results

Experiments are carried out with H.263 video coder. Three QCIF test sequences, Suzie, Mother&Daughter, and Foreman with a Block Error Rate(BER) of 5% $\sim$ 20% are used for the experiment. To simulate the effect of transmission over practical communication channels, errors are introduced randomly in MBs or

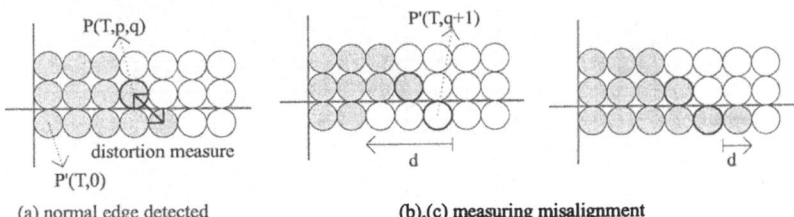

Fig. 5. Measuring edge misalignment

GOBs. Note that sometimes GOBs can be lost since the loss of a GOB header implies the loss of the whole data in the GOB. It is assumed that the concealment process is supported by an appropriate transport format which helps to identify lost or damaged blocks at the decoder. Table 1 shows the comparison of the quality of the recovered images using BMA, MBMA and the proposed method. Fig. 6 displays an example image of 46th frame of the Suzie sequence recovered from 20% block loss. In Fig. 6(c),(e),(g), the distortions incurred by each algorithm are shown and Fig. 6(d),(f),(h) displays enlarged images of some recovered blocks.

In terms of PSNR, the proposed method is about to $0.1 \sim 1(dB)$ better than BMA and outperforms MBMA in most cases. In terms of processing time for the recovery of missing or erroneous MV, the proposed algorithm works faster than MBMA because of two aspects. Firstly, for the edge detection, the proposed approach scans the pixels just above the boundary of the missing or erroneous block, it takes about 1/3 of the calculations needed in MBMA since MBMA calculates the sum of pixel differences along the 3 edge directions. The computation of edge distortion along the detected edge orientations are not of much overhead and can be ignored in comparing the performance, since usually few edges are detected along the boundary pixels. Secondly, scanning for the edge detection is needed only once without respect to the number of candidate motion vectors in the proposed approach. But in MBMA the calculation of pixel differences has to be carried out for every candidate MV. Suppose that k candidate MVs are used for the error concealment, the proposed approach works k times faster than MBMA. In total, the proposed approach can perform $3k$ times faster than MBMA at best.

Table 1. List of PSNR for the Test Sequences

Image	BER(%)	BMA	MBMA	Proposed
Foreman #272	5	35.02	35.11	35.11
	10	34.79	34.98	34.98
	15	34.62	34.63	34.66
	20	32.85	34.25	34.38
Mother& Daughter #15	5	52.65	53.61	53.61
	10	52.21	52.65	52.75
	15	52.45	52.53	52.65
	20	50.63	50.68	50.69
Suzie #46	5	47.39	47.85	47.85
	10	44.26	45.28	45.30
	15	44.05	45.17	45.48
	20	43.51	43.98	44.88

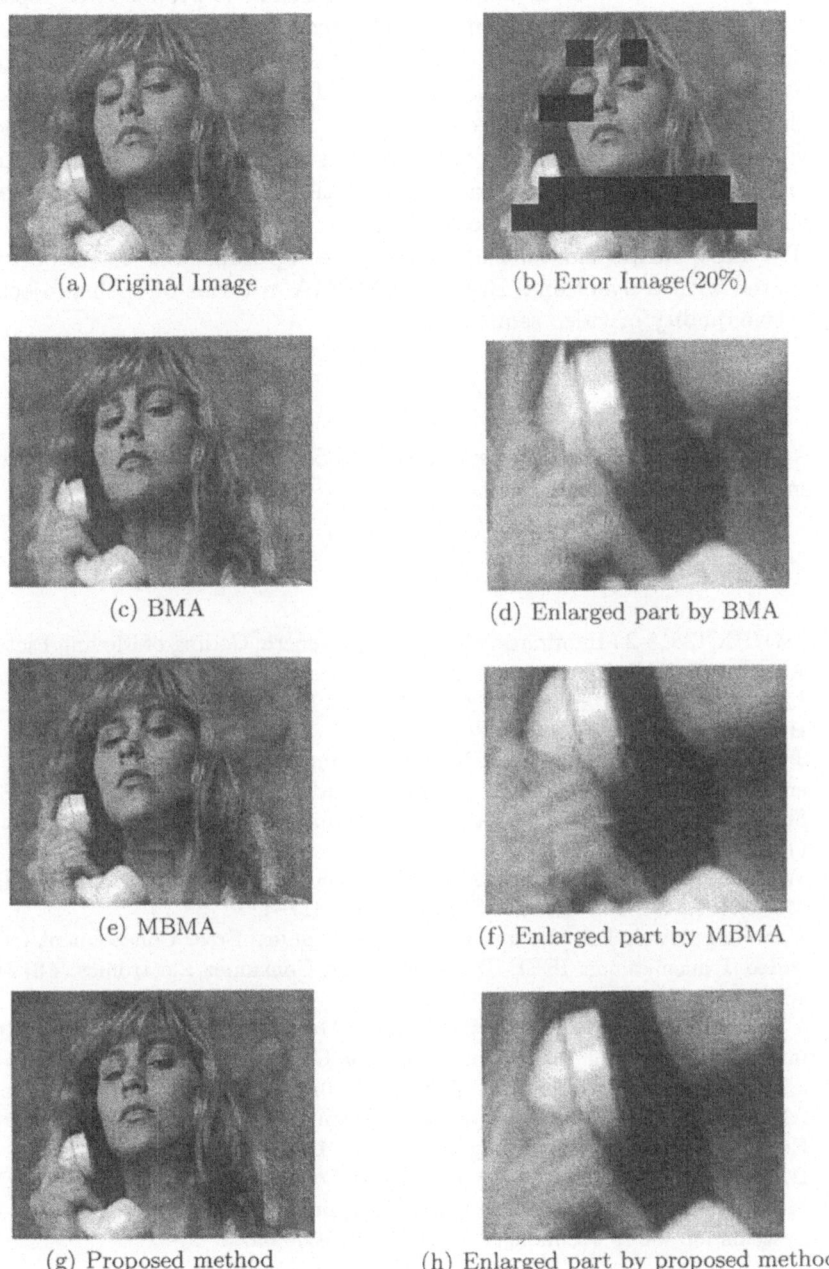

(a) Original Image

(b) Error Image(20%)

(c) BMA

(d) Enlarged part by BMA

(e) MBMA

(f) Enlarged part by MBMA

(g) Proposed method

(h) Enlarged part by proposed method

Fig. 6. Reconstructed images using different computation methods

5   Conclusion

In this paper, a new error concealment algorithm is proposed to repair damaged portions of the video frames in the receiver. Conventional BMA has no consideration for the direction of edges across the boundary. In our approach, the edges are detected across the boundary of the lost or erroneous block and its neighboring blocks. Once the edge direction is decided for each edge detected, only the pixel differences along the expected edges are measured, which results in very few computations, instead of calculating differences between all adjacent pixels on the boundary of the lost block.

The experiments showed that the proposed approach has better performance compared with conventional BMA and MBMA in terms of both subjective and objective quality of video sequences.

Acknowledgement

This work was supported by grant No. R05-2000-000-002800 from the Korea Science & Engineering Foundation.

References

[1] ISO/IEC13818-2.: Information Technology Generic Coding of Moving Pictures and Associated Audio. Draft International Standard. (1994)
[2] ITU-T Recommendation H.263 Version 2, ITU-T SG-16.: Video Coding for Low Bitrate Communication. (1997)
[3] Jong Wook Park, Jong Won Kim and Sang Uk Lee.: DCT Coefficient Recovery Based Error Concealment Technique and its Application to the MPEG-2 Bit Stream Error. IEEE Transactions on Circuits Systems for Video Technology 7 (1997) 845–854
[4] W.-M. Lam, A. R. Reibman, and B. Lin.: Recovery of Lost or Erroneously Received Motion Vectors. In Proc. ICASSP. 5 (1993) 417–420
[5] Jian Feng, Kwok-Tung Lo and Hanssna Mehrpour.: Error Concealment for MEPG Video Transmissions. IEEE Transactions on Consumer Electronics. 43(2) (1997) 183–187
[6] Y. Wang, Qin-Fan Shu and Leonard Shaw.: Maximally Smoothness Image Recovery in Transform Coding. IEEE Transactions on Communications. 41 (1993) 1544–1551
[7] J. S. Hwang, D. K. Park, C. S. Won, J. C. Jung, and S. Y. Kim.: A Concealment Algorithm Based on the Analysis of Transmission Errors or H.263 Bitstream. In Proc. Korean Signal Processing conference. 10(1) (1997) 555–558
[8] H. C. Shyu and J. J. Leou.: Detection and Concealment of Transmission Errors in MPEG-2 Images - A Genetic Algorithm Approach. IEEE Transactions on Circuits Systems for Video Technology. 9(6) (1999) 937–948

Geometric Properties of the 3D Spine Curve

J. M. Sotoca[1], M. Buendía[2], J. M. Iñesta[3], and F. J. Ferri[4]

[1] Dpto. Lenguajes y Sistemas Informáticos. Universidad Jaime I, Campus Riu Sec,
E-12071 Castellón, Spain
sotoca@lsi.uji.es

[2] Unidad de Biofísica, Dpto de Fisiología. Universidad de Valencia, Av., Blasco
Ibáñez, n° 15, E-46010. Valencia, Spain
mateo.buendia@uv.es

[3] Dpto. de Lenguajes y Sistemas Informáticos. Universidad de Alicante. Campus de
San Vicente, E-03071, Alicante, Spain
inesta@dlsi.ua.es

[4] Dpto. de Informática, Universidad de Valencia, Av. Andrés Estellés s/n, E-46100,
(Burjasot) Valencia, Spain
ferri@uv.es

Abstract. Through a 3D reconstruction of the human back surface using structured light techniques, we study the properties of spine curve by means of a set of parameters related to measures commonly applied in medicine. In this way, descriptors for measuring the abnormalities in the projections of the *front* and *sagittal* planes can be computed. We build the spine curve in 3D and analyse the behaviour of the *Frenet frame* when along the curve the deformation processes in idiophatic scoliosis appear.

Keywords: Biomedical pattern analysis, image analysis, structured light.

1 Introduction

Serious deformities in the human spine are present in the 0.3 percent of the population [5]. The most common deformity is *scoliosis*: an abnormal lateral curvature of the spine of congenital origin or caused by trauma or disease of the vertebrae or hip bones. This is first noticed as a result of the changes that occur in the shape of the human back during the adolescent growing season. The characteristic feature is the disfiguring hump, caused by the rotation of the vertebrae and ribs, that is presented together with a lateral bend of the spine.

In some few cases, the deterioration of the spine occurs quickly, so a prevention of the illness is necessary as soon as possible. Unfortunately, the only means of assessment has been unadvisably frequent x-ray examinations. Through a accuracy clinic visualisation on the back surface of the cosmetic deformity, the illness can be diagnosed and the treatment started, although this deformity already involves an important development of the illness. Aiming at this, several methods of surface shape measurements have been previously used, ranging deformation tests, photographic methods, and direct computer input from a special scanner [7, 12, 13].

F.J. Perales et al. (Eds.): IbPRIA 2003, LNCS 2652, pp. 1003–1011, 2003.
© Springer-Verlag Berlin Heidelberg 2003

In the present work, we describe how a non-invasive method like structured light can be used to detect the illness through the study of the spine deformity to the shape of the back surface. We examine how the vertebral deformities reflect on the back surface and what relation do they have to the information obtained with the x-ray images. We make a reconstruction of the spine curve and explore the projections of the curve in the *front* and *sagittal* planes of the body. The intrinsic parameters of the curve and its corresponding properties are also obtained. We use the nomenclature of Ponsetti and Friedman [8] to classify the different types of scoliotic curves[1].

2   Extraction of the Curve Parameters

2.1   Reconstruction of the Back Surface

Through a method based on structured light [1, 11], we obtain a reconstruction of the back surface by means of the deformation of a known structured pattern that is projected over the objects in the scene (object grid). So, we can obtain the 3D position points of the object surface and make the correspondence between points or regions in smooth surfaces as it is the case of human backs.

In order to establish the deformation, and in addition to the object grid, the utilised procedure requires the digitisation of the images of the grid projected on a flat surface (screen) placed, respectively, behind the object (back grid), and in the front of the object (front grid). This method allows to achieve the correspondence of the grid nodes on the three images (back grid, front grid and object grid) and to obtain the values of z (depths) for the nodes in the object grid. This procedure needs to be made just once for each setup for calibration purposes.

In the surface reconstruction phase, we analyse the list of the nodes in the object grid and calculate the co-ordinates of the intersection points of the straight pattern lines for the front grid and back grid images. This way, we get the positions (x, y, z) of the grid nodes as they are projected on the object and we can build a depth map for the grid nodes on the surface of the human back, as it is observed in Fig. 1. The rest of points on the surface are reconstructed by a parametric approximation. The evaluation of the errors during the measurement process have been estimated in less than 4 %.

2.2   Spine Curve Positioning on the Surface

Once we have the back surface depth map, the objective is to obtain the curve that passes over the vertebrae beneath the skin. Two data sources are utilised to obtain this spine curve:

---

[1] This nomenclature makes a classification of the spine shape according to the position of the principal curve in the *front* plane: cervical-thoracic, thoracic, thoraco-lumbar, double major, and lumbar.

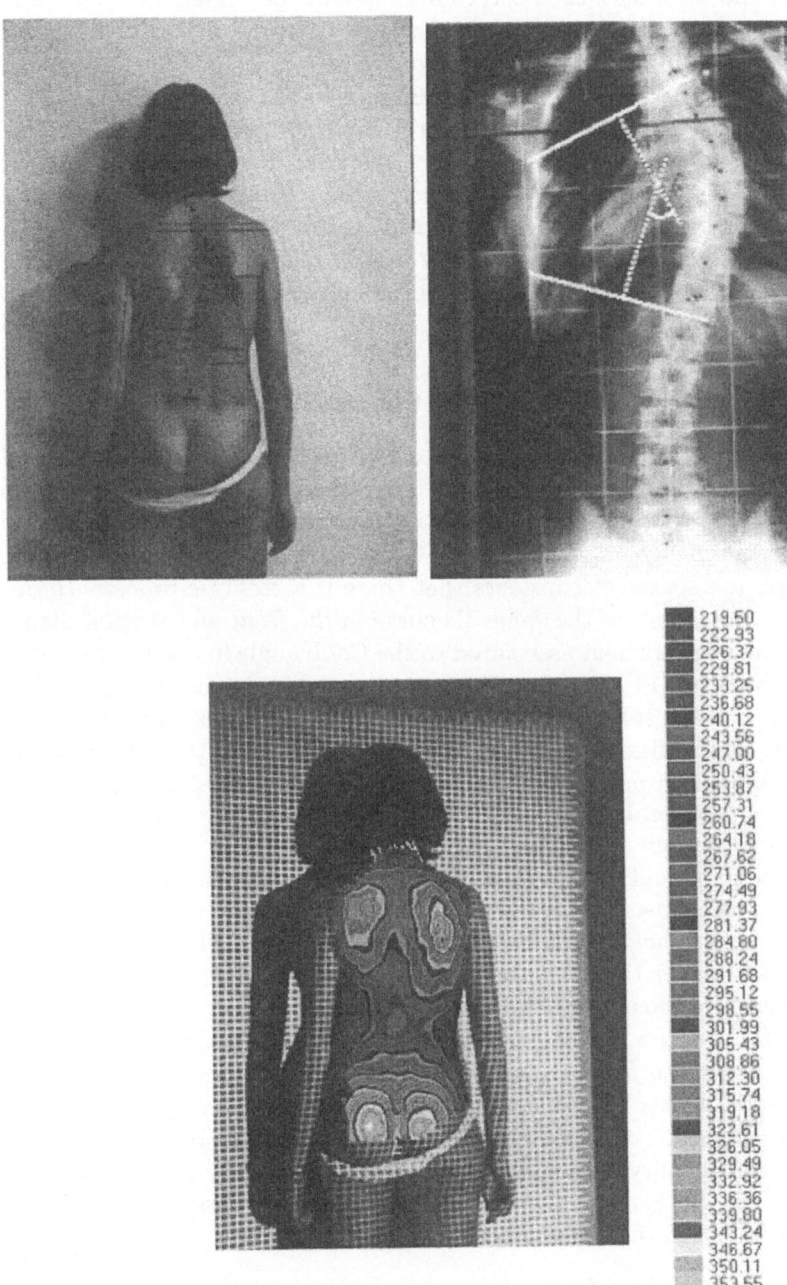

Fig. 1. (Top-left) Clinical image of a patient with a severe thoracic scoliosis. The vertebral spinous processes are marked on the skin. (Top-right) A radiography of the same patient. (Down) Topographic representation of the back surface with the values of z displayed in millimetres (on the right, in colours, not displayed)

1. Locate on the back surface the vertebral spinous processes, from C7, also named the *prominent vertebra*, to the last lumbar vertebra L5[2] (see Fig. 1). In practice, marking the patient takes only one minute and the landmarks can be positioned with an accuracy of ±5 mm.

2. The study of the shape of the spine curve in x-ray images. In this case, we have a real knowledge about the displacements of the vertebrae and their rotations through the projection of the vertebral pedicles. Also, we can locate a centre point for each vertebra in the radiograph (see also Fig. 1) and, by means of an alignment process [3], a transformation of scale, rotation and translation is made to put the points of the spine shape in the x-ray image over our depth map.

2.3   Study of the *Front* and *Sagittal* Planes of the Curve

When the specialists study the x-ray image and assess the lateral displacement of the spine, they utilise the *Cobb angle*, defined as the angle between two vertebral plates: those having a higher and opposite inclination respect to the horizontal plane (see Fig. 1, top-right). So, only if the Cobb angle is larger than 12 degrees in x-ray image, the specialist considers that there is a scoliotic process. In our case, we study projections of the spine 3D curve in the *front* and *sagittal* planes of the body. One measurement associated to the Cobb angle in the *front* plane is the *lateral asymmetry* [14], that is defined as the angle between perpendiculars drawn to the line of the spine at its inflexion points[3]. One problem that appears when detecting these inflexion points is the presence of noise in the control points when an approximation method is applied[4] in the reconstruction of the curve. So, to solve this problem it is necessary to establish which regions in the curve are candidates to contain an inflexion point.

As a first step, we obtain the straight line that joins both extremes in the spine curve and calculate the distance from each point in the curve to the line, fixing a distance threshold of 7 mm as a criterion of normality for the curve. If the distance is bigger than the threshold, we consider that the curve shows a lateral deviation of the spine. The *lateral asymmetry* is given by the absolute value of the sum of two consecutive angles with opposite sign. In Fig. 2(a), the *lateral asymmetry* in the *front* plane is 20.9° in the thoracic region and 13.0° in the lumbar region. Other important angle is the *inclination* angle. This angle quantifies the inclination at the end of the curve in the *front* plane. When this angle is small, the mobility of the L5 vertebra with the sacrum bone compensates this deviation, but if it is severe (> 10 degrees), it causes a possible malfunction of the inferior limbs. In the Fig. 2(a), the *inclination* angle is 5.9°.

---

[2] The vertebrae are enumerated from the head to the hip with the following sequence: Cervical (C1...C7), thoracic or dorsal (D1...D12) and lumbar (L1...L5). The vertebrae C7 and L5 are the extremes of the spine curve considered. Thus, only thoracic and lumbar zones are considered in this work

[3] Given a 2D discrete curve, we define its inflexion points as those where it presents a change in the sign of the curvature.

[4] We apply a cubic B-spline with C_2 continuity.

In the *sagittal* plane, the *kyphosis* angle is measured (curve in the upper back zone) and *lordosis* angle (curve in the lower back). For this, the inflexion points are calculated. In Fig. 2(a) the computed *kyphosis* angle was 49.2° and the *lordosis* angle 45.1°.

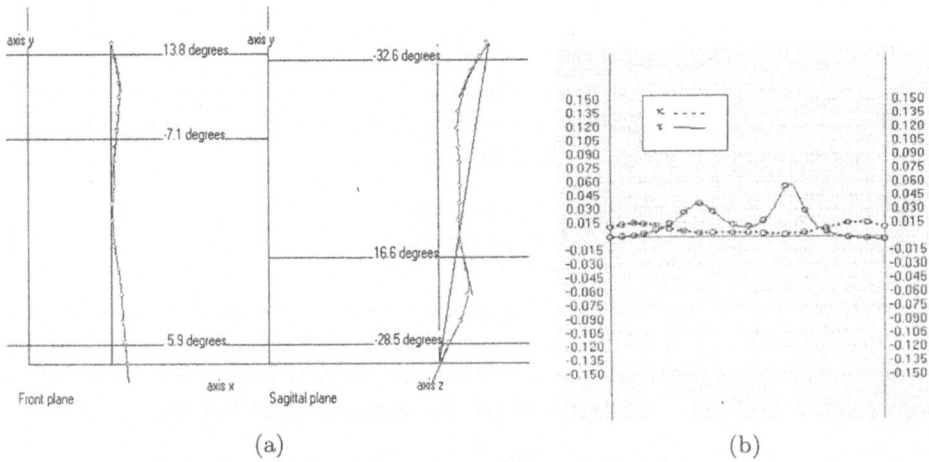

(a)   (b)

Fig. 2. (a) *Front* and *sagittal* planes of the curve for a patient with a thoraco-lumbar scoliosis with thoracic Cobb angle of 24° and lumbar *Cobb* angle of 12°. In the sagittal plane, a flatten zone appears in the transition of the thoracic region to the lumbar region. (b) The dotted line is the *curvature* κ and the solid one is the *torsion* τ. The two peaks that appear in torsion, imply a high rotation in that region of the curve

2.4 Study of the Spine Curve in 3D

Let be $C(u) : [p_i, p_{i+1}] \rightarrow \Re^3, i = 1...n, u \in [0,1]$ a parameterisation of the spine curve. One problem that affects the computation of the invariant parameters of the curve is the existence of errors in the control point positions. So, the curve obtained from the control points must be smooth or the noise of the curvature must be small enough [9, 10]. In our case, we have used a polynomial fitting with regard to the co-ordinates x, y, z and we have computed the coefficients P_x and P_z of the polynomial by least squares, using a threshold in the corresponding correlation index, between the values of the control points and the estimation of the polynomial. The parameterisation of the curve $C(u)$ can be then computerized as:

$$C(u) = \left(\sum_{i=0}^{nx} P_x(i)u^i, u, \sum_{i=0}^{nz} P_z(i)u^i \right) \tag{1}$$

where nx and nz are the degrees of the polynomials. The two invariant parameters in a 3D curve are *curvature* and *torsion*. They can be calculated from an arbitrary parametric curve through the following expressions that use derivatives of the curve parameterisation:

$$\kappa(u) = \frac{||C' \wedge C''||}{||C'||^3} \quad \text{and} \quad \tau(u) = \frac{det[C', C'', C''']}{||C' \wedge C''||} \tag{2}$$

A tangent vector **t** can be defined for each point of the spine curve and the plane that is perpendicular to the curve at that point can also be computed, defining, along with **t**, a natural local reference system called *Frenet frame*. The local system vector is given by the following expressions:

$$\mathbf{t} = \frac{C'}{||C'||} \quad , \quad \mathbf{b} = \frac{C' \wedge C''}{||C' \wedge C''||} \quad , \quad \mathbf{n} = \mathbf{b} \wedge \mathbf{t} , \tag{3}$$

where **b** is the *binormal* vector and **n** is the *normal* vector obtained by a vector product between **b** and **t**. If we consider η and ρ as the angle variations of the vectors **t** and **b**, respectively, we can arrive, by the first order terms of a Taylor expansion, to the following relations for the *curvature* and the *torsion* [6]:

$$\kappa = \frac{\partial \eta}{\partial s} \quad , \quad \tau = \frac{\partial \rho}{\partial s} \tag{4}$$

where s is the arc length. Thus, κ and τ are the angular velocities of **t** and **b**. In this way, the *curvature* gives information about the changes in the orientation of the curve and *torsion* provides information about its rotation. When curves are limited to a plane, the binormal vector is perpendicular to the plane and $\tau = 0$. Through the study of the evolution of κ and τ along the spine curve, we can have a "qualitative description" of how the shape changes affect the properties of the spine curve. With the aim of analysing these variations, Fig. 3 shows a representation of **t**, **b** and **n** in the control points of the curve.

In a normal spine, the curve in the *sagittal* plane has a 'S' shape, with a concave region and other convex one with a point of inflexion where the *torsion* has a peak. This implies a change of direction in the vectors **b** and **n** of about 180°, as can be seen in Fig. 3 (left). The *curvature* also maintains this shape of 'S' and the presence of flatten regions indicates the existence of peaks in the *torsion* as can be seen in Fig. 2(b).

3   Experiments and Results

In this study, we have worked with a sample of 76 patients (42 female and 36 male), where a group of 12 patients, aged from 11 to 18 years, had an idiopathic scoliosis process with the following classification: 4 thoracic, 2 thoraco-lumbar, 1 lumbar and 5 double major curves. For all of them, we made a reconstruction of the surface and a specialist fixed the landmarks on the skin at the detected vertebrae.

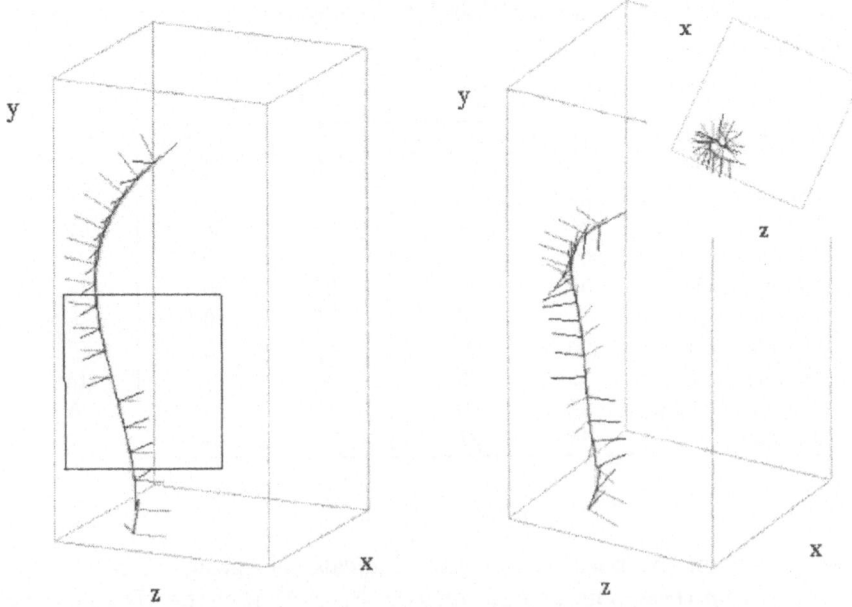

Fig. 3. (Left) A representation of the Frenet frame of a normal spine curve. (Right) Frame evolution for a pathologic spine. In the top-right square, a view from the top is displayed

Some of the studied cases can be observed in the table 1. The spine curve parameters for the thoracic and lumbar regions are displayed both for the *Cobb* angle measured using the classical technique and for the lateral asymmetry extracted through the proposed method. Note that there is a high correlation between the values obtained using both techniques. The correlation index obtained with all the studied cases was $r = 0.89$, being similar to other studies in the literature [4, 14]. This fact supports the diagnostic manually in this measurement.

In the *sagittal* plane, the average value for the *kyphosis* and *lordosis* angles for a group of 30 normal subjects between 12-35 years were 44.5 ± 11.8 and 34.1 ± 10.0 degrees for male and 46.1 ± 11.6 and 39.1 ± 12.6 degrees for female. These values change as a function of age and sex, and allow to establish intervals of normality to detect suspicious cases in the sagittal plane [2].

4   Concluding Remarks and Further Works

We have developed a structured light scheme to obtain a reconstruction of the back function surface. Using this structure, the curve that passes over the main vertebral bodies beneath the skin is obtained, with the aid of a number of land-

Table 1. Values obtained for a number of patients for the Ponsetti classification, the *Cobb* angle, *lateral asymmetry* and its *inclination* angles (all measurements are in degrees)

Curve classif.	Thoracic		Lumbar		
	Cobb	Lat.Asym.	Cobb	Lat.Asym.	inclination
Double major	30	32	20	21	7
Thoracic	50	36	–	–	8
Lumbar	–	–	25	26	12
Thoracic	60	50	28	20	7
Double major	30	26	30	26	14
Double major	18	18	15	16	6
Double major	20	20	15	13	6
Double major	35	25	30	21	12
Thoraco-lumbar	24	20	12	13	6
Thoracic	45	27	–	–	–

marks placed on the back surface that indicate the positions of the spinous processes. From these points, a parametric description of the 3D spine curve is computed.

We have measured some characteristic parameters on the projections of the 3D spine curve in the *front* and *sagittal* planes. We get a description of the deformity of the spine as a function of the *curvature* and *torsion*, from the evolution of the *Frenet frame* along the spine curve.

We have compared this method to a classical measuring method that uses frontal radiographies to measure the spine deviation and obtained good correlations with it. The information obtained by the classical method requires irradiation of the patient and is subjected to human measuring errors.

In this aspect, this work contributes a development in a project of a classifier that uses the information of 3D geometric invariants from the current classifiers based in the front projection of the curve. On the other hand, the obtaining to a automatic reconstruction method without using the manual placing landmarks is under study.

References

[1] Buendía M., Salvador R., Cibrian R. Laguía M. Sotoca J. M.: Determination of the object surface function by structured light: applications to the study of spinal deformities. Med. Phys. Biol. **44** (1999) 75–86

[2] Carr A. J., Jefferson R. J. and Turner-Smith A. R.: Familiar bach shape in adolescent scoliosis. A photogrammetric population study. Acta Orthop. Scand. **62** 2 (1991) 131–135

[3] Cootes T. F., Taylor C. J., Cooper D. H., Grahan J.: Active shape models: Their training and application. Computer Vision and Image Understanding **61** (1995) 38–59

[4] Csongrandi J., Jefferson R. J., Turner-Smith A. R. and Harris J. D.: Surface Topography an spinal deformity IV (eds.): Stokes I. A., Pelelsky I. R., Moreland M. S.
and Fisher G., New York (1988) 21–28

[5] Desmet A. A., Cook L. T., Tarlton M. A.: Assessment of scoliosis using three-
dimensional radiographics measurements. Automedica 4 (1981) 25–36

[6] Farin G.: Curves and surfaces for computer aided geometric design. (eds.): Academic Press, Inc. Harcourt Brace Jovanovich Publishers (1988)

[7] Frobin W., Hierholzer E.: Rasterstereography: a photogrametric method for measurement of body surfaces. Photogrammetric Engineering and Remote Sensing 47
(1982) 1717–1724

[8] Ponsetti I. V. and Friedman B.: Prognosis in idiopathic scoliosis. Journal Bone
Joint Surgery bf 32 A (1950) 381–395

[9] Sapidis N., Kaklis P.: An algorithm for contructing convexity and monotonity
preserving spines in tension. Computer Aided Geometric Design 5 (1988) 127–
137

[10] Sapidis N., Farin G.: Automatic faring algorithm for B-splines curves. Computer
Aided Design 22 (1990) 121–129

[11] Sotoca J. M., Buendía M., Iñesta J. M.: A new structured light calibration method
for large topography. In. Pattern recognition and Applications. Frontiers in Artificial Intelligence and Applications (eds.): Torres M. I. and Sanfeliu A., Amsterdam
(2000) 261–270

[12] Takasaki H.: Moiré Topography. Applied Optics 9 (1970) 1467–1472

[13] Turner-Smith A. R.: A Television/Computer three-dimensional surface shape measurement system. Journal of Biomechanics 21 (1988) 515–529

[14] Turner-Smith A. R., Jefferson R. J.: Analysis and presentation of human back
shape in scoliosis. In. The mathematics of surfaces III (eds.): Handscomb D. C.
Clarendon Press. Oxford (1989) 473–492

Oriented Matroids
for Shape Representation and Indexing

E. Staffetti[1], A. Grau[2], F. Serratosa[3], and A. Sanfeliu[1]

[1] Institut de Robòtica i Informàtica Industrial (CSIC-UPC)
Llorens i Artigas 4-6, 08028 Barcelona Spain
{estaffetti,asanfeliu}@iri.upc.es

[2] Departament d'Enginyeria de Sistemes Automàtica i Informàtica Industrial (UPC)
Pau Gargallo 5, 08028 Barcelona Spain
antoni.grau@upc.es

[3] Departament d' Enginyeria Informàtica i Matemàtiques (URV)
Av. Paisos Catalanes, 26 43007 Tarragona Spain
Francesc.Serratosa@etse.urv.es

Abstract. In this paper a novel method for indexing views of 3D objects is presented. The topological properties of the regions of the segmented images of the objects are used to define an index based on oriented matroid theory. Oriented matroids, which are projective invariants, encode incidence relations and relative position of the elements of the image and give local and global topological information about their spatial distribution. This indexing technique is applied to 3D object hypothesis generation from single views to reduce the number of candidates in object recognition processes.

1 Introduction

In this paper a new method for indexing views of 3D objects is presented. It is applied to 3D object hypothesis generation to reduce the number of candidates in object recognition processes. Given a set of views of different objects, the problem of object recognition using a single image can be regarded as the problem of finding a subset of the set of regions in the image with a relational structure identical to that of a member of the set of views. The standard way to reduce the complexity of model matching is subdividing the problem into a hypothesis generation followed by a verification. To be of interest in object recognition the hypothesis generation should be relatively fast although imprecise in which several possible candidates for matching are generated. In this way the verification can be carried out using a more complex and, therefore, slower procedure [1] over a reduced number of candidates. The hypothesis generation can be made very efficient if it is formulated as an indexing problem where views of a set of 3D objects are stored into a table that is indexed by some function of the views themselves.

In this paper an indexing technique based on oriented matroid theory is presented. More precisely, the topological properties of the regions of the segmented

F.J. Perales et al. (Eds.): IbPRIA 2003, LNCS 2652, pp. 1012–1019, 2003.

views of 3D objects are encoded into a data structure called set of cocircuits. The sets of cocircuits of the different views of a database merged together are used as an index of the database itself. The set of cocircuits, that are one of the several combinatorial data structures called oriented matroids, encode incidence relations and relative position of the elements of the image and give local and global topological information about their spatial distribution. Since index tables are by definition discrete, the discrete nature of the combinatorial structure of the set of cocircuits nicely fits with this technique. This method is employed to the hypothesis generation for 3D object recognition from single views. The principal aspects of oriented matroid theory together with some applications were compiled in 1993 in the comprehensive monograph [2]. For shorter introductions see [3] or [4]. For another approach to shape representation and indexing based on combinatorial geometry see [5].

The paper is organized as follows: in Section 2 oriented matroids are introduced and their invariance properties are illustrated. In Sections 3 the proposed indexing method is described together with the strategy used for hypothesis generation. In Section 4 some experimental results obtained applying the proposed method to 3D object recognition are reported. Finally, Section 5 contains the conclusions.

2   Oriented Matroids

Oriented matroid theory is a broad setting in which the combinatorial properties of geometrical configurations can be described and analyzed. It provides a common generalization of a large number of different mathematical objects usually treated at the level of usual coordinates. In this section oriented matroids will be introduced over arrangements of points using two combinatorial data structures called chirotope and set of cocircuits.

2.1   Oriented Matroids of Arrangements of Points

Given a *point configuration* in $\mathbb{R}^{d-1}$ whose elements are the columns of the matrix $\mathbf{P} = (p_1, p_2, \ldots, p_n)$, the associated *vector configuration* is a finite spanning sequence of vectors $\{x_1, x_2, \ldots, x_n\}$ in $\mathbb{R}^d$ represented as columns of the matrix $X = (x_1, x_2, \ldots, x_n)$ where each point p_i is represented in homogeneous coordinates as $x_i = \binom{p_i}{1}$. To encode the combinatorial properties of the point configuration we can use a data structure called *chirotope* [4] which can be computed using the associated vector configuration X. The *chirotope* of X is the map

$$\chi_X : \{1, 2, \ldots, n\}^d \to \{+, 0, -\}$$
$$(\lambda_1, \lambda_2, \ldots, \lambda_d) \mapsto \text{sign}\left([x_{\lambda_1}, x_{\lambda_2}, \ldots, x_{\lambda_d}]\right)$$

that *assigns to each d-tuple of the vectors of the finite configuration X a sign $+$ or $-$ depending on whether it forms a basis of $\mathbb{R}^d$ having positive or negative

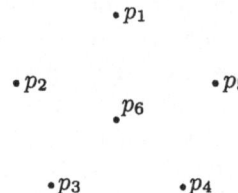

Fig. 1. A planar point configuration

Table 1. Vector configuration that corresponds to the planar point configuration represented in Fig. 1

$x_1 = (0,3,1)$	$x_2 = (-3,1,1)$	$x_3 = (-2,-2,1)$
$x_4 = (2,-2,1)$	$x_5 = (3,1,1)$	$x_6 = (0,0,1)$

orientation, respectively. This function assigns the value 0 to those d-tuples that do not constitute a basis of $\mathbb{R}^d$. The chirotope describes the incidence structure and relative position of the points of the arrangement with respect to the hyperplanes passing through them.

Example 1. Consider the point configuration represented in Fig. 1 whose associated vector configuration X is given in Table 1.

The chirotope χ_X of this vector configuration is given by the orientations listed in Table 2.

The element $\chi(1,2,3) = +$, for instance, indicates that, in the triangle formed by p_1, p_2, and p_3, these points are counterclockwise ordered. These orientations can be rearranged in an equivalent data structure called *set of cocircuits* of X shown in Table 3. In this case, the set of cocircuits of X is the set of all partitions generated by lines passing through two points of the configuration. For example, $(0,0,+,+,+,+)$ means that the points p_3, p_4, p_5, and p_6 lie on the same half plane determined by the line through the points p_1 and p_2. Changing the signs of the set of cocircuits we obtain an equivalent description of the arrangement of points.

Besides chirotopes and sets of cocircuits there are several data structures capable of encoding the combinatorial properties of a point configuration [4]. It

Table 2. Chirotope of the planar point configuration represented in Fig. 1

$\chi(1,2,3) = +$	$\chi(1,2,4) = +$	$\chi(1,2,5) = +$	$\chi(1,2,6) = +$	$\chi(1,3,4) = +$
$\chi(1,3,5) = +$	$\chi(1,3,6) = +$	$\chi(1,4,5) = +$	$\chi(1,4,6) = -$	$\chi(1,5,6) = -$
$\chi(2,3,4) = +$	$\chi(2,3,5) = +$	$\chi(2,3,6) = +$	$\chi(2,4,5) = +$	$\chi(2,4,6) = +$
$\chi(2,5,6) = -$	$\chi(3,4,5) = +$	$\chi(3,4,6) = +$	$\chi(3,5,6) = +$	$\chi(4,5,6) = +$

Table 3. Set of cocircuits of the planar point configuration represented in Fig. 1

$(0,0,+,+,+,+)$	$(0,-,0,+,+,+)$	$(0,-,-,0,+,-)$
$(0,-,-,-,0,-)$	$(0,-,-,+,+,0)$	$(+,0,0,+,+,+)$
$(+,0,-,0,+,+)$	$(+,0,-,-,0,-)$	$(+,0,-,-,+,0)$
$(+,+,0,0,+,+)$	$(+,+,0,-,0,+)$	$(+,+,0,-,-,0)$
$(+,+,+,0,0,+)$	$(-,+,+,0,-,0)$	$(-,-,+,+,0,0)$

can be proven that all of them are equivalent and are referred to as *oriented matroids*.

In the next section a method to represent with an oriented matroid the combinatorial structure of views of three dimensional objects will be presented. It will be used for indexing the image database in which they are stored.

2.2   Oriented Matroid of Arrangements of Regions

Extracting the oriented matroid of a view is not straightforward since the regions that form an image cannot be reduced to points, taking for example their centroids, without losing essential topological information for object recognition. Therefore, in the method presented in this paper the convex hull [6] of each region is used to represent the region itself. Then, pairs of non-overlapped convex regions resulting from this process are considered and their convex hulls are merged. The oriented matroid is extracted based on the spatial location of the other convex regions of the image with respect to the two lines arising when merging the convex hulls of two of them. Consider, for instance, the ordered pair of convex regions (S, T) of the view $v_{1,1}$ of Fig. 3. It is easy to see that the convex hull of these two convex planar non-overlapped polygons is a polygon whose set of vertices is included in the union of the set of vertices of S and T. On the contrary, the set of edges of the convex hull of S and T is not included in the union of their set of edges. Indeed, two new "bridging edges," e_1 and e_2, appear as illustrated in Fig. 2.a. Actually, efficient algorithms for merging convex hulls are based on finding these two edges [7]. Consider the two lines l_1 and l_2 that support e_1 and e_2. They divide the image into three regions, namely the region $\mathcal{R}_{S,T}$ on the right with respect to the pair (S, T), the region $\mathcal{L}_{S,T}$ on the left with respect to the same pair and the region $\mathcal{I}_{S,T}$ comprised between the lines (Fig. 2.b). The shape of the latter varies according to the location of their crossing point with respect to the image. The location of a region U with respect to the ordered couple of regions (S, T) of the image is encoded in the chirotope using a rule derived from the case of planar arrangements of points

$$\chi(S, T, U) = \begin{cases} + & \text{if } U \in \mathcal{L}_{S,T}, \\ 0 & \text{if } U \in \mathcal{I}_{S,T}, \\ - & \text{if } U \in \mathcal{R}_{S,T}. \end{cases}$$

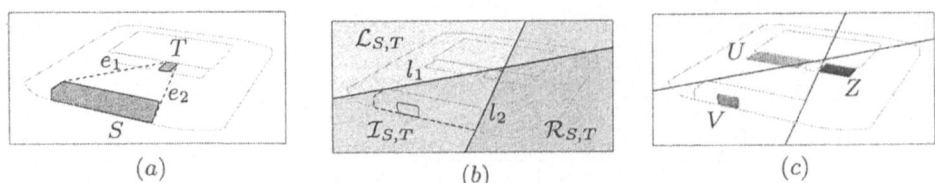

Fig. 2. Steps of encoding of the combinatorial properties of a view of an object into an oriented matroid

It has been implicitly assumed that U is completely contained into either $\mathcal{R}_{S,T}$ $\mathcal{L}_{S,T}$ or $\mathcal{I}_{S,T}$ but in general it can belong to more that one of them. In this case, since the ratio of areas is an affine invariant, introducing an approximation, we can choose the sign based on which region contains the largest portion of the area of U. For instance, if regions U, V and Z are located as in Fig. 2.c we have that $\chi(S,T,U) = +$, $\chi(S,T,V) = 0$ and $\chi(S,T,Z) = -$.

2.3 Invariance of Oriented Matroids

Consider a 3D point configuration and one of its views. The combinatorial structure of the 3D point configuration and that of its 2D perspective projection are related in the following way: if x_0 represents in homogeneous coordinates the center of the camera, p_0, we have that

$$\text{sign}[\bar{x}_i, \bar{x}_j, \bar{x}_k] = \text{sign}[x_i, x_j, x_k, x_0] \tag{1}$$

where x_i, x_j and x_k are the homogeneous coordinates of the 3D points p_i, p_j and p_k, and $\bar{x}_i$, $\bar{x}_j$ and $\bar{x}_k$ are those of the corresponding points in the view, $\bar{p}_i$, $\bar{p}_j$ and $\bar{p}_k$. Equation (1) can be regarded as a projection equation for chirotope. It is easy to see that, whereas the *matrix* that represents in homogeneous coordinates the vertices of a projected set of points is *coordinate-dependent*, an oriented *matroid* is a *coordinate-free* representation. Moreover, the representation of object views based on oriented matroid is a *topological invariant*, that is, an invariant under homeomorphisms. Roughly speaking, this means that the oriented matroid that represents the arrangement of points of a view of an object does not change when the points undergo a continuous transformation that does not change any orientation of the chirotope. This property makes this representation robust to discretization errors of the image as well as to small changes of the point of view that does not change any orientation of the chirotope. Since projective transformations can be regarded as special homeomorphisms, and we can assert that the representation of the projected set of points based on oriented matroids is *projective invariant*. However, since affine and Euclidean transformations are special projective transformations, the oriented matroid of the projected set of points of a view of an object does not change under rotations, translations, and affine transformations of the planar arrangement of points themselves. These considerations can be extended to the case in which

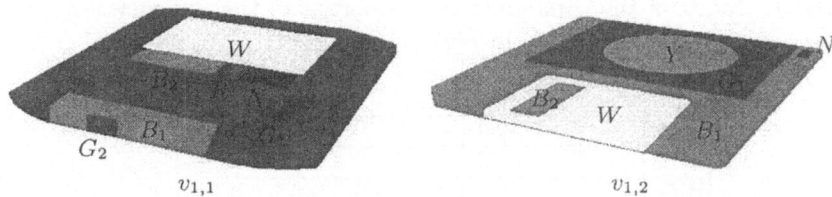

Fig. 3. Two views, of two objects whose combinatorial properties are indexed in Table 4

oriented matroids represent arrangements of planar regions. Therefore, the hypothesis generation method presented in this paper is inherently insensitive to projective, affine and Euclidean transformations of the views.

3   Indexing Views of 3D Objects

This process of indexing a database of views of a set of objects starts with some preliminary choices, namely the number of colors in which the hue is quantized and the number of regions having the same color that will be taken into account. These choices, of course, depend on the properties of the images of the database. Then, the views are segmented according tho these choices the set of cocircuits for each view is computed. Then, the sign combinations of the set of cocircuits of the views of the database are merged together and used for indexing a unique table whose entries are spatial combination of features of regions and the records contains the views that contains that combination.

Example 2. In Fig. 3 two views, $v_{1,1}$ and $v_{1,2}$, of two objects are represented, in which a color quantization with 6 colors white (W), red (R), yellow (Y), green (G), blue (B) and black (N) has been applied and up to two regions with the same color are taken into account. Let (W, R, Y, G, B, N) be the ordered tuple of colors considered. The index of the combinatorial properties of these two views is reported in Table 4, in which an asterisk in the first column indicates that the regions are not completely overlapped. On the contrary, a sign $+$ in the same column, in correspondence with a certain ordered couple of regions (S, T), indicates that S completely contains T, whereas a $-$ denotes that S is contained in T. If they are completely overlapped the corresponding element of the set of cocircuits cannot be computed. An asterisk in the column of the feature U denotes the absence of a region with this feature in the corresponding view of the database. The description of the case of partial overlapping between regions is herein omitted due to space limitations.

3.1   Hypothesis Generation for Object Recognition

Given a database of views of a set of 3D objects and a view v_i of one of them, not necessarily contained in the database, its set of cocircuits is computed. Each

Table 4. Index of the combinatorial properties of the two views $v_{1,1}$ and $v_{1,2}$ of the two objects represented in Fig. 3

	Overlapping	W	R	Y	G_1	G_2	B_1	B_2	N	Views
WR	*	0	0	*	0	0	0	−	+	$v_{1,1}$
WY	*	0	*	0	0	*	0	0	−	$v_{1,2}$
WG_1	−	0	*	*	0	*	*	*	*	$v_{1,1}$
WG_1	*	0	*	0	0	*	0	0	0	$v_{1,2}$
WG_2	*	0	0	*	0	0	+	0	0	$v_{1,1}$
WB_1	*	0	0	*	0	0	0	0	0	$v_{1,1}$
WB_1	−	0	*	*	*	*	0	*	*	$v_{1,2}$
WB_2	*	0	0	*	+	+	+	0	+	$v_{1,1}$
WB_2	+	0	*	*	*	*	*	0	*	$v_{1,2}$
WN	*	0	0	*	−	−	−	−	0	$v_{1,1}$
WN	*	0	*	+	+	*	0	0	0	$v_{1,2}$
RY	*									
RG_1	−	*	0	*	0	*	*	*	*	$v_{1,1}$
$\cdots$	$\cdots$	$\cdots$	$\cdots$	$\cdots$	$\cdots$	$\cdots$	$\cdots$	$\cdots$	$\cdots$	$\cdots$

element of the set of cocircuits is used to access the table that constitutes the index of the database. For each view j of the object k, $v_{j,k}$, found at that address of the table, the elements (i, k) of an image-object views association matrix are increased of 1. The final result of the indexing is therefore an association matrix in which the value of the element (i, k) indicates the strength of the hypothesis of associating the image v_i with the object k of the database. In other words, the view v_i will be associated with the object that has the maximum number of correspondences with v_i in terms of cocircuits. It is easy to see that this method for hypothesis generation, that can be regarded as a qualitative version of the geometric hashing technique [8], is also robust to partial occlusions of the objects. Indeed, if a region of a view is occluded, the set of cocircuits can still be computed and the number of correspondences with the views of the database can still be calculated. In this case, obviously, the selectivity of the method decreases.

4   Experimental Results

To validate our method, four 3D objects composed by colored woody pieces (Fig. 4) have been created. Then, sixteen views of each of them with angular separation of 22.5 degrees have been taken. These images have been segmented using the segmentation method described in [9]. Then, the index of the learning set of eight views per object taken at the angles 0, 45, 90, 135, 180, 225, 270 and 315 have been created. In the recognition process, the set of cocircuits of each image of the test set composed by the eight views not used in the learning process, that is, the views taken at angles: 22.5, 67.5, 115.5, 157.5, 202.5, 247.5, 292.5 and 337.5 degrees, have been calculated. In this experiment, that should

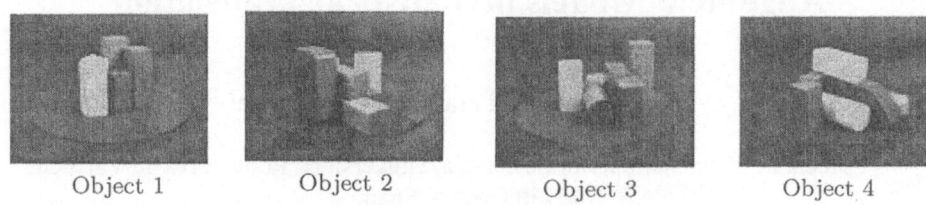

Object 1   Object 2   Object 3   Object 4

Fig. 4. Objects used for the experiments

be regarded as a proof of concept, since the 3D objects employed were not very complex and the images easy to be segmented, all the 32 test views were properly classified.

5 Conclusions

In this paper a new method for indexing views of a set of 3D objects has been presented. It is based on oriented matroids, a combinatorial data structure that captures the local and global topology of the regions of the views. This representation is invariant to projective, affine and Euclidean transformation of the views as well as, intrinsically robust to discretization errors of the image and insensitive to small displacements of the point of view. The experimental results obtained applying this indexing technique to the hypothesis generation in 3D object recognition processes from single views encourage to apply this new method to more complex objects.

References

[1] Serratosa, F., Alquézar, R., Sanfeliu, A.: Function-described for modeling objects represented by attributed graphs. Pattern Recognition **36** (2003) 781–798
[2] Björner, A., Vergnas, M. L., Sturmfels, B., White, N., Ziegler, G. M.: Oriented Matroids. Volume 43 of Encyclopedia of Mathematics and its Applications. Cambridge University Press (1993)
[3] Bokowski, J., Sturmfels, B.: Computational Synthetic Geometry. Volume 1355 of Lecture Notes in Mathematics. Springer–Verlag (1989)
[4] Richter-Gebert, J., Ziegler, G. M.: Oriented matroids. In Goodman, J. E., O'Rourke, J., eds.: Handbook of Discrete and Computational Geometry. CRC Press (1997) 111–132
[5] Carlsson, S.: Combinatorial geometry for shape representation and indexing. In: Proceedings of the International Workshop on Object Representation for Computer Vision. (1996)
[6] O' Rourke, J.: Computational Geometry in C. Cambridge University Press (1999)
[7] Toussaint, G. T.: Solving geometric problems with the rotating calipers. In: Proceedings of IEEE MELECON'83, Athens, Greece (1983)
[8] Lamdan, Y., Schwartz, J. T., Wolfson, H. J.: Affine invariant model-based object recognition. IEEE Transactions on Robotics and Automation **6** (1990)
[9] Comaniciu, D., Meer, P.: Mean shift: A robust approach toward feature space analysis. IEEE Trans. Pattern Anal. Machine Intell. **24** (2002) 603–619

Combining Phrase-Based and Template-Based Alignment Models in Statistical Translation

Jesús Tomás[1] and Francisco Casacuberta[2]

[1] Escuela Politécnica Superior de Gandia, Universidad Politécniva de Valencia,
46730 Gandia, Spain
jtomas@upv.es
[2] Institut Tecnològic d'Informàtica, Universidad Politécniva de Valencia,
46071 Valencia, Spain
fcn@iti.upv.es

Abstract. In statistical machine translation, single-word based models have an important deficiency; they do not take contextual information into account for the translation decision. A possible solution called Phrase-Based, consists in translating a sequence of words instead of a single word. We show how this approach obtains interesting results in some corpora. One shortcoming of the phrase-based alignment models is that they do not have the generalization capability in word reordering. A possible solution could be the template-based approach, which uses sequences of classes of words instead of sequences of words. We present a template-based alignment model that uses a Part Of Speech tagger for word classes. We also propose an improved model that combines both models. The basic idea is that if a sequence of words has been seen in training, the phrase-based model can be used; otherwise, the template-based model can be used. We present the results from different tasks.

1 Introduction

Statistical machine translation has been formalized in [1]. This approach defines a translation model by introducing an alignment, which defines the correspondence between the words of source sentences and target sentences. The optimal parameters of this model are estimated using statistical theory.

The most common statistical translation models can be classified as single-word based (SWB) alignment models. Models of this kind assume than an input word is generated by only one output word [1][10]. This assumption does not correspond to the nature of natural language; in some cases, we need to know a word group in order to obtain a correct translation.

One initiative for overcoming the above-mentioned restriction of single-word models is known as the template-based (TB) approach [5][11]. In this approach, an entire group of adjacent words in the source sentence may be aligned with an entire group of

F.J. Perales et al. (Eds.): IbPRIA 2003, LNCS 2652, pp. 1020-1031, 2003.

adjacent target words. As a result, the context of words has a greater influence and the changes in word order from source to target language can be learned explicitly. A template establishes the reordering between two sequences of word classes. However, the lexical model continues to be based on word-to-word correspondence. An example of this kind of model is the alignment-template model [5]. In this model, the word classes are learned automatically using a bilingual corpus. In this paper, we present a monotone TB model that uses a Part Of Speech tagger for word classes.

Recent works present a simple alternative to these models, the phrase-based (PB) approach [3][7][12]. These methods explicitly learn the probability of a sequence of words in a source sentence being translated to another sequence of words in the target sentence. One shortcoming of the PB alignment models is the generalization capability. If a sequence of words has not been seen in training, the model cannot reorder it properly.

We also propose an improved model that combines PB and TB approaches. The basic idea is that if a sequence of words has been seen in training, the PB model can be used; otherwise, the generalization capability of the TB model can be used.

The organization of the paper is as follows. First, we review the statistical approach to machine translation. Second, we introduce a direct approach to the problem. Then, we revise the PB approach and propose different methods to estimate the parameters. Afterwards, we propose a TB approach that uses a POS tagger for word classes and we show a possible combination of two of the models in question. Finally, we report some experimental results. The system was tested by translating three different tasks.

2   Statistical Translation

2.1   Noisy-Channel Approach

The goal of statistical translation is to translate a given source language sentence $\mathbf{f} = f_1...f_{|\mathbf{f}|}$, to a target sentence $\mathbf{e} = e_1...e_{|\mathbf{e}|}$. The methodology used [1] is based on the definition of a function $\Pr(\mathbf{e}|\mathbf{f})$ that returns the probability of translating the input sentence $\mathbf{f}$ into the output sentence $\mathbf{e}$. Once this function is estimated, the problem can be formulated to compute a sentence $\mathbf{e}$ that maximizes the probability $\Pr(\mathbf{e}|\mathbf{f})$ for a given $\mathbf{f}$. Using Bayes' theorem, we can write:

$$\Pr(\mathbf{e}\,|\,\mathbf{f}) = \frac{\Pr(\mathbf{e})\Pr(\mathbf{f}\,|\,\mathbf{e})}{\Pr(\mathbf{f})} \tag{1}$$

And, therefore, statistical translation can be presented as:

$$\mathbf{e}' = \arg\max_{\mathbf{e}} \Pr(\mathbf{e})\Pr(\mathbf{f}\,|\,\mathbf{e}) \tag{2}$$

Equation (2) summarizes the three following matters to be solved:

An output language model is needed to distinguish valid sentences from invalid sentences in the target language, $\Pr(\mathbf{e})$.

A translation model $\Pr(\mathbf{e}|\mathbf{f})$ must be defined.

An algorithm must be designed to search for the sentence **e** that maximizes this product.

We focus our attention on the translation model, $\Pr(\mathbf{f}|\mathbf{e})$. This probability distribution is too general to be used in a table look-up approach, because there is a huge number of possible values **f**. Therefore, we have to reduce the number of free parameters by reducing the dependencies.

Some models assume that an input word $\mathbf{f}_j$, in position j, is generated by one target word $\mathbf{e}_i$, in position i. Models of this kind are referred to as single-word based alignment models. A possible alignment within **f** and **e** is referred to as variable $\mathbf{a} = a_1 \ldots a_{|\mathbf{f}|}$. If $a_j = i$, the input word in position j is aligned to the output word in position i. As a result, the translation probability can be broken down into a lexicon probability and an alignment probability. In a more general definition of alignment, we can assume that an input word is generated by several words in the output. We can express this kind of alignment by assigning several output words to each input position instead of a single output word: $A = A_1 \ldots A_{|\mathbf{f}|}$ $A_j \subseteq \{i: i=1, .., |\mathbf{e}|\}$.

2.2   Direct Approach in Statistical Translation

Our approach does not follow equation (2). We estimate $\Pr(\mathbf{e}|\mathbf{f})$ directly without using Bayes' theorem [6]. As usual, we can express this likelihood in terms of alignments:

$$\Pr(\mathbf{e} \mid \mathbf{f}) = \sum_{\mathbf{a}} \Pr(\mathbf{e}, \mathbf{a} \mid \mathbf{f}) \tag{3}$$

Without loss of generality, we can write [1]:

$$\Pr(\mathbf{e}, \mathbf{a} \mid \mathbf{f}) = \Pr(I \mid \mathbf{f}) \prod_{i=1}^{I} \left(\Pr(a_i \mid a_1^{i-1}, e_1^{i-1}, I, \mathbf{f}) \Pr(e_i \mid a_1^i, e_1^{i-1}, I, \mathbf{f}) \right) \tag{4}$$

Now, we define an alignment as $\mathbf{a} = a_1 \ldots a_{|\mathbf{e}|}$; if $a_i = j$, the output word in position i is aligned to the input word in position j. If we assume that, e_1^{i-1} is independent of $a_1^i, I, \mathbf{f}$ in the third term of (4), we can write[1]:

$$\Pr(\mathbf{e}, \mathbf{a} \mid \mathbf{f}) = \Pr(I \mid \mathbf{f}) \prod_{i=1}^{I} \overbrace{\frac{1}{\Pr(e_i)} \Pr(e_i \mid e_1^{i-1})}^{\text{language model}} \tag{5}$$

$$\underbrace{\Pr(a_i \mid a_1^{i-1}, e_1^{i-1}, I, \mathbf{f})}_{\text{alignment model}} \underbrace{\Pr(e_i \mid a_1^i, I, \mathbf{f})}_{\text{lexical model}}$$

---

[1] It is easy to demonstrate that $P(a|b,c) = P(a|b)P(a|c)/P(a)$ with b and c being independent events. Thus, if we suppose that e_1^{i-1} is independent of $a_1^i, I, \mathbf{f}$, we can write: $\Pr(e_i \mid a_1^i, e_1^{i-1}, I, \mathbf{f}) = \dfrac{\Pr(e_i \mid e_1^{i-1}) \Pr(e_i \mid a_1^i, I, \mathbf{f})}{\Pr(e_i)}$

As in the standard approach, we have similarly broken down our initial distribution into several distributions: There are three principal distributions: the language model, the alignment model and the lexical model.

3   Monotone Phrase-Based Translation

The principal innovation of the phrase-based (PB) alignment model [3][7][12] is that it attempts to calculate the translation probabilities of word sequences (phrases) rather than of only single words. Figure 1 shows the same sentence written in five different languages.

```
Se requerirá una acción   de la          Comunidad       para la    puesta en práctica
É necessária uma acção    por parte da Comunidade       para pôr    plenamente em prática
Sarà necessaria un'azione della          Comunità        per dare   piena attuazione
Une action est nécessaire au niveau      communautaire afin de     mettre pleinementen œuvre
Action is required        by the         Community       in order to implement fully
```

Fig. 1. Equivalent phrases in a sentence in Spanish, Portuguese, Italian, French and English

As can be seen from this example, we join phrases that are translated together in a natural way. The other property of this translation model is that the alignment between the phrases is monotone-constrained. The example shows how the sentences are monotone-translated.

The generative process, which allows for the translation of a sentence, can be broken down into the following steps: First, the input sentence is segmented into phrases. Then, each phrase is translated to the corresponding output phrase. The output sentence is made by concatenating the output phrases in the same order as in the input phrases.

This model uses a particular kind of alignment that we call *monotone alignment using phrases*.

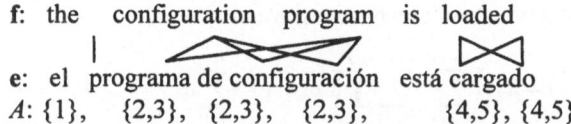

f: the   configuration program is loaded

e: el programa de configuración está cargado
A: {1},   {2,3},   {2,3},   {2,3},   {4,5}, {4,5}

Fig. 2. Example of monotone alignment using phrases

Using the definition of generalized alignment ($A=A_1...A_{|e|}$ $A_i \subseteq \{j: j=1,..,|f|\}$), we can define a *monotone alignment using phrases* if the following holds:

$$(A_i = A_{i+1}) \vee (\forall j_1 \in A_i ; j_2 \in A_{i+1} : j_1 < j_2) \quad \forall i=1..|e|-1 \tag{6}$$

A monotone alignment entails a segmentation of sentences **f** and **e**, in K phrases. We denote these sequences of phrases as: $\tilde{f} = \tilde{f}_1...\tilde{f}_K$ and $\tilde{e} = \tilde{e}_1...\tilde{e}_K$. Thus, we can propose an alternative definition of *monotone alignment using phrases* as the tuple $A=\{\tilde{e},\tilde{f}\}$ with $\tilde{e}$ being a possible breakdown of **e** into phrases; and with $\tilde{f}$ being a possible breakdown of **f** into phrases; with the restriction that the numbers of phrases in $\tilde{e}$ should be identical to $\tilde{f}$. We assume the alignment is monotone, thus the phrase $\tilde{e}_i$ is aligned with the phrase $\tilde{f}_i$, with $i = 1...|\tilde{e}|$. As usual, we can obtain the translation probability by adding the probability of all possible monotone alignments A:

$$\Pr(e|f) = \sum_A \Pr(A|f)\Pr(e|A,f) = \alpha(e)\sum_A \Pr(e|A,f) \tag{7}$$

$$= \alpha(e) \sum_{\tilde{e}:\,\tilde{e}=e} \sum_{\substack{\tilde{f}:\,\tilde{f}=f;\\ |\tilde{e}|=|\tilde{f}|}} \Pr(\tilde{e}|\tilde{f}) \tag{8}$$

In (7), we assume that all alignments have the same probability $\alpha(e)$. This parameter is not relevant for translation and will be omitted. Equation (8) is an alternative expression of equations, where the monotone alignment is explicitly indicated. If we assume that the phrase $\tilde{e}_i$ is produced only by the phrase $\tilde{f}_i$, we can write:

$$\Pr(\tilde{e}|\tilde{f}) = \prod_{i=1}^{|\tilde{e}|} p(\tilde{e}_i|\tilde{f}_i) \tag{9}$$

where the parameter $p(\tilde{e}|\tilde{f})$ estimates the probability that the word group, $\tilde{f}$, be translated to the word group $\tilde{e}$. These are the only parameters of this model.

3.1   Training with a Phrase-Aligned Corpus

In the training phase, we can estimate the parameters of the model by using a parallel corpus, which is aligned sentence to sentence [3][7]. We need to maximize equation (8) subject to the constraints that hold for each $\tilde{f}$:

$$\sum_{\tilde{e}} p(\tilde{e}|\tilde{f}) = 1 \tag{10}$$

Using standard maximization techniques, we obtain [7]:

$$p(\tilde{e}|\tilde{f}) = \lambda_{\tilde{e}}^{-1} \sum_{\tilde{e}:\,\tilde{e}=e} \sum_{\substack{\tilde{f}:\,\tilde{f}=f;\\ |\tilde{e}|=|\tilde{f}|}} \prod_{i=1}^{|\tilde{e}|} p(\tilde{e}_i|\tilde{f}_i) \sum_{i=1}^{|\tilde{e}|} \delta(\tilde{f}=\tilde{f}_i)\delta(\tilde{e}=\tilde{e}_i) \tag{11}$$

where δ is the Kronecker delta function, which is defined as: $\delta\,(true)=1$ y $\delta\,(false)=0$.

The parameters that we are interested in estimating, $p(\tilde{e}|\tilde{f})$, appear on both sides of equation 11. Thus, we need to use the EM algorithm in an iterative procedure [1].

3.2   Training with a Word-Aligned Corpus

The parameters of the model can also be obtained using a word-aligned corpus [12]. We don't have a word-aligned corpus, so we align the corpus automatically using single-word models trained with the free software GIZA++ [6].

This method consists of two steps. In the first step, we extract a set of bilingual phrases from the word aligned corpus. Basically, a bilingual phrase consists of a pair of m consecutive source words that has been aligned with n consecutive target words. Different criteria can define the set of bilingual phrases BP of the sentence pair $(\mathbf{f}; \mathbf{e})$ with alignment $\mathbf{a}^2$. The criteria used (12) is illustrated in Figure 3.

$$BP(\mathbf{f},\mathbf{e},\mathbf{a}) = \left\{ (\mathbf{f}_{j_1}...\mathbf{f}_{j_2}, \mathbf{e}_{i_1}...\mathbf{e}_{i_2}) : \begin{array}{l} \forall j : j_1 \le j \le j_2; (i_1 \le \mathbf{a}_j \le i_2) \vee (\mathbf{a}_j = 0) \\ \forall j : (j < j_1) \vee (j_2 < j); (\mathbf{a}_j < i_1) \vee (i_2 < \mathbf{a}_j) \end{array} \right\} \quad (12)$$

e: configuration program

f: programa de configuración

a: 2   0   1

$BP=\{$configuration-configuración, program-programa,configuration-de configuración, program-programa de, configuration program-programa de configuración$\}$

Fig. 3. Example of extracting a set of bilingual phrases from two aligned sentences

In the second step, we estimate the parameters of the model. This can be done via relative frequencies:

$$t(\tilde{e} \mid \tilde{f}) = \frac{N(\tilde{f}, \tilde{e})}{N(\tilde{f})} \quad (13)$$

where $N(\tilde{f})$ denotes the number of times that phase $\tilde{f}$ has appeared and $N(\tilde{f}, \tilde{e})$ is the number of times that the bilingual phrase $\tilde{f}$-$\tilde{e}$ has appeared. In [12], the noisy-channel approach is used. Therefore, they use the function:

$$t(\tilde{f} \mid \tilde{e}) = \frac{N(\tilde{f}, \tilde{e})}{N(\tilde{e})} \quad (14)$$

We tried another way of estimating the parameters. We needed to maximize (8) subject to the constraint that the monotone alignment in this function be consistent with the training alignment. Using standard maximization techniques we obtain:

$$t(\tilde{e} \mid \tilde{f}) = \lambda_{\tilde{e}}^{-1} \sum_{\tilde{e}:\tilde{e}=e} \sum_{\substack{\tilde{f}:\tilde{f}=f; \\ |\tilde{e}|=|\tilde{f}|}} \prod_{i=1}^{|\tilde{e}|} t(\tilde{e}_i \mid \tilde{f}_i) \sum_{i=1}^{|\tilde{e}|} \delta(\tilde{f} = \tilde{f}_i)\delta(\tilde{e} = \tilde{e}_i)\delta(\tilde{f} - \tilde{e} \in BP(\mathbf{f},\mathbf{e},\mathbf{a})) \quad (15)$$

As in section 1, the parameters can be estimated using the EM algorithm.

4   Monotone Template-Based Translation

The PB approach has one obvious drawback: it does not have generalization capability in word reordering. If we try to translate the English phrase *"configuration pro-*

---

2 GIZA++ provides us noisy-channel alignments. Thus, in this section, we use this kind of alignment.

gram" to Spanish, and this phrase has not been seen in the training, the model can not output the correct sentence *"programa de configuración"*. If we analyze the example, the reason for this word reordering is the POS that each word has in the sentence. Two nouns in English are frequently translated in to Spanish by «2nd noun + *de* + 1st noun». A possible solution could be the template-based (TB) approach, that uses sequences of classes of words instead of sequences of words. We present a TB model that uses a POS tagger for word classes.

The generative process, which allows for the translation of a sentence, can be broken down into the following steps: First, each word is tagged with the corresponding class. Second, the input sentence is segmented into phrases. Then, the corresponding reordering template for each class sequence is selected. The order of the output phrases is the same as the order of the input phrases. Finally, a word is selected for each output position.

As in PB model, we add all possible monotone alignments to obtain the translation probability (as shown in (8)); and we assume that the phrase $\tilde{e}_i$ is produced only by the phrase $\tilde{f}_i$, as shown in (9).

To estimate the translation probability between two phrases $\Pr(\tilde{e} \mid \tilde{f})$, we introduce the concept of template. In our implementation, a template z is the pair (F,R), which describes a possible word reordering R of a word class sequence F.

$$z = (F,R): \quad F_j \in C \quad j=1..|F| \quad R_i \in \mathcal{E} \cup \aleph^+ \quad i=1..|R| \tag{16}$$

where C is the set of input word classes, $\mathcal{E}$ is the output vocabulary and $\aleph^+$ is the set of natural numbers greater than 0.

$$F = JJ \quad NN \quad NN$$
$$R = 3 \quad de \quad 2 \quad 1$$

Fig. 4. Template example between an English phrase and a Spanish phrase

The template example in Figure 4 is used as follows. The input phrase *"new configuration program"* can be tagged as *JJ NN NN* (adjective, noun, noun)[3]. To translate this phrase, we can use a template whose class sequence F matches this sequence. If we use the template in the example, we obtain four words: the first is aligned with the third word in the input, the second is the word *de*, the third is aligned with the second, and the last is aligned with the first. Using the most probable translation for each aligned word, the output phrase *"programa de configuración nuevo"* can be obtained.

We introduce the hidden variable of template z in the phrase translation probability:

$$\Pr(\tilde{e} \mid \tilde{f}) = \sum_z \Pr(z \mid \tilde{f}) \Pr(\tilde{e} \mid z, \tilde{f}) \tag{17}$$

where $\Pr(z \mid \tilde{f})$ is the probability of applying a template given the input phrase; $\Pr(\tilde{e} \mid z, \tilde{f})$ is the probability of the output phrase given the template and the input phrase [5]. We assume that the use of a template depends only on the word class in the input phrase:

---

[3] We use the POS tags defined in [2].

$$\Pr(z \mid \tilde{f}) = p(z \mid C(\tilde{f})) \tag{18}$$

where $C(\tilde{f})$ maps a word sequence to its classes. To estimate the second distribution, we assume that the generation of the word $\tilde{e}_i$ depends only on the position R_i:

$$\Pr(\tilde{e} \mid z, \tilde{f}) = \delta(\mid \tilde{e} \mid = \mid R \mid) \prod_{i=1}^{|\tilde{e}|} \Pr(\tilde{e}_i \mid R_i, \tilde{f}) \tag{19}$$

We use alternative ways on the kind of element in R:

$$\Pr(\tilde{e}_i \mid R_i, \tilde{f}) = \begin{cases} p(\tilde{e}_i \mid \tilde{f}_{R_i}) & \text{if } R_i \in \aleph^+ \\ \delta(\tilde{e}_i = R_i) & \text{if } R_i \in \mathcal{E} \end{cases} \tag{20}$$

If R_i is an alignment index ($R_i \in \aleph^+$), we use the word-to-word translation probability; if R_i is an output word ($R_i \in \mathcal{E}$), the word $\tilde{e}_i$ must be the same as R_i.

This model has only two distributions: $p(z|F)$ probability of applying a template given a class sequence, and $p(e|f)$ word-to-word translation probability.

4.1 Training

We obtain the parameters of this model using a word-aligned corpus. Given a pair of aligned sentences $(\mathbf{f}, \mathbf{e}, \mathbf{a})$: First, each word in the input sentence is tagged with the corresponding POS. Then, the set of bilingual phrases is extracted using the function $BP(\mathbf{f}, \mathbf{e}, \mathbf{a})$. For each bilingual phrase $(\tilde{f}, \tilde{e})$, we extract a template $z=(F,R)$ where:

$$F = C(\tilde{f}) \qquad R_i = \begin{cases} \mathbf{a}_i & \text{if } \mathbf{a}_i \neq 0 \\ \tilde{e}_i & \text{if } \mathbf{a}_i = 0 \end{cases} \qquad \forall i = 1..|\tilde{e}| \tag{21}$$

Figure 5 shows an example of template extraction from a bilingual phrase. Then, the parameters can be estimated using relative frequency:

$$p(z \mid F) = \frac{n(z)}{n(F)} \qquad P(e \mid f) = \frac{n_A(f,e)}{n(f)} \tag{22}$$

where $n(z)$ is the number of times that the template z appears (the same for functions $n(F)$ and $n(f)$), and $n_A(f,e)$ is the number of times that the word f is aligned with e.

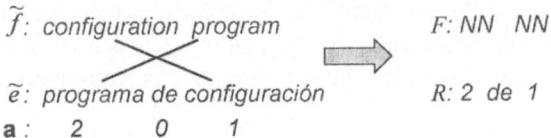

$\tilde{f}$: configuration program   F: NN   NN

$\tilde{e}$: programa de configuración   R: 2 de 1

a :   2   0   1

Fig. 5. Example of template extraction from a bilingual phrase

p(*2* de *1* | NN NN) = 0,226	p(*1 2* | NN NN) = 0,109	p(*2 1* | NN NN) = 0,074
p(*1* | NN NN) = 0.041	p(*2* | NN NN) = 0.039	p(*1 1 2* | NN NN) = 0.035
p(*2 1* | NN NN) = 0,031	p(*2 2 1* | NN NN) = 0.029	p(*2* del *1* | NN NN) = 0.028
p(*2 1* | JJ NN) = 0,294	p(*1 2* | JJ NN) = 0,197	p(de 2 *1* | JJ NN) = 0,068
p(*1* | JJ NN) = 0,058	p(*2* | JJ NN) = 0,038	p(*1* de *2* | JJ NN) = 0,028
p(*2* de *1* | JJ NN) = 0,026	p(*1 1* | JJ NN) = 0,026	p(1 2 2 | JJ NN) = 0,022

Fig. 6. Some template probabilities for two word-class sequences in an English-Spanish task (NN – proper name, JJ – adjective)

5   Combining Phrase-Based and Template-Based Translation

The above models present advantages and disadvantages. The TB model can generalize while the PB cannot. On the other hand, PB model explicitly translates each phrase and is capable of translating some phrases that the TB model cannot.

We consider the two models to be complementary, and so we combine them. The basic idea is that when a phrase is translated, if it has been seen in the training, the PB model is used. Otherwise, the TB model is preferred.

The new model can be defined as a linear combination of these two models:

$$\Pr(\tilde{e} \mid \tilde{f}) = (1-\alpha)p(\tilde{e} \mid \tilde{f}) + \\ \alpha \sum_z p(z \mid C(\tilde{f}))\Pr(\tilde{e} \mid z, \tilde{f}) \tag{23}$$

where α is a factor to adjust the relevance of the two models.

6   Search

The aim of search is to find an approximation to sentence e that maximizes the product Pr(e|f). Our search is based on the stack-decoding algorithm. The basic stack-decoding algorithm searches for only the best alignment, between the sentences **f** and **e** (We will refer to this method as Best alignment). However, in (7), we define the probability of translating **f** to **e** as the sum of all possible alignments. To solve this deficiency, we act as follows: We compute the real probabilities of all the complete hypotheses obtained, and we take the bigger one. (We will refer to it as Add all alignments). [12] proposes extending the search to allow for non-monotone translation. In this extension, all possible reorderings in the output sequence of phrases have the same probability as the monotone one (We will refer to it as Non-monotone).

7   Experimental Results

In order to evaluate the performance of these approaches, we carried out several experiments using tree tasks. The *Xerox* task was compiled using some Xerox technical manuals [9]. This is a reduced-domain task and many phrases in the text have been seen in the training. The *El Periódico* task was obtained from the Internet edition of a general newspaper published daily in Catalan and Spanish. The training corpus was made up of 10 months of the newspaper. The test was obtained from different tasks. The *Hansards* task consists of debates in the Canadian Parliament. This task has a very large vocabulary. Table 1 presents some statistical information about these corpora after the pre-processing phase.

Table 1. Statistical information of the selected corpora for experiments

	Task:	Xerox		El Periódico		Hansards	
	Translation direction:	English	Spanish	Spanish	Catalan	English	French
Training	Sentences pairs	45,493		643,961		137,381	
	Running words	517K	575K	7,180K	7,435K	1,941K	2,130K
	Vocabulary	7,272	9,947	129K	128K	29,479	37,554
Test	Sentences	500		120		250	
	Running words	5,719	6,425	2,211	2,179	2,633	2,805

We selected the trigram model with linear interpolation for the language model.

The results of the translation experiments using the phrase-based approach are summarized in Tables 2 and 3. The main conclusions are that the direct approach produces better translations than the source-channel approach and that adding all possible alignments is better than using the best alignment.

When translating Romanic languages, word reordering is not essential and therefore the PB approach is appropriate. For an unrestricted task, in Spanish-Catalan translation, we obtained better results than some rule-based commercial systems.

Table 2. Translation word-error rate of the PB model for different configurations in the *Xeros* corpus. Default: max. length phrases=14, direct model, add all alignments

Max. length phrases	TWER	parameters	Estimation of parameters	TWER	Search criteria	TWER
6	38.8	678K	Phrase-aligned (11)	33.6	Best alignment	30.5
8	31.2	933K	Direct model (13)	30.1	Add all alignmets	30.1
10	30.6	1,149K	Source chanel (14)	33.9	Non-monotone	33.2
12	30.3	1,328K	Using EM alg. (15)	31.3		
14	30.1	1,475K				

Table 3. Comparison of Spanish-Catalan commercial translators with the PB approach (max. length phrase=3, direct model, monotone search adding all alignments). All references WER correspond to the percentage of words that must be changed in the output in order to obtain a correct translation

Translators	TWER	all references WER	URL
Internostrum	11.9	4.9	www.internostrum.com
Salt	9.9	3.0	www.cultgva.es
Incyta	10.9	3.1	www.incyta.com
Phrase Based Model	10.7	3.8	ttt.gan.upv.es/~jtomas/trad

Table 4 shows the results obtained in the *Hansards* task using PB model, TB model and the integration of two models. We can show how the integration of the two models obtains the best results.

Table 4. Translation word-error rate of the PB model, TB model and integrated model in the *Hansards* corpus (max. length phrases=3, max. length templates=3, direct model, all alignments, α=0.05)

Model	TWER	parameters
Phrase Based	64,9	1,185K
Template Based	68,2	235K
Integrated	63,8	1,420K

8   Conclusion

We have described several approaches for performing statistical machine translation. They are based on monotone alignments using sequences of words. The phrase-based approach is very simple and the search can be performed in reduced time. This method can obtain good translation results in certain tasks such as some reduced-domain tasks or between Romanic languages. For an unrestricted task, in Spanish-Catalan translation, we obtained better results than some rule-based commercial systems. An important drawback of this method is that it does not have generalization capability in word reordering.

We also present a template-based alignment model. This model presents three main differences with the alignment-template model presented in [5]: We use POS for word classes; we use word classes only in the source language; and we translate the sequence of templates in a monotone way.

We think these two models are complementary, and we propose an improved model that consists of a linear combination of these models. We obtained the best results with the combined model.

In the future, we are interested in the exploration of more sophisticated translation models models. We would also like to test the system using other word classes.

Acknowledgements

This work was partially funded by the Spanish CICYT under grant TIC2000-1599-C02 and the IST Programme of the European Union under grant IST-2001-32091.

References

[1]   Brown, P.F., Della Pietra, S., Della Pietra, V., Mercer, R.L.: The Mathematics of Statistical Machine Translation: Parameter Estimation. Computational Linguistics, 19 (1993) 263–311

[2]   Casacuberta, F.: Inference of finite-state transducers by using regular grammars and morphisms. In A.L. Oliveira, editor, Grammatical Inference: Algorithms and Applications, volume 1891 of Lecture Notes in Computer Science, pages 1-14. Springer-Verlag, 2000. 5th International Colloquium Grammatical Inference -ICGI2000-. Lisboa. Portugal. Septiembre

[3]   Marcu, D., Wong W.: A Phrase-Based, Joint Probability Model for Statistical Machine Translation. Proc. of the Conference on Empirical Methods in Natural Language Processing, Philadelphia, PA, July (2002)

[4]   Marcus, M., Kim, G., Marcinkiewicz, M., MacIntyre, R., Bies, A., Ferguson, M., Katz, K., Schasberger, B.: The Penn treebank: Annotating predicate argument structure. In ARPA Human Language Technology Workshop. (1994)

[5]   Och, F.J., Tillmann, C., Ney, H.: Improved alignment models for statistical machine translation. In Proc. Of the Joint SIGDAT Conf. On Empirical Methods in Natural Language Processing and Very Large Corpora, Maryland, USA. (1999) 20-28

[6]   Och, F.J., Ney, H.: Improved Statistical Alignment Models. Proc. of the 38th Annual Meeting of the Association for Computational Linguistics, Hong Kong, China, October (2000)

[7]   Tomás, J., Casacuberta, F.: Monotone Statistical Translation using Word Groups. Proceedings of the Machine Translation Summit VIII, Santiago, Spain (2001)

[8]   Tomás, J., Casacuberta, F.: Binary Feature Classification for Word Disambiguation in Statistical Machine Translation. Proceedings of the 2nd International Workshop on Patter Recognition in Information Systems, Alicante, Spain (2002)

[9]   TT2: TransType2-Computer-Assisted Translation (TT2). Information Society Technologies (IST) Programme. IST-2001-32091 (2002)

[10]   Vogel, S., Ney, H., Tillmann, C.: HMM-Based Alignment in Statistical Word Translation. International conference on Computational Linguistics, Copenhagen, Denmark. (1996)

[11]   Wang, Y., Waibel, A.: Modeling with structures in statistical machine translation. In COLING-ACL'98: 36th Annual Meeting of the Association for Computational Linguistics and 17th Int. Conf. on Computational Linguistics, V2, Montreal, Canada (1998) 1357-1363

[12]   Zens, R., Och, F.J., Ney, H.: Phrase-Based Statistical Machine Translation. In Proc. Conference on Empirical Methods for Natural Language Processing, To appear in Proc. German Conference on Artificial Intelligence (KI 2002), Springer Verlag, (2002)

The Log-polar Image Representation
in Pattern Recognition Tasks*

V. Javier Traver and Filiberto Pla

Dep. de Llenguatges i Sistemes Informàtics,
Universitat Jaume I, E12071-Castelló, Spain
{vtraver,pla}@uji.es

Abstract. This paper is a review of works about the use of the log-polar image model for pattern recognition purposes. Particular attention is paid to the rotation- and scale-invariant pattern recognition problem, which is simplified by the log-polar mapping. In spite of this advantage, ordinary translations become a complicated image transform in the log-polar domain. Two approaches addressing the estimation of translation, rotation and scaling are compared. One of them, developed by the authors, takes advantage of the principles of the active vision paradigm.

1 Introduction

Computer vision often looks at biology for inspiration. This is the case of log-polar images, which follows a foveal model found in some vertebrates, including humans [19]. After these neuro-physiological findings, researchers in artificial vision started to adopt it in their algorithms.

Two main areas where the log-polar model has been adopted are active vision [5] and pattern recognition [28], as it is summarized in the rest of this section. The novel contribution of this paper is as a survey of works on log-polar imagery for pattern recognition, with an emphasis paid in the comparison between a traditional well-known technique (Fourier-Mellin Transform) and an active-vision based approach (developed by the authors) for the problem of similarity motion estimation. After that, rotation and scaling invariances in the log-polar domain and some approaches using them are introduced in Section 2. The problem of dealing with conventional (cartesian) translations in log-polar images is also considered, and two algorithms that can cope with translations combined with scaling and rotation are discussed and compared. Then, in Section 3, applications using the log-polar transform and the benefits brought by it are briefly commented. Finally, at the light of the results surveyed throughout the paper, concluding remarks are drawn in Section 4.

---

* Research partly funded by *Conselleria d'Educació, Cultura i Cincia, Generalitat Valenciana*, under project CTIDIB/2002/333.

F.J. Perales et al. (Eds.): IbPRIA 2003, LNCS 2652, pp. 1032–1040, 2003.
© Springer-Verlag Berlin Heidelberg 2003

Log-polar Images and Active Vision. On the one hand, active vision [1, 2] and foveal sensing are intimately linked to the extent that the term *space-variant active vision* has been coined in the past. One of the favorable properties that log-polar images bring to the field of active vision is a trade-off solution between large field of view, small image size and good resolution at the point of interest. Log-polar images are such that devote a high visual acuity in the center of the field of view, so that foveated objects can be perceived with very good quality. Because resolution decreases exponentially with eccentricity, the size of the log-polar image is small, so that active vision algorithms can exhibit real-time performance. The coarser resolution at the periphery can still be used to detect potentially interesting events that deserve further attention. The topology of log-polar images carry an implicit focus of attention that is particularly useful in vergence control [8] or tracking algorithms [25], because background information becomes less distracting in comparison with uniformly sampled images. Advantages of the log-polar geometry for time-to-impact computation [24], depth estimation [23], or motion stereo [3], among others, have also been studied.

Log-polar Mapping and Pattern Recognition. On the other hand, pattern recognition problems may also benefit from the log-polar representation. This paper focuses on the use of this image model to achieve rotation- and scale-invariant (RSI), or translation-, rotation- and scale-invariant (TRSI) object representations. It is worth noticing an important difference that usually arises between the log-polar images used in active vision applications and those used in recognition tasks. In robotics, there has been a trend to design and use true retina-like sensors (e.g. [29]), or at least, to simulate the log-polar images by software conversion (e.g. [4, 11, 25]) while using cartesian images for the only purpose of the transformation. In this case, we can speak of log-polar *images*. However, practitioners in pattern recognition usually approach the problem from a different perspective, in which it is more appropriate to speak of the log-polar *mapping*, because the transformation is used as a tool. This distinction is fundamental due to its practical consequences:

Image Size. Many recognition problems do not have hard-time constraints, so that devoting a lot of time to process large log-polar images is not really a concern. This is not the case, however, when fast computations are a must.

Biological Motivation. Because log-polar images are obtained as a result of a transformation, cartesian images are still available, and one can make use of both kinds of images, exploiting the best of both worlds. This advantage may be seen as a problem if one is interested in being biologically consistent, or when cartesian images are simply not available.

2   Achieving Invariances

Rotation and Scaling Invariances. It is well-known the fact that rotation and scaling become shifts with the log-polar transform. These properties derive from the topological nature of log-polar images. On the one hand, the *polar* geometry maps angles to shifts along the angular axis of the log-polar image. On the other hand, the *logarithmic* law —which governs the location of receptive fields away from the center of fixation— maps changes of scale to shifts along the radial axis of log-polar images.

Therefore, to estimate a rotation angle or a scale factor, one has only to estimate two shifts: an angular shift and a radial shift, from which the scaling and rotation angle can be derived straightforwardly using the underlying log-polar model. It is worth noticing that some, but not all, of the existing log-polar models actually possess these properties [25]. Therefore, the choice of a log-polar model should take this into account if RSI is a desirable feature.

Pattern Representation and Recognition. Edge invariance (a more suitable name to refer to the RSI of log-polar images) is the key feature exploited in [28] to represent pattern templates. To that end, it is central the *scale and rotation normalization*: rotation normalization is achieved by cyclically shifting the rows of the image by an amount corresponding to the angle of the major axis of the pattern. Scale normalization involves shifting the image down until there is an edge in the bottom row. This work is an enhancement of the normalization method first proposed in [16].

Fourier-Mellin Transform. The Fourier-Mellin Transform (FMT) is a method for making images rotation-, scale- and translation-invariant. The idea is to evaluate the Fourier Transform (FT), then the Log-polar Transform (LPT), and finally another Fourier Transform [20]. This approach relies on the shift theorem of the FT, on the edge-invariance property of the LPT, and on their combination on the appropriate data and in the right order. Through phase correlation, this system can not only determine whether a similar object is in both images, but also to quantify the scaling (α), rotation (ϕ) and translation (d_x, d_y). The overall steps needed in this process are illustrated in Fig. 1, while for specific details, the reader is addressed to Ref. [20].

Another interesting point in [20] is that complex numbers are used to represent color information. Phase correlation performed in this way can discriminate between the different colors of similarly shaped objects. Thus, the argument of the displacement peak —which is complex— is an angle whose value corresponds to the difference in color between the object in the reference image and that in the object image. The advantage of using complex color representation is that the color of the displaced object is calculated as part of the location procedure, with no extra processing.

A log-polar transform on the visibility image (the magnitude of the Fourier transform), is applied in [7], resulting in the so-called *log-polar visibility*. After that, scalings and rotations correspond to shifts. The approach is illustrated in a shift-, scale- and rotation-independent object recognition task. Even though the phase of the Fourier transform is interesting for image representation, an accurate description of the magnitude may also suffice to represent images. In

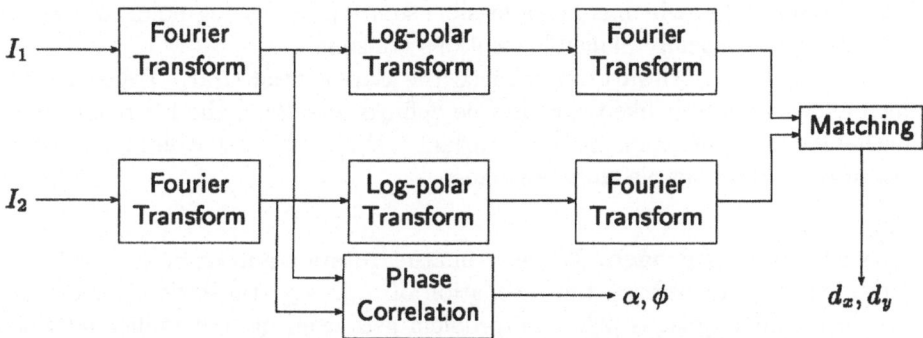

Fig. 1. Fourier-Mellin Transform. The input to the algorithm are two cartesian images I_1, I_2, and the output are the parameters α, ϕ, d_x, and d_y

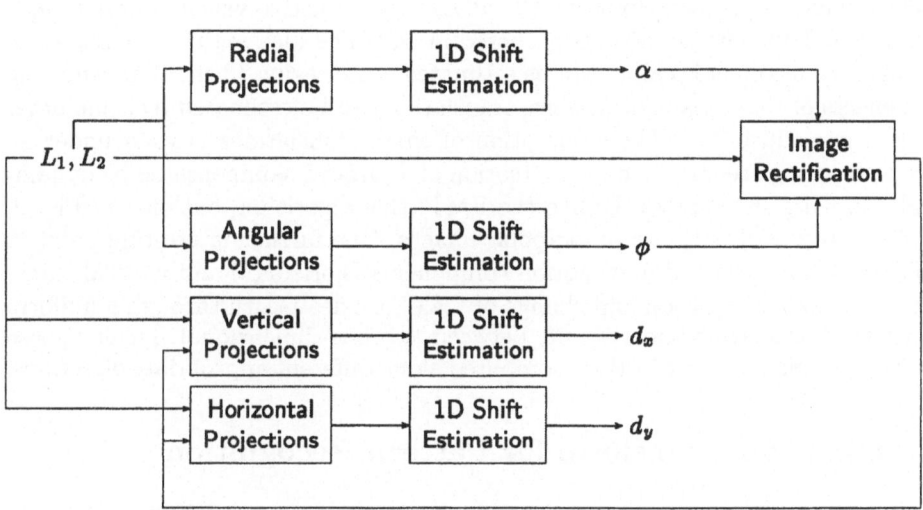

Fig. 2. Two-stage projection-based similarity estimation. The input to the algorithm are two log-polar images L_1, L_2, and the output are the motion estimates (α, ϕ, d_x, d_y)

addition, by using the magnitude of the Fourier transform, the information of the position of the object (which is associated with the phase) is lost, which is an advantage in this particular case.

Exponential Chirp Transform. As can be appreciated, the joint use of the Fourier and the log-polar transforms results in a powerful tool for general object recognition tasks. The main disadvantage of the FT is that the shift invariance does not hold when it is applied directly to a log-polar image. Thus, FMT resorts to cartesian images, which is not a feasible solution if only log-polar images are available, or biologically plausible solutions are sought.

Bonmassar and Schwartz introduced the Exponential Chirp Transform [6], which allows a Fourier-like transform be defined *directly* in the log-polar plane, thus having the benefits of the space-variant architecture and avoiding the drawback of the lack of simple shift invariance.

Active-Vision Approach. While estimating rotation and scaling is facilitated by the log-polar transform, the estimation of ordinary translation is more difficult in log-polar images [26]. The problem gets even more complicated when rotations, scaling and translations are combined.

As we have seen above, the FMT approaches the problem by using both cartesian and log-polar images. This, along with the fact that computationally expensive Fourier transforms are used, makes the FMT an inappropriate solution in many cases. By exploiting the advantages of active vision, another much simpler and efficient solution is proposed in [25]. The idea is that, if translation is small, rotation and scaling can be estimated quite easily. Then, after removing the effects of these transformations, translation can be estimated by some other simple procedure [26]. The assumption of small translations is valid under an active tracking scenario, where the motion of a target is compensated by dynamically moving the camera. Unlike the FMT, this algorithm, outlined in Fig. 2, makes direct and only use of log-polar images. One further interesting point in this proposal is that all four motion components (horizontal and vertical translation, as well as rotation and change of scale) are dealt with through a uniform approach: estimating the 1D shift between two one-dimensional signals. These 1D signals are image projections computed along different appropriate directions.

3 Log-polar Transform for Pattern Recognition

In this section, applications of the LPT are briefly commented. Besides the edge invariance, which the first part of this paper focuses on, other advantages that can be derived from the LPT are mentioned in the subsequent examples.

Straight lines and circles detection. Equations of straight lines and circles take a special form in the log-polar domain [27, 30]. In [30], a point-by-point complex product of the FFT (Fast FT) of the log-polar image with the FFT of a template line, after being mapped back to the spatial domain, yields strong convolution peaks for the most salient straight lines. A similar idea is used for circle detection. Weiman [27] shows that the parameter space of Hough transform has a coordinate system which is identical to the log-polar coordinate system, and stresses the advantages implied by this fact: it simplifies the computations for line recognition, eliminates slope quantization problems, and the so-called *log-Hough* transform is efficient in line and curves detection.

Features recognition by foveation. Lim *et al.*'s work [15] addresses the problem of foveation and feature (line, circle, and ellipse) recognition. An initial open-loop foveation generates a coarse movement (a saccade). Subsequently, a closed-loop foveation involves more accurate movements (micro saccades). What it is important in this work is the observation that when the foveation is accurate, the resultant pattern in log-polar space is always a horizontal line, regardless of the type of feature. This interesting result is used in the closed-loop foveation stage: if the foveation is not accurate, the log-polar mapping will be a slightly curved segment. Additionally, the deviation of this curve from the straight line indicates the amount of error.

Neural networks-based systems. The reduction of information achieved by the log-polar mapping is an attractive feature for researchers in neural networks (NNs), because it allows computationally feasible implementations of NNs for object recognition [18]. In addition, better recognition rates are reported when the input characters are represented by log-polar images than when they are represented by cartesian images because of the more favorable distribution of informative areas [17]. For the recognition of handwritten numerals, two NNs (one working with the input image in *cartesian* coordinates, and the other working in *log-polar* coordinates) are adopted in [14], the latter NN making rotational and scaling invariance possible. By using the interesting principle of *segmentation by recognition*, segmentation plays a key role in a successful recognition of connected cursive handwritten numerals or characters. In [12], a system for recognizing warning and caution traffic signs is described. Two NNs were used: one for color segmentation and the other for traffic sign invariant signature classification. The first 16 Fourier coefficients of the transformed log-polar images of the traffic signs were used as input for the second NN. The system is reported to achieve correct classifications in the presence of rather large noise levels.

Face detection/recognition. A system for face detection and recognition, which uses the log-polar mapping is described in [13]. The face detector encloses the face from the complex scene with a circular boundary and locates the position of the nose. The log-polar mapping is basically used for feature extraction in conjuction with PCA (Principal Component Analysis). The largest circle in the log-polar grid is adjusted to enclose the whole object, to obtain scale normalized feature vectors. Interestingly, the recognition rate is rather less sensitive to the log-polar image resolution than other methods compared in [10]. This robustness of log-polar images to variations in their resolution seems to be in accordance with the insensitiveness of the correlation measures to different image resolutions [4].

Contextualizing features. It is a point deserving some attention that the periphery in log-polar images has been used for two different —and seemingly contradictory— purposes. On the one hand, its coarse resolution allows that information in peripheral areas do not become too distracting, and the relevant information at the fovea becomes "dominating". On the other hand, even though the important information may reside in the high-resolved fovea, image data further away from the fovea may play an important "discriminative" role. In other words, it may help disambiguate the central information, by providing an economic (coarsely resolved) "context" (the surrounding information). To benefit from this more subtle, and less exploited capability, the LPT is found to be ideal in [9] in training NNs for facial features (eyes, nose and mouth) location, as well as in [21, 22], where an active face recognition system is described.

4   Final Remarks

The edge invariance property of log-polar images brings important advantages in rotation- and scale-invariant object recognition. Ordinary translations, which map to a complex transformation in the log-polar domain, can also be properly dealt with by proposed algorithms. The Fourier-Mellin transform, a standard tool to solve the more complex problem of rotation-, scale-, and translation-invariance, has important disadvantages (high computational requirements and the use of both cartesian and log-polar images) which may be overcome by approaches based on the principles of active vision. Other interesting properties, such as small processing time, appropriate coordinate system for feature detection, and inexpensive coarse-resolution context disambiguation, are also advantageous, as demonstrated in practical applications. Finally, it is evident that *active recognition* (pattern recognition under an active vision paradigm), and the use of log-polar imagery within it, is a promising framework to solve both old and new pattern recognition problems.

References

[1] J. Y. Aloimonos, I. Weiss, and A. Bandyopadhyay. Active vision. *Intl. Journal of Computer Vision*, pages 333–356, 1988.

[2] D. H. Ballard. Animate vision. *Artificial Intelligence*, 48:57–86, 1991.

[3] S. L. Bartlett, A. Hampapur, M. J. Huber, D. Kortenkamp, and S. Moezzi. Vision for mobile robots. In J. L. C. Sanz, editor, *Image Technology: Advances in Image Processing, Multimedia and Machine Vision*, pages 1–37. Springer, 1996.

[4] A. Bernardino and J. Santos-Victor. Sensor geometry for dynamic vergence: Characterization and performance analysis. In *Workshop on Performance Characteristics of Vision Algorithms, ECCV*, 1996. (Also as TR 01/96 at VisLab, Lisbon, Portugal).

[5] M. Bolduc and M. D. Levine. A review of biologically motivated space-variant data reduction models for robotic vision. *Computer Vision and Image Understanding (CVIU)*, 69(2):170–184, Feb. 1998.

[6] G. Bonmassar and E. L. Schwartz. Space-variant Fourier analysis: The exponential chirp transform. *IEEE Trans. on Pattern Analysis and Machine Intelligence (PAMI)*, 19(10):1080–1089, Oct. 1997.

[7] L. Capodiferro, R. Cusani, G. Jacovitti, and M. Vascotto. A correlation based technique for shift, scale and rotation independent object identification. In *Intl. Conf. on Acoustics, Speech, and Signal Processing*, volume 1, pages 221–224, 1987.

[8] C. Capurro, F. Panerai, and G. Sandini. Vergence and tracking fusing log-polar images. In *Intl. Conf. on Pattern Recognition (ICPR)*, pages 740–744. IEEE, 1996.

[9] P. Debevec. A neural network for facial feature location. C283 Course report, Berkeley University, http://www.cs.berkeley.edu/~debevec/face_recognition_report.pdf, Fall 1992.

[10] K. Hotta, T. Kurita, and T. Mishima. Scale invariant face recogniton method using spectral features in log-polar image. In *Applications of Digital Image Processing XXII (SPIE Proc.)*, pages 33–43, 1999.

[11] F. Jurie. A new log-polar mapping for space variant imaging. Application to face detection and tracking. *Pattern Recognition*, 32:865–875, 1999.

[12] N. Kehtarnavaz and A. Ahmad. Traffic sign recognition in noisy outdoor scenes. In *IEEE Intl. Conf. on Intelligent Vehicles*, pages 460–565, 1995.

[13] L. H. Koh, S. Ranganath, M. W. Lee, and Y. V. Venkatesth. An integrated face detection and recognition system. In *Intl. Conf. on Image Analysis and Processing (ICIAP)*, Venice, Italy, Sept. 1999.

[14] S. Lee and T. Horprasert. Recognition of handwritten connected numerals based on dual cooperative neural network. In *Intl. Conf. on Neural Networks*, Perth, Australia, Dec. 1995.

[15] F. L. Lim, G. A. W. West, and S. Venkatesh. Use of log polar space for foveation and feature recognition. *IEE Proc. Vis. Image Signal Process.*, 144(6):323–331, Dec. 1997.

[16] L. Massone, G. Sandini, and V. Tagliasco. 'Form-Invariant' topological mapping strategy for 2D shape recognition. *Computer Vision, Graphics, and Image Processing*, 30:169–188, 1985.

[17] Z. Mikrut and G. Augustyn. Influence of the object representation on the results of characters recognition in the car's licence plates. In *5th Conf. on Neural Networks and Soft Computing*, Zakopane, Poland, June 2000.

[18] Z. Mikrut and B. Czwartkowski. Log-Hough space as input for a neural network. In *4th Conf. on Neural Networks and their Applications*, Zakopane, Poland, May 1999.

[19] E. L. Schwartz. Spatial mapping in the primate sensory projection: Analytic structure and relevance to perception. *Biological Cybernetics*, 25:181–194, 1977.

[20] A. L. Thornton. *Color Object Recognition Using a Complex Colour Representation and the Frequency Domain*. PhD thesis, Department of Engineering, The University of Reading, May 1998.

[21] M. Tistarelli. Active/space-variant object recognition. *Image and Vision Computing (IVC)*, 13(3):215–226, Apr. 1995.

[22] M. Tistarelli and E. Grosso. Active vision-based face authentication. *Image and Vision Computing (IVC)*, 18:299–314, 2000.

[23] M. Tistarelli and G. Sandini. Estimation of depth from motion using an anthropomorphic visual sensor. *Image and Vision Computing (IVC)*, 8(4):271–278, Nov. 1990.

[24] M. Tistarelli and G. Sandini. On the advantages of polar and log-polar mapping for direct estimation of time-to-impact from optical flow. *IEEE Trans. on Pattern Analysis and Machine Intelligence (PAMI)*, 15:401–410, 1993.

[25] V. J. Traver. *Motion Estimation Algorithms in Log-polar Images and Application to Monocular Active Tracking*. PhD thesis, Dep. Llenguatges i Sistemes Informàtics, Universitat Jaume I, Castellón (Spain), Sept. 2002.

[26] V. J. Traver and F. Pla. Dealing with 2D translation estimation in log-polar imagery. *Image and Vision Computing (IVC)*, 21(3):145–160, Feb. 2003.

[27] C. F. R. Weiman. Polar exponential sensor arrays unify iconic and Hough space representation. In *SPIE Conf. on Intelligent Robots and Computer Vision VIII: Algorithms and Techniques*, volume 1192, Philadelphia, Nov. 1989.

[28] J. C. Wilson and R. M. Hodgson. Log-polar mapping applied to pattern representation and recognition. *Computer Vision and Image Processing*, pages 245–277, 1992.

[29] R. Wodnicki, G. W. Roberts, and M. D. Levine. A foveated image sensor in standard CMOS technology. In *Custom Integrated Circuits Conf.*, Santa Clara, May 1995.

[30] D. Young. Straight lines and circles in the log-polar image. In *British Machine Vision Conference*, Bristol, UK, Sept. 2000.

Appearance Tracking for Video Surveillance

Javier Varona, Jordi Gonzàlez, F. Xavier Roca, and J. J. Villanueva

Computer Vision Center & Dept. d'Informàtica,
Edifici O, Universitat Autònoma de Barcelona (UAB),
08193 Bellaterra, Spain
{xaviv,poal,xavir,villanueva}@cvc.uab.es
http://www.cvc.uab.es

Abstract. We present an algorithm which tracks multiple objects for video surveillance applications. This algorithm is based on a Bayesian framework and a Particle filter. In order to use this method in practical applications we define a statistical model of the object appearance to build a robust likelihood function. The tracking process is only based on image data, therefore, a previous step to learn the object shape and their motion parameters is not necessary. Using the localization results, we can define a prior density which is used to initialize the algorithm. Finally, our method has been proved successfully in several sequences and its performance is more accurate than classical filters.

1 Introduction

Nowadays, the presence of cameras in streets and buildings is habitual. Human operators control these cameras in order to notify any incidence. However, in most cases, a video surveillance system is composed of a great number of cameras which can not be observed at the same time. Therefore, it is necessary a computer vision system in order to assist humans.

Usually, an automatic video surveillance systems includes the following tasks: locating objects, visual tracking and action recognition. The localization module involves to detect objects into the images. Next, these objects are classified in different categories. The visual tracking task is used to maintain the object trajectories and to prevent localization errors. Lastly, the goal of the action recognition module is to describe what happens in the scene.

The main difficulties of an automatic video surveillance system are the variety of both the scenarios and the acquisition conditions. It is possible to design systems with one or more cameras which can be static or mobile, and different sensors such as color or infrared cameras.

In this paper, we firstly revise the previous work. Subsequently, we define a visual tracking method suitable for video surveillance applications. This method is based on a Bayesian framework and a Particle filter. Also, we define a prior density which allows to use this algorithm for video surveillance. Finally, we present the results of our algorithm and we discuss the conclusions and further work.

F.J. Perales et al. (Eds.): IbPRIA 2003, LNCS 2652, pp. 1041–1048, 2003.

2   Background and Previous Work

There are two main approaches for object detection in automatic video surveillance applications: temporal differences and background subtraction. Frame differencing performs well in real-time[7] but it fails when a tracked object ceases its motion. Background subtraction[10] is based on statistical models to build the appearance model of a static scene. Both methods require the use of a static camera.

Referring to the tracking module, there are works based on a combination of different computer vision algorithms which performs properly in real environments [2, 9]. However, these works are application-based and they can not be generalized for general visual tracking applications. The main difficulty of these visual tracking algorithms is to maintain the object trajectory when new objects appear in the scene or occlusions occur. Therefore it is necessary a process of data association and different application-based heuristics to perform the tracking process.

The Bayesian model for temporal state estimation [3] includes the Kalman filter as a particular case. This approach is used in computer vision to track shapes [4], motion estimation [1] and discrete event recognition [5]. An advantage of the bayesian approach is that it performs data association while doing the prediction-estimation loop. This fact makes feasible its use to track multiple objects[6].

3   Image-Based Tracking: *iTrack*

Based on the Bayesian probabilistic framework, we define an estimation algorithm to track people in video surveillance applications. The basic idea is that our method is just based on image data and it is not necessary to design any previous human body model.

3.1   Bayesian Formulation

Let be $s_t = (x_t, u_t, w_t, M_t)$ the state vector for an object. Where x_t is the position, u_t the velocity, w_t the size, and M_t the appearance of the object (see Fig. 1).

Let be $\mathcal{I}_t = (I_1, \ldots, I_t)$ a sequence of images. The posterior probability density over the parameters of the object state at time t, given a sequence of images is expressed as:

$$p(s_t|\mathcal{I}_t) = \int p(\mathcal{S}_t|\mathcal{I}_t)d\mathcal{S}_{t-1} , \qquad (1)$$

where $\mathcal{S}_t$ is the object state history, $\mathcal{S}_t = (s_1, \ldots, s_t)$. Applying the Bayes rule and the Markov condition we obtain:

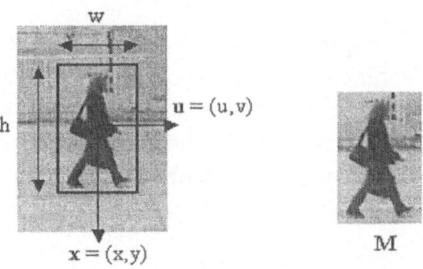

Fig. 1. Object state parameters

$$p(s_t|\mathcal{I}_t) \propto p(\mathbf{I}_t|s_t) \int p(s_t|s_{t-1})p(s_{t-1}|\mathcal{I}_{t-1})ds_{t-1} \ , \tag{2}$$

where $p(\mathbf{I}_t|s_t)$ is the likelihood function. The integral of (2) is referred to as the temporal prior or the prediction, and $p(s_t|s_{t-1})$ is the motion model.

3.2   Motion Model

In order to define the motion model we assume the next independent relations between the state parameters:

$$p(x_t, u_t, w_t, \mathbf{M}_t|x_{t-1}, u_{t-1}, w_{t-1}, \mathbf{M}_{t-1}) =$$
$$p(x_t|x_{t-1}, u_{t-1})p(u_t|u_{t-1})p(w_t|w_{t-1})p(\mathbf{M}_t|\mathbf{M}_{t-1}).$$

We use a smooth motion model for the position, velocity and size parameters:

$$p(x_t|x_{t-1}, u_{t-1}) = \eta(x_t - (x_{t-1} + u_{t-1}), \sigma^x)$$
$$p(u_t|u_{t-1}) = \eta(u_t - u_{t-1}, \sigma^u)$$
$$p(w_t|w_{t-1}) = \eta(w_t - w_{t-1}, \sigma^w) \ ,$$

where $\eta(\mu, \sigma)$ denotes a Gaussian density with mean μ and standard deviation σ. The deviations σ^x, σ^u and σ^w are defined empirically.

To complete the motion model, it is necessary to define the appearance evolution, $p(\mathbf{M}_t|\mathbf{M}_{t-1})$. The brightness constant assumption used in several optical flow algorithms is applied here. Using probabilistic terms, the density for the appearance model is defined as:

$$p(\mathbf{M}_t|\mathbf{M}_{t-1}) = \delta(\mathbf{M}_t - \mathbf{M}_{t-1}) \ , \tag{3}$$

where $\delta(\cdot)$ is a Dirac delta function. This model is also assumed by Sidenbladh et al. in 3D tracking of humans[8].

3.3   Appearance Model for the Likelihood Function

To compute the recursive expression of (2) we need a likelihood function, i.e. $p(\mathbf{I}_t|\boldsymbol{x}_t, \boldsymbol{u}_t, \boldsymbol{w}_t, \mathbf{M}_t)$. This function is the probability of observing the image $\mathbf{I}_t$ given the object parameters. First, we observe that the likelihood function is independent of the velocity parameter. The parameters $\boldsymbol{x}_t$ and $\boldsymbol{w}_t$ define an image region denoted as $\mathbf{I}^p$. Thus, we compare this image region with the object appearance model, $\mathbf{M}_t$, by means of an affine transform to scale both models:

$$\mathbf{R} = \mathbf{A}\mathbf{I}^p \ ,$$

where $\mathbf{A}$ is an affine matrix transform containing translations and scale parameters. Finally, the complete likelihood function is expressed as:

$$p(\mathbf{I}_t|\boldsymbol{x}_t, \boldsymbol{w}_t, \mathbf{M}_t) = p(\mathbf{R}|\mathbf{M}_t) \ , \tag{4}$$

$$p(\mathbf{R}|\mathbf{M}_t) = \frac{1}{N} \sum_{i,j \in \mathbf{R}} p_{ij}(R_{ij}|M_{ij,t}) \ , \tag{5}$$

where N is the number of pixels and p_{ij} is the probability that the appearance of the region pixel (i,j) belongs to the distribution of the appearance model:

$$p_{ij}(R_{ij}|M_{ij,t}) = \eta(R_{ij} - M_{ij,t}, \sigma^M) \ , \tag{6}$$

where $\eta(\cdot)$ is a Gaussian density whose standard deviation, σ^M, is used to model the noise of the adquisition system.

This definition of the likelihood function is robust to outliers because their presence (due to clutter and oclussions) does not penalize the probability measure.

The expression (3) means that the object appearance does not change over time. To maintain a correct appearance model, it is necessary to adjust the model after each estimation step. Once the new state has been estimated, $p(\boldsymbol{s}_t|\mathcal{I}_t)$, we adjust the appearance model using an adaptive rule for each pixel of the model:

$$\mu_{ij,t} = \mu_{ij,t-1} + \alpha(R_{ij,t} - \mu_{ij,t-1}) \ , \tag{7}$$

where $R_{i,j,t}$ is the appearance value of pixel (i,j) of the region obtained with the new state parameters. For the learning coefficient, α, we use the next temporal adjust:

$$\alpha_t = e^{-t} \ . \tag{8}$$

This approximation is established due to the fact that the best estimations are computed during the first frames.

3.4   Algorithm

To make possible the multiple object tracking process by using only one estimator, we need to maintain a multimodal density. Using the CONDENSATION algorithm we can implement the probabilistic model by means of a Particle filter[4]. Therefore, the conditional state density, $p(\mathbf{s}_t|\mathcal{I}_t)$, is represented by a sample set: $\{\mathbf{s}_t^{(n)}\}, n = 1, \ldots, N$. Finally, in order to identify each object, we use an augmented state adding a label, l.

The complete algorithm is showed in Table 1.

Table 1. iTrack algorithm

---

iTrack

The posterior density at time $t-1$ is represented by the sample set, $\{\mathbf{s}_{t-1}^i\}$, where $i = \{1, \ldots, N\}$. Also, the prior density $p(\mathbf{s}_t)$ for time t is assumed to be known at this stage.
Generate the ith sample of N that represents the posterior at time t as follows:

1. **Predict:** Generate a random number, $\alpha \in [0, 1)$ uniformly distributed,
    (a) If $\alpha < r$ use the initilialisation prior, $p(\mathbf{s}_t)$, to generate $\mathbf{s}_t^{i,-}$.
    (b) If $\alpha \geq r$ apply the motion model to the sample $\mathbf{s}_{t-1}^i$:

$$\mathbf{s}_t^{i,-} = p(\mathbf{s}_t|\mathbf{s}_{t-1} = \mathbf{s}_{t-1}^i) \ ,$$

   using the smooth motion model:

$$\mathbf{x}_t^{i,-} = \mathbf{x}_{t-1}^i + \mathbf{u}_{t-1}^i + \xi_x^i \ ,$$
$$\mathbf{u}_t^{i,-} = \mathbf{u}_{t-1}^i + \xi_u^i \ ,$$
$$\mathbf{w}_t^{i,-} = \mathbf{w}_{t-1}^i + \xi_w^i \ ,$$

2. **Correct:** Measure and weight the new sample, $\mathbf{s}_t^{i,-}$, in terms of image data, $\mathbf{I}_t$, using the likelihood funcion of expression (5):

$$\pi_t^i = p(\mathbf{I}_t|\mathbf{x}_t = \mathbf{x}_t^{i,-}, \mathbf{w}_t = \mathbf{w}_t^{i,-}, \mathbf{M}_{t-1}) \ .$$

Once the N samples have been generated, normalize the weights to $\sum_i \pi_t^i = 1$, and build the cumulative probabilities:

$$c_t^0 = 0 \ ,$$
$$c_t^i = c_t^{i-1} + \pi_t^i \quad \forall i = 1, \ldots, N \ .$$

Use the values of the cumulative probabilities to generate by sampling the new samples that represents the posterior at time $t, \{\mathbf{s}_t^i\}$.
For each object, estimate the new state computing the mean of their samples:

$$\hat{\mathbf{s}}_{L,t} = \frac{1}{N_L} \sum_{i,l=L} \mathbf{s}_t^i \ ,$$

where N_L is the number of samples for the object L.
Finally, use the new state to actualize the appearance model.

Table 2. Comparison results

	SAE	MAE
Kalman	680.1809	5.3983
Bayesian	575.2219	4.5653
iTrack	247.2923	1.9626

4   The Prior Density

The prior density is used to initialize the tracking process at the first frame. Subsequently, it is used to initialize new objects while appearing in the scene. We define the prior density by using the Stauffer-Grimson background subtraction method[9] as our localization method. As a result, pixels are classified into two categories: foreground and background. The spatial positions of the foreground pixels are used to model the prior density for the parameter x in terms of a Mixture of Gaussians:

$$p_t(x) = \sum_{k=1}^{B} P(k)p(x|k) \ , \tag{9}$$

where B is the number of blobs located (so $P(k) = 1/B$) and $p(x|k) = \eta(b_k, \Sigma_B)$. b_k is the blob mean position, Σ_B is constant for all the blobs, which is defined a priori. The size parameter w is formulated similarly in terms of the size of the blobs. Finally, the velocity parameter is initially established to zero.

5   Evaluation

First, we compare our method with two tracking approaches which requires a previous feature extraction step: the Kalman Filter and the original Bayesian Filter. Comparison is performed by manually annotating the object position in a sequence. Then we compute the mean absolute error (MAE) and the sum of absolute errors for each method. The results are shown in Table 2.

The results of the expected positions and the marginal density for the x position for different test sequences are shown in Fig. 2.

6   Conclusions

In this paper, we have presented an algorithm which allows multiple objects tracking for video surveillance applications. Our algorithm, called *iTrack* is based on a statistical model of the object appearance and a likelihood function which is suitable enough to handle clutter and occlusions. The algorithm uses a prior density defined from the results of the localization module. Finally, we compare

Fig. 2. Tracking multiple objects

our method with classical approaches to show up that, by considering the object appearance, the filter results are outperformed. Moreover, we should test the algorithm in more complex scenarios in order to be evaluated. However, current visual tracking evaluation methods are not mature enough. Therefore, further work should be addressed to algorithm evaluation.

Acknowledgements

This work has been supported by project TIC2000-0382 of Spanish CICYT.

References

[1] Michael J. Black and David J. Fleet. Probabilistic detection and tracking of motion discontinuities. In *Proceedings International Conference on Computer Vision (ICCV'99)*, Corfu, Greece, 1999.

[2] Ismail Haritaoglu, David Harwood, and Larry S. Davis. W4: Real-time surveillance of people and their activities. *IEEE Trans. Pattern Analysis and Machine Intelligence*, 22(8):809–830, 2000.

[3] Y-C Ho. A bayesian approach to problems in stochastic estimation and control. *IEEE Trans. on Automatic Control*, 9:333–339, 1964.

[4] Michael Isard and Andrew Blake. Condensation: Conditional density propagation for visual tracking. *International Journal of Computer Vision*, 29(1):5–28, 1998.

[5] Michael Isard and Andrew Blake. A mixed-state condensation tracker with automatic model-switching. In *Proceedings of International Conference on Computer Vision (ICCV'98)*, pages 107–112, Mumbai, India, 1998.

[6] Michael Isard and John MacCormick. Bramble: A bayesian multiple-blob tracker. In *Proceedings of International Conference on Computer Vision (ICCV'2001)*, Vancouver, Canada, 2001.

[7] Alan J. Lipton, Hironobu Fujiyoshi, and Raju S. Patil. Moving target classification and tracking from real-time video. In *IEEE Workshop on Applications of Computer Vision (WACV'98)*, pages 8–14, Princenton, NJ, 1998.

[8] H. Sidenbladh, M. Black, and D. Fleet. Stochastic tracking of 3d human figures using 2d image motion. In *Proceedings European Conference Computer Vision (ECCV'2000)*, Dublin, Ireland, 2000.

[9] Chris Stauffer and W.Eric L. Grimson. Learning patterns of activity using real-time tracking. *IEEE Trans. Pattern Analysis and Machine Intelligence*, 22(8):747–757, 2000.

[10] K. Toyama, J. Krumm, B. Brumitt, and B. Meyers. Wallflower: Principles and practice of background maintenance. In *Proceedings International Conference on Computer Vision (ICCV'99)*, pages 255–261, Corfu, Greece, 1999.

Sinusoidal Modelling with Complex Exponentials for Speech and Audio Signals

P. Vera-Candeas[1], N. Ruiz-Reyes[1], D. Martinez-Muñoz[1], J. Curpian-Alonso[1], M. Rosa-Zurera[2], and M. J. Lucena-Lopez[3]

[1] Electronic Department, University of Jaén, Polytechnical School, C/ Alfonso X el Sabio 28
23700 Linares, Jaén, Spain
{pvera,nicolas,damian}@ujaen.es
[2] Signal Theory and Communications Department, University of Alcalá
Polytechnical School, Ctra. Madrid-Barcelona km 33.6
28871 Alcalá de Henares, Madrid, Spain
manuel.rosa@uah.es
[3] Informatics Department, University of Jaén
Polytechnical School, Avda. Madrid 35, 23008 Jaén, Spain
mlucena@ujaen.es

Abstract. In this paper we propose a new approach based on energy-adaptive matching pursuits to improve sinusoidal modelling of speech and audio signals for coding and recognition purposes. To reduce the complexity of the algorithm, an over-complete dictionary composed of complex exponentials is used and an efficient implementation is presented. An analysis-synthesis windows scheme that avoids overlapping is proposed, too. Experimental results show evidence of the advantages of the proposed method for sinusoidal modelling of speech and audio signals compared to some others proposed in the literature.

1 Introduction

The classical sinusoidal or harmonic model [1] comprises an analysis-synthesis framework that represents a signal, $x[n]$, as the sum of a set of K sinusoids with time-varying frequencies, phases, and amplitudes:

$$x[n] \approx \hat{x}[n] = \sum_{k=1}^{K} A_k[n] \cdot cos\left(\omega_k[n] \cdot n + \phi_k[n]\right) \qquad (1)$$

where $A_k[n]$, $\omega_k[n]$ and $\phi_k[n]$ represent the amplitude, frequency and phase of the k-th sinusoid, respectively.

In the literature, different methods have been proposed for estimating the sinusoidal model parameters [2] [3][4][5]. Estimation of parameters is typically accomplished by peak picking the Short-Time Fourier Transform (STFT). Analysis by synthesis is usually used in order to verify the detection of each spectral peak. The length of the analysis frame should be signal dependent so as to achieve an adapted multi-resolution analysis [6].

F.J. Perales et al. (Eds.): IbPRIA 2003, LNCS 2652, pp. 1049–1056, 2003.

The classical harmonic synthesis model expressed in (1) involves a peak-tracking process, which is usually carried out by means of linear interpolation of the amplitudes, while cubic interpolation is used for phases [1][4]. This type of interpolation supposes an important limitation due to the need to overlap adjacent frames so as to track changes in the input signal.

The classical sinusoidal modelling approach only behaves well when it is applied to slow varying tonal signals. When the previous condition does not fulfil, it is advisable the research on new sinusoidal modelling methods, that make possible a better adaptation to the changes in the input signal. In this paper we propose a new method for estimating the parameters of the sinusoidal model, which is based on the matching pursuit algorithm. The method improves the sinusoidal modelling avoiding the sinusoidal parameters interpolation. Further improvements are achieved if windows that do not require overlapping are considered. Good results are obtained with the proposed method when rectangular and trapezoidal windows are used in the analysis and synthesis stages, respectively.

2   Matching Pursuit

The matching pursuit algorithm was introduced by Mallat and Zhang in [7]. So as to explain the basic ideas concerning this algorithm, let's suppose a linear expansion approximating the analyzed signal $x[n]$ in terms of functions $g_i[n]$ chosen from a over-complete dictionary. Let $\mathbf{H}$ be a Hilbert space. We define the over-complete dictionary as a family $D = \{g_i; \ i = 0, 1, \ldots, L\}$ of vectors in $\mathbf{H}$, such as $\|g_i\| = 1$.

The problem of choosing the functions $g_i[n] \in D$ that best approximate the analyzed signal $x[n]$ is computationally very complex. The matching pursuit is a greedy iterative algorithm that offers a sub-optimal solution, where the l^2 norm is used as the approximation metric because of its mathematical convenience. The algorithm is greedy in that at each stage the vector in the dictionary that best matches the current signal is found and subtracted to form a residual. The algorithm then continues on the residual signal. More specifically, in each step of the iterative procedure the vector in set D which gives the largest inner product with the signal ($\langle x[n], g_i[n] \rangle = \sum_{n \in Z} x[n] \cdot g_i^*[n]$) is chosen. The iterative procedure is repeated on the subsequent residual $r^m[n]$:

$$
\begin{aligned}
r^0[n] &= x[n] \\
r^m[n] &= \alpha_{i(m)} \cdot g_{i(m)}[n] + r^{m+1}[n]
\end{aligned}
\tag{2}
$$

where $\alpha_{i(m)}$ is the weight associated to the optimum function (or atom) $g_{i(m)}[n]$ at the m-th iteration.

The orthogonality principle ($\langle r^{m+1}[n], g_{i(m)}[n] \rangle = 0$) allows us to compute the weight α_i^m associated to each element $g_i[n]$ at the m-th iteration:

$$
\alpha_i^m = \frac{\langle r^m[n], g_i[n] \rangle}{\langle g_i[n], g_i[n] \rangle} = \frac{\langle r^m[n], g_i[n] \rangle}{\|g_i[n]\|^2}
\tag{3}
$$

The optimal atom to choose at the m-th iteration can be expressed as:

$$g_{i(m)}[n] = \arg \min_{g_i \in D} \|r^{m+1}[n]\|^2 = \arg \max_{g_i \in D} |\alpha_i^m|^2 \tag{4}$$

The correlations updating procedure is performed as follows:

$$\langle r^{m+1}[n], g_i[n] \rangle = \langle r^m[n], g_i[n] \rangle - \alpha_{i(m)} \cdot \langle g_{i(m)}[n], g_i[n] \rangle \tag{5}$$

The correlations $\langle g_{i(m)}[n], g_i[n] \rangle$ can be pre-calculated and stored, once the over-complete set D has been determined.

Two properties make this algorithm quite suitable for signal representation:

1. The procedure converges to the signal $x[n]$ [7].
2. The signal energy is conserved:

$$\|x[n]\|^2 = \sum_{m=0}^{M-1} |\langle r^m[n], g_{i(m)}[n] \rangle|^2 + \|r^M[n]\|^2 \tag{6}$$

The energy in the residual converges to zero as the number of iterations approaches to infinity [7]. Therefore, energy-adaptive matching pursuits are used in this paper. Although exact reconstruction is possible, the matching pursuit is generally stopped by some desirable criterion to allow low order approximations to the input signal. Some of the more relevant stopping criteria are: 1) after a given number of significant sinusoidal elements are found, 2) when the residual no longer contains components that correlate well with sinusoids, 3) when the error becomes imperceptible to the human ear.

The matching pursuit can be efficiently used for sinusoidal modelling, because it permits the selection of the sinusoidal components that extract most of the energy of a given signal. Furthermore, finite length signals can be analyzed using over-complete sets of elements of the same finite length. From now on, we focus on sinusoidal modelling of finite length signals.

3   Sinusoidal Modelling with Sets of Complex Exponentials

For sinusoidal modelling of finite length signals, the over-complete set D is composed of windowed sinusoidal functions obtained for different values of frequency and phase. We propose the usage of a set of windowed complex exponential functions, instead of the set of windowed sinusoidal functions, in order to reduce the computational complexity. Using windowed complex exponential sets, only the frequency of each exponential function must be determined, which involves a significant reduction of the dictionary size. As shown below, the projection onto the selected complex exponential function contains the information of the phase. Furthermore, each sinusoidal function is a linear combination of two conjugated complex exponentials.

The functions that belong to the considered set can be expressed as follows:

$$g_i[n] = S \cdot w[n] \cdot e^{j\frac{2\pi i}{2L}n}, \quad i = 0, \dots, L \tag{7}$$

The constant S is selected in order to obtain unit-norm functions, $w[n]$ is the N-length analysis window, and $L + 1$ the number of frequencies within the dictionary.

In each iteration, the new residual is calculated according to expression (8):

$$\begin{aligned}
r^{m+1}[n] &= r^m[n] - \alpha_{i(m)} \cdot g_{i(m)}[n] - \alpha^*_{i(m)} \cdot g^*_{i(m)}[n] \\
&= r^m[n] - 2 \cdot Re\{\alpha_{i(m)} \cdot g_{i(m)}[n]\}
\end{aligned} \tag{8}$$

The set of weights at the m-th iteration $\{\alpha_i^m, \ i = 0, 1, \dots, L\}$ can be easily determined applying the orthogonality conditions expressed in (9) to each atom in D:

$$\begin{aligned}
\langle r^{m+1}[n], g_i[n] \rangle &= 0 \\
\langle r^{m+1}[n], g^*_i[n] \rangle &= 0
\end{aligned} \tag{9}$$

Solving these equations, weights $\{\alpha_i^m\}$ are calculated according to equation (10):

$$\alpha_i^m = \frac{\langle r^m[n], g_i[n] \rangle - \langle r^m[n], g_i[n] \rangle^* \langle g^*_i[n], g_i[n] \rangle}{1 - |\langle g^*_i[n], g_i[n] \rangle|^2} \tag{10}$$

By using weights α_i^m, optimal atom $g_{i(m)}[n]$ to be chosen at the m-th iteration can be computed as follows:

$$g_{i(m)}[n] = \arg \min_{g_i \in D} \left\| r^{m+1}[n] \right\|^2 \tag{11}$$

$$g_{i(m)}[n] = \arg \max_{g_i \in D} \left| 2Re\{(\alpha_i^m)^* \cdot \langle r^m[n], g_i[n] \rangle\} - \right. \\
\left. -|\alpha_i^m|^2 \cdot \|g_i[n]\|^2 - Re\{(\alpha_i^m)^2 \cdot \langle g_i[n], g^*_i[n] \rangle\} \right| \tag{12}$$

To update the correlations in (10), we proceed as follows:

$$\langle r^{m+1}, g_i \rangle = \langle r^m, g_i \rangle - \alpha_{i(m)} \cdot \langle g_{i(m)}, g_i \rangle - \alpha^*_{i(m)} \cdot \langle g^*_{i(m)}, g_i \rangle \tag{13}$$

3.1   Efficient Implementation of the Algorithm

Due to the nature of the atoms $g_i[n] \in D$ (complex exponential functions), the correlations required to carry out the matching pursuit can be efficiently computed by applying the Fast Fourier Transform (FFT). So, the correlations between the signal $x[n]$ and the atoms in D are calculated with expression (14):

$$\langle x[n], g_i[n] \rangle = S \cdot \sum_{n=0}^{2L-1} z[n] \cdot e^{-j\frac{2\pi i}{2L}n} = S \cdot Z[i] \tag{14}$$

where $z[n] = x[n] \cdot w[n]$, $Z[i]$ is the $2L$-length DFT of $z[n]$, and $L > N$ in order to assemble an over-complete dictionary.

The initial correlations in (14) can be computed by applying the FFT algorithm, which implies that the signal $x[n]$ must be zero-padded for implementing the $2L$-length FFT.

The correlations between atoms can now be expressed as:

$$\langle g_{i(m)}[n], g_i[n] \rangle = |S|^2 \cdot \sum_{n=0}^{2L-1} u[n] \cdot e^{-j\frac{2\pi(i-i(m))}{2L}n}$$
$$= |S|^2 \cdot U[((i - i(m)))_{2L}] \tag{15}$$

$$\langle g^*_{i(m)}[n], g_i[n] \rangle = |S|^2 \cdot \sum_{n=0}^{2L-1} u[n] \cdot e^{-j\frac{2\pi(i+i(m))}{2L}n}$$
$$= |S|^2 \cdot U[((i + i(m)))_{2L}] \tag{16}$$

where $u[n] = |w[n]|^2$ and $U[i]$ is the $2L$-length DFT of $u[n]$.

From (15) and (16), it is deduced that the correlations between optimum atom $g_{i(m)}[n]$ at the m-th iteration and remaining atoms $g_i[n] \in D$ can also be calculated using the FFT (in this case, $u[n] = |w[n]|^2$). So, this transform can be pre-calculated and stored in order to update the correlations.

The use of a dictionary composed of complex exponential functions involves:

1. The initial correlations can be obtained by a $2L$-length FFT.
2. The correlations between atoms only require a $2L$-length vector in memory.

3.2   The Analysis-Synthesis Windows Scheme for Avoiding Overlapping

In this section the proposed approach for sinusoidal modelling is extended for analyzing non-stationary signals. Non stationary signals can be analyzed in a frame by frame framework, where the signal is windowed in each frame. A sufficient condition of the analysis window to assure the convergence to the analyzed signal is expressed in (17):

$$\sum_l w[n - lP] = 1 \tag{17}$$

where $P \leq N$ represents the hop size. The use of triangular windows is feasible [8, 9], but this choice involves overlapping, which largely increases the number of sinusoids per sample.

In this paper, we propose the usage of windows that complies with (17) avoiding overlapping. So, rectangular windows are considered at analysis, which implies the appearance of block effects (audible artifacts) at the boundaries of adjacent frames. This drawback is solved by extending the synthesis model, in order to synthesize samples that overlap with adjacent frames. The extended frames are windowed using overlapping trapezoidal windows, so that at the transition region between frames the tones of the previous frame disappear and those of the following start to appear. The main advantage of this approach is that overlapping is avoided at the analysis stage, which is a very interesting property for coding and recognition applications.

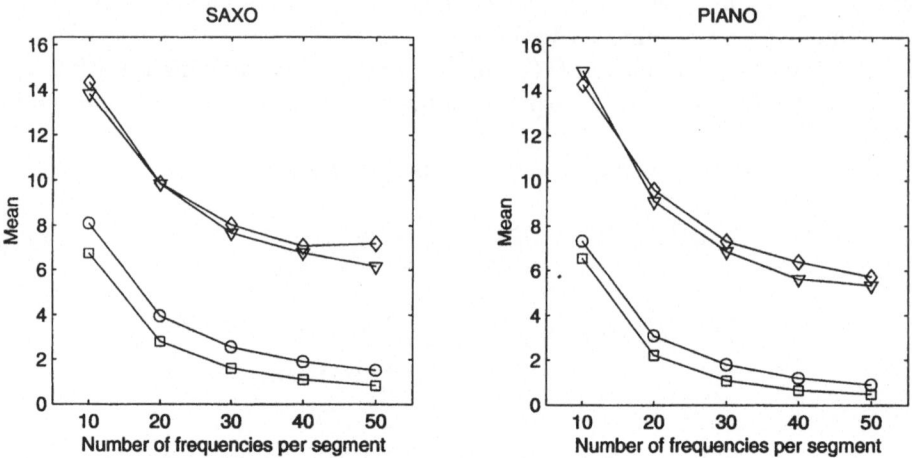

Fig. 1. Variation of the $RSR(\%)$ ratio as the number of sinusoidal components per segment is increased for the four considered methods: A (diamond), B (triangle), C (circle), D (square)

4   Experimental Results

To assess the advantages of the proposed method for sinusoidal modelling, several experiments have been carried out using two CD-quality one channel audio signals with high sinusoidal content:

A. Tone extraction by spectral peak picking, and synthesis by sinusoidal parameters interpolation [1].
B. Tone extraction by matching pursuit, and synthesis by sinusoidal parameters interpolation.
C. Tone extraction by matching pursuit, and triangular windowing in analysis and synthesis [9].
D. Tone extraction by matching pursuit, and box windowing in analysis and trapezoidal windowing in synthesis (the proposed method).

The result presented below have been obtained using an over-complete set of $L + 1 = 4097$ complex exponentials and 1024-length windows.

First of all, figure 1 shows the average value of the Residual to Signal Ratio, expressed in percentage, $RSR(\%)$, when the number of extracted frequencies per segment is increased.

It can be observed that methods C and D perform clearly better than methods A and B. So, a very important conclusion is that the usage of interpolation reduces the performance of sinusoidal modelling.

Figure 2 represents the number of sinusoidal components to be extracted in order to achieve a given percentage of the $RSR(\%)$ ratio for methods labelled C and D. How the use of trapezoidal windowing in synthesis, which makes avoiding overlapping possible, can be appreciated, yielding to the best results.

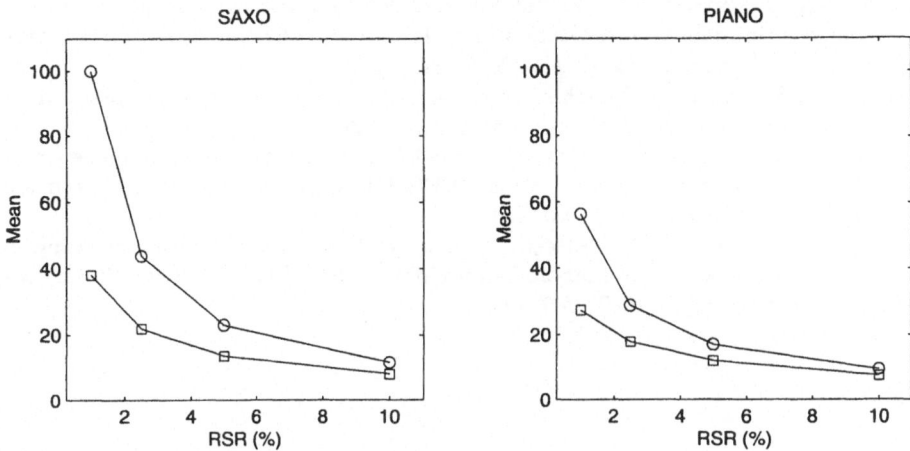

Fig. 2. Number of sinusoidal components to be extracted in order to achieve a fixed $RSR(\%)$ ratio for methods C (circle) and D (square)

5   Conclusions

This paper deals with a new matching pursuit-based method to improve sinusoidal modelling of speech and audio signals for coding and recognition tasks. First of all, the usage of a set of complex exponential functions makes the efficient implementation based on the fast Fourier transform possible. Secondly, this method takes advantage of the possibility of avoiding both interpolation of sinusoidal parameters and overlapping between adjacent frames, applying rectangular and trapezoidal windowing in the analysis and synthesis stage, respectively. The results highlight that the improvement due to the proposed sinusoidal modelling method can be exploited to reduce the amount of data sent to the next signal processing stage, which can be either a speech/audio recognition or coding block.

References

[1] McAulay, R., Quatieri, T.: Speech analysis synthesis based on a sinusoidal representation. IEEE Transaction on Acoustic Speech and Signal Processing **34** (1986) 744–754

[2] Thomson, D.: Spectral estimation and harmonic analysis. Proceedings of the IEEE **70** (1982)

[3] George, E., Smith, M.: Analysis-by-synthesis/overlap-add sinusoidal modeling applied to the analysis and synthesis of musical tones. Journal of the Audio Engineering Society **40** (1992) 497–515

[4] Goodwin, M.: Adaptive signal models: theory, algorithms and audio applications. Kluwer Academic Publishers (1998)

[5] Chang, W., Wang, D.: Perceptual quantisation of lpc excitation parameters. IEE Proc. Vision, Image and Signal Processing **145** (1998) 155–159

[6] Painter, T., Spanias, A.: Perceptual segmentation and component selection in compact sinusoidal representation of audio. Proc. IEEE Int. Conf. on Acoustic, Speech and Signal Processing **5** (2001) 3289–3292

[7] Mallat, S., Zhang, Z.: Matching pursuits with time-frequency dictionaries. IEEE Transaction on Signal Processing **41** (1993) 3397–3415

[8] Verma, T., Meng, T.: Sinusoidal modeling using frame-based perceptually weighted matching pursuits. Proc. IEEE Int. Conf. on Acoustic, Speech and Signal Processing **2** (1999) 981–984

[9] George, E., Smith, M.: Speech analysis/synthesis and modifications using an analysis-by-synthesis/overlap-add sinusoidal model. IEEE Trans. on Speech and Audio Processing **5** (1997) 389–406

Smoothing Techniques for Tree-k-Grammar-Based Natural Language Modeling

Jose L. Verdú-Mas, Jorge Calera-Rubio, and Rafael C. Carrasco*

Departament de Llenguatges i Sistemes Informàtics
Universitat d'Alacant, E-03071 Alacant, Spain
{verdu,carrasco,calera}@dlsi.ua.es

Abstract. In a previous work, a new probabilistic context-free grammar (PCFG) model for natural language parsing derived from a tree bank corpus has been introduced. The model estimates the probabilities according to a generalized k-grammar scheme for trees. It allows for faster parsing, decreases considerably the perplexity of the test samples and tends to give more structured and refined parses. However, it suffers from the problem of incomplete coverage. In this paper, we compare several smoothing techniques such as *backing-off* or *interpolation* that are used to avoid assigning zero probability to any sentence.

1 Introduction

Some previous works ([1], [2], [3]) have explored the performance of parsers based on a probabilistic context-free grammar (PCFG) extracted from a training corpus. The results show that the type of tree representation used in the corpus can have a substantial effect in the estimated likelihood of each sentence or parse tree. According to the conclusions weaker independence assumptions —such as decreasing the number of nodes or increasing the number of node labels— improve the efficiency of the parser. The best results were obtained with offspring annotated labels where each node stores contextual information in the form of the category of the node's parent or the node's descendents. This is in agreement with the observation put forward by Charniak [4] that simple PCFGs, directly obtained from a corpus, largely overgeneralize. This property suggests that, in these models, a large probability mass is assigned to incorrect parses and, therefore, any procedure that concentrates the probability on the correct parses will increase the likelihood of the samples.

In this spirit, a generalization of the classic k-gram models, widely used for string processing [5], was introduced to the case of trees [3]. The PCFG variables are specialized by annotating them with the subtree they generate up to a certain level. In particular, we have studied offspring-annotated models with $k = 3$, that

---

* The authors wish to thank the Spanish CICyT for supporting this work through project TIC2000-1599.

F.J. Perales et al. (Eds.): IbPRIA 2003, LNCS 2652, pp. 1057–1065, 2003.

is, child-annotated models, and we have compared their parsing performance to that of unannotated PCFG –or $k = 2$, in our notation– and of parent-annotated PCFG [2]. The experiments showed that:

- The parsing performance of unannotated model is worse than any annotated model.
- The parsing performance of parent-annotated and child-annotated PCFG are similar.
- Parsers using child-annotated grammars are much faster because the number of possible parse trees considered is drastically reduced; this is, however, not the case with parent-annotated models.
- Child-annotated grammars have a larger number of parameters than parent-annotated PCFG which makes it difficult to estimate them accurately from currently available treebanks.
- Child-annotated models tend to give very structured and refined parses instead of flat parses, a tendency not so strong for parent-annotated grammars.

On the other hand, the smaller ambiguity of child-annotated model leads to unparsable sentences and, then, smoothing is essential in the construction of an efficient tree-k-grammar language model. A language model is a probability distribution over strings $P(s)$ that describes the frequency with which each string s occurs as a sentence in natural text [6].

In this work, we carry out a comparasion of three smoothing techniques. Two of them are well known: linear interpolation and tree-level back-off. In addition, we introduce a new smoothing technique: rule-level back-off. While being relatively simple to implement, we show that all these methods yield good performances with tree-k-grammar language models applied to structural, syntactical or lexical disambiguation.

The experiments were performed using the Wall Street Journal (WSJ) corpus of the University of Pennsylvania [7] modified as described in [4] and [2].

2   The Tree-k-Grammar Model

Recall that k-gram models are stochastic models for the generation of sequences $s_1, s_2, \ldots$ based on conditional probabilities, that is:

1. the probability $P(s_1 s_2 \ldots s_t | M)$ of a sequence in the model M is computed as a product $p_M(s_1) p_M(s_2 | s_1) \cdots p_M(s_t | s_1 s_2 \ldots s_{t-1})$, and
2. the dependence of the probabilities p_M on previous history is assumed to be restricted to the immediate preceding context, in particular, the last $k - 1$ words: $p_M(s_t | s_1 \ldots s_{t-1}) = p_M(s_t | s_{t-k+1} \ldots s_{t-1})$.

Note that in this kind of models, the probability that the observation s_t is generated at time t is computed as a function of the subsequence of length $k - 1$ that immediately precedes s_t (this is called a *state*). However, in the case of trees, it is not obvious what context should be taken in to account. Indeed, there is a natural preference when processing strings (the usual left-to-right order) but

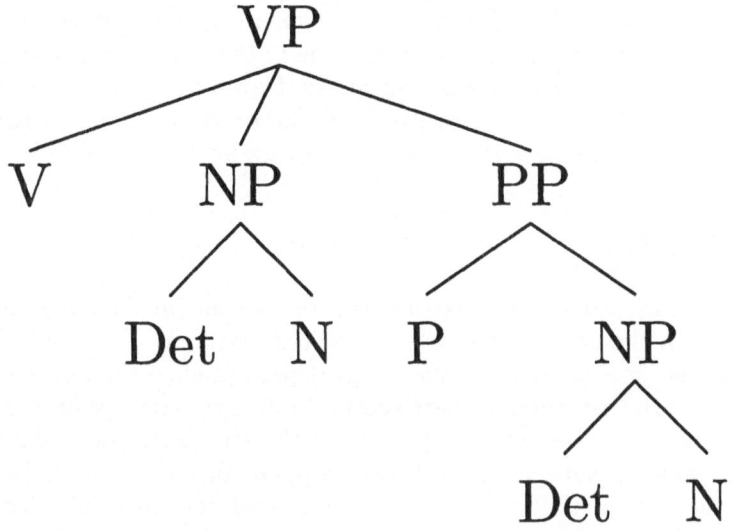

Fig. 1. A sample parse tree of depth 3

there are at least two standard ways of processing trees: ascending (or bottom-up) analysis and descending (or top-down) analysis. Ascending tree automata recognize a wider class of tree languages [8] and, therefore, they allow for richer descriptions.

Therefore, our model will compute the expansion probability for a given node as a function of the subtree of depth $k-2$ that the node generates i.e., every *state* stores a subtree of depth $k-2$ ([3]). In the particular case $k = 2$, only the label of the node is taken into account (this is analogous to the standard bigram model for strings) and the model coincides with the simple rule-counting approach used in treebank grammars. For instance, for the tree depicted in Fig. 1, the following rules are obtained:

$$VP \rightarrow V \ NP \ PP$$
$$NP \rightarrow Det \ N$$
$$PP \rightarrow P \ NP$$

However, in the case $k = 3$, child-annotated model, the expansion probabilities depend on states that are defined by the node label, the number of descendents the node and the sequence of labels in the descendents (if any). Therefore, for the same tree the following rules are obtained in this case:

$$VP_{V,NP,PP} \rightarrow V \ NP_{Det,N} \ PP_{P,NP}$$
$$NP_{Det,N} \rightarrow Det \ N$$
$$PP_{P,NP} \rightarrow P \ NP_{Det,N}$$

where each state has the form $X_{Z_1,...,Z_m}$. This is equivalent to performing a re-labelling of the parse tree before extracting the rules.

It is obvious that the $k = 3$ model incorporate contextual information that is not present in the case $k = 2$ and, then, a higher number of rules for a fixed number of categories is possible. In practice, due to the finite size of the training corpus, the number of rules is always moderate. However, as higher values of k lead to a huge number of possible rules, huge data sets would be necessary in order to have a reliable estimate of the probabilities for values above $k = 3$.

3   Smoothing

Statistical approaches to efficient parsing offer the advantage of making the most likely decision on the basis of available parsed text corpora.

Although the $k = 3$ model yields a good performance (in terms of both parsing and speed), their rules are very specific and, then, some events (subtrees, in our case) in the test set are not present in the training data, yielding zero probabilities. Due to data sparseness, this happens often in reality. However, this is not the case of the $k = 2$ model, with total coverage but with worse performance. This justifies the need for smoothing methods.

In the following, three smoothing techniques are described. Two of them are well known: linear interpolation and tree-level back-off. In addition, we introduce a new smoothing technique: rule-level back-off.

3.1   Linear Interpolation

Smoothing through *linear interpolation* [9] is performed by computing the probability of events as a weighted average of the probabilities given by different models. For instance, the smoothed probability of a $k = 3$ model could be computed as a weighted average of the probability given by the model itself, and that given by the $k = 2$ model, that is,

$$p(t) = \lambda p_3(t) + (1 - \lambda)p_2(t) \tag{1}$$

The mixing parameter $\lambda \in [0,1]$ was chosen to minimize the perplexity of a sample.

3.2   Tree-Level Back-Off

Back-off allows one to combine information from different models. In our case, the highest order model such that the probability of the event is greater than zero is selected. Some care has to be taken in order to preserve normalization.

$$p(t) = \begin{cases} (1 - \lambda)p_3(t) & \text{if } p_3(t) > 0 \\ \Lambda p_2(t) & \text{if } p_3(t) = 0 \end{cases} \tag{2}$$

where

$$\Lambda = \frac{\lambda}{\sum_{t:p_3(t)=0} p_2(t)}. \tag{3}$$

In our experiments, we will assume that a λ may be found such that no sentence s in the test set having a tree with $p_3(t) > 0$ has another tree t' with $p(t') > p(t)$. Therefore, p_2's will only be compared for trees with $p_3(t) = 0$. This leads to the following efficient parsing strategy: $k = 2$ (unannotated, slow) parsing is not launched if the $k = 3$ (annotated, fast) parser returns a tree, because the $k = 3$ tree will win out all $k = 2$ trees; therefore, for parsing purposes, the actual value of λ is irrelevant.

3.3   Rule-Level Back-Off

Our back-off model builds a new PCFG from the rules of the tree-k-grammar models and adding new rules which allow to switch beetween those models. In particular, the new PCFG consists of three different kinds of rules:

1. $k = 3$ rules with modified probability,
2. back-off rules that allow to switch to the lower model, and,
3. modified $k = 2$ rules to switch-back to the higher model.

This is done as follows (for the sake of simplicity, only a kind of binary rules are shown):

1. Add the rules of the $k = 3$ model with probability:

$$p(X_{Y,Z} \to \alpha) = p_3(X_{Y,Z} \to \alpha)(1 - \lambda(X_{Y,Z})) \qquad (4)$$

2. For each non-terminal symbol, $X_{Y,Z}$, of the $k = 3$ model, add a *back-off rule* $X_{Y,Z} \to Y\,Z$ with probability:

$$p(X_{Y,Z} \to Y\ Z) = \frac{\lambda(X_{Y,Z})}{\Lambda(X_{Y,Z})} \qquad (5)$$

where

$$\Lambda(X_{Y,Z}) = 1 - \sum_{X_{Y,Z} \to \alpha_Y \alpha_Z \in \{k=3\}} p_2(Y \to \alpha_Y) p_2(Z \to \alpha_Z) \qquad (6)$$

3. Add the $k = 2$ rules as unary rules, that is, if the rule is $X \to Y\,Z$, then, add $X \to X_{Y,Z}$ with probability:

$$p(X \to X_{Y,Z}) = p_2(X \to Y\ Z) \qquad (7)$$

The grammar is normalized provided that parses of the form $X_{Y,Z} \to Y\,Z \to \alpha_Y \alpha_Z$ are assigned a zero probability if $X_{Y,Z} \to \alpha_Y\,\alpha_Z$ exists in the grammar.

4 Experimental Results

4.1 General Conditions

We have performed experiments to assess the structural disambiguation performance of tree-k-grammar smoothed models as compared to the ones unsmoothed, that is, to compare their relative ability for selecting the best parse tree. To build training corpora and test sets of parse trees, we have used English parse trees from the Penn Treebank, release 3, with small, basically structure-preserving modifications:

- insertion of a root node (ROOT) in all sentences, (as in Charniak [4]) to encompass the sentence and final periods, etc.;
- removal of nonsyntactic annotations (prefixes and suffixes) from constituent labels (for instance, NP-SBJ is reduced to NP);
- removal of empty constituents; and
- collapse of single-child nodes with the parent node when they have the same label (to avoid rules of the form A $\rightarrow$ A which would generate an infinite number of parse trees for some sentences).

In all experiments, the training corpus consisted of all of the trees (41,532) in sections 02 to 22 of the *Wall Street Journal* portion of Penn Treebank, modified as above. This gives a total number of more than 600,000 subtrees. The test set contained all sentences in section 23 having no more than 40 words.

4.2 Structural Disambiguation Results

All grammar models were written as standard context-free grammars, and Earley's probabilistic extended parsing algorithm [10] was used to obtain, for each sentence, the most likely parse that was compared to the corresponding tree in the test set using the customary PARSEVAL evaluation metric [11, 12, p. 432] after eliminating any parent and child annotation of nodes in the most likely tree delivered by the parser. PARSEVAL gives partial credit to incorrect parses by establishing these two measures:

- *labeled precision* (P) is the fraction of correctly-labeled nonterminal bracketings (constituents) in the most likely parse which match the parse in the treebank,
- *labeled recall* (R) is the fraction of brackets in the treebank parse which are found in the most likely parse with the same label, and

As baseline, three non smoothed models were evaluated:

- A standard treebank grammar, with no annotation of node labels ($k=2$), with probabilities for 15,140 rules.
- A child-annotated grammar ($k=3$), with probabilities for 92,830 rules.
- A parent-annotated grammar (PARENT), with probabilities for 23,020 rules.

Table 1. Parsing results with different annotation models: labelled recall R, labelled precision P, fraction of exact matches, fraction of sentences parsed, and average time per sentence in seconds

MODEL	R	P	EXACT	PARSED	t
$k=2$	70.7%	76.1%	10.0%	100%	57
$k=3$	79.6%	74.3%	13.4%	94.6%	7
PARENT	80.0%	81.9%	16.3%	100%	340

Table 2. Parsing results with different smoothed models

MODEL	R	P	EXACT	PARSED	t
M1	80.2%	78.6%	17.4%	100%	57
M2	78.9%	74.2%	17.1%	100%	9.3
M3	82.4%	81.3%	17.5%	100%	68

As expected, the number of rules obtained increases as more information is conveyed by the node label, although this increase is not extreme. On the other hand, as the generalization power decreases, some sentences in the test set become unparsable, that is, they cannot be generated by the grammar. The results in table 1, that were analyzed in detail in [3], show that the parsing performance of parent-annotated and child-annotated PCFG is similar but parsers using child-annotated grammars are much faster because the number of possible parse trees considered is drastically reduced.

Those smoothed models were evaluated:

- A linear interpolated model, M1, as described in section 3.1 with $\lambda = 0.7$ (the value of λ selected to minimize the perplexity).
- A tree-level back-off, M2, as described in section 3.2.
- A rule-level back-off, M3, as described in section 3.3. This model has 92,830 $k = 3$ rules, 15,140 $k = 2$ rules and 10,250 back-off rules. A fixed parameter λ (0.005) was selected to maximize labelled recall and precision).

The results in table 2 show that:

- M2 is the fastest but its performance is worse than that of M1 and M3.
- M1 and M3 parse sentences at a comparable speed but recall and precision are better using M3.

Compared to un-smoothed models, smoothed ones:

- Cover the whole test set ($k = 3$ did not).
- Parsed at reasonable speed (compared to PARENT).
- Achieved acceptable performance ($k = 2$ did not).

5   Conclusions

We have compared several smoothing techniques for tree-k-grammar-based natural language modeling and parsing that are used to avoid assigning zero probability to any sentence. In particular, we have introduced a new smoothing technique: a rule-level back-off that builds a new PCFG from the rules of the tree-k-grammar models and adding new rules which allow to switch beetween those models. The new grammar cover the whole test set and improve the performance in terms of parsing.

References

[1] E. Charniak and G. Carroll. Context-sensitive statistics for improved grammatical language models. In *Proceedings of the 12th National Conference on Artificial Inteligence, AAAI Press*, pages 742–747, Seattle, WA, 1994.

[2] Mark Johnson. PCFG models of linguistic tree representations. *Computational Linguistics*, 24(4):613–632, 1998.

[3] Jose L. Verdu-Mas, Mikel L. Forcada, Rafael C. Carrasco, and Jorge Calera-Rubio. Tree k-grammar models for natural language modelling and parsing. In Terry Caelli, Adnan Amin, Rober P. W.Duin, Mohamed Kamel, and Dick de Ridder, editors, *Proceedings of the Joint IAPR International Workshops on Syntactical and Structural Pattern Recognition and Statistical Pattern Recognition*, volume 2396 of *Lecture Notes in Computer Science*, pages 56–63, Windsor-Canada, 2002. Springer.

[4] E. Charniak. Treebank grammars. In *Proceedings of the Thirteenth National Conference on Artificial Intelligence*, pages 1031–1036. AAAI Press/MIT Press, 1996.

[5] Peter F. Brown, Vincent J. Della Pietra, Peter V. deSouza, Jenifer C. Lai, and Robert L. Mercer. Class-based n-gram models of natural language. *Computational Linguistics*, 18(4):467–479, 1992.

[6] Stanley F. Chen and Joshua Goodman. An empirical study of smoothing techniques for language modeling. In Arivind Joshi and Martha Palmer, editors, *Proceedings of the Thirty-Fourth Annual Meeting of the Association for Computational Linguistics*, pages 310–318, San Francisco, 1996. Morgan Kaufmann Publishers.

[7] Mitchell P. Marcus, Beatrice Santorini, and Mary Ann Marcinkiewicz. Building a large annotated corpus of english: the penn treebank. *Computational Linguistics*, 19:313–330, 1993.

[8] Maurice Nivat and Andreas Podelski. Minimal ascending and descending tree automata. *SIAM Journal on Computing*, 26(1):39–58, 1997.

[9] L. R. Bahl, P. F. Brown, P. V. de Souza, and R. L. Mercer. A tree-based statistical language model for natural language speech recognition. In A. Waibel and K.-F. Lee, editors, *Readings in Speech Recognition*, pages 507–514. Kaufmann, San Mateo, CA, 1990.

[10] Andreas Stolcke. An efficient probabilistic context-free parsing algorithm that computes prefix probabilities. In *Computational Linguistics, MIT Press for the Association for Computational Linguistics*, volume 21. 1995.

[11] Ezra Black, Steven Abney, Dan Flickinger, Claudia Gdaniec, Ralph Grishman, Philip Harrison, Donald Hindle, Robert Ingria, Frederick Jelinek, Judith Klavans, Mark Liberman, Mitch Marcus, Salim Roukos, Beatrice Santorini, and Tomek Strzalkowski. A procedure for quantitatively comparing the syntatic coverage of english grammars. In *Proc. Speech and Natural Language Workshop 1991*, pages 306–311, San Mateo, CA, 1991. Morgan Kauffmann.

[12] Christopher D. Manning and Hinrich Schutze. *Foundations of Statistical Natural Language Processing*. MIT Press, 1999.

Colour Constancy Algorithm Based on the Minimization of the Distance between Colour Histograms*

Jaume Vergés–Llahí and Alberto Sanfeliu

Institut de Robòtica i Informàtica Industrial
Technological Park of Barcelona, U Building
Llorens i Artigas 4-6 2nd Floor, 08028 Barcelona, Spain.
{jverges, asanfeliu}@iri.upc.es

Abstract. Colour is an important clue in many applications in machine vision and image processing. Despite of this, the drawback of colour is its dependence upon illumination changes. Colour constancy aims to provide colour appearance of objects with stability. This paper presents a simple and robust colour constancy algorithm based on a coefficient transformation of the colour coordinates of pixels which goal is to reduce the distance between histograms of two images of similar scenes under different illuminations. Our main contribution is that our algorithm only make use of raw image data contrary to most usual colour constancy algorithms. We show that our approach is able to cope with colour change since it substantially reduces the distance between colour histograms.
Keywords: colour, colour change, colour constancy, colour histograms.

1 Introduction

In a number of applications from machine vision tasks such as object recognition, image indexing and retrieval, to digital photography or new multimedia applications, it is important that colours recorded by a device remain constant under changes in scene illumination.

Hence, a preliminary step when using colour must be to remove the pernicious effect of illumination change. This problem is usually referred in literature as *colour constancy*, i.e., the stability of surface colour appearance under varying illumination conditions.

A great effort has been put lately in solving this problem. Part of the difficulty is due to the fact that this problem is entangled with other confounding phenomena such as the shape of the objects, viewing and illumination geometry besides changes in illumination spectral power distribution and reflectance properties of the imaged objects.

Let us sketch some of the most important approaches and their assumptions. Land [1] assumes that every image contains a white patch. Another assumption

---

* Partially funded by a fellowship of the Government of Catalonia and the CICYT DPI2001-2223.

F.J. Perales et al. (Eds.): IbPRIA 2003, LNCS 2652, pp. 1066-1073, 2003.

[2] is that the average reflectance of all surfaces in a scene is *achromatic*, i.e., gray. In this case, the average colour of the light leaving the surface will be the colour of the incident illumination.

Other authors have tried to exploit features not present in the idealised Mondrian world, such as *specularities* [3], *shadows* [4], or *mutual illumination* [5], to recover information about the scene illumination. As reported in [6], the main drawback of all these algorithms is that their assumptions are often violated in regular images. In the other hand, among the others which work on real images, their performance is still far from being good enough as reported in [7].

An alternative is the set of algorithms which do not try to seek for a unique solution, rather the most *likely* one. For example, the *gamut-mapping* algorithm developed by Forsyth [8] and expanded later by Finlayson [9, 10] selects a solution from the set of all feasible solutions using different selection criteria.

Other authors [11, 12] have posed the problem in a probabilistic framework and, more recently, Sapiro [12] has developed an algorithm based on the probabilistic Hough transform while Finlayson has used this framework in his *colour by correlation* algorithm [6]. The neural network approach [13] to colour constancy can similarly be seen as a method of dealing with the inherent uncertainty of the problem. All these algorithms represent an improvement at solving the colour constancy problem, but some further work must still be done to find a definitive solution [6].

The main problems in colour constancy algorithms are that they should be solely based upon image data rather than on a set of stored data about illuminants which is most of the times difficult to gather or can be inaccurate. Moreover, some approaches using colour, such as image indexing and retrieval, rely enormously on histograms as a mean of describing colour distributions and comparing the appearance of images. Therefore, it seems clear that histogram distance can be a good tool to lead the search for a proper colour transformation which keeps colour as constant as possible.

This paper describes a simple and robust procedure which consists in minimising an *objective function* using a downhill simplex minimization scheme. The objective function gauges the dissimilarities in colour of two images by means of the difference of their colour histograms. The minimization is performed in the space of colour transformations. We used the kind of colour transformations habitual in $2D$ gamut-mapping algorithms, [8–10], which is based on an independent coefficient modifying each colour channel besides of using chromaticity coordinates.

With regard to algorithms such as gamut-mapping [10] or colour by correlation [6], our main contributions consist both in proposing a computational scheme to colour constancy which is completely based on raw image data with no further assumptions about illumination and that of simplifying colour constancy up to a minimization problem driven by a colour measure widely spread in tasks such as image indexing. This way, despite the good performances of the aforementioned approaches, our algorithm also reaches satisfactory results with far fewer *a priori* information under a varied set of illumination.

2   Colour Change Model

Let be I^1 and I^2 two colour images of nearly the same scene taken under different illumination conditions. We take I^2 as the *reference* and our goal will be to find a way to change the colour of pixels of the image I^1 so as to turn them as close as possible to those of image I^2, i.e., to keep the colour of the scene constant.

Since some features such as shape and shading only affect the magnitude of the reflected light but not its colour the use of the *chromaticity coordinates* (r, g) is justified. In the present work, we use the chromaticities defined in [6]:

$$(r_i, g_i) = \left(\frac{R_i}{B_i}, \frac{G_i}{B_i} \right), \quad i = 1, \dots, N \tag{1}$$

where (R_i, G_i, B_i) is the colour response at the ith pixel and N is the number of pixels in an image.

Our colour constancy algorithm is based on computing a transformation of the following form:

$$(r'_i, g'_i) = (\alpha \cdot r_i, \beta \cdot g_i), \quad i = 1, \dots, N \tag{2}$$

where (α, β) are the coefficients that change coordinates r_i and g_i into r'_i and g'_i, respectively. This way, we can denote the transformed imaged from I as $I|_{(\alpha,\beta)}$. This sort of transformation has been successfully used in the 2D gamut mapping algorithm of Finlayson [9, 10, 6] and is based upon the fact that the sensitivity functions of the set of sensors are independent one another.

Provided that the previous model copes with colour change in an adequate way, we now face the problem of computing a proper transformation (α_0, β_0) out of image data. The main idea followed along this work is that from the space of all feasible transformations $\mathcal{T}$ we must take the one that changes colours in image I^1 in a way that most resemble those of the reference I^2. We use the *Swain&Ballard* distance [14] as a mean of computing the colour difference between images I^1 and I^2:

$$dist\left(\mathcal{H}^1, \mathcal{H}^2 \right) = \sum_k \min \left\{ H_k^1, H_k^2 \right\} \in [0, 1] \tag{3}$$

where $\mathcal{H}^1$ and $\mathcal{H}^2$ are the *chromaticity histograms* of images I^1 and I^2, respectively. These histograms take into account of colours for each image.

Consequently, we can now define an *objective function* f which is dependent on (α, β) as follows:

$$f(\alpha, \beta) = dist\left(\mathcal{H}^1|_{(\alpha,\beta)}, \mathcal{H}^2 \right) \tag{4}$$

where $\mathcal{H}^1|_{(\alpha,\beta)}$ is the histogram of the transformed image $I^1|_{(\alpha,\beta)}$ and $\mathcal{H}^2$ that of the reference I^2.

This way, the problem of colour constancy has been translated into a problem of *minimization*, i.e., that of finding the transformation (α_0, β_0) such that:

$$(\alpha_0, \beta_0) = \operatorname*{argmin}_{(\alpha, \beta) \in \mathcal{T}} \{f(\alpha, \beta)\} \tag{5}$$

Once we have a transformation (α_0, β_0), we can recover the true colours of I^1 from the transformed image $I^1\big|_{(\alpha_0,\beta_0)}$ which colours are close to those of image I^2 in the following way:

$$(R_i', G_i', B_i') = (r_i' \cdot B_i, g_i' \cdot B_i, 1 \cdot B_i), \quad i = 1, \ldots, N \tag{6}$$

where (R_i', G_i', B_i') forms the ith pixel of the image $I^1\big|_{(\alpha_0,\beta_0)}$.

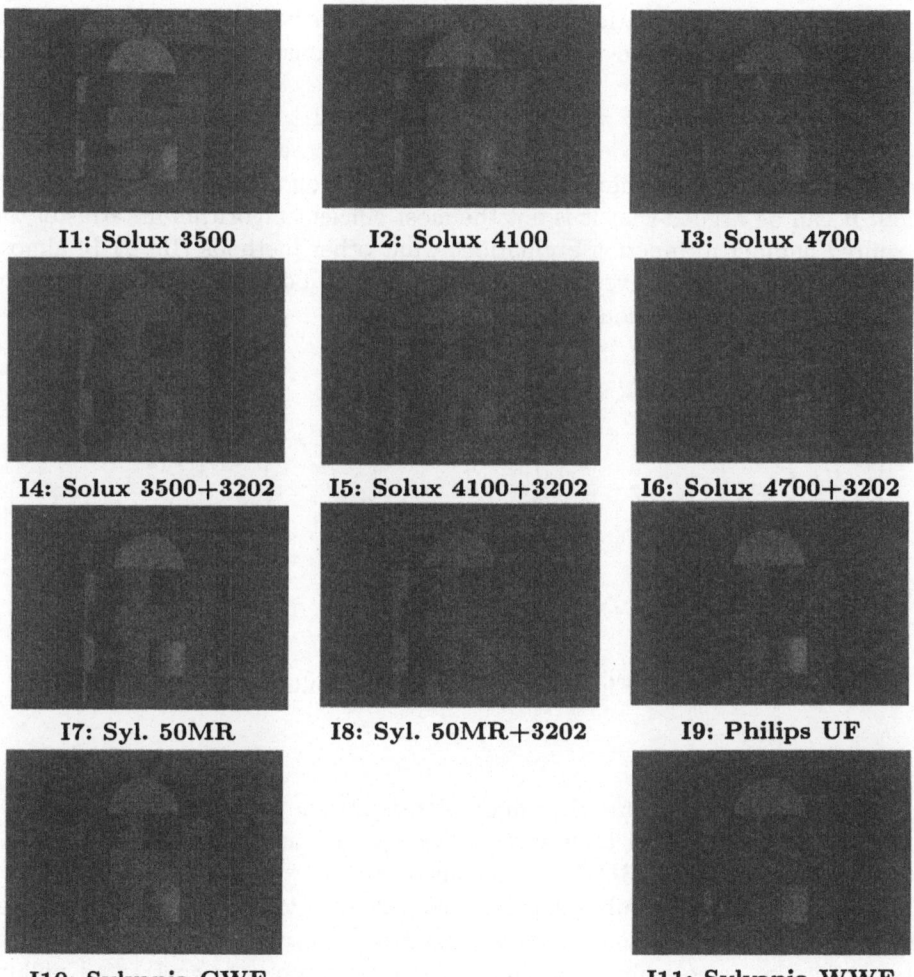

I1: Solux 3500   I2: Solux 4100   I3: Solux 4700

I4: Solux 3500+3202   I5: Solux 4100+3202   I6: Solux 4700+3202

I7: Syl. 50MR   I8: Syl. 50MR+3202   I9: Philips UF

I10: Sylvania CWF   I11: Sylvania WWF

Fig. 1. Set of images.

3   Downhill Simplex Minimization Algorithm

The problem of minimization consists, once a function f depending on one or more independent variables is given, in finding the value of those variables where f takes on a maximum or a minimum value.

Moreover, some methods need to evaluate the derivatives of the function. Despite the fact that algorithms with derivatives are more powerful than those using only the function, they are sometimes computationally expensive or numerically unstable and does not always compensate for the additional calculations.

Due to the precise nature of our problem, where computing the objective function is computationally expensive and derivatives are somewhat unstable because of the discretisation of histograms, it has been clear at once to use of a minimization method which needs no evaluations of the derivatives of the objective function.

The *downhill simplex method* due to Nelder and Mead [15] requires only function evaluations, not derivatives. This method crawls downhill in a straightforward way that makes almost no special assumption about the objective function. It can be argued that it is not the most efficient algorithm in terms of the required number of function evaluations what other methods [15] could almost surely outperform. However, downhill simplex method is extremely robust and needs far lesser information.

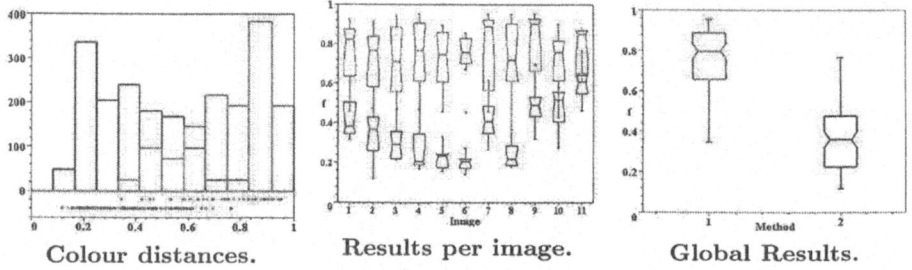

Colour distances.   Results per image.   Global Results.

Fig. 2. Colour constancy results.

A *simplex* is the geometrical figure consisting, in M dimensions, of $M + 1$ points (vertices) and all their interconnecting segments, faces, etc. In $2D$, a simplex is a triangle; in $3D$, it is a tetrahedron.

The goal of the downhill simplex method is to transform an initial guess simplex by means of a set of moves (reflection, contraction and expansion) of its vertices so as to embrace a *valley*. Then the simplex is contracted pulling itself in around the lowest (best) point. As any multidimensional minimization routine, a termination criteria must be given, which can be either the decrease in the function value or the distance the point moved in a step.

As an initial simplex we try the triangle $\mathcal{T} = \{P_0, P_0 + (\lambda, 0), P_0 + (0, \lambda)\}$, where P_0 is the starting point and λ is a constant for the problem's length scale.

Thus, the point $(\alpha_0, \beta_0) \in \mathcal{T}$ found is a (local, at least) minimum of the objective functions f and represents the colour transformation for colour constancy. To likely find a point close to a global minimum, we perform the search at different starting points P_0 of the transformation space and take the better one.

4   Results

In this section, we perform the previous algorithm in a set of 11 images of a scene taken under different illuminations. We compare the algorithm results with the worst performance obtained when no colour constancy algorithm is carried out.

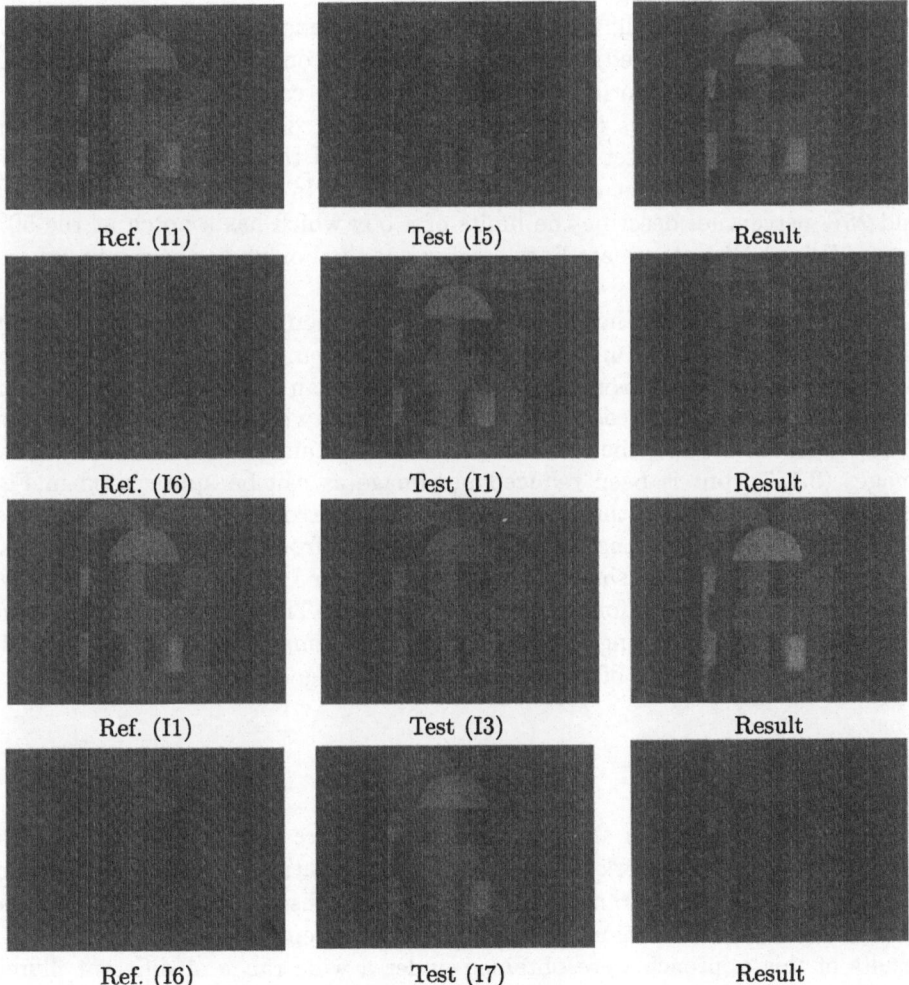

Fig. 3. Some resultant images.

The objects displayed in these images are real block figures of different plain colours. In Fig. 1 we show the set of images. This set belongs to the database of the *Computational Vision Lab* at the *Simon Fraser University* and can be found via Internet at the following URL in http://www.cs.sfu.ca/~colour/.

Objects present shading due to their volumes and shadows because of the direction of the incident light. The nature of the illumination that were used to acquire the images are both bulb and fluorescent lights. Various kinds of daylight bulbs were taken into account, each of different colour temperature (3500K, 4100K and 4700K), as well as a mixture of them.

The experiment consists in taking an image as a reference while computing a colour transformation for the rest of images onto the reference. Afterwards, we compare the colour histograms of these images by means of Eq. (3). This is carried out for every image of the set.

In Fig. 2, we plot in different ways how the distance between colours behave before (blue) and after (red) performing our colour constancy algorithm in order to know whether our algorithm is able to cope with colour constancy.

Leftmost image shows the distributions of the colour histogram distances, while center and rightmost images are box plots of the distances per image of the set and the whole set of images, respectively. In every box plot, the 75% and 25% percentiles describe the limits of a box which has a notch at the 50% percentile as well as there are lines coming out the box up to the minimum and maximum values.

It is clear that there has been a global reduction in the amount of colour distance between images under different illumination, meaning that our colour constancy algorithm is working properly. The mean distance between colour histograms has been decreased from 0.760 to 0.374, which is almost a reduction of the 50%. Meanwhile, the standard deviation remains equal if we take all the images (0.157), but is been reduced per image as can be appreciated in Fig. 2. This means the algorithms is not introducing error in transformed images. Finally, we can say that the median has decreased from 0.797 to 0.359 as well.

Finally, in Fig. 3 we show some images obtained using our algorithm. We place the *reference* image followed by the *test* image. The third image is the *result* obtained after transforming the test image. These images provides a seemingly proof of the performance of the colour constancy algorithm.

5   Conclusions

The present paper's main aim is to show a procedure based on raw image data that allows, in a framework of coefficient transformations of chromaticity coordinates, to find a colour transformation so that the discrepancy in colour caused by variations in illumination conditions over the scene is greatly reduced. The results of this approach were obtained under a wide range of different illuminations and its performance compared to that of the worst case occurred when no colour constancy is applied. We can state that our algorithm improve colour images and provides a way to stabilise colour in front of illumination changes.

References

1. Land, E., McCann, J.: The retinex theory of color vision. Scientific American **6** (1977) 108–129
2. Buchsbaum, G.: A spatial processor model for object colour perception. Journal of Franklin Institute **310** (1980) 1–26
3. Shafer, S.: Using color to separate reflection components. Color Research and Application **10** (1985) 210–218
4. Finlayson, G., Funt, B.: Color constancy with shadows. Perception, Special Issue on the 17th European Conference on Visual Perception **23** (1994) 89–90
5. Funt, B., Drew, M., Ho, J.: Color constancy from mutual reflection. Int. J. Computer Vision **6** (1991) 5–24
6. Finlayson, G., Hordley, S., Hubel, P.: Colour by correlation: A simple, unifying framework for colour constancy. IEEE Trans. on Pattern Analysis and Machine Intelligence **23** (2001) 1209–1221
7. Funt, B., Barnard, K., Martin, L.: Is colour constancy good enough? In: Proc. 5th European Conference Computer Vision. (1998) 445–459
8. Forsyth, D.: A novel algorithm for color constancy. Int. Journal of Computer Vision **5** (1990) 5–36
9. Finlayson, G.: Color in perspective. IEEE Trans. on Pattern Analysis and Machine Intelligence **18** (1996) 1034–1038
10. Finlayson, G., Hordley, S.: Improving gamut mapping color constancy. IEEE Trans. on Image Processing **9** (2000) 1774–1783
11. Brainard, D., Freeman, W.: Bayesian color constancy. J. Opt. Soc. Am. A **14** (1997) 1393–1411
12. Sapiro, G.: Color and illuminant voting. IEEE Trans. on Pattern Analysis and Machine Intelligence **21** (1999) 1210–1215
13. Cardei, V., Funt, B., Barnard, K.: Adaptive illuminant estimation using neural networks. In: Int. Conf. on Artificial Neural Networks. (1998) 749–754
14. Swain, M., Ballard, D.: Indexing via color histograms. In: Proc. Int. Conf. on Computer Vision. (1990) 390–393
15. Press, W., Flannery, B., Teukolsky, S., Vetterling, W.: Numerical Recipes in C: The Art of Scientific Computing. 2on edn. Cambridge University Press (1993)

Video Segmentation for Traffic Monitoring Tasks Based on Pixel-Level Snakes

D. L Vilariño, D. Cabello, X. M. Pardo, and V. M. Brea

Department of Electronics and Computer Science
University of Santiago de Compostela
15782 Santiago de Compostela, Spain
{dlv,diego,pardo,victor}@dec.usc.es
http://www-gva.dec.usc.es

Abstract. In this paper we address a moving object segmentation technique for a video monitoring system. This is approached by means of active contours which appear to be an efficient tool for the spatio-temporal data analysis from 2D image sequences. Particularly we make use of a new active contour concept: the pixel-level snakes whose characteristics allow a high control on the contour evolution and approach topological transformations with a low computational cost. The proposal is focused in the traffic monitoring and the incident detection systems.

1 Introduction

In recent years, applications dealing with automatic surveillance and monitoring have become increasingly important. Traffic monitoring tasks such as detection of anomalies (slow or heavy traffic, vehicles stopped in a crossroad, etc.), classification or counting of automobiles for statistics and forecasts on the traffic fluidity and detection and alert of possible accidents, benefit from automatic systems.

A complete video monitoring system should contain a low-level processing stage in order to detect and segment the moving objects from video sequences; a middle-level processing stage where primitives are extracted and finally a high-level processing stage where the results are interpreted and the suitable actions are carried out (alarm activation, semaphores managing, etc.).

In this paper we focus our attention in the low-level tasks: the moving object detection and segmentation. These probably represent the more critical tasks into the complete system for two reasons: on one hand their efficiency is fundamental to successfully approach the subsequent classification and interpretation steps; on the other hand, this stage acts on a greater volume of data and so it is essential to guarantee the high speed response needed in real-time systems.

The segmentation of moving objects relies on spatio-temporal information extracted from the processing of two or more frames of an image sequence. Like *static* image segmentation the different approaches can be classified in region-based [1, 7], edge-based [11] and clustering algorithms [4]. A good review of the strategies of video segmentation can be found in [14].

F.J. Perales et al. (Eds.): IbPRIA 2003, LNCS 2652, pp. 1074–1081, 2003.

Active contour is a widely acknowledge technique for segmentation and tracking because of its ability to integrate information from different sources and its flexibility. An active contour is an elastic curve which evolves controlled by image features and shape constrains towards the boundaries of the objects of interest. The assumption of the moving objects appearing slightly shifted and/or deformed in two consecutive frames make attractive the application of the active contour techniques to their segmentation. However, to this end it is necessary to give solution to some shortcomings of the active contour approaches:

1. In order to give solution to the complete problem of the location of the desired objects into the scene it is needed to determine the image features suitable for each particular application.
2. The active contours were initially designed as interactive models. For no-interactive applications they must be started close to the structures of interest to guarantee an efficient operation.
3. Due to their parametric nature, the classical active contour techniques cannot split a contour or merge two of them into one. This limits their application to problems where the number of interesting objects and their approximate locations are known *a priori.*
4. All the active contour techniques require to a greater or lesser degree, a high computational cost, which renders them inappropriate for applications needing fast time response.

The two first drawbacks are mainly linked with the particular application and must be approached into this framework. However the other two are inherent to the early active contour techniques which lead to new strategies to solve one or both of two limitations. Among them are the level-set based models which rely on the wave-front propagation with velocity depending on the curvature [10]. This kind of strategies gives a smart solution to the problem of the topological transformations among contours. However, due to their characteristics of evolution they present difficulties to introduce control mechanism and to impose geometric or topological restrictions. The variation of the geodesic active contours clearly outperforms the former level-set based models and in some way reduces the mentioned control limitations [3]. Moreover most of these algorithms require a high computational cost. The reduction of the complexity order lead to strong restrictions in the wave-front evolution like dynamics exclusively compressive or expansive.

Following we propose the use of pixel-level snakes for moving object image segmentation.

2   Pixel-Level Snakes

Pixel-level snakes (PLS) have been first introduced for the task of static image segmentation [12]. PLS are represented as a pixel level discretization in such a way all pixels of the contours evolve independently based on local information. This methodology puts together characteristics from the snake and level-set based approaches in both the contour evolution process and the mechanism for the contour guide. Like level-set based methods and particularly the geodesic models, the contours evolve guided by local information and regularizing terms dependent on the curvature towars (local) minimal distance curves based on a metric defined as a function of the features of interest. On the other hand, like snake models the contour evolution is processed in an *explicit* way: the guiding forces act directly on the curves. This provides a high flexibility and control for the dynamics of the PLS allowing to guide the contour evolution efficiently and to give solution to complex problems as is the case of the topological transformations.

The PLS are represented as sets of connected activated pixels into a binary image called contour image. This has the same size as the original image. The contour evolution is based on an iterative process of activation and deactivation of the contour image pixels according with the guiding information. This includes an external potential, that takes lower values near the edge features and an internal potential, which forces the smoothing of the contour shape.

In Fig. 1 an algorithm for the PLS is showed. The processing of the algorithm is extended along the four cardinal directions. Following we will outline a brief overview of the algorithm. Readers interested in a more detailed description are addressed to [13]. The goal after each iteration is to obtain new thin contours slightly shifted and/or deformed based on the guide information in order to come closer and the final contour which defines the region under interest. The modules involved in this task are the following:

In *IPE*, the internal potential is extracted from the active contours. This is estimated by a recursive low-pass filtering acting on the contour image. The

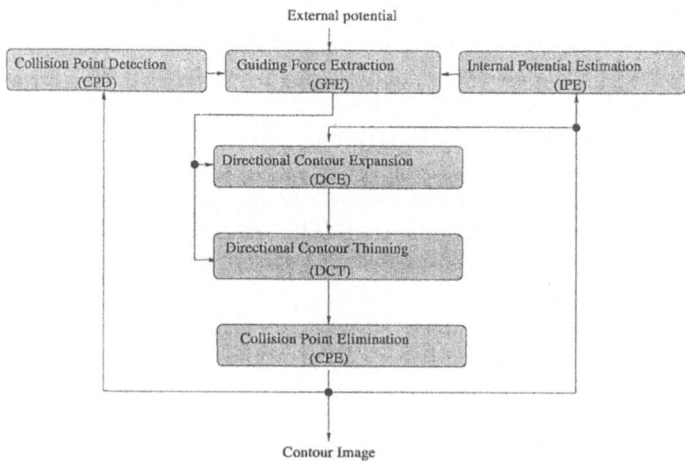

Fig. 1. Block diagram containing all the operations of the pixel-level snake algorithm

result is a real-valued array characterized by lower potential values into the cavities of the contour and higher outside. Therefore a directional gradient operation acting on this array will originate positive internal forces which lead to reduce the local curvature radius and then to smooth the contour shape.

In *GFE*, the components of the guiding forces along the direction under processing are derived from the external and internal potential matrices by simple directional gradient operations. Since a positive force should indicate a valid direction for the contour evolution, only the sign of the guiding forces is needed. Therefore the module of generation of guiding forces should also include a thresholding operation.

In *DCE*, the white pixels into the contour image which are neighbors to black pixels in the direction under processing should be activated if the component of the guiding force for this direction is *positive* in those locations.

In *DCT*, the black pixels into the contour image will be deactivated if the component of the guiding force for this direction is *negative* in those location and this operation does not provoke a rupture in the contour continuity.

When the number of active contours does not coincide with the number of objects into the scene the collision between different contours (or different parts of the same contour) may occur. The pixel-level snakes can handle these situations by foreseeing possible collision between contours and then carrying out a controlled topological transformation.

The first operation is carried out in *CPD* and consists on avoiding the possible collision between contours by the previous estimation of the locations where a collision could occur. This action is relatively easy to approach because the contours move as the effect of activation and deactivation of pixels in the contour image. Thus, the contours evolve pixel to pixel, which allows to estimate the contour location and shape in the next iteration. This operation is carried out by taking as input the binary contour image and returning a binary image with black pixels in those locations where a collision between contours could take place in the next iteration. Therefore, by the projection of this binary map onto the output of the *GFE* module, the operations of activation and deactivation of pixels will be prevented on those conflictive locations and consequently the contour collision will be avoided.

This operation generates a one-pixel wide wall between two contour pieces that otherwise could collide. Now it is possible to take advantages of these *collision points* in order to perform a controlled splitting of the old contours and merging of the new ones. These operations are carried out in the *CPE* block by following three simple steps (Fig. 2). First the set of collision points which can guarantee a correct contour separation by only local operations are selected. Then the splitting of the old contours is carried out by deactivating the neighboring pixels in the direction under processing (vertical direction in the example), to each of those collision points selected in the previous step. Finally the generation of the new contours are made by activating the neighboring pixels in the direction under processing (horizontal direction in the example), to the collision points selected in the previous step.

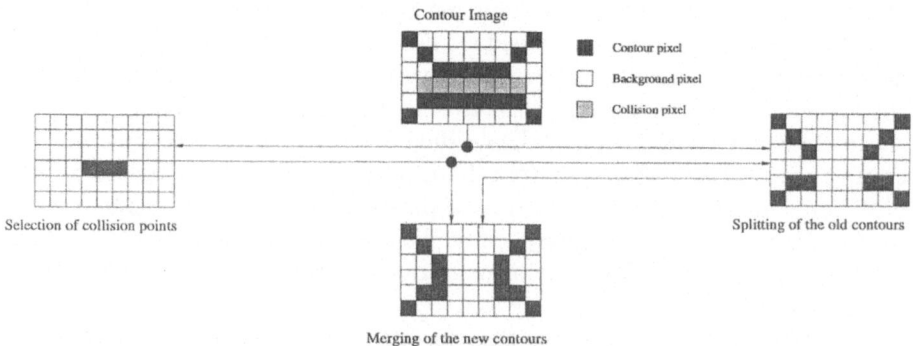

Fig. 2. Example illustrating the operation in the *CPE* module

All the operations of the PLS algorithm can be performed using parallel local operations extended to all pixels of the image. The internal potential estimation and the guiding force extraction (from the external and internal potentials) are supported by simple linear filterings. The remainder processing steps can be implemented as simple hit and miss binary morphological operations together with clemental binary logic operations. Thus it is possible the projection of the algorithm onto architectures like cellular neural networks (CNN) [5]. These constitute a class of recurrent locally coupled array of identical and simple processing elements. Since the coupling between processing elements is exclusively local, the hardware complexity does not increase with the array size. This fact has allowed the hardware implementation of a considerable number of processing elements into a chip [9].

The projection of the PLS-algorithm onto these CNN structures permits to take advantage of the characteristics of massively parallel processing of this kind of architectures. This fact guarantees a fast computation making the pixel-level snakes a valid tool for those applications needing fast time response. We have carried out the projection of the algorithm onto a general purpose continuous-time CNN [8] as well as on a specific purpose discrete-time CNN [2]. Both implementations have demonstrated fast-time response capabilities independent of the number of involved active contours.

3   Tracking with PLS

The moving objects into an image sequence appear slightly shifted/deformed in consecutive slices. Therefore, once the active contours delineate the objects of interest in one frame, the segmentation proceeds on the next frame taking as initial contours the resulting from the previous frame. Thus, the approach of the external potential by local information becomes suitable. However it is needed to provide automatically the first set of initial contours. In some applications this can be achieved by using a rather simple initiation process. This consists

Fig. 3. Example of contour tracking

Fig. 4. Restoration of the control zone after a topological transformation

to fix one (or several) initial contour defining the perimeter of the region to be controlled or situate it into the trajectory of the mobile objects. Thus the moving objects will come close to snakes, contrary to it is usual. This idea is illustrated with an synthetic example in Fig. 3.

We have established a control zone delimited by an active contour with rectangular shape. A potential barrier outside of this location is imposed, so that any object, moving outside the control zone is ignored. However when any of these passes through the limits of the control zone, the active contour reacts delineating it. When the object is completely inside the control zone, a topological transformation generates two new contours from the original active contour. One of these contours delineates the object into the control zone and the another contour restores the control perimeter. This process of restoration, mainly due to the influence of the internal forces, is illustrated in Fig. 4.

Finally another topological transformation occurs when the object goes out the control zone merging again the two active contours into one.

Concerning the external potential, the contours are usually assumed to evolve towards features (edges, motion, motion history) easily obtained by local operators [6]. Once each map is obtained, a diffusion operation (like that in the internal energy estimation) is carried out and the result is added to a weighted version of the edge map. The result is an external potential image guiding the contours towards the boundaries of the moving objects.

In order to illustrate the suitability of our proposal for real applications, Fig. 5 shows an example of moving object segmentation for a control traffic system from a real image sequence[1]. The external potential was derived as before from the difference between each frame and a reference without mobile objects inside the control zone. As it can be seen only those objects going into the control zone are segmented and tracked.

---

[1] Copyright ©1998 by H.H. Nagel. Institut Für Algorithmen und Kognitive Systeme. Fakultät für Informatik, Universität Karlsruhe (TH). Postfach 6980, D-76128 Karlsruhe, Germany. http://i21www.ira.uka.de/.

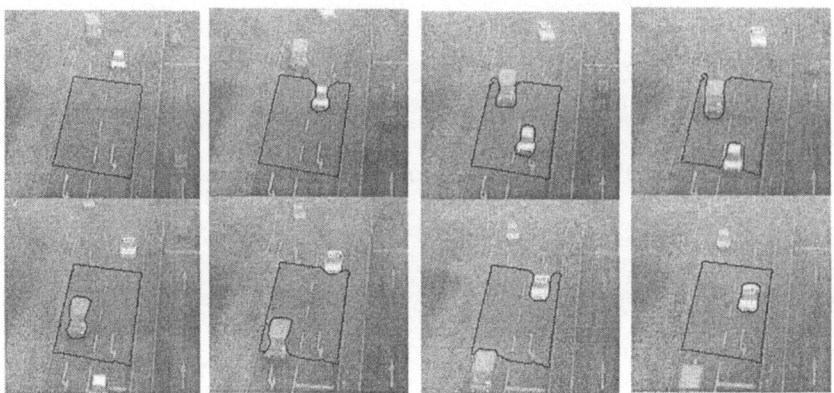

Fig. 5. Example of video segmentation for a traffic monitoring.

4   Conclusions

Active contours seem to be suitable for the segmentation of moving objects from image sequences. To this end it is required a high speed response and the capability of managing topological transformations when an unknown number of objects must be tracked. Pixel-level snakes consist of pixels which can evolve independently based on local information. This allows to guide the evolution of multiple contours efficiently and without extra computational cost as well as to handle their possible topological transformations. The pixel-level snake algorithm can be directly implemented on a massively parallel processing architecture like cellular neural networks which provides the high response speed required to approach video segmentation tasks. Since the contour evolution is based on local guiding information it is necessary to situate the initial contours close to the moving objects. This operation could become as expensive as the contour tracking itself. However for some applications into the video surveillance framework this problem can be easily approached. An initial active contour could delimit the control area and only deform to adapt itself to those objects going through the control zone. In other words: the moving objects go towards the active contours against what it is usual. The preliminary results are very encouraging and suggest that our proposal can bring improvements in the area of video segmentation.

Acknowledgements

This work was supported by the Spanish CICYT under grant TIC2000-0399 and Xunta de Galicia under grant PGIDT01TIC206001PN.

References

[1] A. Alatan, L. Onural, M. Wollborn, R. Mech, E. Tuncel, and T. Sikura. Image sequence analysis for emerging ineteractive multimedia services. the european cost 211 framework. *IEEE Trans. Cir. Syst. Video Tech.*, 8(7):802–813, 1998.

[2] V. M. Brea, A. Paasio, D. L. Vilariño, and D. Cabello. A DTCNN CMOS Implementation of a Pixel-Level Snake Algorithm. In *European Conference on Circuit Theory and Design, ECCTD'01*, pages 269–272, 2001.

[3] V. Caselles, R. Kimmel, and G. Sapiro. Geodesic Active Contours. *International Journal of Computer Vision*, 22(1):61–79, 1997.

[4] R. Castagno, T. Ebrahimi, and M. Kunt. Video Segmentation Based on Multiple Features for Interactive Multimedia Applications. *IEEE Trans. Cir. Syst. Video Tech.*, 8(5):562–571, 1998.

[5] L. O. Chua and L. Yang. Cellular Neural Networks: Theory. *IEEE Trans. Circuits Syst.*, 35:1257–1273, 1988.

[6] L. Czuni and T. Sziranyi. Motion Segmentation and Tracking with Edge Relaxation and Optimization using Fully Parallel Methods in the Cellular Nonlinear Network Architecture. *Real-Time Imaging*, (7):77–95, 2001.

[7] J. B. Kim and H. J. Kim. Efficient Region-based Motion Segmentation for a Video Monitoring System. *Pattern Recognition Letters*, 24:113–128, 2003.

[8] T. Kozek and D. L. Vilariño. An Active Contour Algorithm for Continuous-Time Cellular Neural Networks. *Journal of VLSI Signal Processing Systems*, 23(2/3):403–414, 1999.

[9] G. Liñan, A. Rodriguez-Vazquez, S. Espejo, and R. Dominguez-Castro. ACE16k: A 128x128 Focal Plane Analog Processor with Digital I/O. In *Seventh International Workshop on Cellular Neural Networks and their Applications, CNNA2002*, pages 132–139, 2002.

[10] R. Malladi, J. A. Sethian, and B. C. Vemuri. Shape Modeling with Front Propagation: A Level Set Approach. *IEEE Trans. PAMI*, 17(2):158–174, 1995.

[11] T. Meier and K. N. Ngan. Automatic Segmentation of Moving Objects for Video Object Plane Generation. *IEEE Trans. Cir. Syst. Video Tech.*, 8(5):525–538, 1998.

[12] D. L. Vilariño, D. Cabello, J. M. Pardo, and V. M. Brea. Pixel-Level Snakes. In *International Conference on Pattern Recognition*, volume 1, pages 640–643, 2000.

[13] D. L. Vilariño, D. Cabello, X. M. Pardo, and V. M. Brea. Cellular Neural Networks and Active Contours: A Tool for Image Segmentation. *Image and Vision Computing*, 21(2):189–204, 2003.

[14] D. Zhang and G. Lu. Segmentation of Moving Objects in Image Sequence: A Review. *Circuits, Systems and Signal Processing*, 20(2):143–183, 2001.

Optimal Detection of Symmetry Axis in Digital Chest X-ray Images

Carlos Vinhais[1,2] and Aurélio Campilho[1,3]

[1] INEB – Instituto de Engenharia Biomédica
Laboratório de Sinal e Imagem Biomédica, Campus da FEUP
Rua Roberto Frias, s/n, 4200-465 Porto, Portugal
[2] ISEP - Instituto Superior de Engenharia do Porto, Departamento de Física,
Porto, Portugal
cav@isep.ipp.pt
[3] Universidade do Porto, Faculdade de Engenharia,
Departamento de Engenharia Electrotécnica e Computadores
Porto, Portugal
campilho@fe.up.pt

Abstract. We present a method for detecting the axis of bilateral symmetry in a digital chest X-ray image and subsequently measuring the degree of symmetry of the image. The detection is achieved by analysing rotated-reflected digital chest X-ray images and it is posed as a global optimization problem solved with a probabilistic genetic algorithm (PGA). The global search is initially based on natural peak orientation information related to the orientation of the symmetry axis. Only a few generations of the PGA are needed to achieve convergence to all the images in the database. This method is applied directly on the intensity input image and does not require any prior segmentation.

Keywords. Image Processing, Reflectional Symmetry, Probabilistic Genetic Algorithm

1   Introduction

The detection and measurement of symmetry in natural images is important for their interpretation and understanding, for many areas of science. The approximate symmetry exhibited by human body means that techniques for detecting and measuring symmetry can be particularly useful in medical imaging applications. There are a lot of examples in human anatomy: the ribcage in a single computer tomographic slice, for instance, is symmetrical with respect to a vertical line that passes through the spine. The ribs in a chest X-ray image also appear to be symmetrical with respect to the mediastinum. An image with reflectional symmetry is unchanged if it is reflected about a line, denoted as *reflection-symmetric axis*, for which the left half space is a mirror image of the right half.

F.J. Perales et al. (Eds.): IbPRIA 2003, LNCS 2652, pp. 1082-1089, 2003.

Most research in the field is focused on detecting symmetry on 2D images. Marola [1] presents an algorithm for finding the number and position of the symmetry axes of a symmetric or almost symmetric planar image, by evaluating some rational functions. He also presents a recognition procedure based on the measurements of the degree of symmetry of planar intensity images by superposition or by convolution [2]. Zabrodsky et al. [3] define a continuous symmetry measure to quantify the symmetry of objects. They also present a multi-resolution approach [4] that hierarchically detects symmetry and almost symmetric patterns. O'Mara and Owens [5] use the direction of the principal axes uniquely defined by the centroid and eigenvalues of the covariance matrix of an object, as the initial values of the bilateral symmetry axes. Sun [6] uses a direct correlation method on the gradient information, by using orientation histograms [7], to obtain the direction of the symmetry axis in grey-level images. Shen et al. [8] present a unified method for detecting both reflection and rotation-symmetry of 2D images based on generalized complex moments. Based on these moments, they also formulate the problem of detecting reflectional symmetries as a problem of minimising an asymmetric energy function [9]. Yen and Chan [10] use the Hough transform for detecting skewed and rotational symmetry on a set of points. Zielke et al. [11] look at the vertical or nearly-vertical symmetry axes in the image for car-following.

In this article, the problem of finding the global symmetry of digital chest X-ray images is posed as a global optimization problem, using a probabilistic genetic algorithm (PGA). The symmetry measure to be maximized is well behaved, and is parameterized by the location and orientation of the symmetry axis. The initial solutions in the search space are based on the vertical projection of the digital chest X-ray image. This method is applied directly on the intensity image and does not require any prior segmentation.

2   Measure of Reflectional Symmetry

The detection of reflectional symmetry requires a measure of 2D symmetry, and it is defined as a function of orientation and location of the symmetry axis. The symmetry measure is herein presented.

We represent the original image as the intensity function $f(\mathbf{x}) = f(x,y)$ on the image plane whose coordinates are $\mathbf{x} = (x,y)$. In a new coordinate system $\mathbf{u} = (t,s)$, the rotated image about the origin by the angle θ, and translated by d pixels, parallel to the t axis, is represented as

$$f(\mathbf{u}) = f(\mathbf{R}_\theta \mathbf{x} + \xi) ,$$ (1)

where

$$\mathbf{R}_\theta = \begin{bmatrix} \cos\theta & \sin\theta \\ -\sin\theta & \cos\theta \end{bmatrix}, \quad \xi = \begin{bmatrix} d \\ 0 \end{bmatrix}.$$ (2)

The original image $f(x,y)$ has reflectional symmetry if, in the (t,s) coordinate system, $f(t,s) = f(-t,s)$. A measure of the reflectional symmetry with respect to the s axis is defined as follows:

$$S(\theta,d) = \frac{1}{2} \frac{\iint f(t,s)f(-t,s)dsdt}{\iint f^2(t,s)dsdt} + \frac{1}{2} . \tag{3}$$

The range of $S(\theta,d)$ is from 0 to 1. We may notice that $f(t,s)$ is purely symmetric for $S(\theta,d)=0$ and antisymmetric for $S(\theta,d)=1$. This is a measure similar to the one suggested by Marola [1], and used by Gofman et al. [12]. The detection of the nearly-vertical symmetry in digital chest X-ray images becomes equivalent to finding the global maximum of the symmetry measure $S(\theta,d)$ defined in Eq. (3). A method of extracting reflectional symmetry performing a correlation with the rotated and reflected images has already been proposed by Masuda et al. [13]. However their approach presents high computational cost and memory requirements, since all possible transformations have to be tried. In the next section, we introduce a PGA to solve this global optimization problem, avoiding an exhaustive search for the best transformation.

3   Probabilistic Genetic Algorithm

The symmetry measure $S(\theta,d)$ defined in Eq. (3) is a function of *two* parameters only: the orientation θ of the symmetry axis, and its location d in the x axis of the original image plane. As in the standard genetic algorithm (GA), in the probabilistic genetic algorithm (PGA), each possible solution θ, d is binary encoded over a string of length K, referred to as a *chromosome*, and represents a point in the search space. A chromosome C_i has the following form:

$$\mathbf{C}_i = |c_{i,1},c_{i,2},...,c_{i,K-1},c_{i,K}| c_{i,j} = \{0,1\} . \tag{4}$$

The position of each bit, or *gene*, in the chromosome can be arbitrary. As in the GA, each iteration of the PGA yields a population, or generation of chromosomes. Let N denote the number of chromosomes in each generation, represented as the matrix:

$$\mathbf{C} = \begin{bmatrix} \mathbf{C}_1 \\ \vdots \\ \mathbf{C}_N \end{bmatrix} . \tag{5}$$

The initial population of the PGA can be generated at random. For each chromosome, the goal function defined by Eq. (3) is evaluated. These values are represented as the vector

$$\mathbf{s} = [s_1,\cdots,s_N]^T , \tag{6}$$

and normalized to satisfy $S_i \in [0,1]$.

Each gene j in every chromosome of the next generation is randomly set to "0" or "1", according to the distribution P_j of the values of that gene in the current population, weighted by the values of the goal function:

$$P_j = \frac{\sum\limits_{i=1}^{N} c_{ij} S_i}{\sum\limits_{i=1}^{N} S_i}, \quad j = 1, ..., K \cdot \tag{7}$$

The mutation probability M_j, assigned to each gene in position j in each of the new chromosomes, is based on its diversity by calculating the standard deviation σ of the values of each gene:

$$\sigma_j = \sqrt{\frac{\sum\limits_{i=1}^{N} \left(c_{ij} - \frac{1}{N} \sum\limits_{k=1}^{N} c_{kj} \right)^2}{N}}, \quad j = 1, ..., K \cdot \tag{8}$$

The mutation probability of a gene is made proportional to $0.5-\sigma$, increasing as its diversity decreases:

$$M_j = p_m \cdot \left(0.5 - \sigma_j \right), \quad j = 1, ..., K , \tag{9}$$

where p_m is a parameter to be selected in the range from 0 to 1.

The goal function is evaluated at points represented by the new chromosomes and the best chromosomes in the combined pool of current and new chromosomes are kept for the next generation.

4   The Symmetry Detection Approach

The symmetry measure defined in Eq. (3) is used as the goal function of the PGA described in the previous section. We first process the digital chest X-ray input image, as shown in Fig. 1, in order to define an image windowing for 2D symmetry measure evaluation: the reference intensity of the input image, Fig. 1(a), is ignored by subtracting its local average, Fig. 1(b), and the result is multiplied by a mask defined by the Laplacian of Gaussian (LoG) of the input image, enhancing edge-based regions of interest, producing the image in Fig. 1(c). Because chest X-ray images have symmetry axis nearly-vertical, the initial location of the symmetry axis can be estimated from the maximum of the correlation function between the projection of the local-averaged input image onto the horizontal axis, and its reflection.

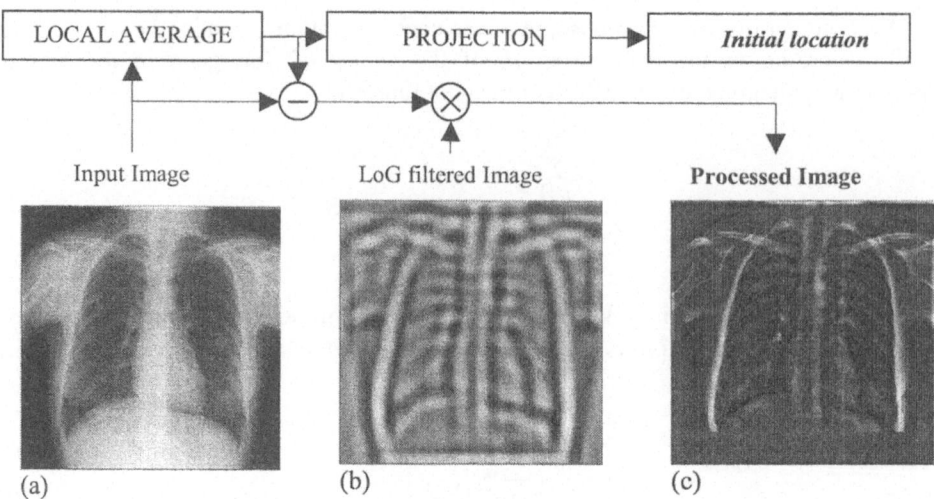

Input Image   LoG filtered Image   Processed Image

(a)   (b)   (c)

Fig. 1. Input image processing blocks for symmetry axis detection: (a) Digital chest X-ray image input; (b) LoG filtered image; (c) Processed input image (a), used as input image of the PGA

The PGA is then used to find the optimal parameters, orientation θ and location d, of the symmetry axis of the input image, as shown in Fig. 2. In order to speed up convergence, the initial generation of the PGA is set randomly around the estimated initial location, obtained from the input image processing.

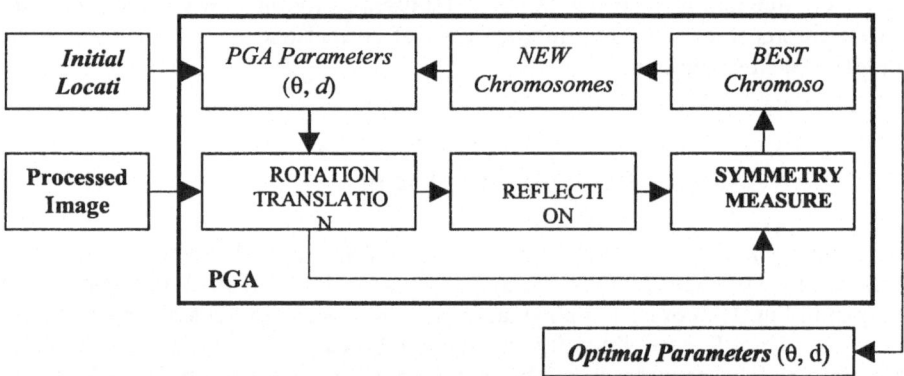

Fig. 2. Processing blocks for PGA optimization of the symmetry axis parameters

The processed image is rotated by an angle θ, translated by d pixels along horizontal axis, and its reflection with respect to vertical axis is obtained, for every chromosome of each generation of the PGA. The symmetry measure $S(\theta,d)$, or degree of similarity of these two images, is calculated via discrete approximation of Eq. (3), and optimized by the PGA.

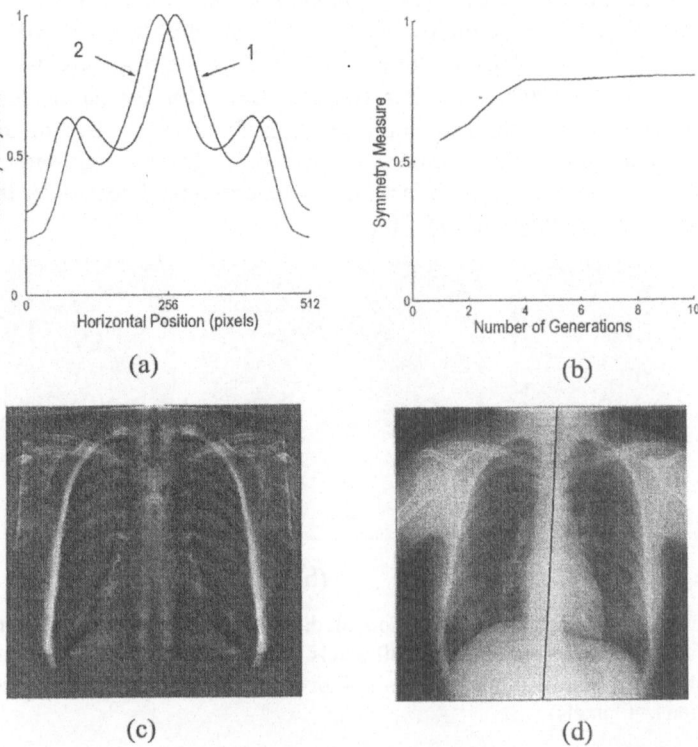

Fig. 3. Results of reflectional symmetry detection of the digital chest X-ray image of Fig. 1. (a) Intensity projection of the local-averaged input image (line 1) onto the horizontal axis of the image, and its reflection (line 2), giving estimated location $d=-13.5$ pixels of the symmetry axis; (b) Convergence of the PGA: maximum symmetry measure value $S=0.803$ achieved after 10 generations; (c) Processed image of Fig. 2(a), rotated and translated using best parameters of the PGA, $\theta=3.2°$ and $d=-14$ pixels, and its reflection superimposed; (d) Original image with axis of reflectional symmetry detected (dark straight line)

5   Results

We implemented the algorithm within the MATLAB^{TM} environment and applied it to several 512×512 digital chest X-ray images. The local average of the input image is obtained with a mean filter of 50 pixels square kernel. A LoG filter of the same size, with standard deviation $\sigma=20$ pixels is then applied to the input image. The processed input image is obtained by multiplying the resulting images of the two filters.

In the PGA, the orientation θ of the symmetry axis is encoded with 7 bits, and the translation d is encoded with 6 bits each, hence the total length of the chromosomes was $K=13$. The number of chromosomes in the beginning and end of each generation was $N=10$, and the number of new chromosomes created in each generation was 15.

The mutation parameter in the PGA was set to $p_m=0.08$. About only 10 generations of the PGA were enough to reach convergence in all the images in the database.

Symmetry detection results for one digital chest X-ray image are shown in Fig. 3. The CPU time for a 512×512 image takes about 3 minutes, in a 700 MHz processor. The convergence of the PGA is shown in Fig. 3(b), with a maximum symmetry measure value S=0.803 achieved after 10 generations, for the parameter set θ=3.2° and d=−14 pixels, with estimated initial location d=−13.5 pixels. For these values, edges of the input image of PGA and the reflected image superimposed, as shown in Fig. 3(c), are well matched. The reflectional symmetry axis detected for this image is shown on the original image, in Fig. 3(d).

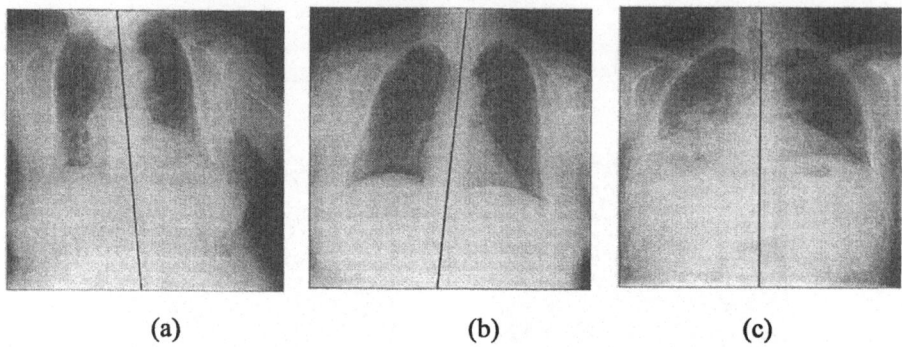

| (a) | (b) | (c) |

Fig. 4. Results of symmetry axis detection of digital chest X-ray images, with symmetry measure (a) S=0.786, for θ=−5.1° and d=30 pixels (initial location d=27 pixels); (b) S=0.702, for θ=5.2° and d=−2 pixels (initial location d=0 pixels); (c) S=0.731, for θ=0° and d=0 pixels (initial location d=0 pixels)

Very similar results, shown in Fig. 4, were obtained for some digital chest X-ray images in the database, after 10 generation of the PGA.

6   Conclusion

We have described a method for extracting the reflectional symmetry axis of digital chest X-ray images, based on the global search of the maximum of a symmetry measure. The search algorithm is implemented by using a probabilistic genetic algorithm, avoiding an exhaustive search for the best transformation of the image, and it is suitable for parallel implementation. This method is applied directly on the intensity valued image and does not need any knowledge of the centroid or any prior segmentation of the input image.

References

[1]   Marola, G.: On the Detection of the Axes of Symmetry of Symmetric and Almost Symmetric Planar Images, *IEEE Transactions on Pattern Analysis and Machine Intelligence*, 11 (1989) 104-108.
[2]   Marola, G.: Using Symmetry for Detecting and Locating Objects in a Picture, *Computer Vision, Graphics and Image Processing*, 46 (1989) 179-195.

[3]   Zabrodsky, H., Peleg, S., Avnir, D.: A Measure of Symmetry Based on Shape Similarity, *Proceedings of Computer Vision and Pattern Recognition*, (1992) 703-706.

[4]   Zabrodsky, H., Peleg, S., Avnir, D.: Hierarchical Symmetry, *Proceedings of International Conference on Pattern Recognition*, III (1992) 9-11.

[5]   O'Mara, D., Owens, R.: Measuring Symmetry in Digital Images, Proceedings of TENCOM '96-IEEE region Ten Conference: Digital Signal Processing Applications, I (1996) 151-156.

[6]   Sun, C.: Symmetry Detection using Gradient Information, *Pattern Recognition Letters*, 16 (9) (1995) 987-996.

[7]   Sun, C., Si, D.: Fast Reflectional Symmetry Detection using Orientation Histograms, *Real-Time Imaging*, 5 (1999) 63-74.

[8]   Shen, D., Ip, H.H.S., Cheung, K.K.T., Teoh, E.K.: Symmetry Detection by Generalized Complex (GC) Moments: a Close-form Solution, *IEEE Transactions on Pattern Analysis and Machine Intelligence*, 21 (5) (1999) 466-476.

[9]   Shen, D., Ip, H.H.S., Teoh, E.K.: An Energy of Asymmetry for Accurate Detection of Global Reflection Axes, *Image and Vision Computing*, 19 (2001) 283-297.

[10]   Yuen, K.S.Y., Chan, W.W.: Two Methods for Detecting Symmetries, *Pattern Recognition Letters*, 15 (1994) 279-286.

[11]   Zielke, T., Brauckmann, M., von Seelen, W.: Intensity and Edge-based Symmetry Detection with an Application to Car-following, *Computer Vision, Graphics and Image Processing: Image Understanding*, 58 (1990) 177-190.

[12]   Gofman, Y., Kiryati, N.: Detecting Symmetry in Grey Level Images: the Global Optimization Approach, *International Journal of Computer Vision (IJCV)*, 29 (1998) 29-45.

[13]   Masuda, T., Yamamoto, K., Yamada, H.: Detection of Partial Symmetry using Correlation with Rotated-reflected Images, *Pattern Recognition*, 26 (8) (1993) 1245-1253.

Low Complexity Motion Estimation Based on Spatio-temporal Correlations

Hyo Sun Yoon and Guee Sang Lee*

Department of Computer Science, Chonnam National University
300 Youngbong-dong, Buk-gu, Kwangju 500-757, Korea
estheryoon@hotmail.com
gslee@chonnam.chonnam.ac.kr

Abstract. To remove temporal redundancy contained in a sequence of images, motion estimation techniques have been developed. However, the high computational complexity of the problem makes such techniques very difficult to be applied to high-resolution applications in a real time environment. For this reason, low complexity motion estimation algorithms are viable solutions. In this paper, we present an efficient algorithm based on exploiting temporally and spatially correlated motion information that defines the search pattern and the location of search starting point adaptively. Experiments show that the speedup improvement of the proposed algorithm over Diamond Search algorithm (DS) and HEXagon-Based Serch (HEXBS) can be up to 2 ~ 3 times faster and the image quality improvement can be better up to 0.1 ~ 1(dB).

1 Introduction

Recently, great interest has been devoted to the study of different approaches in video compressions. The high correlation between successive frames of a video sequence makes it possible to achieve high coding efficiency by reducing the temporal redundancy. Motion estimation (ME) and motion compensation techniques are an important part of most video encoding, since it could significantly affect the compression ratio and the output quality.

The most popular motion estimation and motion compensation method has been the block-based motion estimation, which uses a block matching algorithm (BMA) to find the best matched block from a reference frame. ME based on the block matching is adopted in many existing video coding standards such as H.261/H.263 and MPEG-1/2/4. If the performance in terms of prediction error is the only criterion for BMA, full search block matching algorithm (FS) is the simplest BMA, guaranteeing an exact result. FS can achieve optimal performance by examining all possible points in search area of the reference frame. However, FS is very computationally intensive and it can hardly be applied to any real time applications. Hence, it is inevitable to develop fast motion estimation algorithms for real time video coding applications. Many low complexity

---

* corresponding author

F.J. Perales et al. (Eds.): IbPRIA 2003, LNCS 2652, pp. 1090–1098, 2003.

motion estimation algorithms such as Diamond Search (DS) [1, 2], Three Step Search (TSS)[3], New Three Step Search (NTSS)[4], Four Step Search (FSS)[5], Two Step Search (2SS)[6], Two-dimensional logarithmic search algorithm [7], HEXagon-Based Serch (HEXBS) [8] and the algorithms [9, 10] based on temporal or spatial correlations of motion vectors have been proposed. Regardless of the characteristic of the motion of a block, all these most fast block matching algorithms (FBMAs) use a fixed search pattern and the origin of the search area as a search starting point.

A fixed search pattern and a fixed search starting point results in the use of many checking points to find a good motion vector (MV). To improve the "speed-quality", the motion estimation method we proposed in this paper uses the temporally and spatially correlated motion vectors information to predict a search starting point that reflects the current block's motion trend and to choose a search pattern adaptively. Because a properly predicted search starting point makes the global optimum closer to the predicted starting point, it increases the chance of finding the optimum or near-optimum motion vector with less search points.

In this paper, we proposed an adaptive block matching algorithm based on spatial and temporal correlations. In this algorithm, the motion vector mv_t of the block with the same coordinate in the reference frame and the motion vectors mv_s of neighboring blocks in the current frame are used as predictors to decide a search starting point and a search pattern adaptively for the current block. Specifically, the weighted sum of mv_t and median(mv_s) is computed to get the search starting point and to decide the type of the search pattern.

This paper is organized as follows. Section 2 describes the existing motion estimation algorithms. The proposed algorithm is described in Section 3. Section 4 reports the simulation results and conclusions are given in Section 5.

2   Motion Estimation Algorithms

There are many search algorithms for motion estimation. The full search (FS), the simplest algorithm, examines every point in the search area in the reference frame to find the best match. Clearly, it is optimal in terms of finding the best motion vector, but it is very computationally intensive. Hence, several sub-optimal search algorithms such as DS [1,2], TSS [3], NTSS [4], FSS [5], 2SS [6], Two-dimensional logarithmic search algorithm [7], HEXagon-Based Serch (HEXBS) [8] have been developed. The TSS is a coarse-to-fine search algorithm. The starting step size for search is large and the center of the search is moved in the direction of the best match at the stage, and the step size is reduced by half. In contrast, FSS starts with a fine step size (usually 2) and the center of the search is moved in the direction of the best match without changing the step size, until the best match at that stage is the center itself. The step size is then halved to 1 to find the best match. In other words, in FSS the search process is performed mostly around the original search point (0,0), or it is more center-biased. Based on the characteristics of a center-biased motion vector distribution, NTSS enhanced TSS by using additional search points, which are around the search origin (0,0) of the first step of TSS. The DS is also a center-biased algorithm by exploiting the shape of the motion vector distribution. DS shows the best performance compared to these methods in terms of both average number of search points per motion vector and the PSNR (peak signal to noise ratio) of the predicted image. The DS method uses two diamond search patterns, depicted in Fig. 1. the large diamond search pattern (LDSP) is used for the coarse search. When the centered search position of LDSP show the minimum block distortion, the small diamond search pattern (SDSP) is chosen for the fine search.

(a) Large Diamond Search Pattern (LDSP)   (b) Small Diamond Search Pattern (SDSP)

Fig. 1. Diamond Search Algorithm(DS)

3   The Proposed Algorithm

Since the time interval between successive frames is very short, there are high temporal correlations between successive frames of a video sequence. In other words, the motion of current block is very similar to that of the same coordinate block in the reference frame. And also there are high spatial correlations among the blocks in the same frame. That is to say, the motion of current block is very

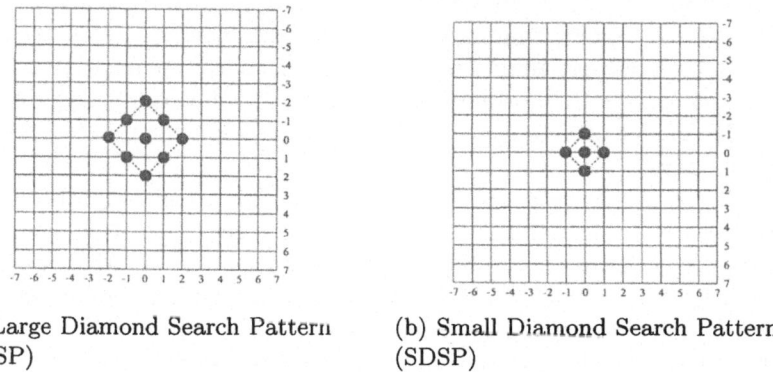

MV_0 : the MV of the same coordinate block in the reference frame
MV_1 : the MV of left block
MV_2 : the MV of above block
MV_0 : the MV of above-right block

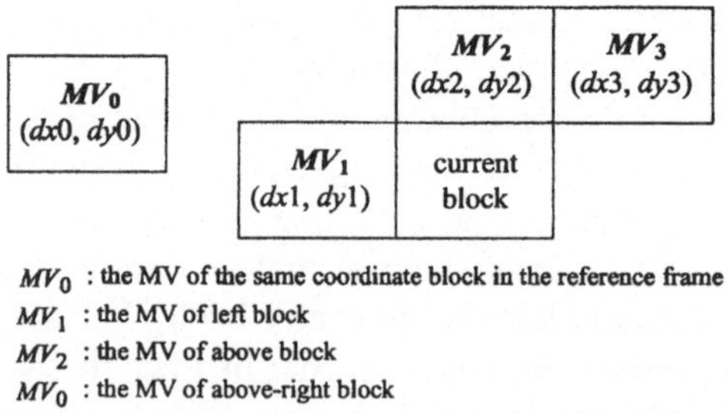

Fig. 2. Blocks for Spatio-Temporal Correlation Information

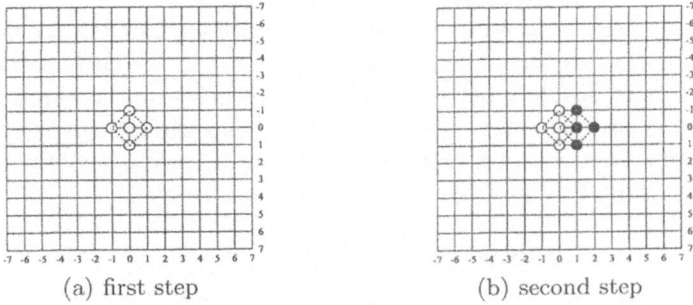

Fig. 3. Small Diamond Search Algorithm(SDSP)

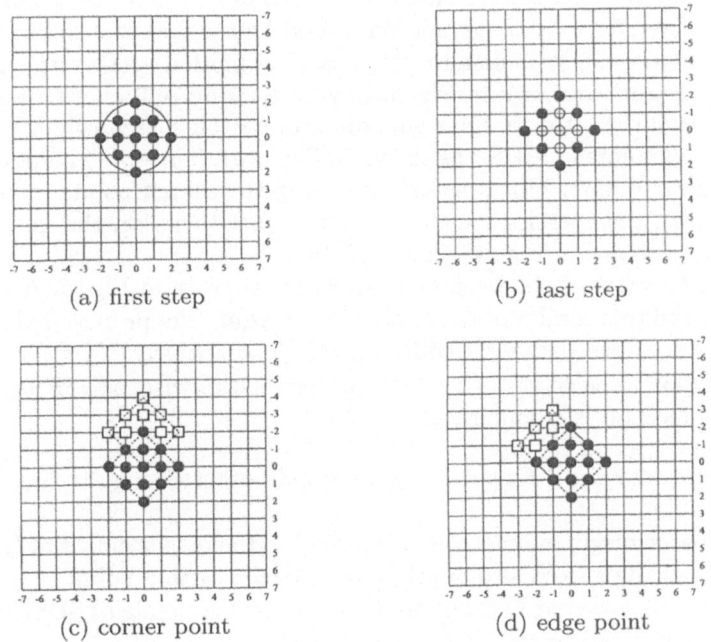

Fig. 4. Modify Diamond Search Algorithm(MDSP)

similar to those of the neighboring blocks in the current frame. If the information of spatially and temporally correlated motion vectors is used to decide the search starting point and the search pattern for the motion estimation, the motion vector will be found with much less number of search points.

In this paper, the motion vector of the same coordinate block in the reference frame and the motion vectors of the neighboring blocks in the current frame are used as predictors to decide a better search starting point and a search pattern adaptively for the current block. The proposed method exploiting spatially and temporally correlated motion vectors depicted in Fig. 2, selects one of two search patterns as illustrated in Fig. 3(a) and Fig. 4(a) adaptively.

$$Px = \lfloor dx0 \times \alpha + median(dx1, dx2, dx3) \times \beta \rfloor \qquad (1)$$

$$Py = \lfloor dy0 \times \alpha + median(dy1, dy2, dy3) \times \beta \rfloor \qquad (2)$$

And then (Px, Py) obtained from Eq. (1–2) is used as a search starting point. (Px, Py) is the weighted sum of the temporal information and the spatial information. In this paper, we experimented with $\alpha = 0.5$ and $\beta = 0.5$. If $\mid Px \mid < 3$ and $\mid Py \mid < 3$, small diamond search pattern (SDSP)[11] as shown in Fig. 3 is selected. In Fig. 3(a), white circles are the initial search points and in Fig. 3(b), black circles are search points added in the second step. Note that the center of black circles is the position which showed the minimum block distortion in the first step. Otherwise, modified diamond search pattern (MDSP) [12], illustrated in Fig. 4 is selected for motion estimation. Based on the fact that about 50%(in large motion case) $\sim$ 98 %(in small motion case) of motion vectors are enclosed in a circular support, as shown in Fig. 4(a), with a radius of 2 pixels around the search origin (0,0)[1,2], the circular support around the search origin becomes the initial search points in MDSP as shown in Fig. 4(a). If one of $\oplus$ points in Fig. 4(b) shows the minimum block distortion among the search points in the first step of Fig. 4(a), the search procedure terminates. Otherwise, the new search points are set as shown in Fig. 4(c) or Fig. 4(d).

The block diagram of the proposed algorithm appears in Fig. 5. According to the spatial and temporal motion vectors information, the proposed algorithm selects a search pattern between SDSP and MDSP adaptively. If $\mid Px \mid < 3$ and $\mid Py \mid < 3$, SDSP is selected as a search pattern. Otherwise, MDSP is chosen. The proposed method is summarized as follows

Step 1 If $\mid Px \mid < 3$ and $\mid Py \mid < 3$, go to Step 2; otherwise, go to Step 3.
Step 2

    I. The search origin in search area is moved to the displacement of (Px, Py). Let's call the moved search origin the search starting point.

    II. SDSP is disposed at (Px, Py), and the 5 checking points of SDSP as seen in Fig. 3(a) are tested. If the minimum block distortion (MBD) point calculated is located at the center position of SDSP, then it is the final solution of the motion vector. otherwise go to III.

    III. If the MBD point calculated is not located at the center position of SDSP, three additional checking points as shown in Fig. 3(b) are used.

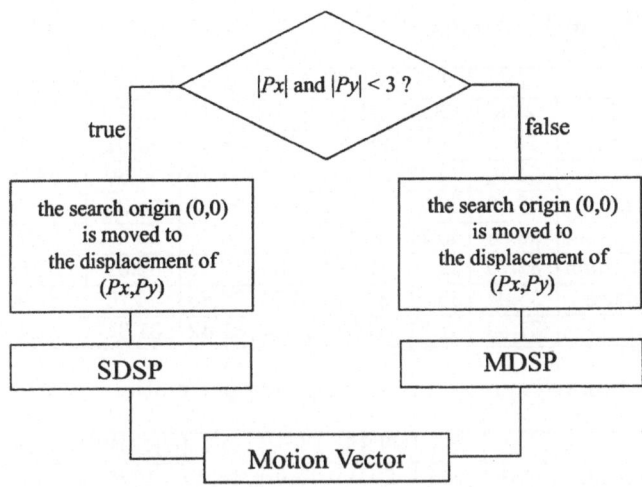

Fig. 5. The block diagram of the proposed algorithm

The MBD point founded in the previous search step is repositioned as the center point to form a new SDSP. If the new MSD point obtained is located at the center position, then it is the final solution of the motion vector. Otherwise, recursively repeated this step

Step 3

    I. The search origin is moved to the displacement of (Px,Py).

   II. MDSP is disposed at (Px,Py), and the 13 checking points of MDSP as seen in Fig. 4(a) are tested. If the MBD point calculated is located at the center position of MDSP or one of $\oplus$ points in Fig. 4 (b), then it is the final solution of the motion vector. otherwise go to III.

 III. If the MBD point is located at the corner of MDSP, eight additional checking points as shown in Fig. 4(c) are used. If the MBD point is located at the edge of MDSP, five additional checking points as shown in Fig. 4(d) are used. And then the MBD point found in the previous search step is repositioned as the center to from a new MDSP. If the MBD point calculated is located at the center position of MDSP or one of $\oplus$ points in Fig. 4(b), then it is the final solution of the motion vector. Otherwise, recursively repeated this step.

4   Simulation Result

In this section, we show the experiment results for the proposed algorithm. We compared FS, NTSS, FSS, 2SS, DS and HEXBS to the proposed method in both of image quality and search speed. Eight QCIF test sequences are used for the experiment: Akiyo, Claire, Carphone, Foreman, Mother and Daughter, Salesman, Stefan and Table. The mean square error (MSE) is used as the block

Table 1. Average PSNR of the test image sequence

	FS	2SS	NTSS	FSS	DS	HEXBS	Proposed
Stefan	23.88	23.85	22.24	22.62	22.77	22.59	23.65
Foreman	29.54	29.24	28.19	28.22	28.66	28.01	29.06
Akiyo	34.50	34.48	34.48	34.33	34.39	34.30	34.50
Table	26.50	26.27	26.5	24.81	25.67	24.90	25.68
Carphone	30.88	30.77	30.14	30.15	30.48	30.07	30.71
Salesman	32.70	32.70	32.69	32.53	32.62	32.51	32.69
Claire	35.05	35.01	34.91	34.74	34.85	34.70	34.94
M&D	31.52	31.51	31.37	31.34	31.42	31.37	31.46

Table 2. Average number of search points per motion vector estimation

	FS	2SS	NTSS	FSS	DS	HEXBS	Proposed
Stefan	961	255	20.0	18.9	16.2	12.9	7.3
Foreman	961	255	19.3	18.6	15.4	11.9	6.4
Akiyo	961	255	17.0	17.0	13.0	11.0	5.0
Table	961	255	19.7	18.7	15.5	12.5	7.5
Carphone	961	255	18.6	17.8	14.4	11.7	6.6
Salesman	961	25	17.1	17.0	13	11.0	5.1
Claire	961	255	17.2	17.08	13.1	11.0	5.1
M&D	961	255	17.3	17.1	13.2	11.1	5.3

distortion measure (BDM). The quality of the predicted image is measured by the peak signal to noise ratio (PSNR), which is defined by

$$MSE = \left(\frac{1}{MN}\right) \sum_{m=1}^{M} \sum_{n=1}^{N} [x(m,n) - \hat{x}(m,n)]^2 \qquad (3)$$

$$PSNR = 10 \, log_{10} \frac{255^2}{MSE} \qquad (4)$$

In Eq. (3), $x(m,n)$ denotes the original image and $\hat{x}(m,n)$ denotes the motion compensated prediction image. From Table 1 and 2, we can see that proposed method is better than DS in terms of both the computational complexity (as measured by the average number of search points per motion vector) and PSNR of the predicted image. In terms of PSNR, the proposed method is about 0.1(dB) better than HEXBS as well as DS in stationary sequences such as Akiyo, Claire, Carphone, Mother and Daughter, Salesman and about $0.5 \sim 1$(dB) in motioned sequences such as Stefan, Table and Foreman in Table 1. The speedup improvement of the proposed method over HEXBS and DS can be up to $2 \sim 3$ times faster. The 2SS shows the performance in PSNR very close to the proposed method, but the proposed method requires less computation by up to more than 30 times on average as shown in Table 2.

5 Conclusion

Based on the temporal and spatial correlation of motion vectors in the reference and current frame, an adaptive block motion estimation method is proposed in this paper. The proposed method chooses a search pattern and a search starting point based on exploiting the temporally and spatially correlated motion vector information. Experiments show that the speedup improvement of the proposed algorithm over DS and HEXBS can be up to $2 \sim 3$ times faster. And the image quality improvement can be better up to $0.1 \sim 1(\text{dB})$. The proposed algorithm reduces the computational complexity compared with previously developed fast BMAs, while maintaining better quality.

Acknowledgement

This study was financially supported by Chonnam National University in the program, 2002.

References

[1] Tham, J. Y., Ranganath, S., Kassim, A. A.: A Novel Unrestricted Center-Biased Diamond Search Algorithm for Block Motion Estimation. IEEE Transactions on Circuits and Systems for Video Technology. **8(4)** (1998) 369–375

[2] Shan, Z., Kai-kuang, M.: A New Diamond Search Algorithm for Fast block Matching Motion Estimation. IEEE Transactions on Image Processing. **9(2)** (2000) 287–290

[3] Koga, T., Iinuma, K., Hirano, Y., Iijim, Y., Ishiguro, T.: Motion compensated interframe coding for video conference. In Proc. NTC81. (1981) C9.6.1–9.6.5

[4] Renxiang, L., Bing, Z., Liou, M. L.: A New Three Step Search Algorithm for Block Motion Estimation. IEEE Transactions on Circuits and Systems for Video Technology. **4(4)** (1994) 438–442

[5] Lai-Man, P., Wing-Chung, M.: A Novel Four-Step Search Algorithm for Fast Block Motion Estimation. IEEE Transactions on Circuits and Systems for Video Technology. **6(3)** (1996) 313–317

[6] Yuk-Ying, C., Neil, W. B.: Fast search block-matching motion estimation algorithm using FPGA. Visual Communication and Image Processing 2000. Proc. SPIE. **4067** (2000) 913–922

[7] Jain, J., Jain, A.: Dispalcement measurement and its application in interframe image coding. IEEE Transactions on Communications. **COM-29** (1981) 1799–1808

[8] Zhu, C., Lin, X., Chau, L. P.: Hexagon based Search Pattern for Fast Block Motion Estimation. IEEE Transactions on Circuits and Systems for Video Technology. **12(5)** (2002) 349–355

[9] Deepak, S. T., Tsuhan, C.: Estimation and Mode Decision for Spatialy Correlated Motion Sequences. IEEE Transactions on Circuits and Systems for Video Technology. **11(10)** (2002) 1098–1107

[10] Xu, J. B., Po, L. M., Cheung, C. K.: Adaptive Motion Tracking Block Matching for Video Coding. IEEE Transactions on Circuits and Systems for Video Technology. **9(7)** (1999) 1025–1029

[11] Guy. C. , Michael. G. , Faouzi. K.: Efficient Motion Vector Estimation and Coding for H.263-based very low bit rate video compression. ITU-T SG 16, Q15-A-45. (1997) 18

[12] Yoon, H. S., Lee. G. S.: Motion Estimation based on Temporal Correlations. EurAisa-ICT. LNCS.**2510** (2002) 75–83

Set-Permutation-Occurrence Matrix Based Texture Segmentation

Reyer Zwiggelaar[1], Lilian Blot[1], David Raba[2], and Erika R.E. Denton[3]

[1] School of Information Systems, University of East Anglia
Norwich, UK
reyer.zwiggelaar@sys.uea.ac.uk
[2] Computer Vision and Robotics Group, University of Girona
Girona, Spain
[3] Department of Breast Imaging, Norfolk and Norwich University Hospital
Norwich, UK

Abstract. We have investigated a combination of statistical modelling and expectation maximisation for a texture based approach to the segmentation of mammographic images. Texture modelling is based on the implicit incorporation of spatial information through the introduction of a set-permutation-occurrence matrix. Statistical modelling is used for data generalisation and noise removal purposes. Expectation maximisation modelling of the spatial information in combination with the statistical modelling is evaluated. The developed segmentation results are used for automatic mammographic risk assessment.

1 Introduction

Texture is one of the least understood areas in computer vision and this lack of understanding is reflected in the ad-hoc approaches taken to date for texture based segmentation techniques. Although no generic texture model has emerged so far a number of problem specific approaches have been developed successfully [1, 2, 3, 4]. Although the described approach is developed with one particular application in mind, we do believe that it is generic within the field of medical image understanding.

Since Wolfe's [5, 6] original investigation into the correlation between mammographic risk (i.e. the risk of developing breast cancer) and the perceived breast density a number of automatic approaches have been developed [7, 8, 9, 10, 11]. Some of these methods are based on grey-level distributions whilst others incorporate some aspect of spatial correlation or texture measure. While all these methods achieve some correlation with manual visual assessment in general they are not good enough to progress to clinical trials. We have investigated a process to separate the relevant background texture from other image structures [8, 12]. This showed that based on only background texture similar classification results could be obtained when compared to results based on the full image information. It is also important to note that the breast density can change over time for a number of reasons [13].

F.J. Perales et al. (Eds.): IbPRIA 2003, LNCS 2652, pp. 1099–1107, 2003.

It is our thesis that the relative size of segmented image regions, representing distinct anatomical tissue classes, is correlated with mammographic risk assessment. Statistical modelling in combination with expectation maximisation (EM) [14] is used for the segmentation of mammographic images. To our knowledge, we introduce a new concept, the set-permutation-occurrence matrix, as a texture feature vector. Realistic texture modelling is possible as spatial information is implicitly incorporated. Statistical modelling has been used as a pre-processing step to generalise the data whilst at the same time remove some noise aspects. Initial results from this automatic segmentation of mammographic images are promising with a good correlation with annotated regions. We show results for automatic mammographic risk assessment [5] and a comparison with expert manual classification is discussed.

To achieve segmentation a number of steps are required: a) information gathering, b) texture feature extraction, c) statistical modelling, d) EM clustering, and e) image segmentation.

2   Methods

A Gaussian mixture model G with k classes is defined as

$$G(x|\varphi) = \sum_{i=1}^{k} w_i g(x|m_i, v_i) \tag{1}$$

where x is an observation vector, φ is a vector with parameters w_i (weight), m_i (mean) and v_i (covariance) for each class, and $g(x|m_i, v_i)$ is defined as

$$g(x|m_i, v_i) = \frac{1}{(\sqrt{2\pi})^n (\sqrt{det(v_i)})} e^{-\frac{(x-m_i)^T v_i^{-1}(x-m_i)}{2}} \tag{2}$$

where $()^T$ indicates the transpose of a vector, v_i^{-1} indicates the inverse of v_i and $det(v_i)$ stands for the determinant of v_i. The *likelihood* function is a function that gives a measure of how well the probability density function defined by the parameters fits the data. If a set of parameter maximises the likelihood, then these parameters will be the optimum set for the given problem. The likelihood function is defined as

$$\mathcal{L}(\varphi) = \prod_{x \in \chi} p(x|\varphi) \tag{3}$$

where χ is the data set and $p(x|\varphi)$ is the probability density function. Here the assumption of independence for all data χ is made. Usually, the *log-likelihood* function is used, mainly to use a sum instead of a product and to reduce the magnitude of the result.

$$\mathcal{L}_{log}(\varphi) = \sum_{x \in \chi} log(p(x|\varphi)) \tag{4}$$

The EM algorithm [14] is a numerical method to estimate a set of parameters that describe a probability distribution, based on data that belongs to this distribution. On each iteration of the algorithm, two steps are performed: first, the E-step evaluates a probability distribution for the data using the parameters of the model estimated on the previous iteration, then the M-step finds the new parameters that maximises the likelihood function. It can be proven mathematically that on each iteration the likelihood increases [14]. One of the problems of the EM algorithm in application to Gaussian Mixture Models is the initialisation [15], with the end results depending on the initial starting point. It is common to select a random starting point of the data set χ for the centre of each class. To make the overall classification more robust we initialise the centre of the class with the result of the *k-Means* algorithm [15].

2.1   Texture Feature

In general the usage of the EM approach for image segmentation is based on the grey-level information at a pixel level with no direct interaction between adjacent pixels. However, it is well known that texture based segmentation should incorporate spatial correlation information. The modelling should not be based on a single grey-level value but incorporates spatial information implicitly. This is why we extract information from a set of points. The information is extracted at several levels of a scale-space representation of the image.

Scale-Space Representation The first step in obtaining the texture features is the generation of an image-stack which is a scale-space representation. At the smallest scale the original grey-level values are used and to obtain the larger scale images we have used a recursive median filter [16], denoted $\otimes$, and a circular structuring element, R (the diameter of the structuring element increases with scale σ). The resulting image-stack is a set of images

$$\bigcup_{\sigma \in \Gamma} \{I_\sigma\} = \bigcup_{\sigma \in \Gamma} \{I \otimes R_\sigma\}, \qquad (5)$$

where Γ is an ordered set of scales. This effectively represents a blurring of the original data and at a particular level in the image-stack only features larger than σ can be found. An alternative representation of the image-stack is given by

$$\bigcup_{\sigma \in \Gamma} \{\bar{I}_\sigma\} = \bigcup_{\sigma \in \Gamma} \{I \otimes R_{\sigma-1} - I \otimes R_\sigma\}, \qquad (6)$$

where Γ is a set of scales. This represents the differences between two scales in I_σ and hence the data in the image-stack at a particular level will only contain features at a particular scale σ.

Sampling Points To capture the texture information over a set of scales a feature vector will need to be extracted from all levels of the image-stack. It can be seen that small size aspects (like noise and small objects) are represented at the top (least amount of smoothing) of the image-stack. On the other hand, large size aspects (large and background objects) are represented at the bottom (after smoothing at the appropriate scale) of the image-stack.

The developed method uses a model that can be seen as a generalisation of normal co-occurrence matrices [1]. Indeed, if we just look at the co-occurrence of grey-level values the information can be captured in matrix format, where the rows and columns represent the grey-level values at two sample points. This process can include a set of points S_{xy}. An example of the points used is shown in Fig. 1. In the experiments described below we have used

$$S_{xy} = \bigcup_{\varepsilon \in D} \{(x, y + \varepsilon), (x + \varepsilon, y)\} \tag{7}$$

where $D = \{-32, -16, -8, -4, -2, 0, 2, 4, 8, 16, 32\}$. This particular set was chosen as it contains short and long range spatial, and directional information. Depending on the level in the scale-space representation this can be used to emphasize small and large scale structures in the image. In the case described here we generate the co-occurrence between all the points in the set of sample points. This is illustrated in Fig. 2 for one particular point, but it should be noted that the same approach is used in a round-robin way or in other words the points are fully connected. When using $\{\overline{I}_\sigma\}$ (a similar notation can be obtained when using $\{I_\sigma\}$), this representation of the texture information in the form of a matrix is given by

$$\overline{\Psi}^\sigma(x, y) = \left[\psi^\sigma_{i,j}\right]_{i,j \in N_g} \tag{8}$$

and

$$\psi^\sigma_{i,j} = \#\left\{(p, p') \in S_{xy} \times S_{xy} \mid \overline{I}_\sigma(p) = i, \overline{I}_\sigma(p') = j\right\} \tag{9}$$

where $\#$ denotes the number of elements in a set and N_g denotes the set of grey-level values. It should be noted that this approach provides a different description than that would be provided by using a set of co-occurrence matrices.

Instead of using the co-occurrence of the grey-level values it is possible to use the occurrence of the grey-level difference. Again, this is using the same set of sample points S_{xy} (see Figs 1 and 2) at each scale (i.e. level in the image-stack). As we are using the occurrence of the grey-level difference values our co-occurrence grey-level value matrix reduces to a vector. When using the difference image-stack representation (see Eq. 6) the feature vector at a single scale is given by

$$\overline{\Phi}^\sigma(x, y) = \left[\phi^\sigma_i\right]_{i \in \delta N_g} \tag{10}$$

where N_g is the set of grey-levels, σ a given scale, δN_g is the set of grey-level differences and

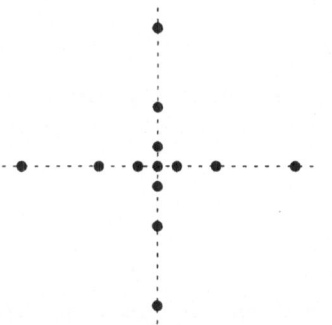

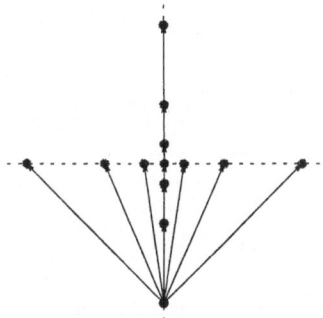

Fig. 1. Sample points S_{xy} **Fig. 2.** Sample points connectivity

$$\phi_i^\sigma = \#\{(p, p') \in S_{xy} \times S_{xy} \mid \overline{I}_\sigma(p) - \overline{I}_\sigma(p') = i\} \tag{11}$$

where, again, $\#$ denotes the number of elements in a set.

One of the main attributes of the feature vector is that descending the original image-stack means that the occurrences of grey-level difference values becomes more localised. In the extreme all grey-level values are identical and the occurrence becomes a delta-function. The story with regard to the difference image-stack is less straight forward. In general the information is sparse and when a structure is present at a particular point and scale the representation changes which is represented as a set of side-bands in the histogram. It should be noted that for a side-band to be regarded as to be caused by an image structure its area should be related to the scale in the image-stack else it can be regarded as noise.

2.2 Statistical Modelling

The texture feature described above is extracted at a pixel level. Combining all the information results in a feature vector which can be used to generate a statistical model. In general such a model is used for noise removal and data generalisation. In this particular case the added bonus of data generalisation is a reduced dimensionality which speeds up the processing. Here we have used principal component analysis [17], but other statistical methods could have been used instead.

The principal components of a set of observation vectors $\{\mathbf{x}_j : j = 1..n\}$ (in our case the texture feature $\overline{\Phi}^\sigma$ or $\overline{\Psi}^\sigma$) are the characteristic vectors, $\mathbf{P}$, of the covariance matrix, $\mathbf{C}$, constructed from the data set. Projecting the data into its principal components generally results in a compact and meaningful representation in which the characteristic vectors associated with the largest characteristic values describe the major modes of data variation. The characteristic values give the variances associated with the principal components. An observation $\mathbf{x}_j$ can be approximated from the principal components using

$$\mathbf{x}_j \approx \mathbf{P}\,\mathbf{b}_j + \mathbf{m}, \qquad\qquad (12)$$

where $\mathbf{m}$ is the average vector and $\mathbf{b}_j$ is a vector of weights. The dimensionality of the data set can be reduced by ignoring the principal components with low (or zero) characteristic values.

3   Results

For evaluation purposes we have used a subset of the Mammographic Images Analysis Society (MIAS) database was used [8, 18]. These are screening xray mammograms, and a detailed account of the database can be found in [18].

Although of interest, it is computationally impractical to base the EM modelling on the original texture feature vector as this has a large number of elements (a high dimensionality) and tends to be sparse. All the results presented in this section are based on a PCA reduced feature vector where we typically capture 95% of the data variation.

Segmentation results for example mammograms are shown in Fig. 3. The original mammograms are shown in Fig. 3a,b. The EM and statistical modelling process take only the breast area into account whilst excluding the pectoral muscle and the background. For the results shown in Fig. 3c-f six classes were used. The selection of six classes is based on an information theoretic approach [19]. In both cases the segmentation process produced plausible results which correlate with the original image.

3.1   Risk Assessment

To evaluate the segmentation results for mammographic risk assessment all the images were assessed by mammographic experts who provided an estimate of the proportion of dense tissue (i.e. high intensity/non-fatty tissue, see also Fig. 3a,b) in each mammogram. The segmentation results, based on EM and statistical modelling using $\{I_\sigma\}$ or $\{\bar{I}_\sigma\}$, can also be used to obtain the relative size of the segmented regions for each class. This feature is used as our classification space. The correlation between the relative region size distribution and the estimated proportion of dense tissue, when using a nearest neighbour classifier on a leave-one-out basis, can be found in Table 1. This shows an agreement for 66% of the mammograms when using $\{I_\sigma\}$. This increases to 86% when using $\{\bar{I}_\sigma\}$. This compares well with an inter-observer agreement of 45%. The intra-observer agreement on the used dataset is 89%.

4   Conclusions

We have shown that a combination of EM and statistical modelling results in a robust approach to the segmentation of mammographic images. We have introduced a texture feature vector based on a set-permutation occurrence matrix

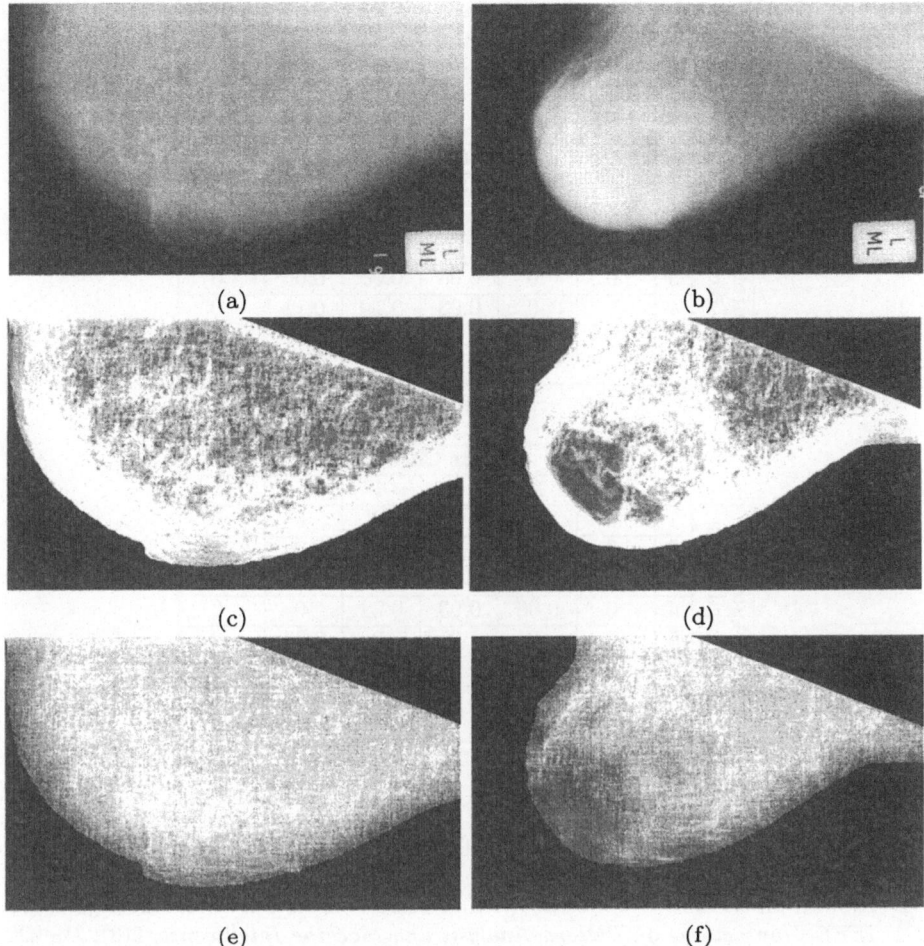

Fig. 3. Original fatty (a) and dense (b) mammographic images. Segmentation results where the EM modelling is based on (c,d) $\{I_\sigma\}$, and (e,f) $\{\bar{I}_\sigma\}$

which captures both spatial and local grey-level information. The use of this type of matrix, especially the size and shape of S_{xy}, will need further development to explore its limitations and full potential. We have shown that the segmentation results can be used to provide valuable information in mammographic assessment of density applications and therefor possibly such as risk assessment.

Acknowledgement

We would like to thank Glynis Wivell for marking the data.

Table 1. Comparison of the density estimate as given by an expert radiologist and automatic segmentation. (a) $\{I_\sigma\}$ and (b) $\{\overline{I}_\sigma\}$. Within the tables the proportion of dense tissue is represented as 1: 0%, 2: 0-10%, 3: 11-25%, 4: 26-50%, 5: 51-75% and 6: 76-100%

		Expert Classification					
		1	2	3	4	5	6
Automatic Classification	1	0	0	0	0	0	0
	2	0	0.22	0	0	0	0
	3	0	0	0.08	0.08	0.06	0
	4	0	0	0.03	0.19	0.11	0
	5	0	0	0.06	0	0.17	0
	6	0	0	0	0	0	0

(a)

		Expert Classification					
		1	2	3	4	5	6
Automatic Classification	1	0	0	0	0	0	0
	2	0	0.17	0	0	0	0
	3	0	0	0.14	0.06	0	0
	4	0	0.06	0.03	0.22	0	0
	5	0	0	0	0	0.33	0
	6	0	0	0	0	0	0

(b)

References

[1] M. W. Haralick. Statistical and structural approaches to texture. *Proceedings of the IEEE*, 67(5):786–804, 1979.

[2] R. W. Conners and C. A. Harlow. A theoretical comparison of texture algorithms. *IEEE Transactions on Pattern Analysis and Machine Intelligence*, 2(3):204–222, 1980.

[3] A. P. Pentland. Fractal-based description of natural scenes. *IEEE Transactions on Pattern Analysis and Machine Intelligence*, 6(6):661–674, 1984.

[4] T. R. Reed and J. M. H. Dubuf. A review of recent texture segmentation and feature-extraction techniques. *Computer Vision, Graphics and Image Processing*, 57(3):359–372, 1993.

[5] J.N Wolfe. Risk for breast cancer development determined by mammographic parenchymal pattern. *Cancer*, 37(5):2486–2492, 1976.

[6] A. M. Oza and N. F. Boyd. Mammographic parenchymal patterns: a marker of breast cancer risk. *Epidemiology Review*, 15:196–208, 1993.

[7] N. Karssemeijer. Automated classification of parenchymal patterns in mammograms. *Phys. Med. Biol.*, 43:365–378, 1998.

[8] L. Blot, E. R. E. Denton, and R. Zwiggelaar. Risk assessment: the use of background texture in mammographic imaging. *6th International Workshop on Digital Mammography*, Bremen, Germany:541–543, 2002.

[9] J. W. Byng, M. J. Yaffe, G. A. Lockwood, L. E. Little, D. L. Tritchler, and N. F. Boyd. Automated analysis of mammographic densities and breast carcinoma risk. *Cancer*, 80(1):66–74, 1997.

[10] J. J. Heine and R. P. Velthuizen. A statistical methodology for mammographic density detection. *Medical Physics*, 27:2644–2651, 2000.

[11] R.Sivaramakrishna, N. A. Obuchowsky, W. A. Chilcote, and K. A. Powell. Automatic segmentation of mammographic density. *Academic Radiology*, 8(3):250–256, 2001.

[12] R. Zwiggelaar. Separating background texture and image structure in mammograms. In *Proceedings of the 10th British Machine Vision Conference*, pages 362–371, Nottingham, UK, 1999.

[13] K. Polyak. On the birth of breast cancer. *Biochimica et Biophysica Acta*, 1552:1–13, 2001.

[14] P. Demster, N. M. Laird, and D. B. Rubin. Maximum likelihood from incomplete data via the em algorithm. *Journal of the Royal Statistical Society B*, 39:1–38, 1977.

[15] P. McKenzie and M. D. Alder. Initialising the em algorithm for use in gaussian mixture modelling. *Proceedings of the International Workshop on Pattern Recognition in Practice IV*, pages 91–105, 1994.

[16] R. Zwiggelaar, T. C. Parr, J. E. Schumm, I. W. Hutt, S. M. Astley, C. J. Taylor, and C. R. M. Boggis. Model-based detection of spiculated lesions in mammograms. *Medical Image Analysis*, 3(1):39–62, 1999.

[17] I. T. Jolliffe. *Principal Component Analysis*. Springer Verlag, 1986.

[18] J. Suckling, J. Parker, D. Dance, S. Astley, I. Hutt, C. Boggis, I. Ricketts, E. Stamatakis, N. Cerneaz, S. Kok, P. Taylor, D. Betal, and J. Savage. The mammographic images analysis society digital mammogram database. In Dance Gale, Astley and Cairns, editors, *Digital Mammography*, pages 375–378. Elsevier, 1994.

[19] R. Zwiggelaar, P. Planiol, J. Marti, R. Marti, L. Blot, E. R. E. Denton, and C. M. E. Rubin. Em texture segmentation of mammographic images. *6th International Workshop on Digital Mammography*, Bremen, Germany:223–227, 2002.

Semi-automatic Segmentation of the Prostate

Reyer Zwiggelaar[1], Yanong Zhu[1], and Stuart Williams[2]

[1] School of Information Systems, University of East Anglia
Norwich, UK
reyer.zwiggelaar@sys.uea.ac.uk
[2] Department of Radiology, Norfolk and Norwich University Hospital
Norwich, UK

Abstract. A semi-automatic method has been developed which segments the prostate in slices of Magnetic Resonance Imaging (MRI) data. The developed approach exploits the characteristics of the anatomical shape of the prostate when represented in a polar transform space. Simple techniques, such as line detection and non-maximum suppression, are used to track the boundary of the prostate. The initial results, based on a small set of data, indicate a good correlation with expert based manual segmentation.

1   Introduction

Prostate cancer is now the most frequently diagnosed male malignancy, with one in every 11 men developing the disease [1]. It is the second most common cause of cancer deaths in men. Patients who present with organ confined disease may be suitable for surgery - radical prostatectomy and bilateral pelvic lymph node dissection. However, once tumour has spread beyond the gland, radical radiotherapy is the preferred option. In advanced disease, hormone deprivation, radiotherapy and chemotherapy all have a role in patient management. The importance of imaging is to determine whether tumour is confined to the gland or whether tumour has spread into the periprostatic tissues. The detection of nodal and bone marrow spread is also important. Magnetic Resonance Imaging (MRI) is now the staging method of choice for cases of proven prostate cancer [2]. It is the most reliable technique for the depiction of the zonal anatomy of the prostate - 70% of tumour arising from the peripheral zone of the gland. Its superior contrast resolution and multiplanar capabilities allow the best chance of detecting extracapsular extension of tumour. Nevertheless, early periprostatic spread can be subtle, with intra-observer discrepancies noted.

The main aim of the developed approach is to improve the assessment of the spread of cancer both within and outside of the gland. MRI provides three-dimensional anatomical information displayed as two-dimensional slices. The overall aim of the project is to investigate the information contained within a number of greylevel profiles which are extracted along straight lines radiating out from the centre of the prostate. The profiles for normal prostates are characteristic showing a number of transitions between anatomical features within the

F.J. Perales et al. (Eds.): IbPRIA 2003, LNCS 2652, pp. 1108–1116, 2003.

gland. When a cancer extends out of the gland, these profiles can be radically changed. To be able to extract these profiles the prostate needs to be segmented. Here we present initial results based on a semi-automatic approach.

2 Data

The main data consists of 20 prostate MRI volumes. All images are obtained on a 1.5 Tesla magnet (Signa, GE Medical Systems, Milwaukee, USA) using a phased array pelvic coil. Field of view 24 × 24 cm, matrix 256 × 512, slice thickness 3mm with an interslice gap of 0.5mm, TR 7800ms, TE 102ms. Fig. 1 shows two typical examples from the data set. In both cases the prostate can be found in the centre of the image. In Fig. 1 on the left there are minor benign hypertrophic changes in the central zone. The peripheral zone architecture is generally preserved, with some patchy loss of the normal high T2 signal, in keeping with some malignant infiltration. There is no extracapsular extension present. In Fig. 1 on the right there are marked benign hypertrophic changes within the central zone, with resultant compression of the peripheral zone to a thin rim of tissue. However, the visible peripheral zone does return reduced signal, suggesting that some tumour is present. Evidence of extracapsular spread is present within the MRI volume (but not on this slice).

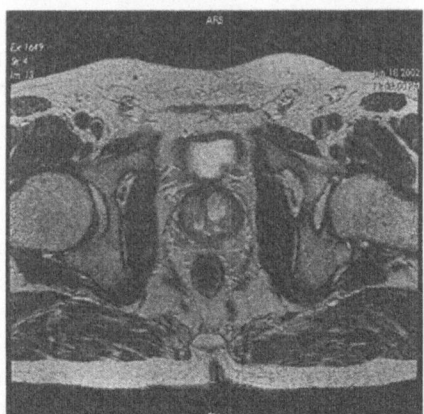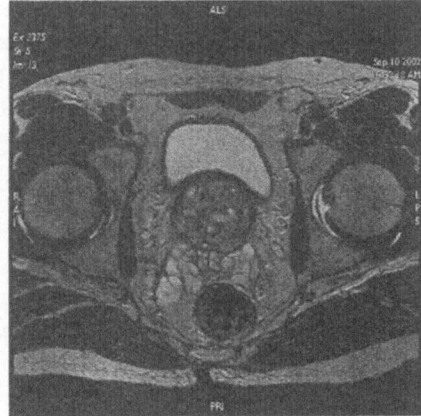

Fig. 1. Axial view prostate MRI examples

3 Methods

A detailed description of the methods used is given. To illustrate the effects of the various steps involved in the segmentation of prostate MRI data typical examples are shown which are based on the axial views shown in Fig. 1.

 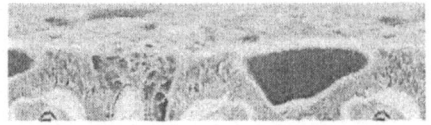

Fig. 2. Polar transforms of the prostate images shown in Fig. 1

The prostate and the surrounding tissue are extracted into a polar transform using

$$x = x_c + r\cos(\theta)$$
$$y = y_c + r\sin(\theta)$$

(1)

where (x, y) is a position in the original image, (r, θ) represents the polar transform space, and (x_c, y_c) represents the centre with respect to which the polar transform is obtained. We have used bilinear interpolation to sample the original data. Bilinear interpolation was used to be able to approximate greylevel values at non-integer (i.e. non-pixel) positions. An example of this, based on the prostate images shown in Fig. 1, is displayed in Fig. 2, where we used $\theta \in [-\pi/4, 9\pi/4]$ and $r \in \langle 0, 128 \rangle$ to define the surrounding tissue. An extended range for θ is used at this initial stage to avoid boundary effects in subsequent steps. In effect we are only interested in the range $\theta \in [0, 2\pi]$. A negative greylevel transform is used, so a dark boundary in the original data is represented as a bright ridge in the polar transform.

Because (x_c, y_c) is within the prostate there should only be one continuous structure across orientations in the polar transform. This continues structure represents the boundary between the prostate and the surrounding tissue. It is expected that if (x_c, y_c) is situated close to the centre of the prostate the distance between (x_c, y_c) and the boundary is more or less constant, which means that in the polar transform representation this forms a horizontal band. To segment the prostate from the other anatomical structures in the image we have to extract the described representation of the boundary in the polar transform.

In the first instance we extract ridges in the polar transform for which we have used Lindeberg's approach [3], which is based on the usage of first and second order directional derivatives. An example of this ridge detection can be found in Fig. 3, which shows a large number of ridges found in the polar transform. Due to the fact that the ridge strength measure produces a probability with values in between zero and one all the ridges with a local high probability value are connected by valleys with lower probability values. This connectivity needs to be removed to extract the prostate boundary.

To achieve this we use non-maximum suppression [4] along the radial direction of the polar transform and the results of this operation based on the curvi-linear structures detected in the polar transform shown in Fig. 3 can be found in Fig. 4. The results are only shown for the $\theta \in [0, 2\pi]$ range. This shows a large number of curvi-linear structures which are unconnected in the vertical

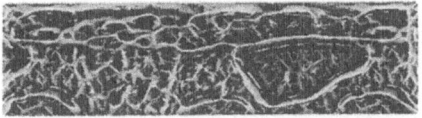

Fig. 3. Ridges detected in the polar transforms of the prostate images shown in Fig. 1

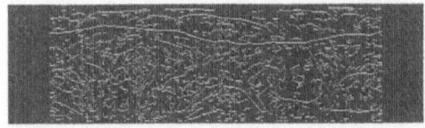
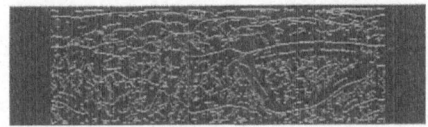

Fig. 4. Non-maximum suppression in the radial direction for the detected ridges in the polar transforms of the prostate images shown in Fig. 1

(the radial) direction. It should be noted that most of the curvi-linear structures are short and only a few longer structures exist.

Subsequently we want to find the one curvi-linear structure that represents the prostate boundary. We use the assumption made above that this is the only structure to appear as a band across all the orientations in the polar transform. To do this we track the curvi-linear structures across the image and select the one with the longest length. To improve the robustness of the selection process the tracking is done both from left to right and visa-versa. The tracking is achieved by considering all radial positions at a zero degree orientation and propagation to the next orientation only occurs if at that orientation there are non-maximum suppression values at the same or plus/minus one radial position. The results of this process for our example polar transform can be found in Fig. 5. Again, the results are only shown for the $\theta \in [0, 2\pi]$ range in the polar transform space. It should be clear that for the left-hand case a curvi-linear structure was found which covers the full $[0, 2\pi]$ range for θ. However, this is not the case for the right-hand side which clearly shows a large gap between two parts of a curvi-linear structure.

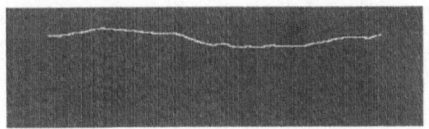
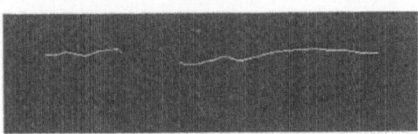

Fig. 5. Selection of the longest curvi-linear structure after non-maximum suppression in the radial direction for the detected ridges in the polar transforms of the prostate images shown in Fig. 1

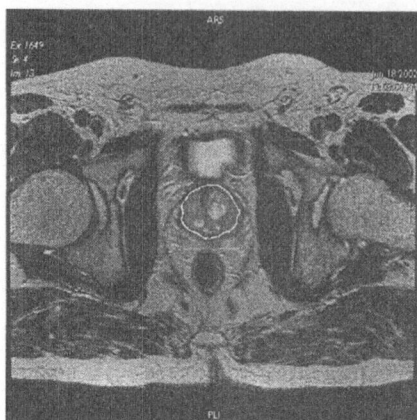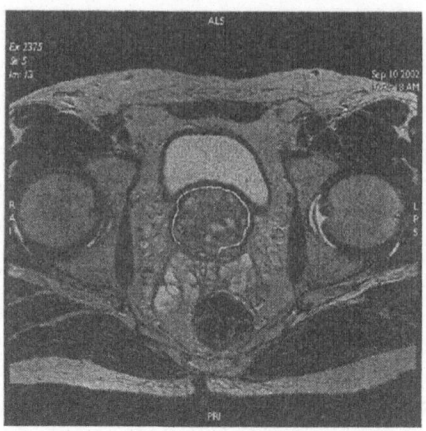

Fig. 6. Segmentation of the prostate in axial MRI views

An inverse polar transform has been used to project the prostate boundary representation from the polar transform back into the original prostate MRI data. The results of this can be found in Fig. 6. It should be clear from these results that only in the left-hand view the prostate is segmented completely. For the right-hand view, only the top half of the prostate has been detected. The non-segmentation of the bottom-half of the prostate is caused by the spread from the central into the peripheral zone.

It should be mentioned that there is a very simplistic approach to obtain an approximation of a complete segmentation if the boundary can not be tracked over the whole range $\theta \in [0, 2\pi]$. In the polar transform the end-points of the parts of the tracked curvi-linear structure can be connected by a straight line. This makes the assumption that the prostate is locally spherical. However, here we have used a slightly more elaborate approach to obtain a boundary over the whole range $\theta \in [0, 2\pi]$. If a complete segmentation is not supported by a single linear structure in the polar transform the non-maximum-suppressed and original greylevel information can be used to obtain a most likely approximation in between the end-points. Within this stage there is a preference to track another linear structure in the non-maximum-suppressed image, but if that is not supported the original greylevel values are used to follow the boundary (using a steepest assent approach). Results of this approach, for the example slices, can be found in Fig. 8.

4   Results

Two aspects of the developed segmentation technique are evaluated. In the first instance we consider the robustness with respect to the central position (x_c, y_c), which is the position that needs to be manually selected. Subsequently, we pro-

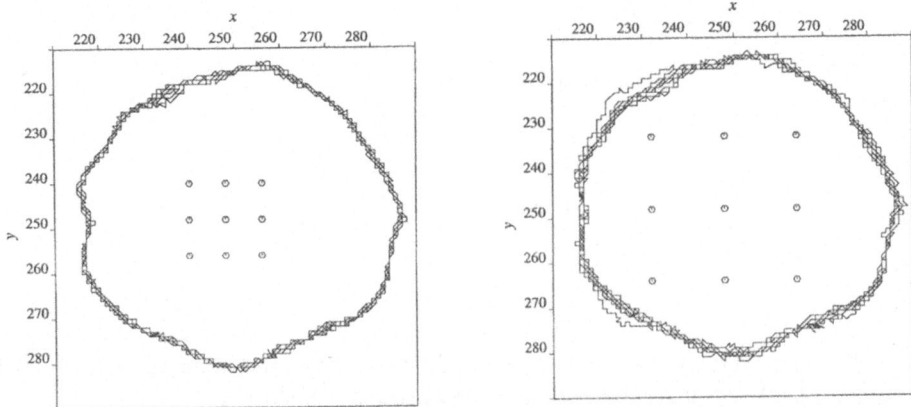

Fig. 7. Segmentation resulting for seventeen different starting positions within the prostate, where (x, y) are pixel positions

vide a comparison of the semi-automatic approach with manual segmentation of the prostate.

4.1   Central Position (x_c, y_c)

To evaluate the robustness of the automatic approach to variation in the position (x_c, y_c) the segmentation was obtained for different values of (x_c, y_c). The segmentation resulting from seventeen different (x_c, y_c) positions can be found in Fig. 7 (the (x_c, y_c) positions used for the two graphs are also indicated). The segmentation resulting from the various values of (x_c, y_c) are all similar, with the difference between segmentations limited to a few pixels at maximum and no difference at some positions of the segmentation. As a result, the centre of gravity of the segmentations is also stable with the variation in position limited by a few pixels in both directions. The consistency in the segmentation is better for the set of positions closer to the centre of the prostate. However, even for the results where the positions of (x_c, y_c) are close to the boundary of the prostate the segmentation results are consistent although the differences between the segmentations can be several pixels. If a point (x_c, y_c) is chosen even closer to the boundary of the prostate the segmentation will fail. It should be noted that the resulting segmentations are realistic and almost independent of (x_c, y_c).

4.2   Comparison with Manual Segmentation

Manual segmentation of the prostate was provided by an expert radiologist. For both axial examples these anatomical boundary annotations can be found in Fig. 8 where they are indicated by a dashed line. For comparison we have included the resulting boundaries based on our semi-automatic approach. A number of aspects should be noted. Firstly, it should be clear that the general shape

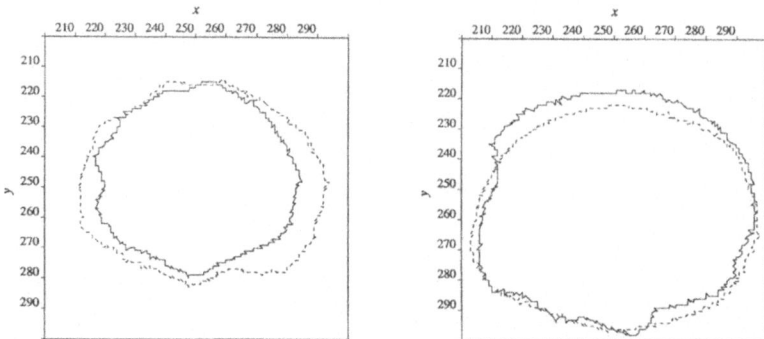

Fig. 8. Comparison between manual (dashed lines) and semi-automatic (continuous lines) segmentation, where (x, y) are pixel positions

of the automatic and manual segmentations are similar. However, it seems that the automatic segmentation approach under-estimates the extent of the prostate. The amount of under-estimation is not consistent along the boundary of the prostate and seems less pronounced at the top-half of the prostate.

In Fig. 9 the comparison of the manual and semi-automatic segmentations are summarised. For all the slices from two volumes (slice number 13 of each volume can be found in Fig. 1) we have determined a measure of overlap between the annotated and automatically segmented regions. The overlap measure Ω is given by [5]

$$\Omega = \frac{TP}{TP + FP + FN},$$ (2)

where TP stands for the area correctly classified as the prostate, FP for the area incorrectly classified as the prostate and FN for the area incorrectly classified as background. For $\Omega = 1$ there is perfect overlap and for $\Omega = 0$ there is no overlap between the annotated and automatically segmented region. The graphs show that the automatic segmentation is closest to the annotations for the most central slices and degrades when moving away from the central slices.

5   Discussion and Conclusions

To date most if the prostate segmentation considers ultrasound [6, 7] and CT [8] as the imaging modality. Only recently has this been extended to include MR imaging [2]. Cootes et al. used prostate segmentation as an examplar in some of their early publications [9]. To our knowledge, no other attempts have been published covering the (semi-) automatic segmentation of prostate MRI data. A direct comparison between these various modalities is currently not possible. Recently there has been some work on the registration of prostate MRI data [10, 11].

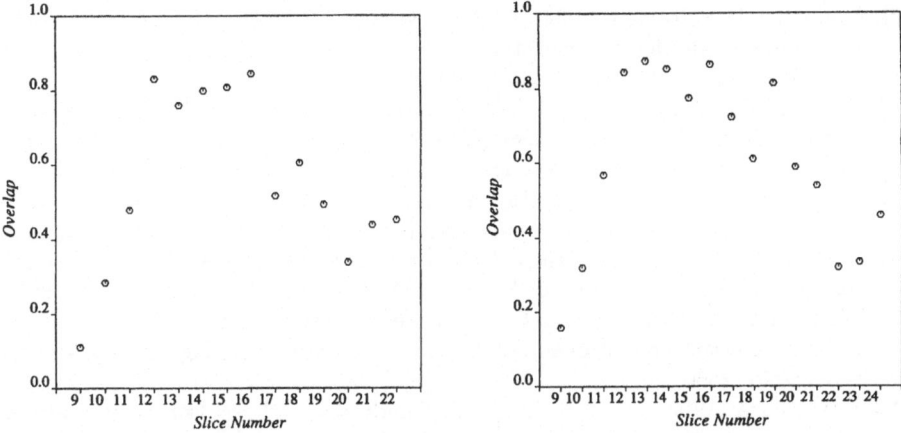

Fig. 9. The overlap, Eq. 2, between the annotated and segmented regions for each MR slice

The next step towards the classification of the prostate (as discussed in Sec. 1) is to use the segmentation as a guide to extract greylevel profiles. It is our thesis that these profiles, in combination with statistical modelling, can be used to classify the prostate and provide a semi-automatic staging tool.

In summary, we have discussed the semi-automatic segmentation of the prostate. The developed approach is based on the usage of simple computer vision techniques in the polar transform of the original MRI data. The extracted boundary can be projected back into the original prostate images. A direct comparison with manual segmentation shows a good correlation, but the semi-automatic approach seems to underestimate the size of the prostate. Although this is a semi-automatic technique, the only parameter that needs to be selected is the position of the centre of the polar transform. It has been shown that the developed technique is robust with respect to variations in this parameters.

References

[1] S. W. Hayward and G. R. Cunha. The prostate: Development and physiology. *Radiologic Clinics of North America*, 38(1):1–15, 2000.
[2] K. K. Yu and H. Hricak. Imaging prostate cancer. *Radiologic Clinics of North America*, 38(1):59–87, 2000.
[3] T. Lindeberg. Edge detection and ridge detection with automatic scale selection. *International Journal of Computer Vision*, 30(2):117–154, 1998.
[4] M. Sonka, V. Hlavac, and R. Boyle. *Image Processing, Analysis and Machine Vision*. Chapman and Hall Publishing, 1993.
[5] B. van Ginneken, A. F. Frangi, J. J. Staal, B. M. ter Haar Romeny, and M. A. Viergever. Active shape model segmentation with optimal features. *IEEE Transactions on Medical Imaging*, 21(8):924–933, 2002.
[6] C. Knoll, M. Alcaniz, V. Grau, C. Monserrat, and M. C. Juan. Outlining of the prostate using snakes with shape restrictions based on the wavelet transform. *Pattern Recognition*, 32(10):1767–1781, 1999.

[7] A. Ghanei, H. Soltanian-Zadeh, A. Ratkewicz, and F. F. Yin. A three-dimensional deformable model for segmentation of human prostate from ultrasound images. *Medical Physics*, 28(10):2147–2153, 2001.

[8] M. Mazonakis, J. Damilakis, H. Varveris, P. Prassopoulos, and N. Gourtsoyiannis. Image segmentation in treatment planning for prostate cancer using the region growing technique. *British Journal of Radiology*, 74(879):243–248, 2001.

[9] T. F. Cootes, A. Hill, and C. J. Taylor. The use of active shape models for locating structures in medical images. *Image and Vision Computing*, 12(6):355–365, 1994.

[10] A. Bharatha, M. Hirose, N. Hata, S. K. Warfield, M. Ferrant, K. H. Zou, E. Suarez-Santana, J. Ruiz-Alzola, A. D'Amico, R. A. Cormack, R. Kikinis, F. A. Jolesz, and C. M. C. Tempany. Evaluation of three-dimensional finite element-based deformable registration of pre- and intraoperative prostate imaging. *Medical Physics*, 28(12):2551–2560, 2001.

[11] B. W. Fei, A. Wheaton, Z. H. Lee, J. L. Duerk, and D. L. Wilson. Automatic mr volume registration and its evaluation for the pelvis and prostate. *Phys. Med. Biol.*, 47(5):823–838, 2002.

Entropy Vector Median Filter

Rastislav Lukac[1], Bogdan Smolka[2],
Konstantinos N. Plataniotis[3] and Anastasios N. Venetsanopoulos[3]

[1] Slovak Image Processing Center,
Jarkova 343, 049 25 Dobsina, Slovak Republic
lukacr@ieee.org
[2] Department of Automatic Control,
Silesian University of Technology, Akademicka 16 Str., 44-101 Gliwice, Poland
bsmolka@ia.polsl.gliwice.pl
[3] Edward S. Rogers Sr. Department of Electrical and Computer Engineering,
University of Toronto, 10 King's College Road, Toronto, Canada
{kostas,anv}@dsp.toronto.edu

Abstract. In this paper, a new adaptive multichannel filter for the detection and removal of impulsive noise, bit errors and outliers in digital color images is provided. The proposed nonlinear filter takes the advantages of the concept of the local entropy contrast and the robust order-statistics theory. The new entropy based vector median is computationally attractive, robust for a wide range of the impulsive noise corruption and significantly improves the signal-detail preservation capability of the standard vector median filter.

1   Introduction

In the image processing applications, the most common processing tasks are noise filtering and image enhancement. Because the final image is often utilized for visual interpretation or for automatic analysis [19], it is important to free the image scene from samples which would endanger the correct recognition of the scene objects.

In the case of color images, it has been widely recognized that the processing of color image data as vector fields is desirable due to the high correlation that exists between the image channels, and that the nonlinear vector processing of color images is the most effective way to filter out noise. In this way, a number of reference vector filters such as vector median filter (VMF) [1], basic vector directional filter (BVDF) [24],[25] and the directional distance filter (DDF) [8] was developed. These nonlinear filters, based on the ordering operation, provide robust estimation in environments corrupted by bit errors, impulsive noise and outliers. In general, the success of the searching for an image close to the undisturbed original, depends on the complexity of the image scene, the nature of the corruption process and also on the adopted measures of the restoration accuracy [2].

F.J. Perales et al. (Eds.): IbPRIA 2003, LNCS 2652, pp. 1117-1125, 2003.
© Springer-Verlag Berlin Heidelberg 2003

2   Well-Known Vector Filters

Let $y(x): Z^l \to Z^m$ represent a multichannel image, where l is an image dimension and m characterizes a number of channels ($m = 3$ for color images). Let $W = \{x_i \in Z^l \; ; \; i = 1, 2..., N\}$ represent a filter window of a finite size N, where $x_1, x_2, ..., x_N$ is a set of noisy samples. Note that the position of the filter window is determined by the central sample $x_{(N+1)/2}$.

In the last decade, a number of nonlinear, multichannel filters, which utilize correlation among multivariate vectors using various distance measures have been proposed [1],[6-12],[16-22]. The most popular nonlinear, multichannel filters are based on the ordering of vectors in a predefined sliding window. The output of these filters is defined as the lowest ranked vector according to a specific ordering technique [1],[17],[19],[20],[26].

In general, the difference between two multichannel samples $x_i = (x_{i1}, x_{i2}, ..., x_{im})$ and $x_j = (x_{j1}, x_{j2}, ..., x_{jm})$ can be quantified through the commonly used Minkowski norm, [19]:

$$\left\| x_i - x_j \right\|_\gamma = \left(\sum_{k=1}^{m} \left| x_{ik} - x_{jk} \right|^\gamma \right)^{\frac{1}{\gamma}} \tag{1}$$

where γ characterizes the specific kind of used norm, m is the dimension (number of channels) of vectors and x_{ik} is the k th element of the sample x_i. Note that the well-known Euclidean distance is obtained for $\gamma = 2$.

Let us consider input sample x_i, $i = 1, 2, ..., N$, associated with the distance measure L_i given by, [1],[19],[20]

$$L_i = \sum_{j=1}^{N} \left\| x_i - x_j \right\|_\gamma \quad \text{for } i = 1, 2, ..., N \tag{2}$$

If the ordering criterion is given by the ordering of distance measures $L_1, L_2, ..., L_N$ and the ordered set is given by

$$L_{(1)} \le L_{(2)} \le ... \le L_{(N)} \tag{3}$$

then the same ordering scheme applied to the input set results in the ordered sequence

$$x_{(1)} \le x_{(2)} \le ... \le x_{(N)} \tag{4}$$

The sample $x_{(1)}$ associated with $\Omega_{(1)}$ represents the VMF output.

3   Proposed Entropy Vector Median

The vector median filter is designed to perform the fixed amount of smoothing. In many applications, it may become an undesired property and in some image areas the vector median filter will introduce too much smoothing and it will blur fine details and even image edges. For that reason, the common problem is how to preserve some desired signal features, when removing efficiently the noise elements. An optimal situation would arise if the filter could be designed so that the desired features would be invariant to the filtering operation and only noise would be affected. Many contributions [3-5],[9-12],[18], [19],[21-23] have provided different solutions on how to minimize the undesired effect of the vector median filtering using fuzzy logic, noise density estimations, subfilter structures and various restrictions imposed on the central sample.

Ideally, the noise reduction filter should be designed in such a way that the noise-free samples should be invariant to the filtering operation and only noise-corrupted pixels should be affected by the filter action. In other words, in the case of noise-free samples, the filter should perform the identity operation (no filtering), whereas noisy samples should be replaced by the VMF. In order to provide the adaptive trade-off between the identity filter and the VMF, we present a new filtering scheme, which makes use of the local entropy of multichannel samples inside the filtering window.

The proposed filter is based on the local contrast entropy proposed by Beghdadi and Khellaf [4]. Let $\{x_1, x_2, ..., x_N\}$ be the set of gray-scale samples inside the filter window of a finite size N. Let us consider that each input sample x_i, for $i = 1, 2, ..., N$, is associated [4] with its contrast C_i defined by:

$$C_i = \frac{|x_i - \mu|}{\mu} = \frac{\Delta_i}{\mu} \tag{5}$$

where Δ_i is the gradient level and μ is the mean of the input set $\{x_1, x_2, ..., x_N\}$. Thus, the local contrast probability is given by two equivalent expressions, [4]:

$$P_i = \frac{C_i}{\sum_{j=1}^{N} C_j} = \frac{C_i}{C_s} \quad \text{and} \quad P_i = \frac{\Delta_i}{\sum_{j=1}^{N} \Delta_j} \tag{6}$$

Any sample x_i, for $i = 1, 2, ..., N$, inside the filter window is considered as noise, if its associated local contrast probability is too high.

Let us consider the multichannel case, where the input set is given by the multichannel samples $\mathbf{x}_1, \mathbf{x}_2, ..., \mathbf{x}_N$. Then, the local contrast probability (6) can be rewritten as follows:

$$P_i = \frac{\left(\sum_{k=1}^{m} |x_{ik} - \mu_k|^\gamma \right)^{\frac{1}{\gamma}}}{\sum_{j=1}^{N} \left(\sum_{k=1}^{m} |x_{jk} - \mu_k|^\gamma \right)^{\frac{1}{\gamma}}} \tag{7}$$

where μ_k is k-th component of the mean $\boldsymbol{\mu} = (\mu_1, \mu_2, ..., \mu_m)$ of the input set $\mathbf{x}_1, \mathbf{x}_2, ..., \mathbf{x}_N$:

$$\mu = \frac{1}{N}\sum_{i=1}^{N}\mathbf{x}_i = \left[\frac{1}{N}\sum_{i=1}^{N}x_{i1}, \frac{1}{N}\sum_{i=1}^{N}x_{i2}, ..., \frac{1}{N}\sum_{i=1}^{N}x_{im} \right] \qquad (8)$$

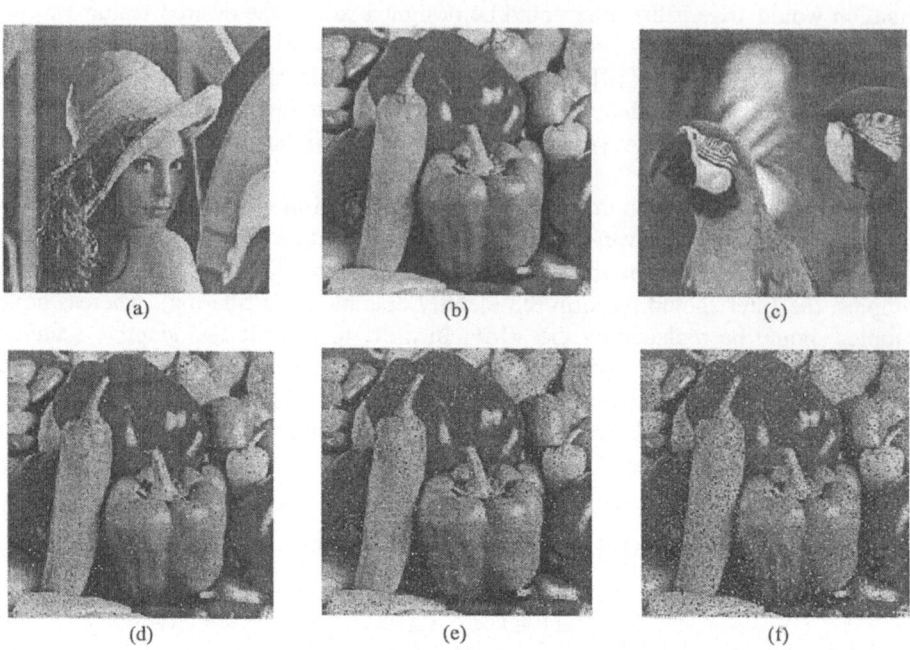

(a)   (b)   (c)

(d)   (e)   (f)

Fig. 1. Test Images. (a) original image Lena, (b) original image Peppers, (c) original image Parrots, (d) noisy image - $p = 0.05$, (e) noisy image - $p = 0.10$, (f) noisy image - $p = 0.20$

Using the entropy definition applied to the input set $\{\mathbf{x}_1, \mathbf{x}_2, ..., \mathbf{x}_N\}$, noisy samples heavily contribute to the entropy defined by

$$H = -\sum_{i=1}^{N} P_i \log P_i \qquad (9)$$

where P_i (7) is the local contrast probability associated with the input vector sample $\mathbf{x}_i$ and N is the window size. In terms of the entropy concept (9), each input sample $\mathbf{x}_i$ is also associated with the local contrast entropy H_i defined as:

$$H_i = -P_i \log P_i \qquad (10)$$

Our purpose is to provide the adaptive threshold to be compared with the local contrast probability. Because each local contrast probability P_i given by (7) is always constrained to be a value between 0 and 1, the adaptive threshold of our approach should be rescaled to the same interval.

Let us assume that each multichannel sample $\mathbf{x}_i$, for $i = 1, 2, ..., N$, is associated with the adaptive threshold β_i expressed as the rate of the local contrast entropy H_i

defined by (10) and the overall entropy H (9) of the input set $\{\mathbf{x}_1, \mathbf{x}_2, ..., \mathbf{x}_N\}$. So, the adaptive threshold β_i is given by

$$\beta_i = \frac{-P_i \log P_i}{H} = \frac{-P_i \log P_i}{-\sum_{j=1}^{N} P_j \log P_j} \tag{11}$$

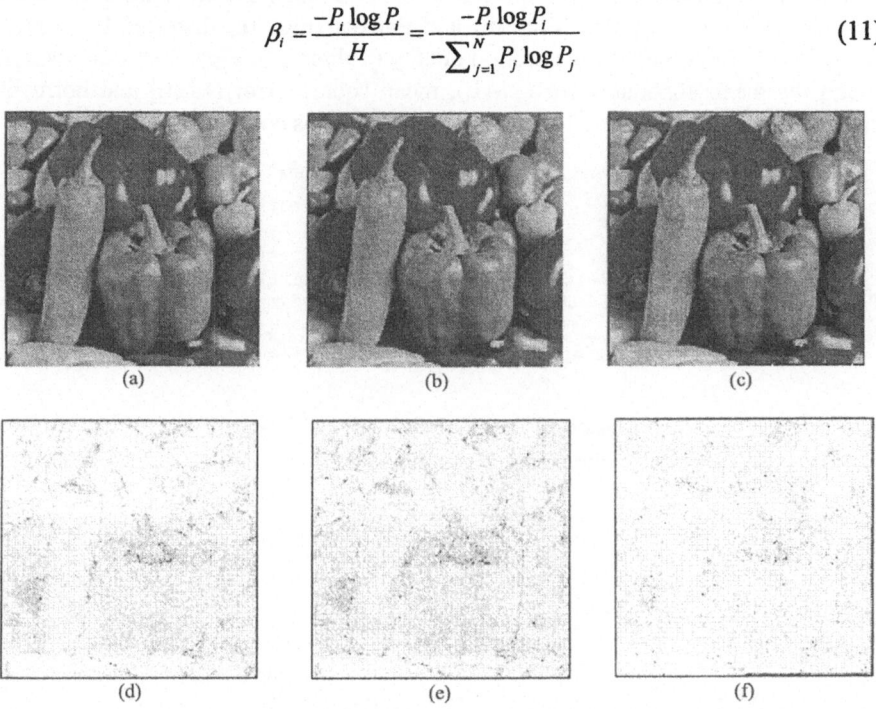

(a)   (b)   (c)

(d)   (e)   (f)

Fig. 2. Achieved results related to the filtering of 10% ($p = 0.10$) impulsive noise. (a) VMF output, (b) BVDF output, (c) output of the proposed method, (d) VMF estimation error, (e) BVDF estimation error, (f) estimation error of the proposed method

Thus, the output of the entropy vector median filter is given by

$$\mathbf{y} = \begin{cases} \mathbf{x}_{(1)} & \text{if } P_{(N+1)/2} \geq \beta_{(N+1)/2} \\ \mathbf{x}_{(N+1)/2} & \text{otherwise} \end{cases} \tag{12}$$

where $\mathbf{y}$ is the filter output, $\mathbf{x}_{(1)}$ is the lowest ranked vector and $\beta_{(N+1)/2}$ is the adaptive threshold associated with the central sample $\mathbf{x}_{(N+1)/2}$.

Besides the filtering efficiency, the proposed method has also the practical advantage, as in the case of noise-free central sample $\mathbf{x}_{(N+1)/2}$, it excludes the time consuming computation of the VMF output. Thus, the computation of the sums of distances to other input samples, the ordering operation and the selection of the VMF output are performed only in the case of impulse detection, which makes the proposed algorithm computationally attractive.

4   Experimental Results

We tested the performance of the presented method using the standard color test images Lena (Fig. 1a), Peppers (Fig. 1b) and Parrots (Fig. 1c) distorted by impulsive noise [2],[19]. The objective restoration quality (Tables 1-2, Figs. 4-6) were evaluated through the mean absolute error (MAE), mean square error (MSE) and normalized color difference (NCD), [19]. The proposed method was compared with vector

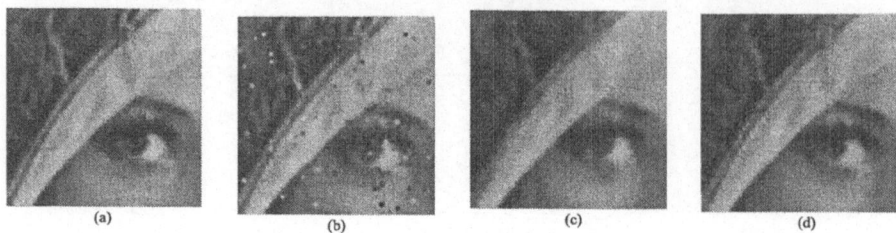

(a)   (b)   (c)   (d)

Fig. 3. Detailed view on the restored Lena image: (a) original image, (b) noisy image $p = 0.05$, (c) VMF output, (d) output of the proposed method

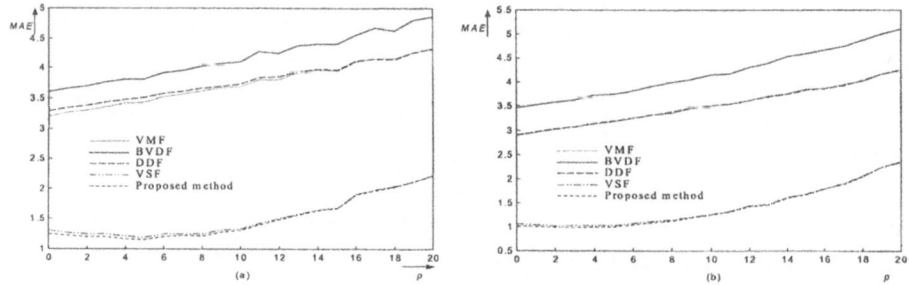

Fig. 4. Mean absolute error (MAE) of the relevant methods in dependence on the probability p of the impulsive noise corruption: (a) test image Lena, (b) test image Peppers

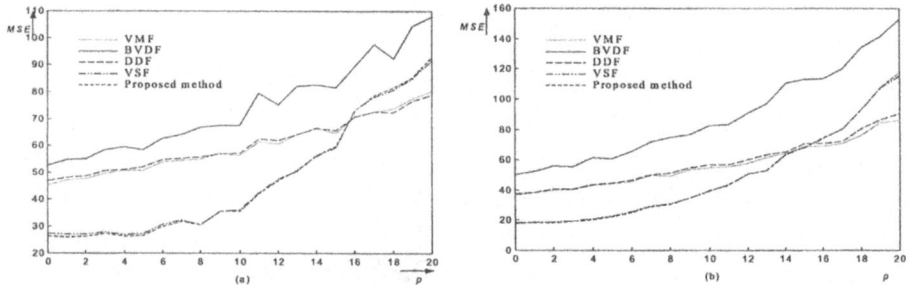

Fig. 5. Mean square error (MSE) of the relevant methods in dependence on the probability p of the impulsive noise corruption: (a) image Lena, (b) image Peppers

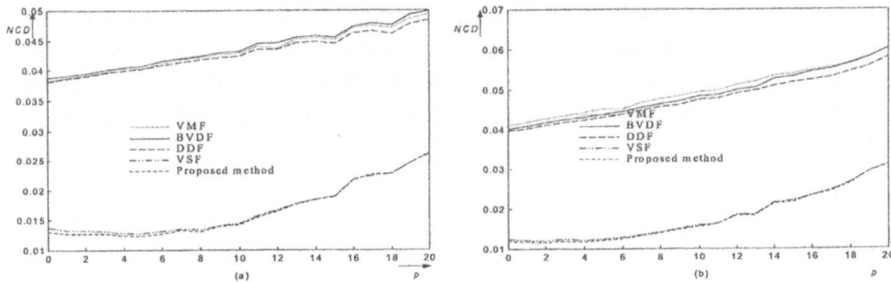

Fig. 6. Normalized color difference (NCD) of the relevant methods in dependence on the probability p of the impulsive noise corruption: (a) test image Lena, (b) test image Peppers

standard filters such as VMF [1], BVDF [24] and DDF [8] and some recently developed adaptive methods such as the vector sigma filter (VSF) [12], adaptive vector directional filter (AVDF) [18] and modified weighted VMF (MWVMF) [21].

It can be seen (Tables 1, Fig.2-6) that the performance of the proposed method is quite good. The proposed entropy vector median outperforms the standard vector filtering schemes with excellent improvements in terms of all used objective quality measures. In many situations, the performance of the proposed method is also better in comparison with adaptive filters (AVDF, MWVMF, VSF). In addition, the proposed method achieves excellent noise attenuation and signal-detail preserving capabilities also for the increased amount of image corruption. This robust behavior of the proposed method is obtained by its fully adaptive structure, so that it requires no optimization and eliminates the undesired properties of the standard vector filtering schemes.

Table 1. Results achieved using the noise corruption probability $p = 0.05$

Image	Lena			Peppers			Parrots		
Method	MAE	MSE	NCD	MAE	MSE	NCD	MAE	MSE	NCD
Noisy	3.762	427.3	0.0445	3.988	486.1	0.0441	3.805	443.6	0.0432
VMF	3.430	50.8	0.0403	3.169	43.9	0.0452	2.669	64.2	0.0132
BVDF	3.818	58.6	0.0407	3.740	60.7	0.0438	3.460	109.0	0.0116
DDF	3.509	52.3	0.0402	3.182	44.6	0.0431	2.645	65.3	0.0117
AVDF	4.301	54.3	0.0483	4.068	51.4	0.0552	3.805	97.3	0.0169
MWVMF	1.312	30.1	0.0158	1.205	23.9	0.0140	1.214	44.5	0.0059
VSF	1.192	27.3	0.0128	1.033	23.0	0.0124	1.081	41.8	0.0041
Proposed	1.155	26.6	0.0124	1.004	22.3	0.0121	1.029	40.2	0.0040

5   Conclusions

This paper focused on adaptive color image filtering using the new entropy based vector median. In order to detect outliers and bit errors present in the input image, the proposed method utilizes the entropy concept applied to multichannel samples inside the filtering sliding window. The new filter outperforms the standard vector median filter and its derivatives like BVDF and DDF. In addition, the complexity of the new methods is significantly lower than that of the above-mentioned well-known standard vector filters. The achieved results show that the new filter is clearly superior to the VMF, BVDF and DDF in terms of all widely used quality measures and the performance of the proposed method is comparable with the best available adaptive vector filters.

References

[1]   Astola, J., Haavisto, P., Neuvo, Y.: Vector Median Filters. Proceedings of the IEEE 78 (1990) 678-689

[2]   Astola, J., Kuosmanen, P.: Fundamentals of Nonlinear Digital Filtering. CRC Press (1997)

[3]   Berstain, R.: Adaptive Nonlinear Filters for Simultaneous Removal of Different Kinds of Noise in Images. IEEE Transactions on Circuits. Sys., Cas-34 (1987) 1275-1291

[4]   Beghdadi, A., Khellaf, K.: A Noise-Filtering Method Using a Local Information Measure. IEEE Transactions on Image Processing, 6 (1997) 879-882

[5]   Chen, T., Wu, H.R.: Adaptive Impulse Detection Using Center-Weighted Median Filters. IEEE Signal Processing Letters, 8 (2001) 1-3

[6]   Gabbouj M., Cheickh F.A., Vector Median-Vector Directional Hybrid Filter for Color Image Restoration. Proceedings of EUSIPCO-96 (1996) 879-881

[7]   Karakos D.G., Trahanias P.E.: Combining Vector Median and Vector Directional Filters: The Directional-Distance Filters, Proc. ICIP-95 (1995) 171-174

[8]   Karakos, D.G., Trahanias, P.E.: Generalized Multichannel Image-Filtering Structure. IEEE Transactions on Image Processing 6 (1997) 1038-1045

[9]   Lukac, R.: Vector LUM Smoothers as Impulse Detector for Color Images. Proc. ECCTD '01 in Espoo, Finland, 3 (2001) 137-140

[10]   Lukac, R.: Adaptive Impulse Noise Filtering by Using Center-Weighted Directional Information. Proc. CGIV'2002 in Poitiers, France, (2002) 86-89

[11]   Lukac, R.: Color Image Filtering by Vector Directional Order-Statistics. Pattern Recognition and Image Analysis 12 (2002) 279-285

[12]   Lukac, R., Smolka, B., Plataniotis, K.N.: Color Sigma Filter. Proc. IWSSIP'02 in Manchester, United Kingdom (2002) 559-565

[13]   Mitra, S.J., Sicuranza, G.L.: Nonlinear Image Processing. Academic Press (2001)

[14]   Peltonen, S., Gabbouj, M., Astola, J.: Nonlinear Filter Design: Methodologies and Challenges. Proc. ISPA'01 in Pula, Croatia (2001) 102-107

[15]   Pitas, I., Venetsanopoulos, A.N.: Nonlinear Digital Filters, Principles and Applications. Kluwer Academic Publishers (1990)

[16]   Pitas, I., Venetsanopoulos, A.N.: Order Statistics in Digital Image Processing. Proceedings of the IEEE, 80 (1992) 1892-1919

[17]   Plataniotis K.N., Androutsos D., Sri V., Venetsanopoulos A.N.: A Nearest Neighbour Multichannel Filter. Electronic Letters, 31 (1995) 1910-1911

[18] Plataniotis, K.N., Androutsos, D., Venetsanopoulos, A.N.: Color Image Processing Using Adaptive Vector Directional Filters. IEEE Transactions on Circuits and Systems II, 45 (1998) 1414-1419

[19] Plataniotis, K.N., Venetsanopoulos, A.N.: Color Image Processing and Applications. Springer Verlag (2000)

[20] Smolka, B., Chydzinski, A., Wojciechowski, K., Plataniotis K.N., Venetsanopoulos, A.N.: On the Reduction of Impulsive Noise in Multichannel Image Processing. Optical Engineering, 40 (2001) 902-908

[21] Smolka, B., Szczepanski, M.K., Plataniotis K.N., Venetsanopoulos, A.N.,: On the Modified Weighted Vector Median Filter. Proceedings of Digital Signal Processing DSP2002, Santorini, Greece, 2 (2002) 939-942

[22] Smolka, B., Lukac, R., Plataniotis, K.N.: New Algorithm for Noise Attenuation in Color Images Based on the Central Weighted Vector Median Filter. Proc. IWSSIP'02 in Manchester, United Kingdom (2002) 544-548

[23] Szczepanski, M., Smolka, B., Plataniotis, K.N. , Venetsanopoulos, A.N.: Robust Filter for Noise Reduction in Color Images. Proc. CGIV'02 in Poitiers, France (2002) 517-522

[24] Trahanias, P.E., Venetsanopoulos, A.N.: Vector Directional Filters - a New Class of Multichannel Image Processing Filters. IEEE Trans. on Image Processing, 2 (1993) 528-534

[25] Trahanias, P.E., Karakos, D., Venetsanopoulos, A.N.: Directional Processing of Color Images: Theory and Experimental Results. IEEE Trans. Image Processing, 5 (1996) 868-881

[26] Tang, K., Astola, J., Neuvo, Y.: Nonlinear Multivariate Image Filtering Techniques. IEEE Transactions on Image Processing 4 (1995) 788-798

That Elusive Diversity in Classifier Ensembles

Ludmila I. Kuncheva

School of Informatics, University of Wales, Bangor
Bangor, Gwynedd, LL57 1UT, United Kingdom
l.i.kuncheva@bangor.ac.uk

Abstract. Is "useful diversity" a myth? Many experiments and the little available theory on diversity in classifier ensembles are either inconclusive, too heavily assumption-bound or openly non-supportive of the intuition that diverse classifiers fare better than non-divers ones. Although a rough general tendency was confirmed in our previous studies, no prominent link appeared between diversity of the ensemble and its accuracy. Diversity alone is a poor predictor of the ensemble accuracy. But there is no agreed definition of diversity to start with! Can we borrow a concept of diversity from biology? How can diversity, as far as we can define and measure it, be used to improve the ensemble? Here we argue that even without a clear-cut definition and theory behind it, studying diversity may prompt viable heuristic solutions. We look into some ways in which diversity can be used in analyzing, selecting or training the ensemble.

1   Introduction

Classifier outputs are combined in an attempt to reach a more accurate decision than that of a carefully designed individual classifier. It is curious that the experts in the field hold diametrically opposite views about our current level of understanding of combining classifiers. In his invited lecture at the 3rd International Workshop on Multiple Classifier Systems, 2002, Ghosh proposes that [5]

> "... our current understanding of ensemble-type multiclassifier systems is now quite mature..."

In an invited book chapter, the same year, Ho states that [8]

> "Many of the above questions are there because we do not yet have a scientific understanding of the classifier combination mechanisms."

Ho proceeds to nominate the stochastic discrimination theory by Kleinberg [9] as the only consistent and theoretically sound explanation of the success of classifier ensembles, criticizing other theories as being incomplete and assumption-dependent. However, as the usual practice invariably shows, ingenious heuristic developments are the heart, the soul and the engine in many branches of science and research.

F.J. Perales et al. (Eds.): IbPRIA 2003, LNCS 2652, pp. 1126–1138, 2003.

This study advocates one such idea: that of measuring diversity and incorporating it into the process of building of the ensemble. We draw upon the somewhat futile efforts hitherto to define, measure and use diversity (our own research in this number!). We are cautious to note that no strong claims are made based on the small experimentation study reported here. The message of this paper is that there is still much room for heuristic in classifier combination, and diversity might be one of the lines for further exploration.

The paper is organized as follows. Section 2 explains diversity and its reincarnations. Section 3 looks into some ways in which diversity has been used in classifier ensembles. In Section 4, an ensemble building version of AdaBoost is proposed, which involves diversity and Section 5 concludes the paper.

2   Diversity

Classifiers in an ensemble should be different from each other, otherwise there is no gain in combining them. Quantifying this difference, named also diversity, orthogonality, complementarity, has been identified as an important research direction by many authors [2, 11, 20, 14, 15]. Measures of the connection between two classifier outputs can be derived from the statistical literature (e.g., [23]). There is less clarity on the subject when three or more classifiers are concerned. There is no strict definition of what is intuitively perceived as diversity. At least not in the vocabulary of machine learning, pattern recognition and computer science in general. Biologists and ecologists have axiomatized their idea of diversity several decades ago. For example, suppose that we are interested in the height of adult gorillas in a certain region of Africa. Consider a population π with a probability measure P associated with it. The measure P defines the distribution of heights for the population. A comprehensive study on diversity in life sciences by Rao [18] gives the following axiomatic definition of a diversity measure.

Let $(\mathcal{X}, \mathcal{B})$ be a measurable space, and let $\mathcal{P}$ be a convex set of probability measures defined on it.[1] A function $H(.)$ mapping $\mathcal{P}$ onto the real line is said to be a **measure of diversity** if it satisfies the following conditions

C1: $H(P) \geq 0$, for any $P \in \mathcal{P}$ and $H(P) = 0$ iff P is degenerate.
C2: H is a concave function of P. [2]

The concavity condition ensures that any mixture of two populations has a higher diversity than the average of the two individual diversities. $H(P_i)$ is the diversity within a population π_i characterized by the probability measure P_i. Rao defines

---

[1] Convexity means that for any $P_1, P_2 \in \mathcal{P}$, and for any $t \in [0, 1]$, $tP_1 + (1-t)P_2 \in \mathcal{P}$.
[2] The concavity here means that for any $P_1, P_2 \in \mathcal{P}$, and for any $t \in [0, 1]$, $H(tP_1 + (1-t)P_2) \geq tH(P_1) + (1-t)H(P_2)$.

$H(P_i)$ to be the averaged **difference** $(\zeta(X_2, X_2))$ between two randomly picked individuals in the population π_i according to the probability measure P_i

$$H(P_i) = \int \zeta(X_1, X_2) P_i(\partial X_1) P_i(\partial X_2). \tag{1}$$

If the two individuals are drawn from two different populations π_i and π_j, then the total diversity will be

$$H(P_i, P_j) = \int \zeta(X_1, X_2) P_i(\partial X_1) P_j(\partial X_2). \tag{2}$$

The **dissimilarity** between the two populations π_i and π_j is then

$$D_{ij} = H(P_i, P_j) - \frac{1}{2}(H(P_i) + H(P_j)). \tag{3}$$

The concavity of H guarantees that D_{ij} will be positive for any two populations and their probability measures. This dissimilarity is based on taking out the diversity coming from each population and leaving only the "pure" diversity due to mixing the two populations.

The distance ζ could be any function that satisfies the axioms for distance (nonnegativity, symmetry and a version of the triangle inequality). We can use the Euclidean distance for quantitative variables and a "matching" type of function for qualitative variables, i.e., $\zeta(X_1, X_2) = 1$ if the two variables have different values and 0, otherwise.

The most useful ideas often drift across sciences and branches thereof. How otherwise would neural networks and evolutionary computation become the powerful algorithmic tools they currently are? Many more algorithms have come about as a mathematical allegory for the underlying biological or physical processes. The question is how can we translate the notion of diversity used successfully in biology, ecology, economics, etc., into the mathematical concept needed in our classifier combining niche?

Our problem can be approached from two different angles as shown in Figure 1, depending on what we decide to be our "gorillas". The variable of interest here is the class label taking values in the set $\Omega = \{\omega_1, \ldots, \omega_c\}$. We suppose we have a data set $\mathbf{Z} = \{\mathbf{z}_1, \ldots, \mathbf{z}_N\}$ on which the L classifiers in the ensemble, $\mathcal{D} = \{D_1, \ldots, D_L\}$, are tested. Each classifier suggests a class label for every data point $\mathbf{z}_j$. Thus a *population* will be a collection of objects (classifiers or data points?) with the respective values of the class label.

We can regard the classifier outputs for a given data point $\mathbf{z}_j$ as a population. The diversity within the population will be the diversity of the ensemble with respect to the particular point in the feature space. The within-population diversity $H(P)$ can be measured by the entropy of the distribution of class labels among the classifiers or by the Gini index. Let P_k be the probability that a randomly chosen member of the population outputs label ω_k ($\sum_{k=1}^c P_k = 1$). Then the Gini diversity within a population of L classifiers is

$$H(P) = G = 1 - \sum_{k=1}^c P_k^2. \tag{4}$$

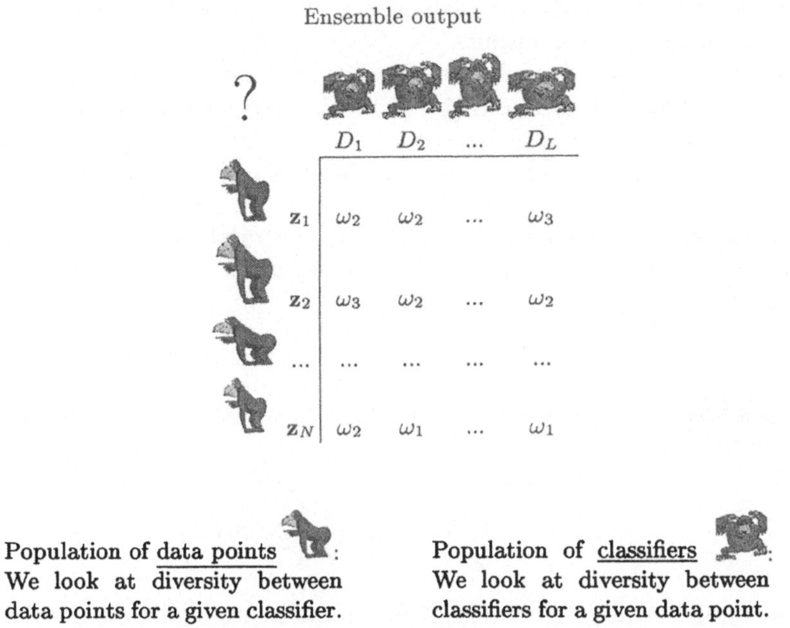

Ensemble output

Fig. 1. Two perspectives on diversity in classifier ensembles

This concept underlies the variance component of the error suggested by Kohavi and Wolpert [10] and is also suggested as a measure of diversity within population by Rao [18]. The data set consists of N such populations, one for each data point. Therefore, the average diversity across the whole feature space is calculated as the average G over the data set **Z**.

The alternative view is to consider the data points as the elements of the population and the classifier as the environment responsible for the distribution of the class labels. In this case, the within-population diversity is not of much use to us; we are interested in the diversity between populations, i.e., between classifiers. Most often we calculate some pairwise measure of diversity and average it across all pairs to get a value for the whole ensemble.

An immediate equivalent of the total diversity $H(P_i, P_j)$, assuming that π_i and π_j are two populations produced by classifiers D_i and D_j is the *measure of disagreement Dis* [13, 7, 22]. We consider the oracle type of outputs from classifiers D_i and D_j, i.e., for every object in the data set, the classifier is either correct (output 1) or wrong (output 0). Then the populations of interest consist of 0's and 1's. We do not assume that the new distribution is simply a mixture of the two distributions. Instead we consider a new space with 4 elements: $00, 01, 10$, and 11. Denote the probabilities for these joint outputs of D_1 (first bit) and D_2 (second bit) as follows $Pr(11) = a$; $Pr(10) = b$; $Pr(01) = c$ and $Pr(00) = d$. The typical choice for the distance as mentioned before is $\zeta(m, n) = 1$, iff $m \neq n$, and 0, otherwise. Then

$$H(P_i, P_j) = \zeta(1,1) \times a + \zeta(1,0) \times b + \zeta(0,1) \times c + \zeta(0,0) \times d = b + c = Dis. \quad (5)$$

This is the expectation of the disagreement between classifiers D_i and D_j in the space of their joint oracle outputs.

However, the disagreement measure does not take out the individual diversities of π_i and π_j as does D_{ij} in (3). An analogue (in spirit) of the dissimilarity measure would be the **kappa** statistic, κ. It measures the agreement between two categorical variables while correcting for chance [4]. For c class labels, κ is defined on the $c \times c$ coincidence matrix M of the two classifiers. The entry $m_{k,s}$ of M is the proportion of the data set (used currently for testing of both D_i and D_j) which D_i labels as ω_k and D_j labels as ω_s. The agreement between D_i and D_j is given by

$$\kappa = \frac{\sum_k m_{kk} - \text{ABC}}{1 - \text{ABC}}, \tag{6}$$

where $\sum_k m_{kk}$ is the observed agreement between the classifiers and 'ABC' is "agreement-by-chance"

$$\text{ABC} = \sum_k \left(\sum_s m_{k,s} \right) \left(\sum_s m_{s,k} \right). \tag{7}$$

Low values of κ signify higher disagreement and hence higher diversity. If calculated on the 2×2 joined oracle output space,

$$\kappa = \frac{2(ac - bd)}{(a+b)(c+d) + (a+c)(b+d)}, \tag{8}$$

The bad news is that despite the large number of proposed measures and formalizations, there is no consensus on what diversity of a classifier ensemble is, which approach should be used to measure it (gorillas = classifiers or gorillas = data points) and what is a good measure of diversity. We will leave this question unanswered here, just acknowledging the "diversity of diversity", and will abstain from strongly advocating one measure or definition over another. In our previous studies we sightly favored the Q statistic (for oracle outputs) [13] because of its: (a) potential sensitivity to small disagreements; (b) value 0 indicating statistical independence; and (c) the relatively small effect of the individual accuracies on the possible range of values of Q. In the rest of this study we draw upon the existing literature and in particular kappa-error plots proposed by Margineantu and Dietterich [16], hence out choice of κ.

3   Using Diversity

The general anticipation is that diversity measures will be helpful in designing the individual classifiers, the ensemble, and the combination method. For this to be possible, there should be a relationship between diversity and the ensemble performance. However, the results from our experiments so far have been disheartening, to say the least [21, 13]. We did not find the desired strong and consistent relationship to guide us into building better ensembles. Although the suspected relationship appears on a large scale, i.e., when diversity spans (uniformly) the whole range of possible values, in practice we are faced with a different picture. Usually the candidates for the ensemble are not very different from one another. This leads to small variations of diversity and also small variations of the accuracy of the ensemble about the individual accuracies. Unfortunately, none of the various diversity measures that we investigated previously (10 measures: 4 pairwise and 6 non-pairwise [13]) appeared to be sensitive enough to detect the changes in the accuracy. This phenomenon is illustrated in Figure 2 showing a typical graph of "accuracy" versus "diversity". A scatterplot of this type was obtained when we simulated classifier outputs with preassigned accuracy (approximately equal for all ensemble members) and preassigned diversity (approximately equal diversity for all pairs). The relationship can easily be spotted on the plot. However, when diversity only varies in a small range, this relationship is blurred (the gray dot and the cloud of classifiers in it).

If we do not enforce diversity, the ensemble is most likely to appear as a dot towards the right side of the graph. For these ensembles, the improvement on the individually best accuracy is usually negligible.

Note that the neat relationship in Figure 2 was obtained under quite artificial circumstances. When the members of the ensemble have different accuracies and different pairwise diversities, such a relationship has not been found. Then is measuring and studying diversity a wasted journey? Several studies which explicitly use diversity to help analyze or build the ensemble offer answers to this skeptical and provocative question.

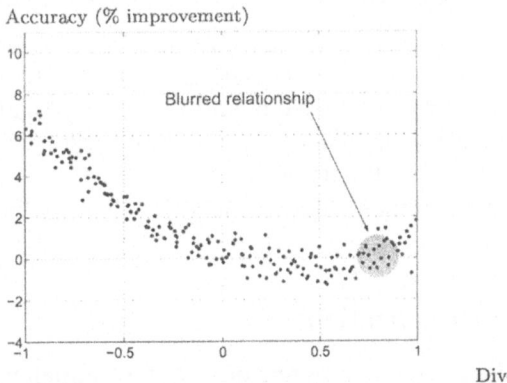

Fig. 2. A typical accuracy-diversity scatterplot. Each point corresponds to an ensemble. The gray dot shows a hypothetical area where ensembles appear most often in real problems

3.1   Diversity for Finding Bounds and Theoretical Relationships

Assume that classifier outputs are estimates of the *posterior probabilities*, $\hat{P}_i(\omega_s|\mathbf{x})$, $s = 1, \ldots, c$, so that the estimate $\hat{P}_i(\omega_s|\mathbf{x})$ satisfies

$$\hat{P}_i(\omega_s|\mathbf{x}) = P(\omega_s|\mathbf{x}) + \eta_s^i(\mathbf{x}), \tag{9}$$

where $\eta_s^i(\mathbf{x})$ is the error for class ω_s made by classifier D_i. The outputs for each class are combined by averaging, or by an order statistic such as minimum, maximum or median. Tumer and Ghosh [24] derive an expression about the added classification error (i.e., the error above the Bayes error) of the team under a set of assumptions

$$E_{add}^{ave} = E_{add}\left(\frac{1 + \delta(L-1)}{L}\right), \tag{10}$$

where E_{add} is the added error of the individual classifiers (all have the same error), and δ is a correlation coefficient (the measure of diversity of the ensemble)[3].

Breiman [1] derives an upper bound on the generalization error of random forests (ensembles of decision trees built according to a simple randomization technology, one possible variant of which is bootstrap sampling) using the averaged pairwise correlation between the ensemble members. The classifiers produce class labels and majority vote is assumed as the combination method. The bound is given by

$$Pr(\text{ generalization error of the ensemble }) \leq \bar{\rho}(1 - s^2)s^2, \tag{11}$$

where $\bar{\rho}$ is the averaged pairwise correlation (our diversity measure)[4], and s is the "strength" of the ensemble. The strength is a measure of accuracy based on the concept of margin. Admittedly the bound is not very tight as it is based on the Chebyshev's inequality but nonetheless it shows the tendency: the higher the diversity (small $\bar{r}ho$), the lower the error.

Both results can be viewed as pieces of that yet missing more general theory of diversity.

3.2   Diversity for Visualization

Diversity measures have been used to find out what is happening in the ensemble. Pękalska and coauthors [17] look at a two-dimensional plot derived from the matrix of pairwise diversity. Each classifier is plotted as a dot in the 2-d space

---

[3] Averaged pairwise correlations between $P_i(\omega_s|\mathbf{x})$ and $P_j(\omega_s|\mathbf{x})$, $i, j = 1, \ldots, L$ are calculated for every s, then weighted by the prior probabilities $\hat{P}(\omega_s)$ and summed.

[4] Since the classifier outputs are labels, therefore categorical, the correlation is calculated between the two oracle outputs. For every data point $\mathbf{z}_j \in \mathbf{Z}$, the output of D_i is taken to be 1 if the suggested label for $\mathbf{z}_j$ matches the true one, and -1, otherwise.

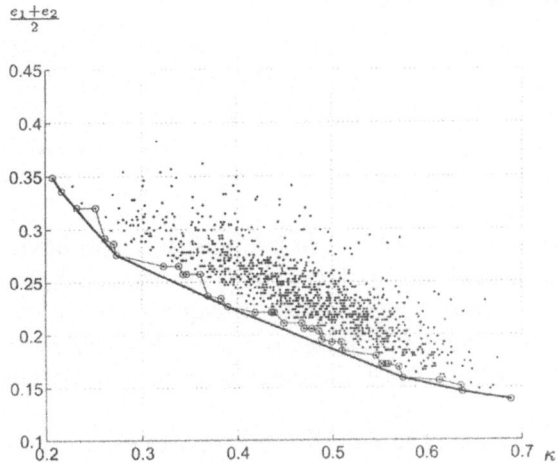

Fig. 3. Kappa-error plot, the convex hull, and the Pareto optimal set of pairs of classifiers

found by Sammon mapping which preserves the "distances" (diversities in our case). The ensemble is a classifier itself and can also be plotted. Any method of combination of the individual outputs can also be mapped. Even more, the oracle classifier (all objects correctly recognized) can be plotted as a point to complete the picture.

Margineantu and Dietterich suggest the kappa-error plots as shown in Figure 3 [16]. Every pair of classifiers is plotted as a dot in a two-dimensional space. The pairwise measure kappa (6) is used as the x-coordinate of the point and the average of the individual training errors of the two classifiers is used as the y-coordinate. Thus there are $L(L-1)/2$ points in the scatterplot. The best pairs are situated in the left bottom part of the plot: they have low error and low kappa (low agreement = high diversity).

The cloud of points shows the pairwise diversity in one ensemble. Margineantu and Dietterich use it to verify that AdaBoost generates more diverse classifiers than Bagging. The example in the figure corresponds to an ensemble of 50 classifiers for the *glass* data set from UCI Machine Repository Database [5]. The shape of the cloud indicates that there is a certain trade-off between the accuracy of the pair and its κ-diversity.

The disagreement measure mentioned before, $Dis = b + c$, was used by Skalak [22] to characterize the diversity between a base classifier and a complementary classifier, and then by Ho [7] for measuring diversity in decision forests.

---

[5] http://www.ics.uci.edu/~mlearn/MLRepository.html

3.3   Overproduce and Select

Several studies try the method of producing a pool of classifiers, usually by bagging (taking bootstrap samples from the data sets and building a classifier on each sample) or boosting (modifying the training set for every new member of the ensemble by putting more "emphasis" on the hard objects). Then a selection procedure is suggested to pick the members of the team which are most diverse or most diverse and accurate.

Giacinto and Roli [6] use the *double fault* measure (probability of both classifiers being incorrect, $DF = d$) and also the Q statistics [19], to form a pairwise diversity matrix for a classifier pool and subsequently to select classifiers that are least related. The selection is carried out using a search method through the set of all pairs of classifiers until the desired number of ensemble members is reached.

Margineantu and Dietterich [16, 3] use kappa to select the ensemble out of the set of classifiers produced by AdaBoost. They call this "ensemble pruning". One proposed technique matches the work by Giacinto and Roli. The pairwise κ's are calculated for the whole ensemble. The pruned ensemble is created by progressively selecting pairs with lowest kappas (highest diversity) until the desired number of classifiers is reached. Since both studies apply greedy algorithms, optimality of the selected ensemble is not guaranteed.

Another interesting strategy of selection is to use the kappa-error plots. As the most desirable pairs of classifiers are situated toward the lower left corner of the plot, Margineantu and Dietterich use the convex hull [16], called kappa-error convex hull pruning. The convex hull of points is depicted in Figure 3 with a thick line.

It might happen that the convex hull contains only a few classifiers on the frontier. Small variations of the estimates of κ and $\frac{e_1+e_2}{2}$ might change the whole frontier, making convex-hull pruning overly sensitive to noise. The number of classifiers in the pruned ensemble cannot be specified in advance. This lack of control on the ensemble size is seen as a defect of the method [16].

Therefore we may look at **Pareto optimality** as an alternative to the convex hull approach. Let $A = \{a_1, \ldots, a_m\}$ be a set of alternatives (pairs in our case) characterized by a set of criteria $C = \{C_1, \ldots, C_M\}$ (low kappa and low error in our case), The Pareto-optimal set $S^* \subseteq S$ contains all non-dominated alternatives. An alternative a_i is non-dominated iff there is no other alternative $a_j \in S$, $j \neq i$, so that a_j is better than a_i on *all* criteria. For the two criteria in our example, the Pareto optimal set will be a superset of the convex hull. The concept is illustrated in Figure 4.

The Pareto-optimal set for the glass data example is depicted in Figure 3 by a thin line joining the circled points in the set.

4   Diversity for Building the Ensemble

Here we only sketch a possible use of diversity during *the process of building of the ensemble*. The motivation is that diversity should step out of the passive role

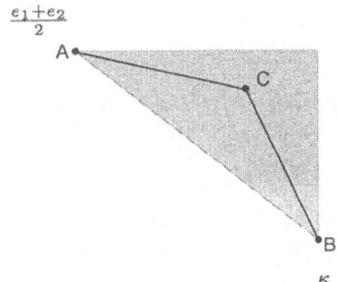

Suppose that points A and B are in the convex hull. Point C is not in the convex hull because it is "behind" the segment AB. However, C is better than A on the error criterion and better than B on the kappa criterion. Therefore C is non-dominated, so it belongs in the Pareto optimal set.

Fig. 4. Illustration of Pareto optimality

of being only a tool for monitoring and should help actively at the design stage. The overproduce-and-select approach discussed earlier is a step in this direction. However, we need to overproduce first. An alternative approach would be to stop the growing of the ensemble when diversity and accuracy satisfy a certain condition.

We take as the starting point the kappa-error diagram and run AdaBoost[6]. The first and the second classifier (D_1 and D_2) will define one single point on the diagram. This point will be the convex hull and the Pareto optimal set of itself. The third classifier, D_3, will place two more points: one for (D_1, D_3) and another for (D_2, D_3). At this step we recalculate the Pareto optimal set. If the points by new classifier have not changed the previous Pareto optimal set, then this classifier is not accepted. Another training set is generated with the same distribution and a new classifier is attempted on it. We run the acceptance check again, and proceed in this manner. A pre-specified parameter T defines the limit number of attempts from the same distribution. When T attempts have been made and a classifier has not been accepted, the procedure stops and the classifier pairs in the last Pareto optimal set are declared to be the ensemble.

Next we give some experimental results with the proposed ensemble construction method. Four data sets were used, three from the UCI and one called "cone-torus"[7]. The characteristics of the data sets are summarized in Table 1.

Table 1. Characteristics of the data sets used

Name	Objects	Classes	Features	Availability
glass	214	6	9	UCI[5]
cone-torus	800	3	2	see footnote 7
liver	345	2	6	UCI[5]
pima	768	2	8	UCI[5]

---

[6] We use AdaBoost in its resampling version: the likelihood of data poins to be selected is modified.

[7] Available at http://www.bangor.ac.uk/~mas00a/Z.txt and Zts.txt, [12].

Table 2. Testing error in % (and ensemble size L), average from 20 splits into 90/10 training/testing

Data set	Classical AdaBoost		Select from 50 (Pareto)		Incorporate diversity, $T = 5$		Incorporate diversity, $T = 10$	
glass	23.18	(50)	25.00	(28.55)	**22.95**	(24.85)	24.09	(34.95)
cone-torus	12.38	(50)	12.56	(33.70)	12.81	(37.00)	**12.25**	(41.50)
liver	30.29	(50)	32.14	(16.45)	32.71	(7.8)	**28.43**	(9.10)
pima	**26.43**	(50)	28.05	(16.40)	29.09	(6.30)	28.64	(8.85)

Table 2 shows the errors (in %) and the number of classifiers in the ensembles for the standard AdaBoost (run up to 50 classifiers), the kappa-error selection from the final ensemble of 50 using Pareto optimality, and the proposed diversity-incorporation method ($T = 5$ and $T = 10$). All the results are the testing averages from 20 runs. At each run we split randomly the data set into 90% training and 10% testing. The same 20 splits were used with each method. The "winner" (smallest error) for each data set is marked in boldface.

As we all know, miracles rarely happen in pattern recognition. If our results appear dramatically better than everybody else's then better double check the code! The results here show that we can sometimes achieve better performance than standard AdaBoost with smaller number of ensemble members. In any case, this part of the paper was not intended as a consistently examined new ensemble building technology. It is instead an illustration of the potential of diversity as an ensemble building aid.

5   Conclusions

This talk looks into diversity again, asking the same old awkward question: do we need to measure and exploit diversity at all? We try to relate the notion of diversity, which appears well channeled in biological and ecological studies, to diversity in combining classifiers. Unfortunately, a straightforward translation is not apparent at this stage, so some analogues from the field of combining classifiers are presented.

Subsequently, the usage of diversity is summarized into four main bullets: for theoretical relationships and limits, for monitoring, for selection from a given pool of classifiers, and for direct use in building the ensemble. The fourth direction seems to be the least researched. The lack of effort can be explained by the discouraging results trying to link unequivocally diversity with the ensemble error for practical purposes. If there is no proven link, then why bother incorporating diversity into the building of the ensemble? For regression and approximation such a link exists, and there are increasing amount of studies on training the members of the ensemble by enforcing negative correlation between the classifier outputs.

However, as argued at the beginning, heuristics sometime produce a surprising escape from what seems to be a dead end. Even without an agreed upon definition, based upon intuition only, diversity can be put to work. Once successful, there should be explanations and maybe a theory that will tell us when, where and how we can make the best of diversity. Will the quest for diversity, now a marginal streak in the research on classifier combination, resurface one day as a major theory for new ensemble creating methods?

Let us return to the experts' disagreement about where we are. My personal view is that we have accumulated quite a lot of unstructured insight on classifier combination. We have a good critical mass of experimental studies and some patchy but exciting theory on different ensemble building and combination methods. So, yes, we know a lot and, no, we don't have the all-explaining theory. This makes our field of research what it is – challenging and entertaining.

Acknowledgements

I wish to thank my colleagues Chris Whitaker, Tim Porter and Catherine Shipp for the inspirational and enjoyable discussions on the subject and in particular on the proposed method.

References

[1] L. Breiman. Random forests. *Machine Learning*, 45:5–32, 2001.

[2] P. Cunningham and J. Carney. Diversity versus quality in classification ensembles based on feature selection. Technical Report TCD-CS-2000-02, Department of Computer Science, Trinity College Dublin, 2000.

[3] T. Dietterich. An experimental comparison of three methods for constructing ensembles of decision trees: bagging, boosting and randomization. *Machine Learning*, 40(2):139–157, 2000.

[4] J. L. Fleiss. *Statistical Methods for Rates and Proportions*. John Wiley & Sons, 1981.

[5] J. Ghosh. Multiclassifier systems: Back to the future. In F. Roli and J. Kittler, editors, *Proc. 3d International Workshop on Multiple Classifier Systems, MCS'02*, volume 2364 of *Lecture Notes in Computer Science*, pages 1–15, Cagliari, Italy, 2002. Springer-Verlag.

[6] G. Giacinto and F. Roli. Design of effective neural network ensembles for image classification processes. *Image Vision and Computing Journal*, 19(9-10):699–707, 2001.

[7] T. K. Ho. The random space method for constructing decision forests. *IEEE Transactions on Pattern Analysis and Machine Intelligence*, 20(8):832–844, 1998.

[8] T. K. Ho. Multiple classifier combination: Lessons and the next steps. In A Kandel and H. Bunke, editors, *Hybrid Methods in Pattern Recognition*, pages 171–198. World Scientific Publishing, 2002.

[9] E. M. Kleinberg. Stochastic discrimination. *Annals of Mathematics and Artificial Intelligence*, 1:207–239, 1990.

[10] R. Kohavi and D. H. Wolpert. Bias plus variance decomposition for zero-one loss functions. In L. Saitta, editor, *Machine Learning: Proc. 13th International Conference*, pages 275–283. Morgan Kaufmann, 1996.

[11] A. Krogh and J. Vedelsby. Neural network ensembles, cross validation and active learning. In G. Tesauro, D. S. Touretzky, and T. K. Leen, editors, *Advances in Neural Information Processing Systems*, volume 7, pages 231–238. MIT Press, Cambridge, MA, 1995.

[12] L. I. Kuncheva. *Fuzzy Classifier Design*. Studies in Fuzziness and Soft Computing. Springer Verlag, Heidelberg, 2000.

[13] L. I. Kuncheva and C. J. Whitaker. Measures of diversity in classifier ensembles. *Machine Learning*, 51:181–207, 2003.

[14] L. Lam. Classifier combinations: implementations and theoretical issues. In J. Kittler and F. Roli, editors, *Multiple Classifier Systems*, volume 1857 of *Lecture Notes in Computer Science*, pages 78–86, Cagliari, Italy, 2000. Springer.

[15] B. Littlewood and D. R. Miller. Conceptual modeling of coincident failures in multiversion software. *IEEE Transactions on Software Engineering*, 15(12):1596–1614, 1989.

[16] D. D. Margineantu and T. G. Dietterich. Pruning adaptive boosting. In *Proc. 14th International Conference on Machine Learning*, pages 378–387, San Francisco, 1997. Morgan Kaufmann.

[17] E. Pękalska, R. P. W. Duin, and M. Skurichina. A discussion on the classifier projection space for classifier combining. In F. Roli and J. Kittler, editors, *Proc. 3d International Workshop on Multiple Classifier Systems, MCS'02*, volume 2364 of *Lecture Notes in Computer Science*, pages 137–148, Cagliari, Italy, 2002. Springer-Verlag.

[18] C. R. Rao. Diversity: Its measurement, decomposition, apportionment and analysis. *Sankya: The Indian Journal of Statistics, Series A*, 44(1):1–22, 1982.

[19] F. Roli, G. Giacinto, and G. Vernazza. Methods for designing multiple classifier systems. In J. Kittler and F. Roli, editors, *Proc. Second International Workshop on Multiple Classifier Systems*, volume 2096 of *Lecture Notes in Computer Science*, pages 78–87, Cambridge, UK, 2001. Springer-Verlag.

[20] B. E. Rosen. Ensemble learning using decorrelated neural networks. *Connection Science*, 8(3/4):373–383, 1996.

[21] C. A. Shipp and L. I. Kuncheva. Relationships between combination methods and measures of diversity in combining classifiers. *Information Fusion*, 3(2):135–148, 2002.

[22] D. B. Skalak. The sources of increased accuracy for two proposed boosting algorithms. In *Proc. American Association for Artificial Intelligence, AAAI-96, Integrating Multiple Learned Models Workshop*, 1996.

[23] P. H. A. Sneath and R. R. Sokal. *Numerical Taxonomy*. W. H. Freeman & Co, 1973.

[24] K. Tumer and J. Ghosh. Linear and order statistics combiners for pattern classification. In A. J. C. Sharkey, editor, *Combining Artificial Neural Nets*, pages 127–161. Springer-Verlag, London, 1999.

Author Index

Lecture Notes in Computer Science

For information about Vols. 1–2590

please contact your bookseller or Springer-Verlag